Text, Cases and Materials on
Medical Law and Ethics

Text, Cases and Materials on Medical Law and Ethics

FOURTH EDITION

Marc Stauch MA (Oxon), Dr jur (Göttingen)
Solicitor, Lecturer and Research Fellow
Leibniz University of Hannover,

and

Kay Wheat BA
Solicitor, Reader in Law
Nottingham Trent University

with

John Tingle BA, Med
Barrister, Reader in Health Care Law,
Nottingham Trent University

Routledge
Taylor & Francis Group

LONDON AND NEW YORK

Fourth Edition published 2012
by Routledge
2 Park Square, Milton Park, Abingdon, Oxon OX14 4RN

Simultaneously published in the USA and Canada
by Routledge
711 Third Avenue, New York, NY 10017

Routledge is an imprint of the Taylor & Francis Group, an informa business

First Edition published by Cavendish Publishing 1998
Third Edition published by Cavendish Publishing 2005

British Library Cataloguing in Publication Data
A catalogue record for this book is available from the British Library

Library of Congress Cataloging in Publication Data
Stauch, Marc.
   Text, cases and materials on medical law and ethics / Marc Stauch and
Kay Wheat with John Tingle.—4th ed.
     p. cm.
   ISBN 978-0-415-58231-5 (hbk)—ISBN 978-0-415-58230-8 (pbk)   1. Medical
laws and legislation—England.   2. Medical care—Law and
legislation—England.   3. Medical ethics.   I. Wheat, Kay.   II. Tingle,
John.   III. Title.   IV. Title: Medical law and ethics.
   KD3395.S73 2011
   344.4204'1—dc23
                                                    2011002330

ISBN: 978-0-415-58231-5 (hbk)
ISBN: 978-0-415-58230-8 (pbk)

Typeset in Joanna
by RefineCatch Limited, Bungay, Suffolk

MIX
Paper from
responsible sources
FSC
www.fsc.org   FSC® C004839

Printed and bound in Great Britain by the MPG Books Group

Outline Contents

Detailed Contents

Preface

Medical law is an exciting and challenging subject, whose dilemmas are the focus of intense and ongoing public debate. The fact that it is a relatively young discipline, which must attempt to keep pace with the constant advance of medical science, makes it of considerable jurisprudential interest. Moreover, the questions which it addresses are ones of fundamental human concern, bearing directly upon the lives of each of us and the shape of the society we inhabit. In this regard, there are few other legal subjects that so clearly display the interaction between law and ethics.

Text, Cases and Materials on Medical Law and Ethics aims to draw together a wide range of material (much of it very recent), including extracts from statutes, judgments and academic commentaries. It is primarily designed for use as a core text by law students taking medical (or health care) law at undergraduate level. However, it is hoped that it may also be of interest to postgraduate students, including those in the burgeoning field of bioethics, as well as to health care professionals.

While the authors take collective responsibility for the book, primary responsibility for the individual chapters was as follows: Marc Stauch, Chapters 3, 6, 7, 8, 11 and 12; Kay Wheat, Chapters 1, 2, 4, 5, 9 and 10.

Crown copyright is reproduced with the permission of the Controller of Her Majesty's Stationery Office. Every effort has been made to trace copyright holders, but if any have been inadvertently overlooked, the publishers will be pleased to make the necessary arrangements.

In this new, fourth edition, we have aimed to take account of developments in the law up until 1 January 2011.

Marc Stauch and Kay Wheat
2011

Acknowledgements

Grateful acknowledgement is made to all the authors and publishers of copyright material which appears in this book, and in particular to the following for permission to reprint material from the sources indicated:

Cambridge University Press for extracts from Keown, John, *Abortion, Doctors and the Law: Some Legal Aspecrs of the Legal Regulation of Abortion in England from 1803 to 1982* (1988), © 1988 Cambridge University Press, reproduced with permission; Maclean, Alastair, *Autonomy, Informed Consent and Medical Law. A Relational Challenge* (2009), ©Alastair Maclean 2009, published by Cambridge University Press, reproduced with permission.

Michael Cavadino for extracts from *Mental Health Law in Context: Doctors' Orders?* (Dartmouth, 1989), pp. 138–41. Reproduced by permission of the author.

Pearson for extracts from Glover, Jonathan, *Causing Deaths and Saving Lives* (Pelican, 1977). Copyright © 1977 Jonathan Glover. By permission of Pearson.

Routledge/Taylor and Francis for extracts from Lamb, David, *Organ Transplants and Ethics* (1990), © 1990 David Lamb; Fennell, Phil, *Treatment without Consent* (1996), © 1996 Phil Fennell. Reproduced by permission of Taylor and Francis Books UK.

Wiley-Blackwell for extracts from Hursthouse, R., *Beginning Lives* (1987), © 1987 Rosalind Hursthouse; Fortin, J., 'Legal protection for the unborn child', *The Modern Law Review*, 51:1 (1988), pp. 54–83; Keown, J., 'The ashes of AIDS and the phoenix of informed consent', *The Modern Law Review*, 52:6 (1989), pp. 790–800; Fox, Marie and McHale, Jean, 'In whose Best Interests?, 60:5 (1997), pp. 700–709; Thomson, J.J. , 'A Defence of Abortion', *Philosophy and Public Affairs*, 1:1 (1971), pp. 47–66.

Hart Publishing for extracts from Stauch, Marc, *The Law of Medical Negligence in England and Germany* (2008), © Marc Stauch 2008. Reproduced by permission of Hart Publishing and the author.

Oxford University Press for extracts from Otklowski, Margaret, *Voluntary Euthanasia and the Common Law* (1997), p. 160, 173, 206, 462; Skegg, P.D.G, *Law, Ethics and Medicine* (1998), p. 40, pp. 110–112; Culver, C.M. and Gert, B., *Philosophy in Medicine* (1982), p. 66, 146; Grubb, Andrew (ed.), *Principles of Medical Law*, 2nd edn (2004); Kuhse, Helga, *The Sanctity-of-life doctrine in Medicine* (1987), pp. 16–20; Downie, R.S., Traditional Medical Ethics and Economics in Health Care: A Critique' in Mooney, Gavin and McGuire, Alistair eds, *Medical Ethics and Economics in Health Care* (1989), pp. 40–55.

BMJ for extracts from Stauch, M., 'Causal authorship and the equality principle: a defence of the acts/omissions distinction in euthanasia', *Journal of Medical Ethics*, 26 (2000), p. 237; Wilkinson, S. and Garrard, E. 'Bodily integrity and the sale of human organs', *Journal of Medical Ethics* (1996) 22, pp. 334.

Harper Collins/Fourth Estate for extracts from Dworkin, R., *Life's Dominion: An Argument About Abortion and Euthanasia* (1993),© Ronald Dworkin 1993; Glover, J. et al, *Report to the European Commission on Reproductive Technologies, Fertility and the Family* (1989), London: Fourth Estate.

Thompson Reuters for extracts from the *Australian Law Journal and Reports*, Section of Health v JWB & SMB (1992), 66, ALJR 300.

Routledge for extracts from Stone, D., *Confidentiality, Access to Health Records and the Human Rights Act* (1998), in Garwood-Gowers, Austen, et al, *Healthcare: The Impact of the Human Rights Act* (1998), London: Cavendish Publishing, 2001.

Every effort has been made to trace and contact copyright holders prior to publication. If notified, the publisher will undertake to rectify any errors or omissions at the earliest opportunity.

Table of Cases

Table of Legislation

Table of Statutory Instruments

Table of Treaties and EU Legislation

Abbreviations

Atlantic Reporter	A
Appeal Cases	AC
Australian Law Journal Reports	ALJR
All England Law Reports	All ER
American Journal of Law and Medicine	Am J Law & Med
British Columbia Law Reports	BCLR
British Medical Journal	BMJ
Butterworths Medico-Legal Reports	BMLR
Californian Appellate Cases	Cal App
Californian Reporter	Cal Rptr
Cambridge Law Journal	CLJ
Chancery Division	Ch
Chancery Division	Ch D
Cox's Criminal Cases	Cox
Criminal Appeal Reports	Cr App R
Criminal Law Review	Crim LR
Current Legal Problems	CLP
Dominion Law Reports	DLR
European Human Rights Reports	EHRR
Family Division	Fam
Family Law	Fam Law
Family Law Reports	FLR
Federal Reporter	F
Industrial Relations Law Reports	IRLR
Journal of Social Welfare Law	J Soc Wel L
Journal of Law and Society	JLS
Journal of Medical Ethics	JME
King's Bench Law Reports	KB
Knight's Industrial Reports	KIR
Law Quarterly Review	LQR
Lloyd's Law Reports: Medical	Lloyd's Rep Med
Massachusetts Supreme Judicial Court Reports	Mass
Medical Law Reports	Med LR
Medical Law Review	Med L Rev
Modern Law Review	MLR
New Jersey Supreme Court Reports	NJ
New Law Journal	NLJ
New Law Journal Reports	NLJR
North Eastern Reporter	NE
North Western Reporter	NW
New York Court of Appeal Reports	NY

New York Supplement	NYS
New Zealand Law Reports	NZLR
Nottingham Law Journal	Nott LJ
New South Wales Law Reports	NSWLR
Ontario Reports	OR
Oxford Journal of Legal Studies	OJLS
Pacific Reporter	P
Pennsylvania District and County Reports	Pa D & C
Public Law	PL
Queen's Bench Law Reports	QB
Road Traffic Reports	RTR
Scots Law Times	SLT
Session Cases	SC
Solicitor's Journal	SJ
Southern Reporter	SO
South Australian State Reports	SASR
South Western Reporter	SW
Supreme Court Reporter	S Ct
Canada Law Reports: Supreme Court	SCR
United States Law Week	USLW
United States Supreme Court Reports	US
Victorian Reports	VR
Weekly Law Reports	WLR
Western Weekly Reports	WWR

Part 1

General Principles

Chapter 1

Introduction to Ethics

Chapter Contents

This chapter will examine the ways in which ethical issues are part of the practice of medicine. In this first section we will look, briefly, at a number of ethical theories and concepts and the ways in which they might relate to medicine. Next, we consider the doctor–patient relationship and the way in which medicine has given rise to particular ways of describing this relationship and its ethical implications. Although it is by no means a clear-cut dichotomy, generally it can be said that many of the problems in medical ethics, and certainly many of the conflicting opinions, are based upon the debate between paternalism and the patient's right to autonomy. First, the view that paternalism is central to the doctor–patient relationship means that because of the doctor's superior knowledge and his ethical obligation to do good, the medical view of what is best for the patient should prevail. The opposing view is that the patient has a right to autonomous decision-making and that this should not be overridden by 'doctor knows best'. Later in the chapter we will study these two different ways of looking at the doctor–patient relationship, question whether it is helpful to use either of these models as frameworks for medical decision-making, and look at alternatives. Finally, we will look at justice and fairness in the allocation of treatment between competing patients when resources dictate that not all can be treated, and at the distribution of health care resources on a national level.

However, although the current chapter looks at general principles, when appropriate, ethical problems in particular areas of medical practice will be examined in other chapters.

1.1 Why Study Ethics?

Why should ethics be so important in medicine? In other fields of activity, such as commerce, ethics plays a small role. As long as business is operated on the right side of the law, little consideration is given to whether it is practised ethically. Although many may protest, for example, that 'it isn't fair' for large supermarkets to put small shops out of business, the 'ethics' of this plays a minor role in the general discourse about such matters, which is much more likely to be concerned with convenience and consumer choice. That is not to say that it is not relevant. It is simply that the language of ethics has not permeated the world of business in the way in which it has the practice of medicine. The reason may be that much of medicine is about issues of life and death: for example, abortion, infertility treatment, the threat to life through negligent treatment, or insufficiency of health resources, the treatment of the terminally ill and so on. Perhaps the heart of the doctor–patient relationship is this: the doctor does things to the body of the patient, thereby invading his physical integrity. This is neither good nor bad in itself, but is instrumentally good if the likely effect is the cure or amelioration of the patient's condition, and if it is done with the real consent and co-operation of the patient. However, in so far as it can be ascertained, it must be done in the patient's best medical interests. If there is no real consent, or if the treatment is unsuitable or negligently carried out, then it could be regarded as a violation of the patient's physical integrity.

Although, as we shall see, there is some argument that the doctor–patient relationship has been wrongly accorded this special status, there is no doubt that since the time of ancient Greece, it has given rise to ethical codes prescribing the extent of the doctor's duties:

Mason, JK and Laurie GT, *Mason and McCall Smith's Law and Medical Ethics*, 8th edn[1]

The Hippocratic Influence

Hippocrates remains as the most famous figure in Greek philosophical medicine but he was not alone and it is probable that the Oath predates his own school. It therefore indicates a prevailing ethos rather than a professorial edict and it is still regarded as the fundamental

---

1   Oxford: OUP, 2011.

governance of the medical profession . . . the Oath lays down a number of guidelines. First, it implies the need for co-ordinated instruction and registration of doctors – the public is to be protected, so far as is possible, from the dabbler or the charlatan. Secondly, it is clearly stated that a doctor is there for the benefit of his patients – to the best of his ability he must do them good and he must do nothing which he knows will cause harm. . . . Thirdly, euthanasia and abortion are proscribed; the reference to lithotomy probably prohibits mutilating operations (castration) but has been taken by many to imply the proper limitation of one's practice to that in which one has expertise. Fourthly, the nature of the doctor–patient relationship is outlined and an undertaking is given not to take advantage of that relationship. Finally, the Oath expresses the doctrine of medical confidentiality.

What is the study of ethics about? The purpose of ethics is to try and find principles for living good lives. It will be seen that there is much overlap between ethical theories, and within each, there are contradictions and tensions. Words such as 'equality', 'rights' and 'liberty' all sound good, and we all like to think that we approve of these things. However, in deciding what we mean by them we may find that we are making all sorts of value judgments and interpretations which suit the end we would like to achieve.

1.1.1 Universalisation and relativism

A fundamental starting point in discussions about ethics is universalisation. This means that one must seek principles that can apply to everyone. Peter Singer describes the way this has permeated ethical thinking:

Singer, P, *Practical Ethics*[2]

From ancient times, philosophers and moralists have expressed the idea that ethical conduct is acceptable from a point of view that is somehow universal. Kant developed this idea into his famous formula: 'Act only on that maxim through which you can at the same time will that it should become a universal law.' Kant's theory has itself been modified and developed by RM Hare, who sees 'universalisability' as a logical feature of moral judgments. The 18th century British philosophers Hutcheson, Hume and Adam Smith appealed to an imaginary 'impartial spectator' as the test of a moral judgment . . . Utilitarians from Jeremy Bentham to JJC Smart take it as axiomatic that in deciding moral issues 'each counts for one and none for more than one'; while John Rawls, a leading contemporary critic of utilitarianism, incorporates essentially the same axiom into his own theory by deriving basic ethical principles from an imaginary choice in which those choosing do not know whether they will be the ones who gain or lose by the principles they select. . . .

This does not mean that a particular ethical judgment must be universally applicable. . . . What it does mean is that in making ethical judgments we go beyond our own likes and dislikes. From an ethical point of view the fact that it is I who benefit from, say, a more equal distribution of income and you, say, who lose by it, is irrelevant. Ethics requires us to go beyond 'I' and 'you' to the universal law, the universalisable judgment, the standpoint of the impartial spectator or ideal observer, or whatever we choose to call it.

Can we use this universal aspect of ethics to derive an ethical theory which will give us guidance about right and wrong? . . . The problem is that if we describe the universal aspect of ethics in bare, formal terms, a wide range of ethical theories, including quite irreconcilable ones, are compatible with this notion of universality; if, on the other hand, we build up our

---

2 Cambridge: CUP, 1979.

description of the universal aspect of ethics so that it leads us ineluctably to one particular ethical theory, we shall be accused of smuggling our own ethical beliefs into our definition of the ethical – and this definition was supposed to be broad enough, and neutral enough, to encompass all serious candidates for the status of 'ethical theory'.

As Singer says, the principle of universalisation has appealed to many and it cannot be said to belong to any particular theory.

See Hart's criticism of Mill, at 1.3.2 ➜

Nevertheless, it is arguable that we approach ethical problems from the standpoint of a white Western man. Increasingly, therefore, there are thinkers who want to move away from this and explore the issues from the perspective of women or of people from different cultures.

We commenced this section with the suggestion that ethical principles should be universal. Some would argue that this does not address the way in which cultural differences might give rise to different ethical norms:

Beauchamp, TL and Walters, L, *Contemporary Issues in Bioethics*[3]

[Cultural] relativists defend their position by appeal to anthropological data indicating that moral rightness and wrongness vary from place to place and that there are no absolute or universal moral standards that could apply to all persons at all times. They add that rightness is contingent on cultural beliefs and that the concepts of rightness and wrongness are there-fore meaningless apart from the specific contexts in which they arise. . . . patterns of culture can only be understood as unique wholes and that moral beliefs about normal behaviour are thus closely connected in a culture to other cultural characteristics, such as language and fundamental political institutions.

Similarly, some feminists have taken the view that the language of moral philosophy is male-centred, and dominated by an undue reverence for 'reason'. This is particularly pertinent to medical ethics, as the medical profession has traditionally been dominated by men, particularly in its upper reaches. It has been said that the traditional approach to medical ethics reinforces the practice of patriarchal medicine and the patriarchal institutions within society (for example, by Susan Sherwin[4]). Some feminist writers have spoken of the need for an 'ethics of care', whereby the emotions have an important role to play in ethical theories.[5] Beauchamp and Childress describe the care ethic as follows:

Beauchamp, TL and Childress, JF, *Principles of Biomedical Ethics*[6]

Having a certain emotional attitude and expressing the appropriate emotion in action are morally relevant factors, just as having the appropriate motive for an action is morally relevant. The person seems morally deficient who acts from rule-governed obligations without appro-priately aligned feelings such as worry when a friend suffers. In addition to expressing their feelings in their responses, agents also need to attend to the feelings of persons toward whom they act. Insight into the needs of others and considerate attentiveness to their circumstances often come from the emotions more than reason.

In the history of human experimentation, for example, those who first recognised that some subjects of research were being brutalised, subjected to misery, or placed at unjustifi-

---

3   Belmont, California: Wadsworth Publishing, 1982.
4   See 'Feminist and medical ethics: two different approaches to contextual ethics', in Bequaert Holmes, H and Purdy, LM, *Feminist Perspectives in Medical Ethics*, Bloomington: Indiana UP, 1992.
5   See Gilligan, C, *In a Different Voice*, Cambridge, Mass: Harvard UP, 1982.
6   Oxford: OUP, 2001.

able risk were persons who were able to feel compassion, disgust, and outrage through insight into the situation of these research subjects. They exhibited emotional discernment of and sensitivity to the feelings of subjects, where others lacked comparable responses. This emphasis on the emotional dimension of the moral life does not reduce moral response to emotional response. Caring also has a cognitive dimension, because it involves insight into and understanding of another's circumstances, needs, and feelings. As Hume pointed out, emotions motivate us and tell us much about a person's character, but human understanding directs us in choosing a path of action.

The care ethic, however, has its weaknesses, in that it is arguable that it is not sufficient as a moral theory. Beauchamp and Childress comment as follows:

Beauchamp, TL and Childress, JF, *Principles of Biomedical Ethics*[7]

On at least some occasions we need an impartial judgment to arbitrate between conflicting moral judgments or feelings. Many who endorse the ethics of care do not want to exclude all impartial judgments and considerations of justice and the public good. But the problem remains about the extent to which this approach can successfully incorporate these moral notions without losing much of its critical thrust and uniqueness. The ethic of care, as Gilligan and others have defended it, recognises that two perspectives exist, but can they be made coherent? . . .

Some feminists [eg Susan Sherwin] have sharply criticised the ethics of care, despite its feminist origins, on the grounds that it attends to women's experiences as givers of care in traditional roles of self-sacrifice, but often neglects their oppression. . . .

. . . without a broader framework, the ethics of care is too confined to the *private* sphere of intimate relationships and may serve to reinforce an uncritical adherence to traditional social patterns of assigning caretaker roles to women.

 SELF-TEST QUESTION

Do you agree that the emphasis on 'care' sets up a potential conflict between rationalism and emotions which is unnecessary and unhelpful in deciding on what is the ethically correct thing to do?

Pattinson states that it is clear that moral 'pluralism' ie that there are different moral standpoints, does in fact exist as a matter of fact. For example, we shall see when issues such as abortion are discussed, even within a fairly homogeneous western society, there are very different views on this. However Pattinson regards this as not being particularly problematic.

Pattinson, SD, *Medical Law and Ethics*[8]

Even in largely secular societies some level of moral consensus is actually quite common. If it were not, no stable polity could exist. It should therefore be no surprise that English legal doctrine actually encompasses many moral values shared by the majority of the population.

---

7   Ibid.
8   London: Sweet & Maxwell, 2006.

Indeed, a more widespread developed-world consensus can be seen in international instruments such as the Helsinki declaration and the innumerable human rights instruments that pepper the international area. These instruments proclaim the universal nature of moral values such as respect for patient autonomy and the democratic process. This still, however, leaves ethical disagreement on many of the issues raised by medical law. . . .

. . . Even *if* moral relativism is to be rejected in favour of objectivism, there are many different variations of moral objectivism.

This brings us to examining some of the different theories.

1.1.2 Consequences v deontological absolutes

One way of deciding whether an action is ethically right or wrong is to look at the consequences of this act; or we might consider it important to look at the consequences of translating this act into an ethical proposition about what should be done generally, ie, by framing an ethical principle which will produce the best consequences. So, for example, we might make a rule about keeping promises which is generally a good thing to do, even though in some circumstances the consequences of breaking a promise may be better than keeping it. Another way is to ask whether the act or principle would be right or wrong *regardless of its consequences*. This leads to a somewhat crude distinction between theories which judge the moral correctness of an action by its consequences alone, and those which state there are certain principles, rights or whatever, which are inviolable, whatever the consequences. However, it is by no means a neat division. With varying degrees of success, most consequentialists try to incorporate certain things such as respect for individual rights into their theories. Those who believe in the paramountcy of absolute values cannot disregard consequences entirely. Advocates of certain principles such as the sanctity of life (one of those so called inviolable principles) may oppose, say, the withdrawal of nutrition from a permanently unconscious patient. However, they may argue that one of the reasons for their view is the 'slippery slope' argument, which says that once a certain course of action is carried out (as here), then the next step will be to withdraw food from a patient who is gravely disabled, but not unconscious. This argument is an appeal to consequentialism.

1.1.2.1 Consequentialism

The theory that the rightness of a course of action is to be judged by its consequences is an attractive one and it is tempting to embrace this view as being self-evidently right. Human actions have outcomes. We believe that we need to know what these are in order to decide what is the right thing to do. However, a moment's reflection will make us realise that whilst it may be correct, as it stands, it is full of holes. First, consequences for whom? If we are looking at types of medical treatment or the allocation of health resources we must ask whether we are looking at these sorts of patients or society as a whole? What sorts of consequences are going to be relevant? If the consequences of treating these patients may be that they will live, but live in pain or be dependent upon others for their most basic needs, is this right?

The most well known consequentialist view is that of utilitarianism. This theory, of whom Jeremy Bentham was one of the earliest exponents, states that ethical principles should produce the greatest happiness for the greatest number of people, and 'happiness' is defined by means of pleasure. The rightness of a decision is judged by deciding whether it produces, on balance, more pleasure than pain. When we consider the treatment of say, very seriously disabled new-born children, we might discount treating them because they will live (we believe) painful lives. But we also tend to think that there is more to life than the pursuit of pleasure and the avoidance of pain. JJC Smart has put forward the example of the 'pleasure machine'.[9] This is a machine that can be

---

9　See Smart JJC and Williams, B, *Utilitarianism: For and Against*, Cambridge: CUP, 1993.

connected to the brain to give pleasure, without the 'inconvenience' of the means of obtaining pleasure, for example, from books, sex, sport and so on. Once we acknowledge the absurdity of this and realise that we do not pursue pleasure as such, but an infinite number of pursuits, the pain-pleasure dichotomy is not so attractive. We tend to think that to be human is to be more than the repository of the sensations of pleasure and pain. Although the most well known utilitarian philosopher, John Stuart Mill, referred to the maximising of pleasure, and described utilitarianism as the 'happiness' theory, he was aware that this might be interpreted as pandering to selfish and, perhaps, base, tastes. Mill tried to deal with this by distinguishing between different kinds of pleasure:

Mill, JS, *Utilitarianism*[10]

It must be admitted . . . that utilitarian writers in general have placed the superiority of mental over bodily pleasures chiefly in the greater permanency, safety, uncostliness, etc, of the former – that is, in their circumstantial advantages rather than in their intrinsic nature. And, on all these points, utilitarians have fully proved their case, but they might have taken the other, and, as it may be called, higher ground, with entire consistency. It is quite compatible with the principle of utility to recognise the fact that some *kinds* of pleasure are more desirable and more valuable than others. It would be absurd that while, in estimating all other things, quality is considered as well as quantity, the estimation of pleasures should be supposed to depend on quantity alone.

Singer describes his own version of utilitarianism, which he claims springs from the universal aspect of ethics. He argues that from this starting point one must look to the interests of others as having equal validity to those of oneself. This means that one must chose a course of action that is most likely to maximise the interests of all those affected. This is utilitarianism, and, Singer says, if we want to go beyond utilitarianism then we need to be provided with good reason for doing this.[11]

Critics of utilitarianism have pointed out that the theory can be upheld and still permit an awful lot of wrongdoing. In other words, the great majority of society can be wealthy and healthy, but a small minority may live in appalling circumstances, with no access whatsoever to basic facilities, such as health care. This is a powerful argument and has led theorists to distinguish between 'act' utilitarianism and 'rule' utilitarianism. Pattinson sums this up as follows:

Pattinson, SD, *Medical Law and Ethics*[12]

Faced with the objection that utilitarianism rides roughshod over widely accepted moral norms and requires endless utility evaluation, another version appeared requiring us to adopt rules that *generally* achieve the best utility balance. . . . Standard act-utilitarianism can have a difficult time considering the consequences of every act. Imagine a doctor faced with a number of patients in need of life-saving donations of organs and tissue in circumstances where there is a suitable but but unwilling potential 'donor' from whom such tissue can be removed relatively safely. For an act-utilitarian set on maxmising utility, the permissibility of removing some tissue . . . to save the lives of four patients will depend on the overall utility balance of so doing. The utility of saving four patients' lives [could be] high enough that in some circumstances the disutility of using an unwilling 'donor' could be outweighed . . . According to supporters of rule-utilitarianism, adopting rules that track the best utility balance, rather than evaluating all individual acts, avoids the need for such calculations and the possibility of concluding that removing these organs is permissible.

---

10 London: Routledge, 1863.
11 Singer, P, *Practical Ethics*, Cambridge: CUP, 1979, p 12.
12 London: Sweet & Maxwell, 2006.

SELF-TEST QUESTION

Do you think that rules can be framed that would satisfy both utilitarians and their opponents?

Although Mill does incorporate concepts such as justice into his form of utilitarianism, is this not coming perilously close to maintaining that there are ideals or principles which are worthy and must be supported regardless of the consequences? Consequentialist theories do not have to be utilitarian, ie, the maximisation of happiness or welfare can be replaced by some other concept of what is good. For example, one may try to incorporate some role for distributive justice. This may be possible, but it is not necessarily part of a consequentialist theory, which may lead us to conclude that judging actions by consequences alone is an insufficient guide to ethical behaviour.

Utilitarianism, however, is an attractive theory when one considers certain specific issues such as the doctor's obligation of confidentiality, where the obligation can be justified on the basis that patients would be less than candid when consulting a doctor if they had doubts that the information would be kept confidential. The fact that the obligation can be broken if it is in the public interest to do so is also an appeal to consequentialism.

It is also arguable that when looking at the provision of healthcare throughout society some form of consequentialist approach is best. Individual treatment decisions may not fare so well under a consequentialist approach, although, for example, Jonathan Baron favours utilitarianism for medical decision-making in general because, he argues, it is all about risks and trade-offs.[13]

1.1.2.2 Deontology/absolutism

Having recognised the inadequacies of consequentialism, John Mackie considers alternatives:

Mackie, JL, *Ethics: Inventing Right and Wrong*[14]

. . . we could reject the consequentialist structure, and develop a moral system built not round the notion of some goal that is to be attained, but rather round the notions of rules or principles of action or duties or rights or virtues, or some combination of these – in a very broad sense, some kind of deontological system. Of course a consequentialist theory will usually give some place to items of all these sorts, but a subordinate place: a utilitarian takes virtues, for example, to be good just because and in so far as they tend to issue in behaviour that increases the general happiness. But in a deontological theory actions of the kinds held to be virtuous are seen as being intrinsically obligatory or admirable, and goodness of character too may be seen as having intrinsic value; actions and characters may have a merit of their own not wholly derived from what they bring about.

The term 'deontology' comes from *deon* – the Greek word for 'duty'. Probably the most well known exponent of this is Immanuel Kant:

---

13 Baron J, *Against Bioethics*, London: MIT, 2006.
14 Harmondsworth: Penguin, 1977.

Paton, HJ, *The Moral Law*[15]

A human action is morally good, not because it is done from immediate inclination – still
less because it is done from self-interest – but because it is done for the sake of duty.

. . .

An action – even if it accords with duty and is in that sense right – is not commonly regarded
as morally good if it is done solely out of self-interest. We may, however, be inclined to attribute
moral goodness to right actions done solely from some immediate inclination – for example,
from a direct impulse of sympathy or generosity. In order to test this we must *isolate* our motives:
we must consider first an action done solely out of inclination and *not* out of duty, and then an
action done solely out of duty and *not* out of inclination. . . . The goodness shown in helping others
is all the more conspicuous if a man does this for the sake of duty at a time when he is fully
occupied with his own troubles and when he is not impelled to do so by his natural inclinations.

Kant's doctrine would be absurd if it meant that the presence of a natural inclination to
good actions (or even of a feeling of satisfaction in doing them) detracted from their moral
worth. . . . He would have avoided the ambiguity if he had said that a man shows moral worth,
not in doing good from inclination, but in doing it for the sake of duty. It is the motive of duty,
not the motive of inclination, that gives moral worth to an action.

Just as happiness was central to Mill's view, it plays a significant role in Kant's philosophy: '. . . the
natural end which all men seek is their own happiness.' However, this happiness will only be
produced, says Kant, if human beings, as rational beings, make rules to govern their own lives and
the lives of others, and have reverence for the moral law. Crucial to Kant's philosophy is the maxim
that no one should be treated merely as a means to an end, but always, as well, as an end in themselves. As we shall see, this Kantian rule is particularly pertinent to issues such as medical research
and organ donation.[16]

Beauchamp and Walters comment on deontological theories as follows:

Beauchamp, TL and Walters, L, *Contemporary Issues in Bioethics*[17]

As an example of differences in utilitarian and deontological thinking, consider a survey
conducted by researchers K Ann Coleman Stolurow and Dale W Moeller. Stolurow and Moeller
were interested in the frequency with which x-rays are routinely used as part of dental
checkups. They conducted a telephone survey of dental offices in the Boston area and found
that in 95% of the offices surveyed x-ray procedures are customarily ordered in connection
with the initial investigation of new patients, and that in nearly half of those offices the procedures employed involve full-mouth x-rays to obtain accurate information. These researchers
misrepresented themselves over the telephone as new residents in the Boston area inquiring
about available dental services and they asked a series of specific questions that followed a
prepared written survey instrument wholly undisclosed to the dentists or their offices. This
misrepresentation apparently contributed significantly to the accuracy of the results, because
the data obtained showed a frequency of dental x-ray use far greater than that reported by an
earlier study in which the researchers did not conceal their purposes.

This use of deception raises ethical issues of whether the researchers violated the moral
rights of the participants or unjustifiably invaded privacy. Many act utilitarians would likely
consider this study justifiable: there are public benefits of obtaining accurate information

---

15 London: Hutchinson University Library, 1948.
16 Baron J, *Against Bioethics*, London: MIT, 2006.
17 Belmont, California: Wadsworth Publishing, 1982.

about dental x-rays. The information, for instance, might form the basis on which the American Dental Association would refocus its ongoing efforts to reduce unnecessary x-ray exposure, from lessening dosage levels to cutting down on the frequency of exposure. . . . A deontologist, by contrast, may find indefensible the deception and invasion of privacy essential to the conduct of the study. In any event, the deontologist will not frame the moral problem exclusively in terms of a weighing of consequences.

We also talk about absolutism, ie the belief in absolute values which can be regarded as inviolable, regardless of what they may bring about in any given set of circumstances. For example, it could be said that torture is *always* wrong. This is illustrated by the prohibition on torture in the Declaration of Tokyo, issued by the World Medical Association:

Declaration of Tokyo 1975 (revised 2006), World Medical Association

1 -The doctor shall not countenance, condone or participate in the practice of torture or other forms of cruel, inhuman or degrading procedures, whatever the offence of which the victim of such procedures is suspected, accused or guilty, and whatever the victim's beliefs or motives, and in all situations, including armed conflict and civil strife. . .

This implies that under no circumstances could torture ever be justified, but it is by no means clear that we can be sure about this. Simmonds gives the following example:

Simmonds, NE, *Central Issues in Jurisprudence*[18]

. . . if a madman had hidden a nuclear device which was set to destroy the whole of South East England at a pre-set time, we might feel justified in torturing him if this really was the only way of discovering the location of the bomb so as to defuse it.

The sanctity of life principle might also be said to be an absolute, but, again, this is questionable. Most people accept the fact that innocent people's lives will be lost in the cause of a just war. In medicine, the right of people to refuse life-saving treatment is respected, even though it conflicts with the sanctity of life principle, and, as we shall see, many doctors believe that it is right not to treat a person if the treatment will not 'benefit' him, even if his death will result because of this.

See Chapter 12 →

This idea that principles can be weighed up against each other depending upon the circumstances is attractive and is reflected in the writings of Ronald Dworkin, who describes the role principles have in legal decision-making.[19] As we shall see, this 'weighing up' of different principles is frequently a feature of medical law cases.

1.1.3 Rights, duties and liberties

When considering absolutist theories we questioned whether there was, for example, a right not to be tortured which could never be overridden. It leads us to try to get to grips with what we mean by rights. Rights are often described in terms of the corresponding duties which go with them. The jurist WN Hohfeld was a well known exponent of this, incorporating into his scheme the role of liberties and powers:

---

18 London: Sweet & Maxwell, 1986.
19 See *Taking Rights Seriously*, London: Duckworth, 1977.

Simmonds, NE, *Central Issues in Jurisprudence*[20]

The idea of strict correlativity between rights (ie, claim-rights) and duties is a controversial one, and the controversy is important for two quite different sets of reasons, which we may summarise as follows:

1   If rights are strictly correlative to duties, then a person has established legal rights only in so far as there are established duties corresponding to those rights. The law on this account has a static appearance: it could be represented as a long list of duties. If, on the other hand, it makes sense to talk of established rights without established correlative – we may think of the law as imposing duties, and perhaps creating new duties, in order to protect established rights. On this account, there may at any one time be established legal rights which are inadequately protected by legal duties: such rights provide a legal reason for creating new legal duties. Seen from this perspective, the law is not static but has an inner dynamic of its own. It is not a long list of duties that is added to whenever moral and policy considerations make this desirable: new duties may be recognised as a response to specifically legal considerations, in the attempt to give better legal protection to established legal rights.

2   Politicians and others make frequent use of the concept of rights. People are said to have rights of this and that kind, and rights are generally regarded as a 'good thing'. But if rights (in this case moral, rather than legal, rights) are correlative to duties, such claims are always open to the question 'on whom do the correlative duties rest?' People are much more willing to assert the existence of rights to various amenities than they are to ascribe specific duties. Moreover, if rights are correlative to duties, we may feel that they are not necessarily an unqualified good: for if rights entail duties, they entail greater restrictions on freedom. If therefore we believe that freedom is a 'good thing' we will not wish to see an unlimited expansion in people's rights (meaning, I repeat, 'claim-rights').

Kant distinguished between perfect and imperfect duties. Paton gives examples of these:

Paton, HJ, *The Moral Law*[21]

A perfect duty is one which admits of no exception in the interests of inclination. Under this heading the examples given are the ban on suicide and on making a false promise in order to receive a loan. We are not entitled to commit suicide because we have a strong inclination to do so, nor are we entitled to pay our debt to one man and not to another because we happen to like him better. In the case of imperfect duties the position is different: we are bound only to adopt the maxim of developing our talents and of helping others, and we are to some extent entitled to decide arbitrarily which persons we will help. There is here a certain 'latitude' or 'playroom' for mere inclination.

In terms of medicine, this could be translated as follows. Doctors are under a perfect duty to be just in the way in which they decide who to treat. They have only an imperfect duty to provide medical treatment to everyone who requests it. Under the Hohfeldian scheme there is no right to medical treatment, only the right to be considered in accordance with just criteria. In the next chapter we refer to the European Social Charter of 1961, which enshrines the 'right to protection of health, and the right to social and medical assistance'. However, as we shall see, in the context of the provision of medical treatment, the clinical discretion of the doctor as to the provision of treatment is paramount.

---

20   London: Sweet & Maxwell, 1986.
21   London: Hutchinson University Library, 1948.

We might look for perfect duties in medical law, or we might consider the question the other way round and ask whether there are any absolute rights. Ronald Dworkin argues that there is a right to be treated with equal respect. Are mentally impaired people to be treated with the same respect as the non-impaired? There are a number of controversial cases where mentally impaired young women have been sterilised for contraceptive purposes even though there was little likelihood of them becoming pregnant.[22] Were they being treated with the same respect as non-impaired women?

The principle of self-determination is frequently asserted in medical law and ethics. It could be said that there is an absolute right to self-determination as long as the person has the capacity to make decisions. We often talk of people being competent to make decisions. Problems may arise in deciding whether the person is competent, but once it is established then the right to physical integrity seems to be inviolable. But could the right still be overridden – for example, in an emergency? As we shall see, this 'right' is overridden when the doctor has no time to consult with, for example, an unconscious patient: he will successfully raise the defence of necessity to an action in battery. However, is it arguable that the right to self-determination has not been overridden at all because the patient was incapable of exercising it? In English law the foetus has no legal 'rights'. We will examine this later, in relation, in particular, to abortion and women who refuse Caesarean section operations, even though the refusal may gravely risk their own lives and the survival of the foetuses. Does the foetus have no rights because it cannot enforce them? If this were the case, then children and the seriously mentally disordered would not have rights, but we often speak about the rights of children and the mentally ill. In one of the sterilisation cases referred to above it was said that a woman's 'right' to reproduce meant nothing to her (Re B (A Minor) (Wardship: Sterilisation).[23] Because of the dangers of dismissing rights in this way, it might be preferable to consider the rights of the incompetent in terms of the duties others have towards them. With regard to children, Carl Wellman states:

Wellman, C, An Approach to Rights[24]

The moral right to freedom of movement contains several other associated elements, but let me mention only one – the State's moral duty to enforce the parental duty of non-interference with the child's freedom of movement. Although this duty is very limited in scope, it can be of crucial importance in extreme cases. Imagine that a parent keeps a young child restrained in a crib so much of the time that the child has no opportunity to learn to walk . . . Under such circumstances, the State would have a moral obligation to intervene in the family and force the parent to cease and desist from such grossly unjustified interference with the freedom of movement of the child. Although this moral duty of the State begins as merely a duty regarding the child, in due course it grows into a moral duty to the child when the child becomes capable of claiming State intervention vis à vis the parent.

Wellman goes on to examine the right of the child to protection. In medical law the tension between granting the child the freedom it needs to develop and the protection it may need will be apparent when we look at the ability of the child to consent to treatment.

Liberty and equality are two other general ethical concepts that are open to a number of different interpretations. In Mill's philosophy they are interdependent. Mill stresses that the liberty of the individual is paramount, and his liberty to pursue his own choices has to be no more than the equal liberty of everyone else. He can only be restrained from any activity which interferes with the liberty of others:

---

22 See *Taking Rights Seriously*, 1977, London: Duckworth
23 [1988] AC 199.
24 Dordrecht: Kluwer Academic, 1997.

Mill, JS, *On Liberty*[25]

The object of this essay is to assert one very simple principle, as entitled to govern absolutely the dealings of society with the individual in the way of compulsion and control, whether the means used be physical force in the form of legal penalties or the moral coercion of public opinion. That principle is that the sole end for which mankind are warranted, individually or collectively, in interfering with the liberty of action of any of their number is self-protection. That the only purpose for which power can be rightfully exercised over any member of a civilised community, against his will, is to prevent harm to others. His own good, either physical or moral, is not a sufficient warrant.

Mill's principle is reflected in the right to self-determination.

1.1.4 Respect for persons

We have referred to Dworkin's equal respect for persons, but do we know what we mean by a person? This may sound like a silly question, but if we pose the question in a different way and ask what we mean by respect for human life it is not an easy one to answer.[26]

Harris asks when human life begins to matter morally and examines the potentiality argument which says that human life begins when the human egg is fertilised, ie when there is the potential for human life:

Harris, J, *The Value of Life*[27]

There are two sorts of difficulty with the potentiality argument which are jointly and severally fatal to it. The first is that the bare fact that something will become X (even if it will inevitably become X, which is far from being the case with the fertilised egg and the adult human being) is not a good reason for treating it now as if it were in fact X. We will all inevitably die, but that is, I suppose, an inadequate reason for treating us now as if we were dead.

The second difficulty is that it is not only the fertilised egg that is potentially a human being. To say that a fertilised egg is potentially a human being is just to say that if certain things happen to it (like implantation), and certain other things do not (like spontaneous abortion), it will eventually become a human being. But the same is also true of the unfertilised egg and the sperm. If certain things happen to the egg (like meeting a sperm) and certain things happen to the sperm (like meeting an egg) and thereafter certain other things do not (like meeting a contraceptive), then they will eventually become a new human being.

It is sometimes objected that it is only the fertilised egg that has all the necessary potential present in one place, so to speak, and it is this that is crucial. It is only when the egg has been fertilised, so the argument goes, that a new unique entity exists that itself has all the potential necessary to become a new human being. This seems plausible enough until we remember that something had the potential to become that fertilised egg; and whatever had that potential, had also the potential to become whatever it is that the fertilised egg has the potential to become!

---

25 Harmondsworth: Penguin, 1982.
26 There are those who argue that respect for life generally is what matters, so that animals should be treated with respect, and this has relevance to medical research and the development of xenotransplantation (animal to human): see Ch 11, and see Singer, P, *Animal Liberation*, New York: Random House, 1990.
27 London: Routledge & Kegan Paul, 1985.

If then we ignore the first difficulty with the potentiality argument, and concede that we are somehow morally required to actualise all human potential, we are all in for a highly exhausting time. And it is clear that if we put the maximal effort into procreation that this imperative demands, our endeavours will ultimately be self-defeating.

Harris goes on to say that what we really value is *a person*:

Harris, J, *The Value of Life*[28]

. . . a person will be any being capable of valuing its own existence. Apart from the advantage of its simplicity, this account has two other major advantages. The first is that it is value- and species-neutral. It does not imply that any particular kind of being or any particular mode of existence is more valuable than any other so long as the individual in question can value its mode of existence. Once this threshold is crossed, no individual is more of a person or more valuable than any other. This concept of the person sets out to identity which individuals and which forms of life have the sort of value and importance that makes appropriate and justifies our according to them the same concern, respect and protections as we grant to one another. And it tries to do so without begging any questions as to the sort of creatures that will be found to qualify.

The second advantage is that it is capable of performing the two tasks we require of a concept of a person. These are that it should give us some grasp of why persons are valuable and make intelligible the moral difference between persons and other beings. The second task is that it should enable us, in principle, to tell persons from non-persons.

On this concept of the person, the moral difference between persons and non-persons lies in the value that people give to their own lives. The reasons it is wrong to kill is that to do so robs that individual of something they value, and of the very thing that makes possible valuing anything at all. To kill a person not only frustrates their wishes for their own futures, but frustrates every wish a person has. Creatures that cannot value their own existence cannot be wronged in this way, for their death deprives them of nothing that they can value.

Of course non-persons can be harmed in other ways, by being subjected to pain for example, and there are good reasons for avoiding subjecting any sentient creatures to pain if this can be avoided.

 SELF-TEST QUESTION

It is important to note that Harris is talking about the *capacity* to value one's own existence, so a new-born child would have that capacity. However, would a foetus also have the capacity?

1.1.5 Justice

By now it will be apparent that the language of morals can slip easily between rights, duties and liberties. The concept of 'justice' is no less an elusive concept. Although its importance usually lies in the realm of politics, it can be relevant both to the wider issues of allocating health resources on a national basis, and when deciding which patients to treat when local resources are limited. This will be examined further at the end of this chapter and in Chapter 2.

See 1.6 and Chapter 2 →

---

28 Ibid.

1.2 The Doctor–Patient Relationship

1.2.1 Beneficence

Doctors are generally regarded as having a positive duty to do good, and as being unique in this regard.[29] However, it is by no means clear that this is the case. Referring to the duty of the doctor as going beyond what can reasonably be expected of everyone else, Downie comments:

> **Downie, RS, 'Traditional medical ethics and economics in health care: a critique', in Mooney, G and McGuire, A (eds), *Medical Ethics and Economics in Health Care*[30]**
>
> [A main ingredient in a code of medical or other professional ethics] consists of some generalised exhortations to care for patients, which can be summed up by saying that the medical and perhaps all the professions are governed to a much greater extent than other jobs by the principle of benevolence. Indeed, Gillon (1986) goes so far as to describe the doctor's duty as one of super-erogatory benevolence, in that it goes beyond what can reasonably be expected of the rest of us.
>
> A short way to dispose of this claim might be to argue that it confuses conceptual points about the definition of the aims of a profession with moral duties; definitional 'oughts' have been confused with moral 'oughts'. Thus, it sounds like a high ideal to say that the doctor ought to care for the health or the welfare of his patient, but in fact this is simply a definition of the job of a doctor. The shepherd *qua* shepherd ought to care for his sheep, the gardener *qua* gardener ought to care for his flower beds and grass, and the pilot *qua* pilot ought to aim at transporting his passengers with safety. These are just definitions of occupations in terms of their aims. Of course, one might say that the person who happens to be a doctor ought to do the best he can as a doctor. Yes, and the person who happens to be a gardener ought to do the best he can for his flower beds. We all ought to work hard in our respective spheres. In other words, if medical ethics is made to seem grander than ordinary morality it is because a conceptual claim has become confused with a perfectly ordinary moral claim.
>
> An argument of this kind is usually thought by doctors to be too superficial. They reply that patients are vulnerable and that health care must be delivered through the uniquely special doctor–patient relationship. But that uniquely special relationship requires a special morality to protect it, and so we need medical ethics as traditionally understood.
>
> Yet what is uniquely special about the doctor–patient relationship? What emerges after any attempt to answer this question is that it is difficult to find a set of necessary and sufficient conditions, which justify the description 'uniquely special' of the doctor–patient relationship. Note to begin with that there is no one relationship which is *the* doctor–patient relationship. For example, an anaesthetist might see a patient once before an operation, but adding this to the anaesthetist's function during an operation hardly creates a 'relationship', and in any case it is certainly different from the 'relationship' which a community health doctor might have with the population who live in a given geographical area. But even waiving this objection and concentrating on certain typical sorts of doctor–patient relationships we cannot easily say what is *uniquely* special about them. Certainly, patients are lacking in information and power when, say, a coronary artery bypass operation is prescribed, but so are most of us when the garage mechanic prescribes an engine transplant! In each case most of us must trust in the knowledge, skills, and good faith of our helpers. Perhaps car engines are not so important as our bodies, but then we also commit the latter to the care of airline pilots and taxi drivers. Again, doctors may have access to our bodies; but teachers, clergymen, and advertisers have access to our minds and can influence to varying degrees our very perceptions of our own identities.

---

29 See Gillon, R, *Philosophical Medical Ethics*, Chichester: John Wiley, 1985.
30 Oxford: OUP, 1998.

The conclusion seems to be that if there are uniquely defining conditions of the doctor–patient relationship they are likely to be trivial and not special in the sense of important, and if there are special or important features they are likely to be shared with a variety of occupations such as the lifeboat service, the police, the clergy, teachers, and many others, some of which are 'professions' and some not. It seems more profitable, then, to drop the whole idea of uniquely special features of the doctor–patient relationship and to draw attention to 'family resemblances' between that relationship and a whole variety of others.

To argue, as I have done, that there is nothing uniquely special about the doctor–patient relationship certainly weakens the claim that there is a need for a special sort of morality. But it does not dispose of it entirely. I wish now to argue that medical ethics as traditionally understood is actually harmful to health care, and that the need is really to drop the traditional approach and to reassert the claims of ordinary morality (Downie and Calman, 1987).

The first respect in which traditional medical ethics has been harmful to health care concerns the distortions it has created in the doctor–patient relationship. For example, traditional codes are expressed in terms of the duties of the doctor, and while this has certainly inspired an idealistic practice it has also created a professional ethos of elitism and paternalism. Thus, generations of medical students have been given the impression that there is an esoteric set of rules – 'medical ethics' – which govern their professional activities. It is easy to extrapolate from this to the conclusion that such a code is different from and superior to ordinary morality. Doctors are not as other men; other men are guided by right and wrong, but doctors have medical ethics. For example, in ordinary life the assumption, if not the reality, is that people speak the truth to each other, but this is not an assumption of those governed by medical ethics; for medical ethics says that the first responsibility of the doctor is to the well being of his patient, and it is generally thought to follow that it is up to the doctor to decide how far, in his opinion, a patient's well being will be furthered by telling the truth. Medical ethics in this respect distorts the doctor–patient relationship, for any true human relationship must have sincerity as its necessary condition, and that condition is discouraged by the attitude built into traditional medical ethics: benevolence (if that is what it is) has swamped sincerity. This criticism might be summed up by saying that the duties of doctors should not be regarded, as they are in the tradition, as duties of benevolence, but rather as duties correlative to the *rights of patients*. To give this emphasis to the doctor–patient relationship is to cut out the distortion caused by the tradition. Indeed, an emphasis on rights – consumer rights, social and political rights, human rights of all kinds – is one moral characteristic of our time.

A second criticism which can be made of the tradition is that its fraternal, inward-looking nature discourages frank and open co-operation with other caring professions. For example, nurses and social workers are not part of the fraternity, so it has been a matter for debate how far they should be admitted into the inner counsels. One consequence of this is inefficiency in the delivery of health care due to uncertainty or lack of co-operation among all the members of a health care team. Where objectives are not shared and discussed among the caring professions there is a diminution of job satisfaction, friction, and a consequent damage to patient care. For example, one member of a team, a nurse, say, may not know how much a patient has been told or what the overall prognosis is. It is then difficult for the nurse to be fully supportive of the patient. This is not good morality.

A third respect in which the traditional approach to medical ethics is deficient is that it suggests that morality is about selected issues, rather than that it is all-pervasive. The discussion of medical ethics has tended to highlight the dramatic issues which happen to be topical at any one time. Although euthanasia, abortion, resuscitation, surrogate motherhood, and human experimentation are undoubtedly important matters, their prominence has obscured the fact that, not just once but many times in the course of a working day, moral stances, value judgments and decisions will result in actions considered to be right or wrong by the doctor.

This is partly, but only partly, due to the uncertain nature of medical diagnosis and prognosis. The doctor, lacking certainty, must estimate what in his opinion is for the total good of the patient. This concept of 'total good' is not just a matter of technical expertise but involves values. For example, let us imagine a 70 year old man who wants to be allowed home soon after an operation. The doctor's judgment here will involve technical expertise, but will also involve economic and value judgments of a total good, including knowledge of the home circumstances and many other factors. Again, whether we do a job only moderately well when we are capable of doing it better is a question of morality, of deciding which direction we want to take. Allowing ourselves to become professionally socialised into routinised working patterns which keep things going but diminish patients' dignity and freedom requires as much a moral justification as a sociological explanation. These moral demands are all-pervasive and inescapable in health care.

Fourth, the traditional distinction between 'medical ethics' and 'private morality' suggests that one can deal with moral questions in a professional context without examining personal values and convictions. But I am arguing that it follows from the inescapable and all-pervasive nature of morality that we encounter moral problems in our personal lives which are not fundamentally different from those we may have to explore in our working environment. Whatever values we may feel to be important to us as individuals are almost certainly influencing and directing the decisions that we make as professional health care workers. If we have or lack the skills which allow us to approach moral dilemmas in a rational and methodical way in ordinary life, this will affect how we attempt to solve moral problems in a professional context. In other words, morality is 'indivisible'.

On the other hand, this fundamental assumption about the 'indivisibility' of morality does not lead to a rejection of the very special place that the maintenance of acceptable professional standards of behaviour must have in the work of people whose primary responsibility is to care for vulnerable fellow men and women. The potential harm that can come to people who are in some ways and by definition dependent on the knowledge and skills of others will undoubtedly heighten the moral concern in situations which, outside the professional context, might not be perceived as quite so threatening or acute. For example, a critical or sarcastic remark, which might be acceptable in ordinary circumstances, could be devastating to a sick person.

Another aspect of the 'indivisibility' of morality is that hospitals and other health care organisations ought not to be immune to general attitudinal changes in society. Moral dilemmas arise frequently from the attempts which the professions make or do not make to accommodate social change. Likewise, what professional people do, or often more pertinently what they would refuse to do, reflects the moral standards of their society in the same way in which actions of the individual doctor or nurse, psychologist or speech therapist, social worker or dietician reflect his or her standards of personal morality. The dilemmas created by social change can be obscured by an emphasis on medical ethics traditionally understood as a product.

A fifth criticism of traditional medical ethics is that it tends to underestimate the fact that medical decisions ought to be made in the real world of technological and economic facts. This point is much stressed in the papers of Mooney and McGuire, and Jennett . . . Traditionally medical ethics tends to be seen in terms of pure moral absolutes – the doctor must do all that is medically possible for his (or her) patient regardless of the cost. I am asserting that in the real world compromises must be made. As an example of compromise we can point to renal dialysis. It is not helpful to say that there is an absolute value on human life if there are two patients who would benefit from dialysis but facilities for treating only one. The moral requirement here is to reflect on the scientific and economic facts of the cases as well as the quality of life of the potential recipients. This point can be expressed in the form of a distinction between compromising our consciences, which is wrong, and conscientious compromises, which consist in making the moral best of a bad job in the light of scientific and economic constraints. This distinction is compatible with the view that in some circumstances no compromises should be made.

These five criticisms of traditional medical ethics . . . suggest that an enlightened medical ethics will be in terms of a 'process' – the process of applying the principles of everyday morality to the scientific and economic complexities of patient care. Moral decisions in medicine are what can be called 'consequential' or 'resultant' in that they arise out of the professional, economic, and legal facts of given cases. Ethics is no substitute for a good diagnosis of the problem, skillfully carried out treatment or clearly communicated information, but equally in doing these things the doctor is at the same time engaging in moral and economic activity.[31]

However, it may be arguable that there is a difference between a doctor and others who provide vital services. It might be said that if a doctor were to refuse to treat in an emergency, he would be the subject of moral condemnation in a way that, say, an off-duty fireman who refused to help in a rescue, would not. It is important to remember that here we are talking about moral, not legal obligations. In the UK, a doctor has no legal obligation to stop at the scene of an accident and treat the injured. If he does, then he is obliged to treat with reasonable skill and care and he may be liable in negligence. The position of a non-medically qualified volunteer who assists at the scene of an accident is exactly the same – it is simply that the standard of care is different. The legal duty not to harm is the same for doctor and lay person alike. Is the doctor's moral obligation different? Harris suggests it is not:

See Chapter 6 ➡

Harris, J, *The Value of Life*[32]

We believe . . . that we should rescue trapped miners and other victims of accidents, or those shipwrecked, or the victims of hijackers of other hostage-takers; and, not least, those who can be rescued only by medical care. Some of these rescues can be performed by anyone who is on hand; others require all sorts of expertise from that of potholers, sailors, miners, engineers, firemen and so on, to specialised military personnel and those with medical skills. Very often, those of us who lack these skills can best help, and thus discharge our obligation to those at risk, by keeping well out of the way. All of this is perhaps obvious enough, but it helps us to see two important features of the obligation of health care professionals. The first is that *there is nothing special about their obligation in particular*. Just as there is no special category of person whose unique and first obligation it is to refrain from inflicting death, injury or suffering on the rest of us, so there is no one who is specially required, morally speaking, to undertake rescues.

It is also illuminating to consider the duty of beneficence in terms of Kant's perfect/imperfect duties. Kant considers generosity or beneficence as imperfect duties, which an individual has no right to demand, as he has a right, for example, to demand justice.

Of course, the doing of 'good' may, in the short term, necessitate the infliction of pain. Beauchamp and McCullough describe the 'balancing exercise' that may arise as follows:

Beauchamp, TL and McCullough, LB, *Medical Ethics*[33]

The basic roles and concepts that give substance to the principle of beneficence in medicine are as follows: the positive benefit the physician is under obligation to seek is the cure of disease and injury if there is a reasonable hope of cure; the harms to be avoided, prevented, or

---

31 © Gavin Mooney and Alistair McGuire 1988. Reprinted from *Medical Ethics and Economics in Health Care* edited by Gavin Mooney and Alistair McGuire (Oxford Medical Publications, 1988) by Oxford University Press.
32 London: Routledge & Kegan Paul, 1985.
33 Englewood Cliffs: Prentice-Hall, 1984.

removed are the pain and suffering of injury and disease. In addition, the physician is enjoined from doing harm. This consideration, too must be included in the beneficence model because physician interventions themselves can inflict unnecessary pain and suffering on patients. The Hippocratic texts hold that inflicting pain and suffering is permissible in those cases in which the physician is attempting to reverse a threat to health, eg, administering an emetic after the accidental ingestion of a poison. Inflicting such pain and suffering on a patient in order to eliminate a deadly substance from the body is justified because the patient is on balance benefited. When the patient cannot be benefited by further intervention, the inflicted pain and suffering is unnecessary and to be avoided. Thus, in its first formulation in Western medical ethics, the beneficence model of moral responsibility adapts the principle of beneficence to patient care by providing a medically oriented account of how to balance goods over harms.

The rosy spectacled view of the special role of beneficence is questioned by Pellegrino and Thomasma:

Pellegrino, ED and Thomasma, DC, *For the Patient's Good: The Restoration of Beneficence in Health Care*[34]

According to the Hippocratic Oath, the physician promises to 'follow that system of regimen which according to my ability and judgment I consider for the benefit of my patients'. Nowhere in the Hippocratic corpus is there any provision for the patient's view of things. In fact, in one place the relationship is described as being between 'one who orders and one who obeys'.

We shall see that this traditional principle, however, may be tempered to take into account the wishes of the patient.

The work of a doctor in the late 20th century is often highly technical in nature, depending upon pharmacy, engineering, computer technology and so on. It might be argued that this diminishes the particular duty of beneficence in some way. Beauchamp and McCullough suggest that it does not:

Beauchamp, TL and McCullough, LB, *Medical Ethics*[35]

In the history of medicine, the physician has primarily functioned in care-giving and comforting roles, with beneficence serving as the moral foundation of these roles. As medical science exploded in the 20th century, medicine was transformed into a more scientific and technical enterprise. Beneficent intervention remains, as ever, the moral foundation of the physician's role, a role powerfully augmented by medical science and technology. These remarkable new capacities created some moral problems in medicine, especially problems concerning the physician's authority, but they did not destroy medicine's tradition of beneficence.

But is this confidence that the traditional role of the physician has not been undermined misplaced? Much of the research which leads to treatment at the disposal of the physician has not been developed by physicians at all. Developments in genetics are a case in point. Once opportunities for genetic manipulation, for example, have been unleashed, how much power does the physician have to resist them?

The principle of beneficence is at work when we consider the doctrine of 'double effect'. Imagine a gravely ill patient in the last stages of terminal cancer. The patient is in pain and only a substantial dose of morphine will relieve the pain. However, such a large dose will also hasten the

---

34 Oxford: OUP, 1988.
35 Englewood Cliffs: Prentice-Hall, 1984.

patient's death. As far as the law is concerned this is not homicide, and as far as medical ethics is concerned, the principle of beneficence means that the doctor's only intention is to do good, ie relieve pain. The fact that death would also be hastened does not undermine the beneficent motive of the doctor. However, as we shall see, there are aspects of medical law where the principle of beneficence is undermined. First, in medical research patients may be subjected to randomised clinical trials (RCTs). This means that some patients will not be receiving any treatment at all but, unknown to them, will be given placebos, so that the researchers can compare their progress with that of the patients who are given drug treatment. It is arguable that this can never be consistent with the principle of beneficence unless the principle is interpreted as meaning beneficence towards patients in the sense of a *general* benefit to the sick. Similarly, it is accepted that doctors may breach their duty of confidentiality in respect of an individual patient in the wider public interest. In these circumstances, it can be argued, the principle of beneficence is only upheld if it is equated with some form of consequentialism.

1.2.2 Non-maleficence

The traditional duty to do good has been accompanied by the obligation to do no harm – *primum non nocere* (first, do no harm). This can be described in terms of Kant's perfect/imperfect duties distinction, ie the obligation not to harm people is a perfect duty whereas the obligation to good is restricted in that it would be impossible to fulfil a duty to benefit everyone and is therefore am imperfect duty.[36]

This principle might, for example, be used to justify the 'acts and omissions' distinction in the law relating to euthanasia. As we shall see, in the case of a very seriously ill patient, a doctor may not be obliged to continue to treat that patient. In other words, he can withdraw or omit to treat, and remain within the confines of the law. This is because the doctor may decide that the treatment is not benefiting the patient. That is consistent with the principle of beneficence because the doctor will say that the treatment is not, or would not, benefit the patient. The omission to treat is acceptable. However, the doctor is not legally permitted to give the patient a lethal injection to bring about death, even when 'natural' death is very close, as, it is argued, it would infringe the principle of non-maleficence. But it is arguable that the lethal injection would not be harmful as it might be the kindest way of treating a patient who is terminally ill and in great pain.

1.2.3 The nature of illness

Why is it necessary to consider this? It could be said that the presence of 'illness' or 'disease' is a straightforward factual matter. However, it is interesting to try and formulate a definition. Culver and Gert review the medical literature and select a number of definitions:

Culver, CM and Gert, B, *Philosophy in Medicine*[37]

Some past definitions of 'disease'
There have been many attempts to set out a formal definition of 'disease,' but among physicians only rarely has a distinction among 'disease', 'illness', 'injury' and related terms been recognised. Consequently, 'illness' is often used interchangeably with 'disease', and injuries are regarded merely as a subclass of diseases. What most of the following authors have

---

36 See Gillon, R, *Philosophical Medical Ethics*, Chichester: John Wiley, p 81, 1985.
37 New York: OUP, 1982.

intended to define is what we call a malady, so that in addition to diseases they have included injuries, illnesses, headaches and the like in their definitions. By not realising what they have done, however, they have often been misled by some particular feature of the term 'disease'.

Some definitions are general, vague, and too inclusive. Thus, a pathology textbook (Peery and Miller, 1971) states:

> Disease is any disturbance of the structure or function of the body or any of its parts; an imbalance between the individual and his environment; a lack of perfect health.

This seems to offer three separate but equivalent definitions. According to the first definition, clipping nails and puberty are diseases, as well as a symptomatic *situs inversus* (right-left reversal of position of bodily organs) and being tied to a chair. The second definition is too vague to be of any use, and the third is circular. A textbook on internal medicine (Talso and Remenchik, 1968) says:

> ... disease may be defined as deprivation or lack of ease, a discomfort or an annoy-ance, or a morbid condition of the body or of some organ or part thereof.

There are similar problems here. Two separate definitions are offered. The first is too sweeping and would include inflation, quarrelsome in-laws, poor television reception, and ill-fitting shoes, while the second is circular and depends on the phrase 'morbid condition', which is merely a synonym for 'disease'.

Most texts on medicine and pathology make no attempt to define disease, which is appro-priate enough since the exercise is irrelevant to their purposes. Thus, it might be said in defence of the above attempts that they were probably not meant to be taken very seriously.

One cluster of definitions which is meant to be taken seriously utilises a dynamic meta-phor in which a person is pictured as constantly interacting and adapting to changes in his environment; disease then corresponds to a failure in that adaptation. An early expression of this definition is found in White's 1926 book, *The Meaning of Disease*:

> Disease can only be that state of the organism that for the time being, at least, is fighting a losing game whether the battle be with temperature, water, micro-organisms, disappointment or what not. In any instance, it may be visualised as the reaction of the organism to some sort of energy impact, addition or deprivation.

Thus, one wrestler held down by another is suffering a disease. A more modern version is found in Engel's 1962 book, *Psychological Development in Health and Disease:*

> When adaptation or adjustment fail and the pre-existing dynamic steady state is disrupted, then a state of disease may be said to exist until a new balance is restored which may again permit the effective interaction with the environment.

Aside from the ambiguities and the question begging inherent in 'adaptation' and 'balance', the emphasis in this definition (and the preceding one) on the deterioration of a previously more normal state seems to rule out all congenital and hereditary diseases . . .

JG Scadding (1959, 1963, 1967) has written a series of papers on the definition of disease. In the most recent of these, he offers the following 'formal definition':

> A disease is the sum of the abnormal phenomena displayed by a group of living organisms in association with a specified common characteristic or set of character-istics by which they differ from the norm for their species in such a way as to place them at a biological disadvantage.

Scadding's definition is an improvement over those previously cited. He explicitly introduces the notion of deviation from a norm for a species which, though it does not deserve the prominence he gives it, is necessary for understanding the essential elements of the concept of malady. His 'biological disadvantage' criterion also points in the right direction but is too vague. Kendell, in a recent paper (1975), interprets 'biological disadvantage' as meaning decreased fertility or longevity. But this does not work. Even Kendell recognises that his revision of Scadding's definition leaves one with the 'rather disconcerting' result that a condition such as psoriasis would not qualify as a disease.

Several recent authors have also correctly identified aspects of disease. Spitzer and Endicott (1978) include in their definition of 'a medical disorder' that it is intrinsically associated with distress, disability, or certain types of disadvantage. We think this definition is on the right track. Goodwin and Guze (1979) consider as a disease 'any condition associated with discomfort, pain, disability, death, or an increased liability to these states, regarded by physicians and the public as properly the responsibility of the medical profession . . .'

Note the concluding phrase 'regarded by physicians and the public as properly the responsibility of the medical profession'. Is 'illness' that which a doctor thinks should be treated? A doctor faced with a hypochondriac may well form the conclusion that the symptoms complained of are imagined and that the person is not ill, and therefore no treatment is given regardless of the fact that the patient may have some organic disorder, which would be treated by another doctor who did not know about the hypochondria. This may sound simplistic, but consider treatment for infertile people. Are they ill? Or diseased? The answer is no, but they receive 'treatment' because doctors think that they should. It may be argued that it is society which decides what conditions merit treatment and what do not, but does that underestimate the power of information and medical technology, concentrated as it is, if not in the hands of doctors exclusively, in the hands of medical science? Society did not demand heart transplants until the first operation had been performed.

 SELF-TEST QUESTION

There is evidence that genes which 'cause' things such as baldness may be isolated and eradicated. This would be a 'medical' procedure. Would it mean that baldness would become an illness?

1.2.4 The medical humanities movement

A similar move away from the scientific emphasis that is so much a part of western medicine is the medical humanities movement. It has been around in the USA for some time, but only for the past four or five years has it found a voice in the UK. A journal 'Medical Humanities' published by the Journal of Medical Ethics aims to promote this:

Greaves, D, and Evans, M, Editorial, (2000) J Med Ethics: Medical Humanities 26(1):

. . . [medical humanities] is a second generational response to the shortcomings of a medical culture dominated by scientific, technical and managerial approaches . . . [there are] two main formulations of medical humanities . . . [t]he first is concerned with complementing medical science and technology through the contrasting perspective of the arts and humanities, but without either side impinging on the other. The second aims to refocus the whole of medicine in relation to an understanding of what it is to be fully human; the reuniting of technical and humanistic knowledge and practice is central to this enterprise.

It is not clear how far the first of these aims is particularly related to medicine unless it is to point up the statement often made: 'medicine is not an exact science'. This relates particularly to the role played by patient psychology in the development of illness and recovery. The second formulation might be a way of moving to what is often described as patient centred medicine, which seeks to emphasise all the non-medical components of medical decision-making, and in particular emphasises communication skills in the doctor–patient relationship.[38] We should also think back to the universalisation/moral relativism debate and how this might relate to this approach. Similarly, we are about to discuss the opposing stances of paternalism and autonomy and conclude that this might be a false dichotomy and that collaborative decision-making takes the best of both these worlds. The 'medical humanities' approach can embrace this.

It is useful to consider these sorts of approaches when making decisions about a patient's capacity to make medical decisions and what might be in the best interests of a patient who lacks capacity.

See Chapter 3

See Chapter 4

1.3 The Case for Paternalism

1.3.1 Introduction

In this and the following sections, we will look at the arguments which may be advanced, respectively, in favour of a paternalistic approach to medicine, and in favour of the primacy of patient autonomy. These two theories are described by Pellegrino and Thomasma:

Pellegrino, ED and Thomasma, DC, *For the Patient's Good: The Restoration of Beneficence in Health Care*[39]

The first, inherited from the Enlightenment, stresses the liberty and autonomy of the individual. It gathered strength in the 19th century in response to the depreciation of personal worth that accompanied the Industrial Revolution. This theory grounds ethics in rights, duties and obligations. The second theory stresses social utility rather than individual autonomy. Ironically, it too gained ascendancy during the Industrial Revolution to counter the social atomism of a purely individualistic ethic. This theory stresses social good, rules of conduct, and social accountability. Mill laid the foundation for such theories when he proposed the principle of autonomy, on the one hand, and the principle of utility, on the other.

Applied to physician–patient relationship, the first theory imposes on the physician the obligation of respect for the patient's self-determination. The second theory requires that the physician act to maximise benefits and goods even if this might demand acting without the patient's consent. It sanctions overriding the patient's autonomous decision if that decision is not judged by the physician to be in the patient's or society's good.

When considering the respective positions of the paternalist and the anti-paternalist, it is important to consider two things. First, as we shall see, the consent of the patient is necessary before any medical treatment can take place. This might be said to reflect the anti-paternalist view. The patient can refuse simple life-saving treatment and there is no mechanism for imposing it upon him. However, at least in English law, the arbiter of what the patient needs to know before he consents or refuses is the doctor. It might be said that this reflects a paternalist viewpoint. Secondly, the patient must be competent, ie have sufficient mental capacity to make a treatment decision. The

---

38 See, for example, Evans, RG, 'Patient centred medicine: reason, emotion, and human spirit? Some philosophical reflections on being with patients' (2003) J Med Ethics: Medical Humanities 29:8.
39 Oxford: OUP, 1988.

doctor will decide whether the patient is competent. If he lacks competence, he may be treated in his 'best interests'. When reading the following, keep these points in mind.

1.3.2 What is paternalism?

When we considered the principle of beneficence, we noted that it is a one-sided principle: the doctor is *doing good to/for the patient*. Beneficence does not mean the same as paternalism (the recognition of the patient's right to self-determination may be part of beneficence), but a narrower view of beneficence is compatible with paternalism. The paternalistic doctor 'knows best' and regards himself as being the best judge as to what is for the patient's own good. It is interesting to consider the duty of beneficence in relation to the parent-child relationship (the term paternalistic meaning to act like a father): although the parent may be said to have a duty of non-maleficence towards his child, does he have a positive duty to do good?

John Harris distinguishes paternalism from moralism:

Harris, J, *The Value of Life*[40]

When health care professionals accept that their first duty is to act always in the best interests of their patients they are in effect saying that they are concerned for the welfare of their patients and that this is in no way inconsistent with manifesting 'respect for persons'. Welfare is not here used as a technical term – it means what it usually means, 'the state or condition of doing or being well', which will include things like happiness, health and living standards.

An initial problem is that concern for the welfare of others is compatible both with paternalism and with moralism. Briefly, paternalism is the belief that it can be right to order the lives of others for their own good, irrespective of their own wishes or judgments. The characteristic cry of the paternalist is: 'Don't do that, it isn't good for you.' *Moralism*, on the other hand, is the belief that it can be right to order the lives of others so that 'morality' may be preserved. The characteristic cry of the moralist is: 'Don't do that, it's wicked.'

Both the paternalist and the moralist are genuinely concerned for the welfare of others. They argue that it cannot be in your interest, nor can it be conducive to your being in a state of doing or being well, if you either do what isn't good for you or act immorally. Despite the genuineness of this moral concern, both paternalism and moralism involve treating the agent as an incompetent. They deny the individual control over her own life and moral destiny and treat her as incompetent to run her own life as she chooses. While both involve genuine concern for the welfare of others, neither can lay claim to demonstrating respect for their wishes.

But although Harris is right in saying that we are not respecting the wishes of the person whom we exhort to do good, or refrain from doing bad, we would nevertheless argue that we are entitled to do it. If you intervene to prevent another from picking someone's pocket, you are certainly not respecting the pickpocket's wishes, but you are not wrong to do this. Cannot we say the same thing about paternalism? The paternalist's argument would be that, although you are not respecting the patient's wishes when he says he does not want a life-saving operation and you go ahead and perform it anyway, nevertheless you are not wrong to save his life.

Hart describes paternalism as the protection of people against themselves, and maintains that, although respect for individual autonomy is very much a part of modern life, there has been a general decline in the belief that we are the best judges of our own best interests. Referring to the libertarian views of JS Mill, Hart says:

---

40 London: Routledge & Kegan Paul, 1985.

Hart, HLA, *Law, Liberty and Morality*[41]

[There is] an increased awareness of a great range of factors which diminish the significance to be attached to an apparently free choice or to consent. Choices may be made or consent given without adequate reflection or appreciation of the consequences; or in pursuit of merely transitory desires; or in various predicaments when the judgment is likely to be clouded; or under inner psychological compulsion; or under pressure by others of a kind too subtle to be susceptible of proof in a law court. Underlying Mill's extreme fear of paternalism there perhaps is a conception of what a normal human being is like which now seems not to correspond to the facts. Mill, in fact, endows him with much of the psychology of a middle-aged man whose desires are relatively fixed, not liable to be artificially stimulated by external influences; who knows what he wants and what gives him satisfaction or happiness; and who pursues these things when he can.

As far as medicine is concerned, this argument states that paternalism is justified when, in the judgment of the doctor, the patient does not exhibit sufficient of the features of Hart's middle-aged man. The patient may be too young; the patient may have limited intelligence or limited education or may have a volatile personality given to acts of impetuosity. The doctor, on the other hand, is educated, impartial, knowledgeable and has only the best interests of the patient at heart. This grading of patients – and in consequence the way in which a doctor is entitled to regard them – is reflected in some of the case law (see, for example, the case of *Sidaway v Board of Governors of the Bethlem Royal Hospital and the Maudsley Hospital*[42] where Lord Diplock[43] states that an educated judge would 'naturally' want to ask questions about the risks of medical treatment before he consented to it).

See Chapter 3

1.3.2.1 Strong and weak paternalism

It is arguable that the above view, ie that some patients do not have sufficient education, etc, to make valid decisions, does not support paternalism in any form, but only where the patient's views are disregarded because of the circumstances, or something in the patient's own character. Writers sometimes refer to the difference as that between 'strong' and 'weak' (or 'limited') paternalism.

Childress describes the justification for limited paternalism as follows:

Childress, JF, *Who Should Decide? Paternalism in Health Care*[44]

The principle of limited paternalism

Parents sometimes override their children's wishes in order to protect them. . . . This example from familial relations yields two conditions that are frequently invoked to justify medical paternalism: (1) the defects, encumbrances, and limitations of a person's decision-making and acting; and (2) the probability of harm to that person unless there is intervention.

If the second condition – probable harm – is held to be sufficient to justify paternalism, apart from the person's incapacity for decision-making, we have extended or strong paternalism. According to this position, paternalistic interventions can be justified when a patient's risk-benefit analysis is unreasonable even though he is competent and his wishes, choices, or actions are informed and voluntary. If, however, the first set of conditions is held to be necessary, we have limited or weak paternalism, which allows paternalistic interventions only when

---

41 Oxford: OUP, 1963.
42 [1985] AC 871.
43 See further Ch 3.
44 Oxford: OUP, 1982.

a person's wishes, choices, or actions are defective because of incompetence, ignorance, or some internal or external constraint.

. . .

If these two conditions are jointly necessary for justified active paternalism, and if only limited paternalism is justified, we are able to express both the principle of beneficence and the principle of respect for persons. In limited paternalism, agents meet the needs of other persons without insulting them. . . .

Since both of these conditions are necessary to justify paternalistic acts, it is possible to start with either one. An apparent reason to start with prevention or removal of harm, or provision of benefit, is that this consideration frequently triggers paternalistic actions. In the order of experience, perception of risk to the patient, apart from intervention, usually precedes and provokes an assessment of the patient's competence to decide. . . . In view of customary medical practice, there are two good reasons for beginning with the patient's incompetence as a necessary condition for justified paternalism. First, to begin with the prevention or removal of harm may appear to give this condition priority and may play into the hands of strong paternalists. Second, even though in practice there may be little interest in the patient's competence unless there are risks, from a moral point of view the assessment of the patient's competence should be somewhat independent of the risks. Otherwise, strong paternalism could masquerade as weak paternalism, since – the argument might go – no competent person would knowingly and voluntarily accept some risks.

Culver and Gert put forward two examples of paternalism, one of which they maintain is justified, the other not:

Culver, CM and Gert, B, *Philosophy in Medicine*[45]

Case 8–1

Mr K was brought to the emergency room by his wife and a police officer. Mrs K had confessed to her husband earlier that evening that she was having an affair with one of his colleagues. He had become acutely agitated and depressed and, after several hours of mounting tension, told her he was going to kill himself so 'you'll have the freedom to have all the lovers you want'. She became frightened and called the police because there were loaded guns in the house and she knew her husband was an impulsive man.

In the emergency room Mr K would do little more than glower at Dr T, his wife, and the officer. He seemed extremely tense and agitated. Dr T decided that for Mr K's own protection he should be hospitalised but Mr K refused. Dr T therefore committed Mr K to the hospital for a 72 hour emergency detention.

How could Dr T attempt to justify his paternalistic commitment of Mr K? He could claim that by depriving Mr K of his freedom, there was a great likelihood that he was preventing the occurrence of a much greater evil: Mr K's death, or serious injury. Dr T could further claim that in his professional experience the overwhelming majority of persons in Mr K's condition who were hospitalised did subsequently recover from their state of agitated depression and acknowledge the irrational character of their former suicidal desires.

Note that Dr T need not claim that self-inflicted death is an evil of such magnitude that paternalistic intervention to prevent it is always justified. Rather, he could claim that it is justified in Mr K's case on several counts. First, Mr K's desire to kill himself seems irrational; while one may explain his desire, using psychodynamic concepts, he appears to have no adequate

---

45 New York: OUP, 1982.

reason for killing himself. An adequate reason would be a belief on his part that his death would result in the avoiding of great evil(s) or the attaining of great goods for himself or others. (His statement to his wife ['You'll have . . . all the lovers you want'] sarcastically expresses an altruistic reason which, even if taken literally, would not be an adequate reason for his suicide.) Second, there is evidence that he suffers from a condition that is well known to be transient. Third, the violation of a moral rule (deprivation of freedom) which Dr T has carried out results in Mr K's suffering a much lesser evil than the evil (death) which Mr K may perpetrate on himself.

But it is not sufficient justification for Dr T merely to show that the evils prevented for Mr K by his paternalistic action outweigh the evils caused to Mr K; he must also be willing to publicly advocate the deprivation of Mr K's freedom in these circumstances. That is, he must be willing to advocate to all rational persons that in these circumstances everyone may be deprived of his freedom for a limited period of time. We believe that, accepting the case as described, not only could Dr T advocate to all rational persons that Mr K may be deprived of his freedom but also that, if they accepted the facts of the case and the conditions of public advocacy, all rational persons would agree with Dr T's judgment completely. Thus, Dr T's paternalistic behaviour is strongly justified.

By contrast, Culver and Gert consider the following:

Case 8–2

Mrs R, a 29 year old mother, is hospitalised with symptoms of abdominal pain, weight loss, weakness, and swelling of the ankles. An extensive medical workup is inconclusive, and exploratory abdominal surgery is carried out which reveals a primary ovarian cancer with extensive spread to other abdominal organs. Her condition is judged to be too far advanced for surgical relief, and her life expectancy is estimated to be at most a few months. Despite her oft-repeated requests to be told 'where I stand and what I face', Dr E tells both the patient and her husband that the diagnosis is still unclear but that he will see her weekly as an out-patient. At the time of discharge she is feeling somewhat better than at admission, and Dr E hopes that the family will have a few happy weeks together before her condition worsens and they must be told the truth.

Dr E's behaviour is clearly paternalistic: he has deceived Mrs R for what he believes is her benefit; he knows that he is violating the moral rule against deception without her consent; and he views her as someone who is competent to give or refuse valid consent to being told the truth.

Dr E could attempt to justify his paternalistic act by claiming that the evil – psychological suffering – he hoped to prevent by his deception is significantly greater than the evil, if any, he caused by lying. While this might be true in this particular case, it is by no means certain. By his deception, Dr E is depriving Mrs R and her family of the opportunity to make those plans that would enable her family to deal more adequately with her death. In the circumstances of this case as described, Mrs R's desire to know the truth is a rational one; in fact, there is no evidence of any irrational behaviour or desires on her part. This contrasts sharply to Mr K's desire to kill himself, which is clearly irrational. Furthermore, although we regard Mr K's desire not to be deprived of freedom, considered in isolation, as a rational one, we would not consider it rational for one to choose a high probability of death over the loss of a few days of freedom

Arguably, we can see a weak form of paternalism operating when we consider our attitude to organ donation and non-therapeutic medical research. It is unlawful in the UK to sell a non-regenerative organ for transplant. Similarly, we prevent anything other than modest payments for those who undergo non-therapeutic research (ie healthy volunteers). Many people who would not regard themselves as paternalists in the context of medical treatment might support these prohibitions on the basis that it is offensive for there to be a 'trade' in

See Chapter ← 11

human organs or for people to sell their bodies for the purposes of research. However, is this not a form of paternalism, albeit one based upon the principle of non-maleficence (as opposed to paternalism in relation to medical treatment which is based upon the principle of beneficence)?

1.3.3 Paternalism and the sanctity of life principle

Both Mill and Kant would accept the sanctity of life principle as this stems from the inherent value of the individual. The duty of beneficence has this principle at its heart. A paternalist might argue that the doctor's duty to do good and to uphold the sanctity of life principle will, on occasion, justifiably, override patient autonomy. For example, in Chapter 3 we look at several cases where the courts have had to consider the refusal by women of consent to Caesarean section operations to deliver their children. It has been held that the women's refusals must be respected, even if there is a strong likelihood that both mother and foetus will not survive. However, there is an argument that the principle of the sanctity of life might, in certain circumstances, override the woman's refusal.

1.3.4 Paternalism and the doctor's duty of beneficence

It might be said that it is bad for those involved in health care to be forced to stand helpless in the face of a refusal of life-saving treatment and witness an unnecessary death. This view might be illustrated by the role of doctors and other health care workers in the treatment of suicide attempts. Someone who attempts to take their own life can be treated without their consent. From what arises the right to override the patient's wish to die? Is it because the true wishes of the patient may not be known (it could be a 'cry for help' or an accident), or is it because of the dominance of the sanctity of life principle? It should be noted that health authorities have been held liable when a patient has committed suicide whilst under their care, if there has been inadequate supervision. 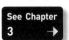 Again, arguably, this is about sanctity of life and beneficence: it is inappropriate that hospitals should be places of avoidable and self-inflicted deaths; they are places for healing and the saving of lives.

See Chapter 3

1.3.5 Paternalism and a duty to oneself?

In Culver and Gert's example of the patient at risk of suicide, it was assumed that paternalism would eventually give way to autonomy. Is there a sustainable ethical argument that one has a duty to oneself to live and to live a healthy life, and, therefore, treatment against one's wishes may be justifiable? It will be recalled that the intuitionist philosopher, WD Ross, said that one of the intuitively good principles was the duty of self-improvement.

Similarly, Kant, whose moral philosophy stated that human life is intrinsically valuable, puts duty before 'natural inclinations'. For example, he thought suicide permissible only if it was to avoid moral degradation. This was based upon the principle that only human beings can uphold the moral law and, therefore, for as long as they are not morally degraded, they have a duty to do that. Would this justify medical paternalism on the basis that the patient has a duty to live a healthy life and if, in the opinion of his doctors, he is not doing so, he must be treated against his will?

1.4 The Case for Patient Autonomy

Paternalism has an old-fashioned ring to it. Two American academics, Pellegrino and Thomasma, comment as follows:

Pellegrino, ED and Thomasma, DC, *For the Patient's Good: The Restoration of Beneficence in Health Care*[46]

The sources of . . . resistance to medical paternalism are many: the political and ethical philosophy of individual rights; the higher educational level of today's public; the latter's awareness of the powers and dangers of medical technology; a distrust of experts; the rise of consumerism; and the moral challenges of the Vietnam War, the civil rights movement, and the campus revolts of the '60s and early '70s. The convergence of these forces has been powerful enough to erode the 2,500 year old tradition of medical status contained in beneficent authoritarianism.

1.4.1 Autonomy

It is in the assertion that the right to autonomous medical decision-making is paramount that Mill's libertarian philosophy is most evident: the only justification for imposing medical treatment on a patient against his will is to prevent harm to others. (In the section on utilitarianism and autonomy we will consider whether non-consensual medical treatment may ever by justified on the basis that it will prevent harm to others, but let us assume for the present that it will not.) Beauchamp and McCullough describe the autonomy principle as being an extension of the right to individual sovereignty to limit the authority of the state:

Beauchamp, TL and McCullough, LB, *Medical Ethics*[47]

Individual sovereignty needs protection for two reasons. First, there is a danger of imbalance in power between the individual and the State (or other parties) in favour of the latter. Individual rights provide a corrective to this imbalance by ensuring that individuals as individuals will be given due consideration and respect. Second, conflicts arise between an individual's perception of his or her best interests and another's perception of those interests. Rights of individual sovereignty protect an individual's freedom to choose his or her best interests.

Much of the debate surrounding the principle of autonomy concerns the right of a patient to refuse life-saving treatment. Earlier we considered how far there may be an obligation to prevent suicide. It is interesting to note that it has been said that the liberty to commit suicide may be seen as 'an index of high civilisation', because the act goes against the most basic of our instincts, that of self-preservation.[48]

1.4.2 The right to self-determination

Is the principle of autonomy equivalent to the right to self-determination? Is this 'right' really a liberty in the sense that there is no claim against anyone in the Hohfeldian sense? Certainly the right to self-determination could not be relied upon to impose duties on others to provide medical treatment.

There is some debate as to whether autonomy is part of the right to privacy. Wellman considers the issue:

Wellman, C, *An Approach to Rights*[49]

. . . how is this right [to privacy] related to personal autonomy? A tempting hypothesis is that autonomy is located within one portion of this right because one of the constitutionally protected areas of privacy is that of private decisions. Thus, even though the right to privacy is not the

---

46 Oxford: OUP, 1988.
47 Englewood Cliffs: Prentice-Hall, 1984.
48 See Alvarez, A, *The Savage God: A Study of Suicide*, London: Weidenfeld & Nicolson, 1971.
49 Dordrecht: Kluwer Academic, 1997.

liberty-right to make and act on private decisions, it includes the claim-right that others not interfere with these private decisions, for any such interference would be an invasion of a protected area of privacy. I very much doubt, however, that this direct and essential connection between privacy and autonomy has ever been recognised by the courts. For one thing, the expression 'a private decision' is conspicuous by its absence from the opinions in the privacy cases, even in *Roe* [*v Wade*] and *Quinlan* that centre on the abortion decision and the decision to refuse medical treatment, respectively. Moreover, this interpretation misrepresents the reasoning of the courts. The argument in *Roe* is not that the abortion decision is constitutionally protected because it is a private decision, but that it is encompassed by the right to privacy because it involves the exercise of one of the fundamental liberties recognised in the US Constitution. Hence, the emphasis is upon how fundamental, not how personal and private, the decision is.

1.4.3 The political approach and the rejection of 'social control'

Those who support the overriding importance of the autonomy principle are lent support by the way in which psychiatry was used in the former Soviet Union, where some political dissidents were diagnosed as being 'psychiatrically ill' and compulsorily detained in hospital. The writer Thomas Szasz, whose work is considered further in Chapter 9, cites this abuse of medicine in a number of his publications.[50] The argument is that illness is a value-laden concept and any form of paternalism runs the risk of doctors branding patients with 'illness' and subsequent treatment. It is easy to see how this abuse can take place with something as nebulous as mental illness, but could this sort of abuse take place in respect of other forms of illness? Perhaps alcoholism, for example, could be so regarded, and 'imperfections' such as baldness might be categorised as illnesses.

1.4.4 Utilitarianism and autonomy

It is interesting to consider the interaction of these two concepts, because both were embraced in the philosophy of JS Mill. His libertarian views imply that one must be free to pursue a conception of life that is conducive to human flourishing. However, is there one conception of the good life, and if not, how do we maximise welfare? Similarly, if one is looking at the consequences of actions, if the exercise of one's autonomy adversely affects other people, then are not the two principles incompatible? In the context of refusal of life-saving treatment, it may be said that the right to self-determination is in conflict with utility because the consequences of the refusal may be bad for the family left behind: the loss of a breadwinner (the family is now dependent upon society for support) and the infliction of grief. It is arguable that this reflects one of the deficiencies in the utilitarian approach: it allows only a limited role for basic rights. Alternatively, it could be said that subjecting people to violation of their physical integrity has worse consequences for society than does respecting their bodily integrity. If this argument were accepted then respect for autonomy would be an essential element of any utilitarian account of medical ethics.

1.4.5 Rationality

Giving effect to autonomy in relation to medical treatment presupposes that the patient is competent to make decisions about such treatment. Do these decisions have to be rational? GEM Anscombe[51] gives an interesting example of having a reason for doing something. She cites the

---

50 See, for example, Szasz, TS, *Law, Liberty and Psychiatry: An Inquiry into the Social Uses of Mental Health Practices*, London: Routledge & Kegan Paul, 1974.
51 See *Intention*, Oxford: Blackwell, 1963.

example of a man who wants a saucer of mud. He is asked whether he wants it to study its chemistry, whether he finds mud aesthetically pleasing, whether he has a practical use for it and so on; he answers all questions in the negative: he just wants a saucer of mud for no reason. Surely we would want to conclude that he doesn't want a saucer of mud at all. By analogy, there would have to be reasons for making decisions about medical treatment. However, these can be, and as we shall see, often are, bizarre. Do we conclude that, because of this, the patient lacks decision-making capacity? As we shall see from examining the case law in Chapter 3, the answer is 'no'. Decision-making capacity may be present despite the fact that a patient holds a number of strange and, apparently unsupportable, beliefs. Perhaps the correct view is that if these beliefs are genuinely held, and form part of the patient's 'world view', then they should be respected. In other words, unlike the man who wants the saucer of mud for no reason whatsoever, the patient has reasons that *make sense to him* and, as such, should be respected.

1.4.6 Autonomy and beneficence

Even the most ardent proponent of the principle of autonomy would accept that it would be wrong to deny someone medical treatment because they were incapable of consenting. If it were otherwise, no mentally incompetent patient would ever receive treatment. However, the argument would be that in the cases of children and adults lacking capacity, such treatment is not contrary to the principle of autonomy because they are not autonomous human beings. Similarly, people suffering from certain forms of mental disorder may be compulsorily detained and treated for that disorder without consent, and it is argued that this is carried out to *restore* their autonomy, and therefore entirely consistent with the principle.

See Chapter 9

1.4.7 Autonomy – a step too far?

Charles Foster has written a provocative book in which he challenges the current ascendancy of the 'autonomy' approach. He acknowledges that the pre-eminence of the concept has roots in a valid objection to the unacceptable face of paternalism, but believes that this has gone too far.

Foster C, Choosing life, choosing death: the tyranny of autonomy in medical ethics and law[52]

Autonomy grew up as a street fighter, and was blooded in some genuinely noble battles against medical paternalism. But like so many rulers with this sort of pedigree, it has quickly forgotten its democratic roots, and grown fat and brutal in power.

Foster argues that the emphasis on autonomy is also illustrated by the paramountcy of clinical judgement in medical decision-making, i.e. noting that this is an example of doctors being able to rely on the importance of their *own* autonomy. He refers to the rare condition of body dysmorphia, whereby some people experience pain and distress in the belief that one or more appendage is alien to them:

The law steadfastly refuses to impose on doctors (other than by contract) any obligation to perform any particular medical treatment. Also, a doctor can choose with whom he enters into a doctor–patient relationship. . .

Since Patient X cannot demand of Doctor Y that procedure Z be performed by Y, can X legitimately complain that his autonomy rights are affected? Since these rules are designed (inter alia) to protect the autonomy rights of Y, that is a complaint that autonomy will be slightly embarrassed to support . . .

---

52 Oxford: Hart, 2009.

Autonomy in the medico-legal arena is (rightly) much more concerned with preventing unwanted violations than in guaranteeing a right to positive benefits. For that reason it has little to say about the vexed business of resource allocation: it is happy to acknowledge that that is the province of other principles. Likewise, it is slow to accept the brief from the patient with body image disorder who begs the surgeon, in autonomy's own language, to remove the objectively normal but subjectively horrific limbs.

Undoubtedly there is an argument that emphasis on autonomy alone or paternalism alone impoverishes medical ethics and that both these can be accommodated within a coherent framework.

1.5 Paternalism v Autonomy – a False Dichotomy?

Using the principle of beneficence, the paternalist will justify treating patients against their will, or withholding information from them which is 'bad for them'. We have seen that, even within the philosophy of autonomy, there may be justified intervention, although the advocate of autonomy would argue that the patient in those cases is not truly autonomous. However, when we look at decision-making capacity, we will find that it is by no means easy to decide whether someone has sufficient capacity to make truly autonomous decisions. It might be thought that this adds fuel to the argument of the paternalists. However, it is arguable that precisely because it can be difficult to assess capacity, it is all the more important to guard against the paternalist declaring someone incapable in order to do what he thinks is best for them. These difficulties might make us wonder whether the traditional opposition of paternalism and autonomy might not give way to something which recognises the best in each of them. Some writers have endeavoured to find a more conciliatory approach, which accommodates both models.

1.5.1 Collaborative decision-making

Pellegrino and Thomasma say that there can never be a single model to describe the doctor–patient relationship adequately. They state that the principle of respect for persons leads to two moral duties:

Pellegrino, ED and Thomasma, DC, *For the Patient's Good: The Restoration of Beneficence in Health Care*[53]

The first is to respect the self-determination or autonomy of others. The second . . . is to help restore that autonomy or help establish it when it is absent. Looked at in this way, beneficence is seen to be a direct consequence of a fundamental moral principle and the guiding duty of medicine. If this is true, then the autonomy model is necessarily incomplete. So, too, is the paternalistic model.

In this regard, other writers have suggested that it would be preferable for medical decision-making to be conceived of as a kind of collaborative effort:

Teff, H, 'Consent to medical procedures: paternalism, self-determination or therapeutic alliance'[54]

It has been argued that the pursuit of a therapeutic alliance, in the sense of a genuine collaborative effort, is desirable in so far as it can facilitate a beneficial outcome. Quite apart from the

---

53 Oxford: OUP, 1988.
54 (1985) 101 LQR 450.

fact that for many medical conditions there is either no specific remedy or the effectiveness of treatment is unknown, the doctor cannot intuitively know precisely what constitutes health or well being for a particular patient. The optimum 'outcome' is not necessarily to be equated with the technically successful result of a given operation, but may embrace a prognosis of the patient's subsequent medical and psychological condition and ability to function, as well as other social and financial considerations where relevant.

When medical procedures, especially invasive ones, are contemplated, doctor–patient relationships are often fraught with uncertainty and ambiguity. There is no *a priori* reason to assume that a doctor or surgeon possesses the kind of psychological or moral insight that would enable him to decide unaided what is most appropriate. The relative importance which patients attach, for example, to quality as against length of life, and to physical integrity or appearance as against diminution of pain, may reflect personal values, circumstances and priorities of which the surgeon, in particular, is initially unaware and may never become sufficiently apprised. It is apparently common practice in English hospitals for the information deemed relevant to patient consent to be provided by 'the most junior and inexperienced doctor, who will not perform the operation and who knows nothing of the likely complications'. . .

1.5.2 A fiduciary relationship

That the doctor–patient relationship might be a fiduciary relationship has yet to be accepted by the English courts (see, for example, the judgment of Lord Scarman in *Sidaway v Board of Governors of the Bethlem Royal Hospital and the Maudsley Hospital*[55]). However, some commentators have suggested that this may be a plausible analysis of the relationship. What is a fiduciary relationship? Peter Bartlett describes it as follows:

Bartlett, P, 'Doctors as fiduciaries: equitable regulation of the doctor–patient relationship'[56]

A fiduciary relationship attracts the attention of equity. The term apparently arose in the 19th century, when a variety of relationships held by equity to be 'on trust' were no longer necessarily flowing from 'trusts' themselves in any meaningful sense. With this motley origin, it is not surprising that fiduciary relationships themselves differ widely in the duties equity imposes on them. Consider the examples of lawyers and trustees. Certainly, one would expect a duty of undivided loyalty to the beneficiary or client in each case, and one would not expect the fiduciary to make a profit from the relationship outside that expressly authorised. There are equally firm differences, however. Unless inconsistent with his or her duty to the court, the lawyer acts on the instructions of the client, even when the instructions do not reflect the lawyer's view of the client's best interest. Trustees, by comparison, act in the beneficiary's best financial interest in any event. Where the beneficiary is in a relatively weak position in the control of the trust, the client is in control of the legal matter.

This has led a number of scholars to argue that it is inappropriate to think of the application of fiduciary relationships as a class at all, but rather specific relationships attracting specific collections of fiduciary duties. . .

Further flexibility is introduced through the distinction between fact-based and status-based fiduciary obligations, the latter being based in relationships traditionally recognised by equity and attracting a broader array of fiduciary obligations, and the former based in specific fact situations and attracting only some fiduciary obligations. The advantage of this approach is that the courts may perceive an increased flexibility to extend obligations beyond the traditional fiduciary situations to offer specific equitable remedies in specific situations, without setting broad precedent.

55 [1985] AC 871.
56 (1997) Med L Rev 193.

Is it arguable that the fiduciary model could remove the paternalism–autonomy divide? For example, could the relationship of trust justify paternalistic treatment as long as the doctor was totally candid with the patient? But there may be an inherent problem here: if the doctor is candid and the patient refuses the treatment, then the 'fiduciary' nature of the relationship does not assist in resolving the problem.

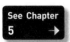 However, it is clear that aspects of the doctor–patient relationship can be fiduciary in nature, such as the duty of confidentiality and, whilst the English courts have been reluctant to accept the model in the context of access to medical records, a fiduciary duty may be applicable.

See Chapter 5 →

 SELF-TEST QUESTION

We will see that when we consider the treatment of children, the current approach of the courts is that some young people under the age of 16 are capable of making decisions about their own medical treatment, but are not capable of refusing treatment that their doctors wish them to have. How do you regard this in the light of the discussion we have just had on paternalism and autonomy?

1.6 Justice in the Allocation of Health Resources

The foregoing sections have considered the treatment of patients when they have not wanted treatment, or where the patients' medical conditions have not been fully revealed to them, or where treatment information has been withheld or restricted. A scenario we have not yet considered consists of a patient requiring treatment, and being refused, or a doctor ready and willing to treat a patient, but unable to do so because of lack of resources.

Most of us would agree that resources should be distributed fairly, or in accordance with justice. However, this bland statement gets us nowhere unless we decide the basis of a fair distribution. Concepts of justice often present three different models for distribution. First, resources may be distributed in accordance with merit. This would mean that the most deserving persons, for example, in terms of moral worth or contribution to society, would receive health care as a matter of priority. Secondly, resources may be distributed 'equally'. However, this presupposes that we have a test for deciding whether the persons concerned are equal. Certainly they are entitled to equal respect and consideration, but that in itself may not be enough. This tempts us to adopt the third model, which is that resources be distributed in accordance with need.

Our ethical dilemmas have previously been about the nature of the doctor–patient relationship in a one to one sense. Now we are looking at the relationship between the doctor and many of his patients. Does this undermine the cosy beneficence model, where the doctor's only concern is to do his best for the patient?

Newdick comments on the issue of clinical freedom and the Hippocratic duty to act in the best interests of patients:

Newdick, C, *Who Should We Treat?*[57]

'Waste' is not a neutral word. Governments, health service managers, doctors, patients, and citizens may each have differing ideas about how resources should be spent. Used as a way of insisting that individual patients receive only the best treatment, it does not undermine the Hippocratic duty to do the best for patients. Many say that doctors should never compromise their

---

57 Oxford: Clarendon Press, 2005.

clinical commitment to the individual. But this notion may positively increase the costs of treatment by highlighting the many excellent, but expensive, new treatments that become available. By contrast . . . health economists stress the need to distribute national resources efficiently and give 'waste' a different meaning. This approach emphasises the clinical benefits to whole communities, rather than to individuals, and could modify the relationship between doctors and patients. . . . The Bristol Inquiry . . . said: 'Against a background of constrained resources, it may not always be right for the individual doctor treating a particular patient to insist on having his, or her way, if the price to be paid is to limit or impair the care available for other patients.'

Clearly, this idea seeks to change the clinical commitment each clinician has to his, or her patient in the interests of patients as a whole. This changes the traditional Hippocratic ideal and its implcations are crucial to the health service we can expect in the future.

It is highly likely in practice that many doctors will frequently have to choose who to treat, or who to treat as a matter of priority, and that this will mean that he is not doing his best for those who are not treated, or not treated in a timely fashion. Some doctors have been frank about these issues and have suggested to their patients that a ballot takes place to decide on priority. Thirty years ago the *Journal of Medical Ethics* reported on the research of Drs Parsons and Lock:

'Editorial' (1980) 6 JME 171:

Who shall die?

Parsons and Lock, disturbed by increasingly inadequate funds for dialysis and transplantation, asked 25 British nephrologists to reject 10 out of 40 realistically described patients, ticking their reasons for rejection from a checklist under the categories of age, marital status, home facilities, underlying disease, and additional disease. All the nephrologists completed the questionnaire except for one who felt unable to accept any of the reasons suggested as valid grounds for rejection. Their responses make important reading. Interestingly, of the 10 patients most generally rejected, 'we found that at least six of them had been successfully treated by our own unit'; and not one of the patients was rejected by all the respondents.

Accepting for the time being that such choices must in practice be made, whereby some individuals are to be allocated life-saving resources while others with the same problem are to be refused them (microallocation or triage) it may be worthwhile distinguishing different criteria upon which such choices might conceivably be made. Perhaps the one most commonly used in practice is that favoured by many of the respondents, notably the medical or technical criterion, whereby triage is based on the probability of successful medical outcome. In clear cases this criterion seems unproblematic; for example, other things being equal, a doctor faced with two patients needing blood transfusion and only enough blood for one would surely be not merely absurd but downright wicked to transfuse the patient with an incompatible blood group when the other's blood group matched that of the available blood. The criterion for proper choice here is quite clearly likelihood of medical success.

The first of the criteria, the probability of successful medical outcome, seems, as the editorial states, unproblematic. However, the example given of the blood transfusion is perhaps too simplistic. It is beyond doubt that in this example there is one, and only one, ethical choice. Indeed there is no ethical dilemma here at all. Many predictions of 'successful medical outcome', however, might be covert value judgments. From time to time the newspapers report cases of smokers being refused heart surgery. Hospitals are at pains to point out that the refusal is not because they are smokers, but because the cardiac specialists state that the surgery will not be a lasting success if the patient, who has no plans to give up smoking, continues to smoke. However, might, at least in part, these decisions be based on other factors?:

'Editorial' (1980) 6 JME 171:

A second criterion for selection might be the candidates' value or disvalue to society; thus those respondents who rejected patients positive for Australia antigen on grounds of the risk to other patients and staff of potentially lethal hepatitis were explicitly or implicitly using this social criterion, as were any respondents who wished to stop treatment on the grounds that resources are being drained by the heavily handicapped and homeless from other less demanding patients.

There may be concern about the restriction on treatment in the cases of elderly people. Doctors may well find it easier to justify this on the basis of successful medical outcome. Is age a good reason for refusing treatment? The following are some of the arguments explored by Harris for and against:

Harris, J, *The Value of Life*[58]

The anti-ageist argument

All of us who wish to go on living have something that each of us values equally, although for each it is different in character, for some a much richer prize than for others, and we none of us know its true extent. This thing is of course 'the rest of our lives'. So long as we do not know the date of our deaths, then for each of us the 'rest of our lives' is of indefinite duration. Whether we are 17 or 70, in perfect health or suffering from a terminal disease, we each have the rest of our lives to lead. So long as we each fervently wish to live out the rest of our lives, however long that turns out to be, then if we do not deserve to die, we each suffer the same injustice if our wishes are deliberately frustrated and we are cut off prematurely. Indeed there may well be a double injustice in deciding that those whose life expectation is short should not benefit from rescue or resuscitation. Suppose I am told today that I have terminal cancer with only approximately six months or so to live, but I want to live until I die, or at least until I decide that life is no longer worth living. Suppose I then am involved in an accident and because my condition is known to my potential rescuers and there are not enough resources to treat all who could immediately be saved I am marked among those who will not be helped. I am then the victim of a double tragedy and a double injustice. I am stricken first by cancer and the knowledge that I have only a short time to live and I'm then stricken again when I'm told that because of my first tragedy a second and more immediate one is to be visited upon me. Because I have once been unlucky I'm now no longer worth saving.

The point is a simple but powerful one. However short or long my life will be, so long as I want to go on living it then I suffer a terrible injustice when that life is prematurely cut short. Imagine a group of people all of an age, say a class of students all in their mid twenties. If fire trapped all in the lecture theatre and only 20 could be rescued in time should the rescuers shout 'youngest first!'? Suppose they had time to debate the question or had been debating it 'academically' before the fire? It would surely seem invidious to deny some what all value so dearly merely because of an accident of birth. It might be argued that age here provides no criterion precisely because although the lifespans of such a group might be expected to vary widely, there would be no way of knowing who was most likely to live longest. But suppose a reliable astrologer could make very realistic estimates or, what amounts to the same thing, suppose the age range of the students to be much greater, say 17 to 55. Does not the invidiousness of selecting by birth-date remain? Should a 17 year old be saved before a 29 year old or she before the 45 year old and should the 55 year old clearly be the last to be saved or the first to be sacrificed?

---

58 London: Routledge & Kegan Paul, 1985.

Our normal intuitions would share this sense of the invidiousness of choosing between our imaginary students by reason of their respective ages, but would start to want to make age relevant at some extremes, say if there were a 2 day old baby and a 90 year old grandmother. We will be returning to discuss a possible basis for this intuition in a moment. However, it is important to be clear that the anti-ageist argument denies the relevance of age or life expectancy as a criterion absolutely. It argues that even if I know for certain that I have only a little space to live, that space, however short, may be very precious to me. Precious, precisely because it is all the time I have left, and just as precious to me on that account as all the time you have left is precious to you, however much those two timespans differ in length. So that where we both want, equally strongly, to go on living, then we each suffer the same injustice when our lives are cut short or are cut further short.

It might seem that someone who would insist on living out the last few months of his life when by 'going quietly' someone else might have the chance to live for a much longer time would be a very selfish person. But this would be true only if the anti-ageist argument is false. It will be true only if it is not plausible to claim that living out the rest of one's life could be equally valuable to the individual whose life it is irrespective of the amount of unelapsed time that is left. And this is of course precisely the usual situation when individuals do not normally have anything but the haziest of ideas as to how long it is that they might have left.

I think the anti-ageist argument has much plausibility. It locates the wrongness of ending an individual's life in the evil of thwarting that person's desire to go on living and argues that it is profoundly unjust to frustrate that desire merely because some of those who have exactly the same desire, held no more strongly, also have a longer life expectancy than the others. However, there are a number of arguments that pull in the opposite direction and these we must now consider.

The fair innings argument

One problem with the anti-ageist argument is our feeling that there is something unfair about a person who has lived a long and happy life hanging on grimly at the end, while someone who has not been so fortunate suffers a related double misfortune, of losing out in a lottery in which his life happened to be in the balance with that of the grim octogenarian. It might be argued that we could accept the part of the anti-ageist argument which focuses on the equal value of unelapsed time, if this could be tempered in some way. How can it be just that someone who has already had more than her fair share of life and its delights should be preferred or even given an equal chance of continued survival with the young person who has not been so favoured? One strategy that seems to take account of our feeling that there is something wrong with taking steps to prolong the lives of the very old at the expense of those much younger is the fair innings argument.

The fair innings argument takes the view that there is some span of years that we consider a reasonable life, a fair innings. Let's say that a fair share of life is the traditional three score and 10, 70 years. Anyone who does not reach 70 suffers, on this view, the injustice of being cut off in their prime. They have missed out on a reasonable share of life; they have been short-changed. Those, however, who do make 70 suffer no such injustice, they have not lost out but rather must consider any additional years a sort of bonus beyond that which could reasonably be hoped for. The fair innings argument requires that everyone be given an equal chance to have a fair innings, to reach the appropriate threshold but, having reached it, they have received their entitlement. The rest of their life is the sort of bonus which may be cancelled when this is necessary to help others reach the threshold.

The attraction of the fair innings argument is that it preserves and incorporates many of the features that made the anti-ageist argument plausible, but allows us to preserve our feeling that the old who have had a good run for their money should not be endlessly propped up at the expense of those who have not had the same chance. We can preserve the conclusion of the anti-ageist argument, that so long as life is equally valued by the person whose life it is, it should be given an equal chance of preservation, and we can go on taking this view until the people in question have reached a fair innings.

There is, however, an important difficulty with the fair innings argument. It is that the very arguments which support the seeing of the threshold at an age which might plausibly be considered to be a reasonable lifespan, equally support the setting of the threshold at any age at all, so long as an argument from fairness can be used to support so doing. Suppose that there is only one place available on the dialysis programme and two patients are in competition for it. One is 30, and the other 40 years of age. The fair innings argument requires that neither be preferred on the grounds of age since both are below the threshold and are entitled to an equal chance of reaching it. If there is no other reason to choose between them we should do something like toss a coin. However, the 30 year old can argue that the considerations which support the fair innings argument require that she be given the place. After all, what's fair about the fair innings argument is precisely that each individual should have an equal chance of enjoying the benefits of a reasonable lifespan. The younger patient can argue that from where she's standing, the age of 40 looks much more reasonable a span than that of 30, and that she should be given the chance to benefit from those 10 extra years.

This argument generalised becomes a reason for always preferring to save younger rather than older people, whatever the age difference, and makes the original anti-ageist argument begin to look again the more attractive line to take. For the younger person can always argue that the older has had a fairer innings, and should now give way. It is difficult to stop whatever span is taken to be a fair innings collapsing towards zero under pressure from those younger candidates who see their innings as less fair than that of those with a larger share.

But perhaps this objection to the fair innings argument is mistaken? If 70 years is a fair innings it does not follow that the nearer a span of life approaches 70 years, the fairer an innings it is. This may be revealed by considering a different sort of threshold. Suppose that most people can run a mile in seven minutes, and that two people are given the opportunity to show that they can run a mile in that time. They both expect to be given seven minutes. However, if one is in fact given only three minutes and the other only four, it's not true that the latter is given a fairer running time: for people with average abilities four minutes is no more realistic a time in which to run a mile than is three. Four minutes is neither a fair threshold in itself, nor a fairer one than three minutes would be.

Nor does the argument that establishes seven minutes as an appropriate threshold lend itself to variation downwards. For that argument just is that seven is the number of minutes that an average adult takes to run a mile. Why then is it different for lifespans? If three score and ten is the number of years available to most people for getting what life has to offer, and is also the number of years people can reasonably expect to have, then it is a misfortune to be allowed anything less, however much less one is allowed, if nothing less than the full span normally suffices for getting what can be got out of life. It's true that the 40 year old gets more time than the 30 year old, but the frame of reference is not time only, but time normally required for a full life.

This objection has some force, but its failure to be a good analogy reveals that two sorts of considerations go to make an innings fair. For while living a full or complete life, just in the sense of experiencing all the ages of man, is one mark of a fair innings, there is also value in living through as many ages as possible. Just as completing the mile is one value, it is not the only one. Runners in the race of life also value ground covered, and generally judge success in terms of distance run.

What the fair innings argument needs to do is to capture and express in a workable form the truth that while it is always a *misfortune* to die when one wants to go on living, it is not a tragedy to die in old age; but it is on the other hand, both a tragedy and a misfortune to be cut off prematurely. Of course, ideas like 'old age' and 'premature death' are inescapably vague, and may vary from society to society, and over time as techniques for postponing death improve. We must also remember that while it may be invidious to choose between a 30 and a 40 year old on the grounds that one has had a fairer innings than the other, it may not be invidious to choose between the 30 and the 65 year old on those grounds.

If we remember, too, that it will remain wrong to end the life of someone who wants to live or to fail to save them, and that the fair innings argument will only operate as a principle of selection where we are forced to choose between lives, then something workable might well be salvaged.

While 'old age' is irredeemably vague, we can tell the old from the young, and even the old from the middle-aged. So that without attempting precise formulation, a reasonable form of the fair innings argument might hold; and might hold that people who had achieved old age or who were closely approaching it would not have their lives further prolonged when this could only be achieved at the cost of the lives of those who were not nearing old age. These categories could be left vague, the idea being that it would be morally defensible to prefer to save the lives of those who 'still had their lives before them' rather than those who had 'already lived full lives'. The criterion to be employed in each case would simply be what reasonable people would say about whether someone had had a fair innings. Where reasonable people would be in no doubt that a particular individual was nearing old age *and* that that person's life could only be further prolonged at the expense of the life of someone that no reasonable person would classify as nearing old age, then the fair innings argument would apply, and it would be justifiable to save the younger candidate.

In cases where reasonable people differed or it seemed likely that they would differ as to whether people fell into one category or the other, then the anti-ageist argument would apply and the inescapable choice would have to be made arbitrarily.

But again it must be emphasised that the fair innings argument would only operate as a counsel of despair, when it was clearly impossible to postpone the deaths of all those who wanted to go on living. In all other circumstances the anti-ageist argument would apply.

One influential proposal for allocating health care resources fairly has been by means of calculating QALYs (quality distinguished life year).[59] John Harris describes this approach as follows:

Harris, J, 'QALYfying the value of life'[60]

1   What are QALYs?

It is important to be as clear as possible as to just what a QALY is and what it might be used for. I cannot do better than let Alan Williams, the architect of QALYs, tell you in his own words:

> The essence of a QALY is that it takes a year of healthy life expectancy to be worth one, but regards a year of unhealthy life expectancy as worth less than one. Its precise value is lower the worse the quality of life of the unhealthy person (which is what the 'quality adjusted' bit is all about). If being dead is worth zero, it is, in principle, possible for a QALY to be negative, ie, for the quality of someone's life to be judged worse than being dead.
>
> The general idea is that a beneficial health care activity is one that generates a positive amount of QALYs, and that an efficient health care activity is one where the

---

59 See, for example, *The Measurement of Health*, published by the Office of Health Economics in 1985; and Williams, A, 'The value of QALYs' (1985) Health and Social Services Journal.

60 (1987) 13 JME 117.

cost-per-QALY is as low as it can be. A high priority health care activity is one where the cost-per-QALY is low, and a low priority activity is one where cost-per-QALY is high.

The plausibility of the QALY derives from the idea that given the choice, a person would prefer a shorter healthier life to a longer period of survival in a state of severe discomfort and disability. The idea that any rational person would endorse this preference provides the moral and political force behind the QALY. Its acceptability as a measurement of health then depends upon its doing all the theoretical tasks assigned to it, and on its being what people want, or would want, for themselves.

Harris subsequently became involved in a debate with John McKie *et al.* about the application of QALYs (a series of articles was published in (1996) 22 JME 204–21). Part of the debate centred on John Rawls's famous 'veil of ignorance' argument in *A Theory of Justice*.[61] Rawls was attempting to find a system of distributive justice whilst accepting the proposition that people tend to be self-interested rather than altruistic. The scenario he envisages is as follows. Imagine that you are one of a number of people who are aware of the way in which the so called laws of economics work, but do not know their place in society. So, for example, you may be rich and powerful, or you may be unemployed with no resources whatsoever. Behind this 'veil of ignorance' you are asked to agree a set of principles which will govern the way in which the benefits and burdens in society are distributed. Assume, too, that you are motivated by self-interest. Rawls argues that because you do not know your position in society you will take care to ensure that conditions for those at the bottom of the pile are as good as possible. Rawls's theory is open to the objection that it assumes that the self-interested person will choose to play safe in this way. It can be argued that those behind the veil might choose to take a gamble. McKie *et al.* state that QALYs would be chosen by those behind the veil of ignorance because QALYs maximise utility. In other words, they take a wider view of self-interest. Harris states that they would not, because the persons behind the veil, ie typical human beings, are cautious risk-averse persons, who would weigh the downside more than the upside. This is a difficult dispute to resolve. Does it depend upon the view one takes of human psychology, and won't there always be at least two views?

Harris also maintains that the problem with the QALY approach is that a person's life is valued more even if the difference in life expectation is very small. For example, the patient who would survive for just two days more than another would be preferred. McKie *et al.* acknowledge this, but point out that Harris's insistence upon treating all needy patients equally means that the patient who would survive for 30 years if treated, and the patient who would survive for two days if treated, would be regarded as equally deserving of that treatment. Is the Harris–McKie debate another example of utility versus absolutism? On the basis of the former, at least the traditional way of looking at utilitarianism, some pretty ruthless decisions could be made about health care rationing. So, for example, the denial of treatment to anyone over 75 years old would provide more resources for younger people who would be in the majority. The utilitarian response would be that such a rule would morally impoverish society, leaving many people to suffer a painful and distressing old age, a spectacle which, far from being good for the majority of younger people, would make them positively unhappy.

Both Harris and McKie agree that any form of resource allocation which creates social divisiveness is wrong. But if the wider issues relating to health are examined, there is a great deal of evidence that poverty and health are inextricably linked. See, for example, Black *et al*, *Inequalities in Health: The Black Report*.[62] The latter produced evidence on the link between health and wealth, and reported that life expectancy at birth was seven years higher in social class one (professional) than

---

61 Oxford: OUP, 1972.
62 Harmondsworth: Penguin, 1982.

in social class five (manual). There is therefore a cogent argument in favour of a redistribution of health resources to redress the imbalance. Furthermore, it points up the fact that 'health care' decisions are strongly linked to economic policy and social justice.

 SELF-TEST QUESTION

When we are looking at allocation of health care resources at a 'macro' level, is a utilitarian approach appropriate, whereas it is not appropriate at the 'micro' level of looking at the treatment of individual patients?

Summary of Key Points

1. Medical ethics particularly highlights the issue of universalisation and how far this can be said to apply when, even within one society, there are many social and cultural attitudes.
2. One of the key distinctions in ethics is between consequentialist ethical theories and those that support absolute duties.
3. The doctor–patient relationship is traditionally said to give rise to special ethical obligations relating to doing good and not doing harm. However, it is questionable as to how far this is the case.
4. Another key distinction which is particularly pertinent in the context of medical ethics is the distinction between treating patients paternalistically and respecting their right to autonomous decision-making, although it is arguable that there is room within medical ethics for both these concepts.
5. Justice is a key ethical concept and is particuarly relevant to the allocation of health care resources.
6. When we are looking at patients and doing what is best for them, are we really only concerned with 'persons' and what exactly is a 'person'?

 Further Reading

Blackburn, S, *Being Good*, Oxford: OUP, 2001.
Campbell, AV, *The Body in Bioethics*, London: Routledge Cavendish, 2009.
Hope, T, *A Very Short Introduction to Medical Ethics*, Oxford: OUP, 2005.
Miola, J, *Medical Ethics and Medical Law*, Oxford: Hart, 2007.
Pence, GE, *Classic cases in medical ethics, accounts of the cases that have shapened and defined medical ethics*, New York: McGraw-Hill Higher Education, 2008.
Singer, P, *Writings on an Ethical Life*, London: Fourth Estate, 2000.

Chapter 2

Health Care in England and Wales

Chapter Contents

2.1 Background

2.1.1 The international framework

The UK is committed under international law to the promotion of its citizens' health and the prevention of disease. The key aspirations to this end are contained in the European Social Charter of 1961 (as revised in 1996), which is an offshoot from the scheme of political and civil rights found in the 1950 European Convention for the Protection of Human Rights and Fundamental Freedoms and is overseen by the same body, the Council of Europe. Articles 11 and 13 of the Social Charter provide as follows:

Article 11 – The right to protection of health

With a view to ensuring the effective exercise of the right to protection of health, the Parties undertake, either directly or in co-operation with public or private organisations, to take appropriate measures designed *inter alia*:

1   to remove as far as possible the causes of ill health;
2   to provide advisory and educational facilities for the promotion of health and the encouragement of individual responsibility in matters of health;
3   to prevent as far as possible epidemic, endemic and other diseases, as well as accidents.

Article 13 – The right to social and medical assistance

With a view to ensuring the effective exercise of the right to social and medical assistance, the Parties undertake:

1   to ensure that any person who is without adequate resources and who is unable to secure such resources either by his own efforts or from other sources, in particular by benefits under a social security scheme, be granted adequate assistance, and, in case of sickness, the care necessitated by his condition;
2   to ensure that persons receiving such assistance shall not, for that reason, suffer from a diminution of their political or social rights. . .

2.1.2 National provisions

Unlike the position in respect of the European Convention on Human Rights, the failure by a state to protect these 'social rights' will not allow one of its citizens to complain to the European Court of Human Rights. However, the broad commitment on this country's part to the goal of access to health care for all is clear, and, in fact, predates the salient international law: it is found in the existence and operation of the National Health Service (NHS), which was established in 1948. They key feature of the NHS is that it was set up, and remains, free at the point of use. The current scheme is set out in the National Health Service Act 2006:

National Health Service Act 2006 c. 41

1 Secretary of State's duty to promote health service

(1)   The Secretary of State must continue the promotion in England of a comprehensive health service designed to secure improvement–
    (a)   in the physical and mental health of the people of England, and
    (b)   in the prevention, diagnosis and treatment of illness.

(2)   The Secretary of State must for that purpose provide or secure the provision of services in accordance with this Act.

(3) The services so provided must be free of charge except in so far as the making and recovery of charges is expressly provided for by or under any enactment, whenever passed.

2 Secretary of State's general power

(1) The Secretary of State may–
  (a) provide such services as he considers appropriate for the purpose of discharging any duty imposed on him by this Act, and
  (b) do anything else which is calculated to facilitate, or is conducive or incidental to, the discharge of such a duty.

. . .

3 Secretary of State's duty as to provision of certain services

(1) The Secretary of State must provide throughout England, to such extent as he considers necessary to meet all reasonable requirements–
  (a) hospital accommodation,
  (b) other accommodation for the purpose of any service provided under this Act,
  (c) medical, dental, ophthalmic, nursing and ambulance services,
  (d) such other services or facilities for the care of pregnant women, women who are breastfeeding and young children as he considers are appropriate as part of the health service,
  (e) such other services or facilities for the prevention of illness, the care of persons suffering from illness and the after-care of persons who have suffered from illness as he considers are appropriate as part of the health service,
  (f) such other services or facilities as are required for the diagnosis and treatment of illness.

. . .

The NHS is a vast public health care system (the largest organisation in Europe), as the following statistics illustrate: in 2002/03 total expenditure was £55.8 billion; in 2007/08 it was £102 billion and in 2008/09 £110 billion. The NHS absorbs 18% of the total public spending in the UK (see www.ukpublicspending.co.uk). Expenditure therefore doubled in the six years from 2002/2003. Nevertheless, the NHS has remained the focus of continued and deeply felt public concern and debate, and the service has, from time to time, been the subject of important reforms. The major controversies have centred on achieving accountability within the NHS in relation to cost of provision and quality of care.

An issue that has recently generated debate is the question of 'top-up' payments to pay for drugs that are not available on the NHS because of cost. The NHS decided that it would be possible for patients in this situation to continue to received their normal NHS care but pay for the particular drug or drugs not funded by the NHS.[1] A lot of the controversy is generated by the fact that usually these are cancer drugs. Emily Jackson discusses some of the arguments for and against this. For example, in favour of top-ups is the argument that people are entitled to the NHS care anyway and it seems churlish to deny them this if they want to pay something extra. The argument against points to the creation of a two-tier health service, one for the poor and one for the better-off. Jackson concludes that with the current developments in pharmaceuticals, top-ups are inevitable, but she describes as 'frankly absurd' the proposal that one way of dealing with the distastefulness of differential treatments being provided on the same hospital ward is to deliver the treatments on

---

1   See, eg, www.telegraph.co.uk/health 12 May 2009.

separate sites.[2] Jackson is surely right here, given that most of these patients will be seriously ill and this sort of fragmented care cannot be good therapy. How far she is right in saying that top-ups are going to be an inevitable feature of the NHS remains to be seen.

We shall next give a little more detail of the structure of the NHS and will then be looking at some of the regulatory mechanisms which have been set up in order to ensure that the NHS delivers both efficient and high-quality care, and how professional regulation operates. The main focus of the remainder of the chapter, however, will be on how far, in law, the individual citizen enjoys a right to obtain the particular treatment he needs.

 SELF-TEST QUESTION

Later in this chapter we look at judicial review cases where patients have challenged the health care decisions within the NHS. Consider now how a patient might be successful within the legal confines of a judicial review action.

2.2 Structure of Health Care in the UK

2.2.1 National Health Service

In economic terms, health care as a commodity has the clear potential for generating an anti-competitive market situation, given that the demand for services is in the hands of the same profession (doctors making patient referrals) as is responsible for its supply.

In a drive to make the NHS more competitive and better serve the interests of patients, under John Major the Conservative Government had experimented with an 'internal market' within the health service. Under this system (set out in the National Health Service and Community Care Act 1990) NHS management and funding were organised on the principle of separating the 'purchasers' and 'providers' of care. The former were local health authorities and GP fund-holders, responsible for assessing the health needs of their local populations or patients and for purchasing the best possible care for them. Providers, such as hospitals, ambulance and community services, were intended to compete among each other for 'contracts' with purchasers to provide the required care services.

However, on assuming office in 1997, the incoming Labour Government quickly signalled its intent to introduce major changes into the NHS. These were highlighted in the Government White Paper, *The New NHS: Modern, Dependable*, Cm 3807.[3] The Labour Government was committed to abolishing the internal market and replacing it with a system of integrated care based on partnerships between NHS bodies and other local agencies. However, that is not to say that the Government were not keen to decentralise the NHS where it could, and proposed the setting up of NHS Foundation Trusts to be run by local managers, staff and members of the public. The intention was to free up the efficient Trusts from over-regulation, and they were set up by the Health and Social Care (Community Health and Standards) Act 2003. Since the change of government in May 2010, more change has been proposed, the latest White Paper being *Equity and Excellence: Liberating the NHS*, Cm 7881.[4] Consultation closed in October 2010. The paper reiterates the general NHS principles: comprehensive service, available to all, free at the point of use, based on need, not ability to pay. It sets out the intentions of putting patients at the heart of everything the NHS does; focusing on continuously improving those things that really matter to patients – the outcome of their healthcare;

---

2 Jackson, E, 'Top-up payments for expensive cancer drugs: rationing, fairness and the NHS' 73(3) (2010) MLR 399.
3 London: TSO, 1997 and *Executive Summary*, London: DoH, 1997.
4 London: TSO, 2010.

and empowering and liberating clinicians to innovate, with the freedom to focus on improving healthcare services. How could anyone disagree with these general aims? However, it is accompanied by implementation of more change; accommodating the concern about funding and the weariness that is induced by the idea of more reorganisation that present the real challenges.

It must be noted that the administrative structure of the NHS differs between the different countries of the UK. The current structure of the NHS in England consists of the government minister, the Secretary of State for Health, who is accountable for the Department of Health which is the government department that the minister oversees. Beneath the Department of Health are ten Strategic Health Authorities whose function is to ensure that the health needs in their area are met, including initiating programmes of improvement. Beneath that level are the NHS Trusts (currently around 125), which essentially provide hospital services, and the Primary Care Trusts (around 150) that arrange the provision of GP services, opticians, dentists and other health workers. Although the provision of GP services is organised by the PCTs, GPs are not employed by the NHS, but are self-employed contractors. Special health authorities are those that provide a single service nationally, such as the NHS Blood and Transplant services. Foundation Trusts, as mentioned above, are NHS Trusts who have acquired this status in a form of management take-over scheme. There are current around 115 Foundation Trusts. There are also Trusts specifically designated to run Mental Health Services and the Ambulance Service.

In Scotland and Wales the structure is far less complicated. In Scotland there are 14 Health Boards which deal with all aspects of patient care and the financing of this. The same applies in Wales, where there are seven Health Boards. There is less fragmentation in Scotland and Wales, due to the fact that internal markets and outsourcing of services are not part of the political culture. Northern Ireland is something of a hybrid.

It should be noted that certain community facilities for disabled people, for example, that are provided by local authorities, are not part of the NHS, and for that reason it is possible to charge for some of these services, but the Health and Social Care Act 2001 section 49 specifically provides that nursing care cannot be subject to charging.

2.2.2 The private sector

The private sector is subject to statutory regulation pursuant to the Care Standards Act 2000. This provides for the National Care Standards Commission, a statutory authority set up under the Act, to operate a system of registration and inspection in respect of private hospitals and residential care homes, and is designed to ensure that patients are offered a suitable standard of care. Moreover, as well as being vulnerable, like their NHS counterparts, to malpractice actions brought in negligence, private hospitals can also be sued for breach of contract.

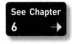

See Chapter 6 →

2.3 Regulating the Quality of Health Care

One perennial concern in relation to the NHS is ensuring that minimum standards are maintained throughout the service in terms of all aspects of provision and care. Clearly, this is also an important way of reducing the expenditure of resources on the fighting and settling of malpractice suits brought by dissatisfied patients (a subject dealt with at length in Chapter 6). In this section, we shall first consider the role of a number of agencies, which oversee and influence the implementation of decision making within the service at the 'macro level' (although the proliferation of these in themselves undermine the above suggestion that expenditure can be significantly reduced), before moving on to address the mechanisms to regulate and provide redress in the context of individual treatment decisions (the 'micro level'). In respect of the latter, there is the possibility for complaints to be brought by aggrieved patients either through

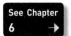

See Chapter 6 →

the complaints system of the NHS or, where unprofessional conduct on the part of a particular member of the NHS medical staff is alleged, through the latter's professional licensing body – in the case of a doctor, the General Medical Council (GMC).

2.3.1 The 'macro' level: the role of regulatory bodies

Ironically, at the same time as the NHS has absorbed more and more of the national budget, and successive governments have grappled with trying to make it 'more efficient' and to cut down bureaucracy, there has been a growth in concerns about improving patient 'safety' and setting up risk management procedures which processes inevitably militate against a reduction in costs. In its 1997 White Paper, The New NHS – Modern, Dependable, Cm 3807,[5] the Government introduced the concept of 'clinical governance', involving the increased use of risk-management techniques and 'evidence-based medicine' 'to assure and improve clinical standards at local level throughout the NHS'. A central role in this initiative was given to two complementary organisations, the National Institute for Clinical Excellence (NICE), and the Commission for Health Improvement (CHI).

NICE began its work as a Special Health Authority on 1 April 1999, pursuant to the National Institute for Clinical Excellence (Establishment and Constitution) Order 1999 SI 1999/220, and became responsible for disseminating 'best practice' guidance to healthcare professionals working within the NHS. The Institute responded to the inquiry into the Bristol heart surgery scandal, in which it was revealed that inept cardiac surgery on children at a Bristol hospital had led to a significant number of extra deaths and disabilities among them.[6] The response outlined its role as advising on management of disease, use of technologies, drawing up guidelines in these areas, and advising on clinical audit. The latter is important, as one of the failings highlighted by the Bristol Inquiry was that there was no adequate process to alert the hospital to their worrying levels of poor outcomes and morbidity.

A network of other organisations grew up (eg the National Patient Safety Agency, and the National Clinical Assessment Authority) to regulate and to improve standards, described by the Department of Health as 'arm's-length' bodies to indicate their degree of independence from the department. However, the plethora of these organisations causes overlap and confusion, and at present there are proposals to 'reconfigure' them.[7] Since 1 April 2005, NICE has joined with the Health Development Agency to become the new National Institute for Health and Clinical Excellence (also to be known as NICE). It is described as 'a single excellence-in-practice organisation' responsible for providing national guidance on the promotion of good health and the prevention and treatment of ill health in three areas: public health; health technologies and clinical practice. NICE guidelines can be controversial as the process of approval of, say a new drug, can be lengthy, and, without approval, patients will not receive it. Unsurprisingly, pharmaceutical companies also have an interest in approval by NICE and have challenged refusals, eg R (on the application of Bristol-Myers Squibb Pharmaceuticals Ltd) v National Institute For Health & Clinical Excellence.[8]

Keith Syrett discusses challenges to NICE decisions by way of judicial review:

Syrett, K, 'Nice work? Rationing, review and the legitimacy problem in the new NHS'[9]

. . . [NICE] may be seen as having two functions. First, it is intended to address the problem of so-called 'postcode prescribing' by reducing 'unacceptable variations in performance and

---

5   London: Department of Health, 1997.
6   Bristol Royal Infirmary Inquiry, The Report of the Public Inquiry into Children's Heart Surgery at the Bristol Royal Infirmary 1984–1995: Learning from Bristol, Cm 5207, London: Department of Health, 2001 – 'the Kennedy Report'.
7   See Reconfiguring the Department of Health's Arm's Length Bodies, London: DoH, 2004.
8   [2009] EWHC 2722 (Admin).
9   [2002]10 Med L Rev 1.

practice' across different regions of the NHS. The controversy which this issue may generate is illustrated by the case of *R v North West Lancashire Health Authority ex p A, D and G*, in which three transsexuals successfully challenged a decision to refuse funding for gender reassignment surgery. It was submitted that 34 out of 41 other authorities made some provision for funding such surgery and that a policy which effectively amounted to a 'blanket ban' in one locality would therefore have the effect that entitlement to treatment would depend upon where the patient lived. The Government's hope is that, by acting as 'a single, national focus for appraisal of significant new and existing interventions' whose recommendations are expected to be followed countrywide, variations – and therefore challenges – of this type will become less frequent as the Institute renders decision-making in the NHS more acceptable by bringing 'greater certainty, greater clarity and greater confidence'.

However, such optimism may be premature because it is clear that NICE has a second role in making 'tough choices' on the allocation of resources. Indeed, notwithstanding assertions to the contrary, the establishment of NICE – especially its technology appraisal function – appears to mark 'the beginning of explicit national rationing' in the NHS. This is significant because it has been powerfully argued that explicit resource allocation decisions are inherently more unstable than decisions which can be presented as based upon clinical necessity, even if these are in reality dictated by resource considerations. The greater visibility of the process thus increases the potential for conflict. This may already be seen in the responses to certain Institute decisions. Refusal to authorise the use of an intervention has been opposed by patients and their representatives. On the other hand, approval has been contested by professionals seeking to preserve their clinical and managerial discretion with the consequence that geographical variations in access to treatment have tended to persist. Elsewhere, patients requiring other services have lost out as resources are diverted to fund 'NICE-approved' interventions. The controversy generated has been manifested in media campaigns, Parliamentary debate and threats of legal action.

The range of interests which may be affected by NICE determinations renders some level of opposition a near-certainty.

In addition to the workings of the above organisations, it should also be noted that a statutory duty to achieve quality in health care is imposed directly upon NHS bodies by s 45 of the Health and Social Care (Community Health and Standards) Act 2003 (replacing s 18 of the Health Act 1999).

The Freedom of Information Act 2000 is also relevant to 'macro' level regulation. This came into force on 1 January 2005 and provides for a public right of acces to information held by public bodies. Information for which disclosure is not provided could be obtained under the Act, but note that (*inter alia*) a request for information can be refused if it would be disproportionately expensive to answer (s 12), the request is vexatious (s 14) and there is a long list of exemptions which include commercial interest, that the information relates to health and safety or is confidential, or if the information is accessible by other means. There is also a public interest exemption.[10]

2.3.2 The 'micro' level: NHS complaints and discipline

A system to deal with complaints brought by patients in respect of their treatment is an important alternative to formal litigation in the courts. The current system (in place since 2009) has two stages. The first stage, known as local resolution, involves complaining to the hospital or trust and getting hold of a copy of the complaints procedure. NHS organisations have a complaints manager

---

10 See Part II of the Act, and see Ch 5 for a discussion of public interest considerations and what 'confidential information' might be.

designated to deal with these. If the patient is still not satisfied then the matter can be referred to the Parliamentary and Health Service Ombudsman, who is independent of the NHS and government. Officers from the Patient Advice and Liaison Service (PALS) are available in all hospitals. They offer confidential advice, support and information on health-related matters to patients, their families and their carers. The Independent Complaints Advocacy Service (ICAS) is a national service that supports people who wish to make a complaint about their NHS care or treatment.

It may become apparent as the result of a complaint (or, indeed, in the course of a malpractice action) that the conduct of a particular medical professional is deserving of censure. In this regard, there are two parallel systems for disciplining the professional concerned. First, disciplinary procedures internal to the NHS may be invoked. However, with regard to these there has been much disquiet because of their time-consuming and costly nature (an estimated £40 million caused just by delay) and, in consequence, a new national disciplinary framework was devised which came into force on 1 June 2005.[11]

See Chapter
◀ 6

2.3.3 Professional regulation and discipline

Of even greater consequence for professionals, their conduct may be investigated by the responsible governing and licensing body for their profession. In respect of doctors this is the GMC,[12] and the equivalent body for nurses is the Nursing and Midwifery Council (NMC). (There are also two general regulatory bodies for health care professionals: the Council for Healthcare Regulatory Excellence and the Health Professions Council, who regulate 15 other bodies of health care professionals such as physiotherapists – a further extension of government's apparently insatiable appetite for regulatory bodies in the field of health care, this time provoked by the Harold Shipman case.) Self-regulatory organisations have a long tradition of enunciating and administering the standards of professional practice to which their members are required to adhere, and their power to discipline and, ultimately, to 'strike off' the register the names of those found guilty of serious misconduct has been codified in statute. In the case of the GMC, the relevant provisions are found in Pt V of the Medical Act 1983 (as amended).

Erasure from the register is clearly a very serious sanction for professionals, in that, henceforth (unless they succeed at some future date in having their names restored to it), they will be deprived of their professional livelihoods. In so far as a doctor is unhappy with the decision of the GMC in this matter, he or she may appeal (pursuant to s 40 of the 1983 Act) to the Privy Council. A case in point, in which the meaning of 'serious professional misconduct' under s 36 of the Act was considered, is that of McCandless v GMC:[13]

McCandless v GMC [1996]

Lord Hoffmann: Dr David McCandless, a general practitioner in Deeside, appeals against a determination and direction of the Professional Conduct Committee of the General Medical Council. At a hearing on 16 March 1995 the Committee found that he was guilty of serious professional misconduct and directed that his name should be erased from the Register of Medical Practitioners.

The charges alleged errors in his diagnoses of three patients and failure to refer them to hospital. Two subsequently died and the other was found on her eventual admission to hospital to be seriously ill. It is not necessary to go further into the details because Mr Mitting, who appeared for Dr McCandless, accepted that the Committee's findings of fact were not open to

---

11 See *Maintaining High Professional Standards in the Modern NHS*, London: DoH, 2005.
12 See www.gmc-uk.org.
13 [1996] 1 WLR 167.

any material dispute. He also accepted that in each case Dr McCandless had been negligent. The chairman of the Committee gave the following brief reasons for its finding that he had been guilty of serious professional misconduct:

> Dr McCandless, the Committee take a very serious view of the evidence which they have heard about the poor standard of medical care which you provided to all three patients in this case. The care which you provided fell deplorably short of the standard which patients are entitled to expect from their general practitioners.

Mr Mitting submits that these reasons reveal an error of law by the Committee. He says that the Committee applied the wrong test for what amounts to serious professional misconduct. It thought that it was enough that the treatment given to the three patients fell 'deplorably short' of the standard which would reasonably be expected. Mr Mitting says that poor treatment is not enough. The doctor may nevertheless have been doing his best. He may have been overworked or just not particularly good at the job. But 'serious professional misconduct' means, he said, conduct which is morally blameworthy. This cannot be determined simply by deciding whether the treatment measured up to an objective standard. One has to look at why the doctor gave the treatment which he did. If it fell short of a reasonable standard because he was, for example, too lazy or drunk to examine the patient properly, then he would be guilty of misconduct. But not if he made an honest mistake.

Their Lordships think that some support can be found for Mr Mitting's submission in old cases on the meaning of 'infamous conduct in a professional respect' – the words which were used in 19th century Medical Acts and which continued to be used until replaced by the words 'serious professional misconduct' in the Medical Act 1969. . .

[However,] . . . the authorities on the old wording do not speak with one voice and . . . they are of little assistance in the interpretation of the new. Secondly, although there remains the single disciplinary offence now styled 'serious professional misconduct', the possible penalties available to the Committee, which used to be confined to the ultimate sanction of erasure, have been extended to include suspension and the imposition of conditions upon practice. This suggests that the offence was intended to include serious cases of negligence. Thirdly, the public has higher expectations of doctors and members of other self-governing professions. Their governing bodies are under a corresponding duty to protect the public against the genially incompetent as well as the deliberate wrongdoers. Fourthly, the meaning of the new wording has been authoritatively stated by this Board in *Doughty v General Dental Council* [1988] AC 164, p 173 in objective terms:

> . . . judged by proper professional standards in the light of the objective facts about the individual patients . . . the dental treatments criticised as unnecessary [were] treatments that no dentist of reasonable skill exercising reasonable care would carry out.

This test appears to their Lordships to be, *mutatis mutandis*, equally applicable to treatment by doctors . . .

Once it is accepted that seriously negligent treatment can amount to serious professional misconduct, then it seems to their Lordships that the appeal must fail. The eminent medical practitioners who sat on the Committee came to the conclusion that Dr McCandless' treatment of his three patients fell deplorably short of the standard to which patients are entitled to expect from general practitioners. In the circumstances, it is scarcely surprising that they concluded that Dr McCandless was guilty of serious professional misconduct. Their Lordships can see no basis for interfering with that conclusion. Nor can they see any ground for interfering with the Committee's decision that the offences merited the penalty of erasure from the register.

Subsequently, in *Roylance v GMC (No 2)*,[14] it was confirmed that, provided there was 'a link with the profession of medicine', serious professional misconduct could extend beyond clinical conduct (that is, the doctor's own carrying out of medical work). The appellant was the chief executive officer of the NHS Trust in Bristol at the centre of the Bristol heart surgery scandal, with responsibility for the particular hospital at which the incompetent cardiac surgeons worked. The GMC struck him off after finding that he had been made aware of concerns about the mortality rate in paediatric cardiac surgery at the hospital and had failed to take adequate action to prevent the surgeons concerned from carrying out operations.

In *R (On the application of Campbell) v GMC*[15] the issue was whether mitigating factors were relevant to a decision as to whether conduct amounted to serious misconduct. The Court of Appeal held that such an approach was flawed; personal mitigating factors were only relevant to the second stage of the procedure, ie the appropriate sanction to be imposed.

In 2002 the Government announced a number of reforms to the GMC, including a new role of regularly revalidating a doctor's licence to practise (to ensure that his practice remains up to date and of a high standard).[16] The GMC has subsequently set up a new system of dealing with complaints, the key feature of which is the separation of functions. The proposal is that the fitness to practise procedures will be divided into two stages: investigation and adjudication. This is to avoid the traditional criticism of certain professional regulatory bodies who could be accused of acting as police, prosecution and judiciary when dealing with their own members. There is also a proposed new validation procedure whereby doctors will require a licence to practise which will be renewed every five years (due to operate from 2012). The new procedures were due to come into force in April 2005. However, the revalidation procedure is based upon fitness to practise in the sense of being medically competent and does not specifically deal with non-clinical misconduct. In consequence, this issue was highlighted by the publication of the Fifth Report on the Harold Shipman case[17] and, following publication, it was decided that the government's Chief Medical Officer should review the new procedures and the April 2005 launch was postponed. The Health and Social Care Act 2008 set up the Office of the Health Professions Adjudicator (OHPA) which was to be the new, independent body set up to ensure clear separation between the investigation of fitness to practise cases by the GMC and the process of determining whether a professional's 'fitness to practise' is impaired. In December 2010, following a consultation exercise, the new Government decided not to proceed with OHPA and to repeal the relevant legislative provisions.

 SELF-TEST QUESTION

Do you agree that, regardless of whatever method is appropriate, it is right to separate the functions of a professional body into investigatory and adjudicatory?

2.3.4 The role of criminal law

Of course, the disciplinary mechanisms with which we have so far been concerned operate alongside, and independently of, the sanctions provided by the legal system in relation to doctors and other persons who, by their conduct, inflict harm upon others. In Chapters 3 and 6 we shall be

---

14 [2000] 1 AC 311.
15 [2005] 1 WLR 3488.
16 See *Reform of the GMC: A Paper for Consultation*, London: DoH, 2002.
17 *The Fifth Report, Safeguarding Patients: Lessons from the Past – Proposals for the Future*, London: Shipman Inquiry, 2004.

focusing upon the civil remedies, in the torts of battery and negligence respectively, available to patients in relation to maltreatment they receive during medical care. However, it is important to note that the criminal law may also be of relevance in some cases. In this regard, where a patient is injured, or simply handled non-consensually, a doctor could in theory be prosecuted for an offence, either in battery at common law, or under the Offences Against the Person Act 1861. Where the patient actually dies, then a charge in murder or manslaughter may be brought, depending on the *mens rea* of the doctor. The former charge, in particular, is a possibility in certain cases of euthanasia.

Although it is generally very rare for criminal charges to be preferred against doctors (it usually not thought to be in the public interest for prosecutions to be brought), the fact that ultimately doctors do not belong to any special category of citizen – and must answer for the serious consequences of deficient conduct – was illustrated by the conviction for manslaughter of an anaesthetist in R v Adomako:[18]

R v Adomako (1994) [19]

Lord Mackay of Clashfern LC: The conviction arose out of the conduct of an eye operation carried out at the Mayday Hospital, Croydon on 4 January 1987. The appellant was, during the latter part of that operation, the anaesthetist in charge of the patient.

The operation was carried out by two surgeons supported by a team of five nurses and a theatre sister. Anaesthesia commenced at about 9.45 am . . .

At approximately 11.05 am a disconnection occurred at the endotracheal tube connection. The supply of oxygen to the patient ceased and this led to cardiac arrest at 11.14 am. During this period the appellant failed to notice or remedy the disconnection.

The appellant first became aware that something was amiss when an alarm sounded on the Dinamap machine, which monitors the patient's blood pressure. From the evidence it appears that some four and a half minutes would have elapsed between the disconnection and the sounding of this alarm. When this alarm sounded the appellant responded in various ways by checking the equipment and by administering atropine to raise the patient's pulse. But at no stage before the cardiac arrest did he check the integrity of the endotracheal tube connection. The disconnection itself was not discovered until after resuscitation measures had been commenced.

For the prosecution it was alleged that the appellant was guilty of gross negligence in failing to notice or respond appropriately to obvious signs that a disconnection had occurred and that the patient had ceased to breathe. In particular the prosecution alleged that the appellant had failed to notice at various stages during the period after disconnection and before the arrest either occurred or became inevitable that the patient's chest was not moving, the dials on the mechanical ventilating machine were not operating, the disconnection in the endotracheal tube, that the alarm on the ventilator was not switched on and that the patient was becoming progressively blue. Further the prosecution alleged that the appellant had noticed but failed to understand the correct significance of the fact that during this period the patient's pulse had dropped and the patient's blood pressure had dropped.

Two expert witnesses gave evidence for the prosecution. Professor Payne described that standard of care as 'abysmal' while Professor Adams stated in that in his view a competent anaesthetist should have recognised the signs of disconnection within 15 seconds and that the appellant's conduct amounted to 'a gross dereliction of care'.

On behalf of the appellant it was conceded at his trial that he had been negligent. The issue was therefore whether his conduct was criminal . . .

---

18 [1994] 5 Med LR 27.
19 [1994] 5 Med LR 27 (Lord Mackay of Clashfern LC, Lords Keith, Goff, Browne-Wilkinson and Woolf).

... [I]n my opinion the ordinary principles of the law of negligence apply to ascertain whether or not the defendant has been in breach of a duty of care towards the victim who has died. If such breach of duty is established the next question is whether that breach of duty caused the death of the victim. If so, the jury must go on to consider whether that breach of duty should be characterised as gross negligence and therefore as a crime. This will depend on the seriousness of the breach of duty committed by the defendant in all the circumstances in which the defendant was placed when it occurred. The jury will have to consider whether the extent to which the defendant's conduct departed from the proper standard of care incumbent upon him, involving as it must have done a risk of death to the patient, was such that it should be judged criminal.

It is true that to a certain extent this involves an element of circularity, but in this branch of the law I do not believe that is fatal to its being correct as a test of how far conduct must depart from accepted standards to be characterised as criminal. This is necessarily a question of degree and an attempt to specify that degree more closely is I think likely to achieve only a spurious precision. The essence of the matter which is supremely a jury question is whether, having regard to the risk of death involved, the conduct of the defendant was so bad in all the circumstances as to amount in their judgment to a criminal act or omission . . .

In my view the summing up of the learned judge in the present case was a model of clarity in analysis of the facts and in setting out the law in a manner which was readily comprehensible by the jury. The summing up was criticised in respect of the inclusion of the following passage ([1991] 2 Med LR 291):

> Of course you will understand it is not for every humble man of the profession to have all that great skill of the great men in Harley Street but, on the other hand, they are not allowed to practise medicine in this country unless they have acquired a certain amount of skill. They are bound to show a reasonable amount of skill according to the circumstances of the case, and you have to judge them on the basis that they are skilled men, but not necessarily so skilled as more skillful men in the profession, and you can only convict them criminally if, in your judgment, they fall below the standard of skill which is the least qualification which any doctor should have. You should only convict a doctor of causing a death by negligence if you think he did something which no reasonably skilled doctor should have done.

The criticism was particularly of the latter part of this quotation in that it was open to the meaning that if the defendant did what no reasonably skilled doctor should have done it was open to the jury to convict him of causing death by negligence. Strictly speaking this passage is concerned with the statement of a necessary condition for a conviction by preventing a conviction unless that condition is satisfied. It is incorrect to treat it as stating a sufficient condition for conviction. In any event I consider that this passage in the context was making the point forcefully that the defendant in this case was not to be judged by the standard of more skilled doctors but by the standard of a reasonably competent doctor. There were many other passages in the summing up which emphasised the need for a high degree of negligence if the jury were to convict and read in that context I consider that the summing up cannot be faulted.

For these reasons I am of the opinion that this appeal should be dismissed . . .

(Lords Keith, Goff, Browne-Wilkinson and Woolf agreed.)

In R v Amit Misra, R v Rajeev Srivastava[20] two doctors who had been convicted of manslaughter by gross negligence appealed. One of their arguments (the other related to the admission of fresh

---

20 [2004] EWCA Crim 2375.

evidence) was that the offence lacked certainty and therefore was incompatible with Articles 7 and 6 of the European Convention on Human Rights. The Court of Appeal rejected this argument, stating that the requirement for legal certainty of an offence was sufficient rather than absolute certainty and the European Convention had not changed this. The question for the jury to decide was whether the behaviour was grossly negligent and consequently criminal and this was a question of fact.

 SELF-TEST QUESTION

Should individual practitioners be prosecuted, or is it preferable that, say, the NHS Trust should be liable to a criminal sanction, instead?

2.4 Access to Health Care

2.4.1 Background – scarcity of NHS resources and setting priorities

Demand for NHS resources has always outstripped supply:

Timmins, N, *NHS 50th Anniversary: A History of the NHS*[21]

The new service uncovered a vast well of unmet need. GPs of the time recall women with prolapsed uteruses, who had been unable to afford the hospital treatment, suddenly pouring into the surgery, along with men with huge hernias held in by trusses. Bevan, who had declared the NHS would 'lift the shadow from millions of homes', had been right.

But there was also some abuse as GPs were inundated with people wanting wigs, or free cotton wool for padding, and free surgical spirit and aspirin. 'One would think the people saved up their illness for the first free day', one GP complained and Bevan himself, when the service had been running for 18 months, declared: 'I shudder to think of the ceaseless cascade of medicine which is pouring down British throats at the present time.'

Nonetheless, the NHS transformed health care – and not just for the poor, who were spared the indignity of means tests, but also for the middle classes, who no longer faced the fear of bills. It did so too for doctors. 'I used to charge 1/6d for a consultation,' one Clydeside GP recalled. 'They laid the money on the desk as they came in. It was all rather embarrassing. I used to charge 2/6d to 7/6d for a visit, the highest rate for foremen and undermanagers. We'd send out the bills, but about a quarter would be bad debts and some you simply didn't bill because you knew they couldn't pay. The NHS thankfully got rid of all that.'

In doing so, however, the service instantly faced the first of the great financial crises which were periodically to mark its history. Spending in the first nine months proved two thirds higher than expected. The sea of unmet need, the sheer difficulty of predicting in advance the costs of the new service, the rising expectations it generated and the costs of medical advance had all combined to blow the early budgets.

If this sounds familiar it is because it is the history of health services the world over. Take medical advance. The first antibiotic – penicillin – had become available, for troops, during the war. But the year 1948 saw new types of penicillin developed. Streptomycin, the first drug to successfully tackle tubercular meningitis – TB in the forties was a major scourge – became available. In both Britain and America, other new antibiotics were developed.

---

21 London: DoH, 1996, p 3.

Clearly, pressures on NHS resources are not simply a consequence of inefficiencies in the way the service is run (the issue that various governmental reforms have sought to address). Rather, in the light of constant advances in medical technology, they are to be regarded as inherent and inescapable in nature. It might be thought that it is the high-tech procedures and relatively short-term drugs for, say, cancer, that swell the NHS budget. Yet, 80 per cent of the total NHS budget goes to the Primary Care Trusts.[22] The availability of drugs to treat heart disease, and an ageing population, mean that many people are routinely prescribed these drugs for many years of their lives. Of course it is not so easy to separate these out because, for example, a heart bypass operation, which is normally very successful, will mean that the patient will subsequently be dependent upon, say, statins that control blood cholesterol for the rest of their lives. On the other hand a lot of health care expenditure will be on routine treatment of, in particular, children and the elderly and is not driven by technology.

In the ten-year NHS plan, launched by the government in July 2000, ambitious targets (backed by increased funding) were laid down for the NHS to achieve in terms of faster patient access to the most effective treatments.

Department of Health, *The NHS Plan, A Plan for Investment, A Plan for Reform*[23]

A3.1 To transform the health and social care system so that it produces faster, fairer services that deliver better health and tackles health inequalities.

Objectives and performance targets

Objective I: improving health outcomes for everyone

A3.2 Reduce substantially the mortality rates from major killers by 2010: from heart disease by at least 40% in people under 75; from cancer by at least 20% in people under 75; and from suicide and undetermined injury by at least 20%. Key to the delivery of this target will be implementing the National Service Frameworks for coronary heart disease and mental health and the National Cancer Plan.

A3.3 Our objective is to narrow the health gap in childhood and throughout life between socio-economic groups and between the most deprived areas and the rest of the country. Specific national targets will be developed in consultation with external stakeholders and experts early in 2001.

Objective II: improving patient and carer experience of the NHS and social services

A3.4 Patients will receive treatment at a time that suits them in accordance with their clinical need: two thirds of all outpatient appointments and inpatient elective admissions will be pre-booked by 2003/04 on the way to 100% pre-booking by 2005.

A3.5 Reduce the maximum wait for an outpatient appointment to three months and the maximum wait for inpatient treatment to 6 months by the end of 2005.

A3.6 To secure year-on-year improvements in patient satisfaction, including standards of cleanliness and food, as measured by independently audited local surveys.

Objective III: effective delivery of appropriate care . . .

Objective IV: fair access

A3.10 Guaranteed access to a primary care professional within 24 hours and to a primary care doctor within 48 hours by 2004.

---

22 www.ukpublicspending.co.uk.
23 London: DoH, 2000.

Objective V: value for money

A3.11 The cost of care commissioned from trusts which perform well against indicators of fair access, quality and responsiveness, will become the benchmark for the NHS. Everyone will be expected to reach the level of the best over the next 5 years, with agreed milestones for 2003/04.

Statement of accountability

A3.12 The Secretary of State for Health is accountable for the delivery of the targets set out in this Public Service Agreement.

However, it is apparent that the above 'agreement' functions primarily to define targets for NHS bodies to aim at, rather than conferring a set of enforceable rights upon patients. In terms of such latter rights, the patient remains dependent upon the action in the courts. What, then, are the available legal mechanisms through which a patient may challenge the denial of NHS treatment?

2.4.2 Judicial Review

Given the public status of the health service, and the constituent bodies within it (that is, health authorities, NHS trusts, etc), a decision not to provide some given treatment may be susceptible to challenge in public law. This means that such a decision, if viewed as *Wednesbury* unreasonable,[24] can be quashed by the courts. Lord Diplock in *Council of Civil Service Unions v Minister for the Civil Service*,[25] described the power of judicial review in the following terms:

Lord Diplock: It applies to a decision which is so outrageous in its defiance of logic or of accepted moral standards that no sensible person who had applied his mind to the question to be decided could have arrived at it. Whether a decision falls within this category is a question that judges by their training and experience should be well equipped to answer, or else there would be something badly wrong with our judicial system.[26]

The test has been slightly refined since the Human Rights Act 1998 came into force, inasmuch as,where Convention Rights are engaged, the courts should look at the degree of interference with those rights when deciding to question the exercise of an administrative discretion on grounds of *Wednesbury* unreasonableness.[27]

In the course of a number of actions brought in judicial review, however, the courts have shown themselves to be unwilling to interfere with decisions of NHS bodies in relation to the treatment of individual patients. In so doing, judges have recognised that the NHS has limited resources and that it is not for them to assume the role of organisers and arbiters of hospital waiting lists.

One of the first cases in which patients invoked judicial review in an attempt to assert a direct right to receive specified health care was that of R v *Secretary of State for Social Services et al ex p Hincks and Others*.[28] It concerned the obligation of the Secretary of State to provide medical services under s 3(1) of the National Health Service Act 1977 (now the National Health Service Act 2006), and in particular whether it imposed an absolute duty on the Secretary of State to provide services regardless of available funding. The wording of the Act (identical in the 2006 Act) is that he should provide services 'to such extent as he considers necessary to meet all reasonable requirements'. Four people who had been on the waiting list for orthopaedic surgery sought a declaration that the Secretary of

---

24 See *Associated Provincial Picture Houses v Wednesbury Corp* [1947] 2 All ER 680.
25 [1985] AC 374.
26 At p 410.
27 See R v *Ministry of Defence ex p Smith* [1996] 1 All ER 257.
28 (1980) 1 BMLR 93.

State was in breach of his duty when plans for additional orthopaedic services at a hospital could not be carried out because of lack of funding. The argument was that, as the additional services had been halted for financial reasons, it was not open to the Secretary of State to argue that he did not consider the additional services necessary. In refusing the declaration, the Court of Appeal stated that the Secretary of State has to have regard to the money made available to him.

In some cases the lives of patients can be seen to be at stake:

R v Central Birmingham HA ex p Walker, R v Secretary of State for Social Services and Another ex p Walker[29]

David Barber Walker was a premature baby who needed a heart operation. He had been cared for in hospital since his birth and was not in any immediate danger. His operation had been postponed on a number of occasions because of a shortage of specially trained nurses in the intensive care unit where he would have to go after the operation. His mother applied for leave to apply for judicial review of the decision to postpone the operation, seeking certiorari to quash the decision to postpone on the ground that it had been arrived at unlawfully and unreasonably, and mandamus to require the authority to carry out the operation. MacPherson J refused to allow the application.

The applicant's appeal to the Court of Appeal (Sir John Donaldson MR, Nicholls LJ and Caulfield J) was dismissed:

Sir John Donaldson MR: It is not for this court, or indeed any court, to substitute its own judgment for the judgment of those who are responsible for the allocation of resources. This court could only intervene where it was satisfied that there was a *prima facie* case, not only of failing to allocate resources in the way in which others would think that resources should be allocated, but of a failure to allocate resources to an extent which was *Wednesbury* unreasonable, if one likes to use the lawyers' jargon, or, in simpler words, which involves a breach of a public law duty ... Even then, of course, the court has to exercise a judicial discretion. It has to take account of all the circumstances of the particular case with which it is concerned.

A later case which considered the meaning of s 3(1) of the NHS Act 1977, and the scope of a health authority's duty to provide medical services, was R v Sheffield HA ex p Seale:

R v Sheffield HA ex p Seale J[30]

Julie Anne Seale sought in vitro fertilisation treatment from the respondent health authority. She was refused it on the grounds that, at 37 years of age, she was outside the age range within which the authority provided such treatment. The decision was challenged on three heads:

Auld J: The first is illegality. As I understand his submission, it is that as the Secretary of State has given no directions or imposed no limitations on the provision of *in vitro* fertilisation, and it is not for the district health authority, once it has committed itself to providing such a service, to restrict that provision ... [if there is a chance] of the treatment being effective. ...

It is not arguable, in my view, that [a district health authority] is bound, simply because it has undertaken to provide such a service, to provide it on demand to any individual patient for whom it may work, regardless of financial and other constraints upon the authority. Accordingly, I reject as unarguable any submission based on illegality here.

---

29 (1987) 3 BMLR 32.
30 (1994) 25 BMLR 1.

In my view it is clear that if the Secretary of State has not limited or given directions as to the way in which such a service, once undertaken, should be provided; the authority providing it is entitled to form a view as to those circumstances and when they justify provision and when they do not.

The second argument . . . [is that the decision] is irrational because it is not founded on any sustainable, clinical approach. . . . I cannot, nor could the court when deciding the matter as a substantive issue, if it came to that, form a view as to the rightness or wrongness of competing medical views on the effective cut-off date for the utility of such treatment. The decision letter does not say that the treatment cannot be effective after the age of 35, but merely that it is 'generally less effective in women aged over 35 years'.

If that is so, can Mr Straker challenge the decision as irrational on the basis that it is absurd to apply the age of 35 years as a blanket cut-off point, taking no account of individual circumstances? His submission is that every case should be considered individually. . . . I cannot say that it is absurd for this authority, acting on advice that the efficacy of this treatment decreases with age and that it is generally less effective after the age of 35, to take that as an appropriate criterion when balancing the need for such a provision against its ability to provide it and all the other services imposed upon it under the legislation.

See Chapter 7 ➜
The application was refused. (On the provision of fertility treatment generally, see further Chapter 7.)

Seale is a useful decision as it shows a slightly less resolute approach being taken to resource allocation issues compared with cases such as *Walker*. Christopher Newdick has commented on the case as follows:

Newdick, C, 'Resource allocation in the NHS'[31]

Although the application was refused on its merits the case distinguishes between 'critical', and other, illnesses. If critical illness necessitates an individual clinical decision of the case the *Wednesbury* test of managerial reasonableness is presumably limited to other areas of elective or optional health care. Note how uncomfortably this approach to clinical merits sits with *Collier*. This case is useful on its own facts for identifying that some care may fall into a category in which a clinical assessment is necessary. It says nothing however, about the components of such a decision, who is responsible for making it, or where the line should be drawn.

It does not, of course, follow from the fact that the patient may sometimes be entitled to have his or her own circumstances and condition clinically assessed, that treatment need actually be provided. Indeed, as a corollary of the general ethical obligation on doctors to act in their patients' best interests, it may be that in a particular case no doctor will be found who is willing to carry it out, for example, where it involves serious side effects for the patient and is believed to be of little or no therapeutic benefit. Certainly, the fact that the patient, where competent, wishes to receive the treatment will usually be a strong indicator that such treatment is in his best interests. Nevertheless, there will be exceptions, especially where terminal illness has been diagnosed, and claims for treatment brought on behalf of incompetent patients may also present difficulties.

A well-known case, which raised issues of this nature, as well as the question of how far financial considerations should play a part in the deliberations of the treatment provider, was that

---

31 (1997) 23(2–3) Am J Law & Med 291.

of R v *Cambridge HA ex p B (A Minor)*. A ten-year-old girl was refused the resources for further remedial treatment. She was suffering from acute myeloid leukaemia. The doctors responsible for her care believed that no further treatment could be usefully given to her beyond palliative care. Her father sought further medical treatment by chemotherapy with a view to a second bone marrow transplant. Taking into account clinical judgement, the nature of the treatment requested and its very low chances of success (it was described by the doctors as 'experimental'), the health authority declined the father's request. He sought judicial review of the health authority's decision, which was granted by Laws J at first instance. The authority appealed:

R v Cambridge HA ex p B (A Minor) [32]

Sir Thomas Bingham MR: First, [the judge] took the view that Dr Zimmern as the decision maker had wrongly failed to have regard to the wishes of the patient, as expressed on behalf of the patient by her family. . . .

It seems to me that the judge's criticism entirely fails to recognise the realities of this situation . . .

[Dr Zimmern] was put under perfectly legitimate, but very obvious, pressure by the family to procure this treatment and he was responding to that pressure. . . . To complain that he did not in terms say that he had regard to the wishes of the patient as expressed by the family, is to shut one's eyes to the reality of the situation with which he was confronted.

The second criticism that is made is of the use of the expression 'experimental' to describe this treatment . . .

The plain fact is that, unlike many courses of medical treatment, this was not one that had a well tried track record of success. It was, on any showing, at the frontier of medical science. That being so, it does not, in my judgment, carry weight to describe this decision as flawed because of the use of this expression.

The third criticism that is made by the judge is of the reference to resources. . . .

. . . Difficult and agonising judgments have to be made as to how a limited budget is best allocated to the maximum advantage of the maximum number of patients. That is not a judgment which the court can make. In my judgment, it is not something that a health authority such as this authority can be fairly criticised for not advancing before the court.

. . .

The fourth criticism which the judge made was that the authority had wrongly treated the problem which they faced as one of spending £75,000 when, in the first instance, the treatment only involved the expenditure of £15,000. . . . It is, of course, true that if the first stage were unsuccessful, then £15,000, or even less than £15,000, would be the maximum that the authority would end up spending. It would not, however, be reasonable for the authority to embark on this expenditure on that basis since, quite plainly, they would have to continue if, having expended the £15,000, it proved successful and the call for the second stage of the treatment came. It was, therefore, an inescapable decision whether they should embark on this process at all.

The treatment was subsequently paid for by an anonymous benefactor, although B eventually died, in March 1996. She did, however, survive well beyond the six to eight weeks' estimate that the health authority had originally given her to live.

Richard Mullender has commented upon the case as follows, stating the Laws J did refer to the 'right to life', although the Court of Appeal did not expressly refer to this:

---

32 (1995) 23 BMLR 1 (Sir Thomas Bingham MR, Sir Stephen Brown P, Simon Brown LJ).

Mullender, R, 'Judicial review and the rule of law'[33]

. . . While the bulk of the judge's analysis concerns the right to life, he, nonetheless, states that the same result can be reached by applying *Wednesbury* and identifies four forms of unreasonableness manifested by the health authority: viz, failure to consider the wishes of B's family, wrongly characterising the treatment sought as 'experimental', failure to explain the priorities that led to the decision not to provide it, and an inaccurate estimate of its cost.

In contrast to the judgment of Laws J, the right to life plays no part in that of Bingham MR, notwithstanding his observing both that 'our society is one in which a very high value is put on human life' and that 'no decision affecting human life . . . can be regarded with other than the greatest seriousness'. While, in the light of these comments, the Master of the Rolls' decision not to invoke the right to life might seem surprising, his not doing so can be explained by his commitment to the principle that, in judicial review proceedings, judges must merely scrutinise the lawfulness of a public body's decision and must not adjudicate upon its merits – a commitment to which he gives emphatic expression thus: '. . . we have one function only, which is to rule upon the lawfulness of decisions. That is a function to which we should strictly confine ourselves.' It is, hence, unsurprising to find him basing his decision not on the right to life, but, rather, on the ground of *Wednesbury* unreasonableness, which specifies a modest standard of review and, thus, leaves public bodies with broad scope for making discretionary decisions. The interpretation placed by Bingham MR on *Wednesbury* diverges radically from that of Laws J: he rescinds the judge's quashing order, identifying as unsustainable all four of the grounds on which the latter found the health authority's denial of treatment to be unreasonable.

The case was decided some time before the Human Rights Act came into force. The application of European Convention Rights is considered below.

The maintenance by a health authority of a policy directly opposed to Department of Health Circulars and advice will – in the absence of the clearest justifying reasons – fail the *Wednesbury* test. This was established in the case of R v North Derbyshire HA ex p Fisher:

R v North Derbyshire HA ex p Fisher[34]

Kenneth Fisher, who suffered from the relapsing/remitting form of multiple sclerosis, challenged the refusal of his health authority, North Derbyshire, to finance his treatment with a new form of drug therapy, beta-interferon, which he had been assessed as suitable to receive by doctors at the NHS trust in Sheffield where he was being treated. North Derbyshire's refusal reflected the view of its own experts that beta-interferon (which was expensive) was of unproven therapeutic benefit, which conflicted with the terms of an NHS Circular, EL (95) 97, in which the NHS Executive asked health authorities to assist in implementing the use of the drug:

Dyson J: [The] lawfulness [of the authority's policy] must be judged in accordance with *Wednesbury* principles against the background of national policy which was set out fully and firmly in the guidance to be found in the Circular. The respondents had to have regard to that national policy. They were not obliged to follow the policy, but if they decided to depart from it, they had to give clear reasons for so doing, and those reasons would have been susceptible to a *Wednesbury* challenge . . . Moreover, if the respondents failed properly to understand the Circular, then their policy would be as defective as if no regard had been paid to the policy at all. It is accepted on behalf of the respondents that they were under a duty to give serious consideration to each

---

33 (1996) 112 LQR 182.
34 [1997] 8 Med LR 327.

aspect of the Circular. Mr Seys Llewllyn submits that the respondents' policy was an honest and conscientious way of managing the introduction into the NHS of the new drug, and was at least consistent with the Circular.

In my judgment the policy was plainly not in accordance with the Circular. The Circular asked for purchasing authorities and providers:

> To develop and implement local arrangements to manage the entry of such drugs into the NHS . . . and in particular to initiate a continued prescribing of beta-interferon through hospitals.

One of the key aims was to 'target the drug appropriately at patients who were most likely to benefit from treatment'. In other words, the Circular was giving guidance as to how most effectively beta-interferon could be introduced into the NHS as a drug to be prescribed to treat patients . . . I do not consider that the respondents' policy could at any time have fairly been described as a reasonable way of giving effect to the Circular. The respondents, like others, no doubt honestly and conscientiously believed that the efficacy of beta-interferon had not been sufficiently tested. The assumption that underpinned the Circular was that it had been sufficiently tested . . . This is not a case in which a health authority departed from the national policy because there were special factors which it considered exceptionally justified departure. . . . The respondents did not take the Circular into account and decide exceptionally not to follow it. They decided to disregard it altogether throughout 1996, because they were opposed to it. That is something which in my judgment they were not entitled to do.

Similarly, in R v North West Lancashire HA ex p A, D and G, the application for judicial review was successful due to another example of a somewhat cavalier attitude of a health authority. Three transsexuals brought an action in judicial review after the respondent health authority refused to fund their gender reassignment surgery. Whilst the health authority had accepted that transsexualism is an illness capable of being dealt with by surgical intervention, the policy formulated to deal with it was based upon the belief of the authority's public health consultant that transsexualism should be dealt with by way of psychiatric intervention only. There was nothing unlawful, in principle, about the authority's policy of according cases of transsexualism lower priority and refusing gender reassignment surgery save in exceptional cases, but here there could be no exceptional circumstances, and that was irrational. As Buxton LJ noted:

R v North West Lancashire HA ex p A, D and G [35]

Buxton LJ: [A]s the evidence in this application demonstrated . . . there is a strong and respectable body of medical opinion that considers gender reassignment procedures to be effective in suitable and properly selected cases . . . I emphasise that the mere fact that a body of medical opinion supports the procedure does not put the health authority under any legal obligation to provide the procedure: the standard here is far removed from the *Bolam* approach in cases of medical negligence. However, where such a body of opinion exists it is in my view not open to a rational health authority simply to determine that a procedure has no proven clinical benefit while giving no indication of why it considers that that is so . . .

I am therefore driven to the conclusion that the health authority has not demonstrated that degree of rational consideration that can reasonably be expected of it before it decides in effect to give no funding at all to a procedure supported by

---

35 Auld, Buxton and May LJJ [1999] Lloyd's Rep Med 399 (CA).

respectable clinicians and psychiatrists, which is said to be necessary in certain cases to relieve extreme mental distress.

R (on the application of Ann Marie Rogers) v Swindon NHS PCT (Respondent) & Secretary of State for Health (Interested Party)[36] concerned a challenge to the decision of the PCT not to fund the drug 'Herceptin' to all women with early stage breast cancer, save in 'exceptional circumstances'. The PCT claimed that this had nothing to do with cost. In consequence, the court could readily find that the policy was irrational, as once the cost factor had been discounted, the only criterion would then relate to the legitimate clinical needs of the patient, and since the PCT had not stipulated and could not stipulate what sorts of circumstances would be 'exceptional', it meant that they did not envisage offering anyone this treatment. A policy adopted by a PCT must genuinely recognise the possibility of an individual meeting its criteria; since there was no conceivable way of distinguishing between eligible individuals, the policy was irrational.

Another basis on which the courts have proven willing to quash decisions by health authorities in judicial review is that of procedural irregularity. Thus, in *R v North and East Devon HA ex p Coughlan*[37] the Court of Appeal held that the respondent authority's planned closure of the severely disabled applicant's care home, contrary to an earlier promise that it would be her home for life, was an unlawful breach of her legitimate expectations. This can be contrasted with the case of *R (On the application of Haggerty and Others) v St Helen's Borough Council*[38] where a similar complaint was made about the closure of a local authority home for the elderly which service was being taken over by a private contractor, but where the application failed on the basis that there had been no promise of 'a home for life'. See also the case of *R v North and East Devon HA ex p Pow*[39] in which a decision to close a hospital was set aside by the High Court (Moses J) due to the health authority's failure to engage in the required consultation process beforehand, and contrast this with *R (on the application of Val Compton (on behalf of Community Action For Savernake Hospital)) v Wiltshire Primary Care Trust*,[40] where a hospital closed after an extensive consultation exercise and the action in judicial review failed.

So far we have been looking at cases in which the judicial review applications have been made against the bodies (usually health authorities) directly responsible for providing or funding treatment. However, this is not the only possibility. In particular, given the increasing tendency for treatment targets and priorities to be set centrally by the Department of Health, the latter too may find its decisions challenged where a link can be shown between such central guidance and the denial of some particular treatment 'on the ground'. This is illustrated by the lengthy attempt by the drug manufacturerr Pfizer to overturn the government's refusal to approve, other than in exceptional circumstances, the prescription of the drug Viagra (otherwise know as silenafil). In *R v Secretary of State for Health ex p Pfizer*[41] the NHS Circular in which this advice was contained (HSC 1998/158) was successfully challenged by Pfizer. Collins J held that this guidance imposed an unreasonable fetter upon the discretion of GPs (the Circular stated that the 'exceptional circumstances' in which the drug could be prescribed had to be cleared with the NHS in advance of prescription). Further, it was in breach of the European 'Transparency Directive' 89/105/EEC. Following this judgment the government took steps to remedy the situation by issuing regulations pursuant to the National Health Service Act 1977 by adding Viagra to the schedule of drugs where availability is limited.[42] Pfizer mounted a second challenge on the ground that this was still in breach of the directive because this states that the criteria to exclude services in such a situation

---

36 [2006] EWCA Civ 392 (CA).
37 [2001] QB 213.
38 [2003] EWHC 803.
39 (1997) 39 BMLR 77, QBD.
40 [2009] EWHC 1824 (Admin).
41 [1999] Lloyd's Rep Med 289.
42 Sch 11, National Health Service (General Medical Services) Regulations 1992 (as amended).

must be available and transparent (Article 7(3)). Pfizer's argument was that the government's statement to the European Commission ostensibly justifying the decision, only referred to cost and did not explain how the treatment of erectile dysfunction should be compared with that for other non-life threatening conditions. The Court of Appeal (R (On the Application of Pfizer Limited) v Secretary of State for Health[43] held that the directive did not require such a statement of competing priorities and therefore there was no breach.[44]

A developing area in the provision of healthcare is the extent to which patients are entitled to require the NHS to fund medical treatment in other Member States of the EU. This brings into play Article 49 of the EC Treaty as it relates to prohibition on restrictions on freedom to provide services and Article 22 of Council Regulation 1408/71 which provides that a person, who is a national of a Member State and is insured under the legislation of the Member State and members of his family residing with him, who is 'authorised by the competent institution to go to the territory of another Member State to receive there the treatment appropriate to his condition', may do so at the expense of the competent institution. Clearly, there could be serious implications for those who wish to seek medical treatment in other EU Member States to avoid waiting lists. In R (on the application of Yvonne Watts) v (1) Bedford Primary Care Trust (2) Secretary of State for Health[45] it was held by the Court of Appeal that Article 49 applied but that a reference would be made to the European Court of Justice for a ruling on the correct interpretation of Article 22 on such as case as this. The decision of the ECJ was that pursuant to Article 22 of the Council Regulation, a patient could go to another member state to receive medical treatment and be reimbursed the cost where there would, on an objective medical assessment of his medical circumstances, be an unacceptable delay before treatment could be provided in the UK. The Court acknowledged that waiting lists could be an acceptable way of managing the supply of health care as long as they were managed on the basis of predetermined clinical priorities R (on the application of Watts) v Bedford Primary Care Trust.[46]

2.4.3 European Convention on Human Rights

In R v North West Lancashire HA ex p A, D and G,[47] considered above, the applicants for judicial review were successful at first instance and the Court of Appeal. However, although the European Convention was canvassed before the courts because it was decided shortly before the Human Rights Act 1998 Act came into force, the Court of Appeal was robust in rejecting what it termed 'unfocused recourse' to the ECHR, and decided the case on the basis of English law principles. As Auld LJ commented:

> **Auld LJ**: As to the European Convention of Human Rights, it is not yet part of our domestic law and is relevant only, in an appropriate case, to the Court's consideration of rationality. Mr Blake indicated that the purpose of his fairly detailed submissions and references to Strasbourg jurisprudence was merely to show that transsexualism is a sufficiently serious condition 'to raise human rights problems'. Such an unfocused recourse to that jurisdiction, whether before or after the statutory absorption of part of the Convention into the law of England and Wales, is not helpful to the Court. Indeed, it is positively unhelpful, cluttering up its consideration of adequate and more precise domestic principles and authorities governing the issues in play. Thus, the deployment of generalised propositions from the ECHR that a person's sexual identity is of sufficient importance to attract the protection of the right to respect for private and family life under

---

43 [2002] EWCA Civ 1566).
44 See Syrett, K, 'Impotence or Importance? Judicial Review in an Era of Explicit NHS Rationing' (2004) 67(2) MLR 289.
45 [2004] EWCA Civ 166.
46 (C–372/04) (2006) ECR I–4325 (ECJ).
47 [1999] Lloyd's Rep Med 399.

Article 8, or that a denial of medical treatment may, if sufficiently serious, amount to 'inhuman or degrading treatment' under Article 3, contributes nothing to resolution of the issues here (see, eg, *Rees v United Kingdom* (1988) 9 EHRR 56; *Cossey v United Kingdom* (1991) 13 EHRR 622; and the dissenting opinion of Judge Pettiti in *B v France* (1992) 16 EHRR 1, pp 40–41). It is common ground in this case that transsexualism is an illness; the issues are whether the Authority's policy for the public funding of treatment of it properly reflects that and whether it makes proper provision for consideration of each application for treatment on its individual merits.

In any event, Article 8 imposes no positive obligations to provide treatment . . . As Hidden J observed, in rejecting similar submissions below:

> The Convention does not give the applicants rights to free healthcare in general or to gender reassignment surgery in particular. Even if the applicants had such a right it would be qualified by the respondent's right to determine healthcare priorities in the light of its limited resources.

It may be somewhat different in cases where life-saving treatment is at issue and the patient's right to life under Art 2 of the ECHR is engaged. However, as Butler-Sloss P noted in *NHS Trust A v M, NHS Trust B v H*,[48] it is clear that the positive obligation upon a state to safeguard life is not an absolute one. In that case, her Ladyship held that, insofar as it accords with respectable medical opinion, a decision to withhold life-sustaining treatment considered not to be in the patient's best interests, would not breach the Article. For a general examination of the role of judicial review in the light of the Human Rights Act 1998, see the judgment of Lord Walker in *R (on the application of Pro-Life Alliance) v BBC*[49] in particular examining the concepts of 'proportionality' and 'margin of appreciation'.

See Chapter 12 →

On the other hand, what does seem clear is that in cases where decisions by health authorities not to fund treatment impinge upon the fundamental interests of patients, the court will subject it to a greater degree of scrutiny in order to be satisfied that it passes the *Wednesbury* test. Phil Fennell, commenting upon the view of the ECHR expressed by the Court of Appeal in *R v North West Lancashire HA ex p A, D and G*, has argued:

Fennell, P, 'Substantive review of decisions to refuse treatment'[50]

An array of arguments based on the European Convention of Human Rights and EU law was given short shrift by their Lordships, their preferred approach being through principles of English administrative law. Although the Court of Appeal judges were unanimous in holding that no Convention rights were engaged here, they nevertheless approached the question from the point of view that a fundamental interest was at stake. Therefore the decision-makers had to substantially consider their decision, and the courts would scrutinise carefully that decision to ensure that they have weighed their justification for interfering with that interest against the importance of the interest. 'Careful scrutiny' may differ in intensity from the 'anxious scrutiny' which has been held appropriate in cases where Convention Rights are engaged. Nevertheless, the basic approach remains as described by Lord Woolf MR in *R v Lord Saville of Newdigate ex p A* [1999] 4 All ER 860, where he said:

> [W]hen a fundamental right such as the right to life is engaged, the options open to a reasonable decision-maker are curtailed. They are curtailed because it is unreasonable to reach a decision which contravenes or could contravene a human right unless there

48 [2001] Fam 348.
49 [2003] UKHL 23.
50 (2000) 8 Med L Rev 129.

are sufficiently significant countervailing considerations. In other words it is not open to the decision-maker to risk interfering with fundamental rights in the absence of compelling justification. Even the broadest discretion is constrained by the need for there to be countervailing circumstances to justify interference with human rights. The courts will anxiously scrutinise the strength of the countervailing circumstances and the degree of interference with the human right involved and then apply the test accepted by Lord Bingham MR in *R v Ministry of Defence ex p Smith* [1996] 1 All ER 257, p 263.

In other words where Convention Rights are engaged, the courts will apply a sliding scale in judging whether to intervene on substantive grounds with the exercise of an administrative discretion on grounds of *Wednesbury* unreasonableness. The more substantial the interference with human rights posed by the decision which is subject to challenge, 'the more the court will require by way of justification before it is satisfied that the decision is reasonable'.

In R v North West Lancashire HA ex p A, D and G,[51] where a 'fundamental interest' rather than a human right was at stake, it was said that a similar sliding scale operated:

The more important the interest of the citizen that the decision affects, the greater will be the degree of consideration that is required of the decision-maker. A decision that, as is the evidence in this case, seriously affects the citizen's health will require substantial consideration, and be subject to careful scrutiny by the court as to its rationality. That will particularly be the case in respect of decisions which involve the refusing of any, or any significant, treatment in respect of an identified and substantial medical condition.

 SELF-TEST QUESTION

Do you think that the reference to a 'fundamental interest' is a useful development in judicial review, or do you think that there is no significant difference between a fundamental interest and a Convention right?

2.4.4 Private law remedies

2.4.4.1 Breach of statutory duty

Rather than bringing a claim in judicial review, could a claimant challenge a decision over health care resource allocation in private law? Jonathan Montgomery addresses the possibility here of an action being maintained for breach of statutory duty, but sees little scope for the successful use of this tort in relation to the National Health Service Act 1977 (and note that the same considerations could apply to s 45 of the Health and Social Care (Community Health and Standards) Act 2003 – see above):

Montgomery, J, *Health Care Law*[52]

In an action for the tort of breach of statutory duty, it is alleged that damage has been caused . . . due to the failure to perform a statutory duty which exists for the benefit of the aggrieved individual, and which parliament intended to be enforceable, . . . by that individual. Thus,

---

51 Per Buxton LJ [1999] Lloyd's Rep Med 399, p 412.
52 Oxford: OUP, 2003.

patients denied services could argue that the NHS body responsible had failed to perform its statutory obligations and had harmed them. . . . However, the courts have shown themselves to be reluctant to permit actions for the breach of duties to provide welfare services, and it is unlikely that such an action could be brought under the NHS Act 1977.

The House of Lords has noted that there has been no case in which statutory social welfare schemes, established for the benefit of the public at large, have been held to give rise to a private law action for damages. Against this authority, there was a suggestion in *R v Ealing DHA ex p Fox* that a specific duty to provide services for discharged mental patients could be spelt out from the provisions of s 3(1) of the NHS Act 1977. It was not necessary for the judge in this case to consider this point, as such a duty was explicitly set out in s 117 of the Mental Health Act 1983. Consequently, it would be dangerous to rely on his comment.

It is possible that the courts will prove themselves less reticent where the statutory duties are more specific, because it is easier to show that the individual was entitled to expect a service to be provided. Thus, a failure to provide after-care services under the Mental Health Act 1983, s 117, might more readily form the basis of an action for breach of statutory duty. There, it will be clear that the individual patient, who has now been discharged, should be receiving help. It is not a general duty owed to the public, but a specific one owed to an identified individual. It may also be possible to use the action for breach of statutory duty where patients are promised specific services after an assessment of their needs, and are then not given them because the relevant authority failed to execute their decision. However, this sort of failure may be more amenable to a claim in negligence.

2.4.4.2 Negligence and health resources

Patients who are denied treatment might also attempt to argue that a health authority or trust has acted carelessly towards them and they have suffered injury as a result. General principles of the law of tort would be applied and the action framed as a malpractice suit (see further Chapter 6). To the extent that treatment is provided, then it is apparent that lack of resources cannot be used as an excuse for failure to reach the requisite standard of care: see *Wilsher v Essex AHA*[53] and *Bull v Devon AHA*.[54] However, it is unlikely that an action in negligence would lie where, due to lack of resources, a decision is taken not to treat in the first place. Certainly, where the NHS body simply refused to make a given facility available, it is difficult to see how any duty of care would arise between it and the patient.

Summary of Key Points

1. The National Health Service, established in 1946, provides a comprehensive health care system which is free at the point of delivery. Its structure has changed on a number of occasions over the years and it is always vulnerable to further structural change by new governments because of its ever-increasing costs. Changes in medicine, technology and an ageing population are the main causes for this.

2. Regulation of the quality of health care consists of internal processes within the NHS which have proliferated as medical litigation has increased. There are bodies that are concerned with risk management and patient safety and NICE will also certify (or refuse to certify) new drugs and other treatments for use in the NHS which makes it a target for judicial review.

3. Complaints about quality of care can be dealt with through the NHS complaints system, and in serious cases applications can be made to the professional bodies that regulate health care professions, such as the General Medical Council.

---

53 [1987] QB 730, CA.
54 [1993] 4 Med LR 117.

4. Patients cannot demand any treatment they wish, but when certain treatments are denied them, eg new and expensive drugs, the patient can ask for the decision to be judicially reviewed.

5. Since the passing of the Human Rights Act 1998 and the incorporation of most of the European Convention on Human Rights into English law, the judicial review test has been slightly modified to accommodate cases where judicial review has been sought on the ground that one or more of the Convention Rights have been interfered with, but on the whole, the courts take a cautious approach to judicial review applications.

Further Reading

Ham, C, *Health Policy in Britain*, Basingstoke: Palgrave Macmillan, 2009.
Newdick, C, *Who Should We Treat?*, Oxford: Clarendon, 2005.
Rhodes, R, Battin, M, and Silvers, A, *Medicine and Social Justice*, Oxford: OUP, 2005.

Chapter 3

Consent to Treatment

Chapter Contents

3.1 Introduction

3.1.1 Background

The requirement that a patient must give a valid consent to medical treatment and its corollary, that it is the patient's prerogative to refuse treatment, even at the cost of his life, are issues at the heart of medical law. It is necessary, therefore, to examine the essential elements which have to be satisfied in order for a patient to give a valid consent. On the other hand, the boundaries and basis of consent also need to be considered: most significantly, asking the patient to consent presupposes that they are autonomously capable of deciding about the treatment they are willing to undergo. In this regard, it has no relevance to those with serious mental disabilities, who lack the necessary mental capacity (ie, understanding) to make such decisions – the rules dealing with the latter are looked at in Chapter 4. Similarly, our discussion of the position of children will be deferred until then.

 See Chapter 4

The present chapter has the following structure. After next considering the ethical underpinnings of consent, we shall, in section 3.2, begin our analysis of the general legal framework by examining the doctor's potential liability if consent is absent (and occasionally even if it is present); we also look there at the rules as to the form and scope of consent. By contrast, section 3.3 addresses some exceptional situations, where (at least, arguably) treatment may proceed without consent. In section 3.4, we then move on to examine what is actually required for a patient to give a valid consent, in terms of capacity, voluntariness, and information. Each of these elements has its complexities, not least the informational requirement, where English law distinguishes between non-disclosures that found an action in battery, and those where the proper cause of action is negligence. In section 3.5 we conclude by looking at the latter type of action, which typically concern a doctor's failure to disclose risks attached to the treatment, and what it is the patient must show in order to obtain compensation.

3.1.2 Ethical Considerations – autonomy and paternalism

In Chapter 1 we looked at the conflict between the patient's right to autonomous decision-making and medical paternalism, and nowhere is this more apparent than in the issue of consent to treatment. Medical treatment, involving as it does an invasion of the

 See Chapter 1

patient's body, takes a prima facie harmful form: its delivery invariably involves a degree of physical restraint and often also entails exposure to harm, or the risk thereof, of a serious nature. This being so, a struggle may ensue between the doctor, who believes that, in the long run, the risks and harm are a price worth paying and the patient, who would rather not be interfered with, even if this makes further debility and premature death more likely. The debate between 'paternalism' and 'patient autonomy' is essentially about whose view should prevail in such circumstances.

It will be recalled that Mill's libertarian philosophy is particularly relevant to the issue of consent:

Mill, JS, *On Liberty*[1]

. . . [T]he only purpose for which power can be rightfully exercised over any member of a civilised community, against his will, is to prevent harm to others. His own good, either physical or moral, is not a sufficient warrant. He cannot rightfully be compelled to do or forbear because it will be better for him to do so, because it will make him happier, because, in the opinions of others, to do so would be wise, or even right.

---

1   (1859): reprint, Harmondsworth: Penguin, 1982.

This approach finds close parallels in the Kantian view that persons are ends in them-selves, not simply means to the ends of other people. On this view, the failure to respect autonomy represents a breach of the duty of respect we owe to others in view of their inherent dignity as rational agents. Sometimes Kant's view of autonomy (as well as that of Mill) has been criticised for involving an overly atomised conception of the individual, but in the following extract Alasdair Maclean defends it against such a charge:

Maclean, A, *Autonomy, Informed Consent and Medical Law – A Relational Challenge*[2]

It is important to recognise that any valuable or useful conception of autonomy grounded in moral person hood and respect for that person hood – both for the actor and for others – must allow and coexist with influences, constraints and obligations arising from the relationships that envelop us. Reducing individuals to isolated atomistic existences undermines the concept of autonomy . . .

Kant's view of autonomy, for all of its problems . . . is essentially relational. Wholly self-regarding decision-making, even if possible, falls foul of both the universalisability formu-lation and the ends/means formulation of Kant's imperative. To live in the context of a social existence means that, in making decisions, the individual should take into account the impact of the decision on at least those others who exist in a close relationship with the individual. The impact on society of a rule that requires only self-regard in making decisions would be as great in severing the social bonds as a rule that permits lying. When applied in the context of health-care, this universal rule would impose on patients a duty to at least take into account the impact of their decision on those others that exist in close relationships with them. There is no reason why this could not be included as a rule of consent.

There are also consequentialist reasons in favour of the need for consent, in terms of the dangers of not having such a rule. These were noted by an American court in the striking case of *McFall v Shimp*,[3] in which a patient required a bone marrow donation to avoid almost certain death. The procedure for donation was virtually risk-free, and if a donation from a suitable donor went ahead, the prognosis was excellent. The patient's cousin had volunteered for a compatibility test, but when the test showed him to be a suitable donor, he declined to undergo further tests or to donate the bone marrow. The patient sought an injunction to compel his cousin to make the donation:

Flaherty J: The common law has consistently held to a rule which provides that one human being is under no legal compulsion to give aid or to take action to save that human being or to rescue. A great deal has been written regarding this rule which, on the surface, appears to be revolting in a moral sense. Introspection, however, will demonstrate that the rule is founded upon the very essence of our free society. It is noteworthy that counsel for the plaintiff has cited authority which has developed in other societies in support of the plaintiff's request in this instance. Our society, contrary to many others, has as its first principle, the respect for the individual, and that society and government exist to protect the individual from being invaded and hurt by another. Many societies adopt a contrary view which has the individual existing to service the society as a whole. In preserving such a society as we have it is bound to happen that great moral conflicts will arise, and will appear harsh in a given instance. In this case, the Chancellor is being asked to force one member of society to undergo a medical procedure which would provide that part of that individual's body would be removed from him and given

2   Cambridge: CUP, 2009.
3   10 Pa D & C (3d) 90 (1978).

to another so that the other could live. Morally, this decision rests with the defendant, and, in the view of the court, the refusal of the defendant is morally indefensible. For our law to compel the defendant to submit to an intrusion of his body would change every concept and principle upon which our society is founded. To do so would defeat the sanctity of the individual, and would impose a rule which would know no limits, and one could not imagine where the line would be drawn.

On the other hand, the situation may be felt to be different, where the therapy stands to benefit the patient, whose consent is at issue: here a doctor could, perhaps, be forgiven for believing that the principle of autonomy should be sacrificed in the best interests of the patient. Indeed, as we saw in Chapter 1, even a strong libertarian such as Mill accepted a limited form of paternalism when it was necessary to intervene temporarily to restore autonomy. However, this is not, perhaps, true paternalism: if autonomy has to be restored, then arguably it could not have been exercised in the first place. More problematic are cases where a patient reaches a decision out of step with their own autonomy considered in the long-term; here a temporary, paternalistically motivated, intervention would arguably also serve the patient's overall autonomy interest. Alisdair Maclean discusses this type of problem as follows:

See Chapter 1

Maclean, A, *Autonomy, Informed Consent and Medical Law – A Relational Challenge*[4]

I argued [earlier] that respect for the patient's autonomy did not permit overriding that person's autonomy in order to protect his or her future autonomy. It might be argued that this is fine as far as defining a general position but that paternalism may still be justifiable in the short term to prevent irrational harm if such decisions are made on a case-by-case basis. The problem with this argument is that it is impossible to isolate cases in this way. As soon as such cases occur they begin to create a more general position and it becomes natural to use each case as a precedent for a new situation with slightly different circumstances so that such a casuistic approach soon starts to resemble a general principle.

This may not completely defeat the casuistic, consequentialist approach if sufficient safe-guards can be established to prevent the slippery slide into a general principle. However, over-riding a person's decision may undermine their confidence in the security of their autonomy. Once one's decision-making has been overridden it implies that the same could happen again, which is problematic – especially when it is a decision that actually matters and the stakes are high – since it threatens to undermine the whole value of autonomy . . .

A further point supporting a non-paternalist position arises from the risk of bad luck. Even with the best will in the world things sometimes go badly. Most, if not all, medical interventions carry some risk, often of quite serious consequences. Since the patient will have to live with those consequences it should be the patient who controls whether or not the treatment is undergone.

Perhaps for these reasons, the law, does not accept paternalism in any form as a permissible argu-ment for imposing treatment upon capable (or competent) patients. At least this is true for adults; as we shall see in Chapter 4, one situation, where the law is prepared to be paternalistic relates to children who purport to refuse treatment with serious implications for their continued life or health; this attitude is captured in the dictum of Ward J in *Re E (A Minor) (Wardship: Medical Treatment)*[5] that 'a court should be slow to let a child martyr himself'.

See Chapter 4

---

4   See n 2, above.
5   [1993] 1 FLR 386.

Conversely, paternalism continues to have legal relevance as providing one justification for an upper limit on what may lawfully be consented to. We shall consider this issue in more detail shortly, under 3.2.1.3.

3.2 The Legal Framework

3.2.1 The protection of bodily integrity

The importance of bodily inviolability is entrenched in the law of Western societies. Every student of medical law is familiar with the statement made by Cardozo J in *Schloendorff v New York Hospitals*:[6]

> **Cardozo J**: Every human being of adult years and sound mind has a right to determine what shall be done with his own body; and a surgeon who performs an operation without his patient's consent, commits an assault . . .

As we shall see below, the English courts have generally also emphasised the primacy of patient autonomy or self-determination and its effect of blocking the doctor's right (and his duty) to invade the patient's bodily integrity so as to treat the patient. This is so, notwithstanding that the treatment might be regarded as in the latter's best interests. In *Airedale NHS Trust v Bland*,[7] Lord Goff commented:

> **Lord Goff of Chieveley**: . . . [I]t is established that the principle of self-determination requires that respect must be given to the wishes of the patient, so that if an adult patient of sound mind refuses, however unreasonably, to consent to treatment or care by which his life would or might be prolonged, the doctors responsible for his care must give effect to his wishes, even though they do not consider it to be in his best interests to do so . . . To this extent, the principle of the sanctity of human life must yield to the principle of self-determination . . . and, for present purposes perhaps more important, the doctor's duty to act in the best interests of his patient must likewise be qualified.

Insofar as the doctor proceeds to treat without consent, he will potentially be liable both in civil and criminal law.

3.2.1.1 Civil law: battery

As regards the position in tort, a valid consent to medical treatment is required because, without it, the doctor will be committing a trespass to the person, ie a battery. The term 'battery' conjures up images of violence, and indeed in *Wilson v Pringle*,[8] the Court of Appeal suggested that the touching must be 'hostile' in order to constitute a battery. However, the reason for this requirement was the need to eliminate actions in battery as a result of things such as physical contact in crowded streets; the Court was thus prepared to adopt a very wide view of hostility so as not to confine it to acts of ill will. In fact the view in *Wilson v Pringle* was later doubted by the House of Lords in *Re F (Mental Patient: Sterilisation)*.[9] There, Lord Goff dealt with the problem of contact in crowded spaces, by stating that there could simply be no liability for physical contact which is generally acceptable in the ordinary conduct of everyday life.

As regards medical treatment, it is clear that this does not fall within such an exception. This is already reflected in early case law, such as *Cull v Royal Surrey County Hospital*,[10] which concerned a

---

6 (1914) 105 NE 92.
7 [1993] AC 789.
8 [1986] 2 All ER 440.
9 [1990] 2 AC 1.
10 (1932) 1 BMJ 1195.

patient who had consented to a medical abortion; the surgeon proceeded during the operation to perform a hysterectomy on the basis that her uterus was in a diseased state, making it dangerous for her to become pregnant again. The patient, who had not given consent to the hysterectomy, was successful in her battery action.

3.2.1.2 Criminal law: maim and statutory assault offences

Battery is a crime as well as a tort, albeit in the latter context the term used for it is 'assault'.[11] In fact, given the nature of non-consensual surgical procedures, it is clear more serious offences than a bare assault may be committed: these include, in cases of non-consensual surgery, the statutory offences of wounding and assault causing grievous bodily harm contrary to ss 18 and 20 of the Offences Against the Person Act 1861. At least this is so in theory, although in practice the DPP is likely to regard charges as not being in the public interest. It is also interesting to contemplate the relevance of the old common law offence of maim. Skegg comments as follows:

Skegg, PDG, *Law, Ethics and Medicine*[12]

In practice, the common law offence of maim has long been supplanted by statutory offences. But it has not been expressly abolished, and a judge has made an extra-judicial statement which suggests that there is at least a theoretical possibility of the offence of maim applying to operations in which a kidney is removed from a healthy living donor, for transplantation into a person who is in need of it. It is therefore desirable to consider the extent to which the offence of maim would apply to medical procedures, and the related issue of whether consent would be effective to prevent liability.

The authorities have long distinguished between acts which permanently disable and weaken a man, rendering him less able in fighting; and acts which simply disfigure. The former are maims, which fall within one category rather than the other . . .

The fact that a particular injury has in the past been classified as a maim need not be decisive in any future case. Changes in military practice, or increased medical knowledge, could lead to certain injuries ceasing to be regarded as maims, and other injuries coming to be regarded as maims . . .

Most medical procedures do not permanently disable a person and render that person less able in fighting. They therefore fall outside even the potential scope of any offence of maim. This is as true of the removal of a healthy kidney for transplantation as it is of the removal of a diseased appendix. But even if a medical procedure did come within the potential scope of an offence of maim, it would not follow that a doctor would commit an offence of maim in going ahead with it. Just as the infliction of a maim was sometimes permitted in self-defence, so a maiming operation would not amount to the offence of maim if there was a good reason for it. Hence, even if castration could still be regarded as coming within the potential scope of maim, it would be justified if performed for a therapeutic purpose.

As Skegg alludes to in this extract, the patient's consent by itself is not always enough to prevent the commission of a crime. This is because the law, for essentially paternalistic reasons, imposes in many situations an upper limit upon the degree of bodily harm to which a person may consent: see *R v Brown et al*.[13] In other words, a person's autonomy to waive his right to bodily integrity is limited.

---

11 The confusion is added to by the fact that in civil law there is a separate tort of assault, which arises from putting another in reasonable fear of a battery.
12 Oxford: Clarendon Press, 1984.
13 [1993] 2 All ER 75.

We shall look further at the situations where consent will fail to provide a defence to maim, or one of the more modern statutory offences, under 3.2.1.3 below. But why, it may be asked in relation to medical treatment, should consent ever be regarded as making a difference? After all, many forms of treatment (such as amputation or radical surgery) will occasion harm well above the normally permitted limit. In *Airedale NHS Trust v Bland*,[14] Lord Mustill addressed this issue as follows:

Lord Mustill:1. *Consent to bodily invasion*. Any invasion of the body of one person by another is potentially both a crime and a tort. At the bottom end of the scale consent is a defence both to a charge of common assault and to a claim in tort. The concentration in most discussions of this topic on this end of the scale has tended to divert attention from the fact that whatever the scope of the civil defence of *volenti non fit injuria* there is a point higher up the scale than common assault at which consent in general ceases to form a defence to a criminal charge. The precise location of this point is at present under consideration by another Committee of your Lordships' House in *Reg v Brown (Anthony)* . . . and I need not explore it here, but that the point exists is beyond question. If one person cuts off the hand of another it is no answer to say that the amputee consented to what was done.

   2. *Proper medical treatment*. How is it that, consistently with the proposition just stated, a doctor can with immunity perform on a consenting patient an act which would be a very serious crime if done by someone else? The answer must be that bodily invasions in the course of proper medical treatment stand completely outside the criminal law. The reason why the consent of the patient is so important is not that it furnishes a defence in itself, but because it is usually essential to the propriety of medical treatment. Thus, if the consent is absent, and is not dispensed with in special circumstances by operation of law, the acts of the doctor lose their immunity.

3.2.1.3 Situations where consent may be insufficient

As just noted, it is apparent that there are certain procedures in respect of which consent is no defence at criminal law. Usually, problems will not arise in relation to medical procedures because these are almost always therapeutic, and thus clearly in the public interest. However, there are a number of interventions which are not therapeutic, and whose acceptability may sometimes be more contentious. The issue of consent to non-therapeutic research and to organ donation will be considered later in Chapters 10 and 11, respectively, which focus on those topics; even more starkly, a person cannot consent to a procedure resulting in his own death. However, two other categories of borderline therapeutic/non-therapeutic, procedure are considered here.

   The first relates to (sometimes radical) surgery carried out for psychological rather than somatic therapeutic reasons. The best-known example is of gender reassignment surgery, which is normally carried out when the patient has exhibited serious and continuing manifestations of the personality of someone of the opposite sex, and is psychologically disturbed by being 'in the wrong body'. Such operations are nowadays regarded as fairly routine, and are performed under the NHS as well as privately. It is thus highly unlikely that a challenge to their legality would succeed; indeed, in its 2003 ruling in *Bellinger v Bellinger*,[15] the House of Lords appears to have taken for granted the lawfulness of this type of surgery. More controversial, on the other hand, remain cases of so-called 'body dysmorphic disorder', where patients suffer from a powerful psychological urge to have healthy parts of their body amputated. In 2000, a considerable media storm followed revelations that a surgeon in Falkirk, Scotland, had performed two amputations on such

---

14 See n 7, above.
15 [2003] 2 All ER 593.

patients, and his health authority subsequently refused to allow further operations of this kind. Tracey Elliott suggests though that, at least in some circumstances, such surgery may be ethically and legally justifiable:

Elliott, T, 'Body Dysmorphic Disorder, Radical Surgery and the Limits of Consent'[16]

These operations generally provoke strong reactions of incredulity, disquiet and even disgust when we learn of them, because we find it difficult to understand why individuals should wish to transform normal, healthy bodies into ones with impairments. Such patients challenge our beliefs with regard to bodily integrity by asserting that they will not feel physically 'whole' until they have had a limb removed, beliefs which are so far removed from what we regard as the norm, that we are suspicious of them and of their motives. Given the maiming nature of the surgery which these 'wannabes' request, questions of diagnosis and treatment must be approached with a great deal of care, and the question of how best to treat such individuals raises a number of ethical difficulties. I suggest that, in the case of a very few 'wannabes', provided that they have capacity to consent, are properly informed about the risks of surgery, all other treatments have proved to be unsuccessful, and a full medical and psychiatric assessment has been undertaken, then amputation may be an appropriate treatment to relieve their suffering.

As to the question of whether a surgeon amputating a healthy limb would commit a criminal offence, a study of the so-called 'medical exception' to the general rule that consent is not a defence to the causing of bodily harm reveals that the limits of the exception are uncertain. The courts have stated that 'proper' or 'reasonable' medical treatment which is consented to by a competent adult is lawful, but have not ruled what the proper limits of surgical intervention are. The term 'surgery' covers a wide variety of procedures. In most cases it will be relatively easy to justify these procedures as being in the public interest, since they are performed for therapeutic reasons. Given that the removal of healthy body parts in gender reassignment surgery in order to treat a severe psychological condition is lawful; might not healthy limb amputation be regarded as being justified upon a similar basis? . . . I suggest that provided that surgery is conducted by appropriately qualified medical practitioners upon adults who have capacity, and who have consented to the procedure, the matter could be regulated by the civil law, and by the medical profession. This would strike an adequate balance between the protection of patients and the public and respect for individual autonomy.

As Elliott also notes, at a lower level, it could be said that even straightforward instances of cosmetic surgery, such as nose reshaping, often lack a legitimating goal, in terms of clear therapeutic benefit. On the other hand, here, where the social consensus is broadly favourable to such interventions, their de facto legality (subject to patient consent) cannot really be doubted.

The second main category of surgical procedures of borderline legality concerns circumcisions carried out for cultural or religious reasons. In most cases, the recipients of such surgery will be infant minors, who, lacking capacity, are unable to consent for themselves. The question of whether their parents may consent for them depends on how far the surgery may be regarded as in their interests; so the question here is whether, in principle, it can be? See Chapter 4 Dealing first with female circumcision, this is a drastic procedure, which results in pain, discomfort, sexual and child birthing difficulties. As a result of a number of well publicised cases, this was criminalised by the Prohibition of Female Circumcision Act 1985, a provision subsequently re-enacted with increased penalties (of up to 14 years' imprisonment) by the Female Genital Mutilation Act 2003.

---

16 (2009) 17 Med L Rev 149.

However, it is apparent that, even in the male, circumcisions, when undergone for religious or cultural reasons, are non-therapeutic, yet they are carried out almost without question. Although failure to be circumcised may inhibit family relationships, it is also said that it is a practice which results in diminished sexual enjoyment. Christopher Price points out that, historically, the practice has been seen as a means of counteracting excessive lust (12th century), and as a preventive for masturbation (19th century England). He also notes that the medical profession justifies carrying out such operations on the basis that they will be performed anyway, and therefore are better done in a clinical setting. He notes that the Bradford Royal Infirmary provide such a service under the NHS. However, he suggests on a number of grounds that the practice should be outlawed:

Price, C, 'Male circumcision: an ethical and legal affront'[17]

Rejoicing in our multicultural society does not mean that we should be blind to practices, whatever their source and motive, which are themselves abusive and discriminatory of others, directly and inevitably diminishing the freedoms, human rights, integrity and dignity of others . . .

The UN Convention on the Rights of the Child makes the position clearer in respect to circumcision. Article 24(3) provides: 'States Parties shall take all effective and appropriate measures with a view to abolishing traditional practices prejudicial to the health of children.' Some have sought to argue that this provision was only aimed at female circumcision; but this argument cannot hold when the Convention is read with the interpretative provisions of the Vienna Convention on the Law of Treaties 1969.

Referring to the conflict with religious freedom, Price states:

Customary international law provides that an individual's exercise of his freedoms can legitimately be restrained when so to exercise them is to damage or deny those freedoms to another. Thus, Art 9(2) of the European Convention on Human Rights provides:

> Freedom to manifest one's religion or beliefs shall be subject only to such limitations as are prescribed by law and are necessary in a democratic society in the interests of public safety, for the protection of public order, health or morals, or *for the protection of the rights and freedoms of others*' (emphasis added).

The Convention thus distinguishes between the unfettered right to freedom of thought, and the more restricted right to manifest one's religion.

. . . Non-therapeutic circumcision is clearly discriminatory, unethical and illegal. Its prehistoric origins, and its kinship with subincision and other forms of penile mutilation, show its essential barbarity . . .

These are strong words, but it is hard to disagree that the procedure is non-therapeutic, and constitutes an assault against the person. Is it tolerated simply to avoid the outcry from the religious communities if action were taken against those who carry it out?

 SELF-TEST QUESTION

Do you think the criminal law has a valid role in limiting the kinds of treatment that may be performed, even with consent, and, if so, where should the line be drawn?

---

17 (1997) *Bulletin of Medical Ethics* (May) 13.

3.2.2 The form of consent

3.2.2.1 Express consent

In both the NHS and in private health care, the patient will be required to sign a consent form. There is a standard form that covers most forms of medical treatment, although modified types of form are used in certain treatments such as sterilisations. (However, in *Taylor v Shropshire Health Authority*,[18] the precise nature of the consent form was described as 'pure window dressing' and the failure to have a specialised consent form at the time was not an indication of negligence.)

By signing the form, it may be thought that the patient is confirming that he has received an explanation of the medical procedures and cannot later deny this. However, in *Chatterton v Gerson*,[19] Bristow J stated:

> **Bristow J**: I should add that getting the patient to sign a pro forma expressing consent to undergo the operation 'the effect and nature of which have been explained to me', as was done here in each case, should be a valuable reminder to everyone of the need for explanation and consent. But it would be no defence to an action based on trespass to the person if no explanation had in fact been given. The consent would have been expressed in form only, not in reality.

This approach has been endorsed by the appeal courts (for example, by Lord Donaldson MR in *Re T (Adult: Refusal of Treatment)*[20]) and is acknowledged by the Department of Health in its *Reference Guide to Consent for Examination or Treatment*,[21] which gives general guidance to NHS doctors and other health care workers:

> 32. The validity of consent does not depend on the form in which it is given. Written consent merely serves as evidence of consent: if the elements of voluntariness, appropriate information and capacity have not been satisfied, a signature on a form will not make consent valid.

The *Reference Guide* goes on to state that the completion of a consent form will, however, be good practice where a significant invasive procedure, such as surgery, is contemplated.

With respect to NHS treatment, there are different consent forms depending on whether the patient is a capable adult, a person with parental responsibility consenting for a minor, etc. The present model NHS consent form for capable adults (Consent form 1), which was introduced in 2002, is shown overleaf.

3.2.2.2 Implied and presumed consent

As we saw above, a signed consent form will not necessarily show that the patient really consented. Conversely, consent may be deemed to have occurred despite the absence of any consent form. Indeed, purely oral consent, at least as regards minor procedures, is commonplace in day-to-day medical practice. Sometimes, the consent may simply be implied – in the absence of words – by the patient's conduct, as in *O'Brien v Cunard Steamship Co*,[22] in which a ship's passenger who held out her arm to be vaccinated was subsequently unable to succeed in battery against the doctor.

Implied consent should not, however, be confused with the concept of 'presumed consent'. The latter does not concern whether, and if so to what, the patient actually consents, but whether, hypothetically (ie if the question were asked of them), it may be assumed they would do so.

---

18 [1998] Lloyd's Rep Med 395.
19 [1981] QB 432.
20 [1992] 3 WLR 782.
21 London: Department of Health, 2nd edn, 2009.
22 28 NE 266 (1891).

[NHS organisation name]
consent form 1

Patient agreement to investigation
or treatment

Patient details (or pre-printed label)

Patient's surname/family name.................................

Patient's first names ....

Date of birth ....

Responsible health professional.................................

Job title ....

NHS number (or other identifier)................................

☐ Male   ☐ Female

Special requirements ....
(eg other language/other communication method)

To be retained in patient's notes

Patient identifier/label

Name of proposed procedure or course of treatment (include brief
explanation if medical term not clear) ....
....
....

Statement of health professional (to be filled in by health professional with
appropriate knowledge of proposed procedure, as specified in consent policy)

I have explained the procedure to the patient. In particular, I have explained:

The intended benefits ....
....
....
Serious or frequently occurring risks ....
....
....
Any extra procedures which may become necessary during the procedure

❑ blood transfusion..

❑ other procedure (please specify) ....
....

I have also discussed what the procedure is likely to involve, the benefits and risks of any
available alternative treatments (including no treatment) and any particular concerns of this
patient.

❑ The following leaflet/tape has been provided ....

This procedure will involve:

❑ general and/or regional anaesthesia   ❑ local anaesthesia   ❑ sedation

Signed:..   Date .. ..
Name (PRINT) ....   Job title ....

Contact details (if patient wishes to discuss options later) ....

Statement of interpreter (where appropriate)

I have interpreted the information above to the patient to the best of my ability and in a way
in which I believe s/he can understand.

Signed ....   Date ....
Name (PRINT) ....

Top copy accepted by patient: yes/no (please ring)

Statement of patient   **Patient identifier/label**

Please read this form carefully. If your treatment has been planned in advance, you should already have your own copy of page 2 which describes the benefits and risks of the proposed treatment. If not, you will be offered a copy now. If you have any further questions, do ask – we are here to help you. You have the right to change your mind at any time, including after you have signed this form.

I agree to the procedure or course of treatment described on this form.

I understand that you cannot give me a guarantee that a particular person will perform the procedure. The person will, however, have appropriate experience.

I understand that I will have the opportunity to discuss the details of anaesthesia with an anaesthetist before the procedure, unless the urgency of my situation prevents this. (This only applies to patients having general or regional anaesthesia.)

I understand that any procedure in addition to those described on this form will only be carried out if it is necessary to save my life or to prevent serious harm to my health.

I have been told about additional procedures which may become necessary during my treatment. I have listed below any procedures **which I do not wish to be carried out** without further discussion. ....
....
....
....

Patient's signature ....   Date...............................
Name (PRINT) ....

A witness should sign below if the patient is unable to sign but has indicated his or her consent. Young people/children may also like a parent to sign here (see notes).

Signature ....   Date ....
Name (PRINT) ....

Confirmation of consent (to be completed by a health professional when the patient is admitted for the procedure, if the patient has signed the form in advance)

On behalf of the team treating the patient, I have confirmed with the patient that s/he has no further questions and wishes the procedure to go ahead.

Signed:...   Date .. ..
Name (PRINT) ....   Job title ....

Important notes: (tick if applicable)

❑   See also advance directive/living will (eg Jehovah's Witness form)

❑   Patient has withdrawn consent (ask patient to sign /date here) ....

Guidance to health professionals (to be read in conjunction with consent policy)

What a consent form is for

This form documents the patient's agreement to go ahead with the investigation or treatment you have proposed. It is not a legal waiver – if patients, for example, do not receive enough information on which to base their decision, then the consent may not be valid, even though the form has been signed. Patients are also entitled to change their mind after signing the form, if they retain capacity to do so. The form should act as an *aide-memoire* to health professionals and patients, by providing a check-list of the kind of information patients should be offered, and by enabling the patient to have a written record of the main points discussed. In no way, however, should the written information provided for the patient be regarded as a substitute for face-to-face discussions with the patient.

The law on consent

See the Department of Health's *Reference guide to consent for examination or treatment* for a comprehensive summary of the law on consent (also available at www.doh.gov.uk/consent).

Who can give consent

Everyone aged 16 or more is presumed to be competent to give consent for themselves, unless the opposite is demonstrated. If a child under the age of 16 has "sufficient understanding and intelligence to enable him or her to understand fully what is proposed", then he or she will be competent to give consent for himself or herself. Young people aged 16 and 17, and legally 'competent' younger children, may therefore sign this form for themselves, but may like a parent to countersign as well. If the child is not able to give consent for himself or herself, some-one with parental responsibility may do so on their behalf and a separate form is available for this purpose. Even where a child is able to give consent for himself or herself, you should always involve those with parental responsibility in the child's care, unless the child specifically asks you not to do so. If a patient is mentally competent to give consent but is physically unable to sign a form, you should complete this form as usual, and ask an independent witness to confirm that the patient has given consent orally or non-verbally.

When NOT to use this form

If the patient is 18 or over and is not legally competent to give consent, you should use form 4 (form for adults who are unable to consent to investigation or treatment) instead of this form. A patient will not be legally competent to give consent if:
- they are unable to comprehend and retain information material to the decision and/or
- they are unable to weigh and use this information in coming to a decision.

You should always take all reasonable steps (for example involving more specialist colleagues) to support a patient in making their own decision, before concluding that they are unable to do so. Relatives **cannot** be asked to sign this form on behalf of an adult who is not legally competent to consent for himself or herself.

Information

Information about what the treatment will involve, its benefits and risks (including side-effects and complications) and the alternatives to the particular procedure proposed, is crucial for patients when making up their minds. The courts have stated that patients should be told about 'significant risks which would affect the judgement of a reasonable patient'. 'Significant' has not been legally defined, but the GMC requires doctors to tell patients about 'serious or frequently occurring' risks. In addition if patients make clear they have particular concerns about certain kinds of risk, you should make sure they are informed about these risks, even if they are very small or rare. You should always answer questions honestly. Sometimes, patients may make it clear that they do not want to have any information about the options, but want you to decide on their behalf. In such circumstances, you should do your best to ensure that the patient receives at least very basic information about what is proposed. Where information is refused, you should document this on page 2 of the form or in the patient's notes.

Accordingly, the concept is not relevant in respect of patients who are in a position to provide consent: here, assumptions (on the part of doctors) as to their wishes will be unnecessary and potentially highhanded. Instead, presumed consent may have a role to play in justifying the treatment of those not (currently) able to consent for themselves. As such, it is considered further in Chapter 4 below.

3.2.3 The scope of consent

3.2.3.1 What was consented to?

Difficulty may arise in relation to deciding exactly what it was to which the patient consented. In the case of *Mohr v Williams*,[23] the defendant tried to argue that the fact that the patient had consented to the operation on her right ear was relevant to the lawfulness of the operation he proceeded to carry out on her other ear. In other words, the suggestion was that the patient had consented to 'an ear operation'. This, however, was rejected by the judge, who found that there was no basis for interpreting the consent in this wide fashion; indeed as he noted, the diseased condition of the patient's left ear was not discovered in the course of an authorised examination of that ear, but in the course of an examination which had not been authorised.

As we have seen, in the model consent form used by the NHS the patient acknowledges that other (unconsented to) procedures will only be carried out if it is necessary to save his life or to prevent serious harm to his health. Even so, it may be queried how far this amounts to a true consent: it is a standard form, which most patients will feel they are unable to object to, so there could be said to be an element of coercion here. How many patients, about to undergo surgery, are likely to delete or alter a standard consent form? Although, it is clearly desirable that there be a legal basis for doctors to perform additional procedures that are necessary in the patient's vital interests, arguably this lies more naturally in the doctrine of necessity, rather than in trying to stretch patient consent. More generally, the disturbing consequences of unduly wide consent forms are illustrated in the case of *Breen v Baker*,[24] where a woman consented to surgery which she believed would be dilatation and curettage, but was subsequently given a total hysterectomy. There was found to be no battery because the consent form stated: 'I agree to leave the nature and extent of the operation to be performed to the discretion of the surgeon.'

Admittedly, the model NHS consent form is much more carefully drafted. Thus, apart from procedures immediately required to safeguard life/prevent serious harm, the form assumes that the patient will be alerted to additional procedures which may become necessary, and have the opportunity to list those he would not wish to take place. Of course, whether the patient has this opportunity in practice will depend on what was actually said to him (and if he knew in essence what was to happen). In *Williamson v East London and City HA and Others*,[25] the claimant underwent surgery following problems with silicone breast implants, and the operation that was eventually performed was a subcutaneous mastectomy. The consent form originally referred to a 'replacement breast prosthesis and right open capsulotomy', procedures less radical than a mastectomy. It seems that after the signing of the form, in a pre-operative examination the surgeon found that the more radical surgery was required: thereupon the hospital altered the consent form, but it was not further signed by the claimant. The claimant successfully recovered against the surgeon in the tort of negligence: it was found that the latter was in breach of duty by not having explained what was proposed to the claimant, and that the consent form was not altered in her presence. Here, it is arguable that battery would have been the more appropriate cause of action.

---

23 (1905) 104 NW 12.
24 (1956) *The Times*, 27 January.
25 [1998] Lloyd's Rep Med 6.

We shall be looking further at the patient's right to information, and the remedies in battery and/or in negligence where this right is breached, in section 3.5 below.

3.2.3.2 The person carrying out treatment

The model NHS consent form requires the patient to acknowledge that the procedure need not be carried out by any particular doctor. There are examples of patients in America who have successfully sued following surgery carried out competently and in accordance with the patient's consent, but performed by a different doctor to that expected by the patient.[26] However, it is implied by the form that if the procedure is not carried out by this doctor, it will be carried out by a doctor. As discussed by Kennedy and Grubb, controversy surrounds the issue of treatment by medical students, or even nurses:

Kennedy, I and Grubb, A, *Medical Law*[27]

There are at least two factual situations . . . which do give rise to legal difficulties if the patient is unaware that the person is a student.

First, a student may, in fact, examine (ie, touch) a patient solely so as to acquire knowledge or experience for himself. The touching plays no part in the care of the patient. In such a circumstance, the consent given by the patient is probably invalid since the identity of the person touching affects the nature of what is being done to the patient, ie, training rather than caring.

Secondly, a student may touch a patient as part of the patient's care. Does the lack of awareness by the patient of the identity of the person touching (identity being status here) affect the validity of the patient's consent? . . . It could be said that the difference between a lay person and a doctor is material whereas the difference between a medical student (presumably supervised) and a doctor is not. In our view, unless the patient suffered harm and could establish that the medical student was negligent, an English court would reject any claim by a patient.

In the case of *R v Richardson*,[28] the Court of Appeal held that there had been a valid consent to treatment by a dentist when, unbeknown to the patient, the dentist had been suspended from practice by the General Dentist Council, and her conviction for assault was, therefore, quashed. There it was accepted that she was practising unlawfully following her suspension. However, this fraud was said not to vitiate the consent to treatment because it had not induced a mistaken belief as to the identity of the person carrying out the treatment, nor had it induced a mistaken belief about the nature and quality of the treatment. The Court of Appeal rejected the Crown's submission that the concept of 'identity' should be extended to cover qualifications or attributes of the dentist. If this were the case, it would distort the everyday meaning of the word 'identity'.

This decision can be contrasted with that of *R v Tabussum*,[29] where the Court of Appeal held that there had not been a valid consent and the defendant's conviction for indecent assault was upheld where he had asked women to take part in a breast cancer survey to enable him to prepare a computer software package for doctors. The three complainants had agreed to the defendant showing them how to self-examine for breast lumps, which involved the removal of their clothes and the defendant touching their breasts. The central issue was that the women believed him to be a doctor. The defendant had no medical qualifications but he was a scientist with experience in the field of breast cancer, and he denied that he had ever represented himself to be medically qualified. He denied that he had any sexual motive, and the Court of Appeal said that, in any event, this was irrelevant.

---

26 See eg *Perna v Pirozzi* 457 A 2d 431 (1983).
27 2nd edn, London: Butterworths, 1994.
28 (1998) 43 BMLR 21.
29 [2000] 2 Cr App R 328.

Clearly, when the Court of Appeal considered the case of *Tabussum*, it had to try and distinguish it from *Richardson*. The court regarded *Richardson* as being decided solely on the question of identity and not the nature and quality of the acts. In *Tabussum*, the consent was given to touching 'for medical purposes'. This consent was valid as to the nature of the acts but, as the women said they would not have consented if they had known he was not medically qualified, the consent was not valid as to the quality. It is hard to reconcile these two cases when they both turned on 'qualifications and attributes'. Further, the disparity is highlighted by the fact that, in the case of *Richardson*, there was a deliberate unlawful act, whereas, at least on the defendant's evidence, in *Tabussum* the defendant was doing exactly what he had told the women concerned.

3.3 Qualifications on the Need for Consent

As previously discussed, the law usually privileges the autonomy interests of (capable adult) patients over and above the paternalistic inclinations of doctors to treat them in (what the doctor regards as) their best interests.[30] It does so by making the patient's consent a necessary condition for the propriety and lawfulness of medical treatment. However, there are some exceptional circumstances in which treatment may occur without consent. These exceptions exist both (arguably) at common law and under statute.

3.3.1 The 'four state interests' at common law

In the first place it might be argued that a patient's refusal of certain forms of treatment can exceptionally be overriden at common law in order to uphold broader interests on the part of the state. The American courts have adverted to such interests. Thus, in the New Jersey case *In the Matter of Claire Conroy*,[31] four state interests with potential for limiting patient rights were identified. These were preserving life, preventing suicide, safeguarding the integrity of the medical profession, and protecting innocent third parties:

> **Schrieber J**: The State's interest in preserving life . . . may be seen as embracing two separate but related concerns: an interest in preserving the life of the particular patient, and an interest in preserving the sanctity of life . . .
>
> While both of these State interests in life are certainly strong, in themselves they will usually not foreclose a competent person from declining life-sustaining medical treatment for himself. This is because the life that the State is seeking to protect in such a situation is the life of the same person who has competently decided to forgo the medical intervention; it is not some other actual or potential life that cannot adequately protect itself . . .
>
> It may be contended that in conjunction with its general interest in preserving life, this State has a particular legislative policy of preventing suicide . . . [However] this State interest in protecting people from direct and purposeful self-destruction is motivated by, if not encompassed within, the State's more basic interest in preserving life. Thus, it is questionable whether it is a distinct State interest worthy of independent consideration.
>
> In any event, declining life-sustaining medical treatment may not properly be viewed as an attempt to commit suicide. Refusing medical treatment merely allows the disease to take its natural course; if death were eventually to occur, it would be the result, primarily, of the underlying disease, and not the result of a self-inflicted injury . . .

---

30 See eg the dictum of Lord Goff in the *Bland* case, at n 7, above.
31 486 A 2d 1209 (1985).

The third State interest that is frequently asserted as a limitation on a competent patient's right to refuse medical treatment is the interest in safeguarding the integrity of the medical profession. This interest is not particularly threatened by permitting competent patients to refuse life-sustaining medical treatment. Medical ethics do not require medical intervention in disease at all costs . . .

Moreover, even if doctors were exhorted to attempt to cure or sustain their patients under all circumstances, that moral and professional imperative, at least in cases of patients who were clearly competent, presumably would not require doctors to go beyond advising the patient of the risks of forgoing treatment and urging the patient to accept the medical intervention . . .

The fourth asserted State interest in overriding a patient's decision about his medical treatment is the interest in protecting innocent third parties who may be harmed by the patient's treatment decision. When the patient's exercise of his free choice could adversely and directly affect the health, safety, or security of others, the patient's right of self-determination must frequently give way. Thus, for example, the courts have required competent adults to undergo medical procedures against their will if necessary to protect the public health . . . or to prevent the emotional and financial abandonment of the patient's minor children: *Application of President and Directors of Georgetown College Inc* 331 F 2d 1000, . . ., cert denied, 377 US 978 . . . (1964) (ordering mother of seven month old infant to submit to blood transfusion over her religious objections because of the mother's 'responsibility to the community to care for her infant'); *Holmes v Silver Cross Hospital* 340 F Supp 125 . . . (1972) (indicating that patient's status as father of a minor child might justify authorising blood transfusions to save his life despite his religious objections).

The categorisation of the four state interests in *Conroy* has been endorsed in a number of subsequent US authorities, and was adopted by Thorpe J (as he then was) in the English High Court in *Secretary of State v Robb*.

Secretary of State v Robb (1995)[32]

The respondent, a prison inmate with a personality disorder, went on hunger strike. The application concerned the question of whether it was lawful for his doctors and nurses to abstain from force feeding him in such circumstances:

Thorpe J: The only reference to the duty of the Home Office in modern authority is the briefest passage in the speech of Lord Keith of Kinkel in *Airedale NHS Trust v Bland* [1993] 1 All ER 821, p 861; [1993] AC 789, p 859, in which he said:

. . . the principle of the sanctity of life . . . is not an absolute one. It does not compel a medical practitioner on pain of criminal sanctions to treat a patient, who will die if he does not, contrary to the express wishes of the patient. It does not authorise forcible feeding of prisoners on hunger strike. It does not compel the temporary keeping alive of patients who are terminally ill where to do so would merely prolong their suffering.

There have been much fuller developments in other common law jurisdictions, particularly in the United States, and all counsel have drawn attention to and relied upon a number of decisions, all of which consider the right of the individual to refuse nutrition in differing circumstances. I will refer only to recent decision in the United States that

---

32 [1995] Fam 127.

is directly concerned with adult prisoners on hunger strike. The most recent, and for me the most helpful, is the decision of the Supreme Court of California, *Thor v Superior Court* 5 Cal 4th 725 (1993). That authority upheld a decision at first instance that the prison authorities failed in their application for an order authorising force feeding of a quadriplegic prison inmate who had determined to refuse food and medical treatment necessary to maintain his life. The conclusion of the court was that the right of self-determination prevailed, but the court recognised that the right of self-determination was not absolute and that there were four specific state interests that might counter-vail. They were specifically: (i) preserving life; (ii) preventing suicide; (iii) maintaining the integrity of the medical profession; and (iv) protecting innocent third parties . . .

These decisions are obviously relevant and helpful in reaching a decision as to how the law stands in this jurisdiction. I consider specifically the four countervailing state interests that were set against the individual's right of self-determination.

The first, namely the interest that the state holds in preserving life, seems to me to be but part and parcel of the balance that must be struck in determining and declaring the right of self-determination. The principle of the sanctity of human life in this jurisdiction is seen to yield to the principle of self-determination. It is within that balance that the consideration of the preservation of life is reflected.

The second countervailing State interest, preventing suicide, is recognisable, but seems to me to be of no application in cases such as this where the refusal of nutrition and medical treatment in the exercise of the right of self-determination does not constitute an act of suicide.

The third consideration of maintaining the integrity of the medical profession is one that I find hard to recognise as a distinct consideration. Medical ethical decisions can be acutely difficult and it is when they are at their most acute that applications for declara-tory relief are made to the High Court. I cannot myself see that this is a distinct consid-eration that requires to be set against the right of self-determination of the individual.

The fourth consideration of protecting innocent third parties is one that is undoubtedly recognised in this jurisdiction, as is evidenced by the decision of Sir Stephen Brown P in *Re S (Adult: Refusal of Medical Treatment)* [1992] 4 All ER 671; [1993] Fam 123 . . .

Admittedly, Thorpe J (as indeed Schrieber J had done in *Conroy*) here distances himself from the proposition that these state interests – at any rate, the first three – would actually justify overriding a patient's competent refusal in a given case; it appears more that the interests are acknowledged in order to be dismissed. Thus in the *Robb* case itself, the Court confirmed the legality of allowing the prisoner to starve himself to death.

Nevertheless, arguably matters are not quite so straightforward as they may here appear. Accordingly, in the following, we briefly consider each putative state interest in turn.

3.3.1.1 Preservation of life

As a general rule, as we have seen, the state's interest in preserving life is regarded as subordinate to the patient's autonomous decision to refuse life-saving treatment. This has been reiterated on many occasions by the courts. In *Re T (An Adult: Medical Treatment)*, Lord Donaldson MR adverted to the conflict between the sanctity of life, which the state will wish to uphold, and the patient's right to self-determination, as follows:

Lord Donaldson MR: This situation gives rise to a conflict between two interests, that of the patient and that of the society in which he lives. The patient's interest consists of his right to self-determination – his right to live his own life how he wishes, even if it will damage his health or lead to his premature death. Society's interest is in upholding the concept that all human life is sacred and that it should be preserved if at all possible. It is well established that in the ultimate the right of the individual is paramount.[33]

Nevertheless, it remains arguable that, in some circumstances, a refusal of life-saving treatment would entail a breach of the sanctity of life principle in so gross a manner, that such a refusal may be overruled. As discussed in 3.3.2, one instance may be if a pregnant woman refused a caesarian section necessary to save both her own life and that of the unborn child.

A second group of cases that may arguably be understood, at least partly, in terms of the state's special interest in preserving life relates to refusal's of life-saving treatment by 'mature minors' (ie older children, of eg 14 and above, who may be judged capable to make decisions about even highly significant medical interventions). As already alluded to, and discussed further in Chapter 4, in such cases the courts have consistently held that, while the child may be able to consent to treatment, he cannot refuse it at serious cost to his health or life.[34]

3.3.1.2 Prevention of suicide

The interest of the state in preventing suicide was considered by the California Court of Appeal in the case of *Bouvia v Superior Court*.[35] Elizabeth Bouvia was a severely disabled quadriplegic, almost totally immobile, and entirely dependent upon others for all her needs. In addition, she was in continual and severe pain. Mentally, however, she was intelligent and aware. She was spoon fed, but found it difficult to take sufficient food orally because of nausea. It was, therefore, decided to feed her by nasogastric tube. She sought a court order that such 'treatment' could be refused (see Chapters 9 and 12 on feeding as treatment), and her right to self-determination was upheld. Associate Justice Beach reviewed the Californian authorities and the Presidential Commission for the Study of Ethical Problems in Medicine and Biomedical and Behavioural Research, and concluded:

> **Beach J**: It is . . . immaterial that the removal of the nasogastric tube will hasten or cause Bouvia's eventual death. Being competent she has the right to live out the remainder of her natural life in dignity and peace. It is precisely the aim and purpose of the many decisions upholding the withdrawal of life support systems to accord and provide as large a measure of dignity, respect and comfort as possible . . .
>
> Overlooking the fact that a desire to terminate one's life is probably the ultimate exercise of one's right to privacy, we find no substantial evidence to support the [trial] court's conclusion [that Bouvia's refusal of tube feeding amounted to a suicide attempt] . . . As a consequence of her changed condition, it is clear she has now merely resigned herself to accept an earlier death, if necessary, rather than live by feedings forced upon her by means of nasogastric tube. Her decision to allow nature to take its course is not equivalent to an election to commit suicide with real parties aiding and abetting therein . . .
>
> Moreover, the trial court seriously erred by basing its decision on the 'motives' behind Elizabeth Bouvia's decision to exercise her rights. If a right exists, it matters not what 'motivates' its exercise. We find nothing in the law to suggest the right to refuse medical treatment may be exercised only if the patient's motives meet someone else's approval. It certainly is not illegal or immoral to prefer a natural, albeit sooner, death than a drugged life attached to a mechanical device.

---

33 See n 20, above.
34 See in particular *Re W (A Minor) (Medical Treatment)* [1992] 3 WLR 758, discussed in Ch 4.
35 179 Cal App 3d 1127 (1986).

These issues relating to positive acts of killing and omissions to treat, will be examined further in Chapter 12. Consider, however, what difference (if any) it would have made if Elizabeth Bouvia had stated categorically that she was refusing food, not because it was difficult for her to swallow, but because she wished to die? On the analysis of Beach J, the motives are irrelevant. However, if that is the case, why was he at pains to point out that she did not intend to kill herself? In the English case of *Ms B v An NHS Trust Hospital*,[36] where a capable patient wished to have her artificial ventilation discontinued, Butler-Sloss P accepted Lord Goff's *dictum* in *Airedale NHS Trust v Bland*, that 'in cases of this kind, there is no question of the patient having committed suicide'.[37]

If, on the other hand, the patient requires life-saving treatment as the result of *self-inflicted* injuries, it is arguable that a doctor may treat him, despite his refusal to consent. As Skegg has written:

Skegg, PDG, *Law, Ethics and Medicine*[38]

Where someone has done something in an apparent attempt to kill himself, doctors will often be justified in taking action to avert the consequences of the action. Prior to the abolition of the offence of suicide, there was no difficulty in explaining the legal basis for a doctor acting to prevent a person from attempting to commit suicide, or to avoid death resulting from such an attempt. Suicide was a felony, so the doctor was simply exercising the general liberty to prevent a felony. [*R v Duffy* [1967] 1 QB 63, p 67] . . . However, since the enactment of the Suicide Act 1961 it has continued to be accepted that doctors are sometimes free – sometimes, indeed, under a duty – to prevent patients from committing suicide.

In some cases, the person who has apparently attempted to commit suicide will be suffering from a mental disorder which prevents the giving or withholding of consent. But in many cases the person will have a sufficient understanding to give, or withhold, consent. This is so, even though the act will often result from a passing impulse or temporary depression, rather than from a rational and fixed decision. If restrained and given assistance, the majority are glad that their action did not result in death. Hence, even if it is accepted that a person should not be prevented from carrying out a calm or a reasoned decision to terminate his own life, there is an overwhelming case for intervention where there is reason to believe that, if given help, the person will be glad he did not kill, or seriously injure, himself. Doctors are constantly intervening in these circumstances and there can be little doubt that, were their conduct to be questioned, the courts would hold it justified.

In fact, there are some cases where it has been held that there is not merely a right (in terms of having immunity from a battery suit), but may even be a duty in negligence on another party to prevent suicide. In *Selfe v Ilford and District Hospital Management Committee*,[39] damages were recovered from the defendant mental hospital after the patient made a further suicide attempt after being admitted following a drug overdose, and in *Kirkham v Chief Constable of Greater Manchester Police*,[40] the Court of Appeal upheld the claim of a widow of a prisoner who killed himself while on remand in custody. The police had failed to pass on to the prison authorities details of the prisoner's suicidal tendencies. More recently, it has been held that, under certain circumstances, the failure to prevent a patient's suicide may in addition infringe his right to life under Art 2 of the European Convention on Human Rights.[41]

---

36 [2002] EWHC Fam 429.
37 See n 7, above.
38 Oxford: Clarendon Press, 1984.
39 (1970) 114 SJ 935.
40 [1990] 2 WLR 987.
41 See *Savage v South Essex Partnership NHS Foundation Trust* [2008] UKHL 74, and [2010] EWHC 865 (QB); but cf *Rabone v Pennine Care NHS Trust* [2010] EWCA Civ 698. This part of the law remains in a state of uncertainty.

The above decisions concerned persons 'of unsound mind' (which arguably equates to a lack of capacity, as discussed below in section 3.4.1). However, in *Reeves v Commissioner of Police of the Metropolis*,[42] the House of Lords held that the police owed a duty of care to take reasonable steps to prevent the suicide of a 'sane' prisoner. The state of mind of the prisoner was irrelevant to the establishment of such a duty. Admittedly *Reeves*, as well as the other cases, related to the failure to prevent/restrain a person's initial self-harming behaviour. But it would arguably be odd if, having imposed a duty at that stage, the law were to deny such a duty (and *a fortiori* the right) to treat of those subsequently rendering medical assistance. In *R (On the Application of Pretty) v Director of Public Prosecutions*,[43] the Divisional Court stated that Art 2 ECHR does not require the state to take positive steps to force life on the unwilling, but nor does it mean that the state is *positively obliged* to stand by and allow someone to take his own life. The clear implication of the court's reasoning is that such intervention would be lawful. But in the subsequent High Court decision of *Re W (Adult: Refusal of Treatment)*,[44] Butler-Sloss P held that the prison authorities were debarred from treating a capable prisoner whose self-inflicted wounds were in danger of causing fatal scepticaemia. As noted in Chapter 12, in a recent case, doctors at a Norfolk hospital similarly felt obliged to allow a young suicidal woman, who attended hospital after overdosing on painkillers, to die, given her refusal of life-saving countermeasures.[45]

 SELF-TEST QUESTION

Following the last case, it was reported that the patient's parents were contemplating legal action against the hospital for its failure to intervene. Summarise the arguments they might be able to use in bringing such a claim.

3.3.1.3 Protecting the integrity of the medical profession

As regards the state interest in protecting the integrity of the medical profession, Schrieber J suggested in *Conroy* that this will not justify overriding a refusal of treatment. However, a different rule would seem to apply in the context of *withdrawing* treatment initiated previously. In the case of *Brophy v New England Sinai Hospital*,[46] a Massachusetts court held that a hospital need not compromise its own principles by withdrawing feeding from a patient in PVS, who had made it clear he would not wish to survive in such a state, but should permit his transfer to another hospital sympathetic to this course. A similar approach can be found in the decision of the English High Court in *Ms B v An NHS Trust Hospital*,[47] in which the patient wished her life-sustaining ventilation to cease. The clinicians treating her had come to like and respect her and could not bring themselves to disconnect the ventilator. The court accepted evidence from a professor of intensive care medicine from another trust that, in his opinion, the patient should be transferred to another hospital which would be willing to accede to her request.

A further controversial question is whether, on related institutional grounds, the state could justify the force-feeding of prisoners on hunger-strike. In *Secretary of State v Robb*,[48] Thorpe J suggested the answer was no, albeit the case was principally concerned with the absence of a duty on the

---

42 [1999] 3 All ER 897.
43 (2001) 151 NLJ 1572 (Div Ct); the point was not considered further when *Pretty* reached the House of Lords.
44 [2002] EWHC Fam 901.
45 See the discussion of the *Wooltorton* case in Ch 12, section 12.3.4.
46 497 NE 2d 626 (1986).
47 See n 36, above.
48 See n 32, above.

authorities to intervene. In fact, arguably such an intervention may be permitted exceptionally to protect the integrity of the judicial system. This was at least hinted at in *R v Collins and Ashworth Hospital Authority ex p Brady*, which concerned the convicted Moors murderer, Ian Brady, who was on hunger strike and who, by way of judicial review, challenged the decision of the hospital to force-feed him. The case was principally about capacity and about the application of the Mental Health Act (MHA) 1983, and is considered further in Chapters 4 and 9, but one of the submissions on behalf of the hospital was that, whatever the statutory position, the patient's right of self-determination is not absolute and can be overridden on public interest grounds. The judge declined to make a finding in this respect, as he found that the patient lacked capacity and that the provisions of the MHA 1983 justified force feeding, but he said, nevertheless:

See Chapters 4 and 9 →

> **Maurice Kay J**: It would be a disappointment to me if I were constrained by authority from finding in favour of [the hospital] on this issue. My impression is that I would not be. Moreover, it would seem to me to be a matter for deep regret if the law has developed to a point in this area where the rights of a patient count for everything and other ethical values and institutional integrity count for nothing.[49]

3.3.1.4 Protection of innocent third parties

It must be said that the purported limtation on treatment refusals 'to protect innocent parties', adverted to in the US *Conroy* case, is of dubious validity. Whilst public health arguments may, in the right circumstances, result in the overriding of a patient's refusal of treatment, in the UK this would have to be by express statutory provision: see section 3.3.4. The cases referred to in *Conroy* relating to the emotional and financial abandonment of children are not in accordance with US or UK law: there is no principle which regards the parents as a means to the ends of their children. Whilst the welfare of the child is paramount in English law, the necessary protection is given, not by compelling parents to care for their children (except financially), but by removing the children from the parents. It is unthinkable that a parent would be ordered to undergo a blood transfusion on the ground that her children would be motherless if she died.

Similarly, the case of *Re S (Adult: Refusal of Medical Treatment)*,[50] referred to by Thorpe J in *Robb* as instancing such a state interest, is also suspect. The case concerned the refusal of a pregnant woman to submit to a Caesarean necessary to save the life of her foetus and her own life. As discussed immediately below, this type of case is not really to be understood as a matter of the court protecting the foetus; rather, to the extent that the decision to intervene may be supportable, this is on a different ground.

3.3.2 Refusals of obstetric intervention

A controversial category of decision, representing something of a testing ground for the principle that the patient must consent to treatment for it to be lawful, concerns cases where a pregnant woman declines medical intervention necessary to prevent serious harm to herself and/or her unborn child. In this regard, in *Re T (Adult: Refusal of Treatment)*,[51] Lord Donaldson MR expressly left open the question as to whether the presence of a viable foetus could oust the normal principle that a capable adult patient may refuse treatment:

> **Lord Donaldson MR**: An adult patient who . . . suffers from no mental incapacity has an absolute right to choose whether to consent to medical treatment, to refuse it or to choose one rather

---

than another of the treatments being offered. The only possible qualification is where the choice may lead to the death of a viable foetus. That is not the case here and if and when it arises, the court will be presented with a novel problem of considerable legal and ethical complexity.

Very soon afterwards, the issue came squarely before the High Court in the case of *Re S (Adult: Refusal of Treatment)*:

Re S (Adult: Refusal of Treatment) (1992)[52]

Mrs S was a 30-year-old 'born-again Christian' in labour with her third child. Her foetus was in a position of 'transverse lie' and it was a practical certainty that, unless an immediate Caesarean section was carried out, her uterus would rupture, killing the child and, very possibly, Mrs S herself. The latter refused the operation, however, on religious grounds:

> **Sir Stephen Brown P**: I have heard the evidence of P, a Fellow of the Royal College of Surgeons, who is in charge of this patient at the hospital. He has given, succinctly and graphically, a description of the condition of this patient. Her situation is desperately serious, as is also the situation of the as yet unborn child. The child is in what is described as a position of 'transverse lie', with the elbow projecting through the cervix and the head being on the right side. There is the gravest risk of a rupture of the uterus if the section is not carried out and the natural labour process is permitted to continue. The evidence of P is that we are concerned with 'minutes rather than hours' and that it is a 'life and death' situation. He has done his best, as have other surgeons and doctors at the hospital, to persuade the mother that the only means of saving her life, and also I emphasise the life of her unborn child, is to carry out a Caesarean section operation. P is emphatic. He says it is absolutely the case that the baby cannot be born alive if a Caesarean operation is not carried out . . .
>
> I have been assisted by Mr Munby QC appearing for the Official Solicitor as *amicus curiae*. The Official Solicitor answered the call of the court within minutes and, although this application only came to the notice of the court officials at 1.30 pm, it has come on for hearing just before 2 o'clock and now at 2.18 pm I propose to make the declaration which is sought. I do so in the knowledge that the fundamental question appears to have been left open by Lord Donaldson MR in *Re T (Adult: Refusal of Medical Treatment)* . . . heard earlier this year in the Court of Appeal, and in the knowledge that there is no English authority which is directly in point. There is, however, some American authority which suggests that if this case were being heard in the American courts the answer would be likely to be in favour of granting a declaration in these circumstances: see *Re AC* (1990) . . . I do not propose to say more at this stage, except that I wholly accept the evidence of P as to the desperate nature of this situation, and that I grant the declaration as sought.

The President referred in his judgment to the American decision of *Re AC*.[53] This was undoubtedly an unfortunate choice of authority. Ian Kennedy has charted the history of that case as follows:

Kennedy, I, *Treat Me Right*[54]

On 10 November 1987, the Court of Appeals of the District of Columbia, in the case of Angela C, approved the lower court's order that a Caesarean section be carried out on a terminally ill

---

52 See n 50, above.
53 573 A 2d 1235 (1990).
54 2nd edn, Oxford: OUP, 1992.

woman with hours or days to live, despite her apparent refusal of permission. The child was in its 26th week of gestation. The mother was heavily sedated and in extremis suffering from a metastatic oxygenic carcinoma in her lung. The operation was performed. The child died two hours thereafter. The mother died two days later. The court in upholding the order held that 'the trial judge did not err in subordinating AC's right against bodily intrusion to the interests of the unborn, [but potentially viable] child'. This was particularly so, the court held, because 'Caesarean section would not significantly affect AC's condition because she had, at best, two days left of sedated life'.

Obviously, 'significantly' assumes great significance here . . .

[Footnote:] *Re AC* was subsequently reheard *en banc* and the Court of Appeals issued a second judgment on 26 April 1990 . . . The court vacated its prior order on the grounds that there had not been a proper finding of fact whether AC was competent, or, if she was not, how 'substituted judgment' was to be applied. The court did, however, decide that the decision of a competent patient or substituted judgment should prevail, even if surgery was refused, in 'virtually all cases' unless there are 'truly extraordinary or compelling reasons to override them', by taking account, for example, of the State's interest in protecting life. At the same time the court did not dissent from, or overrule, a previous decision (1986) of the Superior Court in *Re Madyun* (unreported: published as Appendix to *Re AC*). In *Madyun*, the court authorised surgery on a woman who objected for religious reasons. 'All that stood between the *Madyun* foetus and its independent existence was, put simply, a doctor's scalpel [*sic*]. In these circumstances, the life of the infant inside its mother's womb was entitled to be protected.'

The issue of whether a court should authorise a Caesarean section against the wishes of the pregnant woman gives rise to considerable ethical and legal dilemmas. On the one hand, a situation in which the doctors stood idly by and allowed a mature foetus to rupture its mother's womb would arguably do serious symbolic damage to the concept of the sanctity of life, which any society must maintain. On the other, the thought of doctors carrying out invasive, and potentially risky, therapy upon unwilling patients is deeply troubling to the concept of individual autonomy, another of liberal society's fundamental values. Moreover, the fact that the patients whose rights are infringed in this way are invariably women, opens up the spectre of gender inequality and domination, a problem exacerbated by the time constraints operating which often mean that the women in question lack adequate legal representation.

In the later 1990s a number of further Caesarean cases came before the English courts. In every case, it was declared that the treatment would be lawful. Almost without exception, though, the judges involved based their decisions on a prior determination of fact that the women in question were incapable and could accordingly be treated in their best interests.[55] In one case, *Norfolk and Norwich (NHS) Trust v W*,[56] the patient, who was in labour, denied that she was pregnant at all. Johnson J granted a declaration authorising intervention at common law:

Johnson J: In reliance upon the opinion of the consultant psychiatrist and taking account of the information I had about the statements made by the patient during the course of the day, I held that although she was not suffering from a mental disorder within the meaning of the statute, she lacked the mental competence to make a decision about the treatment that was proposed because she was incapable of weighing up the considerations that were involved. She was called upon to make that decision at a time of acute emotional stress and physical pain in the ordinary course of labour made even more difficult for her because of her own particular mental history.

---

55 See further, the discussion of treating incapable patients in their best interests, in Ch 4, below.
56 [1996] 2 FLR 613.

I held that termination of this labour would be in the best interests of the patient. I was satisfied that unless the patient was delivered of the foetus which she was carrying, whether by way of forceps delivery or by Caesarean section, then her own physical health would be put at risk. This risk would arise if the foetus died because of rupture of the patient's old Caesarean scar or by suffocation in the birth canal. The death of the foetus would have immediate and increasing deleterious effects upon the patient herself leading to serious physical damage and possible death. Termination would end the stress and the pain of her labour, it would avoid the likelihood of damage to her physical health which might have potentially life-threatening consequences and, despite her present view about the foetus, would avoid her feeling any feeling of guilt in the future were she, by her refusal of consent, to cause the death of the foetus.

Throughout this judgment I have referred to 'the foetus' because I wish to emphasise that the focus of my judicial attention was upon the interests of the patient herself and not upon the interests of the foetus which she bore. However, the reality was that the foetus was a fully formed child, capable of normal life if only it could be delivered from the mother . . .

In fact, as Johnson J was hearing this case, another emergency *ex parte* application was brought before him by Rochdale Healthcare NHS Trust in respect of Mrs C, a woman in labour who was similarly refusing to undergo a Caesarean. In finding her incapable (in the course of a two-minute hearing) the judge held that she was unable to 'make any valid decision about anything of even the most trivial kind' owing to the emotional stress and pain of labour. This was despite the evidence from Mrs C's obstetrician that she was, in the latter's opinion, capable.[57]

The preference in these decisions for intervention to be authorised on grounds of the woman's lack of capacity left the principle in Re S (*Adult: Refusal of Treatment*) isolated and doubtful. As we have seen, Sir Stephen Brown P in that case adverted to *dicta* in Lord Donaldson MR's judgment in Re T as to the effect the presence of a viable foetus could have upon refusals of treatment. However, when the House of Lords in *Airedale NHS Trust v Bland* came to restate the general treatment-refusal principle, they did not mention any qualification in such a case. The issue was addressed once more at appellate level by the Court of Appeal in Re MB (*An Adult: Medical Treatment*).

Re MB (An Adult: Medical Treatment) (1997)[58]

Miss MB required a Caesarean section in order to save her foetus from death or serious disability. However, although she agreed to the operation, her 'needle phobia' caused her to panic in the operating theatre and refuse the preliminary anaesthetic. Hollis J granted a declaration that, in these circumstances, it would be lawful to provide her with the treatment in her own best interests and this was upheld, the same evening, by the Court of Appeal. Five weeks later, their Lordships handed down a reserved judgment:

Butler-Sloss LJ (delivering the judgment of the court): All the decisions made in the Caesarean section cases to which we have referred arose in circumstances of urgency or extreme urgency. The evidence was in general limited in scope and the mother was not always represented as a party. With the exception of Re S . . . in all the cases the court decided that the mother did not have the capacity to make the decision. In these extremely worrying situations, it is important to keep in mind the basic principles we have outlined, and the court should approach the crucial question of competence bearing the following considerations in mind. They are not intended to be determinative in every case, for the decision must inevitably depend upon the particular facts before the court:

---

57 See *Rochdale NHS Trust v C* [1997] 1 FCR 274.
58 [1997] 2 FLR 426, CA.

... A competent woman who has the capacity to decide may, for religious reasons, other reasons, for rational or irrational reasons or for no reason at all, choose not to have medical intervention, even though the consequence may be the death or serious handicap of the child she bears, or her own death. In that event the courts do not have the jurisdiction to declare medical intervention lawful and the question of her own best interests, objectively considered, does not arise ...

... Applying these principles to the facts of this case we find:

(1) Miss MB consented to a Caesarean section.
(2) What she refused to accept was not the incision by the surgeon's scalpel but only the prick of the anaesthetist's needle. Capacity is commensurate with the gravity of the decision to be taken.
(3) She could not bring herself to undergo the Caesarean section she desired because, as the evidence established:

> ... a fear of needles ... has got in the way of proceeding with the operation
> ... At the moment of panic ... her fear dominated all ... at the actual point she was not capable of making a decision at all ... at that moment the needle or mask dominated her thinking and made her quite unable to consider anything else.

On that evidence she was incapable of making a decision at all. She was at that moment suffering an impairment of her mental functioning which disabled her. She was temporarily incompetent. In the emergency the doctors would be free to administer the anaesthetic if that were in her best interests.

A feature of some of the cases to which we have referred has been the favourable reaction of the patient who refused treatment to the subsequent medical intervention and the successful outcome. Having noted that, we are none the less sure that however desirable it may be for the mother to be delivered of a live and healthy baby, on this aspect of the appeal it is not a strictly relevant consideration. If therefore the competent mother refuses to have the medical intervention, the doctors may not lawfully do more than attempt to persuade her. If that persuasion is unsuccessful, there are no further steps towards medical intervention to be taken. We recognise that the effect of these conclusions is that there will be situations in which the child may die or may be seriously handicapped because the mother said no and the obstetrician was not able to take the necessary steps to avoid the death or handicap. The mother may indeed later regret the outcome, but the alternative would be an unwarranted invasion of the right of the woman to make the decision.

It is apparent that, though couched in strong terms, the Court of Appeal's endorsement of the principle that, where capable, the woman's autonomy must prevail over her own best interests and those of the foetus, is obiter. On the facts, as we have seen, the Court accepted Hollis J's finding that MB herself was incapable and thus treatment had been lawful. In fact, their Lordships' decision to disapprove the decision in Re S (Adult: Refusal of Treatment) on the basis that, where the woman is capable, the court has no jurisdiction to intervene, is open to criticism:

Stauch, M, 'Court-authorised Caesareans and the principle of patient autonomy'[59]

After considering statutes which deal with the protection of unborn life, together with a number of ECHR and US authorities, the Court of Appeal in Re MB concluded:

> The foetus up to the moment of birth does not have any separate interests capable of being taken into account when a court has to consider an application for a declaration in respect of a Caesarean section operation. The court does not have the jurisdiction to declare that such medical intervention is lawful *to protect the interests of the unborn child* even at the point of birth. [Emphasis added.]

This, it is submitted, is correct so far as it goes. However, at most it follows that the interests of the foetus *per se* are not a sufficient warrant for intervention. Where the court appears, with respect, to have erred is in assuming that a court will therefore never have jurisdiction to declare treatment lawful in such a case, ie, on other grounds. Such a narrow reading of its own powers is contrary to other recent authorities in which doubts over medical treatment have been at issue. In fact, as a judicial tool, declaratory relief has been developed precisely to provide assistance to those, such as doctors, who are faced with urgent ethical dilemmas in situations of legal uncertainty . . . [I]n *Re S (Hospital Order: Court's Jurisdiction)* . . . Sir Thomas Bingham MR suggested that for such relief to be invoked, it was enough that there was 'a serious justiciable issue' before the court. As his Lordship commented, '[t]his is pre-eminently an area in which the common law should respond to social needs as they are manifested, case by case'.

Overriding an autonomous refusal?
Assuming that a court does, in principle, have the requisite jurisdiction to authorise treatment, should it do so against the competent and autonomous refusal of a pregnant woman to permit obstetric intervention? One might think the answer should always be in the negative. After all, an autonomous choice represents a considered value-ordering by the woman of her interests, and recognition of her integrity as an individual implies that we should not second-guess them. This is the more so, given that imposing intervention, while advancing some of her interests, will inevitably set back others. . . .

What [though] of a situation where the refusal of intervention will lead not only to death or serious harm to the foetus but also to the pregnant woman? That, after all, was the situation confronting the English High Court in *Re S*. In general, the courts, while recognising the force of the sanctity of life principle, which is directly implicated here, have given the impression that it is ultimately subordinate to the principle of patient autonomy. . . .

Nevertheless, it does not follow that a person enjoys an unlimited choice over the *manner* of their death, in so far as additional insult to the sanctity of life principle will be entailed. It is, for instance, generally accepted . . . that a doctor is entitled to override a patient's refusal of treatment following a suicide attempt . . . Arguably, a case where a pregnant woman will die without obstetric intervention also possesses features which set it apart from other cases in which life-saving treatment is refused. Most obviously, not only the woman but also her foetus, which (whatever its other attributes) is a potent symbol of life, stands to die. (Indeed, in cases where, without intervention, the woman's womb will rupture there is a sense in which the foetus operates as the instrument of death.) There is, perhaps, also the consideration that such deaths, if allowed, would take place in the maternity wards of hospitals.

In other words, the question of foetal rights or interests in such cases is ultimately something of a 'red herring'.[60] Rather, it is the prospect of the *woman's* death in such circumstances, involving special insult to the sanctity of life principle, that may arguably justify medical intervention.

Subsequently, in *St George's Health Care NHS Trust v S*,[61] the Court of Appeal dealt with an action in judicial review by a woman who had been sectioned under the Mental Health Act 1983 and then

---

60 The legal status of the foetus is considered further in Ch 8, below.
61 [1999] Fam 26.

subjected to an enforced Caesarean. The latter was authorised by a trial judge who was misled by the trust into thinking that the patient was already in labour. In ruling that the latter had been subjected to an unlawful battery, the court reiterated many of the principles it had outlined in the *Re MB* case.

In the last decade, this area of the law has settled down, with no new applications in relation to Caesarian sections coming before the courts. At least in those cases involving the somatic well-being of the foetus alone, it is clear that no legal basis for medical intervention exists. Though normally it is to be expected that the pregnant woman will consent to treatment conducive to her foetus's well-being, her right in principle to refuse remains an important guarantee of her autonomy, especially in the light of continuing advances in foetal diagnostics and therapies, from HIV testing to intra-uterine surgery.

3.3.3 Statutory exceptions to the need for consent

In addition to the common law rules discussed above, there are a number of statutory exceptions to the need normally to obtain a person's consent prior to giving medical treatment and care. The two most important categories of patient, whose consent may be so dispensed with, namely the mentally incapacitated and the mentally ill, will be the subject of Chapters 4 and 9, respectively.

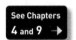 However, there are two further statutory regimes that may also apply in certain circumstances. The first relates to the removal to a place of safety of those who, through age or infirmity, are no longer able to care for themselves:

National Assistance Act 1948

Removal to suitable premises of persons in need of care and attention

47(1) -The following provisions of this section shall have effect for the purposes of securing the necessary care and attention for persons who–

    (a) -are suffering from grave chronic disease or, being aged, infirm or physically incapacitated, are living in insanitary conditions; and

    (b) -are unable to devote to themselves, and are not receiving from other persons, proper care and attention.

(2) -If the medical officer of health certifies in writing to the appropriate authority that he is satisfied after thorough inquiry and consideration that in the interest of any such person as aforesaid residing in the area of the authority, or for preventing injury to the health of, or serious nuisances to, other persons, it is necessary to remove any such person as aforesaid from the premises in which he is residing, the appropriate authority may apply to the court of summary jurisdiction having jurisdiction in the place where the premises are situated for an order under the next following sub-section.

It is, however, questionable how far this provision extends to the administration of medical treatment, as conventionally understood.

Secondly, a patient who suffers from an infectious disease which may pose risks to the health of the community at large may be compulsorily detained and subject to health measures pursuant to Part 2A of the Public Health (Control of Disease) Act 1984 (as amended by the Health and Social Care Act 2008). Section 45G of the amended Act, which entered force in April 2010, provides:

45G Power to order health measures in relation to persons

(1) A justice of the peace may make an order under subsection (2) in relation to a person ("P") if the justice is satisfied that—

    (a) P is or may be infected or contaminated,

    (b)   the infection or contamination is one which presents or could present significant harm to human health,

    (c)   there is a risk that P might infect or contaminate others, and

    (d)   it is necessary to make the order in order to remove or reduce that risk.

(2)   The order may impose on or in relation to P one or more of the following restrictions or requirements—

    (a)   that P submit to medical examination;

    (b)   that P be removed to a hospital or other suitable establishment;

    (c)   that P be detained in a hospital or other suitable establishment;

    (d)   that P be kept in isolation or quarantine;

    (e)   that P be disinfected or decontaminated;

    (f)   that P wear protective clothing;

    (g)   that P provide information or answer questions about P's health or other circumstances;

    (h)   that P's health be monitored and the results reported;

    (i)   that P attend training or advice sessions on how to reduce the risk of infecting or contaminating others;

    (j)   that P be subject to restrictions on where P goes or with whom P has contact;

    (k)   that P abstain from working or trading.

In contrast to the pre-amendment position, the power to make such an order is not limited to cases where the person suffers from a pre-defined 'notifiable disease'; it is enough that he has a contamination or infection that presents or could present a significant risk to human health.[62] At the same time, though, the justification for such compulsory measures is now more clearly the protection of others; in this regard, as appears analogously from s 45E of the Act, the measures at issue may not include treatment for the affected person's own benefit (including vaccination). Instead, the latter's consent here remains necessary.[63]

3.4 The Elements to a Valid Consent

The essential elements to a valid consent to treatment can be summed up as follows:

(a)   the patient must have sufficient understanding, variously described as mental capacity or mental competence, to make the decision;

(b)   the patient must consent to (or refuse) the treatment of his own free will, with no duress or undue influence; and

(c)   the patient must have been given sufficient information about the proposed treatment.

We shall address each of these requirements in turn.

3.4.1 Capacity to consent

In its 1995 report, *Mental Incapacity*, the Law Commission identified three possible alternative approaches to capacity. These are the 'status', 'outcome' and 'functional' approaches. The status

---

62 The concept of a 'notifiable disease' remains relevant in the context of the reporting duties imposed on doctors and others for monitoring the incidence of certain infectious diseases. A list of them is contained in the Health Protection (Notification) Regulations 2010, SI 2010/659.

63 For further information on the new public health regime, see the Department of Health's 2010 health protection legislation guidance, available at www.dh.gov.uk/en/Publicationsandstatistics/Publications/PublicationsPolicyAndGuidance/DH_114510.

approach is most easily explained in relation to children. This would simply state that a person, eg a child under a certain age, lacked capacity and there would be no examination of other issues such as the person's understanding. The Law Commission rejected this in relation to adult patients as being contrary to a policy of encouraging self-determination.

The 'outcome' approach was described by the Law Commission as follows:

Law Commission, *Mental Incapacity*[64]

3.4 An assessor of capacity using the 'outcome' method focuses on the final content of an individual's decision. Any decision which is inconsistent with conventional values, or with which the assessor disagrees, may be classified as incapable. This penalises individuality and demands conformity at the expense of personal autonomy. A number of our respondents argued that an 'outcome' approach is applied by many doctors; if the outcome of the patient's deliberations is to agree with the doctor's recommendations then he or she is taken to have capacity, while if the outcome is to reject a course which the doctor has advised then capacity is found to be absent.

Again, the Law Commission rejected this approach. It must, in fact, be arguable that such an approach would make a nonsense of the whole issue of consent to treatment. To take an outcome approach would mean that the patient's consent would only be required when a doctor did not recommend a type of treatment, but described a number of alternatives to a patient inviting him to decide which to choose. In any situation when there was one recommendation only, a patient who refused it would be deemed to lack capacity, and the treatment could go ahead on the ground that it was in the best interests of the patient to treat him without consent. Not only does it undermine the way in which we have traditionally approached capacity, it would destroy the very basis of the need to obtain a valid consent to treatment at all.

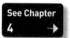

Accordingly, the Law Commission recommended the 'functional' approach. Here, the assessor asks whether an individual is able, at the time when a particular decision has to be made, to understand its nature and effects. The Commission favoured this view not least because it is reflected in the approach the courts have taken. Most notably, in the well-known case of *Gillick v West Norfolk and Wisbech AHA*,[65] the House of Lords, in the context of deciding that girls under the age of 16 would sometimes be able to consent to the provision of contraceptive advice and treatment, had seen the understanding of the particular girl as key. In his speech, Lord Scarman stated:

Lord Scarman: It will be a question of fact whether a child seeking advice has sufficient understanding of what is involved to give a consent valid in law. Until the child achieves the capacity to consent, the parental right to make the decision continues save only in exceptional circumstances . . . When applying these conclusions to contraceptive advice and treatment it has to be borne in mind that there is much that has to be understood by a girl under the age of 16 if she is to have legal capacity to consent to such treatment. It is not enough that she should understand the nature of the advice which is being given: she must also have a sufficient maturity to understand what is involved.

Following *Gillick*, the threshold of capacity needed to consent to medical treatment is sometimes referred to as 'Gillick-competence'. Even so, until the 1990s, there remained surprisingly little authority on the definition of capacity to consent to medical treatment in general. Subsequently, further guidance was given by the High Court in *Re C (Adult: Refusal of Treatment)*, a striking case in a number of ways.

---

64 Report No 231, London: HMSO, 1995.
65 [1986] 1 AC 112; the decision is considered in detail in Ch 4, below.

Re C (Adult: Refusal of Treatment) (1994)[66]

The patient was an elderly man, diagnosed as suffering from paranoid schizophrenia. He had been a patient in Broadmoor special hospital for 30 years. One of his delusional beliefs was that he had been a great doctor who had never failed to cure a patient. He also believed that he had the ability to cure damaged limbs. Following an injury to his foot in 1993, he was diagnosed as suffering from gangrene and the doctors at the local general hospital considered that, unless his foot was amputated, because of the highly toxic nature of gangrene, he was 85% likely to die.

Mr C objected to amputation and made an application to the court for an injunction restraining the health authorities from amputating his foot then *or at any time in the future*. Consent to treatment, other than treatment for the mental disorder, is required even if the patient is mentally ill, as long as he has the necessary capacity,[67] so in this case the decision would turn on C's capacity, regardless of his long history as a patient suffering from what is generally regarded as serious mental illness. Thorpe J held that there is a rebuttable presumption in favour of capacity. C's evidence was that he did not believe the gangrene would kill him, that he had been born into the world with four complete limbs and he intended to go out with those limbs, and that he did not believe that God wanted him to have his foot amputated:

> **Thorpe J**: [Counsels'] submissions divide over the definition of the capacity which enables an individual to refuse treatment. Mr Gordon argues for what he calls the minimal competence test, which he defines as the capacity to understand in broad terms the nature and effect of the proposed treatment. It is common ground that C has the legal capacity to initiate these proceedings without a next friend, within the terms of RSC Ord 80. Mr Gordon contends that the capacity to refuse treatment is no higher and is equally no higher than the capacity to contract. I reject that submission. I think that the question to be decided is whether it has been established that C's capacity is so reduced by his chronic mental illness that he does not sufficiently understand the nature, purpose and effects of the proffered amputation.
>
> I consider helpful Dr Eastman's analysis of the decision making process into three stages: first, comprehending and retaining treatment information, second, believing it and, third, weighing it in the balance to arrive at choice. The Law Commission has proposed a similar approach in para 2.20 of Law Commission Consultation Paper No 129, *Mentally Incapacitated Adults and Decision Making*. Applying that test to my findings on the evidence, I am completely satisfied that the presumption that C has the right of self-determination has not been displaced. Although his general capacity is impaired by schizophrenia, it has not been established that he does not sufficiently understand the nature, purpose and effects of the treatment he refuses. Indeed, I am satisfied that he has understood and retained the relevant treatment information, that in his own way he believes it, and that in the same fashion he has arrived at a clear choice.

The prevalence of paternalism in English medical law had been dealt a blow: the patient's beliefs can be more important than medical opinion. (It is also interesting to note that Mr C did, in fact, respond to more conservative treatment.)

The approach in *Re C* was subsequently approved by the Court of Appeal in the case of *Re MB (Medical Treatment)*,[68] which, as discussed in section 3.3.2, concerned a pregnant woman who refused a Caesarian section after panicking due to 'needle phobia'. The High Court granted a declaration

---

66 [1994] 1 WLR 290.
67 See s63 of the MHA 1983, discussed in Ch 9.
68 See n 58, above.

that it would be lawful to carry out the operation because, on the evidence, the patient was suffering from a temporary impairment to her mental functioning and was, therefore, not capable. This decision was upheld by Court of Appeal:

Butler-Sloss LJ (delivering the judgment of the court):

Conclusions on Capacity to decide

... (1) Every person is presumed to have the capacity to consent to or to refuse medical treatment unless and until that presumption is rebutted ...

... (4) A person lacks capacity if some impairment or disturbance of mental functioning renders the person unable to make a decision whether to consent to or to refuse treatment. That inability to make a decision will occur when:

(a) the patient is unable to comprehend and retain the information which is material to the decision, especially as to the likely consequences of having or not having the treatment in question;

(b) the patient is unable to use the information and weigh it in the balance as part of the process of arriving at the decision. If, as Thorpe J observed in *Re C* ... a compulsive disorder or phobia from which the patient suffers stifles belief in the information presented to her, then the decision may not be a true one. As Lord Cockburn CJ put it in *Banks v Goodfellow* (1870) LR 5 QB 549, p 569:

... one object may be so forced upon the attention of the invalid as to shut out all others that might require consideration.

(5) The 'temporary factors' mentioned by Lord Donaldson MR in *Re T* (confusion, shock, fatigue, pain or drugs) may completely erode capacity but those concerned must be satisfied that such factors are operating to such a degree that the ability to decide is absent.

(6) Another such influence may be panic induced by fear. Again, careful scrutiny of the evidence is necessary because fear of an operation may be a rational reason for refusal to undergo it. Fear may also, however, paralyse the will and thus destroy the capacity to make a decision.

This approach has been applied in a number of subsequent authorities.[69] Indeed, the common law test has now received statutory endorsement in terms of the definition of 'lack of capacity' (the obverse of capacity) contained in the Mental Capacity Act 2005. This provides, in ss 2 and 3, as follows:

Mental Capacity Act 2005

2 People who lack capacity

(1) For the purposes of this Act, a person lacks capacity in relation to a matter if at the material time he is unable to make a decision for himself in relation to the matter because of an impairment of, or a disturbance in the functioning of, the mind or brain.

(2) It does not matter whether the impairment or disturbance is permanent or temporary.

(3) A lack of capacity cannot be established merely by reference to–

(a) a person's age or appearance, or

(b) a condition of his, or an aspect of his behaviour, which might lead others to make unjustified assumptions about his capacity ...

---

69 See eg *St George's Healthcare NHS Trust v S* (n 61 above); *Ms B v An NHS Trust Hospital* (n 36 above); *Re W (Adult: Refusal of Treatment)* (n 44 above).

3 Inability to make decisions

(1) For the purposes of section 2, a person is unable to make a decision for himself if he is unable–
  (a) to understand the information relevant to the decision,
  (b) to retain that information,
  (c) to use or weigh that information as part of the process of making the decision, or
  (d) to communicate his decision (whether by talking, using sign language or any other means).

(2) A person is not to be regarded as unable to understand the information relevant to a decision if he is able to understand an explanation of it given to him in a way that is appropriate to his circumstances (using simple language, visual aids or any other means).

(3) The fact that a person is able to retain the information relevant to a decision for a short period only does not prevent him from being regarded as able to make the decision.

(4) The information relevant to a decision includes information about the reasonably foreseeable consequences of–
  (a) deciding one way or another, or
  (b) failing to make the decision.

As will be apparent, the wording of these provisions owes much to the decision in Re MB, in particular. (One gloss is s 3(1)(d), which allows patients who have capacity in principle, but no means of giving expression to it – ie they are 'locked in' as may happen in rare cases of Guillain Barré syndrome, to be treated as though incapacitated.)

Even so, in practice, the assessment of capacity may be far from straightforward. Such an assessment by its nature requires one person (the assessor) to form a judgment about the 'interior', ie cognitively not directly accessible, mental state of another. The importance in this context of cultural awareness on the part of the assessor was highlighted by Michael Gunn, when examining the Consultation Paper which preceded the Law Commission's Report on Mental Incapacity:

Gunn, M, 'The meaning of incapacity'[70]

It is clearly the case that capacity is a value-laden concept. Undoubtedly, the approach recommended by the Law Commission is one very much within the tradition of Western cultures. Care must therefore be taken in its application to people from other cultures. More specifically, any person assessing the competence of another individual must be aware of their own values so that assumptions and decisions are not made which are unjustifiable. It is the values of the person being assessed which must be respected. The assessor needs to be able to identify where her values vary from those of the person being assessed. Values cannot be removed from any assessment, but assessors of capacity can be educated to be aware of their own values and thus to take care in assessing capacity not to be prejudiced when meeting someone with a different value base.

In the context of medical treatment, it will fall in the first instance to the doctors, at the point of treatment, to make the assessment. The law, as noted above, attempts to provide assistance by directing them to focus separately on such elements as the patient's 'understanding', 'retention', and 'ability to weigh' treatment information.

Nonetheless, as we shall see below, such concepts remain relatively open-textured and fluid.

---

70 (1994) 2 Med L Rev 8.

3.4.2 Assessing capacity

3.4.2.1 The ability to understand and retain information

As we have seen, those caring for the patient must be satisfied that he comprehends or understands the treatment information. The latter must be able to act in an autonomous manner and, as a first step, this requires the abilty to identify and process information relevant to his situation. If radical mistake or confusion besets this process, he will be prevented from making a considered decision. Arguably, however, the notion of 'understanding' can be manipulated to facilitate a finding of incapacity.[71] The question has also been raised – in the context of 'mature minors' (although there is no reason to suppose that the position will differ for adults) – as to whether the requirement of 'understanding' means that the patient must actually understand the nature of the information about the treatment and its consequences, or merely that he is capable of understanding:

Kennedy, I and Grubb, A, *Medical Law*[72]

If the test of understanding is *actual understanding* . . . then whether or not the girl understands *and therefore is competent* to consent may turn on what she is told. Indeed, this seems to have been Lord Donaldson's approach in *Re R* . . . If the girl is not given certain information she may not understand enough, but this would not be the product of any lack of competence but merely that she decided in relative ignorance. It would be an unsatisfactory state of law if doctors could by controlling the information given to a patient thereby grant or deny her competence . . . It must, therefore, be the law that competence is determined by reference to the unvarying conceptual standard of capacity or ability to understand.

A further question relates to whether the patient must have 'first hand' experience in relation to the matters he is required to understand. The answer to this is clearly 'no', as illustrated in *Ms B v An NHS Trust Hospital*.[73] Here the patient was paralysed from the neck downwards, with no prospects of recovery. However, she could be admitted to a spinal rehabilitation unit with a view to rehabilitation into the community. She had declined to participate in this and wanted the ventilator which kept her alive to be disconnected. Dame Butler-Sloss, President of the Family Division, found her to have capacity and, therefore, to be able lawfully to refuse treatment. However, expert evidence on behalf of the trust, which wanted her to go ahead with the rehabilitation, was given by a spinal injuries consultant, who stated that as the patient had not gone through the rehabilitation process she did not have the information necessary to make her decision. This was, rightly, roundly rejected by the President when she said: 'Even in issues of the utmost significance and gravity people, including patients, have to make decisions without experience of the consequences and his requirement is unrealistic.'

As regards the retention of information, an important factor will be the stability of the patient's mental profile. Thus, a fluctuating mental state as in the *Re R* case may impede retention, as can temporary factors such as pain and exhaustion. However, it is important that the latter are stringently defined. As discussed in section 3.3.2 above, there are a number of cases, which concern the refusals of Caesarean sections when, in the course of labour, difficulties have arisen which have put the life of woman and/or foetus at risk. In such cases, there could be a temptation to use a blanket argument that the labour process itself has produced temporary factors which have inhibited

---

71 See Lee, S, 'Towards a jurisprudence of consent', in *Oxford Essays in Jurisprudence*, Oxford: Clarendon, 1987, who argues that few adults could meet Lord Scarman's criteria in relation to a child's understanding, set out in the *Gillick* case (see n 65 above).

72 See n 27, above. The case of *Re R (A Minor) (Wardship: Consent to Medical Treatment)* [1991] 3WLR 592, referred to here, concerned a 15-year-old girl with a fluctuating mental state, who was refusing antipsychotic drugs: see further Ch 4, below.

73 See n 36, above.

understanding and/or retention: see, in particular, the judgment of Johnson J in *Rochdale Healthcare* (NHS) *Trust v C*,[74] where he held that the patient was incapable due to the stress and pain of labour.

In *Re MB(Medical Treatment)*,[75] the Court of Appeal took the opportunity to criticise the evidential basis for Johnson J's finding in the *Rochdale* case. This is not to deny that, on the facts of a given case, there may indeed be evidence of special factors temporarily disruptive of capacity. As we have seen, in *Re MB* itself, the patient's needle-phobia was such a factor.

3.4.2.2 Belief and its effect upon understanding

In *Re C (Adult: Refusal of Treatment)*,[76] Thorpe J treated the patient's ability to believe the treatment information as a distinct element in the test of capacity. Subsequently, however, in *Re MB*, belief was not accorded separate mention, and nor is it adverted to by the new statutory test in s 3 of the Mental Capacity Act 2005. The reason is the difficulty, conceptually, of keeping understanding and belief distinct in this context:[77] to mention belief separately is arguably merely a way of emphasising that the patient must appreciate that the information *pertains to him* (as opposed merely to understanding it abstractly in the way, say, one might follow the plot of a novel).

Accordingly, where a patient has certain delusional beliefs in relation to treatment information, one may sometimes be justified in concluding that he is unable to 'understand' it. In this regard, the Court of Appeal suggested in *Re MB* that 'a misperception of reality (eg the blood is poisoned because it is red) . . . will be more readily accepted to be a disorder of the mind'.[78] It is important to note that what is at issue here are beliefs about the empirical world, where agreed standards exist for demonstrating their falsehood. (By contrast, religiously grounded beliefs, even if of a minority order and regarded by most as wrong headed, will provide no basis for inferences as to their holder's mental capacity.)

An American case, which illustrates a fundamental misperception of reality on the part of the patient, is *State of Tennessee v Northern*:[79]

> **Todd J**: On 24 January 1978 the Tennessee Department of Human Services filed this suit alleging that Mary C Northern was 72 years old, with no available help from relatives; that Miss Northern resided alone under unsatisfactory conditions as a result of which she had been admitted to and was a patient in Nashville General Hospital; that the patient suffered from gangrene of both feet which required the removal of her feet to save her life; that the patient lacked the capacity to appreciate her condition or to consent to necessary surgery . . .
>
> In the present case, this court has found the patient to be lucid and apparently of sound mind generally. However, on the subjects of death and amputation of her feet, her comprehension is blocked, blinded or dimmed to the extent that she is incapable of recognising facts which would be obvious to a person of normal perception. For example, in the presence of this court, the patient looked at her feet and refused to recognise the obvious facts that the flesh was dead, black, shrivelled, rotting and stinking.
>
> The record also discloses that the patient refuses to consider the eventuality of death which is or ought to be obvious in the face of such dire bodily deterioration.
>
> As described by the doctors and observed by this court, the patient wants to live and keep her dead feet, too, and refuses to consider the impossibility of such a desire. In order to avoid the unpleasant experience of facing death and/or loss of feet, her mind or emotions have resorted to

---

74 See n 57, above.
75 See n 58, above.
76 See n 67, above.
77 See also *Local Authority X v MM* [2007] EWHC 2003 (Fam), where Munby J suggested that the need for belief was subsumed within the more general requirements of understanding and ability to weigh the information in the balance.
78 See n 58, above; and see the facts of *An NHS Trust v T (Adult: Refusal of Medical Treatment)* [2004] EWHC 1279 (Fam).
79 563 SW 2d 197 (1978).

the device of denying the unpleasant reality so that, to the patient, the unpleasant reality does not exist. This is the 'delusion' which renders the patient incapable of making a rational decision as to whether to undergo surgery to save her life or to forgo surgery and forfeit her life.

... If, as repeatedly stated, this patient could and would give evidence of a comprehension of the facts of her condition and could and would express her unequivocal desire in the face of such comprehended facts, then her decision, however unreasonable to others, would be accepted and honoured by the courts and by her doctors. The difficulty is that she cannot or will not comprehend the facts.

Accordingly, the court found that the patient was incapable. (See also the decision of the English High Court in *Norfolk and Norwich Healthcare (NHS) Trust v W*,[80] where a patient, who was admitted to hospital in labour, denied that she was pregnant.)

More difficulties arise in cases where a treatment decision by a patient is based upon a mixture of rational and delusional beliefs. The US case of *Re Maida Yetter*[81] provides a good example. Here the patient, a chronic schizophrenic, refused breast surgery, potentially needed to alleviate a malignant condition. It was generally accepted that when surgery was first suggested to her, her reasons for refusing were largely based on fear of surgery, and that she appreciated the consequences of refusal, including death:

Williams J: The doctors recommended that a surgical biopsy be performed together with any additional corrective surgery that would be indicated by the pathology of the biopsy. When this recommendation was first discussed with Mrs Yetter in December of 1972 by her caseworker, Mrs Perhac, who had weekly counselling sessions with Mrs Yetter for more than a year, Mrs Yetter indicated that she would not give her consent to the surgery. Her stated reasons were that she was afraid because of the death of her aunt which followed such surgery and that it was her own body and she did not desire the operation. The caseworker indicated that at this time Mrs Yetter was lucid, rational and appeared to understand the possible consequences of her refusal included death.

Mr Stauffer, who indicated that he visits his sister regularly, and Dr Bischoff, whose direct contacts with Mrs Yetter have been since March 1973, testified that in the last three or four months it has been impossible to discuss the proposed surgery with Mrs Yetter in that, in addition to expressing fear of the operation, she has become delusional in her reasons for not consenting to surgery. Her tendency to become delusional concerning this problem, although no others, was confirmed by Mrs Perhac. The present delusional nature of Mrs Yetter's reasoning concerning the problem was demonstrated at the hearing when Mrs Yetter, in response to questions by the court and counsel, indicated that the operation would interfere with her genital system, affecting her ability to have babies, and would prohibit a movie career. Mrs Yetter is 60 years of age and without children.

... At the hearing Mrs Yetter was alert, interested and obviously meticulous about her personal appearance. She stated that she was afraid of surgery, that the best course of action for her would be to leave her body alone, that surgery might hasten the spread of the disease and do further harm, and she reiterated her fears due to the death of her aunt. On several occasions during the hearing she interjected the statements that she would die if surgery were performed. It is clear that mere commitment to a State hospital for treatment of mental illness does not destroy a person's competency or require the appointment of a guardian of the estate or person: *Ryman* (1940) 139 Pa Superior Ct 212. Mental capacity must be examined on a case by case basis.

80 See n 56, above.
81 96 D & C 2d 619 (1973).

... The testimony of the caseworker with respect to her conversations with Mrs Yetter in December 1972, convinces us that at that time her refusal was informed, conscious of the consequences and would not have been superseded by this court. The ordinary person's refusal to accept medical advice based upon fear is commonly known and while the refusal may be irrational and foolish to an outside observer, it cannot be said to be incompetent in order to permit the State to override the decision.

The obvious difficulty in this proceeding is that in recent months Mrs Yetter's steadfast refusal has been accompanied by delusions which create doubt that her decision is the product of competent, reasoned judgment. However, she has been consistent in expressing the fear that she would die if surgery were performed. The delusions do not appear to us to be her primary reason for rejecting surgery. Are we then to force her to submit to medical treatment because some of her present reasons for refusal are delusional and the result of mental illness? Should we now override her original understanding but irrational decision?

... Upon reflection, balancing the risk involved in our refusal to act in favour of compulsory treatment against giving the greatest possible protection to the individual in furtherance of his own desires, we are unwilling now to overrule Mrs Yetter's original irrational but competent decision.

Arguably, as in this case, where the patient's beliefs concern future events, circumspection is called for before concluding that these are delusional. In *Re C (Adult: Refusal of Treatment)*,[82] the English High Court upheld a treatment refusal, based on similarly 'mixed' beliefs, including some that pertained to the future. Here it should normally be enough that the patient is free of delusion as to the information about his condition and the proposed treatment. Unless the prognosis is such that the doctor believes there is a 100 per cent certainty of death (for example, in the case of a refused blood transfusion), the patient may be told that he has, say, only a 5 per cent chance of survival without treatment, but it is still not unreasonable for him to believe that he will fall into the 5 per cent category.

3.4.2.3 Weighing treatment information in the balance

As noted, the second main requirement, to have capacity, is that the patient is able to 'weigh' the treatment information. One aspect of this is that the patient must be capable of acting volitionally in the light of the information. There have in fact been a number of cases where, although capable, in intellectual terms, of 'understanding', patients have been found incapable due to an impediment in their will. This may be true, for example, in the case of a person suffering from a compulsive disorder. In *Re W (A Minor) (Medical Treatment)*,[83] the Court of Appeal took the view (without deciding the issue) that a 17-year-old girl suffering from anorexia nervosa was probably incapable. One of the symptoms of the condition is that the patient wants to decide herself when to eat:

Lord Donaldson MR: ... [I]t is a feature of anorexia nervosa that it is capable of destroying the ability to make an informed choice. It creates a compulsion to refuse treatment or only to accept treatment which is likely to be ineffective. This attitude is part and parcel of the disease and the more advanced the illness, the more compelling it may become. Where the wishes of the minor are themselves something which the doctors reasonably consider need to be treated in the minor's own best interests, those wishes clearly have a much reduced significance.

In the case of *B v Croydon Health Authority*,[84] a 24-year-old woman with a compulsion to self-harm had been detained under the Mental Health Act 1983. She subsequently suffered serious weight loss

---

82 See n 67, above.
83 See n 34, above.
84 [1994] 2 WLR 294; the case is further discussed in Ch 9.

after refusing further sustenance. Thorpe J held that she was capable, but authorised her force-feeding under the 1983 Act. On appeal, the Court of Appeal was clearly doubtful as to B's capacity:

> **Hoffmann LJ:** I am bound to say that I have some difficulty with the judge's conclusion [that B had capacity at common law]. Reading the letter which Ms B wrote to the hospital at the end of March 1994 and the transcript of her evidence given before the judge on 23 June 1994, I am as impressed as the judge was by her intelligence and self-awareness. It is however this very self-awareness and acute self-analysis which leads me to doubt whether, at the critical time, she could be said to have made a true choice in refusing to eat. In her letter she said: 'My basic need is to be understood why I feel the need to punish myself and at present this is by not eating.' In evidence she said:
>
> > *Q.* Are you being told that you may die if you are not tube fed? *A.* . . . . They told me . . . that they were doing that to save my life.
> > *Q.* Did you understand what they were telling you? *A.* I found it difficult to believe because I felt quite well.
> > *Q.* Yes. Did you want to die? *A.* There are times when you feel so despondent that you do not care whether you live or die but I think deep down I don't. I certainly didn't intend to lose weight. I didn't want to allow myself – I've always enjoyed my food so by denying myself something I endured it as a punishment, but it was never meant as a slow suicide attempt or anything like that.
> > *Q.* Do you think you are running risks in what you are doing? *A.* (Pause). I understand now that with severe loss of weight, as the weight just goes less and less, it does put stress on your heart and risk of heart attack. It is not always easy to believe when you are feeling quite fit really.
> > *Q.* Looking at the matter today, do you appreciate that you are running some risks in what you are doing? *A.* Today I understand why they wanted to tube feed me and I understand that my weight – I can accept that my weight was getting out of hand.
> > *Q.* Yes. *A.* I understand that. As much as some days you just wouldn't – you're crying inside for help but you are so stuck in the routine and self-punishment and that, it's almost like a habit you can't break.
> > *Q.* Yes. *A.* and sometimes you just want somebody to come and break it.
> > *Q.* Yes; how? *A.* I don't know how.
>
> I find it hard to accept that someone who acknowledges that in refusing food at the critical time she did not appreciate the extent to which she was hazarding her life, was crying inside for help but unable to break out of the routine of punishing herself, could be said to be capable of making a true choice as to whether or not to eat.

Subsequently, in R v Collins and Ashworth Hospital Authority ex p Brady,[85] it was found that Ian Brady's inability to weigh up the treatment information meant that he lacked capacity:

> **Maurice Kay J:** . . . [N]otwithstanding the fact that he is a man of well above average intelligence, he has engaged in his battle of wills in such a way that, as a result of his severe personality disorder, he has eschewed the weighing of information and the balancing of the risks and needs to such an extent that . . . his decisions on food refusal and force feeding have been incapacitated.

---

85 See n 49, above.

3.4.2.4 Must there be 'reasons' for the patient's choice?

Generally, as we have seen, even where the consequences of so doing are likely to be very grave, the patient with sufficient understanding may refuse treatment, provided he is capable of balancing the risks of refusal against his other needs. Carrying out this sort of balancing exercise might, on the face of it, require the patient to provide reasons for those needs, and, if necessary, reasons for preferring those needs to taking the recommended medical treatment. However, in *Re T (Adult: Refusal of Treatment)*,[86] Lord Donaldson MR stated that, 'the patient's right of choice exists whether the reasons for making that choice are rational, irrational, unknown or even non-existent'. The denial that the patient need have any reasons for his decision in fact stems from remarks by Lord Templeman in *Sidaway v Board of Governors of the Bethlehem Royal Hospital and the Maudsley Hospital*,[87] and it was reiterated by Butler-Sloss LJ in *Re MB (Medical Treatment)*:

> **Butler-Sloss LJ** (speaking for the Court): A mentally competent patient has an absolute right to refuse to consent to medical treatment for any reason, rational or irrational, or for no reason at all, even where that decision may lead to his or her own death.[88]

The reference to non-existent reasons raises some interesting questions, which we examined in Chapter 1.[89] It will be recalled that when we there discussed 'rational' decision-making, we concluded that if the decision fitted in with the patient's world view, then it should be respected. If this subjective test is adopted, then genuinely held beliefs that fit in with an internally coherent body of thought will not disqualify the patient from decision-making, even if the 'internal coherence' contains a number of bizarre beliefs which can be clearly shown to be unsustainable, for example, Mr C's belief in the *Re C* case that he had once been a successful doctor. Ian Kennedy favours this approach:

See Chapter 1

> **Kennedy, I, 'Consent to treatment: the capable person'[90]**
>
> . . . [I]f the beliefs and values of the patient, though incomprehensible to others, are of long standing and have formed the basis for all the patient's decisions about his life, there is a strong argument to suggest that the doctor should respect and give effect to a patient's decision based on them. That is to say that the doctor should regard such a patient as capable of consenting (or refusing). To argue otherwise would effectively be to rob the patient of his right to his own personality which may be far more serious and destructive than anything that could follow from the patient's decision as regards a particular proposed treatment.

As discussed earlier, the courts are clearly right not to insist that a capable refusal *must* be a rational one (in according with the patient's best interests, objectively considered). For one thing this would rule out refusals based upon religious grounds, which are in practice regarded as among the most respectable reasons for refusing treatment. Indeed, concentration on the rational/irrational raises the image of a neat dichotomy which is misleading. Aside from religious grounds (which are in fact best described as 'non-rational'[91]), many of the factors which influence decisions about medical treatment are difficult to categorise. Thus, is a patient's fear of the pain involved in a given operation irrational?

---

86 See n 20, above.
87 [1985] AC 871.
88 See n 58, above.
89 See 1.4.5 above.
90 In Dyer, C (ed), *Doctors, Patients and the Law*, Oxford: Blackwell Science, 1992.
91 See Stauch, M, 'Rationality and the Refusal of Medical Treatment: a Critique of the Recent Approach of the English Courts' (1995) 21 JME 162.

In *Re JT* (*Adult: Refusal of Medical Treatment*),[92] Wall J found that an adult patient who suffered from mental disability involving learning difficulties and severe behavioural disturbances, such as to have been compulsorily detained under the MHA 1983, had capacity to refuse renal dialysis, without which she would certainly die. He referred to the *Re C* three-stage test, and, upon the evidence, found it to be satisfied. The patient had said that she objected to dialysis and wanted to die. The judge seemed to be particularly impressed with the evidence of the patient's brother who had said that her refusal was 'anything but a flash in the pan' and that, although the family had tried very hard to persuade her to go ahead with the treatment, they now accepted her decision and supported her. However, there is nothing in the case to indicate why she took this view, for example, fear of pain, and arguably, identifying the reason or reasons for refusal of treatment is a good starting point in a decision on capacity. It may well be that in *Re JT* a significant factor was the need for some degree of co-operation on the patient's part in treatment such as dialysis, which is given whilst the patient is conscious, and which takes some time to complete. Clearly, the patient in that case was not going to co-operate, but, of course, that should be irrelevant as far as capacity is concerned.

In other cases, though, and despite the radical rhetoric of decisions such as *Re MB*, it appears that judges will subject the patient's reasons for refusing treatment to considerable scrutiny. An example is provided by *Ms B v An NHS Trust Hospital*,[93] where the question related to whether the paralysed patient was competent to refuse life-sustaining ventilation. Dame Elizabeth Butler-Sloss P (interestingly, the same judge as in *Re MB*) carefully chronicled the evidence before her relating it to Ms B's reasons:

> **Butler-Sloss P:** [39] [Ms B] provided two written statements and gave oral evidence for about an hour and a half. She gave a clear account of her wishes and her feelings. She made it clear in her written and oral evidence that she had never changed her view that she wanted the ventilator withdrawn . . .
>
> [47] She was asked by Mr Francis QC, for the Hospital, whether it was her wish to die, or not to remain alive in her present condition, she replied:
>
>> 'The latter. . . . Given the range of choices, I would want to recover and have my life back, or significant enough recovery to have a better quality of life. I am not convinced from the evidence that that is going to happen, and I find the idea of living like this intolerable.'
>>
>> 'My view [about rehabilitation] is that it offers me no real opportunity to recover physically, that, in actual fact, it will be more teaching me to live with my disability and to make use of the technologies available and that sort of thing, working with the carers. But, actually, I will not recover in any way. That is not acceptable to me.'
>
> [48] She was asked by Mr Francis whether the independence gained through rehabilitation would be of value to her, and said,
>
>> 'I think it is an improvement, certainly. Whether it is sufficient for me or not is where we probably disagree. I don't think it is sufficient, but I can see that it offers opportunities for communication. . . . I think it does make a difference to quality of life, but I do not think it is sufficient for me to want to pursue it.'

Ms B was found to have capacity to refuse further ventilation.

---

92 [1998] 1 FLR 48.
93 See n 36, above.

SELF-TEST QUESTION

How far do the criteria for capacity, from the case law and the MCA 2005, still allow pater-nalistically inclined doctors (and judges) to 'reason backwards' and find patients, who refuse clearly beneficial treatment, incapable?[94]

3.4.3 Consent must be voluntary

The case of *Freeman v Home Office*[95] concerned a prisoner who had been injected with certain drugs, apparently for the treatment of a personality disorder. It gave rise to a number of issues: did the prisoner, as a matter of fact, consent to this treatment, and, more interestingly, could it be argued that a prisoner could not give a valid consent to treatment by a prison medical officer where the officer was not acting in his capacity as a doctor but as a disciplinarian. As to the judge's finding of fact in respect of whether consent had been given, the Court of Appeal refused to disturb this. On the wider point of doctor *qua* disciplinarian, Sir John Donaldson MR stated:

> **Sir John Donaldson MR**: Counsel for the plaintiff submitted that such were the pressures of prison life and discipline that a prisoner could not, as a matter of law, give an effective consent to treatment in any circumstances. This is a somewhat surprising proposition since it would mean that, in the absence of statutory authority, no prison medical officer could ever treat a prisoner. The answer of counsel for the plaintiff was in part that outside medical officers could be brought in, but I am not persuaded that this would reduce the pressures, whatever they may be . . .
>
> The judge expressed his view on this aspect of the argument by saying ([1983] 3 All ER 589, p 597 . . .):
>
>> The right approach, in my judgment, is to say that where, in a prison setting, a doctor has the power to influence a prisoner's situation and prospects, a court must be alive to the risk that what may appear, on the face of it, to be a real consent is not in fact so.
>
> I would accept that as a wholly accurate statement of the law. The judge said that he had borne this in mind throughout the case. The sole question is therefore whether, on the evidence, there was a real consent.

Although *Freeman* endorses the need for particular vigilance when a patient may be in a vulnerable situation, on the evidence in this case, the patient was being administered drugs 'because of his obvious hostility and cantankerous behaviour'. The question arises whether this was treatment at all? The patient had been told that the drugs would 'make him feel like a new man', but there is a very clear indication that the drugs would make him a much easier prisoner to deal with. Arguably, a rather complacent view of the medical interests of prison inmates was also taken in the American case of *Thor v Superior Court*,[96] in which the Supreme Court of California stated:

> There is no reason to believe that the prison environment, with its possible inadequacy of medical and related support services for ill or injured prisoners, inherently jeopardises the voluntariness of a prisoner's decision to forgo life-sustaining treatment. Any individual who suffers a debili-tating or life-threatening disease or injury inevitably faces choices in medical decision making

---

94 For an argument that many of the leading English cases on capacity may be understood in paternalistic terms, see Maclean, A, 'Advance Directives and the Rocky Waters of Anticipatory Decision-Making' (2008) 16 *Med L Rev* 1.

95 [1984] QB 524.

96 5 Cal 4th 725 (1993).

affected or even dictated by his life circumstances, and the prison environment (although in some respects unique) is simply one such circumstance in the individual's personal calculus.

Commenting upon the *Thor* case, Ian Kennedy wrote as follows:

Kennedy, I, 'Commentary on *Thor v Superior Court*'[97]

Medical law as it relates to those in prison is a distinctly murky world. The California Supreme Court could perhaps be excused for not examining in any detail the tensions between the conflicting claims which arise. The impression which is left, however, is one of too great a willingness to defer to the needs of security over the claims of the prisoner, whether to refuse or, just as important, to obtain medical treatment. English law sadly is no less murky. There is, of course, the statement by Lord Keith in the course of his speech in *Bland* [[1993] 1 All ER 821] that concern for the principle of the sanctity of life 'does not authorise forcible feeding of prisoners on hunger strikes'. But the wider questions of the refusal of medical treatment by prisoners, their ability to gain access to treatment and the involuntary treatment of them with, for example, psychotropic drugs are greatly under examined. One obvious reason is the inability to obtain reliable information. The instant case should serve as a reminder that such an examination is long overdue. [See now, *Health Care of Detainees in Police Stations*, 1994, London: BMA.]

Nonetheless, even within the normal setting of patient care (that is, general hospital or GP's surgery), it might be argued that there remains an inherent risk of coercive behaviour on the part of doctors. The issue is discussed by Culver and Gert as follows:

Culver, CM and Gert, B, *Philosophy in Medicine*[98]

Valid consent requires the absence of any coercion by the doctor or the medical staff. Coercion involves any threat of sufficient force that no rational person would reasonably be expected to resist it . . . A threat of this kind means that the person being threatened has been deprived of his freedom and so has an excuse for doing what he has been coerced to do. We do not regard strong recommendations, forcefully given, as coercive. To extend the term 'coercion', so that any pressure by a doctor on a patient to accept the doctor's recommendations would count as coercive, and hence in need of justification, seems to us undesirable. We wish to allow doctors considerable leeway in supporting their views. Patients often have irrational fears that must be overcome, so we do not want to set unrealistic limits. But, given the tremendous authority of doctors and the vulnerable position of patients, no threats of lack of care should be allowed.

Culver and Gert may be right in stating that 'strong recommendations' are not coercive (in the sense of amounting to duress), but given the power imbalance between doctor and patient, and the likelihood of the latter enjoying reduced autonomy due to illness, does the doctor exercise undue influence?

The question of undue influence, here exercised by a relative, was one of the issues considered in the important case of *Re T* (*Adult: Refusal of Medical Treatment*).

Re T (Adult: Refusal of Medical Treatment) (1992)[99]

The 20-year-old patient, who was pregnant, was admitted to hospital after a road accident. The patient's mother was a devout Jehovah's Witness, although the patient herself was not of the

---

97 (1994) 2 Med L Rev 224.
98 New York: OUP, 1982.
99 See n 20, above.

faith. Shortly after being visited by her mother she informed doctors that she did not want a blood transfusion. She asked doctors if there were alternative treatments and was told that there were. Prior to a Caesarean section she signed a form refusing blood transfusions, but was not told that one might be necessary to save her life or prevent serious injury. After the stillbirth of her baby, the patient's condition deteriorated, and the judge at first instance granted a declaration that it would be lawful to administer a blood transfusion:

> **Lord Donaldson MR:** A special problem may arise if at the time the decision is made the patient has been subjected to the influence of some third party. This is by no means to say that the patient is not entitled to receive and indeed invite advice and assistance from others in reaching a decision, particularly from members of the family. But the doctors have to consider whether the decision is really that of the patient. It is wholly acceptable that the patient should have been persuaded by others of the merits of such a decision and have decided accordingly. It matters not how strong the persuasion was, so long as it did not overbear the independence of the patient's decision. The real question in each such case is: does the patient really mean what he says or is he merely saying it for a quiet life, to someone else or because the advice and persuasion to which he has been subjected is such that he can no longer think and decide for himself? In other words, is it a decision expressed in form only, not in reality?
>
> When considering the effect of outside influences, two aspects can be of crucial importance. First, the strength of the will of the patient. One who is very tired, in pain or depressed will be much less able to resist having his will overborne than one who is rested, free from pain and cheerful. Second, the relationship of the 'persuader' to the patient may be of crucial importance. The influence of parents on their children or of one spouse on the other can be, but is by no means necessarily, much stronger than would be the case in other relationships. Persuasion based upon religious belief can also be much more compelling and the fact that arguments based upon religious beliefs are being deployed by someone in a very close relationship with the patient will give them added force and should alert the doctors to the possibility – no more – that the patient's capacity or will to decide has been overborne. In other words the patient may not mean what he says.

Lord Donaldson MR acknowledged that awareness of the possibility of undue influence should not preclude genuine consultation by the patient with others, particularly family members. However, given that the doctors will rarely be privy to these consultations, it is hard to see how they could have sufficient evidence of undue influence, unless this was revealed to them by the patient. It is arguable that the decision in this case should have revolved more around the genuineness of the consent in relation to the information given by the doctors to the patient (that is, risk of death, possibility of no alternative treatment and so on) and/or on the possible temporary incapacity of the patient, rather than on the issue of undue influence.

The position in Re T can be contrasted with that in The Centre for Reproductive Medicine v U,[100] where the consent of a man who was described as able, intelligent and educated, with a responsible job and in good health could not be said to have been obtained under duress. He and his wife were undergoing treatment for infertility. He had withdrawn his consent to the posthumous use of his sperm and unfortunately died unexpectedly soon afterwards. The allegation was that the clinical practice manager had pressurised him into the withdrawal. On the evidence, she had clearly

---

100 [2002] EWCA Civ 565.

warned about the implications of posthumous insemination and would have halted the treatment for further consultation and counselling to take place. At first instance, it was found that the husband had succumbed to the pressure placed on him by the manager, but held that something more than pressure had to be shown; the independence of the patient's decision had to be overborne and that had not taken place in this case. The Court of Appeal upheld the decision.

3.4.4 Informing the patient

Earlier we looked at capacity in terms of the patient's ability to process and act upon information relating to his proposed treatment. Clearly, however, this presupposes something to 'bite upon' in terms of the actual data to be processed: in other words, the patient must also have been provided with information about the treatment in question. It is not uncommon to encounter the expression 'informed consent' as a synonym for consent following the provision to the patient of appropriate information. However, this expression has a number of interpretations (depending on differing views as to what is 'appropriate' and in what legal context) and should be approached with caution.

In fact, as regards the validity of consent to medical treatment, the patient need be informed only as to the latter's nature and purpose. As long as he knows this, much of the further detail can be left out: it does not matter, for example, that a treatment risk that the patient was not informed of later materialises. (It is important, however, to keep in mind that we are here considering the validity of the patient's consent so as to negate a subsequent action in battery, and not whether a doctor may have been *negligent* in not giving certain additional information: as to which, see section 3.5 below).

The distinction between the 'basic' information required for a valid consent – as opposed to the further disclosure of treatment risks (failing which an action may lie in negligence) – was articulated by Bristow J in *Chatterton v Gerson*:[101]

> **Bristow J**: In my judgment, once the patient is informed in broad terms of the nature of the procedure which is intended, and gives her consent, that consent is real, and the cause of the action on which to base a claim for failure to go into risks and implications is negligence, not trespass. Of course, if information is withheld in bad faith, the consent would be vitiated by fraud. Of course, if by some accident, as in a case in the 1940s in the Salford Hundred Court, where a boy was admitted to hospital for tonsillectomy and due to administrative error was circumcised instead, trespass would be the appropriate cause of action against the doctor, though he was as much the victim of the error as the boy. But in my judgment it would be very much against the interests of justice if actions which are really based on a failure by the doctor to perform his duty adequately to inform were pleaded in trespass.

This approach, of limiting 'trespass' or battery to cases where the patient has, in effect, been deliberately misled or told nothing, was initially employed by US courts (see eg, *Canterbury v Spence*[102]) and was endorsed by the House of Lords in *Sidaway v Board of Governors of the Bethlem Royal Hospital and the Maudsley Hospital and Others*.[103] In fact, it is now adopted throughout the common law world. In the case of *Reibl v Hughes*,[104] Laskin CJ in the Supreme Court of Canada commented as follows:

> **Laskin CJ**: I can appreciate the temptation to say that the genuineness of consent to medical treatment depends on proper disclosure of the risks which it entails, but in my view . . . a failure to disclose the attendant risks, however serious, should go to negligence rather than to

---

101 See n 19, above.
102 464 F 2d 772 (1972).
103 See n 87, above.
104 (1980) 114 DLR (3d) 1.

battery. Although such a failure relates to an informed choice of submitting to or refusing recommended and appropriate treatment, it arises as the breach of an anterior duty of due care, comparable in legal obligation to the duty of due care in carrying out the particular treatment to which the patient has consented. It is not a test of the validity of consent.

However, despite its undoubted pedigree, principled reasons for parcelling up the patient's right to information into, on the one hand, that going to the 'nature' of the treatment, and, on the other, that concerning risks, remain elusive.[105] As Laskin CJ acknowledges, a failure to disclose the latter may also seriously impede a patient's autonomous decision-making. Another problem is the requirement that the relevant information need only be in 'broad terms', which may be felt to confer too much discretion upon judges. As Andrew Grubb notes:

Grubb, Andrew (ed), *Principles of Medical Law*[106]

3.97 The information needs to state in 'broad terms' what is to be done to the patient and why. However, this information need not descend into minute, or indeed any, real detail. In practice, judges have considerable leeway in determining what information is relevant to the 'nature and purpose' of a procedure and what is co-lateral to that and, therefore, immaterial to the reality of the patient's consent. For example, it may be enough that the patient knows that a diagnostic procedure of a certain type is to be undertaken, such as a biopsy, and what that involves in terms of contact with the patient and incision. Even if the doctor had been speaking in terms of a partic-ular biopsy such as a muscle biopsy, knowledge of this will be sufficient to amount to a real consent to a bone biopsy carried out at the same time [see *Brushnett v Cowan* [1991] 2 Med LR 271 . . .].

In *Davis v Barking, Havering and Brentwood HA*,[107] the High Court considered the case of a woman who signed a consent form to undergo a general anaesthetic, but, who subsequently received a caudal block (ie an injection of anaesthetising drug into part of the body to interrupt nerve function), and who suffered some damage as a result of this. McCullough J rejected the argument that the failure to obtain consent to this procedure amounted to a battery:

McCullough J: If one is to treat the administration of an injection for analgesic purposes while the patient is generally anaesthetised (eg, the caudal block given to Mrs Davis) as something requiring separate consent, why should separate consent not also be sought for an injection of, for example, morphine to provide analgesia when the patient begins to come round from the general anaesthetic?
  . . . And once this degree of sectionalisation is accepted, how long will it be before the court is invited to say that separate consent should be sought for separate steps in the surgical procedure itself? A sectionalised approach of this kind would encourage – indeed necessitate – what has been called the 'deplorable' prospect of actions being brought in trespass rather than in negligence.

An interesting, related issue concerns the carrying out of unauthorised tests on specimens of bodily fluids or tissue, but where consent to the taking of specimens was given. This is particularly relevant to HIV testing. In April 1994 a number of Harrods' staff had tests carried out on their blood samples without explicit consent (some were also carried out in the face of an express refusal of consent). In the light of this sort of reasoning, would a battery be found to have taken place here?

---

105   Indeed, in many civil law jurisdictions, such as Germany, no distinction is drawn between the two types of information: a failure to disclose risks will equally vitiate consent.
106   2nd edn, Oxford: OUP, 2004.
107   [1993] 4 Med LR 85.

Unfortunately, there has been no judicial consideration of the issue, and expert opinions have differed. The British Medical Association took advice from Michael Sherrard QC and Ian Gatt, who formed the view the explicit consent is necessary, as did Kennedy and Grubb and Gordon Langley QC, whilst Leo Charles QC, advising the Central Committee for Hospital Medical Services, advised that explicit consent was not necessary.

Commenting upon the difference of opinion, with reference to the 'broad nature of the treatment' test in *Chatterton v Gerson*, John Keown states:

Keown, J, 'The ashes of AIDS and the phoenix of informed consent'[108]

The doctor who tells the patient that a sample of blood is to be taken for 'tests' has surely discharged this duty. The fact that he does not inform the patient that one of the tests is for HIV does not alter the general nature of the procedure as part of a process of therapeutic diagnosis.

The Sherrard opinion's invention of a distinction between 'routine' and 'non-routine' tests, a distinction which apparently turns on the seriousness of the consequences of a positive result suffers not only from vagueness (what is meant by 'seriousness' and does the requirement to inform extend to other tests and treatments?) but is unsupported by authority or argument, as are the opinion's assertions of an implied representation by the doctor that he will only do 'routine' tests without express consent, and that this representation vitiates the uninformed patient's consent. Curiously, the most copious use of authority in the opinion is its lengthy quotation from the *dissenting* opinion of Lord Scarman in *Sidaway*. Whereas it is understandable that a distinction could be made between 'therapeutic' and 'non-therapeutic' testing (an example of the latter being where the sample is taken purely as part of a research programme) such as to render the latter a procedure of a different nature to the former, a distinction between 'routine' and 'non-routine' seems to be insupportable.

No less insupportable, with respect, is Kennedy and Grubb's analogy between the removal of a sample of blood for HIV testing and off-the-ball kicks and punches on the sports field, an analogy which can hardly be described as obvious.

It is one thing to say that a person cannot, as a matter of public policy, consent to the deliberate infliction of bodily harm without good reason (and hence to regard off-the-ball kicks and punches as assaults). It is quite another to extend this reasoning to touchings which involve no infliction, deliberate or otherwise, of bodily harm.

Not only is no relevant authority cited to warrant such an extension, but the supporting argument that consent should be required because of the possible far-reaching implications of the test presumably entails the conclusion that on those, doubtless many, occasions when a doctor takes a sample from a patient to perform a test which may have far-reaching implications (such as for cancer) the doctor is guilty of battery if he does not obtain the patient's specific consent to it.

A second argument advanced by Kennedy and Grubb is that *Chatterton* in fact supports their case. They argue that although the doctor need only inform the patient in broad terms of the nature of the procedure, the 'procedure' is not merely the use of the syringe to obtain a blood sample, but to obtain a blood sample for an HIV test. Merely to have assented to a particular touching will not necessarily amount to consent if there is no comprehension of the quality of the touching. In support of this argument they cite the case of *Flattery* (as explained by Dunn LJ in *Sidaway*) and state that it is clear that a woman who consents to sexual intercourse, knowing it is sexual intercourse but believing it is being done as a surgical operation, has not given a valid consent to the intercourse because she is unaware of the underlying quality of the touching . . .

---

108 (1989) 52 MLR 790.

> In sum, *Chatterton* merely requires the patient to be informed in broad terms of the nature of the procedure. The doctor who tells his patient that blood is to be removed for testing, even though he does not say that it is to be tested for HIV, has surely satisfied this requirement.

More generally, an important factor in the courts' eagerness to stress the distinction between battery and negligence is that otherwise a doctor would theoretically be guilty of a criminal offence, as well as a breach of civil law, if he were found to have battered the patient in failing to give sufficient information. Although such a case would be highly unlikely to be prosecuted (as public policy generally militates against imposing criminal liability upon the doctor), a residual stigma carries over to the civil, battery action. An illustration of the judicial unwillingness so to stigmatise a doctor, provided the latter was acting in good faith, may be seen in *Williamson v East London and City HA and Others*.[109] Here, the evidence showed that a patient had not been told that her right breast was to be removed (instead she believed that the operation would replace her silicone breast implant, which had ruptured). Nonetheless, any reference in the judgment to the tort of battery is conspicuously absent: instead Butterfield J awarded the claimant £20,000 for the 'negligent failure on the part of the defendants to acquire her consent to the operative procedure'.

However, while rare, there are cases where doctors have been found to have battered their patients. One example is the Canadian case of *Allan v Mount Sinai Hospital*,[110] in which an anaesthetic injection was given in the patient's left arm, after she had specifically requested that it not be given there. There are also a few English authorities. As noted above, an early example is *Cull v Royal Surrey County Hospital*,[111] in which a patient had consented to an abortion but received a sterilisation in addition. A battery was also found in *Devi v West Midlands RHA*,[112] where the patient, who consented to a repair to a perforation in her uterus, was sterilised by the surgeon, who believed it to be in her best interests. One area where the courts will clearly protect patients is against deliberate deceptions practised upon them by medical professionals acting in bad faith. Thus, in *Appleton v Garrett*,[113] where a dentist represented falsely to his patients that they needed dental treatment and then carried out unnecessary treatment, the court had no hesitation in finding a battery.

 SELF-TEST QUESTION

What of cases where the doctor fails to obtain the patient's consent by mistake (eg the patient's apparent consent is vitiated by incapacity, or the doctor confuses two patients and performs the procedure intended for one on the other). Should these sound in battery or negligence?

3.5 The Duty to Disclose in Negligence

3.5.1 Introduction

As we have just seen, for his consent to be regarded as valid or 'real' (so as to preclude a subsequent action in *battery* against the doctor), the patient need receive only a relatively low amount of information, *viz* as to the 'nature and purpose' of the treatment. However, even where a patient has been

---

109 See n 25, above.
110 (1980) 109 DLR (3d) 634.
111 See n 10, above.
112 (1981) CA Transcript 491.
113 [1997] 8 Med LR 75.

See Chapter 6 →

told this much, he will in some cases still be entitled to claim in *negligence* against the doctor: in particular, he may allege that the doctor failed, in breach of his duty, to disclose a given risk or side-effect of the treatment. We shall be examining medical negligence as a topic in its own right in Chapter 6, but, given the close link between warnings of risks and patient autonomy (does a patient who is ignorant of some serious risk or side-effect of treatment choose autonomously, even if he knows its 'purpose'?), it is useful to deal with the extent of the specific duty on the part of doctors to give such warnings here.

3.5.2 The standard of care in relation to disclosing treatment risks

3.5.2.1 The doctrine of 'informed consent'

The legal question here is, what standard of care does the law impose upon doctors, at the time of obtaining consent, as regards disclosure of risks, side-effects and alternative treatment options? It is in this context that the doctrine of 'informed consent' (in its strict usage: as indicated above, the expression is not always used with sufficient precision) offers one possible answer. The doctrine, which is primarily American, although it has also found widespread acceptance in other parts of the common law world, defines the doctor's duty to disclose risks by reference to the reasonable patient's desire and need to know of them. For this reason the approach is also often termed 'the prudent patient test'.

This approach received its classic exposition in the decision of the US Court of Appeals, District of Columbia circuit, in *Canterbury v Spence*:[114]

> **Robinson J**: There are, in our view, formidable obstacles to acceptance of the notion that the physician's obligation to disclose is either germinated or limited by medical practice. To begin with, the reality of any discernible custom reflecting a professional consensus on communication of option and risk information to patient is open to serious doubt. We sense the danger that what in fact is no custom at all may be taken as an affirmative custom to maintain silence, and that physician witnesses to the so called custom may state merely their personal opinions as to what they or others would do under given conditions. We cannot gloss over the inconsistency between reliance on a general practice respecting divulgence and, on the other hand, realisation that the myriad of variables among patients makes each case so differing that its omission can rationally justified only by the effect of its individual circumstances. Nor can we ignore the fact that to bind the disclosure obligation to medical usage is to arrogate the decision on revelation to the physician alone. Respect for the patient's right of self-determination on particular therapy demands a standard set by law for physicians rather than one which physicians may or may not impose upon themselves . . .
>
> In our view, the patient's right of self-decision shapes the boundaries of the duty to reveal. That right can be effectively exercised only if the physician's communications to the patient, then, must be measured by the patient's need, and that need is the information material to the decision. Thus the test for determining whether a particular peril must be divulged is its materiality to the patient's decision: all risks potentially affecting the decision must be unmasked. And to safeguard the patient's interest in achieving his own determination on treatment, the law must itself set the standard for adequate disclosure.

However, as the court noted, a difficulty with the prudent patient test is in deciding whether it is objective or subjective:

---

114 See n 102, above.

Robinson J: Of necessity, the content of the disclosure rests in the first instance with the physician. Ordinarily it is only he who is in a position to identify particular dangers; always he must make a judgment, in terms of materiality, as to whether and to what extent revelation to the patient is called for. He cannot know with complete exactitude what the patient would consider important to his decision, but on the basis of his medical training and experience he can sense how the average, reasonable patient expectably would react . . .

From these considerations we derive the breadth of the disclosure of risks legally to be required. The scope of the standard is not subjective as to either the physician or the patient; it remains objective with due regard for the patient's informational needs and with suitable leeway for the physician's situation. In broad outline, we agree that '[a] risk is thus material when a reasonable person in what the physician knows or should know to be the patient's position would be likely to attach significance to the risks or cluster of risks in deciding whether or not to forgo the proposed therapy'.

While this retains elements of an objective approach (based around the *reasonable* patient), in another common law jurisdiction, Australia, the courts have accepted an amended definition of 'material risk', whose effect is to create a fully subjective approach. This occurred in the Australian High Court decision of *Rogers v Whitaker*, which concerned a patient who had been almost completely blind in her right eye after a childhood injury. Nearly 40 years later she was referred to an eye surgeon who said that removal of the scar tissue would considerably improve the appearance of the eye and might also restore some sight. He failed to warn her that, as a result of surgery, there was a risk (one in 14,000) of her developing sympathetic ophthalmia in her left, good eye. Unfortunately, this risk materialised, leaving the patient totally blind in the left eye and with none of the hoped-for improvement in the right eye. In finding the surgeon in breach of his duty to warn, Mason CJ stated:

Mason CJ: A risk is material if, in the circumstances of the particular case, a reasonable person in the patient's position, if warned of the risk, would be likely to attach significance to it *or if the medical practitioner is or should reasonably be aware that the particular patient, if warned of the risk, would be likely to attach significance to it*. [Emphasis added][115]

3.5.2.2 The position in the UK

Until quite recently, one could have asserted confidently that the doctrine of informed consent, just described, formed no part of the English law. Instead, English judges could be seen as espousing a rather different approach to the standard of risk disclosure required by doctors to discharge their duty in negligence. This approach was often termed the 'prudent doctor test' and in some ways could be seen as diametrically opposed to the US 'informed consent/prudent patient' test. Its starting point was to link the standard of risk disclosure required of doctors to accepted medical practice: the doctor would not be negligent if his failure to disclose the risk was endorsed by a responsible body of medical opinion: in short, the general *Bolam* test was applied. However, in the light of recent developments, the position now is far less certain. Indeed, the previous dichotomy between the *Bolam*-based, prudent doctor, and the prudent patient approaches arguably no longer exists.

See Chapter ◄ 6

In order to place the newer legal developments in context, we need to begin with *Sidaway v Bethlem Royal Hospital*,[116] the House of Lords judgment from the mid-1980s in which, by a 4:1 majority, their Lordships on the face of it rejected 'informed consent' in favour of the *Bolam*-based approach. (It should also be added that, to this day, *Sidaway* has not been expressly doubted by the courts, let alone overruled.)

---

115 (1992) 109 ALR 625.
116 See n 87, above.

Sidaway v Board of Governors of the Bethlem Royal Hospital and the Maudsley Hospital and Others (1985)[117]

The patient underwent an operation to relieve her recurrent neck pain, which carried an inherent risk (ie even if performed with all reasonable care) of damage to the spinal cord of between 1 and 2%. The patient was not warned of this risk, and when it subsequently material-ised and she became severely disabled, she brought an action in negligence. However, the action failed:

Lord Diplock: My Lords, no convincing reason has in my view been advanced before your Lordships that would justify treating the *Bolam* test as doing anything less than laying down a principle of English law that is comprehensive and applicable to every aspect of the duty of care owed by a doctor to his patient in the exercise of his healing functions as respects that patient. What your Lordships have been asked to do – and it is within your power to do so – is to substitute a new and different rule for that part only of the well established *Bolam* test as comprises a doctor's duty to advise and warn the patient of risks of something going wrong in the surgical or other treatment that he is recommending . . .

My Lords, I venture to think that in making this separation between that part of the duty of care that he owes to each individual patient, which can be described as a duty to advise upon treatment and warn of its risks, the courts have misconceived their functions as the finders of fact in cases depending upon the negligent exercise of professional skill and judgment. In matters of diagnosis and the carrying out of treatment the court is not tempted to put itself in the surgeon's shoes; it has to rely upon and evaluate expert evidence, remembering that it is no part of its task of eval-uation to give effect to any preference it may have for one responsible body of profes-sional opinion over another, provided it is satisfied by the expert evidence that both qualify as responsible bodies of medical opinion . . .

[W]e are concerned here with volunteering unsought information about risks of the proposed treatment failing to achieve the result sought or making the patient's physical or mental condition worse rather than better. The only effect that mention of risks can have on the patient's mind, if it has any at all, can be in the direction of deterring the patient from undergoing the treatment which in the expert opinion of the doctor it is in the patient's interest to undergo. To decide what risks the existence of which a patient should be voluntarily warned and the terms in which such warning, if any, should be given, having regard to the effect that the warning may have, is as much an exercise of professional skill and judgment as any other part of the doctor's comprehensive duty of care to the individual patient, and expert medical evidence on this matter should be treated in just the same way. The *Bolam* test should be applied.

In his speech, Lord Bridge also took a stance which tended to defer to clinical judgment:

Lord Bridge: The important question which this appeal raises is whether the law imposes any, and if so what, different criterion as to the measure of the medical man's duty of care to his patient when giving advice with respect to a proposed course of treatment . . .

There are, it appears to me, at least theoretically, two extreme positions which could be taken. It could be argued that, if the patient's consent is to be fully informed, the doctor must specifically warn him of *all* risks involved in the treatment offered,

---

117   Ibid.

unless he has some sound clinical reason not to do so. Logically, this would seem to be the extreme to which a truly objective criterion of the doctor's duty would lead. Yet this position finds no support from any authority, to which we have been referred, in any jurisdiction. It seems to be generally accepted that there is no need to warn of the risks inherent in all surgery under general anaesthesia. This is variously explained on the ground that the patient may be expected to be aware of such risks or that they are relatively remote. If the law is to impose on the medical profession a duty to warn of risk to secure 'informed consent' independently of accepted medical opinion of what is appropriate, neither of these explanations for confining the duty to special as opposed to general surgical risks seems to me wholly convincing.

At the other extreme it could be argued that, once the doctor has decided what treatment is, on balance of advantages and disadvantages, in the patient's best interest, he should not alarm the patient by volunteering a warning of any risk involved, however grave and substantial, unless specifically asked by the patient. I cannot believe that contemporary medical opinion would support this view, which would effectively exclude the patient's right to decide in the very type of case where it is most important that he should be in a position to exercise that right and, perhaps even more significantly, to seek a second opinion as to whether she should submit himself to the significant risk which has been drawn to his attention.

However, importantly, unlike Lord Diplock, Lord Bridge was prepared to acknowledge some situations in which, notwithstanding its compliance with accepted practice, a failure to disclose a particular risk might still be held to be in breach of duty (in other words, although the starting point, the *Bolam* test would not always furnish the doctor with a complete answer to a charge of negligence):

> **Lord Bridge**: I am of the opinion that the judge might in certain circumstances come to the conclusion that disclosure of a particular risk was so obviously necessary to an informed choice on the part of the patient that no reasonably prudent medical man would fail to make it. The kind of case I have in mind would be an operation involving a substantial risk of grave adverse consequences, as, for example, the 10% risk of a stroke from the operation which was the subject of the Canadian case of *Reibl v Hughes*, 114 DLR (3d) 1. In such a case, in the absence of some cogent clinical reason why the patient should not be informed, a doctor, recognising and respecting his patient's right of decision, could hardly fail to appreciate the necessity for an appropriate warning.

Lord Keith concurred with Lord Bridge; and Lord Templeman, although his speech makes no express reference to the *Bolam* test at all, appears to have taken a similar view. By contrast, Lord Scarman (while agreeing that Mrs Sidaway's appeal failed on its facts) delivered a dissenting judgment on this aspect of the law. His speech accorded much more with the US 'prudent patient' approach:

> **Lord Scarman**: My Lords, I think the *Canterbury* propositions reflect a legal truth which too much judicial reliance on medical judgment tends to obscure. In a medical negligence case where the issue is the advice and information given to the patient as to the treatment proposed, the available options, and the risk, the court is concerned primarily with a patient's right. The doctor's duty arises from his patient's rights. If one considers the scope of the doctor's duty by beginning with the right of the patient to make his own decision whether he will or will not undergo the treatment proposed, the right to be informed of significant risk and the doctor's corresponding duty are easy to understand: for the proper implementation of the right requires that the

doctor be under a duty to inform his patient of the material risks inherent in the treatment . . .

Ideally, the court should ask itself whether in the particular circumstances the risk was such that this particular patient would think it significant if he was told it existed. I would think that, as a matter of ethics, this is the test of the doctor's duty. The law, however, operates not in Utopia but in the world as it is: and such an inquiry would prove in practice to be frustrated by the subjectivity of its aim and purpose. The law can, however, do the next best thing, and require the court to answer the question, what would a reasonably prudent patient think significant if in the situation of this patient? . . .

As we have seen, the *Canterbury v Spence* approach, favoured by Lord Scarman, very much equates the need for information and the right to decide upon its materiality, with the patient's right of self-determination.

Subsequently, though, the English Court of Appeal, in *Gold v Haringey HA*,[118] followed the *Bolam* approach to disclosure of risks, relying upon the unequivocal judgment of Lord Diplock in *Sidaway*. The case related to information given in the context of non-therapeutic treatment, namely a sterilisation carried out for contraceptive purposes: the claimant argued that here the standard of disclosure was higher, and that, notwithstanding normal medical practice, it was negligent not to warn him of the risk of the operation failing. However, in rejecting this argument, the Court held that the *Bolam* test applied in the non-therapeutic context as well.

In another decision, *Blyth v Bloomsbury HA*,[119] the Court of Appeal also applied the *Bolam* test to the issue of the doctor's duty to answer questions put by the patient. The case concerned a patient (a qualified nurse) who was given an injection of the contraceptive Depo-Provera following her pregnancy. She alleged it had caused numerous side effects and maintained that she would not have had the drug if she had known of these. The trial judge had accepted that some of the side effects had been caused by the drug, and that the health authority were negligent in failing to answer inquiries made by her. However, this was reversed upon appeal:

Kerr LJ: The question of what a plaintiff should be told in answer to a general inquiry cannot be divorced from the *Bolam* test, any more than when no such inquiry is made. In both cases the answer must depend upon the circumstances, the nature of the inquiry, the nature of the information which is available, its reliability, relevance, the condition of the patient, and so forth. Any medical evidence directed to what would be the proper answer in the light of responsible medical opinion and practice – that is to say, the *Bolam* test – must in my view equally be placed in the balance in cases where the patient makes some inquiry, in order to decide whether the response was negligent or not.

Neill LJ gave a short judgment supporting this view and Balcombe LJ agreed with both of them. This is a surprising decision given that, in *Sidaway*,[120] Lord Bridge unequivocally posited a duty to answer questions, quite independent of the *Bolam* test. His Lordship had commented:

Lord Bridge: I should perhaps add at this point, although the issue does not strictly arise in this appeal, that, when questioned specifically by a patient of apparently sound mind about risks involved in a particular treatment proposed, the doctor's duty must, in my opinion, be to answer both truthfully and as fully as the questioner requires.

---

118   [1988] 1 QB 481.
119   [1993] 4 Med LR 151.
120   See n 87, above.

In fact even Lord Diplock, the hard-liner in *Sidaway* when it came to *Bolam*, had made the confident assertion that a doctor would tell an inquiring patient 'whatever it was the patient wanted to know'.

However, as alluded to earlier, there have since been developments in the law, which has moved away from a strict *Bolam* approach. Thus the courts have shown themselves more willing to impugn failures by doctors to disclose risk even where there is an accepted practice not to do so.[121] This more pro-patient approach was endorsed by the Court of Appeal in *Pearce v United Bristol Healthcare NHS Trust*.

Pearce v United Bristol Healthcare NHS Trust (1999)[122]

The claimant claimed damages as a result of the stillbirth of her child. The birth was overdue, but the consultant obstetrician advised against inducement or a Caesarean. In giving this advice, he did not warn the claimant of the increased risk of stillbirth as a result of non-intervention (of 0.1 to 0.2%). The Court of Appeal upheld the decision of the trial judge to dismiss her claim. The Court held that *Bolam* was the correct starting point, but Lord Woolf MR, giving the judgment of the court went on to say:

> **Lord Woolf MR**: [21] In a case where it is being alleged that a plaintiff has been deprived of the opportunity to make a proper decision as to what course he or she should take in relation to treatment, it seems to me to be the law . . . that if there is a significant risk which would affect the judgment of a reasonable patient, then in the normal course it is the responsibility of a doctor to inform the patient of that significant risk, if the information is needed so that the patient can determine for him or herself as to what course he or she should adopt.
>
> [22] In the *Sidaway* case Lord Bridge recognises that position. He refers to a 'significant risk' as being a risk of something in the region of 10%. When one refers to a 'significant risk' it is not possible to talk in precise percentages, but I note, and it may be purely coincidental, that one of the expert doctors who gave evidence before the judge gave the following answer in evidence. I refer to the evidence of Mr Pearson:
>
> > A. If she hadn't asked I wouldn't have mentioned the subject as she was already distressed and the risk is excessively small. I generally practise according to the belief that it is not the doctor's duty to warn of very small risks. If the risk, however, was of the order, of 10 per cent, for instance, then of course it would be my duty to warn against such a level of risk.
>
> . . . [24] Turning to the facts of this case, the next question is, therefore, 'Was there a significant risk? To what extent was the risk of Jacqueline being a stillborn child increased by delay?' Miss Edwards, on behalf of the respondent, has referred us to the relevant passages in the transcript. They show that, on any basis, the increased risk of the still birth of Jacqueline, as a result of additional delay, was very small indeed. The statistical material which was available can be broken down into different classes. Even looked at comprehensively it comes to something like 0.1 to 0.2 per cent. The doctors called on behalf of the defendants did not regard that risk as significant, nor do I.

These remarks are somewhat ambiguous. Thus, on one view, *Pearce* could be seen as simply reiterating the approach of Lord Bridge in *Sidaway* (which, despite a good claim to being the majority

---

121 A relatively early example is the judgment of Morland J in *Smith v Tunbridge Wells HA* [1994] 5 Med LR 334.
122 [1999] PIQR P53.

approach, had subsequently been lost sight of by the Court of Appeal in the *Gold* and *Blyth* cases). This is so if Lord Woolf MR's 'a significant risk' is read as equivalent to Lord Bridge's category of 'a substantial risk of grave adverse consequences', which should always be disclosed to the patient. On the other hand, what is new is the Master of the Rolls' reference to the patient's perspective as well ('a significant risk which would affect the judgment of a reasonable patient'), which has echoes of the 'informed consent' doctrine. The ambiguity in the judgment stems from the uncertainty as to how far the risk's effect upon the judgment of a reasonable patient is part of what makes it significant.

Lord Woolf's judgment in the *Pearce* case was cited with approval by the Lord Steyn in House of Lords in its important recent decision in *Chester v Afshar*.[123] The latter case did not directly concern the standard of risk disclosure required of doctors (as the defendant's breach of duty in this regard had already been conceded). Rather, as discussed in part 3.5.3 below, it dealt with problems of causation that may arise in this context. Nonetheless, the *obiter* remarks of the Law Lords in relation to the disclosure of treatment risks are naturally of high persuasive value:

Stauch, M, 'Causation and confusion in respect of medical non-disclosure: *Chester v Afshar*'[124]

In *Chester*, the House of Lords – without expressly doubting *Sidaway* – acknowledged that in the intervening years the law in England too has moved towards recognising the patient's right to know of significant risks to the treatment the doctor is proposing. In his speech, Lord Steyn [at para 14] specifically embraced the language of 'informed consent', noting that, '[t]he court is the final arbiter of what constitutes informed consent. Usually, informed consent will presuppose a general warning by the surgeon of a significant risk of the surgery'. His Lordship approved Lord Woolf MR's dictum in *Pearce v United Bristol Healthcare NHS Trust*, that '. . . if there is a significant risk which would affect the judgment of a reasonable patient, then in the normal course it is the responsibility of a doctor to inform the patient of that significant risk'.

For his part, Lord Hope, who was the only other member of the House to address the issue in detail, was more cautious, and preferred to see in the *Sidaway* decision itself an approach aleady sufficiently protective of patient autonomy. As he noted [at para 54]:

> Lord Templeman said [in *Sidaway*] that he did not subscribe to the theory that the patient is entitled to know everything. Some information might confuse and other information might alarm the patient. So it was for the doctor to decide in the light of his training and experience what needed to be said, and how it should be said. But he went on to add these words . . .: 'At the same time the doctor is not entitled to make the final decision with regard to treatment which may have disadvantages or dangers. Where the patient's health and future are at stake, the patient must make the final decision.'

Lord Hope went on to suggest [at para 55] that, 'the right to make the final decision and the duty of the doctor to inform the patient if the treatment may have special disadvantages or dangers go hand in hand'.

Significantly, as the House of Lords in *Chester* recognised, good practice guidelines promulgated by doctors' own professional organisations nowadays also make clear the rights of patients to be informed of significant treatment risks. Arguably, in the light of this, the old dichotomy between the *Sidaway* 'prudent doctor' and US-style 'informed consent' approaches, has disappeared. This is because, on the logic of the *Bolam* test itself, if responsible accepted

---

123 [2004] UKHL 41.
124 (2005) 14 Nott LJ 66.

practice generally is to disclose risks that a reasonable patient would wish to know about, the failure of a particular doctor to do so in a given case will constitute a breach of duty.

The latest Department of Health guidance to health professionals which accompanies the NHS consent form states:

Department of Health, Good practice in consent implementation guide[125]

The courts have stated that patients should be told about 'significant risks which would affect the judgement of a reasonable patient'. 'Significant' has not been legally defined, but the GMC requires doctors to tell patients about 'serious or frequently occurring' risks. In addition if patients make clear they have particular concerns about certain kinds of risk, you should make sure they are informed about these risks, even if they are very small or rare. You should always answer questions honestly.

As the DoH notes, the General Medical Council has gone further. The latter's 2008 guidance, *Consent: patients and doctors making decisions together*, advises doctors as follows:

General Medical Council, Consent: patients and doctors making decisions together[126]

7. The exchange of information between doctor and patient is central to good decision-making. How much information you share with patients will vary, depending on their individual circumstances. You should tailor your approach to discussions with patients according to:
   (a) their needs, wishes and priorities
   (b) their level of knowledge about, and understanding of, their condition, prognosis and the treatment options
   (c) the nature of their condition
   (d) the complexity of the treatment, and
   (e) the nature and level of risk associated with the investigation or treatment.

8. You should not make assumptions about:
   (a) the information a patient might want or need
   (b) the clinical or other factors a patient might consider significant, or
   (c) a patient's level of knowledge or understanding of what is proposed.

9 You must give patients the information they want or need about:
   (a) the diagnosis and prognosis
   (b) any uncertainties about the diagnosis or prognosis, including options for further investigations
   (c) options for treating or managing the condition, including the option not to treat
   (d) the purpose of any proposed investigation or treatment and what it will involve
   (e) the potential benefits, risks and burdens, and the likelihood of success, for each option; this should include information, if available, about whether the benefits or risks are affected by which organisation or doctor is chosen to provide care
   . . .
   (l) any treatments that you believe have greater potential benefit for the patient than those you or your organisation can offer.

---

125 See: www.dh.gov.uk/prod_consum_dh/groups/dh_digitalassets/@dh/@en/documents/digitalasset/dh_4019061.pdf.
126 London: GMC, June 2008; the guidance is available at: www.gmc-uk.org/static/documents/content/Consent_0510.pdf. For an argument that this is in fact less progressive than the GMC's previous 1998 guidance, see Forvargue, S, and Miola, J, 'One step forward, two steps back? The GMC, the common law and "informed" consent' (2010) 36 JME 494.

10   You should explore these matters with patients, listen to their concerns, ask for and respect their views, and encourage them to ask questions.

3.5.2.3 Disclosure of other information

Besides information as to the risk of suffering iatrogenic injury in the course of treatment, there are also other matters that it may be felt that the patient should be told, in order to reach a properly informed and autonomous decision. One of these relates to the availability of alternative therapies to the treatment being recommended by the doctor. Until recently the issue of the doctor's duty to disclose alternatives remained virtually undiscussed in the English courts; however, the question arose in the High Court case of *Birch v University College London NHS Foundation Trust*.[127] There the claimant, who suffered a stroke in the course of an angiography, a mildly invasive diagnostic procedure, was not told of the alternative of using MRI-imaging, which carried no risks of a stroke.

In finding the Trust liable on the basis of failing to obtain the claimant's properly informed consent, the judge stated:

> **Cranston J**: 74. If patients must be informed of significant risks it is necessary to spell out what, in practice, that encompasses. In this case the defendant informed the patient of the probabilities, the one percent, and the nature of the harm of this risk becoming manifest, the stroke. But these were the objectively significant risks associated with the procedure which was performed, the catheter angiogram. Was it necessary for the defendant to go further and to inform Mrs Birch of comparative risk, how this risk compared with that associated with other imaging procedures, in particular MRI? No authority was cited to this effect but in my judgment there will be circumstances where consistently with Lord Woolf MR's statement of the law in *Pearce v United Bristol Healthcare NHS Trust* the duty to inform a patient of the significant risks will not be discharged unless she is made aware that fewer, or no risks, are associated with another procedure. In other words, unless the patient is informed of the comparative risks of different procedures she will not be in a position to give her fully informed consent to one procedure rather than another. The difficulty is in delineating, in general terms, the circum- stances in which the duty arises to inform of comparative risks. In my judgment, in the special circumstances of Mrs Birch's case, that duty arose.

> . . .

> 77. As a matter of law it is difficult to state in general terms when the duty to inform about compar- ative risk arises. Suffice to say that in my judgment, in the special circumstances of Mrs Birch's case, Mr Kitchen is correct and there was a duty to discuss the comparative risks of the catheter angiography alongside MRI. There is no dispute that that duty was breached since the defendant concedes that comparative risks were not raised. The smallness of the risk associated with cath- eter angiography is irrelevant. The fact is that there was no risk of stroke at all from MRI. What should have occurred is that at Queen Square Mrs Birch should have been given a full and fair explanation of this and of the preference for catheter angiography.

> 78. Mrs Birch's circumstances were unusual. She had been referred to Queen Square by one of its neurologists, but because of a problem with beds she entered a neurosurgical, rather than a neurology, ward. That neurologist, Professor Giovannoni, had specifically recommended an MRI. The Friday night admission notes identified both an MRI and catheter angiography as possibilities for the next day. It was only later that the decision for a catheter angiogram was made. Even then Dr Al-Jeroudi's evidence was that he was suggesting an MRI. Given this

127   [2008] EWHC 2237.

background, where two procedures were open for Mrs Birch, she needed to have explained to her the comparative risks . . .

As Cranston J recognises, the duty to inform of alternatives with lower or other risks is not easy to delineate, which raises a potential issue of legal uncertainty. The issue is also complicated by its relationship to the problem of scarce health care resources: thus here, the reason Mrs Birch did not receive an MRI scan was that the equipment was booked out with other patients. Similarly, should a patient be informed of a, statistically, marginally safer therapy, which costs twice as much to provide? One approach would be to tie the answer to whether the doctor believes the patient is in a position to make effective use of the information. For example, he would tell the patient about non-NHS-funded treatment, if and only if the patient could afford to obtain it privately. However, such an approach may be accused of being both high-handed (in second-guessing the patient's means and priorities) and discriminatory.

Further, complex questions surround the need for factors pertaining to the treating side to be disclosed. For example, should a doctor tell a patient that he has never performed this operation before? It may be thought that the training of surgeons is such that they will always have assisted and observed before carrying out a surgical procedure, and therefore, they will always have 'done' the operation in various ways before taking responsibility for it. However, this will not be the case when new procedures and techniques are developed, for example, keyhole surgery. What sort of disclosure should be made then? It is likely that many patients would be very interested to know that their surgeons had never done this before, particularly if there was alternative treatment (that is, conventional surgery)?

It is also a moot point as to whether there is any obligation to disclose the hospital's success or, crucially, failure rate for the type of treatment proposed. This is particularly pertinent in the light of the GMC proceedings against three doctors at the United Bristol Healthcare Trust.[128] The doctors were found to be in breach of professional standards in continuing to carry out heart operations on babies in the knowledge that the death rates of the children they were treating were well above the average for such operations. The subsequent inquiry into the events chaired by Professor Ian Kennedy,[129] recommended, inter alia, that:

102 Patients are always entitled to know the extent to which a procedure which they are about to undergo is innovative or experimental. They are also entitled to be informed about the experience of the clinician who is to carry out the procedure'.

The second part of this may be thought controversial, in that it could lead to patients refusing care from less experienced clinicians (preventing them from gaining experience, and posing logistical problems for the hospital). Also problematic is the Inquiry's recommendation (no 155), that 'patients and the public must be able to obtain information as to the relative performance of the trust and the services and consultant units within the trust'. It is true that many patients would probably regard such knowledge as of considerable interest and value. However, leaving aside arguments over the interpretation of statistics, the information could potentially be highly sensitive politically (in terms of highlighting geographical inequalities). It might even raise the prospect of patients refusing to be treated in certain hospitals altogether.

3.5.2.4 Therapeutic privilege

'Therapeutic privilege' describes the doctor's potential freedom, as a matter of conscience, not to disclose information that he believes would be damaging to the patient. The issue was considered

---

128 See *GMC v Wisheart and others* (Decision of the GMC's PCC), 18 June 1998.
129 Command Paper: Cm 52, *Learning from Bristol: the report of the public inquiry into children's heart surgery at the Bristol Royal Infirmary 1984–1995*,

in *Canterbury v Spence*,[130] where it was stated that where the patient is likely to become so distraught by medical information that he is incapable of making a rational decision, information may be withheld on the grounds of the doctor's privilege.

In the days when the English courts held to the 'prudent doctor' approach, this issue could be regarded as part of the doctor's general discretion not to disclose risks where this accorded with his clinical instincts. However, now that the informational needs of the reasonable patient increasingly provide the yardstick, recourse to 'therapeutic privilege' to justify non-disclosure in specific instances may become more common. In his minority speech in *Sidaway*, Lord Scarman addressed the scope of this 'defence' and stressed that the burden of proof is on the doctor: ' . . . there is the need that the doctor should have the opportunity of proving that he reasonably believed that disclosure of the risk would be damaging to his patient or contrary to his best interests.'

In *Pearce v United Bristol Healthcare NHS Trust*,[131] Lord Woolf MR can be seen as endorsing the existence of such a privilege in the following passage:

Lord Woolf MR: [23] Obviously the doctor, in determining what to tell a patient, has to take into account all the relevant considerations, which include the ability of the patient to comprehend what he has to say to him or her and the state of the patient at the particular time, both from the physical point of view and an emotional point of view. There can often be situations where a course different from the normal has to be employed.

Similarly, in *Chester v Afshar*,[132] Lord Steyn remarked:

Lord Steyn: [16] A surgeon owes a legal duty to a patient to warn him or her in general terms of possible serious risks involved in the procedure. The only qualification is that there may be wholly exceptional cases where objectively in the best interests of the patient the surgeon may be excused from giving a warning.

 SELF-TEST QUESTION

Is there perhaps a danger here that doctors could invoke therapeutic privilege to avoid disclosing risks of treatment they feel is in the patient's interests to have? If so, how might the privilege be recast to exclude this?

3.5.3 Causation

3.5.3.1 Factual causation

An important consequence of the fact that the law deals with the failure to disclose treatment risks in negligence is that, to succeed in a claim, the patient, besides showing that a given non-disclosure was a breach of duty, must go on to prove causation of damage. As we shall see, when

 we discuss causation in Chapter 6, the first aspect of causation – the so called *factual causa-tion* element – requires that, if the defendant had behaved properly (ie not been in breach), the claimant would not have suffered the injury: this is known as the 'but for test'. In the

---

130   464 F 2d 772 (1972).
131   See n 123, above.
132   See n 124, above.

particular context we are addressing here, ie a breach by a doctor of the duty to warn the patient of risks, the latter must establish that, if he had been properly warned, he would not have gone ahead and had the (injurious) treatment.[133]

As Alisdair Maclean points out, the effect of this requirement is to limit the protection offered by the law to the patient's autonomy interests:

Maclean, A, *Autonomy, Informed Consent and Medical Law – A Relational Challenge*[134]

... [There is an] inconsistency between what the law claims to be the patient's right and what it is prepared to compensate. The law proclaims that the patient can make any decision regardless of reason. However, it is then only prepared to compensate those cases of a failure to disclose where claimants provide credible evidence that they would have made a different decision. To be credible, claimants must provide accessible reasons. This is inconsistent; there is a right to refuse treatment for irrational reasons (or even no reason) but in trying to show causation in a failure-to-disclose case a claimant's purported refusal of treatment must be rational. This arises because of the need to show that the breach of duty caused actual damage. If outcome responsibility were severed from the issue of consent and dealt with separately, the inconsistency would be removed since liability for failure to consent would no longer be dependent on showing that a different decision would have been made and the harm from the risk materialising avoided. Separating consent and outcome responsibility would allow these distinct harms to be dealt with in a less blunt way, which would facilitate a more just response. However, because liability for negligence requires a bad outcome, it cannot entirely separate consent and outcome responsibility.

On the other hand, it may be argued that what is really at issue in such cases is compensation for iatrogenic injury, not the bare insult to autonomy from being exposed unwittingly to the risk of such injury. (Arguably few patients will care very much that they did not know of a risk, which did not in any event materialise; and in other contexts too, private law does not recognise an interest in not being wrongfully exposed to risk *per se*, where no harm results.)

It is apparent that, in resolving the factual causation issue as an evidential matter, the court must determine the truth of assertions by the patient in relation to his own hypothetical conduct. The question of how far it will be guided here by what an objective 'reasonable patient' would have chosen to do in similar circumstances was addressed in *Smith v Barking, Havering and Brentwood HA*.

Smith v Barking, Havering and Brentwood HA (1994)[135]

The claimant was a young woman with a serious spinal condition. Without surgery straightaway she would inevitably develop tetraplegia within a matter of months. However, the surgeon who treated her failed to warn her of the 25% risk of immediate tetraplegia attendant on the operation, which unfortunately materialised:

Hutchison J: There was some discussion as to whether the issue of causation should be approached on what was called the objective or the subjective basis – ie, was the question to be resolved by deciding what a reasonable person in the plaintiff's position would have chosen to do, or by deciding what the plaintiff herself would have chosen to do. In support of the former approach I was referred to the Canadian

---

133 By contrast, it is unclear if causation has to be shown in cases of battery. There, where the wrong is the unlawful treatment, the patient will, on one view, recover automatically for all injuries associated with it: see *Chatterton v Gerson* [1981] QB 432, per Bristow J (*obiter*), but cf. *Abbas v Kenney* (1996) 7 Med LR 47, per Gage J (again *obiter*).

134 See n 2, above.

135 [1994] 5 Med LR 285.

authority of *Reibl v Robert A Hughes* [1980] 2 SCR 880 and in support of the latter to the decision of Hirst J in *Hills v Potter* [1984] 1 WLR 641. Both counsel invited me to accept that in the end the matter must be one for decision on a subjective basis. This must plainly as a matter of principle be right, because the question must be: 'If this plaintiff had been given the advice that she should have been given, would she have decided to undergo the operation or not?'

However, there is a peculiar difficulty involved in this sort of case – not least for the plaintiff herself – in giving, after the adverse outcome of the operation is known, reliable answers as to what she would have decided before the operation had she been given proper advice as to the risks inherent in it. Accordingly, it would, in my judgment, be right in the ordinary case to give particular weight to the objective assessment. If everything points to the fact that a reasonable plaintiff, properly informed, would have assented to the operation, the assertion from the witness box, made after the adverse outcome is known, in a wholly artificial situation and in the knowledge that the outcome of the case depends upon that assertion being maintained, does not carry great weight unless there are extraneous or additional factors to substantiate it. By extraneous or additional factors I mean, and I am not doing more than giving examples, religious or some other firmly held convictions; particular social or domestic considerations justifying a decision not in accordance with what, objectively, seems the right one; assertions in the immediate aftermath of the operation made in a context other than that of a possible claim for damages; in other words, some particular factor which suggests that the plaintiff had grounds for not doing what a reasonable person in her situation might be expected to have done. Of course, the less confidently the judge reaches the conclusion as to what objectively the reasonable patient might be expected to have decided, the more readily will he be persuaded by her subjective evidence.

This subjective approach (looking to what the *particular* patient would have done), which, nevertheless, takes account of objective 'reasonableness' for evidential purposes was approved in *Chester v Afshar* at the Court of Appeal stage,[136] and has also been accepted in Australia.[137] It may, however, be contrasted with the US and Canadian approach, which is to focus simply on how an objective reasonable patient would have behaved.[138] The latter approach, whose effect is that a patient may lose even if able to prove that he, individually, would have refused the treatment, is on the face of things hard to justify.

3.5.3.2 *The problem of* legal *causation*

As noted previously, to establish factual causation the patient must show that, had he known of the risk, he would have declined the course of treatment. However, what of a case where the patient can show they would have initially refused treatment, and hence would have avoided the (random) risk of the injury that occurred, but would ultimately have required that treatment (and, hence, been exposed to the self-same risk) in the future? Such a case creates a problem in terms of so called *legal* causation.

The Australian High Court was confronted with this problem in *Chappel v Hart*,[139] in which the respondent, Mrs Hart, suffered damage to her vocal cord in the course of throat surgery – a risk that the appellant, in breach of duty, had failed to disclose. The respondent accepted that, had she

---

136 [2002] 3 All ER 552.
137 See *Rogers v Whitaker* (n 115, above); *Rosenberg v Percival* (2001) 75 ALJR 734.
138 See eg, the Canadian Supreme Court decision of *Arndt v Smith* [1997] 2 SCR 539.
139 (1998) 72 ALJR 1344.

been warned, she would still have had the surgery, but at a later date. As the minority judges argued, the surgeon's failure had thus merely altered the time and place at which the claimant had been exposed to the risk of injury:

> **Hayne J**: Of course, the respondent did suffer a perforated oesophagus, she did suffer an infection, she did suffer paralysis of the laryngeal nerve. But if she had not attended the hospital on that day, the probabilities are that none of this would have happened. And if the appellant had told her of the risk to her voice, she would not have had the operation when she did. But precisely the same argument would be open if, instead of suffering damage to her voice, as she has, the operating theatre in which her procedure was performed had been struck by lightning, or a runaway truck, and she had been injured. But for the negligent failure to warn she would not have been in harm's way.

However, a majority of the High Court found Dr Chappel liable. Broadly, and without resolving the conceptual problem posed by the minority, it appears to have felt that, since Mrs Hart's injury would almost certainly not otherwise have occurred (ie *factual* causation was present), such injury should on a 'common sense' basis also be attributed to Dr Chappel's failure as a matter of *legal* causation.

Subsequently, in *Chester v Afshar*, the UK House of Lords was required to address exactly the same problem as had vexed the Australian High Court.

Chester v Afshar (2004)[140]

Miss Chester had suffered from progressively worsening back pain for a number of years, and was referred to Mr Afshar, a distinguished consultant neurosurgeon. Although she was apprehensive about operations in general, at consultation the defendant swiftly persuaded her as to the merits of surgery, which he carried out a few days later. Unfortunately, despite being performed with due care, a risk of such surgery, 'cauda equina syndrome' (assessed at one-to-two per cent), materialised, leaving Miss Chester with serious disabilities. The trial judge (Robert Taylor J) found that the defendant had failed to disclose this risk, and that this constituted a breach of duty.

As to causation, the judge found that Miss Chester, if warned, would not have undergone the operation when she did (as she would have wished to seek further medical opinions as to the need for the surgery), albeit she may well have submitted to it in the future. He noted that, 'had she been adequately warned, the operation in question would not have taken place and she would not have suffered damage. In these circumstances, and without more, it seems to me that the necessary causal link is sufficiently established'. The judge accordingly found in favour of Miss Chester, and this was upheld by the Court of Appeal. The defendant appealed to the House of Lords:

> **Lord Steyn:** [13] Counsel for the surgeon submitted that it is contrary to general principles of tort law to award damages when a defendant's wrong has not been proved to have increased the claimant's exposure to risk. He argued that in order to establish causation in a case of a surgeon's failure to warn a patient of a significant risk of injury, the patient must prove both that she would not have consented to run the relevant risk then and there, and that she would not, ultimately, have consented to run the relevant risk. . . .

---

140 See n 124, above.

[18] . . . [I]n the context of attributing legal responsibility, it is necessary to identify precisely the protected legal interests at stake. A rule requiring a doctor to abstain from performing an operation without the informed consent of a patient serves two purposes. It tends to avoid the occurrence of the particular physical injury the risk of which a patient is not prepared to accept . . .

[19] . . . [I]t is a distinctive feature of the present case that but for the surgeon's negligent failure to warn the claimant of the small risk of serious injury the actual injury would not have occurred when it did and the chance of it occurring on a subsequent occasion was very small. It could therefore be said that the breach of the surgeon resulted in the very injury about which the claimant was entitled to be warned.

Lord Hope agreed:

Lord Hope: [86] I start with the proposition that the law which imposed the duty to warn on the doctor has at its heart the right of the patient to make an informed choice as to whether, and if so when and by whom, to be operated on. Patients may have, and are entitled to have, different views about these matters. All sorts of factors may be at work here – the patient's hopes and fears and personal circumstances, the nature of the condition that has to be treated and, above all, the patient's own views about whether the risk is worth running for the benefits that may come if the operation is carried out. . . .

[87] To leave the patient who would find the decision difficult without a remedy, as the normal approach to causation would indicate, would render the duty useless in the cases where it may be needed most. This would discriminate against those who cannot honestly say that they would have declined the operation once and for all if they had been warned. I would find that result unacceptable. The function of the law is to enable rights to be vindicated and to provide remedies when duties have been breached. Unless this is done the duty is a hollow one, stripped of all practical force and devoid of all content. It will have lost its ability to protect the patient and thus to fulfil the only purpose which brought it into existence. On policy grounds therefore I would hold that the test of causation is satisfied in this case. The injury was intimately involved with the duty to warn.

Lord Walker agreed with Lords Steyn and Hope in dismissing Mr Afshar's appeal. However, Lords Bingham and Hoffmann dissented:

Lord Hoffmann: [29] The burden is on a claimant to prove that the defendant's breach of duty caused him damage. Where the breach of duty is a failure to warn of a risk, he must prove that he would have taken the opportunity to avoid or reduce that risk. In the context of the present case, that means proving that she would not have had the operation.

[30] The judge made no finding that she would not have had the operation. He was not invited by the claimant to make such a finding. The claimant argued that as a matter of law it was sufficient that she would not have had the operation at that time or by that surgeon, even though the evidence was that the risk could have been precisely the same if she had it at another time or by another surgeon. A similar argument has been advanced before this House.

[31] In my opinion this argument is about as logical as saying that if one had been told, on entering a casino, that the odds on the number 7 coming up at roulette were only 1 in 37, one would have gone away and come back next week or gone to a

different casino. The question is whether one would have taken the opportunity to avoid or reduce the risk, not whether one would have changed the scenario in some irrelevant detail. The judge found as a fact that the risk would have been precisely the same whether it was done then or later or by that competent surgeon or by another.

[32] It follows that the claimant failed to prove that the defendant's breach of duty caused her loss. On ordinary principles of tort law, the defendant is not liable.

Their Lordships appeared to believe that, allowing recovery by the claimant involved a special departure from the ordinary rules of causation (the disagreement centring on the propriety of such a departure). With respect, it is unfortunate in this regard that the House of Lords failed to distinguish more carefully between *factual* and *legal* causation. Had it done so, it would have been clearer that no radically new principle was involved. There was merely a modest (and justifiable) relaxation of legal causation:

Stauch, M, 'Causation and confusion in respect of medical non-disclosure: *Chester v Afshar*'[141]

It ought to be clear that, in *Chester, factual* causation was present: Mr Afshar's breach, in failing to advise of the risk, had changed the course of events and led to the claimant being injured when, otherwise, she would almost certainly have escaped such injury. As Lord Steyn commented, '. . . but for the surgeon's negligent failure to warn the claimant of the small risk of serious injury the actual injury would not have occurred when it did and the chance of it occurring on a subsequent occasion was very small' . . .

. . . The reason why, once established, factual causation is significant is two-fold. First it prevents the claimant from getting a windfall. It seems right (as the minority in *Chester* suggested, while failing to see that the claimant fulfilled the relevant condition) to reserve substantial damages for cases where the doctor's conduct has altered the course of events and resulted in injury (when otherwise there would very likely have been no injury). Indeed, this is merely an instance of the general requirement, foundational in the tort of negligence, that the claimant must show 'damage' . . . [T]he second, more positive reason why proof of factual causation is significant, this is that it gives rise to a powerful *prima facie* case for compensation: 'if you had behaved properly, I would not have been injured!' Qualifications on liability based upon remoteness/legal causation points are relatively unusual. This is all the more so in cases where the injury intrudes in close temporal proximity to the wrongful act, and was readily foreseeable (both of which were true here) . . .

The further question, as to how far the normal legal causation requirement that the defendant's breach created or added to the risk, should be relaxed in this type of case had been exhaustively discussed in *Chappel v Hart*, a recent case from the High Court of Australia with similar facts, as well as in the meticulous judgment of the Court of Appeal in *Chester* itself. In fact there would seem to be good reasons for such a relaxation. Most importantly, as the majority in the House of Lords recognised, the doctor's duty to inform patients of risks would otherwise be very much attenuated . . .

This is not to say that, in other non-disclosure cases, a claim may not sometimes fail for lack of legal causation. One situation is where the patient's injury stemmed from a *different* risk to the one which

---

141   See n 125, above.

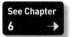

was faultily not disclosed. Admittedly, the few authorities in point are not wholly consistent. Thus in the Scottish decision of *Moyes v Lothian Health Board*[142] the judge appeared to accept that in such circumstances the doctor would remain liable. However, the Court of Appeal's recent judgment in *Thompson v Bradford*[143] would suggest otherwise. As mentioned earlier, we shall look further at issues of causation in medical negligence cases – both factual and legal – in Chapter 6.

Summary of Key Points

1. The requirement that capable (or competent) adult patients consent to their medical treatment is a key principle of medical law, and on the face of it shows the law's commitment to patient autonomy over the desire of doctors to treat in the patient's best interests.
2. A doctor who fails to obtain consent will normally be liable to the patient in civil law for the tort of battery, and also, potentially, in criminal law.
3. Generally speaking, consent is both a necessary and sufficient condition for lawful treatment. However, there are exceptions that run in both directions. Thus some procedures, eg radical surgery with no therapeutic goal, will remain unlawful (in criminal law) despite the patient's consent.
4. Conversely, non-consensual treatment may occasionally be justified on the basis of an overriding public interest. An example is interventions under public health legislation, so far as this is necessary to protect the health of others.
5. It is less clear if there are also bases in common law for treating without consent. A patient's consent presupposes capacity, and the courts in contentious situations (eg where a pregnant woman refuses treatment to save herself/her foetus) have tended to find that the patient is incapable.
6. In fact the test for capacity, as developed by the courts and now encoded in the MCA 2005, is relatively open-textured. It requires that the patient is able to take in and retain treatment information, (believe it), and weigh it in the balance.
7. Besides capacity, two other elements must be present for the patient to give a valid consent. These are voluntariness (ie the patient's decision is free from duress or undue influence) and that the doctor has provided information about the treatment.
8. Even so, only basic information, as to the 'nature and purpose' of the treatment, needs to be given. By contrast, the failure to mention other matters, such as the risks of the procedure, will not affect the patient's consent, though he may be able to bring a subsequent action in negligence.
9. To succed in such an action, the patient must first show the doctor was in breach of duty by not disclosing the relevant risks. In the past, the English courts allowed doctors significant discretion as to which risks to disclose, but this has now altered in favour of an 'informed consent' standard.
10. In addition, it remains necessary for the patient to prove a causal link between the non-disclosure and the injury he has suffered (through the occurrence of the treatment risk). Generally this is satisfied by him showing that he would have declined the treatment, had he known of the risk.

---

142 [1990] 1 Med LR 463; see also *Hepworth v Kerr* [1995] 6 Med LR 139.
143 [2005] EWCA Civ 1439; the facts of the case are discussed in Ch 6, section 6.4.3.

Further Reading

Dworkin, G, *The Theory and Practice of Autonomy*, Cambridge: CUP, 1988.

Elliott, T, 'Body Dysmorphic Disorder, Radical Surgery and the Limits of Consent' (2009) 17 *Medical Law Review* 149.

Gunn, M, 'The Meaning of Incapacity' (1994) 2 *Medical Law Review* 8.

Hockton, A, *The Law of Consent to Medical Treatment*, London: Sweet & Maxwell, 2001 (2nd edn forthcoming, 2011).

Jones, M, 'Informed Consent and Other Fairy Stories' (1999) 7 *Medical Law Review* 103.

Maclean, A, *Autonomy, Informed Consent and Medical Law – A Relational Challenge*, Cambridge: CUP, 2009.

Pattinson, S, 'Consent and Informational Responsibility' (2009) 35 *Journal of Medical Ethics* 176.

Chapter 4

Treating the Incapable Patient

Chapter Contents

4.1 Introduction

There can be no doubt that patients who lack capacity should nevertheless receive medical treatment. However, difficulties arise when considering the legal framework in which treatment decisions are made, and the criteria used to decide on the suitability of treatment.

The treatment of the incapable patient will be considered in later chapters in relation to particular forms of treatment (for example, organ donation; medical research; and – where the patient is terminally ill or gravely incapacitated). In this chapter we will concentrate on the basic legal framework and general principles, making particular reference to so-called non-therapeutic areas relating to the control of fertility by sterilisation and abortion.

See Chapter 11

See Chapter 10

See Chapter 12

The chapter deals with adults and children separately. They are governed by separate legal regimes, and, also, in the case of children, there has always been surrogate decision-making in the form of parental consent. However, this can result in conflicts between the rights and interests of parents and those of incapable children.

We are referring to patients who are 'incapable' but some of the extracts refer to 'incompetent' patients, and this was the more common terminology a few years ago, and, indeed, earlier editions of this book employed it. However, with the passing of the Mental Capacity Act it is more appropriate to use language to reflect this.

As far as incapable adults are concerned, until recently this area was governed entirely by the common law. There is now a statutory scheme under the Mental Capacity Act 2005, but, as case law under the common law will still influence decision-making under the Act, it is helpful to explain the earlier common law situation.

4.2 Incapable Adults

4.2.1 Common law

4.2.1.1 Necessity and common law

At common law the treatment of incapable patients, ie without consent, was potentially a battery. However, the common law developed the defence of necessity (latterly developed into the language of best interests) to avoid the unpalatable consequences of a doctor being civilly and criminally liable in such circumstances. Although the defence of necessity could only be successfully invoked if the treatment was in the best interests of the patient, the defence of necessity was frequently used to refer to emergency treatment carried out on unconscious patients, whilst the best interests defence tended to be referred to when dealing with patients who are permanently lacking in capacity, whether emergency cases or not. It must be stressed, however, that there was no strict dichotomy and, arguably, the distinction is meaningless.

The defence of necessity, therefore, must necessarily entail the doctor acting in the best interests of the patient. The difference lies in the nature of the treatment. In an emergency, the treatment must be confined to that which is necessary to preserve life and limb, when it is impossible to obtain consent. However, the best interests test applied to all forms of medical treatment carried out on permanently incapable patients.

The nature of necessity was examined in the case of Re F (Mental Patient: Sterilisation):

Re F (Mental Patient: Sterilisation) (1990)[1]

Lord Goff: Upon what principle can medical treatment be justified when given without consent? We are searching for a principle upon which, in limited circumstances, recognition may be

---

1   [1990] 2 AC 1, at 73.

given to a need, in the interests of the patient, that treatment should be given to him in circumstances where he is (temporarily or permanently) disabled from consenting to it. It is this criterion of a need which points to the principle of necessity as providing justification . . .

The distinction I have drawn between cases of emergency, and cases where the state of affairs is (more or less) permanent, is relevant in another respect. We are here concerned with medical treatment, and I limit myself to cases of that kind. Where, for example, a surgeon performs an operation without his consent on a patient temporarily rendered unconscious in an accident, he should do no more than is reasonably required, in the best interests of the patient, before he recovers consciousness. I can see no practical difficulty arising from this requirement, which derives from the fact that the patient is expected before long to regain consciousness and can then be consulted about longer term measures. . . .

But where the state of affairs is permanent or semi-permanent, as may be so in the case of a mentally disordered person, there is no point in waiting to obtain the patient's consent. The need to care for him is obvious; and the doctor must then act in the best interests of his patient, just as if he had received his patient's consent so to do. Were this not so, much useful treatment and care could, in theory at least, be denied to the unfortunate. It follows that, on this point, I am unable to accept the view expressed by Neill LJ in the Court of Appeal . . . that the treatment must be shown to have been necessary.

Lord Goff referred to the Canadian case of *Marshall v Curry*,[2] where a patient brought an action in battery against a surgeon who had removed a diseased testicle during the course of a hernia operation. The surgeon tried to argue that it was necessary to remove the testicle because it seriously threatened the health of the patient. In other words, though couched in terms of necessity, the defence, in reality, was that it was in the best interests of the patient to perform this operation. The court held that the removal of the testicle was necessary and that it would have been unreasonable to put the procedure off to a later date. This is a somewhat troubling decision, and was not followed in a later Canadian case. In *Murray v McMurchy*,[3] the patient was a woman who had been sterilised without her consent in the course of a Caesarean section. The defence was that the condition of her uterus was such as to make it dangerous for her to go through another pregnancy. The court held that it would have been reasonable to postpone this operation in order to seek her consent.

4.2.1.2 Common law and the role of the court

It may seem odd, but in English law, until the enactment of the Mental Capacity Act 2005 there was no mechanism whereby someone could be sanctioned to make decisions about medical treatment on behalf of an adult patient. However, this was not always the case. Incapable adults once had protection: there was an inherent power in the courts (known as the *parens patriae* jurisdiction) to act on behalf of the incapacitated adult in very much the same way as minors are still protected today. This is the jurisdiction extant in the Canadian legal process referred to by La Forest J in the judgment in *Re Eve*.[4] However, the royal warrant by which this power was delegated to the courts was revoked shortly after the Mental Health Act 1959 came into force because it was believed that the Act made all necessary provision for mental patients. However, whilst the original Mental Health Act 1983 (since amended) provided for the appointment of a guardian in respect of the patient's financial affairs, no such power was provided for in respect of the personal welfare or health of the patient. *Re F (Mental Patient: Sterilisation)*[5] concerned the sterilisation of a mentally impaired woman aged 36, but said to have an overall mental age of four or five. The case is considered in further detail below but on the subject of the court's

See Chapter 9 ➜

---

2 (1933) 3 DLR 260.
3 (1949) 2 DLR 442.
4 [1986] 2 SCR 388.
5 [1990] 2 AC 1.

role and its inherent declaratory jurisdiction, only Lord Griffiths dissented from the view that an application to the court remains within the discretion of the doctors concerned[6]:

> **Lord Griffiths**: I cannot agree that it is satisfactory to leave this grave decision with all its social implications in the hands of those having the care of the patient with only the expectation that they will have the wisdom to obtain a declaration of lawfulness before the operation is performed. In my view the law ought to be that they must obtain the approval of the court before they sterilise a woman incapable of giving consent and that it is unlawful to sterilise without that consent. I believe that it is open to your Lordships to develop a common law rule to this effect . . .

Similarly, in the earlier case of *Re B (A Minor) (Wardship: Sterilisation*[7]), only Lord Templeman took the view that court approval should always be obtained. However, in the Australian High Court's decision in *Department of Health v JWB and SMB*,[8] although the judges did not express the view that it is mandatory to apply to the court in the case of a therapeutic sterilisation, in the case of a non-therapeutic sterilisation (that is, a sterilisation carried out where the physical health of the patient does not demand it), the court held that it required prior court approval. Although this case and the case of *Re B* concerned children, it is arguable that exactly the same view should be taken in the case of an incapable adult.

Most of the cases using the declaratory jurisdiction have been brought by the health carers involved with the patient. However, it was used in the case of *Re S (Hospital Order: Court's Jurisdiction*[9]) to decide a dispute between the wife and the mistress of an elderly Norwegian who had become incapable following a stroke. Both wife and mistress wanted to care for him. The court held that the declaratory jurisdiction could be used by anyone with a genuine and legitimate interest in obtaining a decision on a serious justiciable issue. The dispute in this case was found to be such an issue. (See also *Re S (Adult's Lack of Capacity: Carer and Residence*).[10])

In *Re F (Adult: Court's Jurisdiction)*,[11] the facts concerned a mentally impaired 18-year-old woman (T). It was agreed that she lacked capacity to make decisions, particularly about the place where she should live. She had been in local authority care, initially with the consent of her parents, but consent to further placement was withdrawn. The local authority sought declarations that it could keep her in similar accommodation and restrict and supervise her contact with her family (previously, she had been neglected and sexually exploited when she had been living at home). An application for guardianship under the MHA 1983 had already been rejected by the Court of Appeal on the basis that she did not satisfy the definition of mental impairment under the Act. However, having reached the age of 18, the wardship jurisdiction was no longer available to the court. The Court of Appeal (*Re F (Mental Health Act: Guardianship)*[12]) held that the common law could 'fill the gap' in the statutory framework. Now, of course, the Mental Capacity Act does this job but it is worth noting the flexibility of the common law.

4.3 The Mental Capacity Act 2005

4.3.1 History

We have seen that the common law provided the legal framework for decision-making in cases of incapacitated patients until very recently. However, the need for a legal framework of protection

6 At p70.
7 [1988] AC 199.
8 (1992) 66 ALJR 300.
9 [1995] 3 All ER 290.
10 [2003] EWHC 1909(Fam).
11 [2000] 2 FLR 512.
12 [2000] 1 FLR 192.

for vulnerable, mentally incapacitated adults had been highlighted by the Law Commission in its report, *Mental Incapacity*, Report no 231.[13] In December 1997, the government published a Green Paper which was closely based upon the Law Commission's report. In 1999 the White Paper, *Making Decisions: the Government's Proposals for Making Decisions on Behalf of Mentally Incapacitated Adults*, Cm 4465,[14] was published. Subsequently there was the draft Mental Incapacity Bill, the draft Mental Capacity Bill (the change of emphasis reflecting the criticisms that 'incapacity' was too negative) and, finally, this resulted in the passing of the Mental Capacity Act 2005. The Act does not apply only to patients as it is used to make decisions about residence or other aspects of personal welfare; it applies to anyone who is incapacitated who has attained the age of 16.

The MCA only applies in England and Wales.

4.3.2 Current Scheme

4.3.2.1 Principles

The Mental Capacity Act contains a number of key principles.

Mental Capacity Act 2005

1 The principles

(1) The following principles apply for the purposes of this Act.

(2) A person must be assumed to have capacity unless it is established that he lacks capacity.

(3) A person is not to be treated as unable to make a decision unless all practicable steps to help him to do so have been taken without success.

(4) A person is not to be treated as unable to make a decision merely because he makes an unwise decision.

(5) An act done, or decision made, under this Act for or on behalf of a person who lacks capacity must be done, or made, in his best interests.

(6) Before the act is done, or the decision is made, regard must be had to whether the purpose for which it is needed can be as effectively achieved in a way that is less restrictive of the person's rights and freedom of action.

These principles reflect a presumption of capacity and the need to help people acquire capacity, and the need to respect actions and wishes which are not necessarily wise, on the basis that we all make unwise decisions, and not to acknowledge this might be regarded as the unacceptable face of paternalism. When there is no capacity then decisions must be taken in the best interests of the person concerned and in a way that least restricts the liberty of the person concerned. Although we are here concerned with patients and medical treatment, the Act applies to all decisions such as where someone lives, what sort of clothes they wear, who they wish to socialise with, and so on.

4.3.2.2 Powers of Attorney and Advance Decisions

Powers of attorney are documents that enable someone to give powers to third parties to make decisions on their behalf. Prior to the Mental Capacity Act it was possible to give someone an 'enduring power of attorney', ie it would continue to be valid if the donor of the power lost capacity. The Mental Capacity Act replaced this with 'lasting powers of attorney' (see s 9 and Sch 1) which widen the remit of the power to cover personal care and treatment. Existing enduring powers of attorney are still valid, and can still be registered, but no new enduring powers can be

---

13 London: HMSO, 1995.
14 London: HMSO, 1999.

created. The Public Guardian heads the administrative function of the Court of Protection (see below) and, *inter alia*, maintains a register of lasting powers of attorney.

The Act also provides for advance decision-making either in oral or written form and these are dealt with in Chapter 12.

See Chapter 12

4.3.3 Human Rights and the Deprivation of Liberty Safeguards

These provisions, contained in ss 4A and 4B and Sch A1 of the Mental Capacity Act 2005, which were inserted by the Mental Health Act 2007, have their origins in a mental health case but they apply to anyone who is having medical treatment or general care eg in a hospital, residential or nursing home, who is deprived in some way of their liberty.

Under the Mental Health Act 1983 there is a provision whereby patients do not have to be detained under compulsory powers in order to receive treatment for mental disorder; they are regarded as informal patients. As they are informal patients, they do not have any right to go to a Mental Health Review Tribunal because they are not detained, ie they are free to leave hospital. It is entirely understandable that patients who are mentally disordered and who also have the capacity to consent to treatment would prefer to have treatment for mental disorder by consenting to it, rather than by having it imposed upon them. However, the difficulty that can arise concerns the patient who does not have capacity. Informal admission under the Mental Health Act 1983, s 131, fell to be considered by the House of Lords in the case of R v *Bournewood Community and Mental Health NHS Trust ex p L*.[15] An autistic patient had been 'informally' admitted to a mental health unit. The psychiatrist felt that formal detention was unnecessary unless the patient resisted treatment. The trust argued that he was an informal patient under s 131 because he had chosen not to leave the hospital. The House of Lords held that it had clearly been intended that patients lacking the capacity to consent could be admitted under s 131. Their Lordships relied heavily on the findings of the Percy Commission, which reported prior to the 1959 Mental Health Act and which had envisaged such admissions as avoiding the stigmatisation of such patients with the label of having been 'sectioned'. Such patients would be admitted for treatment 'in their own best interests'. As we have seen, although this is prior to the Mental Capacity Act of 2005, treatment given 'in the best interests of the patient' was well established by common law. The House of Lords was therefore suggesting that the doctrine of necessity would apply. The case was brought before the European Court of Human Rights. The court held that the patient has been 'detained', and that therefore he was entitled to safeguards that were Article 5 compatible:

HL v United Kingdom (2005)[16]

. . . .

Alleged violation of Article 5(1) of the Convention

. . .

89 It is not disputed that in order to determine whether there has been a deprivation of liberty, the starting point must be the specific situation of the individual concerned and account must be taken of a whole range of factors arising in a particular case such as the type, duration, effects and manner of implementation of the measure in question. The distinction between a deprivation of, and restriction upon, liberty is merely one of degree or intensity and not one of nature or substance.

See Chapter 9

---

15 [1998] 3 All ER 289.
16 (2005) 40 EHRR 32, ECJ.

90 The Court observes that the High Court and the majority of the House of Lords found that the applicant had not been detained during this period while the Court of Appeal and a minority of the House of Lords found that he had. Although this Court will have regard to the domestic courts' related findings of fact, it does not consider itself constrained by their legal conclusions as to whether the applicant was detained or not, not least because the House of Lords considered the question from the point of view of the tort of false imprisonment rather than the Convention concept of 'deprivation of liberty' in Art.5(1), the criteria for assessing those domestic and Convention issues being different.

In this latter respect, considerable emphasis was placed by the domestic courts, and by the Government, on the fact that the applicant was compliant and never attempted, or expressed the wish, to leave. The majority of the House of Lords specifically distinguished actual restraint of a person (which would amount to false imprisonment) and restraint which was conditional upon his seeking to leave (which would not constitute false imprisonment). The Court does not consider such a distinction to be of central importance under the Convention. Nor, for the same reason, can the Court accept as determinative the fact relied on by the Government that the regime applied to the applicant (as a compliant incapacitated patient) did not materially differ from that applied to a person who had the capacity to consent to hospital treatment, neither objecting to their admission to hospital. The Court recalls that the right to liberty is too important in a democratic society for a person to lose the benefit of Convention protection for the single reason that he may have given himself up to be taken into detention, especially when it is not disputed that that person is legally incapable of consenting to, or disagreeing with, the proposed action.

91 Turning therefore to the concrete situation as required by the *Ashingdane* judgment, the Court considers the key factor in the present case to be that the health care professionals treating and managing the applicant exercised complete and effective control over his care and movements from the moment he presented acute behavioural problems on July 22, 1997 to the date he was compulsorily detained on October 29, 1997.

More particularly, the applicant had been resident with his carers for over three years. On July 22, 1997, following a further incident of violent behaviour and self-harm in his day-care centre, the applicant was sedated before being brought to the hospital and subsequently to the IBU, in the latter case supported by two persons. His responsible medical officer (Dr M) was clear that, had the applicant resisted admission or tried to leave thereafter, she would have prevented him from doing so and would have considered his involuntarily committal under s3 of the 1983 Act: indeed, as soon as the Court of Appeal indicated that his appeal would be allowed, he was compulsorily detained under the 1983 Act. The correspondence between the applicant's carers and Dr M reflects both the carer's wish to have the applicant immediately released to their care and, equally, the clear intention of Dr M and the other relevant health-care professionals to exercise strict control over his assessment, treatment, contacts and, notably, movement and residence: the applicant would only be released from the hospital to the care of Mr and Mrs E as and when those professionals considered it appropriate. While the Government suggested that 'there was evidence' that the applicant had not been denied access to his carers, it is clear from the above-noted correspondence that the applicant's contact with his carers was directed and controlled by the hospital, his carers visiting him for the first time after his admission on November 2, 1997.

Accordingly, the concrete situation was that the applicant was under continuous supervision and control and was not free to leave. Any suggestion to the contrary was, in the Court's view, fairly described by Lord Steyn as 'stretching credulity to breaking point' and as a 'fairy tale'.

92 The Court would therefore agree with the applicant that it is not determinative whether the ward was 'locked' or 'lockable' (the evidence before the House of Lords and the Commissioner

appearing to differ in this respect). In this regard, it recalls that the applicant in the *Ashingdane* case was considered to have been 'detained' for the purposes of Art.5(1)(e) even during a period when he was in an open ward with regular unescorted access to the unsecured hospital grounds and unescorted leave outside the hospital.

93 Considerable reliance was placed by the Government on the above-cited *HM v Switzerland* judgment, in which it was held that the placing of an elderly applicant in a foster home, to ensure necessary medical care as well as satisfactory living conditions and hygiene, did not amount to a deprivation of liberty within the meaning of Art.5 of the Convention. However, each case has to be decided on its own particular 'range of factors' and, while there may be similarities between the present and the *HM* case, there are also distinguishing features. In particular, it was not established that *HM* was legally incapable of expressing a view on her position, she had often stated that she was willing to enter the nursing home and, within weeks of being there, she had agreed to stay. This combined with a regime entirely different to that applied to the present applicant (the foster home was an open institution which allowed freedom of movement and encouraged contacts with the outside world) allows a conclusion that the facts of the *HM* case were not of a 'degree' or 'intensity' sufficiently serious to justify the conclusion that she was detained.

The Court also finds a conclusion that the present applicant was detained consistent with the above-cited judgment on which the Government also relied. That case turned on the specific fact that the mother had committed the applicant minor to an institution in the exercise of her parental rights, pursuant to which rights she could have removed the applicant from the hospital at any time. Although the Government noted that the hospital retained responsibility for the present applicant following his release in 1994, the fact that the hospital had to rely on the doctrine of necessity and, subsequently, on the involuntary detention provisions of the 1983 Act demonstrates that the hospital did not have legal authority to act on the applicant's behalf in the same way as Mr Nielsen's mother.

94 The Court therefore concludes that the applicant was 'deprived of his liberty' within the meaning of Art.5(1) of the Convention from July 22, 1997 to October 29, 1997.

The Court did state that whether someone was detained had to be decided on the basis of the specific situation under consideration. This is important because the decision has serious implications for those mentally incapacitated patients and their carers where the patient is not in a place which is registered to take detained patients but in, say, a residential care home. As far as those informal patients in psychiatric hospitals are concerned who lack capacity it is possible that they will be formally detained or discharged.

Following on from this decision, the Mental Health Act 2007 amended the Mental Capacity Act so that such patients could be lawfully deprived of their liberty when it was appropriate to do so.

Mental Capacity Act 2005

4A Restriction on deprivation of liberty

(1) This Act does not authorise any person ("D") to deprive any other person ("P") of his liberty.

(2) But that is subject to–
    (a) the following provisions of this section, and
    (b) section 4B.

(3) D may deprive P of his liberty if, by doing so, D is giving effect to a relevant decision of the court.

(4) A relevant decision of the court is a decision made by an order under section 16(2)(a) in relation to a matter concerning P's personal welfare.

(5)   D may deprive P of his liberty if the deprivation is authorised by Schedule A1 (hospital and care home residents: deprivation of liberty).

4B Deprivation of liberty necessary for life-sustaining treatment etc

(1)   If the following conditions are met, D is authorised to deprive P of his liberty while a decision as respects any relevant issue is sought from the court.

(2)   The first condition is that there is a question about whether D is authorised to deprive P of his liberty under section 4A.

(3)   The second condition is that the deprivation of liberty–

   (a)   is wholly or partly for the purpose of–

      (i)   giving P life-sustaining treatment, or

      (ii)   doing any vital act, or

   (b)   consists wholly or partly of–

      (i)   giving P life-sustaining treatment, or

      (ii)   doing any vital act.

(4)   The third condition is that the deprivation of liberty is necessary in order to–

   (a)   give the life-sustaining treatment, or

   (b)   do the vital act.

(5)   A vital act is any act which the person doing it reasonably believes to be necessary to prevent a serious deterioration in P's condition.

The safeguards apply to anyone aged 18 and over who: suffers from a mental disorder or disability of the mind – such as dementia or a profound learning disability; lacks the capacity to give informed consent to the arrangements made for their care and/or treatment; for whom deprivation of liberty (within the meaning of Art 5 of the ECHR) is considered after an independent assessment to be necessary in their best interests to protect them from harm. The safeguards cover patients in hospitals, and people in care homes registered under the Care Standards Act 2000, whether placed under public or private arrangements and they require a hospital or care home to apply to a supervisory body for authorisation for deprivation of liberty if it finds that a person lacking capacity is being deprived of that liberty or risks being so deprived. The supervisory body is either a local authority or an NHS Primary Care Trust. The upshot of these provisions is that, unless there is a court authorisation, a person can only be deprived of liberty by the 2005 Act where: the deprivation is authorised in accordance with the deprivation of liberty procedures (DOLS) set out in Sch A1 to the 2005 Act; or the deprivation is carried out because it is necessary in order to give life-sustaining treatment, or to carry out a vital act to prevent serious deterioration in the person's condition, while a decision as respects any relevant issue is sought from the court. (The other circumstances where the deprivation is permitted is when it is authorised by an order of the Court of Protection under s16(2)(a) of the 2005 Act.) Section 39A and Sch A1 of the Act provide for Independent Mental Capacity Advocates to be appointed in cases where the person has no one else with whom they might consult about the person's best interests.

Although, it can be seen that the safeguards are designed to protect the interests of an extremely vulnerable group of patients/service users, they have attracted some sharp criticism:

Jones, R, *Mental Health Act Manual*[17]

The Mental Capacity Act 2005 (MCA) is amended by the 2007 Act to provide for a procedure that can be used to authorise the deprivation of liberty of a mentally incapacitated person. The new

---

17   11th edn, London: Sweet and Maxwell, 2008.

procedure, which is intended to sit alongside the powers of compulsion set out in the [Mental Health Act 1983 (MHA)], represents the Government's response to the finding of the European Court of Human Rights in *HL v United Kingdom* (the 'Bournewood' case). The Government could have achieved its objective by making minor amendments to the MHA. Instead, a procedure has been created that is hugely complex, voluminous, badly drafted, overly bureaucratic and difficult to understand, and yet provides mentally incapacitated people with minimum safeguards. If that were not enough, the nature of the relationship between the MHA and the MCA in so far as it relates to the detention of patients is far from clear. This is not surprising given that the two Acts had different sponsoring Government Departments and pursue different policy agendas, one being capacity based and the other focussing on risk. By legislating for parallel legislative regimes, Parliament has created a recipe for confusion which will inevitably result in a lack of consistent practice throughout England and Wales.

Jones is suggesting that because the mental health regime is about protecting people from harm (including harm to oneself), there is a different approach to the capacity cases. However, it is not clear that this is the case, as, without treatment in their best interests, there is potential for a great deal of harm. Presumably Jones is suggesting that, a better way of dealing with this would have been to enable informal patients to have their cases reviewed by Mental Health Review Tribunals as is the case with people who are compulsorily detained under the Act. However, the Deprivation of Liberty Safeguards apply to *all* patients whose liberty is restricted and to those who are confined to, say, residential homes, and some might argue that for them to be reviewed under a Mental Health Act procedure stigmatises them. However, there could have been mechanisms for distinguishing the two procedures and arguably Jones is right in preferring the simpler approach.

The safeguards apply to any form of deprivation of liberty, not just being in a locked unit, so actions such as tying patients/service users to chairs, for example, are a deprivation of liberty, and whilst it might be appropriate to prevent them going outside unsupervised, tying them to a chair might be regarded as too restrictive of their liberty.

Jones is right in referring to these as minimum safeguards because there is no effective 'policing' of the system, and it would not be surprising if many privately owned units did not comply at all.

In *G v E*, the Court of Appeal examined the operation of the safeguards. The appellant brought an action in the Court of Protection alleging that there had been a breach of Art 5 in respect of her brother who had severe learning difficulties, lacked capacity but was not mentally ill. For some time he had lived with his former foster parent, but the local authority removed him from that home to a residential unit without going through the process required by the Mental Capacity Act. The judge at first instance found that this amounted to a breach of his rights under Art 5. However, the judge decided that, despite this, it was open to the court to go on to consider what was in his best interests, and in this case, it was that he remain in the residential unit. The Court of Appeal held that the safeguards did indeed 'plug' the Bournewood gap and that they complied with Art 5. The Court went on to uphold the first instance decision.

G v E (2010)[18]

Sir Nicholas Wall P:

57 . . . We accept Mr. Gordon's submission – indeed, we understand it to be common ground — that the safeguards against arbitrary detention contained in ECHR Article 5 apply to persons lacking capacity. It is our view that MCA 2005 provides a 'procedure prescribed by law' for depriving such persons of their liberty.

---

18 [2010] EWCA Civ 822.

58 . . . [W]e do not think that ECHR Article 5 imposes any threshold conditions which have to be satisfied before a best interests assessment under DOLS can be carried out.

59 With great respect, we think that one of the fallacies in Mr. Westgate's argument is that the European jurisprudence derives exclusively from the fact that in the cases which have reached the ECtHR, the issue has involved alleged mental illness and detention in a psychiatric hospital. In such a case, as the Mental Health Act 1983 requires, a psychiatric opinion that a given person requires detention is essential to justify it. In the instant case, E does not suffer from a psychiatric condition, and is not mentally ill. The evidence of impairment was essentially paediatric . . . In these circumstances, psychiatric evidence is unlikely to be of material assistance at the diagnostic stage.

60 . . . [Incapacitated patients] are, of course, 'of unsound mind' within ECHR Article 5, but in our judgment it plainly does not follow either that they are mentally ill, or that ECHR Article 5 requires psychiatric evidence as a threshold to the deprivation of their liberty. Indeed, learning difficulties often lie outside the expertise of the psychiatrist, but firmly within that of the psychologist.

61 Indeed, in the common case, where the adult concerned is suffering from a chronic condition, expert evidence, in our experience is usually provided by a psychologist or, as here, by a paediatrician. Provided there is credible expert evidence upon which the court can be satisfied that the individual concerned lacks capacity that, in our judgment, is sufficient. It would simply be unreal to require psychiatric evidence in every case, quite apart from the fact that it would, in some cases, be irrelevant. To require such evidence would, in our judgment, make MCA 2005 unworkable.

. . .

64 We also agree with Mr. Gordon that the justification of detention in a case under MCA 2005 is not a medical decision but a decision for the court, to be made in the best interests of the person whom it is sought to detain.

The Court's reference to threshold conditions means that, unlike cases of mental illness, there was no need to provide any psychiatric assessment of the person's learning disability, given that it was accepted by all that he lacked capacity, and therefore, the court could move straight to a decision as to what is in his best interests. The Court accepted that evidence from elsewhere, eg a psychologist, may be necessary to establish lack of capacity, but no evidence was necessary to show that they needed to be deprived of liberty; only that the restrictions placed upon them were in their best interests.

4.3.4 Decision-Making Criteria

4.3.4.1 The therapeutic/non-therapeutic distinction

Most medical procedures performed on mentally incapable patients will be carried out to cure or ameliorate the effects of disease and disorder. However, this will not always be the case. In the case of medical research on healthy volunteers, and the control of fertility (see below), there is no physical or mental disorder which is being treated. It is common to refer to these latter cases as instances of non-therapeutic 'treatment'. Of course, they are not really 'treatment' cases at all. However, when the patient is incapable and the procedure is being carried out on the basis of his 'best interests', the English courts have questioned whether the distinction has any useful purpose.

See Chapter
10 →

The validity of making such a distinction was accepted by the Australian High Court in the case of *Secretary, Department of Health and Community Services v JWB and SMB*. However, although accepting that there is a distinction, all seven judges acknowledged that it was not easy to draw the line. Brennan J suggests the following distinguishing factors:

Secretary, Department of Health and Community Services v JWB and SMB (1992)[19]

Brennan J: It is necessary to define what is meant by therapeutic medical treatment. I would define treatment (including surgery) as therapeutic when it is administered for the chief purpose of preventing, removing or ameliorating a cosmetic deformity, a pathological condition or a psychiatric disorder, provided the treatment is appropriate for and proportionate to the purpose for which it is administered. 'Non-therapeutic' medical treatment is descriptive of treatment which is inappropriate or disproportionate having regard to the cosmetic deformity, pathological condition or psychiatric disorder for which the treatment is administered and of treatment which is administered chiefly for other purposes.

In the Canadian case of Re Eve, the distinction was crucial to the decision of the court. The case concerned a 24-year-old woman suffering from extreme expressive aphasia, which is a condition inhibiting the patient from communicating thoughts and feelings. She was described as being mildly to moderately retarded. It was accepted that she may be able to carry out the physical aspects of child care, but due to her severe lack of communication skills she would not make a suitable mother in the wider sense. As a result of what was described as a close relationship with a male student at the school for retarded adults that she attended, her mother became concerned and wished her daughter to be sterilised:

Re Eve (1986)[20]

La Forest J: . . . [I]t is difficult to imagine a case in which non-therapeutic sterilisation could possibly be of benefit to the person on behalf of whom a court purports to act, let alone one in which that procedure is necessary in his or her best interest. And how are we to weigh the best interests of a person in this troublesome area, keeping in mind that an error is irreversible? Unlike other cases involving the use of the parens patriae jurisdiction, an error cannot be corrected by the subsequent exercise of judicial discretion. That being so, one need only recall Lord Eldon's remark . . . that 'it has always been the principle of this court, not to risk damage to children which it cannot repair' to conclude that non-therapeutic sterilisation may not be authorised in the exercise of the parens patriae jurisdiction.

McQuaid J was, therefore, right in concluding that he had no authority or jurisdiction to grant the application.

In the case of Re B (A Minor) (Wardship: Sterilisation), the distinction was rejected. The child in this case was 17 years old and described as having the mental age of a five or six-year-old. She was in the care of the local authority, and, when it was thought that she was exhibiting signs of some sexual appetite, it applied to the High Court for leave for her to be sterilised. The case eventually reached the House of Lords:

Re B (A Minor) (Wardship: Sterilisation) (1988)[21]

Lord Hailsham of St Marylebone LC: We were also properly referred to the Canadian case of Re Eve . . . I find, with great respect [La Forest J's] conclusions . . . that the procedure of

---

19 (1992) 66 ALJR 300.
20 [1986] 2 SCR 388.
21 [1988] AC 199.

sterilisation 'should never be authorised for non-therapeutic purposes' (my emphasis) totally unconvincing and in startling contradiction to the welfare principle which should be the first and paramount consideration in wardship cases. Moreover, for the purposes of the present appeal I find the distinction he purposes to draw between 'therapeutic' and 'non-therapeutic' purposes of this operation in relation to the facts of the present case above as totally meaningless, and, if meaningful, quite irrelevant to the correct application of the welfare principle.

... To say that the court can never authorise sterilisation of a ward as being in her best interests would be patently wrong. To say that it can only do so if the operation is 'therapeutic' as opposed to 'non-therapeutic' is to divert attention from the true issue, which is whether the operation is in the ward's best interests, and remove it to an area of arid semantic debate as to where the line is to be drawn between 'therapeutic' and 'non-therapeutic' treatment.

Clearly, there is a good argument that the courts should not be fettered by having no discretion to consider 'wider' issues, but, by implication, adopting the therapeutic/non-therapeutic distinction means that these wider issues can be considered, even though, as, in Re Eve, non-therapeutic treatment of a certain nature is rejected.

The case of R v Human Fertilisation and Embryology Authority ex p Blood[22] concerned the legality of using the sperm of the woman's deceased husband after his death. The argument before the court was

See Chapter 7 → about the application of the Human Fertilisation and Embryology Act 1990. However, it was accepted that at least some of the sperm was taken from the man before his death.[23]

Surprisingly, the Court of Appeal passed little comment on the common law, despite the fact that the procedure was non-therapeutic, carried out without consent and, therefore, probably constituted a battery. However, consider the position if the patient would have wished for his sperm to be taken in this way and used after his death (as his widow tried to argue): would it mean that the 'battery' would be transformed into something done in his best interests? Consider also the 'substituted judgment' test, dealt with below.

The case of S v S concerned two disputed cases of paternity. The parents of the children had agreed that blood samples be taken from the children in question for the appropriate tests to be carried out. The Official Solicitor had argued that the blood tests could not be carried out unless it was in the interests of the children. The effect of this decision has been reversed by s 82(3) of the Child Support, Pensions and Social Security Act 2000 which amends s 21(3) of the 1969 Act and allows the court to order the taking of a blood sample for the purposes of resolving paternity disputes where the custodial parent objects, but the general approach of the court can still be applied.

The implications of this are considered further below, but would it be possible to argue that the child has an interest in knowing the identity of his father, and therefore, this 'procedure' would be 'therapeutic' in the sense that it would have psychological benefits for the child? Arguably it would not. It is pure speculation as to the outcome of the paternity dispute and its effect upon the child, and therefore whether it would make him *feel* better is unascertainable. However, this raises a crucial factor in the concept of the 'therapeutic' – the making life better for the person concerned. It must be remembered that we are not talking here about patients. The healthy volunteer in a research programme is not a patient. The mentally handicapped person whom it is proposed to sterilise because she may become pregnant is not a patient (she may or may not live in a hospital, but her residence there would not be because of gynaecological disorder). That is not

---

22 [1997] 2 WLR 806.
23 See Ch 11 for a discussion of the rights anyone may have when tissue is removed from a dead body.

to say that these procedures may never be carried out, but the decision is not a medical decision. It is arguable that it is important to label the procedure as 'non-therapeutic' so as not to lose sight of this.

However, might the converse be the case? We consider below a number of cases where terilisations have been carried out on women for the purposes of 'managing menstruation'. These have been regarded as 'therapeutic' because the purpose was not to render the women sterile. By describing them thus, it could be said that the distinction might be used to mask a real 'non-therapeutic' intention.

 SELF-TEST QUESTION

Leaving aside procedures that are obviously non-therapeutic, such as research on healthy volunteers, do you think that the use of the 'best interests' criterion has made the therapeutic/non-therapeutic distinction irrelevant?

See Chapter
10

4.3.4.2 The 'best interests' test

The Mental Capacity Act 2005 states that one of the principles of the Act is that 'an act done, or a decision made under this Act for or on behalf of a person who lacks capacity must be done, or made, in his best interests' (s 1(5)). Section 4 of the Act deals with the way in which 'best interests' must be determined.

Mental Capacity Act 2005

4 Best interests

(1) In determining for the purposes of this Act what is in a person's best interests, the person making the determination must not make it merely on the basis of–
(a) the person's age or appearance, or
(b) a condition of his, or an aspect of his behaviour, which might lead others to make unjustified assumptions about what might be in his best interests.

(2) The person making the determination must consider all the relevant circumstances and, in particular, take the following steps.

(3) He must consider–
(a) whether it is likely that the person will at some time have capacity in relation to the matter in question, and
(b) if it appears likely that he will, when that is likely to be.

(4) He must, so far as reasonably practicable, permit and encourage the person to participate, or to improve his ability to participate, as fully as possible in any act done for him and any decision affecting him.

(5) Where the determination relates to life-sustaining treatment he must not, in considering whether the treatment is in the best interests of the person concerned, be motivated by a desire to bring about his death.

(6) He must consider, so far as is reasonably ascertainable–
(a) the person's past and present wishes and feelings (and, in particular, any relevant written statement made by him when he had capacity),
(b) the beliefs and values that would be likely to influence his decision if he had capacity, and
(c) the other factors that he would be likely to consider if he were able to do so.

(7) He must take into account, if it is practicable and appropriate to consult them, the views of–
   (a) anyone named by the person as someone to be consulted on the matter in question or on matters of that kind,
   (b) anyone engaged in caring for the person or interested in his welfare,
   (c) any donee of a lasting power of attorney granted by the person, and
   (d) any deputy appointed for the person by the court,

as to what would be in the person's best interests and, in particular, as to the matters mentioned in subsection (6).

(8) The duties imposed by subsections (1) to (7) also apply in relation to the exercise of any powers which–
   (a) are exercisable under a lasting power of attorney, or
   (b) are exercisable by a person under this Act where he reasonably believes that another person lacks capacity.

(9) In the case of an act done, or a decision made, by a person other than the court, there is sufficient compliance with this section if (having complied with the requirements of subsections (1) to (7)) he reasonably believes that what he does or decides is in the best interests of the person concerned.

(10) 'Life-sustaining treatment' means treatment which in the view of a person providing health care for the person concerned is necessary to sustain life.

(11) 'Relevant circumstances' are those–
   (a) of which the person making the determination is aware, and
   (b) which it would be reasonable to regard as relevant.

An argument that has been canvassed is that there can be occasions when it is sufficient to show that a course of action is *not against* the interests of the patient:

S v S (1972)[24]

Lord MacDermott: In exercising what I have called the ancillary jurisdiction in relation to infants the court must also observe and, if need be, exercise its protective jurisdiction. For instance, if the court were satisfied that – as might possibly be the case on rare occasions – a blood test would prejudicially affect the health of the infant it would, no doubt, exercise its discretion against ordering the test. And, again, if the court had reason to believe that the application for a blood test was of a fishing nature, designed for some ulterior motive to call in question the legitimacy, otherwise unimpeached, of a child who had enjoyed a legitimate status, it would be justified in refusing the application. I need not, however, pursue such instances as they do not arise on these appeals. The point to be made is that the protective jurisdiction, if of the nature I have described, would not ordinarily afford ground for refusing a blood test merely because it might, in revealing the truth, prove the infant's illegitimacy in duly constituted paternity proceedings.

Here, it was found that there were no reasons why the tests should not be carried out, as opposed to there being positive reasons in favour. Instead of examining the reasons for the treatment and how these may be for the positive benefit of the patient, the court would be left to decide whether there was any likelihood of detriment to the patient. In practice, might such a change of emphasis be disadvantageous to the patient?

The House of Lords in *Re F* gave no definition of 'best interests', dealing with the case on its particular facts. The lack of judicial guidance was criticised:

---

24 [1972] AC 24.

Kennedy, I, 'Patients, doctors and human rights'[25]

. . . [the best interests test] allows lawyers and courts to persuade themselves and others that theirs is a principled approach to law. Meanwhile, they engage in what to others is clearly a form of '*ad hocery*'. The best interests approach of family law allows the courts to atomise the law, to claim that each case depends on its own facts. The court can then respond intuitively to each case while seeking to legitimate its conclusion by asserting that it is derived from the general principle contained in the best interests formula. In fact, of course, there is no general principle other than the empty rhetoric of best interests; or rather, there is some principle (or principles) but the court is not telling. Obviously the court must be following some principles, otherwise a toss of a coin could decide cases. But these principles, which serve as pointers to what amounts to the best interests, are not articulated by the court. Only the conclusion is set out. The opportunity for reasoned analysis and scrutiny is lost.

This view was supported by Brennan J in his dissenting judgment in the Australian case of:

Department of Health v JWB and SMB[26]

Brennan J:14 . . the best interests approach offers no hierarchy of values which might guide the exercise of a discretionary power to authorise sterilisation, much less any general legal principle which might direct the difficult decisions to be made in this area by parents, guardians, the medical profession and courts. It is arguable that, in a field where the law has not developed, where ethical principles remain controversial and where each case turns on its own facts, the law should not pretend to too great a precision. Better, it might be said, that authority and power be conferred on a suitable repository – whether it be parents or guardians, doctors or the court – to decide these difficult questions according to the repository's view as to the best interests of the child in the particular circumstances of the case. In that way, it can be said, the blunt instrument of legal power will be sharpened according to the exigencies of the occasion. The absence of a community consensus on ethical principles may be thought to support this approach. But it must be remembered that, in the absence of legal rules or a hierarchy of values, the best interests approach depends upon the value system of the decision maker. Absent any rule or guideline, that approach simply creates an unexaminable discretion in the repository of the power.

15 Of course the variable circumstances of each case require evaluation and judicial evaluations of circumstances vary, but the power to authorise sterilisation is so awesome, its exercise is so open to abuse, and the consequences of its exercise are generally so irreversible, that guidelines if not rules should be prescribed to govern it. The courts must attempt the task in the course of, and as a necessary incident in, the exercise of their jurisdiction. That is not to say that the courts should arrogate to themselves the power to authorise sterilisations of intellectually disabled children, but it is to say that it has become the duty of the courts – and, in the present case, specifically the duty of this court – to define the scope of the power to authorise sterilisations of intellectually disabled children and the conditions of exercise of the power, and to determine the repository of the power. The power cannot be left in a state so amorphous that it can be exercised according to the idiosyncratic views of the repository as to the 'best interests' of the child. That approach provides an insubstantial protection of the human dignity of children; it wraps no cloak of protective principle around the intellectually disabled child.

---

25 In Blackburn, R and Taylor, J (eds), *Human Rights for the 1990s*, London: Mansell, 1991, p 90.
26 (1992) 66 ALJR 300.

The potentially broad scope of the best interests test is illustrated in the organ transplant cases, where it has been argued that it may be in the best interests of the donor to be treated as an altruistic member of the wider community.

In *Re M (Child: Refusal of Medical Treatment)*,[27] the patient was a girl of 15 and a half who did not want a heart transplant because she did not want someone else's heart inside her, believing that this would make her 'different'. Dying from heart failure, which was the certain outcome without such a transplant, would not have this effect. Johnson J held that it would be in her best interests to have the operation, notwithstanding that there were risks attached to the operation itself and thereafter, in terms of rejection in the medical sense and rejection by M of further treatment. There was also the risk that she would, for the rest of her life, resent having had the operation imposed upon her. However, balancing these matters against the certainty of death meant that the best interests test was satisfied.

In *JS v An NHS Trust, JA v An NHS Trust*[28] the High Court had to consider the case of two people, aged 18 and 16 respectively, who were suffering from probable variant CJD. Their parents sought a delaration that they lacked capacity and that the proposed treatment was lawful. This treatment was new and untested on human beings. It involved the giving of an infusion surgically under a general anaesthetic. There was no doubt that the patients lacked capacity, but as the treatment was untested, Dame Butler-Sloss was required to consider the application of the *Bolam* test and whether the treatment was in the patients' best interests. She held that a wider view of best interests should be taken in such a case and that the views of the parents and the effect upon them of a refusal to permit the treatment should be taken into account. The declarations were granted. Clearly in this case there was no alternative treatment available and there was no other hope of ameliorating the affects of this progressive and fatal disease. The experts, however, saw the treatment as offering only a very slim chance of improvement. Nevertheless, it must be right not to deny the patients this opportunity on the basis that it was not in their best interests because it could not be shown to have a good chance of success. See also the judgment of Munby J in the case of *R (on the application of Burke) v GMC*[29], discussed in Chapter 12.

Certainly the MCA, section 4, clearly sets out a number of important considerations that must be taken into account when deciding best interests. The MCA Code of Practice expands on section 4 by giving specific examples.[30]

In Scotland, the capacity legislation is different, and, in particular, does not employ the concept of best interests, but instead specifies that any act done in connection with the incapacitated adult is for their 'benefit' and the benefit cannot reasonably be achieved without that intervention (Adults with Incapacity (Scotland) Act 2000, s1(2)). The Explanatory Notes to the Act state that a 'best interests' approach was developed in the context of the law on children and that this is too protective of adults, where it is more appropriate to give weight to the individual's own views. There are a number of ways of regarding these two approaches. The first is to say that 'best interests' has an objective ring to it, ie the individual is being treated as an objectively 'reasonable' person, whereas 'benefit' is looking at the subjective interests of the patient. This might have been the case before the passing of the Mental Capacity Act, but s 4(6) specifically requires the past and present wishes and feelings and beliefs and values of the person to be taken into account when deciding on best interests. The second way of looking at the two concepts is to see it as a semantic distinction only because it would not be possible to decide that something was in someone's best interests if there were no benefit accruing. However, the House of Lords' approach in *S v S*,[31] ie that something could be done if 'it were not against someone's interests', arguably belies this.

---

27 (1999) 52 BMLR 124.
28 [2002] EWHC 2734.
29 [2004] EWHC 1879.
30 Ministry of Justice, Mental Capacity Act Code of Practice, 2007, London: TSO.
31 See n 4 above.

The Scottish approach essentially reflects the 'substituted judgment' test, to which we will now turn.

4.3.4.3 The 'substituted judgment' test

Is it possible to look at the situation from the point of view of the patient, and to make medical decisions on the basis of what he would have wanted, regardless of what may be thought by others to be good for him? The English courts have not adopted the 'substituted judgment' test used by some American courts (see Re Eve[32]). In any event, the test cannot be used when the patient has never had sufficient understanding to form genuine personal opinions on such matters, but is relevant to the status of Advance Directives.

See Chapter
12

The 'substituted judgment' test was considered, and rejected, in *Airedale NHS Trust v Bland*:

Airedale NHS Trust v Bland (1993)[33]

Lord Goff: I wish however to refer at this stage to the approach adopted in most American courts under which the court seeks, in a case in which the patient is incapacitated from expressing any view on the question whether life-prolonging treatment should be withheld in the relevant circumstances, to determine what decision the patient himself would have made had he been able to do so. This is called the substituted judgment test, and it generally involves a detailed inquiry into the patient's views and preferences: see, for example, *Re Quinlan* 70 NJ 10 (1976) and *Belchertown State School Superintendent v Saikewicz* 373 Mass 728 (1977). In later cases concerned with PVS patients it has been held that, in the absence of clear and convincing evidence of the patient's wishes, the surrogate decision maker has to implement as far as possible the decision which the incapable patient would make if he was competent. However, accepting on this point the submission of Mr Lester, I do not consider that any such test forms part of English law in relation to incapable adults, on whose behalf nobody has power to give consent to medical treatment. Certainly, in *F v West Berkshire HA* your Lordships' House adopted a straightforward test based on the best interests of the patient ... Of course, consistent with the best interests test, anything relevant to the application of the test may be taken into account; and, if the personality of the patient is relevant to the application of the test (as it may be in cases where the various relevant factors have to be weighed), it may be taken into account, as was done in *Re J (A Minor) (Wardship: Medical Treatment)* [1990] 3 All ER 930; [1991] Fam 33.

See Chapter
12

It is reasonable to conclude that the views of a patient will not be taken into account if he has never been capable of making an anticipatory decision: his views will be subsumed under the 'best interests' test, (see Chapter 12 on advance decisions).

In any event, s 4(6) now effectively incorporates a form of substituted judgment into the criteria.

4.3.4.4 The *Bolam* test

The test set down in *Bolam v Friern Hospital Management Committee*[34] provides that a doctor will not be negligent if he follows a medical practice which is supported by a responsible body of medical opinion, and recent case law indicates that the 'body' of opinion to support the actions of the doctor can be small (see *Defreitas v O'Brien and Another*[35]). This test has been subjected to much

---

32 [1993] 1 All ER 821 at 872.
33 [1957] 1 WLR 582.
34 [1995] 4 Med LR 108.
35 [1990] 2 AC 1.

criticism on the basis that it results in judicial abstentionism, leaving the standard of care to be set exclusively by a single faction within the medical profession. In the case of *Re F (Mental Patient: Sterilisation),*[36] which concerned a non-therapeutic sterilisation, it was held that decisions by doctors in respect of incapable patients should be judged by the *Bolam* test:

See Chapter 6 →

> **Lord Bridge**: The common law should be readily intelligible to and applicable by all those who undertake the care of persons lacking the capacity to consent to treatment. It would be intolerable for members of the medical, nursing and other professions devoted to the care of the sick that, in caring for those lacking the capacity to consent to treatment they should be put in the dilemma that, if they administer the treatment which they believe to be in the patient's best interests, acting with due skill and care, they run the risk of being held guilty of trespass to the person, but if they withhold that treatment, they may be in breach of a duty of care owed to the patient. If those who undertake responsibility for the care of incapable or unconscious patients administer curative or prophylactic treatment which they believe to be appropriate to the patient's existing condition of disease, injury or bodily malfunction or susceptibility to such a condition in the future, the lawfulness of that treatment should be judged by one standard, not two. It follows that if the professionals in question have acted with due skill and care, judged by the well known test laid down in *Bolam v Friern Hospital Management Committee* [1957] 1 WLR 582, they should be immune from liability in trespass, just as they are immune from liability in negligence. The special considerations which apply in the case of the sterilisation of a woman who is physically perfectly healthy or of an operation upon an organ transplant donor arise only because such treatment cannot be considered either curative or prophylactic.

In the Court of Appeal, the *Bolam* test had been rejected by Neill LJ, with whom Butler-Sloss LJ agreed:

Re F (Mental Patient: Sterilisation) (1990)[37]

> **Neill LJ**: A doctor may defeat a claim in negligence if he establishes that he acted in accordance with a practice accepted at the time as proper by a responsible body of medical opinion skilled in the particular form of treatment in question. This is the test laid down in *Bolam* . . . But to say that it is not negligent to carry out a particular form of treatment does not mean that that treatment is necessary. I would define necessary in this context as that which the general body of medical opinion in the particular speciality would consider to be in the best interests of the patient in order to maintain the health and to secure the well being of the patient. One cannot expect unanimity but it should be possible to say of an operation which is necessary in the relevant sense that it would be unreasonable in the opinion of most experts in the field not to make the operation available to the patient. One must consider the alternatives to an operation and the dangers or disadvantages to which the patient may be exposed if no action is taken. The question becomes: what action does the patient's health and welfare require?

Commenting upon this in the House of Lords, Lord Brandon stated (p 68):

> **Lord Brandon**: With respect to the Court of Appeal, I do not agree that the *Bolam* test is inapplicable to cases of performing operations on, or giving other treatment to, adults incapable to give consent. In order that the performance of such operations on, and the giving of such other

---

36 [1990] 2 AC 1 at 31.
37 London: HMSO, 1995.

treatment to, such adults should be lawful, they must be in their best interests. If doctors were to be required, in deciding whether an operation or other treatment was in the best interests of adults incapable to give consent, to apply some test more stringent than the *Bolam* test, the result would be that such adults would, in some circumstances at least, be deprived of the benefit of medical treatment which adults competent to give consent would enjoy. In my opinion it would be wrong for the law, in its concern to protect such adults, to produce such a result.

Whilst in the context of, say, diagnosis, there is much force in the argument that there should be the same standard of care regardless of whether the patient is capable or incapable, in the context of non-therapeutic treatment the *Bolam* test is not sufficiently rigorous. By its very nature, the decision can only be made on *non-medical* grounds and there is no reason why a doctor should be privileged to make such decisions. Clearly, in certain non-therapeutic cases, the best interests of the patient will be concerned with her best 'social' or 'personal' interests, and the *Bolam* test is far too weak to safeguard these.

The Law Commission considered the relationship of best interests and negligence:

Law Commission, *Mental Incapacity*, Report No 231[38]

3.27 It should be made clear beyond any shadow of a doubt that acting in a person's best interests amounts to something more than not treating that person in a negligent manner. Decisions taken on behalf of a person lacking capacity require a careful, focused consideration of that person as an individual. Judgments as to whether a professional has acted negligently, on the other hand, require a careful, focused consideration of how that particular professional acted as compared with the way in which other reasonably competent professionals would have acted. Lord Mustill, who was both a member of the appellate committee of the House of Lords which decided the case of *Airedale NHS Trust v Bland* and a member of the House of Lords Select Committee on Medical Ethics, said during oral evidence to the latter committee that:

> . . . one of the things that is not very good is that the phrase 'best interests' has been put into play without any description of what it means. This, I think, actually increases the difficulties for the doctors rather than helps to solve them. What is at the back of my mind is whether perhaps Parliament could give some more specific definition of . . . what are the relevant factors . . .

However, it must be noted that the *Bolam* test was not considered in the case of *Re T*, where the Court of Appeal said that the welfare of the child was better served by overriding majority medical opinion (see below). Was this because the *parental* views in the case of a very young child were of greater importance? In the case of an incapacitated adult, would the decision be the same? It is also important to note that, in *Re F*, best interests were rolled up with necessity and it is arguable that this implies a more stringent test than *Bolam*.

Re SL (Adult Patient) (Medical Treatment)[39] concerned a conflict between medical opinion and the opinion of the mother of the incapable adult patient in her care. There were two concerns: that the woman would be become pregnant and that she had heavy periods which caused her distress. The two relevant alternatives were the use of a Mirena coil which would be contraceptive and which would, at the least, reduce menstrual bleeding, and a hysterectomy which would eliminate all bleeding and render the woman permanently incapable of bearing children. The decision of Wall J was that, although medical opinion favoured the less invasive procedure to be tried first, as the hysterectomy, the procedure favoured by the mother and other relatives, was not ruled out by at least

---

38 [2001] Fam 15.
39 [2000] 2 FCR 452.

one of the experts, that satisfied the *Bolam* test, and could be carried out in the woman's best interests. Wall J said: '. . . in my judgment the court is entitled to declare lawful a particular course of treatment if that treatment itself is proper and in the interests of the patient, even if it is not the doctor's first choice.' Furthermore, the *Bolam* test, said the judge, should take into account wider social and emotional factors. These statements, without more, are to be welcomed. Unfortunately, the result in this case was that the judge did not sufficiently take into account the medical evidence. What might be described as a bold resistance to being overly influenced by medical opinion, in the event resulted in him endorsing the most medically invasive option, whilst, at the same time, saying that, since both options satisfied the *Bolam* test, he would make a declaration to that effect and leave the mother to discuss with the doctors what option was to be preferred. The Court of Appeal, in upholding the appeal (not least because it appears that the judge misunderstood some of the medical evidence), endorsed the view that, in considering best interests, the *Bolam* test is incorrect, as a number of medical options can satisfy the *Bolam* test, but the best interests test means that the best option must be chosen. The court also stated that it is for the court to declare what that best option is and not to refer it back to the parties concerned, which must surely be correct, as such cases come before the courts in the first place because of a disagreement between the parties, not on whether treatments are objectively '*Bolam* compatible', but on subjective concerns about the incapacitated person.

Re SL (Adult Patient) (Medical Treatment)

Dame Butler-Sloss: I would suggest that the starting point of any medical decision would be the principles enunciated in the *Bolam* test and that a doctor ought not to make any decision about a patient that does not fall within the broad spectrum of the *Bolam* test. The duty to act in accordance with responsible and competent professional opinion may give the doctor more than one option since there may well be more than one acceptable medical opinion. When the doctor moves on to consider the best interests of the patient he/she has to choose the best option, often from a range of options. As Mr Munby has pointed out, the best interests test ought, logically, to give only one answer.

. . . the *Bolam* test was, in my view, irrelevant to the judicial decision, once the judge was satisfied that the range of options was within the range of acceptable opinion among competent and responsible practitioners. If it was not, I would hope a surgeon would not operate, even if a declaration *was* given by the court.

In my judgment Wall J was in error in his application of the *Bolam* test to his decision-making process . . . He had to declare the lawfulness of the surgical intervention in the context of such an operation being in his judgment in the best interests of the patient. To offer in his judgment the alternatives was not to decide which treatment was the better for S.

The Bolam test, therefore, is not the test as to what is in the best interests of a patient but rather it operates as a form of preliminary filter to exclude treatments and practices that are not accepted within the medical community.

4.3.4.5 Adults and the views of others

In a number of the sterilisation cases we are about to consider, it was argued that the views of the close relatives of the patients were relevant to the final outcome of the cases. However, though taken into account by the courts, as they were in the case of *Re P*, the case concerning a child, the argument that a close relative's views could in any way be determinative has been rejected. In the Canadian case of *Re Eve*,[40] La Forest J stated:

---

40 [1986] 2 SCR 388.

La Forest J: One may sympathise with Mrs E [the adult patient's mother]. To use Heilbron J's phrase, it is easy to understand the natural feelings of a parent's heart. But the *parens patriae* jurisdiction cannot be used for her benefit. Its exercise is confined to doing what is necessary for the benefit and protection of persons under disability like Eve. And a court ... must exercise great caution to avoid being misled by this all too human mixture of emotions and motives.

The relevance of blood ties was considered by the Court of Appeal in the case of *Re S (Hospital Order: Court's Jurisdiction)*. The plaintiff was the patient's cohabitee and the defendant, his son. Hale J held, at first instance, (approved in the Court of Appeal) as follows:

Re S (Hospital Order: Court's Jurisdiction) (1995)[41]

Hale J: Yet although his relationship to the patient is a close one, and his wishes are of course worthy of respect, he has no more legal right to decide the patient's future than has the plaintiff. Indeed, were this to be a Mental Health Act case, the facts might be such that the plaintiff (rather than the wife) would be the patient's nearest relative for the purposes of s 26 of the Mental Health Act 1983.

The Mental Capacity Act incorporates the views of others into the statutory scheme. Section 4(7) states that the views of others must be taken into account, if it is practicable and appropriate to consult them, if they have been named by the incapacited person as someone to be consulted, are engaged in caring for that person, or have been given a power of attorney or have been appointed by the court as a 'deputy' (see below). Letts comments as follows:

Letts, P, 'Mental Capacity Act 2005: The Statutory Principles and Best Interests Test'[42]

The requirement for consultation must be balanced against the right to confidentiality of the person lacking capacity. That right should be protected so that consultation only takes place where relevant and with people whom it is appropriate to consult. For example, it is unlikely to be appropriate to consult anyone who the person had previously indicated should not be involved. However, there may be occasions where it is in the person's best interests for specific information to be disclosed, or where the public interest in disclosure may override the person's private interest in maintaining confidentiality. If professionals are involved in the determination of best interests, they will also need to comply with their own duties of confidentiality in accordance with their professional codes of conduct.

The reference to consulting with people specifically vetoed by the incapacitated person, might lead us to question Letts' view. Thus, to rule this out might mean that crucial information that could help the decision-maker would not be available. Such a course of action would have to be taken cautiously and sensitively in the light of knowledge of the significance of the information, but could not be ruled out altogether.

4.3.4.6 Adults and the role of the court

The MCA applies to all aspects of decision-making on the part of incapacitated patients. Prior to the MCA, the Court of Protection dealt with financial matters; now the Court deals with personal welfare matters too. The powers given to the Court of Protection are contained within Part 2 of the Act. Denzil Lush outlines the new powers.

---

41 [1995] 3 All ER 290, at p 295.
42 [2005] J Mental Health L 150, p 161.

Lush, D, 'The Mental Capacity Act and the new Court of Protection'[43]

In brief, the new Court of Protection will be able to:

- make declarations as to whether or not someone has the capacity to make a particular decision; for example, where professionals disagree on whether someone with learning difficulties has the capacity to refuse major heart surgery;
- make declarations as to the lawfulness or otherwise of any act done, or yet to be done in relation to a person;
- make single, one-off orders; for example the sale of a house and the investment of the proceeds of sale;
- appoint a deputy to make decisions in relation to the matter or matters in which a person lacks the capacity to make a decision;
- resolve various issues involving last powers of attorney;
- make a declaration as to whether an advance decision to refuse treatment exists, is valid, or is applicable to a particular treatment.

The power to make declarations is similar to, though slightly wider than, the present declaratory jurisdiction of the Family Division. . . .

Appointing deputies

. . . the Act provides that, when deciding whether it is in a person's best interests to appoint a deputy, the court should have regard to the principles that (a) a decision by the court is to be preferred to the appointment of a deputy to make a decision, and that (b) the powers conferred on a deputy should be as limited in scope and duration as is reasonably practicable in the circumstances.

This is a good illustration of the operation of the principle of the least restrictive alternative, which requires the existence of alternative courses of action to be investigated and compared, and the preferred course of action to be the one that achieves the desired objective in a manner that interferes least with the rights and freedom of action of the person concerned.

In other words, it may be overly paternalistic and intrusive to appoint someone to act as a deputy when more informal approaches to decision-making will suffice. However, given the somewhat open-textured nature of the Act in terms of who makes decisions and who they consult, even on the most cautious assessment it remained questionable whether the 2005 Act is sufficiently robust.

It is not surprising therefore that there has been public concern. Indeed, since its inception the Court of Protection has attracted considerable unpopularity, particularly in relation to closed-door decisions. When these decisions relate to the personal and financial welfare of incapacitated people, it is in the public interest for these decisions to be made in open court (obviously at the same time protecting the identity of the participants). In particular, enforced medical treatment, rightly, needs some public scrutiny. This may well have influenced the decision of Sir Nicholas Wall to hand down an open judgment in the case of *DH NHS Foundation Trust v PS*[44] concerning a woman aged 55 who had learning difficulties and an overwhelming fear of hospitals and medical treatment. She was deemed not to have mental capacity and unable to make a decision about her treatment. He ruled that she could be given a drug in a glass of Ribena at her home and detained afterwards on a ward for treatment of cancer of the uterus. There was nothing suspect about the case, indeed the application had the support of Mencap, who agreed that this was in the best interests of the patient, but it is essential for the public to be made aware of these cases.[45]

---

43 [2005] J Mental Health L 31, p 36.
44 [2010] EWHC 1217 (Fam).
45 For details of the public concerns, see, eg, www.guardian.co.uk 2 June 2010.

The other point that is important to note is that the creation of the new Court of Protection has removed the inherent jurisdiction of the court to deal with cases where the person is not incapacitated in the strict sense of the word (recall the requirement of 'voluntariness', discussed in Chapter 3). In *A Local Authority v MA NA and SA*[46] it was said: '. . .the inherent jurisdiction can be exercised in relation to a vulnerable adult who, even if not incapacitated by mental disorder or mental illness, is, or is reasonably believed to be, either (i) under constraint or (ii) subject to coercion or undue influence or (iii) for some other reason deprived of the capacity to make the relevant decision, or disabled from making a free choice, or incapacitated or disabled from giving or expressing a real and genuine consent.'[47]

See Chapter
← 3

? SELF-TEST QUESTION

Do you think that the Mental Capacity Act 2005 sufficiently protects vulnerable patients?

4.4 Children

There are special considerations that apply to children. Although this chapter is about patients who lack the capacity to consent, some children are able to consent, but, for the sake of completeness, both capable and incapable children will be dealt with below.

4.4.1 Consent to treatment

Although the English age of majority is 18 years, and up until that date minors are still subject to the jurisdiction of the courts, the Family Law Reform Act 1969 provides that minors who have attained the age of 16 may give a valid consent to medical treatment:

Family Law Reform Act 1969

8(1) -The consent of a minor who has attained the age of 16 years to any surgical, medical or dental treatment which, in the absence of consent, would constitute a trespass to his person, shall be as effective as it would be if he were of full age; and where a minor has by virtue of this section given an effective consent to any treatment it shall not be necessary to obtain any consent for it from his parent or guardian.

Just as mental illness without more will not remove capacity, neither will tender years. The case of *Gillick v West Norfolk and Wisbech AHA*[48] had to consider the capacity of children to consent to treatment. In *Gillick*, it was acknowledged that there was no magic in the age of 16, and that younger children may be able to consent to medical treatment, depending on their level of understanding, that is, what is generally known as 'Gillick competence', or 'Fraser competence'(given that one of the key judgments was given by Lord Fraser and provided guidance on 'competence').

Following concern about the number of under-age pregnancies, the Department of Health and Social Security issued guidance to area health authorities on family planning services containing particular provisions relating to young people. Although it stressed the importance of the parents of children under 16 being involved in the consultation, it went on to say that, in exceptional cases, it was for a

---

46 [2005] EWHC 2942 (Fam).
47 Per Munby J at para 77.
48 [1986] 1 AC 112.

doctor to decide whether to prescribe contraception without informing the parents of the child. Mrs Gillick, who had a number of daughters under the age of 16, sought a declaration that the guidance gave advice which was unlawful and which adversely affected parental rights and duties. Woolf J refused the declaration. Mrs Gillick succeeded before the Court of Appeal. The House of Lords allowed the Department of Health and Social Security's appeal by a majority of 3:2:

Gillick v West Norfolk and Wisbech AHA (1986)[49]

Lord Fraser: It would, therefore, appear that, if the inference which Mrs Gillick's advisers seek to draw from the provisions [of the FLRA 1969] is justified, a minor under the age of 16 has no capacity to authorise any kind of medical advice or treatment or examination of his own body. That seems to me so surprising that I cannot accept it in the absence of clear provisions to that effect. It seems to me verging on the absurd to suggest that a girl or a boy aged 15 could not effectively consent, for example, to have a medical examination of some trivial injury to his body or even to have a broken arm set. Of course the consent of the parents should normally be asked, but they may not be immediately available. Provided the patient, whether a boy or a girl, is capable of understanding what is proposed, and of expressing his or her own wishes, I see no good reason for holding that he or she lacks the capacity to express them validly and effectively and to authorise the medical man to make the examination or give the treatment which he advises. After all, a minor under the age of 16 can, within certain limits, enter into a contract. He or she can also sue and be sued, and can give evidence on oath. Moreover, a girl under 16 can give sufficiently effective consent to sexual intercourse to lead to the legal result that the man involved does not commit the crime of rape – see R v Howard [1966] 1 WLR 13, p 15, when Lord Parker CJ said:

> . . . in the case of a girl under 16, the prosecution, in order to prove rape, must prove either that she physically resisted, or if she did not, that her understanding and knowledge were such that she was not in a position to decide whether to consent or resist . . . there are many girls under 16 who know full well what it is all about and can properly consent.

Accordingly, I am not disposed to hold now, for the first time, that a girl aged less than 16 lacks the power to give valid consent to contraceptive advice or treatment, merely on account of her age.

Lord Fraser suggested a five-point test for doctors contemplating whether to provide such a girl with contraceptive advice and treatment without reference to her parents:

Lord Fraser: . . . [T]he doctor will, in my opinion, be justified in proceeding without the parents' consent or even knowledge provided he is satisfied on the following matters: (1) that the girl (although under 16 years of age) will understand his advice; (2) that he cannot persuade her to inform her parents or to allow him to inform the parents that she is seeking contraceptive advice; (3) that she is very likely to begin or to continue having sexual inter-course with or without contraceptive treatment; (4) that unless she receives contraceptive advice or treatment her physical or mental health or both are likely to suffer; (5) that her best interests require him to give her contraceptive advice, treatment or both without the parental consent.

Lord Scarman, in his judgment, emphasised the increasing autonomy of minors as they approach adulthood:

---

49 (Lords Fraser, Scarman, Bridge, Brandon, and Templeman) [1986] 1 AC 112, HL.

Lord Scarman: . . . . I would hold that as a matter of law the parental right to determine whether or not their minor child below the age of 16 will have medical treatment terminates if and when the child achieves sufficient understanding and intelligence to enable him or her to understand fully what is proposed. It will be a question of fact whether a child seeking advice has sufficient understanding of what is involved to give a consent valid in law. Until the child achieves the capacity to consent, the parental right to make the decision continues save only in exceptional circumstances. Emergency, parental neglect, abandonment of the child or inability to find the parent are examples of exceptional situations justifying the doctor proceeding to treat the child without parental knowledge and consent; but there will arise, no doubt, other exceptional situations in which it will be reasonable for the doctor to proceed without the parent's consent.

When applying these conclusions to contraceptive advice and treatment it has to be borne in mind that there is much that has to be understood by a girl under 16 if she is to have legal capacity to consent to such treatment. It is not enough that she should understand the nature of the advice which is being given: she must also have a sufficient maturity to understand what is involved. There are moral and family questions, especially her relationship with her parents; long term problems associated with the emotional impact of pregnancy and its termination; and there are the risks to health of sexual intercourse at her age, risks which contraception may diminish but cannot eliminate. It follows that a doctor will have to satisfy himself that she is able to appraise these factors before he can safely proceed on the basis that she has capacity at law to consent to contraceptive advice and treatment. And it further follows that ordinarily the proper course will be for him, as the guidance lays down, first to seek to persuade the girl to bring her parents into consultation, and, if she refuses, not to prescribe contraceptive advice and treatment unless he is satisfied that her circumstances are such that he ought to proceed without parental knowledge and consent.

Lord Bridge agreed with Lords Fraser and Scarman. Dissenting judgments were given by Lords Brandon and Templeman. Lord Templeman accepted the general principle that consent is a function of understanding, not status, but dissented on the specific matter of contraceptive advice and treatment:

Lord Templeman: The effect of the consent of the infant depends on the nature of the treatment and the age and understanding of the infant. For example, a doctor with the consent of an intelligent boy or girl of 15 could, in my opinion, safely remove tonsils or a troublesome appendix. But any decision on the part of a girl to practise sex and contraception requires not only knowledge of the facts of life and of the dangers of pregnancy and disease but also an understanding of the emotional and other consequences to her family, her male partner and to herself. I doubt whether a girl under the age of 16 is capable of a balanced judgment to embark on frequent, regular or casual sexual intercourse fortified by the illusion that medical science can protect her in mind and body and ignoring the danger of leaping from childhood to adulthood without the difficult formative transitional experiences of adolescence. There are many things which a girl under 16 needs to practise but sex is not one of them. Parliament could declare this view to be out of date. But in my opinion the statutory provisions discussed in the speech of my noble and learned friend, Lord Fraser of Tullybelton, and the provisions of s 6 of the Sexual Offences Act 1956, indicate that as the law now stands an unmarried girl under 16 is not competent to decide to practise sex and contraception . . .

The position seems to me to be as follows. A doctor is not entitled to decide whether a girl under the age of 16 shall be provided with contraceptive facilities if a parent who is in charge of the girl is ready and willing to make that decision in exercise of parental rights. The doctor is entitled in exceptional circumstances and in emergencies to make provision, normally temporary provision, for contraception but in most cases would be bound to inform the parent of the treatment. The court would not hold the doctor liable for providing contraceptive facilities if the doctor had reasonable grounds for believing that the parent had abandoned or abused parental rights or that there was no parent immediately available for consultation or that there was no parent who was responsible for the girl. But exceptional circumstances and emergencies cannot be expanded into a general discretion for the doctor to provide contraceptive facilities without the knowledge of the parent because of the possibility that a girl to whom contraceptive facilities are not available may irresponsibly court the risk of pregnancy. Such a discretion would enable any girl to obtain contraception on request by threatening to sleep with a man.

Lord Brandon relied on public policy arguments based upon the criminalisation of acts of sex with girls under the age of 16:

Lord Brandon: The Sexual Offences Act 1956 represents the latest pronouncement of parliament on these matters. Sections 5 and 6 provide, so far as material:

> 5 -It is a felony for a man to have unlawful sexual intercourse with a girl under the age of 13.
> 6(1) -It is an offence . . . for a man to have unlawful sexual intercourse with a girl not under the age of 13 but under the age of 16.

Further, by s 37 and Sched 2, the maximum punishment for an offence under s 5 is imprisonment for life, and that for an offence under s 6 imprisonment for two years. Since the passing of the Act of 1956 the distinction between felonies and misdemeanours has been abolished. For the purposes of this case, however, nothing turns on this change of terminology.

My Lords, the inescapable inference from the statutory provisions of the Acts of 1885 and 1956 to which I have referred is that parliament has for the past century regarded, and still regards today, sexual intercourse between a man and a girl under 16 as a serious criminal offence so far as the man who has such intercourse is concerned. So far as the girl is concerned, she does not commit any criminal offence, even if she aids, abets or incites the having of such intercourse. The reason for this, as explained earlier, is that the relevant statutory provisions have been enacted by parliament for the purpose of protecting the girl from herself. The having of such intercourse is, however, unlawful, and the circumstance that the man is guilty of a criminal offence, while the girl is not, cannot alter that situation.

On the footing that the having of sexual intercourse by a man with a girl under 16 is an unlawful act, it follows necessarily that for any person to promote, encourage or facilitate the commission of such an act may itself be a criminal offence, and must, in any event, be contrary to public policy. Nor can it make any difference that the person who promotes, encourages or facilitates the commission of such an act is a parent or a doctor or a social worker.

[T]o give such a girl advice about contraception, to examine her with a view to her using one or more forms of protection, and finally to prescribe contraceptive treatment for her, necessarily involves promoting, encouraging or facilitating the having of sexual intercourse, contrary to public policy, by that girl with a man.

However, as Lord Brandon himself observed, on this logic Mrs Gillick's desire to have the girl's parents involved would also be problematic, since they too would become accessories to an offence. Moreover, it is interesting to reflect upon the earlier judgment of Lord Brandon in the case of R v D,[50] which was cited with approval by both Lords Fraser and Scarman. That judgment clearly implied that a mature child could make decisions about medical treatment. It seems that the nature of the treatment in Gillick influenced Lord Brandon to take a restrictive approach.

---

50 [1984] AC 778.

4.4.2 Refusals of treatment

Although *Gillick* makes it clear that, depending on the nature of the treatment, a child may have the capacity to consent, the case has been interpreted subsequently by the Court of Appeal as relating only to consent and not *refusal*, so that a child's refusal of treatment can still be overridden by his parents or others in *loco parentis*.

The mental health of a 15-year-old girl in the care of the local authority deteriorated and she was placed in an adolescent psychiatric unit. Her condition fluctuated between periods of lucidity and, what was described as 'florid psychotic behaviour'. However, she objected to receiving anti-psychotic drugs, and the local authority applied under the wardship jurisdiction for leave to administer the drugs regardless of her lack of consent. The judge at first instance (Waite J) decided that if she had the necessary capacity, then her refusal could not be overridden, but, on the facts, decided that she lacked capacity. The Court of Appeal accepted that she was not mentally competent due to the fluctuating nature of her mental illness, but went on to assert, *obiter*, that the wardship jurisdiction could not in any event be ousted by the decision of a *Gillick* competent child. The basis of the *Gillick* decision was interpreted by Lord Donaldson:

Re R (A Minor) (Wardship: Consent to Treatment)[51]

Lord Donaldson MR (p 21): . . . [C]onsent by itself creates no obligation to treat. It is merely a key which unlocks a door. Furthermore, whilst in the case of an adult of full capacity there will usually only be one keyholder, namely the patient, in the ordinary family unit where a young child is the patient there will be two key holders, namely the parents, with a several as well as a joint right to turn the key and unlock the door. If the parents disagree, one consenting and the other refusing, the doctor will be presented with a professional and ethical, but not with a legal, problem because, if he has the consent of one authorised person, treatment will not without more constitute a trespass or a criminal assault.

If Mrs Gillick was to succeed in her claim to a declaration that the memorandum of guidance issued by the department was unlawful, she had to show that no child under the age of 16 could be a keyholder in respect of contraception advice and treatment or that the parents' key overrode the child's. As Lord Fraser put it ([1985] 3 All ER 402, p 412; [1986] AC 112, p 173): 'She has to justify the absolute right of veto in a parent.' If she was to succeed in her claim against the area health authority, she had also to show that it was under a duty to inform all medical staff employed by it that Mrs Gillick was exercising that right of veto, but in the light of the House's finding that there was no such right, this additional factor can be ignored.

In the instant appeal Mr James Munby QC, appearing for the Official Solicitor, submits that: (a) if the child has the right to give consent to medical treatment, the parents' right to give or refuse consent is terminated; and (b) the court in the exercise of its wardship jurisdiction is only entitled to step into the shoes of the parents and thus itself has no right to give or refuse consent. Whilst it is true that he seeks to modify the effect of this rather startling submission by suggesting that, if the child's consent or refusal of consent is irrational or misguided, the court will readily infer that in the particular context that individual child is not competent to give or withhold consent, it is necessary to look very carefully at the *Gillick* decision to see whether it supports his argument and, if it does, whether it is binding upon this court.

The key passages upon which Mr Munby relies are to be found in the speech of Lord Scarman ([1985] 3 All ER 402, pp 423–24):

---

51 (Lord Donaldson MR, Staughton and Farquharson LJJ) [1992] Fam 11, CA.

> ... as a matter of law the parental right to determine whether or not their minor child below the age of 16 will have medical treatment terminates if and when the child achieves a sufficient understanding and intelligence to enable him or her to understand fully what is proposed. It will be a question of fact whether a child seeking advice has sufficient understanding of what is involved to give a consent valid in law ...

> ... What Mr Munby's argument overlooks is that Lord Scarman was discussing the parents' right '*to determine* whether or not their minor child below the age of 16 will have medical treat-ment' (my emphasis) and this is the 'parental right' to which he was referring in the latter passage. A right of determination is wider than a right to consent. The parents can only have a right of determination if either the child has no right to consent, ie, is not a keyholder, or the parents hold a master key which could nullify the child's consent. I do not understand Lord Scarman to be saying that, if a child was '*Gillick* competent', to adopt the convenient phrase used in argument, the parents ceased to have an independent right of consent as contrasted with ceasing to have a right of determination, ie, a veto. In a case in which the '*Gillick* compe-tent' child refuses treatment, but the parents consent, that consent enables treatment to be undertaken lawfully, but in no way determines that the child shall be so treated. In a case in which the positions are reversed, it is the child's consent which is the enabling factor and again the parents' refusal of consent is not determinative. If Lord Scarman intended to go further than this and to say that in the case of a '*Gillick* competent' child, a parent has no right either to consent or to refuse consent, his remarks were *obiter*, because the only question in issue was Mrs Gillick's alleged right of veto. Furthermore I consider that they would have been wrong.
>
> One glance at the consequences suffices to show that Lord Scarman cannot have been intending to say that the parental right to consent terminates with the achievement by the child of '*Gillick* competence'. It is fundamental to the speeches of the majority that the capacity to consent will vary from child to child and according to the treatment under consideration, depending upon the sufficiency of his or her intelligence and understanding of that treatment. If the position in law is that upon the achievement of '*Gillick* competence' there is a transfer of the right of consent from parents to child and there can never be a concurrent right in both, doctors would be faced with an intolerable dilemma, particularly when the child was nearing the age of 16, if the parents consented, but the child did not. On pain, if they got it wrong, of being sued for trespass to the person or possibly being charged with a criminal assault, they would have to determine as a matter of law in whom the right of consent resided at the particular time in relation to the particular treatment. I do not believe that that is the law.

The Court of Appeal subsequently considered the status of consent under s 8 of the Family Law Reform Act 1969 in relation to a 16-year-old child's refusal of treatment. It will be seen from the section (see above) that it merely states that there is no need to obtain the consent of a parent or guardian if a child gives consent. However, on the face of it, there is no obligation on a doctor to obtain the consent of the child in preference to that of the parent or guardian.

A 16-year-old girl was suffering from anorexia nervosa and was in the care of the local authority in an adolescent residential unit. Her condition deteriorated and the local authority sought authorisation from the court for removal of the girl to a specialist unit for treatment without her consent. As she had attained the age of 16, she resisted the application on the ground that s 8 of the Family Law Reform Act 1969 conferred on her the same right as an adult to refuse treatment without her consent. Although there is some suggestion in the judgments that, because of her condition, Miss W may not have been competent, the essence of the Court of Appeal's decision was that s 8 did not in any event confer an absolute right upon a child, and could be overridden by the court exercising its inherent jurisdiction:

Re W (A Minor) (Medical Treatment) [52]

Lord Donaldson MR (at p 76):

Is s 8 ambiguous?

The wording of sub-s (1) shows quite clearly that it is addressed to the legal purpose and legal effect of consent to treatment, namely, to prevent such treatment constituting in law a trespass to the person, and that it does so by making the consent of a 16 or 17-year-old as effective as if he were 'of full age'. No question of 'Gillick competence' in common law terms arises. The 16 or 17-year-old is conclusively presumed to be 'Gillick competent' or, alternatively, the test of 'Gillick competence' is bypassed and has no relevance. The argument that W or any other 16 or 17-year-old can, by refusing to consent to treatment, veto the treatment notwithstanding that the doctor has the consent of someone who has parental responsibilities, involves the proposition that s 8 has the further effect of depriving such a person of the power to consent. It certainly does not say so. Indeed if this were its intended effect, it is difficult to see why the sub-section goes on to say that it is not necessary to obtain the parents' consent, rather than providing that such consent, if obtained, should be ineffective. Furthermore, such a construction does not sit easily with sub-s (3), which preserves the common law as it existed immediately before the Act which undoubtedly gave parents an effective power of consent for all children up to the age of 21, the then existing age of consent . . .

The most promising argument in favour of W having an exclusive right to consent to treatment and thus, by refusing consent, to attract the protection of the law on trespass to the person, lies in concentrating upon the words 'as effective as it would be if he were of full age'. If she were of full age her ability to consent would have two separate effects. First, her consent would be fully effective as such. Second, a failure or refusal to give consent would be fully effective as a veto, but only *because no one else would be in a position to consent*. If it is a possible view that s 8 is intended to put a 16 or 17-year-old in exactly the same position as an adult and there is thus some ambiguity, although I do not think that there is, it is a permissible aid to construction to seek to ascertain the mischief at which the section is directed.

The Latey Committee Report

It is common ground that the Family Law Reform Act 1969 was parliament's response to the *Report of the Committee on the Age of Majority*, Cmnd 3342, 1967. The relevant part is contained in paras 474–84. These show that the mischief aimed at was twofold. First, cases were occurring in which young people between 16 and 21 (the then age of majority) were living away from home and wished and needed urgent medical treatment which had not yet reached the emergency stage. Doctors were unable to treat them unless and until their parents had been traced and this could cause unnecessary suffering. Second, difficulties were arising concerning:

> . . . operations whose implications bring up the question of a girl's right to privacy about her sexual life. A particularly difficult situation arises in the case of a girl who is sent to hospital in need of a therapeutic abortion and refuses point blank to enter the hospital unless a guarantee is given that her parents shall not be told about it.

The committee had recommended that the age of majority be reduced to 18 generally. The report, in para 480, records that all the professional bodies which gave evidence recommended that patients aged between 16 and 18 should be able to give an effective consent to treatment and all but the Medical Protection Society recommended that they should also be able to give an effective refusal. The point with which we are concerned was therefore well in the mind of the committee. It did not so recommend. It recommended that:

---

52 (Lord Donaldson MR, Balcombe and Nolan LJJ) [1993] Fam 64, CA.

> *. . . without prejudice to any consent that may otherwise be lawful*, the consent of young persons aged 16 and over to medical or dental treatment shall be as valid as the consent of a person of full age. (Original emphasis.)

Conclusion on s 8

> I am quite unable to accept that parliament in adopting somewhat more prolix language was intending to achieve a result which differed from that recommended by the committee.
>
> On reflection I regret my use in *Re R* . . . of the keyholder analogy because keys can lock as well as unlock. I now prefer the analogy of the legal 'flak jacket' which protects the doctor from claims by the litigious whether he acquires it from his patient who may be a minor over the age of 16, or a '*Gillick* competent' child under that age or from another person having parental responsibilities which include a right to consent to treatment of the minor. Anyone who gives him a flak jacket (that is, consent) may take it back, but the doctor only needs one and so long as he continues to have one he has the legal right to proceed.

It is interesting to compare Lord Donaldson's interpretation of s 8(3) of the 1969 Act with that of Lord Scarman in Gillick. He said that 'sub-s (3) leaves open the question whether the consent of a minor under 16 could be an effective consent', whereas Lord Donaldson interprets it as safeguarding parental rights in cases of minors over 16. In the light of this conflict, it should be noted that in Scottish law a child under the age of 16 has legal capacity to consent to medical treatment if 'he is capable of understanding the nature and possible consequences of the procedure or treatment',[53] and in Houston, Applicant,[54] the Sheriff's Court confirmed that the child's power to consent could not be overridden by a guardian, even though s 5(1) of the Act provides that the guardian of a person under 16 has the same powers after the passing of the Act as before. It was said that it would be illogical to grant a power to consent to medical treatment if this decision could be overridden by a guardian.

Certainly Re R and Re W sit rather uneasily with the Gillick decision. It is hard to see how, for example, Lord Scarman's wide ranging approach to the issue of understanding and the gradual attainment of the age of discretion can simply have been constructed to provide the doctor with protection from legal action. On the other hand, the recommendation of the Latey Committee does appear to support Lord Donaldson's view. However, could it not be argued that the committee was leaving the question open, and that the Gillick decision has since decided the position? The fact that the Report is over 40 years old is also telling. Not surprisingly, the cases have drawn a large amount of critical comment:

Bainham, A, 'The judge and the competent minor'[55]

> [In *Re R*] Lord Donaldson sought to draw a distinction between 'determination' and 'consent', the former being a wider concept than the latter, since it implied a right of veto. In his view, Lord Scarman in *Gillick* was referring to the parent's right to determine whether or not a child should receive medical treatment. . . . There would, according to this interpretation, be concurrent independent rights in parent and child and it would be open to a doctor to act on either consent . . .
>
> There are fundamental objections to this position. It can only work on the assumption that a doctor is dealing solely with the parent or solely with the child and is unaware of any disagreement between them. Where he is aware of a disagreement then, in the absence of judicial intervention, he must choose between the conflicting views. This is so where the parent

---

53 s 2(4) of the Age of Legal Capacity (Scotland) Act 1991.
54 See [1997] 5 Med LR 237.
55 (1992) 108 LQR 194.

is proposing action and the child is objecting, or conversely, where the child is in favour of action and the parent is objecting. If the doctor decides to proceed, or not to proceed, on the basis of the parent's view, he is in reality giving effect to a parental veto over the child's view. He is allowing the parent to 'determine' the matter, and the suggested distinction between 'determination' and 'consent' falls apart. And it is difficult to see how medical personnel seeking to administer drugs with the consent of a parent (or, as here, someone else with parental responsibility) could possibly be unaware of the child's objection. . . .

However Lord Donaldson did not stop there. . . . Section 8(1) of the Family Law Reform Act 1969 provides that where this age has been attained, the child's consent 'to any surgical, medical or dental treatment . . . shall be as effective as it would be if he were of full age' and that 'it shall not be necessary to obtain any consent for it from his parent or guardian'. [Lord Donaldson] adopted a literal interpretation to the effect that, while it was unnecessary for a doctor to secure parental consent in relation to a 16-year-old, there was nothing to preclude him from acting on a parent's consent alone. This flies in the face of the settled interpretation of this provision that it was intended to confer complete autonomy on a young person of this age and that by implication this must outweigh any parental claim to decide.

However, there has also been support for the Court of Appeal's interpretation:

Lowe, N and Juss, S, 'Medical treatment – pragmatism and the search for principle'[56]

[There are] two grounds upon which a child's refusal can be overridden: namely (1) the inability to make an informed judgment, in which case the refusal carries no weight; and (2) where the child is capable of making an informed view, that preference is balanced against the harm to the child's welfare which will ensue if these wishes are observed.

We would support the decisions on either basis because it seems to us wrong for the court to allow a child to refuse treatment that would do him or her irreparable harm. After all, it is perhaps all too easily forgotten that, in the final analysis, a child is still only a child. . . . To those who question how a child can be held able to give a valid consent yet be unable to exercise a power of veto, we would reply that there is a rational distinction to be made between giving consent and withholding it. We must start with the assumption that a doctor will act in the best interests of his patient. Hence, if the doctor believes that a particular treatment is necessary for his patient, it is perfectly rational for the law to facilitate this as easily as possible and hence allow a 'Gillick competent' child to give a valid consent, and also to protect the child against parents opposed to what is professionally considered to be in its best medical interests. In contrast, it is surely right for the law to be reluctant to allow a child of whatever age to be able to veto treatment designed for his or her benefit, particularly if a refusal would lead to the child's death or permanent damage. In other words, the clear and consistent policy of the law is to protect the child against wrong-headed parents and against itself with the final safeguard, as Re W unequivocally establishes, of giving the court the last word in cases of dispute.

On this view, a child may be deemed to be Gillick competent, but still lacking the necessary capacity that an adult would enjoy, to the extent that the outcome of its decision is not deemed to be in its own best interests. However, the support Lowe and Juss seek to derive from the Latey Committee report – that it sought to prevent 'unnecessary pain and suffering' – is in our view not justified. The pain and suffering at issue was caused, not by 'unacceptable' treatment decisions by minors, but

---

56 (1993) 56 MLR 865.

by the fact that – pre-*Gillick* – they had no legal power to make any decisions. The Court of Appeal seems to be substituting the functional view of capacity (at the heart of the later adult case of *Re C (Adult: Refusal of Treatment)*[57]) with a bare 'all or nothing' test: either under or over 18 years of age, either capable or incapable. Whatever view is taken it can be seen that the effect of *Re W*, so far as refusals of treatment are concerned, is to re-establish the very 'status' approach which the House of Lords were at pains to reject in *Gillick* in relation to consent. The 'all or nothing' aspect is illustrated by the train of events during and after the case of *Re E (A Minor) (Wardship: Medical Treatment)*[58], to which the Lowe and Juss refer in the above article. The patient was 15 and, like his parents, a devout Jehovah's Witness. He was suffering from leukaemia, the treatment of which included blood transfusions. Ward J ordered the carrying out of the treatment, which continued until the boy reached 18. At this point he refused further medical treatment and died.

Re L (Medical Treatment: Gillick Competency)[59] concerned a 14-year-old girl who had suffered extensive burns and in the course of the essential surgery to treat them, would require blood transfusions. Without treatment she would die an unpleasant death. She was a Jehovah's Witness and refused consent to the transfusions. Sir Stephen Brown, President (as he then was), whilst noting that counsel's submissions had included a reference to Lord Donaldson's analysis of *Gillick* competence, made his decision on the basis of lack of capacity, as she had limited experience of life and that limited her understanding of 'matters which are as grave as her own present situation'. Arguably, this is just another way of saying that she lacks capacity because she is a child. However, it refers to the grave matters under consideration, and, therefore, she might have sufficient understanding in a less serious situation. Nevertheless, the suggestion might be that, in cases where a religious or similar belief is involved, a child might form views which s/he rejects in adulthood. The difficulty with this approach, however, is that the same argument could be advanced for young adults, or, arguably, all adults.

 SELF-TEST QUESTION

Lowe and Juss say that 'a child is still a child'. But although they would support the decision in *Re E (A Minor) (Wardship: Medical Treatment*[60]*)* above, does not that case demonstrate the inadequacy of the status approach to children, ie one day they are a child and the next they are an adult?

4.4.3 Children and the rights of parents

In *Gillick*, on the subject of parental rights Lord Fraser said:

Gillick v West Norfolk and Wisbech AHA[61]

Lord Fraser (p 171): In practice most wise parents relax their control gradually as the child develops and encourage him or her to become increasingly independent. Moreover, the degree of parental control actually exercised over a particular child does in practice vary considerably according to his understanding and intelligence and it would, in my opinion,

---

57 [1994] 1 WLR 290.
58 [1993] 1 FLR 386.
59 [1998] 2 FLR 810.
60 [1993] 1 FLR 386.
61 [1986] AC 112.

be unrealistic for the courts not to recognise these facts. Social customs change, and the law ought to, and does in fact, have regard to such changes when they are of major importance . . .

In times gone by the father had almost absolute authority over his children until they attained majority. A rather remarkable example of such authority being upheld by the court was *In re Agar-Ellis* (1883) 24 Ch D 317 which was much relied on by the Court of Appeal. The father in that case restricted the communication which his daughter aged 17 was allowed to have with her mother, against whose moral character nothing was alleged, to an extent that would be universally condemned today as quite unreasonable. The case has been much criticised in recent years and, in my opinion, with good reason . . .

. . . In *J v C* [1970] AC 668 Lord Guest and Lord MacDermott referred to the decision in *Agar-Ellis* (1883) 24 Ch D 317 as an example of the almost absolute power asserted by the father over his children before the Judicature Act 1873 and plainly thought such an assertion was out of place at the present time: see Lord MacDermott, pp 703–04. In *Reg v D* [1984] AC 778 Lord Brandon of Oakbrook cited *Agar-Ellis* as an example of the older view of a father's authority which his Lordship and the other members of the House rejected. In my opinion, the view of absolute paternal authority continuing until a child attains majority which was applied in *Agar-Ellis* is so out of line with present day views that it should no longer be treated as having any authority. I regard it as a historical curiosity . . .

Once the rule of the parents' absolute authority over minor children is abandoned, the solution to the problem in this appeal can no longer be found by referring to rigid parental rights at any particular age. The solution depends upon a judgment of what is best for the welfare of the particular child. Nobody doubts, certainly I do not doubt, that in the overwhelming majority of cases the best judges of a child's welfare are his or her parents. Nor do I doubt that any important medical treatment of a child under 16 would normally only be carried out with the parents' approval. That is why it would and should be 'most unusual' for a doctor to advise a child without the knowledge and consent of the parents on contraceptive matters. But, as I have already pointed out, Mrs Gillick has to go further if she is to obtain the first declaration that she seeks. She has to justify the absolute right of veto in a parent. But there may be circumstances in which a doctor is a better judge of the medical advice and treatment which will conduce to a girl's welfare than her parents. It is notorious that children of both sexes are often reluctant to confide in their parents about sexual matters, and the DHSS guidance under consideration shows that to abandon the principle of confidentiality for contraceptive advice to girls under 16 might cause some of them not to seek professional advice at all, with the consequence of exposing them to 'the immediate risks of pregnancy and of sexually transmitted diseases'. No doubt the risk could be avoided if the patient were to abstain from sexual intercourse, and one of the doctor's responsibilities will be to decide whether a particular patient can reasonably be expected to act upon advice to abstain. We were told that in a significant number of cases such abstinence could not reasonably be expected . . .

. . . the doctor will, in my opinion, be justified in proceeding without the parents' consent or even knowledge provided he is satisfied on the following matters: (1) that the girl (although under 16 years of age) will understand his advice; (2) that he cannot persuade her to inform her parents or to allow him to inform the parents that she is seeking contraceptive advice; (3) that she is very likely to begin or to continue having sexual intercourse with or without contraceptive treatment; (4) that unless she receives contraceptive advice or treatment her physical or mental health or both are likely to suffer; (5) that her best interests require him to give her contraceptive advice, treatment or both without the parental consent.

Lord Scarman took a similar view (p 182):

Lord Scarman: Mrs Gillick relies on both the statute law and the case law to establish her proposition that parental consent is in all other circumstances necessary. The only statutory provision directly in point is s 8 of the Family Law Reform Act 1969. Sub-section (1) of the section provides that the consent of a minor who has attained the age of 16 to any surgical, mental or dental treatment which in the absence of consent would constitute a trespass to his person shall be as effective as if he were of full age and that the consent of his parent or guardian need not be obtained. Sub-section (3) of the section provides:

> Nothing in this section shall be construed as making ineffective any consent which would have been effective if this section had not been enacted.

I cannot accept the submission made on Mrs Gillick's behalf that sub-s (1) necessarily implies that prior to its enactment the consent of a minor to medical treatment could not be effective in law. Sub-section (3) leaves open the question whether the consent of a minor under 16 could be an effective consent. Like my noble and learned friend Lord Fraser of Tullybelton, I read the section as clarifying the law without conveying any indication as to what the law was before it was enacted. So far as minors under 16 are concerned, the law today is as it was before the enactment of the section . . .

The law has, therefore, to be found by a search in the judge-made law for the true principle. The legal difficulty is that in our search we find ourselves in a field of medical practice where parental right and a doctor's may point us in different directions. This is not surprising. Three features have emerged in today's society which were not known to our predecessors: (1) contraception as a subject for medical advice and treatment; (2) the increasing independence of young people; and (3) the changed status of women. In times past contraception was rarely a matter for the doctor: but with the development of the contraceptive pill for women it has become part and parcel of everyday medical practice, as it made clear by the department's *Handbook of Contraceptive Practice*, 1984 revision, particularly para 1.2. Family planning services are now available under statutory powers to all without any express limitation as to age or marital status. Young people, once they have attained the age of 16, are capable of consenting to contraceptive treatment, since it is medical treatment: and, however extensive be parental right in the care and upbringing of children, it cannot prevail so as to nullify the 16-year-old's capacity to consent which is now conferred by statute. Furthermore, women have obtained by the availability of the pill a choice of lifestyle with a degree of independence and of opportunity undreamed of until this generation and greater, I would add, than any law of equal opportunity could by itself effect.

The law ignores these developments at its peril . . .

. . . The principle of the law, as I shall endeavour to show, is that parental rights are derived from parental duty and exist only so long as they are needed for the protection of the person and property of the child. The principle has been subjected to certain age limits set by statute for certain purposes: and in some cases the courts have declared an age of discretion at which a child acquires before the age of majority the right to make his (or her) own decision. But these limitations in no way undermine the principle of the law, and should not be allowed to obscure it.

Let me make good, quite shortly, the proposition of principle . . .

. . . It is abundantly plain that the law recognises that there is a right and a duty of parents to determine whether or not to seek medical advice in respect of their child, and, having received advice, to give or withhold consent to medical treatment. The question in the appeal is as to the extent, and duration, of the right and the circumstances in which, outside the two admitted exceptions to which I have earlier referred, it can be overridden by the exercise of medical judgment . . .

Although statute has intervened in respect of a child's capacity to consent to medical treatment from the age of 16 onwards, neither statute nor the case law has ruled on the extent and duration of parental right in respect of children under the age of 16. More specifically, there is no rule yet applied to contraceptive treatment, which has special problems of its own and is a latecomer in medical practice. It is open, therefore, to the House to formulate a rule. The Court of Appeal favoured a fixed age limit of 16, basing themselves on a view of the statute law which I do not share and upon their view of the effect of the older case law which for the reasons already given I cannot accept. They sought to justify the limit by the public interest in the law being certain. Certainty is always an advantage in the law, and in some breaches of the law it is a necessity. But it brings with it an inflexibility and a rigidity which in some branches of the law can obstruct justice, impede the law's development, and stamp upon the law the mark of obsolescence where what is needed is the capacity for development. The law relating to parent and child is concerned with the problems of the growth and maturity of the human personality. If the law should impose upon the process of 'growing up' fixed limits, where nature knows only a continuous process, the price would be artificiality and a lack of realism in an area where the law must be sensitive to human development and social change. If certainty be thought desirable, it is better that the rigid demarcations necessary to achieve it should be laid down by legislation after a full consideration of all the relevant factors than by the courts, confined as they are by the forensic process to the evidence adduced by the parties and to whatever may properly fall within the judicial notice of judges. Unless and until Parliament should think fit to intervene, the courts should establish a principle flexible enough to enable justice to be achieved by its application to the particular circumstances proved by the evidence placed before them . . .

The modern law governing parental right and a child's capacity to make his own decisions was considered in *Reg v D* [1984] AC 778. The House must, in my view, be understood as having in that case accepted that, save where statute otherwise provides, a minor's capacity to make his or her own decision depends upon the minor having sufficient understanding and intelligence to make the decision and is not to be determined by reference to any judicially fixed age limit . . .

In the light of the foregoing I would hold that as a matter of law the parental right to determine whether or not their minor child below the age of 16 will have medical treatment terminates if and when the child achieves a sufficient understanding and intelligence to enable him or her to understand fully what is proposed. It will be a question of fact whether a child seeking advice has sufficient understanding of what is involved to give a consent valid in law. Until the child achieves the capacity to consent, the parental right to make the decision continues save only in exceptional circumstances. Emergency, parental neglect, abandonment of the child, or inability to find the parent are examples of exceptional situations justifying the doctor proceeding to treat the child without parental knowledge and consent: but there will arise, no doubt, other exceptional situations in which it will be reasonable for the doctor to proceed without the parent's consent.

When applying these conclusions to contraceptive advice and treatment it has to be borne in mind that there is much that has to be understood by a girl under the age of 16 if she is to have legal capacity to consent to such treatment. It is not enough that she should understand the nature of the advice which is being given: she must also have a sufficient maturity to understand what is involved. There are moral and family questions, especially her relationship with her parents; long term problems associated with the emotional impact of pregnancy and its termination; and there are the risks to health of sexual intercourse at her age, risks which contraception may diminish but cannot eliminate. It follows that a doctor will have to satisfy himself that she is able to appraise these factors before he can safely proceed upon the basis that she has at law capacity to consent to contraceptive treatment. And it further follows that ordinarily the proper course will be for him, as the guidance lays down, first to seek to persuade the girl to bring her parents into consultation, and if she refuses, not to prescribe contraceptive treatment unless he is satisfied that her circumstances are such that he ought to proceed without parental knowledge and consent.

Most medical decisions made by parents on behalf of their children will be uncontroversial. However, in certain areas, such as the control of fertility, there can be a real conflict between parental wishes and the interests of the child. Bernard M Dickens examines the concept of parental rights:

Dickens, BM, 'Function and limits of parental rights'[62]

The modern function of parental rights, it is proposed, is not to enforce duties children owe their parents, or simply to enforce against third parties powers of custody and control parents enjoy over their children. It is to permit parents to discharge their duties to their children. These duties are not positively to do good, but to avoid harm. It is obvious that to the extent that ill health and, for instance, illiteracy are considered harm, parents are bound by positive duties to provide health care and education. This proposition may be derived from an abundance of case law and legislation. The duty to avoid harm is more elastic, however, since it affords licence to control a child not for its benefit, but in non-beneficial and non-therapeutic ways falling short of causing or risking harm. The issue to be critically addressed is the point at which an exercise of parental choice over a child's management and future is so potentially harmful to the welfare or interests of the child as to require State intervention and possibly a countermanding of parental choice.

Not surprisingly, the courts recognise that there are limits to the rights of a parent. The case of *Re S (A Minor) (Medical Treatment)* is a clear illustration of this. The patient was a young child suffering from T-cell leukaemia, treatable only by chemotherapy which necessitated blood transfusions. The parents of the child were devout Jehovah's Witnesses and therefore were fundamentally opposed to blood transfusions. The local authority invoked the inherent jurisdiction of the court under s 100 of the Children Act 1989, and sought an order permitting such treatment to be given:

Re S (A Minor) (Medical Treatment)[63]

Thorpe J: . . . [T]he test must remain the welfare of the child as the paramount consideration. Specifically, in this case, the choice is not between two medical procedures with similar, if differing, prospects of success. Here the stark choice is between one medical procedure with no prospect of success and one medical treatment with a prospect of success which is put at even.

So, as I put to Mr Daniel in argument: are the religious convictions of the parents to deny their child a 50% chance of survival? Are those convictions to deny him that 50% chance and condemn him to inevitable and early death? Mr Daniel realistically saw that this was an extreme case and one in which it is difficult to pursue the argument that the religious convictions of the parents should deny the child the chance of treatment.

Finally, Mr Daniel invites the court to look ahead to the later years of childhood. If this treatment is applied in the face of parental opposition what would be the difficulties and stresses for S in years to come – parented by parents who believe that his life was prolonged by an ungodly act? Well, that consideration seems to me one that has little foundation in reality. The reality seems to me to be that family reaction will recognise that the

---

62 (1981) 97 LQR 462.
63 [1993] 1 FLR 376.

responsibility for consent was taken from them and, as a judicial act, absolved their conscience of responsibility.

Parental opposition to clinical decisions was considered in the case of Re C (A Minor[64]). The patient was a 16-month-old baby, suffering from spinal muscular atrophy, and said to be seriously disabled and severely emaciated. For a few weeks before the case came before the court, the child had been ventilated to support her own breathing. The opinion of the consultant paediatric neurologist in charge of the child's care was that no further ventilation should take place, and if, following withdrawal of the ventilation, the child should undergo further respiratory arrest, she should not be resuscitated. The evidence was that further respiratory arrest would mean long term ventilator dependency. The parents of the child, who were religious orthodox Jews, were opposed to this. They agreed that ventilation should be withdrawn, but would not agree that no attempt at resuscitation be made. A second medical opinion was obtained which supported the opinion of the treating doctor. Sir Stephen Brown P held that support of the parents' view would be tantamount to requiring doctors to undertake a course of treatment which they were unwilling to do, and no order would be made to this effect. Clinical judgment, however, will not always prevail, as will be seen from the case of Re T (A Minor) (Wardship: Medical Treatment).[65]

In the case of Re S, above, Thorpe J was considering a case where the treatment objected to (the blood transfusion) carried virtually no risk, and nothing more than inconvenience to the child. What about the case of a parent who refuses to agree to a difficult form of treatment which may be lengthy and painful? This was considered in the case of Re T(A Minor) (Wardship: Medical Treatment). The child was born with a serious liver defect and underwent surgery at the age of three and a half weeks. The operation caused pain and distress and was unsuccessful. The medical prognosis was that without a liver transplant the child would not live more than a couple of years. The mother refused consent to a transplant. The child's father (to whom she was not married) agreed with her. Both parents were described as 'health care professionals' with experience of caring for sick children. The mother had moved out of the country at the time of the hearing of the local authority's application for permission for the operation to be carried out. The application had been brought at the behest of the consultants who had treated the child. The judge at first instance granted the application on the basis that it was in the child's best interests for it to be carried out and that the mother was being 'unreasonable'. The Court of Appeal allowed the mother's appeal:

Re T (A Minor) (Wardship: Medical Treatment)[66]

Waite LJ: The law's insistence that the welfare of a child shall be paramount is easily stated and universally applauded, but the present case illustrates, poignantly and dramatically, the difficulties that are encountered when trying to put it into practice. Throughout his clear and able judgment, the judge demonstrated his appreciation of the dilemma to which the case gives rise. Loving and devoted parents have taken, after anxious consideration, a decision to withhold consent to operative transplant treatment. Although it is relatively novel treatment, still unavailable in many countries, doctors of the highest expertise have unanimously recommended it for this child on clinical grounds, taking the view that it involves a relatively minor level of risk which they regard as well worth taking in the child's long term interests (which in this instance include an extension of life itself). The parents' opposition is partly instinctive and (being based on their own awareness of the procedures involved) partly practical. It has

---

64 [1998] 1 Lloyd's Rep Med 1.
65 [1997] 1 All ER 906.
66 [1997] 1 All ER 906.

sufficient cogency to have led one of the principal medical experts in the field of this operation to say that his team would decline to operate without the mother's committed support.

What is the court to do in such a situation? It is not an occasion – even in an age preoccupied with 'rights' – to talk of the rights of a child, or the rights of a parent, or the rights of the court. The cases cited by Butler-Sloss LJ are uncompromising in their assertion that the sole yardstick must be the need to give effect to the demands of paramountcy for the welfare of the child. They establish that there are bound to be occasions when such paramountcy will compel the court, acting as a judicial parent, to substitute the judge's own views as to the claims of child welfare over those of natural parents – even in a case where the views of the latter are supported by qualities of devotion, commitment, love and reason. The judge, after anxious consideration, reached the conclusion that this case provides such an occasion. Was he right to do so?

Of course if his decision was founded on a correct application of legal principle, it is unassailable, however tempted individual members of an appellate court might be to substitute a judgment of our own. These decisions, not least because they are so difficult and finely balanced, are best left to the discretion of the experienced judges who have the task, often a lonely and worrying one, of weighing the numerous delicate elements (including the view taken of the parties and witnesses) which enable a cumulative picture to be formed of the demands of welfare in a particular case, and taking the momentous decision which the child patient cannot take for himself.

In this instance, however, in agreement with Butler-Sloss LJ, I consider that the judge was betrayed into an error of law by his concern with the need to form a judgment about the reasonableness of the mother's approach. An appraisal of parental reasonableness may be appropriate in other areas of family law (in adoption, for example, where it is enjoined by statute), but when it comes to an assessment of the demands of the child patient's welfare, the starting point – and the finishing point too – must always be the judge's own independent assessment of the balance of advantage or disadvantage of the particular medical step under consideration.

In striking that balance, the judge will of course take into account as a relevant, often highly relevant, factor the attitude taken by a natural parent, and that may require examination of his or her motives. But the result of such an inquiry must never be allowed to prove determinative. It is a mistake to view the issue as one in which the clinical advice of doctors is placed in one scale and the reasonableness of the parent's view in the other. Had the judge viewed the evidence more broadly from the standpoint of his own perception of the child's welfare when appraised in all its aspects, he would have been bound, in my view, to take significant account of other elements in the case. Those include the parents' ties in country AB, and – crucially – the evidence of Dr P.

No one disputes that in the aftermath of the operation the child would remain in the primary care of the mother. Dr P maintained a very clear view that – even assuming that the operation proved wholly successful in surgical terms – the child's subsequent development could be injuriously affected if his day to day care depended upon the commitment of a mother who had suffered the turmoil of having her child being compelled against her will to undergo, as a result of a coercive order from the court, a major operation against which her own medical and maternal judgment wholeheartedly rebelled.

All these cases depend on their own facts and render generalisations – tempting though they may be to the legal or social analyst – wholly out of place. It can only be said safely that there is a scale, at one end of which lies the clear case where parental opposition to medical intervention is prompted by scruple or is of a kind which is patently irreconcilable with principles of child health and welfare widely accepted by the generality of mankind; and that at the other end lie highly problematic cases where there is genuine scope for a difference of view between parent and judge. In both situations it is the duty of the judge to allow the court's own opinion to prevail in the perceived paramount interests of the child concerned, but in cases at the latter end of the scale, there must be a likelihood (though never of course a certainty) that the greater the scope for genuine debate between one view and another the stronger will be the inclination of the court to be influenced by a reflection that in the last analysis the best interests of every child include an expectation that difficult decisions affecting the length and quality of its life will be taken for it by the parent to whom its care has been entrusted by nature. I too would allow this appeal.

Is the distinction between the 'welfare of the child' approach and the 'reasonableness of the parent' approach one of semantics only? In other words, was the first instance decision that the mother was being unreasonable only another way of saying that she was not acting in the best interests of the child, and that the Court of Appeal was wrong to disturb the decision?

It is also of some concern that the Court of Appeal was relying too heavily upon the judgment of the mother to whom the child's care 'has been entrusted by nature'. Marie Fox and Jean McHale, referring to Butler-Sloss LJ's judgment, comment as follows:

Fox, M and McHale, J, 'In whose best interests?'[67]

. . . a significant feature is the emphasis in the Court of Appeal judgments on the parents' status as health care professionals, with experience of paediatric care. However it is questionable whether such significance should have been attributed to the parents' profession. It should be noted that, in the context of medical treatment, there is some evidence that health care professionals are actively discouraged from treating their families. However, amongst the professional bodies there appears to be uncertainty about the ethics of the practice. While the General Medical Council and United Kingdom Council for Nursing, Midwifery and Health Visiting do not censure health professionals who treat themselves or their family members, the British Medical Association regards such practice as unethical. In Re T, however, the Court of Appeal drew an implicit distinction between medical treatment on the one hand and 'caring' on the other. This calls into question whether the same objections apply when health professionals are involved in caring for their own children, and what weight their views should carry in this context. Pinpointing the divide between treatment and care is a process fraught with difficulties, especially since caring may be entrusted to either professionals or lay persons. Such difficulties become particularly acute where parents are also health practitioners. Significantly, this policy issue was not addressed in Re T. In part, the Court of Appeal was able to avoid the issue by downplaying the importance of medical opinion. A striking feature of the judgments is that there is virtually no reference to medical evidence. This is in stark contrast to earlier cases, such as Re C and Re J, where a wealth of expert evidence was cited. Indeed, in Re T, greater weight appeared to be placed on a fact sheet published by the Children's Liver Disease Foundation (which highlighted the general complications of liver transplantation, thus endorsing the parental reservations about treatment) than on the specific medical evidence pertaining to this child. Thus, rather than focusing on the evidence which would have justified treatment, the judges focused on the implications for the carers should treatment be authorised against their will. A further point is that the judgments do not clarify whether the significance of the parents' occupations lies simply in their status as health professionals or is derived from their greater competence as decision makers.

---

67 (1997) 60 MLR 700.

Since the legitimacy of according carers an enhanced decision-making role by virtue solely of their status as health care professionals is questionable, we need to explore whether other special features of this case justify the weight accorded to the position of the carers. In this regard Butler-Sloss LJ noted that:

> Some of the objections of the mother, such as the difficulties of the operation itself, turned out . . . to be less important than the mother believed. Underlying those less important objections by the mother was deep-seated concern of the mother as to the benefits to her son of the major invasive surgery and post-operative treatment, the dangers of failure long term as well as short term, the possibility of the need for further transplants, the likely length of life and the impact upon her son of all these concerns.

Thus, the mother's opposition to the procedure is represented as rooted in caring attitudes. Butler-Sloss LJ also refers to 'the enormous significance of the close attachment between the mother and baby'. Yet there are unresolved tensions in this portrayal of the mother. We are given little evidence to support the court's opinion that this mother was exceptionally devoted. Furthermore, even assuming that this representation is accurate, two troublesome issues arise. First, if we accept the court's depiction of her as especially caring, it was surely incumbent upon the judges to examine why she was so reluctant to undertake the care of her son following a procedure which could save his life, particularly in view of her professional expertise in this area. Secondly, there is no exploration of the relationship between caring and reasonableness. It must be doubted whether the decisions of an exceptionally caring parent, even one who is a health professional herself, may automatically be deemed reasonable ones . . .

A further noteworthy point is the manner in which caring was construed as the mother's responsibility rather than that of both the parents. Nowhere in the judgments was the role of the father clearly articulated. In the circumstances this may have been largely because the parents were unmarried so that parental responsibility was vested in the mother alone. Certainly, the effect of the relative marginality of the father was to make it easier for the court to depict the mother as sole carer and then to conflate the interests of mother and child. This occurs most strikingly in the following passage of Butler-Sloss LJ's judgment:

> This mother and child are one for the purpose of this unusual case and the decision of the court to consent to the operation jointly affects the mother and son and it also affects the father. The welfare of this child depends upon his mother.

. . . It may be questioned what the broader implications of this line of reasoning are for the autonomy of the mother in cases where no clinical support exists for her views, with the result that they are not upheld by the court.

Nevertheless, in this case, construing the mother and child as one permitted the Court of Appeal to minimise the potential conflict between the interests of the woman and child. It effectively allowed the court to encompass within the best interests test the interests of the mother as carer as well as the interests of the child. The problem of disentangling the determination of best interests from the question of who decides is rendered still more intractable by the court's reasoning in this case. Thus, it is significant that when Butler-Sloss LJ considered the consequences of upholding the judge's original order that the child should be returned to England for treatment, her emphasis was upon the difficulties and inconvenience of such an outcome for the mother:

> She will have to comply with the court order; return to this country and present the child to one of the hospitals. She will have to arrange to stay in this country for the

foreseeable future . . . If [the father] does not come she will have to manage unaided. How will the mother cope? Can her professionalism overcome her view that her son should not be subjected this distressing procedure? Will she break down? How will the child be affected by the conflict with which the mother may have to cope?

. . . surely the Court of Appeal's approach in this case is exceptional, given that in the Jehovah's Witness cases cited above doctors were prepared to undertake treatment in the face of intransigent parental opposition?

Certainly, there is cause for concern in intertwining the interests of a child and its mother, or indeed a child and its parents. It is difficult to see the difference between *Re T (A Minor) (Wardship: Medical Treatment)*[68] and cases where sincere religious views of caring parents are overridden in the best interests of the child.

In the case of *Re T*, the parents purported to care for their child, despite the potentially tragic consequences of their views holding sway. In a case where the parents simply do not want the child to live, judicial decision-making is more clear cut. The case of *Re B (A Minor) (Wardship: Medical Treatment)*[69] may have been such a case. The child was a newly born Down's syndrome baby who also had an intestinal complaint that required surgery in order for the child to survive. The parents refused consent. Their view was that the child would be better off dead. This may have been because they anticipated a poor life ahead for the child, or it may have been the fact that they did not want a Down's syndrome child. In that case, the Court of Appeal authorised the treatment. Templeman LJ described the choice as a stark one between authorising the operation so that the child may live for 20 or 30 years as a mongoloid, or terminating the life of a mongoloid child because she also has an intestinal complaint.[70]

An interesting contrast to this case is *Re SL(Adult Patient) (Medical Treatment)*.[71] The mother of a 29-year-old woman, with severe learning difficulties, made an application to the court for a declaration in respect of the lawfulness of a proposed sterilisation/hysterectomy. It was anticipated that before long the mother would not be able to continue to care for her daughter and that she would have to go and live in local authority sheltered accommodation. The mother feared that, as her daughter was an attractive woman, she might become pregnant, and also that she was distressed by 'heavy' menstrual bleeding. Three medical options were available. The first was a total hysterectomy (this would render her incapable of bearing children and eliminate menstruation); the second, a sterilisation by clipping of the fallopian tubes (a contraceptive measure, but it would do nothing about menstruation); the third by the fitting of a Mirena coil (contraceptive, with the possibility of reducing or even eliminating menstruation). The mother favoured the first option. The medical evidence all pointed to trying the Mirena coil as a first attempt, but one of the experts stated that, in his opinion, a hysterectomy could be justified even if undertaken at the outset. This seemed to influence the judge, Wall J, who decided that it would be in the woman's best interests, even if it was not the doctors' first choice because, first, the court should decide the best interests question and, secondly, the decision satisfied the *Bolam* test because there was a body of opinion that would undertake the hysterectomy at this, the first stage. The judge then said that as both treatments (the sterilisation was not favoured by anyone) were *Bolam* compliant, he would make a declaration to this effect and leave the mother to discuss with the doctors what was best.

See ◄ 4.3.4.4

This aspect of the case was considered but, here, the issue is the view taken by the Court of Appeal of the mother's wishes. These were based upon the fact that her daughter became very distressed at

68 [1997] 1 All ER 906.
69 [1981] 1 WLR 1421.
70 See Ch 12 for further discussion of this and other cases of gravely incapacitated children.
71 [2000] 2 FCR 452.

the time of her periods, regarding herself as being dirty, and the Mirena coil would not necessarily have any effect upon this. Further, the coil itself had to be inserted under general anaesthetic, and had to be replaced every five years, or more frequently if it became dislodged. The woman had a horror of hospitals and much of this would take place when her mother would not be there to help her. These were understandable concerns, but they did not sway the Court of Appeal. As it happens, in this case, the coil could be tried first and the more invasive method tried later if it did not work. This is unfortunate because, otherwise, the court could have made it more explicit that the interests of this woman and her mother could not be conflated and that might have been an embarrassing contrast with the decision in Re T (A Minor) (Wardship: Medical Treatment).[72]

The question of parental rights was considered in the case of Re P (A Minor), when Butler-Sloss J (as she then was) made an order for the termination of a 15-year-old girl's pregnancy in the face of her parents' opposition. The girl already had a baby and resided in a special mother and baby unit. Her parents wanted to care for the second child she was carrying, and her father objected to abortion on religious grounds:

Re P (A Minor) (1982)[73]

Butler-Sloss J: I would not like it to be thought that because she says she does not want the child her wishes should be given such paramount importance as to mean that for that reason only she should have an abortion. But where her wishes coincide with the facts that she is in danger of injury to her mental health; that she is undoubtedly – when I consider her interests, as I do, as the first and paramount consideration – unable to fulfil her own growing up as a child at her schooling as a consequence of this second pregnancy; where she is endangering the future of her current child; and where I take into account all the aspects of her actual and reasonably foreseeable environment, I have no doubt that this case comes within s 1(a) of the Abortion Act 1967 . . .

I must take into account in considering the welfare of Shirley – and her welfare is what is paramount in my mind because she is a ward of court – and through her the effect on her son of having this unwanted child, the important aspect of her parents. I was helpfully reminded of what had been said in the House of Lords in J v C [1970] AC 668 about the rights and obligations of parents. These parents are in certain difficulties in that they do not have the day to day care of Shirley since she is in care, and they are not able to offer to take over the day to day care of Shirley. In the circumstances, although I must give weight to their feelings as a factor in the case to be taken into consideration, and I must take into account their deeply and sincerely held religious objection, in considering the best interest of the minor as to whether she should have her pregnancy terminated I draw to some extent an analogy with Jehovah's Witnesses and blood transfusions . . . I am satisfied . . . that there is a risk of injury to the mental health of this minor, the factors raised by the grandfather on behalf of himself and his wife – which I have taken into account – cannot weigh in the balance against the needs of this girl so as to prevent the termination which I have decided is necessary in her best interests.

This may be thought to be in stark contrast with the views expressed by Butler-Sloss LJ in the much later case of Re T(A Minor) (Wardship: Medical Treatment)[74] considered above. However, even if it had been in issue, the closeness of the parent/child relationship, which was regarded as so important in Re T, would not have been relevant here as, unlike the case of a young, sick child, there was no question of this child needing her parents to care for her.

---

72 [1997] 1 All ER 906.
73 (1982) 80 LGR 301.
74 [1997] 1 All ER 906.

Note that, in Re P, the judge had to take into account the provisions of the Abortion Act 1967, where, inter alia, there has to be a risk to the health of the pregnant woman. There were, therefore, objective factors that had to be satisfied regardless of the wishes of the child and her parents. However, in abortion cases, it is always arguable that a child who does not want to continue with her pregnancy is going to be mentally damaged if she is compelled to continue it. In the context of other areas of medicine and surgery, however, there have been a number of recent cases where there have been disagreements between the parents, either among themselves or, more often, with the doctors, as to what is the appropriate medical treatment for their children.

See Chapter 8

In Re J (Child's Religious Upbringing and Circumcision),[75] the Court of Appeal refused an application by a child's father that the child be circumcised. The child's parents had separated when he was two and a half and the mother had custody. The father applied for a specific issue order under the Children Act 1989. The Turkish father, who was permanently resident in the UK was a Muslim, but non-practising. Similarly, the child's mother was described as non-practising Church of England. The child went to a secular school. The Court of Appeal upheld the first instance decision that it would not be in the child's best interests, as a non-practising Muslim, to undergo irreversible, non-therapeutic surgery which carried with it pain and the small risk of psychological harm. On the other hand, the same surgery, if agreed by both parents, for religious or cultural reasons, would be lawful.

In C (HIV Test),[76] both parents were agreed that they did not wish their baby to be tested for HIV. The mother was HIV positive and had resisted any form of intervention to prevent transmission of the virus to the child, both during pregnancy and afterwards. The clinical view was that, if the child was infected, there were measures which could be taken to manage the condition and that, if the child was not infected, then immediate cessation of breast feeding would be recommended. The local authority made an application for a specific issue order that the child be tested and this was supported by the Official Solicitor on behalf of the child. The judge at first instance granted the order on the basis that it was in the child's best interests and the Court of Appeal refused leave to appeal, confirming that the wishes of parents could be overruled and approving the judge's evaluation of the medical evidence.

The case of Re MM (A Child) (Medical Treatment)[77] concerned a child's treatment for immunodeficiency by immunoglobin, which doctors recommended. The parents were not prepared to consent to this because treatment received in Russia before the family moved to the UK had been working well and because there had been an early misdiagnosis by the English doctors which had shaken their confidence. In the event, an order was agreed that the immunoglobin treatment be continued, but with the parents closely involved in the decision-making, with liberty for either party to apply to the court for further directions.

The case of Re C (Welfare of Child: Immunisation)[78] was a conjoined case that considered a number of disputes between parents as to whether children should receive the MMR injection which immunised against multiple infectious diseases. There has been some controversy about the safety of the MMR immunisation, and the mothers, with whom the children lived, alleged that it presented unacceptable risks, whereas the fathers argued that there was convincing medical evidence that the benefits outweighed any risks. At first instance the judge made a declaration ordering immunisation of the children. The Court of Appeal upheld the decision on the basis that the judge had properly weighed up the medical evidence, and the Court confirmed that there was no general proposition of law that a court would not order non-essential invasive medical treatment in the face of strong opposition from a child's primary carer.

---

75 (1999) 52 BMLR 82.
76 [1999] 2 FLR 1004.
77 [2000] 1 FLR 224.
78 [2003] EWCA Civ 1148.

4.4.4 Children and the European Convention on Human Rights

The extraordinary circumstances which brought the case of R v Portsmouth Hospital NHS Trust ex p Glass[79] before the courts, came about through a total breakdown of relationships between the doctors and the patient's relatives, such that a fight broke out in which medical staff were punched, kicked and bitten, and three of the patient's relatives were prosecuted and received prison sentences. The patient, David, aged 12, was severely disabled, both mentally and physically, but his family cared for him devotedly and wanted him to live as long as possible. He was hospitalised several times during the summer of 1998, suffering from breathing and digestive problems. The doctors believed he was dying. In October, they wanted to administer diamorphine to relieve distress, but the child's mother refused to consent to this, fearing that sedation was a prelude to death. The doctors went ahead anyway, and a 'Do Not Resuscitate' order was placed on his medical records without consulting his mother. Visiting relatives made strenuous attempts to revive the child, in the course of which the assaults upon the medical staff took place. The child eventually went home and was successfully treated by the family GP. The trust wrote to the child's mother indicating that any future care should be administered by a hospital in Southampton and that it would only deal with him as an emergency admission. The mother sought judicial review of the trust's decision to administer diamorphine in the face of her refusal. Scott-Baker J dismissed the application for judicial review on the basis that the situation which gave rise to the application had now passed; the child was to be admitted to a different hospital and the judicial review mechanism was too blunt a tool for the sensitive and ongoing problems of the type thrown up in such a case. The Court of Appeal agreed and refused leave to appeal, stating that, if future conflicts of 'a grave nature' arose, then declarations could be sought from the court at the appropriate time, rather than trying to anticipate the 'almost infinite' considerations that might arise in the future. The judgment of the Court, given by Lord Woolf MR, whilst peppered with reminders that these cases give rise to sensitive issues, declined to comment on the fact that, in the face of a total breakdown of confidence, the trust did not see fit to bring the matter before the court, when the only course of action which seemed open to the family at that crucial time was, literally, to fight for the child's life.

The case went before the European Court of Human Rights and the decision of that Court (Glass v United Kingdom[80]) was that the decision to impose treatment on David in defiance of his mother's objections gave rise to an interference with the child's Article 8 rights, and in particular his right to physical integrity. Obviously, there are circumstances in which it is right to impose treatment on a child in the face of a parental refusal of consent, as evidenced by the cases above and, under such circumstances, save in emergency situations, UK law requires doctors to seek the intervention of the courts. In the Glass case, failure to do this meant that there had been a breach of Art 8. See also Royal Wolverhampton Hospitals NHS Trust v E and RB and Others,[81] where, it was assumed by the judge that, in circumstances of parental/medical disagreement, an application to the court by the trust was in the best interests of the child patient. In Re S(FC)[82] the House of Lords considered the balancing exercise which must take place when competing Articles of the European Convention are engaged.

Parents are, of course, entitled to use the Human Rights Act 1998 to allege there has been unlawful interference of their Convention rights, but Fortin argues that the phrasing of, in particular, Art 8, encourages parents to argue that these rights are all about protecting adult rights, so, for example, when parents challenge decisions to take their children into care, they focus on their own rights under Art 8. Fortin goes on to examine freedom of the press cases and to look at the balancing act carried out by courts when looking at a child's right to privacy and the freedom of

---

79 [1999] Lloyd's Law Reports 367.
80 (2004) 39 EHRR 15.
81 [2000] 1 FLR 953.
82 [2004] UKHL 47.

the press.[83] Fortin's main argument is that what she refers to as the paramountcy principle, ie s 1 of the Children Act 1989, which states that the welfare of the child is paramount, is the culprit in this situation:

Fortin, J, 'Accommodating children's rights in a post Human Rights Act era'[84]

... there is the assumption that rights and welfare are discrete matters and that therefore issues relating to the child's best interests cannot be introduced in the context of a discussion of his rights. Such a view also underlines the recurring concerns voiced by some family lawyers that by using a rights discourse, those concerned with children's wellbeing would be unable to promote their welfare. Indeed, some of those considering the effect of the HRA on the principles of child law have suggested that a rights-based approach to children's interests might actually conflict with their welfare. But the rights-based approach adopted by the European Convention should surely not be interpreted in manner ignoring the basic premises underpinning rights theories.

... a child's welfare cannot be inconsistent with his rights. Consequently any evidence which a court would traditionally consider when assessing how to accommodate the child's welfare must be accommodated *within* arguments about his rights. In other words, there cannot be two categories of evidence, one relating to the child's rights and another to his welfare.

Perhaps Fortin is unhappy with the welfare principle because it acts like a sort of 'super-right' that overrides the rights of the parents, when she prefers a balancing act between respective rights. In other words, there is a risk that the welfare principle in children cases assumes the same role as best interests in adult cases, where it is arguable that subsuming decisions under these phrases results in an insufficient airing of the issues.

4.4.5 Children and the role of the court

Decisions concerning the treatment of children can come before the court via the Children Act 1989 (specific issue orders under s 8), or via the jurisdiction of the High Court. The wardship jurisdiction must be distinguished from the inherent jurisdiction of the High Court. In the former case parental authority is vested in the court; in the latter the court is dealing only with the particular treatment issue put before it. The inherent jurisdiction of the court may be invoked by local authorities, as the wardship jurisdiction is unavailable to them. Regardless of the nature of the judicial proceedings, the welfare of the child is paramount.

 SELF-TEST QUESTION

Do you agree with Lord Donaldson's interpretation of the *Gillick* case when considering treatment refusals by children?

---

83 See Ch 5 for more discussion of this issue in the context of privacy generally.
84 (2006) 69(3) MLR 299, p 311.

4.5 The Control of Fertility and the Incapable Patient

4.5.1 The therapeutic/non-therapeutic disinction

Sterilisation, abortion and enforced contraception of incapable patients raise profound ethical issues. Furthermore, these procedures are inevitably associated with the practice of eugenics carried out by the Nazis during the 1930s and 1940s. However, as Davies points out, the practice was by no means unknown before this:

Davies, M, *Medical Law*[85]

13.3.1 Historical development of sterilisation

The debate on sterilising the mentally handicapped has been a long, and as the case law will show, a vociferous one. The debate has as its emotive backdrop the history of late 19th and early 20th centuries. The case law will show that the judiciary of a number of common law jurisdictions are aware of the dark side of this history. Sterilisation for eugenic purposes was not a product of Nazi Germany, although that regime was the most horrific expression of the perversion of the concept of eugenics. The theory that the species could be improved or perfected by a cleansing of the gene pool through selective breeding was introduced by Sir Francis Galton at University College London in 1869. It was not long before a number of US State reformatories were using the concept to justify the sterilisation of what were deemed to be those carrying undesirable traits within society . . . One of the best known, and to some most frightening, judicial justifications for the performance of these irreversible operations was found in *Buck v Bell* 274 US 200 (1927). Carrie Buck was described as the 'feeble-minded' daughter of a mother who was herself described (among other things) as 'feeble-minded'. Her proposed sterilisation was challenged on 'due process' grounds as a 'cruel and unusual punishment' under the US Constitution. The Supreme Court's view was that it was not going to be done as a punishment, but as a means to facilitate her freedom within the community. One of the most chilling quotes comes from Mr Justice Oliver Wendell Holmes (p 207):

> We have seen more than once that the public welfare may call upon the best citizens for their lives. It would be strange if it could not call upon those who already sap the strength of the State for these lesser sacrifices, often not felt to be such by those concerned, in order to prevent our being swamped with incapables. It is better for all the world, if instead of waiting to execute degenerate offspring for crime, or to let them starve for their imbecility, society can prevent those who are manifestly unfit from continuing their kind. The principle that sustains compulsory vaccination is broad enough to cover cutting the fallopian tubes. Three generations of imbeciles are enough.

Although, *Buck v Bell* was decided in the 1920s, the issue has not gone away and the controversy remains. The case of *Re B (A Minor)*,[86] which concerned the sterilisation of a mentally handicapped girl, caused a considerable amount of controversy. Michael Freeman, editor of *Medicine, Ethics and the Law*,[87] in a BBC interview, had described the approval of the sterilisation by the Court of Appeal as 'Nazi-like'. In the House of Lords, Lord Hailsham, no doubt bearing in mind this reaction, had sought from the outset to distinguish this case from the practice of eugenics:

---

85 London: Blackstone, 1996, p 262.
86 [1988] 1 AC 199.
87 London: Stevens, 1988.

Re B (A Minor) [88]

Lord Hailsham: There is no doubt that, in the exercise of its wardship jurisdiction, the first and paramount consideration is the well being, welfare, or interests (each expression occasionally used, but each, for this purpose, synonymous) of the human being concerned, that is the ward herself or himself. In this case I believe it to be the only consideration involved. In particular there is no issue of public policy other than the application of the above principle which can conceivably be taken into account, least of all (since the opposite appears to have been considered in some quarters) any question of eugenics.

When the case of *Re F (Mental Patient: Sterilisation)* was in the Court of Appeal, Lord Donaldson had taken the view that sterilisation operations were special cases:

Re F (Mental Patient: Sterilisation) (1990) [89]

Lord Donaldson p 19:

Is sterilisation in a special category?
. . . Mr Munby seeks to persuade us that it is in a special category and in this I think he is right, although I would include in the same category abortion and surgical intervention to enable an incapable adult to donate an organ during lifetime. However, there is a real distinction between medical treatment undertaken with a view to securing abortion or sterilisation and that undertaken for a different purpose, for example the excision of a malignant tumour, which has this incidental result. It is only the former type of treatment which the law regards as being in a special category, probably because of its irreversible and emotive character in the light of the history of our times.

As stated by Lord Donaldson, sterilisation operations can be carried out for exclusively therapeutic purposes, for example, when the ovaries or uterus are damaged or diseased. Those operations do not concern us here. The cases we will examine fall into two categories. First, 'social' sterilisations, where it is proposed to render sterile those who, it is said, are simply incapable of understanding parenthood and caring for a child. Secondly, there have been a number of cases where young women have been sterilised to avoid difficulties with menstruation. Can these properly be called 'therapeutic'?

4.5.2 Non-therapeutic sterilisations

We have considered above whether there is any meaningful distinction between a therapeutic and a non-therapeutic procedure, and saw that La Forest J in the case of *Re Eve* [90] favoured such a distinction. 'Non-therapeutic' sterilisations are those that might be carried out for reasons relating to whether the woman is fit to be a parent. The problem with this is that it necessarily encompasses issues that do not relate to the woman herself but social circumstances. This is fraught with difficulty because while a physically impaired mother may need some assistance in bringing up a child, it is highly unpalatable to think of her being told she cannot have children because of this.

One of the first English cases to examine the issue was *Re D (A Minor) (Wardship: Sterilisation)*. [91] The case concerned an 11-year-old child, who suffered from Sotos syndrome, a condition characterised

---

88 [1988] 1 AC 199at 202.
89 [1990] 2 AC 1.
90 [1986] 2 SCR 388.
91 [1976] 1 All ER 326.

by epilepsy, clumsiness, unusual facial appearance, behavioural problems such as emotional insta-
bility and aggression and impairment of mental function. She was described as having an IQ of 80
(described as 'dull normal'), some reading and writing skills, good conversational skills and the
understanding of a nine or nine and a half year old. An application was made to the court under
the wardship jurisdiction for authorisation of a sterilisation. The reasons are outlined in the
judgment of Heilbron J:

Re D (A Minor) (Wardship: Sterilisation) (1976)[92]

Heilbron J (p 330):

The background to the decision to operate

When Mrs B first realised that she had given birth to a handicapped child, she recalled with
deep concern that, many years before, she had lived near a family who had the misfortune to
have three mentally retarded children, and their plight and their troubled lives had deeply
affected her. She and her husband not unnaturally were extremely worried about D's future, as
at that time they thought D could never improve, and so even when D was a very young child
they decided that when she reached the age of about 18 they would take the necessary steps to
prevent her from having any children, and would apply to have her sterilised. From the decision
made in those early days Mrs B has never resiled, and she has in consequence, over the years,
had several discussions about this operation with Dr Gordon. When D reached puberty by the
age of 10 Mrs B's concern increased, and so she discussed the operation once again with
Dr Gordon on 7 January 1975. Mrs B said, and I accept, that when she reiterated to Dr Gordon
that she would like D sterilised when she was older, the doctor said: 'We can do it now.' This is
indeed confirmed by the doctor in his affidavit when he says that rather than wait any longer the
decision could be taken then. Mrs B agreed that the operation should be performed. She was
very worried lest D might be seduced and possibly give birth to a baby, which might also be
abnormal. She had always believed that D would not, or should not, marry and in any event
would be incapable of bringing up a child. Her anxieties are genuine and understandable.

Dr Gordon took the view that there was a real risk that D might give birth to an abnormal
foetus. I have already referred to some of his other anxieties. As to the possibility of producing
an abnormal child, the evidence of Dr Snodgrass and Dr Newton, the well known consultant
psychiatrist called on behalf of the Official Solicitor, confirmed that there was, as Dr Gordon
stated, an increased risk of such an eventuality. On the other hand, they pointed out that no one
with this particular syndrome had ever been known to have a baby, and it is not therefore
possible to make any precise predictions whether or not they are able to do so.

At that consultation in January Dr Gordon, with Mrs B's agreement, came to a decision
provided that Miss Duncan, the consultant gynaecologist, who is a senior lecturer and gynaecologist to the Sheffield and Northern General Hospital, to whom he referred, concurred in his
recommendation that the operation should be performed. Miss Duncan saw and interviewed
both D and Mrs B on 7 February 1975, but she did not examine the child, and I think there is
little doubt that Miss Duncan did not give very much independent consideration to the wider
implications of this operation, but was content in large measure to rely on Dr Gordon's recommendation and assessment of the situation. She did, however, agree to perform the sterilisation, namely a hysterectomy, and I am satisfied that D was booked to enter hospital on 4 May
for that operation to be carried out on 6 May. No one else was consulted prior to that decision.
It is surprising that Dr T, the child psychiatrist, was not, for, prior to the date of the recommendation, he had on a number of occasions interviewed and examined the child, and his views, as

---

92 [1976] 2 WLR 279.

Dr Gordon later agreed in evidence, must have been of considerable importance in evaluating the numerous problems, medical, social, educational and psychiatric, which such a vital decision involved.

Dr Gordon maintains, however, that his recommendation was one which was based on clinical judgment as a doctor, and that he and the gynaecologist should be the sole judges whether or not it should be performed, provided of course that they had the parent's consent.

Despite Dr Gordon's assertion that his decision should be upheld because it was based on his clinical judgment, he nevertheless, in putting forward his grounds for recommending this operation, stated that such reasons or such grounds were of a twofold character, ie, that they were both medical and social. The medical reasons included the possibility that she might give birth to an abnormal child, that her epilepsy might cause her to harm a child, and that the only satisfactory method of birth control was this operation. The social reasons included his opinion that D would be unable in the future to maintain herself save in a sheltered environment, her inability due to epilepsy and other handicaps to cope with a family if she were to marry, without substantial support, the deterioration in her behaviour for which he said there was no known method of improvement and the possibility that she might have to enter an institution as he alleged for social or criminal reasons in the future. Certain persons concerned with D's welfare, however, took a different view. They were the former and present headmaster of her school, Mrs Hamidi and the social worker involved with the family. They believed that an operation for sterilisation in the case of a minor, particularly a girl of 11, being irreversible and permanent, was a matter of grave concern, and so on 26 March Mrs Hamidi wrote on their behalf and on her own to the senior school medical officer, pointing out in detail the conflict between Mrs B and the school and the welfare services in regard to D's attainments and their concern in regard to the proposed operation, which they pointed out could affect the whole of her future.

On 21 April there was a meeting between Dr Gordon and those professionals working with the child and her family, at which Dr Gordon's social and behavioural reasons for performing this operation were seriously challenged. Dr Gordon, however, refused to acknowledge that these views could possibly be wrong or exaggerated or premature. I think Dr Gordon, whose sincerity cannot be challenged, was persuaded by his emotional involvement with Mrs B's considerable problems and anxieties, and his strong personal views in favour of sterilisation – as he stated in his affidavit, 'Sterilisation is now an emotive word, and we must try to change its image' – to form a less than detached opinion in regard to a number of matters which were not in my view in reality matters of clinical judgment, but which were concerned, to a large extent, with grounds which were other than medical. I feel it is a pity that he was not prepared to accept that others, whose duties, training and skills were directed to the assessment and amelioration of many of these problems, had much to contribute in the formulation of a decision of this gravity.

In my judgment Dr Gordon's views as to D's present and future social and behavioural problems were somewhat exaggerated and mistaken. I think in this area his views were clouded by his resentment at what he considered unjustified interference.

In the event Dr Gordon did not accept the alternative views, and he and Miss Duncan refused to defer the operation despite the grave implications for the child. Mrs Hamidi and the others, therefore, wrote to the area administrator of the health authority requesting an urgent and independent review of this decision. The area administrator consulted the local authority's specialist in community medicine (child health) and he later replied saying that she had made a very careful appraisal of the case, but could not interfere. Mrs Hamidi and her colleagues, however, were not daunted and they thereupon consulted solicitors, and in due course these proceedings got under way. It is only right that I should pay tribute to their courage, persistence and humane concern for this young girl.

. . . I am dealing here with the case of this particular young girl, but the evidence, including that which disclosed that Dr Gordon has recommended and Miss Duncan has performed two prior operations of this nature on handicapped children in Sheffield, indicates the possibility that further consideration may need to be given to this topic, consideration which would involve extensive consultation and debate elsewhere.

Dr Gordon's reason for wishing this operation to be performed was, of course, to prevent D ever having a child. He recognised, as did Mrs B, that there are other methods of achieving that objective, but his view was that D could not satisfactorily manage any form of contraception. Mrs B was concerned lest D might be seduced and become pregnant . . .

Mrs B's genuine concern . . . cannot be disregarded. A body of evidence was produced, therefore, to indicate the advantages and disadvantages of various forms of contraception. I shall not, however, burden this judgment with any detailed examination of it, save to say that I do not accept on the evidence Dr Gordon's contention that this young girl, if and when the time arrived, would not be a suitable subject for one of the various methods described by the doctors . . .

It was common ground that D had sufficient intellectual capacity to marry, in the future of course, and that many people of a like kind are capable of, and do so. Dr Gordon agreed that this being so, she and her future husband would then be the persons most concerned in a question of sterilisation, and such an operation might have a serious and material bearing on a future marriage and its consequences.

The purpose of performing this operation is permanently to prevent the possibility of reproduction. The evidence of Professor Huntingford, consultant and professor of obstetrics and gynaecology at the University of London and at St Bartholomew's Hospital and the London Hospital Medical Colleges, was that in his view such an operation was normally only appropriate for a woman who consented to it, possibly at the conclusion of child-bearing, and then only after careful and anxious consideration by her and her husband of many factors and, what is most important, with full knowledge of all its implications.

Professor Huntingford, Dr Snodgrass and Dr Newton were all agreed that such an operation was not medically indicated in this case, and should not be performed. Dr Snodgrass said he was firmly of the view that it was wrong to perform this operation on an 11-year-old, on the pretext that it would benefit her in the future. Dr Newton said:

> In my opinion sterilisation of a child before the age of consent can only be justified if it is the treatment for some present or inevitable disease. In this case, sterilisation is not a treatment for any of the signs or symptoms of Sotos syndrome, from which she suffers. I am totally against this operation being performed on D.

. . . Dr Gordon, however, maintained that, provided the parent or parents consented, the decision was one made pursuant to the exercise of his clinical judgment, and that no interference could be tolerated in his clinical freedom.

The other consultants did not agree. Their opinion was that a decision to sterilise a child was not entirely within a doctor's clinical judgment, save only when sterilisation was the treatment of choice for some disease, as, for instance, when in order to treat a child and to ensure her direct physical well being, it might be necessary to perform a hysterectomy to remove a malignant uterus. Whilst the side effect of such an operation would be to sterilise, the operation would be performed solely for therapeutic purposes. I entirely accept their opinions. I cannot believe, and the evidence does not warrant the view, that a decision to carry out an operation of this nature performed for non-therapeutic purposes on a minor, can be held to be within the doctor's sole clinical judgment . . .

A review of the whole of the evidence leads me to the conclusion that in a case of a child of 11 years of age, where the evidence shows that her mental and physical condition and attainments have already improved, and where her future prospects are as yet unpredictable, where the evidence also shows that she is unable as yet to understand and appreciate the implications of this operation and could not give a valid or informed consent, but the likelihood is that in later years she will be able to make her own choice, where, I believe, the frustration and resentment of realising (as she would one day) what had happened, could be devastating, an operation of this nature is, in my view, contra-indicated.

Three things in particular are noteworthy: first, the apparent lack of concern by the gynaecologist; secondly, the intransigence of Dr Gordon; and, thirdly, the chance way in which the case came before the court. As far as the first two points are concerned, this case was heard in the days before the decision in Re F (Mental Patient: Sterilisation) which endorsed the Bolam test as the criterion for best interests. However, if the Bolam test had been applied, would the combined opinions of Miss Duncan and Dr Gordon have constituted a responsible body of medical opinion for the purposes of the Bolam test? Even if two opinions were deemed insufficient, it is likely that, if necessary, other doctors could have been found to endorse their views. On an application of the Bolam test (which now has only a preliminary role to play in such cases), would Heilbron J have been able, nevertheless, to reject these opinions on the ground that they were not 'responsible' or that they were 'illogical'? This nicely illustrates the inappropriateness of the Bolam test in the best interests context. The third point, ie the arbitrary way in which the case came to court, is indicative of the time at which it was decided, and attitudes have changed somewhat since 1976. It was 12 years later that the sterilisation of a minor came before the House of Lords. The case of Re B (A Minor) (Wardship: Sterilisation) (the case of 'Jeanette') concerned a 17-year-old girl. She was a voluntary patient in a local authority residential unit. The facts are outlined in the judgment of Lord Oliver:

Re B (A Minor) (Wardship: Sterilisation) (1988)[93]

Lord Oliver p 207 . . . [Jeanette] suffers from what is described as a 'moderate' degree of mental handicap but has a very limited intellectual development. Her ability to understand speech is that of a six-year-old, but her ability to express herself has been described as comparable to that of a two-year-old child. No cause for her mental handicap has been established but the report of Dr Berney, a consultant psychiatrist who gave evidence before the judge, indicates that her epilepsy and the degree of her mental incapacity suggest an underlying abnormality of the brain. It is not envisaged that she will ever be capable of caring for herself in the community or reach a stage where she could return permanently to her mother's care. She is capable of finding her way round a limited locality, of dressing and bathing herself and performing simple household tasks under supervision and she has been taught to cope with menstruation; but the evidence is that she is unlikely to show an improvement in mental capacity beyond that of a six year old child. She has, in the past, shown evidence of extremes of mood and can become violent and aggressive, a phenomenon associated with premenstrual tension. Since the middle of 1986 there has been prescribed for her a drug known as Danazol to help in controlling her irregular periods and relieving premenstrual tension, whilst her epilepsy is controlled by anti-convulsant drugs. She suffers from obesity and an earlier attempt to treat her outbursts of violence with Microgynon 30 (a combined oral contraceptive) had to be abandoned because it produced a significant increase in weight. Another behavioural feature of significance is her high tolerance of pain. There is evidence that she bites her arm and that if injured she interferes with the process of healing by opening and probing the wounds.

---

93 [1988] 1 AC 199.

What prompted the application to the court was the consciousness on the part of her mother and officers of the council responsible for her care that she was beginning to show recognisable signs of sexual awareness and sexual drive exemplified by provocative approaches to male members of the staff and other residents and by touching herself in the genital area. There was thus brought to their attention the obvious risk of pregnancy and the desirability of taking urgent and effective contraceptive measures. Although at present she is subject to effective supervision, her degree of incapacity is not such that it would be thought right that she should, effectively, be institutionalised all her life. The current approach to persons of her degree of incapacity is to allow them as much freedom as is consistent with their own safety and that of other people and although the likelihood is that she will, for the foreseeable future, continue to live at the residential institution, she visits her mother and her siblings at week-ends and will, inevitably, be much less susceptible to supervision when she goes to an adult training centre. At the same time the risks involved in her becoming pregnant are formidable. The evidence of Dr Berney is that there is no prospect of her being capable of forming a long term adult relationship, such as marriage, which is within the capacity of some less mentally handicapped persons. She has displayed no maternal feelings and indeed has an antipathy to small children. Such skills as she has been able to develop are limited to those necessary for caring for herself at the simplest level and there is no prospect of her being capable of raising or caring for a child of her own. If she did give birth to a child it would be essential that it be taken from her for fostering or adoption although her attitude towards children is such that this would not cause her distress. So far as her awareness of her own sexuality is concerned, she has, as has already been mentioned, been taught to manage for herself the necessary hygienic mechanics of menstruation, but it has not been possible to teach her about sexuality in any abstract form. She understands the link between pregnancy and a baby but is unaware of sexual intercourse and its relationship to pregnancy. It is not feasible to discuss contraception with her and even if there should come a time when she becomes capable of understanding the need for contraception, there is no likelihood of her being able to develop the capacity to weigh up the merits of different types of contraception or to make an informed choice in the matter. Should she become pregnant, it would be desirable that the pregnancy should be terminated, but because of her obesity and the irregularity of her periods there is an obvious danger that her condition might not be noticed until it was too late for an abortion to take place safely. On the other hand, the risks if she were permitted to go to full term are serious, for although it is Dr Berney's opinion that she would tolerate the condition of pregnancy without undue distress, the process of delivery would be likely to be traumatic and would cause her to panic. Normal delivery would be likely to require heavy sedation, which could be injurious to the child, so that it might be more appropriate to deliver her by Caesarean section. If this course were adopted, however, past experience of her reaction to injuries suggests that it would be very difficult to prevent her from repeatedly opening up the wound and thus preventing the healing of the post-operative scar. It was against this background and in the light of the increasing freedom which must be allowed her as she grows older and the consequent difficulty of maintaining effective supervision that those having the care of the minor concluded that it was essential in her interests that effective contraceptive measures be taken. Almost all drugs appear to have a bad effect upon her and the view was formed, in which her mother concurred, that the only appropriate course offering complete protection was for her to undergo sterilisation by occluding the fallopian tubes, a relatively minor operation carrying a very small degree of risk to the patient, a very high degree of protection and minimal side effects. There is, however, no possibility that the minor, even if of full age, would herself have the mental capacity to consent to such an operation. Hence the application to the court.

. . . Your Lordships' attention has, quite properly, been directed to the decision of Heilbron J in *In re D (A Minor) (Wardship: Sterilisation)* [1976] Fam 185, a case very different from the instant case, where the evidence indicated that the ward was of an intellectual capacity to marry and would in the future be able to make her own choice. In those circumstances, Heilbron J declined to sanction an operation which involved depriving her of her right to reproduce. That, if I may say so respectfully, was plainly a right decision. But the right to reproduce is of value only if accompanied by the ability to make a choice and in the instant case there is no question of the minor ever being able to make such a choice or indeed to appreciate the need to make one. All the evidence indicates that she will never desire a child and that reproduction would in fact be positively harmful to her.

Was this operation in Jeanette's best interests? Much of the reasoning behind the court's decision was that the operation was necessary to protect her. Lord Oliver said:[94]

> **Lord Oliver**: My Lords, I have thought it right to set out in some detail the background of fact in which this appeal has come before your Lordships' House because it is, in my judgment, essential to appreciate, in considering the welfare of this young woman which it is the duty of the court to protect, the degree of her vulnerability, the urgency of the need to take protective measures and the impossibility of her ever being able at this age or any later age either to consent to any form of operative treatment or to exercise for herself the right of making any informed decision in matters which, in the case of a person less heavily handicapped, would rightly be thought to be matters purely of personal and subjective choice.

Note that, in the judgment of Lord Oliver, he moves from reference to 'provocative gestures' to the 'risk of pregnancy' without pausing to consider that there is no inevitable progression from one to the other. The somewhat hollow ring of the efficacy of this procedure as a protective measure may be, at least in part, related to the fact that it is at odds with much of the evidence. If Jeanette was so limited in her understanding, and this was stressed by carers and judges alike, then the operation was arguably unnecessary for *precisely this very reason*. She would simply never have the opportunity to have sexual intercourse. The concern that she would not be supervised sufficiently at the adult training centre which she was shortly due to attend is not entirely consistent with the negative assertions about her uncontrolled behaviour:

De Cruz, SP, 'Sterilisation, wardship and human rights'[95]

> . . . since Jeanette could not even be allowed on the streets unsupervised, as she could not understand traffic, she would certainly need close and constant attention for a great deal of the time. Admittedly, provided she was indoors, the supervision need not be quite so intensive or intrusive, once this alarming prospect of pregnancy no longer existed. Yet given the prospect of sexual exploitation, of course, sterilisation would give no protection against rape or sexual abuse. Furthermore, the operation would certainly not free her, as Lord Hailsham seemed to imply, from 'incarceration', nor give her the liberty to satisfy the sexual desires she was experiencing, when she would certainly experience difficulties in relationships with the opposite sex. If anything, the ruling accentuates her vulnerability and, tragically, results in her being treated very differently from 'normal' people, which would undermine all the advances made in the last decade or so in the achievements of mental health groups in their efforts to integrate people with mental disabilities into the community at large.

Lord Oliver had said that the concern of the court had been about 'what is in the best interests of this unfortunate young woman and how best she can be given the protection which is essential to

---

94 At p 210.
95 [1988] Fam Law 6.

her future well being so that she may lead as full a life as her intellectual capacity allows'. It is tempting, however, to conclude that the 'full life' was a life which relieved her carers of many of their duties to protect her.

Might someone in Jeanette's position be in need of protection from exploitation from those responsible for her safety? Yet, contrariwise, a sterilisation would effectively and outrageously 'free her up' for exploitation.

In this regard, see the case of *Re LC (Medical Treatment: Sterilisation)*,[96] where an application for authority to perform a sterilisation operation on a 25-year-old mentally impaired woman, came before the court because of her mother's anxiety following an indecent assault upon her by a member of staff at her former residential home. In the event, the operation was not authorised, as the woman was now resident in a home where the care was described as 'of exceptionally high quality', and, on balance, the operation was not justified. Whilst not disputing the correctness of this decision, is it right for the outcome to depend upon the quality of care? If this woman had been in a home where the quality of care was poor, would the operation have been authorised? If so, the woman would have been exposed to a double jeopardy: the imposition of major, invasive and irreversible surgery, together with risk of sexual abuse and exploitation.

It is also questionable that there was any significant likelihood that Jeanette would have become pregnant, as provocative gestures, whatever they may be, are a long way from a willingness to have sexual intercourse.

It is, of course, possible that an incapable patient may not be suited to pregnancy and motherhood. Likewise, in the case of a capable woman there may be circumstances which would mean that pregnancy and motherhood would be similarly undesirable. In such a case would sterilisation be thought to be the only solution, particularly when she was not sexually active, was aged only 17 and her future development was uncertain? Surely, it is highly unlikely that sterilisation would even be considered at that stage in her life. However, it is essential to compare Jeanette with a capable woman, otherwise Jeanette is being treated differently *because of her mental impairment*. The comparison with 'normal' people was made in the dissenting judgment of Brennan J in *Department of Health v JWB and SMB*, where the majority of the High Court of Australia sanctioned a 'non-therapeutic' sterilisation on a 14-year-old girl:

Department of Health v JWB and SMB (1992)[97]

Brennan J:

22 . . . a variety of different purposes may appear which many would regard as of significant value in assessing the 'best interests' of an intellectually disabled child. The purposes which fall into this category can be gathered under the broad description of 'preventative': to prevent the risk of a pregnancy which the child could not properly understand and the concomitant risk of parenthood with responsibilities beyond the capacity of the child to discharge.

These risks are an understandable source of anxiety to parents, guardians and others who have a genuine concern for the welfare of an intellectually disabled child. These are risks which create an understandable anxiety in many parents, guardians and others who have a genuine concern for the welfare of a normal child. In the case of a normal female child, it would be wholly unacceptable to permit sterilisation in order to prevent pregnancy or parenthood, though those events might be thought to be tragedies in particular circumstances by reasonable persons concerned with the welfare of the child. Depending on the circumstances, the use – or, *a fortiori*, the exploitation – of the sexual attributes of a female child may entail tragic

---

96 [1997] 2 FLR 258.
97 (1992) 66 ALJR 300.

consequences, yet the risk or even the likelihood of tragic consequences affords no justification for her sterilisation. What difference does it make that the risk is occasioned by an intellectual disability? The answer to this question depends on the view taken of the proposition earlier set out in the Declaration on the Rights of Mentally Retarded Persons: they are entitled to the same rights as other humans to the maximum degree of feasibility. To accord in full measure the human dignity that is the due of every intellectually disabled girl, her right to retain her capacity to bear a child cannot be made contingent on her imposing no further burdens, causing no more anxiety or creating no further demands. If the law were to adopt a policy of permitting sterilisation in order to avoid the imposition of burdens, the causing of anxiety and the creating of demands, the human rights which foster and protect human dignity in the powerless would lie in the gift of those who are empowered and the law would fail in its function of protecting the weak.

23 ... In any event, though pregnancy be a possibility, sterilisation, once performed, is a certainty. If a non-therapeutic sterilisation could be justified at all, it could be justified only by the need to avoid a tragedy that is imminent and certain. Such a situation bespeaks a failure of care, and sterilisation is not the remedy for the failure. Nor should it be forgotten that pregnancy and motherhood may have a significance for some intellectually disabled girls quite different from the significance attributed by other people. Though others may see her pregnancy and motherhood as a tragedy, she, in her world, may find in those events an enrichment of her life.

Were the alternatives properly explored by the court, and, indeed, by Jeanette's carers? Most forms of contraceptive pill were thought to be unsuitable because of her obesity, although it was argued by the Official Solicitor that insufficient consideration had been given to the use of a progestogen contraceptive pill less likely to have that effect. The prospect of a daily dose, however, was daunting to Jeanette's carers, although other drugs were administered to her for her epilepsy, apparently without undue difficulty. In addition, it was thought undesirable for the contraceptive drug to be administered to her for 30 years or more. De Cruz suggests that the decision may have been made in something approaching indecent haste:

De Cruz, SP, 'Sterilisation, wardship and human rights'[98]

Should the Law Lords have deferred the decision, pending further investigation and observation? The Canadian courts took nearly seven years to decide Eve's case, and it took 16 months for the Supreme Court to produce its judgment, after studying a very wide range of expert opinions and the exhaustive research of the Canadian Law Commission. In their desire not to be faced with a jurisdictional problem once Jeanette reached the age of 18, the English Law Lords only took 28 days to decide the case, but their assumptions about her future conduct may well have led them to discount other possibilities too readily.

As far as adult patients are concerned, the leading case is Re F (Mental Patient: Sterilisation).[99] The facts of that case concerned a female mental patient, a woman in her thirties, who had been assessed as having a mental age of a four to five-year-old. She was a voluntary in-patient in a mental hospital where she had formed what was described as a sexual relationship with a male patient. Both hospital staff, and the patient's mother, felt that she would not be able to cope with childbirth, nor with the subsequent rearing of a child, and that it would, therefore, be in her best interests to be sterilised. A declaration was sought from the court that the proposed sterilisation would be lawful.

---

98 (1988) Fam Law 6.
99 [1990] 2 AC 1.

The unanimous decision of the Court of Appeal and the House of Lords was that the operation was in her best interests.

In both this case and the case of Jeanette, the mental age of the women concerned was a crucial factor. The crude application of intelligence assessments to social and emotional development is questionable:

Lee, R and Morgan, D, 'Sterilisation and mental handicap: sapping the strength of the State?'[100]

The problem of mental age

If the Law Lords appear to have been woefully uninformed as to the reality of the present life for mentally handicapped women, they are also less than convincing in showing an understanding of their capacities. One of the most persistent criticisms of the decision in the professional press concerned the emphasis ascribed to the criteria of mental age, and the use to which this was put. Having stated that Jeanette had a mental age of five or six, the judgments in *Re B* seem to treat Jeanette as if she were simply a child of that age. Jeanette, like all other handicapped people, would be expected to demonstrate different functional abilities across a whole range of skills. Intelligence testing offers little information as to many of these abilities, and in so far as it leads to labels such as 'mental age of five', it misdescribes the mentally handicapped person in a discriminatory fashion. Jeanette may not read at all, unlike many six year olds, but she may consistently outperform most children of that age in terms of socialisation or self-help. In addition, the criterion of 'mental age' was treated as static. Yet, as Woolrych has observed . . . the use of the discredited concept of 'mental age' is disturbing, since current experiences indicate learning potential is dependent on the quality and variety of services available in developing an understanding of issues such as the connection between sex and having babies.

Nor will the concept of mental age shed much light upon Jeanette's biological and emotional state as a 17 year old woman. While it may be difficult to grapple with the concept of a physically mature woman manifesting childlike intelligence in some respects, we must be careful that we do not discount and become repulsed by the notion that this person manifests adult sexual desires. This is a problem facing many parents of mentally handicapped young women.

Can we expect judges to be aware of the controversy which surrounds the notion of mental age? It is used, in part, to justify an irreversible surgical procedure. This procedure eliminates reproductive capacities, infringing what some would claim to be a basic human right. If the courts are to be used to channel issues of controversial ethical dilemmas, and if they are to legitimate their authority to resolve them, then informed judgment is a starting point.

4.5.3 An abuse of human rights?

It was stated in *Re B* that the case was about removing the 'right to reproduce'. Is there such a right? It is often stated that there is: for example, Art 12 of the European Convention on Human Rights enshrines the 'right to marry and found a family':

Freeman, MD (ed), *Medicine, Ethics and the Law*[101]

Why do we have the rights we have and do we have the right to reproduce? One common answer links rights with interests. Such a view was implicit in Bentham and Ihering and is

---

100 (1988) 15 JLS 229.
101 London: Stevens, 1988, p 72.

found in such contemporary writers as Feinberg and McCloskey. Thus, Feinberg writes that 'the sort of beings who can have rights are precisely those who have (or can have) interests'. It is an argument often employed by those who believe that animals have rights. It is also one of the arguments employed by Carby-Hall to demonstrate the Jeanette did not have the right to reproduce. She writes: 'A being can truly be said to have an interest in x, the subject of a potential right, if and only if x will benefit him in the sense of furthering some or all of his present or future desires.' She argues that a necessary condition of possession of a right is at least the capacity to possess the relevant concepts and a desire for that right. Jeanette clearly lacked the former and almost certainly the latter. But is this association of rights and interests justifiable? I think not. What this does not answer is how the having of interests establishes the grounds for having rights. Animals have interests. I have an interest in Middlesex winning the County Cricket Championship. In neither would it make sense to talk of rights. Human beings do not have the same interests. Surely this does not justify an unequal distribution of human rights. I agree with Alan White that 'no valid argument can be given either for including or for excluding children, imbeciles (*inter alia*) . . . as holders of rights on the ground that being capable of having a right ensures or necessitates being capable either of having something in one's interest or of being interested in something. Hence, he concludes, 'the question whether animals, etc . . . can or cannot have interests, either in the sense of something being in their interest or in the sense of their being interested in something, is irrelevant to the question whether they can have rights'.

Freeman is trying to resist the argument that Jeanette had no right to reproduce as long as she was unaware of that so called right. Is awareness of such a right relevant to its existence? If you are deliberately locked in a room and are unaware of this, does it mean that up until the point that you wish to leave you have no right to leave the room? Of course, in the cases of Jeanette and F, it was assumed that they would never wish to leave the room, but it is questionable whether that assumption is justified. Further, the assertion that the right to reproduce meant nothing to her belongs to a dangerous species of argument, that is, 'you have no rights because you are incapable of exercising them, or incapable of exercising them in your own best interests'.

It could be said that there is no right to reproduce because such a right is unenforceable. It might be better to say that one has a right to *attempt* to reproduce. However, viewed in this language, would it make sense to say that in the cases of Jeanette and F, they had no right to attempt, because that presupposes a decision-making capacity which they may not have had? It is doubtful whether this is correct. Many children are produced unintentionally. If one was only endorsing a right to attempt to reproduce, it may be argued that such an unintentional pregnancy was less valuable than others. Might the better view be that of Raanan Gillon who argues that there is a *prima facie* right not to be prevented?[102] The right may not be absolute, but it is arguable that it should only be overridden, in the words of Brennan J, 'to avoid a tragedy that is imminent and certain'.

Is it even necessary to consider the issue in the language of rights? It must be the case that a woman, even if mentally impaired, is entitled to the same amount of respect for her human dignity and physical integrity as any other person. There is a strong argument that subjecting her to invasive surgery on the off-chance that she may become pregnant and 'pregnancy does not mean anything to her', is flouting respect for her dignity as a human being.

The cases of Jeanette and F are very different in at least one important respect. In the case of Jeanette, there was no suggestion that she was sexually active, or indeed, that she wished to be (it does not necessarily follow that she did, despite the so called provocative gestures – again consider

---

102   See 'On sterilising severely mentally handicapped people' (1987) 13 JME 59.

her in comparison with a competent woman). In the case of Re F (Mental Patient: Sterilisation) however, it was said that she was having a sexual relationship. In the Court of Appeal Lord Donaldson stated:

Re F (Mental Patient: Sterilisation) (1990)[103]

Lord Donaldson MR: The particular problem in this case arises out of a relationship F has formed with another patient, P. This is of a sexual nature and probably involves sexual intercourse or something close to it on about two occasions a month . . . There is no evidence of distress or distaste on the part of F. It is probable that she obtains some physical enjoyment. When asked what has happened she replies, 'Nice'. Dr McDonald does not regard P as having the state of mind to make him criminally liable and Dr McDonald certainly does not regard what is happening as sexual molestation. Professor Bicknell made the point that F is quite strong willed and if she does not want something she will not have it. Therefore, whilst there is no direct evidence whether F is a purely passive participant or obtains active enjoyment, I incline to the latter view. There is also evidence that F enjoys a cuddle with those with whom she has some bond. The attitude of F's carers to her relationship with P has been neither to encourage nor discourage it. Although there has been some criticism that this is equivocal, it is, in my judgment, entirely understandable and appropriate.

Some may argue that F needed protecting from this just as much as Jeanette may have needed protecting from sexual exploitation. However, too much 'protection' may interfere with the right to a private life, which, for example, is protected by Article 8 of the European Convention on Human Rights. Many legal mechanisms and social conventions allow competent individuals a considerable measure of privacy. It is generally accepted that mentally impaired people should be afforded similar access to privacy and the means to enjoy pleasurable intimate activities as far as is possible.[104] At least, this is accepted in principle, the practical considerations of providing the necessary facilities are less well worked out. This was acknowledged in Re F by Lord Donaldson MR, p 9: 'There has been a shift from the paternalistic to a much freer approach. Mentally handicapped people have the same needs, feelings and longings as other people, and this is much more frequently acknowledged nowadays than years ago.'

It was argued by the Official Solicitor that the proper course of action was to put an end to the relationship with P, but surely it would have been wrong to deny F the opportunity of sexual enjoyment simply as a contraceptive measure, as this would have been treating her differently from people deemed to have capacity. The desirability of sterilisation as opposed to other forms of contraception, however, does not follow from the desirability of allowing this woman a degree of sexual freedom. What does follow from the case of Re F is that there was a real risk of pregnancy from a sexual relationship which, it appeared, was pleasurable and non-exploitative. The question of obtaining the consent of P (on the assumption that he may have been able to give consent) to the use of contraception, or even vasectomy, was not raised. If P was not capable of consenting, would sterilisation of him have been in his best interests? The decision in Re A (Mental Patient Sterilisation)[105] was anticipated by Douglas, G, in Law, Fertility and Reproduction.[106]

The case concerned A, a 28-year-old Down's syndrome man, who was described as being on the borderline of significant and severe impairment. Although he was supervised by his mother at

---

103   [1990] 2 AC 1at p 9.
104   See, for example, O'Brien, J and Tyne, A, The Principle of Normalisation, London: Campaign for Mentally Handicapped People, 1981.
105   [2000] 1 FLR 549.
106   London: Sweet & Maxwell, 1991.

the time of the application to the court, she was concerned that if her ill health meant that he had to go and live in local authority accommodation, he might have a sexual relationship and would not be able to understand the possible consequences, or cope with them if and when they occurred. The mother applied for a declaration that a vasectomy was in his best interests. There was evidence that the man was sexually aware, but the judge refused the declaration. The Court of Appeal rejected the appeal, holding that male sterilisation on non-therapeutic grounds was not in his best interests. The fact of the birth of a child or disapproval of his conduct would have little effect on him. A further application could be made if he was moved to local authority accommodation and his freedom was unacceptably curtailed to avoid the risk of him fathering a child. However, it was said that, in such circumstances, the likely outcome would be that the female concerned would be subject to extra supervision, rather than him. The Court of Appeal might have gone on to say that the female concerned would probably find herself the subject of court proceedings relating to her own sterilisation. From the point of view of sexual equality, the contrast between this and the female sterilisation cases might give rise to an accusation of unfairness, but doubtless on the application of the best interests test, the decision in ReA is correct.

A difficulty which does arise in this context is that, under s 7 of the Sexual Offences Act 1956, it is an offence to have sexual intercourse with a mental defective (defined as someone with severe impairment of intelligence and social functioning). This may well place obstacles in the way of the sexual liberation of mentally impaired people. It is suggested that the offence, codified over 40 years ago, does not reflect the changes in attitude towards the 'normalisation' of impaired people alluded to above.

Some other sterilisation cases merit attention. In Re W (A Mental Patient) (Sterilisation)[107] Hollis J authorised a sterilisation operation in circumstances where there was no evidence that the woman was involved in any sexual activity. In Re P (A Minor) (Wardship: Sterilisation),[108] the application was in respect of a 17-year-old girl, who was described as having the intellectual development of a six-year-old, but with 'normal' sexual libido. Evidence suggested that she was likely to improve in the development of her 'social' skills. It was also said that pregnancy would be disastrous for her because she would be unlikely agree to an abortion, and to take the child away from her would cause her great distress as she had some maternal feelings. Similarly, in Re X (Adult Patient: Sterilisation),[109] in the case of a severely mentally disabled 31-year-old woman, it was found to be in her best interests to be sterilised when she expressed her desire to have a baby, and had a boyfriend. In B, it will be recalled, the fact that Jeanette had no maternal feelings was of some importance. We are now faced with a situation where the presence of maternal feelings is still disastrous. The question again arises: were these two women being treated the same as women with capacity? An important factor in the case of P was that the type of operation proposed was considered to be reversible. If it was clear that pregnancy would be a disaster, what was the significance of reversibility, if it was not to regard the surgical procedure in the same light as contraceptive measures?

In Re S (Medical Treatment: Adult Sterilisation),[110] Johnson J refused to grant a declaration that it would be lawful to sterilise a 22-year-old woman. Although it was contended that she was vulnerable to sexual exploitation, the judge regarded this as a 'speculative' risk. The invasive procedure of sterilisation with its attendant risk of fatality could not be justified without an identifiable risk of pregnancy. In Re SL (Adult Patient) (Medical Treatment),[111] the Court of Appeal upheld an appeal against a declaration that it would be lawful to carry out a hysterectomy on a patient when there was a less

---

107 [1993] 1 FLR 381.
108 [1989] 1 FLR 182.
109 [1998] 2 FLR 1124.
110 [1998] 1 FLR 944.
111 [2000] 2 FCR 452.

invasive alternative available. It should also be noted in this case that, although the trial judge had found that there was an identifiable risk of pregnancy, in the Court of Appeal this was doubted by Dame Butler-Sloss P. Certainly, the risk in *SL* was 'speculative' and not identifiable, as the woman concerned was still living at home with her mother who carefully supervised her, and whose concerns were all about what might happen in the future.

In *Re F*, Lord Bridge had suggested (at p 52) that doctors may be under a duty to carry out a sterilisation operation, even for what we have described as 'non-therapeutic' reasons, if it was in the best interests of the patient. What is to be made of this suggestion? It is arguable that this could never be the case in respect of non-therapeutic sterilisations, in that the doctor's duty arises from the therapeutic context only.

Finally, it should be noted that failure to consider whether hysterectomies performed on two mentally incapacitated patients were in their best interests has resulted in a finding of serious misconduct by the General Medical Council: *Pembrey v GMC*.[112]

4.5.4 Sterilisation to manage menstruation – therapeutic or non-therapeutic?

In *Re Eve*[113] it was said:

> **La Forest J**: I should perhaps add ... that sterilisation may, on occasion, be necessary as an adjunct to treatment of a serious malady, but I would underline that this, of course, does not allow for subterfuge or for treatment of some marginal medical problem ... The recent British Columbia case of *Re K* (1985) 19 DLR (4th) 255, is at best dangerously close to the limits of the permissible.

The case of *Re K* concerned the authorisation of a sterilisation operation on a child to prevent menstruation occurring because the child had an aversion to blood. There have been several other cases where sterilisation has been advocated as a suitable way of managing menstruation. For example in *Re E (A Minor) (Medical Treatment)*[114] and *Re GF (Medical Treatment)*[115] hysterectomies were authorised in both cases where the women, described as severely handicapped, suffered from excessively heavy periods. In *Re E*, the proposed sterilisation was in respect of a 17-year-old girl. Sir Stephen Brown P held that since it was for therapeutic reasons and not to achieve sterilisation, the parents could consent to the operation, and there was no need for the intervention of the court. In *Re GF*, the woman was an adult. Again, Sir Stephen Brown referred to the therapeutic nature of the procedure, stating that, because of this, there was no need for a declaration as to its lawfulness. It is submitted that the removal of court protection in this way is wrong. It was suggested earlier in this chapter that the therapeutic/non-therapeutic distinction may not always protect the person lacking capacity. Sterilisations carried out for the purposes of 'menstrual management' do achieve sterilisation, even if this was not the purpose. To remove the need for an order of the court is to deny the person valuable protection from non-therapeutic sterilisations being carried out under the guise of 'therapeutic' purposes.

The dangers of such operations being used for non-medical reasons have been considered by Natasha Cica:

---

112 [2003] UKPC 60.
113 [1986] 2 SCR 388.
114 [1991] 2 FLR 585.
115 [1992] 1 FLR 293.

Cica, N, 'Sterilising the intellectually disabled'[116]

Care must . . . be taken in defining when performing a hysterectomy to prevent menstruation may be considered to be 'therapeutic'. It is submitted that four broad principles should govern this category of sterilisation.

1   The procedure should only be described as therapeutic if performed to alleviate or prevent a recognised clinical condition. Merely 'hygienic' purposes should, for the reasons discussed above, be classified as non-therapeutic. The recognised clinical condition may be a physical condition such as a disorder whose symptoms include excessively heavy or painful periods. Or it may be a psychiatric or psychological condition, in which case 'mere' distress or embarrassment would seem to be insufficient. The distress or disturbance suffered by the woman must be sufficiently serious to pose an identifiable danger to her mental health. Again this is necessary to ensure that the woman's best social interests are not confused with her best medical interests. . . .

2   Such a procedure will only be 'therapeutic' if the clinically recognised condition is already present or is virtually certain to arise in the near future. There must be a 'real possibility' that the condition will arise. The less imminent the clinical condition whose treatment is sought by hysterectomy, the more likely the physical, psychiatric or psychological state of the intellectually disabled woman will change and that hysterectomy will not be required.

3   A hysterectomy will only be 'therapeutic' if it is *necessary* for the above purposes, in that it is a treatment of 'last resort'. There must be no alternative, less invasive treatment which would effectively alleviate the condition. The harm done must be proportionate to the risk of harm avoided. Brennan J's notion of 'proportionality' is clearly the guiding principle here.

4   There must be advice from appropriately qualified medical experts that the above conditions are satisfied. Where the health-threatening condition is psychiatric or psychological, expert advice must be given by an appropriately qualified psychiatrist or psychologist. The expert opinions of general practitioners and gynaecologists alone would be insufficient in such cases.

A proposed hysterectomy was declared to be lawful in the case of Re ZM and OS (Sterilisation: Patient's Best Interests),[117] where it was required to be carried out for both contraceptive purposes and for the elimination of menstruation which was painful and caused her great embarrassment. The woman was aged 19, born with Down's syndrome and about to move into a residential unit to achieve more independence. She also had a boyfriend. The procedure was said to be in her best interests, as her periods brought her nothing but pain and discomfort, she would be incapable of looking after a child, and pregnancy and childbirth and the removal of the child would be a catastrophe, as would the emotional and psychological consequences of an abortion.

4.5.5 Abortion and contraception

It was stated in Re SG (A Patient)[118] that the provisions of the Abortion Act 1967 are an adequate safeguard for an incapable woman, and there is no need of court authorisation. It is submitted that they are not. In addition, assuming that the woman (although incapable) has expressed a wish to have the child, there is something highly distasteful

See Chapter
8

116   (1993) 1 Med L Rev 186, p 198.
117   [2000] 1 FLR 523.
118   [1993] 4 Med LR 75.

about forcing her to submit to an abortion. Whilst there may be many occasions when an abortion will be the best course of action for an incapable woman, it is suggested that the vigilance necessary in cases of sterilisation should be present when considering the performance of an abortion.[119]

In *Re SS (Adult: Medical Treatment)*,[120] the court had to consider the case of an adult woman who suffered from schizophrenia and who was detained under the MHA 1983. She was 24 weeks pregnant. Her application to the court sought two declarations: first, that she lacked the capacity to make a decision about the termination of her pregnancy; and, secondly, that it was in her best interests. It was accepted by the Official Solicitor, on her behalf, that she lacked decision-making capacity. As will be seen in Chapter 8, 24 weeks is a significant time in the duration of a pregnancy. Unless certain special conditions apply, terminations cannot take place after this time. Having a termination at such a late time entailed going into labour and giving birth to the unviable foetus. Other factors which were considered relevant by the court were: the woman had already had four children, three of whom lived with the father, the fourth had been given up for adoption; the child would be of mixed race and therefore more difficult to place for adoption; she had expressed a desire for a termination and believed the child to be dead. One psychiatrist who had examined her had to consider the provisions of the Abortion Act 1967 (as amended) and weigh up the likely effect of the baby being removed at birth against the termination of the pregnancy, and concluded that it was not clear that a termination was in her best interests. Another psychiatrist, instructed by the Official Solicitor reported that the woman had said that she would kill herself if she did not have a termination. The woman's responsible medical officer (under the MHA 1983) considered the matter to be so finely balanced that he did not feel he could express an opinion one way or the other. Wall J held that the correct approach was to assess the various risks but, in this case, because the evidence of the medical experts did not come down on one side or another, then it followed that it could not be said that a termination was in her best interests. It was also said that, because the problem of terminating late pregnancies could arise frequently in psychiatric hospitals, each hospital should have a protocol for dealing with them. Two observations can be made. First, it would have been a late termination, that is, later than 24 weeks, and, therefore, different considerations apply as far as complying with the Abortion Act 1967 is concerned. Secondly, the woman had decided that she wanted a termination. Although lacking capacity, her views should be taken into account. If the other matters are finely balanced, there is some merit in saying that her wishes should tilt the balance.

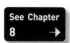

4.5.6 The Mental Capacity Act 2005 to the rescue?

We have already suggested that the safeguards within the Mental Capacity Act might not be tough enough to protect vulnerable people from exploitation. We have also highlighted public disquiet about highly sensitive decisions being made about medical treatment and personal welfare behind the closed doors of the Court of Protection.

It is pertinent therefore, to refer to a recent case where Bodey J was critical of a local authority who wanted a married woman aged 29 with an IQ of 53 to be sedated, taken from her home and have contraception imposed on her against her will. The woman had already had two children that had been taken into care and the local authority did not believe that she (with or without her husband) was capable of developing the necessary 'parenting skills'.

---

119 See, eg, the remarks of Lord Donaldson MR in the Court of Appeal in *Re F (Mental Patient: Sterilisation)* [1990] 2 AC 1 at 19.
120 [2002] 1 FCR 73.

A Local Authority v Mrs A, by her Litigation Friend, the Official Solicitor, Mr A[121]

Bodey J:

77 It is obvious on the facts of this case, that any step towards long-term court imposed contraception by way of physical coercion, with its affinity to enforced sterilisation and shades of social engineering, would raise profound questions about state intervention in private and family life. Whilst the issue of the use of force has not been argued out at this hearing I cannot, on these facts, presently see how it could be acceptable. Following my views expressed along these lines during the hearing, the Local Authority has so formulated its claim that for the moment anyway I am only asked to declare that it would be in the interim best interests of Mrs A to have contraception, if she consents. . . .

78 . . . It is accepted by the Local Authority, that if Mrs A became pregnant, there would be a pre-birth assessment of her and Mr A, and that (whilst it may be possible to speculate) it is impossible to say now what would emerge. It might therefore be concluded that they could with much support bring up a child, or perhaps that a child might be able to be kept within the extended family. Striking a balance of advantage and disadvantage, I do not see that any order at all is justified at this point about contraception. Such an order could only be made on the basis of a gut-feeling that it would be 'kinder' to Mr and Mrs A if Mrs A were to use it, which is not in my judgment an acceptable approach. Even if there were any point in the order sought . . . I certainly do not think the court should intervene at a stage when Mr A has not yet been included in any ability-appropriate discussion or help on the contraception issue; when Mr and Mrs A have not yet had any therapeutic input as a couple about it (as recommended by Dr K), nor about their relationship generally; and when they have not yet had the chance to be helped to understand this judgment. I do not propose therefore to make any order about Mrs A's 'best interests' at this stage. If she were to become pregnant, so be it: matters would take their course in the way I have described, with a pre-birth assessment of Mr and Mrs A's joint parenting abilities and the Local Authority taking such steps on the strength of it as appeared appropriate.

Apart from the last case, all of the cases considered above are prior to the Mental Capacity Act, and some of them go back to the 1970s and 1980s so it might be said that the very real concerns and implications raised by them have gone away in more cautious, and perhaps, more enlightened times. However, the final case shows that, thanks to the developments in contraceptive techniques, less draconian measures than sterilisation might now be the norm; nevertheless, the problem and the impetus to solve it coercively (albeit often well-meaningly), remain the same.

 SELF-TEST QUESTION

The cases we have examined are all prior to the coming into force of the Mental Capacity Act 2005. Do you think that vulnerable patients are now much better protected under the new legislation?

---

121 [[2010] EWHC 1549 (Fam).

Summary of Key Points

1. Prior to the Mental Capacity Act 2005, decisions about medical treatment for adults who lacked capacity were dealt with under the common law of necessity, but this was interpreted as acting in the best interests of the patient. Those common law cases are still relevant in the interpretation of the Mental Capacity Act 2005.

2. The Mental Capacity Act embraces and develops the concept of best interests, and puts it on a statutory footing.

3. The Mental Capacity Act contains provisions (the deprivation of liberty safeguards) that are designed to protect patients, or people in residential units, who might be deprived of liberty because of their mental incapacity.

4. The best interests test can include the substituted judgment test as this forms part of the Mental Capacity Act criteria, but the *Bolam* test does not govern best interests as there can be only one course of action that is in the patient's best interests.

5. Parents can consent to treatment on behalf of their children. The Family Law Reform Act 1969 states that children of the age of 16 can consent to treatment. However, the Court of Appeal has held that until they reach the age of 18 they are still within the jurisdiction of the court, and the same Court has held that they cannot refuse treatment in circumstances where doctors and parents wish them to have it.

6. Certain forms of treatment or procedures that might be regarded as 'non-therapeutic' must be scrutinised carefully when carried out on incapable patients. We have given the control of fertility as an example.

 Further Reading

Bartlett, P, *Blackstone's Guide to the Mental Capacity Act*, 2nd edn, Oxford: OUP, 2008.

Donnelly, M, "Best interests, patient participation and the Mental Capacity Act 2005 (2009) Medical Law Review 17:1.

Elliston, S, *Best Interests of the Child in Healthcare*, New York: Routledge-Cavendish, 2007.

Jones, *Mental Capacity Act Manual*, 3rd edn, London: Sweet & Maxwell, 2008.

Ministry of Justice, Mental Capacity Act Code of Practice, 2007, London: TSO.

Chapter 5

Confidentiality, Privacy and Access to Medical Records

5.1 Confidentiality – the Duty

5.1.1 The ethical obligation

It is not only of academic interest to look at the ethical justifications for the obligation of confidence, it is also important to keep them in mind when examining the circumstances in which the obligation can be lawfully breached, and to consider whether the breaches in question can also be justified on ethical grounds.

As we have seen, the doctrine of utilitarianism assesses the ethics of a course of action on the basis that it will result in the best consequences overall. In the context of confidentiality, therefore, the obligation is justified by the utility of doctors keeping medical information secret. The argument is that if there were no assurance of secrecy, then patients would be reluctant to seek medical advice and treatment, or would be less than frank when doing so. This would, it is argued, have an adverse effect on the health of society. The argument is described by Raanan Gillon:

Gillon, R, *Philosophical Medical Ethics*[1]

Why should doctors from the time of Hippocrates to the present have promised to keep their patients' secrets? If confidentiality is not a moral good in itself what moral good does it serve? The commonest justification for the duty of medical confidentiality is undoubtedly consequentialist: people's better health, welfare, the general good, and overall happiness are more likely to be attained if doctors are fully informed by their patients, and this is more likely if doctors undertake not to disclose their patients' secrets. Conversely, if patients did not believe that doctors would keep their secrets then either they would not divulge embarrassing but potentially medically important information, thus reducing their chances of getting the best medical care, or they would disclose such information and feel anxious and unhappy at the prospect of their secrets being made known.

The utilitarian view is particularly appropriate to confidentiality as it will readily admit that the duty is not absolute and can be breached in certain circumstances. It would be argued that the breach is justified when the utility of disclosure outweighs the utility produced by keeping the confidences. As will be seen, the only legal justification at common law for disclosure is either that the patient has consented, or that it is in the public interest to disclose. The language of the public interest defence has a strong utilitarian flavour: *AG v Guardian Newspapers (No 2)*,[2] *per* Lord Goff:

Lord Goff: . . . although the basis of the law's protection of confidence is that there is a public interest that confidences should be preserved and protected by the law, nevertheless that public interest may be outweighed by some other countervailing public interest which favours disclosure.

As we have already seen, utilitarianism can be contrasted with deontological theories in which duty rather than purpose is the fundamental concept of ethics. Gillon states:

Gillon, R, *Philosophical Medical Ethics*[3]

Deontologists . . . are likely to base their arguments for confidentiality not just (if at all) on welfare considerations but also on the moral principle of respect for autonomy or sometimes on a putatively independent principle of respect for privacy, which is seen as a fundamental

---

1 Chichester: John Wiley, 1986.
2 [1990] AC 109, at 282.
3 See n 1.

moral requirement in itself. Thus, while the principle of medical confidentiality is not defended as a moral end in itself, it is defended by utilitarians and deontologists alike as a means to some morally desirable end [such as] the general welfare, respect for people's autonomy, or respect for their privacy.

Ethical issues arising around the area of confidentiality are reflected in the various ethical codes referred to in Chapter 1. The Hippocratic Oath states: '. . . all that may come to my knowledge in the exercise of my profession or outside of my profession or in daily commerce with men, which ought not to be spread abroad, I will keep secret and will never reveal.' The Declaration of Geneva contains a similar statement.

One grey area surrounds disclosure within the family, ie is a doctor breaching confidences if the disclosure is only made to a spouse? It is here that the interface between law and pragmatism reflects many of the essential difficulties of medical law. What is a doctor to do, say, when faced with a distressed spouse of a terminally ill patient? If the patient has informed the doctor that he does not wish any form of disclosure to the spouse, then although any subsequent conversations with that spouse may be difficult, it is quite clear that the doctor must refuse to discuss his patient's medical condition. However, in the absence of that express request on the part of the patient, under what principle does the doctor justify discussing the patient's medical condition with relatives of the patient? In the case of *Re S (Hospital Orders: Court's Jurisdiction*[4]), it was held that blood ties conferred no right to determine the course of treatment or care, and this would surely extend to the acquisition of confidential information. It seems that the law does not sanction such disclosure, unless one can argue that there is some form of implied or tacit consent.

See Chapter 1

5.1.1.1 The General Medical Council's guidance

The GMC issues guidance to doctors on their obligations in respect of confidentiality, and much of the guidance is co-extensive with general principles of law,[5] but it must be remembered that guidance issued by the General Medical Council (GMC) does not purport to be an account of the law. However, there is no doubt that the guidance has persuasive authority (see *W v Egdell*[6]).

5.1.2 The legal obligation of privacy and the European Convention on Human Rights

A rights-based approach might regard the duty of keeping confidences as a respect for the right to privacy. There is no right to privacy in English common law, although in practice much that is private can be protected in other ways, for example, the tort of trespass, nuisance and so on. Furthermore, the European Convention on Human Rights (ECHR), incorporated into English law by the Human Rights Act 1998, protects the right to a 'private life' (Art 8).

What is the difference between a right to privacy and a right to have confidential information protected? The law imposes a number of requirements in order for a cause of action to arise for breach of confidence, and these criteria mean that, for example, press photographers owe no duty of confidence unless the photography takes place in 'confidential circumstances', or there had been a prior agreement not to publish. If neither of these apply, only a right to privacy can offer protection from publication.

---

4   [1995] 3 All ER 290.
5   General Medical Council, *Confidentiality: Protecting and Providing Information*, London: GMC, 2009.
6   [1990] Ch 359.

Article 8 of the ECHR states:

1   Everyone has the right to respect for his private and family life, his home and his corre-
    spondence.
2   There shall be no interference by a public authority with the exercise of this right except
    such as is in accordance with the law and is necessary in a democratic society in the inter-
    ests of national security, public safety or the economic well being of the country, for the
    prevention of disorder or crime for the protection of health or morals, or for the protection
    of the rights and freedoms of others.

In Z v Finland,[7] the European Court of Human Rights stated:

The protection of personal data, not least medical data, is of fundamental importance to a
person's enjoyment of his or her right to respect for private and family life as guaranteed by
Article 8 of the Convention . . . Without such protection, those in need of medical assistance may
be deterred from revealing such information of a personal and intimate nature as may be necessary in order to receive appropriate treatment and, even, from seeking such assistance, thereby
endangering their own health and in the case of transmissible diseases, that of the community.

The facts were as follows. Mrs Z was the wife of a man who had been accused of attempted
manslaughter by raping his victims and knowingly infecting them with the HIV virus. For evidential
purposes, it was necessary to obtain evidence from Mrs Z's doctors and to obtain her medical
records. The court limited the confidentiality of the trial record to ten years, and in its judgment the
court disclosed Mrs Z's identity. It was common ground that there had been a violation of Mrs Z's
rights under Art 8; the issue for the European Court to decide was whether this could be justified
under Art 8(2). It was accepted that the court action was 'in accordance with the law' so the issue
was whether it was 'necessary in a democratic society'. The taking of evidence from the doctors and
the obtaining of the medical records was held not to breach Art 8(2). However, limiting confidentiality of the trial record to ten years was a disproportionate interference with her right and the
disclosure of her identity was not justified at all. See also I v Finland,[8] where the Court held that it was
fundamental to the right to privacy for states to take positive steps to protect medical confidentiality.
See too the case of Colak v Germany,[9] which is considered in detail below at 5.2.2.6.

In MS v Sweden,[10] medical records relating to a woman's gynaecological condition held by a
clinic had been requested by, and disclosed to, the social security department dealing with a claim
of hers for state industrial injury benefit. She had not been consulted about this, and the European
Court held that this clear breach under Art 8(1) was, nevertheless, justified under Art 8(2) on the
basis that the needs of the state (to avoid paying funds from the public purse to undeserving cases)
were for the economic well-being of the country. It is arguable, however, that it is disproportionate to obtain medical records in this way, without prior reference to the claimant. A more
appropriate way of achieving the same end would have been for such claims to be subject to the
consent of the claimant to the disclosure of all relevant medical records (the case of MS had, at least
in part, given rise to the court action because the records disclosed had contained information
about a wholly irrelevant abortion).

It might be argued that, given the protection of Art 8, the obligation of confidence is redundant. However, the language of confidentiality is still used by the courts.[11] Further, the limitation

---

7   (1998) 25 EHRR 371.
8   (2009) 48 EHRR 31.
9   (07714/01), unreported, March 2009.
10 (1997) 45 BMLR 133.
11 See eg A Health Authority v X and others [2001] EWCA Civ 2014.

placed upon Art 8 by Art 8(2) means that there will be circumstances when there can be justifica-tion for breaching Art 8 and these circumstances will frequently be analogous to the justification for breaching confidences so that the legal framework is still pertinent. In *Rose and another v Secretary of State for Health and Another*[12] the claimants, who had been conceived by artificial insemination, were seeking disclosure of non-identifying information about sperm donors and, where possible, infor-mation that would actually identify such donors. They had requested such information from the Secretary of State who had declined to provide it, and they had commenced an action for judicial review. They argued, first, that the state had an obligation to provide non-identifying information and, secondly, that the state had an obligation to establish a voluntary contact register similar to the contact register available to adopted children. Scott Baker J held that this information engaged Art 8 because such information went to the heart of their identity, and allowed the case to go forward. However, he declined to make a declaration of incompatibility under the Human Rights Act 1998, leaving it open to a court to decide on the basis of the specific facts before it. He did, however, hint strongly that because the donor semen would have been obtained under circumstances of confi-dentiality, Art 8(2) limitations would weigh heavily in the balance. A further example is the case of *R (on the application of John Wooder) v Dr Graham Fegetter and the Mental Health Act Commission*[13] where Potter LJ stated that, on the question of the patient's right to information regarding s 58 treatment under the Mental Health Act (MHA) 1983, there was no need to invoke Art 8 as the common law provides the necessary protection. See the judgments of Lords Nicholl and Waler in *OBG & anor v Allan & others*.[14]

See Chapter
1

5.1.3 The legal obligation of confidentiality

The law of the obligation to keep confidences is not easy to categorise. It is sometimes regarded as an application of equitable principles, sometimes as belonging to the law of tort and/or contract. There is no doubt that the obligation may arise under the law of contract, either expressly or impliedly, but it is clear that it is wider than that. Certainly, as far as medicine is concerned, if it were contract-based only, there would be no legal obligation to keep confidences within the context of National Health Service treatment.[15] There has been much academic debate on the subject:

Gurry, F, *In Breach of Confidence*[16]

The jurisdictional basis of the action for breach of confidence has been a source of lingering uncertainty and controversy. Contract, equity and property have at different times each provided the basis on which the courts have granted relief. In some cases, a mixture of these bases has been relied on. Thus, in *Alperton Rubber Co v Manning* Peterson J referred to the defendant's conduct as 'a breach of trust or confidence, and . . . a breach of the implied provi-sion in all contracts of service that the employee will observe the rules of honesty'; and, in *Prince Albert v Strange*, the court founded the defendants' liability first on property, secondly on a 'breach of trust, confidence or contract'.

The lack of clarity in the law led to a Law Commission inquiry which reported in 1981.[17] The Commission made a number of recommendations, the principal one being that there be a new statutory tort of breach of confidence. No government action has ever been taken on this.

---

12 (2003) 69 BMLR 83.
13 [2002] EWCA Civ 554.
14 [2007] UKHL 21.
15 See *Pfizer Corp v Ministry of Health* [1965] AC 512.
16 Oxford: Clarendon Press, 1984.
17 Law Commission, *Breach of Confidence*, Report No 110, Cmnd 8388, London: HMSO, 1981.

The obligation of confidence, whatever its origin, although not absolute, is free standing, in that the preservation of confidence itself is in the public interest and therefore an end in itself. However, it can conflict with other matters of public interest. It is important to stress that when conflicts arise, they are conflicts between two competing public interests, not between private and public interests:

Scott, R, 'Introduction', in Clarke, L (ed), *Confidentiality and the Law*[18]

The law of confidentiality, like the law of negligence and the law of nuisance, requires a balance to be struck. The balance will, on both sides, involve public and private interests. The newspapers that wanted to publish extracts from *Spycatcher* had private commercial interest in doing so. But there was also a public interest in freedom of speech. On the other side there was a public interest in the protection of the secrets of the security service (no private interest since the litigant was the Government). In the *Francome* case, the plaintiff had a private interest in maintaining the privacy of his telephone conversations but, ranged on the same side, there was a public interest that private telephone conversations should not be the subject of eavesdropping. On the other side, the *Daily Mirror* could rely, in aid of its own private interest, on the public interest in the disclosure of alleged wrongdoing. These are examples to make the point that every case where the law of confidentiality is invoked requires the judge to strike a balance between competing interests.

The essential elements of the law of confidentiality can be summarised by the statement in *AG v Guardian Newspapers* (No 2),[19] per Lord Goff:

Lord Goff: I start with the broad general principle (which I do not intend in any way to be definitive) that a duty of confidence arises when confidential information comes to the knowledge of a person (the confidant) in circumstances where he has notice, or is held to have agreed, that the information is confidential, with the effect that it would be just in all the circumstances that he should be precluded from disclosing the information to others . . .

[In addition to] this broad general principle, there are three limiting principles to which I wish to refer. The first limiting principle (which is rather an expression of the scope of the duty) is highly relevant to this appeal. It is that the principle of confidentiality only applies to information to the extent that it is confidential. In particular, once it has entered what is usually called the public domain (which means no more than that the information in question is so generally accessible that, in all the circumstances, it cannot be regarded as confidential) then, as a general rule, the principle of confidentiality can have no application to it . . .

The second limiting principle is that the duty of confidence applies neither to useless information, nor to trivia . . .

The third limiting principle is of far greater importance. It is that, although the basis of the law's protection of confidence is that there is a public interest that confidences should be preserved and protected by the law, nevertheless that public interest may be outweighed by some other countervailing public interest which favours disclosure.

In *Douglas v Hello Ltd*[20] Sedley LJ said (at 1001) that developments in privacy law mean that the new approach to confidentiality focusses upon the protection of human autonomy and dignity.

---

18 London: LLP, 1990.
19 [1990] AC 109, pp 281–82.
20 [2001] QB 967.

There can be no doubt that the doctor–patient relationship gives rise to an obligation of confidence which fits clearly into the criteria applied generally in the law. Hunter v Mann[21] confirmed such an obligation which was reiterated in AG v Guardian Newspapers (No 2)[22], per Lord Keith:

> **Lord Keith**: The law has long recognised that an obligation of confidence can arise out of particular relationships. Examples are the relationships of doctor and patient, priest and penitent, solicitor and client, banker and customer.

The uncontroversial nature of the obligation, therefore, means that generally problems will only arise when decisions have to be made which will breach the obligation and whether the breach can be justified. Indeed, it may be said that the doctor's duty of confidence is over-determined in that it stems both from the quality of the information and from the circumstances in which it is acquired, each of which is independently sufficient. It follows that, although not usually the subject of litigation, there may be difficulties, first, if the information is not *medical* information and, secondly, if it has been imparted in circumstances other than a doctor–patient consultation.

5.1.3.1 The confidential information

The law on confidentiality will protect a variety of types of information, imparted in a variety of different situations. Information acquired in the confidential circumstances of an employment relationship, for example, will be protected, as will that acquired in the course of an intimate domestic relationship. The latter need not be a marriage, nor even a heterosexual relationship. This was examined in the case of Stephens v Avery,[23] where it was held that information relating to sexual conduct (in that case, a lesbian relationship) could be the subject of a legally enforceable duty of confidentiality.

The case of Campbell v Mirror Group Newspapers Ltd[24] is a good illustration of the way in which 'medical confidentiality' can be wider than that which is engendered in the private consultations between health care professionals and patients. Naomi Campbell, a well-known 'supermodel' brought an action against a newspaper that published photographs of her leaving a clinic where she had been receiving treatment, on the basis that this was a breach of her Art 8 right to privacy under the European Convention. The newspaper argued that prohibition of publication breached Art 10 of the Convention ie freedom of expression. Publication was necessary, it was argued, because she had previously denied having a drug problem, and the photographs showed this to have been a lie. By a majority, the House of Lords found that her privacy had been unjustifiably infringed.

Campbell v Mirror Group Newspapers Ltd[25]

Lord Hope:

Was the information confidential?

88 The information contained in the article consisted of the following five elements: (1) the fact that Miss Campbell was a drug addict; (2) the fact that she was receiving treatment for her addiction; (3) the fact that the treatment which she was receiving was provided by Narcotics Anonymous; (4) details of the treatment—for how long, how frequently and at what times of day she had been receiving it, the nature of it and extent of her commitment to the process; and (5) a visual portrayal by means of photographs of her when she was leaving the place where treatment had been taking place.

---

21 [1974] QB 767.
22 [1990] AC 109, at p 255.
23 [1988] Ch 449.
24 [2004] 2 AC 457.
25 [2004] 2 AC 457, at p 481.

89 The trial judge drew the line between the first two and the last three elements. Mr Caldecott for Miss Campbell said that he was content with this distinction. So the fact that she was a drug addict was open to public comment in view of her denials, although he maintained that this would normally be treated as a medical condition that was entitled to protection. He accepted that the fact that she was receiving treatment for the condition was not in itself intrusive in this context. Moreover disclosure of this fact in itself could not harm her therapy. But he said that the line was crossed as soon as details of the nature and frequency of the treatment were given, especially when these details were accompanied by a covertly taken photograph which showed her leaving one of the places where she had been undertaking it. This was an area of privacy where she was entitled to be protected by an obligation of confidence . . .

98 Where the person is suffering from a condition that is in need of treatment one has to try, in order to assess whether the disclosure would be objectionable, to put oneself into the shoes of a reasonable person who is in need of that treatment. Otherwise the exercise is divorced from its context. The fact that no objection could be taken to disclosure of the first two elements in the article does not mean that they must be left out of account in a consideration as to whether disclosure of the other elements was objectionable. The article must be read as a whole along with the photographs to give a proper perspective to each element. The context was that of a drug addict who was receiving treatment. It is her sensibilities that needed to be taken into account. Critical to this exercise was an assessment of whether disclosure of the details would be liable to disrupt her treatment. It does not require much imagination to appreciate the sense of unease that disclosure of these details would be liable to engender, especially when they were accompanied by a covertly taken photograph. The message that it conveyed was that somebody, somewhere, was following her, was well aware of what was going on and was prepared to disclose the facts to the media. I would expect a drug addict who was trying to benefit from meetings to discuss her problem anonymously with other addicts to find this distressing and highly offensive . . .

124 Any person in Miss Campbell's position, assuming her to be of ordinary sensibilities but assuming also that she had been photographed surreptitiously outside the place where she been receiving therapy for drug addiction, would have known what they were and would have been distressed on seeing the photographs. She would have seen their publication, in conjunction with the article which revealed what she had been doing when she was photographed and other details about her engagement in the therapy, as a gross interference with her right to respect for her private life. In my opinion this additional element in the publication is more than enough to outweigh the right to freedom of expression which the defendants are asserting in this case.

Conclusion

125 Despite the weight that must be given to the right to freedom of expression that the press needs if it is to play its role effectively, I would hold that there was here an infringement of Miss Campbell's right to privacy that cannot be justified. In my opinion publication of the third, fourth and fifth elements in the article (see para 88) was an invasion of that right for which she is entitled to damages. I would allow the appeal and restore the orders that were made by the trial judge.

Information concerning the sexual conduct of a patient, if imparted to a doctor in circumstances of confidentiality, will be protected, even though it is not medical information. The Court of Appeal decision in R v Wilson[26] raises this issue. In that case, the defendant appealed against a

---

26 [1996] 3 WLR 125.

conviction for actual bodily harm under s 47 of the Offences Against the Person Act 1861. He had been charged as a result of marking his wife's buttocks with his initials by use of a hot knife. This was done with her consent and, it appeared from the case reports, at her specific request. Although the appeal was concerned with the applicability of the decision in R v Brown,[27] the implications for medical confidentiality arise from the fact that the matter appears to have come to the attention of the police from a report made to them by her doctor, who became aware of the marks during the course of a medical examination.[28]

If the police were informed of this by the doctor, without the consent of the woman concerned, then here was a potential breach of confidentiality. The fact that the information was not strictly medical would not protect the doctor because, first, on the basis of Stephens v Avery, it has the necessary quality of confidence and, secondly, it was imparted in the circumstances of a medical consultation.

In R v Department of Health ex p Source Informatics Ltd,[29] the Court of Appeal had to decide whether disclosure of patient information which had been anonymised breached the obligation of confidence. The company had obtained anonymised patient data from pharmacists and doctors which had been extracted from prescription forms. The information was used to create a database for the use of pharmaceutical companies. The Department of Health produced guidance which stated that disclosure of anonymised patient information still amounted to a breach of confidence. Source Informatics challenged this by way of judicial review. The judge at first instance took the view that the Department of Health was correct. However, the Court of Appeal allowed the appeal, stating that the touchstone as to whether there has been a breach of confidence is the 'conscience' of the discloser. Arguably, as Fennell points out,[30] it is correct that there is no breach, but the reason is that it is not against the patients' interests and not something to do with the good faith on the part of the discloser. Note that, in 1997, the Department of Health published On the Review of Patient-Identifiable Information (the 'Caldicott Report'),[31] which made a number of recommendations on how to safeguard confidentiality by the anonymisation of the information, and which provides for so-called 'Caldicott guardians' within the NHS to supervise and take responsibility for information systems.

5.1.3.2 The circumstances in which the information is acquired

It may be that it is not clear that the circumstances are such as to amount to 'confidential' circumstances. The inadvertent acquisition of information which clearly has the necessary quality of confidence about it, binds the recipient; see Lord Goff's judgment in AG v Guardian Newspapers (No 2).[32]

The case of R v Wilson is, again, interesting in relation to this point, as it raises the possibility of a doctor being obliged towards a third party when he acquires confidential information in the context of a medical consultation:

Wheat, K, 'Can paternalism ever justify a breach of confidence?'[33]

Extension of duty
Another difficult question raised to which there is no clear answer is the position of the husband of the patient in this case. Could it be argued that the doctor owed him a duty of confidence? Further, would it make any difference if he were also a patient of the doctor? To look at the

---

27 [1993] 2 All ER 75.
28 See (1996) The Times, 5 March and (1996) The Guardian, March, p 5.
29 [2000] 1 All ER 786.
30 (2000) 8 Med L Rev 155.
31 London: Department of Health, 1997.
32 [1990] AC 109, at p 282.
33 (1997) 3(3) Health Care Risk Report 12.

latter question first, if the doctor–patient relationship is to make any difference, then it must be the case that the duty extends to any information obtained about a patient which has the necessary quality of confidence.

It cannot be said with any degree of certainty that this reflects the legal position. Gurry, for example, says that, although the duty is not limited to information acquired directly from the patient but extends to information from other sources, that further information must have been picked up by the doctor by way of his or her position as the patient's doctor. Kennedy and Grubb interpret this as extending to information obtained from third parties who know of the doctor–patient relationship, but pass no comment as to whether it would extend to non-medical information.

Here, the information would not have been obtained by the doctor by virtue of his status as the patient's doctor, but as another patient's doctor, and, although the third party here, namely the wife, would have known about the doctor–patient relationship, the information was not of a medical nature. Given the difficulties, therefore, in arguing that the duty owed is a duty owed *qua* doctor, perhaps it is open to the husband to rely upon the general law of confidentiality and a duty owed to him regardless of him being a patient of the doctor concerned.

. . .

Elements of a breach of confidence action
[Referring to the *Guardian* criteria] [t]here is no difficulty in satisfying the first limb of the test as the information concerned intimate details of a sexual relationship, which will possess the necessary quality of confidence. As to the second limb, although a consultation between doctor and patient will usually impart an obligation of confidence, it is arguable that the circumstances only impart the obligation by the doctor towards the patient . . .

If it is clear from its nature that information is confidential, then a third party should be bound by it (see *Saltman Engineering v Campbell Engineering*[34]), so it is hard to see how the fact that it is not acquired by chance, but in the context of another, different set of confidential circumstances should make any difference.

 SELF-TEST QUESTION

What are the essential differences between the legal concepts of privacy and confidentiality?

5.1.4 Statutory obligations of confidence

Good, utilitarian, public health arguments can sometimes justify a specific emphasis on confidentiality via statutory means. An example of this is contained within the National Health Service (Venereal Disease) Regulations 1974 SI 1974/29:

National Health Service (Venereal Disease) Regulations 1974 SI 1974/29

Confidentiality of information

2   Every NHS Trust . . . shall take all necessary steps to secure that any information capable of identifying an individual obtained with respect to persons examined or treated for any sexually transmitted disease shall not be disclosed except:

---

34 [1963] 3 All ER 413.

(a) for the purpose of communicating that information to a medical practitioner or to a person employed under the direction of a medical practitioner in connection with the treatment of persons suffering from such disease or the prevention of the spread thereof; and

(b) for the purpose of such treatment or prevention.

Kennedy and Grubb comment as follows:

Kennedy, I and Grubb, A, *Medical Law*[35]

This regulation was introduced so as to give statutory emphasis to the obligation of confidence in this area of medical practice.

. . .

A small, but important, point to notice is that the obligation of confidence under the Regulations applies to any disease which is 'sexually transmitted'. If this is so, a patient who is HIV positive may need to look to the common law for protection of his confidence if he became infected by some other means as, for example, if he is a haemophiliac or has otherwise become HIV positive as a result of an infected blood donation. Alternatively a 'sexually transmitted disease' within the Regulations could be said to be one usually transmitted through sexual contact but which may be transmitted by other means. Blood, for example, may be infected with syphilis and transfused into someone who then develops the disease. The disease remains a 'sexually transmitted disease'. On this analysis HIV infection would be within the Regulations regardless of the means of infection. (See *X v Y* [1988] RPC 379, in which Rose J assumes the latter to be the case.)

5.1.5 Incapable patients and confidentiality

5.1.5.1 Children

The ability of children to consent to medical treatment was dealt with in Chapters 3 and 4. The leading case is *Gillick v West Norfolk and Wisbech AHA*,[36] and it is important to remember that this case was about confidentiality as well as consent. It will be recalled that Mrs Gillick objected to a DHSS circular which stated that a doctor, acting in good faith, would not be acting unlawfully if he prescribed contraceptives to a girl under the age of 16 and that, exceptionally, this could be done without informing the child's parents, as the principle of confidentiality applied between a doctor and a patient under the age of 16.

See Chapter 4

As we have seen, the *Gillick* case has been subject to a number of interpretations by the Court of Appeal which have sought to limit its application to one of protection for doctors acting in good faith, rather than an assertion of a child's right to self-determination when he has the necessary capacity. Although these later cases (*Re R (A Minor) (Wardship: Medical Treatment)*[37] and *Re W (A Minor) (Medical Treatment)*[38]) were not about confidentiality, they have implications for this area of medical law. In *Re R*, Lord Donaldson said at p 186:

Lord Donaldson: . . . the judges treated *Gillick*'s case as deciding that a '*Gillick* competent' child has a right to refuse treatment. In this I consider that they were in error. Such a child can consent, but if he or she declines to do so or refuses, consent can be given by someone else

---

35 London: Butterworths, 2000.
36 [1986] AC 112.
37 [1991] 4 All ER 177.
38 [1992] 4 All ER 627.

who has parental rights or responsibilities. The failure or refusal of the 'Gillick competent' child is a very important factor in the doctor's decision whether or not to treat, but does not prevent the necessary consent being obtained from another competent source.

The clear implication of this interpretation is that a doctor, faced with a refusal of medical treatment by a child, is entitled to seek consent from a parent or someone in loco parentis. Suppose, however, the child consents to treatment, but requests that his parents are not informed? Two views can be taken of the implications for confidentiality of Lord Donaldson's interpretation of Gillick. The doctor is protected if, in good faith, he respects the child's confidence, and he cannot have a duty to disclose. If, however, the doctor discloses the matter to the child's parents (let us say, in the course of another consultation), then, one view of Lord Donaldson's interpretation is that he will not be in breach of any duty of confidence owed to the child, because the child's consent to treatment was not based on child autonomy, but on the provision of a 'flak jacket' of legal immunity for the doctor. In other words, the obligation of confidence would be modified in exactly the same way as is the requirement that there be a valid consent. The second view would be that the doctor should respect the child's request, as breaching confidentiality serves no purpose in relation to securing treatment. The latter view is to be preferred, being more consistent with the ethic of confidentiality.

However, if one takes a true autonomy view of Gillick, that is, that a child may be capable of making decisions about medical treatment so that he can refuse rather than consent, then it must be the case that he is entitled to respect of his medical confidences. It may be argued that the doctor is still under an obligation to inform his parents of what is happening because, although the parents will not be responsible for the consequences of medical treatment which they may have opposed if they had been given the opportunity, they will still have general parental responsibility for the child. On the other hand, it was clear from Gillick that some duty of confidentiality was owed. It is no explanation to say, without more, that it depends on the nature of the treatment, because capacity to consent depends upon the understanding by the child of that particular treatment. However, the nature of the treatment may mean there are circumstances where a child is deemed to have sufficient understanding to, say, consent to an abortion. In consequence, even if this conflicts with parental opinion it may be necessary for the parents to be informed of the refusal, and the reasons for it, to enable them to continue to act as parents.

In the context of confidentiality, it is tempting to take the view that Gillick was special on its facts, that is, contraceptive advice, and that there was a strong element of policy in the decision, to avoid teenage pregnancies, and that the Gillick view on consent to other forms of medical treatment and advice would not usually involve a co-extensive view on confidentiality. Jonathan Montgomery comments on the situation in the USA:

Montgomery, J, 'Confidentiality and the immature minor'[39]

The American position
American litigation in the field of birth control and abortion for minors proceeds by considering the extent of constitutional rights to privacy. In *Bellotti v Baird* 443 US 662 (1979) the court was asked to strike down a statute requiring parental consent before a minor was entitled to an abortion. Such a statute, said Powell J in giving the judgment of the court, could not be constitutional because it allowed an agency external to the minor herself to have a veto. A permissible system could be built around the 'mature minor rule'. Under that rule, a girl could go to

---

39 [1987] Fam Law 10.

court in order to have the abortion authorised. If she can prove herself sufficiently mature to take the decision herself, the court will automatically uphold her autonomy. If she cannot prove this, but can show that it would be in her best interests to have the abortion, the court must authorise the procedure. Otherwise the court has a discretion. In these latter circumstances the court may decide that it will be in the best interests of the child to inform her parents.

This position is similar to that which now prevails in English law. It differs in that the person who must decide whether the minor is sufficiently mature to take her own decision is, in this country, a doctor and not a judge. Powell J also considered the issue of confidentiality for the immature minor. He held that the Massachusetts statute before him was only constitutionally valid because under it 'every pregnant minor is entitled in the first instance to go directly to the court for a judicial determination without prior parental notice, consultation or consent' (443 US 662, p 649). Translated into the English context, this would mean that a minor is entitled to approach his or her doctor to have that person determine her capacity to consent to the medical procedures without her parents being informed. If she is found not to have that capacity, she must choose between not receiving the treatment or telling her parents, but that is 'her choice, not the doctor's'.

The general principles enunciated in *Gillick* were revisited in *R (on the application of Sue Axon) v Secretary of State for Health and the Family Planning Association.*[40] In 2004 the Department of Health issued guidance to health care professionals on giving advice and treatment to people under the age of 16 on sexual matters, including contraception, sexually transmitted diseases and abortion. The guidance provided that in cases where the young person was able to understand the advice and its implications but could not be persuaded to notify his or her parents or let the medical professional notify them, then such advice would remain confidential as long as the young person's physical or mental health would not be likely to suffer and the provision of the advice or treatment was in his or her best interests. The guidance also recommended that doctors follow the criteria set out by Lord Fraser in *Gillick*.

The applicant parent in this case sought judicial review on the basis that the guidance was unlawful because people under the age of 16 were not owed the same duty of confidentiality as those over 16, and that there was a breach of Art 8 of the European Convention that protects private life.

Silber J held that there could not be any exception to the duty of confidence owed to a young person as suggested by the applicant. It was important to recognise that, on the whole, a parent was the best person for guiding and advising a young person under the age of 16, that parents had a duty to protect their children, and that secrecy was destructive of family life, but it was also the case that those factors do not override the duty of confidentiality owed. In consequence there was no infringement of the Art 8(1) rights of a young person's parents, and even if there was, such interference could be justified under Art 8(2).

5.1.5.2 Incapable adults

The sensitive issues surrounding medical decision-making on behalf of incapable adults has been examined in Chapter 4. Generally, decisions can be taken, and treatment administered if these are in the patient's best interests. It is arguable that it will always be in the patient's best interests to respect his confidences, unless one or more of the circumstances exist in which confidence can be breached lawfully in respect of a capable adult patient.

---

40 [2006] EWHC 37 (Admin).

SELF-TEST QUESTION

Are patients who lack capacity to make decisions about medical treatment owed the same duty of confidentiality?

5.2 Confidentiality – Breaching Confidences

The duty of confidence is not absolute and there are circumstances in which medical information can be divulged. This part of the chapter will examine these circumstances.

5.2.1 Consent

It may seem trite to say that confidence can be breached with the consent of the patient, but this fell to be considered by the court in the case of C v C.[41] A doctor had refused to disclose details of the respondent's venereal disease, on the basis that it would have been in breach of his duty of confidentiality, despite the fact that both the divorcing petitioner and the respondent (that is, the patient) had requested this:

> **Lewis J**: The question which arises out of these circumstances is: is a doctor, when asked by his patient to give him or her particulars of his or her condition and illness to be used in a court of law, when those particulars are vital to the success or failure of the case, entitled to refuse and in effect to say, 'Go on with your case in the dark and I will tell you in court when I am subpoenaed what my conclusions are'? In the present case the patient asked the doctor to give her this information and asked him also to give the petitioner that same information, with the object of their being placed in a position which would enable them to know whether or not the petitioner had a case against the respondent, in other words, to assist the course of justice. It is, of course, of the greatest importance from every point of view that proper secrecy should be observed in connection with venereal disease clinics, and that nothing should be done to diminish their efficiency or to infringe the confidential relationship existing between doctor and patient. But, in my opinion, those considerations do not justify a doctor in refusing to divulge confidential information to a patient or to any named person or persons when asked by the patient so to do. In the circumstances of this case the information should have been given, and in all cases where the circumstances are similar the doctor is not guilty of any breach of confidence in giving the information asked for.

It is also important to remember that consent must be validly obtained. Given the powerful position of a doctor in the doctor–patient relationship, it is of considerable importance that the patient's consent is obtained scrupulously.

5.2.2 Public interest

Gurry, F, *In Breach of Confidence*[42]

The influence of principles based on the public interest is predominant in the action for breach of confidence. The public interest has two principal roles in the action. In the first place, since

---

41 [1946] 1 All ER 562.
42 Oxford: Clarendon Press, 1984.

it is the law of the land that confidences are enforceable obligations, it is, of course, 'in the public interest that when information is received in confidence – for a limited and restricted purpose, as it always is – it should not be used for other purposes'. The public interest requires that confidences, like contracts, 'be held sacrosanct'. In this role, the public interest operates not only in the private sector, to enforce a confider's right to preserve the confidentiality of information which he entrusts to another, but also in the public sphere, where the public interest in national security or joint ministerial responsibility may require a public official or a Cabinet minister to keep confidential information secret.

But the public interest also has an opposing role which sometimes requires that confidences be broken, and that information which the courts would otherwise protect from disclosure be released for various purposes. The opposing public interests which call for the release of confidential information may be the interests of justice itself, or the disclosure of iniquity, and, wherever such a judicially recognised opposing interest is identified it must 'be put into the scales against the public interest in preserving privacy and protecting confidential information'.

The philosopher, Richard Hare, sums up the picture as follows:

Hare, RM, 'The philosophical basis of psychiatric ethics', in *Essays on Bioethics*[43]

If, for example [a psychiatrist] has as a patient somebody who he knows will be a great deal of trouble to anybody who is so unwise as to employ him, has he any duty to reveal the fact when asked for a medical certificate? Here, as before, it is obviously no use treating the duty of confidentiality to the patient and the duty of candour to the employer as duties on the same level but ranked in order of priority; for it may depend on the case which duty should have precedence. If the patient is an airline pilot and his condition will cause him to lose control of the plane, we may think the public interest paramount; if he is a bank clerk and is merely going to turn up late to work from time to time, we may think that his condition should be concealed.

. . . At the critical level of moral thinking we are bound to be impartial between the interests of all those affected by our own actions. So at this level, we shall have to give no special edge to our patients, but simply ask, in each case we consider, what action would produce the best results for all those affected, treated impartially . . .

The following are examples of public interests which may outweigh the competing public interest in maintaining confidences.

5.2.2.1 Disclosure to maintain the freedom of the press

As we saw above in the case of *Campbell v Mirror Group Newspapers*[44] there is a public interest in the freedom of the press and other forms of media to investigate and report on matters of legitimate public concern. This was examined in the case of X v Y, where the court was unsympathetic to the interests of press freedom, in the face of the protection of the anonymity of patients being treated for AIDS. A health authority sought an injunction restraining a newspaper from publishing the names of two practising doctors who were also being treated for AIDS. The names of the doctors had been given to the newspaper by an employee within the health authority. The issue of freedom of the press was dealt with by Rose J, p 395:

---

43 Oxford: Clarendon Press, 1993.
44 [2004] 2 AC 457.

Rose J: I keep in the forefront of my mind the very important public interest in freedom of the press. And I accept that there is some public interest in knowing that which the defendants seek to publish (in whichever version). But in my judgment those public interests are substantially outweighed when measured against the public interests in relation to loyalty and confidentiality both generally and with particular reference to AIDS patients' hospital records . . . The deprivation of the public of the information sought to be published will be of minimal significance if the injunction is granted; for, without it, all the evidence before me shows that a wide ranging public debate about AIDS generally and about its effect on doctors is taking place among doctors of widely differing views, within and without the BMA, in medical journals and in many newspapers, including *The Observer*, *The Sunday Times* and the *Daily Express*. Indeed, the sterility of the defendants' argument is demonstrated by the edition of the second defendant's own newspaper dated 22 March 1987. It is there expressly stated, purportedly quoting a Mr Milligan, that three general practitioners, two of whom are practising (impliedly in Britain), have AIDS. Paraphrasing Templeman LJ in the *Schering* case, the facts, in the most limited version now sought to be published, have already been made available and may again be made available if they are known otherwise than through the medium of the informer. The risk of identification is only one factor in assessing whether to permit the use of confidential information. In my judgment, to allow publication in the recently suggested restricted form would be to enable both defendants to procure breaches of confidence and then to make their own selection for publication. This would make a mockery of the law's protection of confidentiality when no justifying public interest has been shown.

The authority succeeded on the basis that the doctors needed protection just as any other patient did.

In H *(A Healthcare Worker) v Associated Newspapers Ltd and N (A Health Authority)*,[46] a healthcare worker had been diagnosed as HIV positive and, in injunction proceedings, his former employer, a health authority, was permitted to be named in newspaper reports. The judge had concluded that the risk of identification of the worker did not justify preserving the anonymity of the health authority. The Court of Appeal held that disclosure of the identity of the health authority would enable the worker to be identified and that part of the judge's order was set aside. It was also said, however, that to disclose the particular speciality of the worker did not run such a high risk, and to restrain publication of that would be an unnecessary fetter on the freedom of the press.

In *Re S (A Child) (Identification: Restriction on Publication)*[47] the House of Lords held that no injunction should be made restraining the publication by newspapers of the identity of the defendant in a murder trial in order to protect the privacy of her child (not involved in the criminal proceedings). The freedom of the press to report the progress of a criminal trial without any restraint under the Art 10 of the Convention outweighed the child's rights under Art 8.

5.2.2.2 Disclosure to prevent crime

In the case of X v Y, the health authority unsuccessfully tried to obtain disclosure of the name of the person within the authority who had criminally sold the medical records of the doctors concerned (ie contrary to the Public Bodies Corrupt Practices Act 1889 and the Prevention of Corruption Act 1906). The argument of the authority was based on its alleged duty to prevent crime. The court held that it had no public duty to prosecute crime, and that its real purpose had been to prevent publication, which was prevented on other grounds.[48]

---

45 [1988] RPC 379 p 395.
46 [2002] EWCA Civ 195.
47 [2004] 3 WLR 1129.
48 At p 399.

The protection of the public from crime was considered in *W v Egdell*.[49] The patient was a prisoner in a secure hospital following conviction for a number of killings and woundings, and had made an application to a mental health review tribunal with a view to being transferred to a regional unit. Such a step would be a step towards discharge, and, therefore, the question arose as to whether the patient was still a danger to the public. His legal advisers sought the opinion of an independent psychiatrist, which, it was hoped, could be produced in support of the application. Dr Egdell, however, formed the view that the patient was still dangerous. In the light of this, the patient's application was withdrawn. However, his case was due to be reviewed under the automatic review process, under s 79(1) of the MHA 1983, and Dr Egdell, realising that his report, commissioned confidentially and independently by the patient's legal advisers, would not be included in the notes, sent a copy to the medical director of the hospital and a further copy to the Home Office. The patient brought an action alleging breach of confidence, but the court upheld the breach on the grounds of the public interest, that is, the protection of the public from dangerous criminal acts. The patient failed in his action at first instance and appealed.

W v Egdell[50]

Bingham LJ: The parties were agreed, as I think rightly, that the crucial question was how, on the special facts of the case, the balance should be struck between the public interest in maintaining professional confidences and the public interest in protecting the public against possible violence. Counsel for W submitted that on the facts here the public interest in maintaining confidences was shown to be clearly preponderant. In support of that submission he drew our attention to a number of features of the case, of which the most weighty were perhaps these:

(1) Section 76 of the Mental Health Act 1983 shows a clear parliamentary intention that a restricted patient should be free to seek advice and evidence for the specified purposes from a medical source outside the prison and secure hospital system. Section 129 ensures that the independent doctor may make a full examination and see all relevant documents. The examination may be in private, so that the authorities do not learn what passes between doctor and patient.

(2) The proper functioning of s 76 requires that a patient should feel free to bare his soul and open his mind without reserve to the independent doctor he has retained. This he will not do if a doctor is free, on forming an adverse opinion, to communicate it to those empowered to prevent the patient's release from hospital.

(3) Although the present situation is not one in which W can assert legal professional privilege, and although tribunal proceedings are not strictly adversarial, the considerations which have given rise to legal professional privilege underpin the public interest in preserving confidence in a situation such as the present. A party to a forthcoming application to a tribunal should be free to unburden himself to an adviser he has retained without fearing that any material damaging to his application will find its way without his consent into the hands of a party with interests adverse to his.

(4) Preservation of confidence would be conducive to the public safety: patients would be candid, so that problems such as those highlighted by Dr Egdell would become known, and steps could be taken to explore and if necessary treat the problems without disclosing the report.

(5) It is contrary to the public interest that patients such as W should enjoy rights less extensive than those enjoyed by other members of the public, a result of his judgment

49 [1990] Ch 359.
50 [1990] Ch 359, at p 422.

which the judge expressly accepted (see [1989] 2 WLR 689, p 714; and [1989] 1 All ER 1089, p 1105).

Of these considerations, I accept (1) as a powerful consideration in W's favour. A restricted patient who believes himself unnecessarily confined has, of all members of society, perhaps the greatest need for a professional adviser who is truly independent and reliably discreet. (2) I also, in some measure, accept, subject to the comment that if the patient is unforthcoming, the doctor is bound to be guarded in his opinion. If the patient wishes to enlist the doctor's wholehearted support for his application, he has little choice but to be (or at least convince an expert interviewer that he is being) frank. I see great force in (3). Only the most compelling circumstances could justify a doctor in acting in a way which would injure the immediate interests of his patient, as the patient perceived them, without obtaining his consent. Point (4), if I correctly understand it, did not impress me. Counsel's submissions appeared to suggest that the problems highlighted by Dr Egdell could be explored and if necessary treated without the hospital authorities being told what the problems were thought to be. I do not think this would be very satisfactory. As to (5), I agree that restricted patients should not enjoy rights of confidence less valuable than those enjoyed by other patients save in so far as any breach of confidence can be justified under the stringent terms of r 81(g).

Counsel for Dr Egdell justified his client's disclosure of his report by relying on the risk to the safety of the public if the report were not disclosed. The steps of his argument, briefly summarised, were these:

(1) As a result of his examination Dr Egdell believed that W had a long standing and abnormal interest in dangerous explosives dating from well before his period of acute illness.
(2) Dr Egdell believed that this interest had been overlooked or insufficiently appreciated by those with clinical responsibility for W.
(3) Dr Egdell believed that this interest could throw additional light on W's interest, also long standing and in this instance well documented, in guns and shooting.
(4) Dr Egdell believed that exploration of W's interest in explosives and further exploration of W's interest in guns and shooting might lead to a different and more sinister diagnosis of W's mental condition.
(5) Dr Egdell believed that these explorations could best be conducted in the secure hospital where W was.
(6) Dr Egdell believed that W might possibly be a future danger to members of the public if his interest in firearms and explosives continued after his discharge.
(7) Dr Egdell believed that these matters should be brought to the attention of those responsible for W's care and treatment and for making decisions concerning his transfer and release.

Dr Egdell's good faith was not in issue. Nor were his professional standing and competence. His opinions summarised in (1), (2), (3) and (4) (although not accepted) were not criticised as ill-founded or irrational. Dr Egdell deferred to the greater knowledge of another medical expert relied on by W concerning the regime in a regional secure unit but did not (as I understood) modify his view that the explorations he favoured should take place before transfer . . .

There is one consideration which, in my judgment, as in that of the judge, weighs the balance of public interest decisively in favour of disclosure. It may be shortly put. Where a man has committed multiple killings under the disability of serious mental illness, decisions which may lead directly or indirectly to his release from hospital should not be made unless a responsible authority is properly able to make an informed judgment that the risk of repetition is so small as to be acceptable. A consultant psychiatrist who becomes aware, even in the course of a confidential relationship, of information which leads him, in the exercise of what the court considers a sound professional judgment, to fear that such decisions may be made on the basis of inadequate information and with a real risk of consequent danger to the public is entitled to take such steps as are reasonable in all the circumstances to communicate the grounds of his concern to the responsible authorities. I have no doubt that the judge's decision in favour of Dr Egdell was right on the facts of this case.

The question arises whether this case is different from a case where a dangerous criminal is *at large* and a doctor breaches medical confidentiality to enable him to be taken into custody. It is arguable that there is an important difference. After all, in the *Egdell* case the patient was already the subject of expert medical scrutiny by the doctors at the hospital where he was detained; if those doctors had formed the view that the patient was no longer dangerous (that is, a view contrary to that of Dr Egdell), does not this difference of professional opinion considerably weaken the public interest defence to disclosure? Grubb[51] suggests that it may turn on whether the breaching doctor is basing his view on new facts of which he is aware, and which, without breaching confidence, are not known by the other doctor. If it is merely a difference of opinion based on the same set of facts, then there is a good argument against disclosure.

The public interest defence in the prevention of crime was upheld by the Court of Appeal in the case of *R v Crozier*,[52] where a psychiatrist, instructed by the defendant in an attempted murder case, disclosed his report to the prosecution when he realised that the defence had not produced it in court, when sentence was passed. As a result, the Crown informed the judge of the contents of the report, and the judge quashed the sentence of imprisonment and made a hospital order instead.

There is no doubt that the patient in *W v Egdell*[53] had committed very grave criminal offences. Would fear of less serious offences justify disclosure? Although case law in non-medical areas of confidentiality appears to put all crimes in the same basket (see *Initial Services Ltd v Putterill*[54] and *Malone v Commissioner of Police of the Metropolis (No 2)*,[55] in the Egdell case, the repeated references to the safety of the public – 'In this case the number and nature of the killings by W must inevitably give rise to the gravest concern for the safety of the public'[56] – strongly suggests that the risk of minor crimes being committed would not sway the court in the same way. Furthermore, the non-medical cases generally concern issues of fraud upon the general public (see *British Steel Corp v Granada Television Ltd*).[57]

It should also be noted that in the *Egdell* case, it was said that the risk must be 'real, immediate and serious'.[58] This is important, as it must mean that a doctor acting in good faith and in the genuine belief that there is such a risk, will be in breach of confidence if it transpires that the risk did not amount to one that was real, immediate and serious. Should all three of these requirements be satisfied: what of a risk which is real and serious, but unlikely to materialise for some time?

What of past, undetected criminal offences? The risk of a crime being committed is different to a past crime gone unpunished, the former only a perceived likelihood of criminal activity, the latter a certainty (on the assumption that the doctor is certain). There is a strong argument to say that non-seerious crime should not be disclosed on the basis that the countervailing public interest in maintaining medical confidences outweighs disclosure, as, we suggest, was the case in *Wilson*.

51 3rd edn, *Medical Law*, London: Butterworths, 2000, p 1101.
52 (1990) *The Independent*, 11 May.
53 [1990] Ch 359.
54 [1968] QB 396.
55 [1979] 2 All ER 620.
56 Per Sir Stephen Brown P, at p 846.
57 [1981] 1 All ER 417.
58 Per Sir Stephen Brown P, at p 416.

5.2.2.3 Disclosure to prevent civil wrongs

Gurry[59] reviews the case law, and concludes that disclosure of a *proposed* civil wrong would be in the public interest, but doubts whether the disclosure of a past civil wrong would satisfy this, as 'this would serve only to raise quibbling enmities and thus destroy, rather than advance, the public welfare', whilst in the context of commercial confidences it may be the case that proposed civil wrongs may justify a breach. However, it is hard to envisage the circumstances in which past or future civil wrongs would justify a breach of medical confidences. Medical confidentiality would always override the prevention of civil wrongs because of weightier public interest arguments. In any event, what might be an example of a situation where a doctor would consider breaching confidence to prevent a proposed civil wrong? Perhaps a doctor may consider reporting a patient to his employer if, for example, he has failed to disclose a medical condition on a job application form, for example, psychiatric history (see *O'Brien v Prudential Assurance Co*[60]). It is submitted that this sort of medical busy bodying would be swiftly condemned by the courts and the GMC.

5.2.2.4 Disclosure for the public good

It might be argued that if no wrong, criminal or civil, has been, or is likely to be committed, then disclosure could not possibly be justified. However, there is clear authority for the fact that 'the public good' can be sufficient. The Court of Appeal in *Lion Laboratories v Evans and Express Newspapers*,[61] authorised the publication of internal documents from the manufacturer of the intoximeter that cast doubt upon the accuracy of the machine, which was widely used in the convictions for drink-driving offences. The court held that the possibility of future wrongful convictions raised a matter of legitimate public interest despite the fact that no wrongdoing was involved.

It is possible to envisage countless examples of revelation of medical information for the public good, for example, the publication of information about new drugs and treatments and breakthroughs in medical research may be in the public good. Release of information about the dangers to public health, for example, an outbreak of illness caused by contaminated materials, would, of course, always be in the public good (indeed, the public health authorities would be under a positive duty to do this). However, in most of these cases, there would be no need to name identifiable individuals, so there would be no breach of confidentiality. Nevertheless, if circumstances were such that individuals had to be named, for example, a patient at large suffering from a highly dangerous and contagious disease, identification may be necessary.

In *Woolgar v Chief Constable of Sussex Police*,[62] the Court of Appeal had to decide whether police records could be disclosed to a regulatory body. The appellant was a registered nurse and the former matron of a nursing home. She had been investigated by the police following the death of a patient at the home. There were no criminal charges brought, but this, and other matters, were referred to the United Kingdom Central Council for Nursing, Midwifery and Health Visiting (UKCC), which was the regulatory and disciplinary body for the nursing, midwifery and health visiting professions. The normal practice was, that if there has been a police investigation before the UKCC became involved, the UKCC would contact the police, and with the consent of those who have made statements, obtain copies of those statements. The nurse refused permission for her statement to be released. The court accepted that the statement was confidential on the basis that, if no charges were brought, the person making it is entitled to rely upon it remaining undisclosed. However, the court also decided that there was a sufficiently strong countervailing interest in the release of the statement.[63]

---

59 In *Breach of Confidence*, Oxford: Clarendon, 1984, p 334.
60 [1979] IRLR 140.
61 [1985] QB 526.
62 [1999] Lloyd's Rep Med 335.
63 Note that the UKCC has now been replaced by the Nursing and Midwifery Council (NMC).

Woolgar v Chief Constable of Sussex Police[64]

Kennedy LJ: . . . where a regulatory body such as the UKCC, operating in the field of public health and safety, seeks access to confidential material in the possession of the police, being material which the police are reasonably persuaded is of some relevance to the subject matter of an enquiry being conducted by the regulatory body, then a countervailing public interest is shown to exist which, as in this case, entitles the police to release the material to the regulatory body on the basis that save in so far as it may be used by the regulatory body for the purposes of its own enquiry, the confidentiality which already attaches to the material will be maintained. As Mr Horan said in . . . his skeleton argument:

> A properly and efficiently regulated nursing profession is necessary in the interest of the medical welfare of the country, to keep the public safe, and to protect the rights and freedoms of those vulnerable individuals in need of nursing care.

Putting the matter in Convention terms Lord Lester submitted, and I would accept, that disclosure is necessary in a democratic society in the interests of . . . public safety . . . or . . . for the protection of health or morals, or for the protection of the rights and freedoms of others.

 SELF-TEST QUESTION

Consider the facts of the case of *Distillers Co (Biochemicals) Ltd v Times Newspapers Ltd*,[65] discussed below at 5.2.2.8 and consider whether similar facts, giving rise to a breach of medical confidentiality, would be justified for the public good.

5.2.2.5 Disclosure for the protection of third parties

It might be thought that the protection of third parties would come within the ambit of preventing either a criminal or a civil wrong. However, it may be necessary to disclose medical information when neither of these apply. The case of *Re C (A Minor) (Evidence: Confidential Information)*,[66] concerned the proposed adoption of a one-year-old baby. A day before the hearing, the mother withdrew her consent to the adoption. At an adjourned hearing, the adopting parents' solicitor produced an affidavit sworn voluntarily by the mother's GP, containing evidence of her medical condition and fitness to bring up a child. The mother objected to the admissibility of this evidence as it was a breach of medical confidentiality. She was unsuccessful at first instance, and the case went to the Court of Appeal. Sir Stephen Brown said:[67]

> **Sir Stephen Brown**: It is in fact an unusual case. There is no previous authority which is directly in point, and all the cases which have been cited to the court refer to very different situations. The court is concerned with the proposed adoption of a little child. That is, of course, a very serious matter for the child, as well as being a serious decision for the court to have to make when the mother is withholding her consent. The court should have before it all relevant and significant information which will assist it to make a right decision.
>
> In this case, it is clear that the doctor's affidavit is highly relevant. If it can properly be placed before the judge, then it should be admitted. I consider that this case rests on its own very special facts. Moreover, I have considerable hesitation in reaching a conclusion that there

---

64 [1999] Lloyd's Rep Med 335, CA (Kennedy, Otton and Waller LJJ).
65 [1975] QB 613, at p 266.
66 (1991) 7 BMLR 138.
67 At p 143.

was, in fact, any breach of confidence by the doctor in this case. I observe that it was apparently conceded before the judge that, *prima facie*, there was a breach of confidence. However that may be, in my judgment in this case the doctor was justified in making available her evidence. It may be that it could have been made available to the mother's advisers at an earlier stage, or in some other way, but that is not the issue before this court. In any event, I believe that a judge, if carrying out any balancing exercise, would be fully justified in coming down clearly in favour of admitting this evidence.

It should also be recognised that the disclosure of the material contained in this affidavit was the subject of a restricted disclosure. It was not being made available to the public at large. It was being made available only to the judge who had to decide the application, and to those who were also bound by the confidentiality of the hearing in chambers.

Accordingly, I have no hesitation in reaching the conclusion that the judge was correct to rule that this evidence was admissible and that it should be admitted.

What is of particular interest is the suggestion that the finding at first instance that there had been a breach of confidence, albeit a justified breach, may not have been correct. This was a view supported by both the other appeal judges. This was on the basis that the child was also (or had been) a patient of the doctor. However, in our view this is the wrong approach. To hold that there is no breach is tantamount to saying there was no duty in the first place.

Of course, in all these cases we are looking at *competing* public interests, and the protection of children will frequently justify a refusal of disclosure. In D v National Society for the Prevention of Cruelty to Children,[68] the mother of a child who, it had been alleged, had been abused by her, brought proceedings in negligence against the NSPCC, following the shock-induced illness she had suffered as a result of the society's inspector's call to her home. She alleged that the society had failed to investigate properly the complaint made against her. The society denied negligence and made an application to the court for an order that there should be no discovery of documents which might reveal the identity of the complainant. The House of Lords held that in the interests of the proper functioning of a body such as the NSPCC, charged with the duty of protecting children against ill-treatment, they should have immunity from disclosure, analogously to the guaranteed anonymity of police informers. The case also upheld the principle of disclosure in the interests of the administration of justice.

5.2.2.6 Serious communicable diseases

This is not a separate category of public interest defences, but we are dealing with it separately because of the special concerns about such diseases in the eyes of the general public. It will be recalled that the case of X v Y concerned the doctors who were HIV positive, and whose identities were at risk of being revealed by the press. Conditions such as HIV and AIDS throw the issues raised about medical confidentiality and its breach into very sharp relief because they are very serious, can be easily communicated (the added sexual dimension introduces the scope for dilemmas for doctors, when they know their HIV patient is in a sexual relationship and the other party is unaware of the diagnosis), and these factors mean that the balance between public health issues ie protection of confidentiality, and serious risks to the health of others ie disclosure, can be very fine.

Both HIV and AIDS attract huge stigma. This is partly because there is no cure for AIDS, and although it is too soon to say with any certainty, it is still assumed that an HIV positive person will become ill with AIDS sooner or later. However, many other incurable conditions exist, with prognoses far worse than that of someone recently discovered to be HIV positive, who could well live for 20 years with no sign of AIDS, with the prospect of a cure becoming available in the meantime.

---

68 [1977] All ER 589.

It is suggested that the stigma is as a result of two things: first, the fact that it may be transmitted through sexual activity; and, secondly, the fact that someone with no outward manifestations of illness may nevertheless be carrying a lethal virus. It also carries some stigma because of the erroneous belief, amongst some, that it is exclusive to, or caused by homosexual activities and/or drug use. The stigma has been recognised by disability legislation which is currently contained within the Equality Act 2010. Under Sch 1(6) a diagnosis of HIV is sufficient for someone to be 'disabled' and to acquire protection from discrimination under the Act. Conditions such as HIV/AIDS also have serious insurance implications. The European Court of Human Rights had to consider the issue in *Colak v Germany*.[69] In January 1993 the applicant's partner informed his doctor that he was suffering from AIDS. He did not tell his partner (the applicant) and told the doctor that he must not reveal this either, even though the applicant was also a patient of the doctor. He died in December 1994 (he was also suffering from cancer, which the applicant was aware of, so this presumably masked the AIDS-related illness). In March 1995 the doctor informed the applicant that her partner had died from AIDS. In April 1995 she was diagnosed as HIV positive. She sued her doctor for failure to inform her of her partner's condition and the judge said that, as the doctor has advised her partner to take steps to prevent the spread of the infection and had reasonably believed that he would follow these steps, there was no liability. On appeal to the Frankfurt Court of Appeal, the Court held that there was an error on the part of the doctor in not informing her, but the Court accepted expert evidence that it was likely she was already infected with HIV at the time that the doctor became aware of the situation and therefore the claim failed. In the European Court of Human Rights, the applicant claimed violation of Arts 2, 6 and 8. It was held that (1) there had been no violation of Art 2, as an event that does not result in death may only in exceptional circumstances disclose a violation of Art 2, and the German legal system provided adequate remedies in cases where there is a threat to life; and (2) there had been no violation of Art 8 (by six votes to one), again on the basis that the legal system provided sufficient safeguards of privacy.

(The Art 6 claim was brought because of the destruction of medical files which might have assisted in dealing with the issue of whether she was already HIV positive at the time the doctor acquired the relevant knowledge. It was held that there was no violation because the destruction of the applicant's medical files could not have an impact on the outcome of the case, as it occurred only after the conclusion of the civil proceedings and the files had been available to the domestic courts throughout.)

The following is an extract from the commentary on the case in the *European Human Rights Law Review*:

European Human Rights Law Review 2009 Case Comment

Colak v Germany (77144/01): HIV-patient confidentiality

What is perhaps surprising about this judgment is how little regard is paid to a patient's right to confidentiality and right to privacy under art.8. Although the applicant's complaints were dismissed, the Court accepted the Frankfurt Court of Appeal's assessment that the doctor should have informed the applicant of her partner's condition.

This stands in contrast to the recent case of *I v Finland* (2009) 48 E.H.R.R. 31 [and the earlier case of] *Z v Finland* (1998) 25 E.H.R.R. 371, the Court expressed the view that there must be a weighty public interest reason to justify the disclosure of a person's HIV status; in that case, it was helpful to the prosecution of Z's husband, a sexual offender. Of course, both these cases concern the disclosure of the applicants' HIV status to the wider public. The facts of the present case are distinguishable on the grounds that the disclosure (had it been made) would have been a narrow one to a person at obvious risk of infection.

---

69 (07714/01), unreported, March 2009.

It is very unlikely that this case will provide support to a doctor accused in this country of making an impermissible disclosure. What it does indicate is very different approaches to the issue of patient confidentiality between the United Kingdom and Germany and possible inconsistencies in the Court's own case law.

It will be seen, therefore, that if there is a serious and identifiable risk to a specific individual, such as a spouse or other sexual partner, then disclosure can be made. Recalling the case of Re C (A Minor) (Evidence: Confidential Information)[70], if the partner is also the patient of the doctor, the Court of Appeal suggested there may be no breach (see 5.2.2.5, above).

Whether there could ever be a positive duty to disclose was considered in the Californian case of Reisner v Regents of the University of California,[71] see below at 5.2.6.

5.2.2.7 Genetic information

Like HIV and AIDS, genetic information does not fall into a special 'legal' category, but because of its nature it does throw the public interest issues into sharp relief. The availability of genetic testing does not give rise to any particular issues in relation to the patient who has been tested, as the results are available to that patient as in any other form of test, and the information is, of course, confidential. However, if a patient is found to be carrying an abnormal gene, then the chances are that other members of the patient's family will also be carrying the gene. Should they be told about this? The two sides of the debate are well illustrated by the following books. Laurie argues that when considering whether to disclose such information to relatives, the factors to be considered are the nature of the genetic condition; whether there is any treatment available for the condition; what is the likelihood of the condition developing and how severe is it likely to be; what further testing needs to be done; the precise nature of the information that it is proposed might be disclosed; the likely reaction of the relative and whether disclosure serves the public interest.[72] A different approach is taken by Gilbar who argues that because of its very nature, genetic information, must take into account the family aspects of disclosure and that therefore the usual medical confidentiality approach as taken by Laurie is not appropriate.[73]

It is arguable, however, that it has always been the case that there has been an awareness that certain conditions 'run in families', and that genetic information does little more than confirm this and that the effects of the knowledge should not be exaggerated.

Again, the issue of genetic information raises the question whether there can be a *positive duty* to disclose medical information, which is considered below at 5.2.6.

5.2.2.8 The administration of justice

In the administration of justice there can be conflicts between the public interest in the protection of confidential information and the public interest in parties being able to seek disclosure of confidential communications to assist the presentation of their own cases and to assist the court in adjudication.[74]

In the course of civil proceedings, ss 33 and 34 of the Supreme Court Act 1981 provide for the discovery of documents during the course of a court action (s 34), and, where appropriate, prior to the commencement of proceedings (s 33). The question as to how far documents discovered in the course of legal proceedings may subsequently be published was considered in *Distillers (Biochemicals) Ltd v Times Newspapers Ltd*.[75] The case concerned the drug thalidomide, and in proceedings

---

70 (1991) 7 BMLR 138.
71 See (1997) Med L Rev 250.
72 Laurie, G, *Genetic Privacy: A Challenge to Medico Legal Norms*, Cambridge: Cambridge University Press, 2002.
73 Gilbar R, *The Status of the Family in Law and Bioethics: The Genetic Context*, Dartmouth: Ashgate, 2005.
74 For a very detailed account of this, see McHale, J, *Medical Confidentiality and Legal Privilege*, London: Routledge, 1993.
75 [1975] QB 613.

brought by those injured by the drug, certain documents were ordered to be disclosed. One of the claimants' expert advisers entered into an agreement with the defendants to sell them the documentary information. The claimant company sought an injunction to prevent publication. The injunction was granted on the basis that those who disclosed documents were entitled to the court's protection against any use of the documents otherwise than in the action in which they were disclosed. Talbot J said, p 625:

> **Talbot J**: Whilst, as I have said, the public have a great interest in the thalidomide story (and it is a matter of public interest), and any light thrown onto this matter to obviate any such thing happening again is welcome, nevertheless the defendants have not persuaded me that such use as they proposed to make of the documents which they possess is of greater advantage to the public than the public's interest in the need for the proper administration of justice, to protect the confidentiality of discovery of documents. I would go further and say that I doubt very much whether there is sufficient in the use which the defendants have proposed to raise a public interest which overcomes the plaintiffs' private right to the confidentiality of their documents. In any event I consider that the plaintiffs have established their right (this is not really disputed) and have an arguable case for its protection by an injunction.

In this regard see also *Lewis v Secretary of State for Health & Redfern*,[76] where, under its general powers, the court authorised the disclosure of medical records of certain deceased patients to the Redfern Inquiry into human tissue analysis in nuclear facilities in the UK.

To refer back to the 'public good' justification, it is clear from this case that the court found that the proper administration of justice outweighed any public interest in knowing about the history of the drug thalidomide. Although it is clear that doctors have no immunity from the normal processes of disclosure in court proceedings, in *Hunter v Mann*[77] it was said by Lord Widgery that a doctor who did not wish to answer a question in court because it would involve confidential issues, may point this out to the judge, who should advise as to whether it is necessary to answer the question. See also the Canadian Supreme Court case *M(A) v Ryan*,[78] in which it was confirmed that communications between psychiatrist and patient are not absolutely privileged. Limited disclosure could be sufficient protection.

5.2.2.9 Disclosure in the interests of national security
It is highly unlikely that this could apply to medical information. It is enough to note it as a legitimate area of public interest.

5.2.3 Medical research
It might be thought that there are no special considerations in the case of disclosure in research, but it is different, in that it could be argued that by consenting to take part in research, particularly non-therapeutic research, there was an altruistic motive on the part of the research subject which changes the nature of confidentiality. Perhaps the only special aspect of research and confidentiality is that information may well be disclosed, but anonymously.

---

76 [2008] EWHC 2196 (QB).
77 [1974] 1 QB 767.
78 [1997] SCR 157.

5.2.4 Exchange of information amongst health care workers

This is a grey area. Although it is included here as a particular example of the way in which confidences may be breached, unauthorised exchange of information amongst health care workers may fall foul of the law unless it can be argued that the patient has impliedly consented to this because he knows that he is being cared for by a team of people.

It is instructive, however, to consider into how many pairs of hands medical information may fall. Gillon refers to the investigation by a doctor of a patient's complaint:

Gillon, R, *Philosophical Medical Ethics*[79]

Dr Siegler was 'astonished to learn that at least 25 and possibly as many as 100 health professionals and administrative personnel at our university hospital had access to the patient's record and that all of them had a legitimate need, indeed a professional responsibility, to open and use that chart'.

Note that this was written in 1986. Is it arguable that the larger these numbers become, the less significant the concept of medical confidentiality becomes? Or does it become even more important to bind those increasing numbers of people to secrecy? The NHS has issued a Code of Practice that suggests the latter.[80]

5.2.5 Breaches of confidence justified by statute law

A number of statutory provisions provide for the disclosure of information, and doctors generally are not exempt. The following are examples and it is not an exhaustive list.

National Health Service Act 2006

S 251 Control of patient information

(1) The Secretary of State may by regulations make such provision for and in connection with requiring or regulating the processing of prescribed patient information for medical purposes as he considers necessary or expedient–
    (a) in the interests of improving patient care, or
    (b) in the public interest.

(2) Regulations under subsection (1) may, in particular, make provision–
    (a) for requiring prescribed communications of any nature which contain patient information to be disclosed by health service bodies in prescribed circumstances–
        (i) to the person to whom the information relates,
        (ii) (where it relates to more than one person) to the person to whom it principally relates, or
        (iii) to a prescribed person on behalf of any such person as is mentioned in subparagraph (i) or (ii),
        in such manner as may be prescribed,
    (b) for requiring or authorising the disclosure or other processing of prescribed patient information to or by persons of any prescribed description subject to compliance with

---

79 Chichester: John Wiley, 1986.
80 NHS Contractors: *Confidentiality and Disclosure of Information: General Medical Services, Personal Medical Services and Alternative Provider Medical Services Code of Practice*, Dept of Health, 2005.

any prescribed conditions (including conditions requiring prescribed undertakings to be obtained from such persons as to the processing of such information),

(c) for securing that, where prescribed patient information is processed by a person in accordance with the regulations, anything done by him in so processing the information must be taken to be lawfully done despite any obligation of confidence owed by him in respect of it,

(d) for creating offences punishable on summary conviction by a fine not exceeding level 5 on the standard scale or such other level as is prescribed or for creating other procedures for enforcing any provisions of the regulations.

(3) Subsections (1) and (2) are subject to subsections (4) to (7).

(4) Regulations under subsection (1) may not make provision requiring the processing of confidential patient information for any purpose if it would be reasonably practicable to achieve that purpose otherwise than pursuant to such regulations, having regard to the cost of and the technology available for achieving that purpose.

. . .

(7) Regulations under this section may not make provision for or in connection with the processing of prescribed patient information in a manner inconsistent with any provision made by or under the Data Protection Act 1998 (c 29).

The regulations that were made under earlier legislation continue to apply in this regard (Health Service (Control of Patient Information) Regulations 2002, SI2002/1438).

It can be seen that s 251 is wide and vague, but the counter argument is that this is necessary to enable valuable medical research to be carried out in circumstances where it is not possible to obtain patient consent.

It should be noted that s 19 of the Terrorism Act 2000 creates a criminal offence in respect of failure to disclose information which might be of material assistance in preventing acts of terrorism or in apprehending or securing a prosecution or conviction.

Note the provisions of the Road Traffic Act 1988:

Road Traffic Act 1988, s 172

(2) – Where the driver of a vehicle is alleged to be guilty of an offence to which this section applies–

(a) the person keeping the vehicle shall give such information as to the identity of the driver as he may be required to give by or on behalf of a chief officer of police; and

(b) any other person shall if required as stated above give any information which it is in his power to give and may lead to identification of the driver.

In this sub-section references to the driver of a vehicle include references to the person riding a cycle.

The case of Hunter v Mann[81] examined the extent to which this requirement was applicable to doctors in relation to the forerunner of the 1988 provision, s 168 of the Road Traffic Act 1972. The relevant part of the provision is identical to the 1988 Act. The question to be answered by the Divisional Court was whether a doctor who failed to comply with the provision under s 172(2)(b),above, in respect of information brought to his knowledge in the course of his professional relationship with a patient, was guilty of an offence under s 172(3). The argument on the part of the doctor was that

---

81 [1974] 1 QB 767.

the relevant words should be given a restricted meaning, so as to exclude confidential information, and those in a special position of confidence such as doctors. Boreham J stated:[82]

> **Boreham J**: For my part I cannot find any ground for saying that a restricted meaning should be given. I find the words clear and unequivocal. I accept, as Mr Bingham has suggested, that one should assume that Parliament has passed this Act, and this section in particular, with the existing law in mind. Accepting that, then it seems to me that Parliament must have been conscious of the use of very wide words here and if it had been intended to create exceptions, why then it would have been easy enough to do so. It has not been done. Moreover I ask myself the question: if there is to be a restriction how far is it to go? Where is it to stop? I find it impossible to provide an answer to that question.
>
> In these circumstances I am driven to the conclusion that a doctor acting within his professional capacity, and carrying out his professional duties and responsibilities, is within the words 'any other person' in s 168(2)(b).
>
> . . .
>
> May I say, before leaving this case, that I appreciate the concern of a responsible medical practitioner who feels that he is faced with a conflict of duty. That the defendant was conscious of a conflict and realised his duty, both to society and to his patient, is clear from the finding of the justices, but he may find comfort, although the decision goes against him, from the following. First, that he has only to disclose information which may lead to identification and not other confidential matters; secondly, that the result, in my judgment, is entirely consistent with the rules that the British Medical Association have laid down and from which I have quoted in the course of this judgment.
>
> In the result I have come to the conclusion that the justices were correct and that this appeal, therefore, must be dismissed.

Information must also be disclosed pursuant to the Abortion Regulations 1991 SI 1991/499 for various purposes including the investigation of whether an offence has been committed in relation to abortion, and for bona fide scientific research. Note too the provisions of ss 33 and 34 of the Supreme Court Act 1981, which provide for disclosure of documents during the course of litigation considered above.

 SELF-TEST QUESTION

If the situation is such that disclosure is permissible in the public interest do you think that this means that disclosure can be made to the public at large?

5.2.6 Might there be a common law duty to disclose?

As we have seen in *Hunter v Mann*,[83] a doctor may have a statutory duty to disclose certain information about a patient. However, might there be circumstances in which a common law duty may arise, as opposed to the common law defence which gives a doctor a *discretion* to disclose? This is illustrated by the case of *Tarasoff v Regents of the University of California*.[84] A patient of a psychologist confided that he intended to kill a girl. The psychologist informed the campus police who briefly

---

82 At p 774.
83 [1974] 1 QB 767.
84 17 Cal 3d 425 (1976).

detained the man, releasing him on the basis that he appeared to be rational. He subsequently killed the girl, and her parents sued the University for failing to warn them that their daughter was in danger. By a majority the California Supreme Court upheld their claim:

Tobriner J:

... the adequacy of the therapist's conduct must be measured against the traditional negligence standard of the rendition of reasonable care under the circumstances ... In sum, the therapist owes a legal duty not only to his patient, but also to his patient's would-be victim and is subject in both respects to scrutiny by judge and jury ... Some of the alternatives open to the therapist, such as warning the victim, will not result in the drastic consequences of depriving the patient of his liberty. Weighing the uncertain and conjectural character of the alleged damage done to the patient by such a warning against the peril to the victim's life, we conclude that professional inaccuracy in predicting violence cannot negate the therapist's duty to protect the threatened victim ...

Justice Clark, dissenting, stated:

Clark J:

Overwhelming policy considerations weigh against imposing a duty on psychotherapists to warn a potential victim against harm. While offering virtually no benefit to society, such a duty will frustrate psychiatric treatment, invade fundamental patient rights and increase violence. The importance of psychiatric treatment and its need for confidentiality have been recognised by this court. It is clearly recognised that the very practice of psychiatry vitally depends upon the reputation in the community that the psychiatrist will not tell ... Assurance of confidentiality is important for three reasons:

Deterrence from treatment
First, without substantial assurance of confidentiality, those requiring treatment will be deterred from seeking assistance ...

Full disclosure
Second, the guarantee of confidentiality is essential in eliciting the full disclosure necessary for effective treatment. The psychiatric patient approaches treatment with conscious and unconscious inhibitions against revealing his innermost thoughts ...

Successful treatment
Third, even if the patient fully discloses his thoughts, assurance that the confidential relationship will not be breached is necessary to maintain his trust in his psychiatrist – the very means by which treatment is effected ...

Violence and civil commitment
... Although under existing psychiatric procedures only a relatively few receiving treatment will ever present a risk of violence, the number making threats is huge, and it is the latter group – not just the former – whose treatment will be impaired and whose risk of commitment will be increased.

This approach has been followed in Nebraska, where the duty was to third parties generally and not just people known to the patient (*Lipari v Sears, Roebuck & Co*).[85] However, in the Florida Court of Appeals, there was a refusal to impose liability based upon a defendant's failure to control the

---

85 497 F Supp.185 (D Neb 1980).

See Chapter 6 →

conduct of a third party (*Boynton v Burglass*[86]). It will be seen in Chapter 6 that the case of *Palmer v Tees HA*[87] displayed a similar reluctance. Thomas is highly critical of the decision in *Tarasoff*:

Thomas, M, 'Expanded Liability for Psychiatrists: *Tarasoff* Gone Crazy?[88]

There are several reasons why United Kingdom decision makers should be sceptical about *Tarasoff's* 'enlightened approach'.

Lack of control over patients
In many cases, a psychiatrist will lack the necessary degree of control over a patient to justify the imposition of a duty. For instance, psychiatrists usually have little control over voluntary patients who do not satisfy the criteria for involuntary commitment . . .

Causation problems
. . . it is not clear that the psychologist's failure to warn the victim in *Tarasoff* could be said to have caused the victim's death. Conspicuously, there is no causation analysis in the *Tarasoff* decision.

   . . . To satisfy [the 'but for '] test, the plaintiff would have to prove that had Ms Tarasoff been warned . . . she would have avoided being killed . . . The most that can be said is that, due to the psychologist's failure to warn . . . [she] lost the opportunity to avoid being harmed . . . Based on traditional common law principles of causation, this would be insufficient to establish causation.

Uncertain standard of care
. . . Mosk J stated that a psychiatrist's prediction of violence stands to be examined against 'conformity to standards of the profession'. Yet, one must wonder what common standards the court is referring to, when no such standards exist within the profession itself. Of course, psychiatry has developed a range of risk assessment tools designed to predict dangerousness. However, it appears that there is little consensus within the profession as to what constitutes reasonable practice . . .

Note also the Californian case of *Reisner v Regents of the University of California*,[89] where a doctor was found to have been in breach of a duty of care owed to the sexual partner of a patient who had contracted HIV after receiving a contaminated blood transfusion, which information had been concealed by the doctor concerned. It was said that the patient would have been likely to have warned her sexual partner. However, it was said that third parties who might have become infected by contact with the sexual partner would not be owed a duty of care, on remoteness principles.

5.2.7 To whom should disclosure be made and what should be the extent of that disclosure?
It is well established that even if a breach of confidence may be justified, it may still be actionable if the disclosure goes further than that which is necessary. If, for example, as was alluded to by Bingham LJ, in *W v Egdell*.[90] Dr Egdell had disclosed his report to a newspaper, or commented upon it in a journal article, then this would have been going further than was

---

86 590 So 2d 446.
87 [1999] Lloyd's Rep Med 351.
88 (2009) J Mental Health L 52 2009.
89 See (1997) Med L Rev 250.
90 [1990] Ch 359 at 419.

necessary in the public interest of prevention of crime. The defence of public interest was only available to him in the disclosure to the hospital treating the patient, and the Home Office. Similarly, a doctor who is justified in revealing one aspect of the patient's condition is not thereby justified in revealing other medical information. For example, the revelation that a woman is HIV positive, as we have seen, may occasionally be justified. A doctor who, at the same time, points out that this was discovered in the course of an abortion procedure will be in breach of confidence. However, additional information may be revealed if it is necessary by way of explanation.

The extent of disclosure was the subject of *A Health Authority v X and Others*.[91] The case concerned the release of papers which resulted from a case brought under the Children Act 1989. The health authority sought an order for production of case papers and GP records of two people involved in the case. Munby J had ordered disclosure, subject to express conditions to limit the extent of the disclosure. The health authority appealed against such conditions. One argument advanced on behalf of the health authority was that the NHS would grind to a halt if there were not 'free internal exchange of confidential information'. The Court of Appeal rejected this:

A Health Authority v X and Others[92]

Thorpe LJ: . . . the only real issue in the present appeal is whether the conflict between the private/public interest in the confidentiality of medical records and some other public interest should be decided by the health authority or a judge . . . I accept Mr Pannick's submission that the importance of the resolution of such a conflict requires the independence of a judge. I conclude that the spectres developed by Mr Havers, cost and delay and administrative overload, are no more than speculations which good sense and management can contain.

. . . I conclude that [there was no] error of law or principle that would justify our intervention . . . The judge elected for a cautious approach. In my opinion he was not only entitled but wise to do so.

5.3 Confidentiality – Remedies

5.3.1 Detriment

In *AG v Guardian Newspapers* (No 2)[93], there was no clear stance as to whether there is a need for detriment to be shown in private actions for breach of confidence. Lord Goff, for example, left the question open (pp 281–82). Although there are instances where a patient would suffer pecuniary loss as a result of that breach (for example, disclosure of a medical condition to an employer which results in dismissal), in many cases no quantifiable loss would result. It is arguable that breach of confidence should be actionable *per se*, or that, if detriment is required, the breach itself is a detriment to the patient in the sense that he has been betrayed.

An interesting point arises if we consider inadvertent disclosure. Up until now we have assumed that the act of disclosure has been deliberate. However, if a confidential medical report were to be carelessly lost in a public place, does the patient have to show that damage has resulted from this? In other words would the negligence criterion be applied, that is, that damage must have resulted from the non-deliberate act? This will be examined further in relation to damages.

---

91 [2001] EWCA Civ 2014.
92 [2001] EWCA Civ 2014, CA (Thorpe and Laws LJJ, Harrison J).
93 [1990] AC 109.

5.3.2 Damages

The rather curious New Zealand case of *Furniss v Fitchett*[94] was decided on negligence principles. The facts were as follows. The marriage of a Mr and Mrs Furniss was under a great deal of strain. Both were patients of Dr Fitchett. Mr Furniss asked the doctor to provide him with a letter detailing his wife's psychiatric problems, which he did. It was not marked 'confidential' and the doctor did not know how it was to be used. Just over a year later, it was produced in the course of a court hearing – the first time Mrs Furniss had heard of it. She suffered what is oddly described in the law report as 'shock to the injury of her health'. Leaving aside the difficult issue of what sort of injury this is (the judge referred to it as 'physical' injury), the general negligence criteria were applied in awarding her damages.

In *Cornelius v De Taranto*,[95] the Court of Appeal upheld the decision of the trial judge that a consultant psychiatrist had breached client confidentiality in disclosing a medico-legal report to the patient's GP and another psychiatrist without first obtaining her consent. The report contained defamatory and hurtful material relating to her mental state. Damages of £3,750 were awarded for injury to feelings.

5.3.3 Injunctions

It is important to remember that the injunction is a discretionary remedy and, in the context of breach of confidence, if the information is already in the public domain, there will be no purpose served by an order preventing further publication: see *AG v Guardian Newspapers (No 2)*.[96]

An injunction at the final trial of the action will rarely be granted if there has been no interim injunction when the proceedings are first issued, because if there has been no prior prevention of publication, then by the time of trial, the information will either be well and truly in the public domain, or no longer worth suppressing.

The interim injunction, therefore, is the key weapon in a breach of confidence action. It means that publication will be prevented for what may be a long time before trial. The basis upon which such relief would be granted was set out in *American Cyanamid Co v Ethicon Ltd*,[97] and is generally known as 'the balance of convenience test', where the court has to decide whether either party will suffer irreparable harm and, if both will suffer, who will suffer the most.

5.3.4 The dead

The Hippocratic Oath binds a doctor to keep medical confidences after death, but it is not clear whether there is any legal obligation to keep confidences after the death of the person to whom the duty is owed, after the death of the patient. The common law is not clear as the doctor–patient relationship of confidence no longer exists. Some statutes specifically do not apply to deceased persons (the Data Protection Act 1998) and some do (the Access to Health Records Act 1990). However, ethically, it seems clear that if harm can be caused to relatives then disclosure should be prohibited, subject to their being no countervailing ethical factor.

:

---

94 [1958] NZLR 396.
95 [2002] EMLR 6.
96 [1990] AC 109.
97 [1975] AC 396.

5.4 Confidentiality and the Data Protection Act 1998

The Act was passed to give effect to the European Directive 95/46/EC which requires Member States to implement legislation to protect the right of individuals to privacy with respect to the processing of personal data. As far as medical records are concerned, the Act gives patients the right of access to their medical records, subject to exclusions. It also gives patients the right to ask for necessary corrections to be made to those records. Data will be processed in adherence to the 'Data Protection Principles':

European Directive 95/46/EC

1 Personal data shall be processed fairly and lawfully.
2 Personal data shall be obtained only for one or more specified lawful purposes.
3 Personal data shall be adequate, relevant and not excessive.
4 Personal data shall be accurate and up to date.
5 Personal data shall not be kept for longer than necessary.
6 Personal data shall be processed in accordance with rights of data subjects.
7 Measures shall be taken against unauthorised or unlawful processing and accidental loss or destruction.

David Stone outlines the application of the Act to medical records:

Stone, D, 'Confidentiality, access to health records and the Human Rights Act 1998', in Garwood-Gowers et al, Healthcare: The Impact of the Human Rights Act 1998[98]

The first main purpose of the DPA 1998 is to control the way in which such data are 'processed'. This is a comprehensive term covering almost every conceivable activity in relation to such information. Under s 1(12), processing includes the 'obtaining, recording or holding . . . organisation, adaptation or alteration . . . retrieval, consultation or use . . . disclosure . . . alignment, combination, blocking, erasure or destruction' of data.

A 'data processor' is anybody who does one of these things. It will therefore include hospital staff, GPs and their staff; while a 'data controller' is anybody who determines the purpose for which, or manner in which, the data are processed. This will include NHS organisations and GPs alike. Almost everyone who reads or uses patient records in any way – even putting copies in the post or reading them on screen – will be 'processing' data and will therefore be bound by the provisions of the DPA 1998. This will include not only professional staff but, for example, hospital managers and GP receptionists.

. . . [referring to the first data protection principle] To be 'fair' the data must, in general terms, have been obtained from the patient honestly or in accordance with a legal obligation; the patient must have been told the purposes for which the information is to be processed; and the rules for providing access to the data subject must also have been observed (Sched 1, Pt 2).

The word 'lawfully' is not defined. However, it implies that the processing must not be in breach of any other existing legal restrictions, for example, the common law duty of confidence. This emphasises the point that the DPA 1998 does not replace the common law framework of confidentiality and access, but is an addition to it – albeit a dominant one.

Most importantly, it should be noted that, to be considered fair and lawful, the processing of patient records (as 'sensitive personal data') must meet at least one detailed specific criterion from Sched 2 and at least one from Sched 3. In summary these are:

---

98 London: Cavendish Publishing, 2001.

(a) that the patient has given 'explicit consent' to the processing ('explicit' is not defined, but Guidance from the Data Protection Commissioner suggests that it means that the patient's consent must be absolutely clear, that is, that it should cover the specific purpose of the processing); or

(b) that the processing is necessary for the purposes of exercising or performing a right or obligation imposed by law; or

(c) that it is necessary to protect the vital interests of the patient or another person where consent cannot be given by or on behalf of the patient, or where the data controller cannot reasonably be expected to obtain it or it has been unreasonably withheld; or

(d) that the information has already been deliberately made public by the patient; or

(e) that the processing is necessary for the purpose of actual or prospective legal proceedings, or for obtaining legal advice, or for the purpose of establishing, exercising or defending legal rights; or

(f) that it is necessary for the purposes of 'legitimate interests' pursued by the data controller or the third party to whom the data are to be disclosed, unless disclosure would be unwarranted because it would prejudice the data subject; or

(g) that it is necessary for the administration of justice, or for the exercise of statutory functions; or

(h) that it is necessary for medical purposes (including preventative medicine, diagnosis, research, care, treatment and management of healthcare services), and is carried out by a healthcare professional (as defined in s 69) or by a person who owes the patient an equivalent duty of confidentiality; or

(i) that it is authorised by an Order of the Secretary of State.

For the most part, the processing of patient records will be necessary for medical purposes (Sched 3, para 8), so one can avoid the need for consent in that way. However, one can see areas of uncertainty where important tissues will arise.

. . .

Potential problems

In practical terms, there are a wide range of every day situations in a hospital or surgery in which the legal rights and duties of NHS data controllers may not be clear . . . one example would be where a trust has the opportunity to generate income by selling prescribing data to a data collection company. Will the court necessarily agree with the Court of Appeal's view in the *Source Informatics* case [see 5.1.3 above] that anonymisation is sufficient to dispel any common law duty of confidentiality? Or should the process of anonymising prescriptions be deemed 'processing' for the purposes of the DPA 1998, as the Department of Health seemed to be arguing in that case? If so, what would be the position if the patient had explicitly indicated his/her opposition to such a process? Would Art 8 enable a GP to rely on the legitimate interests exception under Sched 2 to the DPA 1998, where the sole purpose of the exercise was commercial and contractual?

Again, the issue of disclosing information capable of identifying the patient has caused difficulties. The increasing sophistication of information technology has facilitated the production of group studies and the creation of national databases to assist with the treatment and prevention of conditions such as cancer. However, with rare conditions such as CJD, the possibility of a patient being identified even by anonymised information can never be completely eliminated as the GMC's guidance recognises. It is likely that where a legitimate public health purpose can be shown here (for example, under the Public Health (Control of Diseases) Act 1984), the conditions of Art 8 will be adjudged to have been met. However, that is not to say that patients will not challenge the disclosure.

Another possible difficulty might arise from relying on an exemption under Scheds 2 and 3 of the DPA 1998 based on a legal obligation. For instance, under s 35A of the Medical Act 1983, the GMC is entitled to demand disclosure of information from any person in order to assist with the performance of the GMC's functions. But what if the patient is specifically asked first, for example, as a matter of courtesy, and explicitly refuses disclosure out of loyalty to the doctor: does the exemption available to the data controller override the patient's views, or would disclosure be unlawful in the terms of the First Data Protection Principle and Art 8?

Similarly, the Secretary of State is empowered by the DPA 1998 to make Orders in respect of disclosure in a variety of circumstances without the date subject's consent. For example, the Data Protection (Processing of Sensitive Personal Data) Order 2000 [SI 2000/417] allows disclosure of patient records without consent for a range of purposes 'in the substantial public interest', including for the prevention and detection of crime or protecting the public against incompetence or misconduct. The Order falls squarely within Scheds 2 and 3 of the DPA 1998 allowing the disclosure of health records without the a patient's consent; but will such blanket authorisations be considered consistent with the specific reservations set out in Art 8, or will patients be able to challenge them successfully as illegitimate encroachments on the basic principle of right to private and family life?

 SELF-TEST QUESTION

Information about patients goes through the hands of many health care professionals; do you think that this makes issues of confidentiality more or less important?

5.5 Access to Medical Records

5.5.1 Access to medical records – ethical considerations

As a corollary to the duty of confidentiality owed by a doctor to a patient, one could be forgiven for assuming that a patient should have an unfettered right to see his medical records. After all, if a doctor is to be privy to intimate medical information which he has a duty to keep quiet about, but not an absolute duty, then the accuracy of that information should be verifiable at least by the patient concerned. At first sight, it might seem that here there are two discrete patient rights, that is, the right to respect for privacy and the right to know what the doctor is placing in the medical records. However, in practice they are intertwined. The patient's right to protection of confidences must surely extend to the right to know that the information concerned is accurate. Further, the utilitarian argument that the patient will be more candid if confidentiality is protected and that such candour is necessary for the patient's health and that of society generally, also sustains the proposition that a patient should have a right to check the accuracy of that information. (Interestingly, it has been argued that, in order to preserve confidentiality, patients should keep their own medical records.[99])

On the other hand, if the patient has only a discretionary right (or, indeed, no right at all), then this would usually be justified on paternalistic principles. The types of arguments that are advanced in the cause of paternalism, are, for example, that the patient would not understand the records, that they may frighten or confuse him, the doctor would not be able to make 'frank'

---

99 See 'Editorial' (1991) 17 JME 115, and the article in the same edition by Gilhooly, M and McGhee, S, 'Medical records: practicalities and principles of patient possession' (1991) 17 JME 235.

comments about the patient and so on. However, are paternalistic principles justifiable in certain circumstances where revelation of the contents of records may damage the patient or others? It will be seen that both common law and statute favour the paternalistic approach.

5.5.2 Access to medical records – the law

5.5.2.1 Statutory provisions: Data Protection Act; Access to Medical Reports Act 1988

The Access to Health Records Act 1990 was passed as a result of the case of *Gaskin v United Kingdom*,[100] where the European Court of Human Rights held that the UK's refusal to grant a right of access by a patient to his health records was in breach of Art 8 of the European Convention. This has been replaced by the Data Protection Act 1998 in all respects except in relation to deceased persons in respect of which a personal representative can apply for access (s 3(1)(f)).

The Data Protection Act 1998 enables data subjects to have access to data held about them:

Data Protection Act 1998, Part II:

Rights of data subjects and others

7–

(1) Subject to the following provisions of this section and to sections 8 and 9, an individual is entitled–

  (a) to be informed by any data controller whether personal data of which that individual is the data subject are being processed by or on behalf of that data controller;

  (b) if that is the case, to be given by the data controller a description of–

    (i) the personal data of which that individual is the data subject;

    (ii) the purposes for which they are being or are to be processed; and

    (iii) the recipients or classes of recipients to whom they are or may be disclosed;

  (c) to have communicated to him in an intelligible form–

    (i) the information constituting any personal data of which that individual is the data subject; and

    (ii) any information available to the data controller as to the source of those data; and

  (d) where the processing by automatic means of personal data of which that individual is the data subject for the purpose of evaluating matters relating to him such as, for example, his performance at work, his creditworthiness, his reliability or his conduct, has constituted or is likely to constitute the sole basis for any decision significantly affecting him, to be informed by the data controller of the logic involved in that decision-taking.

(2) A data controller is not obliged to supply any information under subsection (1) unless he has received–

  (a) a request in writing; and

  (b) except in prescribed cases, such fee (not exceeding the prescribed maximum) as he may require.

(3) A data controller is not obliged to comply with a request under this section unless he is supplied with such information as he may reasonably require in order to satisfy himself as to the identity of the person making the request and to locate the information which that person seeks.

---

100 (1990) 12 EHRR 36.

(4) Where a data controller cannot comply with the request without disclosing information relating to another individual who can be identified from that information, he is not obliged to comply with the request unless–
   (a) the other individual has consented to the disclosure of the information to the person making the request; or
   (b) it is reasonable in all the circumstances to comply with the request without the consent of the other individual.

(5) In subsection (4) the reference to information relating to another individual includes a reference to information identifying that individual as the source of the information sought by the request; and that subsection is not to be construed as excusing a data controller from communicating so much of the information sought by the request as can be communicated without disclosing the identity of the other individual concerned, whether by the omission of names or other identifying particulars or otherwise.

(6) In determining for the purposes of subsection (4)(b) whether it is reasonable in all the circumstances to comply with the request without the consent of the other individual concerned, regard shall be had, in particular, to–
   (a) any duty of confidentiality owed to the other individual;
   (b) any steps taken by the data controller with a view to seeking the consent of the other individual;
   (c) whether the other individual is capable of giving consent; and
   (d) any express refusal of consent by the other individual.

(7) An individual making a request under this section may, in such cases as may be prescribed, specify that his request is limited to personal data of any prescribed description.

(8) Subject to subsection (4), a data controller shall comply with a request under this section promptly and in any event before the end of the prescribed period beginning with the relevant day.

(9) If a court is satisfied on the application of any person who has made a request under the foregoing provisions of this section that the data controller in question has failed to comply with the request in contravention of those provisions, the court may order him to comply with the request.

(10) In this section–
   –   'prescribed' means prescribed by the Secretary of State by regulations;
   –   'the prescribed maximum' means such amount as may be prescribed;
   –   'the prescribed period' means forty days or such other period as may be prescribed;
   –   'the relevant day', in relation to a request under this section, means the day on which the data controller receives the request or, if later, the first day on which the data controller has both the required fee and the information referred to in subsection (3).

Section 14 entitles the data subject to correct inaccurate information.

The Data Protection (Subject Access Modification) (Health) Order 2000 SI 2000/413 also provides that someone with parental responsibility or appointed by a court to manage someone's affairs cannot obtain access to records if the patient does not wish that information to be disclosed. In addition, access cannot be provided if it identifies another person, other than a health care professional, who has not consented to the disclosure, unless it is reasonable to comply with the request without the consent of that other individual. This provision complies with the European Court decision in *Gaskin v United Kingdom*,[101] where records where withheld on the ground that the social workers objected or could not be traced. The court found that an absolute prohibition on

---

101   (1990) 12 EHRR 36.

disclosure was in breach of Art 8. As will be seen, s 7(6) sets out those matters to be considered in relation to 'reasonableness'.

The Access to Health Records Act 1990 and the Data Protection Act 1984, both contained exemptions, enabling data/record holders to withhold access to medical records in certain circumstances. There are now some exemptions within the 1998 Act itself (for example, relating to the detection of crime). The main medical record exemption in respect of the Data Protection Act 1998 is contained within the Data Protection (Subject Access Modification) (Health) Order 2000 SI 2000/413. Basically, this entitles the health professional concerned to withhold patient records if they consider that disclosure would be likely to cause serious harm to the physical or mental health or condition of the data subject or any other person (Art 5(1)). Before deciding whether this exemption applies, a data controller who is not a health care professional is obliged to consult the health professional responsible for the clinical care of the data subject, or if there is not such a person, someone with the necessary qualifications or experience. Unlike the Access to Health Records Act 1990, there is no specific provision in the Data Protection Act 1998 for applications by, or on behalf of child patients, nor for incompetent adults, although it is assumed by the Data Protection (Subject Access Modification) (Health) Order 2000 SI 2000/413 that these applications can be made.

If the record holder forms the opinion that the information may cause serious harm to the health of the patient or another, access may be excluded to the relevant part of the records. Yet again, this reflects medical paternalism. Further, it makes no sense that access should be refused because it may seriously harm the patient. If the patient is refused access on this ground, is not the refusal itself likely to cause harm? Speculation as to what the records may contain could, and probably would, cause considerable anxiety. Even if one accepts the argument that many patients do not want to know about risks of treatment before consent is given, the same argument cannot apply to access. Patients of sound mind, who have gone to the trouble of making an application, should have their requests respected. Harm caused to third parties raises different issues, which would depend upon the identity of the third party, the type and magnitude of the harm and so on.

Roberts v Nottinghamshire Healthcare NHS Trust[102] concerned an application for disclosure of a medical report under s 7(9) of the Data Protection Act 1998. The applicant was detained in a high security psychiatric hospital following the commission of violent offences. His case was due to be reviewed by a Mental Health Review Tribunal and a report had been prepared by the psychologist who had been treating him. He asked for disclosure of the report, but this was refused on the basis that the Trust did not intend to rely upon the report but on a report from another psychologist. The court held that the Trust had compelling reasons to refuse disclosure and there was no injustice to the applicant because the report would not be used by the Trust and he had the opportunity to have his own psychologist's report presented to the Tribunal. The reasons for non-disclosure were set out in a closed court with only a special advocate present to hear them. McRae comments as follows:

McRae, L, 'Case Comment, Withholding medical records without explanation: a Foucauldian reading of public interest'[103]

It is not a simple task to reconcile the judgment in *Roberts* with substantive and procedural rights. Rule 39.2(3)(c) of the Civil Procedure Rules 1997 states that a hearing, or any part of it, may be conducted in private, if it 'involves confidential information . . . and publicity would damage that confidentiality'. In reaching this decision, the judge will take into account the requirements of Article 6(1) of the Convention (right to a fair and public hearing). Moreover, 'the decision as to whether to hold a hearing in public or in private must be made by the judge conducting the hearing having regard to any *representations* which may have been made to him' [my emphasis].

---

102 [2008] EWHC 1934 (QB).
103 (2009) Med L Rev 438.

In respect of this latter requirement, the judge's decision to hear the exemption relied upon by the defendant in private is baffling. Cranston J suggested that '[f]or the reasons given in Closed Judgment the circumstances here were highly unusual'; yet, one would assume that the more unusual the exemption, the stronger the justification for disclosing it. As it was, Cranston J decided to provide a closed judgment on the sole basis that the NHS Trust had been unwilling up until trial to provide Roberts' solicitors with the exemption it was relying on. In effect, the appropriateness of the exemption was not known *until* the decision to hear the defendant's reasons in private had been reached. Consequently, the justification to 'go private' was borne of the judge's confidence in the defendant's reasons for non-disclosure *apriori*. In an era which is supposed to be increasing the 'transparency' of the administration of justice, this makes the reasoning in *Roberts* dubious.

The Access to Medical Reports Act 1988 confers a right of access to medical reports obtained for employment or insurance purposes. The Act also gives a right for the individual to have access to the report before it is supplied, and provides for the correction by the patient of matters contained in the report. It is important to note that the Act only applies to reports prepared by a medical practitioner who is, or has been, responsible for the clinical care of the individual (s 2(1)). What of the situation where the doctor is nominated by an insurance company or employer, to whom the Act does not apply? Would an obligation of confidence arise? It is submitted that, once the doctor had examined the patient and obtained medical information, without express or implied consent that it would be disclosed, the doctor would owe a duty of confidence. However, would it be easier to conclude that implied consent had been given by attending the medical appointment in the first place? The right under the Act is qualified in the same way as it is under the Data Protection Act 1998. There is a right to apply to the court if access is refused (sub-s (8)).

5.5.2.2 Common law

As has been seen above, there is now a qualified, statutory right of access to medical records, but this does not apply to non-computerised records made prior to 1 November 1991. The common law is still, therefore, of considerable importance. The issue was examined by the Court of Appeal in the case of R v Mid Glamorgan Family Health Services Authority and Another ex p Martin. The facts were as follows. As a young man, the applicant had received psychiatric treatment from doctors employed by the respondents. He had also received assistance from a female social worker, with whom he became infatuated. She was taken off his case, and for some years he had sought access to his medical records, to find out why the social worker had been removed and why he had subsequently been committed under the 1959 Mental Health Act. Access had been refused, on the basis that they were the property of the relevant authority and that disclosure would be damaging to the applicant and to third parties. The applicant's lawyers had responded to the effect that these doctors were in no position to judge whether the applicant would be damaged. Clearly, this was a forceful argument, and it resulted in a compromise offer: the respondents would agree to disclose the records to a medical adviser nominated by him, for that person to decide whether they may be damaging. The offer was refused. The judge at first instance dismissed the application for unmediated disclosure. In the Court of Appeal, the appeal was dismissed:

R v Mid Glamorgan Family Health Services Authority and Another ex p Martin (1995)[104]

Nourse LJ[105] . . . a public body, in fulfilment of its duty to administer its property in accordance with its public purposes, is bound to deal with medical records in the same way as a private

---

104 [1995] 1 WLR 110.
105 At p 116.

doctor. In that regard the observations of Lord Templeman in *Sidaway* [1985] 1 AC 871, p 904, are pertinent:

> I do not subscribe to the theory that the patient is entitled to know everything nor to the theory that the doctor is entitled to decide everything. The relationship between doctor and patient is contractual in origin, the doctor performing services in consideration for fees payable by the patient. The doctor, obedient to the high standards set by the medical profession, impliedly contracts to act at all times in the best interests of the patient. No doctor in his senses would impliedly contract at the same time to give to the patient all the information available to the doctor as a result of the doctor's training and experience and as a result of the doctor's diagnosis of the patient. An obligation to give a patient all the information available to the doctor would often be inconsistent with the doctor's contractual obligation to have regard to the patient's best interests. Some information might confuse, other information might alarm a particular patient. Whenever the occasion arises for the doctor to tell the patient the results of the doctor's diagnosis, the possible methods of treatment and the advantages and disadvantages of the recommended treatment, the doctor must decide in the light of his training and experience and in the light of his knowledge of the patient what should be said and how it should be said.

These observations provide a sensible basis for holding that a doctor, likewise a health authority, as the owner of a patient's medical records, may deny the patient access to them if it is in his best interests to do so, for example if their disclosure would be detrimental to his health.

It is inherent in the views above expressed that I do not accept that a health authority, any more than a private doctor, has an absolute right to deal with medical records in any way that it chooses. As Lord Templeman makes clear, the doctor's general duty, likewise the health authority's, is to act at all times in the best interests of the patient.

The Court also relied on the fact that, although there were a number of statutory rights to access, these were not absolute, and could be wholly or partially excluded in appropriate circumstances. It seems that the Court of Appeal in *Martin* simply accepted the opinion of the consultant psychiatrist and, thence, the respondents' solicitors, that disclosure would be detrimental to the patient. As the above common law *dicta* and legislation show, detriment alone ought to be insufficient.

Is it not the case that the 'serious harm' exception in relation to the patient, however stringently applied, is contrary to patient autonomy? Surely if the patient is competent and suitably warned, he should be entitled to run the risk?

A paternalistic approach was taken by the Australian Supreme Court of New South Wales in the case of *Breen v Williams*, where the doctor's right to decide what it would be good for a patient to know was upheld:

Breen v Williams (1995)[106]

Mahoney JA[107]: . . . *prima facie*, a medical file kept by a doctor is the property of the doctor. . . .

More difficult questions arise in relation to matters such as those particularly referred to by Dr Cashman in the present case, namely, notes taken by the doctor to record the patient's medical history and her signs and symptoms. In one sense such records are made for the purposes of the patient, the making of them is one of the things which the doctor, by his

---

106   [1995] 6 Med LR 385.
107   At p 427.

engagement, may undertake to do. In this sense, the document is created so that there may be a record of what the patient has told the doctor and her signs and symptoms at the time. The record may not merely help in the instant diagnosis and a selection of treatment, it may provide a valuable resource for future purposes. Considered in isolation, a record of this kind, if it were contained in a separate document, would, I think, be the property of the patient.

On the other hand, the doctor may – . . . include with the record of the history and the signs and symptoms of the patient, comments and observations which are made and recorded for the purpose of helping the doctor form the diagnosis and the opinion to be formed as to treatment. There may be observations – Dr Williams used the term 'musings' – which, if standing alone, would ordinarily be the property of the doctor and not of the patient. It is the fact that these things are combined in the documents which illustrates the nature of the problem in a case such as this.

The combination of such things: the history, signs and symptoms on the one hand and the 'musings' and other things on the other hand, may be accidental in the sense that the combination of the two in the one record is not inherent in the process of medical knowledge. But the thrust of Dr Williams' evidence is, I think, that such a combination is not accidental. His evidence suggests that the combination of these two things is inherent in the way medical practice is conducted or, at least in the way he conducts his practice. The trial judge accepted this portion of the doctor's evidence.

If the records kept by the doctor be in this form, then, in my opinion, the records remain the property of the doctor . . .

This decision does not deny that a patient has a right to know the main contents of his records, what it denies to him is the right to look through them and discover his doctor's comments. The reason given for this is that the doctor will be inhibited when making his notes, and that may not be in the patient's interest. It is easy to see that a doctor may feel restrained from making adverse comments relating to, say, genuineness of symptoms, when, for example, referring a patient to another doctor, if he thought that the patient may see this. However, the suspicions must be based upon factual matters such as an inconsistent history of symptoms, and physical examination failing to accord with alleged symptoms, and surely these are matters which the doctor should discuss openly with his patient. Or is it arguable that there is a risk of losing the patient's trust?

However, in *Breen v Williams*, there was a dissenting judgment, by Kirby P, in favour of disclosure, which relied on there being a fiduciary duty owed to the patient. This was following the Canadian Supreme Court decision of *McInerney v MacDonald*.[108] In this case comment was made as follows:

La Forest J (p 421): Information about oneself revealed to a doctor acting in a professional capacity remains, in a fundamental sense, one's own. The doctor's position is one of trust and confidence. The information conveyed is held in a fashion somewhat akin to a trust. While the doctor is the owner of the actual record, the information is to be used by the physician for the benefit of the patient. The confiding of the information to the physician for medical purposes gives rise to an expectation that the patient's interest in and control of the information will continue. The trust-like 'beneficial interest' of the patient in the information indicates that, as a general rule, he or she should have a right of access to the information and that the physician should have a corresponding obligation to provide it.

---

108   (1992) 93 DLR (4th) 415.

5.5.2.3 European Convention on Human Rights

Gaskin v UK[109] confirmed the right of a patient to access his medical records. In *MG v UK*[110] the ECtHR held that the right was not absolute and there could be legitimate restriction on access to protect third parties. In *KH and others v Slovakia*[111] it was held that a request to access records did not have to be justified; on the contrary it was for the record holders to show that there are compelling reasons for refusal.

 SELF-TEST QUESTION

How might the fiduciary duty argument have changed the decision of the Court of Appeal in *Martin*?

Summary of Key Points

1.   The law relating to confidentiality has been refined since the Human Rights Act 1998 whereby Art 8 of the European Convention on Human Rights which protects the right to privacy has become part of domestic law. There are subtle differences between confidentiality and privacy.

2.   Neither the right to protection of confidences nor the right to privacy are absolute and they can be breached in the public interest, or with the consent of the patient.

3.   A countervailing public interest can arise in a wide variety of cases so although it is often about the risk of serious physical or mental harm to an individual, the protection of a free press or a fair judicial system are also compelling public interests.

4.   Unjustified breaches of confidence raise interesting questions as to the precise nature of the damage suffered and how it should be compensated.

5.   There is a difference between a health care professional being able to justify breaching confidence and being *obliged* to do so.

6.   Patients have statutory rights of access to their medical records, and a limited common law right, but there are controversial exceptions to these rights.

Further Reading

Case , P, Confidence matters:The rise and fall of informational autonomy in medical law (2003), *Medical Law Review* 11:208.

Michalowski, S, *Medical Confidentiality and Crime*, Aldershot: Ashgate Dartmouth, 2003.

Stanley, P, *The Law of Confidentiality: a Restatement*, Oxford: Hart Publishing, 2008.

Toulson, R G and Phipps C M, *Confidentiality*, London: Sweet & Maxwell, 2006.

---

109   (1990) 12 EHRR 36.
110   [2002] 3 FCR 413.
111   App 32881/94, judgment April 2009.

Chapter 6

Medical Malpractice

Chapter Contents

6.1 Introduction

Medical malpractice may be defined, broadly, as any unjustified act or failure to act upon the part of a doctor or other health care worker which results in harm to the patient. In this chapter we shall be considering the means, under the civil law, by which a victim of such malpractice may pursue a claim for redress, and the difficulties that lie in his way. (The rare instances in which the doctor may also be the subject of criminal liability have been noted in Chapter 2 at 2.3.4.)

First, what form might the patient's claim take? On the face of it, there would seem to be three possibilities – to sue in tort, either in battery or negligence, or to mount an action for breach of contract. In practice, however, it is the second of these, a negligence action, which offers the only appropriate channel for the vast majority of malpractice claims. The first option, battery, which forms the civil analogue to the crime of assault, generally only arises as a possibility in those rare cases where treatment is carried out without any consent at all. It is no use to the patient who, having given such consent, suffers injury, however poor the execution of the treatment subsequently turns out to be.

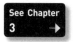

As for the third option, breach of contract, the first thing to note is that this will not assist patients treated under the NHS scheme (that is, the large majority of patients in this country), who provide no consideration in return for the services they receive.[1] What, though, of patients treated in the private sector? Whilst it is true that the latter may sue for breach of contract instead of (or as well as) in negligence, in proving a breach they normally have exactly the same task as their NHS counterparts. This is because it is most unlikely that the doctor will have promised expressly to achieve a specific desired outcome (although for an exceptional American case in point, see *LaFleur v Cornelis*[2]); and otherwise, in implying the terms which govern such contracts, the courts have held the standard of skill and care warranted by the private doctor to be identical to the standard of care required to avoid a claim in negligence. In *Thake v Maurice*,[3] a case in which a patient treated privately sued following the failure of his vasectomy, Neill LJ in the Court of Appeal commented:

> **Neill LJ**: I do not consider that a reasonable person would have expected a responsible medical man to be intending to give a guarantee. Medicine, though a highly skilled profession, is not, and is not generally regarded as being, an exact science. The reasonable man would have expected the defendant to exercise all the special care and skill of a surgeon in that speciality; he would not in my view have expected the defendant to give a guarantee of 100% success.

This common law standard of care is also echoed in s 13 of the Supply of Goods and Services Act 1982, which provides that a person who supplies services in the course of a business must carry them out with reasonable care and skill.

Accordingly, in the remainder of this chapter we shall focus upon actions in medical (or 'clinical') negligence. In order for such actions to succeed, a number of basic elements (familiar from the general tort of negligence) must be made out, that is, the existence of a duty of care, the fact of its breach, and that legally recognised damage was thereby caused. Each raises particular issues in the context of medical negligence, which we shall consider in turn in sections 6.2–6.4, as well as possible defences for the doctor, in section 6.5. In section 6.6 we then address the scheme of 'strict liability' that exists for medicinal products, as 'consumer goods'. Overall, it is notorious that medical negligence claims are frequently hard to prove (as well as costly, time-consuming and traumatic for those involved), and we shall conclude, in section 6.7, by considering the issue of law reform in this area.

---

1   *Appleby v Sleep* [1968] 2 All ER 265. Similarly, it was confirmed in *Reynolds v The Health First Medical Group* [2000] Lloyd's Rep Med 240, that a patient does not have a contractual relationship with his GP.
2   (1979) 28 NBR (2d) 569 (there a cosmetic surgeon promised to improve the appearance of the patient's nose).
3   [1986] QB 644.

6.2 The Duty of Care

6.2.1 The duty to the patient

The patient must establish that the defendant, who may be a doctor, nurse, NHS trust, or a health authority, owed him a legal duty of care. This is generally speaking the easiest element to show. As Michael Jones comments:

Jones, M, *Medical Negligence*[4]

Normally, there will be no difficulty in finding a duty of care owed by the doctor to his patient, at least where the claim is in respect of personal injuries, and this is true even where there is a contractual relationship. The practitioner may also owe a duty of care to the patient in respect of pure financial loss. In addition, there are a number of circumstances where a doctor may also owe a duty of care to a third party arising out of the treatment given to the patient, but the incident and extent of such duties is more problematic.

6.2.1.1 Hospital treatment

The case of *Barnett v Chelsea and Kensington Hospital Management Committee*[5] is authority for the proposition that an open accident and emergency unit has a duty to treat or at least assess the patient. The facts arose after three nightwatchmen, who were taken ill after drinking some tea, went to their local hospital's casualty department, but were sent away without being seen by a doctor. Nield J stated:

Nield J: I turn to consider the nature of the duty which the law imposes on persons in the position of the defendants and their servants and agents. The authorities deal in the main with the duties of doctors, surgeons, consultants, nurses and staff when a person is treated either by a doctor at his surgery or the patient's home or when the patient is treated in or at a hospital. In *Cassidy v Ministry of Health* [1951] 2 KB 343, Denning LJ dealt with the duties of hospital authorities and said:

> In my opinion, authorities who run a hospital, be they local authorities, government boards, or any other corporation, are in law under the self-same duty as the humblest doctor. Whenever they accept a patient for treatment, they must use reasonable care and skill to cure him of his ailment. The hospital authorities cannot, of course, do it by themselves. They have no ears to listen through the stethoscope, and no hands to hold the knife. They must do it by the staff which they employ, and, if their staff are negligent in giving the treatment, they are just as liable for that negligence as is anyone else who employs others to do his duties for him. Is there any possible difference in law, I ask, can there be, between hospital authorities who accept a patient for treatment and railway or shipping authorities who accept a passenger for carriage? None whatever. Once they undertake the task, they come under a duty to use care in the doing of it, and that is so whether they do it for reward or not.

Here the problem is different and no authority bearing directly on it has been cited to me. It is to determine the duty of those who provide and run a casualty department when a person presents himself at that department complaining of illness or injury and before he is treated and received into the hospital wards. This is not a case of a casualty department which closes its doors and says that no patients can be received. The three watchmen entered the defendants' hospital without hindrance, they made complaints to the nurse who received them and

4   London: Sweet & Maxwell, 1996.
5   [1969] 1 QB 428.

she in turn passed those complaints on to the medical casualty officer, and he sent a message through the nurse purporting to advise the three men. Is there, on these facts, shown to be created a relationship between the three watchmen and the hospital staff such as gives rise to a duty of care in the defendants which they owe to the three men?

. . . In my judgment, there was here such a close and direct relationship between the hospital and the watchmen that there was imposed on the hospital a duty of care which they owed to the watchmen. Thus, I have no doubt that Nurse Corbett and Dr Banerjee were under a duty to the deceased to exercise that skill and care which is to be expected of persons in such positions acting reasonably . . .

Individual hospital doctors and nurses are unlikely to be sued directly by the injured patient. A legal claim will normally be made against the hospital/NHS Trust, as the health professional's employer, who will be vicariously liable. This assumes that the negligent doctor or nurse was an employee and was acting in the course of his or her employment. The Department of Health has produced special guidance on handling clinical negligence claims against NHS staff:

Department of Health, *NHS Indemnity – Arrangements for Negligence Claims in the NHS*[6]

Purpose of this document
This document describes the arrangements which apply to handling clinical negligence claims against NHS staff (NHS Indemnity). It updates the guidance given in Health Circular HC (89) 34 . . .

Clinical negligence
Clinical negligence is defined as:

. . . a breach of duty of care by members of the health care professions employed by NHS bodies or by others consequent on decisions or judgments made by members of those professions acting in their professional capacity in the course of their employment, and which are admitted as negligent by the employer or are determined as such through the legal process.

The term health care professional includes hospital doctors, dentists, nurses, midwives, health visitors, pharmacy practitioners, registered ophthalmic or dispensing opticians (working in a hospital setting), members of professions allied to medicine and dentistry, ambulance personnel, laboratory staff and relevant technicians.

Main principles
NHS bodies are vicariously liable for the negligent acts and omissions of their employees and should have arrangements for meeting this liability.

NHS Indemnity applies where:

(a) the negligent health care professional was:
  (i) working under a contract of employment and the negligence occurred in the course of that employment;
  (ii) not working under a contract of employment but was contracted to an NHS body to provide services to persons to whom that NHS body owed a duty of care;
  (iii) neither of the above but otherwise owed a duty of care to the persons injured;
(b) persons, not employed under a contract of employment and who may or may not be a health care professional, who owe a duty of care to the persons injured. These include

---

6   Catalogue No 96 HR 0024, London: DoH, 1996.

locums; medical academic staff with honorary contracts; students; those conducting clinical trials; charitable volunteers; persons undergoing further professional education, training and examinations; students and staff working on income generation projects.

Where these principles apply, NHS bodies should accept full financial liability where negligent harm has occurred, and not seek to recover their costs from the health care professional involved.

Who is not covered

NHS Indemnity does not apply to family health service practitioners working under contracts for services, for example: GPs (including fundholders), general dental practitioners, family dentists, pharmacists or optometrists; other self-employed health care professionals, for example, independent midwives; employees of FHS practices; employees of private hospitals; local education authorities; voluntary agencies . . .

Circumstances covered

NHS Indemnity covers negligent harm caused to patients or healthy volunteers in the following circumstances: whenever they are receiving an established treatment, whether or not in accordance with an agreed guideline or protocol; whenever they are receiving a novel or unusual treatment which, in the judgment of the health care professional, is appropriate for that particular patient; whenever they are subjects as patients or healthy volunteers of clinical research aimed at benefiting patients now or in the future.

In certain circumstances the hospital or NHS Trust may be directly liable for breaching a duty of care they owe to the patient in negligence; in *Wilsher v Essex AHA*,[7] the Court of Appeal suggested that such liability would arise if it were shown that the hospital authorities had filled treatment positions with staff who were unable (through inexperience or otherwise) to cope with the demands made upon them. Direct liability will also arise where the claimant's injury is attributable to some overall failure, of an organisational nature, to provide a safe environment for carrying out treatment. Similarly, in the case of a patient whose treatment is 'farmed out' to a private hospital (an increasing expedient in the drive to cut waiting lists), it is apparent, following *M v Calderdale and Kirklees HA*,[8] that the referring NHS institution remains under a non-delegable duty of care in respect of such treatment.

6.2.1.2 Treatment outside hospital

In relation to general practitioners, who operate outside hospitals, these clearly owe a duty of care to their own patients, that is, those who are registered with them. Moreover, by virtue of the National Health Service (General Medical Services) Regulations 1992,[9] Sch 2, para 4(1)(h), such a practitioner is required, pursuant to his statutory contract with the area Family Health Services Authority, to treat:

(h) persons to whom he may be requested to give treatment which is immediately required owing to an accident or other emergency at any place in his practice area, provided that–
(i)   he is not, at time of the request, relieved of liability to give treatment under para 5; and
(ii) he is not, at the time of the request, relieved, under para 19(2), of his obligation to give treatment personally; and
(iii) he is available to provide such treatment,
and any persons by whom he is requested, and agrees, to give treatment which is immediately required owing to an accident or other emergency at any place in the locality of any

---

7 [1987] QB 730, CA.
8 [1998] Lloyd's Rep 157.
9 SI 1992/635.

FHSA in whose medical list he is included, provided there is no doctor who, at the time of the request, is under an obligation otherwise than under this head to give treatment to that person, or there is such a doctor but, after being requested to attend, he is unable to attend and give treatment immediately required . . .

(Paragraphs 5 and 19(2) of the Schedule relieve the doctor of liability to treat, respectively, in cases where he is elderly or infirm, or another doctor is already present.)

The nature of the duty of care owed in such cases by the practitioner to the patient was considered *obiter* by Stuart-Smith LJ in *Capital and Counties v Hants CC*:[10]

Stuart-Smith LJ: As a general rule a sufficient relationship of proximity will exist when someone possessed of special skill undertakes to apply that skill for the assistance of another person who relies upon such skill and there is direct and substantial reliance by the plaintiff on the defendant's skill (see *Hedley Byrne and Co Ltd v Heller and Partners* and *Henderson v Merrett Syndicates Ltd*). There are many instances of this. The plaintiffs submit that that which is most closely analogous is that of doctor and patient or health authority and patient. There is no doubt that once the relationship of doctor and patient or hospital authority and admitted patient exists, the doctor or the hospital owe a duty to take reasonable care to effect a cure, not merely to prevent further harm. The undertaking is to use the special skills which the doctor and hospital authorities have to treat the patient. In *Cassidy v Ministry of Health (Fahrni, Third Party)* [1951] 1 All ER 574, p 588, Denning LJ said:

> In my opinion, authorities who run a hospital, be they local authorities, government boards, or any other corporation, are in law under the self-same duty as the humblest doctor. Whenever they accept a patient for treatment, they must use reasonable care and skill to cure him of his ailment.

In *Barnett v Chelsea and Kensington Hospital Management Committee* [1968] 1 All ER 1068, Nield J drew a distinction between a casualty department of a hospital that closes its doors and says no patients can be received, in which case he would by inference have held there was no duty of care, and the case before him where the three watchmen who had taken poison entered the hospital and were given erroneous advice, where a duty of care arose.

Likewise, a doctor who happened to witness a road accident will very likely go to the assistance of anyone injured, but he is not under any legal obligation to do so (save in certain limited circumstances which are not relevant) and the relationship of doctor and patient does not arise. If he volunteers his assistance, his only duty as a matter of law is not to make the victim's condition worse.

Subsequently, however, the decision in *Capital and Counties* was distinguished by Lord Woolf MR in *Kent v Griffiths (No 3)*[11] in the context of an ambulance's failure to respond expeditiously to a 999 call made on behalf of a woman who had suffered a serious asthma attack. (The ambulance took nearly 40 minutes to complete a journey that should have taken no more than 20 minutes, and the patient in the meantime suffered a cardiac arrest.) In holding that a duty of care was owed by the ambulance service, his Lordship commented as follows:

Lord Woolf MR: Here what was being provided was a health service. In the case of health services under the 1977 Act the conventional situation is that there is a duty of care. Why should the

---

10 [1997] QB 1004.
11 [2001] QB 36.

position of the ambulance staff be different from that of doctors or nurses? In addition the arguments based on public policy are much weaker in the case of the ambulance service than they are in the case of the police or the fire service. The police and fire services' primary obligation is to the public at large. In protecting a particular victim of crime, the police are performing their more general role of maintaining public order and reducing crime. In the case of fire the fire service will normally be concerned not only to protect a particular property where a fire breaks out but also to prevent fire spreading. In the case of both services, there is therefore a concern to protect the public generally . . . Situations could arise where there is a conflict between the interests of a particular individual and the public at large. But, in the case of the ambulance service in this particular case, the only member of the public who could be adversely affected was the claimant. It was the claimant alone for whom the ambulance had been called.

It remains uncertain how far a similar affirmative duty of rescue (requiring him to assist an ill or injured stranger whom he happens to come across outside his practice) would be imposed upon an individual doctor. This question must now be considered in the light of the courts' obligation, under the Human Rights Act 1998, to develop the common law in line with rights under the European Convention on Human Rights, and in this context, Art 2, safeguarding the right to life may well be relevant. In particular, the person who suffers avoidable injury through the doctor's non-assistance might argue that the law's failure to impose liability upon the latter itself amounts to an infringement of his Art 2 right.[12]

Similar questions arise in relation to examinations carried out by doctors upon persons at the behest of third parties, such as employers or insurance companies. Here the examinee does not become the patient of the doctor in the strict sense: nonetheless, should the latter be placed under a positive duty carefully to diagnose and inform him of any abnormalities (as opposed to having a merely negative duty not to injure him during the examination)? In X (Minors) v Bedfordshire County Council,[13] Lord Browne-Wilkinson suggested obiter that only the negative duty would arise, and this was applied by the Court of Appeal in Kapfunde v Abbey National.[14] The latter case, however, was one of pure economic loss, suffered by a job-applicant who failed to get a job in the light of an unfavourable medical report. By contrast, in the context of physical injury related to a condition negligently overlooked by the examining doctor, it seems likely that a duty would be found. As Andrew Grubb has commented:

Grubb, A (ed), *Principles of Medical Law*[15]

5.119 . . . [I]n principle, applying the well-known *Caparo* test, there is no difficulty in holding the doctor liable for *all* the immediate consequences of a failure to exercise reasonable care and skill in the course of the examination. Consequently, he could be liable for failing (carelessly) to diagnose a medical condition which could have been treated or its symptons alleviated if it had been diagnosed earlier. Injury to the person would be foreseeable and there would be a proximate relationship based upon an implied assumption of responsibility by the doctor. The expectation of both examinee and doctor will usually be that the doctor will perform his professional obligation to the person which would include alerting the person to anything untoward.

---

12 For an instructive Australian decision, in which a doctor, who was in his surgery at the time, was held liable in tort for failing to answer a summons for help from a stranger, see *Lowns v Woods* [1996] Aust Torts Rep 81–376.
13 [1995] 2 AC 633.
14 (1998) 46 BMLR 176.
15 2nd edn, Oxford: OUP, 2004.

6.2.2 The duty in 'wrongful conception/birth' cases

Until a few years ago, English law was prepared, in principle, to award damages to parents for the costs of bringing up healthy children who would not have been born but for negligence on the part of a doctor: see, for example, the Court of Appeal's decision in *Thake v Maurice*,[16] where the defendant failed to advise a husband that the vasectomy that he had been given was liable to reverse spontaneously. However, this area of the law was dramatically altered by the decision of the House of Lords in *McFarlane v Tayside Health*.

McFarlane v Tayside Health Board (2000)[17]

Mr McFarlane, who was married with four children, underwent a vasectomy operation at the defendant's hospital and was told that it had been a success and that he and his wife need no longer use contraception. Subsequently, his wife became pregnant by him again and gave birth to a fifth child. In their negligence action against the board, the couple claimed damages both for the physical discomfort suffered by Mrs McFarlane during her pregnancy, and for the financial costs of bringing up the child:

> **Lord Slynn of Hadley**: My Lords, I do not find real difficulty in deciding the claim for damages in respect of the pregnancy and birth itself. The parents did not want another child for justifiable economic and family reasons; they already had four children. They were entitled lawfully to take steps to make sure that that did not happen, one possible such step being a vasectomy of the husband. It was plainly foreseeable that if the operation did not succeed, or recanalisation of the vas took place, but the husband was told that contraceptive measures were not necessary, the wife might become pregnant. It does not seem to me to be necessary to consider the events of an unwanted conception and birth in terms of 'harm' or 'injury' in its ordinary sense of the words. They were unwanted and known by the health board to be unwanted events. The object of the vasectomy was to prevent them happening. It seems to me that in consequence the wife, if there was negligence, is entitled by way of general damages to be compensated for the pain and discomfort and inconvenience of the unwanted pregnancy and birth and she is also entitled to special damages associated with both – extra medical expenses, clothes for herself and equipment on the birth of the baby . . .
>
> The question remains whether as a matter of legal principle the damages should include, for a child by then loved, loving and fully integrated into the family the cost of shoes at 14 and a dress at 17 and everything that can reasonably be described as necessary for the upbringing of the child until the end of school, university, independence, maturity? . . .
>
> The doctor undertakes a duty of care in regard to the prevention of pregnancy: it does not follow that the duty includes also avoiding the costs of rearing the child if born and accepted into the family. Whereas I have no doubt that there should be compensation for the physical effects of the pregnancy and birth, including of course solatium for consequential suffering by the mother immediately following the birth, I consider that it is not fair, just or reasonable to impose on the doctor or his employer liability for the consequential responsibilities, imposed on or accepted by the parents to bring up a child. The doctor does not assume responsibility for those economic losses. If a client wants to be able to recover such costs he or she must do so by an appropriate contract.

---

16 See n 3 above.
17 [2000] 2 AC 59.

Lord Steyn: It is possible to view the case simply from the perspective of corrective justice. It requires somebody who has harmed another without justification to indemnify the other. On this approach the parents' claim for the cost of bringing up Catherine must succeed. But one may also approach the case from the vantage point of distributive justice. It requires a focus on the just distribution of burdens and losses among members of a society. If the matter is approached in this way, it may become relevant to ask commuters on the Underground the following question: 'Should the parents of an unwanted but healthy child be able to sue the doctor or hospital for compensation equivalent to the cost of bringing up the child for the years of his or her minority, ie until about 18 years?' My Lords, I am firmly of the view that an overwhelming number of ordinary men and women would answer the question with an emphatic 'No'. And the reason for such a response would be an inarticulate premise as to what is morally acceptable and what is not. Like Ognall J in *Jones v Berkshire AHA*, 2 July 1986, they will have in mind that many couples cannot have children and others have the sorrow and burden of looking after a disabled child. The realisation that compensation for financial loss in respect of the upbringing of a child would necessarily have to discriminate between rich and poor would, surely appear unseemly to them. It would also worry them that parents may be put in a position of arguing in court that the unwanted child, which they accepted and care for, is more trouble than it is worth. Instinctively, the traveller on the Underground would consider that the law of tort has no business to provide legal remedies consequent upon the birth of a healthy child, which all of us regard as a valuable and good thing.

Lord Millett: . . . I am persuaded that the costs of bringing Catherine up are not recoverable. I accept the thrust of both the main arguments in favour of dismissing such a claim. In my opinion the law must take the birth of a normal, healthy baby to be a blessing, not a detriment. In truth it is a mixed blessing. It brings joy and sorrow, blessing and responsibility. The advantages and the disadvantages are inseparable. Individuals may choose to regard the balance as unfavourable and take steps to forgo the pleasures as well as the responsibilities of parenthood. They are entitled to decide for themselves where their own interests lie. But society itself must regard the balance as beneficial. It would be repugnant to its own sense of values to do otherwise. It is morally offensive to regard a normal, healthy baby as more trouble and expense than it is worth.

Although the Law Lords did not speak with one voice in *McFarlane*, it is apparent that, where a healthy child is born, damages will be limited to the physical pain and discomfort suffered by the mother during pregnancy. By contrast, no duty of care is owed to the parents in respect of the subsequent costs of maintaining a healthy child. Given both the incalculable benefits to the parents involved, and the policy factors adverted to by Lord Steyn, it was felt that such a birth should simply not sound in damages in tort.[18]

An issue left unresolved by *McFarlane* concerned the problem of parents who, in similar circumstances, have a disabled child. This matter was subsequently considered in *Parkinson v St James and Seacroft University Hospital NHS Trust*,[19] in which, after usefully analysing the diverse speeches in *McFarlane*, the Court of Appeal concluded that the additional costs associated with the child's disability were recoverable. As Brooke LJ commented:

---

18 See also the subsequent decision of the Court of Appeal in *Greenfield v Irwin (A Firm)* [2001] 1 WLR 1279.
19 [2001] 3 WLR 376.

Brooke LJ: . . . (iv) The purpose of the operation was to prevent Mrs P from conceiving any more children, including children with congenital abnormalities, and the surgeon's duty of care is strictly related to the proper fulfilment of that purpose; (v) Parents in Mrs P's position were entitled to recover damages in these circumstances for 15 years between the decisions in *Emeh* and *McFarlane*, so that this is not a radical step forward into the unknown; . . . (vii) If principles of distributive justice are called in aid, I believe that ordinary people would consider that it would be fair for the law to make an award in such a case, provided that it is limited to the extra expenses associated with the child's disability. I can see nothing in any majority reasoning in *McFarlane* to deflect this court from adopting this course, which in my judgment both logic and justice demands.

In another case following *McFarlane*, that of *Rees v Darlington Memorial Hospital NHS Trust*, a majority of the Court of Appeal held that, similarly, a disabled mother who gave birth to a healthy child was entitled to recover the extra costs of child care arising out of her disability. This decision was subsequently taken on appeal by the NHS trust to a specially constituted seven-judge House of Lords.

Rees v Darlington Memorial Hospital NHS Trust (2003)[20]

Ms Rees underwent a sterilisation, due, *inter alia*, to her concern that her severe visual disability would prevent her from being able to care for a child. The operation was performed negligently and she subsequently became pregnant and gave birth to a healthy son. Essentially, the House of Lords was required to consider three points: (i) should it affirm the principle it had laid down four years before in *McFarlane* that damages would not lie for the maintenance of (healthy) children? If so: (iia) did a case, such as this one, involving a disabled parent, comprise an exception to that principle, as *per* the decision of the majority of the Court of Appeal? And – albeit an *obiter* issue: (iib) had the Court of Appeal been right, in the *Parkinson* case, to treat cases of disabled children as an exception to the *McFarlane* principle?

As to the first point, all seven Law Lords upheld the correctness of the decision in *McFarlane*. In his speech Lord Bingham commented on this aspect as follows:

Lord Bingham: [15] In *McFarlane*'s case, your Lordships' House held unanimously that a negligent doctor is not required to meet the cost of bringing up a healthy child born in these circumstances. The language, and to some extent the legal reasoning, employed by each of their Lordships differed. But, however expressed, the underlying perception of all their Lordships was that fairness and reasonableness do not require that the damages payable by a negligent doctor should extend so far. The approach usually adopted in measuring recoverable financial loss is not appropriate when the subject of the legal wrong is the birth of an unintended healthy child and the head of claim is the cost of the whole of the child's upbringing.

[16] I have heard nothing in the submissions advanced on the present appeal to persuade me that this decision by the House was wrong and ought to be revisited. On the contrary, that the negligent doctor or, in most cases, the National Health Service should pay all the costs of bringing up the child seems to me a disproportionate response to the doctor's wrong. It would accord ill with the values society attaches to human life and to parenthood. The birth of a child should not be treated as comparable to a parent suffering a personal injury, with the cost of rearing the child being treated as special damages akin to the financially adverse consequences flowing from the onset of a chronic medical condition.

---

20 [2003] UKHL 52.

On the other hand, a 'gloss' on *McFarlane* was approved by a majority of their Lordships (over the dissents of Lords Steyn and Hope), in the form of permitting a 'conventional award' of £15,000 in such cases to reflect the legal wrong done to claimants in having their wishes to stay childless thwarted.

As to the other issues, the House of Lords reversed, by a bare majority (Lords Steyn, Hope and Hutton dissenting), the decision of the Court of Appeal to award Ms Rees the extra costs of maintaining her healthy child in this case: in short, she was entitled to the £15,000 conventional sum, but nothing more. As to the final, *obiter* question of the position in relation to disabled children, this was left unresolved. Lords Bingham and Nicholls were of the view that here too only the conventional sum should lie, and disapproved the contrary decision of the Court of Appeal in *Parkinson*. By contrast, Lords Steyn, Hope and Hutton supported the recovery of extra costs attributable to maintaining a disabled child (albeit in the context of their dissenting view that a disabled parent should also recover). The two remaining Law Lords, Millett and Scott, left the question open.

In his speech, the latter Law Lord addressed the disabled-child issue as follows:

> **Lord Scott:** [144] I should mention *Parkinson v St James and Seacroft University Hospital NHS Trust* [2001] EWCA Civ 530, [2001] 3 All ER 97, [2002] QB 266. In *Parkinson's* case a sterilisation operation on the claimant was negligently performed. As a result the claimant conceived when she thought, and hoped, she was unable to do so. She declined to have her pregnancy terminated although warned that the child might be born with a disability. The child was born with severe disabilities. The claimant claimed damages for negligence. The Court of Appeal, following *McFarlane's* case up to a point, held that she was entitled to recover damages for the costs of providing for her child's special needs relating to his disabilities but was not entitled to recover the basic costs of his ordinary maintenance.
>
> [145] The question how the *McFarlane* principle should be applied to a case in which the mother is healthy but the child is born with a disability is not one which needs to be resolved on this appeal. In my opinion, however, a distinction may need to be drawn between a case where the avoidance of the birth of a child with a disability is the very reason why the parent or parents sought the medical treatment or services to avoid conception that, in the event, were negligently provided and a case where the medical treatment or services were sought simply to avoid conception. *Parkinson's* case was a case in the latter category. In such a case, where the parents have had no particular reason to fear that if a child is born to them it will suffer from a disability, I do not think there is any sufficient basis for treating the expenses occasioned by the disability as falling outside the principles underlying *McFarlane's* case. The striking of the balance between the burden of rearing the disabled child and the benefit to the parents of the child as a member of their family seems to me as invidious and impossible as in the case of the child born without any disability.

As Lord Scott points out, the disability suffered by the child in the *Parkinson* case was incidental to the hospital's negligence – the medical procedure there was designed to render the claimant sterile, not because she was at any special risk of having a disabled child, but simply for family planning purposes. However, another possible scenario is that the specific purpose of the procedure, whose negligent performance is the subject of a claim, was to avoid the birth of a disabled child. An example is *Hardman v Amin*,[21] where the defendant negligently failed to diagnose the claimant's

---

21 [2000] Lloyd's Rep Med 498.

rubella, thereby depriving her of the opportunity to have an abortion (which, it was accepted, she would have taken). As his Lordship implies, recovery should arguably be permitted in the latter type of ('direct disability') case. In this regard it is interesting to note that, in several such cases, the lower courts have awarded quite generous damages to cover the child's maintenance, not simply the extra costs attendant upon its disability.[22]

 SELF-TEST QUESTION

Do you think that full damages (including for maintenance) should remain payable in respect of disabled children?

6.2.3 The duty to third parties

Interesting questions arise as to how far a doctor will owe a duty to third parties to whom he personally offers no medical care at all. Two broad types of scenario require to be considered. The first ('dangerous patient cases') is where the third party is injured in a foreseeable way through subsequent contact with one of the doctor's patients. The second ('injured patient cases') is where the third party – typically a close relative – suffers secondary harm through the negligence of the doctor in harming the patient.

6.2.3.1 Dangerous patient cases

Suppose that a doctor fails to spot that one of his patients is carrying a contagious disease, and the latter subsequently passes on the infection: does the person he infects have any right of action against the doctor? As a general rule, and in accordance with established principles of tort, a person (A)'s liability for injury caused by another (B) to a third party (C) has tended to depend upon two factors: first, the extent to which B is an involuntary agent in the events which lead to C's injury; and, secondly, the ability on A's part to foresee C's presence in relation to B. Both factors appear to have played a part in the rejection by the Court of Appeal of the claimant's action in the case of *Palmer v Tees HA*.

Palmer v Tees HA (1999)[23]

Mrs Palmer, whose four-year-old daughter, Rosie, was murdered by a psychopath called Armstrong, brought an action against the defendant health authority both in her own name (in respect of the psychiatric illness she suffered) and on behalf of Rosie's estate. Some months prior to committing the murder Armstrong had been treated as an outpatient at the defendant's psychiatric hospital, where he had allegedly told staff that he would kill a child:

Stuart-Smith LJ: Was the judge right to hold that on the facts there was no proximity between the defendants and Rosie or the claimant? Basing himself on the *Dorset Yacht* case and *Hill*'s case the judge held that:

. . . in cases where it is alleged that a defendant by his negligence is responsible for the actions of a third party it must be shown that the victim or injured person was one who came into a special or exceptional or distinctive

---

22 As well as the *Hardman* case, see *Nunnerley v Warrington HA* [2000] PIQR Q69 and *Lee v Taunton and Somerset NHS Trust* [2001] 1 FLR 419 (but cf. *Rand v East Dorset HA* [2000] Lloyd's Rep Med 181).

23 [1999] Lloyd's Rep Med 351, CA.

category of risk from the activities of the third party. It is not sufficient to show that the victim or injured party was one of a wide category of members of the general public.

He held that the potential victim was not identified or identifiable. In the court below Mr Sherman argued that the fact that Rosie and the claimant lived in the same street as Armstrong was sufficient to establish proximity. But he did not rely on this argument before us. Instead he challenged the judge's conclusion stated in the last paragraph. He submitted that in cases of personal injury, it was sufficient that the injury was foreseeable. He relied upon the two passages already cited in paragraphs 16 and 17 above from Lord Oliver's speech in *Caparo* [[1990] 2 AC 605] and Lord Steyn's speech in *Marc Rich* [[1996] AC 211] approving Saville LJ. But in my opinion the judges, in making those statements, did not have in mind the situation which exists here where there is the interposition of the conscious and voluntary act of a third party . . .

[T]he critical decision is that of *Hill v Chief Constable of West Yorkshire* [1989] 1 AC 53 which is a case concerned with personal injury . . .

While there are of course differences between *Hill*'s case and the present, that was a case of the police and not psychiatrists, and the identity of the offender was unknown, the crucial point is that there is no relationship between the defendant and the victim. Mr Sherman relied on the case of *Holgate v Lancashire Mental Hospital Board* [1937] 4 All ER 19. The facts bear a striking resemblance to those in the present case. L was a defective who had been convicted of serious crimes and sentenced to detention during His Majesty's pleasure. In due course he was transferred to the defendant's institution. He was allowed out on licence without any proper inquiry being made, and the licence was subsequently extended. During the period of his extended licence L visited the plaintiff's house and savagely assaulted her. The action was tried by a jury and the report contains the summing-up of Lewis J. It appears to have been assumed that the defendant owed a duty of care to the claimant. The summing-up is concerned only with the issue of want of care . . . The case occurred at a time when the essential elements of a duty of care were much less clearly defined than is the position today. In my judgment the case cannot be reconciled with *Hill* on the question of proximity . . .

An additional reason why in my judgment in this case it is at least necessary for the victim to be identifiable (though as I have indicated it may not be sufficient) to establish proximity, is that it seems to me that the most effective way of providing protection would be to give warning to the victim, his or her parents or social services so that some protective measure can be made. As Mr Moon pointed out, the ability to restrict and restrain a psychiatric patient is subject to considerable restriction under the Mental Health Act 1983 (see particularly section 3) and are not unlimited in time. Moreover treatment, especially drug treatment of the patient, depends on his or her co-operation when an out-patient, and is limited when an in-patient. It may be a somewhat novel approach to the question of proximity, but it seems to me to be a relevant consideration to ask what could the defendant have done to avoid the danger, if the suggested precautions, *ie* committal under section 3 of the Mental Health Act or treatment are likely to be of doubtful effectiveness, and the most effective precaution cannot be taken because the defendant does not know who to warn.

6.2.3.2 Injured patient cases

It is readily apparent that, where a patient is injured or dies as a result of a doctor's negligence, this will have a knock-on effect upon others, in particular the patient's next of kin. The question of the duty of care in the context of breaking bad news to relatives was considered by the Court of Appeal in *Powell and Another v Boldaz and Others*,[24] in which a young boy died after a failure to diagnose Addison's disease:

> **Stuart-Smith LJ**: I turn then to consider whether the pleaded post-death matters can give rise to an action for negligence . . . Mr Powers submits that the duty of care arises under the principles enunciated by Lord Bridge of Harwich in *Caparo Industries plc v Dickman* [1990] 2 AC 605, pp 616E–18F, namely where the following three elements are present:
>
> (a) foreseeability of damage arising from the relevant act or omission;
> (b) a sufficient relationship of proximity between the parties;
> (c) as a matter of legal policy it is fair, just and reasonable that a duty of care should exist.
>
> I propose to consider first whether a sufficient relationship of proximity existed. It must be appreciated that prior to 17 April 1990, although the plaintiffs were patients of the defendants in the sense that they were on their register, the only patient who was seeking medical advice and treatment was Robert. It was to him that the defendants owed a duty of care. The discharge of that duty in the case of a young child will often involve giving advice and instruction to the parents so that they can administer the appropriate medication, observe relevant symptoms and seek further medical assistance if need be. In giving such advice, the doctor obviously owes a duty to be careful. But the duty is owed to the child, not to the parents. As Lord Diplock said in *Sidaway v Governors of Bethlem Royal Hospital* [1985] AC 871, p 890:
>
> > . . . a doctor's duty of care, whether he be a general practitioner or consulting surgeon or physician, is owed to that patient and none other, idiosyncrasies and all.
>
> . . . I do not think that a doctor who has been treating a patient who has died, who tells relatives what has happened, thereby undertakes the doctor–patient relationship towards the relatives. It is a situation that calls for sensitivity, tact and discretion, but the mere fact that the communicator is a doctor, does not, without more, mean that he undertakes the doctor–patient relationship. It is of course possible that the doctor in such a situation may realise that the shock has been so great that some immediate therapy is needed, but even so this situation is probably more akin to the doctor giving emergency treatment to an accident victim, though no doubt it will be a question of fact and degree in each case whether doctor–patient relationships came into existence by the doctor undertaking to treat and heal the person as a patient.

Nonetheless, it is apparent that, where they actually witness the harm occur, relatives may claim as secondary victims of psychiatric injury, subject to satisfying the control mechanisms in *Alcock v Chief Constable of South Yorkshire Police*.[25] In *Allin v City and Hackney HA*,[26] a woman recovered damages for post-traumatic stress disorder caused by being told (falsely) that her baby was dead. More recently, in *North Glamorgan NHS Trust v Walters*,[27] a series of events, which began when the respondent awoke to find her ten-month-old son suffering a seizure and ended with his life-support being terminated some 36 hours later, was held to be a single 'shocking event', entitling her to recover for her pathological grief reaction. Ward LJ held:

> **Ward LJ:** [34] In my judgment the law as presently formulated does permit a realistic view being taken from case to case of what constitutes the necessary 'event'. Our task is not to construe the word as if it had appeared in legislation but to gather the sense of the word in order to inform

---

24 (1997) 39 BMLR 35.
25 [1992] 1 AC 310.
26 [1996] 7 Med LR 167.
27 [2002] EWCA 1792.

the principle to be drawn from the various authorities . . . It is a matter of judgment from case to case depending on the facts and circumstance of each case. In my judgment on the facts of this case there was an inexorable progression from the moment when the fit occurred as a result of the failure of the hospital properly to diagnose and then to treat the baby, the fit causing the brain damage which shortly thereafter made termination of this child's life inevitable and the dreadful climax when the child died in her arms. It is a seamless tale with an obvious beginning and an equally obvious end. It was played out over a period of 36 hours, which for her both at the time and as subsequently recollected was undoubtedly one drawn-out experience.

By contrast, recovery has been denied in cases where, rather than a shock, there is a 'dawning realisation' that one's next of kin will die. Thus, in *Sion v Hampstead HA*,[28] the court rejected the claim of a father whose psychiatric injury was caused by watching his son die over a two-week period.

Finally, albeit in a rather different context, it should be noted that, on grounds of public policy, a doctor will not owe a duty of care to parents in cases where he mistakenly diagnoses child abuse on their part (leading, for example, to the child's temporary removal). As the House of Lords held in *JD v East Berkshire Community Health NHS Trust*,[29] the doctor, provided he acts in good faith, should not be inhibited in the course of his investigations by the prospect of such possible liability: his duty is owed to the child alone.

6.3 The Breach of Duty

6.3.1 The standard of care

6.3.1.1 The ordinary professional

The first point to note is that the standard of care against which the doctor will be judged is not going to be that of the ordinary reasonable man who enjoys no medical expertise. Instead, in holding himself out as possessing the special skills of his profession, the doctor is under a duty to conform to the ordinary standards of that profession. In *Bolam v Friern Hospital Management Committee*,[30] McNair J put this point as follows:

> **McNair J**: How do you test whether [an] act or failure is negligent? In an ordinary case it is generally said that you judge that by the action of the man in the street. He is the ordinary man. In one case it has been said that you judge it by the conduct of the man on the top of a Clapham omnibus. He is the ordinary man. But where you get a situation which involves the use of some special skill or competence, then the test whether there has been negligence or not is not the test of the man on the top of the Clapham omnibus, because he has not got this special skill. The test is the standard of the ordinary skilled man exercising and professing to have that special skill. A man need not possess the highest expert skill at the risk of being found negligent. It is well established law that it is sufficient if he exercises the ordinary skill of an ordinary competent man exercising that particular art.

It is further apparent, however, that doctors will not be treated as an homogenous group in this context. As Lord Bridge noted in *Sidaway v Governors of Bethlem Royal Hospital*:[31]

> **Lord Bridge:** The language of the *Bolam* test clearly requires a different degree of skill from a specialist in his own special field than from a general practitioner. In the field of neuro-surgery

---

28 [1994] 5 Med LR 170; see too *Ward v Leeds Teaching Hospitals NHS Trust* [2004] Lloyd's Rep Med 530.
29 [2005] UKHL 23.
30 [1957] 1 WLR 582.
31 [1985] AC 871; the reference is to Lord President Clyde's speech in the Scottish case of *Hunter v Hanley* (1955) SC 200.

it would be necessary to substitute for Lord President Clyde's phrase 'no doctor of ordinary skill', the phrase 'no neuro-surgeon of ordinary skill'.

The ordinary professional will be expected to keep his knowledge reasonably up-to-date. What counts as 'reasonable' in this context will again vary with the doctor's degree of specialisation. The doctor is not required to read every article in the medical press. In *Crawford v Board of Governors of Charing Cross Hospital*,[32] the Court of Appeal found that there had been no breach of duty when an operative procedure was performed resulting in paralysis, which some months previously had been the subject of an isolated report in *The Lancet*. Nonetheless, the doctor should certainly keep abreast of the most significant developments in his field.[33]

 SELF-TEST QUESTION

What of an operation that is so difficult it requires a surgeon of special skill: would there be negligence if such a surgeon were not used, and, if so, would this be of the health authority (relative to its primary duty of care), or of the 'ordinary' surgeon who operated?

6.3.1.2 Junior doctors

A particular difficulty arises in relation to the level of skill expected of junior medical staff who, ex hypothesi, will lack the experience of the ordinary competent doctor. Here, the courts have felt obliged to follow the reasoning in *Nettleship v Weston*,[34] in which a learner driver was held to be subject to the same standard of care as the reasonably competent and experienced driver. Indeed this principle had already been stated in the early medical negligence case of *Jones v Manchester Corp*,[35] where a patient died after the maladministration of anaesthetic by a doctor qualified for only five months. It was said that 'errors due to inexperience are no defence'. There is an understandably pragmatic aspect to this approach. Courts do not want to apply a sliding scale of standards of care depending upon the subjective attributes of the particular defendant. The liability of junior doctors was subsequently considered by the Court of Appeal in *Wilsher v Essex AHA*.

Wilsher v Essex AHA (1986)[36]

The claimant was a premature baby who was treated in the defendant's ante-natal unit. He was given oxygen by two doctors, both inexperienced. They inserted the catheter through which the oxygen was to be administered, into a vein rather than an artery. This is, apparently, a common mistake and was not due to negligence. The position of the catheter can be checked by use of an x-ray. The doctors, however, failed to notice the mistake, and the senior registrar checking their work also failed to notice. The majority of the Court of Appeal confirmed that there should be a uniform standard of care:

Glidewell LJ: In my view, the law requires the trainee or learner to be judged by the same standard as his more experienced colleagues. If it did not, inexperience would frequently be urged as a defence to an action for professional negligence.

If this test appears unduly harsh in relation to the inexperienced, I should add that, in my view, the inexperienced doctor called upon to exercise a specialist skill will,

---

32 (1953) *The Times*, 8 December.
33 See *Gascoine v Ian Sheridan and Co (A Firm) and Latham* [1994] 5 Med LR 437.
34 [1971] 3 All ER 581.
35 [1952] 2 All ER 125.
36 See n 7 above.

as part of that skill, seek the advice and help of his superiors when he does or may need it. If he does seek such help, he will often have satisfied the test, even though he may himself have made a mistake. It is for this reason that I agree that Dr Wiles was not negligent. He made a mistake in inserting the catheter into a vein, and a second mistake in not recognising the signs that he had done so on the x-ray. But, having done what he thought right, he asked Dr Kawa, the senior registrar, to check what he had done, and Dr Kawa did so. Dr Kawa failed to recognise the indication on the x-ray . . .

As this makes clear, junior doctors are entitled to expect their work to be checked, and, on the facts of the case, were found not to be liable (although the registrar was); indeed, the court suggested that a hospital could be directly liable in negligence if it failed to have a proper system for inspecting the work of junior staff.

Mustill LJ similarly rejected the argument that there should be a subjective standard of care, depending on the doctor's experience:

Mustill LJ: To my mind, this notion of a duty tailored to the actor, rather than to the act which he elects to perform, has no place in the law of tort. Indeed, the defendants did not contend that it could be justified by any reported authority on the general law of tort. Instead, it was suggested that the medical profession is a special case. Public hospital medicine has always been organised so that young doctors and nurses learn on the job. If the hospitals abstained from using inexperienced people, they could not staff their wards and theatres, and the junior staff could never learn. The longer term interests of patients as a whole are best served by maintaining the present system, even if this may diminish the legal rights of the individual patient: for, after all, medicine is about curing, not litigation.

I acknowledge the appeal of this argument, and recognise that a young hospital doctor, who must get on to the wards in order to qualify without necessarily being able to decide what kind of patient he is going to meet, is not in the same position as another professional man who has a real choice whether or not to practise in a particular field. Nevertheless, I cannot accept that there should be a special rule for doctors in public hospitals – I emphasise public, since presumably those employed in private hospitals would be in a different category. Doctors are not the only people who gain their experience, not only from lectures or from watching others perform, but from tackling live clients or customers, and no case was cited to us which suggested that any such variable duty of care was imposed on others in a similar position. To my mind, it would be a false step to subordinate the legitimate expectation of the patient that he will receive from each person concerned with his care a degree of skill appropriate to the task which he undertakes, to an understandable wish to minimise the psychological and financial pressures on hard-pressed young doctors.[37]

By contrast Sir Nicolas Browne-Wilkinson VC, dissenting from the majority view, commented as follows:

Browne-Wilkinson VC: . . . [O]ne of the chief hazards of inexperience is that one does not always know the risks which exist. In my judgment, so long as the English law rests liability on personal fault, a doctor who has properly accepted a post in a hospital in order to gain necessary experience should only be held liable for acts or omissions which a careful doctor with his qualifications and experience would not have done or omitted.

---

37 The case subsequently went to the House of Lords on the issue of causation.

6.3.1.3 Scarce resources and emergencies

Another situation where the courts have insisted on an objective standard of medical care is in the face of arguments based on shortages of health care resources. In practice, such a claim is likely to be brought not against an individual doctor, but directly against a health trust or hospital, in respect of institutional negligence – ie arguing that the overall system of care it operated was flawed. A case in point is that of *Bull v Devon HA*,[38] in which one of the claimant's twins was born brain damaged due to the delay in getting the registrar to attend her. The defendants maintained maternity services on different sites, but only employed a single registrar, and the system for calling him over to assist in the delivery had broken down. The Court of Appeal unanimously held the health authority liable. In his judgment, Mustill LJ commented:

> **Mustill LJ**: The . . . suggested answer [to the claim of negligence] was on these lines: that hospitals such as the Devon and Exeter were in the dilemma of having to supply a maternity service, and yet not disposing of sufficient manpower to provide immediate cover, the more so since the small number of consultants and registrars had to deal with three different sites. They could not be expected to do more than their best, allocating their limited resources as favourably as possible. . . . I have some reservations about this contention, which are not allayed by the submission that hospital medicine is a public service. So it is, but there are other public services in respect of which it is not necessarily an answer to allegations of unsafety that there were insufficient resources to enable the administrators to do everything which they would like to do.

At the same time, what is at issue here is the provision of a minimum level of care. Over and above this a degree of disparity in treatment services will be tolerated between different geographical regions and types of hospital. Thus the fact that a district hospital fails to provide the patient with the level of specialist care he would have received in a university hospital is not itself negligent; the issue will instead be whether, in the light of the patient's condition, it was negligent not to refer him for such specialist care.[39]

An exception to the principle, that a doctor will be judged according to the standard of reasonably experienced doctors in their field, is provided by emergency treatment. Michael Jones has commented as follows on the level of experience expected in the latter context:

Jones, M, *Medical Negligence*[40]

> In an emergency it may well be reasonable for a practitioner inexperienced in a particular treatment to intervene, or indeed for someone lacking medical qualifications to undertake some forms of treatment. For example, a bystander who renders assistance at a road accident does not necessarily hold himself out as qualified to do so. He would be expected to achieve only the standard that could reasonably be expected in the circumstances, which would probably be very low. This approach is clearly borne of the emergency since if there was no urgency, the unqualified person who undertakes treatment which is beyond his competence would be held to the standard to be expected of the reasonably competent and experienced practitioner. A person who holds himself out as trained in first aid must conform to the standards of 'the ordinary skilled first aider exercising and professing to have that special skill of a first aider'.

Secondly, in relation to treatment decisions taken in an emergency, a doctor will not be found negligent simply because the reasonably competent doctor would have made a different decision,

---

38 [1993] 4 Med LR 117.
39 See *Ball v Wirral HA* [2003] Lloyd's Rep Med 165.
40 See n 4 above.

given more time and information. In the case of *Wilson v Swanson*,[41] the Supreme Court of Canada held that there was no negligence when a surgeon had to make an immediate decision whether to operate, and the operation was subsequently found to have been unnecessary. Moreover, the skill itself required in the execution of treatment may be somewhat lower. As Mustill LJ commented in the *Wilsher* case[42]:

> **Mustill LJ**: An emergency may overburden the available resources, and, if an individual is forced by circumstances to do too many things at once, the fact that he does one of them incorrectly should not lightly be taken as negligence.

 SELF-TEST QUESTION

It is sometimes suggested that a doctor who treats in an emergency will only be liable if he actively worsens the patient's situation.[43] Do you think this ought to be the case?

6.3.2 Establishing the breach

6.3.2.1 *Accepted practice – the* 'Bolam *test*'

In determining whether, in a particular case, a doctor has satisfied the appropriate standard of care, the courts will look in the first place to accepted practice within the profession: has the doctor conducted himself in the manner in which other doctors would have conducted themselves in the same circumstances? Of course, medicine is a developing science and new schools of thought as to how best to carry out treatments are constantly emerging. For this reason, the courts do not expect to find uniformity of standard medical practice in any given case. Rather, they ask whether the doctor has conformed with *an* (note the use of the indefinite article) accepted practice within the profession. This approach informed McNair J's direction to the jury in the famous case of *Bolam v Friern Hospital Management Committee*.

Bolam v Friern Hospital Management Committee (1957)[44]

The claimant suffered from clinical depression and it was decided to treat him with electro-convulsive therapy (ECT), which involves passing an electric current through the patient's brain to induce a fit. At the time this was fairly novel treatment and doctors differed as to how best to minimise the risk of the patient suffering bone fractures during the fit. At the hospital where Mr Bolam was treated, a system of manual restraint in which nurses held the patient down, but only by the chin, was in use (two other practices adopted elsewhere involved the use of rigid restraint, and relaxant drugs administered following a general anaesthetic, respectively). Unfortunately, in the plaintiff's case the manual restraint was ineffective and he suffered serious pelvic injuries during treatment:

> **McNair J** (directing the jury): Counsel for the plaintiff put it in this way, that in the case of a medical man, negligence means failure to act in accordance with the standards of reasonably competent medical men at the time. That is a perfectly accurate

---

41 (1956) 5 DLR (2d) 113.
42 See n 7 above.
43 See *Capital and Counties v Hants CC*, n 9 above; but cf *Kent v Griffiths*, n 11 above.
44 [1957] 1 WLR 582.

statement, as long as it is remembered that there may be one or more perfectly proper standards; and if a medical man confirms with one of those proper standards then he is not negligent. Counsel for the plaintiff was also right, in my judgment, in saying that a mere personal belief that a particular technique is best is no defence unless that belief is based on reasonable grounds. That again is unexceptional. But the emphasis which is laid by counsel for the defendants is on this aspect of negligence: he submitted to you that the real question on which you have to make up your mind on each of the three major points to be considered is whether the defendants, in acting in the way in which they did, were acting in accordance with a practice of competent respected professional opinion . . . I myself would . . . put it this way: a doctor is not guilty of negligence if he has acted in accordance with a practice accepted as proper by a responsible body of medical men skilled in that particular art.

In effect, before finding a negligent error of clinical judgment, the court must be satisfied – on the basis of the opinions of other doctors (acting as expert witnesses) – that no reasonable doctor would have acted as the defendant doctor. The *Bolam* test was subsequently approved on several occasions by the House of Lords. An example is found in the leading judgment of Lord Scarman in *Maynard v West Midlands RHA*, a key decision from the 1980s.

Maynard v West Midlands RHA (1984)[45]

The claimant was being treated for a chest complaint. Her consultants believed her probably to have tuberculosis, but, given also the slight chance of Hodgkin's disease, decided to carry out an exploratory diagnostic operation. This confirmed the tuberculosis diagnosis, but unfortunately, due to an inherent risk materialising (without fault on the defendants' part) left the claimant paralysed in one of her vocal cords. At trial, the medical experts were divided over whether the diagnostic operation had been appropriate. The trial judge preferred the view of the claimant's experts that the risk of it not been worth taking, and awarded damages. The defendants' appeal was allowed by the Court of Appeal and the matter reached the House of Lords:

Lord Scarman: The present case may be classifiable as one of clinical judgment. Two distinguished consultants, a physician and a surgeon experienced in the treatment of chest diseases, formed a judgment as to what was, in their opinion, in the best interests of their patient. They recommended that tuberculosis was the most likely diagnosis. But in their opinion, there was an unusual factor, viz, swollen glands in the mediastinum unaccompanied by any evidence of lesion in the lungs. Hodgkin's disease, carcinoma, and sarcoidosis were, therefore, possibilities. The danger they thought was Hodgkin's disease; though unlikely, it was, if present, a killer (as treatment was understood in 1970) unless remedial steps were taken in its early stage. They therefore decided on mediastinoscopy, an operative procedure which would provide them with a biopsy from the swollen gland which could be subjected to immediate microscopic examination. It is said that the evidence of tuberculosis was so strong that it was unreasonable and wrong to defer diagnosis and to put their patient to the risks of the operation. The case against them is not mistake or carelessness in performing the operation which is admitted was properly carried out, but an error of judgment in requiring the operation to be undertaken.

A case which is based on an allegation that a fully considered decision of two consultants in the field of their special skill was negligent clearly presents certain

45 [1984] 1 WLR 634, HL.

difficulties of proof. It is not enough to show that there is a body of competent professional opinion which considered that theirs was a wrong decision, if there also exists a body of professional opinion, equally competent, which supports the decision as reasonable in the circumstances. It is not enough to show that subsequent events show that the operation need never have been performed, if at the time the decision to operate was taken it was reasonable in the sense that a responsible body of medical opinion would have accepted it as proper.

Subsequently, in *Sidaway v Governors of Bethlem Royal Hospital*,[46] the same Law Lord articulated the *Bolam* test in the following terms:

Lord Scarman: The *Bolam* principle may be formulated as a rule that a doctor is not negligent if he acts in accordance with a practice accepted at the time as proper by a responsible body of medical opinion even though other doctors adopt a different practice. In short, the law imposes the duty of care, but the standard of care is a matter of medical judgment.

What are the reasons the courts have for attaching such importance to expert medical opinion in deciding if there has been negligence in a medical case? One has already been mentioned: medicine is recognised as not being an exact science; there may, at any given moment, be two or more perfectly respectable ways of dealing with a particular problem. Indeed one could go further and cite the possibility of competition between different accepted practices as a key element in allowing progress in treatment to be made. *Bolam* itself provides an illustration of this: in the 1950s only one of three schools of thought administered ECT following a general anaesthetic, but nowadays it is invariably done this way. Despite the risks associated with anaesthesia itself, experience ultimately has shown this to be preferable to running the risks of bone fracture associated with either rigid or manual restraint.

Secondly, and more controversially, the courts have arguably also been motivated by the fear of otherwise encouraging an explosion of malpractice litigation and an uncongenial climate for doctors to go about their business of treating patients: as Mustill LJ commented in *Wilsher v EssexAHA*, 'medicine is about curing, not litigation'.[47] This attitude found its most notorious expression in Lord Denning's suggestion (repeated in a number of cases over the years), that an 'error of clinical judgment' could not amount to negligence, a view finally laid to rest in 1981 in the case of *Whitehouse v Jordan*.

Whitehouse v Jordan (1981)[48]

The claimant was born brain damaged, allegedly as a result of the defendant obstetrician's negligence. The latter had made prolonged attempts at normal delivery using forceps before realising this was impossible. The claimant, suing by his mother as next friend, argued that the defendant should have moved more quickly to delivery by Caesarean section.

Lord Edmund Davies: . . . [T]he principal questions calling for decision are: (a) in what manner did Mr Jordan use the forceps? And (b) was that manner consistent with the degree of care which a member of his profession is required by law to exercise? Surprising though it is at this late stage in the development of the law of negligence, counsel for Mr Jordan persisted in submitting that his client should be completely exculpated were the answer to question (b), 'Well, at worst he was guilty of an error of clinical judgment'. My Lords, it is high time that the unacceptability of such an

---

46 See n 31 above.
47 See n 7 above.
48 [1981] 1 WLR 246.

answer be fully exposed. To say that a surgeon committed an error of clinical judgment is wholly ambiguous, for, while some such errors may be completely consistent with the due exercise of professional skill, other acts or omissions in the course of exercising 'clinical judgment' may be so glaringly below proper standards as to make a finding of negligence inevitable. Indeed, I should have regarded this as a truism were it not that, despite the exposure of the 'false antithesis' by Donaldson LJ in his dissenting judgment in the Court of Appeal, counsel for the defendants adhered to it before your Lordships.

But doctors and surgeons fall into no special category, and, to avoid any future disputation of a similar kind, I would have it accepted that the true doctrine was enunciated, and by no means for the first time, by McNair J in *Bolam v Friern Hospital Management Committee* in the following words, which were applied by the Privy Council in *Chin Keow v Government of Malaysia* [1967] 1 WLR 813:

> . . . where you get a situation which involves the use of some special skill or competence, then the test as to whether there has been negligence or not is not the test of the man on the top of a Clapham omnibus because he has not got this special skill. The test is the standard of the ordinary skilled man exercising and professing to have that special skill.

If a surgeon fails to measure up to that standard in any respect ('clinical judgment' or otherwise), he has been negligent and should be so adjudged.

Thirdly, at least in the past, the highly technical nature of some of the information at issue seems to have led judges to defer to the experts in such cases. Thus, in the Court of Appeal case of *Dwyer v Roderick*,[49] May LJ stated:

May LJ: It would be to shut one's eyes to the obvious if one denied that the burden of [establishing a breach of duty on] something more than the mere balance of probabilities was greater when one was investigating the complicated and sophisticated actions of a qualified and experienced doctor than when one was inquiring into the inattention of the driver in a simple running down action.

However, it could be argued that the courts were too ready to mystify medical matters. As Michael Jones comments:

Jones, M, *Medical Negligence*[50]

Where the case does not involve difficult or uncertain questions of medical or surgical treatment, or abstruse or highly technical scientific issues, but is concerned with whether obvious and simple precautions could have been taken, the question of the practice of experts should be largely irrelevant. The courts do not rely on expert rally drivers, for example, to say whether a motorist was negligent.

Moreover, before any question of complying with accepted practice can arise the court must be satisfied on the evidence presented to it that there is a responsible body of professional opinion which supports the practice. It is always open to the court to reject expert evidence applying the ordinary principles of credibility that would be applied in any courtroom, for example, that the evidence is internally contradictory, or that the witness was acting as an advocate rather than an impartial and objective expert.

---

49 (1983) 127 SJ 805.
50 See n 4 above.

In fact, recently the courts have begun to pay greater attention to the proper circumstances for the application of the *Bolam* test. In the case of *Penney v East Kent HA*,[51] it was accepted that where the dispute between the expert witnesses is purely factual in nature (here whether cervical smear slides showed significant abnormalities), the *Bolam* test in fact has no part to play. As Lord Woolf MR commented:

> **Lord Woolf MR**: . . . the *Bolam* test has no application where what the judge is required to do is to make findings of fact. This is so, even where those findings of fact are the subject of conflicting expert evidence. Thus in this case there were three questions which the judge had to answer: What was to be seen in the slides? At the relevant time could a screener exercising reasonable care fail to see what was on the slide? Could a reasonably competent screener, aware of what a screener exercising reasonable care would observe on the slide, treat the slide as negative? Thus, logically the starting point for the experts reasoning was what was on the slides. Except in relation to the slide known as Palmer 2, as to which there was a striking conflict, as a result of a meeting which took place between the experts they were in substantial but by no means total agreement. In so far as they were not in agreement, the judge had the unenviable task of deciding as a matter of fact which of the experts were correct as to what the slides showed. This was a task which required expert evidence. However the evidence having been given, the judge had to make his own finding on the balance of probabilities on this issue of fact in order to proceed to the next step in answering the question of negligence or no negligence. Having come to his own conclusion as to what the slides showed, the judge had, therefore, then to answer the 2nd and 3rd questions in order to decide whether the screener was in breach of duty in giving a negative report. Whether the screener was in breach of duty would depend on the training and the amount of knowledge a screener should have had in order to properly perform his or her task at that time and how easy it was to discern what the judge had found was on the slide. These issues involved both questions of fact and questions of opinion as to the standards of care which the screeners should have exercised.

This more critical approach can be seen as part of a general sea change that has occurred in the courts' attitude towards the *Bolam* test in the past few years. This development is discussed further in the next section.

 SELF-TEST QUESTION:

What of a case where the surgeon's scalpel slips during delicate spinal surgery, leaving the patient paralysed: would the *Bolam* test here be of any application?

6.3.2.2 *Impugning accepted practice – 'new Bolam'*

In Lord Scarman's judgments in the cases of *Maynard* and *Sidaway*,[52] the *Bolam* test appeared to be framed in such a way as to make compliance with an accepted practice a complete defence: that is to say, provided a doctor could show that what he had done complied with such a practice, he could never be found negligent. However, this was never regarded universally as the correct interpretation of the test, and it was one rejected especially vociferously by Commonwealth courts. In the case of F v R, Bollen J, in the Supreme Court of South Australia, commented as follows:

---

51 [2000] Lloyd's Rep Med 41; see also *Marriott v West Midlands HA* [1999] Lloyd's Rep Med 23; *Smith v Southampton University Hospital NHS Trust* [2007] EWCA Civ 387.

52 See nn 45 and 31 above.

Bollen J: Many cases require the calling of expert evidence. These experts frequently express opinions on matters within their field. Sometimes they speak of what is usually done in any activity within that field. Why is the evidence received? It is received to guide or help the court. A court cannot be expected to know the correct procedure for performing a surgical operation. The court cannot be expected to know why a manufacturer should guard against metal fatigue. A court cannot be expected to know how to mix chemicals. And so on. Expert evidence will assist the court. But in the end it is the court which must say whether there was a duty owed and a breach of it. The court will have been guided and assisted by the expert evidence. It will not produce an answer merely at the dictation of the expert evidence. It will afford great weight to the expert evidence . . . But the court does not merely follow expert evidence slavishly to a decision . . . If the court did merely follow the path apparently pointed by expert evidence with no critical consideration of it and the other evidence, it would abdicate its duty to decide, on the evidence, whether in law a duty existed and had not been discharged . . .

. . . I can find nothing in *Bolam v Friern Hospital Management Committee* which justifies any suggestion that evidence of the practice obtaining in the medical profession is automatically decisive of any issue in an action against a surgeon for damages in negligence . . .

. . . I respectfully think that some of the cases in England have concentrated rather too heavily on the practice of the medical profession.[53]

Note what is said here about deciding on the evidence whether the duty had been breached. It is pointing up what has always been the case: that courts *evaluate* the opinion evidence they hear. That English courts, too, ultimately are able to review an accepted practice for its reasonableness and, however distinguished its proponents, may sometimes find it wanting, was confirmed by the House of Lords in *Bolitho v City and Hackney HA*. The latter is the leading modern authority on the application of the *Bolam* test in medical negligence cases.

Bolitho v City and Hackney HA (1997)[54]

The infant claimant was being treated in the defendant's hospital for respiratory difficulties following a serious bout of the croup. Overall his condition appeared to be improving, but on the day in question he suffered two acute episodes in which his breathing was temporarily obstructed. On both occasions the nurse observing him summoned the senior paediatric registrar, however, neither the latter nor her senior house officer responded to the calls. The claimant subsequently suffered a third episode, leading to cardiac arrest and brain damage.

It was accepted for the defendant that the failure of its doctors to attend the claimant amounted to a breach of duty. However, it claimed that, even if they had attended, they would not have instigated the one procedure – intubation – which would have saved him. This was a defence based essentially on lack of causation;[55] however, to succeed it required the court to accept that the hypothetical failure to intubate in such a case would not itself have been a breach of duty. In this regard, the defendant adduced evidence from a number of expert witnesses to the effect that, faced with a patient with the claimant's medical history and symptoms, they too would not intubate:

Lord Browne-Wilkinson: . . . [I]n my view, the court is not bound to hold that a defendant doctor escapes liability for negligent treatment or diagnosis just because he leads evidence from a number of medical experts who are genuinely of the opinion that the defendant's treatment or diagnosis accorded with sound medical practice. In the *Bolam*

---

53 (1983) SASR 189.
54 [1998] AC 232.
55 See further the discussion in 6.4.3.2 below.

case itself, McNair J stated . . . that the defendant had to have acted in accordance with the practice accepted as proper by a 'responsible body of medical men'. Later . . . he referred to 'a standard of practice recognised as proper by a competent *reasonable* body of opinion'. Again, in the passage which I have cited from *Maynard*'s case, Lord Scarman refers to a 'respectable' body of professional opinion. The use of these adjectives – responsible, reasonable and respectable – all show that the court has to be satisfied that the exponents of the body of opinion relied upon can demonstrate that such opinion has a logical basis. In particular in cases involving, as they so often do, the weighing of risks against benefits, the judge before accepting a body of opinion as being responsible, reasonable or respectable, will need to be satisfied that, in forming their views, the experts have directed their minds to the question of comparative risks and benefits and have reached a defensible conclusion on the matter.

There are decisions which demonstrate that the judge is entitled to approach expert professional opinion on this basis. For example, in *Hucks v Cole* (1993) 4 Med LR 393 (a case from 1968), a doctor failed to treat with penicillin a patient who was suffering from septic spots on her skin though he knew them to contain organisms capable of leading to puerperal fever. A number of distinguished doctors gave evidence that they would not, in the circumstances, have treated with penicillin. The Court of Appeal found the defendant to have been negligent. Sachs LJ said, at p 397:

> When the evidence shows that a lacuna in professional practice exists by which risks of grave danger are knowingly taken, then, however small the risk, the court must anxiously examine that lacuna – particularly if the risk can be easily and inexpensively avoided. If the court finds, on an analysis of the reasons given for not taking those precautions that, in the light of current professional knowledge, there is no proper basis for the lacuna, and that it is definitely not reasonable that those risks should have been taken, its function is to state that fact and where necessary to state that it constitutes negligence. In such a case the practice will no doubt thereafter be altered to the benefit of patients. On such occasions the fact that other practitioners would have done the same thing as the defendant practitioner is a very weighty matter to be put on the scales on his behalf; but it is not, as Mr Webster readily conceded, conclusive. The court must be vigilant to see whether the reasons given for putting a patient at risk are valid in the light of any well-known advance in medical knowledge, or whether they stem from a residual adherence to out-of-date ideas.

. . . These decisions demonstrate that in cases of diagnosis or treatment there are cases where, despite a body of professional opinion sanctioning the defendant's conduct, the defendant can properly be held liable for negligence (I am not here considering questions of disclosure of risk). In my judgment that is because, in some cases, it cannot be demonstrated to the judge's satisfaction that the body of opinion relied upon is reasonable or responsible. In the vast majority of cases the fact that distinguished experts in the field are of a particular opinion will demonstrate the reasonableness of that opinion. In particular, where there are questions of assessment of the relative risks and benefits of adopting a particular medical practice, a reasonable view necessarily presupposes that the relative risks and benefits have been weighed by the experts in forming their opinions. But if, in a rare case, it can be demonstrated that the professional opinion is not capable of withstanding logical analysis, the judge is entitled to hold that the body of opinion is not reasonable or responsible.

On the facts, his Lordship (with whose judgment the rest of the House of Lords agreed) held that the hypothetical decision not to intubate the claimant would have been in accord with responsible medical practice:

> **Lord Browne-Wilkinson**: According to the accounts of Sister Sallabank and Nurse Newbold, although Patrick had had two severe respiratory crises, he had recovered quickly from both and for the rest presented as a child who was active and running about. Dr Dinwiddie's view was that these symptoms did not show a progressive respiratory collapse and that there was only a small risk of total respiratory failure. Intubation is not a routine, risk-free process. Dr Roberton described it as 'a major undertaking – an invasive procedure with mortality and morbidity attached – it was an assault'. It involves anaesthetising and ventilating the child. A young child does not tolerate a tube easily 'at any rate for a day or two' and the child unless sedated tends to remove it. In those circumstances it cannot be suggested that it was illogical for Dr Dinwiddie, a most distinguished expert, to favour running what, in his view, was a very small risk of total respiratory collapse rather than to submit Patrick to the invasive procedure of intubation.

It is apparent that, in requiring 'responsible practice' to stand up to logical analysis, Lord Browne-Wilkinson has in mind some form of risk-benefit analysis: the risks inherent in a given procedure must be justified by the benefit it may bring (including the amelioration of any greater risk). However, whilst this may lead to rejection of practices which entail quite unnecessary risks (that is, those where negligible or no benefit is to be gained from running them, as in *Hucks v Cole*[56]), it remains unclear what a judge is to do when faced with evidence of a practice which, say, exposes the patient to a 1 per cent risk of total paralysis but carries a 90 per cent chance of curing the patient's stiff neck. Is such a practice 'illogical'?[57]

In the Court of Appeal in *Bolitho*, Dillon LJ had suggested that before impugning an accepted practice, the court should be satisfied that it was '*Wednesbury* unreasonable'.[58] As we saw in Chapter 2, this test is employed in judicial review proceedings and requires a very high degree of unreasonableness (the practice in question must be perverse or irrational). In so doing, it reflects the courts' reluctance to second guess the decisions of public bodies, which are entrusted with a discretion over how best to implement policy (often involving considerations of finite resources). Such a test would seem an inappropriate basis on which to assess the individual treatment decisions made by doctors, and indeed it finds no place in Lord Browne-Wilkinson's judgment. Nevertheless, arguably the latter's approach is scarcely more favourable to the claimant:

See Chapter 2 →

> **Lord Browne-Wilkinson**: I emphasise that in my view it will very seldom be right for a judge to reach the conclusion that views genuinely held by a competent medical expert are unreasonable. The assessment of medical risks and benefits is a matter of clinical judgment which a judge would not normally be able to make without expert evidence. As the quotation from Lord Scarman [from *Maynard v W Midlands RHA*] makes clear, it would be wrong to allow such assessment to deteriorate into seeking to persuade the judge to prefer one of two views, both of which are capable of being logically supported. It is only where a judge can be satisfied that the body of expert opinion cannot be logically supported at all that such opinion will not provide the bench mark by reference to which the defendant's conduct falls to be assessed.

---

56 [1993] 4 Med LR 393.
57 For the view that professional conduct may in fact be impugned as 'illogical' in a number of scenarios, see Mulheron, R, 'Trumping Bolam: A critical legal analysis of Bolitho's "gloss" ' (2010) 69 CLJ 609.
58 (1993) PIQR P334.

In the years following *Bolitho*, judges following the approach endorsed by Lord Browne-Wilkinson have been cautious. Thus, decisions where a doctor's conduct has been held negligent notwithstanding its compliance with accepted practice remain rare. Nevertheless, one case that seems to have been decided on this basis is *Marriott v West Midlands HA*,[59] in which the trial judge found that, given the risk of neurological deficit, a GP's failure to refer a head injury patient back to hospital for further tests was negligent. As Beldam LJ commented in the Court of Appeal:

> **Beldam LJ**: Having read the evidence of both doctors, I think it is questionable whether either Dr Fell or Dr La Frenais had given evidence from which it was reasonable to infer that their individual approaches were shared by a responsible body of others in their profession. Rather it seems that each was saying what his own approach would have been in the circumstances. It is true that each of them gave evidence of discussing the question with their partners, who (perhaps understandably) did in neither case disagree with their approach. But such evidence fell short of establishing that their views of the appropriate course for Dr Patel to have taken were shared by a body of professional colleagues. However, the judge treated this evidence as if it were evidence of that kind, and she correctly directed herself that it was not open to her simply to prefer the expert evidence of one body of competent professional opinion over that of another where there was a conflict between the experts called by the parties . . . She then subjected that body of opinion to analysis to see whether it can properly be regarded as reasonable. In my view, she was entitled to do so.

A more recent, albeit factually unusual, example of a court finding a breach of duty despite the defendant's compliance with accepted medical practice is *AB v Leeds Teaching Hospital NHS Trust*.[60] This case centred upon the failure of doctors to inform parents that tissue removed from their deceased children for post mortem examinations might subsequently be retained by the hospital. Here, interestingly, the very universality of the practice was regarded as counting against its reasonableness. As Gage J commented:

> **Gage J**: [237] . . . [T]he evidence shows that the practice adopted was blanket practice carried out by virtually all clinicians. In so far as it involved the exercise of a therapeutic judgment it was one which does not appear to have been exercised on a case by case basis. The general view was that such information was unnecessary and likely to be distressing to parents. But there is no evidence that clinicians considered the matter individually with each parent or family. To take an example from the lead claims, although the issue does not arise in their claim, Mr and Mrs Carpenter would, in my judgment, have been quite capable of coping with this information at the time of Daniel's death. In any event, in my opinion, there was very little risk of parents being caused greater distress by being given the additional information. It would have been very simple and easy for a clinician to have provided this information and generally they ought to have done so. If the clinician did not know what was involved in a post-mortem, in my opinion, as Dr Moore said, he ought to have known. In the circumstances, my conclusion is that the practice of not warning parents and in particular a mother that a post-mortem might involve the removal and subsequent retention of an organ cannot be justified as a practice to be adopted in all cases.

6.3.2.3 Departures from accepted practice

Normally, where there is only a single course of treatment recognised by the medical profession (an increasing possibility given the work of the National Institute for Clinical Excellence in disseminating 'best practice' clinical guidelines), it will be practically impossible to demonstrate that the

---

59 [1999] Lloyd's Rep Med 23.
60 [2004] EWHC 644 (QB).

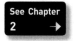
See Chapter
2
practice is illogical and, hence, not reasonable. Arguably, it could be said, even then, that judges might consider practices in other jurisdictions and find that these were superior and should have been adopted by the medical profession here, but this approach was rejected in *Whiteford v Hunter*.[61]

However, how far does the converse apply? That is, will deviation from such practice automatically be regarded as negligent? This issue was addressed in the case of *Clark v MacLennan*.

Clark v MacLennan (1983)[62]

The claimant had recently given birth and was suffering from stress incontinence. The gynaecologist performed a corrective operation one month after the birth of the child. The normal practice was not to perform such operations until at least three months after birth, as the condition often spontaneously resolved itself and there would be less likelihood of haemorrhage. A haemorrhage did, in fact, take place, and despite further surgery, the claimant's condition became permanent. Although evidence was that in very special circumstances the operation might be performed early, this was not an exceptional case. In fact, none of the witnesses knew of a case where the operation had taken place earlier than three months. Contrasting this situation where there is more than one approved practice, Peter Pain J stated:

> **Peter Pain J**: Where . . . there is but one orthodox course of treatment and the doctor chooses to depart from that, his position is different. It is not enough for him to say as to his decision simply that it was based on his clinical judgment. One has to inquire whether he took all proper factors into account which he knew or should have known, and whether his departure from the orthodox course can be justified on the basis of these factors.
>
> The burden of proof lies on the plaintiff. To succeed she must show, first, that there was a breach of duty and, second, that her damages flowed from that breach . . .
>
> . . . [C]ounsel for the plaintiff contended that, if the plaintiff could show: (1) that there was a general practice not to perform an anterior colporrhaphy until at least three months after birth; (2) that one of the reasons for this practice was to protect the patient from the risk of haemorrhage and a breakdown of the repair; (3) that an operation was performed within four weeks; and (4) that haemorrhage occurred and the repair broke down, then the burden of showing that he was not in breach of duty shifted to the defendants.
>
> It must be correct on the basis of *McGhee v National Coal Board* [1973] 1 WLR 1 to say that the burden shifts so far as damages are concerned. But does the burden shift so far as the duty is concerned? Must the medical practitioner justify his departure from the usual practice?
>
> It is very difficult to draw a distinction between the damage and the duty where the duty arises only because of a need to guard against the damage. In *McGhee*'s case it was accepted that there was a breach of duty. In the present case the question of whether there was a breach remains in issue.
>
> It seems to me that it follows from *McGhee* that where there is a situation in which a general duty of care arises and there is a failure to take a precaution, and that very damage occurs against which the precaution is designed to be a protection, then the burden lies on the defendant to show that he was not in breach of duty as well as to show that the damage did not result from his breach of duty.

---

61 (1950) 94 SJ 758.
62 [1983] 1 All ER 416.

Peter Pain J's view that, in cases of departure from approved practice, the burden shifts to the defence to establish non-negligence was subsequently doubted, however, by Mustill LJ in the Court of Appeal in *Wilsher v Essex AHA*:[63]

> **Mustill LJ**: . . . [A]lthough the judge [in *Clark v MacLennan*] indicated that he proposed to decide the case on burden of proof . . . this could be understood as an example of the forensic commonplace that, where one party has, in the course of the trial, hit the ball into the other's court, it is for that other to return it. But the prominence given in the judgment to *McGhee* and the citation from *Clark* in the present case suggest that the judge may have set out to assert a wider proposition, to the effect that in certain kinds of case of which *Clark* and the present action form examples, there is a general burden of proof on the defendant. If this is so, then I must respectfully say that I find nothing in . . . general principle to support it.

In the light of this, it may be more accurate to speak in terms of evidential presumptions: the fact, if it is established, that the defendant failed to act in accordance with accepted practice supports a *prima facie* inference of negligence, which it is then up to the defendant to rebut. Such rebuttal will be more difficult if the accepted practice is universal and is specifically directed against the risk that the defendant, in failing to comply, allowed to materialise. A case in point is that of *Chin Keow v Government of Malaysia*,[64] in which a patient died after the doctor gave her penicillin without checking for the possibility of an allergic reaction. The doctor was unable to give any satisfactory explanation of his failure to observe accepted practice in this regard.

On other occasions, however, the doctor may be able to provide cogent reasons for departing from normal practice. In fact, the importance of giving doctors a certain degree of latitude to try out 'innovative' forms of treatment was noted by Lord Clyde in the pre-*Bolam*, Scottish decision of *Hunter v Hanley*:[65]

> **Lord President Clyde**: . . . [I]n regard to allegations of deviation from ordinary professional practice . . . such a deviation is not necessarily evidence of negligence. Indeed it would be disastrous if this were so, for all inducement to progress in medical science would then be destroyed. Even a substantial deviation from normal practice may be warranted by the particular circumstances. To establish liability by a doctor where deviation from normal practice is alleged, three facts require to be established. First of all it must be proved that there is a usual and normal practice; secondly it must be proved that the defender has not adopted that practice; and thirdly (and this is of crucial importance) it must be established that the course the doctor adopted is one which no professional man of ordinary skill would have taken if he had been acting with ordinary care.

It is important to distinguish here between medical research, which is a planned exercise designed specifically to test a new form of treatment, using control groups and almost always approved by a local ethics committee, and a 'one-off' treatment for a particular patient. We are only concerned at present with the latter situation. There is no doubt that there would be no automatic finding of negligence, if the treatment was innovative. In *Sidaway*[66] Lord Diplock stated:

See Chapter ◀ **10**

> **Lord Diplock**: Those members of the public who seek medical or surgical aid would be badly served by the adoption of any legal principle that would confine the doctor to some

63 See n 7 above.
64 [1967] 1 WLR 813.
65 See n 31 above.
66 See n 31 above.

long-established, well tried method of treatment only, although its past record of success might be small, if he wanted to be confident that he would not run the risk of being held liable in negligence simply because he tried some more modern treatment, and by some unavoidable mischance it failed to heal but did some harm to the patient. This would encourage 'defensive medicine' with a vengeance.

More recently, in Simms v Simms and Another,[67] which concerned the lawfulness of experimental treatment on two young patients dying from variant CJD, Butler-Sloss P commented that, '[t]he Bolam test ought not to be allowed to inhibit medical progress'. In short, doctors should not be afraid to try new treatments when existing ones are not working. Such a constraint would inhibit the development of better treatments, contrary to important utilitarian considerations, and would be contrary to trying to do the best for the individual patient (both of these limbs must be satisfied as utility without more would involve using the patient merely as a means to an end).

There are two important issues here. First (subject to a possible defence of therapeutic privilege), it is suggested that the patient should be fully apprised of the fact that the treatment is innovative and, accordingly, that there may be side effects or other risks that the doctor does not know about.[68] Secondly, the context in which the treatment is given must be considered. In some cases, established treatments may not have been successful, and the patient will, perhaps, agree to accept a 'long shot' chance of success as a last resort. However, what of the situation where other conventional treatments exist and have not been tried? Certainly, in such a case, the patient should be fully informed about these alternatives, associated risks, likely outcomes and so on, but the question must be raised as to whether novel treatment should be given at all. When would such treatment be in the best interests of this patient?

A case in which unjustified 'experimentation' on the part of a doctor was at issue is that of Hepworth v Kerr.[69] The claimant was admitted to hospital in 1979 for a mastoid operation. During the course of the operation, the anaesthetist reduced the patient's blood pressure to a very low level for a period of one and a half hours. The purpose was to create a relatively blood-free operating field in the middle ear. The anaesthetist had been using this technique for some years in around 1,500 cases. However, in the case of this patient the level to which he reduced the blood pressure was 40 mm Hg, when a minimum of 60 mm Hg was strongly indicated in the medical literature. McKinnon J described the defendant as 'plainly negligent':

McKinnon J: As I find, the defendant adopted a new hypotensive anaesthetic technique which, as he knew, had never been attempted routinely before. Other anaesthetists had never gone to such low levels over such long periods. The defendant, as he accepted, was to begin with, at least, plainly experimenting. He expected serious complications such as cerebral or cardiac thrombosis to occur. He was surprised when they did not. He never, however, attempted to embark upon any proper scientific validation of his technique in some 1,500 patients by the time of the plaintiff's operation . . .

I simply cannot, and do not, accept that the defendant was justified in doing what he did without proper scientific validation of his technique.

6.3.3 Proof issues

In every case it is for the claimant to show that the defendant was negligent on the *balance of probabilities* (that is, according to the usual civil burden of proof). As we have seen, in relation to the normative

---

67 [2003] Fam 83.
68 On the doctor's general duty in negligence to disclose treatment risks, see Ch 3 above.
69 [1995] 6 Med LR 139.

question of the *reasonableness* of the defendant's conduct, this makes things very awkward for claimants in cases where medical opinion is divided as to whether such conduct accorded with responsible medical practice or not: see *Maynard v W Midlands RHA*.[70] Following *Bolitho*,[71] it may be said that the onus is squarely on the claimant to show that the conduct in question 'cannot be logically supported at all'.

On other occasions, though, where, as a matter of evidence, it is not clear what such conduct actually consisted of, a claimant may be able to bypass these difficulties by entering a plea of *res ipsa loquitur*. A claimant who enters such a plea (literally 'the thing speaks for itself') alleges that the injury could not have happened *without* negligence and, therefore, throws the ball into the doctor's court to show otherwise. To get this far, he must establish three elements: first, the defendant (either primarily or vicariously) must be in control of the situation prior to injury; secondly, in the ordinary course of events, such injury does not occur; and, finally, the claimant does not have all the facts to show what actually happened. (It is the third aspect which gave rise to the principle in the first place, so as to allow a claimant to sue in circumstances where he cannot properly plead specific allegations of negligence.)

Tort lawyers have long debated whether the principle means, in effect, that the burden of proof is reversed. The favoured view is that it is not. In the Privy Council decision of *Ng Chun Pui v Lee Chuen Tat*,[72] it was said that *res ipsa loquitur* is no more than the use of a Latin maxim to describe the state of the evidence from which it is proper to draw an inference of negligence. In other words, if the claimant asserts that such an accident would not normally happen without negligence, he is merely inviting a finding of negligence earlier in the proceedings than usual.

Two relatively early medical negligence cases in which the principle was invoked are *Roe v Minister of Health*[73] and *Cassidy v Ministry of Health*.[74] In *Roe*, the plaintiffs were paralysed during the course of surgery due to the contamination of their anaesthetic by phenol: the latter had seeped through invisible fissures in the glass storage vessels in which the anaesthetic was stored. Denning LJ commented:

> **Denning LJ**: The judge [at first instance] has said that those facts do not speak for themselves, but I think that they do. They certainly call for an explanation. Each of these men is entitled to say to the hospital: 'While I was in your hands something has been done to me which has wrecked my life. Please explain how this has come to pass.' . . . I approach this case, therefore, on the footing that the hospital authorities and Dr Graham were called on to give an explanation of what has happened.

The defendant was eventually able to establish that, at that time, the danger of such contamination was unknown to science, and accordingly it had not been negligent to fail to guard against it.

In the *Cassidy* case the claimant was admitted for surgery to correct Dupuytren's syndrome which had resulted in the contraction of the third and fourth fingers of his left hand. After surgery the contraction had spread to his two other fingers. The Court of Appeal held that *res ipsa loquitur* applied. It was Denning LJ again who stated:

> **Denning LJ**: If the plaintiff had to prove that some particular doctor or nurse was negligent, he would not be able to do it. But he was not put to that impossible task: he says:
>
> > I went into the hospital to be cured of two stiff fingers. I have come out with four stiff fingers, and my hand is useless. That should not have happened if due care had been used. Explain it, if you can.

---

70 See n 45 above; see also *Ashcroft v Mersey RHA* [1983] 2 All ER 245.
71 See n 54 above.
72 [1988] RTR 298.
73 [1954] 2 QB 66.
74 [1951] 2 KB 343.

Nevertheless, in subsequent cases the courts tended to vacillate on the question of how far, and in what circumstances, the principle should apply in medical negligence cases. The issue was reconsidered by the Court of Appeal in *Ratcliffe v Plymouth and Torbay HA.*

Ratcliffe v Plymouth and Torbay HA (1998)[75]

In September 1989, the claimant underwent a triple arthrodesis of his right ankle, in one of the defendants' hospitals. He received anaesthetic by way of injection into the spine to relieve post-operative pain. Although the operation itself was a success, he was left with a serious neurological defect on the right side from his waist downwards. The defendant was unable to explain how or why this had come about, but the trial judge found the anaesthetist who gave the injection had exercised proper care, and dismissed the claim.

On appeal, the claimant argued the judge should have accorded greater weight to the *res ipsa loquitur* doctrine:

Brooke LJ [*after reviewing the authorities*]: It is now possible to draw some threads out of all this material, by way of explanation of the relevance of the maxim *res ipsa loquitur* to medical negligence cases: (1) In its purest form, the maxim applies where the plaintiff relies on the '*res*' (the thing itself) to raise the inference of negligence, which is supported by ordinary human experience, with no need for expert evidence. (2) In principle, the maxim can be applied in that form in simple situations in the medical negligence field (surgeon cuts off right foot instead of left: swab left in operation site; patient wakes up in the course of surgical operation despite general anaesthetic). (3) In practice, in contested medical negligence cases the evidence of the plaintiff, which establishes the '*res*', is likely to be buttressed by expert evidence to the effect that the matter complained does not ordinarily occur in the absence of negligence. (4) The position may then be reached at the close of the plaintiff's case that the judge would be entitled to infer negligence on the defendant's part unless the defendant adduces evidence which discharges this inference. (5) This evidence may be to the effect that there is a plausible explanation of what may have happened which does not connote any negligence on the defendant's part. The explanation must be a plausible one and not a theoretically or remotely possible one, but the defendant certainly does not have to prove that his explanation is more likely to be correct than any other. If the plaintiff has no other evidence of negligence to rely on, his claim will then fail. (6) Alternatively, the defendant's evidence may satisfy the judge on the balance of probabilities that he did exercise proper care. If the untoward outcome is extremely rare, or is impossible to explain in the light of the current state of medical knowledge, the judge will be bound to exercise great care in evaluating the evidence before making such a finding, but it he does so, the *prima facie* inference of negligence is rebutted and the plaintiff's claim will fail. The reason why the courts are willing to adopt this approach, particularly in very complex cases, is to be found in the judgments of Stuart-Smith and Dillon LJJ in *Delaney v Southmead HA* [1995] 6 Med LR 355. (7) It follows from all this that, although in very simple situations the '*res*' may speak for itself at the end of the lay evidence adduced on behalf of the plaintiff, in practice the inference is then buttressed by expert evidence adduced on his behalf, and if the defendant were to call no evidence, the judge would be deciding the case on inferences he was entitled to draw from the whole of the evidence (including the expert evidence), and not on the application of the maxim in its purest form.

---

75 [1998] Lloyd's Rep Med 162, CA.

In the *Delaney*[76] case, referred to here, Stuart-Smith LJ had commented:

> **Stuart-Smith LJ**: [I]f the human body was a machine where it is possible to see the internal workings and which operates in accordance with the immutable laws of mechanics and with arithmetical precision, I think that the [*res ipsa loquitur*] argument might well be unanswerable. But in spite of the wonders of modern medical science, even at post-mortem not everything is known about an individual human being.

Accordingly, in *Ratcliffe*, the Court of Appeal held that the defendant had defused the force of the *res ipsa loquitur* doctrine on the alternative basis summarised by Brooke LJ in his point (6).[77]

Importantly, though, as his Lordship alludes to in point (5), there may often be a plausible explanation in medical negligence cases (besides the defendant's negligence) as to how the claimant suffered the injury. This indeed constitutes a major limitation on the doctrine's usefulness in this area.[78] As we shall see below, the same phenomenon often also creates problems at the stage of showing factual causation.

6.4 Causation

Assuming that the claimant manages to establish that the defendant doctor was 'negligent' (in the sense of having breached his duty of care), it does not follow that he will succeed in his claim in negligence. A further, and in this context often very troublesome, hurdle remains for him to negotiate in the form of proving causation. Analytically, causation subdivides into two main stages: first, it must be shown that the defendant's breach of duty was a *factual cause* of the claimant's harm; if so, the law must then also deem it to be the *legal cause* (ie the harm must not be so distant from the defendant's breach or unexpected in nature to qualify as 'too remote'). As we shall see, in the context of medical negligence the first of these aspects, especially, may give rise to great difficulty.

6.4.1 Factual causation: the 'but for' test

For the purposes of the tort of negligence, the crucial question is whether the defendant's breach of duty made a difference to (ie was a necessary condition for) the harmful outcome suffered by the claimant. This is generally resolved by means of the so-called 'but for' test. In the well-known words of Denning LJ in the (non-medical negligence) case of *Cork v Kirby Maclean Ltd*,[79] '[i]f you can say that the damage would not have happened but for a particular fault then that fault is in fact a cause of the damage; but if you can say that the damage would have happened just the same, fault or no fault, then the fault is not a cause of the damage'.

A good illustration of the test's application, in the context of medical negligence, is provided by the case of *Barnett v Chelsea and Kensington Hospital Management Committee*.

Barnett v Chelsea & Kensington Hospital Management Committee (1967)[80]

Three nightwatchmen attended the defendant's casualty department complaining of nausea and vomiting after drinking some tea. The casualty doctor on duty negligently failed to see the men and

---

76 [1995] 6 Med LR 355.

77 For a case in which the Court of Appeal rejected the defendant's evidence of due care and inferred negligence on the basis of his failure to detect foetal abnormalities on a scan, see *Lillywhite v University College University Hospitals NHS Trust* [2005] EWCA Civ 1466.

78 In effect, the 'mono-causality' of the claimant's injury, ie that this could only have arisen from a cause within the defendant's control, must already be clear in order to support the inference back to the defendant's lack of care.

79 [1952] 2 All ER 402.

80 See n 5 above.

they were sent away untreated. One of them later died from what it transpired were the effects of arsenic poisoning. In the subsequent action brought by the man's widow, the judge, after holding that the defendant owed a duty of care to the deceased and was in breach, continued as follows:

> **Nield J**: It remains to consider whether it is shown that the deceased's death was caused by that negligence or whether, as the defendants have said, the deceased must have died in any event. In his concluding submission Mr Pain submitted that the casualty officer should have examined the deceased and had he done so he would have caused tests to be made which would have indicated the treatment required and that, since the defendants were at fault in these respects, therefore the onus of proof passed to the defendants to show that the appropriate treatment would have failed, and authorities were cited to me. I find myself unable to accept that argument, and I am of the view that the onus of proof remains upon the plaintiff, and I have in mind (without quoting it) the decision cited by Mr Wilmers in *Bonnington Castings Ltd v Wardlaw* [1956] AC 613 . . . However, were it otherwise and the onus did pass to the defendants, then I would find that they have discharged it, as I would proceed to show. There has been put before me a timetable which I think is of much importance. The deceased attended at the casualty department at five or 10 minutes past eight in the morning. If the casualty officer had got up and dressed and come to see the three men and examined them and decided to admit them, the deceased (and Dr Lockett agreed with this) could not have been in bed in a ward before 11 am. I accept Dr Goulding's evidence that an intravenous drip would not have been set up before 12 noon, and if potassium loss was suspected it could not have been discovered until 12.30 pm. Dr Lockett, dealing with this, said: 'If this man had not been treated until after 12 noon the chances of survival were not good.' Without going in detail into the considerable volume of technical evidence which has been put before me, it seems to me to be the case that when death results from arsenical poisoning it is brought about by two conditions; on the one hand dehydration and on the other disturbance of the enzyme processes. If the principal condition is one of enzyme disturbance – as I am of the view it was here – then the only method of treatment which is likely to succeed is the use of the specific antidote which is commonly called BAL. Dr Goulding said in the course of his evidence: 'The only way to deal with this is to use the specific BAL. I see no reasonable prospect of the deceased being given BAL before the time at which he died' – and at a later point in his evidence – 'I feel that even if fluid loss had been discovered death would have been caused by the enzyme disturbance. Death might have occurred later.' I regard that evidence as very moderate, and it might be a true assessment of the situation to say that there was no chance of BAL being administered before the death of the deceased. For those reasons, I find that the plaintiff has failed to establish, on the balance of probabilities, that the defendants' negligence caused the death of the deceased.

The *Barnett* case is instructive for a number of reasons. For one thing it illustrates the inevitably hypothetical nature of the factual causation enquiry: the court is required to construct a counter-factual parallel series – ie to speculate as to how things would have turned out if the defendant had properly performed his duty. At the same time, the case provides a powerful hint as to why it is that factual causation is often difficult to prove in medical negligence. This is because, in such cases, the claimant – at the time of the doctor's breach – is normally already at risk of suffering an adverse outcome: in the context of a non-treatment case as here, this risk is posed by the illness that led him to seek the doctor's assistance. Here, it is always open to the doctor to argue that the patient's injury was due to the progress of the illness, which, even with all due medical care, could not have been arrested; if that is the case, the risk posed by the doctor's faulty non-treatment will remain just that – it will not have materialised in the sense of playing a necessary part in (ie *causing*) the harm.

As we have seen, it was just this type of argument that Nield J accepted in *Barnett* itself. (It is useful here to contrast the position of defendants in most other negligence scenarios: for example, a negligent motorist is highly unlikely to be able to suggest that the pedestrian whose leg he crushed would have lost the leg in any event through an independent risk materialising.)

 SELF-TEST QUESTION

Why could the hospital in *Barnett* not argue that, on any view, the true cause of Mr Barnett's death was the person who put the arsenic in the tea?

6.4.2 Evidential problems in applying the test

The fact that, in medical negligence cases, the court must normally consider the respective role in the patient's injury of two or more independent risks may generate significant evidential uncertainty. The scientific evidence may be unable to distinguish between the respective risks and determine which of them actually materialised. This is already so in non-treatment cases, such as *Barnett*, where the question, as we saw, is whether the underlying illness was sufficient alone for the injury (ie was untreatable from the start), or whether the omission of proper treatment also played a part. Potentially more complicated still are cases where the patient suffers additional (or 'iatrogenic') injury after negligent treatment is actually provided: here a further possible 'candidate' as the cause of injury will be the known risk from such treatment, even where carefully performed.[81]

6.4.2.1 Multiple risk-exposure and iatrogenic injury – relaxing the 'but for' test?

Outside the medical negligence context, the courts have occasionally allowed recovery on the basis simply that the defendant's conduct exposed the claimant to a 'material risk' of the harm he suffered. A well-known case is *McGhee v National Coal Board*,[82] in which the claimant sued his employer for the dermatitis he contracted following exposure to brick dust at his workplace. Such exposure was not itself negligent, but the defendant had faultily added to it (and hence to the risk of injury) by failing to provide adequate washing facilities. The difficulty lay in determining whether the 'guilty' dust (ie the portion the claimant was exposed to by being unable to wash) had played any causative role. The House of Lords' solution was to assert that, here it was open to a court simply to infer, as a question of fact, that the defendant's breach had materially contributed to the injury. Indeed, in one of the judgments, Lord Wilberforce appeared to go further and suggest that, once the claimant shows the defendant's breach of duty created a risk of harm, the burden of proving that the risk did not materialise and contribute to the harm passes to the defendant.

The question of how far the claimant-friendly approach to resolving such difficulties in *McGhee* should also apply in the field of medical-negligence was faced by the House of Lords in *Wilsher v Essex AHA*.

Wilsher v Essex AHA (1988)[83]

The claimant baby contracted retrolental fibroplasia (RLF), rendering him virtually blind, after treatment in the defendant's post-natal unit. Owing to a breach of duty by hospital staff, he had been over-saturated with oxygen in the first weeks of his life.[84] However, whilst this might,

---

81 See further, Stauch, M, 'Causation, risk and loss of chance in medical negligence' (1997) 17 OJLS 205.
82 [1972] 3 All ER 1008.
83 [1988] AC 1074, HL.
84 On this aspect of the case, *viz* the breach of duty by the staff involved, see the text at n 36 above.

according to some of the evidence, have caused or contributed to the RLF, there were four other natural conditions, all of which had affected the baby, and which could equally have had the same effect. The majority of the Court of Appeal found for the claimant on causation on the basis of Lord Wilberforce's speech in *McGhee*; the defendant appealed:

> **Lord Bridge**: The Court of Appeal, although it felt unable to resolve the primary conflict in the expert evidence as to the causation of Martin's RLF, did make a finding that the levels of PO2 which Martin experienced in consequence of the misplacement of the catheter were of a kind capable of causing RLF. Mustill LJ expressed his anxiety whether 'by making a further finding on an issue where there was a sharp conflict between the expert witnesses, we are going too far in the effort to avoid a retrial' (see [1986] 3 All ER 801, p 825). But he concluded that it was 'legitimate, after rereading the evidence', to make this finding based on 'the weight of the expert evidence'. This finding by the Court of Appeal is challenged by counsel for the authority as one which it was not open to it to make . . . But assuming, as I do for the present, that the finding was properly made, it carried the plaintiff's case no further than to establish that oxygen administered to Martin as a consequence of the negligent failure to detect the misplacement of the catheter was one of a number of possible causes of Martin's RLF.
>
> Mustill LJ subjected the speeches in *McGhee v National Coal Board* [1972] 3 All ER 1008 . . . to a careful scrutiny and analysis and concluded that they established a principle of law which he expressed in the following terms:
>
>> If it is an established fact that conduct of a particular kind creates a risk that injury will be caused to another or increases an existing risk that injury will ensue, and if the two parties stand in such a relationship that the one party owes a duty not to conduct himself in that way, and if the first party does conduct himself in that way, and if the other party does suffer injury of the kind to which the risk related, then the first party is taken to have caused the injury by his breach of duty, even though the existence and extent of the contribution made by the breach cannot be ascertained.
>
> Applying this principle to the finding that the authority's negligence was one of the possible causes of Martin's RLF, he held that this was sufficient to enable the court to conclude that the negligence was 'taken to have caused the injury'. Glidewell LJ reached the same conclusion by substantially the same process of reasoning. Sir Nicolas Browne-Wilkinson VC took the opposite view . . .
>
> Much of the academic discussion to which [*McGhee*] has given rise has focused on the speech of Lord Wilberforce, particularly on two paragraphs. He said:
>
>> . . . First, it is a sound principle that where a person has, by breach of duty of care, created a risk, and injury occurs within the area of that risk, the loss should be borne by him *unless he shows that it had some other cause*. Secondly, from the evidential point of view, one may ask, why should a man who is able to show that his employer should have taken certain precautions, because without them there is a risk, or an added risk, of injury or disease, and who in fact sustains exactly that injury or disease, have to assume the burden of proving more: namely, that it was the addition to the risk, caused by the breach of duty, which caused or materially contributed to the injury? In many cases of which the present is typical, this is impossible to prove, just because honest medical opinion cannot segregate the causes of an illness between compound causes. And if one asks which of the parties,

the workman or the employers should suffer from this inherent evidential difficulty, the answer as a matter in policy or justice should be that it is the creator of the risk who, *ex hypothesi*, must be taken to have foreseen the possibility of damage, who should bear its consequences. (My emphasis.)

He then referred to *Bonnington Castings Ltd v Wardlaw* and *Nicholson v Atlas Steel Foundry and Engineering Co Ltd* and added:

I must say that, at least in the present case, to bridge the evidential gap by inference seems to me something of a fiction, since it was precisely this inference which the medical expert declined to make. But I find in the cases quoted an analogy which suggests the conclusion that, *in the absence of proof that the culpable condition had, in the result, no effect*, the employers should be liable for an injury, squarely within the risk which they created and that they, not the pursuer, should suffer the consequence of the impossibility, foreseeably inherent in the nature of his injury, of segregating the precise consequence of their default. (My emphasis.)

My Lords, it seems to me that both these paragraphs, particularly in the words I have emphasised, amount to saying that, in the circumstances, the burden of proof of causation is reversed and thereby to run counter to the unanimous and emphatic opinions expressed in *Bonnington Castings Ltd v Wardlaw* [1956] 1 All ER 615 . . . to the contrary effect. I find no support in any of the other speeches for the view that the burden of proof is reversed and, in this respect, I think Lord Wilberforce's reasoning must be regarded as expressing a minority opinion.

The conclusion I draw . . . is that *McGhee v National Coal Board* laid down no new principle of law whatever. On the contrary, it affirmed the principle that the onus of proving causation lies on the pursuer or plaintiff. Adopting a robust and pragmatic approach to the undisputed primary facts of the case, the majority concluded that it was a legitimate inference of fact that the defenders' negligence had materially contributed to the pursuer's injury. The decision, in my opinion, is of no greater significance than that and the attempt to extract from it some esoteric principle which in some way modifies, as a matter of law, the nature of the burden of proof of causation which a plaintiff or pursuer must discharge once he has established a relevant breach of duty is a fruitless one.

Subsequently, though, in *Fairchild v Glenhaven Funeral Services*,[85] the view taken of *McGhee* by Lord Bridge in *Wilsher* was itself the subject of reappraisal. In *Fairchild*, which like *McGhee* was a negligence action brought by an employee, the evidential problem in relation to causation was that of multiple possible tortfeasors. The claimant was suffering from mesolethemia, which it was accepted had been caused by inhaling asbestos fibres during his employment. However, he had worked for a number of different companies, each of whom had negligently exposed him to asbestos, and it was not possible now to say, of any particular one, that the fatal inhalation took place while the claimant was working there.

In allowing recovery, the House of Lords regarded *McGhee* as authority for departing from the normal need to satisfy the 'but for' test on the balance of probabilities on the basis of special policy considerations. Where these applied, the proven creation of a material risk of harm (rather than proof the risk actually materialised) should be treated as sufficient for liability. Nonetheless, their Lordships affirmed the correctness of *Wilsher* on its facts. In his speech in *Fairchild*, Lord Hoffmann

---

85 [2002] 3 WLR 89.

was anxious to emphasise that a similar relaxation of causation would not apply in the context of medical negligence:

> **Lord Hoffmann**: [68] The Court of Appeal [in *Wilsher*] treated the causal requirement rule applied in *McGhee* as being of general application . . .
>
> [69] The House of Lords, in a speech by Lord Bridge of Harwich with which all other noble Lords concurred, rejected this broad principle. I would respectfully agree. The principle in *McGhee*'s case is far narrower and I have tried to indicate what its limits are likely to be. It is true that actions for clinical negligence notoriously give rise to difficult questions of causation. But it cannot possibly be said that the duty to take reasonable care in treating patients would be virtually drained of content unless the creation of a material risk of injury were accepted as sufficient to satisfy the causal requirements for liability. And the political and economic arguments involved in the massive increase in the liability of the National Health Service which would have been a consequence of the broad rule favoured by the Court of Appeal in *Wilsher*'s case are far more complicated than the reasons given by Lord Wilberforce [in *McGhee*] for imposing liability upon an employer who has failed to take simple precautions.[86]

However, recently, in *Bailey v Ministry of Defence*,[87] the Court of Appeal permitted a patient to recover damages on the basis of 'material risk' alone. The claimant was left very weak after surgery, partly due to the defendant's negligent aftercare and partly from developing pancreatitis; she later suffered brain damage after choking on a drink. The experts were unable to say whether 'but for' the negligence, she would have avoided this outcome; the pancreatitis by itself may have led to it. In nevertheless awarding damages, the Court distinguished *Wilsher* as dealing with the problem of fixing responsibility between alternative risks, whereas here the negligence and pancreatitis had cumulatively weakened the claimant. The decision may be seen as rather against the grain, in assisting the patient in a doubtful causation case, and it will be interesting to see if it gains approval at the highest level.

6.4.2.2 Misdiagnosis cases – claims for 'loss of chance'?

In *Wilsher* we saw that, due to the over-complexity and lack of clarity of the available evidence, the claimant was unable to show the defendant's breach of duty had played a causative role in his injury. However, in many instances, notably where a doctor's failure to make a prompt or proper diagnosis of a given illness is at issue, the clamant will have evidence as to the effect this has had upon him. Such evidence takes the form of class statistics recording the chances of recovery for patients who *were* properly diagnosed with that illness at a similar stage of progression.

The courts were required to decide whether a claim founded upon such statistical evidence was admissible in the case of *Hotson v East Berkshire AHA*,[88] in which the claimant schoolboy attended the defendant's casualty department after falling from a tree and injuring his hip. The defendant failed, in breach of duty, to carry out an x-ray of the hip and by the time the true extent of the injury was discovered (when the boy returned to hospital several days later) permanent disability was unavoidable. The medical evidence, based on class statistics, was that, even with immediate diagnosis, 75 per cent of patients with such an injury went on to develop permanent disability.

Rather than suing on the basis that the defendant had caused the disability itself (clearly an impossible task, given the need to satisfy the civil standard of proof by showing *on the balance of probabilities* that the failed diagnosis had played a necessary part in it), the claimant restricted his claim to the loss of the residual 25 per cent chance that proper diagnosis would have resulted in successful treatment. At first instance, Simon Brown J accepted that the loss of a substantial chance of this kind

---

86 See also his Lordship's comments, together with those of Lords Scott and Walker, in *Barker v Corus Ltd* [2006] UKHL 20.
87 [2008] EWCA Civ 883.
88 [1987] 1 AC 750.

was actionable and awarded damages assessed at 25 per cent of the full quantum in respect of such an injury, and this approach was upheld in the Court of Appeal:

Sir John Donaldson MR: . . . Mr Whitfield, for the defendants, submits that no causal connection between the negligence and the development of avascular necrosis and consequent disability has been established, since a 25% likelihood fails to achieve the requisite standard of proof. Without that causal connection, there can be no liability in damages based upon that development. In more concrete terms, it is all, ie, £46,000, or nothing – £46,000 if the likelihood of the connection exceeds 50% and otherwise nothing. In the instant case it is nothing . . .

As a matter of common sense, it is unjust that there should be no liability for failure to treat a patient, simply because the chances of a successful cure by that treatment were less than 50%. Nor, by the same token, can it be just that if the chances of a successful cure only marginally exceed 50%, the doctor or his employer should be liable to the same extent as if the treatment could be guaranteed to cure. If this is the law, it is high time that it was changed, assuming that this court has power to do so.

However, the health authority appealed successfully to the House of Lords:

Lord Bridge: The plaintiff's claim was for damages for physical injury and consequential loss alleged to have been caused by the authority's breach of their duty of care. In some cases, perhaps particularly medical negligence cases, causation may be so shrouded in mystery that the court can only measure statistical chances. But that was not so here. On the evidence there was a clear conflict as to what had caused the avascular necrosis. The authority's evidence was that the sole cause was the original traumatic injury to the hip. The plaintiff's evidence, at its highest, was that the delay in treatment was a material contributory cause. This was a conflict, like any other about some relevant past event, which the judge could not avoid resolving on a balance of probabilities. Unless the plaintiff proved on a balance of probabilities that the delayed treatment was at least a material contributory cause of the avascular necrosis he failed on the issue of causation and no question of quantification could arise. But the judge's findings of fact . . . are unmistakably to the effect that on a balance of probabilities the injury caused by the plaintiff's fall left insufficient blood vessels intact to keep the epiphysis alive. This amounts to a finding of fact that the fall was the sole cause of the avascular necrosis.

The upshot is that the appeal must be allowed . . .

Although in *Hotson* their Lordships stopped short of saying that there could never be recovery in medical negligence for loss of chance, they gave little clue as to when it might be allowed. More recently, in *Gregg v Scott*, the House of Lords had another opportunity to consider the merits of a claim framed in this way:

Gregg v Scott (2005)[89]

The claimant, Mr Gregg, consulted Dr Scott in November 1994 about a lump under his arm. The latter assumed it was benign and negligently failed to refer the claimant to hospital for tests. The claimant was subsequently admitted to hospital in January 1996 where it was found that he was suffering from non-Hodgkin's lymphoma. The effect of the 14-month delay in diagnosis was that the cancer had spread and, statistically, Mr Gregg's chance of a 'cure' (defined, medically, as ten-year disease-free survival) had diminished from 42 per cent to 25 per cent. In his action against the doctor, the claimant argued, inter alia, that the lost (or, more accurately,

89 [2005] UKHL 2.

reduced) statistical chance of a cure should itself be compensated for. This basis of the claim would have been allowed by Lord Nicholls:

> **Lord Nicholls**: [21] . . . What the patient loses depends, of course, on the circum-
> stances of the individual case. No doubt in some cases medical opinion will be that,
> given his pre-existing condition, the patient lost nothing by the delay in treatment
> because he never had any realistic prospect of recovery. The doctor's misdiagnosis
> made no significant difference to the patient's prospects of recovery. In other cases
> medical opinion may be that the patient lost everything. Barring unforeseen compli-
> cations he would have made a complete recovery had his condition been diagnosed
> properly and had he then received appropriate treatment.
>
> [22] These two types of case are, in the present context, straightforward. But there
> are also many cases of serious illness or injury where a patient's existing chances of
> recovery fall between these extremes. There are occasions where medical opinion
> will be that, given prompt and appropriate treatment, the outcome was uncertain but
> the patient's prospects of recovery were appreciable, sometimes exceeding 50%,
> sometimes not . . .
>
> [24] Given this uncertainty of outcome, the appropriate characterisation of a patient's
> loss in this type of case must surely be that it comprises the loss of the chance of a
> favourable outcome, rather than the loss of the outcome itself. Justice so requires,
> because this matches medical reality. This recognises what in practice a patient had
> before the doctor's negligence occurred. It recognises what in practice the patient
> lost by reason of that negligence. The doctor's negligence diminished the patient's
> prospects of recovery. And this analysis of a patient's loss accords with the purpose
> of the legal duty of which the doctor was in breach. In short, the purpose of the duty
> is to promote the patient's prospects of recovery by exercising due skill and care in
> diagnosing and treating the patient's condition.
>
> [25] This approach also achieves a basic objective of the law of tort. The common law
> imposes duties and seeks to provide appropriate remedies in the event of a breach of
> duty. If negligent diagnosis or treatment diminishes a patient's prospects of recovery,
> a law which does not recognise this as a wrong calling for redress would be seriously
> deficient today. In respect of the doctors' breach of duty the law would not have
> provided an appropriate remedy.

However, Lord Hoffmann was in the opposite camp. As foreshadowed in his speech in *Fairchild*,[90] one of his Lordship's concerns related to the effect of permitting such claims upon scarce health care resources:

> **Lord Hoffmann**: [84] Academic writers have suggested that in cases of clinical negli-
> gence, the need to prove causation is too restrictive of liability. This argument has
> appealed to judges in some jurisdictions; in some, but not all, of the states of the United
> States and most recently in New South Wales and Ireland: *Rufo v Hosking* . . . [2004]
> NSWCA 391; *Philp v Ryan* . . . [2004] 1 IESC 105. In the present case it is urged that Mr
> Gregg has suffered a wrong and ought to have a remedy. Living for more than 10 years
> is something of great value to him and he should be compensated for the possibility
> that the delay in diagnosis may have reduced his chances of doing so. In effect, the

90 See n 85 above.

Appellant submits that the exceptional rule in *Fairchild* should be generalised and damages awarded in all cases in which the defendant may have caused an injury and has increased the likelihood of the injury being suffered. In the present case, it is alleged that Dr Scott may have caused a reduction in Mr Gregg's expectation of life and that he increased the likelihood that his life would be shortened by the disease.

[85] It should first be noted that adopting such a rule would involve abandoning a good deal of authority. The rule which the House is asked to adopt is the very rule which it rejected in *Wilsher*'s case [1988] AC 1074. Yet *Wilsher*'s case was expressly approved by the House in *Fairchild* [2003] 1 AC 32. *Hotson* [1987] AC 750 too would have to be overruled. Furthermore, the House would be dismantling all the qualifications and restrictions with which it so recently hedged the *Fairchild* exception. There seem to me to be no new arguments or change of circumstances which could justify such a radical departure from precedent . . .

[90] . . . [A] wholesale adoption of possible rather than probable causation as the criterion of liability would be so radical a change in our law as to amount to a legislative act. It would have enormous consequences for insurance companies and the National Health Service.

Lord Phillips and Baroness Hale agreed with Lord Hoffmann in dismissing the claimant's appeal. However, they appear to have been swayed more by the particular factual complexities of the case at hand, and a distrust of the statistical evidence on offer. As the former commented:

Lord Phillips: [189] There are no doubt cases where it is possible to adopt the simple approach of asking to what extent the negligent treatment has reduced the prospects of curing the patient. There are other cases, and this is one, where that simple question is almost impossible to answer . . . The likelihood seems to be that Dr Scott's negligence has not prevented Mr Gregg's cure, but has made that cure more painful.

[190] The complications of this case have persuaded me that it is not a suitable vehicle for introducing into the law of clinical negligence the right to recover damages for the loss of a chance of a cure. Awarding damages for the reduction of the prospect of a cure, when the long term result of treatment is still uncertain, is not a satisfactory exercise. Where medical treatment has resulted in an adverse outcome and negligence has increased the chance of that outcome, there may be a case for permitting a recovery of damages that is proportionate to the increase in the chance of the adverse outcome. That is not a case that has been made out on the present appeal. I would uphold the conventional approach to causation . . .

Gregg v Scott is undoubtedly a difficult case, and one may agree with Lord Phillip's assessment that it did not provide a suitable vehicle for recognising 'loss of chance' claims in medical negligence. A fundamental problem, as their Lordships noted, was that the claimant was still alive nearly 10 years after the original misdiagnosis. Thus (leaving aside, the more painful treatment he had to undergo and his increased mental suffering[91]) he had quite possibly lost nothing, not even a chance. Although statistically it made a difference for 17 per cent of patients with a similar condition whether diagnosis took place at the earlier stage (when it should have) or only later, it appeared increasing likely that the claimant was not in that group. Instead, his case was akin to that of someone who is exposed to a hazardous substance, known to increase the risk of a given harm, but

---

91 As Baroness Hale suggested in her speech, had the claimant put this in his claim, he could have obtained some damages for the more painful treatment.

where as yet no harm has materialised and no one knows whether it will or not (and where it is generally acknowledged that no recovery lies in negligence[92]).

However, returning to the more typical loss of chance scenario illustrated by *Hotson* – where the claimant's injury has already occurred, it is submitted that there such claims should be permitted. Just as in the *Barnett* case,[93] the basic question is whether or not the claimant's medical condition was untreatable from the outset. Would the illness have been sufficient – even despite proper treatment – for the injury, or did the lack of proper treatment also play a necessary part? In such cases, it is strongly arguable that class statistics (where available) bring us significantly closer to the truth than adherence to the balance of probabilities standard of proof:

Stauch, M, *The Law of Medical Negligence in England and Germany – A Comparative Analysis*[94]

[In loss of chance claims] the statistics at issue are derived empirically by reference to how patients with the claimant's condition generally fare (ie with the proper treatment). It is true that this does not offer certainty in a particular case ... Nonetheless, the crucial point is that the traditional balance of probabilities test is no different. In finding that a given patient's condition was *probably* untreatable, the court also draws upon past experience as to how other patients with a similar condition respond to treatment (ie that the majority do not benefit). It does not tell us that the *claimant* individually could not have been helped: he might have been one of the (perhaps substantial) minority, whose condition would have responded. In this context, the use of statistics providing an accurate measure of the opportunity lost as a prequel to an award of proportionate damages, appears significantly fairer than the present 'all or nothing' approach.

Similarly, the fear that allowing claims for proportionate recovery would undermine general principles of causation in personal injury cases is not justified. In the first place, such claims, which depend on the availability of empirical statistical evidence, would normally be confined to medical misdiagnosis cases; ... it is much less likely that such evidence will be at hand where the doctor's mistake actively added to the risks to the patient. Secondly, it is important to reiterate that ... loss of chance claims arise as a response to factual uncertainty (ie in default of individuating evidence as to what would have happened in the particular case). In this regard, the relevant rules operate on a different plane to the substantive law elements, including 'but for' causation.

Thus, following on from the above, it would remain necessary for the (substantive law) requirement of *actual* injury to the claimant to be satisfied – these cases are not about treating exposure to risk per se as a recoverable form of injury. This, it is submitted, was the key difficulty with *Gregg v Scott*, where the claimant's injury (the lost benefit of a cure) had not yet occurred, and it was uncertain whether it would do so in the future ... By contrast, in the most scenarios of this type – such as in *Hotson*– this problem does not arise.

Finally, as to the concern that permitting loss of chance claims could lead to a flood of additional litigation against the NHS, we should be clear that, in terms of overall compensation, no more would be paid out in faulty diagnosis claims than before: this is because, logically the use of statistics as a basis for proportionate recovery 'must cut both ways' [per Baroness Hale in *Gregg v Scott* [2005] UKHL 2, para 225]. Thus a patient who had, say, a 60 per cent chance of benefiting from wrongfully omitted treatment should only receive 60 per cent of damages in respect of his injury, not 100 per cent as at present. It remains true that the total number of claims may increase, as patients will no longer be deterred, as at present, from litigating in cases where their prospects of successful treatment were low. Arguably, to guard against a proliferation of low-value actions, the law (in a pragmatic vein) should demand that the chance lost was a substantial one.

---

92 See *Grieves v F T Everard & Sons* [2007] UKHL 39 (the pleural plaques test case).
93 See the text at n 80 above.
94 Oxford: Hart Publishing, 2008.

6.4.2.3 Human agency in the causal chain

Complications of a different kind arise in cases in which resolving the causal inquiry requires us to decide how a human agent would have behaved in the hypothetical circumstances of no original breach of duty. In contrast to the cases considered previously, in which the causal chain consists only of physical events, such as the progress of an untreated disease, it may well be felt that the balance of probabilities standard of proof remains the most acceptable one here. (To assert that because, in a given situation, X per cent of persons are observed to do A, a particular individual, P, is X per cent likely to do A, would be to take an unduly mechanistic view of human agency.)

As we saw in Chapter 3, a common type of case, which requires us to assess the impact of human agency in the causal chain, is where the doctor fails to advise the patient of a given risk attached to treatment. Here the patient, in order to succeed in his claim, must show that, on the balance of probabilities, he would not have agreed to the treatment had he been properly advised. However, in other cases it is the defendant's hypothetical conduct that will be at issue: this is true in particular where a doctor negligently fails to attend the patient. Assuming that treatment is available which would benefit the patient, would the doctor have administered it? If not, so the doctor might argue, the failure by him to attend made no difference.

See Chapter 3

Here (as with the analogous claim by a patient that, had he known of a risk, he would have refused treatment), the court must first accept the veracity of the doctor's assertion that he would not have given treatment. In *Wisniewski v Central Manchester Health Authority*,[95] the court, in holding that the necessary treatment would probably have been carried out, drew an adverse inference from the doctor's non-appearance in the witness box to back up his contrary assertion. If, though, the doctor's testimony is accepted, then, as Lord Browne-Wilkinson made clear in *Bolitho v City and Hackney HA*, that is not the end of the matter. There is a second question that the court must resolve:

> **Lord Browne-Wilkinson**: Where, as in the present case, a breach of a duty of care is proved or admitted, the burden still lies on the plaintiff to prove that such breach caused the injury suffered: *Bonnington Castings Ltd v Wardlaw* [1956] AC 613; *Wilsher v Essex AHA* [1988] AC 1074. In all cases the primary question is one of fact: did the wrongful act cause the injury? . . . In a case of non-attendance by a doctor, there may be cases in which there is a doubt as to which doctor would have attended if the duty had been fulfilled. But in this case there was no doubt: if the duty had been carried out it would have either been Dr Horn or Dr Rodger, the only two doctors at St Bartholomew's who had responsibility for Patrick and were on duty. Therefore in the present case, the first relevant question is 'what would Dr Horn or Dr Rodger have done if they had attended?' As to Dr Horn, the judge accepted her evidence that she would not have intubated. By inference, although not expressly, the judge must have accepted that Dr Rodger also would not have intubated: as a senior house officer she would not have intubated without the approval of her senior registrar, Dr Horn . . .
>
> However in the present case the answer to the question 'what would have happened?' is not determinative of the issue of causation. At the trial the defendants accepted that if the professional standard of care required any doctor who attended to intubate Patrick, Patrick's claim must succeed. Dr Horn could not escape liability by proving that she would have failed to take the course which any competent doctor would have adopted. A defendant cannot escape liability by saying that the damage would have occurred in any event because he would have committed some other breach of duty thereafter. I have no doubt that this concession was rightly made by the defendants. But there is some difficulty in analysing why it was correct. I adopt the analysis of Hobhouse LJ in *Joyce v Merton, Sutton and Wandsworth HA* [1996] 7 Med LR 1. In commenting on the decision of the Court of Appeal in the present case, he said, p 20:

---

95 [1998] PIQR P324.

Thus a plaintiff can discharge the burden of proof on causation by satisfying the court *either* that the relevant person would in fact have taken the requisite action (although she would not have been at fault if she had not), or that the proper discharge of the relevant person's duty towards the plaintiff required that she take that action. The former alternative calls for no explanation since it is simply the factual proof of the causative effect of the original fault. The latter is slightly more sophisticated: it involves the factual situation that the original fault did not itself cause the injury but that this was because there would have been some further fault on the part of the defendants; the plaintiff proves his case by proving that his injuries would have been avoided if proper care had continued to be taken. In the *Bolitho* case the plaintiff had to prove that the continuing exercise of proper care would have resulted in his being intubated.

There were, therefore, two questions for the judge to decide on causation: (1) 'What would Dr Horn have done, or authorised to be done, if she had attended Patrick?' And: (2) 'If she would not have intubated, would that have been negligent?' The *Bolam* test has no relevance to the first of those questions but is central to the second.

There can be no doubt that, as the majority of the Court of Appeal held, the judge directed himself correctly in accordance with that approach . . . The dissenting judgment of Simon Brown LJ in the Court of Appeal is based on a misreading of the judge's judgment. He treats the judge as having only asked himself one question, namely, the second question. To the extent that the Lord Justice noticed the first question – would Dr Horn have intubated? – he said that the judge was wrong to accept Dr Horn's evidence that she would not have intubated. In my judgment it was for the judge to assess the truth of her evidence on this issue.[96]

Importantly, as this judgment makes clear, where the agent whose hypothetical conduct is called into question is the defendant, such conduct – if it is to be accepted as negativing causation – must in any event fall within the bounds of the non-negligent.

6.4.3 Legal causation/remoteness of damage

Legal causation, or 'remoteness', operates as a further limiting device, which may exclude liability even where the defendant's conduct clearly did play a necessary part in the claimant's injury (ie the factual causation requirement of the 'but for' test has been satisfied). In negligence, the dominant approach of the courts, following the decision of the Privy Council in *The Wagon Mound* (No 1),[97] is to begin by considering the nature of the harm in suit (that is, the damage that actually material-ised) and ask if it was reasonably foreseeable. In other words, was it the risk of *that* harm occurring that made the defendant's conduct faulty?

It is often said that, once the broad 'type' of harm suffered by the claimant was reasonably foreseeable, the fact that its precise manner of upshot or extent may not have been is immaterial. On the other hand, as cases since *The Wagon Mound* demonstrate, given that any harmful outcome can be described at different levels of detail, the question of its foreseeability – and, hence, the defend-ant's liability – will turn on the specificity of the description applied by the court in a particular case. This point has led some commentators to regard the whole remoteness enquiry as merely a cover for the concealed policy choices of judges. Arguably a more cogent approach is to focus not so much on the 'type' of harm that has occurred, but on the further necessary conditions that

---

96 See n 54 above; see also the decision of *Gouldsmith v Mid-Staffs General Hospital NHS Trust* [2007] EWCA Civ 397, in which a majority of the Court of Appeal found the trial judge had failed properly to address the anterior 'would' question: if that is resolved in the patient's favour, the 'should' question will not arise.

97 [1961] AC 388.

(together with the defendant's conduct) completed the causal set for harm in the particular case. Was the possible completion of a causal set that included those further conditions a reason for regarding the conduct as a breach of duty?[98]

In principle, remoteness principles may apply in medical negligence (just as in other negligence cases) to defeat the claimant's action. In *Brown v Lewisham and North Southwark HA*,[99] the claimant, who had undergone heart surgery was negligently discharged from hospital while suffering from a chest infection. Later he was found to have an unsuspected thrombosis, which led to the loss of his leg. The court did not accept that, had he remained in hospital, the leg would have been saved (ie it denied factual causation). However, as Beldam LJ noted in the Court of Appeal, the claimant's action would in any event have failed on remoteness grounds:

> **Beldam LJ**: The public policy of limiting the liability of tortfeasors by the control mechanism of foreseeability seems to me as necessary in cases of medical as in any other type of negligence. I do not see on what policy ground it would be fair or just to hold a doctor [liable] who failed to diagnose an asymptomatic and undetectable illness merely because he was at fault in the management of a correctly diagnosed but unrelated condition. In short, it must be shown that the injury suffered by the patient is within the risk from which it was the doctor's duty to protect him.

Subsequently, this *dictum* was approved in the case of *Thompson v Bradford*,[100] in which the Court of Appeal denied the liability of a doctor for vaccine injuries to a child following immunisation for polio. The doctor had failed to advise the parents that a boil the child had was a contra-indication for the vaccination – advice which would have led to the procedure being postponed. In the event, the boil played a factually causative role in the vaccine damage. Nonetheless, the reason the advice should have been given was not the added risk of such damage (which had been unforeseeable), but the discomfort to the child of vaccinating him in those circumstances.

Overall though, cases of medical negligence claims failing for lack of legal causation are the exception. Usually the courts will refuse to draw fine distinctions between the risk which ought to have been foreseen and that which actually materialised. Thus, in *Hepworth v Kerr*,[101] a doctor was held liable for using an experimental anaesthetic technique on a patient which resulted in a spinal stroke. The risk of inducing a spinal stroke was, in fact not known about, but the risk of a cerebral stroke (making the procedure's use negligent) was. Similarly, in *Wisniewski v Manchester HA*,[102] the defendant tried to deny liability on the basis that, though the claimant's hypoxia during birth – which he had negligently failed to manage – had been foreseeable, the mechanics of it in the particular case (involving a rare instance of a knot in the umbilical cord) had not been. In the Court of Appeal, Brooke LJ commented that to make such a distinction would be an 'affront to common sense, and the law would look an ass'.

As we saw in Chapter 3, the requirement of legal causation may also be relaxed in the context of 'non-disclosure' cases (leading exceptionally to liability for risks over which the doctor had no control at all).[103]

See Chapter 3

6.5 Defences

It must be said that the usual tortious defences are rarely used in medical cases, and, for that reason, are dealt with only briefly. The first possibility is a claim by the doctor/hospital of contributory

---

98   See further, Stauch, M, 'Risk and remoteness of damage in negligence' (2001) 64 MLR 191.
99   [1999] Lloyd's Rep Med 110.
100 [2005] EWCA 1439.
101 See n 69 above.
102 See n 95 above.
103 See further the discussion there of *Chester v Afshar* [2004] UKHL 41.

negligence, to the effect that the patient was also at fault in his conduct, in relation to managing his condition, and this contributed to the injury suffered. If this is accepted, the court may reduce the damages awarded, in accordance with the Law Reform (Contributory Negligence) Act 1945. However, as Grubb and Jones note, the defence has an unattractive feel in the context of medical negligence and will seldom be argued:

Grubb, A, (ed), *Principles of Medical Law*[104]

7.55 Although, in theory, there is no reason why contributory negligence should not apply in a claim for medical negligence, in practice the defence is rarely invoked successfully, and this is reflected in a comparative dearth of cases. It may be that the plea is considered to be inappropriate, given the inequality between the respective positions of doctor and patient. Patients do not generally question the advice or conduct of their doctors, even when they are aware that their condition is deteriorating or not improving. If the patient has ignored the doctor's advice (for example by discharging himself from hospital or failing to return for further treatment) it may be easier to establish the defence. It would have to be shown that a reasonable person would have been aware of the significance of the advice, which will depend on the nature of the advice and whether it was clear to the patient . . .

7.57 The one English reported case in which the claimant's conduct was held to be negligent is *Pidgeon v Doncaster HA* [[2002] Lloyd's Rep Med 130 (Doncaster County Ct)] where a claimant who developed cervical cancer, having been told that the results of a smear test were negative, was held to have been two-thirds contributory negligent in failing to have a further smear test despite frequent reminders. It would also be possible for a plea of contributory negligence to apply in cases where the claimant attempts suicide and a claim is brought against medical staff on the basis of a negligent failure to prevent the suicide attempt . . .

A second possible defence is that of consent, or *volenti non fit injuria*. This is where the defendant argues that the patient had consented to the risk. In a Scottish medical negligence decision, *Sabri-Tabrizi v Lothian Health Board*,[105] it was said that such consent must normally have occurred prior to, and certainly cannot come after, the defendant's breach of duty. It is arguable that this condition would never be satisfied in the context of medical treatment, and there would appear to be no cases where the defence has been argued successfully.

Finally, the defence of illegality, or *ex turpi causa*, may apply where the background events relied on by the claimant in his negligence action disclose criminal wrongdoing on his part. In such cases, the defendant may persuade the court that, as a matter of public policy, it would not be seemly to allow the action. The doctrine will seldom be of any relevance in the medical negligence context. However, the Court of Appeal had recourse to it in *Clunis v Camden and Islington HA*,[106] where the claimant, a mentally ill man imprisoned for manslaughter, alleged that the defendant authority had negligently failed to detain him in time under the Mental Health Act 1983.

6.6 Liability for Defective Medicines

Frequently patients may allege that they were injured, not through negligence on a doctor's part, but by medicinal drugs that they were (properly) given during treatment.

---

104   2nd edn, Oxford: OUP, 2004.
105   (1997) 43 BMLR 190.
106   [1998] 3 All ER 180.

Before they are made available for prescription, medicines are subject to comprehensive licensing requirements pursuant to the Medicines Act 1968. However, the fact that such drugs may sometimes give rise to unpredictable and harmful metabolic reactions was brought poignantly to the public consciousness by the Thalidomide tragedy of the late 1960s and, given the difficulty in proving fault on the part of manufacturers (even the most thorough testing may fail to reveal a particular reaction in advance), provoked calls from both the Law Commission[107] and the Pearson Committee[108] for 'no fault' compensation to be introduced for such injury.

In the event, the emergence of a scheme, dispensing with the need to show fault, had to await initiatives at EC level in relation to defective consumer products generally. As a result of the EC Product Liability Directive,[109] the Government passed Pt I of the Consumer Protection Act 1987, which imposes strict liability upon manufacturers in respect of products put into circulation after 1 March 1988:

. . . 2 Liability for defective products

(1) Subject to the following provisions of this Part, where any damage is caused wholly or partly by a defect in a product, every person to whom sub-s (2) below applies shall be liable for the damage.

(2) This sub-section applies to–
  (a) the producer of the product;
  (b) any person who, by putting his name on the product or using a trade mark or other distinguishing mark in relation to the product, has held himself out to be the producer of the product;
  (c) any person who has imported the product into a Member State from a place outside the Member States in order, in the course of any business of his, to supply it to another.

. . .

3 Meaning of 'defect'

(1) Subject to the following provisions of this section, there is a defect in a product for the purposes of this Part if the safety of the product is not such as persons generally are entitled to expect, and for those purposes 'safety', in relation to a product, shall include safety with respect to products comprised in that product and safety in the context of risks of damage to property, as well as in the context of risks of death or personal injury.

(2) In determining for the purposes of sub-s (1) above what persons generally are entitled to expect in relation to a product, all the circumstances shall be taken into account, including–
  (a) the manner in which, and purposes for which, the product has been marketed, its get-up, the use of any mark in relation to the product and any instructions for, or warnings with respect to, doing or refraining from doing anything with or in relation to the product;
  (b) what might reasonably be expected to be done with or in relation to the product; and
  (c) the time when the product was supplied by its producer to another,
  and nothing in this section shall require a defect to be inferred from the fact alone that the safety of a product which is supplied after that time is greater than the safety of the product in question.

---

107 Report 82, Cmnd 6831, 1977.
108 Cmnd 7054, 1978 (the Pearson Report). A limited pocket of 'no fault liability', namely for injuries resulting from vaccination, was introduced by the Vaccine Damage Payments Act 1979.
109 85/374/EC.

4 Defences

(1)   In any civil proceedings by virtue of this Part against any person ('the person proceeded against') in respect of a defect in a product it shall be a defence for him to show–

. . .(e)   that the state of scientific and technical knowledge at the relevant time was not such that a producer of products of the same description as the product in question might be expected to have discovered the defect if it had existed in his products while they were under his control; . . .

Where a claim is brought under the Act, two key issues for the courts will be the meaning of 'defect' within s 3 of the Act, and the scope of the so-called 'development risk' defence afforded to manufacturers under s 4(1)(e). Both matters were at the heart of the High Court ruling in *A and Others v National Blood Authority*,[110] a class action brought by 114 people who contracted Hepatitis C from contaminated blood supplies. In finding for the claimants, Burton J took the view that, for a 'defect' to arise under s 3, it was enough that the risk of infection was not one that was known and accepted by society generally. As Deards and Twigg-Flesner comment:

Deards, E and Twigg-Flesner, C, 'The Consumer Protection Act 1987: proof at last that it is protecting consumers'[111]

The High Court drew a distinction between 'standard' and 'non-standard' products. 'Standard' products were those that met the design and standard of safety intended by the manufacturer. A 'non-standard' product was a particular unit of the product that did not meet the standard. In *A and Others*, the court stated that the infected blood products were non-standard, that is to say, differed from the standard product intended by the manufacturer. The standard blood products were not inherently defective. In the case of blood transfusions, it was only 1% of the product that 'failed' in that it had been contaminated with the Hepatitis C virus. The court suggested that it might be easier to prove a defect where the product was non-standard, since it would fall to be compared with the standard product. The problem with this argument is that a product is only non-standard if it is defective, but whether it is defective could be affected by whether it is non-standard. Admittedly the court envisaged that a non-standard product was one that was defective in a non-technical, non-Act sense, but there could be cases where even this was disputed, and then a circular argument would result. In respect of non-standard products, the court stated that the consumers' expectations as to safety depended on whether they accepted the non-standard nature of the product.

The High Court confirmed that the factors for assessing the defectiveness listed in section 3 of the Act were not exclusive, and that all relevant circumstances were to be considered. However, it ruled that avoidability of the risk of infection was not a relevant factor. The possibility of avoiding the harmful characteristics by taking precautionary measures, the impracticality, cost and difficulty of taking such measures and the benefit to society of the product were therefore not relevant. On the facts, the risk was known by doctors but was not known and accepted by society generally. The risk of infected blood could therefore not have been accepted by consumers unless they were warned, which they had not been. The infected blood products were therefore defective.

Equally significant was the judge's approach to the 'development risk' defence under s 4(1)(e). Previously, the general view had been that the defence provided a broad escape for manufacturers

---

110   [2001] 3 All ER 289.
111   (2001) 10(2) Nott LJ1.

of products, such as new drugs, whose research and development occurs at the frontiers of scientific knowledge, and where the occasional defect may be regarded as inevitable. Indeed, it was lobbying from the pharmaceutical industry (who argued that, without such a provision, drugs companies would be deterred from developing new products) that led to its inclusion in the EC Directive in the first place. However, in *A and Others*, Burton J interpreted the defence narrowly, holding that it could not be invoked once the risk was known to the defendant (or should have been known in the light of information then accessible to it). The fact that here there was no available test for detecting the presence of Hepatitis C in any specific batch of blood was held to be irrelevant.

Nevertheless, claims under the Act involving medical or medicinal products remain rare. It should also be noted that the payment of compensation is in any event contingent upon causation being shown between the product and injury. Given the frequently opaque nature of causal processes in this area (with plausible causal chains between phenomena often hard to find), this may often be a serious obstacle for claimants. This is especially so in respect of idiosyncratic reactions to a drug on the part of a small minority of users where the degree of regularity between cause (ingesting the drug) and effect (injury), which generally ground causal inferences, will be absent. In the case of *XYZ v Schering Health Care Ltd*,[112] the High Court held that claimants had failed to show the drug they ingested (an oral contraceptive) was capable of causing their injuries, and this has also been the fate of similar actions for medicinal injury at common law.[113]

6.7 Reforming the Law

6.7.1 Problems with the medical litigation system

Medical negligence cases are often very expensive to bring, because of the technical and complex nature of the litigation. Moreover, statistically, far fewer such claims succeed – between 25 and 45 per cent – than the average for negligence actions generally (around 80 per cent).[114] Nevertheless, this has not prevented a major upsurge in such claims over the last 20 years or so, with the public generally appearing less deferential, more aware of their rights, and holding higher expectations of what can and should be achieved on their behalf.

In 1996, the Woolf Report looked critically at medical negligence litigation and found some major problems:

Lord Woolf MR, *Access to Justice: The Final Report to the Lord Chancellor on the Civil Justice System in England and Wales*[115]

Reasons for looking at medical negligence

2   . . . [E]arly in the Inquiry it became increasingly obvious that it was in the area of medical negligence that the civil justice system was failing most conspicuously to meet the needs of litigants in a number of respects:

   (a)   The disproportion between costs and damages in medical negligence is particularly excessive, especially in lower value cases.

   (b)   The delay in resolving claims is more often unacceptable.

   (c)   Unmeritorious cases are often pursued, and clear-cut claims defended, for too long.

   (d)   The success rate is lower than in other personal injury litigation.

   (e)   The suspicion between the parties is more intense and the lack of co-operation frequently greater than in many other areas of litigation.

---

112   [2002] EWHC 1420 (QB).

113   See *Kay v Ayrshire and Arran Health Board* [1987] 2 All ER 417; *Loveday v Renton* [1990] 1 Med LR 117.

114   *Compensation Culture*, HC Constitutional Affairs Committee, Third Report of Session 2005-06, London: TSO, 2006.

115   London: HMSO, 1996.

...5 The difficulty of proving both causation and negligence, which arises more acutely in medical negligence than in other personal injury cases, accounts for much of the excessive cost. The root of the problem, however, lies less in the complexity of the law or procedure than in the climate of mutual suspicion and defensiveness which is still all too prevalent in this area of litigation. Patients feel let down when treatment goes wrong, sometimes because of unrealistic expectations as to what could be achieved. Doctors feel they are under attack from aggrieved patients and react defensively ...

... change of culture

21 The extent of patients' mistrust of doctors and other hospital staff is illustrated by the submission I have received from Action for Victims of Medical Accidents (AVMA). They argue that the real reason for defendants' reluctance to investigate complaints where there is a possibility of legal action is a concern that such an investigation might indeed disclose negligence ...

22 If that mistrust is to be removed, the medical profession and the NHS administration must demonstrate their commitment to patients' well being by adopting a constructive approach to claims handling. It must be clearly accepted that injured patients are entitled to redress, and that professional solidarity or individual self-esteem are not sufficient reasons for resisting or obstructing valid claims.

23 Patients and their representatives, for their part, must recognise that some degree of risk is inherent in all medical treatment, and that even the best practitioners do sometimes make mistakes. They should not pursue unrealistic claims, and should make every effort to resolve disputes without recourse to litigation.

Since then the general Woolf reforms (including stricter pre-trial management and more incentives to settle claims) appear to be having a positive impact on medical litigation; thus there has been some reduction in costs, and an increase in claims settled. Nevertheless, wider anxieties in relation to this area of litigation persist, not least in the light of new data on the overall costs of medical accidents to the NHS. Statistics collated by the NHS Litigation Authority (which handles claims against the NHS) showed total payments in respect of medical negligence (in settlements, awards, and lawyer's fees) to be £235m in 1996–97; by 2009–10 this figure had more than trebled to nearly £800m.[116] Equally, though, it has been recognised that claims brought are merely the tip of the iceberg relative to the actual number of 'preventable adverse events' that occur in the health sector. On the basis of international studies (including the 1990 Harvard Medical Practice Study in the US), it has been estimated that 850,000 adverse outcomes occur in the NHS annually, of which around half are 'preventable'.

One solution, that has been proposed over the years, and was reiterated by Professor Ian Kennedy in his conclusions to the Bristol Royal Infirmary Inquiry,[117] is that we should move away from the common law of tort altogether towards a statutory 'no fault' based system of liability for medical negligence. Some jurisdictions, notably New Zealand and the Scandinavian countries, have been running such schemes for a number of years,[118] with at least some success: certainly, the administration costs are lower than for tort, and it appears that tensions between patients and doctors are reduced; on the other hand problems remain in designing such schemes equitably (to decide who qualifies for compensation, and who does not),[119] and they may potentially become

---

116 See the data on the NHS Litigation Authority website, at www.nhsla.com/home.htm.

117 *Learning from Bristol: the report of the public inquiry into children's heart surgery at the Bristol Royal Infirmary 1984–1995*, Cm 5207, July 2001.

118 More recently, the French have introduced such a scheme: see further Taylor, S, 'Providing Redress for Medical Accidents in France: Conflicting Aims, Effective Solutions?' JEur Tort Law, 2011, forthcoming.

119 For an analysis of the New Zealand scheme, including changes made from time to time to the 'eligibility criteria' in respect of medical injury claims, see Oliphant, K, 'Beyond Misadventure: Compensation for Medical Injuries in New Zealand' (2007) 15 Med L Rev 357

very expensive.[120] Moreover, the difficulties for the claimant associated with proving causation will in any event remain, and his ability to overcome them will determine whether he comes within the no fault scheme at all.

 SELF-TEST QUESTION

In his 2003 Report, *Making Amends* (see below), the CMO proposed a limited no fault scheme to deal with cases of neurologically impaired babies. As an independent research exercise investigate why (so far) this suggestion has not been acted upon.

6.7.2 *Making Amends* and the NHS Redress Act 2006

In 2001, the Department of Health launched a wide-ranging review by the Chief Medical Officer, Sir Liam Donaldson, into the way the law functions in practice in this area, and options for its reform (including the arguments for and against a general 'no fault' scheme). The CMO's Report, *Making Amends*, was published in June 2003:

Chief Medical Officer, *Making Amends: A consultation paper setting out proposals for reforming the approach to clinical negligence in the NHS*[121] – *Summary*

A vision for a successful alternative to the present system
- Any new system should create a climate where:
    - risks of care are reduced and patient safety improves because medical errors and near misses are readily reported, successfully analysed and effective corrective action takes place and is sustained;
    - remedial treatment, care and rehabilitation are available to redress harm and injuries arising from healthcare;
    - any financial compensation is provided fairly and efficiently;
    - payments of compensation act as financial incentives on healthcare organisations and their staff to improve quality and patient safety;
    - the process of compensation does not undermine the strength of the relationship between patient and healthcare professional; . . .

. . . The case for no fault compensation
- The main arguments in favour of 'no fault' compensation are:
    - fairness;
    - speedier resolution of cases;
    - lower administrative and legal costs than court action;
    - increased certainty for claimants on the circumstances in which compensation is payable and increased consistency between claimants;
    - reduced tension between clinicians and claimants;
    - greater willingness by clinicians to report errors and adverse events.

---

120 See CMO, *Making Amends*, London: DoH, 2003. In countries such as Sweden and New Zealand, awards are capped, so that successful claimants only receive a fraction of the damages they would be entitled to under a tort-based system.
121 Ibid. An archived version is available at: www.dh.gov.uk/prod_consum_dh/groups/dh_digitalassets/@dh/@en/documents/digitalasset/dh_4060945.pdf.

The case against no fault compensation

- Critics of no fault compensation schemes argue that:
  - overall costs will be higher than under a tort system;
  - it will open the floodgates to compensation payments and fuel a compensation culture;
  - disputes about causation remain, even if 'fault' is removed;
  - disputes about the amount of damages remain, unless there is a tariff-based approach;
  - it is difficult to distinguish injury from the natural progression of the disease in some cases;
  - explanations and apologies are not necessarily provided in a system which focuses on financial recompense alone;
  - a no fault scheme, in itself, does not improve accountability or ensure learning from adverse events.
- The review specifically considered the option of a comprehensive no-fault compensation system. This was rejected because:
  - a true 'no-fault' scheme would lead to a potentially huge increase in claims and overall costs would be far higher than under the present tort system. Initial estimates suggest that the annual bill could reach £4 billion.
  - to be affordable, compensation would need to be set at a substantially lower level than current tort awards and would not necessarily meet the needs of the harmed patient;
  - it would be difficult to distinguish harm to a patient from the natural progression of a disease;
  - no-fault schemes, of themselves, do not improve processes for learning from error or reduction of harm to patients.

The CMO instead recommended establishing what he christened the 'NHS Redress Scheme', to provide for extra-judicial compensation of low-value claims against the NHS (in which litigation costs often exceed the size of awards). This proposal formed the basis for the NHS Redress Act 2006, which received Royal Assent in late 2006:

1 Power to establish redress scheme

(1) The Secretary of State may by regulations establish a scheme for the purpose of enabling redress to be provided without recourse to civil proceedings in circumstances in which this section applies.

(2) This section applies where under the law of England and Wales qualifying liability in tort on the part of a body or other person . . . arises in connection with the provision, as part of the health service in England, of qualifying services.

. . . (4) The reference in subsection (2) to qualifying liability in tort is to liability in tort owed—

    (a) in respect of or consequent upon personal injury or loss arising out of or in connection with breach of a duty of care owed to any person in connection with the diagnosis of illness, or the care or treatment of any patient, and

    (b) in consequence of any act or omission by a health care professional . . .

2 Application of scheme

(1) Subject to subsection (2), a scheme may make such provision defining its application as the Secretary of State thinks fit.

(2) A scheme must provide that it does not apply in relation to a liability that is or has been the subject of civil proceedings.

3 Redress under scheme

. . . (2) A scheme must provide for redress ordinarily to comprise—

(a) the making of an offer of compensation in satisfaction of any right to bring civil proceedings in respect of the liability concerned,

(b) the giving of an explanation,

(c) the giving of an apology, and

(d) the giving of a report on the action which has been, or will be, taken to prevent similar cases arising, . . .

. . . 6 Proceedings under scheme

. . . (3) A scheme must—

(a) make provision for the findings of an investigation of a case under the scheme to be recorded in a report . . .

The 2006 Act is an enabling statute, laying out the framework of the Redress Scheme, while leaving much of the detail to be fleshed out in regulations to be made by the Secretary of State for Health. However, it gives effect to the CMO's intention that lower-value medical negligence claims should be dealt with outside the courts; such claims will be referred to the NHS Litigation Authority, which will manage the Scheme, for investigation.[122] Where substandard treatment and care is found, it may offer redress (including financial compensation).[123] The patient is not required to accept this, but if he does he will be asked to sign a waiver of subsequent legal proceedings. Besides being thus designed to relieve pressure on the legal system, the Scheme aims to promote risk-management and learning from mistakes: as provided by s6(3), each case arising should be investigated and the subject of a report.[124]

At present the implementing regulations for the Scheme in England remain subject to a lengthy on-going consultation process, so that (as of late 2010) it still remains unclear when it will become operative. By contrast, in Wales, where the relevant consultation process closed in April 2010, its commencement is pending. In fact Wales has since 2005 been operating a mediation scheme of 'Speedy Resolution for Lower Value Clinical Negligence Claims', with some similarities to NHS Redress. Mari Rosser discusses the experiences made with that scheme, as follows:

Rosser, M, 'The changing face of clinical negligence in Wales'[125]

Like all methods of ADR, the scheme is consensual. In summary, the objectives of the scheme are:

- to provide a procedure for quick, proportionate and fair resolution of low value clinical negligence claims against NHS Trusts in Wales;
- to provide for NHS Trusts in Wales to make apologies to patients where the standard of medical care has fallen below the required standard;
- to encourage NHS Trusts in Wales to give patients an explanation for their treatment and medical state;
- to provide a structure for the negotiation and settlement of clinical negligence claims; and
- to encourage Trusts to learn from mistakes to reduce the incidents of clinical negligence claims in the future.

The basis principles are:

- that both the claimant and defendant have agreed that the case is one that meets the scheme criteria;

---

122 The Scheme will apply only to claims arising from hospital care within the NHS, not private health care. Also excluded (by s 1 (6) of the 2006 Act) are 'primary care' from general practitioners, and dental services.

123 The latter is intended to be roughly equivalent to the sum a court might award if the matter went to trial; at present a limit of £20,000 is envisaged.

124 In addition, members of the Scheme (ie NHS hospitals) are required under s 10(3) to 'prepare and publish an annual report about cases involving the member that are dealt with under the scheme and the lessons to be learnt from them'.

125 (2010) 3 JPIL 162.

- it will work to a timetable. . . The maximum period that a claim can take under the scheme is 61 weeks;
- the scheme will provide single jointly instructed experts; . . .

. . . In recommending that the scheme, which was established firstly as a pilot project in February 2005, should be continued as a permanent scheme, the evaluators found that the scheme had been very positively received and was seen as providing a realistic alternative to litigation in the field of clinical negligence. It was seen from the perspective of claimant's solicitors and Welsh Health Legal Services as providing a number of benefits including reduction of costs by the NHS and fixed predictable costs for claimants, access to a relatively inexpensive medical report and a quick resolution of claims.

The evaluators generally considered the scheme successful and fit for purpose and made no significant recommendations for substantial amendments save for further information being provided to patients generally in relation to the availability of the scheme, consideration being given to increasing the fixed fees for medical experts and extension of experts beyond those on the panel at the moment . . .

Given the undoubted success of the Speedy Resolution Scheme it is difficult to understand why the Welsh Assembly Government has not adopted more of its provisions within the draft NHS Redress Regulation (the Regulations). . . . [I]t is the Minister's intention to allow the Speedy Resolution Scheme to continue for the time being alongside NHS Redress . . .

In England there is some concern that, once the NHS Redress Scheme does come into operation, the patient's interests may be insufficiently protected: this stems from the fact that the NHS Litigation Authority, with its interest in keeping costs down, will run the Scheme, as well as the lack of provision for patient legal advice or an appeal procedure.[126]

Summary of Key Points

1. Patients who are injured by medical treatment (either through additional 'iatrogenic' harm or a failure to benefit following a misdiagnosis) may potentially have a claim against the doctor and/or hospital in negligence.
2. Medical negligence actions are a species of the general tort of negligence: in this regard for the patient to succeed, the same basic elements must be established, viz duty of care, breach, and causation of damage.
3. The duty of care element is usually unproblematic, at least where the doctor has accepted the patient for treatment. An exception, deriving from the House of Lords' decision in the *McFarlane* case, relates to the 'loss' occasioned by the birth of a healthy child following negligent contraceptive treatment.
4. In assessing whether a doctor was in breach of duty, his conduct will be measured by the yardstick of a reasonably skilled and experienced practitioner in the relevant field.
5. A controversial question has been how far the doctor may defend himself in such a case by showing that the treatment he gave complied with a practice accepted by other doctors (the so-called 'Bolam test').
6. In the past, it appeared that such an argument would be conclusive against a finding of negligence. However, more recently, in the *Bolitho* case, the House of Lords reiterated that ultimately the judge must be satisfied the practice stands up to 'logical analysis'.

---

126 See Farrell, A-M, and Devaney, S, 'Making Amends or Making Things Worse? Clinical Negligence Reform and Patient Redress in England' (2007) 27 *Legal Studies* 630.

7. As with negligence claims generally, the question of the factual causal link will be decided by the 'but for' test. The fact, though, that the patient was exposed to other risks of injury at the time of treatment, often makes the test very difficult to satisfy in evidential terms.
8. On the whole, the courts have rejected approaches that would relieve the patient of the need to show 'but for' causation to the 'balance of probabilities' proof standard. This includes their dismissal to date of actions for proportional damages based on the patient's 'loss of chance' of a cure.
9. Dissatisfaction has often been expressed with the tort system as a means for compensating medical injury claims. An alternative considered, but so far not taken up in the UK, might be to establish a 'no-fault' compensation scheme for such injury.
10. Following the Chief Medical Officer's 2003 review of medical negligence actions, the Government enacted the NHS Redress Act 2006, laying out the framework for resolving low-value negligence claims against the NHS extra-judicially. At present the scheme is still awaiting implementation.

Further Reading

Donaldson, Sir L (Chief Medical Officer) *Making Amends: A consultation paper setting out proposals for reforming the approach to clinical negligence in the NHS*, London: Dept. of Health, 2003.

Farrell, A-M, and Devaney, S, 'Making Amends or Making Things Worse? Clinical Negligence Reform and Patient Redress in England' (2007) 27 *Legal Studies* 630.

Jones, M, *Medical Negligence* 4th edn, London: Sweet & Maxwell, 2008.

Mulheron, R, 'Trumping *Bolam*: A critical legal analysis of *Bolitho*'s"gloss" ' (2010) 69 *Cambridge Law Journal* 609.

Oliphant, K, 'Beyond Misadventure: Compensation for Medical Injuries in New Zealand' (2007) 15 *Medical Law Review* 357.

Quick, O, 'Outing Medical Errors: Questions of Trust and Responsibility' (2006) 14 *Medical Law Review* 22.

Stauch, M, *The Law of Medical Negligence in England and Germany – A Comparative Analysis*, Oxford: Hart Publishing, 2008.

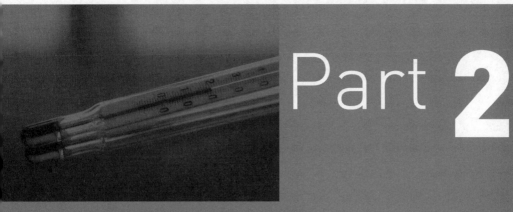

Part 2

Specific Areas in Medical Treatment

Chapter 7

Assisted Reproduction and Embryo Research

Chapter Contents

7.1 Introduction

In the last 30 years, medical science has made significant strides in an area previously largely 'off limits', that of human reproduction. The law, in attempting to regulate these developments, has had to balance many competing interests and viewpoints in an area of particular ethical sensitivity. Four years after the birth, in Britain in 1978, of the world's first 'test tube baby', the Government established a Committee of Inquiry led by the moral philosopher, Dame Mary Warnock, to recommend an appropriate legislative response. The Warnock Committee, which reported in 1984, was well aware of the unprecedented and controversial nature of its remit:

Warnock Committee, *Report of the Committee of Inquiry into Human Fertilisation and Embryology*[1]

1.1   The birth of the first child resulting from the technique of *in vitro* fertilisation in July 1978 was a considerable achievement. The technique, long sought, at last successful, opened up new horizons in the alleviation of infertility and in the science of embryology. It was now possible to observe the very earliest stages of human development, and with these discoveries came the hope of remedying defects at this very early stage. However, there were also anxieties. There was a sense that events were moving too fast for their implications to be assimilated. Society's views on the new techniques were divided between pride in the technological achievement, pleasure at the new-found means to relieve, at least for some, the unhappiness of infertility, and unease at the apparently uncontrolled advance of science, bringing with it new possibilities for manipulating the early stages of human development.

1.2   Against this background of public excitement and concern, this Inquiry was established in July 1982, with the following terms of reference:

To consider recent and potential developments in medicine and science related to human fertilisation and embryology; to consider what policies and safeguards should be applied, including consideration of the social, ethical and legal implications of these developments; and to make recommendations.

In the introduction to her 1985 book, *A Question of Life*, Mary Warnock noted the stormy reception accorded to the report, and a key problem faced by the Committee:

Warnock, M, *A Question of Life*[2]

The Times, on 15 December 1984, carried a dramatic headline. It read 'Warnock: Ethics Undermined'. What followed was a denunciation of the Report of the Committee of Inquiry into Human Embryology ascribed to the Chief Rabbi which was, in fact, moderate in tone compared with some of the abuse to which members of the Inquiry had been, and are still, subjected both collectively and individually, since the publication of our report in July 1984. None of the members of the Inquiry had any doubt that they were concerned with moral issues. But we were not perhaps all of us certain how such issues ought to be approached, and especially how they should be approached by a body set up by Parliament to make recommendations which might lead to legislation. Many of our critics (including, I believe, the Chief Rabbi) have not really addressed themselves to this problem either: the problem of legislation, and its relation to morality, in such controversial fields.

---

1   Cmnd 9314, London: HMSO, 1984.
2   Oxford: Blackwells Press, 1985.

The question of how far, and in what manner, legal regulation of human procreation should occur is undoubtedly one of great complexity. In the remainder of the introduction we shall first briefly survey the principal parties whose interests stand to be affected, before outlining the legal framework that has been put in place in the UK.

7.1.1 The key interests at stake

7.1.1.1 Potential parents

People who wish to be parents and would otherwise be infertile are the most obvious beneficiaries of fertility treatment. As the Warnock Committee commented:

> **Warnock Committee, *Report of the Committee of Inquiry into Human Fertilisation and Embryology*[3]**
>
> 2.2 Childlessness can be a source of stress even to those who have deliberately chosen it. Family and friends often expect a couple to start a family, and express their expectations, either openly or by implication. The family is a valued institution within our present society: within it the human infant receives nurture and protection during its prolonged period of dependence. It is also the place where social behaviour is learnt and where the child develops its own identity and feeling of self-value. Parents likewise feel their identity in society enhanced and confirmed by their role in the family unit. For those who long for children, the realisation that they are unable to found a family can be shattering. It can disrupt their picture of the whole of their future lives. They may feel that they will be unable to fulfil their own and other people's expectations. They may feel themselves excluded from a whole range of human activity and particularly the activities of their child-rearing contemporaries. In addition to social pressures to have children there is, for many, a powerful urge to perpetuate their genes through a new generation. This desire cannot be assuaged by adoption.

As is clear from this extract, the general assumption made by Warnock was that demand for treatment would come mainly if not entirely from infertile, heterosexual couples. In fact, while it is true that such couples account for the majority of demand, a striking phenomenon, especially in more recent years, has been the degree to which homosexual couples and single persons have also recognised the possibilities offered by reproductive technologies to experience parenthood. As we shall see further below (in section 7.4), this has the potential significantly to alter the traditional picture of the family, as has indeed been acknowledged in the latest legislative changes.

7.1.1.2 Gamete providers/surrogates

The success of many fertility treatments depends upon the use of gametes (sperm and eggs) and embryos or, in the case of surrogacy, gestational capacity, provided by third parties, that is, persons who, it is envisaged, will not subsequently play any role in rearing the children born as a result of treatment. A key problem for the law in such cases is to determine how best to regulate the involvement of such third parties (who are the child's genetic or gestational parents). Should they receive money in return for their services? Should they be screened? How should they be counselled? In addition, what sort of obligations may such third parties claims have towards the child? Should they be protected from future contact by a guarantee of anonymity? What, conversely, if a provider later wishes to have contact with the child?

---

3 See n 1 above.

7.1.1.3 Potential children

The answers we give to these last questions clearly have a direct impact on the interests of children who result from infertility treatment involving third party providers. For example, giving gamete providers anonymity will be to deny the child's interest in knowing who one (at least) of its genetic or gestational parents is. In other cases, there may be a conflict between the interests of the potential child and its potential rearing parent(s). A 1989 inquiry into reproductive technologies sponsored by the European Commission, and led by the moral philosopher, Jonathan Glover, commented as follows:

Glover, J et al, Report to the European Commission on Reproductive Technologies, Fertility and the Family[4]

The children are those most deeply affected. Their family circumstances may be unusually complicated: like adopted children, they may have to get used to the fact that at least one of their social parents is not their biological parent. Much more importantly, their very existence results from reproductive help. If they are glad to be alive, they are perhaps the greatest beneficiaries. They are the people who have no say at the time the decisions are taken, and their needs and interests have to be given great weight. Their central need is for a certain kind of home and family . . .

Besides the question of their existence *per se*, another far-reaching issue in respect of the children who result from new reproductive technologies concerns the identities and attributes that they may possess: in particular, some of the new technologies (associated with IVF treatment – see section 7.2) allow for the possibility of selecting between possible children (through choosing which out of a number of embryos to implant) or even of manipulating the characteristics of a given embryo (and hence of the resulting child) that is implanted. As we shall see, these too are matters that have attracted the regulatory attention of the law-maker.

7.1.1.4 Embryos

So far we have been assuming that a child is born following treatment. The position is complicated when we introduce the human embryo (as a separate entity) into the equation. The procedure of *in vitro* fertilisation (IVF), in particular, involves the manipulation of the early human embryo. To work effectively, the procedure typically requires the creation of more embryos than can ever be implanted in the uterus of the woman receiving treatment. There is therefore the question of what to do with such 'spare' embryos; must we simply let them perish? This in itself may be seen as a bad thing. Alternatively should we store them (there are techniques available for freezing early embryos) and, if so, for how long? More radically, should it be permissible to use them for research purposes, and if so under what conditions? And once the possibility of research is conceded, is there any reason not to employ IVF technology specifically to create embryos for research?

These last questions are hugely contentious because they turn partly on a debate of a metaphysical character, viz, do early embryos have any interests in the first place? We return to them in sections 7.2.3 and 7.3 below.

7.1.2 Legal regulation – the Human Fertilisation and Embryology Acts 1990 and 2008

In the light of the interests and putative interests just outlined, how should the law respond? In a liberal democratic state such as the UK, the autonomous activity of individual citizens, each

---

4   London: Fourth Estate, 1989.

pursuing their own ends, is regarded as of central importance, and this gives rise to a strong presumption in favour of respecting procreative liberty. In *A Question of Life*, Mary Warnock had the following to say about the extent to which the law may intrude into the area of assisted reproduction:

Warnock, M, *A Question of Life*[5]

If the question is what measures to remedy infertility should be permitted in this country, the problem may be put in the following form: why should the law intervene to prevent people using whatever methods are possible to enable them to have children? Why should not everybody be entitled to whatever is currently the best and most efficient treatment for infertility? The issues here are quite closely parallel to the issues raised in the 1960s by the Wolfenden Report on homosexuality between consenting males. Ought the law to intervene to make such conduct criminal or ought it not? The famous view of Lord Devlin (*The Enforcement of Morals*, 1959) was that where there is a consensus of opinion against a certain practice among members of the general public (exemplified by the notorious 'man on the Clapham omnibus') then the law must intervene to prevent conduct which is repellent to that public. A shared moral view . . . was the cement that bound society together. . . .

The drawback with Devlin's view is that, increasingly, we are compelled to accept that 'common morality' is a myth. There is no agreed set of principles which everyone, or the majority, or any representative person, believes to be absolutely binding, and especially is this so in areas of moral concern which are radically and genuinely new . . .

Furthermore, any law enacted to render AID a criminal offence, besides going against the moral views of a fair number of the community, would involve, in itself, a disagreeable intrusiveness, for AID is something that can relatively easily be carried out at home, without any medical intervention. For a law to be enforceable, there would need to be a band of snoopers or people ready to pry into the private lives of others, which might well itself constitute a moral wrong . . .

In 1990, Parliament enacted the Human Fertilisation and Embryology Act, which followed many of the recommendations in the Warnock Report; perhaps most importantly, it accepted the need to establish a statutory regulatory authority to oversee continuing developments in this area. Some barriers in the form of absolute prohibitions – backed by criminal sanctions – were established. However, the Act is more notable for its flexibility and its willingness to entrust the new regulatory authority, the Human Fertilisation and Embryology (HFE) Authority, with large amounts of discretion. In his assessment of the impact of the 1990 Act, Jonathan Montgomery suggested 'pragmatism' rather than 'principle' was the guiding impulse behind the new legal regime:

Montgomery, J, 'Rights, restraints and pragmatism'[6]

The nature of the forum in which the debates about infertility treatment and embryo research are to be carried out is structured by a complex web of discretion, restraints control and accountability. The Human Fertilisation and Embryology Authority is to be given powers to oversee the activities of individual health practitioners, and will not be limited to applying standards established by Parliament or government. It will be able, indeed required, to develop its own standards of what is acceptable and proper . . .

Having conferred this considerable flexibility upon the licensing authority, the Government has also reserved a number of powers to reduce it. The boundaries of the power to license may

---

5   See n 2 above.
6   (1991) 54 MLR 524.

be contracted and expanded by regulations. By requiring annual reports to the Secretary of State, detailing both past activities and those projected for the following 12 months, the Act seeks to ensure that the Authority's practice can be monitored (s 7). The reports are to be laid before Parliament by the minister. Nevertheless, pending the exercise of the power to make regulations, considerable trust is placed in the members of the Authority.

The Act permits the Authority to exercise a high degree of control over practitioners. In addition to the power to grant or withhold licences, the Authority will be able to issue mandatory directions (ss 23 and 24). Failure to comply with these directions will sometimes constitute an offence (s 41(2)), but will always empower the Authority to revoke a licence (s 18([2])(c)). Secondly, a code of practice is to be drawn up to provide guidance as to the proper conduct of licensees. This is less coercive than the power to give directions in that disobedience will not in itself constitute an offence, but it may be taken into account by the Authority when considering revocation (s 25).

In summary, the Human Fertilisation and Embryology Authority has been entrusted with considerable powers to determine what embryo research and infertility treatment will be carried out. A system of checks and balances has been created which will allow for the Authority to be accountable to Parliament, but many of the normative principles to be applied will be established neither by the law nor by democratic discussion. In essence, the creation of the Authority is a pragmatic exercise in facilitating medical advances rather than a principled approach to the vindication of rights.

Subsequently, Lord Bingham, in his speech in R (On the Application of Quintavalle) v Secretary of State for Health[7] distinguished three levels of control provided for by the 1990 Act:

Lord Bingham of Cornhill: [4] The Act imposes three levels of control. The highest is that contained in the Act itself. As is apparent, for example from section 3(2) and (3), the Act prohibits certain activities absolutely, a prohibition fortified by a potential penalty of up to ten years' imprisonment (section 41(1)). The next level of control is provided by the Secretary of State, who is empowered to make regulations for certain purposes subject (so far as relevant here) to an affirmative resolution of both Houses of Parliament (section 45(1), (4)). Pursuant to section 3(3)(c) the Secretary of State may make regulations prohibiting the keeping or use of an embryo in specified circumstances. The third level of control is that exercised by the Authority. Section 3(1) prohibits the creation, keeping or use of an embryo except in pursuance of a licence, and the Act contains very detailed provisions governing the grant, revocation and suspension of licences and the conditions to which they may be subject: see, among other references, sections 11–22 of and Schedule 2 to the Act. A power is also conferred on the Authority to give binding directions: sections 23–24.

Overall the scheme of regulation introduced in 1990 has proved successful in reassuring the public that advances in reproductive technology are subject to a degree of scrutiny and control, including by non-medical scientists (the majority of the HFE Authority's members are not scientists), so that practices evoking significant ethical concern are not permitted without more. Nonetheless, recently, in the light both of new scientific developments and changes in social attitudes since 1990, the Government chose to enact further, reforming legislation in the form of the Human Fertilisation and Embryology Act 2008. Unfortunately, the changes have also added significantly to the complexity of the legislation in this area. Marie Fox has commented upon the reform process, and the unwieldy mass of statute it has left in its wake, as follows:

---

7   [2003] UKHL 13.

Fox, M, 'The Human Fertilisation and Embryology Act 2008: Tinkering at the Margins'[8]

The Human Fertilisation and Embryology Act 2008 . . . received royal assent on 13 November 2008, marking the culmination of a protracted reform process. Most of the changes took effect on 1 October 2009, although the revised definitions of parenthood contained in Part 2 of the Act have been effective since April 2009. A final stage of amendments will give effect to parental orders in 2010. Although, as detailed below, many of the changes are to be welcomed, it is questionable how far-reaching their impact will be . . . In part this was due to the strict parameters the government placed on it. It conceived the legislation as an amending statute which, as McCandless and Sheldon note, ensured that 'the key question was not "what model of law do we want?" but rather "what needs to be changed?" ' within the confines of the Human Fertilisation and Embryology Act 1990 . . . The upshot is that a rather clumsy and convoluted mass of legislation now governs the regulation of fertility treatment and embryology research, since the 1990 Act as amended in 2008 must also be read alongside earlier amending legislation. This has led the Department of Health to issue an illustrative amended Act . . ., prompting the question of whether it might not have been preferable to repeal and replace the 1990 Act.

However, it was clear from the outset of the reform process that the government was committed to retaining the core architecture of the 1990 Act. This was unquestionably a landmark piece of legislation which has been emulated elsewhere. Underpinned by the 'twin pillars' of ensuring consent to the use of donated gametes and embryos, and the welfare of children to be born via assisted conception, the 1990 Act established a statutory regulator—the Human Fertilisation and Embryology Authority (the Authority)—to oversee any research or treatment involving creation of human embryos outside the body, or the donation or storage of human gametes. The statutory regime is characterised by a broadly permissive approach to fertility treatment and embryo research, whereby only the most contentious aspects, including human reproductive cloning, are prohibited; other types of treatment and research must be licensed by the Authority.

The 2008 Act is divided into three parts. Part 1 is a purely amending part: it contains a series of provisions that, rather than having stand-alone character, replace and/or add to the terms of the original 1990 Act. In citing the relevant provisions, reference should thus be made to the 'Human Fertilisation and Embryology Act 1990 (as amended)'. As noted by Fox, the complexity of these changes prompted the Department of Health to prepare an illustrative consolidated text of the 1990 Act as amended, which is available on its website.[9] By contrast, Part 2, which sets out new rules determining the parenthood of children born as a result of assisted reproduction, is in effect an autonomous statute, and its sections should be cited as the Human Fertilisation and Embryology Act 2008. Lastly, Part 3 contains a number of miscellaneous provisions (without stand-alone character), including changes to the Surrogacy Arrangements Act 1985.

As before, much of the day-to-day supervision exercised by the HFE Authority over fertility clinics up and down the country (currently over 100, the majority within the private sector) occurs by means of the Code of Practice, which it promulgates. This is currently in its eighth edition (October 2009) and provides detailed guidance on all aspects of the treatment that clinics might wish to provide. Breaches of the Code by a clinic may result in the Authority revoking its licence. Another important function of the Authority is the collection of information pertaining to fertility treatment in the UK. In this regard it has from its inception been required to maintain a register (under s 31 of the HFE Act 1990 (as amended)), recording each case in which a person or persons have received licensed treatment services (including, where donor gametes are used, the identity of

---

8 (2009) 17 Fem Leg Stud 333.
9 See www.dh.gov.uk/en/Publicationsandstatistics/Publications/PublicationsLegislation/DH_080205.

the donor).[10] At the same time, it should be noted that not every type of fertility treatment is covered by the Act: most significantly, the use of 'fertility drugs' to increase ovulation remains unregulated.

In the rest of this chapter, we shall be exploring in more detail the specific solutions adopted by the law in relation to the key areas of licensed fertility treatment. We shall focus, first, in section 7.2 upon IVF treatment involving the creation of an embryo *ex vivo* to be implanted in a woman's uterus for gestation. Although IVF obviously has wide potential applications (it may be used in conjunction with forms of collaborative reproduction involving donated gametes and surrogacy), at this stage the assumption will be that the recipient couple are also the gamete providers. However, another possibility arising from the technique of IVF is of using the embryos so created as objects of research – the ethics and law in relation to such research is the subject of section 7.3. In section 7.4 we then return to the field of assisted reproduction, but move on to address the additional complexities that arise when third party gamete providers are introduced into the picture by procedures such as Artificial Insemination by Donor ('DI') and egg donation. Here, the law must regulate not only the conditions subject to which donation occurs, but provide for the legal status and rights of the resulting children, as against the rearing parent(s) and gamete provider(s). Finally, in section 7.5 we shall look at one area where such third party involvement in reproduction has aroused particular controversy, namely, surrogacy, in which a woman makes use of her gestational capacity to carry a child for others.

 SELF-TEST QUESTION:

Why do you think it is that, unlike other forms of fertility treatment, the use of fertility drugs has not been subject to legal regulation in the UK?

7.2 IVF Treatment

7.2.1 Background

In its report, the Warnock Committee explained the process of IVF (in vitro fertilisation) in the following terms:

Warnock Committee, *Report of the Committee of Inquiry into Human Fertilisation and Embryology*[11]

5.2 – The concept of IVF is simple. A ripe human egg is extracted from the ovary, shortly before it would have been released naturally. Next, the egg is mixed with the semen of the husband or partner, so that fertilisation can occur. The fertilised egg, once it has started to divide, is then transferred back to the mother's uterus. In practice the technique for recovery of the eggs, their culture outside the mother's body, and the transfer of the developing embryo to the uterus has to be carried out under very carefully controlled conditions. The development of laparoscopic techniques during the 1960s made the collection of the egg, in cases where the ovaries were accessible, relatively easy. (Another technique for egg recovery based on ultrasound identification has now been developed.) It was not particularly difficult to fertilise the human egg *in vitro*. The real difficulty related to the implantation of the embryo in the uterus after transfer. A pregnancy achieved in this way must not only survive the normal hazards of implantation of *in vivo* conception, but also the additional problems of IVF and embryo transfer.

---

10 See the HFE Authority's website at www.hfea.gov.uk/fertility-treatment-facts.html. The law governing access to the register in DI cases is discussed further in section 7.4.4 below.

11 See n 1 above.

More is now known about how best to replicate the natural sequence of events, but undoubt-edly achieving a successful implantation is still the most uncertain part of the procedure.

Since the early-1990s a newer variant of IVF has been available, known as intracytoplasmic sperm injection (ICSI): this technique involves injecting a single sperm into the egg and has proven effective in addressing problems of male infertility, including low sperm count and impaired sperm mobility. Today IVF – including ICSI – is increasingly a mainstream treatment: latest HFE Authority figures show that in 2007, 36,861 women underwent a total of 46,829 IVF treatment cycles; over 13,000 children were conceived in this way – around 1.8% of the total number of UK births for that year.[12]

Pursuant to s 3(1) of the HFE Act 1990 (as amended), IVF is a process which may only be carried out under licence from the HFE Authority. Moreover, s 3(2) straightaway places limits upon the nature of the embryos – and gametes – that are used for treatment (ie by being implanted in a female patient):

3 Prohibitions in connection with embryos

(1) No person shall bring about the creation of an embryo except in pursuance of a licence.

. . .

(2) No person shall place in a woman—

(a) an embryo other than a permitted embryo (as defined by section 3ZA), or

(b) any gametes other than permitted eggs or permitted sperm (as so defined)

The definitions of 'permitted eggs, permitted sperm, and permitted embryos' are found in s 3ZA. As is clear from that section, Parliament's concern has been to prohibit scientific interventions that seek to modify the attributes of embryos and gametes (and hence influence the characteristics of the future child):

3ZA Permitted eggs, permitted sperm and permitted embryos

(1) This section has effect for the interpretation of section 3(2).

(2) A permitted egg is one –

(a) which has been produced by or extracted from the ovaries of a woman, and

(b) whose nuclear or mitochondrial DNA has not been altered.

(3) Permitted sperm are sperm –

(a) which have been produced by or extracted from the testes of a man, and

(b) whose nuclear or mitochondrial DNA has not been altered.

(4) An embryo is a permitted embryo if –

(a) it has been created by the fertilisation of a permitted egg by permitted sperm,

(b) no nuclear or mitochondrial DNA of any cell of the embryo has been altered, and

(c) no cell has been added to it other than by division of the embryo's own cells.

We consider further the law as it bears on the potential, during IVF treatment, for doctors to engage in certain forms of embryonic manipulation, in section 7.2.4 below. First, however, we shall look at matters from the perspective of the would-be recipients of IVF treatment, ie the (as will for now be assumed) heterosexual couples, who wish to avail themselves of treatment in order to have a child. What rights do such persons – jointly and singly – enjoy in respect of obtaining treatment, receiving adequate information in relation to it, and controlling the use/disposition of their gametes and any *ex vivo* embryos created with them?

---

12 See www.hfea.gov.uk/ivf-figures-2006.html # 1284.

7.2.2 The potential parents

7.2.2.1 Access to treatment

IVF remains an expensive treatment (a single treatment cycle costs £3,000–4,000 in the UK), and, while there are some fertility clinics within the NHS, the treatment they offer is usually rationed to one cycle per couple, and waiting lists are predictably long. Accordingly, an immediate constraint upon a couple's access to treatment may be the lack of resources needed to fund private treatment. Assuming, though, that a couple has the means, the decision whether actually to provide treatment will be for the individual fertility clinic, acting pursuant to the Code of Practice promulgated by the HFE Authority. Where a couple is refused treatment, para 8.17 of the Code (8th Revision, 2009) makes it clear that reasons should be given to them in writing.

There are two main reasons why treatment might be refused. First, the couple may be medically unsuitable. Secondly, and far more controversially, they may be deemed socially unsuitable as parents. In the latter case, the decision essentially turns on the potential welfare of any child born as a result of treatment. The Glover Report addressed the key arguments in this regard, as follows:

> **Glover, J et al, Report to the European Commission on Reproductive Technologies, Fertility and the Family**[13]
>
> It is hard to know who will be a good or bad parent. But children need warmth and love. Some of the worst cases of cruelty to children would make any humane person wish that those parents stayed childless. It is surely unthinkable that anyone would have wished to help them have children. Of course we cannot easily predict such disasters. But, where there seems a risk, there is a strong reason not to help.
>
> . . . But a distinction has to be drawn between two very different types of case. If it is a question of giving a child to people who will behave with horrifying cruelty, it may be 'a mercy if the child is not born'. On the other hand, perhaps a child with only one parent suffers some disadvantage relative to other children, but few such children would feel life was anywhere near so bad as to wish they had not been born.
>
> A parallel can be drawn with handicap. Some handicaps are so terrible that death can seem a mercy, and it is possible to think it would have been better if the person had not been born. But many handicaps are mild or only moderately severe. No one would think that colour blindness made it better for someone not to have been born. No one would think it wrong to help a couple have a child who would be at risk of colour blindness.
>
> . . . If the disadvantage is only relative, and the child will come nowhere near regretting having been born, it is hard to see how it can be in the interests of the future child for the potential parents to be denied help.

Although, as Glover notes, it seems far-fetched (save in the most extreme cases) to suppose that the interests of the child should dictate that it never exist at all, the HFE Act 1990 (as amended) requires such an assessment to be made. Section 13(5) provides as follows:

> 13(5) A woman shall not be provided with treatment services unless account has been taken of the welfare of any child who may be born as a result of the treatment (including the need of that child for supportive parenting), and of any other child who may be affected by the birth.

The HFE Authority's Code of Practice elaborates on this requirement in para 8.10. Among the matters to which clinics should have regard in deciding whether to provide treatment are the exist-

---

13 See n 4 above.

ence of risk factors for possible abuse of the child, as well as the couple's ability to provide a stable and supportive environment for it.

HFEA Code of Practice[14]

Factors to take into account during the assessment process

8.10 The centre should consider factors that are likely to cause a risk of significant harm or neglect to any child who may be born or to any existing child of the family. These factors include any aspects of the patient's or (if they have one) their partner's:

(a) past or current circumstances that may lead to any child mentioned above experiencing serious physical or psychological harm or neglect, for example:
  (i) previous convictions relating to harming children
  (ii) child protection measures taken regarding existing children, or
  (iii) violence or serious discord in the family environment

(b) past or current circumstances that are likely to lead to an inability to care throughout childhood for any child who may be born, or that are already seriously impairing the care of any existing child of the family, for example:
  (i) mental or physical conditions
  (ii) drug or alcohol abuse
  (iii) medical history, where the medical history indicates that any child who may be born is likely to suffer from a serious medical condition, or
  (iv) circumstances that the centre considers likely to cause serious harm to any child mentioned above.

In so far as infertility treatment is denied to a couple, what, if any, form of legal redress is available to them? In respect of IVF provided by an NHS-funded clinic, a case predating the HFE Act 1990, that of *R v Ethical Committee of St Mary's Hospital (Manchester) ex p Harriott*, suggests that a challenge may lie in judicial review. At the same time, as we saw in Chapter 2, it will generally be no easy matter for the applicant to pass the '*Wednesbury* unreasonable test', and persuade the court to strike down the relevant refusal decision.

See Chapter
◄ 2

R v Ethical Committee of St Mary's Hospital (Manchester) ex p Harriott (1988)[15]

The applicant applied for judicial review after being refused IVF treatment as a result of advice given to her consultant by the hospital's ethical committee. The committee was unhappy with the fact that she and her husband had already been rejected as foster parents on the basis of her alleged poor understanding of parenting and past convictions for prostitution offences:

> **Schiemann J:** Frustrated in her desire to foster and adopt and to conceive by normal means, the applicant wishes to be considered for in vitro fertilisation . . . under the National Health Service. The Health Service – to use an imprecise term for the moment – decided to refuse to give her this treatment. In this application for judicial review she complains of that decision essentially alleging that it was reached by the wrong body: alternatively that she was not given an adequate opportunity to make representations to the decision maker before the decision was taken . . . .
>
> Mr Bell, for the committee, submitted that judicial review does not lie to review any advice given by the committee. As at present advised, I would be doubtful about

---

14 8th edn, London: HFE Authority, 2009. The Code is available on the Authority's website at: www.hfea.gov.uk/code.html.
15 [1988] 1 FLR 512.

accepting that submission in its full breadth. If the committee had advised, for instance, that the IVF unit should in principle refuse all such treatment to anyone who was a Jew or coloured, then I think the courts might well grant a declaration that such a policy was illegal . . . But I do not need to consider that situation in this case. Here the complaint is that the committee's advice was that the consultant must make up her own mind as to whether the treatment should be given. That advice was, in my judgment, unobjectionable.

Subsequently, in R v Sheffield HA ex p Seale,[16] a 37-year-old woman failed to persuade the High Court to quash a health authority's decision to exclude her from its IVF programme on the basis of her age. The judge held that, in view of its limited resources and the lower success rates achieved with older women, the Authority's policy only to treat women below the age of 35 was not irrational.

Increasingly, licensing decisions made by the HFE Authority itself, as they impact on the treatment of a particular patient, have also been the subject of judicial review proceedings. One example is the case of R v Human Fertilisation and Embryology Authority, ex p Assisted Reproduction and Gynaecology Centre and H,[17] in which the applicants – a 46-year-old woman and the clinic treating her – challenged the HFE Authority's policy of only allowing a maximum of three embryos to be placed in women during a single treatment cycle (so as to reduce the risk of multiple pregnancy): the clinic would have wished to transfer five embryos into the patient in this case. However, the Court of Appeal, in upholding Ousely J's dismissal of the action, took the view that the Court had no part to play in the scientific debate and no power to intervene:

Clarke LJ and Wall J: [65] . . . [This] is an area of rapidly developing science in which judicial review has a limited role to play. Disagreements between doctors and scientific bodies in this pioneering field are inevitable. The United Kingdom, through the Act, has opted for a system of licensing and regulation. The Authority is the body which is empowered by Parliament to regulate. Like any public authority, it is open to challenge by way of judicial review, if it exceeds or abuses the powers and responsibilities given to it by Parliament; but where, as is manifest here from an examination of the facts, it considers requests for advice carefully and thoroughly, and produces opinions which are plainly rational, the court, in our judgment, has no part to play in the debate, and certainly no power to intervene to strike down any such decision. The fact that the appellants may disagree with the Authority's advice is neither here nor there.

We shall encounter further cases where applicants have brought judicial review proceedings in respect of decisions by the HFE Authority below: one area where this has occurred is where the Authority has denied the applicant access to treatment with particular gametes or embryos (see 7.2.2.3 below). More generally, the relevance of the Human Rights Act 1998 to this area should also be noted. Thus, as Lord Phillips MR recognised in R v SS for the Home Department, ex p Mellor,[18] denying a person access to fertility treatment will engage their rights under Art 8 (right to respect for family life) and Art 12 (right to found a family) of the ECHR, and require to be justified under Art 8(2).

7.2.2.2 Information and counselling requirements

It is important that adequate information and counselling are provided to a couple prior to them consenting to treatment with IVF. This is necessary so that they can make an informed decision

---

16 (1994) 25 BMLR 1.
17 [2002] EWCA Civ 20.
18 [2001] EWCA Civ 472.

regarding ethically sensitive aspects of the procedure, such as the creation of surplus embryos with little chance of ever developing into fully fledged human beings. Similarly, they should be warned of the high risk that the treatment will fail: it has been estimated that only about 25 per cent of IVF procedures will result in a live birth (and then often only after several failed attempts).

Such information and counselling requirements are outlined in s 13(6) in conjunction with Part 1 of Sch 3ZA of the HFEA 1990 (as amended):

> 13(6)   A woman shall not be provided with treatment services of a kind specified in Part 1 of Schedule 3ZA unless she and any man or woman who is to be treated together with her have been given a suitable opportunity to receive proper counselling about the implications of her being provided with treatment services of that kind, and have been provided with such relevant information as is proper.

. . . SCHEDULE 3ZA

Part 1   Kinds of treatment in relation to which counselling must be offered
. . . 2 The treatment services involve the use of any embryo the creation of which was brought about *in vitro*.

It is also important that the couple are invited to think through and make provision in their consents for various future contingencies that may arise, such as their relationship breaking down or the death of the male partner. As we shall see in 7.2.2.3 below, the failure in some past instances to do so has led to some difficult and sad cases. Accordingly, the amendments to the 1990 Act include – in s 25(2A) – an increased responsibility upon the HFE Authority in its Code of Practice to offer guidance to fertilty clinics, as to the nature of their obligation to patients in respect of information and (the offer of) counselling. In this regard, the present Code of Practice lists the following matters that should be divulged to IVF patients:

HFEA Code of Practice[19]

Information for those seeking treatment
4.2   Before treatment is offered, the centre should give the woman seeking treatment and her partner, if applicable, information about:
  (a)   the centre's policy on selecting patients
  (b)   the centre's statutory duty to take account of the welfare of any resulting or affected child
  (c)   the expected waiting time for treatment
  (d)   fertility treatments available
  (e)   the likely outcomes of the proposed treatment (data provided should include the centre's most recent live birth rate and clinical pregnancy rate per treatment cycle, verified by the HFEA, and the national live birth rate and clinical pregnancy rate per treatment cycle)
  (f)   the nature and potential risks of the treatment, including the risk of children conceived having developmental and birth defects
  (g)   the possible side effects and risks to the woman being treated and any resulting child, including ovarian hyperstimulation syndrome (OHSS)
        . . .
  (i)   the availability of facilities for freezing embryos, and the implications of storing embryos and then using embryos

---

19 See n 14 above.

(j) the importance of informing the treatment centre about the eventual outcome of the treatment (including if no live birth results)

(k) the centre's complaints procedure, and

(l) the nature and potential risks (immediate and longer term) of IVF/ICSI with in vitro matured eggs, including reference to the clinic's experience.

7.2.2.3 Control over the use/disposition of embryos/gametes

One of the cornerstones of the 1990 Act (as amended) consists in the great weight accorded to the consents of the gamete providers in determining what may be done with those gametes and/or any embryos created with them. In establishing a regime in which the providers are invited, following proper counselling, to specify the uses to which the material may be put, the Act reflects a commitment to the autonomy of such providers. The key consent provisions are contained in Sch 3 of the Act:

Schedule 3 – Consent to use or storage of gametes, embryos . . . etc

1   (1) A consent under this Schedule, and any notice under paragraph 4 varying or withdrawing a consent under this Schedule, must be in writing and, subject to sub-paragraph (2), must be signed by the person giving it.

(2) A consent under this Schedule by a person who is unable to sign because of illness, injury or physical disability (a "person unable to sign"), and any notice under paragraph 4 by a person unable to sign varying or withdrawing a consent under this Schedule, is to be taken to comply with the requirement of sub-paragraph (1) as to signature if it is signed at the direction of the person unable to sign, in the presence of the person unable to sign and in the presence of at least one witness who attests the signature.

(3) In this Schedule "effective consent" means a consent under this Schedule which has not been withdrawn.

2   (1) A consent to the use of any embryo must specify one or more of the following purposes –

(a) use in providing treatment services to the person giving consent, or that person and another specified person together,

. . . and may specify conditions subject to which the embryo may be so used.

. . . Variation and withdrawal of consent

4   (1) The terms of any consent under this Schedule may from time to time be varied, and the consent may be withdrawn, by notice given by the person who gave the consent to the person keeping the gametes, human cells, [or] embryo . . . to which the consent is relevant.

(2) . . . the terms of any consent to the use of any embryo cannot be varied, and such consent cannot be withdrawn, once the embryo has been used—

(a) in providing treatment services . . .

. . . In vitro fertilisation and subsequent use of embryo

6   (1) A person's gametes or human cells must not be used to bring about the creation of any embryo in vitro unless there is an effective consent by that person to any embryo, the creation of which may be brought about with the use of those gametes or human cells, being used for one or more of the purposes mentioned in paragraph 2(1)(a), (b) and (c) above.

(2) An embryo the creation of which was brought about in vitro must not be received by any person unless there is an effective consent by each relevant person in relation to the embryo to the use for one or more of the purposes mentioned in paragraph 2(1) . . .

(3) An embryo the creation of which was brought about in vitro must not be used for any purpose unless there is an effective consent by each relevant person in relation to the embryo to the use for that purpose of the embryo and the embryo is used in accordance with those consents.

. . . Storage of gametes and embryos

8   (1) A person's gametes must not be kept in storage unless there is an effective consent by that person to their storage and they are stored in accordance with the consent.

  (2) An embryo the creation of which was brought about in vitro must not be kept in storage unless there is an effective consent, by each relevant person in relation to the embryo, to the storage of the embryo and the embryo is stored in accordance with those consents . . .

As para 1(1) makes clear, for consent to the storage and/or use of gametes and embryos to be effective, it needs to be made in writing and signed by the gamete provider; an exception to the need for a signature is allowed for in para 1(2) in so far as the provider is physically unable to sign due to illness or injury. In fact, following the 2008 amendments to the 1990 Act, it is possible exceptionally for consent to the storage of gametes to be dispensed with: this is, as specified in paras 9 and 10 of Sch 3, where a child or temporarily incapable adult, respectively, is to undergo treatment that may render them infertile, and a registered medical practitioner has certified that in his opinion such storage is in the patient's best interests. Nonetheless, the gametes may not be used for IVF (or other) treatment unless the person, having (re)gained capacity, subsequently gives consent.

Recently, in *Yearworth v North Bristol NHS Trust*,[20] the Court of Appeal held in the context of a negligence claim brought by a number of men against a clinic following the accidental destruction of their sperm, that they could for these purposes be regarded as owning their gametes. As the Court noted, a significant factor was the degree of control they had over the material pursuant to the statutory consent provisions, including the right (through withdrawing consent) to compel its destruction. At the same time, in relation to fertility treatment undertaken by a couple, this approach leaves open the question of what, if any, rights to using the genetic material are enjoyed by the other party to the couple.

There have in fact been several high-profile decisions involving challenges by the other party to the consent provisions in the 1990 Act. One of the first was the well-known case of *R v Human Fertilisation and Embryology Authority ex p Blood*, which concerned the posthumous use of sperm taken from a dying patient.

R v Human Fertilisation and Embryology Authority ex p Blood (1997)[21]

Mrs Blood sought judicial review of the HFE Authority's refusal to license infertility treatment of her with her dead husband's sperm. The sperm had been taken from Mr Blood as he lay in a coma shortly before his death from meningitis and, consequently, none of the written consents to its storage or use (stipulated in the 1990 Act) had been obtained:

Lord Woolf MR:

The position as to storage

Sperm can be used fresh or after it has been preserved. Its life, if not preserved, is extremely limited, a matter of a few hours. If it is preserved then it is being stored for the purposes of the Act and therefore is subject to the requirements of a licence. This is made clear by the definition of keeping or preserving sperm contained in s 2(2). The Act therefore takes the preservation process as the beginning of storage. This is understandable, since preservation involves the processing of gametes, and Parliament has required that this should be done subject to the control of the

---

20 [2009] EWCA Civ 37; the case is discussed further in Ch 11 below.
21 [1997] 2 WLR 806, CA.

licensing process. The result is that in the ordinary way no preservation can take place unless the required written consents exist. This would also apply in the case of the preservation of sperm intended for export unless a particular direction was obtained prior to preservation which permitted the storage to take place notwithstanding that there were not the requisite consents.

It follows that Mr Blood's sperm should not in fact have been preserved and stored. Technically therefore an offence was committed by the licence holder ... There is however no question of any prosecution being brought in the circumstances of this case and no possible criticism can be made of the fact that storage has taken place because Professor Cook of IRT was acting throughout in close consultation with the Authority in a perfectly bona fide manner, in an unexplored legal situation where humanity dictated that the sperm was taken and preserved first, and the legal argument followed. From now on, however, the position will be different, as these proceedings will clarify the legal position. Because this judgment makes it clear that the sperm of Mr Blood has been preserved and stored when it should not have been, this case raises issues as to the lawfulness of the use and export of sperm which should never arise again.

In the special circumstances, it was held that, although Mrs Blood could not be lawfully treated with the sperm in the UK, she was entitled to export it and receive treatment in Belgium pursuant to her rights under Art 59 (now Art 56) of the EC Treaty.[22] She has since had two children as a result.

In so far as gametes are provided and stored pursuant to effective consent, their posthumous use in fertility treatment is allowed for in principle by the Act. In this regard, Sch 3, para 2(2)(b) requires gamete providers to specify what use may be made of their gametes in the event of death, and this may include consent to usage by the other party. However, it is essential that this consent is still effective as at death: a case in point is *Centre for Reproductive Medicine v Mrs U*,[23] where the respondent widow's husband, after initially agreeing to the posthumous use of his sperm to treat his wife in the event of his death, later revoked this consent. The Court of Appeal, having rejected the respondent's argument that the clinic had unduly influenced her husband's change of mind, held that she was not entitled to use the sperm.

As the *Mrs U* case illustrates, where the requisite consents were obtained at the outset, they remain inherently revocable at the initiative of either gamete provider. Moreover, even if the gametes have subsequently been mixed with those of the other party to the couple to form an embryo, the effective and continuing consent of both parties are required for its use in treatment. Apart from the death of one of the gamete providers, the other main problem – as regards a party's ability to use such gametes (or embryos created with them) in order to have a child – will be presented by relationship-breakdown. Here, the withdrawal of the consent of the other party to the continued storage of any embryo formed with his or her gametes will entail that further storage (and *a fortiori* use in IVF treatment) are impermissible: see Sch 3, paras 4(1) and 6(2). The validity of these statutory provisions was the subject of legal challenge in *Evans v Amicus Healthcare Ltd*:

Evans v Amicus Healthcare Ltd (2004)[24]

The claimant, Ms Evans, had a number of eggs harvested from her at the defendant clinic in October 2001 following the diagnosis of ovarian cancer. As, at the time, the cryopreservation of

---

22 See also the recent, unusual case of *L v HFE Authority* [2008] EWHC 2149, permitting a woman to export sperm from her deceased husband, extracted after his death pursuant to an erroneous court order.

23 [2002] EWCA Civ 565.

24 [2004] EWCA Civ 727, CA.

eggs was not yet possible, they were mixed with the sperm of her then partner, Mr Johnston, and the resulting embryos stored by the defendant. In May 2002, the relationship between the claimant and Mr Johnston broke down. The claimant attempted to resist the embryos' destruction by arguing, *inter alia*, that Mr Johnston was estopped from revoking his consent:

> **Thorpe and Sedley LJJ:** [35] In relation to his estoppel ground . . . Mr Tolson [counsel for Ms Evans] sought to develop the submission that Mr Johnston had concealed his ambivalence, thereby inducing Ms Evans to go forward with him into couple treatment. Mr Tolson submitted that had she known his true state of mind and feeling she would have appreciated the risks of his withdrawing consent and, perhaps, elected for fertilisation of her eggs with donor sperm.
>
> . . . [37] [T]he clear policy of the Act is to ensure continuing consent from the commencement of treatment to the point of implant. Consent may be given subject to conditions. Consent may be varied. Consent may be withdrawn. Against that background the court should be extremely slow to recognise or to create a principle of waiver that would conflict with the Parliamentary scheme.
>
> . . . [41] In our judgment therefore, Mr Johnston was entitled by the terms of the Act to withdraw his consent as and when he did. The effect of his withdrawal of consent is to prevent both the use and the continued storage of the embryo fertilised with his sperm. Future treatment of the appellant would not be 'treatment together' with Mr Johnston.

In the alternative, Ms Evans contended that the HFEA 1990, by permitting such revocation, was incompatible with her rights under Art 8 ECHR:

> **Arden LJ:**
>
> **Article 8**
>
> [108] It is common ground that Article 8, which has already been set out by Thorpe and Sedley LJJ, is engaged because Ms Evans' bodily integrity (private life) is affected. I do not consider that she could assert any right to family life with a future child whose embryo has not yet been transferred to her . . . The assumption made by all parties is that Article 8 is engaged to the extent that the 1990 Act purports to regulate any right they would otherwise have to use an embryo . . .
>
> [109] The next question is whether the interference is justified under Article 8(2). In the 1990 Act Parliament has taken the view that each genetic parent should have the right to withdraw their consent for as long as possible. It was not inevitable that Parliament should take that view. Subject to the possible effect of the Convention, Parliament could have taken the view that, as in sexual intercourse, a man's procreative liberty should end with the donation of sperm but that, in the light of the woman's unique role in making the embryo a child, she should have the right to determine the fate of the embryo. But Parliament did not take that view. Nor did Parliament take the view that the court should have any power to dispense with the requirement for consent of both parties, even when circumstances occur which were not envisaged when the original arrangements were made.
>
> [110] Like Thorpe and Sedley LJJ, I consider that the imposition of an invariable and ongoing requirement for consent in the 1990 Act in the present type of situation satisfies Article 8(2) of the Convention. . . . As this is a sensitive area of ethical judgment, the balance to be struck between the parties must primarily be a matter for Parliament: see the passage from the speech of Lord Nicholls in *Wilson v First County Trust Ltd (No. 2)* [2004] . . . Parliament has taken the view that no-one should have

power to override the need for a genetic parent's consent. The wisdom of not having such a power is, in my judgment, illustrated by the facts of this case. The personal circumstances of the parties are different from what they were at the outset of treatment, and it would be difficult for a court to judge whether the effect of Mr Johnston's withdrawal of his consent on Ms Evans is greater than the effect that the invalidation of that withdrawal of consent would have on Mr Johnston. The court has no point of reference by which to make that sort of evaluation. The fact is that each person has a right to be protected against interference with their private life. That is an aspect of the principle of self-determination or personal autonomy . . .

Ms Evans subsequently appealed to the European Court of Human Rights in Strasbourg; however, in dismissing her action, the Court noted that, at the European level too, there was no consensus as to how to resolve the conflicting Art 8 rights of the parties in such a case. In this context, the majority of the Court was of the view that the approach adopted in the HFE Act – incorporating the need for their joint consent – was a permissible one.[25]

In the wake of the *Evans* case, the 2008 amendments to the HFE Act have included a change to the relevant consent provisions. Thus Sch 3, para 4A of the 1990 Act (as amended) now provides for a 12-month 'cooling off' period, where one party withdraws consent to the storage of an embryo created with his/her and the other party's gametes. During this time, the embryo may not be destroyed without the other party's agreement. Nor, however, may any other use be made of it.

 SELF-TEST QUESTION

Do you think it is appropriate, in the context of assisted reproduction (in contrast to non-assisted conception), for the interests in procreating (or not) of the female and male gamete providers to enjoy equal weight?

7.2.3 The embryo

7.2.3.1 Status issues

From what has been said above, in relation to the primacy granted to the wishes of gamete providers in determining the use made of the resulting embryos, it might appear that the embryo's own status is an entirely subordinate one. This is partly true; as we have just seen, the consequence of a gamete provider withdrawing consent to storage of an embryo is the latter's inevitable destruction. Nevertheless, as we shall see when we look at embryo research (see section 7.3 below), there are important limits on the freedom of action of medical scientists so far as the treatment of embryos is concerned. The ambivalence of the law on the early embryo was foreshadowed in the Warnock Report. After describing the initial stages of embryonic development, the report side-stepped the question of what moral inferences were to be drawn:

---

25 *Evans v United Kingdom* (2006) 46 EHRR 321.

Warnock Committee, Report of the Committee of Inquiry into Human Fertilisation and Embryology[26]

The starting point for discussion

11.8 It was the development of IVF that, for the first time, gave rise to the possibility that human embryos might be brought into existence which might have no chance to implant because they were not transferred to a uterus and hence no chance to be born as human beings. This inevitably led to an examination of the moral rights of the embryo.

11.9 Some people hold that if an embryo is human and alive, it follows that it should not be deprived of a chance for development, and therefore it should not be used for research. They would give moral approval to IVF if, and only if, each embryo produced were to be transferred to a uterus. Others, while in no way denying that human embryos are alive (and they would concede that eggs and sperm are also alive), hold that embryos are not yet human persons and that if it could be decided when an embryo becomes a person, it could also be decided when it might, or might not, be permissible for research to be undertaken. Although the questions of when life or personhood begin appear to be questions of fact susceptible of straightforward answers, we hold that the answers to such questions in fact are complex amalgams of factual and moral judgments. Instead of trying to answer these questions directly we have therefore gone straight to the question of how it is right to treat the human embryo. We have considered what status ought to be accorded to the human embryo, and the answer we give must necessarily be in terms of ethical or moral principles.

In the American case of *Davis v Davis*,[27] which involved a custody battle over frozen embryos, the Tennessee Supreme Court was concerned with the question of whether embryos should be categorised as 'persons' or 'property' or as having an interim, *sui generis* legal status. In his judgment, Daughtrey J discussed the position as follows:

Daughtrey J: To our way of thinking, the most helpful discussion on this point is found not in the minuscule number of legal opinions that have involved 'frozen embryos', but in the ethical standards set by the American Fertility Society, as follows:

> Three major ethical positions have been articulated in the debate over pre-embryo status. At one extreme is the view of the pre-embryo as a human subject after fertilisation, which requires that it be accorded the rights of a person. This position entails an obligation to provide an opportunity for implantation to occur and tends to ban any action before transfer that might harm the pre-embryo or that is not immediately therapeutic, such as freezing and some pre-embryo research.
>
> At the opposite extreme is the view that the pre-embryo has a status no different from any other human tissue. With the consent of those who have decision making authority over the pre-embryo, no limits should be imposed on actions taken with pre-embryos.
>
> A third view – one that is most widely held – takes an intermediate position between the other two. It holds that the pre-embryo deserves respect greater than that accorded to human tissue but not the respect accorded to actual persons. The pre-embryo is due greater respect than other human tissue because of its potential to become a person and because of its symbolic meaning for many people. Yet, it should not be treated as a person, because it has not yet developed the features of

---

26 See n 1 above.
27 842 SW 2d 588 (1992).

> personhood, is not yet established as developmentally individual, and may never realise its biologic potential . . .
>
> We conclude that pre-embryos are not, strictly speaking, either 'persons' or 'property', but occupy an interim category that entitles them to special respect because of their potential for human life.

The position in England as regards the existence of property rights in embryos remains uncertain. As noted earlier, in *Yearworth v North Bristol NHS Trust*[28] the Court of Appeal was prepared to recognise such rights in gametes for the purposes of a negligence action against a clinic, which had lost them. Though the judgment did not expressly address the position as to embryos, in some ways its logic could be read as extending to them − at least in a case where a couple jointly wished to sue a clinic responsible for their destruction. On the other hand, the courts might well recoil from the symbolic implications of categorising nascent human organisms in terms of property.

What is clear, by contrast, is the embryo's lack of personhood under English law. In *Evans v Amicus Healthcare Ltd*,[29] the Court of Appeal, in denying that the embryo was a legal person for the purposes of Art 2 of the ECHR, commented as follows:

> **Thorpe and Sedley LJJ:** [19] . . . In our domestic law it has been repeatedly held that a foetus prior to the moment of birth does not have independent rights or interests: see *Re F (In Utero)* . . . and *Re MB (Medical Treatment)*. . . . Thus even more clearly can there be no independent rights or interests in stored embryos. In this respect our law is not inconsistent with the decisions of the ECHR. Article 2 protects the right to life. No Convention jurisprudence extends the right to an embryo, much less to one which at the material point of time is non-viable. Mr Tolson was prepared to accept that the Article 2 right would fail if both gamete providers wanted the embryo destroyed. Yet, as was pointed out to him, the right to life, where it exists, cannot be waived by its possessor, let alone by others. This simply illustrates the fallacy of invoking Article 2 in the present argument. Ms Evans' case is not about the right to life; it is about the right to bring life into being.

(See also the discussion of the status of the foetus in Chapter 8 below.)

7.2.3.2 The storage of embryos and gametes

As we have already seen, the consent of gamete providers must be obtained in order to continue to store their gametes/embryos in accordance with the Act. Such storage is possible in relation to both embryos and gametes (though egg storage is still in its infancy) by means of 'cryopreservation' (freezing). Nevertheless (assuming that valid consents are in force), should there be any absolute time limit beyond which the material in question may in any event not be kept?

The Warnock Committee recommended the need for an upper time limit to storage, on grounds both of the possible (albeit speculative) risk of physical harm to children born from embryos after extended storage, and the increased risk of gamete providers dying or falling into disagreement over the period in question. The HFEA 1990, as originally enacted, reflected these concerns in stipulating in maximum storage periods of 10 years for gametes and five years for embryos. After the expiry of these periods, the clinics storing the material were required to 'allow it to perish'. However, subsequently, it was felt desirable to extend the limit in respect of embryos: this was especially so in cases where gametes were taken from a female provider prior to therapy for cancer, where it is medically preferable to wait for as long as possible after such therapy before implanting her with any embryo formed with them.

---

28 See n 20 above.
29 See n 24 above.

Accordingly, s 14(4) of the HFEA 1990 (as amended) now provides – subject to the specification by the gamete providers of a lesser period – for a ten-year storage period for embryos as well. Indeed, pursuant to the Human Fertilisation and Embryology (Statutory Storage Period for Embryos and Gametes) Regulations 2009,[30] the latter limit itself may be exceeded, eg in cases where a woman is due to undergo some other treatment, for example, radiotherapy, interfering with her fertility. Here, reg 3 allows for ten-year extensions to storage to be made where the gamete providers' original consents provided this and a medical practitioner certifies in writing that one of them is, or is likely to become, prematurely infertile. This is subject to a long-stop period of 55 years from original storage (which admittedly is difficult to imagine applying in practice).

7.2.3.3 Embryo testing and selection

As we have seen, the process of IVF treatment consists of two main stages: first, the creation of one or more *ex vivo* embryos; secondly, the implantion of these in the female patient's uterus for gestation to birth. One possibility this separation opens up is of screening embryos in the interim so as to identify those with genetic defects, either of a kind that will prevent a live birth, or as will lead to a future child with a serious genetic disorder. However, other more controversial possibilities also exist, such as screening to identify embryos that would provide a tissue match for an existing sick child ('saviour siblings'), or of identifying and selecting embryos on social grounds, including on the basis of sex. We look in turn at how the law currently deals with these various issues.

7.2.3.3.1 *Pre-implantation genetic diagnosis to eliminate disease*

The practice of 'pre-implantation genetic diagnosis' (PGD) involves testing embryos for specific genetic diseases – only embryos free of genes associated with the disease will be implanted, while the others are discarded. In 1999, the HFE Authority and Advisory Committee on Genetic Testing published a report, *Pre-Implantation Genetic Diagnosis*, which concluded that the practice was ethically sound, at least in the case of serious genetic diseases such as cystic fibrosis. An analogy can be invoked here with abortion on grounds of serious foetal handicap, which is also widely regarded as permissible. In fact, in terms of the implications for the 'sanctity of life', not to mention the health of the putative mother, the discard of an embryo prior to implantation may well be thought preferable to the termination an already existing pregnancy. Indeed it is clear that some couples (notably, those who have previously had a genetically disabled child) will resort to IVF precisely because of the possibility of testing.

Arguably more controversial was the HFE Authority's decision in 2006 to license PGD in order to identify embryos with genes that would not cause disability at birth, but significantly increase the child's risk of developing an inherited form of cancer later in life. Here the effect is to 'screen out' persons who potentially could enjoy many years of disease-free existence. Nonetheless, the permissibility of such screening – as well as that designed to eliminate more immediate genetic disabilities – is confirmed by the 2008 amendments to the HFE Act 1990. Schedule 2 of the Act now provides that:

Schedule 2 – Activities that may be licensed under the 1990 Act

Licences for treatment

. . . *Embryo testing*

1ZA (1) A licence . . . cannot authorise the testing of an embryo, except for one or more of the following purposes–
   (a) establishing whether the embryo has a gene, chromosome or mitochondrial abnormality that may affect its capacity to result in a live birth.

---

30 SI 2009/1582.

> (b) in a case where there is a particular risk that the embryo may have any gene, chromosome or mitochondrion abnormality, establishing whether it has that abnormality or any other gene, chromosome or mitochondrion abnormality,
>
> . . .
>
> (2) A licence . . . cannot authorise the testing of embryos for the purpose mentioned in sub-paragraph (1)(b) unless the Authority is satisfied–
> (a) in relation to the abnormality of which there is a particular risk, and
> (b) in relation to any other abnormality for which testing is to be authorised under sub-paragraph (1)(b), that there is a significant risk that a person with the abnormality will have or develop a serious physical or mental disability, a serious illness or any other serious medical condition.

7.2.3.3.2 'Saviour siblings'

A particular application of PGD, which has evoked controversy, is its use – in conjunction with tissue typing – to try to create a so-called 'saviour sibling' (ie a new child whose tissue is compatible with that of an existing sick child of the same couple). In 2002, the HFE Authority licensed a clinic in Nottingham to carry out treatment designed to enable a couple, Mr and Mrs Hashmi, to produce a child who would be a tissue donor for one of their children, Zain, who suffered from beta-thalassaemia – a serious genetic blood disorder. Subsequently, in R (*On the Application of Josephine Quintavalle on Behalf of CORE*) v HFEA,[31] this decision was challenged by the pressure group, CORE (Comment on Reproductive Ethics). In arguing that such testing fell outside the scope of the Authority's licensing powers, CORE relied on the (former) wording of Sch 2, para 1 of the 1990 Act, which provided that a licensed activity must be necessary or desirable for the purpose of providing 'treatment services'. It contended that these provisions should be construed narrowly as assisting a woman physically to carry a child, but not a child with specific genetic attributes.

Although CORE's argument succeeded at first instance, it was rejected by the Court of Appeal and the House of Lords, which saw the provisions as conferring a discretion upon the Authority in such cases. Following the 2008 amendments to the HFE Act 1990, Sch 2, para 1ZA (1)(d) now expressly provides for the legality of tissue typing to determine an embryo's compatibility to act as a donor for a sick sibling, as follows:

> **Licences for treatment**
>
> . . . *Embryo testing*
>
> 1ZA (1) A licence under paragraph 1 cannot authorise the testing of an embryo, except for one or more of the following purposes—
>
> ̄   . . . (d) in a case where a person ('the sibling') who is the child of the persons whose gametes are used to bring about the creation of the embryo (or of either of those persons) suffers from a serious medical condition which could be treated by umbilical cord blood stem cells, bone marrow or other tissue of any resulting child, establishing whether the tissue of any resulting child would be compatible with that of the sibling.

Nonetheless, as later made clear in para 1ZA (4), tissue typing will not be permitted in relation to the proposed creation of a child to serve as a whole organ donor for a sibling.

In fact, the HFE Authority has remained cautious in granting treatment licences in such cases; generally it must be satisfied both that the condition of the existing child is serious or life-threatening and that other reasonable possibilities of treatment and/or sources of tissue have been

---

31 [2005] UKHL 28.

exhausted.[32] Originally, a further requirement imposed by the Authority was that the tested embryos should themselves be at risk of developing the condition affecting the existing child. For this reason it refused, in the summer of 2002, to grant a licence to carry out PGD and tissue-typing in the case of a couple, the Whitakers, who wanted a child to provide a tissue match for their three-year-old son, who had Diamond Blackfan anaemia. (The crucial difference between their case and the Hashmis' was that the anaemia was sporadic rather than congenital, so that any further embryos produced by them were not at special risk of having it.) However, this requirement – which the Authority attempted to justify by reference to the speculative risk to embryos from PGD itself – was subject to strong criticism,[33] and was abandoned in 2004.

7.2.3.3.3 Sex selection

Another controversial and significant possibility that has arisen out of developments in reproductive technology is that of testing *ex vivo* embryos (and more recently, sperm alone) in order to determine the sex of the potential child. How far should this practice be permitted for merely social (as opposed to medical) reasons? The Warnock Report had the following to say:

Warnock Committee, Report of the Committee of Inquiry into Human Fertilisation and Embryology[34]

Other reasons for sex selection

9.11 – So far we have discussed the use of sex selection in a clinical context, where it would be practised solely for the purpose of avoiding hereditary sex-linked disorders. We see no reason why, if a method of selecting the sex of a child before fertilisation is developed, this should not be offered to couples who have good medical reasons for choosing the sex of their child. But if an efficient and easy method of ensuring the conception of a child of a particular sex became available, it is likely that some couples would wish to make use of it for purely social reasons. Such a practice would obviously affect the individual family and the children involved, and would also have implications for society as a whole. It is impossible to predict, either in the long or the short term, the likely effects of such a practice on the ratio of males to females within society. It is often suggested that a majority of couples would choose that their first child was male, and if this happened, it could have important social implications, since there is considerable evidence that the first born sibling may enjoy certain advantages over younger siblings. It would have particular implications for the role of women in society, although some would argue that these effects would today be less damaging than they might have been a hundred years ago. These important considerations make the Inquiry dubious about the use of sex selection techniques on a wide scale, but because of the difficulty of predicting the outcome of any such trend we have not found it possible to make any positive recommendations on this issue. Nevertheless, we consider that the whole question of the acceptability of sex selection should be kept under review.

As originally enacted in 1990, the HFE Act left the possibility of licensing sex selection to the discretion of the HFE Authority. In 1993, following a process of consultation, the Authority decided that such selection for non-medical reasons was unethical and should not be carried out. In October 2000, it was reported that a Scottish couple, Mr and Mrs Masterton, who had four sons and had lost their only daughter in an accident, were preparing to challenge the HFE Authority in judicial review over its refusal to grant their fertility clinic the requisite licence to perform sex selection on their embryos to try for a girl. However, that case did not progress, and the HFE

---

32 HFEA Code of Practice, 8th edn (2009) para 10.22.
33 See Sheldon, S, and Wilkinson, S, 'Hashmi and Whitaker: an unjustifiable and misguided distinction?' (2004) 12 Med L Rev 137.
34 See n 1 above.

Authoriry later reaffirmed its opposition to the practice of social sex selection in its report, *Sex Selection: Options for Regulation*,[35] and in successive Codes of Practice.

As noted by the Warnock Report, one concern regarding sex selection is the uncertain effects it would have, were it to be widely employed, upon the ratio of the sexes in society. Admittedly, this problem could be side-stepped, were permissible sex selection to be limited to cases of 'family balancing' (where the couple already have one or more child of the other sex). Nonetheless, as Stephen Wilkinson argues in the following extract, an objection that remains here relates to the sexual stereotyping involved:

Wilkinson, S, 'Sexism, Sex Selection and "Family Balancing" '[36]

As with 'regular' sex selection, whether 'family balancing' involves stereotyping depends on what exactly it is that the parents are aiming at. If what they want is a 'balance' of plainly biological features (if they want half their children to be capable of beard growth and other half to develop breasts, for example), then (as explained previously) while we may think that this is weird or objectionable in other ways, it does not seem to involve sex-stereotyping, for the desired sex-linked characteristics really are biologically determined. If, on the other hand, the sort of 'balance' that they are after is less clearly related to biology and more to do with character traits that may or may not be determined by physical sex, then there is a significant risk that the parents are guilty of stereotyping. It seems then that such stereotyping is as likely in the case of 'family balancing' sex selection as it is in 'regular' sex selection. Consider these two cases. Family A want all of their children to have aggression and sporting prowess and so select all boys; Family B want half their children to have aggression and sporting prowess, and the other half to be caring and musical, and so use ('family balancing') selection to have half boys and half girls. Whatever the general merits of these choices, it seems clear that, as far as sex-stereotyping is concerned, the families are in the very same position; both are guilty of sex-stereotyping.

In fact, the 2008 changes to the HFE Act 1990 have now removed from the HFE Authority the possibility of licensing social sex selection, and instead contain a statutory prohibition of the practice. Schedule 2, para 1ZB of the 1990 Act (as amended) states:

Licences for treatment

. . . Sex selection

1ZB

(1) A licence under paragraph 1 cannot authorise any practice designed to secure that any resulting child will be of one sex rather than the other.

. . .

(3) Sub-paragraph (1) does not prevent the authorisation of any other practices designed to secure that any resulting child will be of one sex rather than the other in a case where there is a particular risk that a woman will give birth to a child who will have or develop –

(a) a gender-related serious physical or mental disability,

(b) a gender-related serious illness, or

(c) any other gender-related serious medical condition.

(4) For the purposes of sub-paragraph (3), a physical or mental disability, illness or other medical condition is gender-related if the Authority is satisfied that –

(a) it affects only one sex, or

(b) it affects one sex significantly more than the other.

---

35 London: HFEA, 2003; available at: www.hfea.gov.uk/docs/Final_sex_selection_main_report.pdf.
36 (2008) 16 *Med L Rev* 369.

As is apparent from sub para 1ZB(3) (and as previously allowed by the HFE Authority) sex selection remains permissible for medical reasons, in particular to avoid/reduce the risk of transmitting a serious sex-specific genetic disease. For example, where a couple are known to be transmitters of the genes for haemophilia – and assuming testing cannot determine which of their embryos have these – it would be lawful to screen out all the male embryos (as only male children are at risk of actually developing the condition).

7.2.3.3.4 Other bases for selection

So far the only genes that can be identified with any certainty are those for some genetic diseases and for sex. However, in the future it may become possible to identify genes that contribute to other attributes such as intelligence, musicality, or aggression (assuming they have some genetic as opposed to purely social basis). If this were to occur, should the testing of embryos for the relevant genes – enabling parents to use the information to choose which embryos to have implanted – be permitted? This possibility, leading to the creation of what are popularly termed 'designer babies', was the subject of a report by the Nuffield Council on Bioethics in 2002, which found against the practice, *inter alia*, on the basis that it could negatively affect the attitude of parents towards their children:

Nuffield Council on Bioethics, *Genetics and Human Behaviour. The Ethical Context*[37]

Summary and Recommendations . . .

At present, parents accept their children as they find them in an attitude of 'natural humility' to the unchosen results of procreation. This attitude is an important feature of parental love, the love that parents owe to their children as individuals in their own right; for this is a love that does not have to be earned and is not dependent on a child having characteristics that the parents hoped for. Parental love which includes this element of natural humility is, therefore, incompatible with the will to control. It is not compatible with attempts to interfere in the life of a child except where the interference is in the child's own interest. Equally, it is not compatible with the practice of prenatal selection which seeks to identify, as a basis for choice, genetic predispositions for enhanced abilities or special character traits. For this is an attempt to determine the kind of child one will have – which is precisely not the unconditional, loving acceptance of whatever child one turns out to have.

Given that we are dealing here with only speculative possibilities, and since the likely small effects of individual genes may make accurate predictions of future behaviour very difficult, it is hard to evaluate the disagreement between the contrasting positions. In particular, it may be that the contrast between the affirmation of a right to procreative autonomy and the defence of natural humility is too simple. It might turn out that there are possibilities for modest applications of PGD in relation to the traits considered in this Report which would not seriously undermine the present relationship between parents and their children. *While not entirely persuaded by this conservative line of argument, we do accept that, at present, the case for permitting prenatal selection based on the identification of genetic predispositions for enhanced abilities remains to be made. We recommend, therefore, that the technique of preimplantation genetic diagnosis, which is currently restricted to serious diseases and disorders, should not be extended to include behavioural traits in the normal range such as intelligence, sexual orientation and personality traits* (para 13.78).

On the other hand, other commentators have defended such hypothetical selection on consequentialist grounds. Julian Savelescu argues that it is consonant with the demands of 'procreative

---

37 (2002); the full report is available at www.nuffieldbioethics.org/go/browseablepublications/geneticsandhb/report_354.html.

beneficence' – which requires parents to select, as between possible children, those with the greatest chance of having the best life (ie containing the most well-being). He goes on to dismiss two objections that are often raised to the approach:

Savelescu, J, 'Procreative Beneficence: Why we should select the best children'[38]

1. *Harm to the child*: One common objection to genetic selection for non-disease traits is that it results in harm to the child. There are various versions of this objection, which include the harm which arises from excessive and overbearing parental expectations, using the child as a means, and not treating it as an end, and closing off possible future options on the basis of the information provided (failing to respect the child's 'right to an open future').

There are a number of responses. Firstly, in some cases, it is possible to deny that the harms will be significant. Parents come to love the child whom they have (even a child with a serious disability). Moreover, some have argued that counselling can reduce excessive expectations.

Secondly, we can accept some risk of a child experiencing some state of reduced well-being in cases of selection. One variant of the harm to child objection is: 'If you select embryo A, it might still get asthma, or worse, cancer, or have a much worse life than B, and you would be responsible.' . . . [However,] you have not harmed A unless A's life is not worth living (hardly plausible) because A would not have existed if you had acted otherwise. A is not made worse off than A would otherwise have been, since without the selection, A would not have existed.

2. *Inequality*: One objection to Procreative Beneficence is that it will maintain or increase inequality. For example, it is often argued that selection for sex, intelligence, favourable physical or psychological traits, etc all contribute to inequality in society . . .

. . . Even if the Disability Discrimination Claim were true, it would be a drastic step in favour of equality to inflict a higher risk of having a child with a disability on a couple (who do not want a child with a disability) to promote social equality.

. . . There are better ways to make statements about the equality of people with disability (e.g., we could direct savings from selection against embryos/fetuses with genetic abnormalities to improving well-being of existing people with disabilities).

These arguments extend to selection for non-disease genes. It is not disease which is important but its impact on well-being. In so far as a non-disease gene such as a gene for intelligence impacts on a person's well-being, parents have a reason to select for it, even if inequality results.

As noted, at present it is not possible to link attributes such as intelligence to genes in this way and the HFE Act 1990 (as amended) does not contain any express provisions on the matter – instead, the question of whether to license such practices would remain with the HFE Authority, which, given the public ambivalence towards the idea of 'designer babies', may be expected to act cautiously. Interestingly, in another context the Act (as amended) appears to give some endorsement to Savelescu's more radical approach. This is in relation to a prohibition it contains on selecting on social grounds in favour of embryos (or gamete donors) with genes for conditions that are commonly perceived as disabling (the situations contemplated are of deaf couples who might wish to select embryos with the genes for deafness, dwarf couples those with the genes for dwarfism, etc). Section 13(9) of the HFEA 1990 (as amended) provides:

Section 13 Conditions of licences for treatment

. . . (9) Persons or embryos that are known to have a gene, chromosome or mitochondrion abnormality involving a significant risk that a person with the abnormality will have or develop–

---

38 (2001) 15 Bioethics 413.

(a) a serious physical or mental disability,

(b) a serious illness, or

(c) any other serious medical condition,

must not be preferred to those that are not known to have such an abnormality.

As Savelescu notes, such a prohibition – which runs counter to the procreative liberty of the couple, as well as arguments based on diminishing inequality in society – cannot easily be justified by reference to the harm to a hypothetical child who is born with the relevant disability, since otherwise (ie in a case where a non-disabled embryo is selected) that particular child would not exist at all. Instead, its justification appears to be based on something akin to procreative beneficence.

7.2.3.4 Embryonic manipulations

In 7.2.3.3 above, we looked at the use of PGD and the selection between embryos with different attributes it makes possible. However, another possibility – as yet in its scientific infancy – concerns the genetic modification of embryos. This may take the form of 'genetic engineering', in which certain genes are added or replaced, resulting in a new individual, possessing new or enhanced genetic characteristics. Another possibility, and so far more scientifically feasible, is that of 'reproductive cloning', in which a child is produced who is the genetic copy of an existing person. We consider the ethical and legal issues in each case below.

7.2.3.4.1 Genetic engineering

The practice of modifying the genetic content of an embryo is often termed 'positive genetic engineering' (in contrast to the more 'negative' process of selecting embryos from a pool, and discarding those without a particular charateristic, looked at in 7.2.3.3). Sometimes, the manipulation may be aimed at enhancing some desired genetic charateristic; alternatively, it may be done to remove defective genes – known as 'gene therapy' – in a case where embryo selection is not available, eg because all of a couple's embryos are affected by the defect. In either case such manipulations are generally perceived as ethically problematic. The Glover Report in 1989 commented on the issue as follows:

Glover, J et al, Report to the European Commission on Reproductive Technologies,
Fertility and the Family[39]

Safe gene therapy is not yet with us. But it is better to start thinking about the implications of likely technological developments before they arrive. The stage when a technology seems too remote to be worth thinking about has been followed so often by abrupt transition to the stage when it is already out of control . . .

There are real causes for concern about positive genetic engineering, and it is worth bringing them into sharper focus.

One concern is perhaps obvious to any late 20th century European. This is the danger of giving new technological powers to a government with a programme of racist eugenics, or perhaps to one which had some other, not 'race' linked, category of people it regarded as less than fully human. In our countries there is nearly universal revulsion against this kind of outlook. But technology once developed is always available, and it is hard to be sure that such an outlook will never return.

Another cause for concern is not the deliberate use of genetic engineering for perverted ends, but the accidental side effects of well intentioned uses. One problem is that we may overlook some genetic linkage between different characteristics. In choosing, say, genes for high intelligence, we may find we have inadvertently also chosen genes for high levels of

---

39 See n 4 above.

aggression or depression. All technology carries with it the risk of mistakes and unwanted side effects. Here the 'mistakes' will be human beings. There is also the risk of disasters which are irreversible: 'mistaken' genes would be passed on to future generations.

Another problem is that if certain characteristics were frequently selected, those who did not have them might come to be seen as inferior. It may be hard to keep the decent reluctance to see people in terms of some competitive rank ordering, when, in another part of our mind, we are ranking characteristics which may be available for our children.

There are also enormous problems about who would take the decisions. These problems are sometimes gestured at by describing the choice as 'playing God', with the implication that it would take a great deal of presumption to put oneself forward as qualified to choose the genes of another person.

Perhaps, if there were great benefits, we would overcome our reluctance to play God in this way. But there would remain the question of whose decision it should be. Many shudder at the idea of some central government committee taking such decisions. The alternative of parents choosing for their children is much more attractive. But that too has huge unsolved problems. Could parents not sometimes choose disastrously for their children? And suppose too many parents chose the same characteristics? What social limits to their choice would be set, and by what means?

. . . This adds up to a case for saying that positive human genetic engineering is unethical now (or when it becomes available) and will remain so at least until policies have been worked out to cope with the huge problems it raises.

Some of these problems are also present in the case of 'negatively' selecting between embryos on the basis of social charateristics (see 7.2.3.3.4). However, a specific additional one is the risk, noted by Glover, that genetic modifications could have unintended side-effects, damaging the resulting child and/or future generations.

Under the HFE Act 1990 (as amended), genetic engineering (including gene therapy) – assuming it becomes scientifically feasible – remains prohibited pursuant to ss3 and 3ZA, which only countenance the implantation of 'permitted' (ie non-modified) embryos and gametes:

3 Prohibitions in connection with embryos

. . . (2) No person shall place in a woman—

(a) an embryo other than a permitted embryo (as defined by section 3ZA), or

(b) any gametes other than permitted eggs or permitted sperm (as so defined).

. . .

3ZA Permitted eggs, permitted sperm and permitted embryos

(1) This section has effect for the interpretation of section 3(2).

(2) A permitted egg is one –

(a) which has been produced by or extracted from the ovaries of a woman, and

(b) whose nuclear or mitochondrial DNA has not been altered.

(3) Permitted sperm are sperm –

(a) which have been produced by or extracted from the testes of a man, and

(b) whose nuclear or mitochondrial DNA has not been altered.

(4) An embryo is a permitted embryo if –

(a) it has been created by the fertilisation of a permitted egg by permitted sperm,

(b) no nuclear or mitochondrial DNA of any cell of the embryo has been altered, and

(c) no cell has been added to it other than by division of the embryo's own cells.

. . .

7.2.3.4.2 Reproductive cloning

Reproductive cloning entails, first, that an embryo is created which is a genetic copy of an existing individual (through nucleus substitution or cell nuclear replacement) and, secondly, that it is implanted in a woman to be gestated to term. Although in its infancy, such cloning has already successfully been carried out on some mammals. Most famously, 'Dolly' the sheep was produced by CNR cloning at the Roslin Institute, Edinburgh in 1997, and since then other animals have been cloned around the world in the same way.

The notion that human beings might also be cloned in this fashion undoubtedly evokes widespread fear and repugnance. Some of the concerns surrounding reproductive cloning are directly consequentialist in form (relating to the potential well-being, physical or psychological, of the individuals who result from cloning; indeed, the experience with cloned animals, including Dolly the sheep, is that these often suffer from ill-health and die prematurely. Even so – as with embryo selection (though unlike positive genetic engineering) – the invocation of harm in this context may encounter the response that the life of the cloned person is still unlikely to be so bad, for him to prefer (hypothetically) never to have existed at all. Nor are arguments based on the denial of genetic individuality to clones ultimately persuasive, given the widespread existence of identical twins. On the other hand, other objections to the practice of a more intuitive character remain: probably an important aspect, as with other instances of genetic engineering, is the foreboding that, if people were 'manufactured' in this way, deep-rooted notions of human dignity (and perhaps the sanctity of human life itself) might be placed in jeopardy.[40]

As to the law, the HFE Act 1990, as originally enacted, placed a ban on the creation of human clones by nucleus substitution: specifically, (ex) s 3(3)(d) prohibited 'replacing a nucleus of a cell of an embryo' with a nucleus from another person. However, the Parliamentary Draftsman did not foresee the emergence of the newer CNR form of cloning: here a nucleus taken from an adult human is introduced into an unfertilised egg (as opposed to an embryo). Indeed, in R (*On the Application of Bruno Quintavalle on Behalf of Pro-Life Alliance*) v *Secretary of State for Health*,[41] the High Court found that CNR cloning fell outside the scope of the 1990 Act altogether, meaning not only was it not prohibited, but that the HFE Authority was powerless to control it by licence. In immediate response to that decision (later reversed by the higher courts[42]), Parliament enacted a short Act, the Human Reproductive Cloning Act 2001, to make it clear that CNR-produced embryos could not be used for reproductive cloning. Section 1(1) of the 2001 Act provided:

1 The offence

(1)   A person who places in a woman a human embryo which has been created otherwise than by fertilisation is guilty of an offence.

In fact, the 2001 Act has now been repealed as part of the 2008 amendments to the HFE Act 1990. This is because, pursuant to ss 3 and 3ZA of the amended Act (see section 7.2.1 above), a CNR-produced embryo is not a 'permitted embryo' and so could not in any event be implanted in a woman.

At the same time, it should be emphasised that the above provisions do not prevent the creation of cloned embryos by CNR for research purposes (so-called 'therapeutic cloning'), a matter looked at further in section 7.3.3 below.

---

40   See Robertson, J, 'Liberty, identity, and human cloning' (1998) 76 Texas L Rev 1371, for a careful analysis of the various issues.
41   [2001] EWHC Admin 918.
42   See n 7 above.

SELF-TEST QUESTION

If it is acceptable for parents to use PGD to prevent a child suffering a significant genetic disadvantage, then (once this is safe) should they not equally have access to techniques of genetic enhancement, to advantage the child?

7.3 Embryo Research

7.3.1 Background

The creation of human embryos *ex vivo* opens up significant opportunities for the conduct of medical research. Nevertheless, for many people the possibility of such research is one of the most troubling aspects of the advance in reproductive technology, more so than, for example, simply allowing spare or unwanted embryos – left over from IVF treatment – to perish. Why this should be so is a complex question, which is inextricably linked to our attitudes towards unborn human life in general. In *A Question of Life*, Mary Warnock commented as follows:

Warnock, M, *A Question of Life*[43]

There was, however, a more testing kind of question [than the issue of regulating fertility treatment], infinitely more important, in my opinion.

This was the question of research using human embryos . . . Utilitarianism could . . . by itself, provide no solution, simply because the very question at issue was whether or not embryos count as those whose harms and benefits, pleasures and pains, have to be thrown into the balance to be weighed against the benefits or harms to society as a whole. But here we had, it seemed, an issue on which legislation must be foreseen, and must be enacted quickly. No one felt inclined to argue that the decision whether or not to embark on research with the use of human embryos was a matter of personal conscience, as they might in the case of [donor insemination], surrogacy, or, for that matter, homosexuality between adults. Everyone agreed that this was a matter on which there must be legislation, and that whether and to what extent embryos should be used must be a decision for the law.

It is certainly true that the moral permissibility of embryo research turns upon the issue of the embryo's moral status in a particularly direct way. This is because, unlike the case of 'spare embryos' allowed to perish following IVF treatment carried out for an infertile couple, or that of embryos/foetuses destroyed through abortion, the rights/interests of identifiable, fully fledged individuals are not directly implicated. To the extent that the view of embryo-as-person is rejected, such research may appear acceptable in principle. On the other hand, as argued by John Robertson, other problems – notably the symbolic damage it may cause – remain:

See Chapter 8

Robertson, JA, *Children of Choice*[44]

. . . [C]reating embryos for research and then discard deserves protection only if other important interests are served that justify whatever symbolic costs deliberate creation and discard of embryos entails. The purpose here is to increase knowledge of how to treat infertility, improve contraception, and treat or prevent cancer or birth defects. With cryopreservation of

---

43 See n 2 above.
44 Ewing, New Jersey: Princeton UP, 1994.

extra embryos limiting the number donated for research, a policy against creating embryos solely for research and discard could greatly limit the amount of embryo research. Research with embryos would then occur only with spare embryos created as a byproduct of IVF treatment of infertility, which may be too few to meet all research needs, with the result that important research across a range of fields is lost. The symbolic benefits of protecting embryos from being created solely for research purposes does not appear to justify this loss. If the embryo is so rudimentary that research on excess, discarded embryos does not harm them and is permissible, there would appear to be no additional harm to embryos from creating them for this purpose only. In both cases research will occur at the same stage of development, and thus no added harm would occur from deliberate creation of embryos for research purposes.

Opponents, however, would argue that additional symbolic harm arises from creating embryos solely to be vehicles of research and then discarded. Additional symbolic harm results because creating embryos with the intent to discard them demonstrates a profound disrespect for the earliest stages of human life. This practice permits human life to be created, manipulated, and discarded for utilitarian purposes, without regard to the embryo's own interests or potential. The deliberateness of the act – creating new human life only to destroy it – is thus viewed as symbolically more offensive than research on excess embryos created as a byproduct of the IVF process of treating infertility.

7.3.2 The 1990 Legal Framework

Although, as noted in section 7.2.3.1, the Warnock Committee avoided taking a view as to the personhood or otherwise of the embryo, it concluded that 'the status of the embryo is a matter of fundamental principle which should be enshrined in legislation' (para 11.17). This recommendation was followed in the HFE Act 1990, which in s 3(3)(a) prohibited 'keeping or using' an embryo after the appearance of the 'primitive streak'. According to s 3(4) this was deemed to occur no later than 14 days after the initial creation of the embryo (not counting any periods of storage). The effect of these provisions was thus to outlaw any research on embryos more than two weeks old.

As the Warnock Report had noted, the formation of the primitive streak marks that stage in embryonic development when a new individual entity is first discernible:

> **Warnock Committee, *Report of the Committee of Inquiry into Human Fertilisation and Embryology*[45]**
>
> 11.5 The first of these features is the primitive streak, which appears as a heaping up of cells at one end of the embryonic disc on the 14th or 15th day after fertilisation. Two primitive streaks may form in a single embryonic disc. This is the latest stage at which identical twins can occur. The primitive streak is the first of several identifiable features which develop in and from the embryonic disc during the succeeding days, a period of very rapid change in the embryonic configuration. By the 17th day the neural groove appears and by the 22nd to 23rd day this has developed to become the neural folds, which in turn start to fuse and form the recognisable antecedent of the spinal cord.

As for research on embryos within the first 14 days, this could be carried out (with the consent of the gamete providers) subject to the researcher having a research licence from the HFE Authority.

---

45 See n 1 above.

In granting a licence the Authority needed to be satisfied that the research was 'necessary or desirable' for one of the purposes specified in Sch 2, para 3 of the 1990 Act. Originally these included promoting infertility treatment, increasing knowledge about congenital diseases, and improving techniques of contraception.

Subsequently, in 2001, several new research purposes were added by Statutory Instrument,[46] which included increasing knowledge about, and developing treatments for, serious disease. The reason for this change (which followed a report by the Chief Medical Officer's Expert Group, *Stem Cell Research: Medical Progress with Responsibility*[47]) was to allow research into embryonic stem cells, including those generated by the technique of CNR (Cell Nuclear Transfer). Possibly, in the future, this technique could be used, in conjunction with cells taken from particular patients, to clone replacement organs and tissue for them. As the Human Genetics Advisory Commission (HGAC) and the HFE Authority commented in their report, *Cloning Issues in Reproduction, Science and Medicine*:

HGAC and HFE Authority, *Cloning Issues in Reproduction, Science and Medicine*[48]

5.3 The most likely objective of a research project involving the use of CNR would be to create a cultured cell line for the purposes of cell or tissue therapy. People who have tissues or organs damaged by injury or disease (eg, skin, heart muscle, nervous tissue) could provide their own somatic nuclei and, by using these to replace nuclei in their own or donated eggs, individual stem cells (not embryos) could be produced in culture. These cells could then be induced (by exposure to appropriate growth factors) to form whichever type of cell or tissue was required for therapeutic purposes with no risk of tissue rejection and no need for treatment of the patient with immunosuppressive drugs.

As noted in section 7.2.3.4, CNR is a form of cloning in which a nucleus from an adult human cell is placed in an unfertilised, denucleated egg. The egg is then stimulated artificially to begin the process of division and embryo-formation. As we saw, the legality of CNR cloning – and the HFE Authority's ability to regulate it – was the subject of legal challenge in R (*On the Application of Bruno Quintavalle on Behalf of Pro-Life Alliance*) v *Secretary of State for Health*.[49] Ultimately the lawfulness of the procedure was confirmed by the higher courts, and the House of Lords Select Committee on *Stem Cell Research*, which reported in 2002, gave the HFE Authority the 'green light' to begin licensing such research. At the same time the Committee stressed the need for fully informed consent from the donors of the genetic material, and that the 14-day time limit on all forms of research involving human embryos should remain.[50]

A further, controversial, matter in relation to stem cell research following CNR cloning, relates to the technique's reliance in many cases (given the shortage of human eggs) on denucleated animal eggs – leading to the creation of embryos containing some mitochondrial animal DNA. In 2008 the question of whether these amounted to hybrid animal-human embryos (prohibited by the terms of the 1990 Act) was the subject of another (unsuccessful) legal challenge by the pressure group CORE.[51] As we shall see below, the use of such embryos for stem-cell research was subsequently an issue addressed by the amendments made to the HFE Act in 2008.

---

46 Human Fertilisation and Embryology (Research Purposes) Regulations 2001, SI 2001/188. As discussed in section 7.3.3, the Regulations have now been superseded by the 2008 amendments to the HFE Act 1990.
47 London: Department of Health, 2000.
48 HGAC & HFEA, London: December 1998.
49 [2003] UKHL 13; see text at nn 41–42 above.
50 The full report is available at www.parliament.the-stationery-office.co.uk/pa/ld200102/ldselect/ldstem/83/8301.htm.
51 R (*on the application of Quintavalle and CLC*) v *HFEA* [2008] EWHC 3395 (Admin).

7.3.3 Embryo Research following the 2008 Amendments to the HFE Act

7.3.3.1 Permissible research purposes

The 2008 changes to the HFE Act have consolidated and extended the purposes for which licensed research may be conducted upon embryos. These are listed in Sch 2, para 3A as follows:

3A (1) A licence under paragraph 3 cannot authorise any activity unless the activity appears to the Authority–

   (a) to be necessary or desirable for any of the purposes specified in sub-paragraph (2) ('the principal purposes'),

   (b) to be necessary or desirable for the purpose of providing knowledge that, in the view of the Authority, may be capable of being applied for the purposes specified in sub-paragraph (2)(a) or (b), or

   (c) to be necessary or desirable for such other purposes as may be specified in regulations.

(2) The principal purposes are–

   (a) increasing knowledge about serious disease or other serious medical conditions,

   (b) developing treatments for serious disease or other serious medical conditions,

   (c) increasing knowledge about the causes of any congenital disease or congenital medical condition that does not fall within paragraph (a),

   (d) promoting advances in the treatment of infertility,

   (e) increasing knowledge about the causes of miscarriage,

   (f) developing more effective techniques of contraception,

   (g) developing methods for detecting the presence of gene, chromosome or mitochondrion abnormalities in embryos before implantation, or

   (h) increasing knowledge about the development of embryos.

Here, the references in sub-para (2) to research aimed at improving knowledge of and treatments for 'other serious medical conditions' (as well as disease in the narrower sense) makes it clear that new treatments for spinal cord injuries are now a permissible goal of research – this could potentially be an important application for stem-cell replacement therapy. At the same time, as sub-para (1) stipulates, the HFE Authority may only grant a licence in cases where it is satisfied that the proposed research is necessary or desirable for promoting one of the purposes. Indeed, this is augmented by a yet stricter necessity test in Sch 2, sub-para 3(5), which provides that: 'No licence under this paragraph is to be granted unless the Authority is satisfied that any proposed use of embryos or human admixed embryos is necessary for the purposes of the research.'

The effect of this last provision is that the HFE Authority must be satisfied that the research could not be carried out effectively using non-embryonic materials. This condition may become harder to satisfy in the future in the light of recent scientific progress in using adult cells, reprogrammed to behave like embryonic stem-cells, as a substitute for the latter. At present, though, the need in general for recourse to embryonic cells in this area of science remains.

7.3.3.2 The use of 'human admixed embryos' in stem-cell research

As noted earlier, the comparative shortage of human eggs has led to pressure to employ eggs from animals (such as cows, mice or rabbits) to create embryos by CNR-cloning for use in stem-cell research. In fact the resulting embryos will be largely human, since as part of the cloning process, the animal nucleus of the egg is removed and replaced by a human cell. Nonetheless, some mitochondrial animal DNA will remain in the outer membrane of the egg.

The question of whether the creation of such 'hybrid' embryos, ostensibly prohibited by the 1990 Act (albeit not in the specific context of CNR-cloning – which did not then exist), should be permitted, was the subject of fierce public and parliamentary debate in the run-up to the 2008 amendments to the Act. Originally, the Government itself favoured a ban on such creations; however, due to arguments brought to bear by the scientific lobby, it changed its view and accepted an amendent to the Bill (which became the 2008 Act) as it passed through Parliament.[52] In the result, s4A of the HFE Act 1990 (as amended) provides for the creation of hybrid embryos for research – which it terms 'human admixed embryos' – as follows:

4 A Prohibitions in connection with genetic material not of human origin

(2) No person shall—

(a)   mix human gametes with animal gametes,

(b)   bring about the creation of a human admixed embryo, or

(c)   keep or use a human admixed embryo,

except in pursuance of a licence.

. . .

(6) For the purposes of this Act a human admixed embryo is—

(a)   an embryo created by replacing the nucleus of an animal egg or of an animal cell, or two animal pronuclei, with—

    (i)   two human pronuclei,

    (ii)   one nucleus of a human gamete or of any other human cell, or

    (iii) one human gamete or other human cell,

(b)   any other embryo created by using—

    (i)   human gametes and animal gametes, or

    (ii)   one human pronucleus and one animal pronucleus,

(c)   a human embryo that has been altered by the introduction of any sequence of nuclear or mitochondrial DNA of an animal into one or more cells of the embryo,

(d)   a human embryo that has been altered by the introduction of one or more animal cells, or

(e)   any embryo not falling within paragraphs (a) to (d) which contains both nuclear or mito-chondrial DNA of a human and nuclear or mitochondrial DNA of an animal ('animal DNA') but in which the animal DNA is not predominant.

The terms of this provision are in fact of wider application than to CNR-cloned embryos using denucleated animal eggs (covered under s 4A(6)(a)). Thus, as per sub-s(6)(b), it is apparent that other forms of hybrid – this time composed of equal amounts of animal and human DNA – will also qualify as 'human admixed embryos', and may thus be created under licence. On the other hand, what is equally clear is that their only possible use would be in research: the placing of such embryos in a woman (or for that matter in an animal) for gestation is expressly forbidden by s 4A(1) and (4), respectively. Nor, for good measure, will such an embryo meet the definition of 'permitted embryo' under s3ZA of the Act (see section 7.2.3.4 above).

7.3.3.3 Time limits and consent issues

As discussed in section 7.3.2, following the recommendations of the Warnock Report, the original 1990 Act prohibited research upon human embryos that are older than 14 days. This time-limit has been retained in the amendments to the 1990 Act (under s3(3)), while s4A(3) also extends it to human admixed embryos:

4A (3) A licence cannot authorise keeping or using a human admixed embryo after the earliest of the following—

(a)   the appearance of the primitive streak, or

---

52 See Fox, M, 'The Human Fertilisation and Embryology Act 2008: Tinkering at the Margins', n 8 above.

(b) the end of the period of 14 days beginning with the day on which the process of creating the human admixed embryo began, but not counting any time during which the human admixed embryo is stored.

A final important issue in relation to embryo research concerns the consent of the (human) gamete providers to the use of their genetic material in this way. In line with the generally strict consent requirements that characterise the HFE legislative scheme (see 7.2.2.3), here too the 1990 Act (as amended) stipulates in Sch 3, para 2 the need, normally, for fully informed written consent on the part of the providers. In relation to research involving stem cells the HFE Authority's Code of Practice (8th edn) suggests in para 22.7 that providers should be made aware that their consent will allow use to be made of their cells indefinitely (including after their death). Equally, they should appreciate that they personally are extremely unlikely to benefit (either medically or financially) from the research.

Nonetheless the HFE Act 1990 (as amended) provides for an exception to the need for consent in relation to mentally incapacitated persons, where research using their cells may increase knowledge into and/or treatments for a condition or disease from which they suffer. As provided for in Sch 3, paras 15B *et seq* this is subject to a number of limiting conditions, including that the research cannot be carried out equally effectively using the cells of competent persons:

Adults lacking capacity: exemption relating to use of human cells etc.

15B (1) If, in relation to the proposed use under a licence of the human cells of a person who has attained the age of 18 years ('P'), the Authority is satisfied–

(a) that the conditions in paragraph 15C are met, . . .

the Authority may in the licence authorise the application of this paragraph in relation to P.

(2) Where a licence authorises the application of this paragraph, this Schedule does not require the consent of P–

(a) to the use (whether during P's life or after P's death) of P's human cells to bring about the creation in vitro of an embryo or human admixed embryo for use for the purposes of a project of research, . . .

Consent to use of human cells etc. not required: adult lacking capacity

15C (1) The conditions referred to in paragraph 15B(1)(a) are as follows.

(2) Condition A is that P suffers from, or is likely to develop, a serious disease, a serious physical or mental disability or any other serious medical condition.

(3) Condition B is that P lacks capacity to consent to the use of P's human cells to bring about the creation in vitro of an embryo or human admixed embryo for use for the purposes of a project of research.

(4) Condition C is that the person responsible under the licence has no reason to believe that P had refused such consent at a time when P had that capacity.

(5) Condition D is that it appears unlikely that P will at some time have that capacity.

(6) Condition E is that any embryo or human admixed embryo to be created in vitro is to be used for the purposes of a project of research which is intended to increase knowledge about–

(a) the disease, disability or medical condition mentioned in sub-paragraph (2) or any similar disease, disability or medical condition, or

(b) the treatment of, or care of persons affected by, that disease, disability or medical condition or any similar disease, disability or medical condition.

(7) Condition F is that there are reasonable grounds for believing that research of comparable effectiveness cannot be carried out if the only human cells that can be used to bring about the creation in vitro of embryos or human admixed embryos for use for the purposes of the project are the human cells of persons who–

(a) have attained the age of 18 years and have capacity to consent to the use of their human cells to bring about the creation in vitro of an embryo or human admixed embryo for use for the purposes of the project, or

(b) have not attained that age but are competent to deal with the issue of consent to such use of their human cells.

In the case of children under the age of 18, provisions dispensing with the need for consent are found in Sch 3, para 15A, which allow for parental consent instead (subject to similar, stringent conditions).

 SELF-TEST QUESTION:

Do the consent provisions in the HFE legislation, as regards what kind of research gamete providers permit their genetic material to be used for, serve any real purpose (in terms of protecting some recognisable interest)?

7.4 Collaborative Reproduction

7.4.1 Background

The term 'collaborative reproduction' (borrowed from John Robertson[53]) describes situations in which a third party (who will have no parental role in nurturing the child) assists in the production of the child. Such assistance may come either through the donation of gametes and embryos, or (in the case of a woman) the provision of her uterus to gestate the child. The latter practice, known as surrogacy, raises particular problems and will accordingly be dealt with separately in section 7.5 below. For the time being we shall restrict our discussion to issues centring on gamete/embryo donation; useful summaries of the key techniques can be found in the Warnock Report:

> **Warnock Committee,** *Report of the Committee of Inquiry into Human Fertilisation and Embryology*[54]
>
> **I Artificial insemination**
>
> 4.1 The term artificial insemination (AI) is used to refer to the placing of semen inside a woman's vagina or uterus by means other than sexual intercourse. The principle of this tech-nique has been known for centuries in the veterinary context. The simplicity of artificial insem-ination contrasts sharply with the technical complexity of more recent developments such as *in vitro* fertilisation. It begins with the collection of semen from the husband or a donor, through masturbation. The semen is either placed in the upper part of the vagina next to the cervix or injected into the uterus through a fine catheter. Insemination is undertaken near the predicted time of ovulation, the time in a woman's menstrual cycle when she has the highest chance of conceiving. The semen used may be fresh or it may have been previously frozen and thawed before use . . .
>
> **II Artificial insemination by donor (AID)**
>
> 4.6 Artificial insemination by donor (AID) may be used when investigations have shown the husband to be sterile or to have significantly reduced fertility, or it may be used for the avoid-

---

53 See Robertson, J, *Children of Choice*, n 44 above.
54 See n 1 above.

ance of hereditary diseases when these are carried by the male . . . In this procedure the woman is inseminated with semen from a donor. [NB: *Today the more common term for this type of treatment is 'Donor Insemination' (DI).*]

. . .

III Egg donation

6.1 Egg donation . . . may help those women who cannot themselves produce an egg. It may also help those who would be candidates for IVF except that in their case egg collection is impossible because their ovaries are inaccessible. About 5% of infertile couples might benefit from the technique. A mature egg is recovered from a fertile woman donor, for example, during sterilisation, and is fertilised *in vitro*, using the semen of the husband of the infertile woman. The resulting embryo is then transferred to the patient's uterus. If it implants she may then carry the pregnancy to term. There are other situations where eggs might be donated. When a woman is herself undergoing infertility treatment and several eggs have been recovered from her, she may be prepared to donate one or more eggs to another woman whose infertility can be treated only by egg donation.

. . .

IV Embryo donation

7.1 Embryo donation would help the same groups of women who might benefit from egg donation and, more particularly, the even smaller number whose husbands are also infertile. Embryo donation may take two forms. One involves the donation of both egg and semen. The donated egg is fertilised *in vitro* with donated semen and the resulting embryo transferred to a woman who is unable to produce an egg herself and whose husband is infertile. The second method, known as lavage, does not involve removing the egg by surgical intervention. Instead the egg is released naturally from the ovary at the normal time in the donor's menstrual cycle. At the predicted time of ovulation she is artificially inseminated with semen from the husband of the infertile woman (or from a donor if the husband is also infertile). Some three to four days later, before the start of implantation, the donor's uterus is 'washed out' and any embryo retrieved is then transferred to the uterus of the infertile woman. If the embryo implants successfully the recipient carries the pregnancy to term.

According to statistics published by the HFE Authority, licensed donor-assisted conception has to date been responsible for the births of some 20,000 children in the UK. However, the proportion of such births relative to the total number of children resulting from licensed fertility treatment has declined significantly; thus, for example, in 1992 there were 1,703 births involving donated gametes/embryos, and 2,031 live births not involving donation; in 2006, the respective figures were 1,128 and 9,610.[55] As the HFE Authority has noted, a key reason for this change has been the development of the newer ICSI variant of IVF treatment (see section 7.2.1 above), which has reduced the need for recourse to donated sperm. Instead it appears that today, where donated sperm is used, this is often to provide children for women in single-sex partnerships.

The potential for techniques of collaborative reproduction to alter the traditional picture of the heterosexual, two-parent family is one – though not the only – reason why this field of medicine tends to generate controversy. As John Robertson has written:

Robertson, JA, *Children of Choice*[56]

Resort to donor gametes or surrogates is not an easy choice for infertile couples. The decision arises after previous efforts at pregnancy have failed, thus confronting the couple with the fact

---

55 See www.hfea.gov.uk/donor-conception-births.html.
56 See n 44 above.

of one or both partners' infertility. A collaborative technique is chosen because it offers an opportunity to have a child who is the biologic offspring of one or, in the case of egg donation and gestational surrogacy, both partners. Yet collaborative reproduction occurs in an uncertain ethical, legal, and social milieu, where social practices and legal rules are still largely unclear.

A basic commitment to procreative liberty – to the freedom to have and rear offspring – should presumptively protect most forms of collaborative reproduction. After all, collaborative reproduction occurs for the same reason as IVF: the couple is infertile and cannot produce offspring. They need donor or surrogate assistance if they are to have children. Even if both rearing partners are not reproducing in the strict genetic sense, at least one partner will have a genetic or gestational relationship with their child. The same techniques may also be sought by a single woman or a same-sex couple that wishes to have offspring. In a few cases, donor gametes are used to avoid genetic handicap in offspring.

Despite its clear link to procreative choice, collaborative reproduction often generates controversy and even calls for prohibition. Collaborative reproduction is problematic because it intrudes a third party a donor or surrogate – into the usual situation of two party parenthood, and separates or deconstructs the traditional genetic, gestational, and social unity of reproduction. A child could in theory end up with three different biologic parents (a genetic mother, a gestational mother, a genetic father) and two separate rearing parents, with various combinations among them. Such collaboration risks confusing offspring about who their 'true' parent is and creating conflict about parental rights and duties.

In what follows we consider the law on gamete and/or embryo donation as it bears in turn on the interests of the immediate parties to such an enterprise, namely the potential nurturing parent(s), the gamete donor(s), and any child who is born as a result. This is an area of law that has been sensitive to shifting social attitudes, and, as we shall see, there have been some significant changes in recent years – not least in the 2008 amendments to the HFE legislation – which have rebalanced (and to a degree reconceptualised) the key interests at stake.

7.4.2 The potential nurturing parent(s)

7.4.2.1 Access to treatment

Pursuant to s 4(1) of HFEA 1990 (as amended), infertility treatment involving the use of third party gametes may only be carried out under licence. (The same condition applies to donated embryos by virtue of s 3 of the Act.) The first major issue is who should be eligible for such treatment? In particular, should it be limited to those in a traditional heterosexual marriage who are unable to reproduce by reason of medical infertility, or may it be given also to single persons or homosexual couples whose 'infertility' results from their lifestyle? The Warnock Committee had the following to say on the matter:

Warnock Committee, *Report of the Committee of Inquiry into Human Fertilisation and Embryology*[57]

2.9 . . . [T]he various techniques for assisted reproduction offer not only a remedy for infertility, but also offer the fertile single woman or lesbian couple the chance of parenthood without the direct involvement of a male partner. To judge from the evidence, many believe that the interests of the child dictate that it should be born into a home where there is a loving, stable,

---

57 See n 1 above.

heterosexual relationship and that, therefore, the *deliberate* creation of a child for a woman who is not a partner in such a relationship is morally wrong. On the other side some expressed the view that a single woman or lesbian couple have a right under the European Convention to have children even though those children may have no legal father. It is further argued that it is already accepted that a single person, whether man or woman, can in certain circumstances provide a suitable environment for a child, since the existence of single adoptive parents is specifically provided for in the Children Act 1975.

2.10 In the same way that a single woman may believe she has a right to motherhood, so a single man may feel he has a right to fatherhood. Though the feminist position is perhaps more frequently publicised, we were told of a group of single, mainly homosexual, men who were campaigning for the right to bring up a child. Their primary aim at present is to obtain in practice equal rights in the adoption field, but they are also well aware of the potential of surrogacy for providing a single man with a child that is genetically his. There have been cases in other countries of surrogacy in such circumstances. It can be argued that, as a matter of sex equality, if single women are not totally barred from parenthood, then neither should single men be so barred.

2.11 We have considered these arguments, but, nevertheless, we believe that as a general rule it is better for children to be born into a two-parent family, with both father and mother, although we recognise that it is impossible to predict with any certainty how lasting such a relationship will be.

Although the Warnock Committee stopped short of making specific recommendations on this point, its attitudes were reflected by the insertion into the HFE Act 1990 of s 13(5), which – as originally drafted – required the clinic, in considering the welfare of the future child, 'to have regard to [its] need . . . for a father'. This provision, with its clear bias against lesbian couples, remained controversial, and in practice was ignored by clinics. (As noted in 7.2.2.1 above, the general idea underlying s 13(5) that the potential child's welfare may dictate that it should never exist at all, is implausible save in extreme cases, and the marginal disadvantage (if any) of having two female parents is clearly not one of them.)

As one of the 2008 changes to the 1990 Act, this aspect of s 13(5) has now been replaced by the requirement on clinics to take account of the child's need for 'supportive parenting'. This has been elaborated on in para 8.11 of the HFE Authority in its Code of Practice as follows:

HFEA Code of Practice

8.11 When considering a child's need for supportive parenting, centres should consider the following definition:

'Supportive parenting is a commitment to the health, well being and development of the child. It is presumed that all prospective parents will be supportive parents, in the absence of any reasonable cause for concern that any child who may be born, or any other child, may be at risk of significant harm or neglect. Where centres have concern as to whether this commitment exists, they may wish to take account of wider family and social networks within which the child will be raised.'

Also pertinent here is the non-discrimination provision contained in para 8.7 of the Code:

8.7 Those seeking treatment are entitled to a fair assessment. The centre is expected to consider the wishes of all those involved, and the assessment must be done in a non-discriminatory way.

In particular, patients should not be discriminated against on grounds of gender, race, disability, sexual orientation, religious belief or age.[58]

As was suggested in 7.2.2.1, in respect of a couple seeking fertility treatment for themselves, an action in judicial review may lie against refusal of treatment by an NHS clinic: see Ex p Harriott (1988),[59] and this avenue would clearly be available also to a lesbian couple, seeking treatment with donor sperm. As noted too, following the enactment of the Human Rights Act 1998, the right to found a family – including through recourse to fertility treatment – has been recognised by the courts as protected by the European Convention on Human Rights: R v SS for the Home Department, ex p Mellor (2002),[60] and a decision to deny treatment will require justification under Art 8(2) ECHR. In principle, a judicial review action could thus be brought by a single woman – in particular if a clinic were to interpret 13(5), and its invocation of 'supportive parenting', in such a way as to mandate a refusal of treatment. It is arguable that such a 'blanket approach' to what is already a philosophically shaky provision could not be justified; more defensible, given the general impor- tance attached to motherhood, might be such a policy in respect of single or homosexual males – but here too the arguments are by no means clear-cut.[61]

At the same time, a more general, underlying constraint on the ability of persons to procure fertility treatment should not be forgotten, namely the requirement that they can pay for it. At present, only a minority of clinics offering such treatment are financed as part of the National Health Service, and waiting lists are predictably long. In this regard, the main concern of NHS clinics presented with, for example, a single woman desiring fertility treatment, is likely to be whether their limited resources should be expended on those who are 'socially' as opposed to 'medically' infertile.[62]

7.4.2.2 Counselling and information requirements

As in the case of a couple seeking IVF treatment using their own gametes (see 7.2.2.2), those seeking treatment involving donated gametes are required to be offered counselling pursuant to s 13(6) of the 1990 Act. However, in addition, s 13A will apply, which (in conjunction with Part II of Sch 3ZA) sets out specific counselling and information requirements in cases where the husband or partner of the carrying mother will – in agreeing to her treatment – be signalling their willing- ness to be a legal parent of the child. Arguably, the need for counselling in such a case is particu- larly pressing. The parents must of necessity accept the fact of their infertility as a couple and, where the infertility is specifically attributable to one partner, the latter's possible reaction to nurturing a child not genetically his or her own must be canvassed.

In respect of egg donation, which commonly occurs within families (eg between sisters), the identity of the donor will often be known to the nurturing parents. In other cases, they will be provided with non-identifying information that nevertheless gives them an idea of the donor's genetic characteristics. According to the HFE Authority Code of Practice:

HFEA Code of Practice

20.1 The centre should give people seeking treatment with donated gametes or embryos:

a)   relevant non-identifying information about donors whose gametes are available to them, including the goodwill message and the pen-portrait (if available), and

---

58 See n 14 above.
59 See n 15 above.
60 See n 18 above.
61 An added complication for solely male applicants is their need to use a surrogacy arrangement. Surrogacy is looked at in section 7.5 below.
62 The prioritising of the clinically infertile is presupposed by the relevant NICE guidance, Fertility: assessment and treatment of people with fertility problems (Clinical Guideline 11, February 2004).

b) relevant information about genetic inheritance and, in particular, the likelihood of inheriting physical characteristics from the donor.

Under paras 20.3 and 20.4, clinics should also inform the prospective parents of the genetic and other screening that has occurred in relation to the donated gametes (including the limitations on such screening).

A key further issue in this field concerns how the parents later approach the subject of the child's genetic identity with the child. Admittedly this problem does not arise in the increasing proportion of cases where same-sex female couples or single women, make use of gamete donation; here it will be clear to the child that its genetic and nurturing parents differ. However, in cases involving heterosexual couples, the evidence in the 20 years since the enactment of the HFE Act 1990 is that most parents who make use of such treatment do not tell the child; this is arguably no longer a tenable position, given the recent abolition of donor anonymity (see 7.4.3.2 below), as well as the increasing importance for a person's medical treatment of accurate genetic information derived from their family history.

In this regard, the 2008 changes to the 1990 Act stop short of compelling the nurturing parents to inform the child of the use of donated gametes in its conception – that itself might well be thought an intrusive and heavy-handed approach. However, s 13(6C) places clinics under a duty to make clear to the parents the desirability of being open with their children in this matter:

Conditions of licences for treatment

13 (6C) In the case of treatment services falling within paragraph 1 of Schedule 3ZA (use of gametes of a person not receiving those services) or paragraph 3 of that Schedule (use of embryo taken from a woman not receiving those services), the information provided by virtue of subsection (6) or (6A) must include such information as is proper about–

(a) the importance of informing any resulting child at an early age that the child results from the gametes of a person who is not a parent of the child, and

(b) suitable methods of informing such a child of that fact.

The HFE Authority's Code of Practice elaborates upon this requirement in paras 20.7 and 20.8, as follows:

HFEA Code of Practice[63]

20.7 The centre should tell people who seek treatment with donated gametes or embryos that it is best for any resulting child to be told about their origin early in childhood. There is evidence that finding out suddenly, later in life, about donor origins can be emotionally damaging to children and to family relations.

20.8 The centre should encourage and prepare patients to be open with their children from an early age about how they were conceived. The centre should give patients information about how counselling may allow them to explore the implications of treatment, in particular how information may be shared with any resultant children.

7.4.2.3 Legal status vis à vis child

It is self-evident that a couple (or, indeed, a single person) that seeks fertility treatment, involving the use of third party gametes/embryos, will be concerned about the legitimacy of any child born as a result. Indeed, the attitude of the law towards this issue may be one of the most significant factors taken into account by would-be nurturing parents when deciding whether to opt for

---

63 See n 14 above.

treatment in the first place. The original response of the legislature was contained in ss 27–28 of the HFEA 1990, and these provisions continue to remain valid for parents treated with donated gametes or embryos prior to April 2009. As regards treatment after that date, new rules, set out in ss 33–47 (comprising the self-standing Part II) of the HFE Act 2008 operate. In what follows we shall consider both the old and new legal positions, but with an emphasis on the innovations (and their rationale), contained in the 2008 Act.

7.4.2.3.1 Legal motherhood

First, as regards motherhood, the effect of s27 of the 1990 Act is that the woman who received the gametes or embryo, and gestated the child to term, is its legal mother. This applies whether or not she had her treatment in the UK or elsewhere. Conversely, in no case will the egg or embryo donor be regarded as the mother. The only ways to effect a subsequent change in status, are through adoption proceedings or by obtaining a parental order.

This approach has been re-enacted, in respect of post-April 2009 fertility treatment, by s 33 of the HFE Act 2008:

33 Meaning of 'mother'

(1) The woman who is carrying or has carried a child as a result of the placing in her of an embryo or of sperm and eggs, and no other woman, is to be treated as the mother of the child.

(2) Subsection (1) does not apply to any child to the extent that the child is treated by virtue of adoption as not being the woman's child.

(3) Subsection (1) applies whether the woman was in the United Kingdom or elsewhere at the time of the placing in her of the embryo or the sperm and eggs.

By contrast, matters are more complex in relation to determining the child's legal father. Here it is useful to consider the 1990 and 2008 Acts separately, as they bear respectively upon pre- and post-April 2009 instances of collaborative reproduction:

7.4.2.3.2 Fatherhood in cases before April 2009

The rules under s 28 of the HFE Act 1990 drew (draw) a distinction according to whether or not the woman treated with donated gametes or embryos was married at the time. If so, under s 28(2) the presumption of legitimacy applied, making her husband the legal father of the child, unless it was shown that he did not consent to the treatment. In respect of unmarried women, s 28(3)(a) conferred fatherhood upon the man together with whom the woman sought out fertility treatment. In other cases, eg where she received the treatment alone, the child would be legally fatherless: s 28(6) expressly made clear that the donor who provided the sperm would not be considered the child's father.

The fatherhood provisions in the 1990 Act have occupied the courts on more than one occasion. Thus in the well-known case of The Leeds Teaching Hospitals NHS Trust v Mr A, Mrs A et al,[64] the High Court was required to consider the effect of s 28(2) in circumstances – scarcely foreseeable by the parliamentary draftsman – of a mistake at a fertility clinic, which led to a woman, Mrs A, receiving sperm not as planned from Mr A, her husband, but from a Mr B. For his part, Mr B had given his sperm for the treatment of his wife, Mrs B. In determining the paternity of the resulting twins, Dame Elizabeth Butler-Sloss P held that the mistake as to the identity of the embryos vitiated Mr A's consent so that he was not the father under s 28(2). Instead, Mr B was their father at common law (it would have been otherwise if Mr B had been a sperm donor – there s 28(6)(a) would have removed his paternity; however, he had not consented to the use of his sperm to treat anyone but Mrs B).

---

64 [2003] EWHC 259 (Fam).

Difficulty also arose in relation to s 28(3), with its recourse to the concept of 'treatment services provided for [the woman] and a man together' to impute fatherhood to unmarried partners. In *Evans v Amicus Healthcare Ltd*, Thorpe and Sedley LJJ interpreted this to mean 'the couple are united in their pursuit of treatment, whatever may otherwise be the nature of the relationship between them'.[65] However, the case of *Re D (a child appearing by her guardian ad litem) (Respondent)*[66] highlights the potential for residual uncertainty. Here a woman received IVF treatment, involving donor sperm at a licensed fertility clinic after she and her partner had provided the requisite consents. She later returned for a further course of treatment, accompanied by a man whom the clinic took to be the original partner (and did not ask to re-consent), but who was in fact a different man. When that treatment resulted in the birth of a child, the original partner argued that, as the consent-provider, he was the baby's father under s 28(3). Though it rejected this contention, the House of Lords acknowledged the Act's vagueness here; Lord Walker commented:

Lord Walker of Gestingthorpe: [25]. The . . . problem is understanding what the [section] means in a case where the woman eventually becomes pregnant as a result of IVF with embryos created with donor sperm. In a case of that sort the infertile male partner does not receive any positive treatment of any kind (although he may have undergone tests, and received counselling, at an earlier stage). This problem would arise regardless of the duration of the treatment, but protracted treatment may exacerbate it, since the feelings and perceptions of the two partners, and the degree to which the man actively supports the woman may change in the course of treatment . . .

7.4.2.3.3 *Fatherhood (and female parenthood) in cases after April 2009*

As noted, Part II of the HFE Act 2008 has introduced some changes to the law governing the fatherhood (or – in the case of a lesbian couple – 'female parenthood') of children conceived/implanted using donated gametes/embryos after April 2009. As before, in cases where the woman (referred to in the new provisions as 'W') is married at the time of the treatment, her husband will be deemed the father of the child unless it is shown he did not consent to it. Section 35 of the HFE Act 2008 provides:

35 Woman married at time of treatment
(1) If—
    (a) at the time of the placing in her of the embryo or of the sperm and eggs or of her artificial insemination, W was a party to a marriage, and
    (b) the creation of the embryo carried by her was not brought about with the sperm of the other party to the marriage,
    Then . . . the other party to the marriage is to be treated as the father of the child unless it is shown that he did not consent to the placing in her of the embryo or the sperm and eggs or to her artificial insemination (as the case may be).
(2) This section applies whether W was in the United Kingdom or elsewhere at the time mentioned in subsection (1)(a).

However, in cases where the woman is unmarried, the 2008 Act has abandoned the old test that focused on the man with whom she was 'treated together' – which, as noted, sometimes created difficulty – in favour of a more rigorous 'contract-based' approach. Under the latter, 'the agreed fatherhood conditions' must be satisfied, requiring written notices of consent from both parties (prior to the treatment cycle) to the man being treated as the father:

---

65 See n 24 above (para [29]).
66 [2005] UKHL 33.

36 Treatment provided to woman where agreed fatherhood conditions apply

If no man is treated by virtue of section 35 as the father of the child and no woman is treated by virtue of section 42 as a parent of the child but—

(a) the embryo or the sperm and eggs were placed in W, or W was artificially inseminated, in the course of treatment services provided in the United Kingdom by a person to whom a licence applies,

(b) at the time when the embryo or the sperm and eggs were placed in W, or W was artificially inseminated, the agreed fatherhood conditions (as set out in section 37) were satisfied in relation to a man, in relation to treatment provided to W under the licence,

(c) the man remained alive at that time, and

(d) the creation of the embryo carried by W was not brought about with the man's sperm,

then, subject to section 38(2) to (4), the man is to be treated as the father of the child.

37 The agreed fatherhood conditions

(1) The agreed fatherhood conditions referred to in section 36(b) are met in relation to a man ('M') in relation to treatment provided to W under a licence if, but only if,—

(a) M has given the person responsible a notice stating that he consents to being treated as the father of any child resulting from treatment provided to W under the licence,

(b) W has given the person responsible a notice stating that she consents to M being so treated,

(c) neither M nor W has, since giving notice under paragraph (a) or (b), given the person responsible notice of the withdrawal of M's or W's consent to M being so treated,

(d) W has not, since the giving of the notice under paragraph (b), given the person responsible—

(i) a further notice under that paragraph stating that she consents to another man being treated as the father of any resulting child, or

(ii) a notice under section 44(1)(b) stating that she consents to a woman being treated as a parent of any resulting child, and

(e) W and M are not within prohibited degrees of relationship in relation to each other.

As is apparent from s 36(a), a prerequisite for the agreed fatherhood conditions to apply is that the woman receives treatment in a licensed UK clinic. In this regard, the 2008 Act continues the policy of the 1990 Act in discouraging recourse by couples (or single women) to 'do-it-yourself' methods of donation, where the legal father would remain the sperm provider at common law. Otherwise, though, the provisions are notable in allowing the woman to select any man she wishes to be the child's father (provided he agrees); there is no requirement that they be living together, or indeed in any form of relationship. The only limitation, as per s 37(1)(e), is that the man must not be within the prohibited degrees of relationship to her – eg the woman could not choose her brother to be her child's father.

A further innovation in the 2008 Act is to allow legal parenthood in DI cases to be conferred on a second woman (typically the mother's lesbian partner). As with heterosexual couples, the 2008 Act distinguishes between cases where the mother and the other woman are in a legal civil partnership (akin to marriage), and those where they are not. In the former situation, s 42 provides (analogously to s 35 for married women) that the mother's civil partner will automatically be the child's second parent, unless it is shown that she (the civil partner) did not consent to the treatment. In other cases, where there is no civil partnership, the second woman may enjoy legal parenthood subject to the fulfilment of the 'agreed female parenthood conditions' in ss 43–44 of the 2008 Act. These mirror the 'agreed fatherhood conditions' for unmarried men in ss 36–37 of the Act in being based on the existence of written notices of consent from both parties. Here too the rules on prohibited degrees of relationship will apply: thus (under s 44(1)(e)) the mother may not choose, eg, her sister to be the child's second parent.

As noted earlier, the evidence nowadays is that increasingly it is lesbian, rather than hetero-sexual, couples, who are the main recipients of treatment with donated gametes, and in this regard the 2008 Act may be seen as incorporating timely changes that reflect modern social attitudes. At the same time the legislation holds fast to the traditional idea that a child can have no more than two parents. Julie McCandless and Sally Sheldon have commented upon this aspect as follows:

McCandless, J and Sheldon, S, 'The Human Fertilisation and Embryology Act (2008) and the Tenacity of the Sexual Family Form'[67]

The two parent model retains a grip on the law which appears to have out lived any inevitable relationship between legal parenthood and either biological fact or marital convention. Significantly, while the reform of section 13(5) ensured that there was sustained attention to the question of whether a child could flourish equally well without a father (either in a single parent family or raised by a same sex couple), this reform process saw no discussion of the question of whether, if two parents are better than one, three parents might be better than (or, at least, as good as) two. In other contexts, family law has developed increasingly flexible and creative ways of recognising a range of adults as of significance to a child. To take just two examples: parental responsibility can be awarded to any number of adults and current adoption practice seeks to maintain links with birth parents alongside those with legal/social parents. Yet it seems that notwithstanding this greater flexibility, there remains something special about the legal status of parent and registration as such on a birth certificate. The question of whether, in certain circumstances, more than two parents might be legally recognised was raised by just one respondent early in the Government consultation process regarding how the 1990 Act should be reformed and, although noted in two consecutive interventions in the House of Lords debates, was not subject to any further elaboration. . . . [T]he Department of Health told us that they had mooted the possibility of a child having three legal parents in the early stages of the reform process and discussed it with the Office for National Statistics. The idea was rejected on the basis that the consequences of such a change were too far reaching and controversial, potentially 'hijacking' the reform process and jeopardising the Bill.

In the context of lesbian relationships, where couples might consider having one partner provide the egg and – following IVF using donated sperm – the other carry the embryo to term, it is apparent from s 33 of the 2008 Act that the latter alone will be the child's mother. As s 47 makes clear, the egg provider may be the second female parent, but only where she is the mother's civil partner, or the agreed female parenthood conditions are met:

47 Woman not to be other parent merely because of egg donation
A woman is not to be treated as the parent of a child whom she is not carrying and has not carried, except where she is so treated—
(a) by virtue of section 42 or 43, ...

7.4.3 The gamete donors

The ethical and legal issues in relation to the third party donors who provide their gametes in order for others to be treated may conveniently be divided into two parts. First, how should they be treated at the initial point of recruitment, and secondly, what role, if any, should they be accorded after the birth of any child which, genetically, is theirs?

---

67 (2010) 73 MLR 175.

7.4.3.1 Recruitment, screening and information issues

As countenanced by the HFE Act 1990, the recruitment of gamete donors in the UK originally took place under a significant shroud of secrecy, at least as regard sperm donation, whose main source was students in medical schools. The policy of according donors anonymity was based on a recommendation of the Warnock Report, which was concerned that otherwise, men might be put off from being donors, thus placing the DI programme in jeopardy. (As regards egg donation – which entails some discomfort and risk – anonymity has generally been less of an issue: the donor was often someone known to the infertile woman, such as a sister, wishing to help for altruistic reasons.)

As discussed further under section 7.4.4, the policy of donor anonymity was abandoned in April 2005 as no longer consonant with modern perceptions of the interests of children, conceived in this way, in knowing of their genetic identity. Interestingly, contrary to the original fears, the statistics in relation to gamete donation collected by the HFE Authority, show a significant increase since then in the number of registered donors (both male and female).[68] Added to that is the point, noted in section 7.4.1, that today donated gametes play less of a role (both in absolute and relative terms) in fertility treatment, due to scientific advances in helping (heterosexual) couples conceive using their own gametes.

Subject to any lower limit specified by the donor, his or her gametes may be used to conceive children for up to ten families.[69] As regards the matter of paying gamete donors, s 12 of the HFE Act 1990 (as amended) states:

12 General conditions

(1) The following shall be conditions of any licence granted under this Act–

... (e) that no money or other benefit shall be given or received in respect of any supply of gametes, embryos or human admixed embryos unless authorised by Directions . . .

In the past, Directions (issued by the HFE Authority) provided for a standard payment of £15 per donation; however since 2006 this is no longer so.[70] The present Directions merely allow compensation for reasonable out-of-pocket expenses (such as the standard costs of travelling to the clinic). Nonetheless, egg donors may still receive a very considerable benefit in kind, in terms of receiving their own IVF treatment at a reduced rate. The pros and cons of this practice (known as 'egg sharing') were considered in the 'SEED Report', undertaken by the HFE Authority in 2006, which concluded that, though not free from difficulty, it was on balance justified in order to ensure an adequate supply of eggs:

SEED Report – A report on the Human Fertilisation & Embryology Authority's review of sperm, egg and embryo donation in the United Kingdom[71]

6.10 Many opponents of egg sharing clearly regard the value of the compensation offered to the egg provider as equivalent to a substantial payment amounting to a significant inducement to her to give up her eggs. One way of stating this argument is that the offer of discounted treatment encourages the egg provider to ignore the consequences and possible risks of donation and therefore invalidates her consent to the procedure. However, if an egg provider's judgement were really obscured by the promise of free treatment, one might expect to find evidence of people complaining about this afterwards, or at least that some egg providers later regret giving up their eggs.

---

68 See 'new donor registrations 1992-2008', at www.hfea.gov.uk/3411.html.
69 HFEA Code of Practice (8th edn, 2009) para 11.35.
70 Policy changed following the recommendations of the SEED Report, n 71 below.
71 HFEA: London, 2005. The full report is available at www.hfea.gov.uk/docs/SEEDReport05.pdf.

6.11 Such evidence is scant, but even where it does exist this might not be a decisive objection, as long as the majority derive considerable benefit from the procedure (and as long as every effort has been made to ensure that their consent is properly informed and their choice is uncoerced). The argument that almost any adverse consequence is sufficient to prohibit a practice which brings great general benefit seems disproportionate. In any case, subsequent regret is not in itself evidence of vitiated consent (people often freely do things which they later wish they had not done) and may often have more to do with people's changing values than the impairment of their judgement or the constraint of their consent.

. . . 6.14 Having debated these and many other arguments at length, it is our view that the opponents of compensated egg sharing have not succeeded in arguing that the alleged harms are proximate, likely or significant enough to amount to a sufficient or compelling reason to prohibit the practice. Having said this, we acknowledge that it will remain necessary to ensure that egg sharing, whether compensated or not, is managed in such a way as to minimise the acknowledged potential for adverse effects for those involved. We intend to keep egg sharing in general under review, in particular evidence of the emotional consequences for women participating in egg sharing arrangements, about which there is as yet little available.

Other significant issues concern the screening and informing of donors. The need for enquiry into the donor's medical history, and testing of the gametes, so as to reduce the risk to the recipient woman and/or potential children from infectious disease or genetic defects is clear, and is the subject of detailed guidance in the current Code of Practice (at paras 11.06–11.17). However, matters are more complex when it comes to the screening/selection of donors for their positive attributes. The Warnock Report in 1984 commented unfavourably upon the practice, in parts of the USA, of offering the nurturing parents a choice of donors, as follows:

Warnock Committee, *Report of the Committee of Inquiry into Human Fertilisation and Embryology*[72]

4.19 It is the practice of some clinics in the USA to provide detailed descriptions of donors, and to permit couples to exercise choice as to the donor they would prefer. In the evidence there was some support for the use of such descriptions. It is argued that they would provide information and reassurance for the parents and, at a later date, for the child. They might also be of benefit to the donor, as an indication that he is valued for his own sake. A detailed description also offers some choice to the woman who is to have the child, and lack of such choice can be said to diminish the importance of the woman's right to choose the father of her child.

4.20 The contrary view, also expressed in the evidence, is that detailed donor profiles would introduce the donor as a person in his own right. It is also argued that the use of profiles devalues the child who may seem to be wanted only if certain specifications are met, and this may become a source of disappointment to the parents if their expectations are unfulfilled.

The Committe instead felt that information provided to the rearing parent(s) should be limited to that needed for their reassurance, such as the donor's ethnic group and genetic health (para 4.21). For a while the HFE Authority operated a more liberal policy, which encouraged donors to provide non-identifying biographical information about themselves to be passed on to prospective parents and, ultimately, future children. However, the SEED report in 2005 noted doubts about the value of 'donor-recipient matching', in which parents look for donors with particular attributes (and the

---

72 See n 1 above.

unclear implications for the welfare of the child),[73] presaging a return to a more Warnock-style approach.

For their part, donors should also receive full information at the time of giving their consent to the extraction and use of their gametes (under Sch 3 para 5 of the HFE Act 1990 (as amended)). The HFE Authority Code elaborates upon this requirement as follows:

HFEA Code of Practice[74]

11.24 Before any consents or samples are obtained from a prospective donor, the recruiting centre should provide information about:

a) the screening that will be done, and why it is necessary

b) the possibility that the screening may reveal unsuspected conditions (eg, low sperm count, genetic anomalies or HIV infection) and the practical implications

c) the scope and limitations of the genetic testing that will be done and the implications for the donor and their family

d) the importance of informing the recruiting centre of any medical information that may come to light after donation that may have health implications for any woman who receives treatment with those gametes or for any child born as a result of such treatment

e) the procedure used to collect gametes, including any discomfort, pain and risk to the donor (eg, from the use of superovulatory drugs)

f) the legal parenthood of any child born as a result of their donation

h) what information about the donor must be collected by the centre and held on the HFEA Register.

Where a would-be donor is considered unsuitable to donate, paras 11.18–11.19 of the Code state that they should receive a sensitive explanation as to the reasons, as well as an offer of counselling.

7.4.3.2 Legal status and contact in respect of resulting children

As we saw in section 7.4.2, the effect of the parenthood rules in ss 33–47 HFE Act 2008 (and for pre-2009 births, ss 27–28 of the 1990 Act) is that all parental rights and obligations, in relation to children born out of licensed DI treatment, inhere in the recipient(s) of the gametes, not the donor(s). However, this leaves the question of how other aspects of the relationship between the donor and the child conceived with his or her gametes should be managed. First and foremost, should they be made aware of each other's identity at all?

Originally, as noted in 7.4.3.1, the HFE Act 1990 incorporated a policy of donor anonymity: though the HFE Authority has from the outset been required to include information in its register, linking gamete providers with resulting children, the latter's access to this information was previously strictly controlled. As further discussed in section 7.4.4, this changed with enactment of the HFE (Disclosure of Donor Information) Regulations 2004:[75] for gamete dononations prior to April 2005, these allowed detailed information about the donor to be provided to the child, albeit not such as would identify the donor. (This reflected s 31(5) of the 1990 Act, which stipulated that regulations could not retrospectively require a donor's identity to be divulged – ie where he had donated under the assumption of anonymity.) By contrast, children born from gametes donated after 31 March 2005, were given the right, on reaching 18, to discover the identity of the donor.

These changes have been built upon further in the 2008 amendments to the 1990 Act, which for the first time also accord donors the right to some information concerning children born using their gametes. Pursuant to s 31ZD of the 1990 Act (as amended):

---

73 See n 71 above, recommendation 2.7.
74 See n 14 above.
75 SI 2004/1511.

31ZD Provision to donor of information about resulting children

(1) This section applies where a person ('the donor') has consented under Schedule 3 (whether before or after the coming into force of this section) to–

(a) the use of the donor's gametes, or an embryo the creation of which was brought about using the donor's gametes, for the purposes of treatment services provided under a licence, . . .

. . . (3) The donor may by notice request the appropriate person to give the donor notice stating–

(a) the number of persons of whom the donor is not a parent but would or might, but for the relevant statutory provisions, be a parent by virtue of the use of the gametes or embryos to which the consent relates,

(b) the sex of each of those persons, and

(c) the year of birth of each of those persons.

As is apparent, the above does not entitle donors to receive identifying information in respect of children conceived with their gametes. The only way they could learn the specific identity of such a child is if the latter (where conceived after March 2005) were later to access the register and initiate contact: this is discussed insection 7.4.4 below.

Finally, it should be noted that the HFE legislation provides that in certain circumstances the donor may potentially be liable to the child in a civil action for damages. The details of when this might be the case are considered further under 7.4.4.2.

7.4.4 The child

7.4.4.1 Establishing genetic identity

It is apparent from the foregoing discussion that, while in 1990 the law gave a nod to the interests of prospective children (in s 13(5) of the HFEA 1990), these were until recently largely subordinated to those of the other key players in the collaborative reproductive process, that is, the nurturing parents and gamete providers. In particular, the latter parties' interests in preserving anonymity/confidentiality were allowed to prevail over any interest the child might have in knowing of its provenance. In fact, even prior to the original HFE Act, the Glover Report had commented on the potentially deleterious psychological consequences of policy of anonymity for the child as follows:

> **Glover, J et al, Report to the European Commission on Reproductive Technologies, Fertility and the Family**[76]
>
> Our sense of who we are is bound up with the story we tell about ourselves. A life where the biological parents are unknown is like a novel with the first chapter missing. Also there are the marked similarities between children and their biological parents. The child may wonder who is the person, perhaps among those passed in the street, who has that degree of closeness.
>
> On the other hand, for young children who know who the semen donor was, there may be problems about their identity. They may see neither person as being unambiguously their father. This suggests that it may not be in the children's interest to be told who the donor is at an early age, but is not a point against a system of the Swedish type, setting the right to know at the age of 18. And, since the legal right to know need not be exercised, no child loses anything by it. Since some people care so much about their origins, seeing them as an important part of their identity, the interests of the children count strongly in favour of the right to know . . .

---

76 See n 4 above.

In the wake of the enactment of the Human Rights Act 1998, the question also arose more directly as to whether the policy of donor anonymity was compatible with the ECHR rights of children conceived with donated gametes. This was partially tested in the case of *Rose and Another v Secretary of State for Health*,[77] in which two 'DI children' obtained a declaration that their interest in obtaining information about the sperm donor engaged Art 8 of the ECHR. Scott Baker J commented:

> **Scott Baker J:** [47] It is to my mind entirely understandable that [DI] children should wish to know about their origins and in particular to learn what they can about their biological father or, in the case of egg donation, their biological mother. The extent to which this matters will vary from individual to individual. In some instances, as in the case of the Claimant Joanna Rose, the information will be of massive importance. I do not find this at all surprising bearing in mind the lessons that have been learnt from adoption. A human being is a human being whatever the circumstances of his conception and a [DI] child is entitled to establish a picture of his identity as much as anyone else. We live in a much more open society than even 20 years ago. Secrecy nowadays has to be justified where previously it did not.

Though the Court was not asked to decide the further question of whether anonymity could be justified under Art 8(2) ECHR (as necessary to protect the donor's rights, etc), the Government decided shortly afterwards to abandon the previous policy. As noted in section 7.4.3.2, this occurred through Regulations enacted in 2004, and this shift has since been cemented (and expanded on) by the 2008 amendments to the HFE Act 1990.

The relevant section of the HFE Act 1990 (as amended) now provides as follows:

31ZA Request for information as to genetic parentage etc.
(1) A person who has attained the age of 16 ('the applicant') may by notice to the Authority require the Authority to comply with a request under subsection (2).
(2) The applicant may request the Authority to give the applicant notice stating whether or not the information contained in the register shows that a person ('the donor') other than a parent of the applicant would or might, but for the relevant statutory provisions, be the parent of the applicant, and if it does show that–
    (a) giving the applicant so much of that information as relates to the donor as the Authority is required by regulations to give (but no other information), or
    (b) stating whether or not that information shows that there are other persons of whom the donor is not the parent but would or might, but for the relevant statutory provisions, be the parent and if so–
        (i) the number of those other persons,
        (ii) the sex of each of them, and
        (iii) the year of birth of each of them.
(3) The Authority shall comply with a request under subsection (2) if–
    (a) the information contained in the register shows that the applicant is a relevant individual, and
    (b) the applicant has been given a suitable opportunity to receive proper counselling about the implications of compliance with the request.
(4) Where a request is made under subsection (2)(a) and the applicant has not attained the age of 18 when the applicant gives notice to the Authority under subsection (1), regulations can not require the Authority to give the applicant any information which identifies the donor.

---

77 [2002] EWHC 1593 (Admin).

(5) Regulations cannot require the Authority to give any information as to the identity of a person whose gametes have been used or from whom an embryo has been taken if a person to whom a licence applied was provided with the information at a time when the Authority could not have been required to give information of the kind in question.

The effect of these provisions is that children aged 16 or over may request detailed non-identifying information about the donor held by the HFE Authority. For children born using gametes donated after 31 March 2005 (the date specified in the 2004 Regulations), the donor's identity itself can be revealed once they reach the age of 18. By contrast, as s 31ZA(5) makes clear, children conceived with gametes donated before this date will not normally be entitled to identifying information: as noted in section 7.4.3(b) this is to protect the donor's legitimate expectation of anonymity at the time they donated.[78]

It is now also possible, pursuant to s 31ZE of the HFE Act 1990 (as amended), for DI children aged 18 or above to obtain identifying information as to their genetic half-siblings (ie other children conceived using gametes from the same donor), subject to the half-sibling agreeing to the release of this information. Excluded from this section, though, are situations where the half-sibling is the donor's own legitimate child. Clearly, one circumstance in which it will be of particular importance for half-siblings to be aware of each other's identity is where there is otherwise a risk of them entering into an incestuous relationship. This is catered for specifically by s 31ZB (which re-enacts provisions already contained in the original 1990 Act), as follows:

31ZB Request for information as to intended spouse etc.
(1) Subject to subsection (4), a person ('the applicant') may by notice to the Authority require the Authority to comply with a request under subsection (2).
(2) The applicant may request the Authority to give the applicant notice stating whether or not information contained in the register shows that, but for the relevant statutory provisions, the applicant would or might be related to a person specified in the request ('the specified person') as–
  (a) a person whom the applicant proposes to marry,
  (b) a person with whom the applicant proposes to enter into a civil partnership, or
  (c) a person with whom the applicant is in an intimate physical relationship or with whom the applicant proposes to enter into an intimate physical relationship.

Here the information may be disclosed (subject to the other party's consent) to applicants from the age of 16 upwards, and may (in contrast to s 31ZE) extend to parties who are the donor's children. On the other hand, this section – as indeed do the rest of the information access provisions under the Act – presupposes that the DI child is aware he or she was conceived in this way in the first place, and as we saw in 7.4.2.2, this may often not be the case.

7.4.4.2 Redress against the gamete donor
In one situation, even in 1990, it was contemplated that full disclosure (that is, which identifies the individual gamete donor) could occur, namely in prospect of a legal suit by the child against the donor. In this regard, s 35 of the 1990 Act (as amended) provides:

35 Disclosure in interests of justice: congenital disabilities, etc
(1) Where for the purpose of instituting proceedings under section 1 of the Congenital Disabilities (Civil Liability) Act 1976 (civil liability to child born disabled) it is necessary to

---

78 Though if they wish, pre-April 2005 donors can register themselves as identifiable under s 31ZF of the HFE Act 1990 (as amended).

identify a person who would or might be the parent of a child but for the relevant statutory provisions, the court may, on the application of the child, make an order requiring the Authority to disclose any information contained in the register kept in pursuance of section 31 of this Act identifying that person.

. . . (2A) In subsection (1) . . . 'the relevant statutory provisions' means–

(a)   sections 27 to 29 of this Act, and

(b)   sections 33 to 47 of the Human Fertilisation and Embryology Act 2008.

Such disclosure is part of a cluster of provisions designed to afford remedies to children injured prenatally in the course of fertility treatment provided to one or both of their parents. Gillian Douglas explains the effect of these provisions as follows:

Douglas, G, *Law, Fertility and Reproduction*[79]

English law does not usually permit a child to bring an action for 'wrongful life' which is a claim that he or she should never have been born. However, a handicapped child who claims that his or her birth resulted from defective gametes being used, or a defective embryo being wrongly transferred, has now been given a right of action under [s 1A of] the Congenital Disabilities (Civil Liability) Act 1976, which was originally enacted to deal with cases concerning prenatal injury.

That legislation was amended by the 1990 Act, to make clear that a child may sue under it where he or she is born disabled, and the disability results from an act or omission in course of the selection, or the keeping or use outside the body, of the embryo . . . or of the gametes used to bring about the creation of the embryo . . .

Where the *donor* of the gametes fails to reveal infection or genetic disease, it will be more difficult for the child to bring a claim. Of course, in most cases, there would be no advantage to the child to sue the donor rather than the doctor, who will carry insurance. But where a condition cannot be revealed by testing, so that the doctor would not be at fault, the child might wish to seek redress from the donor. The anonymity of the donor may in such a case be overridden, by the child applying to the court for an order under s 35 . . .

As Douglas notes, the existence of such a remedy is not without its puzzles: in particular affording a remedy to a child who, but for the relevant impugned conduct, would not have been conceived,

appears vulnerable to philosophical objections – and the problem of quantifying loss – identified by the Court of Appeal in its 'wrongful life' judgment in *Mackay v Essex AHA*.[80] To date, however, the point remains untested, as a claim using the section has yet to be brought.

See Chapter 8 →

❓ SELF-TEST QUESTION

Are the new parenthood provisions in the HFE Act 2008, really much of an improvement over the rules found in the HFE Act 1990?

---

79   London: Sweet & Maxwell, 1991.

80   [1982] QB 1166.

7.5 Surrogacy

7.5.1 Background

Surrogacy describes the practice whereby one woman (the 'surrogate mother') agrees to carry a child on behalf of another person or couple ('the commissioning parent(s)'), with the intention that, following birth, it will be handed over to the latter for nurturing. Most often, the commissioning parents will be a heterosexual couple, where the female partner is unable to bear children. However, in principle a single person or homosexual couple could also make use of the practice. While often the surrogate mother will expect to be paid for her services, this is not always true: sometimes 'altruistic surrogacy' occurs, such as where a woman agrees to carry a child for her infertile sister.

A further distinction that is often drawn is between cases of 'partial' and 'total' (or IVF) surrogacy: in the former, the surrogate mother is inseminated with sperm from the commissioning father, and will thus herself be the genetic (as well as the gestational) mother of the child. By contrast, in total surrogacy, another woman's egg will be used, usually from the commissioning mother (if she is able to produce one), which is then implanted in the surrogate following IVF. In this situation, the surrogate mother will not be genetically related to the child.

The number of surrogacy arrangements in the UK remains small (constituting a tiny proportion of fertility treatment overall): figures from the HFE Authority show that in 2006, out of nearly 40,000 women treated, in just 61 cases was this pursuant to a (total) surrogacy arrangement, resulting in 15 live births.[81] Nonetheless, the practice has long excited a disproportionate amount of ethical and legal controversy. In 1984 the Warnock Report made clear its hostility to surrogacy, including on deontological grounds: 'that people should treat others as a means to their own ends, however desirable the consequences, must always be liable to moral objection' (para 8.17). A few years later Glover, reporting to the EC Commission, provided a summary of the main arguments for and against the practice, as follows:

Glover, J et al, Report to the European Commission on Reproductive Technologies, Fertility and the Family[82]

1 The case for surrogacy

Part of the case is straightforward. Surrogacy relieves childlessness. For women who have had repeated miscarriages, or who suffer from conditions making pregnancy dangerous, surrogacy may be the only hope of having a child.

Another, more problematic, argument appeals to the interests of the child who would not have existed without surrogacy.

Another argument appeals to liberty. Some strong justification is needed for preventing people from bearing children to help their sisters or friends. And a similar strong justification is needed for preventing people freely contracting to do this for someone for money. This argument relates to the legality of surrogacy, but does nothing to show that surrogacy is a good thing in itself. The central case for that has to rest on relieving the burden of childlessness.

2 The case against surrogacy

(a) *The children*: One line of thought appeals to the rights of the child. It appears in the Catholic document issued by the Congregation for the Doctrine of the Faith, which says that surrogacy 'offends the dignity and the right of the child to be conceived, carried in the womb, brought into the world and brought up by his own parents'.

---

81 See *Fertility treatment in 2006 – a statistical analysis*, at www.hfea.gov.uk/5777.html. Admittedly, the overall number of such arrangements, including partial surrogacy following (unlicensed) DIY insemination, is likely to be somewhat higher.

82 See n 4 above.

This case seems to us not overwhelming. Even if the child has a strong interest in being created sexually, to call this a right is to claim that it trumps any interests of the childless couple. This requires that being the child of a surrogate is such an indignity that, by comparison, relieving any degree of the potential parents' misery is to count for nothing. We have not found the powerful supporting argument this would need.

The objection is made even weaker by a further problem. For the potential child, the alternative to surrogacy may be non-existence. It seems unlikely that the child will see surrogacy as so bad as to wish he or she had not been born at all. The 'right' looks like one the child will later be glad was not respected. It is hard to see the case for giving this supposed interest any weight at all, let alone for saying that it justifies leaving people unwillingly childless.

Another argument appeals to the psychological effects of surrogacy on the child. If the surrogacy is paid for there is a danger that the child will think he or she has been bought. Also, it is sometimes suggested that surrogacy breaks a bond formed by the time of birth. Dr John Marks, the chairman of the British Medical Association, has said: 'By the time a baby is born there is a bond between the mother and the child. With surrogacy you break that bond. You are depriving the child of one natural parent. We think that is wrong.' ((1987) *The Guardian*, 8 May) . . .

The surrogate mother may well feel a bond between herself and the child. But is there reason to believe in any bond in the other direction before birth? Or could this be an illusion created by projecting the mother's feelings on to the foetus? If the child's feelings are a reason against surrogacy, the baby has to have, by the time of birth, highly specific feelings towards the particular woman who bears him. The evidence for this can charitably be described as slight.

Suppose, for the sake of argument, that there is such a bond. It is then undesirable to break it. But, where it is broken, is the child so harmed that it would have been better if he or she had not been born? For this is what banning surrogacy on these grounds seems to imply. We do not have such drastic thoughts about people who are adopted. The British Medical Association's Board of Science is quoted as saying that while adoption may be 'the next best thing' for a child facing an uncertain future, any arrangement where a surrogate mother hands over the child 'dooms it to second best from the start' ((1987) *The Independent*, 8 May). But is it obvious here that no life at all is preferable to 'second best'?

(b) *Conflicts*: The conflicts sometimes arising between the potential parents and the surrogate mother may harm the child, and this is part of the case against surrogacy.

(c) *Effects on the family*: Perhaps introducing a third party so intimately into the process of having children may weaken the institution of the family . . .

(d) *The surrogate mother*: The position of the surrogate mother varies, according to whether she is bearing a child to help a sister or friend, or has made a commercial arrangement. There is the criticism that surrogacy is an invasion of her bodily integrity. This criticism may be weaker if she willingly agreed than if she was forced into it by money problems. Sometimes she may bitterly regret having agreed to give away the baby. As we have seen, there is a danger of her being exploited. Financial pressures may put her in a weak position to resist contractual conditions which give little weight to her interests.

Another important motive for volunteering to act as a surrogate seems to be the desire for friendship with the parents-to-be. As this is usually exactly what the parents-to-be do not want, it is an illusory objective. She wants friendship: she is treated as a provider of a service, and afterwards dismissed . . .

At the same time, it is important to keep the questions of the moral and legal permissibility of surrogacy separate. For its part, the law must distinguish in its response between two different moments in time; it must first determine how far it is legitimate to discourage, or indeed prohibit, the formation of surrogacy arrangements in the first place. Secondly, however, in so far as its strictures at this earlier stage are ignored and a surrogacy arrangement results in pregnancy, the law must attribute rights and duties to the participants and, if they are in dispute, adjudicate between them. In doing so, of course, the position of any resulting child must be resolved. These two distinct stages were recognised by Latey J in one of the first surrogacy cases to reach the English courts:

Re C (A Minor) (Wardship: Surrogacy) (1985)[83]

A partial surrogacy arrangement, negotiated by an agency, was entered into between an American commissioning couple and a British woman, Kim Cotton (who was married with three children of her own). Following the successful birth of a child, it was clear that Mrs Cotton was happy to relinquish all parental rights in respect of it. The commissioning father issued a wardship summons in order to obtain custody, which was duly granted:

Latey J: First and foremost, and at the heart of the prerogative jurisdiction in wardship, is what is best for the child or children concerned. That and nothing else. Plainly the methods used to produce a child, as this baby has been, and the commercial aspects of it, raise difficult and delicate problems of ethics, morality and social desirability. These problems are under active consideration elsewhere.

Are they relevant in arriving at a decision on what now and, so far as one can tell, in the future is best for this child? If they are relevant, it is incumbent on the court to do its best to evaluate and balance them.

In my judgment, however, they are not relevant. The baby is here. All that matters is what is best for her now that she is here and not how she arrived. If it be said (though it has not been said during these hearings) that because the father and his wife entered into these arrangements it is some indication of their unsuitability as parents, I should reject any such suggestion. If what they did was wrong (and I am not saying that it was), they did it in total innocence. . . .

So, what is best for this baby? Her natural mother does not ask for her. Should she go into Mr and Mrs A's care and be brought up by them? Or should some other arrangement be made for her, such as long term fostering with or without adoption as an end?

The factors can be briefly stated. Mr A is the baby's father and he wants her, as does his wife. The baby's mother does not want her. Mr and Mrs A are a couple in their 30s. They are devoted to each other. They are both professional people, highly qualified. They have a very nice home in the country and another in a town. Materially they can give the baby a very good upbringing. But, far more importantly, they are both excellently equipped to meet the baby's emotional needs. They are most warm, caring, sensible people, as well as highly intelligent. When the time comes to answer the child's questions, they will be able to do so with professional advice if they feel they need it. Looking at this child's well being, physical and emotional, who better to have her care? No one.

Clearly, the two stages are often not separate in practice: the anticipated response of the law at the second stage will almost certainly have an impact on the parties' decision to risk entering into the arrangement in the first place. Nevertheless, for expository purposes, it is useful to look at each in turn.

---

83 [1985] FLR 846.

7.5.2 Entering into Surrogacy Arrangements

Following adverse media reaction to the *Re C* case, and in the light of the recommendations of the Warnock Committee, Parliament enacted the Surrogacy Arrangements Act (SAA) 1985:

1 Meaning of 'surrogate mother', 'surrogacy arrangement' and other terms

(1) The following provisions shall have effect for the interpretation of this Act.

(2) 'Surrogate mother' means a woman who carries a child in pursuance of an arrangement—

    (a) made before she began to carry the child, and

    (b) made with a view to any child carried in pursuance of it being handed over to, and the parental rights being exercised (so far as practicable) by, another person or other persons.

(3) An arrangement is a surrogacy arrangement if, were a woman to whom the arrangement relates to carry a child in pursuance of it, she would be a surrogate mother.

. . .

1A Surrogacy arrangements unenforceable

No surrogacy arrangement is enforceable by or against any of the persons making it.

2 Negotiating surrogacy arrangements on a commercial basis, etc

(1) No person shall on a commercial basis do any of the following acts in the United Kingdom, that is–

    (a) initiate any negotiations with a view to the making of a surrogacy arrangement;

    (aa) take part in any negotiations with a view to the making of a surrogacy arrangement,

    (b) offer or agree to negotiate the making of a surrogacy arrangement; or

    (c) compile any information with a view to its use in making, or negotiating the making of, surrogacy arrangements,

and no person shall in the United Kingdom knowingly cause another to do any of those acts on a commercial basis.

(2) A person who contravenes sub-s (1) above is guilty of an offence; but it is not a contravention of that sub-section–

    (a) for a woman, with a view to becoming a surrogate mother herself, to do any act mentioned in that sub-section or to cause such an act to be done; or

    (b) for any person, with a view to a surrogate mother carrying a child for him, to do such an act or to cause such an act to be done.

(2A) A non-profit making body does not contravene subsection (1) merely because—

    (a) the body does an act falling within subsection (1)(a) or (c) in respect of which any reasonable payment is at any time received by it or another, or

    (b) it does an act falling within subsection (1)(a) or (c) with a view to any reasonable payment being received by it or another in respect of facilitating the making of any surrogacy arrangement.

. . . (2C) Any reference in subsection (2A) or (2B) to a reasonable payment in respect of the doing of an act by a non-profit making body is a reference to a payment not exceeding the body's costs reasonably attributable to the doing of the act.

Here s1A, which provides that a surrogacy arrangement will be void (as a contract in private law), was inserted in 1990 by an amending section in the original HFE Act. Otherwise, though, the main thrust of the 1985 Act – in terms of the criminal prohibitions in s 2 – is against the commercial facilitators of surrogacy arrangements, notably agencies which profit from brokering between the commissioning couple and potential surrogate. In this regard, s 3 of the Act extends liability to the advertisement of their services.

By contrast, under s 2(2), immunity from criminal liability is conferred upon the immediate parties to the arrangement, viz the surrogate mother and commissioning couple (as per the rules of statutory interpretation, the reference to 'him' in s 2(2)(b) includes 'her'). Moreover, under s 2(3), the payment of monies to the surrogate herself is not unlawful. This reflected the view of the Warnock Committee that it would be undesirable for the birth of a child through surrogacy to be tainted with criminality. In addition, the operation of charitable brokering organisations in this field has not been prohibited. Indeed, their position has recently been strengthened by the insertion of s 2(2A)–(2C) into the Act (by s 59 of the HFE Act 2008), permitting them to charge a fee for their reasonable expenses.

It is important to note too that the 1985 Act is not aimed at doctors (or fertility clinics) who receive a fee for medically facilitating a surrogate pregnancy by carrying out IVF or AID treatment on the surrogate. Accordingly (assuming the clinic has the appropriate licence to carry out such treatment under the HFE legislation), they would commit no offence. Indeed, the provision of medical treatment ancillary to surrogacy has increasingly gained acceptance within the medical profession: thus the BMA in its report, *Changing Conceptions of Motherhood, The Practice of Surrogacy in Britain*,[84] has recognised surrogacy as 'an acceptable treatment of last resort'. The HFE Authority, in its Code of Practice, has similarly acknowledged the modern-day reality of surrogacy arrangements. The latter in paras 14.1–14.3, places its focus upon the additional information that clinics, involved in surrogacy treatments, should provide to the parties:

HFEA Code of Practice

14.1 In addition to providing relevant information about gamete donation, the centre should give those involved in surrogacy arrangements information about the effect of the Parental Orders provisions in the HFE Act 2008. These state that parental rights and obligations in respect of surrogacy arrangements may be transferred from the birth parents to those who commissioned the surrogacy arrangement, as long as certain conditions are met.

14.2 The centre should advise patients that surrogacy arrangements are unenforceable and that they should seek legal advice about this.

14.3 The centre should advise patients intending to travel to another country for the purpose of entering into a surrogacy arrangement not to do so until they have sought legal advice about:
a)   legal parenthood of the prospective child, and
b)   the adoption or parental orders procedures for that country.

The courts too have changed their attitude towards surrogacy. From an initially censorious stance (in *A v C* from 1978 the Court of Appeal referred to such an arrangement as 'a kind of baby-farming operation of a wholly distasteful and lamentable kind'[85]), judges have recently evinced more sympathy towards those having recourse to the practice. In *Briody v St Helen's and Knowsley AHA*,[86] the Court of Appeal was required to consider whether the claimant, who had lost her womb as a result of medical negligence, should also receive damages to fund the costs of a surrogacy arrangement. While rejecting this on the facts (given the claimant's very slim chance of successfully so having a child), the Court demonstrated an open-minded approach to surrogacy in general. Hale LJ commented as follows:

---

84 London: BMA, 1996.
85 [1985] FLR 445, *per* Cumming-Bruce LJ (the case was decided in 1978).
86 [2001] EWCA Civ 1010.

Hale LJ: [14] . . . [W]hile there is general agreement that commercial agencies and advertising should be banned, that surrogacy for convenience or social rather than medical reasons is unacceptable, and that the agreement should be unenforceable, there is little discernible consensus on anything else. Lord Winston's view was that opinion was turning against surrogacy, and that was certainly his experience at his hospital, but if anything the tone of official publications since Warnock has been more sympathetic. Professor Craft's view was certainly different . . .

[16] . . . I find it impossible to say that the proposals which the claimant now wishes to pursue are contrary to public policy . . . She fulfils the criteria for permissible surrogacy laid down both by the Human Fertilisation and Embryology Authority and the BMA: she has no other way of having a baby because she has no womb. She has found a surrogate mother through perfectly lawful means with whom she proposes to make a lawful, although unenforceable, arrangement.

It is nevertheless true that surrogacy arrangements, and their optimal legal regulation, continue to pose difficult questions. In 1997, the Government commissioned an inquiry (headed by Professor Margaret Brazier) into the arrangements for payments and regulation under the 1985 Act. The ensuing report, *Surrogacy: Review for Health Ministers of Current Arrangements for Payment and Regulation*,[87] recommended a number of changes to the existing law. In particular, it felt that payment to surrogate mothers should be more closely controlled to ensure that only genuine expenses were covered and that the (charitable) agencies involved in negotiating surrogacy arrangements should be required to operate in accordance with a Code of Practice drawn up by the Department of Health. However, the Government subsequently chose not act upon these recommendations.

7.5.3 Resolving Surrogacy Arrangements

As regards the law's involvement in surrogacy arrangements at the second stage, namely once the child is born, two possibilities need to be considered. First, the parties to the arrangement may have fallen into dispute as to who should nurture it. Secondly, in so far as there is no dispute (that is, the surrogate mother is willing to hand over the child and the commissioning parents are happy to accept it and to pay the agreed fee), there remains the need to legitimate the child.

7.5.3.1 Where the parties are in dispute

Sometimes the surrogate, during the course of her pregnancy, may decide that she is not, after all, prepared to go through with the agreement to hand over the child after birth. In the early case of *A v C*,[88] the Court of Appeal upheld the trial judge's ruling that the surrogacy agreement providing, *inter alia*, for this handing over, was void on grounds of public policy. As noted above, when enacting the HFEA 1990, Parliament also inserted s 1A into the SAA 1985, to reinforce the voidness of such arrangements. Nevertheless, this point will not in itself be determinative of the outcome in a given surrogacy dispute. The reason is that what is now generally at issue is the future of a child: is it to be brought up by the surrogate who gestated it, or the couple who commissioned it (and to whom it may be partly or wholly genetically related)? Thus, in principle, and notwithstanding the voidness of their contractual rights, it might seem that the commissioning parents could win custody.

An analogy could be drawn here with cases of marital break-up in which the custody of a child is at issue. The courts, in dealing with such matters as residence and contact, will, in accordance

---

87 Cm 4068, London: Department of Health, 1998.
88 See n 85 above.

with the provisions of the Children Act 1989, regard the welfare of the child as paramount. This approach can indeed already be seen at work in the pre-Children Act case of *Re P* (*Minors*):

Re P (Minors) (1987)[89]

Mrs P, a divorcée with one son of her own, entered into an arrangement with Mr B to bear his child and hand it over to him and his wife, Mrs B. As her pregnancy progressed, she began to have doubts about honouring the agreement and these hardened following the birth of twins. Although upset about disappointing Mr and Mrs B, she ultimately refused to hand the twins over. The latter were made wards of court:

> **Sir John Arnold P:** In this, as in any other wardship dispute, the welfare of the children, or child, concerned is the first and paramount consideration which the court must, by statute, take into account, and that is what I do.
>
> These children have been, up to their present age of approximately five months, with, quite consistently, their mother and in those circumstances there must necessarily have been some bonding of those children with their mother and that is undoubtedly coupled with the fact that she is their mother, a matter which weighs predominantly in the balance in favour of leaving the children with their mother, but there are other factors which weigh in the opposite balance and which, as is said by Mr B through his counsel, outweigh the advantages of leaving the children with their mother, and it is that balancing exercise which the court is required to perform . . .
>
> What then are the factors which the court should take into account? I have already mentioned on the side of Mrs P the matters which weigh heavily in the balance are the fact of her maternity, that she bore the children and carried them for the term of their gestation and that ever since she has conferred upon them the maternal care which they have enjoyed and has done so successfully. The key social worker in the case who has given evidence testifies to the satisfactory nature of the care which Mrs P has conferred upon the children and this assessment is specifically accepted by Mr B as being an accurate one. I start, therefore, from the position that these babies have bonded with their mother in a state of domestic care by her of a satisfactory nature and I now turn to the factors which are said to outweigh those advantages, so as to guide the court upon the proper exercise of the balancing function to the conclusion that the children ought to be taken away from Mrs P, and passed over, under suitable arrangements, to Mr and Mrs B. They are principally as follows. It is said, and said quite correctly, that the shape of the B family is the better shape of a family in which these children might be brought up, because it contains a father as well as a mother and that is undoubtedly true. Next, it is said that the material circumstances of the B family are such that they exhibit a far larger degree of affluence than can be demonstrated by Mrs P. That, also, is undoubtedly true. Then it is said that the intellectual quality of the environment of the B's home and the stimulus which would be afforded to these babies, if they were to grow up in that home, would be greater than the corresponding features in the home of Mrs P . . .
>
> Then it is said that the religious comfort and support which the B's derive from their Church is greater than anything of that sort available to Mrs P. How far that is true, I simply do not know. I do know that the B's are practising Christians and do derive advantages from that circumstance, but nobody asked Mrs P about this and I am not disposed to assume that she lacks that sort of comfort and support in the

---

89 [1987] 2 FLR 421.

absence of any investigation by way of cross-examination to lay the foundations for such a conclusion. Then it is said, and there is something in this, that the problems which might arise from the circumstance that these children who are, of course, congenitally derived from the semen of Mr B and bear traces of Mr B's Asiatic origin would be more easily understood and discussed and reconciled in the household of Mr and Mrs B, a household with an Asiatic ethnic background, than they would be if they arose in relation to these children while they were situated in the home of Mrs P, which is in an English village and which has no non-English connections . . .

As regards [these] factors, they are, in the aggregate, weighty, but I do not think, having given my very best effort to the evaluation of the case dispassionately on both sides, that they ought to be taken to outweigh the advantages to these children of preserving the link with the mother to whom they are bonded and who has, as is amply testified, exercised over them a satisfactory level of maternal care, and accordingly it is, I think, the duty of the court to award the care and control of these babies to their mother.

This case suggests that there is a presumption that the welfare of the child is best served by leaving it with the surrogate mother. This is all the more so, given the inevitable delay, following the birth of the child, in such disputes coming before the courts, during which time the child may well have bonded with her.

The surrogate's position has since been strengthened by the parenthood provisions in the HFE legislation. In this regard, one should recall that at birth it is she – as the gestational mother – who, under s 27 HFEA 1990 and now s 33 HFE Act 2008, is the child's legal mother. This is so whether or not it is a case of partial or total surrogacy (ie whether her own egg or that of the commissioning mother was used). Equally, the effect of the rules is that the commissioning father – even where his sperm was used – will not be the legal father.[90] Accordingly, the onus from the outset will be upon the commissioning parents to persuade the court that there is some compelling justification for upsetting the status quo.

A rare case in which the latter succeeded in doing so is Re N (a child).[91] Here the evidence showed that from the beginning, the surrogate had set out to deceive the commissioning couple into believing that she intended to hand the child over to them at birth – in fact she wanted the child for herself. Thorpe LJ noted:

Thorpe LJ: [4] The judge's findings in relation to the history are perhaps largely superfluous for this afternoon's disposal of the appeal, but in very broad terms he rejected the evidence of the P's and commended the responsibility of the J's. In particular, and crucially, he found that the P's had deliberately embarked on a path of deception, driven by Mrs P's compulsive desire to bear a child or further children, and that she had never had any other objective than to obtain insemination by surrogacy, with the single purpose of acquiring for herself, and her family, another child. This was crucially important, since it informed the review of the experts and the review of the judge of the medium and long-term future of N, if the responsibility for his future care were left with the P's.

[5] The judge had the considerable advantage of two reports from Dr Eia Arsen of the Marlborough Day Clinic. His expertise in this field, forensic child and adolescent psychiatry, is second to none, and the judge was clearly guided by him to his ultimate conclusion. Dr Arsen

---

90 Under ss 35–37 HFE Act 2008; often the child at birth will be legally fatherless, eg where the surrogate is unmarried and the agreed fatherhood conditions do not apply.
91 [2007] EWCA Civ 1053.

had been instructed by the guardian ad litem, and the guardian ad litem fully supported Dr Arsen's conclusions, as well as expressing her independent expert view that, of the two options that the judge surveyed, the better for N was the future offered by the J's. So, given those ingredients, the judge's ultimate conclusion could not have been surprising to any of the professionals in the case, even if it was unexpected by the P's.

In these circumstances (and despite the fact that by the time of the hearing N, the child, had been living with the Ps for 18 months) the Court of Appeal upheld the order of Coleridge J in the High Court, granting residency to Mr J, the commissioning father (who was also the genetic father) and his wife.

Such exceptional cases aside, it is suggested that the courts will normally prefer to allow the child to remain with the surrogate. For one thing, they would not wish to send out a signal to surrogate mothers who, while pregnant, change their minds about handing over the child, that it could subsequently be taken from them against their will. As the Glover Report argues, this could be bad for the child. Instead, the Report suggests that 'the possibility of the surrogate mother changing her mind should be accepted by the [commissioning] couple as one of the risks of this way of trying to overcome childlessness.'[92]

7.5.3.2 Where the parties are agreed

On the face of it, things should be simpler where there is consensus between the surrogate and commissioning couple that the child be handed over. However, as we shall see, despite special statutory rules designed to assist the parties in transferring the parentage of the child, in a significant proportion of cases – in particular those involving cross-border surrogacy arrangements – serious difficulties may remain.

Starting with the relevant statutory provision, s 54 of the HFE Act 2008 allows the commissioning couple to apply for a parental order in a non-contentious surrogacy case. This is a swifter and notably less bureaucratic process than the alternative of adopting the child.[93] Nonetheless, for such an order to be granted, a variety of conditions need to be satisfied:

54 Parental orders

(1) On an application made by two people ('the applicants'), the court may make an order providing for a child to be treated in law as the child of the applicants if—

    (a) the child has been carried by a woman who is not one of the applicants, as a result of the placing in her of an embryo or sperm and eggs or her artificial insemination,

    (b) the gametes of at least one of the applicants were used to bring about the creation of the embryo, and

    (c) the conditions in subsections (2) to (8) are satisfied.

(2) The applicants must be—

    (a) husband and wife,

    (b) civil partners of each other, or

    (c) two persons who are living as partners in an enduring family relationship and are not within prohibited degrees of relationship in relation to each other.

(3) Except in a case falling within subsection (11), the applicants must apply for the order during the period of 6 months beginning with the day on which the child is born.

(4) At the time of the application and the making of the order—

    (a) the child's home must be with the applicants, and

---

92 See n 4 above.
93 Under the Adoption and Children Act 2002.

    (b)   either or both of the applicants must be domiciled in the United Kingdom or in the Channel Islands or the Isle of Man.

(5)   At the time of the making of the order both the applicants must have attained the age of 18.

(6)   The court must be satisfied that both—

    (a)   the woman who carried the child, and

    (b)   any other person who is a parent of the child but is not one of the applicants (including any man who is the father by virtue of section 35 or 36 or any woman who is a parent by virtue of section 42 or 43),

    have freely, and with full understanding of what is involved, agreed unconditionally to the making of the order.

(7)   Subsection (6) does not require the agreement of a person who cannot be found or is incapable of giving agreement; and the agreement of the woman who carried the child is ineffective for the purpose of that subsection if given by her less than six weeks after the child's birth.

(8)   The court must be satisfied that no money or other benefit (other than for expenses reasonably incurred) has been given or received by either of the applicants for or in consideration of—

    (a)   the making of the order,

    (b)   any agreement required by subsection (6),

    (c)   the handing over of the child to the applicants, or

    (d)   the making of arrangements with a view to the making of the order,

unless authorised by the court.

This provision replaces the rules as to parental orders contained in s 30 of the HFE Act 1990. In fact the only significant change (under sub-s (2)) is that, whereas under the 1990 Act, the applicants (ie the commissioning parents) had to be married to one another, now co-habiting couples and homosexual couples are also able to apply (as before, however, a single person may not obtain such an order).

The requirement in sub-ss (6)–(7) that the surrogate must consent to the order, and that such consent is not valid where given less than six weeks after the birth of the child, is clearly there to protect the surrogate's position. Less obviously defensible is the apparent double-standard applied by sub-s (8) requiring on the one hand the court to be satisfied that the surrogate was unpaid, but on the other allowing it retrospectively to authorise any such payment. In practice, given the court will have the child's welfare as its paramount concern, it is difficult to imagine circumstances when – as a prerequisite for making the desired order – it would fail to do this.

The High Court had to consider the effect of the previous (identical) rules in s 30 of the 1990 Act, including the possibility of authorising payment to the surrogate, in the case of Re Q (Parental Order):

Re Q (Parental Order) (1996)[94]

Baby Q was born in the summer of 1995 as a result of a total surrogacy arrangement. The unmarried surrogate, Miss A, received IVF treatment at a licensed clinic, and was paid £8,280 to cover her expenses and loss of earnings. Although she developed a strong attachment to the child she was carrying and equivocated about handing it over, she ultimately decided to go through with the agreement. The commissioning couple applied for a parental order:

---

94 [1996] 1 FLR 369.

Johnson J: Turning belatedly to the particular application made to me, I am satisfied that the statutory requirements are all complied with. . . .

The first relates to the consent of the carrying mother. She had entered into the procedure with the best of intentions, but when the time came to relinquish the child that she had carried so devotedly, she was overcome with doubt and at first declined to give her consent. This reaction is natural and was contemplated by parliament in stipulating that the carrying mother is to be given at least six weeks after the birth to make her decision before she can give a binding consent. One of the duties of the guardian *ad litem* under the Family Proceedings Courts (Children Act 1989) (Amendment) Rules 1994 is to investigate the circumstance of the carrying mother's consent.

It may be of interest if I quote *verbatim* from the guardian's report:

> I have visited Miss A twice in order to ascertain her wishes in this matter and to try and clarify the issues around her agreement to the order. Miss A explained how she came to offer herself as a surrogate mother due to seeing the anguish of infertile friends and how she had never thought she would have difficulty parting with the baby she bore. When she received details of Mr and Mrs B she immediately warmed to them and these first good impressions were confirmed when she met them. Miss A has two children of her own and they are both aware of this child's whereabouts . . .; they always knew that the baby would not be living with them. At about 28 weeks Miss A experienced some bleeding and was admitted to hospital. She questioned for the first time what she was doing and feels that it was only at this stage that the baby began to feel like a real person to her and that she began to bond with her. Notwithstanding this first period of questioning she decided to carry through handing over the baby to Mr and Mrs B and remained of this view until after the birth. . . . In talking to Miss A, it is clear that the depth of feeling she experienced towards her baby took her by surprise. She said that she felt no different toward this baby at her birth than she had felt towards her other children and had not really been prepared for this. It is clear that Miss A felt emotionally torn in half by the separation from the baby. With time, however, and as her own body settled after the birth, so she was able to think more clearly about the issues and this is why she decided to give her agreement. I prepared an agreement form for her to sign on my second visit and she did this willingly and in a positive and definite manner. She fully understands the effects of a parental order, understanding that she loses all parental responsibility, and wishes the order to be made as soon as possible. She does not now wish to attend court herself for the hearing.

This account of the feelings of this carrying mother shows the sensitivity and, indeed, difficulty of the task of the guardian *ad litem* in these cases. . . .

Secondly, I had to consider whether or not I should authorise payments totalling £8,280 which had been made to Miss A by Mr and Mrs B.

I hold that such authorisation can be given retrospectively. In so doing I follow the decision of Latey J in *Re Adoption Application (Payment for Adoption)* (1987) . . . which was concerned with a similar provision in the Adoption Act 1976.

The guardian told me that she had at first thought that this amount seemed rather high but on further inquiry she concluded that the payments were understandable. £3,280 was made up of payments to cover clothes, daily trips to the doctor for injections, child care provision of her own children during some of those visits and similar related expenses. A further £5,000 was a payment to compensate Miss A for loss of earnings. Given the circumstances of the pregnancy and her potential earnings of £15,000 [per annum], I joined with the guardian in concluding that the payment was reasonable and, retrospectively, I gave authority for it.

Since this case was decided, the courts have sanctioned the payment of increasingly high sums to surrogate mothers. In Re C (A Child),[95] a payment of £12,000 was authorised by the High Court in similar circumstances; more recently, in Re X & Y (foreign surrogacy),[96] Hedley J granted a parental order (including the authorisation of payment) in a case in which a British couple paid a Ukrainian woman no less than £23,000 to put down as a deposit on a flat in return for bearing them twins following an IVF surrogacy (using the commissioning father's sperm and a donor egg).

The Re X & Y case was complicated by the fact that, while under Ukrainian law, the British couple were the twins' legal parents at birth, under British law this was not the case: as we have seen, the effect of the HFE Act(s) is that the surrogate was their mother and her husband, rather than the commissioning (and genetic) father, their father. The disturbing implications of this case, that children born through a foreign surrogacy may potentially be left both parentless and stateless, are commented on by Theis, Gamble and Ghevaert, as follows:

Theis, L, Gamble, N, and Ghevaert, L, Re X and Y (Foreign Surrogacy): 'A Trek Through A Thorn Forest'[97]

Though the facts of this case may seem unusual, the prospect of other children being born into similar complications is worrying. The numbers of British people travelling abroad for fertility treatment (including surrogacy) are growing fast, driven by ease of access to information about foreign fertility services via the internet, cost, the acute shortage of egg donors in the UK, the lifting of anonymity for donors, and public policy restrictions which prohibit commercial surrogacy and advertisements for surrogate mothers. Hedley J acknowledged this trend saying, at para [26]: 'As babies become less available for adoption and given the withdrawal of donor confidentiality (wholly justifiable, of course, from the child's perspective), more and more couples are likely to be tempted to follow the applicants' path to commercial surrogacy in those places where it is lawful, of which there may be many'.

This suggests that some of the problems with the law highlighted by this case (as well as the lack of good quality public information) should be addressed as a matter of urgency. Surrogacy was an issue not looked at in detail as part of the government's review of fertility laws last year, though the government did suggest in Parliament that it was minded to review surrogacy separately. Hedley J noted, at para [29]: 'It is no part of the court's function to express views on that, save perhaps to observe that some of the issues thrown up in this case may highlight the wisdom of holding such a review.'

The language is moderate but Hedley J is right: surrogacy law urgently needs a review. What Re X and Y has demonstrated so graphically is how complex and difficult the current law is for British children born through foreign surrogacy, and at the same time how the law fails in practice to uphold the public policy of discouraging payments for childbirth. Parliament needs to take a fresh look at surrogacy and find a more effective legal solution fit for the twenty-first century. In the meantime, anyone contemplating foreign surrogacy (and their legal advisers) should proceed with extreme caution lest they too find themselves on 'a trek through a thorn forest'.

---

95 [2002] 1 FLR 1008.
96 [2008] EWHC (Fam) 3030.
97 [2009] Family Law 239.

Although, as we have seen, the HFE Act 2008 has added to the parties who are eligible to apply under s 54 for a parental order in cases of surrogacy, the above problem has not been addressed.

Difficulties may also occur in the opposite situation, that is where a foreign commissioning couple avails itself of the services of a British surrogate. Here the couple will not satisfy the requisite UK residency condition to allow them to apply for a parental order. Instead, as occurred in the case of *Re G (Surrogacy: Foreign Domicile)*[98] – involving a commissioning couple from Turkey – the couple will be forced back upon the more cumbersome alternative of applying for adoption, pursuant to the Adoption and Children Act 2002.

 SELF-TEST QUESTION

Has the time now come for wholesale reform of the law in respect of surrogacy, and if so, what form should the main changes take?

Summary of Key Points

1. The Human Fertilisation and Embryology Act 1990 (as amended in 2008) provides detailed regulation in respect of most aspects of fertility treatment. One of its key achievements was to set up the HFE Authority, responsible for the detailed supervision and licensing of UK fertility clinics.

2. Great importance is attached by the Act both to the consent of the gamete providers and to the welfare of children born as a result of fertility treatment. The stringency of the consent provisions especially has provoked several (in most cases unsuccessful) legal challenges to the Act in recent years.

3. Another concern of the legislation is to rein in the more extreme possibilities of scientific technology (reproductive cloning, genetic engineering, etc), where it is deemed that public opinion is not yet ready for them. Some of the 2008 changes to the 1990 Act address scientific techniques unknown in 1990.

4. One controversial question is how far genetic modifications may be undertaken that will affect the characteristics of the resulting child. At present, some 'selecting out' of embryos is permitted (chiefly on account of genetic defects); by contrast, positive manipulations of the embryo are prohibited.

5. As regards the related issue of embryo research, the law has adopted a compromise position: research is permitted within the first 14 days if necessary for one of the defined statutory purposes (including attempting to develop treatments for serious disease by using embryonic stem-cells).

6. A separate set of complexities emerge in relation to using donor gametes to provide children for infertile persons or couples ('collaborative reproduction'). Here one matter is the need for the law to resolve the question of who, between the donors and the recipients of treatment, are the the legal parents.

7. In the light of experience with the 1990 rules, as well as changes in social attitudes (particularly as regards the potential for homosexual couples to use donor gametes to found a family), these parenthood rules have been amended: they are now contained in (the self-standing part of) the HFE Act 2008.

---

98 [2007] EWHC 2814 (Fam).

8.   A second issue relates to the degree of contact (if any) that the children should have with the donor. Until 2005, the law pursued a policy of 'donor anonymity'; however, since then the position has changed, so that the child may later access the HFE Authority register showing who the donor was.

9.   One especially contentious area of collaborative reproduction is surrogacy, in which a woman agrees to bear a child for others – normally for payment. Here the law (in the 1985 Surrogacy Arrangements Act) attempted to clamp down on commercialisation in this area by banning profit-making agencies.

10.   At the same time, the practice itself – as well as the surrogate's ability to charge for her services – remains lawful. Overall, this form of assisted reproduction appears poorly and inconsistently regulated; a particular challenge is posed by the increasing number of cross-border surrogacies.

Further Reading

Fox, M, 'The Human Fertilisation and Embryology Act 2008: Tinkering at the Margins' (2009) *Feminist Legal Studies* 333.

Freeman, M, 'Does Surrogacy have a future after Brazier?' (1999) 7 *Medical Law Review* 1.

Glover, J, *Choosing Children: Genes, Disability and Design*, Oxford: Clarendon Press, 2006.

Jackson, E, *Regulating Reproduction: Law, Technology and Autonomy*, Oxford: Hart Publishing, 2001.

Robertson, J, *Children of Choice*, Ewing, New Jersey: Princeton UP, 1994.

Robertson, J, 'Liberty, identity, and human cloning' (1998) 76 *Texas Law Review* 1371.

Chapter 8

Abortion and Pre-Natal Harm

8.1 Introduction

By contrast with the issues examined in Chapter 7, in which the law has had, in the main, to respond to novel problems created by recent advances in medical technology, abortion as a procedure has existed for centuries. Nevertheless, it remains one of the most intractable and emotive topics within the province of medical law. Broadly speaking, 'abortion' denotes the practice of terminating a pregnancy in such a way as to destroy the life of the foetus being carried by the pregnant woman. In the case of abortions carried out early in pregnancy on non-viable foetuses, the fact that the foetus is expelled from the womb is sufficient for its death. In other cases, where the foetus is more mature (and capable of surviving outside the womb), additional steps will be taken to ensure that it dies prior to delivery. Either way, it is apparent that the practice stands in direct opposition to the major forms of fertility treatment considered in the last chapter. There, the intention is normally to produce a pregnancy resulting in a successful live birth. Here, the intention is to bring an existing pregnancy to an end without the live birth of the child. In another sense, however, there is a close relationship between the practices in that they both implicate (albeit in opposing ways) reproductive freedom. As John Robertson notes:

Robertson, JA, *Children of Choice*[1]

An essential distinction is between the freedom to avoid reproduction and the freedom to reproduce. When people talk of reproductive rights, they usually have one or the other aspect in mind. Because different interests and justifications underlie each, and countervailing interests for limiting each aspect vary, recognition of one aspect does not necessarily mean that the other will also be respected; nor does limitation of one mean that the other can also be denied.

However, there is a mirroring or reciprocal relationship here. Denial of one type of reproductive liberty necessarily implicates the other. If a woman is not able to avoid reproduction through contraception or abortion, she may end up reproducing, with all the burdens that unwanted reproduction entails. Similarly, if one is denied the liberty to reproduce . . . one is forced to avoid reproduction, thus experiencing the loss that absence of progeny brings. By extending reproductive options, new reproductive technologies present challenges to both aspects of procreative choice.

Gillian Douglas has explored the background to the right to avoid reproduction claimed for individuals as follows:

Douglas, G, *Law, Fertility and Reproduction*[2]

Methods, effective or not, for avoiding conception or childbirth are probably as old as civilisation itself, and various remedies to alleviate childlessness are probably of equal antiquity. To what extent have individuals been at liberty to make use of these? The former, certainly, have always been forthrightly condemned by the Roman Catholic Church, drawing originally upon the Jewish view that the duty to procreate through marriage is the first of all commandments. Sex became associated by St Augustine with sin, and could only be justified by procreation. Aquinas considered that to dissociate sex from procreation was to act against nature and therefore to sin.

The breaking down of this religious influence and the rise of a rights-based political philosophy in the West during the 18th and 19th centuries, utilised first by men and then by women, enabled individuals to challenge these old ideas and control of sexual behaviour. Since

---

1　Ewing, NJ: Princeton UP, 1994.
2　London: Sweet & Maxwell, 1991.

women are the central actors in reproduction, it is not surprising to find that the first wave of feminism in the 19th century was in part characterised by a desire to enable women to restrict their childbearing, albeit mainly to ensure that they could be better mothers to a few children, rather than poor mothers to too many. The possibility of a right to control one's reproductive capacity through contraception is more likely to be a female than a male concern because of the consequences for the woman where such a possibility is not permitted. In this century, the modern wave of feminism has demanded such a freedom directly, as an aspect of a general desire to gain autonomy and control over one's own body.

In this chapter, we shall first consider the principal moral arguments for and against abortion, together with the additional factors which influence the legal response to what many regard as an ethical impasse. Next, in section 8.2, the present state of the law will be analysed, including, in section 8.3, the implications for the parties most directly affected by the practice. Lastly, in section 8.4 the discussion will move beyond the question of abortion to address the legal position in relation to other forms of avoidable pre-natal harm.

8.1.1 The moral debate

Traditionally, the debate as to the rights and wrongs of abortion has been couched in terms of the 'right to life' of the foetus versus the pregnant woman's 'right to choose' whether or not to bear a child. In many cases, the position a person takes in this debate will depend upon the underlying moral status they accord to the human foetus. As Rosalind Hursthouse writes:

Hursthouse, R, *Beginning Lives*[3]

The simplest view on the issue of abortion, the one often expressed explicitly or implicitly by non-philosophers in letters to newspapers, discussions on the wireless and so on, is that the moral rights and wrongs of abortion can be unproblematically settled by determining the moral status of the foetus. Hence it is common to find people on the conservative side insisting that the foetus is an unborn baby and hence that abortion is infanticide or murder and absolutely wrong, while people on the opposite side insist that the foetus is just a clump of living cells and hence that abortion is merely an operation which removes some part of one's body and hence is morally innocuous.

Now it is certainly true that the question of the moral status of the foetus is important, for according to what its status is, different arguments will bear upon the rights and wrongs of abortion. If, as conservatives believe, the foetus has the same moral status as a baby, then the mother's moral right to abortion is, to say the least, problematic; if there were any such right, a quite particular case would have to be made out for it. If, on the other hand, the foetus has the same moral status as, say, a kidney, then the argument for the mother's moral right to abortion could proceed, quite generally, as an argument concerning the right, of both women and men, to decide what happens to their own bodies.

The physical attributes of the foetus and the developmental process that it undergoes during pregnancy are, as we saw in the previous chapter, agreed upon. What is controverted is the moral inferences as to its status that should be drawn from the physical facts. The two key contrasting views, the 'theological' and 'personhood' approaches, are discussed by Jane Fortin in the following extract, along with a middle position put forward by Michael Lockwood:

---

3   Oxford: Blackwells, 1987.

Fortin, J, 'Legal protection for the unborn child'[4]

... [M]ost philosophers argue that the point in time when human life begins is quite distinct from and less relevant than when a human 'person' comes into existence. The advantage of this approach is that it avoids the 'speciesism' involved in maintaining that all human life automatically has a greater intrinsic value and right to protection than that of any other species. Instead, it concentrates on those aspects of human life that merit such preferment. Thus whilst few would claim that a human sperm or unfertilised egg merits greater protection than a 10 week old kitten, most would accept without question the automatic right to life of a 10 year old child. This is because the child has become a person and as such, his life has an intrinsic value both to himself and others. Arguably then, there is little reason for extending legal protection to human life until 'a person' comes into existence. If this argument is accepted, it becomes vital to establish a clear definition of 'personhood'; no easy matter when moral philosophers show little accord in their choice of essential attributes to be displayed by a 'person'.

Perhaps the most widely known to the general public is the traditional Roman Catholic approach to the question. This is a metaphysical one which, in its strictest form, maintains that a human person comes into existence at the moment of the ovum being fertilised. At this moment of 'ensoulment', the fertilised ovum becomes infused with a rational soul of its own and this theory of immediate animation is widely believed to embody the official teaching of the Roman Catholic Church . . .

Many moral philosophers reject the metaphysical approach to personhood which is so often associated with the Roman Catholic Church. In their view personhood is not defined by reference to the presence or otherwise of an immaterial human soul but by reference to a complicated combination of mental and or physical properties. . . . Inevitably, many proponents of such a combination of properties, find it impossible to accept that a human foetus can be deemed a person and worthy of protection; consequently, in their view, there can be no moral objection to abortion, however late. Indeed, Michael Tooley lucidly presents the argument that since even a newly born child lacks these properties, infanticide is not morally objectionable.

. . . Although many would find Tooley's conclusion distasteful, its logic cannot be denied. A possible way of avoiding some, but not all, of these problems is to maintain three clear distinctions. Thus Michael Lockwood distinguishes between human organisms, human beings and persons. In this way, depending on the definition of 'human being', a newly born infant might be classified as such, with certain consequential rights, despite its not having attained the status of personhood. Lockwood uses the term 'human being' to describe what 'you and I are essentially, what we can neither become nor cease to be, without ceasing to exist'. Thus, in his view, this concept revolves round that of personal identity, which underlies 'certain discernible continuities' such as memory and personality – those unchanging elements in a human being which establishes his own unique blueprint. Accordingly, the concept of identity is established not by the continuities themselves but by those elements underlying them . . .

In his view, it is only when the brain develops to this extent, that a human embryo can be said to have become a human being. Only then does it become able to sustain distinctively mental processes, thereby justifying certain protection. Lockwood himself feels that it is impossible to be precise over the point in time when this occurs. Nevertheless, on the basis of the existing, albeit sparse, scientific evidence, he suggests that an appropriate marker might be 10 weeks' gestation. Lockwood's analysis is attractively clear and less cold blooded than that of Tooley. Moreover, it has the advantage of allowing both the unborn and the newly born child to have a measure of protection as human beings, without claiming either to be a fully fledged person.

---

4 (1988) 51 MLR 54.

However, it is apparent that all three views described by Fortin require some commitment to unprovable 'metaphysical' premises. As Margaret Brazier has noted:

Brazier, M, 'The challenge for Parliament'[5]

The difficulty is that the dispute is itself incapable of any conclusive resolution. Perception of the status of the embryo derives in many cases from the presence or absence of religious belief. Most, but not all, proponents of the belief that the embryo is from fertilisation a genetically unique individual as fully human as you or I, rest that belief, at least in part, on the embryo's potential possession of an immortal, immaterial soul ... Many, but again by no means all, proponents of allowing research on embryos deny or doubt the existence of the soul.

Thus the argument on abortion becomes for opponents: 'How can the law permit the wanton destruction of human life?' And supporters of liberal abortion laws respond: 'By what right do you seek to impose your personal unprovable claims about God and the soul on others?' The dispute reaches stalemate ... The humanity of the embryo is unproven and unprovable. But that acts both ways. Just as I cannot prove that humanity was divinely created and that each and every one of us possesses an immortal soul, so it cannot be proved that it is not so. Admitting the possibility of the soul, the moment of ensoulment cannot be proved. Nothing more or less can be concluded about the full humanity of the embryo save to say that the cases for and against are, to borrow a Scottish term, not proven.

Rather than attempting to found the moral status of the foetus on any particular attribute it possesses as it now is, an increasingly popular approach is to stress the potential (understood in terms of how it would develop naturally, other things equal) that the foetus has to become a person in the future. However, this concept stands in need of significant clarification if it is to bear any real moral weight. As Glover notes:

Glover, J et al, Report to the European Commission on Reproductive Technologies, Fertility and the Family[6]

Perhaps what matters is not some property an embryo now has, but what it has the potential to become. This claim seems to imply that disposing of an embryo is wrong because it prevents the existence of a particular developed person, namely the one the embryo would have become. But this argument rules out contraception. You are a particular developed person, and contraception would have prevented your existence. The apparently innocuous word 'potential' turns out to be very slippery.

To avoid ruling out contraception, potentiality has to be interpreted differently. Perhaps the destruction of potential is not just a matter of the loss of a future developed person, but also the loss of something that has got a certain distance on the way there: the programme is already in existence, as all the genes are present. But this leaves some unanswered questions. If the properties an embryo now has do not generate a right to life, and the argument about one less future person does not do so either, why should combining the two considerations give the desired result? Of course a compound can have properties not possessed by its individual ingredients, but in this case some account is needed of the moral chemistry involved ...

It is accordingly important to consider whether there may be alternative ways to understand the debate which allow conclusions about the morality of abortion which do not depend on views

---

5   In Dyson, A and Harris, J (eds), *Experiments on Embryos*, London: Routledge, 1990.
6   London: Fourth Estate, 1989.

about the status of the foetus. Two very different, but equally bold, attempts to recouch the abortion debate to precisely this end have been made, respectively, by Judith Jarvis Thomson and Ronald Dworkin. Taking Thomson's argument first, in a celebrated article 'A defense of abortion', she suggested that, even if, for the sake of argument, we were to grant the foetus equal moral status to adult human persons, abortion would remain morally permissible in a large number of circumstances, given the prior right of the pregnant woman to exercise control over her body:

Thomson, JJ, 'A defense of abortion'[7]

Most opposition to abortion relies on the premise that the foetus is a human being, a person, from the moment of conception. . . .

. . . How, precisely, are we supposed to get from there to the conclusion that abortion is morally impermissible? Opponents of abortion commonly spend most of their time establishing that the foetus is a person, and hardly any time explaining the step from there to the impermissibility of abortion. Perhaps they think the step too simple and obvious to require much comment. Or perhaps instead they are simply being economical in argument. Many of those who defend abortion rely on the premise that the foetus is not a person, but only a bit of tissue that will become a person at birth; and why pay out more arguments than you have to? Whatever the explanation, I suggest that the step they take is neither easy nor obvious, that it calls for closer examination than it is commonly given, and that when we do give it this closer examination we shall feel inclined to reject it.

I propose, then, that we grant that the foetus is a person from the moment of conception. How does the argument go from here? Something like this, I take it. Every person has a right to life. So the foetus has a right to life. No doubt the mother has a right to decide what shall happen in and to her body; everyone would grant that. But surely a person's right to life is stronger and more stringent than the mother's right to decide what happens in and to her body, and so outweighs it. So the foetus may not be killed; an abortion may not be performed.

It sounds plausible. But now let me ask you to imagine this. You wake up in the morning and find yourself back to back in bed with an unconscious violinist. A famous unconscious violinist. He has been found to have a fatal kidney ailment, and the Society of Music Lovers has canvassed all the available medical records and found that you alone have the right blood type to help. They have therefore kidnapped you, and last night the violinist's circulatory system was plugged into yours, so that your kidneys can be used to extract poisons from his blood as well as your own. The director of the hospital now tells you: 'Look, we're sorry the Society of Music Lovers did this to you – we would never have permitted it if we had known. But still, they did it, and the violinist now is plugged into you. To unplug you would be to kill him. But never mind, it's only for nine months. By then he will have recovered from his ailment, and can safely be unplugged from you.' Is it morally incumbent on you to accede to this situation? No doubt it would be very nice of you if you did, a great kindness. But do you have to accede to it? What if it were not nine months, but nine years? Or longer still? What if the director of the hospital says: 'Tough luck, I agree, but you've now got to stay in bed, with the violinist plugged into you, for the rest of your life. Because remember this. All persons have a right to life, and violinists are persons. Granted you have a right to decide what happens in and to your body, but a person's right to life outweighs your right to decide what happens in and to your body. So you cannot ever be unplugged from him.' I imagine you would regard this as outrageous, which suggests that something really is wrong with that plausible-sounding argument I mentioned a moment ago.

---

7   (1971) 1 *Philosophy and Public Affairs* 1.

In this case, of course, you were kidnapped; you didn't volunteer for the operation that plugged the violinist into your kidneys. Can those who oppose abortion on the ground I mentioned make an exception for a pregnancy due to rape? Certainly. They can say that persons have a right to life only if they didn't come into existence because of rape; or they can say that all persons have a right to life, but that some have less of a right to life than others, in particular, that those who came into existence because of rape have less. But these statements have a rather unpleasant sound. Surely the question of whether you have a right to life at all, or how much of it you have, shouldn't turn on the question of whether or not you are the product of a rape.

Despite its ingenuity, there are a number of difficulties with Thomson's argument. First, whilst it may well permit abortion in cases of rape (where the woman has not given the foetus a 'right' to the use of her body), it is not clear that it can be extended to pregnancy which results from consensual sex. As Hursthouse notes:

Hursthouse, R, *Beginning Lives*[8]

Thomson asserts it as a premise that a woman cannot be said to have given the foetus the right to use her body if she is pregnant because of rape. Plausibly the pregnancy must result from voluntary intercourse . . . However this still leaves a very large number of cases; does Thomson agree that in all cases of pregnancy due to voluntary intercourse in full knowledge of the facts of life the mother could be said to have given the foetus the right to use her body – that the intercourse, as it were, amounts to an offer to have one's body thus used?

She clearly does not, but her argument at this point depends on two rather unsatisfactory analogies. In one she imagines that children come about by people-seeds taking root in one's carpet; this may happen even if one has gone to great trouble to try to prevent it by putting fine mesh screens over one's windows. In the other analogy, she does not consider children, but how people might acquire a right to use my house, and says it would be absurd to suppose that someone had acquired it by just blundering in, through a window I had happened to open, behind bars I had installed to keep people out which happened to have a defect. In each case I go to some trouble to try to keep people-seeds or people out; in each case there is supposed to be a way that would guarantee keeping them out, say with sealed windows, but it cannot be said that I am responsible for their being in my house and that hence they have a right to it simply because I do not go in for this extreme measure.

These analogies are obviously supposed to be with contraception; despite the woman's efforts not to become pregnant, she does. Given that she was trying not to, her voluntary intercourse cannot count as an offer, conferring a right, to have her body used by the foetus. But the difficulty with the people-seed analogy is that, because it is so far-fetched, it lacks all the background that enables one (sometimes) to make up one's mind. Do these people-seeds just root for nine months? What are the available alternatives to uprooting and killing them – can they be transplanted, can you swap your house for nine months with someone who wants children . . .? The difficulty with the other analogy is that it misses out the crucial aspect of the foetus being dependent on the use of the woman's body for its survival . . .

Secondly, there remains the problem that abortions are typically carried out by a third party, the doctor, and it may be argued that conceiving of abortion in terms of a conflict of maternal-foetal rights cannot settle the question of what would be an appropriate moral response on the part of

---

8   See n 3 above.

such a third party. Finally, and more generally, Thomson's narrow focus on rights may be felt to obscure other ways in which an action is morally problematic. In particular, it does not follow, from the mere fact that the foetus lacks a right to use the woman's body, that abortion is morally innocuous. This appears to be recognised by Thomson herself:

Thomson, JJ, 'A defense of abortion'[9]

We surely must all grant that there may be cases in which it would be morally indecent to detach a person from your body at the cost of his life. Suppose you learn that what the violinist needs is not nine years of your life, but only one hour: all you need do to save his life is to spend one hour in that bed with him. Suppose also that letting him use your kidneys for that one hour would not affect your health in the slightest. Admittedly you were kidnapped. Admittedly you did not give anyone permission to plug him into you. Nevertheless it seems to me plain you *ought* to allow him to use your kidneys for that hour – it would be indecent to refuse.

In a telling contribution to the abortion debate, Ronald Dworkin attempted to bridge the gap between the 'pro-life' and 'pro-choice' positions by identifying an important piece of common ground between the two camps. In particular, he argued that both conservatives and liberals share a common commitment to the sanctity of human life:

Dworkin, R, *Life's Dominion: An Argument About Abortion and Euthanasia*[10]

Both conservatives and liberals assume that in some circumstances abortion is more serious and more likely to be unjustifiable than in others. Notably, both agree that a late term abortion is graver than an early term one. We cannot explain this shared conviction simply on the ground that foetuses more closely resemble infants as pregnancy continues. People believe that abortion is not just emotionally more difficult but morally worse the later in pregnancy it occurs, and increasing resemblance alone has no moral significance. Nor can we explain the shared conviction by noticing that at some point in pregnancy a foetus becomes sentient. Most people think that abortion is morally worse early in the second trimester – well before sentience is possible – than early in the first one . . . Foetal development is a continuing creative process, a process that has barely begun at the instant of conception. Indeed, since genetic individuation is not yet complete at that point, we might say that the development of a unique human being has not started until approximately 14 days later, at implantation. But after implantation, as foetal growth continues, the natural investment that would be wasted in an abortion grows steadily larger and more significant.

Human and divine

So our sense that frustration rather than just loss compromises the inviolability of human life does seem helpful in explaining what unites most people about abortion. The more difficult question is whether it also helps in explaining what divides them . . .

Suppose parents discover, early in the mother's pregnancy, that the foetus is genetically so deformed that the life it would lead after birth will inevitably be both short and sharply limited. They must decide whether it is a worse frustration of life if the gravely deformed foetus were to die at once – wasting the miracle of its creation and its development so far – or if it were to continue to grow in utero, to be born, and to live only a short and crippled life. We know that people divide about that question, and we now have a way to describe the division. On one view,

---

9 See n 7 above.
10 London: Harper Collins, 1993.

immediate death of the foetus, even in a case like this one, is a more terrible frustration of the miracle of life than even a sharply diminished and brief infant life would be, for the latter would at least redeem some small part, however limited, of the natural investment. On the rival view, it would be a worse frustration of life to allow this foetal life to continue, because that would add, to the sad waste of a deformed human's biological creation, the further, heartbreaking waste of personal emotional investments made in that life by others, but principally by the child himself, before his inevitable early death.

We should therefore consider this hypothesis: though almost everyone accepts the abstract principle that it is intrinsically bad when human life, once begun, is frustrated, people disagree about the best answer to the question of whether avoidable premature death is always or invariably the most serious possible frustration of life. Very conservative opinion, on this hypothesis, is grounded in the conviction that immediate death is inevitably a more serious frustration than any option that postpones death, even at the cost of greater frustration in other respects. Liberal opinion, on the same hypothesis, is grounded in the opposite conviction: that in some cases, at least, a choice for premature death minimises the frustration of life and is therefore not a compromise of the principle that human life is sacred but, on the contrary, best respects that principle . . .

Although enlightening, Dworkin's inclusive strategy is not likely to satisfy everybody. In particular, in the metaphysical assumptions he makes about the foetus he appears to be far closer to the liberal than the conservative position. Even if he is right that some conservatives oppose abortion on the 'detached' ground that it frustrates life in the abstract, there will inevitably remain others whose opposition is derived from specific beliefs about foetuses which are not amenable to any compromise. Equally, it is likely that some adherents of a liberal-feminist persuasion will not be convinced that the foetus is to be regarded as any more sacred than other parts of the woman's body tissue. Nevertheless, it is probable that Dworkin's view is one that, empirically speaking, accurately reflects a broad consensus of opinion in our society today.

 SELF-TEST QUESTION

Which of the arguments considered above do you personally find most persuasive?

8.1.2 Abortion and legislation

The point that questions as to the morality of a practice must be distinguished from the rightness of legislating against the same was noted in Chapter 7. In relation to abortion, the salient arguments are well put by Rosalind Hursthouse:

See Chapter 7

Hursthouse, R, *Beginning Lives*[11]

The confusion of questions about morality and legislation is particularly common in arguments about abortion . . . One reason why the questions become readily confused in debate is because of the tactics of opposition. Many people, particularly women, do think there is something wrong about having an abortion, that it is not a morally innocuous matter, but also think that the current abortion laws are if anything still too restrictive, and find it difficult to articulate

11 See n 3 above.

their position on the morality of abortion without, apparently betraying the feminist campaign concerning legislation. To give an inch on 'a woman's right to choose', to suggest even for a moment that having an abortion is not only 'exercising that right' (which sounds fine) but also 'ending a human life' (which sounds like homicide) or even 'ending a potential human life' (which sounds at least serious) is to play into the hands of the conservatives.

What happens to the conservative and the liberal sides of the debate once the distinction between questions of morality and questions of legislation is drawn? In theory, drawing the distinction opens up the possibility of four different positions.

Morality of abortion	Laws on abortion	Position
Wrong	Restrictive	Conservative
Innocuous	Restrictive	'Totalitarian'
Innocuous	Liberal	Liberal/radical
Wrong	Liberal	Liberal/moderate

The 'totalitarian' position is of merely theoretical interest. (It might be occupied by someone in an underpopulated country, indifferent both to women's rights and to appeals to the sanctity of life, who thought it was necessary to increase the population quickly.) The first position is a familiar one. It is well known that the conservative position on legislation about abortion is based on a corresponding conservative position about its morality. According to the conservative view, abortion is morally wrong because it is the taking of human life, and hence, like any other case of homicide, justifiable in only a restricted range of circumstances, which should be laid down by law.

It is the possibility of two distinct liberal positions, which for want of better labels I will henceforth distinguish as the 'radical' and the 'moderate', which is not so familiar, and much that is said on the liberal side about women's rights leaves it quite unclear which of two views about the morality of abortion its supporters hold. Do they hold that abortion is morally quite innocuous – and hence that to have laws restricting women's access is as absurd and punitive as having laws which decreed, say, that women (though not men) were forbidden to cut their hair or smoke? Or do they agree with the conservatives that it is a morally very serious matter but hold that nevertheless the suffering and lack of freedom that women must at present undergo when abortion is not legally available not only justify but require our having laws which permit this wrong to be done whenever the woman wishes it? Is abortion a necessary evil as things are at present, or not an evil at all?

As this suggests, at a pragmatic level any lawmaker must consider the likely effect of laws which (for whatever reason) straightforwardly prohibited abortion. Experience, in both this country as well as in many others, has indeed tended to show that, rather than curtailing the practice, abortion will simply be driven underground.

8.2 The Legal Position

8.2.1 Criminal law provisions

Abortion in the UK remains *prima facie* a criminal offence. Historically, the influence of the canon law of the Christian Church played an important part in the emergent common law on the subject. John Keown has charted this influence as follows:

Keown, J, *Abortion, Doctors and the Law*[12]

... [T]he weight of available authority supports the view that the common law prohibited abortion, at the latest, after the foetus had become 'quick' or 'animated'. Animation was believed to occur when the foetus 'quickened' in the womb. An incident of the second trimester of pregnancy, quickening marks the first maternal perception of foetal movement. In associating the origin of life with quickening, the law betrayed both pragmatic and metaphysical influences. The former concerned the need to prove, in any prosecution for abortion, that the woman had been pregnant and that the foetus had been killed by the abortifacient act. Evidence of quickening would clearly facilitate prosecution. The metaphysical influence upon the law was the popular theory, originated by Aristotle and perpetuated by Galen, that human life began at the point of 'animation'. This theory was espoused by the canon law of the Christian Church and thence it found its way into the developing common law.

The criminal law of abortion achieved its modern form only in the mid-19th century. As JK Mason has written:

Mason, JK, *Medico-Legal Aspects of Reproduction and Parenthood*[13]

The recognition of variable foetal rights has fluctuated in British law. The influence of medieval teaching was still apparent in 1803 when procuring the miscarriage of a woman who was 'quick with child' was a statutory offence subject to capital punishment. Abortion at an earlier state of gestation carried a lesser penalty, although it is difficult now to see much advantage to the culprit of a sentence of up to 14 years' transportation; nevertheless, the distinction was clearly meaningful at the time. The law remained the same until 1861 when the Offences Against the Person Act came into being. This introduced two major changes – first, the death penalty was replaced by potential penal servitude for life and, secondly, any distinction as to foetal age was abolished. The 1861 Act remains the definitive law in England, Wales and Northern Ireland ...

Section 58 of the Offences Against the Person Act (OAPA) 1861 provides as follows:

58 Administering drugs or using instruments to procure abortion

Every woman, being with child, who, with intent to procure her own miscarriage, shall administer to herself any poison or other noxious thing, or shall unlawfully use any instrument or other means whatsoever with the like intent, and whosoever, with intent to procure the miscarriage of any woman, whether she be or be not with child, shall unlawfully administer to her or cause to be taken by her any poison or other noxious thing, or shall unlawfully use any instrument or other means whatsoever with the like intent, shall be guilty of felony, and being convicted thereof shall be liable to be kept in penal servitude for life.

Furthermore, s 59 of the Act prohibits various ancillary acts designed to facilitate the commission of the offence:

59 Procuring drugs, etc, to cause abortion

Whosoever shall unlawfully supply or procure any poison or other noxious thing, or any instrument or thing whatsoever, knowing that the same is intended to be unlawfully used or employed

---

12 Cambridge: CUP, 1988.
13 Aldershot: Dartmouth, 1990.

with intent to procure the miscarriage of any woman, whether she be or be not with child, shall be guilty of a misdemeanour, and being convicted thereof shall be liable to be kept in penal servitude.

It will be noted that the Act does not speak in terms of 'carrying out an abortion', but rather of 'procuring a miscarriage'. This (although it remains undefined) is arguably a narrower concept, which would apparently leave certain forms of foetal killing lawful, namely those where the woman does not 'miscarry' as a result of the procedure. The most startling example would be a situation in which the foetus is destroyed once the woman is already in labour: no miscarriage occurs here, but equally the foetus, even one which has partially emerged from the womb, does not yet enjoy the protection of the criminal law against homicide. The existence of such a legal *lacuna* was deplored by Talbot J in charging a jury at Liverpool in 1928, and his comments led to the passing of a further piece of legislation, the Infant Life (Preservation) Act (IL(P)A) 1929. Section 1(1) of the 1929 Act created a new offence of 'child destruction':

1 Punishment for child destruction

(1)   Subject as hereinafter in this sub-section provided, any person who, with intent to destroy the life of a child capable of being born alive, by any wilful act causes a child to die before it has an existence independent of its mother, shall be guilty of felony, to wit, of child destruction, and shall be liable on conviction thereof on indictment to penal servitude for life:

   Provided that no person shall be found guilty of an offence under this section unless it is proved that the act which caused the death of the child was not done in good faith for the purpose only of preserving the life of the mother.

Although, as noted, the primary purpose of this provision was the protection of the foetus during the course of its birth, it is apparent that its effect goes further by extending such protection back in time to the point in the pregnancy at which the foetus became 'capable of being born alive'. By virtue of s 1(2) of the Act, this is rebuttably presumed to be at 28 weeks' gestation:

1(2)   –For the purposes of this Act, evidence that a woman had at any material time been pregnant for a period of 28 weeks or more shall be *prima facie* proof that she was at that time pregnant of a child capable of being born alive.

Thus, the 1861 and 1929 Acts operate to some extent in overlap: a termination carried out on a foetus capable of being born alive will, in so far as it occurs by way of a miscarriage, be an offence under both statutes. By contrast, only the 1861 Act applies to the younger, non-viable foetus and, conversely, only the 1929 Act to a foetus already in the course of its birth.

8.2.2 Defences to abortion prior to 1967

Section 1(1) of the ILPA 1929 contains an express proviso to the effect that no offence is committed by a person who causes the death of the foetus in order to save the life of the pregnant woman. This provision was included because, before the development of modern Caesarean sections, the craniotomy (crushing the foetus's skull) was a standard medical procedure to deal with cases where normal delivery was not medically possible. It is apparent, however, that no similar defence was provided for in the OAPA 1861 in relation to procuring a miscarriage. A question that long remained open, therefore, was whether a doctor who terminated a pregnancy at this earlier stage in order to save the pregnant woman's life was necessarily guilty of an offence under the 1861 Act. The issue finally came before a court in 1938 in the case of R v Bourne.

R v Bourne (1938)[14]

A 14 year old girl became pregnant as a result of a brutal rape. Mr Bourne, an eminent gynae-cologist, made public his intention to perform an abortion on the girl and, having obtained the consent of her parents, duly did so. He was charged with procuring a miscarriage contrary to s 58 of the OAPA 1861. In his defence, could a similar proviso to that found in the ILPA 1929 be read into the section and, if so, what was its scope?

> **Macnaghten J**: No such proviso is in fact set out in s 58 of the Offences Against the Person Act 1861; but the words of that section are that any person who 'unlawfully' uses an instrument with intent to procure miscarriage shall be guilty of felony. In my opinion the word 'unlawfully' is not, in that section, a meaningless word. I think it imports the meaning expressed by the proviso in s 1, sub-s (1) of the Infant Life (Preservation) Act 1929, and that s 58 of the Offences Against the Person Act 1861 must be read as if the words making it an offence to use an instrument with intent to procure a miscarriage were qualified by a similar proviso.
>
> In this case, therefore, my direction to you in law is this – that the burden rests on the Crown to satisfy you beyond reasonable doubt that the defendant did not procure the miscarriage of the girl in good faith for the purpose only of preserving her life . . .
>
> What then is the meaning to be given to the words 'for the purpose of preserving the life of the mother'? There has been much discussion in this case as to the differ-ence between danger to life and danger to health. It may be that you are more fortu-nate than I am, but I confess that I have found it difficult to understand what the discussion really meant, since life depends upon health, and it may be that health is so gravely impaired that death results. A question was asked by the learned Attorney General in the course of his cross-examination of Mr Bourne. 'I suggest to you, Mr Bourne,' said the Attorney General, 'that there is a perfectly clear line – there may be border-line cases – there is a clear line of distinction between danger to health and danger to life'. The answer of Mr Bourne was: 'I cannot agree without qualifying it; I cannot say just yes or no. I can say there is a large group whose health may be damaged, but whose life almost certainly will not be sacrificed. There is another group at the other end whose life will be definitely in very great danger.' And then he adds:
>
>> There is a large body of material between those two extremes in which it is not really possible to say how far life will be in danger, but we find, of course, that the health is depressed to such an extent that life is shortened, such as in cardiac cases, so that you may say that their life is in danger, because death might occur within measurable distance of the time of their labour.
>
> If that view commends itself to you, you will not accept the suggestion that there is a clear line of distinction between danger to health and danger to life. Mr Oliver wanted you to give what he called a wide and liberal meaning to the words 'for the purpose of preserving the life of the mother'. I should prefer the word 'reasonable' to the words 'wide and liberal'. I think you should take a reasonable view of those words.

---

14 [1939] 1 KB 687.

It is not contended that those words mean merely for the purpose of saving the mother from instant death. There are cases, we are told, where it is reasonably certain that a pregnant woman will not be able to deliver the child which is in her womb and survive. In such a case where the doctor anticipates, basing his opinion upon the experience of the profession, that the child cannot be delivered without the death of the mother, it is obvious that the sooner the operation is performed the better. The law does not require the doctor to wait until the unfortunate woman is in peril of immediate death. In such a case he is not only entitled, but it is his duty to perform the operation with a view to saving her life.

Mr Bourne was acquitted by the jury.

Although an important decision, the law still continued to remain in a state of some uncertainty. Unsurprisingly, given the prospect of criminal prosecution and possible conviction, many doctors would only intervene in the clearest cases of risk to the woman's life. In the meantime, the practice of illegal and unhygienic backstreet abortions thrived, leading not infrequently to serious injury to the pregnant woman, or even her death. In the light of this situation, and with the arrival of the more permissive social climate of the 1960s, pressure built up in favour of legislative reform. This culminated in the enactment of the Abortion Act of 1967.

 SELF-TEST QUESTION

In Northern Ireland, where the 1967 Act was never enacted, the law is still governed by *R v Bourne*: as a short independent research exercise, examine later developments in the case law there and summarise your findings.

8.2.3 The Abortion Act 1967

It is important to be clear at the outset that the Abortion Act 1967 has not replaced the pre-existing criminal law statutes on abortion. Rather, its effect is to provide a medical practitioner who carries out an abortion within its terms with a statutory immunity to such criminal prosecution. Originally, only liability under the 1861 Act was excluded; however, the Abortion Act was amended in 1990 (by s 37 of the Human Fertilisation and Embryology Act), to also exclude liability for child destruction under the 1929 IL(P)A. The effect was a further liberalisation of the law, as terminations could now be carried out on later, viable foetuses, including where the pregnant woman's life was not at risk – notably for foetal disability.

The relevant terms of the 1967 Act (as amended) are set out in s 1 as follows:

1 Medical termination of pregnancy

(1) Subject to the provisions of this section, a person shall not be guilty of an offence under the law relating to abortion when a pregnancy is terminated by a registered medical practitioner if two registered medical practitioners are of the opinion, formed in good faith–

(a) that the pregnancy has not exceeded its 24th week and that the continuance of the pregnancy would involve risk, greater than if the pregnancy were terminated, of injury to the physical or mental health of the pregnant woman or any existing children of her family; or

(b) that the termination is necessary to prevent grave permanent injury to the physical or mental health of the pregnant woman; or

(c) that the continuance of the pregnancy would involve risk to the life of the pregnant woman, greater than if the pregnancy were terminated; or

    (d)   that there is a substantial risk that if the child were born it would suffer from such physical or mental abnormalities as to be seriously handicapped.

(2)   In determining whether the continuance of a pregnancy would involve such risk of injury to health as is mentioned in para (a) or (b) of sub-s (1) of this section, account may be taken of the pregnant woman's actual or reasonably foreseeable environment.

(3)   Except as provided by sub-s (4) of this section, any treatment for the termination of pregnancy must be carried out in a hospital vested in the Secretary of State for the purposes of his functions under the National Health Service Act 2006 or the National Health Service (Scotland) Act 1978 . . . or in a place approved for the purposes of this section by the Secretary of State. . . .

(4)   Sub-section (3) of this section, and so much of sub-s (1) as relates to the opinion of two registered medical practitioners, shall not apply to the termination of a pregnancy by a registered medical practitioner in a case where he is of the opinion, formed in good faith, that the termination is immediately necessary to save the life or to prevent grave permanent injury to the physical or mental health of the pregnant woman.

In the following we consider each of the four grounds for termination mentioned in s 1(1) in turn.

8.2.3.1 . . . risk . . . of injury to the physical or mental health of the pregnant woman or any existing children of her family

This ground is used to justify the great majority of abortions carried out in Britain. It is widest in scope and the suggestion that it permits abortions on 'social' as well as strictly 'medical' grounds is given weight by the fact that, besides risks to the pregnant woman, those to the existing children of her family may also be considered. Similarly, s 1(2) of the Act provides that account may here be taken of the woman's environment. It is apparent that the risks in question need not be substantial; it is enough that they exceed the risk to the woman (and/or her existing children) of carrying out the termination. This has led to an argument that since, statistically, an abortion carried out in the first 12 weeks of pregnancy poses fewer health risks to the woman than carrying the foetus to term, the Act will invariably permit such early terminations. Jonathan Montgomery has commented upon the operation of ground 1(1)(a) as follows:

Montgomery, J, *Health Care Law*[15]

While this ground clearly refers to health matters, it has been described as a 'social' ground, because doctors may take account of the woman's actual or foreseeable environment when they assess the risks involved. This means that the inconvenience of having a child may provide a basis for an abortion. It has been argued that this makes it lawful to terminate a pregnancy on the basis of the sex of the foetus where the social and cultural pressures upon a woman to produce a child of a particular sex are strong.

The majority of induced abortions are performed under s 1(1)(a) . . . This overwhelming pattern of 'social' abortions has led to the 1967 Act being criticised for allowing abortion on demand. This assertion is based on the practice of some doctors who argue that there is statistical evidence that carrying a foetus to term is more dangerous to the woman than terminating the pregnancy in its early stages. This enables them to hold that s 1(1)(a) is made out whenever a woman is pregnant. This argument has never been tested in the courts, but it appears that

---

15 Oxford: OUP, 1997.

doctors have given 'pregnancy' as the sole reason for believing that termination is less risky than continuing without being prosecuted.

However, it is apparent that the fact that proceeding to term poses some risk to the woman is not, in itself, a sufficient reason for termination. Rather, the doctor must perform a balancing operation in respect of the patient and determine that termination itself carries a lower risk: it is after all possible that, in a particular case, the risks of termination may in fact be greater than those attached to continuance, for example, where the woman may subsequently suffer some form of psychological reaction. This need to identify the risks running both ways suggests that the doctor's role requires him to engage in more than mere statistical 'rubber stamping'. In this context, the BMA in its guidance, *The Law and Ethics of Abortion*, notes:

BMA, *The Law and Ethics of Abortion*[16]

The Abortion Act requires doctors to make an assessment in the context of each case. They must assess the potential impact of the pregnancy and birth on the woman's physical and mental health and the well-being of existing siblings. Blanket rules cannot be applied to such sensitive and difficult decisions, which require an understanding of the woman's individual needs. A decision to terminate a pregnancy is never an easy one. In making these decisions, patients and doctors should ensure that the decision is supported by appropriate information and counselling about the options and implications.

Importantly, unlike the other grounds under s 1(1), ground (a) contains a time limit: it may only be invoked in so far as the pregnancy has not exceeded its 24th week. This limit was introduced in the 1990 amendments to compensate for the fact that the same amendments removed the effect of the IL(P)A 1929, which had previously supplied a rough upper time limit to lawful abortions (in terms of the child's viability).[17] The practical difficulties, though, in applying a precise time limit in such cases have been noted by Andrew Grubb:

Grubb, A, 'The new law of abortion: clarification or ambiguity'[18]

Section 1(1)(a) does not specify the point in time which starts the clock running in calculating the 24 weeks. There are four possibilities: (A) the first day of the woman's last period; (B) the date of conception (up to 14 days later); (C) the date of implantation (up to 10 days later); and (D) the first day of the woman's first missed period (about four weeks after (A)).

In England the medical profession calculates the length of gestation of a baby on the basis of (A) because it is the most certain date of any of these alternatives. Options (B) and (C), namely the date of conception and the date the fertilised egg implants into the woman, by contrast, cannot be known for certain. But there are difficulties with option (D), because although the first day of the woman's first missed period is certain, it may be quite misleading to indicate length of pregnancy where, for example, following conception during the last week of a cycle the woman does not miss the next period but only the one that follows. The date calculated on the basis of (D) could be about five weeks after conception has actually occurred.

Consequently, when does time start to run? The law might accept the medical profession's approach because of the certainty it would achieve. More importantly, however, it might be accepted because it is the basis upon which parliament introduced the 24 week time limit in

16 London: BMA, November 2007. See www.bma.org.uk/images/lawethicsabortionnov07_tcm41-146867.pdf.
17 As noted in section 8.2.2 above, the 1929 Act itself allowed for late-term feticide in case of imminent risk to the woman's life.
18 [1991] Crim LR 659.

s 1(1)(a) . . . . On that basis, in order to conform to the underlying premise that a foetus which is capable of surviving should not be aborted on the ground in s 1(1)(a), the time limit should actually be 22 weeks or even less.

8.2.3.2 . . . termination necessary to prevent grave permanent injury to the physical or mental health of the pregnant woman

This ground contains no time limit and, by virtue of s 1(4), may be invoked in an emergency by a single doctor without waiting for a second certificate. Arguably, it simply codifies the common law defence available to the doctor who performs a therapeutic abortion designed to avoid serious harm to the woman, as established in R v Bourne. There is, however, one oddity. In speaking of the termination being 'necessary', the ground appears to require foresight by the doctor of such harm as a practical certainty, yet s 1(2) (which applies to this ground as well as (a) above) implies that a mere 'risk' of such injury will be sufficient. Whilst, doubtless, at some point a high enough risk may be treated, analytically, as forming a practical certainty, the term usually denotes something rather less than this.

8.2.3.3 . . . risk to the life of the pregnant woman, greater than if the pregnancy were terminated

Like ground (b) above, this ground may be used in an emergency by a single doctor. Although ground (c) specifically refers to risk to 'life', in practice a large measure of overlap may be expected between the two grounds. This is because, as was apparent in R v Bourne, it may be difficult to say, as a matter of evidence, where grave injury to health ceases and risk to life begins. Moreover, given that – as in the case of ground (a) – the doctor is required to conduct a simple balancing of risks to determine whether a termination is justified, ground (c) may actually be easier to employ: the risk to the woman's life in continuing to term need not be substantial provided that it exceeds the risk involved in abortion. Ironically, the risks at issue are likely to be more readily quantifiable than the somewhat diffuse harms contemplated under ground (a), so it may be here that a 'statistical argument' would have the greatest purchase. For example, suppose that a doctor assesses the risk to the life of the woman in giving birth at one in 8,000. Provided the risk attached to termination is even lower, say, one in 10,000, an abortion would apparently be justified here. Since, in contrast with ground (a), no time limit is placed on terminations under this ground, it appears that an abortion in the circumstances just described could, in theory, take place until birth.

8.2.3.4 . . . substantial risk that if the child were born it would suffer from such physical or mental abnormalities as to be seriously handicapped

In common with the first three grounds, there are significant difficulties in interpreting the precise application and scope of this ground. On the face of it, however, it differs from the others in being directed to the welfare of the foetus rather than that of the pregnant woman. Derek Morgan has argued for a strict interpretation of the ground, allowing its use only in cases of 'foetal euthanasia', that is to say where termination is in the foetus's best interests:

Morgan, D, 'Abortion: the unexamined ground'[19]

Section 1(1)[(d)] requires that the physician decide that there is a 'substantial' risk that the physical or mental abnormalities are such that the child if born would be 'seriously' handicapped . . .

One immediate analogy which could be drawn is that of the severely handicapped neonate who if its condition had been known, might have been aborted under s 1(1)[(d)]. In two recent

---

19 [1990] Crim LR 687.

cases, the Court of Appeal has had to consider in what, if any, circumstances a severely handi-capped infant might be allowed to die. In *In Re C* the court was concerned with a baby born with an unusually severe form of hydrocephalus and with a poorly formed brain structure. She was physically handicapped, including generalised spastic cerebral palsy of all limbs, probable blindness and deafness and an inability to absorb food. In the first judgment of its kind, the High Court acknowledged and condoned the paediatric practice of managing some neonates towards their death rather than striving with heroic interventions to save or treat at all costs . . .

Re C amplified the earlier judgment of the Court of Appeal in *Re B*. There, the court had established, first, that these cases could only proceed under a 'best interests' test (in that case of the ward). And secondly, the court held that only in a case where the prognosis established that the child's life was going to be 'demonstrably . . . so awful', and where there was no lingering doubt about that future, could a non-treatment order be contemplated. Lords Justices Templeman and Dunn observed that this would include cases of severe proved damage such that the court would be driven to conclude that non-treatment was appropriate. This would not be the case, however, where the prognosis or information about the damage was 'still so imponderable' that it would be wrong for the baby to be allowed to die.

The attempt to invoke an analogy between the severely disabled foetus (even at term) and the similarly afflicted neonate is weakened, however, by the fact that, in another crucial respect, the law clearly regards the two situations as very different. In particular, whereas the foetus remains vulnerable to active measures to destroy it, the most that is permitted in relation to the neonate is the passive withholding of measures that would otherwise prolong its life. The view that this ground, like the others, in fact goes principally to the parents' interests, is supported by the history

See Chapter 12 →

behind the 1990 amendments, which removed the time limits restricting the abortion of handicapped foetuses 'capable of being born alive'. The 1988 Select Committee of the House of Lords had the following to say on the issue:

House of Lords Select Committee, *Report of the Select Committee on the Infant Life (Preservation) Bill*[20]

41 Although abortions on ground 4, that is to say, a substantial risk that the child if born would suffer from such abnormalities as to be seriously handicapped, are only a small proportion of the total abortions, they comprise most of the abortions performed after 24 weeks . . . It is these late abortions which would be made more difficult to obtain if an upper limit of 24 weeks were to be imposed, and they represent in the opinion of the Committee a highly important factor. Whether an abortion is desired or justified in such a case will depend to a large extent on the degree of abnormality which is diagnosed and the circumstances and attitude of the parents. Although a severely handicapped child is often the cause of crisis and disaster, there are other cases where even severe handicap has been the means of inspiring love and care within the family, and even the strengthening of character and family ties. At its worst, a child severely affected by spina bifida may be not only mentally retarded, but also severely paralysed so as to be unable to walk, doubly incontinent, deaf and blind. It is obvious that the birth of such a child will constitute an immediate crisis for parents and doctors. Although some women elect never-theless to have severely handicapped children, the Committee have received evidence that the cumulative effect on families of years of caring for a totally dependent child can be devastating, and when the parents die the child must all too often be institutionalised, with traumatic effects. Ante-natal care is rightly directed to the detection of mothers who are subject to these risks, and counselling must always be available, though the choice will be the mother's.

---

20 HL Paper No 50, London: HMSO, 1987–88.

As we have seen, s 1(1)(d) speaks of the foetus suffering from 'such mental or physical abnormalities as to be seriously handicapped'. This undoubted vagueness is compounded by the fact that the section requires only 'a substantial risk' of such abnormalities, which again leaves room for semantic disagreement. Significantly, if the 'parental interests' interpretation of s 1(1)(d) is correct, it suggests these terms should be understood subjectively – ie in the light of the meanings assigned to them by the foetus' mother/parents.

This view arguably finds support in the 2003 case of *Jepson v Chief Constable of West Mercia Police*,[21] which arose after it was revealed that s 1(1)(d) had been used to carry out an abortion at more than 24 weeks upon a foetus with a cleft palate. The claimant, a Church of England curate, sought judicial review of the police's decision not to prosecute the doctors involved, as well as a declaration that a cleft palate was not capable of constituting a serious handicap within the section. Although it eventually gave leave to proceed, the Divisional High Court made it clear that in its view the claimant had little chance of succeeding at trial, and the action was subsequently dropped. Rosamund Scott has commented upon the proceedings as follows:

Scott, R, 'Interpreting the Disability Ground of the Abortion Act'[22]

The claimant in *Jepson* contended that a key error of law surrounding the abortion in that case was 'that the medical practitioners who signed the certificate . . . took into account the views of the parents involved' and 'that . . . in relation to the decision in question, the parents' views, as a matter of law, could have no weight'. Certainly the Act states that two doctors must be 'of the opinion, formed in good faith' that the impairment is serious. Whether two doctors can decide in good faith that the condition is serious and mean, in so doing, 'serious for this woman or couple' is a crucial question. Doctors could decide that a woman's or couple's views as to seriousness are relevant to their opinion of whether the condition of seriousness is satisfied if they consider that the purpose of the disability section of the Act, at least in some cases, is to protect parents by giving them choice.

. . . [T]he basis of this section has recently been reconsidered by Sally Sheldon and Stephen Wilkinson [(2001) 9 Med L Rev 85]. They argue that, because very few foetuses aborted under this ground would have lives of little or no quality if born, most abortions under this section cannot be seen as protecting the foetus from such a life. Rather, in most cases in which this section is invoked, the real concern is with the woman's or parents' interests. This is a moral argument as to the legal interpretation of this section of the Act.

The legal objection to this argument, originally explored by Derek Morgan, is that a 'parental interests' interpretation of section 1(1)(d) of the Act would essentially repeat section 1(1)(a) of the Act, making section 1(1)(d) redundant. Sheldon and Wilkinson observe that, from an ethical viewpoint, it may simply be that there is more than one justification for this section. . . .

Of course, section 1(1)(d) can never be entirely redundant in that, unlike section 1(1)(a), it allows terminations up until birth. Apart from this point and more fundamentally, it may be that as a society we have not necessarily been honest about whose interests the disability section of the Act is capable of protecting: it is to some degree taboo to say that parents have an interest in choosing to accept or avoid the birth of an impaired child and those debating the Act in Parliament may well have sensed this.

In its 2010 report, *Termination of Pregnancy for Fetal Abnormality in England, Scotland and Wales*,[23] the Royal College of Obstetricians and Gynaecologists expressed the view that it would be impractical to

---

21 [2003] EWHC 3318 (Admin).
22 (2005) 64CLJ 388.
23 See www.rcog.org.uk/files/rcog-corp/TerminationPregnancyReport18May2010.pdf.

produce an objective list of conditions constituting serious handicap, given the difficulty of predicting the long-term impact of an abnormality on a child or its family.

 SELF-TEST QUESTIONS

Why is it that Parliament in 1967 did not simply repeal the earlier criminal law statutes on abortion?
       How far is it true that the main change to the law made by the 1967 Act was to permit abortion for foetal disability?

8.3 Implications of the Law

8.3.1 The involved parties

Given the legal framework sketched above, what rights are enjoyed by the key actors in the abortion process? We begin by considering the position of the pregnant woman.

8.3.1.1 The pregnant woman

The general view is that the 1967 Act gives the pregnant woman no right to demand an abortion. As Jonathan Montgomery notes:

Montgomery, J, *Health Care Law*[24]

. . . [I]t does not follow from the fact that doctors are in practice usually immune from prosecution that the Abortion Act 1967 provides for abortion on demand. The Act does not provide women with rights to terminate their pregnancy. Instead, it leaves them dependent upon finding a doctor who will co-operate with their wishes. This means that women who can afford to go to private clinics will usually have little difficulty obtaining a legal abortion. Those reliant on NHS provision, however, are faced with considerable variation between the practice of different doctors. Consequently, there is considerable disparity in the degree to which abortions are readily available both between and within different areas of the country. Official statistics showed that in 1973 only 10% of those seeking an abortion in Walsall were able to get one through the NHS, while in Oxford the figure was 79%.

It is therefore doctors who control access to abortions. Women's access to abortions is dependent on the ethical position of individual doctors and is vulnerable to prejudices of an essentially white middle class profession. Norrie has pointed out that terminations sought because the child is the 'wrong' sex are as justifiable under the Act as those because the pregnancy is inconvenient for economic or career reasons. However, the former is far less likely to be accepted by the medical profession. The Abortion Act 1967 may allow doctors to offer abortion on demand in the early stages of pregnancy, but it does not secure it for women.

It is certainly true that nowhere in the Abortion Act 1967 is there to be found any express right to an abortion and, in this omission, it could be argued that it is a less liberal measure than similar laws in many other jurisdictions. In the USA, for example, the effect of the decisions of the Supreme Court in *Roe v Wade* and *Planned Parenthood v Casey* is that, until viability, state laws placing undue

---

24 See n 15 above.

obstacles in the path of abortion will infringe the woman's constitutionally protected right to privacy.[25] However, although English law, thus, inhibits (at least in symbolic terms) a woman's freedom to terminate her pregnancy, it could be asked whether abortion differs in this respect from any other form of medical treatment available in this country. After all, it is well established that a patient cannot insist upon a particular procedure if the doctor does not believe it to be medically indicated as in the patient's best interests.[26]

In fact, in practice, the wishes of the pregnant woman will usually be the principal factor in persuading doctors to certify an abortion's legality within the Act, at least ones to be carried out in the first trimester. This is borne out by empirical studies into the way in which women who undergo abortions perceive their experience. Ellie Lee has chronicled the accounts of some young women who sought access to UK abortion services as follows:

Lee, E, 'Young Women, Pregnancy, and Abortion in Britain: A Discussion of Law in Practice'[27]

. . . [M]ost young women made a decision about what the outcome of the pregnancy should be before seeing a doctor. This did not mean there was no perceived need for discussion, 'I made my decision straight away. I didn't really need to think about it . . . She [the GP] talked it over for a while with me so it was good'.

It was quite straight cut, it wasn't the right time . . . the doctor was really helpful . . . he asked me what I wanted to do . . . and we'd spoken for a little bit and I said that I didn't really want it and so he went through the procedure and what I had to do . . . he told me exactly what was going to happen . . . so he made me feel a bit easier, that I didn't have to do it on my own, didn't have to find out about it on my own.

These accounts show that the experience of referral was positive where referrers provided clear information about what obtaining an abortion entails. As another interviewee explained, the GP she saw was, '. . . really good' because, '. . . he did get me referred quick, and he did sit down and say what the risks were, what could happen and what couldn't happen'. Information provision was experienced positively not simply because it meant specific questions were answered and it was made clear how abortion could be obtained. It was also of psychological significance, in that it legitimized and normalized requesting abortion.

However, as regards second trimester terminations, more resistance from the medical profession was apparent:

Others who thought their pregnancy had progressed beyond the first trimester (12 weeks) . . . commented that the referral process was difficult. One, who ended up continuing her pregnancy, recounted, 'I wanted an abortion . . . she was like saying, "I don't know if they can do it at that many weeks" (14) . . . '. As a result of taking further advice from her GP and a friend, another obtained an NHS funded abortion at 16 weeks through an independent provider. However, her first port of call was her local family planning clinic: '(S)he didn't even help, she just said, "yeah, it's most probably going to be too late . . . you'll have to look for antenatal care" ', she recounted, of the doctor. Three others also indicated they had the impression it would be very difficult to get a second trimester procedure.

---

25 410 US 113 (1976) and 112 S Ct 2791 (1992). The US Supreme Court's recent decision in *Gonzales v Carhart*, 550 US 124 (2007) does not detract from these principles, being concerned solely with the prohibition of a particular, problematic, late-abortion technique.

26 See eg *R v Cambridge HA ex p B* (1995) 23 BMLR 1.

27 (2004) 18 Int'l JL Pol'y&Fam 283.

This is interesting because, so far as the Abortion Act is concerned, most such terminations would still fall within the ambit of the social ground for abortion (under s 1(1)(a)), with its cut-off of 24 weeks: this suggests that the doctor's own intuitions play a greater role in such cases than the positive legal framework. Be that as it may, the BMA in its briefing paper, *The Law and Ethics of Abortion*, encourages doctors to adopt a facilitative approach, with the pregnant woman at the centre of their concerns:

BMA, *The Law and Ethics of Abortion*[28]

In the 1970s and 1980s the BMA approved policy statements supporting the 1967 Abortion Act as 'a practical and humane piece of legislation' and calling for its expansion to Northern Ireland. The BMA does not consider that abortion is unethical but as with any act having profound moral implications, the justifications must be commensurate with the consequences. Patients are entitled to receive objective medical advice regardless of their doctor's personal views for or against abortion. Furthermore, a doctor could be sued for damages if, because of a failure to refer, a delay is caused which results in the woman being unable to obtain a termination.

As the BMA paper notes, as with other patients who can show that they were improperly denied medical treatment, a pregnant woman prevented from having an abortion through a doctor's failure to certify it under the Abortion Act, may potentially have an *ex post facto* claim in negligence. Though, as we saw in Chapter 6, substantive awards in cases of 'wrongful birth' are no longer available for the birth of a healthy child, the woman remains entitled to damages arising from continued pregnancy, as well as a 'solatium' for the denial of procreative autonomy.[29] In cases where the child is born disabled, significantly higher compensation is payable. Indeed, over the years a number of successful negligence actions have been brought by women who have argued that they should have been given the opportunity to have an abortion on the ground of foetal handicap unders 1(1)(d) of the 1967 Act. An example is the case of *Mackay v Essex AHA*, in which Griffiths LJ expressly suggested that the medical profession is under a duty to advise the pregnant woman of 'her right to have an abortion and the pros and cons of doing so'.[30]

See Chapter 6 →

By contrast, in so far as a pregnant woman, who is a competent adult, chooses not to abort her foetus, it is clear that the law will not make her do so. At first glance, this assertion may seem to be a straightforward application of the principle that competent adults must always consent to medical procedures carried out upon them. However, this is to ignore the possible use of indirect legal means to pressurise women to opt for terminations in certain cases. For example, in the context of an action for wrongful birth, might a woman be denied compensation for the costs of raising a disabled child on the basis that her failure to have a termination was 'unreasonable'? This question was at the heart of the case of *Emeh v Kensington and Chelsea AHA*:

Emeh v Kensington and Chelsea AHA (1985)[31]

The claimant, who already had four children, underwent a voluntary sterilisation at the defendant's hospital. The operation was negligently performed and the plaintiff subsequently became pregnant, only discovering this fact when her foetus was of 17–20 weeks' gestation. She

---

28 See footnote 16 above.
29 *Rees v Darlington Memorial Hospital NHS Trust* [2003] UKHL 52; see further, Ch 6 section 6.2.2 above.
30 [1982] QB 1166. The case is further considered in section 8.4.1 in relation to the child's attempt to claim for 'wrongful life', which unlike the mother's action in 'wrongful birth' was not allowed to proceed.
31 [1985] QB 1012, CA.

refused the defendant's offer of an abortion and later gave birth to a disabled child. At first instance, Park J denied her claim for the costs of raising the child, finding that her failure to have the abortion amounted to a *novus actus interveniens*, which eclipsed the defendant's earlier negligence and made her the author of her loss. The claimant successfully appealed:

> **Slade LJ**: The judge, in saying that her failure to obtain an abortion was so unreasonable as to eclipse the defendants' wrongdoing, was, I think, really saying that the defendants had the right to expect that, if they had not performed the operation properly, she would procure an abortion, even if she did not become aware of its existence until nearly 20 weeks of her pregnancy had elapsed.
>
> I do not, for my part, think that the defendants had the right to expect any such thing. By their own negligence, they faced her with the very dilemma which she had sought to avoid by having herself sterilised.
>
> For the reasons which I have attempted to give, I think that they could and should have reasonably foreseen that if, as a consequence of the negligent performance of the operation she should find herself pregnant again, particularly after some months of pregnancy, she might well decide to keep the child. Indeed, for my part I would go even a little further. Save in the most exceptional circumstances, I cannot think it right that the court should ever declare it unreasonable for a woman to decline to have an abortion in a case where there is no evidence that there were any medical or psychiatric grounds for terminating the particular pregnancy. And no such evidence has been drawn to our attention relating to this particular pregnancy of the plaintiff in the present case.

8.3.1.2 The foetus

Self-evidently, the existence of the regime under the 1967 Abortion Act, permitting legal abortion in a large number of circumstances, means that the foetus has no legal right to life. In this regard, Jane Fortin has written as follows:

Fortin, J, 'Legal protection for the unborn child'[32]

. . . [T]he abortion legislation has contrived a situation whereby a decision to terminate the life of the foetus can be reached by two doctors in consultation only with the mother. There is thus no possibility of anyone intervening on behalf of the foetus, to ensure that adequate consideration has been given to its particular stage of physical and mental development, in order to assess the precise degree of its increasing 'humanness' and whether it warrants protection against its mother's desire for an abortion.

In this context, there is a stark contrast between the legal protection accorded to the unborn and to the newly born. In relation to the latter, however premature, the wardship jurisdiction can be used to cast an immediate cloak of protection over the child, thereby ensuring that fundamentally important decisions relating to the child's future can be considered dispassionately by the High Court. Thus, in the case of *Re B*, the Court of Appeal authorised a life-giving operation on a Down's syndrome child, against the wishes of its parents who had rejected it. By contrast, it is clear from the decisions in *Paton* and *C v S* that although an abortion has a fatal effect on the unborn child, intervention by a third party would be impossible even if in his view the abortion decision has been reached erroneously . . .

Despite the heavy responsibility for interpreting the 1967 Act imposed on the medical profession, it is surprising that the Act contains no guidance to them as to the factors to

---

32 (1988) 51 MLR 54.

consider when deciding whether to approve an abortion. The omission of any direction specifically requiring the doctors to consider the interests of the foetus itself, when deciding whether to approve the abortion, implies that the abortion is a purely medical matter relating only to the mother herself and devoid of any moral implications relating to the foetus.

As Fortin notes elsewhere, the perceived need to safeguard the interests of the pregnant woman has led the courts to deny that the foetus, in utero, enjoys any legal personality. This important point lay behind the decision of the High Court in the case of *Paton v Trustees of British Pregnancy Advisory Services*.

Paton v Trustees of British Pregnancy Advisory Services (1979)[33]

The claimant sought an injunction restraining his wife from having an abortion under the Abortion Act 1967. Although she had obtained the required certificates from two doctors that she satisfied one of the statutory grounds, the plaintiff alleged that she was in fact acting in *male fides*. As a starting point, the plaintiff needed to establish *locus standi* to bring his action, either in his own right or as 'next friend' of the foetus:

> **Sir George Baker P**: The first question is whether this plaintiff has a right at all. The foetus cannot, in English law, in my view, have a right of its own at least until it is born and has a separate existence from its mother. That permeates the whole of the civil law of this country (I except the criminal law, which is now irrelevant), and is, indeed, the basis of the decisions in those countries where law is founded on the common law, that is to say, in America, Canada, Australia and, I have no doubt, in others.
>
> For a long time there was great controversy whether, after birth, a child could have a right of action in respect of pre-natal injury . . . but it was universally accepted, and has since been accepted, that in order to have a right the foetus must be born and be a child. There was only one known possible exception . . . an American case, *White v Yup* . . ., where a wrongful 'death' of an eight month old viable foetus, stillborn as a consequence of injury, led an American court to allow a cause of action, but there can be no doubt, in my view, that in England and Wales the foetus has no right of action, no right at all, until birth. The succession cases have been mentioned. There is no difference. From conception the child may have succession rights by what has been called a 'fictional construction', but the child must be subsequently born alive: see per Lord Russell of Killowen in *Elliot v Lord Joicey* . . .

The approach of the High Court in *Paton* was subsequently endorsed by the Court of Appeal, outside the context of abortion, in the case of *Re F (In Utero)*.

Re F (In Utero) (1988)[34]

A woman with a history of psychiatric problems was 38 weeks pregnant when she absconded from the residential care home in which she lived. Her local authority, which was responsible for her care, sought to make her unborn child a ward of court as a preliminary to further measures to protect its health at this late stage in the pregnancy:

---

33 [1979] QB 276.
34 [1988] Fam 122.

May LJ: Even though this is a case in which, on its facts, I would exercise the [wardship] jurisdiction if I had it, in the absence of authority I am driven to the conclusion that the court does not have the jurisdiction contended for. I respectfully agree with the dictum from the judgment of Sir George Baker P in the *Paton* case . . .

Secondly, I respectfully agree with the judge below in this case that to accept such jurisdiction and yet to apply the principle that it is the interest of the child which is to be predominant is bound to create conflict between the existing legal interests of the mother and those of the unborn child, and that it is most undesirable that this should occur . . .

Staughton LJ: I agree that this appeal should be dismissed. In their notice of appeal the local authority seek orders as follows:

(1) The tipstaff do seek and detain in a suitable place the defendant and do report her whereabouts to the plaintiffs and the court.

(2) The defendant do not leave the jurisdiction so long as she remains pregnant and further following the birth of the said child do not remove the said child from the jurisdiction.

(3) The defendant do forthwith surrender her passport or other travel document to the court.

(4) The defendant do attend forthwith such hospital suitable for the delivery of the said unborn child as the plaintiffs in their discretion direct.

It will be observed that all are orders directed at the mother, as in the nature of things they must be until the child is born.

When the wardship jurisdiction of the High Court is exercised, the rights, duties and powers of the natural parents are taken over or superseded by the orders of the court. Until a child is delivered it is not, in my judgment, possible for that to happen. The court cannot care for a child, or order that others should do so, until the child is born; only the mother can.

In the wake of the decision in *Paton v Trustees of British Pregnancy Advisory Services*, Mr Paton took his case to Strasbourg; however, he failed to persuade the European Commission on Human Rights that the foetus's right to life is protected under Art 2 of the European Convention on Human Rights (ECHR).[35] The Commission's view was that, given the intimate connection between the foetus's life and that of the pregnant woman, any such right must in any event be limited in cases where the latter's life and health are at stake. More recently, in *Vo v France*,[36] the European Court of Human Rights (ECtHR), after noting the lack of consensus in ECHR signatory states as to the nature and status of the foetus, held that unborn life need not be treated as within the ambit of Art 2 of the ECHR. Thus, the degree of legal protection to be accorded to the foetus (in particular by criminal law) was a matter for each individual state.[37]

On the other hand, it should not be concluded that a foetus enjoys no protection at all in English law. It is rather that its interests are subordinated to those of full legal subjects – ie persons already born. Especially in the context of abortion, where there is a conflict between its interests and those of the pregnant woman, the law will accord priority to the woman. (The degree to which the foetus is protected in other circumstances is explored in section 8.4 below.)

---

35 *Paton v UK* (1980) 3 EHRR 408.
36 (2004) 2 FCR 577.
37 Presently, the ECtHR is considering its decision in *A,B & C v Ireland* (25579/05), on how far criminal law protection of the foetus, in the form of restrictive abortion laws, is compatible with the woman's ECHR rights.

8.3.1.3 The father

It is well established that, under English law, the father of a foetus cannot prevent a pregnant woman from having an abortion and, indeed, has no right even to be consulted over her proposed course of action. As we have seen, this was made clear in *Paton v Trustees of British Pregnancy Advisory Services*:[38]

> **Sir George Baker P**: The father's case must . . . depend upon a right which he has himself. I would say a word about the illegitimate, usually called the putative, but I prefer myself to refer to the illegitimate father. Although American decisions to which I have been referred concern illegitimate fathers, and statutory provisions about them, it seems to me that in this country the illegitimate father can have no rights whatsoever except those given to him by statute. That was clearly the common law. One provision which makes an inroad into this is s 14 of the Guardianship of Minors Act 1971, s 9(1) and some other sections of that Act which apply to illegitimate children, giving the illegitimate father or mother the right to apply for the custody of or access to an illegitimate child. But the equality of parental rights provision in s 1(1) of the Guardianship Act 1973 expressly does not apply in relation to a minor who is illegitimate: see s 1(7).
>
> . . . [T]his plaintiff must, in my opinion, bring his case, if he can, squarely within the framework of the fact that he is a husband. It is, of course, very common for spouses to seek injunctions for personal protection in the matrimonial courts during the pendency of or, indeed, after divorce actions, but the basic reason for the non-molestation injunction often granted in the family courts is to protect the other spouse or the living children, and to ensure that no undue pressure is put upon one or other of the spouses during the pendency of the case and during the breaking up of the marriage . . .
>
> The law is that the court cannot and would not seek to enforce or restrain by injunction matrimonial obligations, if they be obligations, such as sexual intercourse or contraception (a non-molestation injunction given during the pendency of divorce proceedings could, of course, cover attempted intercourse). No court would ever grant an injunction to stop sterilisation or vasectomy. Personal family relationships in marriage cannot be enforced by the order of a court. An injunction in such circumstances was described by Judge Mager in *Jones v Smith* . . . in the District Court of Appeal of Florida as 'ludicrous'.
>
> I ask the question, 'If an injunction were ordered, what could be the remedy?' and I do not think I need say any more than that no judge could even consider sending a husband or wife to prison for breaking such an order. That, of itself, seems to me to cover the application here; this husband cannot by law stop his wife by injunction from having what is now accepted to be a lawful abortion within the terms of the Abortion Act 1967.

In his action before the European Commission of Human Rights, Mr Paton argued that his right to 'respect for family life' under Art 8 of the ECHR had been infringed. In dismissing this claim, however, the Commission noted that Art 8(2) specifically limits that right in so far as necessary to protect the rights of another person (here the pregnant woman).[39] The view taken in *Paton* as to the father's lack of status has been endorsed by the courts on a number of occasions since, including by the Court of Appeal in *C v S*.[40]

8.3.1.4 The doctor/health care worker

As will have been apparent in the discussion of s 1(1) of the Abortion Act 1967 above, the Act gives doctors a very wide discretion in determining whether the one of the grounds for lawful

---

38 See n 33 above.
39 See n 35 above.
40 [1988] QB 135; see also the Scottish decision of *Kelly v Kelly* 1997 SLT 896.

termination has been met. Writing in *The Lancet* in 1971, IM Ingram suggested that the wording of the Act is indeed so wide as to be meaningless, and, though the 1990 amendments to the Act have moved the key provisions around, it is apparent that they have not introduced any greater precision. What safeguards are there, then, to prevent a doctor from abusing his discretion? John Keown has discussed this issue as follows:

Keown, J, *Abortion, Doctors and the Law*[41]

During the parliamentary debates on his Bill, Mr Steel [the Act's sponsor] said that it was necessary for such a measure as his to contain 'safeguards' against abuse, and he pointed to three 'essential and new' safeguards in his Bill: the requirements of certification of opinions, notification of abortions, and approval of premises where the operations were to be performed. To what extent have these safeguards, which he said would prevent abuse of the Act, operated as a check on excessively permissive interpretation of s 1?

... The Abortion Regulations 1968 came into effect on the same day as the Abortion Act in discharge of the statutory duty placed on the minister by s 2(1) of the Act. Section 3 of the Regulations deals with the certification of the practitioner's opinions. ...

This Regulation undoubtedly represents a restriction on the practitioner's freedom in that it introduces a formality which he must observe, on pain of a fine. However, certification hardly restricts the exercise of medical discretion, for although it ensures a second opinion it requires neither the second practitioner to be of a particular status nor limits the number of practitioners who may be approached for a second opinion. It does not even require the second practitioner to see the patient ...

As a safeguard against abuse of medical discretion, therefore, certification is only of limited effectiveness. Its main virtue is in ensuring a second opinion, but this had been standard practice well before the enactment of the Regulations, among both reputable and disreputable practitioners. Although the ostensible function of certification is the protection of the patient, it also serves the interests of the practitioner by helping to protect him from suspicion of impropriety.

If certification is only a limited safeguard against abuse of the Act, what of notification? This safeguard was built into the Act in the form of s 2(1)(b), and its requirements are specified in s 4 of the Regulations. Section 4(1) requires the operating practitioner to notify the abortion to the CMO [Chief Medical Officer] within seven days, including in the notification form such information as is specified in Sched 2 to the Regulations.

Unlike certification, notification did represent a significant innovation in this area of medical practice, for whereas it had long been usual to obtain a second opinion, practitioners had not previously reported the operation to a third party. Moreover, failure to notify might, like failure to certify, involve the practitioner in liability under s 2(3) of the Act, and also in suspicion of illegal abortion.

However, the effectiveness of notification as a safeguard is also limited, for, just as a practitioner could certify an illegal abortion as falling within the terms of the Act, so too could he notify such an operation as having been performed within the Act, and it would be extremely difficult to prove the absence of good faith.

The procedure for certification under the Act as amended is now dealt with in the Abortion Regulations 1991, made under s 2 of the Act. The Regulations provide, in s 3, as follows:

---

41 See n 12 above.

Certificate of opinion

3 (1) Any opinion to which s 1 of the Act refers shall be certified–

    (a) in the case of a pregnancy terminated in accordance with s 1(1) of the Act, in the form set out in Part I of Sched 1 to these Regulations; and

    (b) in the case of a pregnancy terminated in accordance with s 1(4) of the Act, in the form set out in Part II of that Schedule.

(2) Any certificate of an opinion referred to in s 1(1) of the Act shall be given before the commencement of the treatment for the termination of the pregnancy to which it relates.

(3) Any certificate of an opinion referred to in s 1(4) of the Act shall be given before the commencement of the treatment for the termination of the pregnancy to which it relates or, if that is not reasonably practicable, not later than 24 hours after such termination.

(4) Any such certificate as is referred to in paras (2) and (3) of this Regulation shall be preserved by the practitioner who terminated the pregnancy to which it relates for a period of not less than three years beginning with the date of the termination.

(5) A certificate which is no longer to be preserved shall be destroyed by the person in whose custody it then is.

A rare case in which a doctor's performance of an abortion was impugned, on the basis that he had not formed the view in good faith that the termination came within one of the grounds under the 1967 Act, was that of R v Smith (John):

R v Smith (John) (1973)[42]

Dr Smith performed an abortion on a young woman, allegedly without either satisfying himself that continuance of her pregnancy would involve a risk greater than termination to her mental or physical health, or obtaining the requisite second opinion. The matter came to light because, following the operation, the patient became ill, and it was she who subsequently acted as the main prosecution witness. After his conviction by a jury of procuring a miscarriage contrary to s 58 of the OAPA 1861, Dr Smith appealed:

Scarman LJ: The [1967] Act, though it renders lawful abortions that before its enactment would not have been lawful, does not depart from the basic principle of the common law as declared in *R v Bourne*, namely that the legality of an abortion depends on the opinion of a doctor. It has introduced the safeguard of two opinions: but, if they are formed in good faith by the time the operation is undertaken, the abortion is lawful. Thus, a great social responsibility is firmly placed by the law on the shoulders of the medical profession . . .

On 28 April 1970 at the Hayward Nursing Home a Miss Rodgers underwent an operation performed by the appellant, the initial purpose of which was to terminate her pregnancy. The prosecution's case is that he was not acting in good faith; he had not formed a *bona fide* opinion as to the balance of risk between termination and continuation of her pregnancy, that is to say, that the continuance would involve risk to her physical or mental health greater than if it were terminated. The appellant's defence was twofold: he said that he formed an honest opinion as to the need for an abortion, but that when he had the girl on the operating table, he found she was starting an inevitable abortion. Thus according to him, his operation became not a termination, but a facilitating and tidying up of an inevitable abortion – a natural process which had already begun. If this be the truth, the prosecution concedes

---

42 [1973] 1 WLR 1510.

that the operation would be lawful without the need of recourse to the Abortion Act 1967.

In arguing the appeal, counsel for the appellant directed the greater part of his argument not to the issue of inevitable abortion but to that of his client's good faith in deciding to terminate Miss Rodgers' pregnancy. But the course of the trial was somewhat different. The presence of an inevitable abortion already beginning when he operated was at the forefront of the doctor's defence. Professor Fairweather, the specialist called for the Crown, directed most of his evidence to this issue. No doubt both the Crown and the defence appreciated – correctly, we think – that, if the appellant was disbelieved when he said he found an inevitable abortion, his credit would be so undermined that he was unlikely to be believed when he asserted that his decision to terminate was taken only after he had formed an opinion in good faith as to the balance of risk. Nevertheless the two lines of defence merited, as indeed at trial they received, separate attention . . .

The case against the appellant relied on the evidence of Miss Rodgers and of police officers who interviewed the appellant in November and December 1970 and March 1971. Professor Fairweather, a distinguished gynaecologist, gave evidence on the question as to the likelihood of an inevitable abortion when there had been no history of pain or bleeding; he thought it unusual but possible. In reply to the recorder he emphasised the need for careful inquiry when the reason for abortion was injury to mental health and agreed that the 1967 Act could be abused. Both defendants and Dr Davis gave evidence. The trial was a long one and culminated in a lengthy summing up.

Was the verdict unsafe? Counsel for the appellant took a great number of detailed points in his attack on the trial and the summing up. But, as he put it, his central submission was that a finding of bad faith against a doctor, when it relates to the forming of a medical opinion, cannot be safe or satisfactory unless supported by medical evidence pointing overwhelmingly to the lack of good faith . . .

The question of good faith is essentially one for the jury to determine on the totality of the evidence. A medical view put forward in evidence by one or more doctors as to the good faith of another doctor's opinion is no substitute for the verdict of the jury. An opinion may be absurd professionally and yet formed in good faith; conversely an opinion may be one which a doctor could have entertained and yet in the particular circumstances of a case may be found either to have been formed in bad faith or not to have been formed at all. Although the 1967 Act has imposed a great responsibility on doctors, it has not ousted the function of the jury. If a case is brought to trial which calls in question the *bona fides* of a doctor, the jury, not the medical profession, must decide the issue. The risk of abuse, by some, of the protection afforded by the Act was recognised as a genuine risk by Professor Fairweather. In the instant case it was for the jury to determine whether the appellant had or had not abused the protection afforded him by the Act. By leaving the ultimate question to a jury, the law retains its ability to protect society from an abuse of the Act.

This case, which is undoubtedly an unusual one, appears, on the face of it, to be at odds with subsequent judicial reluctance – evident in Sir George Baker P's comments in *Paton v British Pregnancy Advisory Services*[43] – to scrutinise the doctor's *bona fides* in applying the terms of the Abortion Act 1967:

Sir George Baker P: The case which was first put forward to me a week ago, and indeed is to be found in the writ, is that the wife had no proper legal grounds for seeking a termination of

---

43 See n 33 above.

her pregnancy and that, indeed, not to mince words, she was being spiteful, vindictive and utterly unreasonable in seeking so to do. It now appears I need not go into the evidence in the affidavits because it is accepted and common ground that the provisions of the Act have been complied with, the necessary certificate has been given by two doctors and everything is lawfully set for the abortion . . .

The case put to me finally by Mr Rankin . . . is that while he cannot say here that there is any suggestion of a criminal abortion, nevertheless if doctors did not hold their views, or come to their conclusions in good faith, which would be an issue triable by a jury (see *R v Smith (John)* . . .), then this plaintiff might recover an injunction. That is not accepted by Mr Denny. It is unnecessary for me to decide that academic question because it does not arise in this case. My own view is that it would be quite impossible for the courts in any event to supervise the operation of the Abortion Act 1967. The great social responsibility is firmly placed by the law upon the shoulders of the medical profession: see per Scarman LJ in *R v Smith (John)*. . . .

. . . The two doctors have given a certificate. It is not and cannot be suggested that the certificate was given in other than good faith and it seems to me that there is the end of the matter in English law.

More recently, in R v Dixon[44] a doctor who continued with a hysterectomy upon a patient whose pregnancy only came to light during the operation, was similarly charged with an offence under s 58 of the OAPA 1861. On this occasion, the doctor's defence that he had acted in good faith to preserve the woman from grave permanent injury to her mental health (within s 1(1)(b) of the Abortion Act 1967) was accepted by the jury. While the doctor's evidence may appear flimsy ('in view of this lady's age, her very recent history of deliberate suicide attempt by overdose . . . and her express wish for hysterectomy, we felt an emergency termination of pregnancy would be justified'), the case highlights the reluctance of juries to criminalise the practice of the modern abortion doctor.

As discussed in section 8.3.1.1, an opposing, and ironically perhaps more effective, brake upon a doctor's discretion under the 1967 Act may consist in the potential ability of the pregnant woman to sue in negligence in so far as the doctor *fails* to assist her in having an abortion. As yet this remains untested in the courts: so far all of the cases relating to 'wrongful birth' have involved unwitting rather than deliberate failures to refer patients for an abortion.[45] However, it appears likely that – excepting cases of express reliance on conscientious objection, considered below – a doctor who for any but the most cogent reasons failed to assist a woman in obtaining a desired abortion, would fail the *Bolam* test, and hence open himself up to liability. As noted, the BMA has warned its members about this possibility.[46]

As just alluded to, a residual and important issue issue in relation to the doctor is how far he may in fact refuse to participate in an abortion on grounds of conscience. This question is dealt with in s 4 of the Abortion Act 1967:

4 Conscientious objection to participation in treatment

(1) Subject to sub-s (2) of this section, no person shall be under any duty, whether by contract or by any statutory or other legal requirement, to participate in any treatment authorised by this Act to which he has a conscientious objection, provided that in any legal proceedings the burden of proof of conscientious objection shall rest on the person claiming to rely on it.

---

44 R v Dixon (Reginald) (1995) (unreported).
45 See Ch 6 above. Typically, cases involve negligent failure to diagnose that the patient was pregnant and/or that the foetus is suffering from disability.
46 See n 28 above.

(2) Nothing in sub-s (1) of this section shall affect any duty to participate in treatment which is necessary to save the life or to prevent grave permanent injury to the physical or mental health of a pregnant woman.

As is apparent from s 4(2) above, this provision cannot be relied upon by a doctor called upon to perform an abortion in an emergency. The question (in non-emergency situations) of who, apart from the treating doctor, may rely on the conscientious objection clause, came before the House of Lords in 1988 in *Janaway v Salford HA*.

Janaway v Salford HA (1988)[47]

The claimant, a Roman Catholic, lost her job working as a secretary for the defendant health authority after refusing to type a letter of referral in respect of an abortion patient. She brought an action for unfair dismissal on the basis that her refusal was protected under s 4(1) of the Abortion Act 1967:

> **Lord Keith**: The applicant claims the protection of s 4(1). The issue in the case turns on the true construction of the words in that sub-section 'participate in any treatment authorised by this Act'. For the applicant it is maintained that the words cover taking part in any arrangements preliminary to and intended to bring about medical or surgical measures aimed at terminating a pregnancy, including the typing of letters referring a patient to a consultant. The health authority argues that the meaning of the words is limited to taking part in the actual procedures undertaken at the hospital or other approved place with a view to the termination of a pregnancy . . .
>
> The argument for the applicant proceeds on the lines that the acts attracting the protection afforded by s 4(1) are intended to be co-extensive with those which are authorised by s 1(1) and which in the absence of that provision would be criminal. The criminal law about accessories treats one who aids and abets, counsels or procures a criminal act as liable to the same extent as a principal actor. In the absence of s 1(1) the applicant by typing a letter of referral would be counselling or procuring an abortion, or at least helping to do so, and subject to a possible defence on the principle of *R v Bourne* . . . would be criminally liable. Therefore any requirement to type such a letter is relieved, in the face of a conscientious objection, by s 4(1).
>
> The majority of the Court of Appeal (Slade and Stocker LJJ) accepted the main thrust of the applicant's argument, to the effect that s 1(1) and s 4(1) are co-extensive, but decided against her on the ground that her intention in typing a letter of referral would not be to assist in procuring an abortion but merely to carry out the obligations of her employment. In their view the typing of such a letter by the applicant would not be a criminal offence in the absence of s 1(1).
>
> Nolan J, however, and Balcombe LJ in the Court of Appeal rejected the applicant's main argument. They accepted the argument for the health authority that on a proper construction the word 'participate' in s 4(1) did not import the whole concept of principal and accessory residing in the criminal law, but in its ordinary and natural meaning referred to actually taking part in treatment administered in a hospital or other approved place in accordance with s 1(3), for the purpose of terminating a pregnancy.
>
> In my opinion Nolan J and Balcombe LJ were right to reach the conclusion they did. I agree entirely with their view about the natural meaning of the word

---

47 [1989] AC 537.

'participate' in this context. Although the word is commonly used to describe the activities of accessories in the criminal law field, it is not a term of art there. It is in any event not being used in a criminal context in s 4(1). *Ex hypothesi* treatment for termination of a pregnancy under s 1 is not criminal. I do not consider that parliament can reasonably have intended by its use to import all the technicalities of the criminal law about principal and accessory, which can on occasion raise very nice questions about whether someone is guilty as an accessory. Such niceties would be very difficult of solution for an ordinary health authority. If parliament had intended the result contended for by the applicant, it could have procured it very clearly and easily by referring to participation 'in anything authorised by this Act' instead of 'in any treatment [so] authorised'. It is to be observed that s 4 appears to represent something of a compromise in relation to conscientious objection. One who believes all abortion to be morally wrong would conscientiously object even to such treatment as is mentioned in sub-s (2), yet the sub-section would not allow the objection to receive effect.

On this basis the House of Lords found that Mrs Janaway's actions were too ancillary to the abortion procedure to bring her within the scope of the conscientious objection clause.[48] At the same time the position of other facilitative agents, in particular the GP who might be asked to provide a second certificate as to an abortion falling within one of the statutory grounds, was left open. As Lord Keith continued:

> **Lord Keith**: A certain amount of argument was addressed to the Abortion Regulations 1968 SI 1968/390, which, *inter alia*, set out the form of certificate, known as the 'Green Form', to be signed by two registered medical practitioners in pursuance of s 1(1)(a) of the Act, and to the position in relation to s 4(1) of practitioners who might be required to sign such a certificate. The Regulations do not appear to contemplate that the signing of the certificate would form part of treatment for the termination of pregnancy, since reg 3(2) provides:
>
>> Any certificate of an opinion referred to in s 1(1) of the Act shall be given before the commencement of the treatment for the termination of the pregnancy to which it relates.
>
> It does not appear whether or not there are any circumstances under which a doctor might be under any legal duty to sign a green form, so as to place in difficulties one who had a conscientious objection to doing so. The fact that during the 20 years that the Act of 1967 has been in force no problem seems to have surfaced in this connection may indicate that in practice none exists. So I do not think it appropriate to express any opinion on the matter.

More recently, in *Barr v Matthews*,[49] Alliott J expressed the view that 'once a termination of pregnancy is recognised as an option, the doctor invoking the conscientious objection clause should refer the patient to a colleague at once'. This is echoed in current GMC guidance, which addresses doctors in the following terms:

---

48 Arguably, a person in Mrs Janaway's position today could invoke the protection afforded by the Employment Equality (Religion or Belief) Regulations 2003 (SI 2003/2660): see Addison, N, 'The Right not to Participate in Abortion' CMQ (Nov 2008).
49 (1999) 52 BMLR 217.

GMC, *Personal Beliefs and Medical Practice*[50]

21 Patients may ask you to perform, advise on, or refer them for a treatment or procedure which is not prohibited by law or statutory code of practice in the country where you work, but to which you have a conscientious objection. In such cases you must tell patients of their right to see another doctor with whom they can discuss their situation and ensure that they have sufficient information to exercise that right. In deciding whether the patient has sufficient information, you must explore with the patient what information they might already have, or need.

22 In the circumstances described in paragraph 21, if the patient cannot readily make their own arrangements to see another doctor you must ensure that arrangements are made, without delay, for another doctor to take over their care. You must not obstruct patients from accessing services or leave them with nowhere to turn. Whatever your personal beliefs may be about the procedure in question, you must be respectful of the patient's dignity and views.

 SELF-TEST QUESTION

Do you think that the father of the foetus should be accorded greater rights (such as a right to be consulted by the pregnant woman) in cases of abortion?

8.3.2 Forms of termination raising special issues

We conclude our examination of abortion by considering a number of procedures, in relation to the practice, that have generated particular legal or ethical concerns.

8.3.2.1 Pre-implantation terminations

What is the legality of a measure which prevents a newly formed embryo from implanting in the woman's uterus in the first place? In particular, is it the case here that a 'miscarriage' is procured contrary to the terms of the OAPA 1861? Margaret Brazier has commented on this question as follows:

Brazier, M, *Medicine, Patients and the Law*[51]

The 1967 Act envisaged that once a diagnosis of pregnancy had been made, the doctor faced with a request for an abortion would then consider and weigh any risk to the woman or the child. But there is a drug approved for general use which will, if taken by a woman within 72 hours of intercourse, ensure that any fertilised ovum will not implant in the womb. This, inaptly named, 'morning after' pill is not the only means by which a fertilised ovum (egg) may be disposed of at a stage before pregnancy can be confirmed. An intra-uterine device (IUD) fitted within a similar time after intercourse will have the same effect.

Are such methods lawful? They raise the question of where the line is to be drawn between contraception and abortion. . . . The crucial legal issue . . . is whether a procedure which prevents implantation is an act done to procure a miscarriage so as to make the doctor liable for criminal abortion . . . The argument that prevention of implantation is no offence runs thus.

---

50 GMC (March 2008). See www.gmc-uk.org/static/documents/content/Personal_Beliefs.pdf.
51 2nd edn, Harmondsworth: Penguin, 1992.

There is no carriage of a child by a woman before implantation takes place, and so to prevent that event even occurring cannot be an act done to procure a miscarriage. Many fertilised ova fail to implant naturally and no one then suggests that a miscarriage has occurred. The opponents of post-coital birth control reply that the fertilised ovum is present within the body of the woman; she carries it within her. . . .

No successful prosecution has ever been brought in respect of either the 'morning after' pill, or the use of an IUD, as means of post-coital birth control. In 1983 the Attorney General expressed his opinion that prior to implantation there is no pregnancy and so means used to prevent implantation do not constitute procuring miscarriage. In 1991 a judge dismissed a prosecution for criminal abortion based on the insertion of an IUD agreeing with the Attorney General that until implantation there is no pregnancy. The Attorney General's ruling is persuasive, but not binding on his successors. The matter remains unresolved by higher judicial authority. In practice, however, doctors are prescribing the 'morning after' pill without any pretence of applying the criteria laid down in the Abortion Act.

In spring 2002, the Society for the Protection of the Unborn Child brought judicial review proceedings against the decision by the Secretary of State for Health to allow the sale of the morning after pill in chemists, without prescription. In dismissing the application, Munby J held that 'the prescription, supply, administration or use of the morning after pill does not – cannot – involve the commission of any offence under either s 58 or s 59 of the 1861 Act': see R v Secretary of State for Health ex p Smeaton.[52]

8.3.2.2 Selective reduction

As we saw above, in Chapter 7, certain forms of fertility treatment, IVF or (more often) the use of super-ovulatory drugs, may result in a multiple pregnancy in which the woman carries more foetuses than can safely be brought to term. The term 'selective reduction' refers to the practice, in such a pregnancy, of deliberately terminating the lives of some of the foetuses in order to improve the survival chances of those that remain. Andrew Grubb has discussed the legal problems posed by the practice as follows:

Grubb, A, 'The new law of abortion: clarification or ambiguity'[53]

Modern medicine has developed techniques whereby a multiple pregnancy may be reduced by killing one or more foetuses *in utero*. This has become particularly important in cases where infertility treatment has led to a multiple pregnancy. The greater the number of foetuses carried by a woman, the greater is the risk to her health during pregnancy and at delivery. Equally, in these circumstances there is the risk of foetal mortality and of foetal handicap, including cerebral palsy, blindness and mental retardation. . . .

It was not clear under the law prior to 1 April 1991 whether selective reduction and selective foeticide were covered by the abortion legislation. It could be argued that in cases where the 'reduced' foetus(es) is not expelled there is not a 'miscarriage' within the terms of s 58 of the Offences Against the Person Act 1861. The better view is, however, that the term 'miscarriage' does not require expulsion of the contents of the womb but merely that some or all of the contents cease to be carried alive within it. This would bring both procedures within s 58 of the 1861 Act. In any event, the argument overlooks the fact that ultimately, the withered and dead products of the foetus will be expelled at the time the remaining foetuses are delivered.

52 [2002] EWHC 610 (Admin).
53 See n 18 above.

A further complication was raised as to whether selective reduction was a 'termination of pregnancy' within the Abortion Act 1967 because the woman is still pregnant in the sense that one or more of the healthy foetuses remains after the procedure. If there was no termination of pregnancy, then the procedure could never be lawful, because what was being done would not fall within the wording of the Abortion Act. There would be a crime but no possible defence.

In the light of these uncertainties, when Parliament came to amend the Abortion Act in 1990 a new s 5(2) was introduced specifically to deal with the practice:

5 (2) -For the purposes of the law relating to abortion, anything done with intent to procure a woman's miscarriage (or, in the case of a woman carrying more than one foetus, her miscarriage of any foetus) is unlawfully done unless authorised by s 1 of this Act and, in the case of a woman carrying more than one foetus, anything done with intent to procure her miscarriage of any foetus is authorised by that section if–

(a) the ground for termination of the pregnancy specified in sub-s (1)(d) of that section applies in relation to any foetus and the thing is done for the purpose of procuring the miscarriage of that foetus; or

(b) any of the other grounds for termination of the pregnancy specified in that section applies.

It is apparent that the effect of this provision is that selective reduction will be lawful either to protect the health or life of the pregnant woman (in which case the foetus(es) for destruction may be randomly chosen) or to terminate the life of a particular foetus on the s 1(1)(d) ground of foetal handicap.

8.3.2.3 Drug-induced abortions

When the Abortion Act 1967 was first enacted, medical abortion invariably necessitated the surgical removal of the foetus by a qualified doctor. For this reason, s 1(1) confers immunity from criminal liability only where abortion is carried out by 'a registered medical practitioner'. Developments in abortion techniques since then, particularly the availability of new 'abortifacient' drugs, now allow others, besides doctors, to take a much more direct role in terminating pregnancy. How far will they be protected by the terms of the 1967 Act? The issue, in relation to nursing staff, was considered by the House of Lords in the case of *Royal College of Nursing of UK v DHSS*.

Royal College of Nursing of United Kingdom v DHSS (1981)[54]

The RCN became concerned over the potential liability of its members in relation to the practice of using the drug Prostaglandin to carry out many abortions. The drug acts by stimulating contractions in the uterus, leading to the expulsion of the foetus. Here, whilst a doctor will perform the initial insertion of a catheter into the pregnant woman's uterus, the drug itself is later fed through the catheter by a nurse. The College sought a declaration that a Department of Health circular authorising the practice was wrong in law:

Lord Keith: Section 1(1) of the Act of 1967 can operate to relieve a person from guilt of an offence under the law relating to abortion only 'when a pregnancy is terminated by a registered medical practitioner'. Certain other conditions must also be satisfied, but no question about these arises in the present case. The sole issue is whether the

---

54 [1981] AC 800.

words I have quoted cover the situation where abortion has been brought about as a result of the procedure under consideration.

The argument for the respondents is, in essence, that the words of the sub-section do not apply because the pregnancy has not been terminated by any registered medical practitioner, but by the nurse who did the act or acts which directly resulted in the administration to the pregnant woman of the abortifacient drugs.

In my opinion this argument involves placing an unduly restricted and unintended meaning on the words 'when a pregnancy is terminated'. It seems to me that these words, in their context, are not referring to the mere physical occurrence of termination. The sidenote to s 1 is 'Medical termination of pregnancy'. 'Termination of pregnancy' is an expression commonly used, perhaps rather more by medical people than by laymen, to describe in neutral and unemotive terms the bringing about of an abortion. So used, it is capable of covering the whole process designed to lead to that result, and in my view it does so in the present context. Other provisions of the Act make it clear that termination of pregnancy is envisaged as being a process of treatment. Section 1(3) provides that, subject to an exception for cases of emergency, 'treatment for the termination of pregnancy' must be carried out in a National Health Service hospital or a place for the time being approved by the minister. There are similar references to treatment for the termination of pregnancy in s 3, which governs the application of the Act to visiting forces. Then by s 4(1) it is provided that no person shall be under any duty 'to participate in any treatment authorised by this Act to which he has a conscientious objection'. This appears clearly to recognise that what is authorised by s 1(1) in relation to the termination of pregnancy is a process of treatment leading to that result . . .

Given that the termination of pregnancy under contemplation in s 1(1) includes the whole process of treatment involved therein, it remains to consider whether, on the facts of this case, the termination can properly be regarded as being 'by a registered medical practitioner'. In my opinion this question is to be answered affirmatively. The doctor has responsibility for the whole process and is in charge of it throughout. It is he who decides that it is to be carried out. He personally performs essential parts of it which are such as to necessitate the application of his particular skill. The nurse's actions are done under his direct written instructions. In the circumstances I find it impossible to hold that the doctor's role is other than that of a principal, and I think he would be very surprised to hear that the nurse was the principal and he himself only an accessory. It is true that it is the nurse's action which leads directly to the introduction of abortifacient drugs into the system of the patient, but that action is done in a ministerial capacity and on the doctor's orders. Even if it were right to regard the nurse as a principal, it seems to me inevitable that the doctor should also be so regarded. If both the doctor and the nurse were principals, the provisions of the sub-section would be still satisfied, because the pregnancy would have been terminated by the doctor notwithstanding that it had also been terminated by the nurse.

I therefore conclude that termination of pregnancy by means of the procedures under consideration is authorised by the terms of s 1(1). This conclusion is the more satisfactory as it appears to me to be fully in accordance with that part of the policy and purpose of the Act which was directed to securing that socially acceptable abortions should be carried out under the safest conditions attainable. One may also feel some relief that it is unnecessary to reach a decision involving the very large numbers of medical practitioners and others who have participated in the relevant procedures over several years past should now be revealed as guilty of criminal offences.

Lord Roskill: Learned counsel for the respondents did not shrink from the anomalies which would necessarily flow from the acceptance of his submission and the construction adopted by the majority of the Court of Appeal. There was, he said, only a limited qualification engrafted upon an otherwise unchanged criminal law and in 1967 parliament had legislated by reference to the surgical techniques of abortion as they then were and not for other techniques of abortion as they might subsequently be evolved. Pressed to say whether a new method must not be adopted which involved less risk to the patient, he replied that any such new method would only be lawful if the doctor were present throughout, a view which would seemingly make unrealistic demands upon medical manpower since no one suggested that each of the seven steps taken by the nurse, to which I have already referred, was not well within the capacity of someone possessed of the qualifications and experience which such a nurse would necessarily possess.

Whilst the decision of the House of Lords (by a narrow 3:2 majority) means that nursing staff involved in abortions enjoy the same statutory protection as doctors, the problem of who else might benefit has now arisen following the development of a further abortifacient drug, RU-486 or Mifepristone. This drug is similar in its operation to Prostaglandin but is significantly easier to administer. Indeed, the drug could, in principle, be made available on prescription in tablet form to be taken by pregnant women who remain out-patients. As part of the 1990 amendments to the Abortion Act, a new s 1(3A) was specifically introduced to allow the Health Secretary to authorise GPs' surgeries as a 'class of place' where Mifepristone could be administered (previously, under s 1(3), treatment to terminate a pregnancy could only be given at NHS or other hospitals approved by the Secretary):

1 (3A) The power under subsection (3) of this section to approve a place includes power, in relation to treatment consisting primarily in the use of such medicines as may be specified in the approval and carried out in such manner as may be so specified, to approve a class of places.

Nevertheless, as Kennedy and Grubb point out, a further difficulty remains:

Kennedy, I and Grubb, A, *Medical Law*[55]

[Mifepristone] is prescribed by a doctor, dispensed by a pharmacist, but administered to herself by the pregnant woman. In this situation who terminates the pregnancy?

There are two possible situations which might arise. First, the termination is only completed after the woman has returned to the hospital some 36 to 48 hours later after the Prostaglandin pessary has been inserted. Here, undoubtedly the termination would be by the doctor even if the Prostaglandin were given by a nurse under his supervision (*Royal College of Nursing* case). This is not problematic for the law. However, the alternative situation that might arise is.

Suppose, instead, the effects of Mifepristone occur before the woman returns to the hospital for the Prostaglandin pessary. In 55% of cases bleeding (and therefore, the potential for a 'miscarriage') occur within 48 hours of administering Mifepristone. In a proportion of cases (about 3%) termination will occur before readmission. In our view, in this situation it must be the pregnant woman and not the doctor who terminates the pregnancy. It is she who does the last voluntary act necessary to effect the termination. Legally, the situation is

---

55 2nd edn, London: Butterworths, 1994.

analogous to a case where a doctor provides the means (eg, pills) for a patient to kill himself. It is the patient who commits suicide . . .

However, an argument which would challenge this view could be mounted on the basis of the *Royal College of Nursing* case. There, the House of Lords . . . extended 'medical practitioner' to include all acts performed by the medical team for whom the doctor is responsible . . .

Could this wider notion of 'termination by a registered medical practitioner covering all action for which the doctor takes responsibility' (or 'charge') help in the case of Mifepristone? In one sense, a doctor does have responsibility for the patient throughout the treatment. However, it is a different kind of responsibility from that contemplated in the *Royal College of Nursing* case. In that case the responsibility denoted the right to control those who acted on his behalf in a professional capacity. In the case of Mifepristone . . . the relationship is neither one of control nor one where the patient (in administering the drug to herself) can be said to act on the doctor's behalf or be in his charge.

The issue was recently tested in *British Pregnancy Advisory Service v Secretary of State for Health*,[56] in which the applicant argued that where the woman self-administers the drug at home, it would still be the doctor (and not the woman) who had carried out the termination; and this was thus permissible under the 1967 Act. However, Supperstone J disagreed and refused a declaration to that effect. The upshot is that (as had previously been the case) the use of Mifepristone, and of a similar, newer drug, Misoprostol, requires their administration by – or at least under the supervision of – nursing staff in approved hospitals/clinics.

8.3.2.4 Late-term abortions

As noted, in some circumstances the Abortion Act 1967 (as amended) permits termination of pregnancy up until birth, namely under grounds (b), (c) and (d). Such late terminations are extremely rare,[57] and, due to restrictions in the licences granted to private abortion clinics (imposed by the Secretary of State pursuant to s 1(3) of the Act), may only be carried out in NHS hospitals. In practice, it is the last of the grounds, foetal handicap, which is almost always invoked in such circumstances.

By contrast with early abortions, where abortifacient drugs may be used, late abortions normally require surgical intervention. Of course, the intention of the doctor is that the foetus will not survive the abortion process; however, unless measures are taken to kill the foetus while still inside the womb, there is a real chance that it will be born alive. What is the legal position of the doctor, in such circumstances, where the foetus only dies some time after delivery? In *AG's Reference (No 3 of 1994)*[58] the House of Lords considered a reference in respect of the acquittal for murder (on the directions of the trial judge) of a man who had stabbed his pregnant girlfriend in the abdomen. (The woman went into labour soon after the attack and, although the child was delivered alive, it died 120 days later due to its severe prematurity.) In reversing the decision of the Court of Appeal that a murder charge could lie in such circumstances, their Lordships were nevertheless extremely cautious to limit their response to the facts in hand (involving an intention by the respondent to harm the pregnant woman). Lord Mustill commented that he 'would wish to proceed with particular care in relation to allegations of murder stemming from an injury to the foetus unaccompanied by any causative injury to the mother'. Given this present lack of certainty in the law, the doctor responsible for a late abortion would be well advised to take the greatest care that the foetus dies while it is still inside the womb.

---

56 [2011] EWHC 235 (Admin).
57 The abortion statistics published by the Department of Health for 2009, show that of the 189,100 terminations carried out on England and Wales residents that year, only 136 involved foetuses of 24 weeks and over. The statistics are available at www.dh.gov.uk/dr_consum_dh/groups/dh_digitalassets/documents/digitalasset/dh_116336.pdf.
58 [1997] 3 WLR 421.

Another issue in relation to late-term abortions relates to the potential capacity of the foetus to feel pain. Evidence as to this matter is conflicting, but there is reason to think that, by 26 weeks' gestation, the foetal nervous system is sufficiently developed for it to do so.[59] On this basis, one of the arguments the claimant wished to use in the *Jepson* case,[60] was that the foetus at this stage should receive protection under Art 3 of the ECHR (right not to be subjected to torture or inhuman and degrading treatment). This argument in itself is problematic, as arguably reliance on Convention rights presupposes that an entity is at least a rights-bearer for the purposes of Art 2 of the Convention, which as we have seen with foetuses is not the case.[61] Nonetheless, as the BMA notes, in ethical terms this is a matter in respect of which abortion doctors certainly should exercise caution:

BMA, *The Law and Ethics of Abortion*[62]

. . . Fetal pain

Whether, and at what stage, a fetus feels pain has been a matter of much debate and past practice has been partly influenced by Department of Health advice. Interpretation of the evidence on fetal pain is conflicting with some arguing that the fetus has the potential to feel pain at ten weeks' gestation, others arguing that it is unlikely to feel pain before 26 weeks gestation and still others arguing for some unspecified gestational period in between.

There is clearly a need for further research to provide more conclusive evidence about the experiences and sensations of the fetus *in utero*. In the meantime the BMA recommends that, when carrying out any surgical procedures (whether an abortion or a therapeutic intervention) on the fetus *in utero*, due consideration must be given to appropriate measures for minimising the risk of pain. This should include an assessment of the most recent evidence available. Even if there is no incontrovertible evidence that fetuses feel pain the use of pain relief, when carrying out invasive procedures, may help to relieve the anxiety of the parents and of health professionals.

8.3.3 Moving to a 'counselling model'?

Though, as we have seen, abortion in England and Wales remains technically subject to medical control, in practice a liberal approach prevails, which comes close in practice to 'abortion on demand'. This is reflected in abortion rates among the highest in Western Europe. Although around 90 per cent of terminations take place in the first trimester, the law is more permissive than that in many other countries in respect of later abortions. This, plus the fact of the more than usually restrictive abortion policy operated by its close neighbour, Ireland, have also made Britain subject to a degree of 'abortion tourism'.[63]

At the same time, there appears to be little appetite for law reform, which many politicians fear would simply provoke divisive and insoluble debate. On this view, the existing 1967 Act, in treating abortion as a 'medical question' for doctors to rule on, has functioned well in depoliticising the issue, avoiding the polarities ('pro-life' vs 'pro-choice') that have disfigured abortion discourse in countries such as the US. The downside, though, is a vaguely-worded statute, with arguably something of a disjunction between its terms and how it is applied in practice. A further

---

59 Glover, V, and Fisk, NM, 'Foetal Pain: Implications for Research and Practice' (1999) 106 British J of Obstet and Gyn 881.
60 See n 21 above.
61 See n 36 above, and the discussion by Scott, n 22 above.
62 See n 16 above.
63   In 2009, around 6,700 abortions carried out in England and Wales involved non-residents: see n 57 above.

concern is that the Act – in medicalising the issue – remains bound to a paternalistic approach, which fails to treat the pregnant woman sufficiently as the author of her decision.

In the following extract, Sjef Gevers, referring to the comparative law work of Eser and Koch,[64] notes three broad models on which countries around the world have premised their abortion laws:

Gevers, S, 'Abortion Legislation and the Future of the "Counseling Model" '[65]

If there is any medico-legal issue on which it seems virtually impossible to reach consensus, it is abortion. Over the last decades, abortion law has been highly debated in many countries, also in Europe, but it has turned out to be hard to reconcile the opposing views . . .

Whereas – at the normative level – there is the tension between the 'pro life' and the 'pro choice' approach to abortion, at the practical level, the situation is more complex. In all countries, abortions take place, even where the law prohibits them. According to the World Health Organisation, an estimated 46 million pregnancies end in induced abortion each year; as nearly 20 million of these are estimated to be unsafe, safe abortion services with adequate equipment and well trained staff need to be available so that women can have rapid access to these services, at least within the limits allowed by the law.

Often, medicine plays an important role in bridging the gap between 'pro life'and 'pro choice' on the one hand and between normative beliefs and practical necessities on the other. According to the WHO report, most countries allow abortion when pregnancy poses a threat to the woman's physical or mental health (medical indication model), making doctors 'gatekeepers' of abortion. Other countries have taken a further step in liberalising criminal statutes that prohibit abortion, and have enacted laws that allow for it on request of the woman at least in the first term of pregnancy (time limitation model).

In their important, comparative work on abortion and the law, Eser and Koch observe that a third model of legislation has emerged, i.e. the so-called 'conflict (or emergency) oriented discourse model'. Basically, this refers to regulations in which the law establishes grounds (such as certain emergencies) for allowing abortions but leaves the determination of whether such grounds exist ultimately to the judgment and the discretion of the woman. She is expected, however, to make a careful decision, to weigh the alternatives and to be willing to be counseled in doing so. Because of this latter aspect, this model is also referred to as the 'counseling model'. In their recent book, the authors not only notice that this approach is adopted by legal reformers to a growing extent but also argue that it is the best way to do justice to the conflicting values involved.

Within this rubric, abortion law in England and Wales currently illustrates – at least on paper – the 'medical indication' approach. Nonetheless, as Charles Foster argues, if at some stage the Abortion Act 1967 were to be subject to reform, the need for greater counselling and informed consent is a matter on which both those disposed to support and oppose the practice may find a measure of agreement:

Foster, C, 'A Lost Opportunity'[66]

1967 is a long time ago. Medicine has moved on. We now know a good deal more about the effect of abortion on the bodies of foetuses, on the bodies and minds of women, on the psyches of doctors and nurses, on the bank accounts of abortion providers, and on the ethics of the

---

64 Eser, A, and Koch, HG, *Abortion and the Law: from international comparison to legal policy*, The Hague: TMC Asser Press, 2005.
65 (2006) 13 Eur J Health L 27.
66 (2008) 158 NLJ, Issue 7326.

medical profession as a whole. It was amended, rather tentatively, by the Human Fertilisation and Embryology Act 1990. Whatever one's view of the ethics, abortion matters. Surely it is hard to contend coherently that it does not deserve a review?

Although [the Abortion Act] 1967 itself made no express provision for it, informed consent is plainly vitally important. Abortion sometimes seems to exist on a tiny island, terribly isolated from the rest of the law of consent. It is a significant procedure. Most would agree that it can cause prematurity in subsequent pregnancies and debilitating guilt: some argue for a link between abortion and lasting depression . . . Whatever one makes of this evidence, the magnitude of the risks and the significance of the possible sequelae would, in any comparable area of medicine or surgery, make detailed counselling mandatory. And yet all the indications are that abortion counselling, if it occurs at all, is generally cursory. . . . The pro-abortionists are right: we do need an informed consent clause in [the Act]. All sensible people should be 'pro-choice' in the sense of being pro-informed-choice.

 SELF-TEST QUESTION

Can the relative lack of attention to the patient's consent in relation to abortion, in contrast to that which it receives in cases of assisted reproduction, be rationalised?

See Chapter 7

8.4 Pre-Natal Harm Beyond the Abortion Context

8.4.1 General principles

Beyond the context of abortion, it is readily apparent that injuries may be caused to a foetus in utero which subsequently lead to it being born disabled. The question of whether a child damaged in this way can, after it is born, bring an action against the person responsible has created a surprising amount of difficulty for the common law. Nevertheless, in respect of children born after 21 July 1976, such a child has been given a statutory right to recover damages under the Congenital Disabilities (Civil Liability) Act 1976. Section 1 of this Act provides as follows:

1 Civil liability to child born disabled

(1) If a child is born disabled as the result of such an occurrence before its birth as is mentioned in sub-s (2) below, and a person (other than the child's own mother) is under this section answerable to the child in respect of the occurrence, the child's disabilities are to be regarded as damage resulting from the wrongful act of that person and actionable accordingly at the suit of the child.

(2) An occurrence to which this section applies is one which–

    (a) affected either parent of the child in his or her ability to have a normal, healthy child; or

    (b) affected the mother during her pregnancy, or affected her or the child in the course of its birth, so that the child is born with disabilities which would not otherwise have been present.

(3) Subject to the following sub-sections, a person (here referred to as 'the defendant') is answerable to the child if he was liable in tort to the parent or would, if sued in due time have been so; and it is no answer that there could not have been such liability because the parent suffered no actionable injury, if there was a breach of legal duty which, accompanied by injury, would have given rise to the liability.

(4) In the case of an occurrence preceding the time of conception, the defendant is not answerable to the child if at that time either or both of the parents knew the risk of their

child being born disabled (that it to say, the particular risk created by the occurrence); but should it be the child's father who is the defendant, this sub-section does not apply if he knew of the risk and the mother did not.

(5) The defendant is not answerable to the child, for anything he did or omitted to do when responsible in a professional capacity for treating or advising the parent, if he took reasonable care having due regard to then received professional opinion applicable to the particular class of case; but this does not mean that he is answerable only because he departed from received opinion.

(6) Liability to the child under this section may be treated as having been excluded or limited by contract made with the parent affected, to the same extent and subject to the same restrictions as liability in the parent's own case; and a contract term which could have been set up by the defendant in an action by the parent, so as to exclude or limit his liability to him or her, operates in the defendant's favour to the same, but no greater, extent in an action under this section by the child.

(7) If in the child's action under this section it is shown that the parent affected shared the responsibility for the child being born disabled, the damages are to be reduced to such extent as the court thinks just and equitable having regard to the extent of the parent's responsibility.

The effect of s 1(3) above is to found the child's action upon the concept of 'derivative liability', ie, it may only bring a claim in so far as the occurrence which caused its injuries involved a breach of duty by the tort feasor to one of its parents. Subsequently, in *Burton v Islington HA*, the Court of Appeal had to tackle head on the problem at common law of how it is that a duty in tort can be owed to an entity which has no legal personality. In finding for the claimant, Dillon LJ relied extensively upon Commonwealth authority, in particular the decision of the Supreme Court of Victoria in *Watt v Rama*.[67]

Burton v Islington HA (1992)[68]

The claimant was born disabled as a result of an invasive gynaecological procedure carried out upon her mother early on in the pregnancy: the defendant had negligently failed to carry out a pregnancy test before performing the procedure. As these events occurred prior to the enactment of the 1976 Act, the Court was required to consider the legal position at common law.

Dillon LJ: The main Commonwealth case from a country with a common law jurisdiction is *Watt v Rama* . . . which has since been accepted by other appellate courts in Australia as a correct statement of the law, that is to say the common law of Australia. That was a case which arose out of injuries in a motor accident. The leading judgment is that of Winneke CJ and Pape J. It is founded on an analysis – in my judgment, correct – of the tort of negligence by reference to decisions of the House of Lords and the Privy Council and certain Australian decisions. . . . I can take up that judgment, at pp 358–59:

> The real question posed for our decision is not whether an action lies in respect of pre-natal injuries but whether a plaintiff born with injuries caused by the pre-natal neglect of the defendant has a cause of action in negligence against him in respect of such injuries. To this question the defendant answers 'No', because at the time of his neglect the plaintiff was

---

67 (1972) VR 353.
68 [1993] QB 204, CA.

not in existence as a living person, had no separate existence apart from her mother, was not capable of suing to assert a legal right, and was not a legal person to whom he could be under a duty.

There is then reference to well known authorities like *Donoghue v Stevenson* [1932] AC 562; *Dorset Yacht Co Ltd v Home Office* [1970] AC 1004; *Bourhill (Hay) v Young* [1943] AC 92 . . . After the citations the judgment continues, at pp 360–61:

> Those circumstances, accordingly, constituted a potential relationship capable of imposing a duty on the defendant in relation to the child if and when born. On the birth the relationship crystallised and out of it arose a duty on the defendant in relation to the child. On the facts which for present purposes must be assumed, the child was born with injuries caused by the act or neglect of the defendant in the driving of his car. But as the child could not in the very nature of things acquire rights correlative to a duty until it became by birth a living person, and as it was not until then that it could sustain injuries as a living person, it was, we think, at that stage that the duty arising out of the relationship was attached to the defendant, and it was at that stage that the defendant was, on the assumption that his act or omission in the driving of the car constituted a failure to take reasonable care, in breach of the duty to take reasonable care to avoid injury to the child . . .

With respect, the analysis endorsed by Dillon LJ appears to confuse breach of duty with the damage which is thereby caused. It might be simpler to accept that legal duties can be owed to the unborn child, as a potential person, even though the corresponding right of such an entity to bring a claim remains contingent upon its subsequent birth. Indeed, this seems to have been an unspoken assumption in many medical negligence claims: see, for example, *Whitehouse v Jordan*.[69]

Ultimately, all that is being allowed in these cases is that a damaged child may recover damages where, but for the defendant's negligence, it would have been born undamaged. A claim, on the other hand, by such a child who, but for the defendant's negligence would never have been born at all, would form an inadmissible action for 'wrongful life'. Such a claim was considered, and rejected, by the Court of Appeal in *Mackay v Essex AHA*:

Mackay v Essex AHA (1982)[70]

The claimant's mother was infected with German measles while pregnant with the claimant. The latter claimed, *inter alia*, that the defendant doctor had negligently failed to advise her mother of the desirability of an abortion, and (given that her mother would have accepted such advice) she had consequently suffered damage by 'entry into a life in which her injuries are highly debilitating, and distress, loss and damage':

> **Stephenson LJ**: There is no doubt that this child could legally have been deprived of life by the mother's undergoing an abortion with the doctor's advice and help. So the law recognises a difference between the life of a foetus and the life of those who have been born. But because a doctor can lawfully by statute do to a foetus what he cannot lawfully do to a person who has been born, it does not follow that he is under a legal

---

69 [1981] 1 All ER 267. This case is looked at in Ch 6, above.
70 [1982] QB 1166, CA.

obligation to a foetus to do it and terminate its life, or that the foetus has a legal right to die . . .

To impose such a duty towards the child would, in my opinion, make a further inroad on the sanctity of human life which would be contrary to public policy. It would mean regarding the life of a handicapped child as not only less valuable than the life of a normal child, but so much less valuable that it was not worth preserving, and it would even mean that a doctor would be obliged to pay damages to a child infected with rubella before birth who was in fact born with some mercifully trivial abnormality. These are the consequences of the necessary basic assumption that a child has a right to be born whole or not at all, not to be born unless it can be born perfect or 'normal', whatever that may mean. Added to that objection must be the opening of the courts to claims by children born handicapped against their mothers for not having an abortion . . .

Finally, there is the nature of the injury and damage which the court is being asked to ascertain and evaluate.

The only duty of care which courts of law can recognise and enforce are duties owed to those who can be compensated for loss by those who owe the duties, in most cases, including cases of personal injury, by money damages which will as far as possible put the injured party in the condition in which he or she was before being injured. The only way in which a child injured in the womb can be compensated in damages is by measuring what it has lost, which is the difference between the value of its life as a whole and healthy normal child and the value of its life as an injured child. But to make those who have not injured the child pay for that difference is to treat them as if they have injured the child, when all they have done is not having taken steps to prevent its being born injured by another cause.

The only loss for which those who have not injured the child can be held liable to compensate the child is the difference between its condition as a result of their allowing it to be born alive and injured and its condition if its embryonic life had been ended before its life in the world had begun. But how can a court of law evaluate that second condition and so measure the loss to the child? Even if a court were competent to decide between the conflicting views of theologians and philosophers and to assume an 'after life' or non-existence as the basis for the comparison, how can a judge put a value on the one or the other, compare either alternative with the injured child's life in this world and determine that the child has lost anything, without the means of knowing what, if anything, it has gained?

Griffiths LJ: To my mind, the most compelling reason to reject this cause of action is the intolerable and insoluble problem it would create in the assessment of damage. The basis of damages for personal injury is the comparison between the state of the plaintiff before he was injured and his condition after he was injured. This is often a hard enough task in all conscience and it has an element of artificiality about it, for who can say that there is any sensible correlation between pain and money? Nevertheless, the courts have been able to produce a broad tariff that appears at the moment to be acceptable to society as doing rough justice. But the whole exercise, difficult as it is, is anchored in the first place to the condition of the plaintiff before the injury which the court can comprehend and evaluate. In a claim for wrongful life how does the court begin to make an assessment? The plaintiff does not say, 'But for your negligence I would have been born uninjured'. The plaintiff says, 'But for your negligence I would never have been born'. The court then has to compare the state of the plaintiff with non-existence, of which the court can know nothing; this I regard as an impossible task.

Nonetheless, two points should be made. First, as noted earlier in this chapter, the mother/parents of the child will still be able to claim damages for 'wrongful conception/birth'.[71] Secondly, in one situation, the exclusion of liability in *Mackay* has been statutorily overruled, namely for children born disabled after licensed fertility treatment. Here the Human Fertilisation and Embryology Act 1990 amended the CD(CL)A 1976 to provide that the child (including one who would not otherwise have existed) has a remedy against the person (the fertility clinic, or possibly a gamete donor), whose negligence led to the disability.[72]

8.4.2 Harm caused by the child's mother

It is important to note that, except in the case of negligent driving (allowed for in s 2 of the Act) no action will lie under the 1976 Act where the pre-natal injuries arose through the negligence of the child's mother. The policy grounds underlying this immunity are discussed by Jane Fortin as follows:

Fortin, J, 'Legal protection for the unborn child'[73]

By making liability to the child depend on liability to the parent, th[e] formula [of derivative liability] excludes a wide range of negligent acts and omissions on the part of the mother. Some would say that circumstances like those arising in the *Berkshire* case indicate quite clearly that the existence of maternal tortious liability would be a useful means of controlling the mother's ante-natal behaviour. Nevertheless, the Law Commission rejected the proposition that a child might sue its mother for pre-natal injuries caused by her negligence, largely on the social policy grounds that the existence of such a right of action would have deleterious effects on family cohesion. In particular, the mother might become vulnerable to litigation brought on behalf of her child, claiming that it was her failure to give up cigarette smoking or alcohol or to follow the latest dietary ante-natal regime that had caused the child's disablement. Moreover, the existence of such a cause of action might well fuel a matrimonial or parental conflict. . . .

Nevertheless, the Law Commission was satisfied that different considerations applied to cases of pre-natal injury caused by a road accident, where the existence of third party insurance would prevent any risk of a child's claim against its mother causing family conflicts. Consequently, despite the unborn child's lack of legal personality, the 1976 Act does impose on the pregnant mother a duty of care in relation to it, but only in the context of driving a motor vehicle. . . .

Despite the inconsistency of the exception relating to maternal liability for negligent driving, the 1976 Act maintains the general principle of the civil law that the unborn child has no legal personality. It is arguable that this principle is acquiring an element of unreality, particularly when the 1976 Act itself and now the *Berkshire* case, clearly adhere to the proposition that a child's development is a continuing process that commences at conception not birth.

In the case of *D v Berkshire CC*,[74] referred to by Fortin, the House of Lords held that events prior to a child's birth (which led to it being born with drug withdrawal symptoms) could properly be taken into account by magistrates when making a care order.

In general, it might seem paradoxical, given the relative ease with which the pregnant woman may dispose of her foetus altogether through abortion, that the law should concern itself with

---

71 See text at n 30 above.
72 s1A Congenital Disabilities (Civil Liability) Act 1976; see further the discussion in Ch 7, at section 7.4.4.2.
73 See n 4 above.
74 [1987] 1 All ER 20, HL.

'lesser harms' it may suffer as a result of her behaviour while pregnant. However, the point is, of course, that in the latter case alone there will be an existing person whose interests have been adversely affected by her conduct. The highly contentious question of whether, in cases of this sort, the criminal law might be invoked to afford protection to the foetus, is addressed by John Robertson:

Robertson, JA, *Children of Choice*[75]

Given the foreseeable impact of certain pre-natal acts or omissions on the welfare of offspring, one cannot reasonably argue that women and men have no pre-natal obligation to avoid harm to children they choose to bring into the world. The more contested question is what public policies and legal options should be pursued to prevent pre-natal harm to offspring. The choice ranges from education and access to treatment to post-birth sanctions and pre-natal imposition of treatment on pregnant women. Because procreative liberty is not involved, and because the conduct in question poses serious harm to offspring, coercive sanctions are not in principle excluded. However, as we shall see, the better policy in most cases will be to rely on information, education, and access to treatment . . .

Opponents of prosecution also see a grave threat to personal privacy and civil liberties. If illegal drug use during pregnancy is independently punishable, then anything with the slightest pre-natal risk to offspring could be punished as pre-natal child abuse. Women could be prosecuted for smoking or drinking even moderate amounts of alcohol at any time during pregnancy, because even a few drinks might lower IQ points, and smoking increases the risk of prematurity and low birth weight. In the worst-case scenario, special pregnancy police will be commissioned to monitor women for pregnancies, and then surveil their behaviour; if they err, they are then stigmatised, shamed, fined, or incarcerated. Margaret Atwood's *The Handmaid's Tale*, a chilling novel of women forced to serve the needs of a repressive dictatorship, starts sounding much less fanciful than it appears to be . . .

All these points deserve considered attention. They explain why prosecutions have been largely unsuccessful, are widely opposed, and are unlikely to be a key factor in preventing pre-natal harm. They also show why education, treatment, and services are the more desirable and most effective avenue for public policy.

Despite the drawbacks of a criminal approach, however, these criticisms do not establish that criminal sanctions should never be imposed on persons who culpably harm offspring by pre-natal conduct. When culpability is established, criminal law theory easily includes pre-natal as well as post-natal conduct that harms offspring. For example, Lord Coke in the 17th century recognised criminal liability for pre-natal actions that caused post-natal death.

In some cases, the only effective means of preventing harm to the future person that a given foetus will become, may take the form of *ex ante* coercive restraint of the pregnant woman. However, this raises even greater problems of civil liberty and sexual equality than *ex post facto* sanctions. As we saw earlier, in Re F (in utero), the Court of Appeal recoiled from the implications of making a foetus a ward of court, in order to allow it to direct restraining orders at the mother.[76]

Admittedly, in Re F (in utero), the risk to the child was not directly quantifiable; it might be argued that different considerations should apply where the mother's conduct, if allowed to continue, is nearly certain to damage her child. A situation of this kind arose in Canada in *Winnipeg Child & Family Services v DFG*,[77] in which the Supreme Court of Canada was required to decide whether

---

75 See n 1 above.
76 See n 34 above.
77 [1997] 3 SCR 925.

to allow restraint against a woman in her fifth month of pregnancy, who was addicted to glue-sniffing. As a result of this addiction, she had already had two severely disabled children:

McLachlin J: [41] . . . While the law may properly impose responsibility for the consequences of addictive behaviour, like drunkenness, the policy question remains of whether extending a duty of care in tort in this particular situation as the remedy for redressing problems which are caused by addiction is a wise option. Given the lack of control pregnant women have over many of these harmful behaviours, it is doubtful whether recognizing a duty of care to refrain from them will significantly affect their choices. As a result, the general deterrent value of the proposed new duty of care is questionable.

[42] Recognizing a duty of care in relation to the lifestyle of the pregnant woman would also increase the level of outside scrutiny that she would be subjected to. Partners, parents, friends, and neighbours are among the potential classes of people who might monitor the pregnant woman's actions to ensure that they remained within the legal parameters. Difficulty in determining what conduct is and is not permissible might be expected to give rise to conflicts between the interested persons and the pregnant woman or even between the interested persons themselves. This raises the possibility of conflict which may exacerbate the pregnant woman's condition (and thus the fetus') rather than improve it.

[43] If it could be predicted with some certainty that all these negative effects of extending tort liability to the lifestyle choices of pregnant women would in fact diminish the problem of injured infants, the change might nevertheless arguably be justified. But the evidence before this Court fails to establish this. It is far from clear that the proposed tort duty will decrease the incidence of substance-injured children. Indeed, the evidence suggests that such a duty might have negative effects on the health of infants. No clear consensus emerges from the debate on the question of whether ordering women into 'places of safety' and mandating medical treatment provide the best solution or, on the contrary, create additional problems.

Accordingly, the Court refused to issue a restraining order, and it is suggested that in England the outcome of such a case would be the same.

As discussed in Chapter 3, it is now also clear the English courts will not intervene in the case of a competent adult woman's refusal of a caesarian section, or other procedure, the doctors advise as in the vital interests of her foetus.[78] In such cases, as we have seen, the foetus has no legal interests of its own, and the patient's right to refuse consent to unwanted medical treatment is regarded as absolute.

See Chapter 3

Summary of Key Points

1. Abortion has long been an area of intractable moral debate. The pro and contra positions on the practice are often referred to as 'pro-choice', stressing the pregnant woman's right to decide what happens in her body, and 'pro-life', which appeals to the interests of the foetus.
2. For the law-maker, besides trying to find an acceptable middle-ground in this debate, there is the need to consider the likely adverse consequences of any law that radically restricted access to abortion, in terms of driving it underground.
3. Under current UK law abortion remains an offence under s 58 Offences Against the Person Act 1861 (which criminalises 'procuring a miscarriage'). In addition, the killing of an older, viable foetus is punishable as 'child destruction' under the Infant Life (Preservation) Act 1929.

78 See *Re MB (Adult: Refusal of Medical Treatment)* [1997] 2 FLR 426, CA; the case is considered in Ch 3 above.

4. The 1929 Act gave a defence to a doctor who terminated the life of a foetus in order to save the life of the mother; subsequently, the courts held that a doctor who carried out an abortion to protect the mother from a significant risk to life had a similar defence to a charge under the 1861 Act.

5. Since the entry into force of the Abortion Act 1967, the grounds for lawful abortion have been widened. A doctor who terminates a pregnancy under one of these – and conforms with the further statutory requirements (including certification by a second doctor) is protected from criminal prosecution.

6. Following amendment in 1990, four such grounds appear in the 1967 Act. The most widely used is the so-called 'social ground', which permits abortion up to 24 weeks where the continuance of the pregnancy poses greater risk to the woman and/or her existing children than its termination.

7. The other grounds encompass situations of serious risk to the woman's health or life, as well as – more controversially – the prospect of foetal disability. These grounds may be used to carry out terminations up to birth (though in practice it is rare for abortions to occur after 24 weeks).

8. Though the effect of the legal position is thus to deny the pregnant woman a right to an abortion (she must persuade the doctor(s) she falls within one of the statutory grounds), in practice she is unlikely to face difficulty in obtaining one: each year nearly 200,000 abortions take place in England and Wales.

9. Outside the abortion context, the foetus enjoys legal protection, if born alive, but disabled due to a damaging event while in utero: here it may bring an action under the Congenital Disabilities (Civil Liability) Act 1976. However, the Act largely excludes the possibility of it suing its mother.

10. More generally, the law in denying legal personality to the foetus, has shown its unwillingness to curtail the pregnant woman's autonomy. This appears to include cases where the woman engages in activity that poses a risk to the life or health of the foetus.

📖 Further Reading

BMA, *The Law and Ethics of Abortion*, London, London (available at www.bma.org.uk/images/lawethicsabortionnov07_tcm41-146867.pdf).

Fortin, J, 'Legal protection for the unborn child' (1988) 51 *Modern Law Review* 54.

Gevers, S, 'Abortion Legislation and the Future of the "Counseling Model" ' (2006) 13 *European Journal of Health Law* 27.

Hursthouse, R, *Beginning Lives*, Oxford: Blackwells, 1987.

RCOG, *Termination of Pregnancy for Fetal Abnormality in England, Scotland and Wales*, London, 2010 (available at www.rcog.org.uk/files/rcog-corp/TerminationPregnancyReport18May2010.pdf).

Sheldon, S, *Beyond Control: Medical Power and Abortion Law*, London: Pluto Press, 1997.

Chapter 9

Mental Health Law

Chapter Contents

9.1 Background

9.1.1 Introduction

Mental disorder cannot be treated like any other form of medical disorder. First of all, there are special difficulties involved in deciding precisely what we mean when we say that someone is mentally 'disordered'. Perhaps this is inevitable, given the nebulous nature of mental disorders and their overlap with antisocial behaviour, the holding of bizarre beliefs, and eccentric lifestyles. In addition, the mentally ill are often stigmatised and misunderstood. Furthermore, the Mental Health Act (MHA) 1983 provides for the compulsory detention of both criminal offenders and non-offenders. It is clear, therefore, that mental health law raises distinct ethical and legal issues.

Leaving aside the special problems that can arise when dealing with the mentally ill criminal offender, it is generally accepted that compulsorily detaining someone who has committed no offence is probably the most serious interference with civil liberties that a state can impose. In consequence, its ethical underpinning must be beyond reproach, and the mechanism which allows this to be done should be open to the most searching scrutiny. We are concerned here with balancing, on the one hand, the rights of the individual, and, on the other hand, both the utilitarian desire to protect the community at large, and the paternalistic impulse to protect the individual from harming himself. This is reflected in the Mental Health Act 1983, by which compulsory civil detention, either for assessment or treatment, is permitted when the patient is suffering from mental disorder and ought to be detained either to protect themselves or others (the latter being a mixture of paternalism and community protection).

9.1.2 European Convention on Human Rights

Although the Human Rights Act 1998 might be used to some effect, where appropriate, in most areas of medical law, it is particularly pertinent to mental health law because of the power of the state to detain, without consent, people who have been diagnosed as suffering from a number of forms of mental disorder. Article 5 is particularly relevant.

Article 5 (right to liberty and security) provides that:

> 1 . . . No one shall be deprived of his liberty save in the following cases and in accordance with a procedure prescribed by law:
>
> . . .
>
> (e) the lawful detention of persons for the prevention of the spreading of infectious diseases, of persons of unsound mind, alcoholics or drug addicts of vagrants
>
> . . .
>
> 4 Everyone who is deprived of his liberty by arrest or detention shall be entitled to take proceedings by which the lawfulness of his detention shall be decided speedily by a court and his release ordered if the detention is not lawful.

The European Court of Human Rights, in *Winterwerp v Netherlands*,[1] set out the conditions which a national government has to satisfy in order for detention on the ground of 'unsoundness of mind' to apply:

1 except in emergency cases, a true mental disorder has been established by objective medical expertise;
2 the detention must be effected in accordance with a procedure prescribed by law;

---

1 (1979) 2 EHRR 387.

3   the mental disorder is of a kind or degree warranting compulsory confinement;

4   the validity of continued confinement depends upon the persistence of such a disorder.

In *Aerts v Belgium*,[2] the European Court held that the detention of a mentally disordered person will only be lawful in terms of Art 5 if effected in a hospital, clinic or other appropriate institution.

Article 6 (right to a fair trial) has some application if a patient is claiming that his rights have been contravened, for example, under Art 5, and he has not been given the opportunity of putting his case before a court. Article 3 (the prohibition on torture or inhuman or degrading treatment or punishment) has been used successfully in the context of treatment in prison of a suicidal prisoner who was deemed to be vulnerable and who was not given the appropriate care in a medical, as opposed to a penal, context (*Keenan v United Kingdom*[3]). Articles of the Convention will be referred to, where appropriate, below.

The most significant mental health ECHR case in recent times was *HL v United Kingdom*[4] which concerned 'informal patients' under the Act, ie patients who were not compulsorily detained because they were compliant. UK law was found to be incompatible with Art 5. The case is dealt with in detail below at 9.5.3.4 and in Chapter 4 at 4.3.3.

See Chapter 4

9.1.3 What is mental disorder?

The wording of the original Mental Health Act 1983 referred to mental disorder, mental illness, psychopathic disorder and mental impairment. The new revised Act simply refers to mental disorder. Mental illness is often thought to consist of more serious aspects of disorder such as schizophrenia, but there is no definition of these general phrases, either in the medical or legal literature. There have been a number of writers who have questioned the existence of mental illness, or at least, questioned whether it is a *medical* condition. Interestingly, these views have been harnessed to both right and left wing perspectives. The American doctor and writer, Thomas Szasz, is one of the most well known proponents and approaches it from a libertarian analysis. His view is that *all* illness has a *physical* pathology, and the psychiatrist must be either a malevolent meddler or a benevolent, but misguided healer; he sees psychiatry as a study of personal conduct. Szasz maintains that psychiatric interventions are directed at moral, rather than medical problems, the view he takes is that of the psychiatrist as malevolent meddler. Szasz's pithy summary of his thesis is uncompromising:

Szasz, T, *The Myth of Mental Illness: Foundations of a Theory of Personal Conduct*[5]

Summary

The principal arguments advanced in this book and their implications may be summarised as follows.

1   Strictly speaking, disease or illness can affect only the body; hence, there can be no mental illness.

2   'Mental illness' is a metaphor. Minds can be 'sick' only in the sense that jokes are 'sick' or economies are 'sick'.

3   Psychiatric diagnoses are stigmatising labels, phrased to resemble medical diagnoses and applied to persons whose behaviour annoys or offends others.

---

2   (2000) 29 EHRR 50.
3   (2001) 33 EHRR 38.
4   (2005) 40 EHRR 32, ECtHR.
5   Revised edn, New York: Harper and Row, 1974.

4   Those who suffer from and complain of their own behaviour are usually classified as 'neurotic'; those whose behaviour makes others suffer, and about whom others complain, are usually classified as 'psychotic'.

5   Mental illness is not something a person has, but is something he does or is.

6   If there is no mental illness there can be no hospitalisation, treatment, or cure for it. Of course, people may change their behaviour or personality, with or without psychiatric intervention. Such intervention is nowadays called 'treatment', and the change, if it proceeds in a direction approved by society, 'recovery' or 'cure'.

7   The introduction of psychiatric considerations into the administration of the criminal law – for example, the insanity plea and verdict, diagnoses of mental incompetence to stand trial, and so forth, corrupt the law and victimise the subject on whose behalf they are ostensibly employed.

8   Personal conduct is always rule-following, strategic, meaningful. Patterns of interpersonal and social relations may be regarded and analysed as if they were games, the behaviour of the players being governed by explicit or tacit game rules.

9   In most types of voluntary psychotherapy, the therapist tries to elucidate the inexplicit game rules by which the client conducts himself; and to help the client scrutinise the goals and values of the life games he plays.

10 There is no medical, moral, or legal justification for involuntary psychiatric interventions. They are crimes against humanity.

Szasz has continued to maintain his basic contentions:

Szasz, T, 'Psychiatric diagnosis, psychiatric power and psychiatric abuse'[6]

Psychiatric practice, as the term implies, is a practical, not a theoretical, enterprise. Accordingly, so long as psychiatrists continue to assign the role of mental patient to persons against their will, that fact will remain a fundamental characteristic of psychiatric practice . . .

Art historians, drama critics, musicologists, and many other scholars also make subjective classifications. However, lacking State-sanctioned power over persons, their classifications do not lead to anyone's being deprived of life, liberty, or property. Surely, the plastic surgeon's classification of beauty is subjective. But because the plastic surgeon cannot treat his or her patient without the patient's consent, there cannot be any political abuse of plastic surgery. It is as simple, and inconvenient, as that.

Whilst not doubting the sincerity of Szasz's views, it is easy to see how they might be attractive to those who wish to reduce public spending on the care of those diagnosed as being mentally ill.

The British psychoanalyst, the late RD Laing, whose most well known publication is *The Divided Self*,[7] took a different approach, and did not deny the existence of mental 'illness', but saw it as the reaction of a normal person to abnormal social pressures, for example, oppressive family situations. He related the experience of mental illness very much to being out of kilter with the social norm. It is not difficult to see how this approach might be used in libertarian and even anarchistic arguments against traditional social organisations. It must, however, be said that, interesting though theories such as those of Szasz and Laing are, they were never brought into the mainstream of psychiatry.[8]

---

6   (1994) 20 JME 135–38.
7   Harmondsworth: Penguin, 1959, reissued 1990.
8   See also Horwitz A and Wakefield J, *The Loss of Sadness: How Psychiatry Transformed Normal Sorrow into Depressive Disorder*, New York: OUP, 2007.

However, although most people would not dispute the existence of mental illness, there is an inevitable difference between patients who are physically ill, and patients who are mentally ill, in that it is by no means agreed what is meant by *mental* illness. Although there may be some dispute about areas of physical illness, generally, it is acknowledged that one can point to examples of physical 'normality', but clearly it would be futile to attempt to define a psychologically normal person. Whilst it is accepted that there can be desirable deviations from the physical norm (for example, athletic prowess), we are used to thinking of most significant deviations from the physical 'norm' as being undesirable. However, significant deviations from the psychological 'norm' can be *much better* than the norm, for example, in intellectual ability or capacity for forgiveness and compassion. Furthermore, in the case of physical characteristics, it is easier to decide whether the deviation is desirable or not, not least because mental qualities are essentially part of personal identity.

One of the few cases to consider the definitional issue is *W v L*,[9] where the Court of Appeal considered whether a young man was 'mentally ill' following a series of acts of violence and cruelty. He had hanged a puppy, strangled a terrier with wire, made a cat inhale ammonia and then cut its throat, and had put another cat in the gas oven. When he turned his attention away from family pets, and threatened his wife with a knife and offered other forms of violence towards her, he was admitted as an emergency under the provisions of the Mental Health Act 1959. Both Denning MR and Orr LJ accepted the medical evidence that the patient was psychotic, and did not consider the meaning of the expression 'mentally ill'. However, Lawton LJ made these observations[10]:

> **Lawton LJ**: The facts of this case show how difficult the fitting of particular instances into the statutory classification can be. Lord Denning MR and Orr LJ have pointed out that there is no definition of 'mental illness'. The words are ordinary words of the English language. They have no particular medical significance. They have no particular legal significance. How should the court construe them? The answer in my judgment is to be found in the advice which Lord Reid recently gave in *Cozens v Brutus* [1973] AC 854, p 861 namely, that ordinary words of the English language should be construed in the way that ordinary sensible people would construe them. That being, in my judgment, the right test, then I ask myself, what would the ordinary sensible person have said about the patient's condition in this case if he had been informed of his behaviour to the dogs, the cat and his wife? In my judgment such a person would have said: 'Well, the fellow is obviously mentally ill'. If that be right, then, although the case may fall within the definition of 'psychopathic disorder' in s 4(4), it also falls within the classification of 'mental illness'; and there is the added medical fact that when the EEG was taken there were indications of a clinical character showing some abnormality of the brain. It is that application of the sensible person's assessment of the condition, plus the medical indication, which in my judgment brought the case within the classification of mental illness, and justified the finding of the county court judge.

If it is the case that the words 'mental illness' are ordinary words and *have no particular medical significance*, what are the implications of this? In some ways this is an extraordinary conclusion, because if it has no medical significance, what significance does it have? The 'any normal person can see he's ill' definition of mental illness is a worrying one, and it adds fuel to the arguments of people such as Szasz.

On the difficulty of making precise medical classifications of mental disorders, see the House of Lords case of R (*On the Application of B*) v *Ashworth Hospital Authority*.[11]

---

9 [1974] QB 711.
10 At pp 718–19.
11 [2005] UKHL 20.

If one looks at the two main psychiatric diagnostic manuals published by the American Psychiatric Association and the World Health Organisation,[12] it will be seen that the symptoms of all known psychiatric disorders are described in some detail, but, not surprisingly, 'mental disorder or mental illness' as such are not considered.

It should also be noted that those with learning disabilites can be brought within the remit of the Act and that the concept of 'learning disability' has replaced 'mental impairment' in the revised MHA. This is discussed further below.

 SELF-TEST QUESTION

Do you think that it would be preferable to define mental disorder in terms of unacceptable behaviour on the part of the patient? If so, how would you decide what is acceptable?

9.1.4 Justifying detention

The Percy Commission, which reported before the MHA 1959, stated that it was wrong to detain someone compulsorily, before they had committed any criminal offence:

Lord Percy of Newcastle, *Report of the Royal Commission on the Law relating to Mental Illness and Mental Deficiency*, Cmd 169[13], (the Percy Commission), para 348

Preventive detention under the ordinary criminal law may only be applied to offenders over a certain age who have a definite criminal record of a certain number of convictions for serious offences; and even preventive detention lasts only for a fixed period, after which the prisoner must be released even if it is almost certain that he will then commit further crimes. If one is to apply preventive control to psychopathic patients under wider conditions than these, one is in effect applying to them preventive detention in hospital in circumstances which would not justify preventive detention in prison under the criminal law. Whether or not special forms of control are justified on these grounds depends on how accurate the diagnosis of the patient's condition and the prognosis of his future behaviour is likely to be, and on the extent to which it is fair to assume that the risks to society from persons suffering from these forms of mental abnormality are greater than the risks which society runs from criminals who are not considered to be mentally abnormal.

Apart from having to be suffering from some form of mental disorder, the person compulsorily detained under the Act for assessment 'ought to be so detained in the interests of his own health or safety or with a view to the protection of other persons' (s 2(2)(b)), and in the case of a person compulsorily detained for treatment, it must be '*necessary* for the health or safety of the patient or for the protection of other persons that he should receive such treatment and it cannot be provided unless he is detained under this section' (s 3(2)(c)). It will be seen that the 'protection' condition is wider in the case of admission for assessment, being 'ought to be so detained in the interests of' as opposed to 'necessary for' and this is hardly surprising. However, it is not clear as to what sort of risks must be involved for patients and/or third parties.

---

12 *Diagnostic and Statistical Manual of Mental Disorders*, Washington DC: American Psychiatric Press, 2000 and *The Classification of Mental and Behavioural Disorders*, Geneva: World Health Organisation, 1992, known as DSM IV Revised and ICD–10, respectively.

13 London: HMSO, 1954–57.

The Code of Practice contains no guidance on the safety of the patient; perhaps it is thought to be self-evident, but the assessment of the risk and the probability of the risk turning into reality must surely be of central importance. There is guidance on health risk which states:

Department of Health and Welsh Office, *Code of Practice, Mental Health Act 1983,*[14] para 4.6

Factors to consider – the health or safety of the patient

4.6 Factors to be considered in deciding whether patients should be detained for their own health or safety include:

- The evidence suggesting that patients are at risk of:
  - suicide;
  - self-harm;
  - self-neglect or being unable to look after their own health or safety; or
  - jeopardising their own health or safety accidentally, recklessly or unintentionally;

  or that their mental disorder is otherwise putting their health or safety at risk:
- any evidence suggesting that the patient's mental health will deteriorate if they do not receive treatment;
- the reliability of such evidence, including what is known of the history of the patient's mental disorder;
- the views of the patient and of any carers, relatives or close friends, especially those living with the patient, about the likely course of the disorder and the possibility of it improving;
- the patient's own skills and experience in managing their condition;
- the potential benefits of treatment, which should be weighed against any adverse effects that being detailed might have on the patient's wellbeing; and
- whether other methods of managing the risk are available.

Is the desire to protect from self-harm paternalistic and unsustainable? It can be argued that there is no interference with the positive freedom of the individual because there is a competing right held by the patient himself. The argument states that a person in ill health has reduced capacities to act and therefore less ability to make effective choices. In other words the patient will be *more free* as a result of the paternalistic intervention. Cavadino gives a good account of the civil libertarian, and other issues raised by the treatment of the mentally ill.

Cavadino, M, *Mental Health Law in Context*[15]

. . . liberal thinkers such as Isaiah Berlin (1969) have usually adopted the 'negative concept of freedom'. Negative freedom is defined as the absence of coercion or constraint imposed on the individual by other people. (I use the word 'liberty' to mean freedom in this negative sense.) In this sense, everyone who is not prevented from doing so by other people is equally free to run a mile in under four minutes or to dine at the Ritz Hotel, although only some people (those fast enough, or rich enough) actually can.

There is, however, a rival concept of freedom which also has its adherents. 'Freedom in the positive sense' may be defined as 'the ability to make effective choices about one's own life'. In this positive sense, I am not free to run a mile in under four minutes, or to dine at the Ritz in my present financial circumstances. For to be 'positively free' is to be actually able to perform the action in question, not simply to be unconstrained by other people or by the law.

---

14 London: HMSO, 2008.
15 Aldershot: Dartmouth, 1989.

To be sure, negative freedom (absence of constraint) is necessary in order to have positive freedom; but to be positively free additionally requires, first, the physical and psychological capacities to carry out the action or course of action in question; and second, access to any material resources necessary to perform the action. So I am not free to dine at the Ritz if I cannot physically get there or cannot afford it.

Surely liberal theory of any kind – even those which emphasise the importance of 'negative freedom' – must presuppose that 'positive freedom' is of value. For what else is the point of valuing negative freedom (as liberalism does) if this negative freedom does not actually enable people to make real, effective choices? For all that some liberals vehemently insist on employing the negative definition of freedom, it must be 'positive freedom' which is the intrinsically valuable commodity to human beings, with 'negative freedom' only of instrumental value in so far as it is conducive to real ability to choose. In short, if negative freedom is to be valued, this can only be because positive freedom is of more fundamental value.

If we accept that positive freedom is of value, and necessarily is of value to every human being, then any defensible philosophy of morality must accept as a basic principle that every individual has an equal right to maximum positive freedom. This is the 'positive freedom principle' (PFP). I suggest that this principle provides a much more consistent and coherent approach than liberal theories typically do . . .

The presumption in favour of liberty must be a strong one. For as is generally accepted over a wide spectrum of political views, States and other powerful authorities have a distressing tendency to restrict liberty excessively (thereby depriving people of the positive freedom to which they are entitled). Given this, there are good reasons for holding (as liberalism does) that people should not be deprived of substantial liberty without strong justification being adduced. Thus it is indeed right that laws should be framed to protect negative freedom with clear criteria and adequate procedural safeguards.

What should the criteria for deprivation of liberty be? First, it is clear that the protection of others can in principle be a valid justification for deprivation of liberty. The potential victims of violent assault have a right to personal safety which comes into competition with the right to liberty of the potential detainee, since the infliction of injury represents an unjustified diminution of the positive freedom of the victim. The injured person's real abilities to act are diminished by injury and totally extinguished by death, because injury and death reduce or remove a person's physical capacities.

This is not to say, however, that people may be justly deprived of liberty without further ado if there is any evidence or belief, however slight, that they might be dangerous to others. The nature of the risk to others must be assessed together with its likelihood of eventuating. As Dworkin has suggested, we 'should treat a man against his will only when the danger he presents is vivid' [Dworkin, R, *Taking Rights Seriously*, 1978, London: Duckworth, p 11]. It also follows from the strength of the presumption in favour of liberty that cogent evidence of the patient's dangerousness should normally be adduced under conditions of due process before detention can be justified. (And incidentally, as we saw in Chapter 8, a psychiatrist's assessment that a patient is dangerous is by no means always 'cogent evidence'; due process requires that such evidence should be carefully scrutinised to assess its validity.)

What about parentalism [paternalism]? Here again a case can be made for interfering with the individual's (negative) liberty on the ground that there is a more important competing right to be protected. In this case, however, the competing right is not one owned by some other individual, but by the patient, the same person who has the right to liberty. If the intervention results in the preservation or promotion of the health of the patient, this could result overall in the maximisation of the patient's positive freedom. For a person in ill health has reduced capacities to act, and consequently less ability to make effective choices : . .

(Note that this argument is not a utilitarian one. It does not rest on the contention that the patient will be happier or will suffer less if the intervention occurs. It argues that the patient will be more free overall if parentalism is allowed.)

This is a persuasive justification, but it depends upon much sharper definitions of self-harm, and the possibility of accurate diagnoses which at present we do not have.

As to the protection of others, it may be accepted even on strong libertarian grounds that detention of someone who, for example violently assaults others, is consistent with the concept of the freedom of the individual as the patient will be seriously interfering with their liberty. However, in the Act itself the requirement regarding harm to others is weak: there is no suggestion that the severity of the harm, and likelihood of the risk are relevant.

The Code of Practice deals with the protection of others, and it is clear from this that, whilst it includes the protection of others from psychological as well as physical harm, risk to property is not enough:

Department of Health and Welsh Office, *Code of Practice, Mental Health Act 1983*,[16] para 4.7

4.7 In considering whether detention is necessary for the protection of other people, the factors to consider are the nature of the risk to other people arising from the patient's mental disorder, the likelihood that harm will result and the severity of any potential harm, taking into account:

- that it is not always possible to differentiate risk of harm to the patient from the risk of harm to others;
- the reliability of the available evidence, including any relevant details of the patient's clincial history and past behaviour, such as contact with other agencies and (where relevant) criminal convictions and cautions;
- the willingness and ability of those who live with the patient and those who provide care and support to the patient to cope with and manage the risk; and
- whether other methods of managing the risk are available.

4.8 Harm to other people includes psychological as well as physical harm.

Price comments on the notion of dangerous as follows:

Price, DPT, 'Civil commitment of the mentally ill: compelling arguments for reform'[17]

Dangerousness is a social construct, it is not a psychiatric phenomenon and thus not peculiarly within the competence of psychiatrists to assess in individual cases. In any event, the problems in predicting dangerousness are immense. Almost all studies of predictive accuracy show that there are likely to be more false positives than true positives in any defined population. This is hardly surprising in view of the (relative) rarity of violent conduct and the fact that violent or dangerous conduct is at least partly a product of a person's environment (in other words it is situation specific). Some studies have shown very substantial over predictions of dangerousness by psychiatrists, which is partially due to the understandable tendency to err on what can be considered from one perspective as 'the safe side'. The potential for erosion of civil liberties through the unwarranted removal of liberty is then clear.

In 2000, government proposals for reform of the 1983 Act envisaged more draconian measures for 'dangerous' patients, see below at 9.1.5.

---

16 London: HMSO, 2008.
17 (1994) 2 Med L Rev 321.

9.1.5 History of statutory control

Brenda Hoggett sets out the development of the law relating to the control of mentally disordered people. After describing the provisions of the Lunacy Act 1890 and the Mental Treatment Act 1930, she goes on:

Hoggett, B, *Mental Health Law*[18]

Until the 1959 Act . . . there were three different types of patient in mental illness hospitals – voluntary and temporary patients under the 1930 Act and patients certified under the various procedures in the 1890 Act. For mental 'defectives' there was a totally different, if rather less complex, set of procedures under the Mental Deficiency Acts of 1913 and 1927. These did not include a voluntary status, but the institutions were not expressly prohibited from taking patients without formality. After 1952, this was officially encouraged for short stays, and the Percy Commission recommended that it could be extended to long stay patients without waiting for legislation. In . . . the 1959 Act, a determined effort was made to break down the rigid legal boundaries and integrate the separate legal systems relating to 'lunacy' and 'mental deficiency'.

Two developments lay behind much of the Percy Commission's thinking. First was the introduction of the National Health Service in 1948 . . . The Commission believed that there was no longer any need for strict legal control over public hospitals. Further, as improvements depend upon the availability of resources, full responsibility should rest with the government department which controlled the allocation of resources within the health service as a whole. The Board of Control could safely be abolished, and with it the legal segregation of mental hospitals from the main stream of hospital development.

Second was the great optimism about the advances in medical treatment for the major mental illnesses, through psycho-surgery, electro-convulsive therapy and above all the new breed of psychotropic drugs, the major tranquillisers. These made it possible for increasing numbers of seriously disordered patients to be discharged into the community or treated on clinical wards in ordinary hospital conditions. It no longer seemed necessary for the law to assume that these patients were inevitably different from the physically sick or injured. For the most part, they could be admitted to hospital in just the same way. Compulsory procedures could be kept only for those for whom they were absolutely necessary. Once in hospital, their treatment and care could be left in the hands of the medical profession. As many as possible would be discharged back into the community just like other patients.

Hence, removing the legal controls over mental patients was inextricably linked with removing the legal controls over their doctors. The 1983 Act was mainly concerned to reimpose some of the latter.

In 1998, the Government set up a 'scoping study review committee' to examine the provisions of the 1983 Act, to take soundings from experts and interested parties and to prepare a report, outlining recommendations for reform. The committee reported in July 1999 (known as the 'Richardson Report') and, in November 1999, the Government issued a Green Paper.[19] Peay describes the Green Paper that followed the Richardson Report which had been patient-focussed, as a 'squandered opportunity'.[20]

In 1999, another consultation document was issued by the Department of Health and the Home Office, *Managing Dangerous People with Severe Personality Disorder*. This was largely in response to the public outcry following the murders committed by Michael Stone, an allegedly 'untreatable'

---

18 4th edn, London: Sweet & Maxwell, 1996.
19 *Reform of the Mental Health Act 1983: Proposals for Reform*, Cm 4480, London: DoH, 1999.
20 See Peay, J, 'Report of the Mental Health Act 1983:Squandering an Opportunity?' (2000) J Mental Health L 5.

personality disordered patient who had been released into the community. Subsequently, a White Paper was issued, *Reforming The Mental Health Act*.[21] In 2002 a draft Mental Health Bill was issued, which gave rise to much criticism that it was too draconian in its measures to deal with people who were classified as personality disordered and dangerous.

Debate continued through Bills that were introduced in 2002 and 2004, which were abandoned, and in 2006 another Bill was produced that subsequently became the Mental Health Act 2007. Essentially, it made some amendments to the 1983 Act in certain key areas, but much of the Act remains the same. Certainly there has been no root and branch reform that had been hoped for by parties on all sides of the debate.

The main changes are as follows.

1. In order to be detained under the Act, patients now have to be suffering from 'mental disorder' ie the other definitions have gone.
2. The 'treatability requirement' has gone. Previously, in order to justify admitting a patient for treatment under s 3, if the patient was suffering from non-severe mental impairment or psychopathic disorder then there had to be available treatment that was likely to alleviate or prevent a deterioration of his condition. This was controversial because arguably such a requirement should apply to all patients. It is also problematic because patients suffering from 'psychopathic disorder' (defined as a 'disorder or disability of mind . . . which results in abnormally aggressive or seriously irresponsible conduct . . .' and which, in terms of the diagnostic manuals, is more properly referred to as 'antisocial personality disorder') are often very difficult patients to deal with, and there could be a temptation to declare them to be untreatable in order to discharge them from hospital. That is not to say that there is no genuine debate as to how far such patients can be treated. However, the interpretation of 'treatment' under the Act has been very wide indeed. We will examine this issue in due course.
3. The Act now provides for compulsory treatment in the community which is an attempt to avoid the 'revolving door' syndrome whereby patients are detained under the Act, treated successfully, released into the community, only to suffer relapse when they fail to take the stabilising medication.
4. The Act also provides for an independent advocacy scheme for detained patients who have no other form of representation.

The main elements of the revised legislation are set out below. For a detailed and exhaustive examination of the statutory provisions, readers are advised to consult Richard Jones's excellent guide to the Act.[22]

9.2 Detention

9.2.1 Mental disorder

Brief and somewhat unhelpful definitions of mental disorder and the other conditions referred to in the Act are contained within s 1:

1 Application of Act: 'mental disorder'
(1) The provisions of this Act shall have effect with respect to the reception, care and treatment of mentally disordered patients, the management of their property and other related matters

---

21 Cm 5016–1, London: Department of Health and the Home Office, 2000.
22 *Mental Health Act Manual*, 13th edn, London: Sweet & Maxwell, 2010.

(2)   In this Act–
'mental disorder' means any disorder or disability of mind and 'mentally disordered' shall be
   construed accordingly . . .

   . . .

Under s 1(3) of the Act, definitions exclude alcohol or drug dependency without more. The *Review of the Mental Health Act 1959*, carried out by the Department of Health and Social Security[23] concluded that it was inappropriate to regard such problems as mental disorders. Note that Art 5 of the European Convention provides for detention of persons who are alcoholic or addicted to drugs, although the Act does not permit this, without more. It has been recognised that, where there is a 'dual diagnosis' of people with both mental illness and either drug or alcohol problems, there is a risk that they can fall between the mental health services, and substance misuse services. The Department of Health has issued guidance for both providers on 'dual diagnosis'.[24]

In *St George's Healthcare NHS Trust v S*,[25] there had been an attempt to use the provisions of the Act to detain a pregnant woman and perform a non-consensual Caesarean section. She had attended a GP practice when 36 weeks pregnant, not having previously sought antenatal care. She had pre-eclampsia and was advised that she should be admitted to hospital for an induced delivery. She refused this, wanting her baby to be born naturally. A social worker became involved and an application was made under s 2 of the Act (compulsory detention in hospital for 'assessment'). The Court of Appeal was highly critical of the way in which the case was handled from both the point of view of the law and medicine (even the way in which the court procedure was used was flawed). For example, the hospital sought legal advice because it was erroneously believed that treatment could not be given under a s 2 admission. The doctor assessing the patient found her to have capacity, although subsequently reconsidered this and amended her note to say that her mental state may be affecting her capacity. The mental state referred to was diagnosed as moderate depression. After approval by the court (the judge having been erroneously informed that it was a 'life and death situation' with only minutes to spare), the child was delivered by Caesarean section. The following day the woman was examined again, and the consultant found 'no current abnormalities in her mental state'. The s 2 order was discharged. The Court of Appeal granted judicial review and stated that someone not suffering from mental disorder could not be detained under the MHA 1983 against his will merely because his thinking process was unusual and contrary to the views of the overwhelming majority of the community. It was clear that the purpose of detention was to manage her pregnancy and confinement and not to assess and treat a mental condition.

In *Winterwerp v Netherlands*,[26] when referring to the rather quaint expression in Art 5 – 'persons of unsound mind' – the ECtHR held that this term is constantly evolving in the light of developments in psychiatry and in society's attitude to mental illness.

The old expression of 'mental impairment' is no longer used in the Act since the 2007 reforms. The new expression is 'learning disability'.

Mental Health Act 1983

1 Application of Act: 'mental disorder'

(2A) But a person with learning disability shall not be considered by reason of that disability to be –

---

23 Cmnd 7320, London: HMSO, 1978.
24 *Mental health policy implementation guide: Dual diagnosis good practice guide* (Dept of Health, May 2002).
25 [1998] 3 All ER 673.
26 (1979) 2 EHRR 387.

(a) suffering from mental disorder for [certain purposes]

... unless that disability is associated with abnormally aggressive or seriously irrespon-sible conduct on his part.

The certain purposes referred to above include all compulsory admissions except admission under s 2 for assessment which is for a maximum of 28 days and is non-renewable. For all other compulsory detentions the learning disability must be associated with antisocial behaviour of an 'abnormal' nature.

The question of what constitutes 'seriously irresponsible conduct' was raised in *Re F* (*Mental Health Act: Guardianship*).[27] The Court of Appeal held that a 17-year-old's desire to return to her home where she had been severely neglected and sexually exploited was not 'seriously irresponsible'. It was said that the expression should be interpreted as relating to a significant risk of harm to self or others.

 SELF-TEST QUESTION

Do you agree with the argument that there should only be compulsory detention if the patient is a risk to the health and safety of others, and not to him/herself?

9.2.2 Key parties involved

The Act refers to a number of key personnel who are empowered to take action in respect of patients liable to be detained. Under s 11 of the Act, applications for compulsory admission may be made either by an approved mental health professional or by the patient's nearest relative.

9.2.2.1 Approved mental health professionals

Under s 114 of the Act, the local authority must appoint a 'sufficient number of approved mental health professionals for the purpose of discharging the functions conferred upon them'. Under the 1959 Act the same functions were carried out by mental welfare officers; under the 1983 Act prior to 2007 the functions were carried out by approved social workers:

13 Duty of approved mental health professionals to make applications for admission or guardianship

[(1) If a local social services authority have reason to think that an application for admission to hospital or a guardianship application may need to be made in respect of a patient within their area, they shall make arrangements for an approved mental health professional to consider the patient's case on their behalf.

(1A) If that professional is–

(a) satisfied that such an application ought to be made in respect of the patient; and

(b) of the opinion, having regard to any wishes expressed by relatives of the patient or any other relevant circumstances, that it is necessary or proper for the application to be made by him,

he shall make the application.

(1B) Subsection (1C) below applies where–

---

27 [2000] 1 FLR 192.

(a) a local social services authority makes arrangements under subsection (1) above in respect of a patient;

(b) an application for admission for assessment is made under subsection (1A) above in respect of the patient;

(c) while the patient is liable to be detained in pursuance of that application, the authority have reason to think that an application for admission for treatment may need to be made in respect of the patient; and

(d) the patient is not within the area of the authority.

(1C) Where this subsection applies, subsection (1) above shall be construed as requiring the authority to make arrangements under that subsection in place of the authority mentioned there.]

(2) Before making an application for the admission of a patient to hospital an [approved mental health professional] shall interview the patient in a suitable manner and satisfy himself that detention in a hospital is in all the circumstances of the case the most appropriate way of providing the care and medical treatment of which the patient stands in need.

[(3) An application under subsection (1A) above may be made outside the area of the local social services authority on whose behalf the approved mental health professional is considering the patient's case.

(4) It shall be the duty of a local social services authority, if so required by the nearest relative of a patient residing in their area, to [make arrangements under subsection (1) above for an approved mental health professional to consider the patient's case] with a view to making an application for his admission to hospital; and if in any such case [that professional] decides not to make an application he shall inform the nearest relative of his reasons in writing.

It will be seen from the following (s 13) that the approved mental health professional's duty is described as being personal to them and not as a functionary of the local authority which has appointed them, ie see the wording of sub-s (1A). See also *St George's Healthcare NHS Trust v S*.[28]

9.2.2.2 Nearest relative

Under some of the early reform proposals, the nearest relative provisions would be abolished in favour of a nominated person, the identity of whom being, to some extent, under the control of the patient. In the European Court case of *JT v United Kingdom*,[29] where the patient alleged that there was an infringement of her Art 8 right as the legislation did not provide for her to 'change' her nearest relative, the UK government responded (to the satisfaction of the court) that this would be reformed. The same point was taken in the case of R (*On the Application of M*) v *Secretary of State for Health*,[30] where the nearest relative provisions (not open to challenge by the patient) were declared to be incompatible with the HRA 1998, Art 8. In consequence, under s29(3), patients will now be able to apply to the county court to displace their nearest relative on the ground that they are unsuitable to act.

The nearest relative is defined by s 26 of the Act:

26.— Definition of 'relative' and 'nearest relative'.

(1) In this Part of this Act 'relative' means any of the following persons:—

   (a)   husband or wife [or civil partner];

28 [1998] 3 All ER 673, at 694.
29 [2000] 1 FLR 909.
30 [2003] EWHC 1094.

(b)   son or daughter;

(c)   father or mother;

(d)   brother or sister;

(e)   grandparent;

(f)   grandchild;

(g)   uncle or aunt;

(h)   nephew or niece.

(2)   In deducing relationships for the purposes of this section, any relationship of the half-blood shall be treated as a relationship of the whole blood, and an illegitimate person shall be treated as the legitimate child of [. . .]

[(a)   his mother, and

(b)   if his father has parental responsibility for him within the meaning of <u>section 3</u> of the <u>Children Act 1989</u>, his father.]

(3)   In this Part of this Act, subject to the provisions of this section and to the following provisions of this Part of this Act, the 'nearest relative' means the person first described in subsection (1) above who is for the time being surviving, relatives of the whole blood being preferred to relatives of the same description of the half-blood and the elder or eldest of two or more relatives described in any paragraph of that subsection being preferred to the other or others of those relatives, regardless of sex.

(4)   Subject to the provisions of this section and to the following provisions of this Part of this Act, where the patient ordinarily resides with or is cared for by one or more of his relatives (or, if he is for the time being an in-patient in a hospital, he last ordinarily resided with or was cared for by one or more of his relatives) his nearest relative shall be determined—

(a)   by giving preference to that relative or those relatives over the other or others; and

(b)   as between two or more such relatives, in accordance with subsection (3) above.

The definition does not include spouses who are separated and provision is also made for cohabitees and other persons with whom the patient has been residing to be treated as relatives (sub-ss (5)–(7)). It is possible for persons who do not come within the ambit of s 26 nevertheless still to act in the capacity of a nearest relative. The nearest relative may forfeit status, and can authorise another person to act, or that person can be appointed by the county court to be the patient's nearest relative, under s 29:

29 . . .

(3)   An application for an order under this section may be made upon any of the following grounds, that is to say—

(a)   that the patient has no nearest relative within the meaning of this Act, or that it is not reasonably practicable to ascertain whether he has such a relative, or who that relative is;

(b)   that the nearest relative of the patient is incapable of acting as such by reason of mental disorder or other illness;

(c)   that the nearest relative of the patient unreasonably objects to the making of an application for admission for treatment or a guardianship application in respect of the patient; [. . .]

(d)   that the nearest relative of the patient has exercised without due regard to the welfare of the patient or the interests of the public his power to discharge the patient [. . .] under this Part of this Act, or is likely to do so [; or]

[(e)   that the nearest relative of the patient is otherwise not a suitable person to act as such.]

In *W v L*,[31] the Court of Appeal had to consider the meaning of s 29(3)(c), that is, when does a nearest relative *unreasonably* object?

> **Lord Denning MR** (p 717): This brings me to the final question: is the wife unreasonable in objecting to the making of an application for the husband's detention? . . . if you look at it from her own point of view, she may not be unreasonable. But I do not think it correct to look at it from her own point of view. The proper test is to ask what a reasonable woman in her place would do in all the circumstances of the case.

9.2.2.3 Doctors

Applications must, of course, be supported by medical recommendations. An application under s 2 (admission for assessment), s 3 (admission for treatment) or s 7 (reception into guardianship) requires two medical recommendations. An application under s 4 (emergency) needs only one recommendation. The doctor in charge of the patient's treatment is referred to as the 'responsible clinician'.

9.2.3 The categories of admission

9.2.3.1 Admission for assessment – s 2

Section 2 of the MHA 1983 states as follows:

> **2 Admission for assessment**
>
> (2) An application for admission for assessment may be made in respect of a patient on the grounds that–
>
> > (a) he is suffering from mental disorder of a nature or degree which warrants the detention of the patient in a hospital for assessment (or for assessment followed by medical treatment) for at least a limited period; and
> >
> > (b) he ought to be so detained in the interests of his own health or safety or with a view to the protection of other persons.
>
> . . .
>
> (4) Subject to the provisions of s 29(4) below, a patient admitted to hospital in pursuance of an application for admission for assessment may be detained for a period not exceeding 28 days beginning with the day on which he is admitted, but shall not be detained after the expiration of that period unless before it has expired he has become liable to be detained by virtue of a subsequent application, order or direction under the following provisions of this Act.

It should be noted that, under s 11(3) if the application is made by an approved mental health professional, he must inform the nearest relative that an application is to be made. There is no requirement in respect of a s 2 admission for the approved mental health professional to have *consulted* with the relative (see s 11(4)), but under s 13(1), the social worker must have regard to any wishes expressed by the relative when deciding whether to make the application. There is no illegality if it subsequently transpires that the patient is not suffering from mental disorder at all (R v *Kirklees Metropolitan BC ex p* C[32]).

---

31 [1974] QB 711.
32 [1993] 2 FLR 187.

Admission under s 2 is for 28 days only, and s 2(4) states that the patient 'shall not be detained after the expiration of that period unless before it has expired he has become liable to be detained by virtue of a subsequent application, order or direction under the following provisions of this Act'. Clearly, this means that it is not renewable, and it may be argued that no subsequent s 2 application could be made. However, in R v South Western Hospital Managers ex p M,[33] it was held that the discretion of an approved social worker (as they were then called) could not be fettered by the earlier decision of a Mental Health Review Tribunal to discharge a s 2 patient, albeit in this case, to pursue a subsequent application under s 3 (admission for treatment). Laws J stated that such decisions by the social workers, doctors and hospital managers would be amenable to applications for judicial review. It seems therefore that a further s 2 application, made immediately after the expiry of an earlier one, would be judicially reviewable, but, on the reasoning employed by Laws J would not be automatically regarded as unlawful on the face of the statute.

A similar issue came up in R v East London and City Mental Health NHS Trust ex p Brandenburg,[34] in relation to the discharge of a patient by a Mental Health Tribunal following a s 2 admission. The patient was redetained on the day before the discharge was due to take place. The Court of Appeal held that there did not have to be a change of circumstances to justify this under the Act, but the decision to discharge must be given great weight. A decision to redetain where there was no change of circumstances, would have to be made in the light of facts known to the doctors and not to the tribunal, otherwise the decision of the tribunal would prevail. The House of Lords rejected an appeal, but it was stated by Lord Bingham that an ASW (approved social worker as they were then called) may not lawfully apply for the admission of a patient whose discharge has been ordered by a tribunal unless s/he has formed the reasonable and bona fide opinion that s/he has information not known to the tribunal which puts a signficantly different complexion on the case as compared with that which was before the tribunal.[35]

A related point is the question of 'assessment' and when it is appropriate to admit for that reason. In B v Barking Havering and Brentwood Community Healthcare NHS Trust,[36] it was said that assessment could be an important part of evaluating treatment. This would mean that a patient could be admitted for assessment under s 2 where a diagnosis of his condition had already been made. Admitting someone under s 2, however, and then failing to undertake any form of assessment would be unlawful.[37]

9.2.3.2 Admission for treatment – s 3

Long-term admission is sanctioned under s 3 of the Act.

3 Admission for treatment

. . .

(2) An application for admission for treatment may be made in respect of a patient on the grounds that–

(a) he is suffering from mental disorder of a nature or degree which makes it appropriate for him to receive medical treatment in a hospital; and

. . .

(c) it is necessary for the health or safety of the patient or for the protection of other persons that he should receive such treatment and it cannot be provided unless he is detained under this section . . .

---

33 [1994] 1 All ER 161.
34 [2001] EWCA Civ 239.
35 [2003] UKHL 58. See also R (On the Application of Wirral Health Authority and Wirral BC) v Dr Finnegan and DE [2001] EWCA Admin 312.
36 [1999] 1 FLR 106.
37 See St George's Healthcare NHS Trust v S [1999] Fam 26.

It can be argued that applications under s 3 are, more often than not, unnecessary. Why should this be the case? Although there is no obligation to do so, an application in respect of a patient who has not been formally sectioned before, will usually be under s 2 of the Act. This means that for up to 28 days a patient can be observed, and, if necessary, treated. After the lapse of this period of time, therefore, the patient may be a lot 'better' than when first admitted, and therefore more amenable to remaining as a voluntary patient, rather than by invoking the provisions of s 3.

The use – or abuse – of the wording of s 3 was considered in the case of *R v Hallstrom and Another ex p W (No 2)*. In that case, an admission under s 3 was made, and almost immediately the patient was discharged under s 17 (a provision of the Act which enables the responsible clinician to grant leave of absence to any patient liable to be detained). The purpose was to allow compulsory treatment within the community. McCullough J said:[38]

R v Hallstrom and Another ex p W (No 2)[39]

McCullough J: It stretches the concept of 'admission for treatment' too far to say that it covers admission for only so long as it is necessary to enable leave of absence to be granted after which the necessary treatment will begin. 'Admission for treatment' under s 3 is intended for those whose condition is believed to require a period of treatment as an in-patient. It may be that such patients will also be thought to require a period of out-patient treatment thereafter, but the concept of 'admission for treatment' has no applicability to those whom it is intended to admit and detain for a purely nominal period, during which no necessary treatment will be given.

This principle was, in the words of Phil Fennell, distinguished almost to the point of extinction in the case of *R (On the Application of DR) v Merseycare NHS Trust*.[40] In that case, the claimant alleged that the renewal of her detention under s 20(2) of the Act was only appropriate when a patient's treatment plan was for treatment as an 'in-patient'. In her case, the proposal was that she be treated as an 'out-patient'. Her application for judicial review was rejected on the basis that 'any distinction between treatment at a hospital and in a hospital was too subtle'. It is also important to note here that, since the 1983 Act was passed, there has been a move away from treatment in hospital to treatment in the community, a change based upon a desire to avoid the institutionalisation of patients and to allow an appropriate degree of autonomy. However, as demonstrated, in effect, the interpretation of the requirement under the unamended legislation that the patient's condition 'warrants the detention of him in a hospital' has included hospital out-patient treatment, so that treatment can effectively be carried out in the community without the use of the newly introduced Community Treatment Orders.

The interpretation of 'the nature or degree' of the disorder warranting hospital treatment was considered in *R v The Mental Health Review Tribunal for the South Thames Region ex p Smith*.[41] It was said that this would be satisfied in the case of a patient whose symptoms are adequately controlled by medication, but who has stopped taking medication and whose history is such that a significant deterioration can be expected as a result of this. This not uncommon scenario (and results in what is often described as the 'revolving door' of admission/discharge/admission), was considered by the Court of Appeal in relation to the application of the HRA 1998 in the case of *R (On the Application of H) v Mental Health Review Tribunal, North and North East London Region*.[42] It was said that the continued

---

38 At p 315.
39 [1986] 2 All ER 306.
40 [2002] All ER(D) 28. See Commentary [2003] Med L Rev382.
41 [1999] COD 148.
42 [2001] EWCA Civ 415.

detention of such a patient was not contrary to Art 5(1)(e) of the ECHR (no one shall be deprived of his liberty save in (*inter alia*) the lawful detention of persons of unsound mind and in accordance with a procedure prescribed by law). There was no contravention as long as the detention was a proportionate response having regard to the risks that would be involved in discharge.

9.2.3.3 Admission for assessment in emergencies – s 4

Section 4 of the Act states as follows:

4 Admission for assessment in cases of emergency

(1) In any case of urgent necessity, an application for admission for assessment may be made in respect of a patient in accordance with the following provisions of this section, and any application so made is in this Act referred to as 'an emergency application'.

(2) An emergency application may be made either by an approved mental health professional or by the nearest relative of the patient; and every such application shall include a state- ment that it is of urgent necessity for the patient to be admitted and detained under s 2 above, and that compliance with the provisions of this Part of this Act relating to applica- tions under that section would involve undesirable delay.

(3) An emergency application shall be sufficient in the first instance if founded on one of the medical recommendations required by s 2 above, given, if practicable, by a practitioner who has previous acquaintance with the patient and otherwise complying with the require- ments of s 12 below so far as applicable to a single recommendation, and verifying the statement referred to in sub-s (2) above.

(4) An emergency application shall cease to have effect on the expiration of a period of 72 hours from the time when the patient is admitted to the hospital unless–

(a) the second medical recommendation required by s 2 above is given and received by the managers within that period; and

(b) that recommendation and the recommendation referred to in sub-s (3) above together comply with all the requirements of s 12 below (other than the requirement as to the time of signature of the second recommendation).

Although it may be accepted that there will be cases which are genuine emergencies and where a streamlined admission procedure is necessary, some may find cause for concern if such a proce- dure is used frequently. Further, it is important to keep in mind the wording of the section: it should not be used where it is simply more convenient to admit in this way, and obtain a second recommendation once the patient is in hospital so that the patient can then be admitted under s 2 or s 3. These concerns were considered in the 1978 *Review of the 1959 Mental Health Act*:

Review of the 1959 Mental Health Act[43]

Emergency admission for observation (s 29)

2.3 –Section 29 provides, in a case of urgent necessity, for the compulsory admission to hospital of a patient for observation. Twelve thousand people were admitted in this way in 1976. An application can be made by any relative (as defined by the Act) or by a Mental Welfare Officer, on the basis of a recommendation by any doctor. The section authorises detention for up to 72 hours only, unless the second medical recommendation which is required . . . is obtained within that period. The intention of the 1959 Act was that . . . s 29 should be used only in emer- gencies when there was not enough time to obtain the second medical recommendation.

---

43 Cmnd 7320, London: HMSO, 1978, para 1.17.

Section 29 has however been invoked more frequently than originally envisaged, and it has become the most widely used form of compulsory admission. There is also wide regional variation in its use. The Government hopes that the increasing development of the 24 hour crisis intervention services envisaged in the White Paper 'Better Services for the Mentally Ill' will in time reduce the need for such admissions, by enabling some emergencies to be contained without the need for compulsory admission to hospital or alternatively for two medical assessments to be provided. However, given the present constraints on manpower and resources, it is accepted that there is a continuing need for a statutory emergency procedure. While there is a good deal of support in comments on the Consultative Document for developing 24 hour crisis intervention services and for the view that these would reduce the use of s 29, it was also argued that, however fully developed, crisis intervention services could never adequately replace s 29 powers, particularly in rural areas. Comments included the point that s 29 allows for a short assessment or 'cooling off' period which can often lead to discharge within 72 hours or to the person staying in hospital as an informal patient.

It should be noted that treatment cannot be given to a patient admitted under this section under Part IV of the Act (that is, without his consent) so the patient is in the same position as a voluntary patient to whom treatment cannot be given without consent if they have capacity. These emergency powers do not contravene the HRA 1998, because the ECHR's procedural safeguards do not apply in emergency situations (*Winterwerp v Netherlands*[44]).

9.2.3.4 Guardianship – s 7

The requirements of s 7 are such that a patient over the age of 16 can be made the subject of a guardianship order if he is suffering from mental disorder of a nature or degree which warrants his reception into guardianship. The powers of the guardian are to require specified residence; to require attendance for medical treatment, education and training, and to require access to the patient.

A person received into guardianship is not a person who is 'liable to be detained' for the purposes of s 56, and therefore the Part IV provisions as to treatment do not apply; that is, the patient cannot be treated for the mental disorder against his will (see 9.4, below).

Both Art 5 (right to liberty) and Art 6 (right to a fair trial) apply to guardianship. There is no contravention of Art 6 because there is a right to appeal to a Mental Health Review Tribunal. As far as Art 5 is concerned, this applies even though the patient is not directly physically restrained. Restrictions as to dwelling place, etc, are also capable of contravening Art 5 (*Ashingdanev United Kingdom*[45]).

Guardianship is used infrequently (see the House of Commons Health Committee, *Report on Community Supervision Orders*[46]), and, given that substantial resources would be necessary to 'police' the system successfully, there must be doubts as to its usefulness. Mike Fisher, referring to the Social Services Research Group Study, carried out 1985–86, notes that during that 12-month period, the 63 incidents of guardianship constituted less than 1 per centof all detentions under the Act.[47] It might be thought that now there is the provision to provide treatment in the community, there would be no need to retain the power to make someone the subject of guardianship. However, guardianship is not about medical treatment, but about general personal care and, in that respect, it can be argued that it still retains a role.

---

44 (1979) 2 EHRR 387.
45 (1985) 7 EHRR 528.
46 London: HMSO, 1992–93.
47 See Fisher, M, 'Guardianship under the mental health legislation: a review' [1988] J Soc Wel L 316.

9.2.3.5 The detention of inpatients – s 5

5 Application in respect of patient already in hospital

(1) An application for the admission of a patient to a hospital may be made under this Part of this Act notwithstanding that the patient is already an in-patient in that hospital or, in the case of an application for admission for treatment that the patient is for the time being liable to be detained in the hospital in pursuance of an application for admission for assessment; and where an application is so made the patient shall be treated for the purposes of this Part of this Act as if he had been admitted to the hospital at the time when that application was received by the managers.

(2) If, in the case of a patient who is an in-patient in a hospital, it appears to the registered medical practitioner in charge of the treatment of the patient that an application ought to be made under this Part of this Act for the admission of the patient to hospital, he may furnish to the managers a report in writing to that effect; and in any such case the patient may be detained in the hospital for a period of 72 hours from the time when the report is so furnished.

. . .

The purpose of s 5 is to enable a hospital to detain a voluntary patient who decides that he is going to leave the hospital. Where the provisions of s 5(2) and (4) are used, the patient cannot be treated without consent, that is, the patient is specifically excluded from the provisions of Part IV by s 56 of the Act.

9.2.3.6 Informal admission – s 131

Patients can be informally admitted under the Act, that is, they are voluntary patients, and, as such are free to leave at any time. As we saw in Chapter 4, following the case of *HL v United Kingdom*[48] in the European Court of Human Rights, the Mental Health Act 2007 amended the Mental Capacity Act 2005 by introducing the Deprivation of Liberty Safeguards and, of course, these apply to informal psychiatric patients just as much as they apply to non-psychiatric patients and residents in care homes.

See Chapter 4

9.2.3.7 Miscellaneous powers

Under s 17 of the Act, a detained patient may be granted leave of absence subject to such conditions as the responsible clinician thinks necessary in the interests of the patient or for the protection of others. It should be noted that such a person is still liable to be detained, so that both the consent to treatment provisions of the Act and the HRA 1998 apply.

Finally, it must be noted that there are a number of powers under the Act conferred upon the police and social workers. Under s 115, an approved mental health professional may enter and inspect any premises if he has reasonable cause to believe that a mentally disordered person living there is not under proper care. Under s 136, a police officer may remove a person to a place of safety if he finds, in a public place, a person who appears to be suffering from mental disorder and to be in immediate need of care or control. Such a person can be detained to a maximum period of 72 hours to enable him to be examined by a doctor and interviewed by an approved mental health professional. Section 135 provides for the issue of warrants to search for and remove patients to a place of safety, so that persons believed to be suffering from mental disorder can be removed from private premises too. The power given to approved mental health professionals under s 115 does not enable them to force entry, and in such circumstances it would be necessary to obtain a warrant under s 135.

---

48 (2005) 40 EHRR 32.

9.2.4 Detention via the criminal justice system

A detailed examination of this area would involve consideration of criminological matters and penal policy which are outside the scope of this book. However, it is important to remember that many patients compulsorily detained have arrived in that state via criminal sentences. For an account of the criminal provisions see Bartlett and Sandland.[49]

9.3 Non-Medical Treatment

Part IV of the Act deals specifically with medical treatment. However, the Act is silent on issues such as the management of difficult patients, the extent to which they can be physically restrained, secluded and searched. In *Pountney v Griffiths*,[50] the House of Lords said that detention under the Act (the 1959 Act at that time), necessarily involves the exercise of control and discipline.

Department of Health and Welsh Office, *Mental Health Code of Practice*[51]

Personal and other searches

16.10 Hospital managers should ensure that there is an operational policy on searching patients detained under the Act, their belongings and surroundings and their visitors. When preparing the policy, hospital managers should consider the position of informal patients.

16.11 The policy should be based on the folowing clear principles:

- the intention is to create and maintain a therapeutic environment in which treatment may take place and to ensure the security of the premises and the safety of patients, staff and the public;
- the authority to conduct a search of a person or their property is controlled by law, and it is important that hospital staff are aware of whether they have legal authoirty to carry out any such search;
- searching should be proportionate to the identified risk and should involve the minimum possible intrusion into the person's privacy; and
- all searches will be undertaken with due regard to and respect for the person's dignity.

This approved use of routine and random searching for no particular reason was considered by the Court of Appeal in *R v Broadmoor Special Hospital Authority and Another ex p S and Others*.[52] Prior to 1997, Broadmoor's policy had been to search patients only when there had been a reason to do so. However, the policy was changed after a patient had attacked a priest with a heavy object which he had hidden on his person. In consequence, the search policy was amended to permit random searches, without consent or cause and, if necessary, overriding medical opinion against its exercise (presumably such opinion would be based upon the issue of 'trust'). The Court of Appeal confirmed the lawfulness of the policy on the basis that prisoners held in a special hospital such as Broadmoor were there because of their dangerous, violent or criminal propensities, and the policy was necessary in order to maintain a safe therapeutic environment.

---

49 Bartlett, P and Sandland, R, *Mental Health Law: Policy and Practice*, Oxford: OUP, 2003, Ch 6.
50 [1976] AC 314.
51 London: HMSO, 2008.
52 [1998] COD 199.

Seclusion was considered by the Court of Appeal in *Colonel Munjaz v Mersey Care NHS Trust* (1) *The Secretary of State for Health* and (2) *The National Association for Mental Health* (MIND), *and S v Airedale NHS Trust and* (1) *The Secretary of State for Health and* (2) *The National Association for Mental Health* (MIND).[53] The following principles emerged: the power to seclude is derived from the statutory power to detain and the common law justification of necessity; if the power is exercised in this way it will not amount to the tort of false imprisonment; seclusion is capable of being 'medical treatment'; it can amount to inhuman or degrading treatment or punishment under Art 3 of the ECHR but would have to reach a minimum level of severity; it would infringe Art 8 but could be justified under Art 8(2); if a hospital's actions breached the Code of Practice, an action in judicial review would lie.

Section 134 of the Act permits inspection and withholding of a detained patient's outgoing and incoming mail. Article 8 of the ECHR, which protects the right to respect for private life, specifically refers to protection of correspondence, so would it be possible to use the HRA 1998 to challenge this? First, it must be said that, under the Act, the restrictions on mail are not unqualified. Except in cases where the addressee has requested that communications from the patient to him should be withheld, the restrictions apply only to hospitals at which high security psychiatric services are provided and, secondly, they can only be imposed if it is necessary to do so in the interests of the safety of the patient or for the protection of other persons. This is likely to be proportionate and to satisfy Art 8(2), that is, 'to be necessary in a democratic society in the interests of public safety . . . for the prevention of disorder or crime, for the protection of heath or morals, or for the protection of the rights and freedoms of others'. Furthermore, the restriction does not apply to mail sent (*inter alia*) to 'any legally qualified persons instructed by the patient to act as his legal adviser'.[54] Further, this exception should also have the effect of avoiding any potential breach of Art 6, which protects the right to a fair trial.

Article 8 was considered in *R v Ashworth Hospital Authority ex p E*,[55] where it was held that the decision to refuse the request of a male patient to dress as a woman was lawful. The restrictions on dress were justified in terms of a pressing social need (the risk of disguise to facilitate abscondment was one reason) and it was proportionate.

9.4 Medical Treatment

9.4.1 Consent to treatment

As we saw in Chapter 3, adult patients in possession of the necessary decision making capacity have the right to refuse even life-saving medical treatment for any physical condition from which they may be suffering. However, in the case of patients detained under the Act, treatment for the mental disorder itself requires neither their express nor their implied consent (s 63). This is subject to exceptions contained within ss 57, 58 and 58A for certain types of treatment, and subject to s 62 which deals with urgent treatment. Consent, however, is required of voluntary patients (s 56(1) and (2)). These exceptions are examined in detail below but, first, the nature of treatment for mental disorder must be considered.

See Chapter
◄ 3

9.4.1.2 Treatment not needing the patient's consent

63 Treatment not requiring consent

The consent of a patient shall not be required for any medical treatment given to him for the mental disorder from which he is suffering, not being treatment falling within ss 57,58 or 58A

---

53 [2003] EWCA Civ 1036.
54 See *Valle v Finland* (2000) unreported, 16 March, where restrictions on telephone calls to a psychiatric patient's legal adviser were found to be unjustified.
55 [2002] QBD, Admin Court, Richards J, 19 December 2001.

above, if the treatment is given by or under the direction of the approved clinician in charge of the treatment.

The implication is that treatment for other purposes, ie, the patient's physical disorders, remains governed by the common law. The interpretation of what constitutes the medical treatment for the mental disorder from which the patient is suffering has recently been given a very wide interpretation by the courts. The Act defines medical treatment as including 'nursing, and also includes care, habilitation and rehabilitation under medical supervision' (s 145(1)), but there is no guidance as to how this should relate to the mental disorder from which the patient is suffering, and in the case of B v Croydon HA, the Court of Appeal interpreted this so as to permit a wide range of acts ancillary to the core treatment. The case concerned a s 3 patient, suffering from a psychopathic disorder, which, it was found, was treatable only by psychoanalytical psychotherapy. The patient made various attempts to harm herself, and when these were discovered and prevented, she decided that she would refuse to eat. The health authority decided to force feed her without her consent, and she applied to the court for an injunction to restrain them. At first instance the court refused this on the basis that it was treatment for the mental disorder and therefore, by reason of s 63, did not require her consent. The Court of Appeal upheld this.

It was accepted that, because of the 'treatability' requirement in s 3 (which has been removed since reform in 2007) (see 9.1.5, above), it would not have been lawful to detain her unless her condition was treatable. However, it was held that it did not follow that every act which formed part of treatment as defined by s 145(1) must, in itself, be likely to alleviate or prevent a deterioration of the disorder. The nasogastric feeding would be a form of concurrent care. Hoffmann LJ said:

B v Croydon HA[56]

Hoffmann LJ: Mr Gordon says that food is a medicine. He draws our attention to the fact that some special foods (for example, gluten-free rice cookies for coeliacs) may be obtained on prescription. In my view, however, this is not relevant to whether food is a medicine within the meaning of s 58. The section is concerned with medicines administered as treatment for mental disorder. The words 'by any means' in the opening phrase show that one identifies a medicine by its chemical composition and not by whether it is administered to the patient through a tube down his throat or by being put before him on a plate. Even gluten-free rice cookies are not administered for mental disorder and in my judgment ordinary food in liquid form, such as would be used in tube feeding, is not a medicine within the meaning of s 58.

That brings one back to the question of whether tube feeding would have been treatment for the mental disorder from which Ms B was suffering. My initial reaction was that it could not be. Ms B suffers from a psychopathic disorder which, according to the evidence, is incapable of treatment except by psychoanalytical psychotherapy. How can giving her food be treatment for that disorder? Mr Gordon says that it cannot. It may be a prerequisite to a treatment for mental disorder or it may be treatment for a consequence of the mental disorder, but it is not treatment of the disorder itself. He draws attention to s 3 of the Act, which specifies the grounds upon which a person suffering from a psychopathic disorder may be detained. It is not enough that the disorder must be 'of a nature or degree which makes it appropriate for him to receive medical treatment in a hospital' (sub-s (2)(a)). The proposed treatment must be 'likely to alleviate or prevent a deterioration of his condition' (sub-s (2)(b)) and it must be 'necessary for the health or safety of the patient or for the protection of other persons that he should receive such

---

56 [1994] 2 WLR 294, at p 297.

treatment' (sub-s (2)(c)). So Mr Gordon says that the patient cannot lawfully be detained unless the proposed treatment will alleviate or prevent a deterioration of his condition. No less should be required of the treatment which can be given without his consent under s 63.

This is a powerful submission. But I have come to the conclusion that it is too atomistic. It requires every individual element of the treatment being given to the patient to be directed to his mental condition. But in my view this test applies only to the treatment as a whole. Section 145(1) gives a wide definition to the term 'medical treatment'. It includes 'nursing, and also includes care, habilitation and rehabilitation under medical supervision'. So a range of acts ancillary to the core treatment fall within the definition. I accept that by virtue of s 3(2)(b) a patient with a psycho-pathic disorder cannot be detained unless the proposed treatment, taken as a whole, is 'likely to alleviate or prevent a deterioration of his condition'. In my view, contrary to the submission of Mr Francis, 'condition' in this paragraph means the mental disorder on grounds of which the application for his admission and detention has been made. It follows that if there was no proposed treatment for Ms B's psychopathic disorder, s 63 could not have been invoked to justify feeding her by nasogastric tube. Indeed, it would not be lawful to detain her at all.

It does not however follow that every act which forms part of that treatment within the wide definition in s 145(1) must in itself be likely to alleviate or prevent a deterioration of that disorder. Nursing and care concurrent with the core treatment or as a necessary prerequisite to such treatment or to prevent the patient from causing harm to himself or to alleviate the consequences of the disorder are in my view all capable of being ancillary to a treatment calcu-lated to alleviate or prevent a deterioration of the psychopathic disorder. It would seem to me strange if a hospital could, without the patient's consent, give him treatment directed to allevi-ating a psychopathic disorder showing itself in suicidal tendencies, but not without such consent be able to treat the consequences of a suicide attempt. In my judgment the term 'medical treatment . . . for the mental disorder' in s 63 includes such ancillary acts.

Mr Francis was, I think, right to draw our attention to s 62 as throwing some light upon the question. Sections 57 and 58 place special restrictions upon the use of particular 'forms of medical treatment for mental disorder', surgical operations for destroying brain tissue or implanting hormones (s 57), electro-convulsive therapy and drugs (s 58). There are special procedures which must be followed before these treatments can be given. But s 62(1) says that in certain specified cases of emergency, these special rules need not be complied with. They include:

. . . any treatment–

(a)   which is immediately necessary to save the patient's life; or
(b)   . . .
(c)   which (not being irreversible or hazardous) is immediately necessary to alleviate serious suffering by the patient; or
(d)   which (not being irreversible or hazardous) is immediately necessary and repre-sents the minimum interference necessary to prevent the patient from behaving violently or being a danger to himself or to others.

Mr Francis says, in my view rightly, that these emergency cases are not primarily concerned with a direct alleviation or the prevention of a deterioration of the mental disorder. The danger to the patient's life or the likelihood of serious suffering or the patient being a danger to himself or others are more likely to be the results of symptoms of the disorder. Nevertheless, the treatment of such symptoms is assumed by s 62 to be a 'form of medical treatment for mental disorder', since otherwise it would not have come within ss 57 or 58 in the first place.

I therefore agree with Ewbank J in *In re KB (An Adult) (Mental Patient: Medical Treatment)* (1994) 19 BMLR 144, p 146 when he said of the tube feeding of an anorexic: '. . . relieving symp-toms is just as much a part of treatment as relieving the underlying cause.' To similar effect is the judgment of Stuart-White J, quoted by Sir Stephen Brown P in *Riverside Mental Health NHS Trust v Fox* [1994] 1 FLR 614, p 619. The decision in *In re C (Adult: Refusal of Treatment)* [1994] 1 WLR 290, in which a schizophrenic was held entitled to refuse treatment for gangrene, is distinguishable. The gangrene was entirely unconnected with the mental disorder.

Mr Gordon said that if the meaning of 'medical treatment for mental disorder' was wide enough to include ancillary forms of treatment, s 63 would involve a breach of the Convention for the Protection of Human Rights and Fundamental Freedoms, Cmnd 8969, 1953. He referred us to *Herczegfalvy v Austria* (1992) 15 EHRR 437 in which the court said, p 485, that a measure constituting an interference with private life and therefore *prima facie* contrary to Art 8(1) (like involuntary tube feeding) can only be justified under Art 8(2) if, among the other requirements of that article, its terms are sufficiently precise to enable the individual 'to foresee its consequences for him'. This requirement is necessary to prevent such measures from being a source of arbitrary official power, contrary to the rule of law. In my judgment s 63 amply satisfies this test. There is no conceptual vagueness about the notion of treating the symptoms or consequences of a mental disorder, although naturally there will be borderline cases. But there is no question of an exercise of arbitrary power.

This is arguably a disturbing decision, widening as it does the ambit of non-consensual treatment. Note, also, that this case has been followed in *Re VS (Adult: Mental Disorder*[57]*)*, and, even more controversially, in the case of *Tameside and Glossop Acute Services Trust v CH*,[58] where it was held that the performance of a Caesarean section was treatment for mental disorder under s 63:[59]

Wall J: Is the question of inducing the defendant's labour and/or causing her to be delivered of her child by Caesarean section 'entirely unconnected' with her mental disorder? At first blush, it might appear difficult to say that performance of a Caesarean section is medical treatment for the defendant's mental disorder: I am, however, satisfied that on the facts of this case so to hold would be 'too atomistic a view', to use Hoffmann LJ's phrase in the passage from *B v Croydon HA* which I have cited and the reasoning of which I respectfully adopt.

There are several strands in the evidence which, in my judgment, bring the proposed treatment within s 63 of the Act. First, there is the proposition that an ancillary reason for the induction and, if necessary, the birth by Caesarean section is to prevent a deterioration in the defendant's mental state. Secondly, there is the clear evidence of Dr M that in order for the treatment of her schizophrenia to be effective, it is necessary for her to give birth to a live baby. Thirdly, the overall structure of her treatment requires her to receive strong antipsychotic medication. The administration of that treatment has been necessarily interrupted by her pregnancy and cannot be resumed until her child is born. It is not, therefore, I think, stretching language unduly to say that achievement of a successful outcome of her pregnancy is a necessary part of the overall treatment of her mental disorder. Treatment of C's gangrene was not likely to affect his mental condition: the manner in which the delivery of the defendant's child is treated is likely to have a direct effect on her mental state.

However, the Court of Appeal confirmed in *St George's Healthcare NHS Trust v S*[60] that s 63 cannot be used to force upon patients medical procedures that are totally unconnected with mental disorder. Nevertheless, it was said that s 63 may apply to the treatment of any condition which is integral to the mental disorder which means that it does not specifically overrule the *Tameside* case. It is

---

57 [1995] 3 Med LR 292.
58 [1996] 1 FLR 762.
59 At p 775.
60 [1998] 3 All ER 673.

arguable that it is still possible for virtually any form of treatment to be given for mental disorder and that the *St George's* case failed from the point of view of s 63, largely because of inadequate diagnosis and assessment of mental disorder, which, in turn, stemmed from the fact that the real purpose of the action was management of the pregnancy.

Treatment under s 63 was considered in the case of *R v Collins and Ashworth Hospital Authority ex p Brady*.[61] It was found that force feeding was treatment under s 63 because the hunger strike was a manifestation or symptom of the patient's personality disorder (the patient was also found to lack capacity so could, in any event, be treated in his best interests). The responsible medical officer had formed the view that the hunger strike was 'a florid example of his psychopathology in action' which stemmed from aspects of his personality such as self-importance and desire to control. The judge was also required to consider the appropriate test for the lawfulness of treatment under s 63. The argument on behalf of Brady had been that the court must be satisfied that the treatment actually was treatment for mental disorder and not just that the doctor had reasonable grounds for considering it to be, that is, the test in *Khawaja v Secretary of State for the Home Department*,[62] rather than '*Wednesbury* unreasonableness' (*Associated Provincial Picture House v Wednesbury Corp*[63]). The court rejected this argument and held that the correct test was the 'super-*Wednesbury*' test, that is, the more substantial the interference with human rights, the more the court would require by way of justification.[64] However, the judge went on to say:

See Chapter 3

R v Collins and Ashworth Hospital Authority ex p Brady

Maurice Kay J: I am entirely satisfied that [the doctor's diagnosis] satisfies both tests. On any view, and to a high degree of probability, section 63 was triggered because what arose was the need to medical treatment for the mental disorder from which the applicant was and is suffering. The hunger strike is a manifestation or symptom of the personality disorder. The fact (if such it be) that a person without mental disorder could reach the same decision on a rational basis in similar circumstances does not avail the applicant because he reached and persists in his decision because of his personality disorder.

The issue was examined in a slightly different context (where the patient had been detained under the criminal provisions of the Act and was subject to a Hospital and Restriction Order under ss 37 and 41) in the case of *R (On the Application of B) v Ashworth Hospital Authority*.[65] The House of Lords held that it was not unlawful for the patient to receive treatment under s 63 for a 'mental disorder' in respect of which he had not been 'classified'. A contrary decision would certainly have sat uneasily alongside the case of *B v Croydon*.[66]

 SELF-TEST QUESTION

Do you agree that 'force feeding' can be regarded as 'treatment for mental disorder'?

9.4.2 Exceptional treatment not covered by s 63

9.4.2.1 Section 57 – consent and a second opinion

This section covers the most drastic forms of treatment for mental disorder. It covers psycho-surgery and any other form of treatment specified by the Secretary of State (at present the only

---

61 [2000] Lloyd's Rep Med 355.
62 [1984] 1 AC 74.
63 [1947] 2 All ER 680.
64 *R v Ministry of Defence ex p Smith* [1996] QB 517.
65 [2005] UKHL 20.
66 [1994] 2 WLR 294.

treatment pursuant to this is surgical implantation of hormones to reduce the male sex drive). It should be noted that, given that consent is necessary as well as a second medical opinion, it is not possible to treat a patient under s 57 who lacks capacity.

9.4.2.2 Sections 58 and 58A – consent or a second opinion

Section 58 specifies treatment which requires consent or a second opinion. The treatment covered by s 58 is medication administered over a period of three months or more. The section empowers the Secretary of State to make regulations to cover other treatment under this section. Section 58A deals with electroconvulsive therapy or any other treatment that is specified by regulations made by the 'appropriate national authority'.

It must be noted that this section does little to protect the patient's right to refuse treatment; it merely adds a safeguard by requiring that, in so far as the patient refuses, two doctors must recommend a course of treatment rather than one. Phil Fennell reports the results of a survey of second opinions carried out in 1992 (note that SOAD means Second Opinion Appointed Doctor):

Fennell, P, *Treatment Without Consent*[67]

Concerns of the 1970s and early 1980s led to the introduction of express legal provision for treatment without consent, which had previously been so much taken for granted as part of clinical authority that mentioning it did not even occur to legislators. By the 1980s it was necessary to spell it out. Part IV upheld the position of the RMO as in charge of a detained patient's treatment, and defined powers to treat without consent, subject to a second opinion procedure. If the personnel with power to decide whether or not to treat without consent had changed, did Part IV result in a change in the substance of these decisions? One clear incursion on clinical authority was that psychosurgery would no longer be allowed without valid consent. Another was that the decision of the SOAD to refuse permission was binding on the RMO and there was no appeal to the MHAC. Set against this is the fact that the second opinion is medical. Although there is a duty on the SOAD to consult other professionals, on occasion these are staff in occupations with little to do with patient care, and often nurses and others were brought in to 'get to know' the patient before being consulted. The test for giving the treatment, likelihood of benefit or prevention of deterioration, used in combination with the *Bolam* test, creates a presumption in favour of the RMO's judgment. Not surprisingly, the concordance rate for s 58 opinions is high. The 1992 survey showed that the main cases where authority was withheld for clinical reasons involved ECT or the 'new' antipsychotic Clozaril, because it was felt that other less drastic treatments should be given time to work. There was even one case, the *Pimozide* case, where the second opinion may have been a life saver. The survey also shows the extent of psychiatry's continued reliance on ECT, and in particular the strikingly high numbers of middle aged and elderly women who have the treatment. In this the pattern of the past is being followed, for women have traditionally been in the majority of those receiving radical treatment, whether it be clitoridectomy, ovariotomy, lobotomy, chemical shock, comas or ECT.

Perhaps the most important indicator of the effect on the substance of clinical decisions, and of the resilience of the experimental spirit, is the extent to which SOADs authorised high dose medication. The BNF recommended dose levels, used loosely as a yardstick in the second opinion process, are viewed by some psychiatrists as too low, and resistance to central prescription remains strong. The fact that 12% of medicine second opinions involved doses above [British National Formulary – BNF] limits does not suggest a significant interference with clinical authority. A poignant reminder of psychiatry's limitations were the numbers of

---

67 London: Routledge, 1996.

patients in the MHAC 1 survey who had been on high doses of medication for years and who showed no improvement, remaining totally inaccessible (61 out of 232). Could it be that their medication contributed to their poor mental state?

Since s 58 offers no real protection to the patient, no real purpose of this provision is discernible.

In R v Feggetter and Another ex p Wooder,[68] the Court of Appeal said that a SOAD should give adequate reasons when certifying s 58 treatment and these should be communicated to the patient unless this would be likely to cause serious harm to the physical or mental health of the patient or any other person. In R (On the Application of Wilkinson) v RMO Broadmoor Hospital, the Mental Health Act Commission SOAD Doctor and the Secretary of State for Health[69] the Court of Appeal held that a patient who was opposed to treatment under section 58 could apply for judicial review on the question as to whether his rights under Arts 2, 3 and 8 of the Convention were violated, or could raise an action in tort for assault against the Special Health Authority. In order for the court to reach a decision it would be necessary for the doctors concerned to give evidence and be subjected to cross-examination.

9.4.2.3 Urgent treatment under s 62

Under s 62 urgent treatment, normally subject to the additional requirements of ss 57, 58, or 58A, may be given without satisfying those conditions, and if it is a form of treatment for which consent was required and that consent is subsequently withdrawn, treatment can continue under these provisions if it is thought that discontinuance of the treatment would cause serious suffering to the patient:

62 Urgent treatment

(1) Sections 57 and 58 above shall not apply to any treatment–

    (a) which is immediately necessary to save the patient's life; or

    (b) which (not being irreversible) is immediately necessary to prevent a serious deterioration of his condition; or

    (c) which (not being irreversible or hazardous) is immediately necessary to alleviate serious suffering by the patient; or

    (d) which (not being irreversible or hazardous) is immediately necessary and represents the minimum interference necessary to prevent the patient from behaving violently or being a danger to himself or to others.

(1A) Section 58A above, in so far as it relates to electro-convulsive therapy by virtue of subsection (1)(b) of that section, shall not apply to any treatment which falls within paragraph (a) or (b) of subsection (1) above.

(1B) Section 58A above, in so far as it relates to a form of treatment specified by virtue of subsection (1)(b) of that section, shall not aply to any treatent which falls within such of paragraphs (a) to (d) of subsection (1) above as may be specified in regulations under that section.

(2) Sections 60 and 61(3) above shall not preclude the continuation of any treatment or of treatment under any plan pending compliance with s 57 or 58 above if the approved clinician in charge of the treatment considers that the discontinuance of the treatment or of treatment under the plan would cause serious suffering to the patient.

(3) For the purposes of this section treatment is irreversible if it has unfavourable irreversible physical or psychological consequences and hazardous if it entails significant physical hazard.

---

68 [2002] EWCA Civ 554.
69 [2002] 1 WLR 419.

Where the treatment is ECT (s 58A) urgent treatment can only be given if either of the grounds in paras (a) or (b) apply. In practice, it will only be treatment under s 58 and s 58A to which this section will apply, as the nature of s 57 treatments (at present, psychosurgery and surgical implantation of hormones to reduce the male sex drive) are unlikely to comply with sub-s (1)(a)–(d) in terms of hazard and/or irreversibility. The section would therefore be most likely to be used in the administration of medicine under s 58, when the three-month period was about to elapse, and a second opinion could not be obtained. These occasions should be rare, genuine emergencies. However, in practice the situation may be very different as treatment may be given to those who lack capacity as consent does not have to be obtained and this section can apply to patients who have been admitted under s 4 of the Act as an emergency.

Bickle et al[70] carried out an audit of urgent treatment administered at Rampton High Security Hospital from 2000 to 2005, in total 107 occasions. They reviewed the treatment against the standards from the then relevant Code of Practice and found compliance with this. The other standard they reviewed it against was the recommendation from the Mental Health Act Commission which said that generally a second opinion should be obtained, and there was around 50 per cent compliance with this. However, they found this to mean that the standard was close to being met.

9.4.3 Community Treatment Orders

Community Treatment Orders (CTOs) were introduced by the Mental Health Act 2007. They were designed to tackle the well-known 'revolving door' problem whereby patients enter hospital, are stabilised and discharged, then go on to no longer take medication, become ill again and return to hospital.

17A Community treatment orders

(1) The responsible clinician may by order in writing discharge a detained patient from hospital subject to his being liable to recall in accordance with section 17E below.

(2) A detained patient is a patient who is liable to be detained in a hospital in pursuance of an application for admission for treatment.

(3) An order under subsection (1) above is referred to in this Act as a 'community treatment order'.

(4) The responsible clinician may not make a community treatment order unless–
　(a) in his opinion, the relevant criteria are met; and
　(b) an approved mental health professional states in writing–
　　(i) that he agrees with that opinion; and
　　(ii) that it is appropriate to make the order–

(5) The relevant criteria are–
　(a) the patient is suffering from mental disorder of a nature or degree which makes it appropriate for him to receive medical treatment;
　(b) it is necessary for his health or safety or for the protection of other persons that he should receive such treatment;
　(c) subject to his being liable to be recalled as mentioned in paragraph (d) below, such treatment can be provided without his continuing to be detained in a hospital;
　(d) it is necessary that the responsible clinician should be able to exercise the power under section 17E(1) below to recall the patient to hospital; and
　(e) appropriate medical treatment is available for him.

---

70 Bickle, A et al, 'Audit of Statutory Urgent Treatment at a High Security Hospital'(2008) J Mental Health L 66.

(6) In determining whether the criterion in subsection (5)(d) above is met, the responsible clinician shall, in particular, consider, having regard to the patient's history of mental disorder and any other relevant factors, what risk there would be of a deterioration of the patient's condition if he were not detained in a hospital (as a result, for example, of his refusing or neglecting to receive the medical treatment he requires for his mental disorder).

CTOs can only be made in respect of patients who have been discharged from hospital having been detained under s 3 or the criminal provisions of the Act, so they do not apply to voluntary patients or s 2 patients. The approved mental health professional (AMHP) and the responsible clinician (RC) have to be satisfied that the patient is suffering from a mental disorder of a nature or to a degree that makes it appropriate for them to receive medical treatment, and that it is necessary for the patient's health or safety, or for the protection of others, that the patient should receive such treatment, and that, subject to the powers of recall, the treatment can be provided in the community. The power of recall must be *necessary*, and, self-evidently, appropriate medical treatment is available. There are two compulsory conditions and these are that, where necessary, the patient makes themselves available for examination by the RC when/if the RC is considering whether to remove the CTO; and secondly, that, where necessary, the patient makes themselves available for examination by a second opinion doctor.

Other conditions can be imposed, but only if they are necessary or appropriate to ensure the patient receives treatment that prevents harm to self or others. A residence requirement for example might be imposed. Although the patient does not have to agree to a CTO, it is unlikely that they would be discharged from hospital without this.

The order is initially for six months but is renewable. If it is renewed the patient has to be examined and the AMHP has to agree to renewal.

Hoyer and Ferris examine CTOs (they refer to the process as 'Outpatient Commitment' – 'OC') and refer to two models: those that are imposed as a condition of leave and those that are invoked as an alternative to hospitalisation. The model under the 1983 Act is the former. Hoyer and Ferris, however, cite some empirical evidence in support of the latter model being the most successful. Referring to this distinction, they state that 'a wide interpretation' of the legal requirements for OC can muddy the waters:

Hoyer, G, and Ferris, R J, Outpatient Commitment. Some Reflections on Ideology, Practice and Implications for Research[71]

The legal criteria are such that OC can only be imposed on patients suffering from a 'Serious mental disorder', usually understood as synonymous with a psychotic condition. In a Supreme Court verdict of 1993, however, the courts ruled that patients who were taking antipsychotics would have manifested psychotic symptoms if they were not taking medication. Thus they were legally to be regarded as still suffering from a serious mental disorder so long as they were taking antipsychotic medication(s), and could accordingly be placed under an OC order, in spite of a lack – for the time being – of any sign of psychotic symptoms. Thus the patient is being coerced to receive continuing treatment with medication in the absence of overt psychotic symptoms, because of a presumption that serious mental disorder persists, and despite the fact that most patients will have retained competency to accept or refuse treatment. This problem is not unique to Norway, but represents a fundamental problem regarding OC legislation and its implementation.

---

71 (2001) J Mental Health L 56, at 60.

Certainly, the assumption of the court in this case that without the medication the patient would have been psychotic is worrying, as that could result in OC or CTOs in perpetuity.

In R (on the application of H) v Mental Health Review Tribunal[72] it was held that a conditional discharge, conditional upon complying with medication, did not amount to a compulsion that interfered with a patient's right to refuse medication (as he would have that right when not detained under the Act). Of course now that CTOs are available, a refusal to agree to a treatment regime that was a condition of the CTO could result in the patient's recall.

9.4.4 Human rights and treatment without consent

Psychiatrists, as has been seen, have very wide powers to treat without consent. The interests of the wider community may justify detention, but can they justify treatment? It is arguable that most treatment will be consented to because after the initial treatment, the patient is compliant and will therefore consent to subsequent treatment. But in the case of a refusal, why should we make treatment compulsory?

Given that a patient can refuse life-sustaining treatment for physical illness, if mentally competent, what is the argument for saying that the mentally ill patient cannot refuse treatment of mental illness? The 1959 Mental Health Act did not deal with the issue of consent to treatment, and it was thought that detention was sufficient to suspend the need to obtain a patient's consent.

During the passage through Parliament of the 1983 Mental Health Act, a justification for being able to treat without consent was given by the Minister of Health in the debate on the proposal in parliamentary committee:

Special Standing Committee on the Mental Health (Amendment) Bill (Parliamentary Session 1981–82), 29 June 1982

. . . those who looked after them (those forcibly detained) would have to gaze on them knowing perfectly well that some treatment could be given to alleviate their suffering and distress and enable them eventually to recover their liberty. Hospitals are places of treatment . . .

This reasoning relies upon the fact that, by detaining someone against their will on the ground that they are ill, means that it is in the interests of them regaining their liberty that they receive treatment to enable them to do just this. It has to be admitted that this argument has a certain force. What is clear is that the reason cannot be that, by definition, the mental patient is incompetent because of the vagueness of the definition of mental illness, and indeed, case law confirms that a

long term mental patient can refuse life-sustaining treatment for a physical condition. The question is whether the patient has the capacity to understand the particular form of treatment.

 SELF-TEST QUESTION

If a patient is capable of consenting to treatment, they should also be able to refuse treatment. Why should this be different for mental health patients?

---

72 [2007] EWHC 884.

9.5 Safeguarding the Patient

9.5.1 Discharge of the patient under s 23

Section 23 states:

23 Discharge of patients

. . .

(2) An order for discharge may be made in respect of a patient–
   (a) where the patient is liable to be detained in a hospital in pursuance of an application for admission for assessment or for treatment by the responsible medical officer, by the managers or by the nearest relative of the patient;
   (b) where the patient is subject to guardianship, by the responsible medical officer, by the responsible local social services authority or by the nearest relative of the patient.

It should be noted that, under s 23, these are powers, and not duties, and therefore a patient cannot claim that, for example, once he ceased to be a danger to self, or others, he should be discharged under s 23.

In *Johnson v United Kingdom*,[73] the European Court of Human Rights held that, even if there is no longer justification under the Act for detention, this does not mean that the patient must be discharged immediately if he still poses a risk to others. Discharge can be delayed until after-care facilities have been put in place. But, see *R v Camden and Islington HA ex p K*,[74] and s 117 of the Act, see 9.6, below. (See also *R v Nottinghamshire Healthcare NHS Trust and Others ex p IH*[75] and *R v Mental Health Review Tribunal, North and East London Region ex p H*.[76])

There can be no doubt that the powers of civil detention under the Act have great potential for abuse. The importance of protective procedures, therefore, cannot be over-estimated.

9.5.2 The Mental Health Act Commission

Section 120 of the Act deals with the general protection of detained patients:

120 General protection of detained patients

(1) The Secretary of State shall keep under review the exercise of the powers and the discharge of the duties conferred or imposed by this Act so far as relating to the detention of patients or to patients liable to be detained under this Act and shall make arrangements for persons authorised by him in that behalf–
   (a) to visit and interview in private patients detained under this Act in hospitals and registered establishments and community patients in hospitals and establishments of any description . . . and
   (b) to investigate:
      (i) any complaint made by a person in respect of a matter that occurred while he was detained under this Act . . . and which he considers has not been satisfactorily dealt with . . .; and

---

73 (1997) 27 EHRR 296.
74 [2001] EWCA Civ 240.
75 [2001] EWHC Admin 1037.
76 (2001) unreported, 28 March.

(ii) any other complaint as to the exercise of the powers or the discharge of the duties conferred or imposed by this Act in respect of a person who is or has been so detained or is or has been a community patient.

The Commission carries out the functions under s 120(1) and (4), together with functions under s 61 of the Act (review of treatment given under s 57(2) and s 58(3)(b)). The Commission was established under s 11 of the National Health Service Act 1977, and s 121 of the MHA 1983 provides for its continuance. In addition to the above, the Commission appoints medical practitioners and other persons for the purposes of providing second opinions and verifying consent to treatment under Part IV of the Act and examines reports on that treatment; submits proposals for inclusion in the Code of Practice; submits proposals in relation to s 57 treatments, and produces a biennial report on its activities. There are about 90 commissioners, made up of doctors, nurses, social workers and lawyers.

It is important to note that the Commission's powers do not extend to voluntary patients, but only to those who are formally detained under the Act. Note the decision in *R v Bournewood Community and Mental Health NHS Trust ex p L*[77] and the discussion in Chapter 4.

9.5.3 Challenging detention

The powers of the Commission are not designed to provide a mechanism for challenging the validity of the compulsory admission itself. There are, however, a number of ways in which a compulsorily detained patient may gain his liberty, both under the Act itself, and by the use of the common law.

9.5.3.1 Mental Health Review Tribunals

A statutory framework for challenging compulsory admissions was first introduced by the 1959 Act following the recommendations made by the Royal Commission (the Percy Commission 9.1.4 above, see para 438). Under s 66, patients, including those admitted for assessment, can apply to a Tribunal for a review of their case. The nearest relative also has a right to apply. There is also an automatic review process, under s 68, whereby hospital managers must refer to a Tribunal any patient admitted for treatment who has not exercised his right to apply within the first six months. They must also refer any patient admitted for treatment if his detention is renewed and three years have gone by since the case was last considered by a tribunal.

Mental Health Review tribunals consist of at least one 'legal member', one 'medical member' and the third must be neither a legal nor a medical member. Procedures are governed by the Mental Health Review Tribunals Rules.

Decisions of Mental Health Review tribunals are susceptible to the judicial review test if no reasonable tribunal would come to such a decision (*R v Mental Health Review Tribunal for West Midlands and North West ex p Ashworth Hospital Authority and Others*).[78]

9.5.3.2 Habeas corpus

It may be thought that, since the introduction of the right to apply to a Mental Health Review tribunal, this ancient remedy would have little application. However, it has continued to be used, and was given approval as, in certain circumstances, the only remedy for an unlawfully detained patient.[79] Nevertheless, challenges are more likely to be made by way of judicial review, particularly since the enactment of the HRA 1998.

---

77 [1998] 3 All ER 289.
78 [2001] EWHC Admin 901.
79 See *Re S-C (Mental Patient: Habeas Corpus)* [1996] 1 FLR 548.

In M v South West London & St George's Mental Health NHS Trust,[80] the appellant was a woman who had been detained under s 2 of the Act, suffering from a number of psychiatric conditions. Whilst in hospital she was found to need treatment for a physical disorder and was transferred to a general hospital for treatment. It was thought by her psychiatrist that she should be detained under s 3 of the Act because she was a danger to herself and others, and a social worker and another psychiatrist went to the hospital to examine and interview her. The patient was uncooperative but it was decided to detain her under s 3. The patient applied for a writ of habeas corpus on the basis that the formal requirements for detention under the Act had not been met and that the court should determine this by hearing evidence about disputed matters of fact. The judge rejected this argument and concluded that the 'interview' with the patient had been sufficient to comply with the statutory requirements, and dismissed her application for habeas corpus. The Court of Appeal upheld this and also confirmed that there was nothing in the legislation that required cooperation on the part of the patient. This must be the case because by its very nature, compulsory detention is primarily there to deal with uncooperative patients.

9.5.3.3 Judicial review

Although Gunn's views were expressed some time ago, judicial review remains an important remedy.

> **Gunn, M, 'Judicial review of hospital admissions and treatment in the community under the Mental Health Act 1983'[81]**
>
> The right to apply for judicial review forms, along with an application for a writ of habeas corpus, a vital way in which the patient can complain about the original admission. Indeed, they form the only way, if it is right that a Mental Health Review Tribunal cannot consider the validity of the initial admission to hospital, as one member of the Court of Appeal, Ackner LJ, said in passing. It is important, therefore, to emphasise that a Mental Health Review Tribunal apparently can only decide whether a person should continue to be detained in hospital by considering whether the conditions justifying detention exist at the time the Tribunal sees the patient. Although judicial review and habeas corpus do permit consideration of the original admission decision, neither provide a form of appeal on the merits of the decision: neither can question whether the decision was right or wrong. Instead they concentrate on whether the doctors, social workers and nearest relatives had the legal power to admit the patient; they consider whether the discretion that the professionals have was exercised in a proper manner; for example, did they take all relevant factors into account?

See too the cases of R v Hallstrom and Another ex p W[82] and R v Gardner and Another ex p L.[83]

In R v Mental Health Review Tribunal and Another ex p KB and Others,[84] it was held that commonplace delays in hearings before the Mental Health Review tribunal breached the right to a speedy hearing under Art 5(4) of the ECHR.[85]

9.5.3.4 Article 5 of the European Convention on Human Rights

One of the issues in the Bournewood case was the adequacy or otherwise of the judicial review (and habeas corpus) procedures to safeguard the patient's Art 5 rights:

---

80 [2008] EWCA Civ 1112.
81 [1986] J Soc Wel L 290.
82 [1986] 2 All ER 306.
83 [1986] 1 QB 1090.
84 (2002) 152 NLJ 672.
85 See also R v Mental Health Review Tribunal South West Region ex p C [2002] 1 WLR 176.

HL v United Kingdom (2005) 40 EHRR 32, European Court of Human Rights

. . .

Lawfulness and protection against arbitrary detention

. . .

136 The Government mainly argued that an application for leave to apply for judicial review of the decision to admit and detain, including a writ of habeas corpus, constituted a review fulfilling the requirements of Art.5(4) of the Convention. The applicant disagreed.

137 The Court considers that the starting-point must be the above-cited X v United Kingdom judgment where the Court found that the review conducted in habeas corpus proceedings was insufficient for the purposes of Art.5(4) as not being wide enough to bear on those conditions which were essential for the 'lawful' detention of a person on the basis of unsoundness of mind since it did not allow a determination of the merits of the question as to whether the mental disorder persisted. The Court is not persuaded by the Government's argument that the X case can be distinguished because it concerned detention pursuant to a statutory power: no authority has been cited and no other material adduced to indicate that the courts' review of detention based on the common law doctrine of necessity would indeed have been more intrusive.

138 Nor does the Court find convincing the Government's reliance on the development of the 'super- Wednesbury' principles of judicial review prior to the entry into force of the Human Rights Act 1998 in October 2000. Those principles were outlined and applied in the domestic judgment in the above-cited case of R v Ministry of Defence Ex p Smith. In the subsequent application to this Court by the same applicant, it was found that, even if his essential complaints under Art.8 of the Convention had been considered by the domestic courts, the threshold at which those courts could have found to be irrational the impugned policy prohibiting homo-sexuals from the armed forces had been placed so high that it effectively excluded any consid-eration by the domestic courts of the question whether the interference with the applicants' rights answered a pressing social need or was proportionate to the national security and public order aims pursued, principles which lay at the heart of the Court's analysis of complaints under Art.8 of the Convention. The Court concluded that the remedy of judicial review, even on a 'super-Wednesbury' basis, could not therefore constitute an effective remedy (within the meaning of Art.13) for a breach of Mr Smith's rights under Art.8.

139 The Court considers that it can be equally concluded for the purposes of Art.5(4) (the lex specialis vis-à-vis Art.13 in terms of entitlement to a review of the lawfulness of detention) that, even with the application of the 'super-Wednesbury' principles on judicial review, the bar of unreasonableness would at the time of the applicant's domestic proceedings have been placed so high as effectively to exclude any adequate examination of the merits of the clinical views as to the persistence of mental illness justifying detention. This is indeed confirmed by the decision of the Court of Appeal, in a case where the necessity of medical treatment was contested by the patient, that pre-incorporation judicial review of necessity in accordance with 'the super- Wednesbury' criteria was not sufficiently intrusive to constitute an adequate examination of the merits of the relevant medical decisions.

140 For these reasons, the Court finds that the requirements of Art.5(4) were not satisfied, as suggested by the Government, by judicial review and habeas corpus proceedings. It is not necessary therefore to examine the applicant's additional submissions that those proceedings did not satisfy the requirements of that Article because, inter alia, the burden of proof was on the detainee or because such proceedings did not provide 'speedy' and 'periodic control' at 'reasonable intervals'.

141 The Government also contended, without elaboration, that a dissatisfied patient could bring a civil claim for damages for negligence, false imprisonment and for trespass to the person (technical assault consequent on detention for treatment) which actions would be 'likely' to cause the hospital to justify its treatment of the patient without consent. The Government then proposed, without further detail, that the applicant could have invoked the declaratory jurisdiction of the High Court. However, the applicant did not allege that the relevant health professionals were negligent but rather that they had been incorrect in their diagnoses. His own action in false imprisonment and assault did not involve the submission of expert evidence by each of the parties or any assessment by the courts of that expertise and no case, decided at or around the relevant time, has been cited where such expertise was requested or such a merits review was carried out. As to seeking declaratory relief from the High Court, the Government has not cited any case decided around the relevant time where the High Court accepted that there was a 'serious justiciable issue' to be examined by it in a case such as the present one where the patient was readmitted and detained for assessment and treatment (which treatment was not of an exceptional nature) on the basis of a consensus amongst the health professionals that admission was necessary.

142 In such circumstances, the Court concludes that it has not been demonstrated that the applicant had available to him a procedure which satisfied the requirements of Art.5(4) of the Convention. There has been therefore a violation of this provision.

In R (H) v *Secretary of State for Health*[86] the respondent (M), who was severely mentally disabled, had been detained in hospital under s 2 of the Act. She had not applied to the mental health review tribunal within the first 14 days, as was her right. The hospital wished to arrange for M to be received into guardianship under s 7 of the Act but M's mother, as her nearest relative, objected. An application was made to the county court to displace her mother and appoint an acting nearest relative under s 29 of the Act. The county court proceedings took longer than expected, which meant that M was detained under the s 2 order well beyond the usual 28 days. The issue before the House of Lords was whether this meant that s 2 was incompatible with Art 5(4) of the Convention where a patient had a right to apply to a Tribunal but did not have the capacity to do so, and whether s 29(4), which has the effect of extending the s 2 detention until it is resolved, is incompatible with the convention. The Court of Appeal had held that there was incompatibility.

The House of Lords granted the appeal and held that there was no authority that implied into Art5(4) the requirement of judicial review in every case where the patient was unable to make his own application. Hospital managers had a statutory duty to take steps to ensure that a patient understood their rights under the provisions of their detention. Even if a patient's nearest relative had no independent right of application there was much that they could do to put the patient's case before a judicial authority. In this case, M's mother had been able to challenge every important decision. She had also initiated the reference (under s 67(1) of the Act) to the secretary of state after it became clear that her daughter was to be kept in hospital longer than 28 days. A Mental Health Review tribunal was best suited to determining the merits of a patient's detention, and doing so in a way that was convenient to the patient, readily accessible and comparatively quick.

---

86 [2005] UKHL 60.

R (H) v Secretary of State for Health[87]

Baroness Hale of Richmond

32 . . . while judicial review and/or habeas corpus may be one way of securing compliance with the patient's article 5(4) rights, this would be much more satisfactorily achieved either by a speedy determination of the county court proceedings or by a Secretary of State's reference under section 67. Either way, however, the means exist of operating section 29(4) in a way which is compatible with the patient's rights. It follows that the section itself cannot be incompatible, although the action or inaction of the authorities under it may be so.

Conclusion

33 For these reasons, my Lords, I would decline to hold that either section 2 or section 29(4) is incompatible with article 5(4) of the Convention in the respects identified by the Court of Appeal. I would therefore allow this appeal and set aside the declarations.

This unsatisfactorily vague approach to protection illustrates the point that Richardson and Machin make when they suggest that there is something anti-therapeutic about the judicial review process and that the latter's emphasis on procedure creates an uneasy conflict.

Richardson G and Machin, D, A Clash of Values? Mental Health Review Tribunals and Judicial Review[88]

If the classic conflict between law and psychiatry, between autonomy and welfare, were to be reflected in the judicial review case law we might expect to see the reviewing courts assiduously protecting those aspects of patient autonomy which had not been unambiguously restricted by statute. The case law relating both to the discharge criteria and to tribunal powers denies that expectation.

For other comments as to judicial review of Human Rights Act challenges, see *R v Responsible Medical Officer Broadmoor Hospital and Others ex p Wilkinson*.[89] Judicial review also applies to private psychiatric hospitals: *R v Partnerships in Care Ltd ex p A*.[90]

9.6 A Right to Treatment for Mental Disorder?

Because of the civil liberty issues that it raises, much of the concern surrounding patient rights is to do with the patient's right to liberty unless there are compelling reasons to the contrary. However, it can also be asked whether a mentally ill patient has a right to be treated.

In terms of medical treatment generally, there have been a number of attempts over the years to persuade courts to intervene when limited health care resources within the UK National Health Service have resulted in the denial of treatment to physically ill patients.[91] The conclusion to be drawn from these cases is that unless there is irrationality or procedural impropriety, the courts will not intervene. There is, therefore, very limited scope in making a challenge, and none in respect of *clinical* judgment.

However, the element of public protection in mental health law means that treatment for physical illness and treatment for psychiatric illness are not exactly comparable. There have been a

---

87 Ibid.
88 [1999] J Mental Health L 3, at 11.
89 [2002] 1 WLR 419.
90 [2002] EWHC 529.
91 See Ch 2 and, for example, the cases of *R v Secretary of State for Social Services ex p Hincks* (1980) 1 BMLR 93; *R v Central Birmingham HA ex p Walker* (1987) 3 BMLR 32; and *R v Cambridge HA ex p B* [1995] 2 All ER 129.

number of recent incidents when members of the public have been injured and even killed by ex-psychiatric patients, and there has been something of an outcry that the persons concerned were not receiving treatment, or not receiving in-patient treatment.[92] However, in this regard, note the case of *Clunis v Camden and Islington HA*,[93] where the Court of Appeal held that there was no liability of a discharging health authority towards a patient who subsequently killed a member of the public (the *Jonathan Zito* case). This was based upon the fact that the action was grounded in the patient's own illegal act, so that *ex turpi causa non oritur action* applied, and upon the court's decision that the obligation under s 117 of the Act to provide patient after care did not give rise to an obligation at common law.[94]

Judicial review was brought to allege a violation of the patient's rights under Art 5 in the case of *R v Secretary of State for the Home Department and another ex p IH*.[95] A Mental Health Review tribunal had been satisfied that the patient should be discharged, but subject to suitable s 117 supervision within the community. There were difficulties in finding suitable supervision and discharge was deferred. The patient made an aplication for judicial review and, at the suggestion of the court, the case went before another tribunal. The decision of this tribunal was that it was approriprate for the patient to be detained in hospital. The allegations of the patient were twofold: first that his rights under Art 5(4) had been violated (this requires a speedy review of lawfulness of detention). He succeeded in this respect. However, the more interesting aspect of his application concerned Art 5(1)(e), which provides for detention of patients of unsound mind. The patient argued that this should be interpreted as providing for detention *only in circumstances in which the level of security represents a proportionate response to the risk posed by the patient*. In other words, he was asking for a gloss to be placed on the provision to reflect the European law concept of proportionality. The House of Lords rejected this, and distinguished the ECtHR case of *Johnson v UK*,[96] where an applicant's discharge had been delayed because suitable accommodation could not be found and, in circumstances where there was no doubt that the patient was no longer ill. Here, the difficulty in finding suitable aftercare was based upon the fact that the psychiatric services who would have been responsible for aftercare disagreed with discharge into the community as 'being clinically inappropriate'.

A patient is unlikely to request to be compulsorily detained under the Act, but could request to be informally admitted (s 131). For the purposes of this, the patient would have no more rights than a patient who demanded to be admitted to hospital for the treatment of physical illness. The decision would be based upon clinical judgment, and in the absence of judicially reviewable procedural irregularity, the courts would not intervene.

After the discharge of a patient detained under s 3 (or under certain criminal provisions, under ss 37, 47 or 48 of the Act, for detention), there is a duty on both the local health authority and the local social services authority to provide, in co-operation with the relevant voluntary agencies, after-care services until both are satisfied that the patient no longer needs them (s 117): this is a duty in respect of the individual patient rather than to the mentally disordered generally.

Given the concern about the discharge of potentially dangerous patients mentioned above, it is interesting to speculate on the nature of this duty and whether it does impose a heavier onus on health care providers in the field of mental health than on their counterparts who are providing treatment for physical illnesses. This was considered in the case of *R v Ealing District HA ex p Fox*,[97] where a health authority refused to provide psychiatric supervision for a patient who had been

---

92 See, for example, newspaper reports in (1994) *The Independent*, 16 September; and (1995) *The Guardian*, 28 July; and (1997) *The Guardian*, 30 May.
93 [1998] 2 WLR 902.
94 See Jones, MA, 'The violent mentally disordered patient: who cares?' (1998) 14(2) *Professional Negligence* 99.
95 [2003] UKHL 59.
96 (1997) 27 EHRR 296.
97 [1993] 3 All ER 170.

conditionally discharged by a Mental Health Review Tribunal subject to receiving psychiatric supervision in the community. In this case, the judge held that the health authority had erred in law in not attempting with all reasonable expedition and diligence to make arrangements so as to enable the patient to comply with arrangements *'required by a Mental Health Review Tribunal'*.[98] However, does this mean that if Tribunals are prepared to attach such conditions to discharge orders that they will be enforceable? The answer to this is in the negative. In *Fox*, it was said that there should have been a reference back to the Tribunal, presumably with a view to amendment, and that duties owed to the patient could only be enforced by alleging procedural defectiveness through the mechanism of judicial review, which, as we have seen, are important, but limited in scope. In *R v Mental Health Review Tribunal ex p H*,[99] the Court of Appeal confirmed that a tribunal does not have the power to make orders against local and health authorities compelling them to implement any particular s 117 after care plan. Furthermore, in *R v Camden and Islington HA ex p K*,[100] the Court of Appeal confirmed that s 117 does not impose an absolute obligation on authorities to satisfy any conditions imposed by a tribunal on the discharge of a patient.

In other words, as with treatment for physical illness, the courts will defer to clinical judgment and will not compel treatment to be given, as long as the decision to refuse to treat has been taken in a procedurally sound way. In this particular case the authority's consultant psychiatrist was doubtful that supervision in the community would work. However, the judge said that the health authority is bound to continue to seek to provide the necessary treatment, either from its own resources or from elsewhere, and if it cannot do so, then the matter should be referred back to the Mental Health Review Tribunal to reconsider the discharge condition. However, suppose there was not clinical doubt, but simply lack of the appropriate resources to provide the treatment? After all, the reason for the failure to provide medical treatment is more likely to be lack of financial resources than anything else (although in the case of *R v Cambridge HA ex p B*,[101] resources were in issue, but the stress was upon the likelihood of success of the treatment). The question of resources was raised in the case of *R v Hertfordshire CC ex p Three Rivers DC*.[102] This was about the level of provision in the community under the National Health Service and Community Care Act 1990, which imposes a duty upon the local social services authority to assess the needs of, *inter alia*, discharged mental patients. It was held in that case that identifying the level and nature of the service to be provided may be constrained by available resources and that these constraints could properly be taken into account when identifying the appropriate level of service provision.

The conclusion is, therefore, that ultimately there is no 'right' to treatment for the psychiatrically ill any more than there is for the physically ill. The only right is to be considered for treatment and given the appropriate clinical assessment.

 SELF-TEST QUESTION

Do you think that psychiatric patients should have some entitlement to treatment that other patients should not have?

---

98   Per Otten J, emphasis added.
99   [2000] 1 WLR 1323.
100   [2001] EWCA Civ 240.
101   [1995] 2 All ER 129.
102   (1992) 90 LGR 526.

9.7 Liability towards Patients

9.7.1 Criminal liability

The ordinary criminal law does, of course, apply to psychiatric patients, and in addition there are a number of specific statutory offences relating to ill treatment of patients and forgery of documentation for the purposes of detention, and these can be found in Part IX of the Act.

9.7.2 Civil liability

9.7.2.1 False imprisonment

In addition to the remedies discussed above, a patient unlawfully detained may pursue a civil claim for false imprisonment, and, if successful, obtain an award of damages. In the case of *Furber v Kratter*,[103] the patient succeeded despite the fact that the original detention was lawful. It was held that the substitution of a harsher regime than at first prescribed could constitute false imprisonment.

9.7.2.2 Battery and negligence

The same principles of common law negligence apply to the treatment of psychiatric patients. If it can be shown that those treating a potentially suicidal patient failed to supervise and treat in accordance with the appropriate standard of care, then the claimant will succeed: see *Selfe v Ilford and District Hospital Management Committee*.[104] *Kirkham v The Chief Constable of the Greater Manchester Police*[105] concerned a successful suicide in police custody. The widow of the person concerned succeeded in her claim. The Court of Appeal rejected the argument that the defence of *volenti* could apply: it was held that, as the person was clinically depressed, his judgment was too impaired in order for this to succeed. The latter point is of some interest: it is accepted that mental disorder itself does not mean that a patient is incapable as far as medical decision making is concerned. Refusal of life-saving treatment by such a patient, unless it can be shown that the treatment is for the mental disorder itself,[106] is acceptable. However, a positive act of suicide in *Kirkham* should have been prevented on the basis of clinical impairment of judgment. Is there an illogicality here, or are we simply back to the distinction between positive acts, and omissions to take certain courses of action?

The liability of doctors and nurses to supervise suicidal patients was considered in the case of *Selfe v Ilford Hospital Management Committee*, where damages were awarded when there was found to be an unacceptable level of supervision. The clinical judgment of a psychiatrist was examined by the Supreme Court of Canada in the case of *Villemure v l'Hopital Notre-Dame et al* where a 'Bolam' argument as to what other doctors would have done was rejected. The majority decision approved the following finding of the trial judge:

Villemure v l'Hopital Notre-Dame et al[107]

The court is unable to accept the opinion of Drs Fortin and Saucier. It may be that they would have done exactly what Dr Turcot did. Had they done so, in the opinion of the court they would have been wrong and negligent. It is no answer to say it is impossible absolutely to prevent a person from committing suicide unless he is placed in a straitjacket. This of course is obvious. But it is surely possible to prevent him from committing suicide for 30 hours and until a

---

103 (1988) *The Times*, 21 July.
104 (1970) 114 SJ 935.
105 [1990] 2 QB 283.
106 See the case of *B v Croydon HA* [1994] 2 WLR 294, see 9.4.1.2, above.
107 (1972) 31 DLR (3d) 454.

sufficient investigation has been made into his condition to be able more accurately to diagnose his true situation. The court also rejects Dr Saucier's view that there were many factors which indicated that the patient's condition was not nearly as serious as might at first have been thought. The facts as proven of what happened prior to the entry into the hospital, coupled with the incidents in the hospital, indicate to the court rather a situation which should have made both Dr Turcot and the nurses take particular care of the deceased.

In the context of civil liability, mention must be made of a form of statutory immunity contained within s 139(1) of the Act:

139 (1) No person shall be liable, whether on the ground of want of jurisdiction or on any other ground, to any civil or criminal proceedings to which he would have been liable apart from this section in respect of any act purporting to be done in pursuance of this Act or any regulations or rules made under this Act, or in, or in pursuance of anything done in, the discharge of func- tions conferred by any other enactment on the authority having jurisdiction under Part VII of this Act, unless the act was done in bad faith or without reasonable care.

It will be seen that the reference to 'without reasonable care' means that this section gives no immunity against an action in negligence. However, under s 139(2), leave of a High Court judge is required to bring an action in the first place. Gunn concludes that, in order to bring an action for judicial review, a patient does not have to allege bad faith or lack of reasonable care.[108]

9.7.2.3 A violation of Article 2 of the European Convention on Human Rights?

In *Savage v South Essex Partnership NHS Foundation Trust* (MIND and others intervening) the House of Lords had to consider the application of Art 2 of the Convention with regard to a situation where a detained mental patient absconded from hospital and killed herself:

Savage v South Essex Partnership NHS Foundation Trust (MIND and others intervening)[109]

Lord Rodger of Earlsferry

19 Fundamentally, article 2 requires a state to have in place a structure of laws which will help to protect life. In *Osman v United Kingdom* 29 EHRR 245, 305, para 115, the European court identified the 'primary duty' of a state under the article as being:

'to secure the right to life by putting in place effective criminal law provisions to deter the commission of offences against the person backed up by law-enforcement machinery for the prevention, suppression and sanctioning of breaches of such provisions.'

But, as the parties in Osman's case recognised, the state's duty goes further, and article 2 : 'may also imply in certain well defined circumstances a positive obligation on the authorities to take preventive operational measures to protect an individual whose life is at risk from the criminal acts of another individual.'

. . .

68 In terms of article 2, health authorities are under an over-arching obligation to protect the lives of patients in their hospitals. In order to fulfil that obligation, and depending on the circumstances, they may require to fulfil a number of complementary obligations.

---

108 Gunn, M, 'Judicial review of hospital admissions and treatment in the community under the Mental Health Act 1983' [1986] J Soc Wel L 290.

109 [2009] 2 WLR 115.

69 In the first place, the duty to protect the lives of patients requires health authorities to ensure that the hospitals for which they are responsible employ competent staff and that they are trained to a high professional standard. In addition, the authorities must ensure that the hospitals adopt systems of work which will protect the lives of patients. Failure to perform these general obligations may result in a violation of article 2. If, for example, a health authority fails to ensure that a hospital puts in place a proper system for supervising mentally ill patients and, as a result, a patient is able to commit suicide, the health authority will have violated the patient's right to life under article 2.

70 Even though a health authority employed competent staff and ensured that they were trained to a high professional standard, a doctor, for example, might still treat a patient negligently and the patient might die as a result. In that situation, there would be no violation of article 2 since the health authority would have done all that the article required of it to protect the patient's life. Nevertheless, the doctor would be personally liable in damages for the death and the health authority would be vicariously liable for her negligence . . .

71 The same approach would apply if a mental hospital had established an appropriate system for supervising patients and all that happened was that, on a particular occasion, a nurse negligently left his post and a patient took the opportunity to commit suicide. There would be no violation of any obligation under article 2, since the health authority would have done all that the article required of it. But, again, the nurse would be personally liable in damages for the death and the health authority would be vicariously liable too.

72 Finally, article 2 imposes a further 'operational' obligation on health authorities and their hospital staff. This obligation is distinct from, and additional to, the authorities' more general obligations. The operational obligation arises only if members of staff know or ought to know that a particular patient presents a 'real and immediate' risk of suicide. In these circumstances article 2 requires them to do all that can reasonably be expected to prevent the patient from committing suicide. If they fail to do this, not only will they and the health authorities be liable in negligence, but there will also be a violation of the operational obligation under article 2 to protect the patient's life. . . .

9.8 Mental Health Law and Mental Capacity

We looked at the operation of the Mental Capacity Act 2005 in Chapter 4. The capacity and mental health regimes are separate, and patients who are 'incapable' under the MCA can be treated in their best interests for both physical and mental illness. Szmukler, Daw and Dawson maintain that there should be new legislation that would govern all non-consensual treatments. Dawson is a New Zealand academic, and they acknowledge that the current discrete approaches to capacity and to mental health are also reflected in schemes in Australasia as well as the UK. They believe that the best of both approaches should be fused:

See Chapter 4 ←

Szmukler, G, Daw R and Dawson J, 'A model law fusing incapacity and mental health legislation'[110]

The 'fusion' framework

The alternative approach that we advocate is to abandon the two-track approach, and, instead, to fuse the two together into a single comprehensive involuntary treatment scheme, which

---

110 [2010] Special edn J Mental Health L 11, 12.

preserves the strengths of each. A major strength of non-consensual treatment schemes that are based on incapacity principles is the respect shown for the autonomy of those patients who retain their capacity; but these schemes are, nevertheless, often weak on the regulation of emergency treatment powers, detention in hospital, and forced treatment. These are the areas, in contrast, in which civil commitment schemes are strong. The use of force, and the detention and involuntary treatment of objecting patients, is clearly authorised and regulated by mental health legislation. We therefore advocate a legal regime that retains the strengths of both, but still relies squarely on the incapacity of the person to make necessary care or treatment decisions as the primary justification for intervention in their life.

Our proposed 'fusion' legislation deals with all persons who lack capacity who may require treatment or care; compulsory powers will only affect a subset of those covered. Provisions for the treatment and care of informal patients include safeguards for those requiring 'serious medical treatment', protections for informal patients in residential care, and requirements for informal patients lacking capacity who need to be 'deprived of their liberty' in their best interests. A single regime is thus provided that specifies the conditions for both treatment under compulsion and treatment under circumstances amounting to a 'deprivation of liberty'.

... The basic criterion for intervention under 'fused' legislation is incapacity to make necessary treatment decisions.

... [the patient] enters a staggered compulsory assessment process ...

... Comprehensive review and accountability mechanisms ... apply. All involuntary patients must have ready access to rights advice and to independent review of their status before a court or tribunal. A substitute decision-maker for treatment is appointed.

... involuntary treatment is restricted to patients who lack capacity. This does not preclude involuntary treatment for the protection of others, which is permitted ... first, where treatment for the protection of others is in the patient's best interests, and second, where in the course of providing treatment in the best interests of the patient, there arises a risk of harm to others.

Certainly, this proposal demonstrates coherence of approach. However, is it satisfactory that capable patients who would currently be detained under a mental health regime, who pose a danger to themselves or others, can only be treated without consent if it is in their best interests to be so treated? It is effectively saying that their refusal of consent can be overridden in their best interests if they are a danger to others, which is roughly how the current scheme operates, albeit that the words 'best interests' are not explicitly used. Undoubtedly, supporters of the current scheme would say that it would be unthinkable to be providing treatment that is not in the best interests of the patient.

Summary of Key Points

1. Mental health law is considered a discrete area of medical law for two main reasons. First, there are difficulties in defining 'mental health' or defining 'mental disorder', as these are inextricably bound up with personality, and 'norms' are much harder to find. Secondly, some forms of mental disorder can result in behaviours that are socially unacceptable and sometimes dangerous, and in consequence the general medical principle that patients can only be treated with their consent or in their best interests if they lack the ability to give consent has not been applied to cases where the patient is a serious risk to themselves or others.

2. There has been much debate surrounding the above issues, ranging from asserting that some, if not all, mental illness is a fiction, to more moderate concerns about how compulsory

detention of mentally disordered patients can be justified, particularly if they have the capacity to make treatment decisions.

3.   Mental health law raises important human rights questions, particularly in relation to Art 5 of the European Convention on Human Rights, and the deprivation of liberty. Under Art (5)(1)(e) lawful detention of persons of unsound mind is permitted in principle, and case law has refined the requirements that must be fulfilled in order to be compliant with the Convention.

4.   There are statutory schemes in many parts of the world that permit detention by reason of mental disorder if there is a risk of harm to self or others, and in England and Wales the Mental Health Act 1983 is such a scheme. It provides for compulsory detention for assessment in hospital, for treatment, detention in an emergency, detention of an informal in-patient and also for treatment within the community.

5.   Mental health hospital regimes raise special considerations both in terms of general treatment with regard to respect for privacy and the provision of a therapeutic environment, and in terms of medical treatment itself. As far as the latter is concerned the Mental Health Act 1983 provides, in certain circumstances, for treatment without the consent of the patient.

6.   Ways of challenging detention under the Act include statutory Mental Health Review Tribunals and common law remedies of judicial review and habeas corpus.

7.   Patients might argue that they have a right to treatment if they are liable to be detained in hospital against their will as a result of their disorder.

8.   Special issues can arise in relation to the prevention of suicide and other self-harm.

📖 Further Reading

Bartlett, P and Sandland, R, 3rd edn, *Mental Health Law: Policy and Practice*, Oxford: Oxford University Press, 2007.

Fennell, P, *Treatment Without Consent: Law, Psychiatry and the Treatment of Mentally Disordered People since 1945*, London: Routledge, 1996.

Jones, R, 13th edn, *Mental Health Act Manual*, London: Sweet & Maxwell, 2010.

Journal of Mental Health Law, Special Edition, 2010.

Peay, J, *Decisions and Dilemmas*, Oxford: Hart Publishing, 2003.

Richardson, G, 'Autonomy, guardianship and mental disorder: one problem, two solutions,' Modern Law Review, (2002) 65, 702.

Chapter 10

Medical Research

Chapter Contents

10.1 Introduction

10.1.1 Background

New therapies are constantly being developed in the battle against sickness and disease, and advances are not merely desired, but expected by society at large. However, their achievement inevitably involves carrying out previously untried treatment upon human subjects, with attendant uncertainty as to the treatment's capacity to harm rather than benefit the subjects in question.

In this chapter, we are concerned with the legal and ethical issues presented by medical research. To this end, we look first at the scientific methodology of research, and examine the key ethical dilemmas raised by such practices. The remaining sections then consider the legal and quasi-legal constraints that operate upon the researcher; in particular the need for research to be subject to independent ethical review: the requirement that the subject consent to research; the various voluntary codes which seek to impose further safeguards in this field; and the issue of *ex post facto* compensation for those injured during the course of research.

It should be borne in mind that medical research gives rise to issues that have been discussed in other chapters such as confidentiality and privacy, human tissue and assisted reproduction.

10.1.2 The importance of scientific advancement

There is a school of thought that says there is an obligation to carry out research, for the advancement of society generally, or, even if there is no such positive obligation, there is a right not to be unduly fettered in pursuing that scientific enquiry. Medical research is just one form of scientific enquiry which is generally thought to be a good thing. However, there is a particular resonance in the field of medicine because of the the impact and potential impact upon the control of disease and pain and discomfort. The personal benefits to patients therefore make endorsement of this form of scientific enquiry rather different from the benefits that can be obtained from advances in, say, civil engineering techniques, however important these might prove to be for society as a whole.

John Harris is typically robust in his advocacy of the importance of medical research, to the extent that he argues that we have a moral duty to participate in medical research:

Harris, J, 'Scientific research is a moral duty'[1]

Let me present the question in its starkest form: is there a moral obligation to undertake, support and even to participate in serious scientific research? If there is, does that obligation require not only that beneficial research be undertaken but also that 'we', as individuals and 'we' as societies be willing to support and even participate in research where necessary? Thus far the overwhelming answer given to this question has been 'no', and research has almost universally been treated with suspicion and even hostility by the vast majority of all those concerned with the ethics and regulation of research.

. . .

Two separate but complementary lines of argument underpin a powerful obligation to pursue, support, and participate in scientific research.

. . .

The first is one of the most powerful obligations that we have, the obligation not to harm others. Where our actions will, or may probably prevent serious harm then if we can reasonably (given the balance of risk and burden to ourselves and benefit to others) we clearly should act because to fail to do so is to accept responsibility for the harm that then occurs. . . .

---

1   (2005) 31 *Journal of Medical Ethics* 242.

Because medical research is a necessary component of relieving [medical needs] in many circumstances furthering medical research becomes a moral obligation. . . . Second, the obligation also flows from an appeal to basic fairness. This is sometimes expressed as an appeal to the unfairness of being a 'free rider'. We all benefit from the existence of the social practice of medical research. Many of us would not be here if infant mortality had not been brought under control, or antibiotics had not been invented.

. . .

[There is a concept of] 'mandatory contribution to public goods'. All British citizens between 18 and 70 are liable for jury service. They may be called, and unless excused by the court, must serve. This may involve a minimum of 10 days but sometimes months of daily confinement in a jury box or room, whether they consent or not. However, although all are liable for service only some are actually called. If someone is called and fails to appear they may be fined. Participation in, or facilitation of, this public good is mandatory. There are many senses in which participation in vaccine or drug trials involve features relevantly analogous to jury service.

 SELF-TEST QUESTION

Is Harris's view merely treating human beings as means to further the interests of others, and does this fit in with our more conventional view of medical ethics?

10.1.3 Defining 'research'

Scientific research may be defined, very broadly, as any systematic inquiry aimed at discovering new facts about the way things in the world around us behave. In the case of medical research, the object of such inquiry is usually improving the efficacy of medical treatments. This includes the development of new forms of treatment and the ways in which medical treatments can be more effectively administered. The scope of research is wider than might be thought. Often people think only about the testing of new drug treatments, but, for example, research is often carried out in the field of preventative medicine where lifestyle choices might be the subject of medical research, where research can be carried out by simply observing doctor/patient interactions, or by the use of questionnaires and interviews with health care professionals or patients, and so on. Frequently methodologies give rise to minimal risk to the participants, but they can raise quite sensitive issues, and even if the questions do not raise such issues, they will almost always give rise to ethical matters such as privacy and confidentiality of information which must be considered in the ethical review process.

It is important to emphasise the deliberate and systematic nature of the research enterprise. Plomer comments as follows:

Plomer, A, *The Law and Ethics of Medical Research: International Bioethics and Human Rights*[2]

The distinction between experimental treatment and research is particularly significant in respect of the specification of the legal obligations imposed on researchers, with the risk that the categorisation of an intervention or procedure as innovative or experimental 'treatment','therapy' or 'practice' could be used to justify a lower level of legal protection on

---

2 London: Cavendish Publishing, 2005.

levels of information and disclosure of risks than those appropriate for research, notwith-standing the fact that the effects and risks of an innovative or experimental procedure by definition are yet to be proven. Undoubtedly, the recipient of an innovative or experimental treatment or therapy, like a participant in a therapeutic medical research program, potentially stands to derive a health benefit from the intervention *if* the anticipated, unproven health benefits materialise.

Plomer refers to the case of *Simms v Simms*[3] which concerned proposed invasive brain surgery on a young person with CJD. The procedure had never been tested on humans but there was no other possible treatment for this condition. The High Court authorised the surgery, simply as a form of experimental treatment. Although this form of experiment needs to be controlled in the sense that there must be fully informed consent or court authorisation, and it must be used in quite specific circumstances (mostly as a measure of last resort), it is not controlled by the regulatory frame-works of research ethics. However, experience with such treatment (often referred to as 'innova-tive therapy') may subsequently form the 'jumping off point' for proper research (especially if it turns out to be highly effective), but it lacks the necessary systematic and repetitive quality to count as research; equally its level of scientific probity remains fairly low.

Significantly, from the doctor's point of view, the desire in such cases is solely to benefit the individual patient being treated in this way. Of course, he may foresee the likelihood of gaining new knowledge in the process, but this merely equates to a wider intention on his part to acquire it (contrast therapeutic research where it is part of his desire). The upshot is that there is no conflict between the doctor *qua* doctor and *qua* scientist: he acts as the former alone. In such a case, it is also submitted that (subject to gaining proper consent) the doctor may also run higher risks on the patient's behalf than those permissible in the context of research. This is because the intended beneficiary of the treatment is the patient alone; he is not being used as a means to any further end.

The key components to 'research' that requires some form of ethical approval is that there is either some form of risk to the participant, and/or that the procedure requires consent in the knowledge that it is a research project.

Without the emphasis on the systematic aspect of research, one might be inclined to regard all medical treatment as constituting 'research', given that our store of knowledge will inevitably increase in the course of providing it. As John Marshall comments:

Marshall, J, 'The case against experimentation'[4]

. . . [In] one sense any medical intervention is research. Giving an aspirin to a patient, though done thousands and thousands of times, may on the thousand-and-oneth [*sic*] occasion produce some unexpected, unpredictable result because of idiosyncrasies in that patient. Therefore, when people talk on the one hand about certain orthodox procedures which they do without thinking and, on the other hand, about unorthodox procedures, it is clear that there is a difference in degree but never a difference in kind. Anything that is done, any intervention in another person, can have unexpected and unpredictable results. But it is not about that that we are really talking in this context.

The other area which ought to be distinguished is that of improving therapy. Again, people think that there is a certain standard way of doing appendectomies, or coronary bypass proce-dures, that there is a certain standard way of treating people with respiratory failure. But medi-cine is always engaged in the business of improving therapy, and improving therapy is often on

---

3   [2003] 2 WLR 1465.
4   In Dyson, A and Harris, J (eds), *Experiments on Embryos*, London: Routledge, 1989.

a research basis. When you try to modify some procedure because you think it might work better in a different way, you are engaged in a form of research, a form of inquiry

It is generally accepted that, in scientific terms, randomised control trials (RCTs) represent the ideal form of medical research. The basic idea is that subjects are randomly divided into different groups. One will be offered the treatment under research, and another (the 'control group') will not. As is evident from the following extract written by Charles Fried in 1974, many therapies that are considered standard today were once the subject of RCTs to establish their efficacy:

Fried, C, *Medical Experimentation – Personal Integrity and Social Policy*[5]

Coronary bypass surgery

In recent years techniques have been developed for bypassing regions of serious atherosclerotic blockage in the major coronary arteries . . . There have, however, been serious questions raised regarding the efficacy of this technique in certain cases of coronary artery disease

In order to evaluate the claims for coronary bypass surgery in various categories of disease, a number of hospitals throughout the country have instituted randomised clinical trials. In one trial, participants are referred by their physician to cardiologists in the participating hospital. The participants are told that a study is being conducted in which they are involved, that they will receive the best available treatment for their case, and that they are free not to join in or stay in the study. Although they know of the alternative therapies, only if they ask are they told that the choice is determined by a randomising scheme.

The scientific utility of randomisation is derived from the elimination, through the randomisation process, of potential bias in observing and interpreting the results of the treatment. In particular, some patients will not be receiving any active drug at all, but will be randomised into a group that is receiving a placebo. The term 'placebo' used here refers to an inert substance, such as a 'dummy' pill, which is given to a subject so that he is unaware that he is in the control group not receiving the therapy under research. Patients are normally aware that they might be receiving the active treatment or a placebo. This is meant to deal with the beneficial effects of a patient simply believing that they are, or might be, receiving a genuine therapy designed to make them better. Indeed the placebo affect can influence the interpretation of trial outcomes, so a lot of clinical trials take place 'double blind' so that the researcher does not know which control groups are which. The use of placebo drugs has been well established over many years as a good research tool, but, of course, other treatments might be subject to placebo use. There are instances of research being carried out involving placebo surgery, where the patient undergoes some form of surgical intervention (cutting open the body and suturing it without doing anything further, for example). The ethical issue with the use of placebo drugs is that the patient might benefit from an active drug, but at least the placebo is not actively harmful. In surgery (even under local anaesthetic only) there is a form of harm taking place.

As Sarah Hewlett notes, from the point of view of participants in clinical trials, a measure of inconvenience, and indeed risk, will be entailed:

Hewlett, S, 'Consent to clinical research – adequately voluntary or substantially influenced?'[6]

The scientific gold standard for clinical research is the randomised controlled trial (RCT) which attempts to establish statistically the risk-benefit ratio of the drug by reducing bias and

---

5   Amsterdam: North-Holland Publishing, 1974.
6   (1996) 22 JME 232.

controlling for variables. This it does by controlling the selection of well characterised groups of patients, randomising them into treatment groups, using standardised outcome measurements performed by blinded assessors, and stipulating a population size powerful enough to answer the question being asked. Although not without criticisms the RCT is a credible test of safety and efficacy within the medical world and some would say it would be unethical to introduce a new drug without RCT data.

Patients participating in an RCT will usually need to attend hospital regularly for safety and efficacy assessments . . . Such visits may take several hours and their frequency varies from every few days to every month, as does the duration of the RCT (from a few days to several years). Neither the safety nor the efficacy of the drug is yet proven and in addition the patient may receive a placebo during the course of the study. When taken together these are not inconsiderable inconveniences for the patient and although hopefully kept to minimum impact, there is sometimes an element of risk.

It should also be noted that clinical trials do not necessarily involve the use of placebos as a standard treatment might be being compared with the trial drug where the standard treatment is inadequate in some way.

 SELF-TEST QUESTION

Is there something inherently unethical about the use of placebos?

Concern has been expressed about patient understanding of RCTs:

Ames, J and Thurston, M, 'Trials and treatments: some reflections on informed consent and the role of research ethics committees'[7]

Key features of the methodology of RCTs are:

- There is uncertainty about which of two, or more treatments is most effective in treating a particular condition, a circumstance likely to occur when at least one of the treatments is new or has been amended in some way;
- The trial is designed to discover which of the treatments in the trial is most effective;
- The method of allocating patients to one of the treatments is based on randomization, rather that clinical judgement.

Patients who have participated in RCTs, however, have produced somewhat different accounts of their methodology.

. . .

The authors of an influential study (Snowden C, Garcia J, Elbourne D. Making sense of randomization : responses of parents of critically ill babies to random allocation of treatment in a clinical trial. Soc Sci Med 1997; 45(9): 1337–1355) identified four areas where the accounts of 37 parents, who had consented to their seriously-ill babies partcipating in a neonatal RCT, differed from the rationale for RCTs outlined above.

Firstly, the word trial was portayed by some parents to refer to a treatment that was being tried-out. Opportunities for the treatment to be tried out were stated by some to be limited and,

---

7 (2008) 4(3) *Research Ethics Review* 95–100.

hence, randomization was used in order to decide which babies would receive the treatment. In these accounts, the term 'trial' was employed as a synonym for 'treatment'. Secondly, some parents expressed the belief that their babies were being chosen for a treatment, rather than for inclusion in a trial comparing two treatments. The issue for them was whether their baby would be selected as suitable for the specified treatment. Thirdly, some parents said that they knew that the experimental treatment was available in other countries and, hence, their accounts did not display an understanding of the principle of uncertainty surrounding the two treatments in the trial. Fourthly, for parents whose child was not responding to the standard treatment, the authors argued that the hope afforded by the experimental treatment made it desirable for its own sake. To be included in the trial, yet randomized out of receiving the experimental treatment, was described as difficult for these parents . . .

Parents' reported expectations were that clinicians would offer the best treatment suitable for their baby. This was inaccurate in the context of a randomized controlled trial.

Research proposals can be quite complex, particularly with regard to justifying the research methodology and providing suitable statistical analysis. The question arises as to how far the scientific validity of the research can be challenged. In this chapter we are concerned with the regulation of research from the point of view of ethics. The questions that are important for people carrying out an ethical review of scientific projects normally relate to such things as fully informed consent, the level of risk to the participants that is acceptable, the amount of protection afforded to the identities and personal information of the participants. The question of whether the science makes it a worthwhile project in the first place is outside the remit of ethical review, except in cases where the science is so flawed the project will be a waste of the time of participants, or where there is another way of achieving the same results without the level of risk and/or intrusion involved in the proposal under consideration.

 SELF-TEST QUESTION

Do you think that people should be paid to take part in medical research?

10.1.4 Therapeutic and non-therapeutic research

The distinction between therapeutic and non-therapeutic research is central to any discussion of the ethical and legal issues surrounding medical research. This does not go to the methodology of the research process (RCTs may equally be used for both), but derives from the two main classes of research subject on whom research may be carried out, and to what end. Both, of course, must be contrasted with experimental treatment or innovative therapy, as discussed above. Despite this well-used distinction, there are circumstances in which 'therapeutic' can mean benefit to patients in general rather than the individual.

10.1.4.1 Therapeutic

This type of research is defined as that which is carried out on patients with the direct potential for beneficial results in respect of their illness. The researcher (who is in a doctor–patient relationship with the subject) will commonly be attempting to establish whether a new treatment is more effective than existing therapy that is available for that condition. It is significant here that the doctor/researcher has what is termed a 'dual-intention': he desires both the attainment of new knowledge *and* benefits for the individual patient/subject, although as far as the latter is concerned, in many cases it might be more accurate to say that the benefit might be for patients suffering from that condition as a whole.

10.1.4.2 Non-therapeutic

In contrast to the therapeutic form, non-therapeutic research denotes that which is carried out on volunteers (either drawn from the public or, perhaps, those hospitalised with unrelated conditions) and offers no hope of benefiting them personally. It often takes place in relation to new drug treatments in order to establish toxicity levels or any side effects. Here, the researcher is in the position of scientist alone: he does not owe duties to the research subject qua patient, and intends only the gaining of knowledge.

Although these two categories may admit of some blurring, they have been recognised for legal and ethical purposes as distinct and are addressed separately in Codes such as the Declaration of Helsinki.

Non-therapeutic research can take place in the context of all forms of medical treatments, but it is in the field of clinical drug trials that the most risk lies and which can give rise to considerable controversy. Trials of new drugs are divided into a number of phases. Prior to human testing, drugs are tested on animals to ascertain minimum safety levels. Although this gives rise to considerable emotional responses and protestation, this chapter is not concerned with non-human aspects of research. The first phase for our purposes is the 'first in human' phase, where the new drug is tested on healthy volunteers. This phase of a clinical trial has been highlighted in the UK by the tragic events that occurred at Northwick Park Hospital, London, in 2006. The drug concerned, TGN1412, was an anti-inflamatory drug developed at a German University, which had set up a biotechnology company, TeGenero, to develop it, and this company contracted with Parexel to conduct the clincial trial on this drug in the UK. Parexel carries out a number of functions with regard to servicing the pharmaceutical industry. This structure is described in detail because TeGenero subsequently became insolvent. Questions arise as to liability and ability to pay compensation for injury, and this will be discussed further at 10.5 below.

As a result of their participation in this trial six young men suffered serious adverse reactions to the drug, which resulted in multiple organ failure. Five of them were able to be discharged from hospital after two months, but the sixth suffered pneumonia and septicaemia, as well as organ failure. One of the volunteers had several toes and fingers amputated as a result of gangrene. It was, in short, a catastrophe, and they commenced proceedings against Parexel for compensation.

Prior to this trial Pamela Ferguson had carried out research to try and ascertain the motivations of healthy volunteers who participate in such trials. She obtained data from 65 volunteers and the seven potential motivations specified were: that it was 'something to do'; curiosity; helping others; a way to obtain health checks; the social contact involved; being part of a team; and financial reasons. On this last reason, Ferguson comments as follows:

Ferguson, Pamela R, 'Clinical Trials and Healthy Volunteers'[8]

Twenty years ago, the [Royal College of Physicians] warned that financial incentives 'may over-persuade individuals, including students, who have low incomes, and may promote the "professional volunteer" '. Several newspaper reports of the TGN1412 trial emphasised that the men were to be paid £2,000 for their participation, and that some people were able to earn £13,000 a year by volunteering for drug studies. One author has warned of the dangers of 'inappropriate rewards or inducements', concluding: 'It may be very difficult for the poor . . . to say no to a risky project if they are offered valuable commodities in exchange for participating'. As Table 2 shows, money was indeed the main motivating factor in the Tayside study, with 80% of volunteers regarding 'financial reasons' as relevant (35%) or highly relevant (45%). One might have expected that the percentage of volunteers who regarded payment as irrelevant to be very low, yet almost one-fifth of participants claimed that the money they would be paid was of no

---

8   (2008) Spring *Medical Law Review*, 16m.

relevance in their decision to take part. Some of these volunteers claimed that they were unaware of the amount of their fee, or indeed that any payment was involved.

. . . In the Tayside study, the fees ranged from £185/£200 to £650/£750. Interestingly, four volunteers mis-stated the amount they were to be paid: one of those in a trial with a fee of £200 stated that he believed that he would be paid £100, and another in the same trial thought he would be paid only £50. A participant who was to be paid £375 thought she would be given £350, whereas another thought the fee was £400 when it was actually £750 . . . . Somewhat surprisingly, three of these had rated financial reasons as a 'highly relevant' motivation. Participants were asked to state whether they thought the fee they were getting was 'a reasonable amount', 'too much' or 'too little' . . . the majority (77%) thought that the fee they were to be paid was a reasonable one, 12% thought that it was too little and 6% thought that they were being paid too much money.

10.1.5 The concept of risk

As already mentioned, medical research, at least where its focus is on invasive forms of therapy, exposes the human research subject to a degree of *additional* risk. Additional, that is to say, to the risks attendant upon receiving treatment where no research is being carried out. Why is this, and what meaning may be ascribed to the concept of risk itself, in this context?

We may begin by recognising that there is always a residual uncertainty, when carrying out any invasive medical procedure, as to whether the patient may in fact be harmed in the process. Given the complexity of each individual human metabolism, we can never be 100 per cent sure in advance that a particular drug will not react with some feature (perhaps of a highly idiosyncratic order) in that metabolism, perhaps with disastrous consequences. Nevertheless, the more often we give the treatment in question, the better the picture we build up of the drug's causal properties, including any such propensity to do harm, and, if so, with what frequency and magnitude.

Clearly, in the case of research involving novel treatment, we will lack this (relative) certainty: the very fact that a particular treatment is untried means that we have no databank of experience as to how the treatment in question has acted upon patients in the past. Although, by the very nature of things, the precise degree of risk presented to a research subject through their participation is thus difficult to quantify, the following rough categories have been proposed:

Nicholson, RH (ed), *Research on Children*[9]

Table 5.6 Risk equivalents

British definition	Negligible	Minimal	More than minimal
American definition	Minimal	Minor increase over minimal	Greater than minor increase over minimal
Risk of death	Less than 1 per million	1 to 100 per million	Greater than 100 per million
Risk of major complication	Less than 10 per million	10 to 1,000 per million	Greater than 1,000 per million
Risk of minor complication	Less than 1 per thousand	1 to 100 per thousand	Greater than 100 per thousand

Despite their tentative character, as we shall see, these categories are often considered ethically significant in furnishing acceptable parameters within which research may take place.

---

9   Oxford: OUP, 1986.

10.2 The Ethics of Good Research Practice

10.2.1 Human Rights

Although, as we have seen, nearly all medical research involves some extra degree of risk to the research subject, without it medical science would be unable to progress properly. This raises a classic dilemma (similar to that in relation to the use of body tissue and organs from live donors): under what conditions and to what extent is it permissible to treat a person (the research subject) as a means to an end (here, greater medical knowledge)?

See Chapter 11

The need for some form of response, at an international level, to this question became dramatically apparent in the wake of the Second World War when, at the Nuremberg Trials, Nazi doctors were revealed to have performed a catalogue of horrific medical experiments on inmates of concentration camps, causing terrible suffering and death.

In the course of their judgment, the judges at Nuremberg articulated a set of parameters within which they felt research might acceptably take place. This has become known as the Nuremberg Code. This was followed, in 1964, by the World Medical Association's Declaration of Helsinki, which deals with the issues in a lengthier and more systematic fashion. As will be seen, the Declaration consists of a preamble followed by two parts: Part B sets out basic principles which apply to all forms of medical research and Part C applies specifically to medical research combined with medical care, that is, therapeutic research. Three themes dominate: the research must be scientifically sound, it must satisfy the proportionality test (that is, risks to the subject should be commensurate with the expected benefits of carrying the research out), and there must be the greatest possible respect at all times for the integrity of the research subject:

Declaration of Helsinki (1964) (as amended – most recently in October 2008 at the 59th Assembly of the World Medical Association in Seoul)

A

1. The World Medical Association (WMA) has developed the Declaration of Helsinki as a statement of ethical principles for medical research involving human subjects, including research on identifiable human material and data.
   The Declaration is intended to be read as a whole and each of its constituent paragraphs should not be applied without consideration of all other relevant paragraphs.

2. Although the Declaration is addressed primarily to physicians, the WMA encourages other participants in medical research involving human subjects to adopt these principles.

3. It is the duty of the physician to promote and safeguard the health of patients, including those who are involved in medical research. The physician's knowledge and conscience are dedicated to the fulfilment of this duty.

4. The Declaration of Geneva of the WMA binds the physician with the words, 'The health of my patient will be my first consideration,' and the International Code of Medical Ethics declares that, 'A physician shall act in the patient's best interest when providing medical care.'

5. Medical progress is based on research that ultimately must include studies involving human subjects. Populations that are under represented in medical research should be provided appropriate access to participation in research.

6. In medical research involving human subjects, the well-being of the individual research subject must take precedence over all other interests.

7. The primary purpose of medical research involving human subjects is to understand the causes, development and effects of diseases and improve preventive, diagnostic and therapeutic interventions (methods, procedures and treatments). Even the best current interventions must be evaluated continually through research for their safety, effectiveness, efficiency, accessibility and quality.

8. In medical practice and in medical research, most interventions involve risks and burdens.

9. Medical research is subject to ethical standards that promote respect for all human subjects and protect their health and rights. Some research populations are particularly vulnerable and need special protection. These include those who cannot give or refuse consent for themselves and those who may be vulnerable to coercion or undue influence.

10. Physicians should consider the ethical, legal and regulatory norms and standards for research involving human subjects in their own countries as well as applicable international norms and standards. No national or international ethical, legal or regulatory requirement should reduce or eliminate any of the protections for research subjects set forth in this Declaration.

B BASIC PRINCIPLES FOR ALL MEDICAL RESEARCH

11. It is the duty of physicians who participate in medical research to protect the life, health, dignity, integrity, right to self-determination, privacy, and confidentiality of personal information of research subjects.

12. Medical research involving human subjects must conform to generally accepted scientific principles, be based on a thorough knowledge of the scientific literature, other relevant sources of information, and adequate laboratory and, as appropriate, animal experimentation. The welfare of animals used for research must be respected.

13. Appropriate caution must be exercised in the conduct of medical research that may harm the environment.

14. The design and performance of each research study involving human subjects must be clearly described in a research protocol. The protocol should contain a statement of the ethical considerations involved and should indicate how the principles in this Declaration have been addressed. The protocol should include information regarding funding, sponsors, institutional affiliations, other potential conflicts of interest, incentives for subjects and provisions for treating and/or compensating subjects who are harmed as a consequence of participation in the research study. The protocol should describe arrangements for post-study access by study subjects to interventions identified as beneficial in the study or access to other appropriate care or benefits.

15. The research protocol must be submitted for consideration, comment, guidance and approval to a research ethics committee before the study begins. This committee must be independent of the researcher, the sponsor and any other undue influence. It must take into consideration the laws and regulations of the country or countries in which the research is to be performed as well as applicable international norms and standards but these must not be allowed to reduce or eliminate any of the protections for research subjects set forth in this Declaration. The committee must have the right to monitor ongoing studies. The researcher must provide monitoring information to the committee, especially information about any serious adverse events. No change to the protocol may be made without consideration and approval by the committee.

16. Medical research involving human subjects must be conducted only by individuals with the appropriate scientific training and qualifications. Research on patients or healthy volunteers requires the supervision of a competent and appropriately qualified physician or other health care professional. The responsibility for the protection of research subjects must always rest with the physician or other health care professional and never the research subjects, even though they have given consent.

17. Medical research involving a disadvantaged or vulnerable population or community is only justified if the research is responsive to the health needs and priorities of this population or community and if there is a reasonable likelihood that this population or community stands to benefit from the results of the research.

18. Every medical research study involving human subjects must be preceded by careful assessment of predictable risks and burdens to the individuals and communities involved in the research in comparison with foreseeable benefits to them and to other individuals or communities affected by the condition under investigation.

19. Every clinical trial must be registered in a publicly accessible database before recruitment of the first subject.

20. Physicians may not participate in a research study involving human subjects unless they are confident that the risks involved have been adequately assessed and can be satisfactorily managed. Physicians must immediately stop a study when the risks are found to outweigh the potential benefits or when there is conclusive proof of positive and beneficial results.

21. Medical research involving human subjects may only be conducted if the importance of the objective outweighs the inherent risks and burdens to the research subjects.

22. Participation by competent individuals as subjects in medical research must be voluntary. Although it may be appropriate to consult family members or community leaders, no competent individual may be enrolled in a research study unless he or she freely agrees.

23. Every precaution must be taken to protect the privacy of research subjects and the confidentiality of their personal information and to minimize the impact of the study on their physical, mental and social integrity.

24. In medical research involving competent human subjects, each potential subject must be adequately informed of the aims, methods, sources of funding, any possible conflicts of interest, institutional affiliations of the researcher, the anticipated benefits and potential risks of the study and the discomfort it may entail, and any other relevant aspects of the study. The potential subject must be informed of the right to refuse to participate in the study or to withdraw consent to participate at any time without reprisal. Special attention should be given to the specific information needs of individual potential subjects as well as to the methods used to deliver the information. After ensuring that the potential subject has understood the information, the physician or another appropriately qualified individual must then seek the potential subject's freely-given informed consent, preferably in writing. If the consent cannot be expressed in writing, the non-written consent must be formally documented and witnessed.

25. For medical research using identifiable human material or data, physicians must normally seek consent for the collection, analysis, storage and/or reuse. There may be situations where consent would be impossible or impractical to obtain for such research or would pose a threat to the validity of the research. In such situations the research may be done only after consideration and approval of a research ethics committee.

26. When seeking informed consent for participation in a research study the physician should be particularly cautious if the potential subject is in a dependent relationship with the physician or may consent under duress. In such situations the informed consent should be sought by an appropriately qualified individual who is completely independent of this relationship.

27. For a potential research subject who is incompetent, the physician must seek informed consent from the legally authorized representative. These individuals must not be included in a research study that has no likelihood of benefit for them unless it is intended to promote the health of the population represented by the potential subject, the research cannot instead be performed with competent persons, and the research entails only minimal risk and minimal burden.

28. When a potential research subject who is deemed incompetent is able to give assent to decisions about participation in research, the physician must seek that assent in addition to the consent of the legally authorized representative. The potential subject's dissent should be respected.

29. Research involving subjects who are physically or mentally incapable of giving consent, for example, unconscious patients, may be done only if the physical or mental condition that prevents giving informed consent is a necessary characteristic of the research population. In such circumstances the physician should seek informed consent from the legally authorized representative. If no such representative is available and if the research cannot be delayed, the study may proceed without informed consent provided that the specific reasons for involving subjects with a condition that renders them unable to give informed consent have been stated in the research protocol and the study has been approved by a research ethics committee. Consent to remain in the research should be obtained as soon as possible from the subject or a legally authorized representative.

30. Authors, editors and publishers all have ethical obligations with regard to the publication of the results of research. Authors have a duty to make publicly available the results of their research on human subjects and are accountable for the completeness and accuracy of their reports. They should adhere to accepted guidelines for ethical reporting. Negative and inconclusive as well as positive results should be published or otherwise made publicly available. Sources of funding, institutional affiliations and conflicts of interest should be declared in the publication. Reports of research not in accordance with the principles of this Declaration should not be accepted for publication.

C ADDITIONAL PRINCIPLES FOR MEDICAL RESEARCH COMBINED WITH MEDICAL CARE

31. The physician may combine medical research with medical care only to the extent that the research is justified by its potential preventive, diagnostic or therapeutic value and if the physician has good reason to believe that participation in the research study will not adversely affect the health of the patients who serve as research subjects.

32. The benefits, risks, burdens and effectiveness of a new intervention must be tested against those of the best current proven intervention, except in the following circumstances:
    - The use of placebo, or no treatment, is acceptable in studies where no current proven intervention exists; or
    - Where for compelling and scientifically sound methodological reasons the use of placebo is necessary to determine the efficacy or safety of an intervention and the patients who receive placebo or no treatment will not be subject to any risk of serious or irreversible harm. Extreme care must be taken to avoid abuse of this option.

33. At the conclusion of the study, patients entered into the study are entitled to be informed about the outcome of the study and to share any benefits that result from it, for example, access to interventions identified as beneficial in the study or to other appropriate care or benefits.

34. The physician must fully inform the patient which aspects of the care are related to the research. The refusal of a patient to participate in a study or the patient's decision to withdraw from the study must never interfere with the patient-physician relationship.

35. In the treatment of a patient, where proven interventions do not exist or have been ineffective, the physician, after seeking expert advice, with informed consent from the patient or a legally authorized representative, may use an unproven intervention if in the physician's judgement it offers hope of saving life, re-establishing health or alleviating suffering. Where possible, this intervention should be made the object of research, designed to evaluate its safety and efficacy. In all cases, new information should be recorded and, where appropriate, made publicly available.

Comment should be made on para 2 of this latest version of the Helsinki Declaration that recognises the fact that although the primary concern of the World Medical Association is the behaviour of doctors, medical research involves people from many other disciplines, and that these principles also apply to them. The Declaration has acted as a template for the various domestic codes, which have subsequently been drafted in respect of particular areas of research practice worldwide. In Europe the Convention on Human Rights and Biomedicine (CHRB) (note that the UK is not a signatory to this at the moment), drawn up by the Council of Europe, states the following on the subject of scientific research:

Convention for the Protection of Human Rights and Dignity of the Human Being with regard to the Application of Biology: Convention on Human Rights and Biomedicine (Council of Europe, 1997): Chapter V – Scientific research

Article 15 – General rule
Scientific research in the field of biology and medicine shall be carried out freely, subject to the provisions of this Convention and the other legal provisions ensuring the protection of the human being.

Article 16 – Protection of persons undergoing research
Research on a person may only be undertaken if all the following conditions are met:
i   there is no alternative of comparable effectiveness to research on humans;
ii   the risks which may be incurred by that person are not disproportionate to the potential benefits of the research;
iii the research project has been approved by the competent body after independent examination of its scientific merit, including assessment of the importance of the aim of the research, and multidisciplinary review of its ethical acceptability,
iv   the persons undergoing research have been informed of their rights and the safeguards prescribed by law for their protection;
v   the necessary consent as provided for under Article 5 has been given expressly, specifically and is documented. Such consent may be freely withdrawn at any time.

Article 17 – Protection of persons not able to consent to research
1   Research on a person without the capacity to consent as stipulated in Article 5 may be undertaken only if all the following conditions are met:
    i   the conditions laid down in Article 16, sub-paragraphs i to iv, are fulfilled;
    ii   the results of the research have the potential to produce real and direct benefit to his or her health;
    iii research of comparable effectiveness cannot be carried out on individuals capable of giving consent;
    iv   the necessary authorisation provided for under Article 6 has been given specifically and in writing; and
    v   the person concerned does not object.

2   Exceptionally and under the protective conditions prescribed by law, where the research has not the potential to produce results of direct benefit to the health of the person concerned, such research may be authorised subject to the conditions laid down in paragraph 1, sub-paragraphs i, iii, iv and v above, and to the following additional conditions:
    i   the research has the aim of contributing, through significant improvement in the scientific understanding of the individual's condition, disease or disorder, to the ultimate attainment of results capable of conferring benefit to the person concerned or to other persons in the same age category or afflicted with the same disease or disorder or having the same condition;
    ii   the research entails only minimal risk and minimal burden for the individual concerned.

Article 18 – Research on embryos *in vitro*

1   Where the law allows research on embryos *in vitro*, it shall ensure adequate protection of the embryo.

2   The creation of human embryos for research purposes is prohibited.

10.2.2 The duty of doctor/researcher

Our concern in this section is the duties of an ethical nature that the doctor/researcher may be held to owe to the research subject. In accordance with the central distinction, outlined above, between therapeutic and non-therapeutic research, we shall deal separately with the duties which exist in each case.

10.2.2.1 Duties to patients

Can therapeutic research, and the additional risks it entails, be reconciled (and if so, how far) with the doctor's pledge under the Hippocratic Oath to do the best for each of his patients? In itself, this question admits of an affirmative answer: the higher risks can be balanced against the hope that a new therapy will bring increased benefits for the patients so treated. However, matters are complicated by the use, in Randomised Control Trials, of randomisation to determine the treatment given to each patient. For here it might well be argued that the doctor has abdicated his duty to tailor the treatment he provides to the latter's individual needs. The question of how far the patient's fully informed consent could provide a justification, is analysed by Charles Fried:

Fried, C, *Medical Experimentation – Personal Integrity and Social Policy*[10]

Should [the patient] be told that he is receiving that therapy which in the judgment of his physicians is the best available in his case, or should he be told more fully that his therapy is being determined by some randomising device in furtherance of a medical experiment? In the case where the choice between the two treatments is not in equipoise, the failure to disclose the existence of the RCT adds insult to injury since it plainly withholds information which any patient should find relevant and indeed the basis for considering a change of doctors. The non-disclosure is deceptive because it fails to reveal that the patient's interests are, to some extent, being sacrificed for the sake of the experimental design and thus, the wider social good. That sacrifice might be the overt one of exposing the patient to the risk of a treatment which in the present state of knowledge is somewhat less favoured, or the less overt one of not inquiring fully into his particular circumstances (including his particular value system) in order to determine whether the balance of probabilities is in equipoise in his particular case. There are two justifications for non-disclosure frequently offered: (1) that the distress this would cause the patient would be therapeutically undesirable; and (2) that the disclosure would endanger the experiment by introducing a disturbing element or even by causing the patient to withhold his consent. Both justifications are inadequate to show that non-disclosure does not sacrifice some interest of the subject. Both justifications beg this question, since they assume that the choice by randomisation is proper, and thus they assume that limiting disclosure in order to facilitate this kind of experimentation is proper.

However, Fried does not acknowledge that it is in the interests of the researcher to tell the patient that the trial is 'blind', because knowledge of the treatment arm into which the patient has been

---

10 Amsterdam: North-Holland Publishing, 1974.

placed can influence the outcome of the trial itself. Furthermore, as already noted, a lot of trials are 'double blind', in the sense that neither researcher nor patient has this knowledge.

10.2.2.2 Duties to volunteers

As previously noted, the researcher who carries out non-therapeutic research on volunteers has no doctor–patient relationship with his subject. Nevertheless, this does not entail the absence of ethical duties on his part towards the latter. In some ways, indeed, it may heighten the ethical obligation.

Exceptionally a doctor may rely on the doctrine of 'therapeutic privilege'[11] to avoid informing a patient of his participation in therapeutic research; no such argument is admissible in relation to volunteers.

10.3 Consent to Research

Whereas research upon embryos may only be carried out under licence pursuant to the Human Fertilisation and Embryology Act 1990,[12] and that upon animals is regulated by the Animals (Scientific Procedures) Act 1968, there are no similar statutory safeguards operative in respect of research upon (full) human beings. Perhaps the major reason for this is that the human research subject is thought able to protect himself adequately against abuse by the researcher through the mechanism of consent at common law. How far is this really so? Although we have examined consent to treatment in some detail,[13] medical research gives rise to some special considerations. For example, in relation to general treatment, consent may sometimes simply be inferred from the surrounding circumstances, as when a patient submits to a medical examination. In the context of therapeutic research, the additional (and cloaked) intention of the doctor/researcher means that the subject's consent cannot be so inferred.

It will be recalled that the three elements to a valid consent are capacity, voluntariness and information, and each will be examined in relation to therapeutic and non-therapeutic research, respectively.

10.3.1 Therapeutic research

10.3.1.1 The competent patient

The first issue here is to determine whether the subject has genuine capacity to consent. In this regard, could it be argued that the latter must possess a more sophisticated understanding than someone who is receiving 'ordinary' medical treatment? In one sense, the answer is 'yes', because the issues in a research project may be quite complex, but there is no real difference of criteria. Consent to general treatment requires an ability to understand the nature of the treatment and this general principle applies equally to therapeutic research.

More problematic, however, may be the requirement for such consent to be free from coercion. This is because there is a danger that pressure (real or perceived) may be placed upon a patient to agree to participate in a clinical trial for fear of not receiving the best treatment in the face of a refusal. Sarah Hewlett comments on this problem as follows:

---

11 See Ch 3, above.
12 See Ch 7, above.
13 See Ch 3, above.

Hewlett, S, 'Consent to clinical research – adequately voluntary or substantially influenced?'[14]

Influences or controlling influences?

So strong is [the trust in doctors] that patients may agree to anything the doctor suggests and even the invitation to participate may be viewed as a recommendation rather than a request. Patients may feel flattered by the request and under an obligation to help because of past care received.

For many patients the relationship is an unequal one, with the doctor being perceived as a powerful figure on whom they depend, making it difficult for them to take an unnaturally dominant role and refuse the doctor's request. Patients may fear that if they do so, the doctor will be displeased and their future care will be jeopardised. Patients may view clinical research as a means of access to care (which may be true for patients in countries where many people do not have health care insurance) and may also equate the frequent safety visits with improved care.

She suggests that one way of dealing with this is to introduce a system of patient advocates, funded by the NHS and trained and supervised by research ethics committees. The problem with this is the cost of such an exercise. In particular, members of research ethics committees are not paid, and to give them the additional responsibility of training and supervising patient advocates would bring a call for payment and have an adverse effect on recruitment of members of such committees.

The Royal College of Physicians confirms in its Guidance[15] that patients must feel free to decline to participate and assured that the refusal will not put them at a disadvantage, (paras 7.4 et seq). Note, below, the provisions of s 33 of the Mental Capacity Act 2005 which reflect this, as do the Medicines for Human Use (Clinical Trials) Regulations 2004.

There is concern that certain groups in particular may be vulnerable to exploitation in the field of research. It will be recalled that this was examined in Chapter 3, above.[16]. In relation to prisoners, Mason and McCall Smith comment as follows:

Mason, JK and McCall Smith, RA, *Law and Medical Ethics*[17]

. . . the use of prisoners exposes many ethical issues essentially based on the arguments that some advantage, even if only imagined, must accrue to the prisoner participating in a trial; that advantage may be so great as to induce the prisoner to volunteer for research which involves greater discomfort or risk than would be accepted by a free man and, in particular, it may compromise his inalienable right to withdraw from the experiment. The arguments are not, however, entirely one way – it is possible to be paternalistic in an attempt to preserve people's autonomy. Thus, prisoners could well resent protective attitudes on the grounds that it is their right to dispose of their bodies and to take such risks as they please that is being compromised. This could be the subject of lengthy debate, but we would suggest that the conditions in today's prisons are such that any process which provides some relief deserves, at least, a sympathetic evaluation and, secondly, that many prisoners might be therapeutically benefited through helping society. But it is also felt that experiments on prisoners should be particularly rigidly

---

14 (1996) 22 JME 232.
15 *Research Involving Patients*, London: RCP, 1990.
16 See the cases of *Freeman v Home Office* [1984] 1 All ER 1036 and *Kaimowitz v Michigan Department of Mental Health* 42 USLW 2063 (1973).
17 3rd edn, London: Butterworths, 1991.

controlled by ethical committees which should always contain lay members with experience in criminology . . .

However, given the concerns we address later about the lack of sanctions given to ethics committees, it may be doubted as to whether they really can 'rigidly control' such a situation. The Declaration of Helsinki at para 17 states that research involving a disadvantaged or vulnerable population can only be justified if it is responsive to the health needs of that particular population.

A further major issue in respect of therapeutic research carried out upon competent patients concerns the amount of information to which they are legally entitled. We have seen that a battery will be committed if the patient is not informed of the broad nature of an intended medical procedure. Kennedy and Grubb comment as follows:

Kennedy, I and Grubb, A, *Medical Law*[18]

One view, and it is ours, is that where there is a dual intention on the part of the doctor, ie, to treat and to conduct research, any failure to inform the patient concerning *both* of these intentions and their possible consequences would amount in law to a battery. This is because in the absence of such knowledge the patient will have assented to a procedure which is materially different in its nature from that which the doctor intends to carry out. To put it another way, research adds a further component to the quality of the consent that the law requires.

. . . A court may insist on the patient being informed of three particular matters in addition to this generalised intention. Each of them is an aspect of those interests of the patient which the law of battery seeks to protect. The patient must be informed: (1) that he may refuse to take part in the research project or may at any time withdraw from the research and that in either case if he does so he will suffer no adverse consequences in terms of the treatment he will then receive; (2) that the nature of the research may be such that he may be a member of a control group in a trial which is intended to evaluate the efficacy of a new therapy; (3) that the trial is a randomised controlled trial (RCT) if it be such.

As regards (2), one consequence of being a member of a control group could be that the patient does not receive the form of treatment which subsequently proves to be the more efficacious. To meet this ethical difficulty researchers ordinarily would be expected to provide for periodic examination of the emerging data. It is our view that a patient's consent is not informed for the purpose of the tort of battery unless he is made aware of this periodic review.

As regards (3), randomisation means that a treatment regime is assigned to a patient randomly without regard to the particular circumstances of that patient, his needs, his preferences or the preferences of his doctor. Again, it is our view that a patient may volunteer for such a trial but his consent is only valid if he is given the opportunity of knowing it is randomised and he is aware of what this means.

As redrafted over the years, the Declaration of Helsinki has placed greater emphasis upon informed consent (see paras 24–26, 34) than it did in the 1964 version which provided for circumstances in which the physician might consider it essential not to obtain informed consent (para II (5)), but even so the 2008 version does not expressly refer to disclosure of the precise nature and use of an RCT. There could be circumstances in which therapeutic privilege could be used to avoid giving full details to patients of the precise nature of the trial. However, as Kennedy and Grubb point out, if the patient would be caused distress by the knowledge that he is in a clinical trial, this is an argument for excluding him from the trial, not for including him without his knowledge. As yet,

18 3rd edn, London: Butterworths, 2000.

however, the position has not been tested in the courts. The cases of *Sidaway v Board of Governors of the Bethlem Royal Hospital and the Maudsley Hospital*[19] and *Chester v Afshar*[20] are pertinent here. As we have seen in Chapter 3, *Chester* confirmed that the patient has a right to be informed of any risks that would have affected the decision of the reasonable patient in his/her circumstances. The same conclusion must be drawn, even more forceably, in a case where there is an objective (here, research) other than the well being of the patient. However, even in *Chester* it was acknowledged that there could be circumstances where therapeutic privilege might apply, and in *Sidaway* Lord Scarman had stated the same thing. In the USA, where there is Federal law that regulates medical research, the doctrine of therapeutic privilege is acknowledged.[21] Given that, at least in part, the purpose of therapeutic research is to offer some benefit to the patient, is it not inevitable that something akin to therapeutic privilege will exist? A report from Peter Hamilton, the Sheriff in Aberdeen, however, highlights a case, where the patient had been positively misled:

See Chapter 3 ➡

Hamilton, P (Sheriff), 'Sheriff's Report, Aberdeen'[22]

28 January 1997

In 1993, while recovering from a fractured hip, Mrs Phyllis Moffit was recruited into a clinical trial after receiving the following revised patient information sheet:

> Dear . . .
>
> We are asking patients who have had a hip fracture in the past if they will take part in a research project. The aim is to try to prevent their unaffected hip from breaking at a later date.
>
> In order to do this, we would like to have the opportunity to inject your unaffected hip (the one you have not broken) with a material which we think would actually strengthen the bone. It is composed of crystals of calcium, very like bone, and a protein which is known to stimulate bone growth.
>
> We know there is a one in five chance that you might break the other hip within four years, and therefore there would be great benefits if the injection were to be successful. We are not aware of any significant risks associated with this injection.
>
> If you agree to this injection, you will be admitted to Woodend Hospital. It will be done under a local anaesthetic in the operating theatre. It will involve having a small cut (about half an inch) made in your unaffected hip and the material being injected into your hip bone. This is not a painful procedure and should not inconvenience or incapacitate you in any way. This will not affect your mobility . . .

Mrs Moffit died in August 1994 of heart failure while under sedation for the experimental hip surgery. The heart failure was caused by an unsuspected aneurysm of the coronary artery. In this case, the statistic quoted in the information sheet as to the likelihood of a second hip fracture was based upon inconclusive evidence and had indeed been changed from an earlier sheet in which the chance was described as 'one in 10 over two years'. The victim's daughter gave evidence that the alarm her mother had felt on reading this was the chief reason she had agreed to participate in the research. Moreover, the research proposal approved by the local research ethics committee (LREC) had not mentioned the need for sedation of subjects as initially it had not been thought that the procedure would be painful. Whilst the researchers had become aware that this would in fact be required some time prior to recruiting Mrs Moffit, they failed either to amend the information

---

19 [1985] AC 871.
20 [2004] UKHL 41.
21 See Myers, D, *The Human Body and the Law*, Edinburgh: Edinburgh UP, 1990.
22 (1997) *Bulletin of Medical Ethics* 22.

sheet or to inform the LREC. Finally, although the patient here was recovering from a fractured hip, it may be queried whether this was really *therapeutic* research at all.

10.3.1.2 The incapable patient

Both the Declaration of Helsinki and the European Convention on Human Rights permit a limited amount of research on those patients who are not capable of giving a valid consent.[23] Some would argue that this is ethically unacceptable, on the basis that without consent the incapable are being used as a means to the ends of others unless there are direct benefits to the incapable patient. Garwood-Gowers uses a 'slippery slope' argument.

> ### Garwood-Gowers, A, 'Vindicating the right to bodily security of the incapable in research' – Part 2[24]
>
> Of course it might in theory be possible to argue that if it is legitimate to trade off the right to bodily security vis-à-vis the needs of others in extreme circumstances then participation of incompetent adults in medical research is one such extreme circumstance. However, for common arguments to the effect that we need to dilute protection to make progress in relation to conditions like Alzheimer's disease, one could substitute the argument that we need to dilute protection of all classes of person to facilitate greater extraction of bodily material to help meet the need for transplantation and general biotechnological advancement. Or, more specifically, we could substitute the argument that we need to dilute protection of insensate dying persons to facilitate the need to prepare their body for use in transplantation, medical research or medical education after their death.

It is suggested that this argument breaks down in the way that all slippery slope arguments do by taking something that is fairly innocuous (such as allowing incapable adults who suffer from Alzheimer's disease to participate in a risk-free observation exercise), and concluding this will mean that society is, in consequence, incapable of preventing this leading to wholescale involuntary euthanasia and organ-harvesting. However, writers such as Garwood-Gowers might rightly argue that such an observation exercise, whilst not interfering with bodily integrity, is not innocuous, because it is a breach of privacy. As we have seen in Chapter 5, the legal right to privacy is subject to a number of wide exceptions, and this might well fall into the 'protection of health' exception, but there is still an argument that from an ethical point of view, it is an unacceptable breach. It goes to whether one is prepared to use a consequentialist argument or not. Undoubtedly such an argument is powerful in the need to investigate serious illness such as Alzheimer's disease.

See Chapter 5

10.3.1.2.1 Children

Does s 8 of the Family Law Reform Act 1969[25] apply to research? The section refers to 'any surgical, medical or dental treatment', and it has been argued[26] that this does not cover treatment which includes a research component. This would mean that the age of 16 would have no significance as far as consent of the child is concerned, but presumably the concept of *Gillick* competence would apply. The guidelines issued by the professional bodies such as the Royal College of Paediatrics and the British Medical Association acknowledge that children can consent to *therapeutic* research. The

---

23 See principles 24–26 above, at 10.2.1.
24 (2006) *Journal of Mental Health Law* 17.
25 See Ch 3, above.
26 By, for example, Kennedy and Grubb in *Medical Law*, 3rd edn, London: Butterworths, 2000.

European Directive on Clinical Trials[27] acknowledges the necessity of carrying out research on children, but only when the research in question cannot be carried out on adults. It is important to note that there is a real need for research on children, because even if a clinical trial has found a drug to be effective and safe in adults, it does not mean to say that it will be safe or efficacious in children. Frequently medicines are prescribed for children 'off label', which means that they have not been licensed for use in children. However, children are not just small adults; they have different physiological and psychological characteristics, and there are certain diseases that are specific to childhood.

In the House of Lords case of S v S[28] the Court had to consider whether it was appropriate to order a blood test on a child for the purposes of establishing paternity when the mother of the child was refusing to consent. Lord Reid said that it was 'not against the interests of the child' for this to be done. The implication for therapeutic research appears to be that the therapeutic aspect of the treatment means that it would not be contrary to the child's interests. However, if we consider randomised control tests, where the child may be getting no treatment at all, and where the choice as to whether the child is treated is not made on clinical grounds, can it still be argued that this is not contrary to the interests of the child?

10.3.1.2.2 Incapable adults

As we have seen, until the enactment of the Mental Capacity Act 2005 there was no provision in English law for proxy decision making in medical and personal welfare matters. However, the new legislation not only applies to bona fide medical treatment but also extends to providing for medical research to be carried out on incapable adults. The Law Commission had recommended that research on incapable adults should be permitted[29] but this recommendation was not followed up in the Mental Incapacity Bill. It was however taken up again when the Mental Capacity Bill was drafted following the pre-legislative scrutiny of the Joint Committee.[30]

Mental Capacity Act 2005

30 Research

(1) Intrusive research carried out on, or in relation to, a person who lacks capacity to consent to it is unlawful unless it is carried out–
  (a) as part of a research project which is for the time being approved by the appropriate body for the purposes of this Act in accordance with section 31, and
  (b) in accordance with sections 32 and 33.

(2) Research is intrusive if it is of a kind that would be unlawful if it was carried out–
  (a) on or in relation to a person who had capacity to consent to it, but
  (b) without his consent.

(3) A clinical trial which is subject to the provisions of clinical trials regulations is not to be treated as research for the purposes of this section.

(4) 'Appropriate body', in relation to a research project, means the person, committee or other body specified in regulations made by the appropriate authority as the appropriate body in relation to a project of the kind in question.

(5) 'Clinical trials regulations' means–
  (a) the Medicines for Human Use (Clinical Trials) Regulations 2004 (S.I. 2004/1031) and any other regulations replacing those regulations or amending them, and

---

27 See below, at 10.4.
28 [1970] 3 All ER 107.
29 Law Commission Report 231 (1995).
30 Reports HL Paper 189-I & HC 1983-I.

(b)   any other regulations relating to clinical trials and designated by the Secretary of State as clinical trials regulations for the purposes of this section.

(6)   In this section, section 32 and section 34, 'appropriate authority' means–
   (a)   in relation to the carrying out of research in England, the Secretary of State, and
   (b)   in relation to the carrying out of research in Wales, the National Assembly for Wales.

31 Requirements for approval

(1)   The appropriate body may not approve a research project for the purposes of this Act unless satisfied that the following requirements will be met in relation to research carried out as part of the project on, or in relation to, a person who lacks capacity to consent to taking part in the project ('P').

(2)   The research must be connected with–
   (a)   an impairing condition affecting P, or
   (b)   its treatment.

(3)   'Impairing condition' means a condition which is (or may be) attributable to, or which causes or contributes to (or may cause or contribute to), the impairment of, or disturbance in the functioning of, the mind or brain.

(4)   There must be reasonable grounds for believing that research of comparable effectiveness cannot be carried out if the project has to be confined to, or relate only to, persons who have capacity to consent to taking part in it.

(5)   The research must–
   (a)   have the potential to benefit P without imposing on P a burden that is disproportionate to the potential benefit to P, or
   (b)   be intended to provide knowledge of the causes or treatment of, or of the care of persons affected by, the same or a similar condition.

(6)   If the research falls within paragraph (b) of subsection (5) but not within paragraph (a), there must be reasonable grounds for believing–
   (a)   that the risk to P from taking part in the project is likely to be negligible, and
   (b)   that anything done to, or in relation to, P will not–
      (i)   interfere with P's freedom of action or privacy in a significant way, or
      (ii)   be unduly invasive or restrictive.

(7)   There must be reasonable arrangements in place for ensuring that the requirements of sections 32 and 33 will be met.

Section 32 provides for consultation with carers.

The following are some observations on these provisions. First, it will be seen that 'intrusive' research is research that would constitute a battery if it were carried out without consent, so that mere observation of a mentally incapacitated person would not constitute intrusive research. Secondly, the Act does not apply to clinical trials as these are covered by the Medicines for Human Use (Clinical Trials) Regulations 2004 (see below). Secondly, the key provisions of s 31(1) to (4) should be carefully noted. The research must be connected with either an impairing condition which affects the incompetent patient, or its treatment, and the condition must be one which causes some impairment or functioning of the mind or brain. In other words, the research could not be on a physical condition that affects the patient, as such a physical condition might affect those who are competent to provide the necessary consent. Nevertheless although we are referring to patients here, there is no requirement that the 'patient' is 'suffering' or acutely ill, merely that they have an impairment, so it is not strictly speaking correct to think of them as 'patients'. Interestingly this neatly conflates the patient/healthy volunteer distinction, arguably to the detriment of the research subject, whether described as a patient or not.

Further, under s 31(5) the research must either have the potential to benefit the patient (without imposing a disproportion burden), or to be beneficial to other persons affected by the same or similar conditions. It is arguable that the second part of the justification is unethical as it means that research which is not of benefit to the incapable person can be carried out. However, this might be countered by s 31(6) which states that in these circumstances there must be reasonable grounds for believing that the risk is negligible and that it will not interfere with the patient's 'freedom of action or privacy in a significant way' or 'be unduly invasive or restrictive'. The key ethical point here is whether these provisions are sufficient to justify actions which might well constitute a battery upon a capable person who refused consent. For the protection of the patient it is important that s 31(6)(b) is construed so that both (i) and (ii) have to be satisfied and not be construed as justifiable alternatives. The Explanatory notes to the Bill did indicate that the type of research typical to sub-s(6) might include indirect research on medical notes, or on human tissue already taken for other purposes, or may include interviews or questionnaires about health- or social-care with the patient or his carers or limited observation of him. This is interesting given the views expressed by the Law Commission, see 10.3.2.2.2 below, and the Commission's acknowledgement of the risk to the dignity and privacy of the research participant when they were incapable and the research was non-therapeutic. Here we have a situation where provision is made quite clearly for this sort of research to be carried out on participants when it is not of benefit to them, ie it is non-therapeutic.

Section 33 provides additional safeguards and s 34 deals with loss of capacity during a research project:

33 Additional safeguards

(1) This section applies in relation to a person who is taking part in an approved research project even though he lacks capacity to consent to taking part.

(2) Nothing may be done to, or in relation to, him in the course of the research–
   (a) to which he appears to object (whether by showing signs of resistance or otherwise) except where what is being done is intended to protect him from harm or to reduce or prevent pain or discomfort, or
   (b) which would be contrary to–
      (i) an advance decision of his which has effect, or
      (ii) any other form of statement made by him and not subsequently withdrawn,

   of which R is aware.

(3) The interests of the person must be assumed to outweigh those of science and society.

(4) If he indicates (in any way) that he wishes to be withdrawn from the project he must be withdrawn without delay.

(5) P must be withdrawn from the project, without delay, if at any time the person conducting the research has reasonable grounds for believing that one or more of the requirements set out in section 31(2) to (7) is no longer met in relation to research being carried out on, or in relation to, P.

(6) But neither subsection (4) nor subsection (5) requires treatment that P has been receiving as part of the project to be discontinued if R has reasonable grounds for believing that there would be a significant risk to P's health if it were discontinued.

34 Loss of capacity during research project

(1) This section applies where a person ('P')–
   (a) has consented to take part in a research project begun before the commencement of section 30, but
   (b) before the conclusion of the project, loses capacity to consent to continue to take part in it.

(2)   The appropriate authority may by regulations provide that, despite P's loss of capacity, research of a prescribed kind may be carried out on, or in relation to, P if–

    (a)   the project satisfies prescribed requirements,

    (b)   any information or material relating to P which is used in the research is of a prescribed description and was obtained before P's loss of capacity, and

    (c)   the person conducting the project takes in relation to P such steps as may be prescribed for the purpose of protecting him.

(3)   The regulations may, in particular,–

    (a)   make provision about when, for the purposes of the regulations, a project is to be treated as having begun;

    (b)   include provision similar to any made by section 31, 32 or 33.

 SELF-TEST QUESTION

Would you wish to restrict non-therapeutic research being carried out on people who lack capacity, and if so, how would you do this?

10.3.2 Non-therapeutic research

10.3.2.1 The capable volunteer

Given that we are not considering *treatment* at all, should the test of capacity to consent be different in this context? The test, it is suggested, will be the same. The volunteer will still be required to understand the nature of the procedure and any risks involved, and weigh up the risks of the procedure with the advantage of participating (either financial, or psychological well being because of the potential benefits to others).

However, just as there may be a temptation for a doctor, who wishes to treat a refusing patient in the latter's own interests, to regard such a patient as *incapable*, here, where a researcher needs healthy volunteers to assist in what he believes to be valuable research, the opposite temptation may arise: that is to say, the researcher may be over-ready to find an assenting volunteer capable. It is clear that vigilance is needed to protect individuals from unwarranted physical interference in both cases.

Difficulties also arise in the context of ensuring that consent to participate is truly voluntary. This is especially true of volunteers, who are already in hospital for unrelated treatment, and who may feel unable to refuse 'secondment' into a trial if approached by their doctor. Another potential group of research subjects, vulnerable in a somewhat different way, are the poor. Although the financial inducements are relatively modest, the sums may tempt those on low incomes. For example, advertisements in *The Big Issue* (a publication sold on the streets by the homeless) invite volunteers for medical research (stating that they are 'all approved by ethics committees'), for £100. See the extract from Ferguson at 10.1.4.2 above.

The next requirement, once again, is that the research subject be properly informed of the risks attendant upon participating in the research. Clearly, therapeutic privilege can have no part to play in research on healthy volunteers. In the Canadian case of *Halushka v University of Saskatchewan*[31] it was stated:

---

31   (1965) 52 WWR 608.

Hall JA: The example of risks being properly hidden from a patient when it is important that he should not worry can have no application in the field of research. The subject of medical experimentation is entitled to a full and frank disclosure of all the facts, probabilities and opinions which a reasonable man might be expected to consider before giving his consent.

To what extent would the UK courts similarly distinguish non-therapeutic from therapeutic research in this context? In the post-*Sidaway* case of *Gold v Haringey HA*,[32] the Court of Appeal held that disclosure, in the context of non-therapeutic treatment, was just as much governed by the *Bolam* test (as now refined by the cases of *Bolitho v City and Hackney Health Authority*[33] and *Chester v Afshar*[34]) as advice given in the course of therapy. However, it is probable that this question is of theoretical interest only since, as noted earlier in our discussion of therapeutic research, the *Bolam* test itself would surely impose the duty to obtain fully informed consent upon the researcher (all guidance, including the Declaration of Helsinki, is unanimously to this effect).

10.3.2.2 The incapable volunteer

The expression 'incapable volunteer' is, of course, a contradiction in terms. If the person is incapable, then, by definition, he is unable to volunteer. However, others may 'volunteer' on his behalf, and this undoubtedly generates some of the most contentious ethical and legal issues in medical research. Indeed it may be felt that there is an argument for prohibiting any form of non-therapeutic research on those who lack the capacity to consent.

10.3.2.2.1 Children

It is generally thought ethically acceptable, in certain circumstances, to carry out non-therapeutic research upon children. That is certainly the view taken by such bodies as the Royal College of Paediatricians and the Royal College of Physicians, whose guidelines offer very similar advice here to that covering therapeutic research on patients. In the case of mature minors, there is an assumption that *Gillick* competence will apply. (Clearly, s 8 of the Family Law Reform Act 1969 will not apply to 16 and 17-year-olds in this context.) However, should children really be able to consent at all to non-therapeutic measures on *Gillick* principles? It is suggested here that the answer is 'yes', at least where the risks involved are negligible or minimal. After all, mature minors are capable of giving consent to major medical interventions, such as surgery, which may require them to comprehend and balance much higher risks.

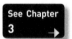

Interesting issues arise when the child is incapable of consenting, and the parent consents on the child's behalf. Robert Redmon tackles arguments which state that children in such research are being used merely as 'ends' and sees participation as part of the child's wider development as a moral being, even though the research is not for the benefit of the child's immediate health:

Redmon, R, 'How children can be respected as "ends" yet still be used as subjects in non-therapeutic research' [35]

If the child is old enough, she may enjoy seeing how this aspect of science functions, and her participation may aid her education. Also, this participation can be seen as part of her moral education.

However, these particular benefits – scientific and moral education – are of a different nature from most others (money, health, prestige, etc). To aid in the development of intellectual and,

32 [1987] 2 All ER 888.
33 [1998] AC 232.
34 [2004] UKHL 41.
35 (1986) 12 JME 77.

especially, moral abilities (or sensitivities) is to aid in the development of the individual's autonomy. For Kant, a person was only free when she was doing the morally praiseworthy thing (acting from 'a good will'). A development of a 'good will' (notwithstanding Kant's view that such a will is 'non-empirical' and thus, in some sense, innate) is a step towards being an ultimate 'end'.

Citing a piece by Hans Jonas ('Philosophical reflections on experimenting with human subjects' (1969) *Daedalus* (Spring) 219), Redmon favours the approach whereby, if the goals of the subject are the same as the researcher, then the subject is not being merely used. This he refers to as an 'identification of interests':

Redmon, R, 'How children can be respected as "ends" yet still be used as subjects in non-therapeutic research'[36]

It does make sense . . . to ask how a person with a particular moral outlook, particular values, virtues and vices, would act. Thus the prediction of how the child will later view his participation must be made by those in the child's family, in particular by his parents. Their consent should be based upon their own values and the expectation that the child will share, to some extent, in them. They might reasonably expect, for example, that their child may later, as an adult, have an interest in the welfare of children whom the research may benefit. Their child will probably be a parent himself. They should also . . . be present during all stages of the research, and be involved in it as much as possible. This will help confirm their judgment that their child will later 'identify' with the research project.

My 'Kantian deliberations' thus lead to a tentative conclusion: if we can reasonably expect this child to 'identify' (in Jonas' sense) with the goals of the research when she is an adult, and that the identification will be strong enough to outweigh the harm of the knowledge of being used by her parents, and if the child (if old enough) assents, and if the possibility of harm is slight ('minimal risk'), then such research is permissible.

Could it be argued, in the light of this (and echoing the approach taken in the case of S v S[37]), that parental consent to enter their child into non-therapeutic research involving minimal risk is not contrary to the child's best interests? In the US case of *Curran v Bosze*,[38] it was suggested that 'individual altruism in an abstract theoretical sense' was an insufficient basis for regarding a non-therapeutic procedure as in a child's best interests.[39] Significantly, in that case, however, the children's mother opposed the procedure in issue.

10.3.2.2.2 Adults

It is arguable that non-therapeutic research on the incapable adult is always wrong, both morally, and in law, as it constitutes a battery. (Contrast the position of children, where at least a parent may (and must) consent on their behalf.) At the very least, additional safeguards should be necessary. The Law Commission in its report, *Mental Incapacity*, commented as follows:

Law Commission, *Mental Incapacity*, Report No 231[40]

6.29 'Non-therapeutic' research . . . does not claim to offer any direct or immediate benefit to the participant. Such procedures may well be scientifically and ethically acceptable to those who are qualified to decide such matters. If, however, the participant lacks capacity to consent

---

36 (1986) 12 JME 77.
37 [1970] 3 All ER 107.
38 566 NE 2d 1319 (1990).
39 See Ch11, below.
40 London: HMSO, 1995.

to his or her participation, and the procedure cannot be justified under the doctrine of necessity, then any person who touches or restrains that participant is committing an unlawful battery. The simple fact is that the researcher is making no claim to be acting in the best interests of that individual person and does not therefore come within the rules of law set out in Re F. It was made abundantly clear to us on consultation, however, that non-therapeutic research projects of this nature are regularly taking place. We were told of a research project into the organic manifestations of Alzheimer's disease which involves the administration of radioactive isotopes to sufferers, followed by extensive testing of blood and bodily functions. Another project was said to involve the examination of written patients' records, although they are unable to consent to this examination. In some cases relatives are asked to 'consent' to what is proposed, and do so. It appears that some funding bodies and ethics committees stipulate for consent by a relative where the research participant cannot consent. As a matter of law, such 'consent' is meaningless. It appears that the question of the legality of non-therapeutic research procedures is regularly misunderstood or ignored by those who design, fund and approve the projects.

6.30 A number of our respondents expressed concern about non-invasive research based on observations, photography or videoing of participants (sometimes covertly). We accept that questions of dignity and privacy arise in such situations where the project is not designed to benefit the research participant.

6.31 We suggested in our consultation paper that the balance of expert opinion favours the participation of people unable to consent in even non-therapeutic research projects, subject to strict criteria. The majority of our consultees argued that there is an ethical case for such participation. This case turns on the desirability of eradicating painful and distressing disabilities, where progress can be achieved without harming research subjects . . .

We recommend that research which is unlikely to benefit a participant, or whose benefit is likely to be long delayed, should be lawful in relation to a person without capacity to consent if (1) the research is into an incapacitating condition with which the participant is or may be affected and (2) certain statutory procedures are complied with. (Draft Bill, cl 11(1).)

The Commission, therefore, took the view that one of the essential conditions of non-therapeutic research taking place on an incapable person is that the person has the condition which the research is seeking to alleviate. Nevertheless, as the Law Commission's report noted, non-therapeutic research on incompetent patients does occur and, indeed, the Medical Research Council's guidelines, The Ethical Conduct of Research on the Mentally Incapacitated, 1991, in this respect mirror its Guidance on incompetent minors: such research may be carried out provided the hoped-for knowledge is unprocurable by other means and risk to the subject is no more than minimal. Furthermore, para 24 of the Declaration of Helsinki (see above) expressly acknowledges that this may take place as it is contained within section B, which is not restricted to therapeutic research. It is also anticipated by Art 17(2) of the European Convention on Human Rights and Biomedicine which states that exceptionally, and under condition as that are protectible by law, non-therapeutic research can be carrried out on incapable adults. Nevertheless, it is still pertinent to ask how such research can satisfy the 'best interests' requirement laid down in Re F. Admittedly, the courts have been prepared to construe best interests quite widely in some cases (see especially the discussion of Re Y (An Adult Patient) (Transplant: Bone Marrow)[41]), but only to the extent that some form of benefit can be shown to accrue directly to the individual concerned. The problem stems from the issue discussed above at 10.4.1 where we acknowledged that the therapeutic/non-therapeutic divide is not a distinct dichotomy. Certainly under the MCA 2005 the patient has to have been diagnosed with the condition concerned, but the research does not have to benefit the research subject personally (see s 31[5][b] MCA, 10.3.1.2.2 above).

See Chapter 11 →

---

41 (1996) BMLR 111.

10.4 The Regulation of Research in the UK

Until relatively recently, medical research has been subject to the common law, and clinical trials have been subject to the Medicines Act 1968. However, the enactment of the European Clinical Trials Directive 2001/20 EC prompted the government to issue regulations to govern the conduct of clinical trials. Not all research, however, is concerned with the investigation of medicinal products and research that lies outside this ambit will still be governed by a mixture of the common law, any constraints imposed by ethics committees, and any quasi-statutory guidance from the relevant bodies (see below).

10.4.1 Common law

10.4.1.1 Contract

There are two contractual relations that are relevant to medical research. First, there is the contract between the research subject and the researcher, and secondly, the contract between the sponsor of the research (for example a drug manufacturer), and the researcher, or investigator. Ian Dodds-Smith comments as follows:

Dodds-Smith, I, 'Clinical research'[42]

The sponsor's obligations to the investigator

The contract between the sponsor/manufacturer and the investigator will govern the legal relationship between them. Ideally, to avoid uncertainty and possible unnecessary dispute, the agreement should be in writing and clearly expressed. There is no model format for such contracts – they may be and often are contained in a letter. The overriding concern, however, is that they should be unambiguous and contain all the crucial details relating to the protocol to be adopted, information to be made available about the test product, reporting of adverse drug reactions, the duration of the study, the maintenance of patient confidentiality, the publication of results, liability for injury to subjects and the fee for the study. Under English law, certain conditions are implied additionally into any contract for services. These include that the service will be performed with reasonable care and skill and in a reasonable period. There are also rules under statute which may restrict the ability of the parties to exclude their liability for damages for personal injury caused by negligence.

The sponsor's obligations to the research subject

Contract

The Declaration of Helsinki does not address the matter of how the subject/sponsor relationship might be structured or recorded. In general, the sponsor and a patient subject do not enter into a direct contractual arrangement. However, where studies are to be conducted upon healthy volunteers, a form of contract may and usually will exist. In 1970 the Association of the British Pharmaceutical Industry (ABPI) published a report to which a simple form of written contract was appended. In 1986 the Royal College of Physicians issued a report on healthy volunteer studies in which it advocated the use of a 'simple form of contract' mainly to ensure that the subject would be compensated for any injury occurring during a trial. In the appendix to the report the college provided a checklist of matters which should be considered when drawing up such a contract. In 1988, the ABPI published revised Guidelines for medical experiments in non-patient human volunteers which contained both a model patient information form and draft

---

42 In Dyer, C (ed), *Doctors, Patients and the Law*, Oxford: Blackwell Science, 1992, p 146.

provisions for a volunteer agreement and consent form and stated that all volunteers 'must sign a simple form of agreement' . . . with the sponsor or outside research establishment.

As Dodds-Smith states, in relation to the contract between sponsor and investigator, certain terms are implied into the contract. These terms will also apply to any contract between sponsor and research subject. Although when the patient is receiving NHS treatment, there will not be a contract, a contractual situation must arise, within the NHS as well as elsewhere, in the case of healthy volunteers (in the context of non-therapeutic research), as they are not being treated pursuant to a statutory obligation. Clearly, s2(1) of the Unfair Contract Terms Act 1977 would prevent any such contract excluding liability for damages for negligently caused death or personal injury, and there would be an implied term that the research would be carried out with reasonable skill and care.

Although, for the purposes of the research subject bringing an action for injuries suffered, the contents of the contract may well be important, in the context of the research subject failing to participate, or withdrawing part way through the research, would a court enforce such a contract? The answer must surely be that it is unenforceable from the point of view of the researcher. Damages would be unquantifiable, and an order for specific performance repugnant.

10.4.1.2 Tort

The torts of battery and negligence will apply to those who participate in medical research. These have already been considered in relation to consent, and will be looked at again, in the context of recovering compensation for injuries, see Section 10.5.

10.4.1.3 Criminal law

It is important to recall that battery is a crime as well as a tort, and that statutory criminal offences may apply in the appropriate circumstances. Whilst, in the normal course of medical research, the criminal law would be unlikely to be invoked, note the US case of *Hyman v Jewish Chronic Disease Hospital*,[43] where doctors injected live cancer cells into 22 patients, not only without their consent, but by leading them to believe that the injections were part of their normal treatment. The Medical Association Review Board found the doctors guilty of fraudulent and deceitful conduct, but no criminal proceedings were taken. There is some precedent in English law in the case of *R v Burdee*,[44] where a doctor who had prescribed cold water foot baths and a three-day fast for a sick patient who subsequently died, was convicted of manslaughter. (As has previously been noted, however, something which is experimentation at best, and quackery at worst, is not research in the accepted sense of the term.)

See Chapter 3 →

10.4.2 Statutory provisions in relation to clinical trials

The European Clinical Trials Directive 2001/20 EC governs the regulation of clinical trials of medicines and has been transposed into UK law by the Medicines for Human Use (Clinical Trials) Regulations 2004 which replace the clinical trial provisions of the Medicines Act 1968 and regulations made thereunder. These came into force on 1 May 2004. The Medicines and Healthcare Products Regulatory Agency is the regulatory body that oversees the operation of the Regulations.

The aim of the Directive is to simplify and harmonise the regulation of clinical trials. There are two main aspects to this: the establishment of a clear procedure for dealing with clinical trials and the facilitation of effective co-ordination of clinical trials throughout Europe. Whilst the protection of trial participants is given importance it seems that the advancement of medical research and the

---

43 251 NYS 2d 818 (1964).
44 (1916) 25 Cox 598.

promotion of the internal market in medicinal products are key to the impetus behind the Directive. As well as the regulation of research it also deals with manufacturing standards. For our purposes the important part of the Regulations is Schedule 1 (implementing Art 3(2) of the Directive) and this deals with consent to participation. As far as capable adults are concerned, the conditons are: that the subject has had an interview with the investigator, or another member of the investigating team, in which s/he has been given the opportunity to understand the objectives, risks and inconveniences of the trial and conditions under which it is to be conducted; that he has been informed of his right to withdraw from the trial at any time; that he has given his 'informed consent' to participating and that this can be withdrawn at any time without resulting in detriment; and that he has been given a contact point for further information.

As far as children are concerned, the Schedule provides for a hierarchy of consent on behalf of the child, commencing with a parent or person with parental responsibility. The others are personal legal representatives and professional legal representatives (i.e. someone nominated by the relevant health care provider) but consent can only be taken from these in emergencies. There are similar provisions for incapable adults. Obviously a parent has no relevance in the latter case, qua parent, but the personal legal representative is someone suitable to act as the legal representative by virtue of their relationship with the adult concerned, and who is not connected with the conduct of the trial. The following provisions contained within Schedule 1 relate to the principles of good clinical practice and the protection of clinical trial subjects:

PART 2

CONDITIONS AND PRINCIPLES WHICH APPLY TO ALL CLINICAL TRIALS

Principles based on International Conference on Harmonisation GCP Guideline

1. Clinical trials shall be conducted in accordance with the ethical principles that have their origin in the Declaration of Helsinki, and that are consistent with good clinical practice and the requirements of these Regulations.
2. Before the trial is initiated, foreseeable risks and inconveniences have been weighed against the anticipated benefit for the individual trial subject and other present and future patients. A trial should be initiated and continued only if the anticipated benefits justify the risks.
3. The rights, safety, and well-being of the trial subjects are the most important considerations and shall prevail over interests of science and society .
4. The available non-clinical and clinical information on an investigational medicinal product shall be adequate to support the clinical trial.
5. Clinical trials shall be scientifically sound, and described in a clear, detailed protocol.
6. A trial shall be conducted in compliance with the protocol that has a favourable opinion from an ethics committee.
7. The medical care given to, and medical decisions made on behalf of, subjects shall always be the responsibility of an appropriately qualified doctor or, when appropriate, of a qualified dentist.
8. Each individual involved in conducting a trial shall be qualified by education, training, and experience to perform his or her respective task(s).
9. Subject to the other provisions of this Schedule relating to consent, freely given informed consent shall be obtained from every subject prior to clinical trial participation.
10. All clinical trial information shall be recorded, handled, and stored in a way that allows its accurate reporting, interpretation and verification.
11. The confidentiality of records that could identify subjects shall be protected, respecting the privacy and confidentiality rules in accordance with the requirements of the Data Protection Act 1998 and the law relating to confidentiality.

12. Investigational medicinal products used in the trial shall be –

(a) manufactured or imported, and handled and stored, in accordance with the principles and guidelines of good manufacturing practice, and

(b) used in accordance with the approved protocol.

13. Systems with procedures that assure the quality of every aspect of the trial shall be implemented.

Conditions based on Article 3 of the Directive

14. A trial shall be initiated only if an ethics committee and the licensing authority comes to the conclusion that the anticipated therapeutic and public health benefits justify the risks and may be continued only if compliance with this requirement is permanently monitored.

15. The rights of each subject to physical and mental integrity, to privacy and to the protection of the data concerning him in accordance with the Data Protection Act 1998 are safeguarded.

16. Provision has been made for insurance or indemnity to cover the liability of the investigator and sponsor which may arise in relation to the clinical trial.

PART 3

CONDITIONS WHICH APPLY IN RELATION TO AN ADULT ABLE TO CONSENT OR WHO HAS GIVEN CONSENT PRIOR TO THE ONSET OF INCAPACITY

1. The subject has had an interview with the investigator, or another member of the investigating team, in which he has been given the opportunity to understand the objectives, risks and inconveniences of the trial and the conditions under which it is to be conducted.

2. The subject has been informed of his right to withdraw from the trial at any time.

3. The subject has given his informed consent to taking part in the trial.

4. The subject may, without being subject to any resulting detriment, withdraw from the clinical trial at any time by revoking his informed consent.

5. The subject has been provided with a contact point where he may obtain further information about the trial.

PART 4

CONDITIONS AND PRINCIPLES WHICH APPLY IN RELATION TO A MINOR

Conditions

1. Subject to paragraph 6, a person with parental responsibility for the minor or, if by reason of the emergency nature of the treatment provided as part of the trial no such person can be contacted prior to the proposed inclusion of the subject in the trial, a legal representative for the minor has had an interview with the investigator, or another member of the investigating team, in which he has been given the opportunity to understand the objectives, risks and inconveniences of the trial and the conditions under which it is to be conducted.

2. That person or legal representative has been provided with a contact point where he may obtain further information about the trial.

3. That person or legal representative has been informed of the right to withdraw the minor from the trial at any time.

4. That person or legal representative has given his informed consent to the minor taking part in the trial.

5. That person with parental responsibility or the legal representative may, without the minor being subject to any resulting detriment, withdraw the minor from the trial at any time by revoking his informed consent.

6. The minor has received information according to his capacity of understanding, from staff with experience with minors, regarding the trial, its risks and its benefits.

7. The explicit wish of a minor who is capable of forming an opinion and assessing the information referred to in the previous paragraph to refuse participation in, or to be withdrawn from, the clinical trial at any time is considered by the investigator.

8. No incentives or financial inducements are given –
   (a) to the minor; or
   (b) to a person with parental responsibility for that minor or, as the case may be, the minor's legal representative,
   except provision for compensation in the event of injury or loss.

9. The clinical trial relates directly to a clinical condition from which the minor suffers or is of such a nature that it can only be carried out on minors.

10. Some direct benefit for the group of patients involved in the clinical trial is to be obtained from that trial.

11. The clinical trial is necessary to validate data obtained –
    (a) in other clinical trials involving persons able to give informed consent, or
    (b) by other research methods.

12. The corresponding scientific guidelines of the European Medicines Agency are followed.

Principles

13. Informed consent given by a person with parental responsibility or a legal representative to a minor taking part in a clinical trial shall represent the minor's presumed will.

14. The clinical trial has been designed to minimise pain, discomfort, fear and any other foreseeable risk in relation to the disease and the minor's stage of development.

15. The risk threshold and the degree of distress have to be specially defined and constantly monitored.

16. The interests of the patient always prevail over those of science and society.

PART 5

CONDITIONS AND PRINCIPLES WHICH APPLY IN RELATION TO AN INCAPACITATED ADULT

Conditions

1. The subject's legal representative has had an interview with the investigator, or another member of the investigating team, in which he has been given the opportunity to understand the objectives, risks and inconveniences of the trial and the conditions under which it is to be conducted.

2. The legal representative has been provided with a contact point where he may obtain further information about the trial.

3. The legal representative has been informed of the right to withdraw the subject from the trial at any time.

4. The legal representative has given his informed consent to the subject taking part in the trial.

5. The legal representative may, without the subject being subject to any resulting detriment, withdraw the subject from the trial at any time by revoking his informed consent.

6. The subject has received information according to his capacity of understanding regarding the trial, its risks and its benefits.

7. The explicit wish of a subject who is capable of forming an opinion and assessing the information referred to in the previous paragraph to refuse participation in, or to be withdrawn from, the clinical trial at any time is considered by the investigator.

8. No incentives or financial inducements are given to the subject or their legal representative, except provision for compensation in the event of injury or loss.

9. There are grounds for expecting that administering the medicinal product to be tested in the trial will produce a benefit to the subject outweighing the risks or produce no risk at all.

10. The clinical trial is essential to validate data obtained –
    (a) in other clinical trials involving persons able to give informed consent, or
    (b) by other research methods.

11. The clinical trial relates directly to a life-threatening or debilitating clinical condition from which the subject suffers.

Principles

12. Informed consent given by a legal representative to an incapacitated adult in a clinical trial shall represent that adult's presumed will.

13. The clinical trial has been designed to minimise pain, discomfort, fear and any other foreseeable risk in relation to the disease and the cognitive abilities of the patient.

14. The risk threshold and the degree of distress have to be specially defined and constantly monitored.

15. The interests of the patient always prevail over those of science and society.

A comparison should be made between the conditions placed upon clinical trials concerning adults who lack capacity and the conditions that are contained in the Mental Capacity Act 2005. Put simply conditions are much more stringent in relation to clinical trials, notably in the case of clinical trials the requirement that the trial relates directly to a 'life-threatening or debilitating clinical condition from which the subject suffers'.[45] Whilst conditions such as Alzeimer's disease would be covered by this, mere mental impairment would not.

10.4.3 UK specific regulation

This is governed by the Medicines for Human Use (Clinical Trials) Regulations 2004 SI 2001/1031 and, in England, the Governance Arrangements for NHS Research Ethics Committees and the Research Governance Framework for Health and Social Care, 2001, as amended in 2005. There are very similar framework documents for Northern Ireland, Scotland and Wales. The ethics of medical research is regulated via independent Research Ethics Committees in accordance with the Declaration of Helsinki states as one of its basic principles that the design and performance of all research trials should be subject to scrutiny by 'a specially appointed ethical review committee which must be independent of the investigator, the sponsor or any other kind of undue influence' (para 15 at section 10.2.1 above). In addition to these, the Research Ethics Committee must consider other regulatory conditions such as the Mental Capacity Act 2005 and the Human Tissue Act 2004.

The 2001 guidance deals with the composition of a Research Ethics Committee as follows:

Department of Health, *Governance Arrangements for NHS Research Ethics Committees*, 2001

6   Composition of an REC

6.1 An REC should have sufficient members to guarantee the presence of a quorum (see 6.11) at each meeting. The maximum should be 18 members. This should allow for a sufficiently

---

45 See para 11 above.

broad range of experience and expertise, so that the scientific, clinical and methodological aspects of a research proposal can be reconciled with the welfare of research participants, and with broader ethical implications.

6.2 Overall the REC should have a balanced age and gender distribution. Members should be drawn from both sexes and from a wide range of age groups. Every effort should also be made to recruit members from black and ethnic minority backgrounds, as well as people with disabilities. This should apply to both expert and lay members.

6.3 RECs should be constituted to contain a mixture of 'expert' and 'lay' members. At least three members must be independent of any organisation where research under ethical review is likely to take place.

Expert members

6.4 The 'expert' members of the committee shall be chosen to ensure that the REC has the following expertise:

  relevant methodological and ethical expertise in:
  - clinical research;
  - non-clinical research;
  - qualitative or other research methods applicable to health services, social science and social care research,
  clinical practice including:
  - hospital and community staff (medical, nursing and other);
  - general practice,
  statistics relevant to research.

Lay members

6.5 At least one third of the membership shall be 'lay' members who are independent of the NHS, either as employees or in a non-executive role, and whose primary personal or professional interest is not in a research area.

6.6 The 'lay' membership can include non-medical clinical staff who have not practised their profession for a period of at least five years.

6.7 At least half of the 'lay' members must be persons who are not, and never have been, either health or social care professionals, and who have never been involved in carrying out research involving human participants, their tissue or data.[46]

 SELF-TEST QUESTION

Do you think that research participants should be able to sue REC members if they suffer damage as a result of participating in medical research that has been approved by a REC?

It can be questioned as to exactly what sort of experience is required of an REC member, as it raises the question of the very function of the committee. The Department of Health guidance states baldly that the purpose of the committee is 'to consider the ethics of proposed research projects

---

46 London: DOH, 2001.

within the NHS'. Matters that they should have regard to, as a minimum, in doing so are as follows:

Department of Health, *Governance Arrangements for NHS Research Ethics Committees*, 2001

Requirements for a favourable opinion

9.12 Before giving a favourable opinion, the REC should be adequately reassured about the following issues as applicable:

9.13 *Scientific design and conduct of the study*

    a   the appropriateness of the study design in relation to the objectives of the study, the statistical methodology (including sample size calculation where appropriate), and the potential for reaching sound conclusions with the smallest number of research participants

    b   the justification of predictable risks and inconveniences weighed against the anticipated benefits for the research participants, other present and future patients, and the concerned communities

    c   the justification for use of control arms in trials, (whether placebo or active comparator), and the randomisation process to be used

    d   criteria for prematurely withdrawing research participants

    e   criteria for suspending or terminating the research as a whole

    f   the adequacy of provisions made for monitoring and auditing the conduct of the research, including the constitution of a data safety monitoring committee (DSMC)

    g   the adequacy of the research site, including the supporting staff, available facilities, and emergency procedures. For multi-centre research, these locality issues will be considered separately from the ethical review of the research proposal itself

    h   the manner in which the results of the research will be reported and published.

9.14 *Recruitment of research participants*

    a   the characteristics of the population from which the participants will be drawn (including gender, age, literacy, culture, economic status and ethnicity) and the justification for any decisions made in this respect

    b   the means by which initial contact and recruitment is to be conducted

    c   the means by which full information is to be conveyed to potential research participants or their representatives

    d   inclusion criteria for research participants

    e   exclusion criteria for research participants.

9.15 *Care and protection of research participants*

    a   the safety of any intervention to be used in the proposed research

    b   the suitability of the investigator(s)'s qualifications and experience for ensuring good conduct of the proposed study

    c   any plans to withdraw or withhold standard therapies or clinical management protocols for the purpose of the research, and the justification for such action

    d   the health and social care to be provided to research participants during and after the course of the research

    e   the adequacy of health and social supervision and psychosocial support for the research participants

    f   steps to be taken if research participants voluntarily withdraw during the course of the research g   the criteria for extended access to, the emergency use of, and/or the compassionate use of study products

h   the arrangements, if appropriate, for informing the research participant's general practitioner, including procedures for seeking the participant's consent to do so

i   a description of any plans to make the study product available to the research participants following the research

j   a description of any financial costs to research participants

k   the rewards and compensations (if any) for research participants (including money, services and/or gifts)

l   whether there is provision in proportion to the risk for compensation/treatment in the case of injury/disability/death of a research participant attributable to participation in the research; the insurance and indemnity arrangements

m   the nature and size of any grants, payments or other reward to be made to any researchers or research hosts

n   circumstances that might lead to conflicts of interest that may affect the independent judgement of the researcher(s).

9.16 *Protection of research participants' confidentiality*

a   a description of the persons who will have access to personal data of the research participants, including medical records and biological samples

b   the measures taken to ensure the confidentiality and security of personal information concerning research participants

c   the extent to which the information will be anonymised

d   how the data/samples will be obtained, and the purposes for which they will be used

e   how long the data/samples will be kept

f   to which countries, if any, the data/samples will be sent

g   the adequacy of the process for obtaining consent for the above.

9.17 *Informed consent process*

a   a full description of the process for obtaining informed consent, including the identification of those responsible for obtaining consent, the time-frame in which it will occur, and the process for ensuring consent has not been withdrawn

b   the adequacy, completeness and understandability of written and oral information to be given to the research participants, and, when appropriate, their legally acceptable representatives

c   clear justification for the intention to include in the research individuals who cannot consent, and a full account of the arrangements for obtaining consent or authorization for the participation of such individuals

d   assurances that research participants will receive information that becomes available during the course of the research relevant to their participation (including their rights, safety and well being)

e   the provisions made for receiving and responding to queries and complaints from research participants or their representatives during the course of a research project.

9.18 *Community considerations*

a   the impact and relevance of the research on the local community and on the concerned communities from which the research participants are drawn

b   the steps which had been taken to consult with the concerned communities during the course of designing the research c   the extent to which the research contributes to capacity building, such as the enhancement of local healthcare, research, and the ability to respond to public health needs

   d   a description of the availability and affordability of any successful study product to the concerned communities following the research

   e   the manner in which the results of the research will be made available to the research participants and the concerned communities.[47]

Some might argue that the 'expert' committee members will tend to dominate discussion and be instrumental in the final decision.[48]

Regulation 12 of the Medicines for Human Use (Clinical Trials) Regulations 2004 prohibits anyone from commencing or conducting a clinical trial, recruiting subjects or advertising to recruit subjects to be in a trial unless certain contitions are met. Specifically, such a trial can only be started or conducted if it has been authorised by the Medicines and Healthcare Products Regulatory Agency and approved by an ethics committee.

What would be the legal consequences of a breach of the above guidelines? Certainly, any researcher employed by the NHS who was in breach would be liable to dismissal or other form of discipline, but would a patient or healthy volunteer have any right of redress? It is likely that the breach would be akin to a breach of statutory duty, in the sense that it would not necessarily give rise to a private law right in itself. However, if the patient suffered injury, then failure to obtain REC approval might point towards negligence, although the problem of causation would remain. Another problem, highlighted by the case involving Mrs Moffit,[49] arises where, though initially obtaining approval in the proper way, a researcher fails to keep the Committee apprised of changes in the execution of a project.

As will be seen from para 3.1, ethical approval for non-NHS research is not specifically required. However, even if the private sector can, in theory, ignore RECs, in practice, because of the effect upon insurance and legal liability generally (not to mention publication), researchers will want to obtain approval of their projects, and para 3.2 makes provision for this. Furthermore, as far as clinical trials are concerned, Regulation 12 of the Medicines for Human Use (Clinical Trials) Regulations 2004 applies to non-NHS trials.

Members of RECs are indemnified by the NHS in respect of any action brought by a research subject alleging that they have been damaged as a result of the decision of the ethics committee, as long as they have not acted in bad faith, or been deceitful or grossly negligent. Damage can of course include damage that has occurred as a result of breach of, say, confidentiality. In the vast majority of cases, any injury they have received will be as a result of the execution of the research, eg wrong dosages, keeping patients in the research when they have experienced an adverse reaction, inadequate monitoring and so on. However, it is possible that approval is given to research that does not have sufficient safeguards attached to it, eg specific 'stopping rules' that require the participant to be taken out of a trial at clinically appropriate times, and if damage results the ethics committee might be liable. Of course, in order to show that the committee has been negligent, there has to be a duty owed to the research participants in the first place, and the usual tort considerations apply, which principally relate to the proximity of the relationship and the issue of whether it is just and reasonable to impose a duty in the first place. Given the protective remit of the REC it would be hard to argue that no duty was owed. Pattinson endorses this view but goes on to say:

---

47 London: DoH, 2001.
48 See McNeill, PM, *The Ethics and Politics of Human Experimentation*, Cambridge: Press Syndicate of the University of Cambridge, 1993.
49 See 10.3.1.1, above.

Pattinson, SD, *Medical Law and Ethics*[50]

. . . the majority of REC approvals of research protocols are not straightforwardly analogous to those situations where assumptions of responsibility have previously been imposed, as protocols do not usually identify specific individual participants and the participants might not even be aware of the existence of the REC. Consider, for example, *Kent v Griffith* [2001] QB 36, where the ambulance service was held to owe a duty to provide an ambulance for the claimant within a reasonable time *because* it had accepted a call dealing with a *named individual* and had thereby *discouraged others* from providing alternative means of transport to the hospital. Thus, while there are clearly circumstances where a duty of care will be owed, the courts are unlikely to impose a blanket duty. In any event . . . proving breach and causation are onerous obstacles to overcome.

It has been stated by Christopher Roy-Toole that, under the European Clinical Trials Directive, ethics committees have an obligation to ensure the *legality* of the proposed trial as well as giving ethical approval:

Roy-Toole, C, 'Illegality in the research protocol: the duty of research ethics committees under the 2001 Clinical Trials Directive'[51]

There is no value in an ethics committee unless it can and does protect the research subject from the illegality of research, and especially if the legal rights of the subject are violated by it. The expression of a legal opinion by an ethics committee would be the clearest way of protecting these rights. Instead, if that committee has concerns about the legality of the research, [the Governance Arrangements for Research Ethics Committees] seems to contemplate a situation in which it can merely recommend that a researcher obtain legal advice in order to clarify the matter . . . If the committee gives a favourable opinion before the researcher has obtained that legal advice, it has expressly endorsed research that might be illegal. Furthermore, what is the committee supposed to do if a researcher resumes his application armed with a sponsor's legal advice that the committee knows to be wrong?

. . . if an ethics committee rejects a protocol for its illegality, paragraph 9.11 [of the Governance Arrangements] would expose the committee to the allegation that it had gone beyond its proper function in providing what is, in effect, a legal opinion.

. . .

Article 2 of the 2001 Directive defines the legal duty of the REC. It stipulates that it is their responsibility to protect the rights, safety and wellbeing of human subjects involved in a trial. It is obvious and unassailable from the context in which it appears that this referece to 'rights' includes the legal rights of the subject. What else could it mean?

Arguably, Roy-Toole overstates the case. The phrase in the Directive could be referring to the rights of the patient in terms of the right to have any research in which s/he participates subjected to ethical scrutiny. The expression 'rights' is much more likely to mean rights under the various international and national agreements such as the Declaration of Helsinki which constitute general statements and the rights which a REC are meant to safeguard when they ethically review the research. In any event, Roy-Toole does not adequately distinguish between the rights of the participant, even if these are interpreted as all-encompassing legal rights, and the general concept of 'legality' which is much wider. For example a piece of research could be ethical but for a reason

---

50 London: Sweet & Maxwell, 2006.
51 (2008) 4(3) *Research Ethics Review* 111–16.

relating to, say, the terms of a lease the research could not lawfully be carried out on the premises where it is proposed to do it (clinical trials in non-NHS establishments have to be approved by a REC). The fact that research can be entirely lawful but unethical just reinforces this point. A good example of this is the availability of insurance to provide compensation if the participant is injured. Biggs states:

Biggs, H, *Healthcare Research Ethics and Law*[52]

Under the Clinical Trials Regulations it is a requirement that all clinical trials include provision for 'insurance or indemnity to cover the liability of the investigator and sponsor which may arise in relation to the clinical trial' . . . This is incorporated into reg15(5) of the Clinical Trials Regulations which stipulates that:

> In preparing its opinion, the committee shall consider, in particular, the following matters:
>
> . . .
>
> (i) provision for indemnity or compensation in the event of injury or death attributable to the clinical trial;
>
> (j) any insurance or indemnity to cover the liability of the investigator or sponsor. . .

Clearly, it is easy for an REC to establish the existence of insurance (but not, of course, that it will be renewed if it expires before the research has been completed), but not so easy to satisfy itself that the insurance is adequate. In the case of the large pharmaceutical companies this is not of great concern because they will have the resources to pay regardless of insurance, but some of the companies are relatively small. As was seen above in relation to the Northwick Park research, the company set up to develop the drug became insolvent (See section 10.1.4.2 above).

 SELF-TEST QUESTION

Do you think that the regulation of medical research might stifle innovation that could result in much needed medical advances?

10.5 Compensation for Injuries Arising from Research

10.5.1 Compensation at common law

A patient who is entered in a clinical trial without giving his properly informed consent may arguably have an action against the doctor in battery; this would perhaps be most likely in the case of a volunteer involved in non-therapeutic research. Failing an action in battery, however, an action in negligence may lie and could arise in two main ways, albeit in both cases the subject must show some tangible injury. In the first case, the trial itself may be properly conducted, but the doctor/researcher (whilst providing enough basic facts to escape an action in battery) fall below his duty of care in the amount of information he divulges to his subject, and the latter is able to show that, if properly informed, he would not have participated in the trial.

In the second case, the trial itself, in terms of design or execution, may turn out to be defective in some way. An additional issue which arises here is whether, to the extent that the defect was

---

52 London: Routledge, 2010.

something which the REC, in approving the trial, should have noticed, the members of that Committee could be joined as defendants in any action. The standard terms and conditions of appointment of REC members now state that the Strategic Health Authority who will take full responsibility for members' actions in the course of the performance of their duties as members of the REC excepting actions taken in bad faith, wilful default or gross negligence.

10.5.2 'No fault' compensation?

Whatever form his action takes, the injured research subject (like his 'pure' patient counterpart) will have substantial hurdles to overcome, both in relation to the breach of duty question and causation. However, an ethical argument for treating research subjects more favourably than other patients injured in the course of treatment is that, just as society at large stands to benefit from any advances in medical knowledge that the research may secure, so it should bear the costs of mishaps along the way. Accordingly, it has frequently been urged that those injured in the course of medical research should be compensated on a 'no fault' basis. A direct analogy can be invoked here with persons injured in the course of a community-wide vaccination programme, who are entitled to 'no fault' compensation under the Vaccine Damage Payments Act 1979:

1   Payments to persons severely disabled by vaccination

(1)   If, on consideration of a claim, the Secretary of State is satisfied–
   (a)   that a person is, or was immediately before his death, severely disabled as a result of vaccination against any of the diseases to which this Act applies; and
   (b)   that the conditions of entitlement which are applicable in accordance with s 2 below are fulfilled,
   he shall in accordance with this Act make a payment of the relevant statutory sum to or for the benefit of that person or to his personal representatives.

In its 1978 Report, the Royal Commission on Civil Liability and Compensation for Personal Injury (the Pearson Committee), recommended that a similar scheme of compensation be established for injuries in the course of medical research. Whilst this recommendation has not been acted upon by Parliament, the DoH's REC Guidelines mention the existence of provision for *ex gratia* compensation as a relevant factor in the sanctioning of trials (para 9.15(1)).

In every case, of course, it remains necessary for the research subject to demonstrate that his injuries were caused by participation in the trial. This may be by no means easy to do: after all, research will be taking place precisely because the causal properties of the new treatment (including its propensity to do harm) are unclear. Sometimes, to be sure, the claimant's case will be a strong one, for example where everyone in the trial is similarly affected. However, where the claimant's injury is a more isolated occurrence, a court may well take the view that some unknown, independent cause was, just as likely, at work.[53]

10.5.3 Drug-induced injury

One area in which the use of research subjects has attracted particular attention is in relation to the testing of new drugs and pharmaceutical products. There is a heightened sense here (engendered both by the power imbalance between subject and drug company and by the latter's pre-eminently economic motivation), that volunteers and patients participating in such trials require protection.

---

53   See, in this regard, the case of *Loveday v Renton* [1990] 1 Med LR 117 referred to in Ch 6, above.

In fact, the Association of the British Pharmaceutical Industry, has issued Guidelines, that recommended that *ex gratia* compensation should be paid in cases where injury results. These ABPI Guidelines are echoed by guidance at EU level.[54]

Finally, in cases of drug-induced injury, the subject may also wish to bring an action under the Consumer Protection Act 1987. The issues in relation to the use of this Act have been addressed in Chapter 6, above.

Summary of Key Points

1. The need to scrutinise medical research must be examined in the light of the importance of scientific research and the public expectation of medical advances.
2. The nature of medical research methodologies is important in deciding on what is ethically permissible, in particular the use of placebos and randomised controlled trials.
3. Human rights play a central role in medical research, in particular in the Declaration of Helsinki.
4. It is important to examine the distinctions between therapeutic and non-therapeutic research and innovative treatment.
5. Legal duties are owed to research participants, and these will vary according to whether the research is therapeutic or non-therapeutic.
6. The consent aspects of research must be examined in relation to research on children and incapable adults and also the differences between consent in therapeutic and consent in non-therapeutic research.
7. Medical research is heavily regulated at both the European and the domestic level, and in the composition and functions/duties of research ethics committees (RECs)
8. There are difficulties in awarding compensation for injuries caused by research if it is not caused by general negligence principles.

Further Reading

Biggs, H, *Healthcare Research Ethics and Law*, London: Routledge, 2010.

Cheung, P, *Public Trust in Medical Research*, Oxford: Radcliffe, 2008.

Foster, C, *The Ethics of Medical Research on Humans*, London: Cambridge University Press, 2001.

Morrison, D, 'A holistic approach to clinical and research decision-making', (2005) Medical Law Review 13:45.

Plomer, A, *The Law and Ethics of Medical Research: International Bioethics and Human Rights*, London: Cavendish Publishing, 2004.

---

54 See *Detailed Guidance for the Request for Authorisation of a Clinical Trial on a Medicinal Product for Human use to the Competent Authorities, Notification of Substantial Amendments and Declaration of the End of the Trial* (2010).

Chapter 11

Organ Transplantation

Chapter Contents

11.1 Introduction

Organ transplantation is undoubtedly one of the triumphs of modern medicine. The procedure has become increasingly routine as a means of saving and improving the quality of the lives of thousands of people each year. The history of this programme, and the manner in which it has expanded to encompass an increasing variety of organs and other body tissue, has been chronicled by David Lamb:

Lamb, D, *Organ Transplants and Ethics*[1]

The idea of taking bone, skin, or organs from one person and transplanting them into another has been a subject of fascination and intrigue since earliest times. Yet until the 20th century the dream of creating a healthy whole person by transplantation remained in the realm of mythology and the miraculous. Early attempts at blood transfusion met with no success until knowledge of different blood types and their mutual compatibility or incompatibility was discovered. This meant that many attempts at blood transfusion during the 18th century resulted in charges of homicide before several European courts outlawed the practice. However, blood transfusion was widely used in the 1914–18 war when blood banks were created to store blood. This, perhaps, was one of the most important features in the early stages of the history of transplantation. . . .

Transplantation of non-vital organs has steadily increased during the 20th century. Skin grafts began in the late 1920s. This procedure is usually applied as a temporary measure in cases of burns. Recent experiments with cultured skin, however, suggest that procurement from donors may one day be unnecessary. Under appropriate conditions skin can be stored and there are now skin and bone banks, where bone is stored for treatment of the skeletal system. . . .

The modern transplant era, however, began with the transplantation of non-regenerating vital organs in the 1950s, but its antecedents can be traced back to the turn of the century when Dr Alexis Carrel and Dr Charles C Guthrie developed the technique of suturing blood vessels. Then, in 1902, an Austrian surgeon, Dr Emmerick Ullman, removed a kidney from a dog and kept it functioning in the body of another dog for a few days. The eventual failure of this transplant revealed the problem of rejection, and it was discovered in further experiments that successful transplants depend on a close genetic resemblance between donor and recipient . . .

The major breakthrough in understanding rejection had to wait until Dr Peter Medawar, winner of the 1960 Nobel Prize, explained how the body's immunisation system recognises foreign bodies that enter it by means of markers or antigens, and then rejects foreign matter by means of the production of antibodies. This knowledge led to the development of tissue-typing, where the donor's and recipient's tissues are examined with a view to compatibility. . . . Throughout the 1960s and 1970s drugs were developed which lessened the organism's ability to develop antibodies. But many of these had the unfortunate effect of weakening the recipient's immune system. However, a major breakthrough occurred in 1983 when a Swiss pharmaceutical company produced Cyclosporin, which selectively inhibits the rejection of foreign tissues without damaging their ability to combat viruses and bacteria. The ability to control tissue rejection marks the transition from the era of transplantation as an experimental therapy to the era of organ transplantation as routine therapy.

---

1 London: Routledge, 1990.

However, despite compelling evidence that such transplants are not only of significant therapeutic benefit to the majority of recipients but highly cost effective (in allowing savings in other, more expensive forms of treatment, for example, dialysis), this is an area which remains fraught with ethical difficulty. This is especially so as the demand for donor organs continues markedly to outstrip supply. As New *et al* note:

New, B, *et al, A Question of Give and Take*[2]

The transplanting of organs from one human to another is a medical intervention which 50 years ago would have seemed a suitable topic for a science fiction novel. And yet, in the 1990s, kidney transplants are the treatment of choice for end-stage renal disease, and heart and liver transplants offer the only chance of life for thousands of people across the world with chronic heart or liver failure. It is an operation which attracts intense media attention, particularly when children's lives are at stake. However, the reason for such attention is often particularly poignant, involving a race against time for a suitable donor.

The legal framework within which transplantation takes place – the general law as to the removal, retention and use of human materials – was subject to important review and change in the form of the Human Tissue Act 2004, which entered force in 2006. The background to the Act, which again illustrates the sensitivity of this whole area of medical activity, is set out in the explanatory notes issued by the Department of Health:

Explanatory Notes to the Human Tissue Act 2004[3]

4. The purpose of the Act is to provide a consistent legislative framework for issues relating to whole body donation and the taking, storage and use of human organs and tissue. It will make consent the fundamental principle underpinning the lawful storage and use of human bodies, body parts, organs and tissue and the removal of material from the bodies of deceased persons. It will set up an over-arching authority which is intended to rationalise existing regulation of activities like transplantation and anatomical examination, and will introduce regulation of other activities like *post mortem* examinations, and the storage of human material for education, training and research. It is intended to achieve a balance between the rights and expectations of individuals and families, and broader considerations, such as the importance of research, education, training, pathology and public health surveillance to the population as a whole.

5. The Act arose from concern raised by events at Bristol Royal Infirmary and the Royal Liverpool Children's Hospital (Alder Hey) 1999–2000. The *Kennedy* and *Redfern* inquiries at these hospitals established that organs and tissue from children who had died had often been removed, stored and used without proper consent. A subsequent census by the Chief Medical Officer for England (2000) and the *Isaacs Report* (2003) showed that storage and use of organs and tissue from both adults and children without proper consent has been widespread in the past. It also became clear that the current law in this area was not comprehensive, nor as clear and consistent as it might be for professionals or for the families involved . . .

In this chapter our main focus will remain the law as it pertains to organ transplants (although at times we shall touch upon wider issues arising from the use of human material). In sections 11.2

---

2   London: Kings Fund Institute, 1994.
3   London: Department of Health, Crown Copyright, 2004.

to 11.4, we look at the various sources from which organs may be obtained, including live donors and deceased human donors, and the ethical and legal issues raised in each case. In section 11.5 we then consider the (relatively novel) legal problem of what status to accord to extracted body parts, before addressing the rights of the donee of such material in section 11.6. Lastly, in section 11.7, we examine possible measures of law reform that aim to increase the number of organs available for transplantation.

11.2 Transplants from Living Donors

11.2.1 Background

The world's first successful kidney transplant, which took place in Boston in 1954, involved a live donation between identical twins. Indeed, until the development of powerful new immuno-suppressant drugs in the early 1980s, live donation between close relatives was preferred in order to reduce the chance of organ rejection by the donee. Although, since then, live donations have decreased as a proportion of total organ transplants (2008–09 statistics from 'NHS Blood and Transport' show that in the UK live donors accounted for just over a quarter of solid organ transplants), the numbers have been rising in actual terms: that year there were 961 such transplants, an increase of 12 per cent over the previous year.[4] Moreover, certain tissues, such as bone marrow and skin, are invariably obtained from live donors.

The major ethical issue here is similar to that considered in the last chapter in relation to medical research, ie how far is it permissible to expose a person to harm, or the risk of harm, in order to benefit another? Just as in the case of research, the question exposes a conflict between two differing systems of moral philosophy. As Price and Garwood-Gowers observe:

Price, DPT and Garwood-Gowers, A, 'Transplantation from minors: are children other people's medicine?'[5]

By virtue of the fact that removal of the material from the donor is primarily for the prospective benefit of another individual, the whole issue of living donation of body materials for transplantation raises starkly the conflict between the two fundamental philosophical theories, deontological theory and consequentialist theory. Few areas of law highlight this conflict as keenly as deontological theory, of which Immanuel Kant is the prime exponent, which seeks to guide our actions by reference to overriding moral imperatives and insists that as part of a respect for persons their intrinsic moral worth dictates that they should not be used merely as a means to another's ends. By contrast, consequentialist approaches, of which utilitarianism is the pre-eminent example, attempt to judge the rightness or wrongness of an action according to the consequences which flow from it. The action which maximises happiness and minimises suffering is the preferred one. Clearly, on a utilitarian calculus the pendulum swings further in favour of donation than on a deontological approach in so far as the risks from donating even a paired organ are generally fairly modest, whereas transplanting such an organ has the potential to improve the quality (and duration) of life of the recipient dramatically.

The Kantian approach, with its emphasis on the primacy of human autonomy, may well be preferred here. On the other hand, as suggested in Chapter 1, the conflict between the two systems

---

4   See www.organdonation.nhs.uk/ukt/statistics/transplant_activity_report/current_activity_reports/ukt/2008_09/transplant_activity_uk_2008-09.pdf.
5   (1995) 1 *Contemporary Issues in the Law* 1.

largely disappears once it is realised that any plausible form of utilitarianism must also accord great weight to individual autonomy (albeit as an instrumental rather than intrinsic value): a society in which persons could have their organs forcibly extracted for the benefit of others would be a perilous and miserable one indeed.

That having been said, an interesting question concerns how far autonomy in this area should be completely unfettered. This is relevant where a person actively wishes to donate an organ even though the consequences to them will be serious harm or death. The Nuffield Council on Bioethics has expressed its conclusions on this matter as follows:

Nuffield Council on Bioethics, *Human Tissue: Ethical and Legal Issues*[6]

6.4 We identify the avoidance and limitation of injury as a basic requirement for any type of use of human tissue to be ethically acceptable. Avoidance and limitation of injury can be seen as expressing a central element of the undefined, yet widely endorsed, demand for respect for the human body and for respect for human dignity. In paras 6.7–6.16 we identify and elaborate this basic requirement which makes types of use of human tissue ethically acceptable.

6.5 We note, however, that the avoidance and limitation of injury is a complex requirement, and that in certain circumstances, injury can be avoided or limited only by inflicting injury. In our view, the only circumstance in which inflicting injury is acceptable is when it is done to avoid greater injury. It is this that justifies much medical treatment, and action taken in self defence and in other situations. This principle is also useful in evaluating proposed uses of human tissue.

6.6 Although we identify the avoidance and limitation of injury as basic to acceptable use of human tissue, there are other important considerations. For example, consent of those from whom tissue is taken (patient, donor) or of relatives (post mortem) is important. Consent, however, is not the primary consideration. In particular, consent cannot justify injury: for example, killing or maiming cannot be justified by the victim being willing . . .

Avoidance and limitation of injury

6.7 It is not easy to state the underlying rationale for viewing these and other sorts of action as unacceptable. The difficulty is in part that many people see these actions as wrong, repugnant or repellent for multiple reasons, about some of which there is no agreement. The most widely accepted reasons, however, often stress that these sorts of action fail to respect others or to accord them dignity, that they injure human beings by treating them as things, as less than human, as objects for use. Although all these phrases are vague, there is considerable agreement about a central range of injurious activity that would constitute disrespect for human beings and for human dignity . . .

A related issue, touched upon in section 11.7 below, is how far a person should be entitled to benefit financially from the provision of his or her body parts?

11.2.2 The position at common law

11.2.2.1 The capable donor and the limits of consent

As a minimum, the donor must, where adult and capable, always consent to the removal of an organ. This is simply an application of the general rule that the consent of such a person is needed

---

6   London: Nuffield Council on Bioethics, 1995.

to any medical procedure. In this context, however, there may well be doubts about one of the preconditions for valid consent being present, namely freedom from coercion or undue influence. This is especially so in the vast majority of cases where the donation is between two members of the same family. As we saw in Chapter 3, the Court of Appeal was obliged to consider the effect of institutionalised power relationships upon the reality of consent in the case of *Freeman v Home Office* (No 2).[7] Nevertheless, there is a suspicion that, in the case of related live transplants, the courts do not wish to get involved in determining such matters, and are instead leaving the question to the doctors.

See Chapter 3 ➡

Be that as it may, a further question long unresolved at judicial level was whether the removal of an organ for transplant by a surgeon would in any event remain a criminal assault, ie *notwithstanding* the donor's consent. Writing in 1970, Gerald Dworkin commented on this issue as follows:

Dworkin, G, 'The law relating to organ transplantation in England'[8]

. . . [M]any surgical operations are *prima facie* unlawful. Without further justification not only would operations be criminal acts, but they would also be unlawful in the civil law and surgeons might be liable to pay compensation for the consequences of their acts, even though they had exercised all reasonable care. What are the criteria, then, which convert unlawful acts into lawful surgical operations? In some countries the criminal codes absolve from responsibility persons who perform in good faith and with reasonable care and skill a surgical operation upon another person, with his consent and for his benefit, if the performance of the operation is reasonable in the circumstances. No such provision appears in any United Kingdom legislation but it is clear, of course, that surgery, within limits, is a perfectly legal activity. Sir James Fitzjames Stephen formulated the general proposition that 'everyone has a right to consent to the infliction of any bodily injury in the nature of a surgical operation upon himself' and stated that although he knew of no authority for this, the existence of surgery as a profession assumed its truth.

Dworkin suggested four conditions that would need to be satisfied for surgery in general, and donor-organ removal in particular, to be lawful:

(i) *The patient must give a full, free and informed consent.* The importance of consent cannot be overemphasised . . . It is clear that, in any common law jurisdiction, the general principle is that a patient should be informed of all the material facts relating to the operation which would enable a reasonable person to weigh up the risks and benefits and arrive at a rational decision whether or not to undergo the operation. Also, there should be no unfair pressure upon the patient which induces him to give his consent in spite of all the risks.

(ii) *The operation must be therapeutic: it must be expressly for the patient's benefit.* The major distinguishing feature between surgical operations and unlawful mutilation is, of course, that all surgical operations are allegedly in the medical interests of the patient. Coke refers to a case in 1603 where 'a young and lustie rogue prevailed upon a friend to cut off his left hand, so that he might be better able to beg'. Both were found guilty of the crime of maim; today, they would also be criminally liable. In the criminal codes of some countries, the provisions concerning surgical operations expressly state that they must be for the patient's benefit; in other countries this, until recently, has been accepted as being obvious.

---

7 [1984] 1 All ER 1036.
8 (1970) 33 MLR 353.

(iii) *There must be lawful justification.* This is a relatively unexplored and open ended requirement. Ethical and social questions are more relevant here and the courts may occasionally use this rubric to extend the law to meet new circumstances. Most surgical operations
are lawful . . . There are other surgical operations, only arguably of therapeutic benefit to
the patient, where the courts nevertheless may be tempted to emphasise their lawful
justification. It is unlikely that the courts would condemn circumcision as unlawful. No
doubt the ritual circumcision of Jewish infants could be upheld on grounds of religious
toleration, although circumcision for non-religious reasons would have to be accepted on
wider public policy grounds.

(iv) Generally, the operation must be performed by a person with appropriate medical skills . . .

It is suggested that, rather than each being necessary in its own right, condition (ii) would tend
now to be regarded as a particular application of the more general principle contained in (iii). In
the present context (as opposed to therapeutic surgery), it is all-important to look at the reason
why the operation is taking place: removal for transplantation is a socially recognised good and is
lawfully justified; removal for other purposes, for example, because the person whose organ it was
wanted to taste it, would remain a battery. A further requirement, given that no therapeutic benefit
will accrue to the donor, appears to be that such removal not expose the donor to an unreasonable
amount of harm (or a significant risk thereof). In this regard, the media reported in February 1996
that doctors had refused the request of a father that his remaining kidney be transplanted into his
chronically ill son and he be placed on dialysis instead. He had previously given up his first kidney
to his other son.

It follows *a fortiori* from what has just been said that the law will not sanction the removal of
vital organs where the consequence for the donor will be death. In his above article Gerald Dworkin
cites the comment, made extra-judicially by Edmund Davies LJ to the effect that he would:

. . . be surprised if a surgeon were successfully sued for trespass to the person or convicted of
causing bodily harm to one of full age and intelligence who freely consented to act as donor
always provided that the operation did not present unreasonable risk to the donor's life or
health. That proviso is essential. A man may declare himself ready to die for another, but the
surgeon must not take him at his word.[9]

In such a case, the surgeon would be guilty of murder (or, at the very least, manslaughter). For this
reason, transplants involving live donors are generally limited to tissues such as bone marrow,
blood, and (more recently) liver lobes, which are all capable of regenerating; or kidneys, of which
most people have a 'spare'. The only exception relates to so called 'domino transplants' of hearts
which may occur following the donor's own receipt of a heart-lung transplant.

11.2.2.2 The incapable donor

The legal position, until quite recently, was less clear in relation to the lawfulness of using incapable
adults as donors. Such persons are by definition incapable of giving their consent; rather, as the
House of Lords made clear in its decision in *Re F (Mental Patient: Sterilisation)*,[10] they may be subjected
to medical intervention only in so far as the procedure is in their best interests. Can donating an
organ be regarded as in the donor's (as opposed to the donee's) best interests? An important US
case in point is *Strunk v Strunk*,[11] where an affirmative answer was given by the Kentucky Court of

---

9 'A Legal Look at Transplants', 633 Proc Roy Soc Med, Vol 62, July 1969.
10 [1990] 2 AC 1; this case is discussed in Ch 4.
11 445 SW 2d 145 (1969).

Appeals: it authorised a kidney transplant from Jerry, a 27-year-old man with a mental age of six, to his 28-year-old brother after hearing psychiatric evidence of the 'extremely traumatic effect' his brother's death would have upon him.

The question subsequently arose for determination by an English court in the case of *Re Y (An Adult Patient) (Transplant: Bone Marrow)*:

Re Y (Adult Patient) (Transplant: Bone Marrow)[12]

Miss Y was 25 years old and had been severely mentally and physically disabled from birth. She had lived in care since the age of 10. Her sister, aged 36, who suffered from pre-leukaemic bone marrow disorder, sought a declaration that it would be lawful to perform blood tests and possible bone marrow extraction upon Miss Y, despite the latter's inability to consent:

Connell J: The taking of blood tests and the harvesting of bone marrow from the defendant who is incapable of giving informed consent would amount to assaults upon the defendant and would therefore be illegal unless shown to be in the best interests of the defendant and therefore lawful.

The test to be applied in a case such as this is to ask whether the evidence shows that it is in the best interests of the defendant for such procedures to take place. The fact that such a process would obviously benefit the plaintiff is not relevant unless, as a result of the defendant helping the plaintiff in that way, the best interests of the defendant are served.

The approach is as set out in the case of *Re F (Mental Patient: Sterilisation)* [1990] 2 AC 1 . . . a non-therapeutic sterilisation case. Thus, the giving of medical treatment to mentally disordered adult patients is, save as to treatment for their mental disorder under the Mental Health Act 1983, governed by common law. The lawfulness of the action depends upon whether the treatment is in the best interests of the patient . . .

This case is different from the case of *Re F* because it involves the concept of donation of bone marrow by a donor who is incapable of giving consent where a significant benefit will flow to another person. There was no other person in *Re F* who would have benefited directly as a result of the declaration sought, the benefits of sterilisation attaching solely to the mentally incapacitated subject of the application.

Nonetheless, I am satisfied that the root question remains the same, namely, whether the procedures here envisaged will benefit the defendant and accordingly benefits which may flow to the plaintiff are relevant only in so far as they have a positive effect upon the best interests of the defendant . . .

The information provided by those who now care for the defendant in the residential home make it apparent that the defendant benefits from the visits which she receives from her family and from her occasional involvement in family events, for example, the wedding of one of her sisters, particularly because these visits maintain for her a link with the outside world which is helpful to her and which would otherwise be lost to her. . . .

If the plaintiff dies, this is bound to have an adverse effect upon her mother who already suffers from significant ill health. One lay witness took the gloomy view that this event would prove fatal to the mother, but in any event her ability to visit the defendant would be handicapped significantly, not only by a likely deterioration in her

12 (1996) 35 BMLR 111 (Fam Div).

health, but also by the need which would then arise for her to look after her only grandchild, E.

In this situation, the defendant would clearly be harmed by the reduction in or loss of contact to her mother. Accordingly, it is to the benefit of the defendant that she should act as donor to her sister, because in this way her positive relationship with her mother is most likely to be prolonged. Further, if the transplant occurs, this is likely to improve the defendant's relationship with her mother who in her heart clearly wishes it to take place and also to improve her relationship with the plaintiff who will be eternally grateful to her.

This case shows the court adopting a wide interpretation of 'best interests'; it is not somatic health alone which is relevant, but the wider interests a person has as part of the social community. (This approach is also in line with decisions relating to sterilisation discussed in Chapter 4.) Nevertheless, there are important limits on invoking the test in order to justify organ extraction, especially where the organ is non-regenerative. As Andrew Grubb has commented:

See Chapter 4

Grubb, A, 'Commentary on Re Y'[13]

Of course, the judge recognised that it was insufficient for him merely to identify a 'benefit' to Miss Y without weighing against this any detriment that she might suffer by undergoing the procedures. However, the risks inherent in the procedures – the general anaesthetic and the removal of two pints of bone marrow – were regarded as 'very small' (one in 10,000 risk of death) and non-existent (as bone marrow is regenerative) respectively. Further any pain that might arise from the harvesting could be controlled by morphine. And, of course, there could be a detriment by not undergoing the procedure . . . In Re Y, Connell J referred to the 'harm' Miss Y would suffer (directly and indirectly) from the death of her sister although the evidence never elevated this to the level of psychiatric injury.

Limitations in future cases. Given the weaknesses in the evidence which have been suggested above, Re Y could be seen as giving a 'green light' to support donations by [incapable] adults and children in the future. This would, I think, be a misreading of the case and not Connell J's intention for a number of reasons.

First, the case is probably an unusual one in that it concerned a procedure which does have minimal risks for the donor. Given the need to weigh the benefits of the procedure against the risks of doing it, it is not likely that a court would contemplate donation of non-regenerative tissue such as a kidney. Connell J suggested as much when he remarked that his decision should not be considered 'a useful precedent in cases where the surgery involved is more intrusive'. While the long term risks of having one kidney are not great, they do exist and the nature of the procedure suggests that it would be difficult to satisfy the 'best interests' test . . .

Secondly, the courts will undoubtedly look for evidence of a 'close relationship' which will be damaged if the donee patient dies. It is most unlikely, therefore, that the court would contemplate even a minimally risky procedure if the donor's mental disability or if the child's age prevented them forming such a relationship. Donations by babies and the severely mentally disabled may thus be out of court.

The common law position is left broadly intact by the statutory framework for the mentally incapable, introduced by the Mental Capacity Act 2005. Thus, while the Code of Practice under the

---

13 (1996) 4 Med L Rev 204.

Act states that proposed cases of organ or bone marrow extraction should be referred to the Court of Protection, it expressly leaves the door open for court approval of such procedures, as follows:

Mental Capacity Act 2005, Code of Practice[14]

8.20 Cases involving organ or bone marrow donation by a person who lacks capacity to consent should also be referred to the Court of Protection. Such cases involve medical procedures being performed on a person who lacks capacity to consent but which would benefit a third party (though would not necessarily directly or physically benefit the person who lacks capacity). However, sometimes such procedures may be in the person's overall best interests. . . . For example, the person might receive emotional, social and psychological benefits as a result of the help they have given, and in some cases the person may experience only minimal physical discomfort.

11.2.2.3 Child donors

In contrast to the position with incapable adults, there is no English authority directly on the question of live organ donation by minors. Moreover, this issue raises a number of further complications. First, in the case of older children who satisfy the test of 'Gillick competence', can they consent in their own right to act as donors? The answer, in principle, would appear to be yes. As Lord Donaldson MR noted, *obiter*, in *Re W (A Minor) (Medical Treatment)*:[15]

Lord Donaldson MR: [Section 8 of the Family Law Reform Act 1969 establishing the presumption that a minor of 16 years can consent to medical treatment] extends not only to treatment, but also to diagnostic procedures (see sub-s (2)). It does not, however, extend to the donation of organs or blood since, so far as the donor is concerned, these do not constitute either treatment or diagnosis. I cannot remember to what extent organ donation was common in 1967, but the Latey Committee expressly recommended that only 18 year olds and older should be authorised by statute to consent to giving blood. . . . It seems that parliament accepted this recommendation, although I doubt whether blood donation will create any problem as a *'Gillick* competent' minor of any age would be able to give consent under the common law.

Organ transplants are quite different and, as a matter of law, doctors would have to secure the consent of someone with the right to consent on behalf of a donor under the age of 18 or, if they relied upon the consent of the minor himself or herself, be satisfied that the minor was *'Gillick* competent' in the context of so serious a procedure which would not benefit the minor. This would be a highly improbable conclusion. But this is only to look at the question as a matter of law. Medical ethics also enter into the question. The doctor has a professional duty to act in the best interests of his patient and to advise accordingly. It is inconceivable that he should proceed in reliance solely upon the consent of an under-age patient, however *'Gillick* competent', in the absence of supporting parental consent and equally inconceivable that he should proceed in the absence of the patient's consent. In any event he will need to seek the opinions of other doctors and may be well advised to apply to the court for guidance, as recommended by Lord Templeman in a different context in *Re B (A Minor) (Wardship: Sterilisation)* . . .

---

14 London: TSO, 2007; see www.opsi.gov.uk/acts/acts2005/related/ukpgacop_20050009_en.pdf.
15 [1992] 3 WLR 758.

Lord Donaldson MR suggests here that it would be 'inconceivable' both that extraction would go ahead without parental consent *and* that it could occur solely on the basis of the latter (a necessary caveat in the light of his Lordship's 'flak jacket' approach to consent in his decision in the case).

In the case of children who lack capacity, it is apparent that the parents must normally give proxy consent to any form of medical intervention upon them. Indeed, in the American case of *Bonner v Moran*[16] a doctor who failed to obtain parental consent was held liable in battery after taking skin grafts from a 15-year-old boy to treat the latter's badly burnt cousin. On the other hand, it is clear that parental authorisation of such an intervention will not guarantee that it is lawful. Rather, as Lord Scarman made clear in *Gillick v W Norfolk and Wisbech HA*,[17] the parent's power to consent is one they should exercise exclusively for the child's benefit.

In its 2009 Code of Practice, the Human Tissue Authority offers the following guidance where the involvement of a child donor is contemplated:

Human Tissue Authority, *Code of Practice 1 – Consent*[18]

140. Children may consent to a proposed medical procedure or the storage and use of their tissue if they are competent [capable] to do so. In the *Gillick* case, the court held that a child was considered competent to give valid consent to a proposed intervention if they had sufficient intelligence and understanding to enable them fully to understand what was involved . . .

141. If a child consents to a procedure, then this consent carries over into adulthood unless they explicitly withdraw it.

142. Under the Children Act 1989, a person who has parental responsibility . . . for the child may consent on their behalf only if the child has not made a decision either way; and the child:

is not competent to do so; or

is competent to do so, but is unwilling to make that decision.

. . . 144. Where there is any dispute between persons with parental responsibility or any doubt as to the child's best interests, the matter should be referred to court for approval . . .

145. Even if the child is competent to consent, it is good practice to consult the person who has parental responsibility for the child and to involve them in the process of the child making a decision. However, it should be emphasised that, if the child is competent, the decision to consent must be the child's. Information about a competent young person should only be disclosed to the person with parental responsibility for the child with the child's consent. It is also essential to make sure that a child has consented voluntarily and has not been unduly influenced by anyone else.

In fact, it appears that bone marrow donation between minor siblings occurs fairly routinely on the basis of parental consent. In relation to more intrusive and risky procedures, such as solid organ donation, it is much less likely that this would suffice. Rather, as suggested by the HTA Code of Practice, the matter would almost certainly be brought before the court for a declaration of lawfulness. In the USA, there have been a number of cases where such declarations have been granted:

---

16 126 F 2d 121 (1941) (USCA DC).

17 [1986] 1 AC 112.

18 See www.hta.gov.uk/legislationpoliciesandcodesofpractice/codesofpractice/code1consent.cfm. The role of the Authority is discussed in section 11.2.3.

see, for example *Hart v Brown*,[19] which concerned a kidney transplant between seven-year-old identical twins. By contrast, the Illinois Supreme Court refused to make one in the case of *Curran v Bosze*:

Curran v Bosze[20]

The plaintiff was the former wife of the defendant and mother of three-and-a-half-year-old twins by him. The defendant's 12-year-old son from a previous marriage was dying from leukaemia and the defendant brought a petition requiring her to submit the twins to a blood test to establish compatibility with the 12-year-old with a view to a subsequent bone marrow transplant:

> **Calvo J**: In each of the foregoing cases where consent to the kidney transplant was authorised, regardless whether the authority to consent was to be exercised by the court, a parent or a guardian, the key inquiry was the presence or absence of a benefit to the potential donor. Notwithstanding the language used by the courts in reaching their determination that a transplant may or may not occur, the standard by which the determination was made was whether the transplant would be in the best interest of the child or incompetent [incapable] person.
>
> The primary benefit to the donor in these cases arises from the relationship existing between the donor and recipient. In *Strunk* [*v Strunk*], the donor lived in a State institution. The recipient was a brother who served as the donor's only connection with the outside world. In both *Hart* [*v Brown*] and *Little* [*v Little*], there was evidence that the sibling relationship between the donor and recipient was close. In each of these cases, both parents had given their consent . . .
>
> We hold that a parent or guardian may give consent on behalf of a minor daughter or son for the child to donate bone marrow to a sibling, only when to do so would be in the minor's best interest.
>
> The evidence reveals three critical factors which are necessary to a determination that it will be in the best interests of a child to donate bone marrow to a sibling. First, the parent who consents on behalf of the child must be informed of the risks and benefits inherent in the bone marrow harvesting procedure to the child.
>
> Second, there must be emotional support available to the child from the person or persons who take care of the child. The testimony reveals that a child who is to undergo general anaesthesia and the bone marrow harvesting procedure needs the emotional support of a person whom the child loves and trusts. A child who is to donate bone marrow is required to go to an unfamiliar place and meet with unfamiliar people. Depending upon the age of the child, he or she may or may not understand what is to happen. The evidence establishes that the presence and emotional support by the child's caretaker is important to ease the fears associated with such an unfamiliar procedure.
>
> Third, there must be an existing, close relationship between the donor and recipient. The evidence clearly shows that there is no physical benefit to a donor child. If there is any benefit to a child who donates bone marrow to a sibling it will be a psychological benefit. According to the evidence, the psychological benefit is not simply one of personal, individual altruism in an abstract theoretical sense, although that may be a factor.

---

19 289 A 2d 386 (1972).
20 566 NE 2d 1319 (1990).

The psychological benefit is grounded firmly in the fact that the donor and recipient are known to each other as family. Only where there is an existing relationship between a healthy child and his or her ill sister or brother may a psychological benefit to the child from donating bone marrow to a sibling realistically be found to exist. . . .

This court shares the opinion of the circuit court that Jean Pierre's situation evokes sympathy from all who've heard [it]. No matter how small the hope that a bone marrow transplant will cure Jean Pierre, the fact remains that without the transplant, Jean Pierre will almost certainly die. The sympathy felt by this court, the circuit court, and all those who have learned of Jean Pierre's tragic situation cannot, however, obscure the fact that, under the circumstances presented in the case at bar, it neither would be proper under existing law nor in the best interests of the three and a half year old twins for the twins to participate in the bone marrow harvesting procedure.

 SELF-TEST QUESTION

Given the primacy of autonomy in other contexts (eg a patient's right to reject life-saving treatment), is the law not unduly paternalistic in its refusal to countenance a person's considered decision to donate, say, their heart in order to save their dying child?

11.2.3 Statutory limitations on live organ donation

11.2.3.1 'Appropriate consent' to storage and use of organs and tissue

The Human Tissue Act 2004 has introduced a new statutory regime of consent (termed by the Act 'appropriate consent') needed before human organs and tissue may be used and/or stored, including for transplantation. Nominally, the Act leaves it to the common law to determine the lawfulness of the prior *removal* of such material from live donors. However, in practice the new regime will already operate – in duplication with the common law – at the point of removal. Not only does removal here precede the material's use for transplantation but, as noted earlier, in legal terms such an intended use is essential. In other words, the failure to have obtained statutory consent (to subsequent use and/or storage) before removing an organ will render the removal itself unlawful at common law.

The relevant consent provisions of the 2004 Act, so far as they relate to live donors, are as follows:

Human Tissue Act 2004

2 'Appropriate consent': children

(1) This section makes provision for the interpretation of 'appropriate consent' in section 1 in relation to an activity involving the body, or material from the body, of a person who is a child or has died a child ('the child concerned').

(2) Subject to subsection (3), where the child concerned is alive, 'appropriate consent' means his consent.

(3) Where–

(a) the child concerned is alive,

(b) neither a decision of his to consent to the activity, nor a decision of his not to consent to it, is in force, and

(c)   either he is not competent to deal with the issue of consent in relation to the activity or, though he is competent to deal with that issue, he fails to do so,

'appropriate consent' means the consent of a person who has parental responsibility for him. . . .

3 'Appropriate consent': adults

(1)   This section makes provision for the interpretation of 'appropriate consent' in section 1 in relation to an activity involving the body, or material from the body, of a person who is an adult or has died an adult ('the person concerned').

(2)   Where the person concerned is alive, 'appropriate consent' means his consent. . . .

6 Activities involving material from adults who lack capacity to consent

Where–

(a)   an activity of a kind mentioned in section 1(1)(d) or (f) involves material from the body of a person who–

   (i)   is an adult, and

   (ii)   lacks capacity to consent to the activity, and

(b)   neither a decision of his to consent to the activity, nor a decision of his not to consent to it, is in force,

there shall for the purposes of this Part be deemed to be consent of his to the activity if it is done in circumstances of a kind specified by regulations made by the Secretary of State.

As previously noted, these provisions operate on top of the existing common law requirements in relation to the lawful removal of material, and simply add a further safeguard. Thus, for example, as regards the use of material from an incapable child, s 2(3), providing for consent by a person with parental responsibility, in duplicating the common law requirement, in no way detracts from the requirement at common law for the removal procedure (and hence the consent thereto) also to be in the child's best interests.

Section 6 of the Act provides for the Health Secretary to make regulations to address the issue of consent in relation to incapable adults. This was done in 2006 in the form of the Human Tissue Act 2004 (Persons who Lack Capacity to Consent and Transplants) Regulations 2006,[21] which introduce special procedural requirements for such cases. These are discussed further in 11.2.3(c) below.

11.2.3.2 The prohibition on organ (and tissue) trafficking

Following a well publicised scandal in the late 1980s, in which it was revealed that a Harley Street clinic was paying impoverished Turkish donors up to £3,000 for their spare kidneys, Parliament enacted the Human Organ Transplants Act 1989. This prohibited commercial dealings in organs (which were defined by the Act to include non-regenerative body parts, such as kidneys, but not regenerative tissues such as bone marrow or blood). The 1989 Act was repealed by the 2004 Human Tissue Act, which, in re-enacting the salient prohibitions, extended them to cover other forms of human tissue too. Section 32 provides as follows:

Human Tissue Act 2004

Trafficking

32 Prohibition of commercial dealings in human material for transplantation

(1)   A person commits an offence if he–

---

21 SI 2006/1659.

(a) gives or receives a reward for the supply of, or for an offer to supply, any controlled material;

(b) seeks to find a person willing to supply any controlled material for reward;

(c) offers to supply any controlled material for reward;

(d) initiates or negotiates any arrangement involving the giving of a reward for the supply of, or for an offer to supply, any controlled material;

(e) takes part in the management or control of a body of persons corporate or unincorporate whose activities consist of or include the initiation or negotiation of such arrangements.

(2) Without prejudice to subsection (1)(b) and (c), a person commits an offence if he causes to be published or distributed, or knowingly publishes or distributes, an advertisement–

(a) inviting persons to supply, or offering to supply, any controlled material for reward, or

(b) indicating that the advertiser is willing to initiate or negotiate any such arrangement as is mentioned in subsection (1)(d).

. . . (6) For the purposes of subsections (1) and (2), payment in money or money's worth to the holder of a licence shall be treated as not being a reward where–

(a) it is in consideration for transporting, removing, preparing, preserving or storing controlled material, and

(b) its receipt by the holder of the licence is not expressly prohibited by the terms of the licence.

(7) References in subsections (1) and (2) to reward, in relation to the supply of any controlled material, do not include payment in money or money's worth for defraying or reimbursing–

(a) any expenses incurred in, or in connection with, transporting, removing, preparing, preserving or storing the material,

(b) any liability incurred in respect of–

(i) expenses incurred by a third party in, or in connection with, any of the activities mentioned in paragraph (a), or

(ii) a payment in relation to which subsection (6) has effect, or

(c) any expenses or loss of earnings incurred by the person from whose body the material comes so far as reasonably and directly attributable to his supplying the material from his body.

(8) For the purposes of this section, controlled material is any material which–

(a) consists of or includes human cells,

(b) is, or is intended to be removed, from a human body,

(c) is intended to be used for the purpose of transplantation, and

(d) is not of a kind excepted under subsection (9).

(9) The following kinds of material are excepted–

(a) gametes,

(b) embryos, and

(c) material which is the subject of property because of an application of human skill . . .

Gametes and embryos are excepted on the basis that they are subject to their own regulatory regime under the Human Fertilisation and Embryology Act 1990 (as amended). However, otherwise it is apparent that the definition of controlled material under sub-s (8) is very wide and will encompass all cellular matter, including blood used for transfusions. It should also be noted that the immediate participants in the arrangement, ie the donor and donee of the material are also caught by the section (contrast other statutes, such as the Surrogacy Arrangements Act 1985, where on public policy grounds, the immediate parties, are granted an immunity: in the case of

See Chapter 7 →

trading in organs, clearly it was felt there were no such grounds). However, as stated in s 32(c), the donor's reasonable expenses and/or loss of earnings as a result of donating will not count as a 'reward', and thus can lawfully be paid.

Sub-sections 32(4) and (5) provide for offences under the section to be punishable by stiff penalties, including (in the case of a breach of sub-s (1)) by a term of imprisonment of up to three years.

11.2.3.3 Further restrictions on live transplants – the role of the Human Tissue Authority

In addition to prohibiting commercial dealings, Parliament, when it passed the 1989 Human Organ Transplants Act, evinced a general concern about live donations between persons not genetically related. Accordingly, it created a special authority, the Unrelated Live Transplants Regulatory Authority, and provided that, to be lawful, such transplants had first to be approved by this authority. Nonetheless, the basis for singling out the unrelated donor for special protection in this way was never very convincing: arguably it is, if anyone, the related donor who may be vulnerable to illicit pressure to donate. As Kennedy and Grubb pointed out in their analysis of the 1989 legislation:

Kennedy, I and Grubb, A, *Medical Law*[22]

. . . Parliament was concerned that the donation be entirely altruistic and presumes that this will be so in the case of those who are 'genetically related' whereas it may not be otherwise. It is fair to ask, however, if the key to altruism is close family ties, why should a spouse be treated as a stranger? Furthermore, grandparents and grandchildren are genetically related and may surely be presumed to act as altruistically as those included within the Act, yet they too are excluded as if they were strangers. It cannot be that a grandparent is necessarily too old to be a donor because someone may be a grandparent at 40!

By contrast, if altruism is the key, why should parliament restrict unregulated donation to the genetically related? It could be said that intrafamily donations may well be the product of severe social pressure ('coercion') rather than altruism . . . In some jurisdictions, consequently, legislation prohibits the removal of non-regenerative tissue from a minor for the purpose of transplantation, recognising the danger of pressure within the family (see, for example, s 14(1) of the Human Tissue Act 1982 in Victoria, Australia).

Under the Human Tissue Act 2004, while special safeguards in relation to live transplants remain, the distinction between genetically related and unrelated donors has been largely removed. Instead, all proposed transplants – related and unrelated alike – must be referred for approval to the new Human Tissue Authority.[23] The relevant provision of the 2004 Act, s 33, is as follows:

Human Tissue Act 2004

Transplants

33 Restriction on transplants involving a live donor

(1) Subject to subsections (3) and (5), a person commits an offence if–
    (a) he removes any transplantable material from the body of a living person intending that the material be used for the purpose of transplantation, and

---

22 2nd edn, London: Butterworths, 1994.

23 The Authority was set up under ss 13 ff of the HTA 2004. For details of its work (which extends to the licensing of virtually all activities involving the use human tissue, not just organ donation), including the codes of practice it operates, see www.hta.gov.uk/.

    (b)   when he removes the material, he knows, or might reasonably be expected to know, that the person from whose body he removes the material is alive.

 (2)   Subject to subsections (3) and (5), a person commits an offence if–

    (a)   he uses for the purpose of transplantation any transplantable material which has come from the body of a living person, and

    (b)   when he does so, he knows, or might reasonably be expected to know, that the transplantable material has come from the body of a living person.

 (3)   The Secretary of State may by regulations provide that subsection (1) or (2) shall not apply in a case where–

    (a)   the Authority is satisfied–

       (i)   that no reward has been or is to be given in contravention of section 32, and

       (ii)   that such other conditions as are specified in the regulations are satisfied, and

    (b)   such other requirements as are specified in the regulations are complied with.

 (4)   Regulations under subsection (3) shall include provision for decisions of the Authority in relation to matters which fall to be decided by it under the regulations to be subject, in such circumstances as the regulations may provide, to reconsideration in accordance with such procedure as the regulations may provide.

 (5)   Where under subsection (3) an exception from subsection (1) or (2) is in force, a person does not commit an offence under that subsection if he reasonably believes that the exception applies. . . .

 (7)   In this section–

    . . . 'transplantable material' means material of a description specified by regulations made by the Secretary of State.

The regulations referred to, the Human Tissue Act 2004 (Persons who Lack Capacity to Consent and Transplants) Regulations 2006 (which notwithstanding their title cover both capable and incapable donors)[24] were introduced in September 2006. After defining 'transplantable material' in reg 10 to include organs or part organs,[25] as well as – in the case of children and incapable adults – bone marrow and peripheral blood stem cells, reg 11 goes on to provide:

Human Tissue Act 2004 (Persons who Lack Capacity to Consent and Transplants) Regulations 2006

Cases in which restriction on transplants involving a live donor is disapplied

11—(1) Section 33(1) and (2) of the Act (offences relating to transplants involving a live donor) shall not apply in any case involving transplantable material from the body of a living person ('the donor') if the requirements of paragraphs (2) to (6) are met.

 (2)   A registered medical practitioner who has clinical responsibility for the donor must have caused the matter to be referred to the Authority.

 (3)   The Authority must be satisfied that—

    (a)   no reward has been or is to be given in contravention of section 32 of the Act (prohibition of commercial dealings in human material for transplantation), and

    (b)   when the transplantable material is removed—

       (i)   consent for its removal for the purpose of transplantation has been given, or

       (ii)   its removal for that purpose is otherwise lawful.

---

24 See n 21 above.
25 reg 10(2) makes an exception for 'domino transplants' (see 11.2.2(a) above), which accordingly do not require approval by the Authority.

(4)   The Authority must take the report referred to in paragraph (6) into account in making its decision under paragraph (3).

. . .

(6)   Subject to paragraph (7), one or more qualified persons must have conducted separate interviews with each of the following—

(a)   the donor,

(b)   if different from the donor, the person giving consent, and

(c)   the recipient,

and reported to the Authority on the matters specified in paragraphs (8) and (9).

(7)   Paragraph (6) does not apply in any case where the removal of the transplantable material for the purpose of transplantation is authorised by an order made in any legal proceedings before a court.

(8)   The matters that must be covered in the report of each interview under paragraph (6) are—

(a)   any evidence of duress or coercion affecting the decision to give consent,

(b)   any evidence of an offer of a reward, and

(c)   any difficulties of communication with the person interviewed and an explanation of how those difficulties were overcome.

(9)   The following matters must be covered in the report of the interview with the donor and, where relevant, the other person giving consent—

(a)   the information given to the person interviewed as to the nature of the medical procedure for, and the risk involved in, the removal of the transplantable material,

(b)   the full name of the person who gave that information and his qualification to give it, and

(c)   the capacity of the person interviewed to understand—

(i)   the nature of the medical procedure and the risk involved, and

(ii)   that the consent may be withdrawn at any time before the removal of the transplantable material.

As well as needing to be satisfied that no payment has occurred, the Authority is thus directed to pay close attention to the consent aspects of the arrangement. In this regard it will require an independent assessor to carry out interviews with both the donor and recipient of the organ, covering such matters as possible coercion, the donor's knowledge of the risks and ability to understand them, etc. The decision to allow the transplant will then normally be taken by a 'HTA transport approvals team'; however, under reg 12, a panel of at least three Authority members is required to decide cases involving children or incapable adults, as well as ones of 'non-directed altruistic', 'paired' or 'pooled' donations. The meanings of the latter terms are elucidated in reg 12(5) of the 2006 Regulations:

12–(5) In this regulation—

'non-directed altruistic donation' means the removal (in circumstances not amounting to a paired or pooled donation) of transplantable material from a donor for transplant to a person who is not genetically related to the donor or known to him;

'paired donations' means an arrangement under which—

(a)   transplantable material is removed from a donor ('D') for transplant to a person who is not genetically related or known to D, and

(b)   transplantable material is removed from another person for transplant to a person who is genetically related or known to D;

and

'pooled donations' means a series of paired donations of transplantable material, each of which is linked to another in the same series (for example, transplantable material from D is transplanted to the wife of another person ('E'), transplantable material from E is transplanted to the partner of a third person ('F') and transplantable material from F is transplanted to D's son).

Paired live donation arises as an option where one person (D1) would like to donate to a specific person (R1), but is prevented from doing so by tissue incompatibility. In such a case, the solution is to find another similar couple (D2 and R2) and – assuming their respective compatibility – for D1 to donate to R2 in return for D2 donating to R1; pooled donation involves the same process with more than two couples. In 2006, NHS Blood and Transplant began setting up a paired/pooled donation matching scheme,[26] and the Human Tissue Authority has already approved a number of such arrangements, including the first pooled kidney donation in late 2009.[27]

 SELF-TEST QUESTION

In the light of the need for the donor to provide valid consent to extraction at common law, do the further consent formalities in the 2004 Act, including the requirement of HT Authority approval, serve any purpose?

11.3 Transplants from Deceased Donors
11.3.1 Background

As noted earlier, the development of new immuno-suppressant drugs within the last 30 years has diminished the importance of donor-recipient compatibility and permitted the increased use of cadaveric transplants. Currently, around two-thirds of kidneys transplanted in the UK are obtained in this way and the practice enjoys a number of practical advantages. Most obviously, there is no difficulty in terms of exposing the dead donor to harm (or the risk of harm) and a total harvesting of organs is therefore possible, including the heart, lungs, pancreas, and corneas. On the other hand, some distinct problems are also created, notably the need for the organs to be removed fairly rapidly after death, if they are to be of any use. This raises the issue not only of who may authorise such removal, but also the larger question of how it is proper to treat the recently deceased human corpse. David Lamb has commented on this latter issue as follows:

Lamb, D, *Organ Transplants and Ethics*[28]

Although respect for the deceased takes different forms in different cultures, for the most part violation of the body's integrity for therapeutic purposes, such as organ transplantation, is not regarded as disrespect. At least no Western Church has adopted an unfavourable stance towards organ removal. Jewish, Christian, and Buddhist countries, despite prohibitions on the

---

26 See further: www.uktransplant.org.uk/ukt/about_transplants/organ_allocation/kidney_(renal)/living_donation/paired_pooled_donation.jsp.
27 See HTA Press Release, 8 March 2010, at www.hta.gov.uk/newsandevents/htanews.cfm/837-First-pooled-transplants-performed-in-the-UK.html.
28 See n 1 above.

mutilation of corpses, permit cadaveric transplants provided prior consent of the deceased – or family consent – has been obtained.

The respect accorded to dead bodies in the Muslim faith rules out the study of anatomy on indigenous corpses. Post mortems are rare in Islamic countries. But in 1982 organ donation after death was declared *halal* (permissible) by the Senior 'Ulama' Commission, the highest religious authority in such matters, in Saudi Arabia . . .

Nevertheless, there are sources of resistance to organ transplantation which deserve consideration. An important aspect of resistance to routine harvesting of cadaveric organs is the symbolic role which is assigned to the dead body. This role should not be underestimated, even though the interests of the living may outweigh those of the dead. Joel Feinberg . . . cites a case which brings out the importance of such symbolism. In 1978 the Department of Transport in the USA contracted with several university laboratories to test designs for automobiles in actual crashes at varying velocities. Dummies had proven unsatisfactory. Some researchers – with the consent of the relatives – had substituted human cadavers. After a public outcry the tests were stopped, despite the Department of Transport's protest that such a decision would set back progress on safety protection for years. The grounds for the prohibition of these tests were that 'the use of human cadavers for vehicle safety research violated fundamental notions of morality and human dignity' . . .

The issue at stake appears to concern the symbolic role of the human cadaver. Violent assault on a cadaver is an assault on the important symbolic role assigned to the newly dead.

According to Feinberg, symbolic fears of this kind, though culturally significant, should not outweigh the imperative to save lives. Certainly objections to the routine salvaging of cadaveric organs based on symbolic fears should not impede research to improve life expectancy. To drive home this point Feinberg draws an analogy with William James' story of a Russian aristocrat who wept over a fictional tragedy in a theatre while her coachman froze to death outside in her carriage. In such cases the symbolic has outweighed the real.

There is merit in Feinberg's argument. But in reply it must be stressed that symbols are important to the very fabric of society. A society with no symbolic values for the dead is little short of savagery. Moreover, a body is not just a symbol. The newly dead continue as a presence, which is why they are referred to as deceased. The absence of the life that once existed has a very real presence . . .

Arguably, such symbolic concerns contributed to the furore in the wake of the revelations at Bristol and Alder Hey as to the non-consensual retention of organs from deceased children. As noted earlier, a result of these scandals has been the Human Tissue Act 2004, which aims to clarify the law governing the treatment of human materials generally. We shall look at the effect of the new Act in relation to cadaveric organ transplants shortly. First, though, we consider two residual matters of common law that remain important.

11.3.2 Dealing with the recently deceased

11.3.2.1 Establishing death

Traditionally, death was defined in terms of cessation of cardiovascular function, that is, the person had no pulse, was not breathing, etc. Advances in medical technology have rendered this approach obsolete: the features in question, though closely aligned with death, are no longer either sufficient or necessary for it (a person may be revived from the above state or, conversely, have the relevant functions sustained mechanically in the absence of all brain activity). Accordingly, a new definition of death was put forward in Guidelines issued by the Medical Royal Colleges in 1976.[29] Death is now equated with irreversible loss of brainstem function: the brainstem, which is the last part of the brain to die off, is necessary both for any possibility of awareness (the upper brainstem) and for spontaneous reflexes such as respiration (lower brainstem).

Although this new concept of death (referred to interchangeably as 'brainstem death' or simply 'brain death') has not been incorporated into legislation, it was accepted by the High Court in the 1992 case of *Re A*:

Re A[30]

A was a 19-month-old infant who was admitted to hospital with serious head injuries following a domestic incident. He was placed upon a ventilator but showed no signs of recovery. The hospital, after carrying out the diagnostic tests laid down by the MRC Guidelines, was satisfied that A was dead and applied for a declaration allowing his removal from the ventilator:

Johnson J: On 20 January – that is last Monday – the consultant removed A briefly from the ventilator to see whether he was capable of supporting himself without the ventilator. When she did so she heard slight gasping noises which led her to believe that A was not brainstem dead according to criteria now generally accepted in medical circles.

The precise definition of death has been the subject of recommendations by both the Royal College of Surgeons and the Royal College of Physicians and a working party of the British Paediatric Association. Applying the criteria laid down by her profession the consultant concluded on 20 January that A was not then brainstem dead. On the following day she again carried out the tests which are necessary to determine whether the necessary criteria are satisfied. The consultant described those tests to me and she explained to me that each one was satisfied. The tests lasted overall about half an hour. . . .

On the same day the consultant had arranged for a colleague consultant paediatric neurologist to carry out the same tests that she had, herself, carried out the previous day with a view to confirming or otherwise the validity of her own professional conclusion. Under professional guidelines it was not necessary for her to seek a second opinion in that way, but she decided that in the particular circumstances of the case it would be a wise thing for her to do. Accordingly, the tests were carried out again on Wednesday of last week, 22 January, by this colleague who reached the same conclusion as had been reached by the first consultant. Both doctors were at pains to exclude other possibilities for A's state, including the possibility of his suffering from extreme hypothermia or some abnormality of his biochemistry. Moreover, they tested for drugs, lest his brainstem function should have been suppressed by the administration of some drug of which they had not been aware . . .

Both doctors concluded that A was brainstem dead . . .

It is now Monday 27 January. I have no hesitation at all in holding that A has been dead since Tuesday of last week, 21 January.

The current Code of Practice in relation to diagnosing brain stem death, issued by the Academy of Medical Royal Colleges in 2008,[31] reiterates the earlier Medical Royal Colleges guidance.

---

29 (1976) 2 BMJ 1187.
30 [1992] 3 Med LR 303 (Fam Div).
31 See www.aomrc.org.uk/publications/reports-guidance/doc_download/42-a-code-of-practice-for-the-diagnosis-and-confirmation-of-death.html.

11.3.2.2 Elective ventilation

The ability to establish the fact of death swiftly, but nevertheless with an appropriate degree of certainty, is important in the context of transplanting organs where, to maximise the chances of success, removal should generally take place as soon as possible. Before death is positively verified, the removal cannot of course come into question; even so, once the doctors are certain that a patient will not survive, there are other, earlier steps they might wish to take in order to preserve his organs pending their removal after death has been confirmed.

The problem here is that the patient will be – if not already dead – in an irreversible coma, and thus can, as an incapable person, only be treated in his own best interests. Concerns as to the legality of medical interventions upon patients in this situation led to the halting of a technique for organ retrieval previously deployed in the South West of England with some success. The background to the procedure in question, known as 'elective ventilation', and the debate it aroused, are described by David Price:

Price, DPT, 'Organ transplant initiatives: the twilight zone'[32]

In 1988 the Royal Devon and Exeter Hospital became the first British hospital to develop an E[lective] V[entilation] protocol. Patients in deep irreversible coma and believed to be dying imminently of intracranial haemorrhage were transferred to intensive care, with relatives' consent, so that artificial ventilation could be commenced immediately respiratory arrest occurred and until brain (stem) death tests could be satisfied. However, in October 1994, the Health Departments of England and Wales issued guidelines stating that EV for transplantation purposes constituted an unlawful battery – being non-therapeutic and not done in the best interests of the individual. This . . . is probably an accurate perception of the present common law. Although an alternative 'not against the interests of the individual' test has been occasionally employed in relation to non-therapeutic procedures performed on minors, such a standard has yet to be legally employed in respect of a mentally incompetent [incapable] adult person in a similar context . . .

The meaning of death

By contrast with the majority view across all disciplines, the clinicians who developed the Exeter protocol argue that the process of dying is not prolonged by EV, as the patient is already dead – one is ventilating a corpse . . . Riad, from Exeter, has said, 'The procedure causes no harm to the patient as ventilation is instituted at the time of respiratory arrest which is the consequence of brain death . . . Therefore it is important not to institute EV before respiratory arrest' . . .

Supporters of the Exeter protocol argue that cessation of respiration is (necessary and sufficient) evidence that the patient has already succumbed to brain death – the question is whether this is so . . .

Judicial acceptance

. . . [A]lthough there is no definition of death in English law, brain stem death established in accordance with the agreed criteria incorporated in the code of practice of the medical royal colleges has been accepted as establishing legal as well as 'medical' death. However, whilst this constitutes judicial acceptance of these tests, it does not necessarily indicate that this is the sole criterion for the determination of death in law . . . Re A illustrates that death can be legally declared to have occurred according to brain death criteria before two sets of tests have been completed and death has been confirmed. . . . The code of practice, although highly influential, does not have the force of law . . .

---

32 (1997) 23 JME 170.

In effect, proponents of the Exeter protocol argued that in some cases (where patients had received direct injury to the brain stem), brain stem death should be recognised as preceding – and causing – cessation of respiration, rather than vice versa: accordingly, they could already at that point be ventilated simply to facilitate organ harvesting. Nonetheless, the diagnostic uncertainties involved, plus evidence of a risk of putting patients with residual brain-stem function into a PVS, have meant that 'elective ventilation', in terms of *commencing* ventilation of comatose and dying patients with a view to subsequent organ extraction, is no longer practised.

What, by contrast, is regarded as ethically and legally acceptable is the *continuing* life-support of patients initially placed on the ventilator on therapeutic grounds, in order to prolong the dying process until the transplant team is on hand. (Extraction will then take place once brain-stem death has been diagnosed, including – in an increasing number of cases – after cessation of ventilation as a 'non-heart-beating donation'.[33]) In these cases, where the incapable, dying patient previously expressed the wish to be an organ donor, such measures may be considered in their best interests, which, as per the 2005 Mental Capacity Act, may be influenced by the patient's previous wishes and values.[34] In this context, the Department of Health's Organ Donation Taskforce, in its 2008 Report, *Legal issues relevant to non-heartbeating donation*, advises as follows:

DoH, *Legal issues relevant to non-heartbeating donation*[35]

. . . Maintenance of life-sustaining treatment

. . . 6.11 Decisions to carry out such interventions must be made in line with the MCA. If a person wanted to be an organ donor and such steps facilitate donation, then this will mean that these steps may be considered to be in that person's best interests. However, these considerations must be weighed against any significant risk of harm in maintaining each treatment and any distress that may be caused to the family by certain procedures, before determining if such steps would be in their best interests.

. . . 6.14 Anything that places the person at risk of serious harm . . . or distress . . . is unlikely ever to be in the person's best interests in this situation. A clinician would need strong and compelling reasons to consider these types of actions and would be recommended to seek a declaration from the Court of Protection in relation to the person's best interests before doing so.

. . . Timing and location of withdrawal of treatments

6.15 Decisions about the timing of withdrawal of treatment must be made in the person's best interests. It is generally understood and accepted that there is some flexibility in timing, for example to allow family members to be present or to make sure the relevant health professionals are available to oversee the donation process . . .

6.16 It is necessary to begin organ retrieval very soon after death has been declared. In practice this means that the surgical retrieval team must be ready and an operating theatre available before cardio-respiratory support is withdrawn. Because it commonly takes some hours for arrangements for retrieval to be completed, this requires withdrawal of cardio-respiratory support to be delayed if NHBD is to be possible. For similar reasons, local circumstances may necessitate moving the patient to a different location within the hospital . . .

---

33 According to the statistics from NHS Blood and Transplant – see n 4 above – non-heart-beating donors accounted for 288 of the 900 deceased solid organ donors in 2008/09, an increase of 44% over the previous year.

34 s 4(6) MCA 2005; see further the discussion in Ch 12, at p 595.

35 London: Department of Health, 2008, Crown copyright.

6.17 Again, it will be necessary for clinicians to assess whether such actions are in the best interests of the potential donor. If the person wanted to donate, then in many cases, because these steps facilitate donation, they may be considered to be in that person's best interests. The decision-maker must therefore consider whether this is something the person wanted to happen, whether the actions would cause any harm or distress to the person, or whether there was any significant risk of such an occurrence . . .

As regards the Human Tissue Act 2004, this specifically allows, in s 43, for doctors to take steps to preserve cadaveric organs for transplantation. However, this provision is directed to potential donors whose death has already been confirmed (it relates to the legality of measures taken after this point, but before 'appropriate consent' has been obtained to the organs' removal and use: see further 11.3.3.2 below.

11.3.3 Authorising the removal and use of organs

11.3.3.1 Historical background

In 1970 Gerald Dworkin commented upon the shortcomings in previous law in this area, and the consequent need for more recent statutory intervention, as follows:

Dworkin, G, 'The law relating to organ transplantation in England'[36]

(a) *Common law.* The common law position concerning corpses is curious but relatively well established. A corpse cannot ordinarily be the subject of ownership. Usually the executor or next of kin will have lawful possession of the body and there is a duty to arrange for burial at the earliest opportunity. It follows that, at common law, a man cannot by his will, or otherwise, legally determine what shall happen with his body after his death, although in most cases his wishes concerning the disposal of his body will be observed. That does not, of itself, authorise organs to be taken from corpses for the purpose of transplantation.

(b) *Statute.* The need for human bodies for medical purposes is not new: bodies have always been required for anatomical teaching and research. But any attempt on the part of persons in possession of a body to sell it, even for the purpose of dissection, was unlawful; the bodies of persons convicted of murder were alone capable of being used for dissection. The scandals of body snatching and the publicity of the murder trial of Burke and Hare led to the passing of the Anatomy Act 1832, which enabled bodies to be supplied legally to medical schools for the purpose of anatomical examination. The demand for corpses was then successfully met for over a century.

It is only in recent times that the medical profession realised that the law relating to cadavers was far too restrictive. The successful development of the corneal graft operation focused attention on the lack of supply of eyes and the inability of potential donors to bequeath their eyes for such purposes. In a little debated, but carefully prepared, piece of legislation the Corneal Grafting Act 1952 (the wording of which to some extent followed the Anatomy Act 1832) was passed authorising the use of eyes of deceased persons for therapeutic purposes. This Act quickly proved to be too narrow, for it did not enable any other part of the body to be removed. However, once this kind of provision was on the statute book, it was much easier to extend it. The Human Tissue Act 1961 replaced the 1952 Act and authorised, in certain circumstances, *'the use of the body or any specified part of the body after death for therapeutic purposes or for purposes of medical education or research'*.

---

36 See n 8 above.

The Human Tissue Act 1961 allowed organs to be removed by the hospital (in lawful possession of the body) for transplant where the deceased had made an express request to that effect. Alternatively, in the absence of such a request, removal was authorised where reasonable inquiry revealed no objection to the same either by the deceased or by his spouse/surviving relatives. Nonetheless, significant vagaries remained in the statutory provisions, including as to the scope of 'any surviving relative', and what amounted to the making by the hospital of 'such reasonable inquiry as may be practicable'. More seriously, even if a breach of the statute could be demonstrated – eg the parents of the deceased were present but simply not asked if they objected to organ removal – the Act failed to provide for any offence to be committed.[37]

The lack of effective legal penalties for taking cadaveric organs without reference to the relatives may well have contributed to the Alder Hey scandal in the late 1990s, in which it was revealed that organs of deceased children had routinely been taken and stored without their parents' knowledge. The subsequent public inquiry into those events accordingly recommended urgent amendment of the 1961 Act to provide for criminal, and possibly also civil law sanctions:

The Royal Liverpool Children's Inquiry Report[38]

We respectfully recommend that:

- The Department of Health, the Royal Colleges and medical schools shall instruct members of the medical profession in the precise terms and provisions of the Human Tissue Act 1961, on the basis of our analysis, and the need for strict compliance.
- The Human Tissue Act 1961 shall be amended to provide a test of fully informed consent for the lawful post mortem examination and retention of parts of the bodies of deceased persons. While we have concluded that there has been little difference between 'lack of objection' and 'informed consent' in practical terms for the next of kin, it is important that the law and future practice are brought into line and updated.
- The class of persons relevant to the obtaining of fully informed consent shall be defined as the 'next of kin'.
- The class of 'any surviving relative' shall no longer be relevant to post mortem examination.
- There shall be a programme of health education for the public relevant to the medical need for continued post mortem examination and access to organs and samples for therapeutic, educational and research purposes.
- The Department of Health, the Royal Colleges and medical schools shall provide training for all those involved in obtaining fully informed consent.
- The Human Tissue Act 1961 shall be amended to impose a criminal penalty by way of fine for breach of its provisions in order to encourage future compliance.
- Guidelines relating to the requirements of the Human Tissue Act 1961 and the obtaining of fully informed consent shall be drawn up and provision made for breach to result in disciplinary proceedings which could lead to suspension, dismissal or financial penalty.

The Human Rights Act 1998 makes provision for an effective remedy other than in criminal proceedings. If breaches of the Human Tissue Act 1961 amount to breaches of the Human Rights Act 1998 consideration shall be given to incorporating a financial remedy with the Human Tissue Act 1961 itself. If necessary, reference should be made to the Law Commission.

---

37 Subsequently, in *AB v Leeds Teaching Hospital NHS Trust* [2004] EWHC 644 – an action brought by parents affected by the Alder Hey Scandal – the High Court recognised a remedy in negligence (in the form of damages for psychiatric injury).

38 London: HMSO, 2001.

In the event, Parliament opted to repeal the 1961 Act altogether, and include cadaveric organ trans-plantation as one of the matters covered in the new Human Tissue Act 2004, which entered force in 2006.

11.3.3.2 The effect of the Human Tissue Act 2004

As noted earlier, the 2004 Act establishes a comprehensive regulatory regime in relation to the removal, storage and/or use of human tissue, with wider implications than for transplantation alone (indeed, the Alder Hey scandal itself did not involve any issues of transplantation). However, transplantation is one of the scheduled purposes caught by the Act, in respect of which 'appropriate consent' will now be required. We have already examined the relevant sections as they bear upon live donors. As regards cadaveric donors, the salient terms of the Act are as follows:

Human Tissue Act 2004

2 'Appropriate consent': children

(1) This section makes provision for the interpretation of 'appropriate consent' in section 1 in relation to an activity involving the body, or material from the body, of a person who is a child or has died a child ('the child concerned') . . .

(7) Where the child concerned has died . . . 'appropriate consent' means–
  (a) if a decision of his to consent to the activity, or a decision of his not to consent to it, was in force immediately before he died, his consent;
  (b) if paragraph (a) does not apply–
    (i)   the consent of a person who had parental responsibility for him immediately before he died, or
    (ii) where no person had parental responsibility for him immediately before he died, the consent of a person who stood in a qualifying relationship to him at that time.

3 'Appropriate consent': adults

(1) This section makes provision for the interpretation of 'appropriate consent' in section 1 in relation to an activity involving the body, or material from the body, of a person who is an adult or has died an adult ('the person concerned') . . .

(6) Where the person concerned has died . . . 'appropriate consent' means–
  (a) if a decision of his to consent to the activity, or a decision of his not to consent to it, was in force immediately before he died, his consent;
  (b) if–
    (i)   paragraph (a) does not apply, and
    (ii) he has appointed a person or persons under section 4 to deal after his death with the issue of consent in relation to the activity,
    consent given under the appointment;
  (c) if neither paragraph (a) nor paragraph (b) applies, the consent of a person who stood in a qualifying relationship to him immediately before he died.

(7) Where the person concerned has appointed a person or persons under section 4 to deal after his death with the issue of consent in relation to the activity, the appointment shall be disregarded for the purposes of subsection (6) if no one is able to give consent under it.

(8) If it is not reasonably practicable to communicate with a person appointed under section 4 within the time available if consent in relation to the activity is to be acted on, he shall be treated for the purposes of subsection (7) as not able to give consent under the appointment in relation to it.

4 Nominated representatives

(1) An adult may appoint one or more persons to represent him after his death in relation to consent for the purposes of section 1.

(2) An appointment under this section may be general or limited to consent in relation to such one or more activities as may be specified in the appointment.

(3) An appointment under this section may be made orally or in writing . . .

These requirements are elaborated upon in the Human Tissue Authority's Code of Practice 2 on solid organ donation. As regards the position of deceased adults, the latter states:

HTA, *Code of Practice 2 – Donation of Organs*[39]

Consent – adults

96. The HT Act makes clear that where an adult made a decision to, or not to, consent to organ donation taking place after their death, then that consent is sufficient for the activity to be lawful.

97. In cases of potential deceased donation, the transplant coordinator or delegated person should be approached at an early stage and asked to determine whether the deceased person had consented to donate their organs after death. This should be done before partners, relatives or close friends are approached.

98. Trained staff should determine whether the deceased person had given consent for organ donation by checking relevant sources, such as the Organ Donor Register. If consent is established, those close to the deceased should be told.

99. If no records are held, an approach should be made to the deceased person's partner, relatives or close friends by a transplant coordinator or a member of the team who cared for the person, or both together, to establish any known decision of the deceased person to consent (or not) to donation.

100. Once it is known that the deceased person consented to donation, the matter should be discussed sensitively with those close to the deceased. They should be encouraged to recognise the wishes of the deceased and it should be made clear, if necessary, that they do not have the legal right to veto or overrule their wishes. There may nevertheless be cases in which donation is considered inappropriate and each case should be assessed individually.

101. If the deceased person's wishes are unknown and donation is a possibility, trained healthcare professionals should raise the subject of donation with the appropriate partner, relative/s or close friend/s. This approach should be made as sensitively as possible and provide enough information to allow a decision to be reached. Once a decision has been made, it must be respected.

102. If the deceased person's wishes are not known and they were an adult who had appointed a person to deal with the use of their body after death, then consent can be given by that nominated representative . . .

103. If the deceased person's wishes are not known, and they had not appointed a nominated representative, consent can be given by a person who was in a qualifying relationship immediately before the death . . .

---

39 See www.hta.gov.uk/legislationpoliciesandcodesofpractice/codesofpractice/code2donationoforgans.cfm.

As the Code notes, where the deceased consented, the relatives should still be consulted, but if necessary also informed that they do not have a right to veto the use of the organs. Where the deceased did not consent (or refuse), then there are two mechanisms through which their organs may nevertheless be taken; the first is if the deceased appointed a nominated representative under s 4 of the 2004 Act, and the latter consents – as the Code of Practice makes clear, such a consent cannot be overridden by the relatives.[40]

Secondly, in the absence of a nominated representative, appropriate consent may be given by someone in a 'qualifying relationship'. Such persons are defined in s 54(9) of the Act as 'spouse, partner, parent, child, brother, sister, grandparent, grandchild, child of a brother or sister, step-father, stepmother, half-brother, half-sister and friend of long standing'. In practice a ranking is applied: in this regard the 2004 Act enjoined the Human Tissue Authority to provide in its Code of Practice as follows:

Human Tissue Act 2004

27 Provision with respect to consent

(1) The duty under section 26(3) [viz, to deal with consent issues in its Code of Practice] shall have effect, in particular, to require the Authority to lay down the standards expected in relation to the obtaining of consent where consent falls by virtue of section 2(7)(b)(ii) or 3(6)(c) to be obtained from a person in a qualifying relationship . . .

(4) The qualifying relationships for the purpose of sections 2(7)(b)(ii) and 3(6)(c) should be ranked in the following order–

    (a) spouse or partner;

    (b) parent or child;

    (c) brother or sister;

    (d) grandparent or grandchild;

    (e) child of a person falling within paragraph (c);

    (f) stepfather or stepmother;

    (g) half-brother or half-sister;

    (h) friend of longstanding.

(5) Relationships in the same paragraph of subsection (4) should be accorded equal ranking.

(6) Consent should be obtained from the person whose relationship to the person concerned is accorded the highest ranking in accordance with subsections (4) and (5) . . .

In the case of deceased children, the rules are similar: if capable, the deceased would himself have been able consent; if he did not do so, a person with parental responsibility should be asked, and failing such a person, then somebody in a qualifying relationship.[41] For both adults and children, if a dispute arises between persons of equal rank, the Code of Practice, while suggesting the need for sensitive discussion, states that the organs may be taken and used on the basis of just a single consent.[42] However, as stipulated by s 28 of the 2004 Act, a breach of the Code of Practice will not by itself render the party in breach liable to prosecution.

Unlike the Human Tissue Act 1961, which failed to provide any sanction for non-compliance, the 2004 Act makes clear that the use of material without 'appropriate consent' is a criminal offence. Section 5 provides as follows:

---

40 HTA: *Code of Practice 2*, para 107.
41 Ibid, paras 115 ff.
42 Ibid, para 113.

Human Tissue Act 2004:

5 Prohibition of activities without consent etc

(1) A person commits an offence if, without appropriate consent, he does an activity to which subsection (1), (2) or (3) of section 1 applies, unless he reasonably believes–

    (a) that he does the activity with appropriate consent, or

    (b) that what he does is not an activity to which the subsection applies . . .

(7) A person guilty of an offence under this section shall be liable–

    (a) on summary conviction to a fine not exceeding the statutory maximum;

    (b) on conviction on indictment–

        (i) to imprisonment for a term not exceeding 3 years, or

        (ii) to a fine, or

        (iii) to both.

 SELF-TEST QUESTION

What would the position be if the doctors, in taking an organ, ignore the ranking in s 27(4) of the 2004 Act, and obtain the consent of the deceased's half-brother, rather than of his wife: will they have committed an offence or be otherwise liable?

11.3.3.3 Further issues – conditional and directed donation

In general, it should be noted that, under s 1(1) of the 2004 Act, the presence of 'appropriate consent' merely makes it lawful for the hospital to remove material from the deceased and use it for a stipulated scheduled purpose, including for transplantation. There is, however, no obligation upon it to do so. Most obviously, the organs in question may not be medically suitable for donation; more problematically, even where the deceased expressed the wish to donate in a donor card, the relatives in their distress may voice objections, and the doctors then feel unable ethically to proceed: this appears to have occurred quite often under the (in this respect identical regime of) the 1961 Human Tissue Act, and even though the Code of Practice under the 2004 Act is more robust, in advising doctors to tell the relatives they have no veto rights,[43] it is questionable how far this will alter clinical practice.

A few years ago, media reports into an incident in the North of England highlighted a somewhat different concern, namely the practice of 'conditional donation' in which the relatives, or indeed the deceased, have sought to impose conditions upon the donation of the deceased's organs – in that case that they should only go to a white person. In its subsequent report into the incident, the Department of Health rejected as unethical the possibility of any such conditional donation:

Department of Health, *An Investigation into Conditional Organ Donation: The Report of the Panel*[44]

6.1 This was a very unfortunate incident. It should not have happened. In the Panel's view to attach any condition to a donation is unacceptable, because it offends against the fundamental principle that organs are donated altruistically and should go to patients in the greatest need. The Panel consider that racist conditions are completely abhorrent, as well as being unacceptable under the Race Relations Act . . .

---

43 Ibid, para 100.
44 London: Department of Health, 2000.

6.4 In saying this, the Panel are conscious that one consequence of a decision not to accept organs might be that seriously ill potential recipients might die before other organs become available. This is therefore a hard judgement to make. The Panel are, however, convinced that it is the right one, morally as well as legally. The Panel have been interested to discover that the vast majority of those they have talked to in the course of their investigation, patient groups as well as clinicians, take the same view.

6.5 This is not true of everyone, however. Some very strongly believe that the overriding principle should be the saving of lives. In their view any conditions should be accepted if the consequence is that more organs become available than would otherwise be the case. The Panel do not accept this argument.

In this case, the racist nature of the donor's condition made it relatively easy for the DoH Panel to reject this form of donation as unethical. However, in other circumstances, the ethics of the situation may be more complex: in particular, what of a case where the deceased attaches as a condition of donation that one or more of their organs should be used to treat a particular person or persons? As we saw in section 11.2, this kind of 'directed' donation is the norm in the context of transplants from living donors; however in relation to cadaveric donation, the default position is of 'unconditional' donation, according to an ethic of disinterested altruism, ensuring that organs are allocated purely on the basis of greatest medical need. Two questions are how far this ethical position is open to challenge, particularly in the light of the quite different approach to living donation; and secondly, whether the recent change to the law (in the form of the 'appropriate consent' requirements in the 2004 Act) may unwittingly have served to undermine it?

As regards the first issue, controversy was generated in 2008 by media reports into the case of Laura Ashworth, a young woman who, prior to her sudden death from asthma, intended to apply to the Human Tissue Authority to act as a living kidney donor for her mother, who had suffered renal failure. Laura had also registered as a deceased donor, and following her death, her organs were in fact given to anonymous recipients on the basis of medical need. This was despite her family telling the hospital staff she would have wanted a kidney to go to her mother. The incident prompted the Authority to issue a statement in response:

Human Tissue Authority, *Statement on directed donations of organs after death*[45]

. . . The central principle of matching and allocating organs from the deceased is that they are allocated to the person on the UK waiting list who is most in need and who is the best match with the donor. This is regardless of gender, race, religion or any other factor. The ethics of this position have long been supported by the government and professionals working in the field.

In line with this central principle, a person cannot choose to whom their organ can be given when they die; nor can their family. However, the HTA recognises that there may be exceptional situations when this rule might be reconsidered, but the importance of maintaining the central principle means that such exceptional situations would need to be considered with the greatest care before any part of the current rules were to be changed.

Subsequently, in March 2010, NHS Blood and Transplant, together with the Authority, issued a new policy document, *Requested Allocation of a Deceased Donor Organ*, in which it acknowledged that exceptionally, the previous wishes of the deceased to donate to a specified individual could be taken into account: this was subject though to the donor having registered to donate on an

---

45 HTA Statement 14 April 2008.

unconditional basis, and secondly that no one else was in 'desperately urgent clinical need' of the organ.[46]

As to the effect of the Human Tissue Act 2004, it is arguable that, with its new regime of appropriate consent, it has actually (if unintentionally) put greater power in the hands of deceased donors and/or their relatives to attach conditions to donation, which – if not adhered to – may lead to the potential liability of the medical staff. This argument is explored by Cronin and Douglas as follows:

Cronin, AJ, and Douglas, JF, 'Directed and Conditional Deceased Organ Donations: Laws and Misconceptions'[47]

[P]aragraph 105 [of the HTA Code] states:

Consent can be:
- General, i.e. if someone consents to the use of tissue for research, it need not be limited to a particular object
- Specific, i.e. a person limits their consent – a sample can only be used for research into a particular condition
- Both general and specific, i.e. a general consent subject to specific exceptions.

It is true that the examples given by the 2006 Code seem to refer to cases of proposed tissue retention for research: but both the 2004 Act and the Code make it clear that, in section 3, 'general provision is made for adults to consent to the use of their material for a range of purposes, including research and organ transplantation'. If consent is not required to be unrestricted, or 'generic' in the context of donations for research, the same *must* apply to consent for deceased organ donation for transplantation since neither the 2004 Act nor the Codes make any distinction as to the nature of the consent involved in these two situations. In 2009, a Revised Code of Practice not only restated the difference between generic and specific consent but also emphasized that it should be *valid*, i.e. given voluntarily by an 'appropriately informed' and [capable] person . . .

The conclusion from this interpretation of consent is clear but disconcerting. If a donor's consent has been limited to specific situations, it follows that any allocation of organs contrary to such limitations vitiates that consent and amounts to dealing with the organs without consent . . . [In such a case] [NHS Blood and Transplant, Organ and Transplantation Directorate] (or any other organ user] is *not* free to accept the donation while ignoring the restriction . . . To do so would be an offence under section 5 of the Act. It has been argued already that conditional and directed donations have never been illegal per se, as they are not prohibited by any law. But, even if a restriction were held to be illegal (e.g. under the Race Relations Acts), it does not follow that it could then be disregarded for the purposes of establishing consent to unconditional donation. On the contrary, like any other qualification, it would tend to vitiate the donor's consent, raising the prospect of criminal liability as a result.

A further, interesting question that follows on from this, is whether in such circumstances of a conditional directed donation (ie where the deceased consents to donate a given organ to a specified individual only), the medical staff/organ procurement agency would remain free simply to refuse to use the organ on those conditions. For, at least where the organ would have been medically suitable for the nominated recipient, such a refusal could arguably expose them to a civil law action by the latter in negligence. This possibility is considered further in section 11.6.1 below.

---

46 See www.dh.gov.uk/prod_consum_dh/groups/dh_digitalassets/@dh/@en/@ps/documents/digitalasset/dh_114803.pdf.
47 (2010) 18 Med L Rev 275.

11.4 Other Sources of Organs/Tissue

As well as living and deceased human donors, there are a number of other possible sources of supply of organs and tissue that may offer themselves. As transplant technology continues to advance, some of these can be expected to assume increasing importance in the future.

11.4.1 Foetal tissue transplants

Recent developments in medical science have revealed the possibility of using live brain cells, harvested from aborted foetuses of 10–14 weeks' gestation, to treat certain degenerative brain disorders, notably Parkinson's and Alzheimer's disease. In the future, foetal pancreatic cells may also be used in the treatment of some forms of diabetes. In contrast to the issue of embryo research looked at in Chapter 7, the focus here is on the usage of *in vivo* foetuses. The ethical difficulty that this gives rise to, and the entanglement of this issue with the abortion debate, is explored by David Lamb:

Lamb, D, *Organ Transplants and Ethics*[48]

What are the chief ethical objections to foetal tissue research and transplants? There are three closely related objections. First, it is argued that killing and then dissecting a foetus is an abuse to the developing human being. The second objection is that engaging in such practices will brutalise those who perform this work, and the third objection is that it will encourage abortions and even motivate conceptions with the express intention to abort . . . In addition to these objections are ethical problems concerning the authorisation of embryo tissue research and transplantation.

The . . . objections are so closely related that they can be dealt with together. The issue they relate to is the morality of voluntary termination of pregnancy. . . . In short, if voluntary termination is wrong, then so are actions which depend on it, and at least some degree of guilt by association is incurred by those who seek to benefit from the killing of a foetus. Moreover, an assurance that no foetus is ever dissected prior to death would be of no consequence. For on these terms the issue turns on the rightness or wrongness of killing the foetus in the first place . . .

On these terms, it would seem that if the arguments against voluntary terminations are persuasive, then the only scope for ethical discussion on foetal tissue transplantation is whether it is morally acceptable to use material from spontaneous abortions. The problem is that material from the latter is less reliable than from voluntary abortions. This is because the possibility of foetal abnormality is too high, and because of various problems concerning the time lag between the actual death of the foetus and its expulsion from the uterus. In any case, most miscarriages occur too early for viable transplantation.

But given the obvious benefits of foetal cadaver research and transplantation, can these virtues be separated from what some people see as the immorality of elected abortion? According to the foregoing discussion the rights and wrongs of abortion and foetal tissue research and transplantation stand or fall together. Yet despite an obvious causal relationship between them, this is not necessarily the case. It could be argued that even if abortion is regarded as wrong, discussions concerning the ethical status of research on embryos and possible transplantation of foetal tissue are an independent issue. The UK Committee, chaired by John Polkinghorne (1989), outlined a 'separation principle' according to which there must be

---

48 See n 1 above.

'a separation of the supply of foetal tissue from its use'. This is to ensure that the need for foetal tissue does not influence decisions to have abortions. One consequence of this principle was the recommendation that whilst informed maternal consent is required for the use of foetal tissue, the woman concerned should have no knowledge of what happens to it.

What is the ethical basis of a separation principle? [John] Robertson, who maintains that the abortion issue and the ethics of foetal research can be treated separately, suggests an analogy with transplant organs taken from homicide victims. If consent is obtained, then the victim's organs can be retrieved and distributed to recipients without any suggestion that the surgeon who has received the heart, lung, or kidneys, was an accomplice to murder, even if he or she was aware of the source. By the same token medical students, who use cadavers of murder victims in anatomy, cannot be associated with a crime. Moreover, research on legally obtained cadavers of murder victims cannot, in any way, be said to be responsible for the brutalisation of the researchers or contribute to an increase in the homicide rate. 'One may benefit from another's evil act without applauding or approving of that evil', says Robertson . . .

The Polkinghorne Report referred to here was presented in 1989 by a Committee of Inquiry, chaired by the Revd John Polkinghorne, into the research use of such foetuses. It set out its 'separation principle' as follows:

Polkinghorne Committee, *Review of Guidance on the Research Use of Foetuses and Foetal Tissue*[49]

4.1 We have taken the view that, whatever one's ethical opinion about abortion itself, it does not follow that morally there is an absolute prohibition on the ethical use of foetuses or foetal tissue from lawful abortion. We have argued that the termination of pregnancy and the subsequent use of foetal tissue should be recognised as separate moral questions and we regard it as of great importance that the separation of these moral issues should be reflected in the procedures employed. Accordingly, we have recommended that great care should be taken to separate the decisions relating to abortion and to the subsequent use of foetal material. The prior decision to carry out an abortion should be reached without consideration of the benefits of subsequent use. . . .

4.2 It has been argued that knowledge of the use of foetal tissue could influence mothers' decisions to have their pregnancies terminated. It has been suggested that the use of foetal tissue could place women under pressure when reaching a decision or result in more abortions taking place. It has even been put to us that someone could become pregnant in order to make a foetus available for medical use. In our view, pregnancy undertaken to such an end would be an ethically unacceptable use of the foetus as an instrument (treating it as a 'thing'). It is not possible fully to discern people's motivations, but it is possible to limit the degree to which morally dubious wishes can be implemented. To this end we recommend, not only the separation of the decisions relating to abortion and the subsequent use of foetal tissue, but also procedures which will make it impossible for a mother to specify that foetal tissue, which she makes available, should be used in a particular way.

A related question is whether the consent of the mother of the foetus should in fact be sought in these circumstances. David Lamb comments on this as follows:

---

49 Cm 762, London: HMSO, 1989.

Lamb, D, *Organ Transplants and Ethics*[50]

It might be argued that having decided to terminate her pregnancy, she has foregone any rights concerning the foetal disposal. [John] Harris argues that there is no moral basis for seeking the mother's consent over what happens to an aborted foetus. 'Has she not already abdicated responsibility for the foetus by opting for abortion?' asks Harris . . . Moreover, when the aborted foetus cannot live, or is already dead, Harris sees no moral requirement to seek maternal consent:

> If experimenters ask her for, and are given, permission to experiment on the foetus this permission will not absolve them from the responsibility of deciding for themselves whether such a course of action is ethically sound. And if she withholds permission, we must ask what gives her the right to decide that others should not benefit from the research or from transplantation . . .

Harris is equally dismissive of the view that the mother has quasi property rights by virtue of the fact that the foetus is growing inside her. Deadly and infectious viruses may grow in someone's body without any claim that they are in some way 'owned' by the being who plays host to them. Furthermore, if it were established that a foetus were a person, then prohibitions against slavery would rule out property rights over the foetus . . .

In contrast Robertson argues that the case for denying the mother's control is not persuasive: 'As a product of her body and potential heir that she has for her own compelling reasons chosen to abort, she may care deeply about whether foetal remains are contributed to research or therapy to help others' . . . Thus, although:

> . . . she cannot insist that foetal remains be used for transplant because no donor has the right to require that intended donees accept anatomical gifts, but she should retain the existing legal right to veto use of foetal remains for transplant research or therapy. Her consent to donation of foetal tissue should be routinely sought.

Now the case for giving the woman control, on Robertson's terms, seems to rest on the analogy with organ donation, such as live kidney donation. But this analogy is complicated by the suggestion that, by undergoing voluntary termination for family planning purposes, her interest in the foetus ceases with its removal. In electing an abortion, she is, on these terms, expressing an overriding interest in a premature separation from the foetus, consequently terminating any potential interest which could apply to the foetus. Having fulfilled her primary interest, further interest in the foetus would be foregone . . .

For its part, the Polkinghorne Committee took the view that the woman's informed consent should always be obtained:

Polkinghorne Committee, *Review of Guidance on the Research Use of Foetuses and Foetal Tissue*[51]

2.8 . . . The use of foetal tissue from terminations of pregnancy has been justified by analogy with the use of human organs which have become available as a result of morally questionable circumstances, such as careless accident or even murder. However, it has been suggested that this analogy is imperfect, since in the case of abortions the one who consents to the use of the material (the mother) is also the one who has brought about its availability by her decision

---

50 See n 1 above.
51 See n 49 above.

to seek the termination of the existence of her foetus. Some have argued that this decision abrogates the mother's subsequent rights in relation to her foetus. Again, this is an opinion to which the Committee has given careful consideration, but once more it is one that we are unable to accept. Because abortion is a decision of moral ambiguity and perplexity for many, reached only through a conflict of considerations, it seems too harsh a judgment of the mother's relation to her foetus to suppose that she is no longer in a special position with regard to it, following an abortion.

The position that the pregnant woman must consent to the use of aborted foetal tissue is also that reflected in the Human Tissue Authority's Code of Practice on Consent, which though resiles from a significant aspect of the Polkinghorne Committee's 'separation principle':

HTA, *Code of Practice 1 – Consent*[52]

157. The law does not distinguish between fetal tissue and other tissue from the living; fetal tissue is regarded as the mother's tissue. Consequently, fetal tissue is subject to the same consent requirements under the HT Act as all other tissue from the living . . .

159. It should be noted that the reference to fetal tissue within this code does not include stillbirths (babies born dead after 24 weeks gestation), or neonatal deaths (babies or fetuses of any gestational age which are born showing signs of life and die before the age of 28 days). Obtaining consent for the removal, storage or use of the tissue of babies from stillbirths or neonatal deaths should be handled in accordance with provisions for gaining consent for use of the tissue of the deceased . . .

160. It is recognised that, in the absence of specific legal requirements, guidance on the use of fetuses and fetal tissue for research has been derived from the 1989 Review of the Guidance on the Use of Fetuses and Fetal Material, also known as the Polkinghorne Guidelines. A number of aspects of the Polkinghorne Guidelines are outside the remit of the HTA and of this code of practice. However, it should be noted that guidance within the Polkinghorne guidelines which recommended that in the context of giving consent, women should not know the purpose for which the fetus would be used, or whether it would be used at all, is now superseded by guidance within this code on valid consent, which must be based on the person's understanding of what the activity involves . . .

 SELF-TEST QUESTION

In the light of the change in para 160 of the HTA Code, is it possible a woman could now enter into and terminate a pregnancy, with a view to the foetal tissue being used to treat a particular person, eg her sick husband?

11.4.2 Xenotransplantation

Recently, significant research effort has gone into the possibility of xenografting, literally the use of organs and tissue taken from non-human animals. Previously, though such transplants were occasionally tried (a well-known case from 1984 concerned a Californian infant, baby Fae, who

---

52 See n 18 above.

survived for three weeks with a baboon's heart), there was a formidable difficulty in the way of lasting success in the form of inevitable tissue rejection by the donee. However, there now seem real prospects of overcoming this problem by genetically engineering certain breeds of animals specifically for transplant purposes.

The Nuffield Council of Bioethics, in its 1996 report, *Animal to Human Transplants: The Ethics of Xenotransplantation*, charted some of the obstacles in the way of carrying out such transplants on a wide scale:

Nuffield Council on Bioethics, *Animal to Human Transplants: The Ethics of Xenotransplantation*[53]

10.9 Even if some use of animals for medical purposes can be justified in principle, their use for xenotransplantation raises specific issues that need further consideration. Particular concerns are raised by the use of primates, such as baboons . . . The high degree of evolutionary related-ness between human beings and primates both suggests that xenotransplantation of primate organs and tissue might be successful and also raises questions about whether it is ethical to use primates in ways that it is not considered acceptable to use human beings. Certainly, any harm suffered by primates should be given great weight. This position is reflected in the prin-ciples underlying current practice in the UK. *The Working Party endorses the special protection afforded to primates used for medical and scientific purposes.* . . .

10.12 Given the ethical concerns raised by the use of primates for xenotransplantation, atten-tion has turned to developing the pig as an alternative source of organs and tissue. As discussed below, in the view of the Working Party, the use of pigs for xenotransplantation raises fewer ethical concerns. To develop the use of primates for xenotransplantation, when there is an ethically acceptable alternative, would not be justifiable. *The Working Party recommends that non-primate species should be regarded as the source animals of choice for xenotransplantation.* However, possibilities for alleviating the organ shortage which do not involve the use of animals, such as increased donation of human organs, and the development of artificial organs and tissue, should be actively pursued. . . .

Transmission of infectious diseases

. . . 10.25 It is not possible to predict or quantify the risk that xenotransplantation will result in the emergence of new human diseases. But in the worst case, the consequences could be far-reaching and difficult to control. The principle of precaution requires that action is taken to avoid risks in advance of certainty about their nature. It suggests that the burden of proof should lie with those developing the technology to demonstrate that it will not cause serious harm. *The Working Party concluded that the risks associated with possible transmission of infectious diseases as a consequence of xenotransplantation have not been adequately dealt with. It would not be ethical therefore to begin clinical trials of xenotransplantation involving human beings . . .*

In 1997 a government inquiry, chaired by Professor Ian Kennedy, also took the view that, because of the unknown risks associated with infectious diseases passing from animal to human, clinical trials should be delayed. Subsequently the Government established the Xenotransplantation Interim Regulatory Authority to keep the situation under review, but this body was wound up in 2006 in favour of regulation by Department of Health guidance. The latter, while allowing the possibility of xenotransplantation as part of a controlled research project, stipulates strict conditions designed to minimise the attendant risks:

---

53 London: Nuffield Council on Bioethics, 1996.

Department of Health, *Xenotransplantation Guidance*[54]

The Department of Health considers that further development of xenotransplantation should take place in line with international recommendations and guidance. It is recommended that anyone considering xenotransplantation be familiar with these.

Key recommendations include those from the Council of Europe, the European Medicines Agency (EMEA), the Food and Drug Administration (FDA), and the World Health Organisation (WHO).

Common themes across all the international recommendations are that:

- Xenotransplantation should only take place when there is an adequate regulatory framework in place;
- Risks of transmission of known or unknown infections from animal to human should be minimised;
- Traceability and ongoing surveillance of patients is essential;
- Public debate in this area should be encouraged.

The major issue around xenotransplantation is one of public safety, particularly the risk that infectious disease/agents might be transmitted from the animal tissue to the recipient and potentially to the wider population. Much attention is focused on the possibility that [porcine] endogenous retroviruses (which exist harmlessly in animals) may be transferred into humans and become activated – potentially spreading new diseases to the human population. Investigators/researchers will need to bear this in mind as a key factor for consideration by any authorising committee and the regulator . . .

The Government believes that it is right to explore the potential of xenotransplantation in a cautious, stepwise fashion. It is extremely important to carry out a xenotransplant procedure in a controlled research context. Clearly, the wellbeing of the individuals concerned, and the safety of the public in general, must be foremost in the consideration of any proposal to undertake a xenotransplantation procedure. No xenotransplantation procedures involving humans will be allowed to take place unless the approving body is fully satisfied that the evidence put forward is sufficient to justify the particular procedure proposed.

Concerns in respect of animal–human infections have increased still further in the wake of the recent emergence of avian flu, not to mention the 2009 swine flu pandemic. In the light of this it is unsurprising that at present there appear world-wide to be no clinical trials involving xenotransplantation. Indeed, it could be argued that, given the unquantifiable risks of proceeding, and the availability of reasonable alternatives, the time has now come for xenotransplantation trials to be prohibited. As Forvargue and Ost write:

Forvargue, S, and Ost, S, 'When should precaution prevail? Interests in (public) health, the risk of harm, and xenotransplantation'[55]

Given the impossibility of measuring the risks of xenotransplantation and the 'histories of lentiviruses and prions have taught us about the untameable distances between the laboratory, the spread of infectious diseases and public health', a better approach would be to avoid taking the risk to ensure that needless harm is not created. This may seem unnecessarily precautionary but as there are alternatives to xenotransplantation including reforming the existing

---

54 Department of Health, 12 December 2006; see www.dh.gov.uk/en/Publicationsandstatistics/Publications/PublicationsPolicyAndGuidance/DH_063075.

55 (2010) 18 Med L Rev 302.

allotransplant recovery systems and structures and the promise of stem cells, there is no need to create this risk in the first place. In the light of the limited pre-clinical survival times, uncertainty as to the ability of genetically engineered pig organs to support human life, the potentially catastrophic risks, and the difficulties in identifying, managing, and controlling those risks, it is unclear why some still view xenotransplantation as a viable solution to the shortage of organs. In this environment, the public interest in health and state obligations to protect public health require the state to prohibit clinical xenotransplantation.

11.4.3 Mechanical organs

Whilst artificial implants and other devices have long been a mainstay of modern medical science (for example, hip replacements, pacemakers, etc) in terms of organs, the successful design and manufacture of full organs has proven more difficult. Until very recently, the only organ that it appeared feasible to reproduce in mechanical form was the heart. David Lamb chronicles the history of such devices, and the ethical problems to which their use gives rise, as follows:

Lamb, D, *Organ Transplants and Ethics*[56]

The idea of a totally implantable artificial heart was first mooted in 1964, when the USA National Heart Institute drew up a plan for the construction of a prototype and obtained financial support from Congress for the project. The researchers were unrealistically optimistic, for they looked forward to the mass production and implantation of artificial hearts by 1970 . . . Despite some limited success with animals, artificial implants into humans did not achieve any significant results. One major problem is the high incidence of strokes and chronic infections, which has not been overcome. The first human implantation of an artificial heart was performed in Texas in 1969 on a dying patient, Haskelle Karp, who survived for a further 65 hours with it before receiving a human heart. He died shortly after. In 1977 a woman in Zurich survived for two days with an artificial heart . . . The initial belief that an artificial heart might function as a permanent replacement has given way to more realistic therapy. Artificial hearts are presently used, in a limited sense, as 'bridges' to assist survival until a donor becomes available. As of January 1987, some 17 US transplant centres were using artificial heart 'bridges', and 63 patients had been implanted with such a device . . . The number of artificial hearts and ventricular assistance devices currently functioning as bridges is 200 worldwide . . .

The deeper ethical and philosophical aspects of artificial heart implants surfaced in the widely discussed case of Dr Barney Clark, a retired American dentist who received an artificial heart in 1982. Dr Clark's own defective heart was replaced with a device made of polyurethane. The motor driving the heart was too large to be implanted, so it was placed in a cart which the patient had to push around. He lived for 112 days, and his death was caused by the failure of most of his other organs, but not by the failure of the heart, which went on pumping blood to a mass of dead organs, thus demonstrating the separability of the heart function from the mechanism of death. The longest survivor with an artificial heart was William Schroeder, who lived for 620 days, but during that time he suffered four strokes and developed chronic infections which sapped his strength . . .

The suffering endured by Barney Clark and William Schroeder and their families certainly raises ethical problems concerning the extent to which doctors should strive to maintain life. But this limited success may bring hope for the future; hope that an artificial heart is not an impossible dream, and that with sufficient technological improvements artificial implants could reduce waiting lists for human organs.

---

56 See n 1 above.

In the wake of technological developments, increasing use is now made of artificial hearts, either as bridging devices until a donor of a natural heart is found, or to supplement the workings of the patient's own damaged heart. In general the therapeutical results have been very positive: a ten-year pilot study published in the US in 2004 showed that patients who receive such devices have a much higher chance of surviving to transplant and beyond.[57]

Advances in this field continue apace. Thus in 2008 French scientists announced that a permanent artificial heart they are developing is likely to be ready for clinical testing in 2011.[58] More recently, in September 2010, scientists in San Francisco unveiled a prototype model for an artificial kidney that in the future could eliminate the need for dialysis, and which is expected to be ready for testing in five-to-seven years.

11.5 The Status of Extracted Material
11.5.1 The requirements of the Human Tissue Act 2004

As noted, the 2004 Act established a new authority, the Human Tissue Authority, to be responsible for licensing various activities in relation to extracted human material (whether taken from the living or the deceased). Section 16 provides as follows:

Human Tissue Act 2004:

Licensing

16 Licence requirement

(1) No person shall do an activity to which this section applies otherwise than under the authority of a licence granted for the purposes of this section.

(2) This section applies to the following activities–

(a) the carrying-out of an anatomical examination;

(b) the making of a post-mortem examination;

(c) the removal from the body of a deceased person (otherwise than in the course of an activity mentioned in paragraph (a) or (b)) of relevant material of which the body consists or which it contains, for use for a scheduled purpose other than transplantation;

(d) the storage of an anatomical specimen;

(e) the storage (in any case not falling within paragraph (d)) of–

(i) the body of a deceased person, or

(ii) relevant material which has come from a human body,

for use for a scheduled purpose;

(f) the use, for the purpose of public display, of–

(i) the body of a deceased person, or

(ii) relevant material which has come from the body of a deceased person . . .

(7) In subsection (2)–

(a) references to storage do not include storage which is incidental to transportation, and

(b) 'relevant material', in relation to use for the scheduled purpose of transplantation, does not include blood or anything derived from blood.

---

57 Copeland, JG, et al, 'Cardiac Replacement with a Total Artificial Heart as a Bridge to Transplantation' [2004] *New England Journal of Medicine*; 351: 859–67.

58 See www.guardian.co.uk/science/2008/oct/28/artificial-human-heart-trial-2011.

Organ transplantation is a scheduled purpose (under Sch 1 of the Act). The effect of this provision, so far as relevant to that purpose, is that, while the organs' removal need not be licensed, their storage will need to be (although this excludes storage in the course of transportation). This will admittedly have little impact in relation to 'organs' in the narrower sense of solid matter, such as kidneys, etc, which are not presently capable of storage in any event, but will affect holdings of tissue including bone marrow. Licensees will be required to adhere to good practice guidelines issued by the Human Tissue Authority, which will in due course incorporate EU-wide standards of quality assurance and safety, as laid down in the EC Tissues and Cells Directive (2004/23/EC). The storage of blood for transfusion is excluded, being subject to its own regulatory regime pursuant to a separate EC Directive (2002/98/EC).

The framework of regulation instituted by the 2004 Act, and especially its creation of a special authority with responsibility for licensing and disseminating codes of practice, is clearly modelled upon the regime established in relation to reproductive medicine by the Human Fertilisation and Embryology Act 1990. In fact, for a time the Government planned to merge the Human Tissue Authority with the Human Fertilisation and Embryology Authority; in the event though this idea was abandoned as overly complicated.

See Chapter 7 →

11.5.2 The question of property rights

The phenomenon of organ and tissue transplantation, and the practice of removing tissue for medical purposes including donation, give rise to interesting questions as to the status of such material. Is it susceptible of ownership, and, if so, who enjoys the relevant property rights? It is convenient to look at the position in relation to deceased persons first, and then move on to look at ownership of body parts taken from living persons.

11.5.2.1 Rights in the body of a deceased person (or parts taken therefrom)

Traditionally, English law took the view that there were no property rights in the human corpse.[59] The origins of this rule, as well as the development of an exception for cases where the corpse, or body parts taken therefrom, is subject to alteration through human skill, were recently analysed by the Court of Appeal in its decision in *Yearworth v North Bristol NHS Trust*:[60]

> **Lord Judge CJ** (delivering the judgment of the Court): **A human corpse**
>
> [31] In his Institutes of the Laws of England, mostly published in 1641, after his death, Sir Edward Coke wrote . . . that the 'buriall of the Cadaver is nullius in bonis [in the goods of no one] and belongs to Ecclesiastical cognizance'. In his Commentaries on the Laws of England, published in 1765, Sir William Blackstone wrote . . . that:
>
> > '. . . though the heir has a property in the monuments and escutcheons of his ancestors, yet he has none in their bodies or ashes; nor can he bring any civil action against such as indecently at least, if not impiously, violate and disturb their remains, when dead and buried. [But] if any one in taking up a dead body steals the shroud or other apparel, it will be felony; for the property thereof remains in the executor, or whoever was at the charge of the funeral.'
>
> There were at least three reasons for the rule that a corpse was incapable of being owned. First, in that there could be no ownership of a human body when alive, why should death trigger

---

59 *Williams v Williams* [1882] 20 Ch D 659.
60 [2009] EWCA Civ 37.

ownership of it? Second, as implied by Coke and Blackstone, the body was the temple of the Holy Ghost and it would be sacrilegious to do other than to bury it and let it remain buried: see for example, *In Re Estate of Johnson 7 NYS 2d 81* (1938) . . Third, it was strongly in the interests of public health not to allow persons to make cross-claims to the ownership of a corpse: in the words of Higgins J in his dissenting judgment in *Doodeward v. Spence* in the High Court of Australia [(1908) 6 CLR 406], there was an 'imperious necessity for speedy burial'.

. . .

[33] . . . [I]in *Doodeward* . . . [t]he body of a still-born two-headed baby was preserved in spirits by the doctor who had been attending its mother; upon the doctor's death it was sold and later came into the possession of C, who exhibited it for profit as a curiosity. D, a police officer, seized it with a view to its burial. C's action for detinue succeeded. Griffith CJ said:

'[W]hen a person has by the lawful exercise of work or skill so dealt with a human body or part of a human body in his lawful possession that it has acquired some attributes differentiating it from a mere corpse awaiting burial, he acquires a right to retain possession of it . . .'

Although evidently disgusted by C's exhibition of a 'dead-born foetal monster', Barton J agreed. Higgins J dissented on the footing that there could be no ownership of a human corpse.

Parts of a human corpse

[34] In relation to parts of a human corpse our courts have recently built upon the exception, recognised in *Doodeward*, to the principle that there can be no ownership of a human corpse.

[35] First there was the decision of this court in *Dobson v. North Tyneside Health Authority and Another* [1996] 4 A ll ER 474 [in which] Peter Gibson LJ held . . . that the decision in *Doodeward* was (at least arguably) correct. . . .

[36] The issue was also addressed in the Court of Appeal, Criminal Division, in *R v. Kelly and Lindsay* [1998] 3 All ER 741. The defendants appealed against their conviction (and sentence) for theft of human body parts which had been preserved or fixed and had come into the possession of the Royal College of Surgeons, by which they had been used in training surgeons. Their appeals against conviction, founded upon a submission that body parts could not be property and thus the subject of theft, were dismissed. In giving the judgment of the court Rose LJ said in a valuable passage . . .:

'We accept that, however questionable the historical origins of the principle, it has now been the common law for 150 years at least that neither a corpse nor parts of a corpse are in themselves and without more capable of being property protected by rights . . .
. . . [But] parts of a corpse are capable of being property within section 4 of the Theft Act 1968 if they have acquired different attributes by virtue of the application of skill, such as dissection or preservation techniques, for exhibition or teaching purposes . . .
Furthermore, the common law does not stand still. It may be that if, on some future occasion, the question arises, the courts will hold that human body parts are capable of being property for the purposes of section 4, even without the acquisition of different attributes, if they have a use or significance beyond their mere existence. This may be so if, for example, they are intended for use in an organ transplant operation, for the extraction of DNA or, for that matter, as an exhibit in a trial . . .'

11.5.2.2 Rights in body parts taken from the living

We now need to consider the problem of body parts taken from a living person. Here matters are complicated by the fact that the latter, himself, may be felt to have a *prima facie* claim upon such material. This indeed was the question at issue in the *Yearworth*[61] case itself, which involved a compensation claim brought by a number of men whose frozen sperm was negligently destroyed by the defendant fertility clinic. In finding that, for the purposes of their negligence action, the men had property in their sperm, the Court of Appeal held:

See Chapter 7 →

> **Lord Judge CJ:** [45] We conclude:
>
> (a) In this jurisdiction developments in medical science now require a re-analysis of the common law's treatment of and approach to the issue of ownership of parts or products of a living human body, whether for present purposes (viz. an action in negligence) or otherwise.
>
> (b) The present claims relate to products of a living human body intended for use by the persons whose bodies have generated them. In these appeals we are not invited to consider whether there is any significant difference between such claims and those in which the products are intended for use by other persons, for example donated products in respect of which claims might be brought by the donors or even perhaps by any donees permissibly specified by the donors.
>
> . . .
>
> (f) In our judgment, for the purposes of their claims in negligence, the men had ownership of the sperm which they ejaculated:
>
> (i) By their bodies, they alone generated and ejaculated the sperm.
>
> (ii) The sole object of their ejaculation of the sperm was that, in certain events, it might later be used for their benefit . . . It is true that, by confining all storage of sperm and all use of stored sperm to licence-holders, the [Human Fertilisation and Embryology Act 1990] has effected a compulsory interposition of professional judgment between the wishes of the men and the use of the sperm . . . For two reasons, however, the absence of their ability to 'direct' its use does not in our view derogate from their ownership. First, there are numerous statutes which limit a person's ability to use his property – for example a land-owner's ability to build on his land or to evict his tenant at the end of the tenancy or a pharmacist's ability to sell his medicines – without eliminating his ownership of it. Second, by its provisions for consent, the Act assiduously preserves the ability of the men to direct that the sperm be not used in a certain way: their negative control over its use remains absolute.
>
> . . . (v) In reaching our conclusion that the men had ownership of the sperm for the purposes of their present claims, we are fortified by the precise correlation between the primary, if circumscribed, rights of the men in relation to the sperm, namely in relation to its future use, and the consequence of the Trust's breach of duty, namely preclusion of its future use.

In the upshot, there now appear two separate bases for acquiring property rights in body parts. The first, which applies to material from the deceased and living alike, is where the material is subject to some process or application. Here, third parties in lawful possession, such as medical personnel, may acquire rights in the material; indeed, this principle receives statutory recognition in s 32(9)(c) Human Tissue Act 2004, which excludes from the prohibition on commercial dealings,

---

61 Ibid.

'material which is the subject of property because of an application of human skill'. Secondly, as regards material from living persons, this may, as held in *Yearworth*, be regarded as the property of the donor of the tissue, insofar as he retains a legitimate interest in its use for his own benefit.

The difficult question remains, though, of what happens when such third party and first party claims are in conflict? This is a matter of huge practical significance given the scope for the commercial exploitation of human tissue, including through its use to develop cell-lines with lucrative future applications. The problem of how to balance the interests of the parties, as well as take account of wider social interests, underlay the well-known decision of the Supreme Court of California in *Moore v Regents of University of California*.[62] In that case, the plaintiff had his spleen removed during treatment for leukaemia. Unbeknown to him, the doctors then used it to generate a cell line from which a highly profitable drug was produced. Moore subsequently brought a claim, inter alia, in conversion (on the basis that he retained ownership) in order to secure a share of the profits. However, the Court rejected this head of the claim, essentially for policy reasons:

> **Panelli J (for the majority)**: Research on human cells plays a critical role in medical research. This is so because researchers are increasingly able to isolate naturally occurring, medically useful biological substances and to produce useful quantities of such substances through genetic engineering. These efforts are beginning to bear fruit. Products developed through biotechnology that have already been approved for marketing in this country include treatments and tests for leukemia, cancer, diabetes, dwarfism, hepatitis-B, kidney transplant rejection, emphysema, osteoporosis, ulcers, anemia, infertility, and gynecological tumors, to name but a few. . . .
>
> The extension of conversion law into this area will hinder research by restricting access to the necessary raw materials. Thousands of human cell lines already exist in tissue repositories, such as the American Type Culture Collection and those operated by the National Institutes of Health and the American Cancer Society. . . . At present, human cell lines are routinely copied and distributed to other researchers for experimental purposes, usually free of charge. This exchange of scientific materials, which still is relatively free and efficient, will surely be compromised if each cell sample becomes the potential subject matter of a lawsuit . . .
>
> **Mosk J (dissenting)**: [O]ur society acknowledges a profound ethical imperative to respect the human body as the physical and temporal expression of the unique human persona. One manifestation of that respect is our prohibition against direct abuse of the body by torture or other forms of cruel or unusual punishment. Another is our prohibition against indirect abuse of the body by its economic exploitation . . . for the sole benefit of another person. The most abhorrent form of such exploitation, of course, was the institution of slavery. Lesser forms, such as indentured servitude or even debtor's prison, have also disappeared. Yet their specter haunts the laboratories and boardrooms of today's biotechnological research-industrial complex. It arises wherever scientists or industrialists claim, as defendants claim here, the right to appropriate and exploit a patient's tissue for their sole economic benefit – the right, in other words, to freely mine or harvest valuable physical properties of the patient's body . . .

The decision in the *Moore* case remains controversial, and following the Court of Appeal decision in *Yearworth* it is possible the courts in England might take a different view of the claimant's rights.[63] Nonetheless, as Herring and Chau argue, it is far from clear that according the donor property in his material offers the best solution:

---

62 793 Pd 479 (1990).
63 The Court in *Yearworth* (n 60 above) noted the existence of 'trenchant dissents' in *Moore*.

Herring, J, and Chau, P-L, 'My Body, Your Body, Our Bodies'[64]

To some, *Moore* shows the problem with not adopting the property approach. Vast sums of money were made by the scientists, but the person who made 'everything possible' was left with nothing. A property approach would ensure he was adequately rewarded. The difficulty is that the property approach might ensure he was over-rewarded. On the facts, if we regarded the DNA sequence as his and therefore accept he has a claim to the money produced from his property, then in theory he should be entitled to all the proceeds. There is a danger that valuable research into stem cell lines and DNA will be hindered if patients are able to claim an interest in the products . . . The door might be opened to a lawyer's goldmine as weeks are spent in the courtroom attempting to ascertain whose bodily material was used in the creation of a particular product. It may be that the *Moore* decision is complicated by the fact that the research on Moore's body parts was carried out without his consent and permission. The decision left this deception without any form of sanction. . . .

The real issue is money. To some, to give an individual whose body by chance carries a useful DNA sequence a share in millions of dollars is iniquitous. On the other hand, is it any less iniquitous that the money should end up in the hands of the scientists who may have put little effort into the discovery? And some people are able to make large sums of money from their outward appearance which may simply be an accident of DNA. Some have suggested that genetic information that creates a useful product should be seen as owned by the community and the money put to projects that benefit the community . . .

We all benefit from the existence of the social practice of medical research. Many of us would not be here if infant mortality had not been brought under control, or antibiotics had not been invented. Most of us will continue to benefit from these and other medical advances (and indeed other advances such as clean drinking water and sanitation). Since we accept these benefits, we have an obligation in justice to contribute to the social practice which produces them.

It could be argued that, just as it was unlucky chance that Moore contracted leukemia, requiring his (successful) treatment, it was lucky chance that exploitable material was inside him. Here, a financial reward to the patient may well appear inconsistent. After all, a fundamental aim of any equitable system of health care – from which Moore himself benefited – is to even out, not encourage, inequalities arising from the 'natural lottery'.

 SELF-TEST QUESTION

If body parts were recognised generally as the property of the person whose body they come from, would this mean persons could sell their organs and tissue on the open market? If so, is this a prospect we should embrace or reject?

11.6 The Interests of the Organ Recipient

11.6.1 The putative recipient

We begin by looking at the position of the potential recipient of a transplant organ, prior to the transplant actually taking place. First it is clear that, even if he desperately needs the organ to

---

64 (2007) 15 Med L Rev 34; for a different view, see Nwabueze, R, 'Donated Organs, Property Rights, and the Remedial Quagmire' (2008) 16 Med L Rev 201.

survive, and a compatible donor is identified, he cannot require the latter to submit to non-consensual extraction. A well-known case in point is *McFall v Shimp*,[65] discussed in Chapter 3 above. In that case an American court refused to compel a man to undergo a bone-marrow transplant in order to save his dying cousin. While Flaherty J took the view that the man's refusal to submit voluntarily was morally indefensible, he was not prepared to recognise a legal duty to donate, which would fly in the face of the stress placed by liberal society on the inviolability of the individual. It is virtually certain that an English court, faced with a similar predicament, would come to the same conclusion.

The legal position is less clear, however, in cases where the organ has already been removed from the donor. In such cases, it is arguable that, as discussed in section 11.5.2, the organ may enjoy the status of property. This possibility was alluded to by Rose LJ in *R v Kelly and Lindsay*,[66] and Remigius Nwabueze has argued such an approach would offer the best means of addressing problems relating to damaged or misdirected organs:

Nwabueze, R, 'Donated Organs, Property Rights, and the Remedial Quagmire'[67]

Transplantation technology brought with it a significantly different dimension to property claims over the human body and body parts. Unforeseen problems may arise in the course of moving organs across state and local borders and through several authorised hands en route to the recipient. Although people within the organ transfer network (physicians, nurses, administrators and technicians) appreciate the need for optimal levels of care and competence, human fallibility remains an undermining factor with enormous potential for injury. For instance, an organ donated and prepared for transplantation might be damaged by poor preservation techniques or inefficient handling. Likewise, an organ donated by A for transplantation to B might be intentionally or negligently redirected to C . . . Such challenges have exacerbated with the development of organ transplantation as a routine medical procedure. It is important that a legal system should have clear rules for dealing with such problems . . . A claim in negligence is surely one of the possible causes of action, though problems relating to causation and proof of damage remain formidable. The focus here, however, is on the property liability of a defendant in the above hypothetical scenario.

Property claims to body parts donated for transplantation are qualitatively different from other contexts in which property rights have been asserted with respect to the human body and parts of it . . . More than emotional pain, a misdirected organ causes some real, physical deprivation. The claimant will complain about not only his or her mental agony but also the loss of a physical organ directed to him or her . . . The claimant has lost something whose physical embodiment shares some of the characteristics of ordinary forms of property and would, accordingly, be reasonable to expect a proprietary redress.

In the US, a claim by a disappointed putative recipient (after the organ earmarked for him by the deceased donor was given to another person) was the subject of litigation in *Colavito v New York Organ Donor Network*.[68] In *Colavito* (No 2), the court dealing with the matter expressed a preference for a property-based analysis; however in *Colavito* (No 3), this approach was rejected by the New York Court of Appeals, which saw the remedy in such a case as lying in negligence. On the facts, though, the plaintiff's claim failed as he would not in any event have been a compatible recipient for the material.

---

65 10 Pa D & C (3d) 90 (1978).
66 [1999] QB 621.
67 See n 64 above.
68 *Colavito v New York Organ Donor Network* (No 2) 438 F 3d 214 (2006); *Colavito* (No 3) 8 NY3d 43 (2006).

As discussed in 11.3.3 above, in the UK the practice of directed donation from deceased (as opposed to living) donors is currently opposed by guidelines maintained by NHS Blood and Transplant, which see it as contrary to the desired ethic of altruism. However, as suggested in the article by Cronin and Douglas, this policy may no longer consonant with the regime of 'appropriate consent' under the 2004 Human Tissue Act. In a case where a donor opted for directed donation, and the procurement agency failed to abide by his wishes (eg by allowing the organ to perish), it is quite possible that – subject to establishing compatibility – the English courts would grant the putative recipient a remedy in negligence.[69] Such a claim appears even stronger in the case of a misdirected live transplant.

11.6.2 The actual recipient

11.6.2.1 Redress for injury against the surgeon/procurement agency

As we have seen, some organ transplant therapy (especially that involving animal or artificial implants) remains highly experimental in nature. It has been argued by JK Mason that, just as the donor cannot consent to the extraction of an organ if it is likely to cause them serious harm, 'it is equally unlawful to consent to accept an organ in the certainty or near certainty that it would be fatal to do so'.[70] We respectfully doubt whether, so far as a 'near certainty' is involved, this is correct: a one in a thousand chance of life is surely better – other things equal – than no chance at all. At the same time, problematic questions of consent may arise, at least at an ethical level. As Forvargue and Ost note in the context of possible participation in a xenotransplantation trial:

Forvargue, S, and Ost, S, 'When should precaution prevail? Interests in (public) health, the risk of harm, and xenotransplantation'[71]

In order to fulfil the positive obligation of autonomy, which requires '[r]espectful treatment in disclosing information and actions that foster autonomous decision making', the surgeon performing the xenotransplant must provide the necessary information for a person to make an informed decision. This will not be easy given the limited information available on xenotransplantation. And an individual consenting to participate in a xenotransplant trial might not be truly exercising individual autonomy because it will lead to such a severe infringement of their personal autonomy in the future. Is it possible to give fully informed consent to as-of-yet unexperienced severe liberty limiting measures which could include a lifelong surveillance and monitoring regime, remaining within it, refraining from having children, and compulsory post-mortems?

Similar doubts surrounding consent may arise in respect of the unknown psychological effects of participating in recently developed transplant procedures affecting the outward appearance of the recipient, such as face or hand transplants.

What is, by contrast clearer is that insofar as a transplant surgeon performs the operation without due care and, in so doing causes harm to the recipient, the standard principles of negligence will apply to afford the latter a remedy. An allegation of negligence may also be framed against the agency or authority which procured the organ for transplantation. This will be so if the organ itself turns out to be defective in some way, notably if the donee is exposed to a virus, such as HIV or

---

69 It is unclear why, as intimated by Nwabueze (n 67 above), causation and damage should pose a special problem: the putative recipient will generally be quantifiably worse off than if he had received the organ.

70 In Dyer, C (ed), *Doctors, Patients and the Law*, Oxford: Blackwells, 1992, 122.

71 See n 55 above.

hepatitis, that the donor was carrying. The Nuffield Council on Bioethics has considered some of the special problems that might face a recipient claimant in such a case as follows:

Nuffield Council on Bioethics, *Human Tissue: Ethical and Legal Issues*[72]

12.53 -Standards of care change from time to time: what was not negligence in 1990 may well be negligence in 1995. As knowledge, and the perception of risks and their avoidance, improve, so too do the obligations imposed upon those who work in these areas. For example, at one time far less was known than today about the various contaminants in blood products: HIV, hepatitis, syphilis, malaria and toxoplasmosis; and methods of screening or heat treating blood products were not so prevalent. There may have been no negligence liability on the supplier of defective blood had a person then been contaminated with an HIV virus. The situation would be different today, when the norm is to test for such viruses. But what of other viruses? Does an obligation to screen for all known viruses arise as soon as the risk of their presence becomes known? The view has been expressed that as:

> . . . more and more minor contaminants of recombinant DNA derived human growth hormone are being identified which are biologically active and pose no safety problem . . . the effort and expense in identifying them and then measuring them on a batch-to-batch basis may be out of proportion to the public health risk.

-As long as no adverse consequences follow, that argument may appear to be sound. But what happens if a virus which is deliberately neglected turns out to be far more potent than was anticipated? This has been an issue with hepatitis C: could it be said to be negligent to take a professional, and considered, decision not to screen for this virus even when its presence but not its full potency were known? And what of such bodies as the Committee on the Safety of Medicines and the Licensing Authority . . . should they be liable for failure to act earlier to impose higher standards of care? In the last resort, it will be for the courts to weigh up all the factors and decide whether the balance struck was reasonable . . .

The Nuffield Council also considered whether a claimant might be able to bring an action under the Consumer Protection Act 1987:

12.57 -A product is 'defective' when it does not provide the safety which a person is entitled to expect, taking all the circumstances into account. Thus, instructions for use, contraindications and warnings and supplied information in one form or another may in some cases assist in determining whether the product was 'defective'. Contaminated blood supplied to patients, or a defective organ used for transplantation, are likely to be regarded as 'defective products' regardless of the information which is given to patients.

12.58 -Liability is imposed upon producers, including manufacturers, importers and suppliers of such products. It is likely that human tissue would be regarded as 'products' for these purposes. This was recommended by the Pearson Royal Commission in 1978. Human tissue used for medical purposes, although not strictly manufactured, would possess the 'essential characteristics attributable to an industrial or other process'.

12.59 -Although these strict liability provisions are an improvement on the negligence action, there are still many difficult hurdles which an injured person has to face before liability can be established. The two most difficult are the so called 'development-risk' defence and, once again, causation.[73]

---

72 See n 6 above.
73 Ibid.

With regard to the residual hurdles under the 1987 Act mentioned in para 12.59, the development risk defence may no longer pose such an obstacle to claimants in the light of the 2001 ruling in *A and Others v National Blood Authority*,[74] which arose out of the supply of blood contaminated with the Hepatitis C virus.

See Chapter 6 →

Lastly, it should be noted that other forms of action, besides those just mentioned, may be available against the procurement agency in appropriate cases. In the American case of *Ashcraft v King*,[75] the plaintiff recovered in battery after receiving HIV infected blood from an anonymous donor; she had stipulated that she wanted blood obtained only from members of her immediate family. Equally, in France the director of a procurement agency was charged with manslaughter after a patient, who had received an infected corneal graft, died of rabies.

11.6.2.2 Redress against the organ donor

Because of limitations in current screening techniques, it is possible for infected tissue to fail to be identified even though the procurement agency took all reasonable precautions. In such a case a donee, injured through the use of such tissue, would have an action, if at all, only against the original donor of the material: it may be that the latter was (or should have been) aware of their infected status and/or failed to reply honestly to the inquiries of the procurement agency.

In a number of US and Commonwealth cases, the courts have been unsympathetic to the donee's cause. In *Rasmussen v South Florida Blood Service*,[76] in which the plaintiff became infected with HIV following a blood transfusion, public policy in favour of the preservation of donor anonymity was said to outweigh the donee's rights in the matter:

> **Barkett J**: The threat posed by the disclosure of the donors' identities goes far beyond the immediate discomfort occasioned by a third party probing into sensitive areas of the donors' lives. Disclosure of donor identities in any context involving AIDS could be extremely disruptive and even devastating to the individual donor. If the requested information is released, and petitioner queries the donors' friends and fellow employees, it will be functionally impossible to prevent occasional references to AIDS . . .
>
> We wish to emphasise that although the importance of protecting the privacy of donor information does not depend on the special stigma associated with AIDS, public response to the disease does make this a more critical matter. By the very nature of this case, disclosure of donor identities is disclosure in a damaging context. We conclude, therefore, that the disclosure sought here implicates constitutionally protected privacy interests.
>
> Our analysis of the interests to be served by denying discovery does not end with the effects of disclosure on the private lives of the 51 donors implicated in this case. Society has a vital interest in maintaining a strong volunteer blood supply, a task that has become more difficult with the emergence of AIDS. The donor population has been reduced by the necessary exclusion of potential blood donors through AIDS screening and testing procedures as well as by the unnecessary reduction in the donor population as a result of the widespread fear that donation itself can transmit the disease. In light of this, it is clearly 'in the public interest to discourage any serious disincentive to volunteer blood donation'. Because there is little doubt that the prospect of inquiry into one's private life and potential association with AIDS will deter blood donation, we conclude that society's interest in a strong and healthy blood supply will be furthered by the denial of discovery in this case.

---

74 [2001] 3 All ER 289.
75 278 Cal Rptr 900 (1991).
76 500 So 2d 533 (1987).

A similar conclusion was reached in the Scottish case of *AB v Scottish National Blood Transfusion Service*.[77] However, in other cases some relaxation of this strict anonymity requirement has been allowed in favour of a rule of 'cloaked disclosure'.[78] Even so, the point of doing this is to assist a plaintiff where there is a suspicion that the *procurement agency* may have been negligent in allowing the blood through. Indeed, as one of the conditions for receiving such information, the plaintiff has had to undertake not to sue the donor directly.

 SELF-TEST QUESTION

Could it not be argued against the recipient (in at least some cases) that he is in any event better off than if he had not received the organ/tissue at all, and accordingly has not suffered any damage?

11.7 Tackling the Shortage in Organs

Transplant activity is increasingly constrained by the shortage of organs, a phenomenon affecting every country which has developed the ability to undertake this form of surgery. Quite possibly uniquely, doctors and surgeons are prevented from alleviating suffering and avoiding death by the shortage of a particular physical resource – a human organ. Figures from NHS Blood and Transplant[79] show that in September 2010, there were around 8,000 persons on the National Transplant 'active' waiting list for a transplant (the active list only includes persons with a reasonable chance of receiving an organ; the overall number of persons who could benefit from the procedure is far higher). Given the poignant consequence of a significant number of avoidable deaths, often of quite young people, it is natural that much attention has been focused on the possibility of remedying this shortfall through legal reform. In terms of the possible sources of organs and tissue identified above, cadaveric transplants seem *prima facie* to be the type where such reform may have the greatest chance of achieving positive results.

11.7.1 Addressing the shortfall in cadaveric organs

The system, under the Human Tissue Act, with its emphasis on 'appropriate consent', either from the deceased or someone else empowered by the Act to give it, may be described as an 'opt in' scheme: in default of 'appropriate consent', material may not be taken or used. The reason for this approach, which is stricter than the regime it replaced under the 1961 Human Tissue Act (which simply required enquiry of relatives who could be reasonably located, to check they did not object) may be understood in the context of the scandals that formed the background to the new Act.

Nonetheless, a move to a more liberal 'opt out' approach to organ donation, based on the presumed consent of the donor unless he made known his objections while alive, has long been advocated by the BMA and, both during and after the passage of the 2004 Act, several MPs pressed for such a scheme. Key questions remain, though, as to the degree of public support such a move would enjoy, and whether it would actually increase organ donation rates. One should also be

77 1993 SLT 36.

78 See *Snyder v Mekhjian* 593 A 2d 318 (1991); *PD v Australian Red Cross Society (NSW Div)* (1993) 30 NSWLR 376.

79 NHS Blood and Transplant publishes weekly statistics, including numbers of persons registered for a transplant, and operations taking place, at www.uktransplant.org.uk/ukt/statistics/latest_statistics/latest_statistics.jsp.

aware that, as the 1994 Kings Fund Institute report notes by reference to practices in other jurisdictions, 'presumed consent' itself is not a single approach, but comes in alternative forms:

New, B, et al, *A Question of Give and Take*[80]

Changing the law on gaining consent

Of particular interest to policy makers has been the various legal frameworks within which procurement takes place. The UK, along with Germany, the Netherlands, Italy, Canada, Australia and New Zealand, have what might broadly be termed 'opting in' legal systems. Two other systems have generated much interest in the literature: presumed consent – also known as opting out – and required request.

Presumed consent

Presumed consent schemes have been introduced into many countries, although attempts to enact such legislation in the UK have always failed, the latest being the Transplantation of Human Organs Bill 1993. The international legislation falls into several categories. The purest version of the law allows automatic removal except in a situation in which the deceased has expressed an objection during his or her lifetime. This 'strict' type of presumed consent procedure applies in Austria where organs can be removed provided in his or her life, the person concerned has not expressed an objection. The views of close relatives are not taken into account . . .

A slightly less strict version of presumed consent operates in Belgium where, if there is no explicit objection by the deceased, the relatives are allowed to object but the medical profession are under no obligation to seek their views. The relatives must initiate the process under these circumstances . . .

Other, still weaker, schemes allow removal unless the deceased has made an explicit or informal objection at any time. Such a formulation of the law effectively requires that the relatives are consulted in order to glean the wishes of the deceased. Although it is formally the views of the deceased whilst alive which are being sought, such schemes allow the relatives to object on the deceased's behalf. France and Spain operate presumed consent legislation of this kind . . .

Finally, a scheme in operation in Singapore provides for the automatic exclusion of certain categories of potential donor, including non-citizens and Muslims . . . Muslims can, however, donate their organs if they wish, by pledging their organs whilst alive or if their relatives consent . . .

In 2009, a research review carried out for NICE by the Health Technology Assessment programme found notably higher rates of cadaveric transplants in countries with presumed consent approaches, such as Belgium and Austria, than in the UK. Interestingly, the country with the highest rate (with 34.3 donors per million of population annually, compared to just 13.2 in the UK) was Spain: the latter has a 'soft' version of presumed consent, which allows the relatives to object, but apparently in practice only around 20 per cent do so. As the HTA programme review concludes:

Rithalia, A, et al, *A systematic review of presumed consent systems for deceased organ donation*[81]

1. Presumed consent alone is unlikely to explain the variation in organ donation rates between different countries. A combination of legislation, availability of donors, transplantation system

---

80 See n 2 above.
81 *Health Technology Assessment* 2009: Vol 13, issue 26. The review can be accessed at www.hta.ac.uk/fullmono/mon1326.pdf.

organisation and infrastructure, wealth and investment in health care, as well as underlying public attitudes to and awareness of organ donation and transplantation, may all play a role, although the relative importance of each is unclear. The between-country comparison studies overall point to presumed consent law being associated with increased organ donation rates (even when other factors are accounted for) although it cannot be inferred from this that the introduction of presumed consent legislation per se leads to an increase in donation rates. The before-and-after studies suggest an increase in donation rates following the introduction of presumed consent legislation; however, it is not possible to rule out the influence of other factors on donation rates.

2. It is important to note that the survey evidence is incomplete and the variation in attitudes between surveys may reflect differences in methods and the phrasing of questions. Some surveys suggest a lack of public support for presumed consent, both in the UK and in other countries; however, more recent UK surveys provide evidence of support for presumed consent.

Implications for policy

. . . The available evidence suggests that presumed consent legislation is associated with an increase in organ donation rates, although the size of the association varied between studies. Other factors also appear to be associated with organ donation rates, such as transplant capacity and GDP and health expenditure per capita. It is therefore important to consider such factors when attempting to predict the impact of changing to a presumed consent system. It is also important to take into account the likely public response to presumed consent should legislation be changed. The limited and incomplete evidence available from surveys suggests variable levels of support. In addition, consideration needs to be given to potential variation in attitudes between different socio-demographic subgroups.

Arguably, in this area, legal change unaccompanied by any corresponding change in cultural values (notably the pre-eminence accorded to the views of relatives), or commitment of greater technical resources to organ retrieval, is unlikely to decrease appreciably the shortfall in donor organs. As Bernard Teo has observed:

Teo, B, 'Strategies of organ procurement'[82]

What strategy of organ procurement a society ought to adopt depends on its willingness to expend resources for its transplant programme(s), ie, after the requirements of social priorities have been considered. If it chooses to ration resources for these programme(s), then it is arguably wiser to adopt a less efficient but ethically preferable strategy of expressed consent or its variants. The system would most likely yield a limited quantity of organs which would probably remain comfortably within the resources allocated for the programme(s). What would be the purpose of adopting a more efficient organ procurement policy when the number of procedures capable of being performed would be constrained by limitations in other resources? . . .

Perhaps France is a case in point. In his report on the French organ transplant and procurement programmes, Arthur Caplan noted that concerns for the rising costs of health care have created a less than enthusiastic commitment of its scarce medical resources to its transplant programmes. Restrictions in the availability of resources for transplants have placed '. . . severe limits both in terms of personnel and hospital space on the number of

---

82 (1992) 6 *Bioethics* 113.

transplants of all types that can now be performed'. . . . Thus, it is arguable that France ought not to have adopted presumed consent without prior consideration of the extent to which it is prepared to support its transplant programmes. . . .

Even as a society contemplates the adoption of presumed consent, it ought to consider another important factor: political feasibility. . . . The French people hold a strong belief in the rights of families relative to cadaver disposal. French doctors find it 'psychologically intoler-able to remove tissues from a body without obtaining the permission of the next of kin' . . . In practice, France's presumed consent policy, ie of not requiring familial consent, exists only on paper.

A similar conclusion was reached by the Organ Donation Taskforce (an arm of NHS Blood and Transplant) in its 2008 Report, *Organs for Transplant*.[83] While rejecting the adoption of a 'presumed consent' model, it outlined 14 recommendations directed to organisational and logistical aspects of organ retrieval, including UK-wide co-ordination and improved education of medical personnel and the public, which, in its view could produce a 50 per cent increase in deceased donations within five years.

11.7.2 Creating a market in organs?

The shortfall in organs could probably be eradicated at one stroke if we were prepared to sanction commercial dealings in them. However, such a possibility undoubtedly arouses widespread repug-nance. The main arguments against permitting a market in organs are explored by Wilkinson and Garrard, who find them less convincing than often supposed:

Wilkinson, S and Garrard, E, 'Bodily integrity and the sale of human organs'[84]

There seem to us to be four standard objections to permitting organ sale, each of which we regard as ultimately unconvincing:

Pain and risk

The first is simply that the organ seller is subjected to an extremely high level of pain and risk. This in itself, though, can't be sufficient to justify a ban on organ sale, since we don't in general think that it's wrong to pay people for doing dangerous things. (There are numerous examples of this: firefighters, astronauts, miners and divers, to name but a few.) Common forms of 'risky labour' are often more dangerous than organ sale, but are regarded as heroic, rather than condemned; it is seen as quite proper to reward those who do them. And this difference in attitude can't be justified in terms of the good consequences that 'risky labour' produces, since the consequences of an organ sale (typically, saving a life) may be just as good or better.

Exploitation and commodification

The second worry is that the relationship between the buyer and seller is likely to be exploita-tive and to either cause or constitute an unacceptable *commodification* of the seller and/or her body. Brecher, for example, describes trading in human kidneys (along with many other practices) as 'exploitation based on making a commodity of human beings'.

There are two problems with this objection. First, although organ sale does necessarily involve treating a human body part as a commodity, there is no reason to suppose that this is

---

83 London: Department of Health, January 2008. The report is available at www.dh.gov.uk/prod_consum_dh/groups/ dh_digitalassets/@dh/@en/documents/digitalasset/dh_082120.pdf.
84 (1996) 22 JME 334.

necessarily exploitative. Would we really regard it as exploitative if the organ seller were wealthy, educated, rational and well informed and got paid £1,000,000 for her organ? Second, we do, in fact, permit many practices which are at least as exploitative and 'commodifying' as organ sale (for example, poorly paid labour). Of course, this doesn't show that exploitation and commodification are acceptable. But it *does* show that they aren't a special problem for organ sale and that they alone can't explain why organ sale is seen as more offensive than (say) low wages. . . .

Undermining the practice of free donation

Another objection to permitting organ sale is that to do so would undermine the practice of free donation. Abouna *et al*, for example, claim that there is 'considerable evidence to indicate that marketing in human organs will eventually deprecate and destroy the present willingness of members of the public to donate their organs out of altruism'. There are two distinct worries here. The first is a purely practical one. If payment is allowed, then virtually all donors will begin to expect payment and so voluntary donations will cease. The second is that allowing payment for organs would deprive people of an opportunity to participate in 'giving' relationships with one another: relationships which have some ethical or social value, independently of their practical consequences.

Taking the second worry first, it is sufficient to point out that the mere permissibility of sale doesn't itself prevent people from donating (although it might, of course, encourage them to sell rather than donate). Organ givers are at liberty to waive their fee and, in a sense, the possibility of sale allows the (free) donor to be even more generous than she could otherwise have been; for not only does she give up her organ, but she gives up her fee as well.

As regards the first worry, it seems that there's no compelling reason to believe that organ sale would undermine the practice of free donation. After all, professional social work and charitable social work co-exist. Also, if organ sale led to a significant overall increase in the supply of organs, this would more than compensate for the reduced number of free organs. But in any case, it is far from clear that there is a significant practice of free donation to be undermined . . . Given the high level of pain and risk involved, free donation (except by relatives, who might well waive the fee, if it were offered) is very unlikely to take place anyway.

Concerns about autonomy and consent

It is generally agreed that the absence of coercion and manipulation is required for genuine consent. And the final objection we consider is that no one could ever be in a position autonomously to consent to selling an organ such as a kidney, since the process would be so unpleasant and/or dangerous that only someone who was coerced or manipulated would agree to it. One virtue of this objection is that it would explain why we're more concerned about organ selling than the selling of blood and certain other body products. In the case of the latter, the level of pain and/or risk is very low, and so the need for coercion and manipulation is much less.

This objection does, indeed, raise a serious practical worry about the possibility of organ sellers being coerced, and it is certainly true that, were organ sale to be permitted, rigorous safeguards aimed at ensuring fully informed consent in every case would be required. But does organ sale necessarily involve coercion or manipulation? It seems not, since even a wealthy, informed and rational agent might consent to it (without coercion or manipulation) if the price were high enough. Would we want to say, in such a case, that the person hadn't really consented? (Of course, with a broad enough conception of manipulation, the answer to this question might be 'yes', but we would question whether so broad a conception would be able to do any ethical work, since too many things would be counted as manipulative.)

Also, given that organ sale is less unpleasant and dangerous than many accepted forms of 'risky labour', were we to take this objection seriously, then a wide range of accepted practices should be condemned on similar grounds.

Ultimately, our reluctance to treat irreplaceable bodily parts as commodities which may be the subject of buying and selling seems to be grounded both in an intrinsic sense of respect for persons as ends in themselves, and in fears as to the moral climate of any society in which organised trading in organs became the norm. As Bernard Teo writes:

Teo, B, 'Strategies of organ procurement'[85]

. . . [T]he human body is not like other things. Since human bodiliness is intrinsically tied to human personality and identity, it follows that respect for the human person would also be intrinsically tied to respect for the human body and its parts. In every culture and society, the instinctive revulsion and strong moral aversion toward treating the human body as property and commodity in both religious and secular attitudes is shown by the special respect accorded to the body in elaborate ceremonies and rituals surrounding death and burial. They are signs of respect and reverence for the person who lived. There seems to be that intuitive instinct that the human body has a special moral significance that cannot be equated with other things or commodities. Leon Kass, a physician and philosopher, has warned against trivialising human embodiment. Because human dignity is intrinsically linked to human embodiment, treating the body and its parts as commodities would be to strip the human body of its proper dignity. It would be morally intolerable therefore if human body parts are treated as objects for payment and as commodities of exchange in the market place. Thus it is arguable that placing a monetary value on human body parts would be ethically unacceptable.

Furthermore, in a society where cherished communal values such as altruism and giving are encouraged and cultivated, legalising a commercial market for organs and paying for them would dissolve communal bonds and relationships based on goodwill and altruism. It would transform them into one of contractual buying and selling. . . . The wisdom of paying for organs and allowing commercialisation is therefore highly questionable even for the lofty purpose of saving lives.

As noted earlier, under the law in the UK as it stands, commercial dealing in organs (both from live donors and cadavers) is a criminal offence under s 32 of the Human Tissue Act 2004.

Summary of Key Points

1.   Organ transplantaion, particularly since the development of modern immuno-suppressant drugs, is a technique with great potential for saving and improving the quality of human lives. However it is subject to a number of ethical and legal doubts and qualifications, which have partly contributed to the shortage of transplant organs.

2.   At present the main sources of organs are live or deceased human donors. As regards the former, the key issues at common law concern the validity of the donor's consent, including how far a person is entitled legally to expose himself to harm or the risk of harm.

3.   In relation to organs taken from deceased donors, the main common law questions relate to how far patients who are near death may already be treated with a view to taking their organs after death. Subsequently, their death must also be established in legal terms.

4.   For both types of transplant, the common law has been significantly supplemented by statute, now in the form of the Human Tissue Act 2004. The Act established the Human Tissue Authority to oversee transplants (and other activities involving the use of human tissue).

---

85 See n 82 above.

5. The 2004 Act re-enacts previous statute law prohibiting commercial dealings in organs ('organ trafficking'). Those engaging in such practices (including the donor and recipient directly involved) may be liable to imprisonment for up to three years.

6. A further, key requirement introduced by the 2004 Act, is the need for 'appropriate consent' by the donor. In the context of deceased organ donation this also addresses the need, where the donor himself did not express a wish, for the surviving relatives to consent instead. Failure to obtain such consent is made a criminal offence.

7. The 2004 Act has not resolved every issue: one area of uncertainty is the enforceability of conditional or directed donations from deceased donors. As regards living donors, directed donations are the norm, but the Human Tissue Authority, together with NHS Blood and Transplant, oppose them in relation to the deceased.

8. A further, controversial issue concerns the status of organs and tissue following extraction from the donor. Does such material amount to property and if so to whom does it belong? These questions, which may have significant commercial implications, were addressed (though not fully clarified) by the Court of Appeal in the *Yearworth* case.

9. There remains a significant shortfall in transplant organs in the UK. Given the cost in human lives, there is an overriding social imperative to address this, including through law reform. Possibilities include moving from the current 'opt in' system for deceased donation (in the Human Tissue Act 2004) to a system based on presumed consent.

10. At present, though, a shift to a presumed consent model remains off the political agenda. Still less likely is that commercial dealings in organs would ever be legalised. This is a prospect that most people view with apprehension, given the dangers of exploitation and commodification of the human body.

Further Reading

Cronin, A, and Douglas, J, 'Directed and conditional deceased donors organ donations: laws and misconceptions' (2010) 18 *Medical Law Review* 275.

Herring, J, and Chau, P-L, 'My body, your body, our bodies' (2007) 15 *Medical Law Review* 34.

Hoppe, N, *Bioequity – Property and the Human Body*, Farnham: Ashgate, 2009.

Journal of Medical Ethics (2003) Vol 29, no 3, Special issue on organ donation (June 2003).

Lamb, D, *Organ Transplants and Ethics*, London: Routledge, 1990.

Organ Donation Taskforce, *Organs for Transplant*, London: Department of Health, January 2008.

Price, D, 'The Human Tissue Act 2004' (2005) 68 *Modern Law Review* 798.

Chapter 12

Euthanasia

Chapter Contents

12.1 Introduction

12.1.1 What is euthanasia?

Euthanasia (literally 'an easeful death', from the Greek) describes the practice of bringing about death in a manner that causes the least amount of suffering to the patient. The term is sometimes used narrowly to refer only to the taking of life by active means, for example, the giving of a lethal injection to a patient whose life is full of unbearable pain.

However, in common with much of the academic literature, we here employ the term more widely, also to encompass situations in which a doctor, intending his patient's death, omits to provide life-prolonging treatment: we thus distinguish between 'active' euthanasia and 'passive' euthanasia (the latter involving such an omission). Whilst this is ultimately a matter of semantics, the reader should be alert, especially when reading judgments, as to whether the narrower or wider usage has been adopted in a particular instance. In addition to the active/passive distinction, the practice of euthanasia may also be characterised as 'voluntary' or 'non-voluntary' depending on whether the patient was mentally capable to request it or not.

12.1.2 Ethical background: the value of human life

12.1.2.1 Sanctity of Life

What makes the issue of euthanasia so morally contentious is the enormous value which we place upon human life. In the following extract, Helga Kuhse charts the historical framework in which respect for individual human life attained centrality in Western thought, as well as noting the difficulties encountered by the view in an increasingly secular age:

Kuhse, H, *The Sanctity-of-Life Doctrine in Medicine*[1]

Every society known to us subscribes to some principle or principles involving respect for human life. As Georgia Harkness puts it:

> In every society there appears to be an elemental reverence for life which makes the deliberate killing of another person a punishable offence. In all societies there are exceptions . . . yet aversion to murder is probably the most universal of all moral attitudes.

But if aversion to murder, or wrongful killing, is universal, there have been great variations between cultural traditions as to what constitutes wrongful killing.

If we turn to the roots of our Western tradition, we find that in Greek and Roman times not all human life was regarded as inviolable and worthy of protection. Slaves and 'barbarians' did not have a full right to life, and human sacrifices and gladiatorial combat were acceptable at different times. Spartan law required that deformed infants be put to death; for Plato, infanticide is one of the regular institutions of the ideal State; Aristotle regards abortion as a desirable option; and the Stoic philosopher Seneca writes unapologetically: 'Unnatural progeny we destroy; we drown even children who at birth are weakly and abnormal.'

. . . And whilst there were deviations from these views . . ., it is probably correct to say that such practices as abortion, infanticide, suicide, and euthanasia were less proscribed in ancient times than they are today. There has been a gradual expansion of the circle protecting human life, outlawing not only the killing of slaves or 'barbarians', gladiatorial combat, and human sacrifice, but also abortion, infanticide, and euthanasia.

---

1   Oxford: Clarendon Press, 1987.

Most historians of Western morals agree that the rise of Judaism and even more of Christianity contributed greatly to the general feeling that human life is valuable and worthy of respect.

WEH Lecky gives the now classical account of the sanctity of human life in his *History of European Morals*:

> Considered as immortal beings, destined for the extremes of happiness or of misery, and united to one another by a special community of redemption, the first and most manifest duty of the Christian man was to look upon his fellow men as sacred beings and from this notion grew up the eminently Christian idea of the sanctity of human life . . . it was one of the most important services of Christianity that besides quickening greatly our benevolent affections it definitely and dogmatically asserted the sinfulness of all destruction of human life as a matter of amusement, or of simple convenience, and thereby formed a new standard higher than any which then existed in the world . . . This minute and scrupulous care for human life and virtue in the humblest form, in the slave, the gladiator, the savage, or the infant, was indeed wholly foreign to the genius of Paganism. It was produced by the Christian doctrine of the inestimable value of each immortal soul.

. . . Whilst it is today no longer generally believed that life has sanctity in the religious sense, the ethical attitudes to which these religious beliefs gave rise still find expression in the deep-seated belief that human life, irrespective of its quality or kind, is absolutely inviolable and equally valuable; and that we must never take life – either our own or that of anyone else – because life is not ours to do with as we see fit.

Kuhse here associates the 'sanctity of life' doctrine, in its strongest form, with the view that human life is of absolute value and should, where possible, be maintained at any cost, including the cost to the individual whose life it is. Thus, it is impermissible to shorten (or fail to extend) life, by however small an amount and irrespective of any suffering endured by the person concerned.[2]

12.1.2.2 Quality of life

A number of contemporary philosophers have argued that, in making decisions about ending life, we should instead be prepared to deploy overt quality of life considerations.[3] Human life is no longer to be regarded as possessing intrinsic value *per se*; rather, what makes life valuable is, crudely, the life-holder's capacity for pleasurable states of consciousness. As Kuhse notes, this value is enhanced where the individual in question is a person with a sense of existing over time and capable of valuing their existence:

Kuhse, H, *The Sanctity-of-Life Doctrine in Medicine*[4]

. . . [W]hat is it that gives value to human life, but not – or not to the same degree – to the lives of other living things? Two answers are possible. The first answer is that human life has sanctity simply because it is human life, that is, because it is the life of a member of the species *Homo sapiens*. The second answer is that human life has special value because humans are self-aware, rational, autonomous, purposeful, moral beings, with hopes, ambitions, life purposes, ideals, and so on . . . Any of these qualities, or a combination of them, could serve as

---

2   For an argument that the 'sanctity of life' approach is in reality more flexible, see Keown, J, 'Restoring moral and intellectual shape to the law after *Bland*' (1997) 113 LQR 481.
3   See, e.g., Glover, J, *Causing Death and Saving Lives*, Harmondsworth: Penguin, 1977; Harris, J, *The Value of Life*, London: Routledge & Kegan Paul, 1985.
4   See n 1 above.

a basis for a moral distinction between human beings and lettuces or chickens. That such distinguishing qualities are needed is clear: for if the value of life were based on 'mere life', rather than on one or more of the above characteristics, then every life including the earthworm's or the lettuce's would be equally valuable.

It is not difficult to see that the second answer does point to a morally relevant difference between some lives and others. For example, it is quite plausible to hold that the life of a self-aware, rational, purposeful being that sees itself as existing over time is more valuable than the life of an entity or being who lacks these characteristics. But if one takes this approach, then one is not saying that human life has sanctity, but rather that rationality, the capacity to be self-aware, moral or purposeful, and so on, have 'sanctity'. Of course, one may still hold . . . that human life has sanctity or special worth, but only in so far as it is a precondition for ration-ality, purposiveness, or whatever else one takes the valuable characteristic to be. One would not, on this view, be able to argue that the lives of all members of the human species have special value – for example, the lives of the irreversibly comatose, or the lives of severely brain-damaged new-born infants. The second approach, then, does not give us a reason for preserving all human lives, and cannot serve as the basis for the view that all human lives, irrespective of their quality or kind, are equally valuable . . .

In cases where the individual whose life is at stake is mentally capable, there is also the argument that it should be for them alone to decide if and when the quality of that life is so low that it should end; this is consistent with respecting their autonomy. In this context an appeal is often made to a capable person's (moral) 'right to die', and this has underpinned campaigns to have 'active volun-tary euthansia' legalised. As Margaret Otlowski writes:

Otlowski, M, *Voluntary Euthanasia and the Common Law*[5]

The main argument in support of the legalisation of active voluntary euthanasia is based on the principle of autonomy or the right of self-determination. According to this principle, each person has value and is worthy of respect, is the bearer of basic rights and freedoms, and is the final determinant of his or her destiny . . .

Proponents argue that the maintenance of the current legal prohibition on active volun-tary euthanasia is an unjustifiable infringement of the liberty of those persons who would choose to be killed. It has been argued that to deny active voluntary euthanasia is a form of tyranny; an attempt to control the life of a person who has his or her own autonomous view about how that life should go, and that this consitutes an ultimate denial of respect for persons. According to proponents of euthanasia, in order to uphold the patient's interest in self-determination, doctors should be free to act upon the request of an informed and mentally capable patient for active voluntary euthansia without fear of criminal liability.

12.1.2.3 The 'Qualified' Sanctity of Life Approach

We now turn to a position which may be regarded as a compromise between the sanctity and quality of life approaches. This 'qualified' sanctity doctrine agrees with the fully fledged sanctity approach that there is something special about human life, such that it is not reducible to the sum of the life-holder's states of consciousness. The respect due to such life is reflected in a (virtual) prohibition on active steps by third parties, including doctors, to terminate it. This prohibition extends to cases where a capable patient requests help in dying. On the other hand, the doctrine is more relaxed about allowing quality of life considerations to determine when third parties need

5   Oxford: Clarendon Press, 1997.

not act to prolong life, ie allowing death by omission. This attitude can be broadly summed up by reference to the Victorian poet AH Clough's sardonic lines: '. . . thou shalt not kill, but need'st not strive officiously to keep alive'.

It is this position that has been adopted by the common law. In the Court of Appeal in *Airedale NHS Trust v Bland*[6] Hoffmann LJ articulated it in the following terms:

> **Hoffmann LJ:** In my view the choice which the law makes must reassure people that the courts do have full respect for life, but that they do not pursue the principle to the point at which it has become almost empty of any real content and when it involves the sacrifice of other important values such as human dignity and freedom of choice. I think that such reassurance can be provided by a decision, properly explained, to allow Anthony Bland to die . . . Is this answer affected by the proposed manner of his death? Some might say that as he is going to die, it does not matter how. Why wait for him to expire for lack of food or be carried off by an untreated infection? Would it not be more humane simply to give him a lethal injection? No one in this case is suggesting that Anthony Bland should be given a lethal injection. But there is concern about ceasing to supply food as against, for example, ceasing to treat an infection with antibiotics. Is there any real distinction? In order to come to terms with our intuitive feelings about whether there is a distinction, I must start by considering why most of us would be appalled if he was given a lethal injection. It is, I think, connected with our view that the sanctity of life entails its inviolability by an outsider. Subject to exceptions like self-defence, human life is inviolate even if the person in question has consented to its violation. That is why although suicide is not a crime, assisting someone to commit suicide is. It follows that, even if we think Anthony Bland would have consented, we would not be entitled to end his life by a lethal injection.
>
> On the other hand, we recognise that, one way or another, life must come to an end. We do not impose on outsiders an unqualified duty to do everything possible to prolong life as long as possible. I think that the principle of inviolability explains why, although we accept that in certain cases it is right to allow a person to die (and the debate so far has been over whether this is such a case) we hold without qualification that no one may introduce an external agency with the intention of causing death.

This approach was subsequently affirmed by the House of Lords in the same case, although not without a degree of soul searching:

> **Lord Goff:** I must however stress, at this point, that the law draws a crucial distinction between cases in which a doctor decides not to provide, or to continue to provide, for his patient treatment or care which could or might prolong his life, and those in which he decides, for example by administering a lethal drug, actively to bring his patient's life to an end . . . [T]he former may be lawful, either because the doctor is giving effect to his patient's wishes by withholding the treatment or care, or even in certain circumstances in which . . . the patient is incapacitated from stating whether or not he gives his consent. But it is not lawful for a doctor to administer a drug to his patient to bring about his death, even though that course is prompted by a humanitarian desire to end his suffering, however great that suffering may be: see *R v Cox* (1992) . . . So to act is to cross the Rubicon which runs between on the one hand the care of the living patient and on the other hand euthanasia – actively causing his death to avoid or to end his suffering.
>
> **Lord Browne-Wilkinson:** Finally, the conclusion I have reached will appear to some to be almost irrational. How can it be lawful to allow a patient to die slowly, though painlessly, over a period of weeks from lack of food but unlawful to produce his immediate death by a lethal

6   [1993] AC 789.

injection, thereby saving his family from yet another ordeal to add to the tragedy that has already struck them? I find it difficult to find a moral answer to that question. But it is undoubtedly the law and nothing I have said casts doubt on the proposition that the doing of a positive act with the intention of ending life is and remains murder.

As already noted, the law's position represents a compromise: as such it has been attacked, on the one hand, by commentators, such as John Keown who, from the full 'sanctity' position, believe it has already gone too far in allowing the intended and avoidable deaths of certain patients through omission; and on the other, by adherents to the quality of life position who regard the law, in prohibiting active steps to terminate life even where this is the patient's express wish, as not going far enough. In this regard a central focus of criticism (for both sets of critics) has been the alleged incoherence of the acts/omissions distinction underpinning the law.

We shall return to the question of whether the acts/omissions distinction provides a tenable foundation for the law on euthanasia in section 12.5, when we address arguments and initiatives in favour of law reform. First, though, we shall consider the law as it currently stands. We begin in section 12.2 by examining the prohibition on doctors (and others) on actively taking life, including the question of how far it is always adhered to in practice. We then go on to consider the law's approach to cases of passive euthansia – first, in section 12.3, in respect of capable patients; and then, in section 12.4, in respect of the incapable: in what circumstances are doctors permitted to allow such patients to die?

 SELF-TEST QUESTION

If the quality of life approach were to inform the law in this area, would it mean that doctors would be required to kill their patients on demand?

12.2 Active Euthanasia and Assisted Suicide

12.2.1 The prohibition on taking life

The intentional taking of a patient's life by a doctor, including as a response to the patient's wishes, will amount to the crime of murder. In this context the doctor's motive for acting (to spare the patient pain), as distinct from his intention (to cause death) will be irrelevant. A well-known case illustrating this point is that of R v Cox:

***R v Cox* (1992)**[7]

Dr Cox injected a 70-year-old patient, Lillian Boyes, with the lethal poison potassium chloride, after she pleaded with him to put her out of her misery; she was *in extremis*, suffering from the terminal stages of rheumatoid arthritis, and her pain was beyond the control of analgesic drugs. He was charged only with her attempted murder on the basis that, given her condition, Mrs Boyes' death at that time could in fact have been due to her illness rather than the poison (her body had been cremated without a post-mortem):

Ognall J (directing the jury): This is a sad and testing case for all of us involved. The reason is obvious. A distinguished professional man of unblemished reputation and

---

7   (1992) 12 BMLR 38.

character is now on trial, and the allegation is that he behaved in a way which is a clear repudiation of a doctor's lifelong professional duty, namely to save and not to take life.

Even the prosecution case acknowledged that he did so only because he was prompted by deep distress at Lillian Boyes' condition; by a belief that she was totally beyond recall and by an intense compassion for her fearful suffering. Nonetheless, members of the jury, if he injected her with potassium chloride for the primary purpose of killing her, of hastening her death, he is guilty of the offence charged. You are therefore tested to the utmost, members of the jury, for you must do your best to put emotion to one side. You must try this case impartially and objectively. You 12 ladies and gentlemen represent the public interest in ensuring that, where it is surely proved, no man of whatever situation or in whatever circumstance can place himself above the law . . .

You must understand, members of the jury, that in this highly emotional situation, neither the express wishes of the patient nor of her loving and devoted family can affect the position. Lillian Boyes was fully entitled to decline any further active medical treatment and to specify that thereafter she should only receive painkillers. She did that on 11 August. That was her absolute right and the doctors and nursing staff were obliged to respect her wishes. A young senior house officer, Dr Byrne, gave evidence before you. He told you that on that day when Lillian Boyes had said 'no more active intervention, please, only painkillers from now on', he had said to her, in effect: 'Thus far and no further. We will stop your positive medical treatment, we will confine ourselves to giving you only analgesics, only painkillers, but we cannot accede to your request that we give you something to kill you.'

Dr Cox was convicted of attempted murder. However, he did not receive a jail sentence, and also escaped a ban from the GMC, instead being placed under supervision for 12 months. In fact, the conviction itself was a rarity. In other cases, where doctors have been charged in connection with causing the deaths of terminally ill patients in order to end their exteme suffering, juries have generally refused to convict.[8]

It fact, it seems that doctors in practice not infrequently aid the incurably ill to die, but that most cases are never investigated, let alone prosecuted, because of lack of evidence and/or any prospect of obtaining a conviction. As David Price comments:

Price, D, 'What Shape to Euthanasia after *Bland*? Historical, Contemporary and Future Paradigms'[9]

Whilst the medical profession continues to maintain its traditional resistance to the legalisation of both physician-assisted suicide and voluntary euthanasia, not only is there considerably less unanimity amongst members of its representative organisations than at any point in time, but a British Social Attitudes survey conducted in early 2007 revealed that 80 per cent of the public would support doctors assisting terminally ill patients to die if they so requested. The debate becomes increasingly urgent. It has been claimed that approximately 18,000 people in Britain are medically assisted to die annually in any event, and that the deaths of approximately 2,800 patients are a consequence of either voluntary euthanasia or the ending of life without an explicit request from the patient. Moreover, the number of clinical decisions bearing on this estate is expanding rapidly due to substantial demographic trends towards a larger elderly and potentially infirm population . . .

---

8   See eg *R v Carr*, *The Times*, 30 December 1986.
9   (2009) 125 LQR 142.

12.2.2 Medicines which shorten life

One reason doctors, in treating the terminally ill, in practice have significant discretion in taking measures that shorten life is due to the existence of the so-called 'Adams defence'. According to this, a doctor is entitled to administer powerful analgesic (pain-killing) drugs, such as diamorphine, to such patients, even though these drugs, ingested in large doses, have the known side-effect of accelerating death.

The existence of this exception (that is, the fact that a doctor who prescribes such drugs to control pain, though foreseeing his patient's earlier death, will not be guilty of murder) was established in the case of R v Bodkin Adams:

R v Bodkin Adams (1957)[10]

Dr Bodkin Adams was charged with murder after increasing the dosage of opiates for an elderly stroke patient, who left him a Rolls-Royce and a chest of silver in her will. Devlin J, commenting upon the doctor's defence that his primary purpose had been to dull the patient's sensation of pain, gave the following direction to the jury:

> **Devlin J**: . . . [A] doctor who is aiding the sick and the dying [need not] calculate in minutes, or even in hours, and perhaps not in days or weeks, the effect upon a patient's life of the medicines which he administers or else be in peril of a charge of murder. If the first purpose of medicine, the restoration of health, can no longer be achieved there is still much for a doctor to do, and he is entitled to do all that is proper and necessary to relieve pain and suffering, even if the measures he takes may incidentally shorten life. That is not because there is any special defence for medical men; it is not because doctors are put into any category different from other citizens for this purpose. The law is the same for all, and what I have said to you rests simply upon this: no act is murder which does not cause death. 'Cause' means nothing philosophical or technical or scientific. It means what you 12 men and women sitting as a jury in the jury box would regard in a common sense way as the cause . . . If, for example, because a doctor has done something or has omitted to do something death occurs, it can be scientifically proved – if it could – at 11 o'clock instead of 12 o'clock, or even on Monday instead of Tuesday, no people of common sense would say, 'Oh, the doctor caused her death'. They would say the cause of her death was the illness or the injury, or whatever it was, which brought her into hospital, and the proper medical treatment that is administered and that has an incidental effect of determining the exact moment of death, or may have, is not the cause of death in any sensible use of the term. But it remains the fact, and it remains the law, that no doctor, nor any man, no more in the case of the dying man than of the healthy, has the right deliberately to cut the thread of life.

The notion that, in such a case, the doctor may be regarded as not having caused the patient's death is, with respect, difficult to accept: after all, usually it is clear that 'but for' the administration of morphine, the patient would have lived somewhat longer, and nor will legal causation (in terms of foreseeability) be in issue. More recently, in the Cox case,[11] Ognall J preferred to concentrate upon the doctor's intention as providing the key to his possible exculpation:

> **Ognall J**: We all appreciate that some medical treatment, whether of a positive, therapeutic character or solely of an analgesic kind – by which I mean designed solely to alleviate pain and

---

10 [1957] Crim LR 365.
11 See n 7 above.

suffering – some treatment carries with it a serious risk to the health or even the life of the patient. Doctors are frequently confronted with, no doubt, distressing dilemmas. They have to make up their minds as to whether the risk, even to the life of their patient, attendant upon their contemplated form of treatment, is such that the risk is, or is not, medically justified. If a doctor genuinely believes that a certain course is beneficial to his patient, either therapeutically or analgesically, then even though he recognises that that course carries with it a risk to life, he is fully entitled, nonetheless, to pursue it. If in those circumstances the patient dies, nobody could possibly suggest that in that situation the doctor was guilty of murder or attempted murder . . .

There can be no doubt that the use of drugs to reduce pain and suffering will often be fully justified notwithstanding that it will, in fact, hasten the moment of death. What can never be lawful is the use of drugs with purpose of hastening the moment of death.

And so, in deciding Dr Cox's intention, the distinction the law requires you to draw is this. Is it proved that in giving that injection, in that form and in those amounts, Dr Cox's primary purpose was to bring the life of Lillian Boyes to an end?

If it was, then he is guilty. If, on the other hand, it was, or may have been, his primary purpose in acting as he did to alleviate her pain and suffering, then he is not guilty. That is so even though he recognised that, in fulfilling that primary purpose, he might or even would hasten the moment of her death. . . .

The apparent reliance of this way of regarding the *Bodkin Adams* defence on the principle of double effect (a Catholic doctrine, which has the support of advocates of the full sanctity of life position, but is rejected by other commentators), has given rise to much debate. Normally, intention in the criminal law is established through straightforward foresight that a given outcome will be the likely effect of one's act.[12] In this situation, though, the law is exceptionally prepared to limit its focus to the primary intention of the doctor, that is to say, the desire to relieve the patient's pain.

The upshot is that, provided the doctor administers life-ending drugs that at the same time have some analgesic effect (cf Dr Cox, who used potassium chloride, a drug with no such effect), he or she would seem, as a practical matter, to be safe from criminal liability for murder. As Suzanne Ost notes:

Ost, S, 'Euthanasia and the Defence of Necessity: Advocating a More Appropriate Legal Response'[13]

Undoubtedly, the physician is likely to know what his primary intent was in administering the drug in question, yet how can the jury truly know whether the intent was to relieve suffering rather than cause death? When a certain act can be carried out with more than one intent, perhaps the most we can ascertain as objective actors is what these different intents could be, rather than what the primary intent actually is . . .

Significantly, in the light of such concerns, the question of whether the doctrine provides an effective means of establishing the physician's intent has been addressed by a recent study involving 683 Australian general surgeons. Two hundred and forty-seven of these surgeons stated that when administering drugs in order to relieve a patient's suffering, they had administered a greater dosage than they felt necessary to relieve symptoms with the intention of hastening death. Interestingly, the authors of the study raise the question of whether the only distinction between these surgeons and the other participants in the study is that they reported their own mental state differently. This leads to a further related criticism of the utilisation of

---

12 R v *Woollin* [1999] 1 AC 82.
13 (2005) Crim L Rev 355.

the doctrine of double effect in English law. The legal application of the doctrine undoubtedly requires reliance upon physicians to truthfully report their primary intent. Yet, if a physician did administer lethal treatment with a primary intent to cause death, can we really expect him to reveal this truth, given the legal consequences of this revelation?

As Ost goes on to ask, 'by utilising the doctrine . . . are we not skating around the issue of the intent behind administering lethal doses of pain-alleviating treatment towards the end of life instead of tackling it head on?' In her view, it would be preferable to see the doctrine as affording a defence (based on necessity) to the doctor, notwithstanding his intention to cause death. In its 2005 paper, 'A New Homicide Act for England and Wales' the Law Commission appears to go along with this, endorsing Kennedy and Grubb's suggestion that in such cases the doctor indeed intends the patient's death, but 'the intention is not culpable . . . because the law permits the doctor to do the act in question'.[14]

Leaving aside its precise doctrinal justification, it is apparent that the *Adams* defence forms an established part of the common law. Nonetheless, its limited ambit should be emphasised: it applies to cases where the patient in any case (without analgesia) only has a comparatively short time to live, and would otherwise experience significant suffering. The latter will ordinarily be physical in nature; however, in a case brought in 1997 by a woman, Annie Lindsell, dying from motor neurone disease, Sir Stephen Brown, President of the Family Division of the High Court, confirmed that the defence protects doctors who prescribe such analgesics to ease their patients' mental torment (although this was not made the subject of a formal declaration).[15]

12.2.3 The separation of a non-viable conjoined twin

In 2001, a further inroad was made into the distinction between active and passive euthanasia to the extent that, in one particular set of circumstances, the Court of Appeal sanctioned an act (separation surgery) whose inevitable consequence was to terminate a patient's life. This step was taken in the well-known case of the conjoined twins, *Re A (Children)*.

Re A (Children) (Conjoined Twins: Surgical Separation) (2001)[16]

Jodie and Mary were conjoined twin girls who were born joined at the pelvis. The medical evidence was that Jodie sustained the life of Mary (whose own heart and lungs did not function) by circulating oxygenated blood through a common artery, and that, if they were not separated, Jodie's heart would eventually fail and they would both die within a few months. The hospital wished to perform separation surgery, which would enable Jodie to lead a relatively normal life (though Mary would die almost immediately), but the parents refused to consent on religious grounds. In the High Court, Johnson J granted a declaration that the hospital could lawfully carry out the surgery in both twins' best interests. The parents appealed:

> **Robert Walker LJ**: Every member of the court has been deeply troubled by this case, but we have to decide it in accordance with the principles of existing law as we perceive them to apply to this unprecedented situation. I will summarise my conclusions as to the applicable principles as simply as I can.
>
> (i) The feelings of the twins' parents are entitled to great respect, especially so far as they are based on religious convictions. But as the matter has been referred

---

14 Law Commission, Consultation Paper No 177, para 4.87. See www.lawcom.gov.uk/docs/cp177_web.pdf.
15 *Lindsell v Holmes, The Guardian*, 29 October 1997.
16 [2001] Fam 147, CA.

to the court the court cannot escape the responsibility of deciding the matter to the best of its judgment as to the twins' best interests.

(ii)   The judge erred in law in equating the proposed surgical operation with the discontinuance of medical treatment (as by disconnecting a heart-lung machine). Therefore the Court of Appeal must form its own view.

(iii) Mary has a right to life, under the common law of England (based as it is on Judaeo-Christian foundations) and under the European Convention on Human Rights. It would be unlawful to kill Mary intentionally, that is to undertake an operation with the primary purpose of killing her.

(iv)   But Jodie also has a right to life.

(v)   Every human being's right to life carries with it, as an intrinsic part of it, rights of bodily integrity and autonomy – the right to have one's own body whole and intact and (on reaching an age of understanding) to take decisions about one's own body.

(vi)   By a rare and tragic mischance, Mary and Jodie have both been deprived of the bodily integrity and autonomy which is their natural right. There is a strong presumption that an operation to separate them would be in the best interests of each of them.

(vii) In this case the purpose of the operation would be to separate the twins and so give Jodie a reasonably good prospect of a long and reasonably normal life. Mary's death would not be the purpose of the operation, although it would be its inevitable consequence. The operation would give her, even in death, bodily integrity as a human being. She would die, not because she was intentionally killed, but because her own body cannot sustain her life.

(viii) Continued life, whether long or short, would hold nothing for Mary except possible pain and discomfort, if indeed she can feel anything at all.

(ix)   The proposed operation would therefore be in the best interests of each of the twins. The decision does not require the court to value one life above another.

(x)   The proposed operation would not be unlawful. It would involve the positive act of invasive surgery and Mary's death would be foreseen as an inevitable consequence of an operation which is intended, and is necessary, to save Jodie's life. But Mary's death would not be the purpose or intention of the surgery, and she would die because tragically her body, on its own, is not and never has been viable.

I would therefore dismiss this appeal.

The Court of Appeal's judgment runs to over 100 pages, and the three Lord Justices, while agreeing in the result, justify their conclusions in different ways. Thus, whereas Robert Walker LJ (relying on the doctrine of 'double effect') suggested that the doctors who performed the operation would not intend Mary's death, both Ward and Brooke LJJ applied the criminal law approach to intention set out by the House of Lords in *R v Woollin*,[17] and found that there would be intent.

For his part, Ward LJ thought that an argument based on self-defence could be used to justify the doctors' intervention on behalf of Jodie, but was not supported in this by Brooke or Robert Walker LJJ. Moreover, although all three members of the Court took the view that Mary's killing could be justified on the basis of the doctrine of necessity, they appear to have differed as to the precise ambit of this doctrine in the criminal law. Ward LJ, in particular, was careful to limit his decision to the particular circumstances of the case:

17 See n 12 above.

Ward LJ: In my judgment, the appeal must be dismissed. Lest it be thought that this decision could become authority for wider propositions, such as that a doctor, once he has determined that a patient cannot survive, can kill the patient, it is important to restate the unique circumstances for which this case is authority. They are that it must be impossible to preserve the life of X without bringing about the death of Y, that Y by his or her very continued existence will inevitably bring about the death of X within a short period of time, and that X is capable of living an independent life but Y is incapable under any circumstances, including all forms of medical intervention, of viable independent existence. As I said at the beginning of this judgment, this is a very unique case.

An extensive academic literature has been generated by this case. For a selection, see the special edition of the *Medical Law Review* devoted to it.[18]

12.2.4 Assisted suicide

In respect of patients who are not already dying, or though dying are not in pain, the doctor is clearly not permitted to do anything that directly shortens life. How far, though, may he furnish the means to allow such patients to kill themselves? It is evident that a doctor who acts thus is not guilty of murder; even one who, say, in the case of a paralysed patient, places a lethal pill in the latter's mouth will (provided the patient knows what is in the pill) at most have assisted in the patient's suicide. The reason is that the latter's voluntary and informed action of swallowing the pill operates as a *novus actus interveniens* which breaks the chain of causation between the doctor's previous act of providing the pill and the patient's death.

Here, notwithstanding that suicide itself is not a crime, the doctor will be guilty of the offence of 'assisting suicide' contrary to s 2 of the Suicide Act 1961:

2 Criminal liability for complicity in another's suicide

(1) A person who aids, abets, counsels or procures the suicide of another, or an attempt by another to commit suicide, shall be liable on conviction on indictment to imprisonment for a term not exceeding 14 years.

(2) If on the trial of an indictment for murder or manslaughter it is proved that the accused aided, abetted, counselled or procured the suicide of the person in question, the jury may find him guilty of that offence.

. . .

(4) No proceedings shall be instituted for an offence under this section except by or with the consent of the Director of Public Prosecutions.

The key reasons for retaining the offence of assisted suicide are apparent from the following passage of Sopinka J's judgment in the Canadian Supreme Court case of *Rodriguez v AG of British Columbia*,[19] in which he refers to the Canadian Law Reform Commission's discussion of the question as follows:

Sopinka J: The Law Reform Commission had discussed in the Working Paper the possibility of the decriminalisation of assisted suicide in the following terms . . .:

First of all, the prohibition . . . is not restricted solely to the case of the terminally ill patient, for whom we can only have sympathy, or solely to his physician or a member

---

18 (2001) 9(3) Med L Rev.
19 (1993) 82 BCLR (2d) 273 (Canadian Sup Ct).

of his family who helps him to put an end to his suffering. [It] is more general and applies to a variety of situations for which it is much more difficult to feel sympathy. Consider, for example, a recent incident, that of inciting to mass suicide. What of the person who takes advantage of another's depressed state to encourage him to commit suicide, for his own financial benefit? What of the person who, knowing an adolescent's suicidal tendencies, provides him with large enough quantities of drugs to kill him? The accomplice in these cases cannot be considered morally blameless. Nor can one conclude that the criminal law should not punish such conduct. To decriminalise completely the act of aiding, abetting or counselling suicide would therefore not be a valid legislative policy . . .

It can be seen, therefore, that while the Law Reform Commission of Canada had great sympathy for the plight of those who wish to end their lives so as to avoid significant suffering, it was not prepared to recognise that the active assistance of a third party in carrying out this desire should be condoned, even for the terminally ill. The basis for this refusal is twofold it seems – first, the active participation by one individual in the death of another is intrinsically morally and legally wrong, and second, there is no certainty that abuses can be prevented by anything less than a complete prohibition. Creating an exception for the terminally ill might therefore frustrate the purpose of the legislation of protecting the vulnerable because adequate guidelines to control abuse are difficult or impossible to develop.

In the UK, the House of Lords Select Committee on Medical Ethics (1994) similarly recommended that the prohibition on assisting suicide should remain.[20] Nonetheless, this is an issue that, especially in the light of European human rights law, remains on the political and legal agenda. The English courts were first required to rule on the compatibility of the provisions of the Suicide Act 1961 with the rights of the putative suicide under the European Convention on Human Rights (ECHR) in R (On the Application of Pretty) v DPP:

R (On the Application of Pretty) v DPP (2002)[21]

Dianne Pretty was suffering from the terminal stages of motor neurone disease. Rather than await death through suffocation or starvation (the natural outcome of the disease), she wished to commit suicide, but, due to her condition, needed help to do so. Her husband was willing to assist her, provided that the Director of Public Prosecutions undertook not to prosecute him under s 2 of the Suicide Act 1961. When the DPP refused to do so, Mrs Pretty brought an action in judicial review proceedings, arguing that s 2 of the 1961 Act contravened her ECHR rights, in particular those under Art 2 (the right to life), Art 3 (the right not to suffer inhuman or degrading treatment) and Art 8 (the right to private and family life):

Lord Steyn: [41] This is the first occasion on which the House of Lords has been asked to consider the question of assisted suicide by a terminally ill individual . . . For her to succeed it is not enough to show that the European Convention allows member states to legalise assisted suicide. She must establish that at least that part of section 2(1) of the 1961 Act which makes aiding or abetting suicide a crime is in conflict with her Convention rights. In other words, she must persuade the House that the European Convention compels member states of the Council of Europe to legalise assisted suicide.

---

20 *Report of the Select Committee on Medical Ethics*, HL Paper No 21, 1994.
21 [2002] 1 AC 800.

... Policy grounds

[57] If section 2 of the 1961 Act is held to be incompatible with the European Convention, a right to commit assisted suicide would not be doctor assisted and would not be subject to safeguards introduced in the Netherlands. In a valuable essay Professor Michael Freeman trenchantly observed 'A repeal of section 2 of the Suicide Act 1961, without more, would not be rational policy-making. We would need a 'Death with Dignity' Act to fill the lacuna': 'Death, dying and the Human Rights Act 1998' (1999) 52 CLP 218, at 237. That must be right. In our parliamentary democracy, and I apprehend in many member states of the Council of Europe, such a fundamental change cannot be brought about by judicial creativity. If it is to be considered at all, it requires a detailed and effective regulatory proposal. In these circumstances it is difficult to see how a process of interpretation of Convention rights can yield a result with all the necessary in-built protections. Essentially, it must be a matter for democratic debate and decision-making by legislatures.

The specific articles

... [59] ... Counsel for Mrs Pretty argued that article 2 and in particular its first sentence acknowledges that it is for the individual to choose whether to live or die and that it protects her right of self-determination in relation to issues of life and death. This interpretation is not sustainable. The purpose of article 2(1) is clear. It enunciates the principle of the sanctity of life and provides a guarantee that no individual 'shall be deprived of life' by means of intentional human intervention. The interpretation now put forward is the exact opposite viz a right of Mrs Pretty to end her life by means of intentional human intervention. Nothing in the article or the jurisprudence of the European Court of Human Rights can assist Mrs Pretty's case on this article.

[60] ... The core of counsel's argument [under Art 3] is that ... the state's obligations are to take effective steps to ensure that no one shall be subjected to inhuman or degrading treatment. For my part article 3 is not engaged. The word 'treatment' must take its colour from the context in which it appears. While I would not wish to give a narrow interpretation to what may constitute degrading treatment, the concept appears singularly inapt to convey the idea that the state must guarantee to individuals a right to die with the deliberate assistance of third parties. So radical a step, infringing the sanctity of life principle, would have required far more explicit wording

[61] ... Counsel submitted that [Art 8] explicitly recognises the principle of the personal autonomy of every individual. He argues that this principle necessarily involves a guarantee as against the state of the right to choose when and how to die. None of the decisions cited in regard to article 8 assist this argument. It must fail on the ground that the guarantee under article 8 prohibits interference with the way in which an individual leads his life and it does not relate to the manner in which he wishes to die.

... [68] ... The logic of the European Convention does not justify the conclusion that the House must rule that a state is obliged to legalise assisted suicide. It does not require the state to repeal a provision such as section 2(1) of the 1961 Act. On the other hand, it is open to a democratic legislature to introduce such a measure. Our Parliament, if so minded, may therefore repeal section 2(1) and put in its place a regulated system for assisted suicide (presumably doctor assisted) with appropriate safeguards.

The other Law Lords agreed with Lord Steyn in dismissing Mrs Pretty's application. Subsequently, she appealed to the European Court of Human Rights in Strasbourg, which agreed with the House of Lords that Arts 2 and 3 had no application to the case. However, it endorsed the minority view of Lord Hope (on this point) that Mrs Pretty's right under Art 8 of the ECHR was engaged:

> [65] The very essence of the Convention is respect for human dignity and human freedom. Without in any way negating the principle of sanctity of life protected under the Convention, the Court considers that it is under article 8 that notions of the quality of life take on significance. In an era of growing medical sophistication combined with longer life expectancies, many people are concerned that they should not be forced to linger on in old age or in states of advanced physical or mental decrepitude which conflict with strongly held ideas of self and personal identity.[22]

At the same time, the European Court of Human Rights held that the interference in this right – in terms of the prohibition on assisted suicide – was justified under Art 8(2) of the ECHR, namely as necessary in order to protect the rights of others – ie vulnerable persons who might otherwise feel pressure to agree to suicide. In this regard, the Court noted that s 2(4) of the 1961 Act already provides for some flexibility in genuinely 'hard cases' (involving circumstances such as those in Pretty), by making prosecution under s 2 subject to the consent of the DPP.

Whilst the Court thus dismissed Mrs Pretty's action against the UK Government, the legal position in such cases remained dangerously uncertain from the point of view of those contemplating helping others to commit suicide: when would the DPP exercise his discretion under s 2(4) not to prosecute them, and when not? Against this background the House of Lords was required to rule again on the compatibility of the law in this area with the ECHR in the case of R (On the Application of Purdy) v DPP.

R (On the Application of Purdy) v DPP (2009)[23]

Debbie Purdy was suffering from incurable, progressive multiple schlerosis. She wished to be able to end her life at a point when she judged it no longer bearable, by travelling to a country such as Switzerland, where assisted suicide is lawful; however, she would need the assistance of her husband to make the journey. Unlike Mrs Pretty, she did not seek an undertaking from the DPP that her husband would not be prosecuted under the 1961 Act; but she argued that, pursuant to Art 8 of the ECHR, she at least had a right to more detailed information from the DPP as to the factors that would influence his decision whether to prosecute.

> **Lord Hope**: [26] It must be emphasised at the outset that it is no part of our function to change the law in order to decriminalise assisted suicide. If changes are to be made, as to which I express no opinion, this must be a matter for Parliament . . . We do not venture into that arena, nor would it be right for us to do so. Our function as judges is to say what the law is and, if it is uncertain, to do what we can to clarify it . . .
>
> [28] Lord Pannick Q.C. for Ms Purdy directed his argument to s.2(4) of the 1961 Act, which provides that no proceedings shall be instituted for an offence under that section except by or with the consent of the Director of Public Prosecutions, and to her right to respect for her private life under art.8(1) of the European Convention for the Protection of Human Rights and Fundamental Freedoms . . . He submits, first, that the

---

22 Pretty v United Kingdom (2002) 35 EHRR 1.
23 [2009] UKHL 45.

prohibition in s.2(1) of the 1961 Act constitutes an interference with Ms Purdy's right to respect for her private life under art.8(1) of the European Convention on Human Rights; and, second, that this interference is not 'in accordance with the law' as required by art.8(2), in the absence of an offence-specific policy by the Director of Public Prosecutions which sets out the factors that will be taken into account by him and Crown Prosecutors acting on his behalf in deciding under s.2(4) of the 1961 Act whether or not it is in the public interest to bring a prosecution under that section . . .

[40] The Convention principle of legality requires the court to address itself to three distinct questions. The first is whether there is a legal basis in domestic law for the restriction. The second is whether the law or rule in question is sufficiently accessible to the individual who is affected by the restriction, and sufficiently precise to enable him to understand its scope and foresee the consequences of his actions so that he can regulate his conduct without breaking the law. The third is whether, assuming that these two requirements are satisfied, it is nevertheless open to the criticism that it is being applied in a way that is arbitrary because, for example, it has been resorted to in bad faith or in a way that is not proportionate . . .

[41] The word 'law' in this context is to be understood in its substantive sense, not its formal one . . . A law which confers a discretion is not in itself inconsistent with this requirement, provided the scope of the discretion and the manner of its exercise are indicated with sufficient clarity to give the individual protection against interference which is arbitrary . . .

[46] . . . Consistency of practice is especially important here. The issue is without doubt both sensitive and controversial. Many people view legally assisted suicide as an appalling concept which undermines the fundamental human right to life itself. On the other hand there are those, like Ms Purdy, who firmly believe that the right to life includes the right to end one's own life when one can still do so with dignity. Crown Prosecutors to whom the decision-taking function is delegated need to be given the clearest possible instructions as to the factors which they must have regard to when they are performing it. The police, who exercise an important discretion as to whether or not to bring a case to the attention of the Crown Prosecutors, need guidance also if they are to avoid the criticism that their decision-taking is arbitrary. Important too is the general policy of the law that the Attorney-General and the Director only intervene to direct a prosecution when they consider it in the public interest to do so.

. . . [56] I would therefore allow the appeal and require the Director to promulgate an offence-specific policy identifying the facts and circumstances which he will take into account in deciding, in a case such as that which Ms Purdy's case exemplifies, whether or not to consent to a prosecution under s.2(1) of the 1961 Act.

Following this decision, the DPP in February 2010 issued guidance on his policy in respect of prosecuting cases of assisted suicide. Among the public interest factors mentioned as militating against prosecution are that the victim had a settled and informed wish to die, and that the assisting person was motivated wholly by compassion.[24] In contrast, a factor in favour of prosecution is that the assisting person was acting in his or her capacity as a medical doctor, nurse, or other healthcare professional.[25] Clearly, then, physician-assisted suicide is intended to remain off-limits; however,

---

24 DPP, 'Policy for Prosecutors in Respect of Cases of Encouraging or Assisting Suicide', para 45: 1 & 2. The full guidance may be found at www.cps.gov.uk/publications/prosecution/assisted_suicide_policy.html.
25 Ibid, para 43: 14.

it could be argued that a doctor's neutrality and expertise would provide an important safeguard in such cases. The question of whether assisted suicide should be the subject of full-scale legislative reform, which includes provision for physician involvement, is addressed in section 12.5 below.

 SELF-TEST QUESTION

If a doctor, intending to end a patient's life, were to inject him with a massive dose of morphine, how likely, as a practical matter, is a conviction for murder?

12.3 Passive Euthanasia: Capable Patients

12.3.1 Background

Our concern here is with the more flexible attitude taken by the qualified sanctity of life doctrine in respect of omissions to provide life-sustaining treatment (reflected in the 'need'st not strive officiously' part of AH Clough's couplet).

A preliminary question is what conduct, in the context of providing medical care, will be regarded in law as an *omission* rather than an *act*? For example, a common means of sustaining the life of a critically ill patient in hospital is to place him on a ventilator. If, in a given case, a doctor decides that there is no hope of recovery and switches the machine off, could he not be said to have acted to bring about the patient's death? Lord Goff, however, forcefully rejected this possibility in the *Bland*[26] case:

> **Lord Goff**: Why is it that the doctor who gives his patient a lethal injection which kills him commits an unlawful act and indeed is guilty of murder, whereas a doctor who, by discontinuing life support, allows his patient to die, may not act unlawfully – and will not do so, if he commits no breach of duty to his patient? Professor Glanville Williams has suggested (see his *Textbook of Criminal Law . . .*) that the reason is that what the doctor does when he switches off a life support machine 'is in substance not an act but an omission to struggle', and that 'the omission is not a breach of duty by the doctor, because he is not obliged to continue in a hopeless case'.
>
> I agree that the doctor's conduct in discontinuing life support can properly be categorised as an omission. It is true that it may be difficult to describe what the doctor actually does as an omission, for example where he takes some positive step to bring the life support to an end. But discontinuation of life support is, for present purposes, no different from not initiating life support in the first place. In each case, the doctor is simply allowing his patient to die in the sense that he is desisting from taking a step which might, in certain circumstances, prevent his patient from dying as a result of his pre-existing condition; and as a matter of general principle an omission such as this will not be unlawful unless it constitutes a breach of duty to the patient. I also agree that the doctor's conduct is to be differentiated from that of, for example, an interloper who maliciously switches off a life support machine because, although the interloper may perform exactly the same act as the doctor who discontinues life support, his doing so constitutes interference with the life-prolonging treatment then being administered by the doctor. Accordingly, whereas the doctor, in discontinuing life support, is simply allowing his patient to die of his pre-existing condition, the interloper is actively intervening to stop the doctor from prolonging the patient's life, and such conduct cannot possibly be categorised as an omission.

---

26 See n 6 above.

It is apparent that, for these purposes, the description of a given piece of conduct by the doctor as an *act* turns not upon a narrow criterion of voluntary physical movement, but rather upon whether what he has done amounts to an interference with the natural course of events. Whereas the doctor, in stopping life support, simply brings to a close his own previous and continuing interference in nature, the malicious interloper does interfere in (and hence 'acts' relative to) the life-sustaining regime – a sort of second 'nature' created and maintained by the doctor.

The principle that conduct engaged in by the medical staff in the process of withdrawing treatment will not amount to an act in legal terms, is implicit in the High Court decision in the case of *Ms B v An NHS Hospital Trust*,[27] in which a hospital was held to be acting unlawfully in continuing to ventilate a capable patient, who was paralysed from the neck down, and no longer wished to be kept alive. At the same time, the President of the Family Division acknowledged the psychological difficulties faced by the treating team in the case:

> **Dame Elizabeth Butler-Sloss P**: [58] It was clear from their evidence that both the treating clinicians were deeply distressed by the dilemma which had faced them over the year that Ms B had spent in the ICU. They knew her well and respected and liked her. They considered her to be capable to make decisions about her medical treatment. They could not, however, bring themselves to contemplate that they should be part of bringing Ms B's life to an end by the dramatic, (my word), step of turning off the ventilator. As I listened to the evidence of each of them I had the greatest possible sympathy for their position.

Accordingly, the hospital was ordered to arrange for Ms B's transfer to another facility where the medical staff would be prepared to switch off the ventilator sustaining her life.

For similar reasons it makes no difference whether the doctors decide to withhold medical treatment from the outset or, having begun to treat the patient, elect to withdraw it at a later stage: in both cases what is at stake is an omission. As Lord Lowry commented in *Airedale NHS Trust v Bland*:[28]

> **Lord Lowry**: I do not believe that there is a valid legal distinction between the omission to treat a patient and the abandonment of treatment which has been commenced, since to recognise such a distinction could quite illogically confer on a doctor who had refained from treatment an immunity which did not benefit a doctor who had embarked on treatment in order to see whether it might help the patient and had abandoned the treatment when it was seen not to do so.

At the same time, it certainly does not follow that, provided his conduct can be characterised as an omission, the doctor has a free hand in allowing death to occur. The reason why this is not so, and the manner in which the doctor's position differs in this respect from that of the average citizen, is evident from the following passage from Lord Browne-Wilkinson's speech in *Bland*:

> **Lord Browne-Wilkinson**: It is the submission of the Official Solicitor that the withdrawal of artificial feeding would constitute murder. The Official Solicitor has been criticised for using emotive language in this case. In my judgment this criticism is misplaced: much the most difficult question is indeed whether the proposed course of action is, in law, murder notwithstanding the best motives from which everyone concerned is acting.
>
> Murder consists of causing the death of another with intent so to do. What is proposed in the present case is to adopt a course with the intention of bringing about Anthony Bland's death. As to the element of intention or *mens rea*, in my judgment there can be no real doubt

---

27 [2002] EWHC 429 (Fam).
28 See n 6 above.

that it is present in this case: the whole purpose of stopping artificial feeding is to bring about the death of Anthony Bland.

As to the guilty act, or *actus reus*, the criminal law draws a distinction between the commission of a positive act which causes death and the omission to do an act which would have prevented death. In general an omission to prevent death is not an actus reus and cannot give rise to a conviction for murder. But where the accused was under a duty to the deceased to do the act which he omitted to do, such omission can constitute the actus reus of homicide, either murder (*R v Gibbins* (1918) 13 Cr App R 134) or manslaughter (*R v Stone* [1977] QB 354) depending upon the *mens rea* of the accused . . .

It is apparent, then, that the lawfulness of passive euthanasia revolves around the question: 'When is the doctor released from his normal duty to treat?' In answering this, we shall look first, in the remainder of this section, at the position of those patients who remain capable to decide whether they wish to receive life-sustaining treatment, or who have codified their previous capable wishes in an advance directive ('passive voluntary euthanasia'). In section 12.4 we then go on to consider the question of permitting death through non-treatment in the case of those patients who have never expressed a capable and/or sufficiently clear view on the subject ('passive non-voluntary euthanasia').

12.3.2 The patient who wishes to be kept alive

Insofar as a capable patient wishes to receive life-sustaining treatment, then the doctor will virtually always be obligated to provide it, at least where the treatment is one that is medically established. This principle lay at the heart of the case of R (*On the Application of Burke*) v GMC:

R (On the Application of Burke) v GMC (2005)[29]

Mr Burke suffered from a cerebellar ataxia, a terminal degenerative condition that at some point would require him to receive artificial nutrition and hydration (ANH) to prolong his life: he would thereupon remain conscious and capable for a considerable time until the disease reached its final stages. He was concerned by the tenor of the GMC's Guidance to doctors, which implied that unless the patient was actively *refusing* ANH, its continuation was a matter of medical discretion, and challenged the Guidance's legality in relation both to the common law and his rights under the ECHR.

At first instance,[30] Munby J agreed that the Guidance had attached too little weight to the patient's right, reinforced by ECHR considerations, to require life-prolonging ANH, and ruled it unlawful in a number of respects. However, this ruling was reversed by the Court of Appeal, which emphasised that the patient was amply protected by the existing common law, and that nothing in the GMC's Guidance should be read as detracting from this:

Lord Phillips MR (delivering the judgment of the Court): [31] . . .Autonomy and the right of self-determination do not entitle the patient to insist on receiving a particular medical treatment regardless of the nature of the treatment. Insofar as a doctor has a legal obligation to provide treatment this cannot be founded simply upon the fact that the patient demands it. The source of the duty lies elsewhere.

[32] So far as ANH is concerned, there is no need to look far for the duty to provide this. Once a patient is accepted into a hospital, the medical staff come under a posi-

---

29 [2005] EWCA Civ 1003.
30 [2004] EWHC 1879 (Admin).

tive duty at common law to care for the patient. The authorities cited by Munby J at paragraphs 82 to 87 under the heading *The duty to care* establish this proposition, if authority is needed. A fundamental aspect of this positive duty of care is a duty to take such steps as are reasonable to keep the patient alive. Where ANH is necessary to keep the patient alive, the duty of care will normally require the doctors to supply ANH. This duty will not, however, override the competent patient's wish not to receive ANH. Where the competent patient makes it plain that he or she wishes to be kept alive by ANH, this will not be the source of the duty to provide it. The patient's wish will merely underscore that duty.

[33] Insofar as the law has recognised that the duty to keep a patient alive by administering ANH or other life-prolonging treatment is not absolute, the exceptions have been restricted to the following situations: (1) where the competent patient refuses to receive ANH and (2) where the patient is not competent and it is not considered to be in the best interests of the patient to be artificially kept alive. It is with the second exception that the law has had most difficulty. The courts have accepted that where life involves an extreme degree of pain, discomfort or indignity to a patient, who is sentient but not competent and who has manifested no wish to be kept alive, these circumstances may absolve the doctors of the positive duty to keep the patient alive. Equally the courts have recognised that there may be no duty to keep alive a patient who is in a persistent vegetative state ('PVS'). In each of these examples the facts of the individual case may make it difficult to decide whether the duty to keep the patient alive persists.

[34] No such difficulty arises, however, in the situation that has caused Mr Burke concern, that of the competent patient who, regardless of the pain, suffering or indignity of his condition, makes it plain that he wishes to be kept alive. No authority lends the slightest countenance to the suggestion that the duty on the doctors to take reasonable steps to keep the patient alive in such circumstances may not persist. Indeed, it seems to us that for a doctor deliberately to interrupt life-prolonging treatment in the face of a competent patient's expressed wish to be kept alive, with the intention of thereby terminating the patient's life, would leave the doctor with no answer to a charge of murder.

Accordingly, where straightforward treatment such as ANH is at issue, the doctor has a near-absolute duty to provide it as part of his duty to treat his patients in their best interests: the interests in question will be strongly coloured by the patient's wish to be kept alive. On the other hand, as the Court of Appeal in Burke recognised, there could exceptionally be cases, eg where a patient asks for treatment that will marginally prolong his life but at the cost of severe suffering, where the doctor may legitimately refuse to administer the treatment:

Lord Phillips MR: [54] There is one situation where the provision of ANH will not be clinically indicated that is not relevant to Mr Burke's concern but which received a disproportionate amount of attention in this case. In the last stage of life the provision of ANH not only may not prolong life, but may even hasten death. Unchallenged evidence from Professor Higginson illustrated the latter proposition. At this stage, whether to administer ANH will be a clinical decision which is likely to turn on whether or not it has a palliative effect or is likely to produce adverse reactions. It is only in this situation that, assuming the patient remains competent, a patient's expressed wish that ANH be continued might conflict with the doctor's view that this is not clinically indicated.

[55] . . . Clearly the doctor would need to have regard to any distress that might be caused as a result of overriding the expressed wish of the patient. Ultimately, however, a patient cannot demand that a doctor administer a treatment which the doctor considers is adverse to the patient's clinical needs. This said, we consider that the scenario that we have just described is extremely unlikely to arise in practice.

Mr Burke's subsequent application to the European Court of Human Rights was ruled inadmissible. The Court found that he had not shown a real and imminent risk that ANH would be withdrawn, thereby infringing his right to life under Art 2 ECHR.[31]

A further, complicating feature in some cases where a capable patient requests a particular form of treatment to prolong his life for as long as possible is of possible resource constraints in the background. For here the doctor's accession to the wishes of one patient will necessarily impact upon the treatment of other patients. The problem of limited resources – and its interaction, in the case of potentially life-prolonging treatment, with the patient's right to life – has been discussed above in Chapter 2, in relation to the public law applications of patients to receive the cancer drug, Herceptin.[32] We shall also return to the issue in section 12.4.3, in relation to the issue of keeping alive incapable patients, with no or minimal awareness.

12.3.3 Refusals of life-sustaining treatment

As we saw in Chapter 3, it is a cardinal principle of medical law that, in respect of a capable adult patient, treatment may generally not be administered without consent; this is so even in a situation in which, without the treatment, the patient will die. In this regard, Lord Goff commented in *Airedale NHS Trust v Bland* that:

[I]t is established that the principle of self-determination requires that respect must be given to the wishes of the patient, so that if an adult patient of sound mind refuses, however unreasonably, to consent to treatment or care by which his life would or might be prolonged, the doctors responsible for his care must give effect to his wishes, even though they do not consider it to be in his best interests to do so . . . To this extent, the principle of the sanctity of human life must yield to the principle of self-determination . . .

Subsequently, the principle formed the *ratio* in the High Court decisions in *Re C (Adult: Refusal of Treatment)*[33] and *Secretary of State v Robb*.[34] Indeed, in *Ms B v An NHS Hospital Trust*[35] it underlay the decision, referred to earlier, that a capable, paralysed woman had the right to require her life-sustaining ventilator to be switched off.

On the other hand, as mentioned in Chapter 3, it may be that the right to refuse treatment is tempered in certain circumstances by overriding state interests, including the prevention of suicide.[36] In this regard, a natural question to ask is why refusals of life-saving treatment are not construed in general as attempts at suicide which doctors are entitled to thwart? This issue has been discussed by David Price as follows:

---

31 ECtHR: Application 19807/06.
32 Ch2, 64 ff above.
33 [1994] 1 All ER 819.
34 [1995] 2 WLR 722.
35 See n 27 above.
36 Ch3, 89 ff above.

Price, D, 'Assisted suicide and refusing medical treatment: linguistics, morals and legal contortions'[37]

Does a patient intend to die when he or she refuses further medical treatment definitely resulting in death? The courts typically adopt a narrow construction of intention in this context, equating it with desire, yet seemingly then deny the self-evident truth. In *Bouvia v Superior Court*, for instance, a 28 year old mentally capable quadriplegic woman with cerebral palsy and crippling arthritis, who required others to feed her, refused to allow further food to be administered to her. The trial court said:

> It is fairly clear from the evidence and the court cannot close its eyes to the fact that [petitioner] during her stay in defendant hospital, and for some time prior thereto, had formed an intent to die. She voiced this desire to a member of staff of defendant hospital.

The California Court of Appeal, however, disagreed finding that there was no such intent to die . . . It is arguable though that Elizabeth Bouvia did intend to die, even in the sense of wanting to do so – she plainly stated her desire to starve herself to death . . .

[C]ould it nevertheless be asserted that suicide is incapable of being committed by an omission? It is submitted that, contrary to the views of Glanville Williams, the fact that the patient is (on one view) merely passive and does nothing positive to cause the death is not to the point. One can seemingly commit suicide by failing to act, by deliberately failing to feed oneself for instance. In the Supreme Court of the United States in *Cruzan v Director, Missouri Health Department* . . ., Scalia J stated that:

> . . . it would not make much sense to say that one may not kill oneself by walking into the sea, but may sit on the beach until submerged by the incoming tide.

He later added:

> Starving oneself to death is no different from putting a gun to one's temple as far as the common law definition of suicide is concerned; the cause of death in both cases is the suicide's conscious decision to 'put an end to his own existence'.

It is indeed difficult to see what justification could be advanced for a distinction to be drawn between acts and omissions here. The individual is clearly terminating his own life deliberately by either means – it is the ends not the means which are the essence of suicide.

Despite the cogency of these arguments, the English courts have made it clear that they will not equate refusals of life-saving medical treatment with suicide: thus in the *Bland* case, Lord Goff stated (*obiter*) that:

> I wish to add that, in cases of this kind, there is no question of the patient having committed suicide, nor therefore of the doctor having aided or abetted him in doing so. It is simply that the patient has, as he is entitled to do, declined to consent to treatment which might or would have the effect of prolonging his life, and the doctor has, in accordance with his duty, complied with his patient's wishes.

It is apparent that, in making such judgments, the courts (in accordance with their 'qualified sanctity of life' approach) do in fact regard the acts/omissions distinction as crucial: the person who passively declines a life-saving opportunity is distinguished from one who actively engineers his own end. The upshot in the great majority of refusal-of-treatment cases involving capable patients

---

37 (1996) 4 Med L Rev 370.

is that, as Lord Goff noted in *Bland*, 'the doctor's duty to act in the best interests of his patient must likewise be qualified'.

12.3.4 Advance decisions

A significant issue, in relation to refusals of treatment, is how far a patient while still capable may provide for the possibility (or in the case of a progressive condition that will have this effect, inevitability) of his future incompetence and make an anticipatory refusal of life-saving medical treatment. How far will such a refusal subsequently bind a doctor who wishes to treat the patient, who in the interim has become incapable?

The use of advance decisions (often also referred to as 'advance directives' or 'refusals', and colloquially known as 'living wills') to refuse future treatment began in North America; a good illustration of their operation is provided by the decision in the Canadian case of *Malette v Shulman*:

Malette v Shulman (1990)[38]

The claimant was a Jehovah's Witness who was admitted to hospital unconscious following a road accident. She was found to be carrying a card which (translated from French into English) read as follows:

No blood transfusion!
As one of Jehovah's Witnesses with firm religious convictions, I request that no blood or blood products be administered to me under any circumstances. I fully realise the implications of this position, but I have resolutely decided to obey the Bible command: 'Keep abstaining . . . from blood' (Acts 15:28, 29). However, I have no religious objection to the use of non-blood alternatives, such as Dextran, Haemaccel, PVP, Ringer's Lactate or saline solution.

However, the defendant doctor carried out a life-saving blood transfusion:

Robins JA: On the facts of the present case, Dr Shulman was clearly faced with an emergency. He had an unconscious, critically ill patient on his hands who, in his opinion, needed blood transfusions to save her life or preserve her health. If there were no Jehovah's Witness card he undoubtedly would have been entitled to administer blood transfusions as part of the emergency treatment and could not have been held liable for so doing. In those circumstances he would have had no indication that the transfusions would have been refused had the patient then been able to make her wishes known and, accordingly, no reason to expect that, as a reasonable person, she would not consent to the transfusions.

. . . Here, the patient, anticipating an emergency in which she might be unable to make decisions about her health care contemporaneous with the emergency, has given explicit instructions that blood transfusions constitute an unacceptable medical intervention and are not to be administered to her. Once the emergency arises, is the doctor nonetheless entitled to administer transfusions on the basis of his honest belief that they are needed to save a patient's life?

The answer, in my opinion, is clearly no. A doctor is not free to disregard a patient's advance instructions any more than he would be free to disregard instructions given at the time of the emergency. The law does not prohibit a patient from withholding consent to emergency medical treatment, nor does the law prohibit a

---

38 (1990) 72 OR (2d) 417 (Ontario Court of Appeal).

doctor from following his patient's instructions. While the law may disregard the absence of consent in limited emergency circumstances, it otherwise supports the right of capable adults to make decisions concerning their own health care by imposing civil liability on those who perform medical treatment without consent.

The claimant was awarded C$20,000 in damages.

In England, the concept of advance decisions was supported by the Court of Appeal in *Re T (Adult: Refusal of Medical Treatment)*,[39] where Lord Donaldson MR commented as follows:

Lord Donaldson MR: There seems to be a view in the medical profession that in such emergency circumstances the next of kin should be asked to consent on behalf of the patient and that, if possible, treatment should be postponed until that consent has been obtained. This is a misconception because the next of kin has no legal right either to consent or to refuse consent. This is not to say that it is an undesirable practice if the interests of the patient will not be adversely affected by any consequential delay. I say this because contact with the next of kin may reveal that the patient has made an anticipatory choice which, if clearly established and applicable in the circumstances – two major 'ifs' – would bind the practitioner.

Subsequently, the High Court upheld the binding effect of the wishes of a patient not to receive future treatment at a time when no longer capable in *Re C (Adult: Refusal of Treatment)*.[40] In that case, as discussed in Chapter 3,[41] Thorpe J granted an injunction, preventing doctors from amputating the gangrenous leg of a paranoid schizophrenic (who was nevertheless adjudged capable), which was drafted so as to include the period after the patient had lost competence.

See Chapters ← 3

Another example is furnished by the case of *Re AK (Medical Treatment: Consent)*.[42] Here the patient suffered from a neuro-muscular disease causing rapid muscle degeneration; at the time of the Court application he was only able to communicate with the doctors treating him by blinking one of his eyes. Hughes J upheld his wish that, once this last means of communication had disappeared, his artificial ventilation should cease and he be allowed to die. Indeed the judge suggested that the law (in favour of such a step) was sufficiently clear that a formal declaration may not have been necessary.

Although the effect of advance decisions was thus accepted by the common law, in at least some cases there may be felt to be a tension between the interests of the capable maker of the decision and the incapable person they later become. This can occur in cases of long-term, irreversible incompetence, eg through moderate brain injury, or an illness such as dementia, where the patient nevertheless continues to derive pleasure from their existence: here it does not seem self-evidently right that the later, incapable patient should be denied lifesaving treatment on the basis of previous wishes made when, mentally, the patient was a significantly different personality. As the following extract makes clear, it is at any event an approach whose justification involves accepting arguments of some philosophical complexity:

Kuczewski, MG, 'Whose will is it, anyway? A discussion of advance directives, personal identity and consensus in medical ethics'[43]

Living wills are attempts by the capable person to make treatment decisions for her future based upon her present, rather than future, interests. It may be wrong to base how we treat a patient on interests the person previously possessed rather than her current ones. As [John] Robertson

---

39 [1992] 4 All ER 649.
40 See n 33 above.
41 Ch 3, p 101 above.
42 [2001] 1 FLR 129.
43 (1994) 8 *Bioethics* 27.

states, 'The values and interests of the capable person no longer are relevant to someone who has lost the rational structure on which those values and interests rested'. Robertson wishes his critique to apply only to situations that involve an incapable conscious patient. This limitation occurs, presumably, because permanently unconscious patients do not possess significant enough interests to generate a morally weighty conflict with their previous wishes . . .

We need to keep in mind that this is not a mere abstract philosophical word game. . . It is not empirically obvious why interests in dignity, the financial well being of one's family, bodily integrity, and so on, should be said to survive and be applicable to a person who either no longer exists or cannot cognise and presently appreciate these values. Although present practices regarding the use of living wills may go on despite the failure to justify their employment philosophically, such failure would mean that the consensus was forged on a fictitious account of self-determination. Thus, those who argued in the pre-consensus years for the primacy of the best interest standard as the sole standard of decision-making would actually be correct . . .

Kuczewski goes on to argue that the interests of the formerly capable person do survive, not in a personal, but rather in a communal or institutional sense. Accordingly, that person's advance decision should be respected:

[A]n individual's interest in dignity, privacy, and bodily integrity is encoded in his living will, in the memory of others, and even in their perceptions of the situation at the time of one's incompetence. . . . The body that belongs to the incapable patient at t2 is in some sense 'mine' because other persons will call it by my name and make the story of what happens to it a chapter of the story they tell about 'me'. As such, I attempt to make that chapter embody the values which are presently mine. Through the same type of act of will by which I commit to live today in accordance with dignity, so also, I commit that my final chapter shall embody those values . . .

In its 1995 report, *Mental Incapacity*,[44] the Law Commission recommended that the legal effect of advance decisions be enshrined in legislation and this has now occurred by virtue of ss 24–26 of the Mental Capacity Act 2005, which came into effect on 1 October 2007:

Mental Capacity Act 2005:

24 Advance decisions to refuse treatment: general

(1) 'Advance decision' means a decision made by a person ('P'), after he has reached 18 and when he has capacity to do so, that if—

    (a) at a later time and in such circumstances as he may specify, a specified treatment is proposed to be carried out or continued by a person providing health care for him, and

    (b) at that time he lacks capacity to consent to the carrying out or continuation of the treatment,

the specified treatment is not to be carried out or continued.

. . .

25 Validity and applicability of advance decisions

(1) An advance decision does not affect the liability which a person may incur for carrying out or continuing a treatment in relation to P unless the decision is at the material time—

    (a) valid, and

    (b) applicable to the treatment.

. . .

---

44 (1995) Law Com No 231.

(5) An advance decision is not applicable to life-sustaining treatment unless—

  (a) the decision is verified by a statement by P to the effect that it is to apply to that treatment even if life is at risk, and

  (b) the decision and statement comply with subsection (6).

(6) A decision or statement complies with this subsection only if—

  (a) it is in writing,

  (b) it is signed by P or by another person in P's presence and by P's direction,

  (c) the signature is made or acknowledged by P in the presence of a witness, and

  (d) the witness signs it, or acknowledges his signature, in P's presence.

. . .

26 Effect of advance decisions

(1) If P has made an advance decision which is-

  (a) valid, and

  (b) applicable to a treatment,

  the decision has effect as if he had made it, and had had capacity to make it, at the time when the question arises whether the treatment should be carried out or continued.

(2) A person does not incur liability for carrying out or continuing the treatment unless, at the time, he is satisfied that an advance decision exists which is valid and applicable to the treatment.

(3) A person does not incur liability for the consequences of withholding or withdrawing a treatment from P if, at the time, he reasonably believes that an advance decision exists which is valid and applicable to the treatment.

(4) The court may make a declaration as to whether an advance decision—

  (a) exists;

  (b) is valid;

  (c) is applicable to a treatment.

(5) Nothing in an apparent advance decision stops a person–

  (a) providing life-sustaining treatment, or

  (b) doing any act he reasonably believes to be necessary to prevent a serious deterioration in P's condition,

while a decision as respects any relevant issue is sought from the court.

Broadly, these provisions seek to codify the pre-existing legal position at common law. An advance decision to refuse treatment may be made by a person aged 18 or over at a time when he is capable, which binds the treating team beyond the onset of incompetence (and thus stops them from providing treatment), just as a contemporaneous, capable refusal would. However, in s 25 of the Act, the operation of the decision in this way is made subject to two significant requirements, namely that the decision is 'valid', and that it is 'applicable' in the relevant circumstances. These requirements are explained in the Explanatory Notes to the Act prepared by the Department of Consitutional Affairs and Department of Health as follows:

Explanatory Notes to the Mental Capacity Act[45]

. . . Section 25: Validity and applicability of advance decisions

86. This introduces the two important safeguards of validity and applicability in relation to advance decisions to refuse treatment.

---

45 London: TSO, 2005.

87. To be valid the advance decision must not have been withdrawn or overridden by a subsequent LPA giving a donee the authority to consent or refuse consent to the treatment. . . Also, if the person has acted in a way that is clearly inconsistent with the advance decision remaining his fixed decision, then the advance decision is invalid. An example of an inconsistent action might be a former Jehovah's Witness converting to Islam and marrying a Muslim man. Even if she had forgotten to destroy a written advance decision refusing blood transfusion, her actions could be taken into account in determining whether that earlier refusal remained her fixed decision.

88. An advance decision will not be applicable if the person actually has capacity to make the decision when the treatment concerned is proposed. It will also not be applicable to treatments, or in circumstances, not specified in the decision. Furthermore the decision will not be applicable if there are reasonable grounds for believing that the current circumstances were not anticipated by the person and, if they had been anticipated by him, would have affected his decision. For example, there may be new medications available that radically change the outlook for a particular condition and make treatment much less burdensome than was previously the case.

As para 87 states, an advance decision will not be valid if, subsequent to it, the patient confers authority upon another person (the 'donee') under a lasting power of attorney to make decisions in relation to his medical treatment. The general manner in which LPAs operate in relation to the treatment of the incapable has been discussed in Chapter 4.[46] Here, though, it is important to emphasise that the donee does not thereby gain the power, previously enjoyed by the patient (as encoded in the decision), to refuse treatment that the doctors regard as objectively indicated. Rather, the donee must at all times make treatment decisions that accord with the incapable person's best interests.

See Chapter 4 →

The paragraph goes on to note that an advance decision will also be invalid under s 25 MCA 2005 if the patient has subsequently behaved inconsistently with the beliefs that underlay the decision. The example it gives is modelled on the pre-MCA 2005 case of *HE v A Hospital NHS Trust and AE*.[47] There, a young woman was unconscious with serious heart problems, and required surgery including the use of blood products in order to survive. She had been brought up a Muslim, but – together with her mother – subsequently became a Jehovah's Witness and at that time (in February 2001) signed an advance directive rejecting the use of blood products. Although by the time of the proposed surgery (in April 2003) all the indications were that she had reverted to the Muslim faith, her mother insisted that the hospital abide by the directive 'despite the greatly increased risk of death'. In declaring the use of blood products during surgery lawful, Munby J held that the the burden of proof was on those asserting the continued applicability of a directive and that, given that life was at stake, the evidence offered would need especially close and anxious scrutiny.

Section 25(5)–(6) of the 2005 Act outlines a number of additional formalities that must be satisfied for an advance decision to apply to the refusal of life-sustaining treatment. Here the decision must be in writing and signed by the patient (or his nominee in his presence) and witnessed by one other person. It must further include an statement by the patient that the refusal is intended to apply even where non-treatment will put life at risk (according to the *Explanatory Notes*, this includes the life of an unborn foetus). Here the 2005 Act is stricter than the previous common law (which did not insist on such formalities), and this gave rise to the problem of how to deal with advance decisions, which purported to refuse life-sustaining treatment, made prior to 1 October 2007. This difficulty has been

---

46 Ch4, p 140 above.
47 [2003] EWHC 1017 (Fam).

partially addressed by a statutory instrument, the Mental Capacity Act 2005 (Transitional and Consequential Provisions) Order 2007. According to Art 5 of the Order, where an advance refusal of life-sustaining decision predates 1 October 2007, and the patient has since lacked capacity to make a new decision, the refusal – in order to be binding – need not contain an express statement that it extends to life-threatening situations, and nor need it be signed and witnessed. However, the condition that it should be in writing (as now required by s 25 (6)(a) of the 2005 Act) has not been waived.

Section 26 of the Act details the effect that the existence of an advance decision has upon the rights and duties of the doctors treating the patient. Provided the decision is valid and applicable, then, as noted, it will bind the doctors just like a capable, contemporaneous refusal. Accordingly, continued treatment would amount to a battery and possibly also lead to a charge of criminal assault. What, however, where there is uncertainty in the minds of the doctors as to whether the decision really is valid and/or applicable? This is addressed in s 26(2), which states that the doctor will not be liable for giving treatment unless he is satisfied that it meets the relevant tests. Equally, under s 26(3) he will not be liable for withholding treatment (in accordance with the advance decision) where he reasonably believes that the decision is valid and applicable. These provisions, and the fact that the doctor's belief in the validity and applicability of the decision, but not the converse, has to be reasonable, are discussed by Alasdair Maclean, who argues that, in encouraging the doctor to treat in cases of any doubt, they betray a bias against patient autonomy:

Maclean, A, 'Advance Directives and the Rocky Waters of Anticipatory Decision-Making'[48]

Under section 26, healthcare professionals are protected from liability for treating patients when they are not 'satisfied that an advance decision exists which is valid and applicable to the treatment'. On the face of it, this provision gives them considerable discretion, as there is no specific requirement that their satisfaction must be objectively reasonable. Given that the belief in the existence of an advance directive is explicitly required to be reasonable, it is likely that the courts will interpret section 26(2) as not implicitly requiring the professional's satisfaction to be reasonable. This places significant power in the professional's hands and makes any advance directive inherently more vulnerable. As the Code of Practice notes, it 'is ultimately the responsibility of the healthcare professional who is in charge of the person's care' to determine whether there is a valid and applicable advance directive.

Where there is any doubt about the validity or applicability of the advance directive then the professional may apply to the court for clarification. Under section 42(4) of the Act, any professional dealing with an incapacitated adult has a duty to 'have regard to' the Code of Practice. The Code gives the professional initial discretion, but when 'genuine doubt or disagreement' persists, it states that the Court of Protection may make a declaration. However, healthcare professionals are not obliged by the terms of the statute to refer the matter to court. The Code emphasises that the professional should be looking to determine the validity and scope of the advance directive rather than overrule it. However, the test of satisfaction, which might be interpreted as meaning 'convinced', could be applied stringently. As such, it would swallow up the possibility of doubt: if there is any doubt, then the professional cannot be satisfied and so may legitimately treat the patient. Furthermore, the test of 'satisfaction' is subject only to the honest discretion of the professional and there is no requirement that it be reasonable. This puts pressure on the professional to treat and only the most certain of directives may survive. As with the other provisions, section 26(2), and section 26(3) protect healthcare professionals from liability, facilitate the provision of healthcare and safeguard patient welfare but do little for precedent autonomy.

---

48 (2008) 16 Med L Rev 1.

As noted here, in cases of dispute as to the validity and/or applicability of an advance decision, the matter may (albeit not 'must') be referred to the Court of Protection to make a declaration on the issue, and in the meantime treatment to sustain life or prevent a serious deterioration in health remain permissible under s 26(5). In a case from late 2009, which attracted media concern, it was reported that doctors had felt obliged to respect the written advance refusal of life-saving treatment by a young woman, Kerrie Wooltorton, who attended hospital after poisoning herself. In fact, it is not clear if her written refusal complied with the statutory formalities to be a binding decision within the MCA 2005; indeed the doctors appear to have been swayed more by the contemporaneous oral refusal of Ms Wooltorton, who on attendance remained conscious and, in the doctors' view, capable.[49]

Finally, insofar as an advance decision is found not to be binding, this does not mean that it will lose all significance: rather, as stated in para 9.45 of the MCA 2005 Code of Practice,[50] it may still be regarded as an expression of the patient's former wishes and as such relevant in determining his best interests.[51] The paragraph also reminds health professionals not to 'assume that because an advance decision is either invalid or not applicable, they should always provide the specified treatment (including life-sustaining treatment) – they must base this decision on what is in the person's best interests'.

 SELF-TEST QUESTION

Will a doctor who switches off a life support machine have performed active or passive euthanasia? If it is the latter, could the doctor still be guilty of murder anyway?

12.4 Passive Euthanasia: Incapable Patients

12.4.1 Background

In addressing the question of when life-saving treatment may be withheld or withdrawn from the incapable patient (in the absence of a valid and applicable advance decision), we are within the province of *non-voluntary* passive euthanasia. As already noted, the crucial issue here is the extent of the doctor's duty to employ life-prolonging measures in respect of his patient. It is clear that common sense has never regarded this duty as an absolute one. Nevertheless, the first significant English authority in point is a Court of Appeal decision from 1981:

Re B (A Minor) (Wardship: Medical Treatment) (1981)[52]

B was a baby girl born with Down's syndrome and also suffering from an intestinal blockage. Without an operation to remove the blockage, she would die within a few days. Her parents, however, refused to consent to the treatment and B was made a ward of court. The judge at first instance initially authorised treatment, but revoked his order after speaking to the parents and also hearing that the surgeon appointed to the case was unwilling to operate contrary to their wishes. The health authority appealed:

---

49 See Sheila McLean's comment at http://blogs.bmj.com/bmj/2009/10/01/sheila-mclean-on-advance-directives-and-the-case-of-kerrie-wooltorton/. The question of whether in such a case the doctors could be justified in overriding a patient's treatment refusal is considered in Ch 3, pp 89 ff above.
50 London: TSO, 2007.
51 See s4(6) MCA 2005.
52 [1981] 1 WLR 1421, CA.

Templeman LJ: There may be cases, I know not, of severe proved damage where the future is so certain and where the life of the child is so bound to be full of pain and suffering that the court might be driven to a different conclusion, but in the present case the choice which lies before the court is this: whether to allow an operation to take place which may result in the child living for 20 or 30 years as a mongoloid or whether (and I think this must be brutally the result) to terminate the life of a mongoloid child because she also has an intestinal complaint. Faced with that choice I have no doubt that it is the duty of this court to decide that the child must live. The judge was much affected by the reasons given by the parents and came to the conclusion that their wishes ought to be respected. In my judgment he erred in that the duty of the court is to decide whether it is in the interests of the child that an operation should take place. The evidence in this case only goes to show that if the operation takes place and is successful then the child may live the normal span of a mongoloid child with the handicaps and defects and life of a mongol child, and it is not for this court to say that life of that description ought to be extinguished.

Accordingly the appeal must be allowed and the local authority must be authorised themselves to authorise and direct the operation to be carried out on the little girl.

This decision is an important one, not least because it renders doubtful a well-known criminal case of about the same time, R v Arthur,[53] in which a doctor was acquitted of attempting to murder a Down's syndrome baby (whose parents did not wish it to live) after ordering treatment to be withheld: the effect of Re B is that, whatever the parents' views, doctors will generally be obliged to treat babies with the standard disabilities associated with Down's syndrome. However, although Templeman LJ recognised *obiter* the possibility that, in other cases of more drastic disability, treatment could be withheld, it remained unclear in what circumstances this would be so.

Subsequently, some light was shed on this problem in Re C (A Minor) (Wardship: Medical Treatment),[54] where the Court of Appeal authorised the withdrawal of treatment from a severely brain-damaged baby said to be 'dying' in any event. The decisive step, in favour of a more open endorsement of passive euthanasia in extreme cases, came shortly afterwards in the seminal case of Re J:

Re J (A Minor) (Wardship: Medical Treatment) (1990)[55]

J was a five-month-old baby who suffered severe brain damage as a result of his grossly premature birth. He was profoundly disabled, both mentally and physically, and was unlikely to develop even the most basic functions. He had collapsed on a number of occasions since his birth and the court, pursuant to its wardship jurisdiction, was asked to decide if mechanical ventilation of J should occur in the event of a further collapse:

Lord Donaldson MR: Of the three neonatalogists who have been concerned with [J's] care, the most optimistic is Dr W. His view is that J is likely to develop serious spastic quadriplegia, that is to say, paralysis of both his arms and legs. It is debatable whether he will ever be able to sit up or to hold his head upright. J appears to be blind, although there is a possibility that some degree of sight may return. He is likely to be deaf. He may be able to make sounds which reflect his mood, but he is unlikely

---

53 (1981) 12 BMLR 1.
54 [1989] 2 All ER 782, CA.
55 [1991] 1 Fam 33, CA.

ever to be able to speak, even to the extent of saying Mum or Dad. It is highly unlikely that he will develop even limited intellectual abilities. Most unfortunately of all, there is a likelihood that he will be able to feel pain to the same extent as a normal baby, because pain is a very basic response. It is possible that he may achieve the ability to smile and to cry. Finally, as one might expect, his life expectancy has been considerably reduced, at most into his late teens, but even Dr W would expect him to die long before then . . .

The issue here is whether it would be in the best interests of the child to put him on a mechanical ventilator and subject him to all the associated processes of intensive care, if at some future time he could not continue breathing unaided . . .

The basis of the doctors' recommendations, approved by the judge, was that mechanical ventilation is itself an invasive procedure which, together with its essential accompaniments, such as the introduction of a nasogastric tube, drips which have to be re-sited and constant blood sampling, would cause the child distress. Furthermore, the procedures involve taking active measures which carry their own hazards, not only to life but in terms of causing even greater brain damage. This had to be balanced against what could possibly be achieved by the adoption of such active treatment. The chances of preserving the child's life might be improved, although even this was not certain, and account had to be taken of the extremely poor quality of life at present enjoyed by the child, the fact that he had already been ventilated for exceptionally long periods, the unfavourable prognosis with or without ventilation and a recognition that if the question of reventilation ever arose, his situation would have deteriorated still further.

The Court of Appeal accordingly upheld the decision of the High Court that further ventilation aimed at prolonging J's life should not occur.

12.4.2 The role of the court

In both the *Re B* and *Re J* cases, the final decision – in the first case to authorise treatment, in the second to withhold it – was taken by the court pursuant to its wardship jurisdiction in relation to minors under the age of 18 years. Indeed it may well be thought that, given the very serious consequences for the involved parties when the proposed withdrawal of life-prolonging treatment is at issue (the death of the patient; the possible criminal liability of the doctor), such cases should always be decided by a judge. Nonetheless, as discussed in Chapter 4, in the case of incapable adults, the old *parens patriae* jurisdiction, which had permitted the courts to make such decisions was removed in 1959 by a legislative oversight.[56] As noted there, the courts responded creatively to this difficulty by developing the so-called 'declaratory jurisdiction' of the High Court. This allowed courts to hear applications in serious cases impinging on the welfare of incapable (or putatively incapable) patients and declare – that is, *confirm* – that the proposed course of action in respect of them was lawful, or not.

See Chapter 4 →

At the same time, since such a declaration did not as such alter the legal position (making something lawful that was previously unlawful), it followed that those with the care of the incapable did not, as a formal matter, need to seek one: they might simply proceed to treat (or remove treatment), and simply take the risk that their conduct would later be attacked as unlawful. Even so, as noted in Chapter 4, in cases of serious or controversial medical treatment, it increasingly became good practice for the doctors to apply to the High Court for a declaration, such that

---

56 Ch 4, p 138 above.

not doing so could lead to a charge of serious professional misconduct. In context of life-prolonging treatment, as made clear by House of Lords in *Airedale NHS Trust v Bland*, one situation where good practice demanded that the doctors seek a declaration was prior to withdrawing ANH from a patient in PVS (see further 12.4.4 below).

Subsequently, in R (*on the application of Burke*) v GMC, Munby J at first instance[57] suggested that, in the light of ECHR considerations, what had previously been a matter of good practice, was now in certain circumstances a legal requirement: the failure to involve the court would violate the patient's right to respect for private and family life under Art 8 ECHR. He derived this view in particular from the European Court of Human Right's ruling in *Glass v UK*.[58] His interpretation was rejected, however, in forthright terms by the Court of Appeal in *Burke*,[59] which was dismissive as to the significance of the *Glass* ruling (suggesting the ECtHR had misunderstood the applicable English law):

Lord Phillips MR: [75] Munby J . . . concluded that [*Glass v UK*] converted what had previously been only 'a matter of good practice' into 'a matter of legal requirement' by reason of the Human Rights Act 1998 (judgment paragraph 210). He observed that this was 'a significant and potentially very important change'. If the judge was correct we would concur. Accordingly it is necessary to consider *Glass* with some care.

[76] The application in *Glass* was brought by a mother on behalf of her small child. The complaint related to the treatment of the child when in hospital. The doctors thought that the child was dying and administered diamorphine by way of palliative despite the objections of the mother, who thought that the intention of this treatment was to hasten the child's death. The disagreement culminated in a fight in the hospital and the removal of the child by the mother. The child recovered. The mother also complained that the doctors had imposed a 'do not resuscitate' direction in relation to the child without her consent, but the ECtHR did not give separate consideration to this complaint. They treated the case as one of the imposition of invasive treatment on a child contrary to the wishes of its parent.

[77] The ECtHR gave detailed consideration to the position under English law, as this was presented to the court. The ECtHR understood the position to be as follows. As a general proposition, medical treatment of a child requires the authorisation of the child's parents. Where the parents do not consent, the court can authorise such treatment. The doctors can, however, lawfully impose treatment without the consent of the parents or the authorisation of the court in a situation of emergency. . . .

[78] In these circumstances the ECtHR identified the critical issue as whether the child's treatment had been administered in circumstances of emergency which justified the failure on the part of the hospital to seek the approval of the court. . . .

[79] After considering the facts, the ECtHR concluded that the mother had not consented to the administration to her child of diamorphine and that, when this became apparent to the doctors, they had ample time to get the court to resolve the position . . .

[80] This was not a decision which made 'a significant and potentially very important change in English law'. The ECtHR did no more than consider the implications of the doctors' conduct in the light of what the ECtHR understood to be English law. The true position is that the court does not 'authorise' treatment that would otherwise be unlawful. The court makes a declaration as to whether or not proposed treatment, or the withdrawal of treatment, will be lawful. Good practice may require medical practitioners to seek such a declaration where the legality of proposed treatment is in doubt. This is not, however, something that they are required to do as a matter of law. For these reasons Declaration 6 made by Munby J misstated the law.

---

57 See n 29 above.
58 [2004] 1 FCR 553.
59 See n 30 above.

As discussed in Chapter 4,[60] since the coming into force of the Mental Capacity Act 2005, the new Court of Protection has been invested with jurisdiction to make (as opposed to merely confirm the lawfulness of) decisions as to the medical treatment of incapable adults: under s 17(1)(d) MCA the Court's powers extend to 'giving or refusing consent to the carrying out or continuation of a treatment by a person providing medical care for P'. Nonetheless, the preliminary question as to when exactly the responsible carers are required to approach the Court for a decision – as opposed to taking it themselves – is arguably no clearer than before. The MCA Code of Practice, after reiterating the need to seek court approval in cases where it is proposed to withdraw ANH from patients in PVS, has the following to say:

Mental Capacity Act 2005: Code of Practice[61]

Serious healthcare and treatment decisions

8.18 Prior to the Act coming into force, the courts decided that some decisions relating to the provision of medical treatment were so serious that in each case, an application should be made to the court for a declaration that the proposed action was lawful before that action was taken. Cases involving any of the following decisions should therefore be brought before a court:

– decisions about the proposed withholding or withdrawal of artificial nutrition and hydration (ANH) from patients in a permanent vegetative state (PVS) . . .

– all other cases where there is a doubt or dispute about whether a particular treatment will be in a person's best interests.

8.19 The case law requirement to seek a declaration in cases involving the withholding or withdrawing of artificial nutrition and hydration to people in a permanent vegetative state is unaffected by the Act and as a matter of practice, these cases should be put to the Court of Protection for approval. . . .

8.23 Other cases likely to be referred to the court include those involving ethical dilemmas in untested areas (such as innovative treatments for variant CJD), or where there are otherwise irresolvable conflicts between healthcare staff, or between staff and family members.

8.24 There are also a few types of cases that should generally be dealt with by the court, since other dispute resolution methods are unlikely to be appropriate . . . This includes, for example, cases where it is unclear whether proposed serious and/or invasive medical treatment is likely to be in the best interests of the person who lacks capacity to consent.

It appears then that, following the Act, the expectation remains that in most cases, the decision to withdraw life-prolonging treatment will be made by the doctors in consultation with the relatives. It is only exceptionally, where the factors telling in favour and against the decision are finely poised and/or a sharp conflict of views arises between the doctors and relatives that the matter should go to the Court of Protection (and, as before, the 'should' here seems to denote a matter of good practice). While, arguably, it is appropriate that the need for formal court hearings, with the attendant stress for all sides, should be minimised, it seems that – as the Court of Appeal hints in para 69 of its *Burke* judgment – costs and court time are also factors in the law's reticence in requiring applications.

---

60 Ch4, pp 157 ff above.
61 See n 50 above; see also the guidance contained in the Court of Protection's Practice Direction 9E, at www.hmcourts-service. gov.uk/cms/files/09E_-_Serious_Medical_Treatment_PD.pdf.

12.4.3 Reaching the decision: the best interests test

How, then, should the decision-maker (be they the doctors, or a judge) go about deciding when it is no longer appropriate for life-sustaining treatment to be provided? In *Re J* the Court of Appeal invoked the 'best interests' of the infant as the justification for not prolonging his life by further mechanical ventilation. We have previously encountered the 'best interests' test in the context of decisions to provide incapable patients with treatment of a non-life-saving nature, most notably in sterilisation cases involving mentally disabled women.[62] In itself the test lacks substance: it is merely a direction that, in reaching the decision whether to treat, the decider should objectively weigh up the factors in favour of treatment against those which militate against it. The factors themselves, and their respective weighting, clearly stand in need of further specification.

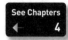
See Chapters 4

An initial question, however, is whether such a balancing exercise can be meaningfully performed at all in a context in which one of the options (non-treatment) leads to death. This point was taken by counsel for the Official Solicitor in the *Re J* case:[63]

> **Lord Donaldson MR**: [James Munby QC's] first, or absolutist, submission is that a court is never justified in withholding consent to treatment which could enable a child to survive a life-threatening condition, whatever the pain or other side effects inherent in the treatment, and whatever the quality of the life which it would experience thereafter. . . .
>
> In support of this submission, Mr Munby draws attention to the decision of this court in *McKay v Essex HA* . . . There a child suffered severe and irreversible damage before birth, as a result of her mother contracting rubella (German measles). She sued the health authority [inter alia] . . . on [the] basis . . . that her mother should have been advised to seek an abortion and that, if this advice had been given and accepted, she would never have been born at all. The damages claimed under this head were necessarily based upon a comparison between her actual condition and her condition if, as a result of an abortion, she had never been born at all. . . .
>
> . . . I do not regard this decision as providing us with either guidance or assistance in the context of the present problem. The child was claiming damages, and the decision was that no monetary comparison could be made between the two states.
>
> **Taylor LJ**: Despite the court's inability to compare a life afflicted by the most severe disability with death, the unknown, I am of the view that there must be extreme cases in which the court is entitled to say: 'The life which this treatment would prolong would be so cruel as to be intolerable.' If, for example, a child was so damaged as to have negligible use of its faculties and the only way of preserving its life was by the continuous administration of extremely painful treatment such that the child either would be in continuous agony or would have to be so sedated continuously as to have no conscious life at all, I cannot think Mr Munby's absolute test should apply to require the treatment to be given. In those circumstances, without there being any question of deliberately ending the life or shortening it, I consider the court is entitled in the best interests of the child to say that deliberate steps should not be taken artificially to prolong its miserable lifespan.

Assuming that a balancing exercise is possible, it will nevertheless be somewhat different in nature from the comparative assessment of benefits and burdens (the patient's *life with treatment* against her *life without treatment*) familiar from decisions dealing with such matters as sterilisation. In the latter type of case, one can imagine that decisions may sometimes be finely weighted, ultimately turning on apparently marginal differences. By contrast, where without treatment death will occur, the

---

62 See Ch 4, Section 4.5 above.
63 See n 55 above.

courts will brook no such ambiguity: not only must a life be truly awful for death to seem preferable, but the residual force of the (qualified) sanctity of life principle here asserts itself:

> **Taylor LJ**: Three preliminary principles are not in dispute. First, it is settled law that the court's prime and paramount consideration must be the best interests of the child . . .
>
> Secondly, the court's high respect for the sanctity of human life imposes a strong presumption in favour of taking all steps capable of preserving it, save in exceptional circumstances. The problem is to define those circumstances.
>
> Thirdly, and as a corollary to the second principle, it cannot be too strongly emphasised that the court never sanctions steps to terminate life. That would be unlawful. There is no question of approving, even in a case of the most horrendous disability, a course aimed at terminating life or accelerating death. The court is concerned only with the circumstances in which steps should not be taken to prolong life.

What, then, will be the substantive factors relevant to a decision that it is not in a patient's best interests to have his or her life prolonged? Lord Donaldson MR suggested that 'the critical equation . . . cannot be done with mathematical or any precision'. Balcombe LJ also commented as follows:

> **Balcombe LJ**: . . . I would deprecate any attempt by this court to lay down . . . an all-embracing test, since the circumstances of these tragic cases are so infinitely various. I do not know of any demand by the judges who have to deal with these cases at first instance for this court to assist them by laying down any test beyond that which is already the law: that the interests of the ward are the first and paramount consideration . . .

On the other hand, Taylor LJ was prepared to be more expansive:

> **Taylor LJ**: I consider the correct approach is for the court to judge the quality of life the child would have to endure if given the treatment, and decide whether in all the circumstances such a life would be so afflicted as to be intolerable to that child. I say 'to that child' because the test should not be whether the life would be tolerable to the decider. The test must be whether the child in question, if capable of exercising sound judgment, would consider the life tolerable. This is the approach adopted by McKenzie J in *Re Superintendent of Family and Child Service and Dawson* . . . It takes account of the strong instinct to preserve one's life even in circumstances which an outsider, not himself at risk of death, might consider unacceptable. The circumstances to be considered would, in appropriate cases, include the degree of existing disability and any additional suffering or aggravation of the disability which the treatment itself would superimpose. In an accident case, as opposed to one involving disablement from birth, the child's pre-accident quality of life and its perception of what has been lost may also be factors relevant to whether the residual life would be intolerable to that child.

Subsequently, Taylor LJ's approach was applied by the High Court in *Re R (Adult: Medical Treatment)*.[64] There the patient was a 23-year-old man who had been born with a serious malformation of the brain and cerebral palsy. He was described as being in a 'low-awareness state' with roughly the perception and cognitive faculties of a new-born infant. During 1995 he was admitted to hospital on no fewer than five occasions and his weight dropped to five stone. The NHS trust responsible for his care sought a declaration that it would be lawful to withhold cardio-pulmonary resuscitation if he collapsed and, subject to the views of his doctors and parents at the relevant time, anti-

---

64 [1996] 2 FLR 99.

biotics in the face of a life-threatening infection. In granting the declaration, Sir Stephen Brown P commented:

> **Sir Stephen Brown P**: The principle of law to be applied in this case is that of the 'best interests of the patient' as made clear by the Court of Appeal in *Re J (A Minor) (Wardship: Medical Treatment)* . . . In the course of his judgment . . . Taylor LJ said:
>
>> I consider the correct approach is for the court to judge the quality of life the child would have to endure if given the treatment, and decide whether in all the circumstances such a life would be so afflicted as to be intolerable to that child.
>
> Although this present case concerns a handicapped adult and not a child who is a ward of court the overriding principle in my judgment is the same.

At first instance in R (*On the Application of Burke*) *v GMC*,[65] Munby J (who as James Munby QC had acted as Counsel in the *Re J* case) favoured the recognition of 'intolerability' as providing the general touchstone of best interests in the context of withdrawing medical treatment from a sentient incapable patient. However, in reversing that judgment, the Court of Appeal was critical of the attempt to define best interests in such cases by means of a single test:

> **Lord Phillips MR**: [58] There are tragic cases where treatment can prolong life for an indeterminate period, but only at a cost of great suffering while life continues. Such a case was *In re J (a Minor) (Wardship: Medical Treatment)*. . . . There are other cases, and these are much more common, where a patient has lost competence in the final stages of life and where ANH may prolong these final stages, but at an adverse cost so far as comfort and dignity are concerned, sometimes resulting in the patient's last days being spent in a hospital ward rather than at home, with family around.
>
> . . .
>
> [62] . . .The suggestion that the touchstone of 'best interests' is the 'intolerability' of continued life has, understandably given rise to concern. The test of whether it is in the best interests of the patient to provide or continue ANH must depend on the particular circumstances. The two situations that we have considered above are very different. As to the approach to be adopted in the former, this court dealt with that in *Re J* and we do not think that it is appropriate to review what the court there said in a context that is purely hypothetical.
>
> [63] As to the approach to best interests where a patient is close to death, it seems to us that the judge himself recognised that 'intolerability' was not the test of best interests. At paragraph 104 he said:
>
>> 'where the patient is dying, the goal may properly be to ease suffering and, where appropriate, to "ease the passing" rather than to achieve a short prolongation of life.'
>
> We agree. We do not think it possible to attempt to define what is in the best interests of a patient by a single test, applicable in all circumstances . . .[66]

Shortly afterwards in 2005, in *Wyatt v Portsmouth NHS Trust*,[67] the Court of Appeal was required to rule in a dispute between the doctors, who did not wish to mechanically ventilate a seriously premature and disabled baby girl if she suffered an infection, and the baby's parents, who wanted every effort to be made to prolong her life. In the judgment, Wall LJ, speaking for the Court, gave

---

65 See n 29 above.
66 See n 30 above.
67 [2005] EWCA Civ 1181.

the following advice to trial judges hearing cases where it is proposed to withdraw treatment from severely disabled infants:

> **Wall LJ** (delivering the judgment of the Court): [87] In our judgment, the intellectual milestones for the judge in a case such as the present are . . . simple although the ultimate decision will frequently be extremely difficult. The judge must decide what is in the child's best interests. In making that decision the welfare of the child is paramount, and the judge must look at the question from the assumed point of view of the patient (*In re J* [1991] Fam 33). There is a strong presumption in favour of a course of action which will prolong life, but that presumption is not irrebuttable (*In re J*). The term 'best interests' encompasses medical, emotional, and all other welfare issues (*In re A* [2000] 1FLR 549). The court must conduct a balancing exercise in which all the relevant factors are weighed (*In re J*) and a helpful way of undertaking this exercise is to draw up a balance sheet (*In re A*).
>
> [88] Inevitably, whilst cases involving the treatment of children will fall into recognised categories, no two cases are the same, and the individual cases will inevitably be highly fact-specific. In this context any criteria which seek to circumscribe the best interests tests are, we think, to be avoided. As Thorpe LJ said in *In re S* [2001] Fam 15: 'it would be undesirable and probably impossible to set bounds to what is relevant to a welfare determination.'
>
> . . .
>
> [91] We do not, however, dismiss 'intolerability' as a factor altogether. As we have already stated, we agree with Hedley J that whilst 'intolerable to the child' should not be seen either as a gloss on or a supplementary guide to best interests, it is, as he said, a valuable guide in the search for best interests in this kind of case.

In the *Wyatt* case, the courts agreed with the medical view that, given the baby's serious disabilities and limited capacity to develop, it would not be in her best interests to subject her to further invasive treatment. As discussed in Chapter 4, where disputes arise over what is best for incapable children, the medical opinion of the doctors will nearly always carry the day.[68] As Anne Morris argues, in the context of decisions to withdraw treatment from disabled infants, the parents' emotional stake in the continued life of their child may be seen as counting against them, and not always correctly.

See Chapter 4 ➡

Morris, A, 'Selective Treatment of Irreversibly Impaired Infants'[69]

. . . [W]hile neonatologists in the UK consider it important to involve parents in the decision-making process . . . there is also a view that the ultimate decision must be that of the clinician. This derives both from the idea that it is implicit in a professional context that the practitioner takes responsibility for her actions, and from the belief that the parents should not perceive that they alone decide whether their child should live or die. This 'ownership' of the ultimate decision may again privilege medical considerations, while also allowing the personal non-clinical views of the doctor to carry greater weight . . . However, while disagreements between parents and health care professionals may be rare, they can be profound.

Some disagreements may arise from easily identifiable causes, as with parental adherence to a particular religious belief. Others may result from an inability to comprehend the severity of the problems or unwillingness on the part of the family to accept a bleak prognosis in the face of incontrovertible medical and scientific evidence. There are, however, cases

---

68 Ch 4, section 4.4.3 above.
69 (2009) 17 Med L Rev 347.

where it seems that the dispute is rather more complex. Although the Wyatt parents held strong Christian beliefs and were reported to be awaiting 'a miracle', they saw a different child from the one identified solely in medical terms. They recognized her disabilities, but challenged the medical opinion that Charlotte was going to die. Charlotte's survival, however, was itself problematic. Was she 'condemned' to a quality of life that is on any reckoning suboptimal and might be termed 'unbearable', or is she lucky to be alive? Who judges?

... Once the dispute reaches court, the risk is that non-compliant parents are seen as well-intentioned but lacking the necessary objectivity and/or technical knowledge. The temptation to see parental opinion as wishful thinking is clear in a number of cases including *Wyatt* ...

An unusual example of the court siding with the parents and favouring the continuance of life-prolonging treatment that the doctors did not consider to be in a child's best interests, is provided by *An NHS Trust v MB*.[70] There, MB was an 18-month-old boy, who suffered from spinal muscular atrophy, a degenerative muscle-wasting disease. By the time of the hearing, he was completely paralysed and reliant on mechanical ventilation to breath. It was unclear to what extent he was impaired mentally, but, on the basis of the parents' evidence, Holman J was prepared to assume that he derived pleasure from activities such as listening to stories or watching DVDs. His Lordship applied the 'balance sheet' approach to determining MB's best interests, endorsed by the Court of Appeal in *Wyatt*, and made the following observations:

Holman J: [58] The test is one of best interests, and the task of the court is to balance all the factors. The Court of Appeal have suggested that the best and safest way of reliably doing this is to draw up a list on which are specifically identified, on the one hand, the benefits or advantages and, on the other hand, the burdens or disadvantages of continuing or discontinuing the treatment in question. At a relatively early stage of this hearing I therefore asked each advocate to draw up and submit to me their respective proposed lists, and they kindly did so. It has been an enormously useful discipline, both during evidence (when the lists were used as a kind of check list), the argument and now as I reach my decision and prepare this judgment. I would like, as an aside, to suggest that in similar cases each party should prepare such lists as part of their preparation of the case. The lists can always be added to, or amended, in the light of the evidence, as happened in this case.

. . .

[102] It is impossible to put a mathematical or any other value on the benefits. But they are precious and real and they are the benefits, and only benefits, that M was destined to gain from his life. I do not consider that from one day to the next all the routine discomfort, distress and pain that the doctors describe (but not the ones I have now excluded) outweigh those benefits so that I can say that it is in his best interests that those benefits, and life itself, should immediately end. On the contrary, I positively consider that as his life does still have benefits, and is his life, it should be enabled to continue, subject to excluding the treatment I have identified.

Accordingly, the judge refused the NHS trust's application for a declaration that it would be lawful in MB's best interests immediately to discontinue treatment, though he agreed that, if and when these became necessary, further painful interventions to prolong his life, such as cardio-pulmanory resuscitation, should not be undertaken.

As we saw in Chapter 4, on other occasions it may be the doctors who wish to provide treatment – including life-prolonging treatment – to an incapable patient, in the face of objections from the patient's relatives. Earlier in this chapter, we saw that this

See Chapter
4

---

occurred in the case of *Re B*, in which the parents of a child with Down's syndrome did not wish her to survive. Another case where the relatives disputed that treatment should occur, this time involving an incapable adult, is *W Healthcare NHS Trust v H*:

W Healthcare NHS Trust v H (2004)[71]

The trust caring for KH, a 59-year-old woman in the final stages of multiple sclerosis, obtained a declaration that it would be lawful to reinsert her feeding tube (PEG), which had become detached. KH had been incapable, due to the effects of her illness, for at least 20 years and was now only minimally conscious, being unable to recognise her family or to utter more than the occasional word. Physically, most of her bodily functions had ceased to work and she required 24-hour care to survive. In their appeal, KH's family presented evidence that she had made it clear, when still capable, that she would not wish to be kept alive in her present condition.

Brooke LJ: [14] In a case like this there are three tests that have to be applied. First, is the patient capable of taking an informed decision for herself? I need not pause on that test. It is agreed that KH is not so capable and has not been so capable for many years.

[15] The next question when what is being proposed amounts to a trespass is whether there is a clear exposition of the patient's wishes before she became incapable, which is capable in law of amounting to a direction as to how she wishes to be treated when no longer capable of taking decisions for herself. . . .

. . . [21] I am of the clear view that the judge was correct in finding that there was not an advance directive which was sufficiently clear to amount to a direction that she preferred to be deprived of food and drink for a period of time which would lead to her death in all circumstances. There is no evidence that she was aware of the nature of this choice, or the unpleasantness or otherwise of death by starvation, and it would be departing from established principles of English law if one was to hold that there was an advance directive which was established and relevant in the circumstances in the present case, despite the very strong expression of her wishes which came through in the evidence.

[22] One is then left with stage 3, which is where the patient's best interests lie . . .

[23] . . . If the House of Lords in 1990 had come down in favour of substituted choice so that the law of England was that the court should put itself in the shoes of the patient and do its best to make a choice now, then we would be applying a different test, and one which might well be more favourable to the family than the test which the law requires us to apply.

[27] The way that the judge came to the conclusion was that in KH's present state he was unable to say that life prolonging treatment would provide no benefit, and that death by, in effect, starvation would be even less dignified than the death which she will face in due course if kept artificially alive for more weeks or months or possibly years.

[28] The judgment is not ours to make. This is a court of appeal. The balance is for the judge of first instance to assess, and this court can only interfere on well recognised grounds if the judge has misdirected himself in law or there are reasons why we are entitled to fault the exercise of the judgment he concluded.

---

71 [2004] EWCA Civ 1324.

This decision provides another example of the courts favouring medical opinion as to the patient's best interests over the contrary views of the patient's family. However, the case is also interesting for the way in which the Court dealt with the question as to how far KH's own previous wishes (not to be kept alive in a severely debilitated state) were relevant to the question of whether such treatment was nevertheless in her best interests. In the result the court decided that, once it was established that those wishes did not amount to a valid advance directive, they could not be determinative. In passing, though, Brooke LJ noted (in para 23) an alternative to the best interests approach, potentially available in such a case (and which might well have favoured the views of KH's family), namely the test of substituted judgment.

As noted in Chapter 4,[72] this test directs attention to the hypothetical wishes of the incapable person. It does so by asking whether the patient himself (were he magically restored for a split second to his former state of competence) would wish to receive treatment in his present circumstances. This approach has been used in a number of American cases involving the withdrawal of treatment from incapable patients, for example, Re Quinlan;[73] however, in Airedale NHS Trust v Bland,[74] the House of Lords disparaged the test's application in English law:

> **Lord Mustill:** The second method, which is adopted if the evidence is insufficient to justify an inference of what the patient chose in the past so that it can be projected to the present, involves the appointment of a surrogate to make on behalf of the patient the choice which he believes the patient would now make if able to do so. For this purpose the surrogate builds up a picture of the patient's former character, feelings, convictions and so on from which the putative choice is deduced. This process may perhaps have some justification where the patient is sentient but unable to communicate a choice, but it breaks down totally in a case such as the present. To postulate a patient who is in such a condition that he cannot know that there is a choice to be made, or indeed know anything at all, and then ask whether he would have chosen to terminate his life because that condition made it no longer worth living is surely meaningless, as is very clearly shown by the lengths to which the court was driven in *Superintendent of Belchertown State School v Saikewicz* 370 NE 2d 417. The idea is simply a fiction, which I would not be willing to adopt even if there were in the case of Anthony Bland any materials upon which a surrogate could act, which as far as I can see there are not.

Subsequent to the decision in *Bland*, the Law Commission, in its Report on Mental Incapacity, also rejected a pure substituted judgment approach. However, it recommended that the patient's past wishes should be treated as a relevant factor in determining his best interests:

Law Commission, *Mental Incapacity*[75]

3.28 – We recommend that in deciding what is in a person's best interests regard should be had to:

(1) the ascertainable past and present wishes and feelings of the person concerned, and the factors that person would consider if able to do so;

(2) the need to permit and encourage the person to participate, or to improve his or her ability to participate, as fully as possible in anything done for and any decision affecting him or her;

(3) the views of other people whom it is appropriate and practicable to consult about the person's wishes and feelings and what would be in his or her best interests;

---

72 Ch 4, p 153 above.
73 70 NJ 10 (1976) (New Jersey Sup Ct).
74 See n 6 above; see too the comments of Lord Goff in the case, cited in Ch 4, at p 153.
75 See n 44 above.

(4) whether the purpose for which any action or decision is required can be as effectively achieved in a manner less restrictive of the person's freedom of action. (Draft Bill, cl 3(2).)

Wishes, feelings and putative factors

3.29 –This first element in the checklist establishes the importance of individual views. Realistically, the former views of a person who is without capacity cannot in every case be determinative of the decision which is now to be made. Past wishes and feelings may in any event conflict with feelings the person is still able to express in spite of incapacity. People who cannot make decisions can still experience pleasure and distress. Present wishes and feelings must therefore be taken into account, where necessary balanced with past wishes and feelings. One of the failings of a pure 'substituted judgment' model is the unhelpful idea that a person who cannot make a decision should be treated as if his or her capacity were perfect and unimpaired, and as if present emotions need not also be considered.

These recommendations are broadly reflected in the Mental Capacity Act 2005. As part of the exercise to determine an incapable person's best interests under s 4(6), the decision-maker is required to consider, 'so far as is reasonably ascertainable (a) the person's past and present wishes and feelings (and, in particular, any relevant written statement made by him when he had capacity), (b) the beliefs and values that would be likely to influence his decision if he had capacity, and (c) the other factors that he would be likely to consider if he were able to do so'.

Finally, the Court of Appeal's decision in the *W Healthcare* case[76] may be seen as an illustration of Taylor LJ's dictum in the *Re J* case,[77] that 'the court's high respect for the sanctity of human life imposes a strong presumption in favour of taking all steps capable of preserving it'. Subsequently, the Mental Capacity Bill 2004 proposed to incorporate this presumption into the 'best interests' test: cl 4(5) stated that, '[the decision-maker] must, where the determination relates to life-sustaining treatment, begin by assuming that it will be in the person's interests for his life to continue'. However, this clause was altered late in the day, and s 4(5) of the 2005 Act now reads rather differently:

Mental Capacity Act 2005

4 Best interests

. . . (5) Where the determination relates to life-sustaining treatment [the person making the determination] must not, in considering whether the treatment is in the best interests of the person concerned, be motivated by a desire to bring about his death.

This is a peculiar provision. On the one hand it acknowledges that removal of life-sustaining treatment may sometimes be in a person's best interests. On the other, it attempts to exclude wrongly motivated determinations by the decision-maker. It is hard to see though what the decision-maker's subjective attitude has to do with the fact (if established) that treatment is no longer in a given patient's interests. At least if taken at face value, the subsection has, as John Coggon notes, the potential to create a significant dilemma for doctors:

Coggon, J, 'Ignoring the moral and intellectual shape of the law after *Bland*: the unintended side-effect of a sorry compromise'[78]

It is simply a fact, I would suggest, that a doctor may well feel that a patient's best interests would be served by death. Clearly that provides no justification of itself for killing. But no justification is

---

76 See n 71 above.
77 See n 55 above.
78 (2007) 27 *Legal Studies* 110.

required where the doctor is anyway doing what he is morally and legally required to do, indeed what he is paid to do: treat (or cease to treat) the patient in accordance with the patient's interests. So, let us return to a new variant of our rejigged hypothetical example.

Imagine that a doctor has a patient whose best interests would be served by a withdrawal of treatment: the treatment is excessively burdensome on a valid sanctity-of-life approach. The doctor pities the patient and feels that the patient would be better off dead, and has death in his mind as one of his motives for desiring to withdraw the treatment.

Our doctor is now faced with a legal as well as a moral dilemma, which is imposed by s 4(5). If he fails to cease treating the patient he is acting unlawfully because the Act requires him to treat the patient in accordance with 'objective' best interests. If, on the other hand, he does cease the treatment, he would be acting unlawfully by violating the doctrine of the sanctity of life. This is not a semantic game; it is a logical consequence of s 4(5).

It remains to be seen how the courts will interpret the sub-section in practice.

12.4.4 The problem of patients in PVS

So far our concern has been with patients who have been sentient (ie capable of experience) but severely impaired. Here it has arguably made sense to conduct a form of comparative exercise in which their (intolerable) quality of life is measured against death (conceived of as permanent unconsciousness). We must now consider a second category of patient for whom no such exercise appears possible, viz, those who, while still alive, become permanently insensate. As Jonathan Glover remarks, citing the idealist philosopher, Arthur Schopenhauer, in subjective terms such patients are already dead:

Glover, J, *Causing Death and Saving Lives*[79]

I have no way of refuting someone who holds that being alive, even though unconscious, is intrinsically valuable. But it is a view that will seem unattractive to those of us who, in our own case, see a life of permanent coma as in no way preferable to death. From the subjective point of view, there is nothing to choose between the two. Schopenhauer saw this clearly when he said of the destruction of the body:

But actually we feel this destruction only in the evils of illness or of old age; on the other hand, for the *subject*, death itself consists merely in the moment when consciousness vanishes, since the activity of the brain ceases. The extension of the stoppage to all the other parts of the organism which follows this is really already an event after death. Therefore, in a subjective respect, death concerns only consciousness.

Legally, of course, such patients are alive: as we saw in Chapter 11, death is regarded in law as occurring only when the whole of an individual's brainstem has perished. The brainstem is divided into upper and lower parts, the former, together with the cerebral cortex, being necessary for consciousness while the latter controls the body's automatic functions such as breathing, swallowing and other basic reflexes. When the brain is starved of oxygen, the lower brainstem is the last part of it to die, a fact which may give rise to a permanently insensate condition known, medically, as a permanent (formerly 'persistent') vegetative state or 'PVS'. Although there are no precise figures, it has been estimated that in the UK there are around 850 patients with this condition, and a further 2,500 who are in a minimally consciousness 'near PVS' state.[80]

See Chapter 11

---

79 See n 3 above.
80 Jennett, B in Laureys, S (ed), *The Boundaries of Consciousness*, Amsterdam: Elsevier, 2005, 537.

The issue of whether a patient diagnosed as being in PVS should be subject to a life-sustaining regime of treatment and care fell to be decided by the House of Lords in the most famous passive euthanasia case in English law to date, *Airedale NHS Trust v Bland*:

Airedale NHS Trust v Bland (1993)[81]

Tony Bland suffered massive and irreversible brain damage in the Hillsborough football disaster in April 1989. He had lain in a PVS for more than three years and the medical evidence was unanimous that he would never regain any form of awareness. The trust caring for him applied, with his parents' approval, for a declaration that it would be lawful to withhold further life-prolonging treatment and care (artificial nutrition and hydration as well as antibiotics) from him, thus, allowing him to die. The declaration was granted by the High Court, and this was unanimously affirmed by the Court of Appeal and by the House of Lords:

> **Lord Keith of Kinkel**: The broad issue raised by the appeal is stated by the parties to be: 'In what circumstances, if ever, can those having a duty to feed an invalid lawfully stop doing so?' The immediate issue, however, is whether in the particular circumstances of Anthony Bland's case those in charge of it would be acting lawfully if they discontinued the particular measures, including feeding by nasogastric tube, which are now being used to maintain Anthony Bland in his existing condition . . .
>
> It is argued for the respondents, supported by the *amicus curiae*, that his best interests favour discontinuance. I feel some doubt about this way of putting the matter. In *Re F (Mental Patient: Sterilisation)* [1990] 2 AC 1 this House held that it would be lawful to sterilise a female mental patient who was incapable of giving consent to the procedure. The ground of the decision was that sterilisation would be in the patient's best interests because her life would be fuller and more agreeable if she were sterilised than if she were not. In *Re J (A Minor) (Wardship: Medical Treatment)* [1991] Fam 33 the Court of Appeal held it to be lawful to withhold life-saving treatment from a very young child in circumstances where the child's life, if saved, would be one irredeemably racked by pain and agony. In both cases it was possible to make a value judgment, as to the consequences to a sensate being, of in the one case withholding and in the other case administering the treatment in question. In the case of a permanently insensate being, who if continuing to live would never experience the slightest actual discomfort, it is difficult, if not impossible, to make any relevant comparison between continued existence and the absence of it. It is, however, perhaps permissible to say that to an individual with no cognitive capacity whatever, and no prospect of ever recovering any such capacity in this world, it must be a matter of complete indifference whether he lives or dies.
>
> Where one individual has assumed responsibility for the care of another who cannot look after himself or herself, whether as a medical practitioner or otherwise, that responsibility cannot lawfully be shed unless arrangements are made for the responsibility to be taken over by someone else. Thus a person having charge of a baby who fails to feed it, so that it dies, will be guilty at least of manslaughter. The same is true of one having charge of an adult who is frail and cannot look after herself: *R v Stone* [1977] QB 354. It was argued for the guardian *ad litem*, by analogy with that case, that here the doctors in charge of Anthony Bland had a continuing duty to feed him by means of the nasogastric tube and that if they failed to carry out that duty they were guilty of manslaughter, if not murder. This was coupled with the argument that

---

81 See n 6 above.

feeding by means of the nasogastric tube was not medical treatment at all, but simply feeding, indistinguishable from feeding by normal means. As regards this latter argument, I am of opinion that regard should be had to the whole regime, including the artificial feeding, which at present keeps Anthony Bland alive. That regime amounts to medical treatment and care, and it is incorrect to direct attention exclusively to the fact that nourishment is being provided. In any event, the administration of nourishment by the means adopted involves the application of a medical technique. But it is, of course, true that in general it would not be lawful for a medical practitioner who assumed responsibility for the care of an unconscious patient simply to give up treatment in circumstances where continuance of it would confer some benefit on the patient. On the other hand a medical practitioner is under no duty to continue to treat such a patient where a large body of informed and responsible medical opinion is to the effect that no benefit at all would be conferred by continuance. Existence in a vegetative state with no prospect of recovery is by that opinion regarded as not being a benefit, and that, if not unarguably correct, at least forms a proper basis for the decision to discontinue treatment and care: *Bolam v Friern Hospital Management Committee* [1957] 1 WLR 582. . . .

Given that existence in the persistent vegetative state is not a benefit to the patient, it remains to consider whether the principle of the sanctity of life, which it is the concern of the State, and the judiciary as one of the arms of the State, to maintain, requires this House to hold that the judgment of the Court of Appeal was incorrect. In my opinion it does not. The principle is not an absolute one. It does not compel a medical practitioner on pain of criminal sanctions to treat a patient, who will die if he does not, contrary to the express wishes of the patient. It does not authorise forcible feeding of prisoners on hunger strike. It does not compel the temporary keeping alive of patients who are terminally ill where to do so would merely prolong their suffering. On the other hand it forbids the taking of active measures to cut short the life of a terminally ill patient. In my judgment it does no violence to the principle to hold that it is lawful to cease to give medical treatment and care to a PVS patient who has been in that state for over three years, considering that to do so involves invasive manipulation of the patient's body to which he has not consented and which confers no benefit upon him . . .

My Lords, for these reasons, which are substantially the same as those set out in the speech delivered by my noble and learned friend, Lord Goff of Chieveley, with which I agree, I would dismiss the appeal.

As we have seen, there is a philosophical problem in applying the best interests approach to a patient who will never again enjoy any form of experience. For such patients, rather than offering any prospect of release from suffering, death must, as Lord Keith recognised, be a matter of pure indifference. Thus, it might well be argued, it cannot be in their best interests. In the Court of Appeal in *Bland*, Hoffmann LJ, drawing on Ronald Dworkin's work, *Life's Dominion*,[82] addressed this difficulty by suggesting that patients in PVS do in fact retain certain interests (*critical* – as opposed to *experiential* – interests in Dworkinian terms) and that these are served by allowing them to die:

Hoffmann LJ: Counsel for the Official Solicitor argued that however vestigial Anthony Bland's life might be, one could not assume that he would choose to die. Being unconscious, he felt no pain or humiliation and therefore had no interests which suffered from his being kept alive.

---

82 Dworkin, R, *Life's Dominion*, New York: Knopf, 1993.

Anthony Bland was in fact indifferent to whether he lived or died and there was nothing to put in the balance against the intrinsic value of his life.

I think that the fallacy in this argument is that it assumes that we have no interests except in those things of which we have conscious experience. But this does not accord with most people's intuitive feelings about their lives and deaths. At least a part of the reason why we honour the wishes of the dead about the distribution of their property is that we think it would wrong them not to do so, despite the fact that we believe that they will never know that their will has been ignored. Most people would like an honourable and dignified death and we think it wrong to dishonour their deaths, even when they are unconscious that this is happening. We pay respect to their dead bodies and to their memory because we think it an offence against the dead themselves if we do not. Once again I am not concerned to analyse the rationality of these feelings. It is enough that they are deeply rooted in our ways of thinking and that the law cannot possibly ignore them. Thus I think that counsel for the Official Solicitor offers a seriously incomplete picture of Anthony Bland's interests when he confines them to animal feelings of pain or pleasure. It is demeaning to the human spirit to say that, being unconscious, he can have no interest in his personal privacy and dignity, in how he lives or dies . . .

This argument has a slightly metaphysical flavour and was not adopted in the House of Lords. Instead, as reflected in Lord Keith's judgment, their Lordships preferred to look at the question from the opposite direction and ask if *treatment* was a benefit to the patient. This approach found its most robust expression in the speech of Lord Mustill:

Lord Mustill: [Anthony Bland] feels no pain and suffers no mental anguish. Stress was laid in argument on the damage to his personal dignity by the continuation of the present medical regime, and on the progressive erosion of the family's happy recollections by month after month of distressing and hopeless care. Considerations of this kind will no doubt carry great weight when parliament comes to consider the whole question in the round. But it seems to me to be stretching the concept of personal rights beyond breaking point to say that Anthony Bland has an interest in ending these sources of others' distress. Unlike the conscious patient he does not know what is happening to his body, and cannot be affronted by it; he does not know of his family's continuing sorrow. By ending his life the doctors will not relieve him of a burden become intolerable, for others carry the burden and he has none. What other considerations could make it better for him to die now rather than later? None that we can measure, for of death we know nothing. The distressing truth which must not be shirked is that the proposed conduct is not in the best interests of Anthony Bland, for he has no best interests of any kind.

Best interests: the termination of treatment

After much expression of negative opinions I turn to an argument which in my judgment is logically defensible and consistent with the existing law. In essence it turns the previous argument on its head by directing the inquiry to the interests of the patient, not in the termination of life but in the continuation of his treatment. It runs as follows: (i) the cessation of nourishment and hydration is an omission not an act; (ii) accordingly, the cessation will not be a criminal act unless the doctors are under a present duty to continue the regime; (iii) at the time when Anthony Bland came into the care of the doctors, decisions had to be made about his care which he was unable to make for himself. In accordance with *Re F* [1990] 2 AC 1 these decisions were to be made in his best interests. Since the possibility that he might recover still existed his best interests required that he should be supported in the hope that this would happen. These best interests justified the application of the necessary regime without his consent; (iv) all hope of recovery has now been abandoned. Thus, although the termination of his life is not in the best interests of Anthony Bland, his best interests in being kept alive have also disappeared, taking with them the justification for the non-consensual regime and the correlative duty to keep it in being; (v) since there is no longer a duty to provide nourishment and hydration, failure to do so cannot be a criminal offence.

However, although unassailable as a matter of logic, this analysis may be thought to attach too little weight to the general presumption, underpinning the qualified sanctity of life principle, that life should be preserved unless death is unambiguously preferable. Moreover, point (iv) appears to imply that the continuing treatment of a PVS patient in such a case will acually be an unlawful battery.[83]

It is unlikely that in practice doctors and relatives involved in the care of patients in PVS would accept any interpretation of the law that required them to cease treatment (as opposed to sometimes permitting them to do so). As noted in section 12.2 above, a special safeguard that applies to such cases is that, as a matter of good practice, they should be brought to court for a judicial hearing as to the lawfulness of withdrawing treatment (typically, ANH). Following a recommendation to this effect in *Bland* itself, this requirement of good practice was included in a Practice Note issued by the Official Solicitor. Since the coming into force of the Mental Capacity Act 2005, and as specified in Practice Direction 9E of the Court of Protection, the requirement also applies to patients not strictly in PVS, but who are in a state of minimal consciousness.

In the nearly 20 years since the *Bland* decision, there has been a small but steady trickle of applications to court in such cases. In some of these the relatives were divided and/or opposed to the view of the doctors as to whether treatment should continue;[84] in other cases doubts were raised as to whether the patient's diagnosis really conformed to a PVS.[85] Nonetheless, insofar as medical opinion supported such a course, the courts in such cases have invariably approved the proposed withdrawal of treatment as in the patient's best interests. Recently, though, new doubts have surfaced as to the accuracy of diagnosing PVS, fuelled by the discovery that the administration of a drug, Zolpidem, may in some cases allow patients, previously thought to be in PVS, to recover some level of consciousness. This development was acknowledged by the High Court in the case of *An NHS Trust v J*,[86] which concerned a woman who had been in a PVS for some three years after suffering a stroke. Here, Sir Mark Potter P agreed with the Official Solicitor (but against the wishes of J's family) that, before finally withdrawing ANH, a short course of Zolpidem should be tried upon her. In the event, though, the drug did not have any positive effect, and the court thereupon authorised the withdrawal ANH to allow her to die.

Another recent development adding to the difficulty in resolving PVS cases, relates to research done with functional magnetic resonance imaging (fMRI), which may open up the possibility of communicating with patients ostensibly in PVS. The implications of this are discussed by Skene et al in the following article:

Skene, L, et al, 'Neuroimaging and the Withdrawal of Life-Sustaining Treatment from Patients in Vegetative State'[87]

. . . [R]ecent research by Professor Adrian Owen suggests that some patients in VS may be able to follow instructions leading to a pattern of brain activity that can be observed by fMRI . . . Two of [his] patients . . . manifested characteristic changes on brain scanning after being instructed to imagine playing tennis. Both . . . had been diagnosed as being in VS at the time, but both subsequently improved clinically to the point where they inconsistently manifested behavioural responses to stimuli and thereby met the criteria for M[inimally] C[onscious] S[tate] . . .

---

83 Dicta to this effect can also be found in the speeches in *Bland* of Lords Browne-Wilkinson and Lowry.
84 See eg *Re G (Persistent Vegetative State)* [1995] 2 FCR 46; *An NHS Trust v D* [2005] EWHC 2349 (Fam).
85 See eg *Frenchay Healthcare NHS Trust v S* [1994] 2 All ER 403.
86 [2006] EWHC 3152 (Fam).
87 Med L Rev 17 (2009) 245.

It is at least conceivable that future research will show that some patients who respond to fMRI may be able to use this or a similar technique to communicate and make their wishes known, though it seems unlikely on the basis of what we know about the nature of the global brain injury in patients in VS. If such a form of communication were established with some brain-damaged patients, it would certainly be relevant, especially if the patient wanted treatment to be stopped. However, it would probably not be determinative, even concerning the withdrawal of treatment, as the meaning of a response to fMRI and its significance in assessing the competence of the patient are so uncertain . . .

Courts have held in a number of cases that it is lawful not to provide life-sustaining treatment if it is 'futile', justifying this on the ground of the patient's best interests. As Lord Goff said in Bland, 'if the treatment is futile . . . it is no longer in the best interests of the patient to continue it' . . . While there is reasonable consensus among health professionals and in the case law about the permissibility of withdrawing life-sustaining treatment from patients in VS, there is much less agreement about MCS . . .

One might question whether the possibility of a very small change in the patient's condition . . . is sufficient to warrant the continuation of treatment that would otherwise be withdrawn, given the remote chance that the patient will ever make a reasonable recovery. Also, as argued above, it should not be assumed that minimal consciousness would give us more reason to keep such patients alive; the reverse may be true. In such a life, unlike in VS, a patient clearly has interests, including an interest not to suffer, that might be compromised by continued existence, something not true of other patients in VS.

12.4.5 Residual questions

12.4.5.1 Non-medical reasons for the withdrawal of life-sustaining medical treatment – scarce resources and/or impracticability

The discussion in this chapter has so far ignored the fact that, in keeping alive patients who enjoy a low (or, in the case of someone in PVS, non-existent) quality of life, there is an 'opportunity cost', in the sense that scarce resources are expended which might otherwise be utilised upon people with a greater capacity to benefit from them. In *Re J (A Minor) (Wardship: Medical Treatment)*[88] the Court of Appeal quashed the trial judge's order that the health authority treat a severely disabled baby. Balcombe LJ stated:

> **Balcombe LJ**: I would also stress the absolute undesirability of the court making an order which may have the effect of compelling a doctor or health authority to make available scarce resources (both human and material) to a particular child, without knowing whether or not there are other patients to whom those resources might more advantageously be devoted. Lord Donaldson MR has set out in his reasons the condition of J and his very limited future prospects. The effect of the order of Waite J, had it not been immediately stayed by this court, might have been to require the health authority to put J on a ventilator in an intensive care unit, and thereby possibly to deny the benefit of those limited resources to a child who was much more likely than J to benefit from them. At the very least it would in those circumstances have required the health authority to make a further application to the court to vary or discharge the injunction.

In *Airedale NHS Trust v Bland*[89] the fact that resource allocation is ultimately an issue that must be faced up to was noted by Lord Mustill:

---

88 [1992] 4 All ER 614; this case should not be confused with the slightly earlier CA decision of the same name.
89 See n 6 above.

Lord Mustill: Threaded through the technical arguments addressed to the House were the strands of a much wider position, that it is in the best interests of the community at large that Anthony Bland's life should now end. The doctors have done all they can. Nothing will be gained by going on and much will be lost. The distress of the family will get steadily worse. The strain on the devotion of a medical staff charged with the care of a patient whose condition will never improve, who may live for years and who does not even recognise that he is being cared for, will continue to mount. The large resources of skill, labour and money now being devoted to Anthony Bland might in the opinion of many be more fruitfully employed in improving the condition of other patients, who if treated may have useful, healthy and enjoyable lives for years to come.

This argument was never squarely put, although hinted at from time to time. In social terms it has great force, and it will have to be faced in the end. But this is not a task which the courts can possibly undertake. A social cost-benefit analysis of this kind, which would have to embrace 'mercy killing' to which exactly the same considerations apply, must be for parliament alone, and the outcome of it is at present quite impossible to foresee. Until the nettle is grasped, we must struggle on with the existing law, imperfect as it is.

In his speech, Lord Browne Wilkinson similarly stated that 'it is not legitimate for a judge in reaching a view as to what is for the benefit of the one individual whose life is in issue to take into account the wider practical issues as to allocation of limited financial resources'. Rather, as he suggested, the inclusion of scarce resources as a permissible basis for withdrawing treatment would have to be a matter for Parliament. So far, Parliament has (not surprisingly) steered clear of the issue. As discussed in Chapter 2,[90] resource considerations will play a part earlier, in deciding, at the macro-level, whether a particular form of treatment should be made available on the NHS.

See Chapter ← 2

As to impracticability as a reason for withdrawing life-sustaining treatment., this was alluded to at first instance in R (*On the Application of Burke*) *v GMC*.[91] There, Munby J suggested that this may comprise a further category (besides the PVS type of case, where continued treatment may be said to be futile, and the class of case looked at in section 12.4.3, of sentient incapable patients, in which continued treatment will be disproportionately burdensome). By way of illustration, he posited a case in which 'the patient, although incapable, strongly objects and is not prepared to submit to the relevant procedure . . .'.

This type of situation occurred in the case of *Re D (Medical Treatment: Mentally Disabled Patient)*,[92] where a long-term psychiatric patient required ongoing dialysis treatment for renal failure. The patient was refusing to cooperate and sometimes had to be anaesthetised for the treatment to take place. In the circumstances, the High Court ruled that the continued imposition of dialysis was not in the patient's best interests. However, a stricter approach may be found in the subsequent case of *An Hospital NHS Trust v S and others*. Here, the question for the High Court related to the medical care of an 18-year-old with serious mental disabilities, who had suffered end stage renal failure. In holding that further, invasive treatment (possibly including a kidney transplant) should not be ruled out on 'non-medical grounds', Dame Elizabeth Butler-Sloss P commented as follows:

Butler-Sloss P: [64] The medical situation cannot, of course, be considered in isolation. There is no doubt that S's severe learning disability militates against explanations other than the simplest. I recognise the complexity of the operation and the probability of emergency recall to

---

90 Ch 2, section 2.4.1 above.
91 See n 29 above.
92 [1998] 2 FLR 22.

hospital on more than one occasion. I recognise the real concerns about the risk of infection and the likely need for one, or possibly even several, biopsies and the added difficulties for S to have an immediate biopsy, since he is on warfarin. The very real concerns of the Hospital Trust are, however, mainly based upon the consequences of emergency surgery on an autistic boy without any preparation of any kind. However, an emergency admission to hospital followed by life-saving surgery and treatment would be a traumatic experience for anyone. For an autistic boy, as I have set out above, it must have been extremely distressing and he reacted accordingly . . . With some preparation and with the support of a person or people in whom he had trust, in my view, and despite the opposite conclusions of the medical and nursing team at the Hospital Trust, S ought to be manageable post operation. The need for blood tests, the use of needles and the likelihood of several returns to hospital post operation, do not seem to me to be insuperable obstacles. On balance, however, if the medical reasons for a kidney transplantation are in his favour, and alternative methods of dialysis are no longer viable, in my judgment, a kidney trans-plantation ought not to be rejected on the grounds of his inability to understand the purpose and consequences of the operation or concerns about his management.[93]

12.4.5.2 The impact of the ECHR

Today such questions must also be assessed through the prism of human rights jurisprudence centred upon the European Convention on Human Rights (as incorporated into UK law by the Human Rights Act 1998). Earlier, in section 12.2, we saw how arguments based on the ECHR have been used by capable patients, who wish to assert their freedom to (be helped to) die, without interference by the state. In the context of the decision to withdraw treatment from incapable patients resulting in their deaths, two ECHR rights come to the fore, namely Art 2 (the right to life), and Art 3 (the right not to be subjected to torture or inhuman and degrading treatment). At first sight the articles may appear to require continued treatment: in the context of the withdrawal of ANH, it might be argued that death by dehydration is inhuman and degrading. These issues were addressed in the following decision by the President of the Family Division in 2001:

NHS Trust A v M, NHS Trust B v H (2001)[94]

Mrs M and Mrs H were two patients who had been in PVS for three years, and nine months, respectively. The applicant hospital trusts, supported by the women's families, applied for declarations that, notwithstanding the HRA 1998, it would be lawful to discontinue artificial nutrition and hydration in respect of each of them. In granting the declarations, Butler-Sloss P analysed the effect of the ECHR as follows:

Butler-Sloss P: If a decision to cease medical treatment in the best interests of the patient is to be characterised as intentional deprivation of life, in view of the absolute nature of the prohibition on intentional killing, [Counsel] submitted that there would be a duty in every case to take steps to keep a terminally ill patient alive by all means possible, and to continue those steps indefinitely, until the patient's body could no longer sustain treatment, irrespective of the circumstances or the prognosis. I agree with [Counsel] that such an interpretation of article 2 [the right to life] cannot be correct.

Although the intention in withdrawing artificial nutrition and hydration in PVS cases is to hasten death, in my judgment the phrase 'deprivation of life' must import a deliberate act, as opposed to an omission, by someone acting on behalf of the state,

---

93 [2003] EWHC 365 (Fam).
94 [2001] Fam 348.

which results in death. A responsible decision by a medical team not to provide treatment at the initial stage could not amount to intentional deprivation of life by the state. . . .

The analysis of these issues by the House of Lords in *Bland's* case [1993] AC 789 is entirely in accordance with the Convention case law on article 2 and is applicable to the distinction between negative and positive obligations . . .

However, article 2 also contains a positive obligation, to take adequate and appropriate steps to safeguard life: see *Osman v United Kingdom* (1998) 29 EHRR 245, 305 [Even so] that positive obligation upon a state to protect life is not absolute . . . The court held in the *Osman* case . . .:

> For the court, and having regard to the nature of the right protected by article 2, a right fundamental in the scheme of the Convention, it is sufficient for an applicant to show that the authorities did not do all that could be reasonably expected of them to avoid a real and immediate risk to life of which they have or ought to have knowledge. This is a question which can only be answered in the light of all the circumstances of any particular case.

The standard applied by the European Court of Human Rights bears a close resemblance to the standard adopted in the domestic law of negligence and approximates to the obligation recognised by the English courts in the *Bolam* test . . .: see *Airedale NHS Trust v Bland* . . . In a case where a responsible clinical decision is made to withhold treatment, on the grounds that it is not in the patient's best interests, and that clinical decision is made in accordance with a respectable body of medical opinion, the state's positive obligation under article 2 is, in my view, discharged.

In *Widmer v Switzerland* (unreported) the Commission considered the claim that there was negligent failure on the part of the hospital to treat the applicant's father. The Commission rejected the petition and said that 'the idea that the right of any person to life is protected by law requires the state . . . to take all reasonable steps to protect life'. It considered that Switzerland in its legislation had taken sufficient steps to carry out the duty imposed upon it by article 2. The court in *Osman v United Kingdom* . . . said that the positive obligation under article 2 'must be interpreted in a way which does not impose an impossible or disproportionate burden on the authorities'.

As regards Art 3, the President held that this had no application to patients in a state of non-awareness.

> On the assumption that article 3 requires to be considered, I am satisfied that the proposed withdrawal of treatment from these two patients has been thoroughly and anxiously considered by a number of experts in the field of PVS patients and is in accordance with the practice of a responsible body of medical opinion. The withdrawal is for a benign purpose in accordance with the best interests of the patients not to continue life-saving treatment; it is legitimate and appropriate that the residual treatment be continued until death. I am, moreover, satisfied that article 3 requires the victim to be aware of the inhuman and degrading treatment which he or she is experiencing or at least to be in a state of physical or mental suffering. An insensate patient suffering from permanent vegetative state has no feelings and no comprehension of the treatment accorded to him or her. Article 3 does not in my judgment apply to these two cases.

This decision is strongly to the effect that the principles developed by the common law prior to the enactment of the HRA 1998 remain good law.

In NHS Trust A v M, NHS Trust B v H, the point at issue was whether Art 3 militated *against* the withdrawal of treatment. On the other hand, at least where the patient retains some awareness, Art 3 might also lend itself to use the other way round – ie, it could be argued that in some circumstances the *provision* of invasive medical treatment amounts to inhuman or degrading treatment. This possibility was adverted to in *A NHS Trust v D*,[95] where, in deciding doctors need not mechanically ventilate a severely disabled 19-month-old child with incurable lung disease, Cazalet J cited Strasbourg jurisprudence in which Art 3 was held to include the right to die with dignity.[96] His Lordship stated that, 'It is that right . . . which is to be protected through the declaration that I propose to make in this case'.

In *Pretty v DPP*,[97] the attempt was made to invoke Art 3 in a similar fashion. As will be recalled (see 12.2.4 above) that case concerned an application by a capable patient in the final stages of motor neurone disease, who wished her husband to be allowed to assist her suicide: her argument (as to Art 3) was that the DPP's failure to countenance this would have the effect of consigning her to a prolonged and painful death through her illness. In rejecting this argument, though, Lord Bingham was of the view that the taking of steps by the state to safeguard or prolong life, if they engage Art 3 at all, may be justified by reference to Art 2 ECHR:

> **Lord Bingham** [13] Article 3 enshrines one of the fundamental values of democratic societies and its prohibition of the proscribed treatment is absolute: *D v United Kingdom* . . . Article 3 is, as I think, complementary to article 2. As article 2 requires states to respect and safeguard the lives of individuals within their jurisdiction, so article 3 obliges them to respect the physical and human integrity of such individuals. There is in my opinion nothing in article 3 which bears on an individual's right to live or to choose not to live. That is not its sphere of application; indeed, as is clear from *X v Germany* . . ., a state may on occasion be justified in inflicting treatment which would otherwise be in breach of article 3 in order to serve the ends of article 2.

Pretty itself did not in any event concern the provision by the state of life-prolonging treatment. And subsequently, in the case of *W Healthcare NHS Trust v H*,[98] which would have offered a direct opportunity to consider the point, Art 3 does not appear to have been pleaded. Had it been, the Court of Appeal would have had to decide whether the continued treatment of KH, prolonging her life in a severely compromised state, was more inimical to her Convention rights than the process (if ANH were withdrawn) of dying from dehydration.

 SELF-TEST QUESTIONS

1. In what kinds of situation will 'intolerability' *not* be the appropriate touchstone in determining that it is no longer in an incapable patient's best interests to receive life-sustaining treatment?
2. Why do patients in PVS receive more protection from the law (in terms of the need for the withdrawal of treatment to be judicially sanctioned) than other incapable patients?

---

95 [2000] Lloyd's Rep Med 411.
96 D v UK (1997) 24 EHRR 423.
97 See n 21 above.
98 See n 71 above.

12.5 Reforming the Law

12.5.1 Background – critiquing the current law

As discussed in 12.1 above, the 'qualified sanctity of life' approach taken by English law draws heavily upon the so-called 'acts/omissions distinction'. Doctors are accorded some flexibility, in allowing death to occur (through removing treatment), but – leaving aside the special case of palliative care for those patients already dying – are not permitted to take positive measures to shorten life.

At first sight the 'acts/omissions' distinction has an intuitive plausibility: it generally strikes people as worse to bring about a bad result by acting, as opposed to failing to prevent the same thing occurring 'naturally'. Nonetheless, the distinction has attracted criticism from ethicists and philosophers. As John Keown has observed: 'There is surely no significant moral difference between a doctor intentionally killing a patient by, say, choking the patient, and by deliberately failing to stop the patient from choking, when the doctor could easily do so, precisely so that the patient should die'.[99] Similarly, James Rachels has produced a pair of well-known, and colourful, hypothetical cases to deny the relevance of whether death is caused by action or inaction:

Rachels, J, *Active and Passive Euthanasia*'[100]

One reason why so many people think that there is an important moral difference between active and passive euthanasia is that they think killing someone is morally worse than letting someone die. But is it? Is killing, in itself, worse than letting die? To investigate this issue, two cases may be considered that are exactly alike except that one involves killing whereas the other involves letting someone die. Then, it can be asked whether this difference makes any difference to the moral assessments. It is important that the cases be exactly alike, except for this one difference, since otherwise one cannot be confident that it is this difference and not some other that accounts for any variation in the assessments of the two cases. So, let us consider this pair of cases:

In the first, Smith stands to gain a large inheritance if anything should happen to his six-year-old cousin. One evening while the child is taking his bath, Smith sneaks into the bathroom and drowns the child, and then arranges things so that it will look like an accident.

In the second, Jones also stands to gain if anything should happen to his six-year-old cousin. Like Smith, Jones sneaks in planning to drown the child in his bath. However, just as he enters the bathroom Jones sees the child slip and hit his head, and fall face down in the water. Jones is delighted; he stands by, ready to push the child's head back under if it is necessary, but it is not necessary. With only a little thrashing about, the child drowns all by himself, 'accidentally,' as Jones watches and does nothing.

Now Smith killed the child, whereas Jones 'merely' let the child die. That is the only difference between them. Did either man behave better, from a moral point of view? If the difference between killing and letting die were in itself a morally important matter, one should say that Jones's behavior was less reprehensible than Smith's. But does one really want to say that? I think not.

It is certainly true that in many cases the intention of an agent and the consequences of his conduct, in the context of bringing about the death of another individual, will be the same whether active or passive means are adopted. However, a residual difference can be found in the causal relationship between the agent and the death. Arguably, the causal authorship of the doctor who actively kills his patient makes his conduct problematic in a sense not shared (at least where the duty to treat has ceased) by the doctor whose non-intervention results in his patient's death. The problem resides in the first doctor's breaching of the 'equality principle':

---

99 *Euthanasia, Ethics and Public Policy*, Cambridge: CUP, 2002.
100 (1975) 292 *New England Journal of Medicine* 78.

Stauch, M, 'Causal authorship and the equality principle: a defence of
the acts/omissions distinction in euthanasia'[101]

. . . The failure to provide someone with medical assistance cannot by itself cause that person's death: he must first be in need of life-saving treatment through illness or otherwise. In fact, the agent who fails, through omission, to prevent death is allowing the completion (his non-intervention is *necessary* for this) of a pre-existing causal set for that outcome. By contrast, the agent who causes death by an act, for example by administering a lethal injection, typically instigates a causal set for the same result: his act is *sufficient* to produce it in conjunction with normal background conditions alone . . .

According to [the equality principle], the life of each individual has an equal claim to a minimum respect by possessing irreducible value (ie, a value that cannot be fully cashed out in terms of the life-holder's own states of consciousness, pleasurable or otherwise). An agent who engages in active euthanasia (even at the behest of the 'victim') fails to show this respect, for, in assuming authorship over that other's death, he automatically accords his own life an ontological priority: he draws upon his own resources (for which his life is, of course, a precondition) in such a way as to extinguish the life of the other. This breaching of the equality principle amounts, it is submitted, to a prima facie reason against any killing, and one which persists even if, in all the circumstances, we are disposed morally to excuse a *particular* killing. Consider, for example, the following hypothetical case proposed by Dan Brock:

> A patient is dying from terminal cancer, undergoing great suffering that cannot be relieved without so sedating him that he is unable to relate in any way to others. This patient prepared an advance directive at an early stage of his disease indicating that in circumstances like this he wanted to have his life ended either by direct means or by withdrawing life-sustaining treatment. In a recent lucid moment he reaffirmed the directive. The attending physician and the patient's family are in agreement that the patient's desire to die ought now to be granted.

Brock offers two alternative conclusions to this case. In the first, the man's wife places a pillow over his face and asphyxiates him while he is asleep. In the second, the man develops breathing problems (while unconscious) and needs placing on a respirator to prolong his life. His wife, who is present and knows this, fails to alert the medical staff and the man dies. Brock goes on to ask if there is 'any reason why what the wife does in the first instance is morally (as opposed to legally) worse or different to what she does in the second instance?' The answer (and remember we are not being asked whether, in the first instance as well, we should not morally excuse her action) is surely simply that in the first instance, by assuming authorship over the man's death, she infringes the equality principle. In the second instance she does not.

This may admittedly be thought a rather thin distinction, standing in need of further argument as to why the equality principle itself matters. On one view the latter is linked to an outmoded theological picture of the world. As David Price remarks:

Price, D, 'What Shape to Euthanasia after *Bland*? Historical,
Contemporary and Future Paradigms'[102]

People . . . commonly feel that death should be 'natural', not controlled nor contrived by human agency. But whilst a theological or spiritual account of the world shaped by a higher force coun-

---

101   (2000) 26 J Med Ethics 237.
102   See n 9 above.

sels against interventions interfering with the natural design, a secular view finds difficulties in the notion of the sanctity of the natural order. On a Darwinian, evolutionary plane, nature lacks a harmony or purpose of its own shaped by any intelligent force, and thus to speak of 'interfering' with nature is vacuous. It has, moreover, nothing to do with the right or the good. Radcliffe-Richards nevertheless observes that 'there is still a strong tendency for non-religious people to think of nature as taking the place of God in specifying how the world should be, and of evolution as producing progress of all kinds'; 'vestigial religion' as Rachels refers to it.

Another point is that, as we saw in section 12.2.2 above, the law as it already stands countenances the practice of the active administration of life-shortening palliative drugs to the terminally ill. If so, why, it may be asked, not take the short further step of permitting the use of non-palliative lethal drugs?

Leaving aside the question of whether the acts/omissions distinction is ultimately coherent, it is apparent that policy arguments play an important part in the law's prohibition of active euthanasia. Jonathan Glover has commented on this point as follows:

Glover, J, *Causing Death and Saving Lives*[103]

One [objection to abandoning the prohibition] is the suggestion that, if voluntary [active] euthanasia were known to be an option, people might put pressure on their burdensome relations to volunteer. It is hard to evaluate this objection. It seems to me rather implausible, but perhaps I am being too optimistic. In advance of trying a voluntary euthanasia policy, we do not know how people would behave. (Is there any evidence of such pressures in a country where voluntary euthanasia is not illegal?)

A related objection is that, even without pressure being brought by relations, people who felt they were a burden might think that, although they had lives worth living, they ought to volunteer for euthanasia. This gains some support from the fact that there have been cases of suicide by people whose motive was a reluctance to be a burden on others. Part of the difficulty of evaluating this objection is that it is hard to predict how widespread such feelings would be. Another difficulty is the more fundamental uncertainty about whether it is right in such a case to override the person's autonomy. Where he is wrong in thinking he is a burden, he should not be given euthanasia, but should be persuaded of the truth. (It seems possible that, with so much talk of old people almost as though they were members of another species, many old people who are loved and wanted members of a family do have unnecessary fears that they are a nuisance to the others.) But there are sometimes cases where a person who is old or ill does put a great strain on a family, and where he sees this and would rather die than have the situation continue, it is not obvious that a paternalist refusal to carry out his wishes is justified.

Another possible bad side effect of voluntary euthanasia concerns the treatment of dying patients. Is there a danger that allowing such a policy would hamper the development of the kind of terminal care which would make euthanasia unnecessary? The policy of total rejection of euthanasia may have the advantage of strengthening people's commitment to developing more humane and imaginative forms of terminal care. Certainly some of the most sensitive and impressive work here, such as that of Cicely Saunders and others, has been done in the context of a principled refusal to comply with euthanasia requests. But it is not clear that voluntary euthanasia would seem an alternative rather than a supplement to better terminal care. A hospital with a voluntary euthanasia policy could still have a staff that did all they could to make euthanasia requests unnecessary. The view that voluntary euthanasia would be

---

103   See n 3 above.

accepted as an easy alternative to improved care underrates the deep revulsion against killing which most people have, and which often seems especially strong among those in professions like nursing. (Perhaps this is again too optimistic. Is there any clear evidence relevant to this?)

However, if pragmatic policy reasons, rather than any fundamental ethical principle are seen as underlying the present law, then, as Glover implies, this turns the reform issue into an essentially empirical question: would the consequences of reform be worse than the ills that the reform is designed to cure? In section 12.5.2 we look at two key reform options to allow doctors to participate actively in their patients' deaths, as well as the experience of other countries where these options have been tried.

12.5.2 The key reform options

12.5.2.1 Legalising active voluntary euthanasia

The most radical option would be to legislate so as to make it lawful, in certain circumstances, for doctors to kill their patients. Supporters of such a step, such as the pressure group 'Dignity in Dying' (formerly the Voluntary Euthanasia Society) generally agree that one precondition should be that the patient has made a capable request to be killed: by contrast, active non-voluntary euthanasia has not been widely mooted as an option. Though one might pause to ask why not – if one rejects the significance of the acts/omissions distinction, then why should it matter whether, say, a PVS patient is given a lethal injection or allowed to die through removal of ANH – there appears to be a strong tabu at work here, possibly due to historical association with Nazi eugenic practices.

In drafting acceptable legislation, though, two other questions remain. First, what other conditions (besides the patient's capable request) should be required to be satisfied for active euthanasia to arise as an option? Secondly, what practical safeguards are needed to minimise the potential for abuse (such as the risk, noted by Glover, that the sick and elderly may be pressurised to opt for it, and/or of possible slippage towards the non-voluntary euthanasia of incapable patients)? The first question is discussed by Margaret Otlowski in the following extract:

Otlowski, M, *Voluntary Euthanasia and the Common Law*[104]

An initial question which arises is whether it is appropriate to have any reference to the condition of the patient as a precondition for eligibility for active voluntary euthanasia. Taking a very liberal view of self-determination, it could be argued that all patients who have decision-making capacity should be free to seek active euthanasia, regardless of their medical condition. However . . . [t]he focus of this work is on the contemporary understanding of euthanasia, that is, euthanasia in the medical context in circumstances where the patient is suffering from some illness or disability, and it is in this area that there are problems with law and practice which need to be addressed. . . .

A number of the legislative proposals . . . have proceeded on the basis that the patient must be in a 'terminal' state before he or she is eligible . . . However, proposals of this kind are arguably too limited in their operation, and would not permit active voluntary euthanasia in respect of an incurable and suffering patient who is not expected to die from his or her condition. . . .

One possibility is to include incurability as a criterion . . . [I]t is less arbitrary and uncertain in its application and leaves greater scope to the patient to determine whether active voluntary euthanasia is an appropriate option. However, in view of the wide variety of possible incurable

---

104   See n 5 above.

conditions ranging from the trivial to the life-threatening, it would be necessary to stipulate that the condition of which the patient complains must be objectively serious.

It is instructive in this context to have regard to the Netherland' criteria for active voluntary euthanasia which simply require that there must be 'physical or mental suffering which the sufferer finds unbearable'. This clearly implies that the patient's suffering stems from a physical or mental condition, but there is no stipulation as to the nature or seriousness of that condition. This formulation has the advantage of conceptual simplicity and avoids the need to determine the state of the patient's condition (whether it be 'terminal' or 'incurable'). It does, however, represent an expansion of the range of potentially eligible candidates for active voluntary euthanasia; theoretically, any physical or mental condition would suffice . . .

Some proposals for legalization also refer to the presence of pain as an additional requirement alongside other preconditions. It would be impossible to gauge objectively the extent of pain that a patient is experiencing, so as with the notion of 'suffering', a patient's pain would have to be subjectively assessed. However, it could be argued that the reference to pain is, in any event, inappropriate. With the development of palliative care, the situation has now been reached where most pain can be relieved. Moreover, experience has shown that the presence of pain is rarely of itself a reason for a patient to request active euthanasia.

Here Otlowski refers to the situation in the Netherlands, where active voluntary euthanasia is permitted in cases of 'unbearable suffering'. This was initially made possible by the courts, which, starting in the 1970s, developed guidelines for doctors to follow in such cases, compliance with which would foreclose prosecution under Dutch criminal law. In 2001 the position was formalised by the Termination of Life on Request and Assisted Suicide (Review Procedures) Act. Under s 2 of this Act, a doctor will be protected from prosection where – following consultation with another doctor – he is satisfied that the patient: is in a state of lasting and unbearable suffering; is fully informed as to his condition, prospects and options; and has an enduring and voluntary wish to die. The Act also establishes certain safeguards, notably that the doctor be present at the death and report it to the municipal coroner for assessment by a regional review committee (as to whether the relevant criteria were satisfied).

The effects and implications of the Dutch law in this area have sparked an intense (if ultimately inconclusive) debate among commentators, who have vied to produce statistics showing that abuse (in terms of non-compliance with all of the eligibility requirements and/or reporting safeguards) is/is not occurring. In fact, the significance accorded to instances of non-compliance will inevitably be influenced in part by the commentator's underlying views as to the rights and wrongs of active euthanasia. Moreover, as Otlowski observes, failure to comply with the formal law on euthanasia is just as likely to occur – if not more so – in countries where the practice remains prohibited:

Otlowski, M, *Voluntary Euthanasia and the Common Law*

. . . [C]oncern regarding the adequacy of safeguards must be interpreted in the light of current practice. As was noted in an earlier chapter, there is incontrovertible evidence to suggest that active voluntary euthanasia is to some extent already being performed, but in a totally unregulated fashion. Thus, the current situation inevitably involves some risk of abuse, and there is good reason to believe that the legalization of the practice, with appropriate regulatory procedures, would in fact reduce the possibility of covert improper practices. It would, however, be naive to suggest that a proposal for the legalization of active voluntary euthanasia would be completely free of risk. All existing laws are potentially open to abuse, and a law permitting the practice of active voluntary euthanasia would be no exception. Looking at the situation realistically, the aim of legislation legalizing active voluntary euthanasia would be to minimize the risk of abuse by the imposition of stringent safeguards regulating the practice.

Overall, the number of deaths occurring in Holland as a result of active euthanasia appears to have remained fairly constant (thus in 2005 there were around 8,400 requests for active euthanasia, of which some 2,400 were granted).[105] Arguably, more noteworthy is the change in social attitudes that appears to have occurred since (or because of?) the legal acceptance of active voluntary euthanasia. A survey carried out in the wake of the 2002 *Brongersma* case,[106] in which a physician was convicted of assisting the death of a former politician, who was 'tired of life' (but did not satisfy the 'unbearable suffering' test in the 2001 Act), found that nearly half of the population supported the doctor's actions. In early 2010 it was reported that a citizens' initiative, 'Out of Free Will', whose members include prominent figures from politics and the arts, has begun to campaign for the right of all Dutch citizens aged over 70, who are 'tired of life', to have the legal right to be helped to die.

A further point to note is that, while primarily concerned with active voluntary euthanasia, in one category of case Dutch law also permits active non-voluntary euthanasia: this is in relation to severely disabled neonates in respect of whom it has been decided to withdraw life-prolonging medical care (ie they have already been selected for passive euthansia). As Suzanne Ost explains, by reference to the discussion of this practice found in Griffiths *et al*:

Ost, S, Review of Griffiths, Weyers and Adams, *Euthanasia and the Law in Europe*[107]

The Dutch approach to this matter has been discussed by the Nuffield Council on Bioethics' Working Party on Critical Decisions in Fetal and Neonatal Medicine, who unreservedly rejected 'the active ending of neonatal life even when that life is "intolerable" ' . . . The most crucial requirements in order for such practice to be lawful in the Netherlands are that there must have already been a legitimate decision made to withdraw or withhold life-sustaining treatment and that both parents must agree to the termination of life on the basis of the baby's current unbearable and hopeless suffering . . . Termination of life is justifiable because following the withholding or withdrawal of treatment, death is not going to take place immediately. The doctor must comply with 'due care norms'. . . The authors refer to research studies that indicate that almost all neonatal end-of-life practice that occurs in the Netherlands is in the form of withholding and withdrawing treatment and that the active termination of life is very rare, although the statistics from national surveys indicate higher figures . . . It is of note that in 2007, a national committee of experts was created specifically to advise the prosecutorial authorities on the matter of the active termination of neonatal life, to receive doctors' reports of cases where such practice has occurred and pass its conclusions on to the authorities . . . One of the conclusions that the reader can draw from the authors' analysis here is that a country moving towards legalisation of euthanasia must also be prepared to reassess the reasons for prohibiting other even more sensitive forms of [medical behaviour that potentially shortens life]. It must be decided whether it is possible to justify placing a dividing line between euthanasia and the termination of neonatal life, for instance, so that the former becomes lawful while the latter does not. The answer to this question will depend, in large part, upon the legitimating values and principles that lie behind the proposals to decriminalise euthanasia within that particular society.

---

105 Pasman, HR *et al*, 'Concept of unbearable suffering in context of ungranted requests for euthanasia: qualitative interviews with patients and physicians' BMJ 2009; 339: b4362.
106 Dutch Supreme Court, 24.12.2002; NJ 2003/167.
107 (2009) 17 Med L Rev 118.

Subsequently, Belgium (in 2002) and Luxembourg (in 2009) have legislated to permit active voluntary euthanasia in circumstances similar to those recognised by Dutch law. However, in almost every other country in the world the prohibition on active euthanasia currently remains.

12.5.2.2 Legalising physician-assisted suicide

Physician-assisted suicide presents itself as a less radical alternative to active voluntary euthanasia. As discussed in section 12.2.4 above, what is at issue here is a preparatory act by the doctor – such as placing a lethal pill in the patient's mouth or (if the patient cannot swallow) wiring him up to an intravenous drip: it is the patient himself who then performs the final, death-bringing act (swallowing the pill, activating the drip, etc). As we saw earlier, English law already treats this as a separate category of case: the doctor who so behaves will not be guilty of murder (as with active euthanasia), but rather of an offence under s 2 of the 1961 Suicide Act.

Some of the arguments for decriminalising assisted suicide are discussed as follows by Margaret Otlowski:

Otlowski, M, *Voluntary Euthanasia and the Common Law*[108]

The possibility of legalization of doctor-assisted suicide has been advanced by a number of commentators and organizations and is seen by many as a preferable alternative to any change with regard to active voluntary euthanasia. Indeed, as noted earlier, the citizen-initiated referendum in the State of Oregon for legislation permitting physician-assisted suicide was passed by a majority of voters, whereas similar efforts in other states for far-reaching change have failed. A number of arguments have been put forward in support of this method of reform. An obvious advantage is that patients genuinely wishing to commit suicide would have the benefit of appropriate medical information and assistance in achieving that result. This would reduce many of the risks associated with patient suicide; for example that the patient's diagnosis and prognosis are inadequately confirmed, and that the means chosen for suicide will be unreliable or inappropriately used . . . Another advantage which is claimed in respect of this particular option is that acceptance of doctor-assisted suicide would at least provide some guarantee of the voluntariness of the patient's decision . . . It is reasoned that where the patient is capable of performing the death-inducing act, there is no justification for others to do what that patient can do for him or herself.

The US state of Oregon legislated to permit physician-assisted suicide in the Death With Dignity Act 1994, which entered into force in 1998. The Act, which is limited to residents of Oregon, allows terminally ill patients with a likely prognosis of less than six-months to live to obtain a prescription of a lethal drug. The process is subject to numerous safeguards, including the following responsibilities that are imposed on the patient's doctor by s 3 of the Act:

The Oregon Death With Dignity Act 1994, s3

(1) The attending physician shall:

    (a) Make the initial determination of whether a patient has a terminal disease, is capable, and has made the request voluntarily;

    (b) Request that the patient demonstrate Oregon residency. . .;

    (c) To ensure that the patient is making an informed decision, inform the patient of:

        (A) His or her medical diagnosis;

        (B) His or her prognosis;

---

108   See n 5 above.

(C) The potential risks associated with taking the medication to be prescribed;

(D) The probable result of taking the medication to be prescribed; and

(E) The feasible alternatives, including, but not limited to, comfort care, hospice care and pain control;

(d) Refer the patient to a consulting physician for medical confirmation of the diagnosis, and for a determination that the patient is capable and acting voluntarily;

(e) Refer the patient for counseling if appropriate. . .;

(f) Recommend that the patient notify next of kin;

(g) Counsel the patient about the importance of having another person present when the patient takes the medication . . . and of not taking the medication in a public place;

(h) Inform the patient that he or she has an opportunity to rescind the request at any time and in any manner, and offer the patient an opportunity to rescind at the end of the 15 day waiting period. . .;

(i) Verify, immediately prior to writing the prescription for medication . . . that the patient is making an informed decision;

(j) Fulfill the medical record documentation requirements. . .;

. . .

An interesting perspective on the way the Act operates in practice, including the type of patient making use of it, can be found in the annual reports on it published by the Oregon state government. The 2009 report provides the following snapshot:

Death With Dignity Act – 2009 Annual Report; Summary[109]

- During 2009, 95 prescriptions for lethal medications were written under the provisions of the DWDA compared to 88 during 2008. . . Of these, 53 patients took the medications, 30 died of their underlying illness, and 12 were alive at the end of 2009. In addition, six patients with earlier prescriptions died from taking the medications, resulting in a total of 59 DWDA deaths during 2009. This corresponds to an estimated 19.3 DWDA deaths per 10,000 total deaths.

- Fifty-five physicians wrote the 95 prescriptions (range 1–6).

- Since the law was passed in 1997, 460 patients have died from ingesting medications prescribed under the Death with Dignity Act.

- As in prior years, most participants were between 55 and 84 years of age (78.0%), white (98.3%), well-educated (48.3% had at least a baccalaureate degree), and had cancer (79.7%). Patients who died in 2009 were slightly older (median age 76 years) than in previous years (median age 70 years).

- Most patients died at home (98.3%); and most were enrolled in hospice care (91.5%) at time of death.

- In 2009, 98.7% of patients had some form of health care insurance. Compared to previous years, the number of patients who had private insurance (84.7%) was much greater than in previous years (66.8%), and the number of patients who had only Medicare or Medicaid insurance was much less (13.6% compared to 32.0%).

- As in previous years, the most frequently mentioned end-of-life concerns were: loss of autonomy (96.6%), loss of dignity (91.5%), and decreasing ability to participate in activities that made life enjoyable (86.4%).

- In 2009, none of the 59 patients were referred for formal psychiatric or psychological evaluation. Prescribing physicians were present at the time of ingestion for 3 (5.1%)

---

109 Oregon Department of Human Services (2010); see www.oregon.gov/DHS/ph/pas/docs/year12.pdf?ga=t.

patients compared to 22.6% in previous years; the prescribing physician was present at the time of death for one patient. The time from ingestion until death ranged from 2 minutes to 4½ days (104 hours).

- During 2009, one referral was made to the Oregon Medical Board for failing to submit a witnessed written consent form.

In 2008 Washington became the second US state to legislate to allow physician-assisted suicide; as in Oregon, its availability is limited to terminally ill patients with less than six months to live.

As is well-known, in Europe assisted suicide for the ill and dying is lawful in Switzerland. Indeed in recent years a small but increasing number of British citizens have been travelling there to end their lives in this way. (It will be recalled that the background to the *Purdy* case was the applicant's wish for her husband to be able to accompany her on the journey without risk of prosecution under the 1961 Suicide Act.) However, it should be noted that, in contrast to the position in Oregon, there is no specific Swiss legislation on the matter: it is simply that the Swiss Criminal Code only prohibits cases of 'selfish' assisted suicide (ie where the assister will gain personally in some way from the death). Accordingly, in other cases, where the assister can show that they acted from motives of altruism, no offence will be committed.

It also follows that in Switzerland physicians do not have any privileged role in relation to assisting suicide – in principle any person may do so. Nor are there any qualifying conditions that the person to be assisted must satisfy, in terms of being terminally ill or subject to unbearable suffering. It is enough that the patient has expressed the capable wish to die. In a decision in 2006 the Swiss Federal Supreme Court confirmed that assisted suicide would be lawful in the case of those suffering from mental illness, provided that this was not due to temporary and treatable factors, but reflected a 'rational and well-considered' decision to put an end to their further suffering. In such cases this would need to be established by a full psychiatric evaluation.

The implications of the relatively unregulated situation in Switzerland, as well as the attitudes of doctors there to assisting in suicide, are explored by Hurst and Mauron in the following extract:

Hurst, SA and Mauron, A 'Assisted Suicide and Euthanasia in Switzerland: Allowing a Role for Non-Physicians'[110]

The Swiss Academy of Medical Sciences states in its ethical recommendations that assisted suicide is 'not a part of a physician's activity.' This statement is ambiguous. It has usually been understood to mean that physicians should not assist suicide and was paraphrased in 2002 in a joint statement by the Swiss Medical Association and the Swiss Nurses Association. But the statement from the Swiss Academy of Medical Sciences has also been understood to place assisted suicide outside the purview of professional oversight, and to refer physicians, as citizens, to the law. This allows them, like other citizens, to altruistically assist suicide. In fact, even if it is understood to discourage physicians from assisting suicide, legally it leaves physicians with the same discretion as any citizen to altruistically assist suicide.

In practice, many physicians oppose assisted suicide and euthanasia, and hospitals have barred assisted suicide from their premises. Some physicians, however, do assist suicides and some advocate the decriminalisation of euthanasia. The arguments advanced are the same as in other countries. Opponents argue that killing patients violates physicians' professional integrity and endangers the doctor patient relationship. Proponents see assisted suicide and euthanasia as part of a caring response to intractable human suffering. In 2001, the Swiss parliament rejected a bill that would have barred physicians from assisting suicide . . .

---

110 (2003) 326 BMJ 271.

> Assisted suicide is a controversial topic in Switzerland, but data on public attitudes . . . are scarce . . . In a 1999 survey of the Swiss public, 82% of 1000 respondents agreed that 'a person suffering from an incurable disease and who is in intolerable physical and psychological suffering has the right to ask for death and to obtain help for this purpose.' Of these, 68% considered that physicians should provide this help . . .
>
> No validated statistics exist for assisted suicides in Switzerland. These deaths are not differentiated from unassisted suicides in official records. According to the president of one of the Swiss right to die societies, around 1800 requests for assisted suicides are made each year. Two thirds are rejected after screening. Half of the remaining people die of other causes, leaving about 300 suicides assisted by these societies annually. This constitutes around 0.45% of deaths in Switzerland . . . Individuals outside these societies may assist additional suicides. In comparison, reported assisted suicide in Oregon represents 0.09% of deaths . . .

In recent years a number of assisted dying associations have established themselves in Switzerland, which help persons who wish to commit suicide by arranging a consultation with a doctor (to obtain the required drugs) and for them to ingest the drugs in a supervised environment. Nonetheless, the activities of such groups remain controversial, not least their willingness to arrange suicide for those who are simply tired of life, as opposed to seriously ill or suffering: it has been estimated that around a quarter of cases fall into this category; also striking is the over-representation of women among applicants for suicide.[111]

12.5.3 Current Developments in the UK

In the wake of the Bland case, a Select Committee of the House of Lords was established to look into the current state of English law in relation to euthanasia. Whilst endorsing steps to facilitate the practice of passive euthanasia, such as by encouraging the greater use of advance directives, the Committee was of the view that both assisted suicide and active euthanasia should remain offences, the latter continuing to be treated as murder:

House of Lords Select Committee, *Report of the Select Committee on Medical Ethics*[112]

236 The right to refuse treatment is far removed from the right to request assistance in dying. We spent a long time considering the very strongly held and sincerely expressed views of those witnesses who advocated voluntary [active] euthanasia. Many of us have had the experience of relatives or friends whose dying days were less than peaceful or uplifting, or whose final stages of life were so disfigured that the loved one already seemed lost to us, or who were simply weary of life. Our thinking must inevitably be coloured by such experience. The accounts we received from individual members of the public about such experiences were particularly moving, as were the letters from those who themselves longed for the release of an early death. Our thinking must also be coloured by the wish of every individual for a peaceful and easy death, without prolonged suffering, and by a reluctance to contemplate the possibility of severe dementia or dependence. We gave much thought too to Professor [Ronald] Dworkin's opinion that, for those without religious belief, the individual is best able to decide what manner of death is fitting to the life that has been lived.

237 Ultimately, however, we do not believe that these arguments are sufficient reason to weaken society's prohibition of intentional killing. That prohibition is the cornerstone of law

---

111 Fischer, S et al, 'Suicide assisted by two Swiss right-to-die organisations' (2008) 34 J Med Ethics 810.
112 See n 20 above.

and social relationships. It protects each of us impartially, embodying the belief that all are equal. We do not wish that protection to be diminished and we therefore recommend that there be no change in the law to permit euthanasia. We acknowledge that there may be individual cases in which euthanasia may be seen by some to be appropriate. But individual cases cannot reasonably establish the foundation of a policy which would have such serious and widespread repercussions. Moreover dying is not only a personal or individual affair. The death of a person affects the lives of others, often in ways and to an extent that cannot be foreseen. We believe that the issue of euthanasia is one in which the interest of the individual cannot be separated from the interest of society as a whole.

In 2003, however, in the wake of developments in Holland, Belgium and Oregon, and the public debate at home unleashed by the *Diane Pretty* case, the issue of law reform once again appeared on the UK parliamentary agenda. In that year the Labour peer, Lord Joffe introduced a private member's bill, the Assisted Dying for Terminally Ill Bill, modelled on the Oregon Death with Dignity Act. Subject to various qualifying conditions being satisfied, terminally ill patients experiencing unbearable suffering would have access to 'assisted dying': this was defined as a doctor providing the means for the patient to commit suicide or, if the patient was physically unable to do so, directly ending the patient's life. Subsequently the Bill was considered by a House of Lords Select Committee under the Chairmanship of the former Lord Chancellor, Lord Mackay.

In its Report the Committee – while accepting that there had been a shift in UK public opinion, with more people open to the idea of medical assistance in dying – was critical of the Bill's merging of assisted suicide and voluntary active euthanasia, which it felt would encourage a higher take-up on assisted death than needed as a genuine last resort:

Select Committee on the Assisted Dying for the Terminally Ill Bill[113]

243. Lord Joffe's Bill seeks to legalise not only medical assistance with suicide but also, in cases where self-administration of lethal medication is not possible, voluntary euthanasia. We have visited two places—Oregon and The Netherlands—which have gone down different roads in this regard and which show widely different death rates from this source. In Oregon less than 1 in 700 deaths is currently attributable to assisted suicide, whereas in The Netherlands the figure is more than 1 in 40, less than 10% of which are from assisted suicide while over 90% are as a result of voluntary euthanasia . . .

244. There was general agreement among our witnesses that the number of people who might be regarded as serious about ending their lives, who are not psychiatrically ill and who are unlikely to be deflected from their purpose is very small indeed and comprises to a large extent terminally ill people who have strong personalities and a history of being in control of their lives and whose suffering derives more from the fact of their terminal illness and from the loss of control which this involves than from the symptoms of their disease. If therefore it should be accepted by the House that there is a case for such exceptional individuals to be afforded assistance to end their lives, consideration would need to be given to how the parameters of any new law could be set in such a way as to ensure that the take-up rate is limited to such people . . . The much smaller numbers of deaths in countries where only assisted suicide is legal suggests strongly that such a restriction, with its emphasis on the individual taking responsibility for the final stage of ending his or her life, has the effect of making those who are minded to end their lives think very carefully before taking action to give effect to their wishes.

---

113   HL Paper 86-I, London: TSO, 2005.

245. . . . From the evidence we have received it is clear that, while there are indeed some doctors who support a change in the law [to permit voluntary euthanasia], the medical profession as a whole is at best ambivalent on the subject and in many cases opposed. On the other hand, it appears that there would be rather less unhappiness about a law which is limited in its scope to assisted suicide . . .

Subsequently Lord Joffe introduced an amended version of the Bill so that, as in the case of Oregon, it was restricted to allowing cases of physician-assisted suicide. However, at its second reading in May 2006, the House of Lords voted by 148 votes to 100 against its progression. One reason was the 'slippery slope' fear that such a reform would clear the way towards voluntary active euthanasia in the future. Subsequently, in July 2009 the House of Lords also rejected an amendment to the Coroners and Justice Bill proposed by Lord Falconer of Thoroton, which sought to remove cases from the ambit of the Suicide Act 1961 in which a person accompanies a patient to a jurisdiction where this is lawful, for them to receive assistance in dying. This would have been subject to two doctors certifying that the patient was terminally ill and had capacity to make the decision.

Nonetheless, it is unlikely, following *Purdy v DPP*,[114] that these issues are going to go away. First, the current restriction upon physician involvement in assisted suicides appears arbitrary. Secondly, now that assisted suicide is *de facto* lawful, there will inevitably be pressure from those patients who wish to die, but lack the means to commit suicide: they may well argue that they are being discriminated against on the basis of their physical incapacity. In this regard it was reported in July 2010 that a British man, Tony Nicklinson, left paralysed following a stroke, was preparing to challenge the present law prohibiting his wife from killing him at his request.

SELF-TEST QUESTION

Especially in the light of 'suicide tourism' within Europe, would it now be preferable for the UK to legalise assisted suicide? If so, what are the key provisions that should be included in any relevant statute?

Summary of Key Points

(1) Euthanasia may be defined as the practice of bringing about an easeful death for the patient. In its active form this involves the use of positive means to cause death. By contrast, passive euthanasia occurs where a doctor deliberately withholds or withdraws life-sustaining treatment.

(2) Under English law as it stands, active euthanasia is unlawful, and generally treated as murder. This prohibition on killing, which persists even where the patient himself wishes to die, reflects the (qualified) sanctity of life principle, which treats human life as inviolable.

(3) However, by way of an important qualification, doctors are permitted to prescribe powerful analgesic drugs to terminally ill patients, even though they foresee that such drugs will shorten the patient's life. This common law exception was recognised in 1957 in the case of R v (Bodkin) Adams.

(4) In other cases where, rather than acting directly to cause death, the doctor provides the means for the patient to kill himself, the doctor will be liable for the offence of assisted suicide. This remains punishable under the Suicide Act 1961, with up to 14 years' imprisonment.

---

114 See n 23 above.

(5) The legal position in respect of passive euthanasia is generally more flexible: as confirmed by the House of Lords in 1993 in *Airedale NHS Trust v Bland*, insofar as the *prima facie* duty to treat has lapsed, the doctor may withdraw life-sustaining treatment to allow the patient's death.

(6) One such situation is where a capable patient refuses consent to further treatment. Here the doctor who continues to prolong the patient's life will commit a battery. Nor does it matter if in discontinuing treatment, the doctor 'acts' (in the narrow sense), eg by detaching a tube. Legally this will count as an omission.

(7) As set out in the 2005 Mental Capacity Act, a formerly capable patient may encode a treatment refusal in an advance decision. Provided the decision is found to be both valid and applicable, it will bind the doctors to cease maintaining the life of the (now incapable) patient.

(8) In respect of incapable patients, where there is no binding advance decision, life-sustaining treatment may be withdrawn insofar as it is no longer in the patient's best interests (passive involuntary euthanasia). In some cases, notably where the decision relates to a patient in PVS, an application should be made to the Court of Protection under the Mental Capacity Act.

(9) In other cases, concerning sensate and suffering incapable patients, and where there is no dispute between the doctors and the relatives, the decision may be taken without court involvement.

(10) In recent years, particularly given the lawfulness of active euthanasia and assisted suicide in certain other countries, there has been pressure in the UK in the direction of law reform. However, significant concerns remain as to the implications of this and so far change has been resisted.

 Further Reading

Greasley, K, '*R (Purdy) v DPP* and the case for wilful blindness' (2010) 30 *Oxford Journal of Legal Studies* 301.

Huxtable, R, *Euthanasia, Ethics and the Law: From Conflict to Compromise*, Abingdon: Routledge-Cavendish, 2007.

Keown, J, *Euthanasia, Ethics and Public Policy*, Cambridge: Cambridge University Press, 2002.

Lewis, P, 'Euthanasia in Belgium five years after legalisation' (2009) 16 *European Journal of Health Law* 125.

Otlowski, M, *Voluntary Euthanasia and the Common Law*, Oxford: OUP, 1997.

Price, D, 'What Shape to Euthanasia after *Bland*? Historical, Contemporary and Future Paradigms' (2009) 125 *Law Quarterly Review* 142.

Index